LOUD & PROUD
PRESTON NORTH END

Dedicated to Maria Rigby and Angela Payne,
for their tolerance and understanding

Loud & Proud
Preston North End FC

The Complete Story of the Lilywhites

By

Ian Rigby and Mike Payne

'A Book for the Fans, by the Fans.'

Palatine Books, 2005

Copyright © Ian Rigby and Mike Payne 1999, 2005

First published by Carnegie Publishing Ltd, 1999

This revised and extended edition published in 2005 by
Palatine Books,
Carnegie House,
Chatsworth Road,
Lancaster LA1 4SL
www.palatinebooks.com

All rights reserved
Unauthorised duplication contravenes existing laws

ISBN 10: 1-874181-31-4
ISBN 13: 978-1-874181-31-6

The publishers acknowledge, with gratitude, the permission to use the Preston crest
which was kindly granted by Preston City Council.

Typeset by Carnegie Book Production
Printed and bound by The Alden Press, Oxford

Contents

		page
Foreword, by Sir Tom Finney		vii
Ian Rigby, by Mike Payne		viii
Mike Payne, by Ian Rigby		ix
Acknowledgements		x
Proud Preston: an introduction by Mike Payne		xi
Life in Preston at around the time Preston North End came into being		xii
In the beginning ... Pre-league Preston North End		xiii
Major William Sudell		xix

Season	Division	P	W	D	L	F	A	Pts	Position	
1888–1889	ONE	22	18	4	0	74	15	40	CHAMPIONS	1
1889–1890	ONE	22	15	3	4	71	30	33	CHAMPIONS	3
1890–1891	ONE	22	12	3	7	44	23	27	RUNNERS-UP	5
1891–1892	ONE	26	18	1	7	61	31	37	RUNNERS-UP	7
1892–1893	ONE	30	17	3	10	57	39	37	RUNNERS-UP	9
1893–1894	ONE	30	10	3	17	44	56	23	14th	12
1894–1895	ONE	30	15	5	10	62	46	35	4th	14
1895–1896	ONE	30	11	6	13	44	48	28	9th	16
1896–1897	ONE	30	11	12	7	55	40	34	4th	19
1897–1898	ONE	30	8	8	14	35	43	24	12th	21
1898–1899	ONE	34	10	9	15	44	47	29	15th	23
1899–1900	ONE	34	12	4	18	38	48	28	16th	25
1900–1901	ONE	34	9	7	18	49	75	25	17th RELEGATED	27
1901–1902	TWO	34	18	6	10	71	32	42	3rd	29
1902–1903	TWO	34	13	10	11	56	40	36	7th	31
1903–1904	TWO	34	20	10	4	62	24	50	CHAMPIONS	33
1904–1905	ONE	34	13	10	11	42	37	36	8th	35
1905–1906	ONE	38	17	13	8	54	39	47	RUNNERS-UP	38
1906–1907	ONE	38	14	7	17	44	57	35	14th	40
1907–1908	ONE	38	12	12	14	47	53	36	12th	43
1908–1909	ONE	38	13	11	14	48	44	37	10th	46
1909–1910	ONE	38	15	5	18	52	58	35	12th	49
1910–1911	ONE	38	12	11	15	40	49	35	14th	51
1911–1912	ONE	38	13	7	18	40	57	33	19th RELEGATED	53
1912–1913	TWO	38	19	15	4	56	33	53	CHAMPIONS	55
1913–1914	ONE	38	12	6	20	52	69	30	19th RELEGATED	58
1914–1915	TWO	38	20	10	8	61	42	50	RUNNERS-UP	61
League suspended due to First World War										64
1919–1920	ONE	42	14	10	18	57	73	38	19th	68
1920–1921	ONE	42	15	9	18	61	65	39	16th	70
1921–1922	ONE	42	13	12	17	42	65	38	16th	73
1922–1923	ONE	42	13	11	18	60	64	37	16th	76
1923–1924	ONE	42	12	10	20	52	67	34	18th	79
1924–1925	ONE	42	10	6	26	37	74	26	21st RELEGATED	82
1925–1926	TWO	42	18	7	17	71	84	43	12th	85
1926–1927	TWO	42	20	9	13	74	72	49	6th	88
1927–1928	TWO	42	22	9	11	100	66	53	4th	91
1928–1929	TWO	42	15	9	18	78	79	39	13th	94
1929–1930	TWO	42	13	11	18	65	80	37	16th	97

Season	Division	P	W	D	L	F	A	Pts	Position	
1930–1931	TWO	42	17	11	14	83	64	45	7th	100
1931–1932	TWO	42	16	10	16	75	77	42	13th	103
1932–1933	TWO	42	16	10	16	74	70	42	9th	106
1933–1934	TWO	42	23	6	13	71	52	52	RUNNERS-UP	109
1934–1935	ONE	42	15	12	15	62	67	42	11th	112
1935–1936	ONE	42	18	8	16	67	64	44	7th	115
1936–1937	ONE	42	14	13	15	56	67	41	14th	118
1937–1938	ONE	42	16	17	9	64	44	49	3rd	121
1938–1939	ONE	42	16	12	14	63	59	44	9th	126
League suspended due to Second World War										129
1946–1947	ONE	42	18	11	13	76	74	47	7th	133
1947–1948	ONE	42	20	7	15	67	68	47	7th	136
1948–1949	ONE	42	11	11	20	62	75	33	21st RELEGATED	139
1949–1950	TWO	42	18	9	15	60	49	45	6th	142
1950–1951	TWO	42	26	5	11	91	49	57	CHAMPIONS	145
1951–1952	ONE	42	17	12	13	74	54	46	7th	150
1952–1953	ONE	42	21	12	9	85	60	54	RUNNERS-UP	153
1953–1954	ONE	42	19	5	18	87	58	43	11th	156
1954–1955	ONE	42	16	8	18	83	64	40	14th	161
1955–1956	ONE	42	14	8	20	73	72	36	19th	164
1956–1957	ONE	42	23	10	9	84	56	56	3rd	167
1957–1958	ONE	42	26	7	9	100	51	59	RUNNERS-UP	170
1958–1959	ONE	42	17	7	18	70	77	41	12th	173
1959–1960	ONE	42	16	12	14	79	76	44	9th	176
1960–1961	ONE	42	10	10	22	43	71	30	22nd RELEGATED	181
1961–1962	TWO	42	15	10	17	55	57	40	10th	184
1962–1963	TWO	42	13	11	18	59	74	37	17th	187
1963–1964	TWO	42	23	10	9	79	54	56	3rd	190
1964–1965	TWO	42	14	13	15	76	81	41	12th	193
1965–1966	TWO	42	11	15	16	62	70	37	17th	196
1966–1967	TWO	42	16	7	19	65	67	39	13th	199
1967–1968	TWO	42	12	11	19	43	65	35	20th	202
1968–1969	TWO	42	12	15	15	38	44	39	14th	205
1969–1970	TWO	42	8	12	22	43	63	28	22nd RELEGATED	208
1970–1971	THREE	46	22	17	7	63	39	61	CHAMPIONS	211
1971–1972	TWO	42	12	12	18	52	58	36	18th	214
1972–1973	TWO	42	11	12	19	37	64	34	19th	217
1973–1974	TWO	42	9	14	19	40	62	31*	21st RELEGATED	219
1974–1975	THREE	46	19	11	16	63	56	49	9th	222
1975–1976	THREE	46	19	10	17	62	57	48	8th	225
1976–1977	THREE	46	21	12	13	64	43	54	6th	228
1977–1978	THREE	46	20	16	10	63	38	56	3rd PROMOTED	231
1978–1979	TWO	42	12	18	12	59	57	42	7th	234
1979–1980	TWO	42	12	19	11	56	52	43	10th	237
1980–1981	TWO	42	11	14	17	41	62	36	20th RELEGATED	242
1981–1982†	THREE	46	16	13	17	50	56	61	14th	245
1982–1983	THREE	46	15	13	18	60	69	58	16th	248
1983–1984	THREE	46	15	11	20	66	66	56	16th	251
1984–1985	THREE	46	13	7	26	51	100	46	23rd RELEGATED	254
1985–1986	FOUR	46	11	10	25	54	89	43	23rd Re-elected	257
1986–1987	FOUR	46	26	12	8	72	47	90	RUNNERS-UP	260
1987–1988	THREE	46	15	13	18	48	59	58	16th	263
1988–1989	THREE	46	19	15	12	79	60	72	6th Play-offs	266
1989–1990	THREE	46	14	10	22	65	79	52	19th	269
1990–1991	THREE	46	15	11	20	54	67	56	17th	276

1991–1992	THREE	46	15	12	19	61	72	57	17th		279
1992–1993	TWO (New)	46	13	8	25	65	94	47	21st RELEGATED		282
1993–1994	THREE (New)	42	18	13	11	79	60	67	5th Play-offs		285
1994–1995	THREE	42	19	10	13	58	41	67	5th Play-offs		290
1995–1996	THREE	46	23	17	6	78	38	86	CHAMPIONS		294
1996–1997	TWO	46	18	7	21	49	55	61	15th		299
1997–1998	TWO	46	15	14	17	56	56	59	15th		302
1998–1999	TWO	46	22	13	11	78	50	79	5th Play-offs		305
1999–2000	TWO	46	28	11	7	74	37	95	CHAMPIONS		308
2000–2001	ONE	46	23	9	14	64	52	78	4th Play-off Finalist		311
2001–2002	ONE	46	20	12	14	71	59	72	8th		314
2002–2003	ONE	46	16	13	17	68	70	61	12th		317
2003–2004	ONE	46	15	14	17	69	71	59	15th		320
2004–2005	ONE	46	21	12	13	67	58	75	5th Play-off Finalist		323

The Play-offs 326
Roll of Honour 330
Postscript 332

* One point deducted for fielding an ineligible player   † First season of three points for a win

Up to and including season 2004–2005 Preston North End's total record has been: Played 4,316; Won 1,682; Drawn 1,076; Lost 1,558; Goals for 6,505; Goals against 6,150; Total points 4,864.*

Foreword
by Sir Tom Finney OBE, CBE

I did not hesitate when approached to write a foreword for this book, which is a very comprehensive historical account of my club, Preston North End. *Proud Preston* will not only bring memories flooding back to followers of North End, but also to supporters of other clubs, as over one hundred match reports are uniquely featured in the book. The authors, both avid fans, have tried to be unbiased which reflects in their choice of the games covered. The reproduction of photographs, especially the older ones, help bring the Club's history to life. This book, which is a very enjoyable read, for young and old alike, is quite an achievement, I fully recommend it.

Best Wishes
Tom Finney

Sir Tom Finney
President of Preston North End Football Club

Ian Rigby

by Mike Payne

I have never met anyone so dedicated to one club, as Ian is, or one who has such a passion for Preston North End's history. Ian has spent most of his life researching every aspect of the club's existence and if you want to know who made the cup of tea at half-time in the FA Cup final of 1922, and what their middle name was, then Ian is probably the man to ask. When it comes to North End, nothing is too great a task for this born and bred Prestonian who first saw the light of day at the Sharoe Green Hospital on Watling Street Road in July 1951. Significantly, PNE almost won the League Championship in the first season after Ian was born, so maybe this had some influence on his passionate interest. And also significantly, throughout his life Ian has always lived within a mile and a half of Deepdale! For many years now he has become the unofficial historian for the club and many's the time he has spent long hours researching a supporter's enquiry about a long lost relative who had one game for the reserves back in 1898. Nine times out of ten Ian will find the answer too! He has now been married to his lovely wife Maria for 35 years, and she has been forever indulgent and supportive of her husband's hobby. She once found him sound asleep on the sitting room sofa at about three in the morning, with his North End records and scraps all around him, and the TV and fire still switched on! You see, when Ian gets his teeth into something to do with North End the small matter of going to bed is forgotten. Ian's three children, Suzanna, John Carlo and David have long since given up trying to understand their dad's passion for North End, but each of them are definitely fans of the club because of Ian. It has been a delight for me to work with Ian on this project, as his attention to detail is what makes him different from other club statisticians and why this book is such a good one. Quite a few football history books are full of inaccuracies but this book on North End is unique in that every fact has been checked, double-checked and treble checked for authenticity. As an added bonus for me Ian handles everything with his wonderfully dry Lancashire sense of humour, which often has me in stitches during our endless phone conversations. Above all North End could not have a more genuine or nice man to deal with the enquiries about the club's history. The perfect role for Ian came about when he was one of the founder members of the now hugely successful PNE Former Player's Association. This association is now thriving and boasts over 200 members. Ian is the secretary of the organisation and all the members think the world of him. This book is a tribute to all the people who have made Preston North End Football Club into what it is today, but it is also a tribute to Ian, and one man's love for his team.

Mike Payne

Mike Payne

by Ian Rigby

I first met Mike through our mutual love for Preston North End and after getting to know him I realised that football fans all have their own reasons for supporting their particular chosen team. In his case he chose North End because his favourite player at the time, Tom Finney, played for the club. Surprisingly, after Tom retired, Mike's affection for the club remained and over the years it has grown and grown, and rarely has anyone supported the club so fervently. Because he lives over 200 miles from Deepdale he does not see them play as often as he would like, and it is probably just as well because he gets very, very nervous when he does watch them. But he has been to Deepdale on a few occasions and he loves every minute of the experience. He has no ties with the town, although, and whisper this softly, his lovely wife of 37 years, Angela, was born in Blackburn! And yet, despite this lack of connection with Preston, there are few people I know who have as wide a knowledge of the club's history than Mike. He has a daughter, Rebecca, who is married to James, and they have since fulfilled Mike's greatest ambition by providing two gorgeous grandchildren, Matthew and Imogen. Mike has tried desperately to convert Matthew, who is football mad, into supporting North End. He is winning the battle. Mike's pride and joy, apart from Angie and the family of course, are his PNE scrapbooks. They have been lovingly compiled over nearly 50 years and I defy anyone to better his collection. This patient and meticulous effort has given Mike a unique record of North End's match by match history and these scrapbooks have been invaluable in the compilation of this book. Over recent years, I have been able to introduce Mike to several former players and the look of excitement on his face when he meets them is a picture. I have asked him why he supports North End so passionately? After all, as a schoolboy he lived on the Isle of Wight, over 300 miles from Preston! It is a difficult question for Mike to answer, suffice to say that Preston North End has been, and is, a huge part of his life and he can't imagine it without them. By his own admission the club has given him much pleasure, and heartache, over the years, and he is absolutely delighted that circumstances have given him the chance to share in the writing of this book. For Mike it really has been a labour of love and he believes passionately in the illustrious history of the men who made Preston North End football club. His other passion is the non-league game, which he also loves, and give him an FA Cup-tie between North End and Newport Isle of Wight FC (his hometown) at Deepdale and play Roy Orbison songs at the half-time break and that would be Mike's idea of heaven.

Ian Rigby

Acknowledgements

Although this book has been compiled by the two authors many other people have, sometimes unwittingly, played a part in contributing to the book and we would like to thank the following, in particular, for their help.

Firstly, Viator, Ajax, Perseus, Walter Pilkington, Norman Shakeshaft, Paul Agnew and Brian Ellis, whose work in reporting North End's daily fortunes has been magnificent and without whom this historic record would not have been possible.

To Preston City Council for use of the Town Badge and to the Harris Reference Library for access to their comprehensive records.

To the *Lancashire Evening Post* who offered access to their records and photographs.

To the Football League for access to their records.

To the late Ted Griffith, a former PNE Director, and Mrs E. Griffith.

To Sir Tom Finney for being Sir Tom!

To the staff of the *Preston Citizen* for recent photographs.

To Karen Pearson and Sharon Gifford, both avid North End fans, for agreeing to the use of their photographs.

To Carnegie Publishing for their continued faith in this project and especially Mark Keating and Adam Gregory for their unstinting efforts and patience in dealing with two fussy and cantankerous old geezers who were obsessed with Preston North End!

To Peter Reed and Howard Talbot for the photography.

To Bob Bond for allowing us to use his remarkable caricatures.

And finally, to the numerous players, officials, administration staff and fans of Preston North End F.C., past and present, who have given their all to the club and provided the many memories recorded in this book. Those memories have been treasured by the authors.

Proud Preston

An introduction by Mike Payne

When Ian Rigby and I decided to put together the story of Preston North End's illustrious and rich history, we had no idea how it would grip our imagination over the next few years. We had been working on the build up to this book for most of our lives, both of us being lifelong fans of the club. Ian, who lives in Preston, is probably the leading authority on North End's history and has dedicated his life to improving his vast knowledge on everything and anything to do with his local team. I, meanwhile, began my life on the Isle of Wight, which could hardly be further from Preston. But as a schoolboy I hooked my allegiance on to a certain master footballer named Finney, and for as long as I can remember Preston North End results are the most important in my life.

In the late 1950s (or early 1960s in Ian's case as he is younger than me), after we had learned to write, we began keeping records of our favourite team and much of what you find in these pages has been trawled from the archives which we have both so patiently cultivated. Many of the pieces we researched were written in our schoolboy hand-writing of many years ago.

Ian and I met over 20 years ago through our mutual love of this famous old club, and we immediately realised that there was a bond between us. We were both as mad as each other for North End. The similarities in our lives has also been uncanny at times; even our daughters had their honeymoons in the same place! With different husbands of course. Continuing the coincidences even more recently, we were both made redundant from our jobs at around the same time, me after 32 years with the same company and Ian after a long time in engineering. The ups and mainly downs of our football club during the time we have given them our support has taken its toll on us, and as middle age gives way to the twilight years, we thought we had better share our knowledge with the many fans of the Lilywhites around the world. The club has an amazing story and every conceivable emotion has been experienced by those fans who, like us, have supported the club for forty years or more.

In the pages of this new edition of the book we have tried to cover every aspect of the history of North End and incorporated many fascinating facts along the way. So much more has happened in the six seasons since the first edition was published in the autumn of 1999, and the interest in the club has climbed to new heights. It is not just a statistical record, although every league and cup match is recorded in full detail. We have also tried to add many social history aspects of the football club, the town – and now, of course, city – of Preston, as well as including pieces, which made Ian and myself smile. A keen sense of humour is another thing we share.

Preston North End Football Club was a Founder Member of the Football League and the very first League Champions, a fact that can never be taken away from them. We hope this lovingly compiled history does the club's status in the game justice. During our research one thing that comes across all the time is the players pride at playing for the world-renowned Deepdale club. In January 1998 Ian Rigby was one of the founder members of the PNE Former Players' Association, which is now a flourishing concern with over 200 ex-players registered. Ian and his fellow committee members regularly arrange events on behalf of the Association and those events give the fans of North End the chance to meet up with some of the stars of this book. The players love to reminisce about their days at Deepdale because of that pride they had in playing for the Lilywhites.

Proud Preston was a nickname earned many years ago by a very talented team, and Proud has become synonymous with the town of Preston. One thing is certain: all Prestonians can be proud of the heritage and achievements of their football team.

Please enjoy this trip down memory lane.

Life in Preston

at around the time that Preston North End came into being

Living in Preston in the 1870s and 1880s was quite a bit different to how people live there today. Things we take for granted now were unheard of then, such as electric light, cars, television, etc. Telephones were just starting up and, indeed, one of the first telephone systems in this country was set up in Preston by 1881. The main form of transport between towns was the growing railway train system, but the landscape they travelled through would have looked very different, too, with Deepdale just a field on the edge of town. In January 1875, the month North End first leased their ground, there was an outbreak of foot and mouth in the area, so it was much more rural than it is now. William Sudell once lived in one of the four-house St George's Terrace on Deepdale Road, close to Gutteridge School, which wasn't built until 1904. In those days his house would have looked out on to green fields, a little different to the view today from the terrace that still survives. Sudell later moved to the Manor House on Holme Slack Lane, which apparently hasn't survived.

The *Lancashire Evening Post* is an institution in Preston today, but before that newspaper began in 1886 as the *Lancashire Daily Post*, the public had other papers to read. The *Preston Chronicle* was printed every Saturday morning, whilst the *Preston Guardian* and *Preston Herald* were both published twice a week, on Wednesdays and Saturdays. There were around 91,500 people living in Preston in 1880 and the environment around them would have dictated the occupations of many. For instance, believe it or not, there were 460 'beer houses' in the town, if you include hotels, inns and taverns. The town also boasted twenty different cotton manufacturers, 57 cow keepers, 63 cloggers and 39 tobacconists! So, the average

Prestonian probably dressed in cotton suits, wore designer clogs, ate steak for dinner and drank and smoked themselves to a standstill!

Meanwhile, crime was such that newspapers were forced to report in 1875 that the Mayor of Woodstock was fined one pound for keeping his public house, the King's Arms Inn, open for one hour beyond the legal time for closing. What a heinous crime! And Richard Horne fell foul of the law in 1880 when he was fined five shillings, plus costs, 'for riding without reins' (look mum, no hands!). The defendant ran his horse into a cart that was travelling in the opposite direction. Then there was the more serious crime, like the time that Francis Holmes, an overlooker of weavers, was committed to gaol for two calendar months, without the option of paying a fine, for brutally kicking a young woman when, according to the defendant, he was really trying to kick his wife, to whom he had just given a black eye!

In May 1880, the month North End were formed as a football team, Newsome's Circus came to town and the first notes of a cuckoo was heard in the Deepdale neighbourhood. The Zulu War in South Africa had just ended and it was reported that it had cost this country a staggering £5,230,323. An unbelievable amount now, let alone in those days. Apparently £2,500 of those costs was for stationery. Sadly the war to end all wars had yet to come.

Overall, though, life was good for the gentle folk of Preston and the attraction of outside entertainment, such as sport, was increasingly becoming an important part of their lives. They were soon to take to football with great enthusiasm and they had lots to look forward to.

In the beginning ...

Pre-League Preston North End

From all the information available it would seem that the origins of the Preston North End Football Club that we know today stemmed from a cricket match! During the Preston Guild Year of 1862 a full day's cricket was played by a group of men on the Ashton Marsh on that year's Whit Monday. Those cricketers were known to have been linked with the schools around the Wellfield Road and Bow Lane area of the town, but little did they realise at the time that this would be the start of something special.

The cricket team continued to play each summer until 1867, when the Preston Town Council opened up a new stretch of land for use by the community and called it Moor Park. The Ashton Marsh lads moved to the new pitches on the park and it would seem that the name of 'North End' first appeared around this time. Some publications state that North End were originally named 'Nelson' and during that first cricket season on the newly opened Moor Park it was changed to North End. But this is difficult to believe as both North End and Nelson were playing their cricket on the park during those summer months of 1867. A local newspaper, the *Preston Guardian*, gives reports on the games played, with North End receiving quite substantial write-ups while Nelson only warranted minimal coverage. If Nelson had changed their name to North End, then how do we explain that both clubs were playing independently around the same time?

It was fairly obvious that the North End club had been so named purely due to being situated at the north end of the town. The club progressed well and on 21 January 1875 the members made what turned out to be a momentous decision. They decided to lease a field at Deepdale, and over 130 years later they are still there. So far, the North End club had only played cricket in the summer, but in 1876 the first signs of a change of direction occurred. Rugby football was experimented with as a winter sport for the cricketers to play, with the first match coming on 21 October 1876 when they lost to Preston Olympic. Early rugby players included, J. Singleton, J. Wilson, W. Sudell, T. Wadeson, H. Cartmell, J. Hulme, W. Charnley, J. Wadeson, W. Wadeson, J. Naylor, J. Major, T. Parkinson, C. Towers and Messrs Horridge and Welsh. Unfortunately the idea met with little success as the local Preston Grasshoppers side were well estab-

lished as the top team with the oval ball. But North End continued to play cricket, with some athletics meetings, in the summer months and rugby through the winter for the next couple of years while a new sport started to spread across the country.

Rules for organised association football, with a round ball, had been agreed in October 1863 after the game's origins had been founded in the public schools much earlier. But it was from 1863 that the game really began to take shape, with the foundation of the Football Association at the Freemasons' Tavern, Great Queen Street, Lincoln's Inn Fields, in London. The game had initially been mainly southern based, but it had spread north to Nottingham and Sheffield, and new clubs were starting to spring up all over. The game had already started in Scotland, too, something that would eventually be very important to North End, and Queens Park were already a prominent force. The Lancashire Football Association did not appear until the 1870s and in 1872 the first FA Cup was contested. The new trophy cost £20 to buy and only 15 teams entered, most of which came from the Home Counties. The two exceptions were Donnington School from Lincoln and Queen's Park from Scotland. The latter reportedly sent one guinea (£1.05) towards the cost of the trophy and then went on to play The Wanderers club, from London, in the final. The match ended 0–0 but because the Scottish club could not afford another trip to London for a replay the trophy was awarded to The Wanderers.

The game developed quickly after that first FA Cup final and it soon took a hold in East Lancashire. The top sides in this part of the county were Blackburn Rovers, Darwen and Blackburn Olympic, but at this stage there was no sign of Preston joining this select band. Instead, North End continued with rugby as the main winter sport but during the 1878–79 season they made their first tentative steps into this new phenomenon.

During that season North End played 15 games, 14 at rugby and one under the new association rules. The rugby had gone well, with ten wins, two draws and only two defeats, and with the team amassing 43 tries along the way. The one game of soccer, as it was to become known, was an experimental match played at Deepdale on 5 October

1878. Without doubt this is the first ever football match that Preston North End played, and it is worth recording the players who took part. They were: H. Turner, (goalkeeper), W. Sudell, J. Sefton, T. Charnley, T. Wadeson, J. Wadeson, C. Miller, T. Parkinson, F. Dodgson, R. Green and H. S. Cartmell who was the Captain and Secretary. The game, against Eagley, was lost 1–0, with the winning goal being a deflected own goal. On the same day the second team were playing rugby against Preston Rangers. A few weeks later, a game aided by a form of electric light was also played at Deepdale, advertised as North End *vs.* Rovers. But this was actually a rugby match played against Preston Rovers. Rugby was to continue as the main winter sport until January 1880. In all probability Preston North End's final rugby game came during this month, when a rival local outfit called Olympic were visiting Deepdale. Things became a little overheated when a maul ensued after a controversial refereeing decision. North End's captain was so incensed that he led his team off the pitch in protest. The following May the club made its biggest decision to date.

It was clear by now that the influence that association football was having on the country was beginning to take effect in Preston. A general meeting of the members of the North End Cricket and Football Club was held at the Deepdale Hotel on 3 May 1880 with Mr William Sudell, who had joined the club in August 1867, occupying the chair. Mr Sudell, a mill manager, was to have a huge influence over the club during the next few years and if ever a man nurtured a dream it was William Sudell. At that crucial meeting it was resolved 'that the club should join the Lancashire Association Football Union, and henceforth play soccer under their rules.' It was also resolved that the name of the club be altered to, 'Preston Athletic Society and North End Cricket and Football Club'. It was to be the most defining moment in the formation of Preston North End as we know it today. There was obviously much enthusiasm for sport in the area and the club was already becoming a focal point for the local community. They had been organising an annual 'North End Sports Day' since 1876.

The autumn of 1880 saw the start of the first year that the club played football throughout the season and ten games are recorded. North End entered the Lancashire Cup for the first time, losing their opening tie 6–0 to Turton, a team from the Bolton area. Some of the other results did not go too well, either, including a 16–0 mauling at the hands of the experienced Blackburn Rovers side. When North End played Darwen they scored their first goal, although unfortunately Darwen scored 14! But the man who holds the honour of scoring North End's first ever goal was one Harry Cartmell, and a crowd of between seven and eight hundred people saw the match. The press had reported, 'that it was the first game of real importance in Preston's first season'. But football was very different in those days, and it is also reported that Cartmell was one of *six* forwards in a formation of 2–2–6! No wonder they let in 14! It was soon obvious that Preston had a steep learning curve to climb and there was much work to do if they wanted to compete on an equal basis with teams like Blackburn Rovers or Darwen. Preston's first win came against Cox Green of Bolton when they won 3–0. William Sudell was in goal for the match and he often played in those early games. For the record the twin centre-forwards, Ainsworth and Nuttall (2) scored the goals. But there were a lot of determined characters involved with North End at the time and other early committee members included, John Woods, William Naylor, Walter Pomfret, William Turner, John Parkinson, Harry Cartmell, Fred Woods, John Sumner, William Whiteside, Thomas Banks, Bethal Robinson, R. Green, W. H. Hulme and J. Milner. Most of these gentlemen had been involved from the beginning and were players in both the rugby and cricket teams. Some even went on to play in the football team and, egged on by a determined Mr Sudell, the club started to make progress. Throughout their history Preston North End have had 'influential local men' involved with the club and in the early 1880s W. E. M. Tomlinson Esquire, was the club's President, and he was also a Member of Parliament. Two years later, the Mayor of Preston, Mr J. Forshaw, replaced Tomlinson as President.

On the football playing front North End were fast learners. Using the maxim that practice makes perfect they threw their energies into playing more and more games. The 1881–82 season saw a significant shift towards making football the number one sport at Deepdale. Fixtures were more than doubled in number and results showed some improvement. They included a 12–3 win over Stackstead Working Men's Club in the Lancashire Cup. However, North End did have a problem with the goalkeeping position at the start of this new season, using five different players in the first five games. They tried Sharp, who had previously played at centre-forward and on the left wing, Parkinson, Chadwick, James Cookson and even William Sudell was given a go. This problem position continued to cause headaches until October 1882, when William Joy came along and made the position his own for a while. Another significant event in 1881–82 showed just how the popularity of the club was growing as new members joined. North End decided to start up a reserve team and the first recorded match for PNE reserves came on New Year's Day, 1882, when Preston lost 5–1 to Preston Parker Street, a team that was later renamed Preston Swifts.

By the time the club's third football season of 1882–83 came along the organisation and performances had risen to a much higher standard. Around this time North End started to advertise their forthcoming games for the first time in the local newspapers, with an admission price of threepence. It showed the increased interest that was being shown in the game that people would pay to go and watch football. During this year 37 fixtures were fulfilled, including, for the first time, two games against Scottish opposition. The connection with Scotland would prove very productive for the club over the next few years, and of course, eventually would give them some of their greatest players. From 1880 to 1883 James McDade played for the club and he is recognised as the first Scotsman in a long line of acquisitions from o'er the border. The affinity with Scotland is something the club has retained right up to the present day. Whenever North End have done well there has invariably been Scotsmen deeply involved and in most seasons there has been a strong Scottish presence.

The first of those significant Scots began to arrive in the 1883–84 season. Some of them would go on to achieve immortality as the 'Old Invincibles.' In many ways this was the start of the build-up to that first ever League Championship, although it was still five years away. But the North End committee knew that they had to find a better class of player if they wanted to make inroads against the bigger teams of the day. The names of some of the players who arrived during this season certainly emphasised that quest for talent. Nick Ross, David Russell, George Drummond, Jimmy Ross, Jack Gordon, Sandy Robertson, Johnny Graham and Sam Thomson all arrived at Deepdale in this defining season. It was no coincidence that Preston's results began to improve drastically, and even the reserves had a good season that year. They won 16 out of 27 games, scoring 123 goals in the process. How did Preston attract this calibre of player? An incident which happened later that season would reveal all. Preston were drawn against Upton Park (London) in the FA Cup and the Londoners protested to the FA, before the match, that Preston were paying their players, a practice of professionalism that was severely outlawed at the time. After the game, which was drawn 1–1 after extra time, the FA decided to disqualify Preston from the competition, upholding Upton Park's protest. William Sudell,

by now known as Major Sudell due to his involvement with the local Rifle Corps, was summoned by the FA, with his fellow club representatives, to answer the charges against his club. But rather than argue against the charges, Sudell stunned everyone by admitting them, and in the club's defence he said, 'Wherever there was a crowd at any sport there was professionalism'. Sudell was cross-examined for nearly two hours, along with his four unnamed colleagues, but strangely neither the treasurer nor the secretary was called upon. The FA also never asked to examine the 'books' though they were readily available. Ironically, the Upton Park representative expressed his club's willingness to pay the whole of the expenses incurred by the Preston deputation visiting London for the meeting. In the end Sudell's stance certainly rocked the game, so much so that not long after this case the FA had a rethink, and professionalism in football was legalised. So, Preston North End have always been credited with being the first professional football team, although almost certainly they had not been the only team to pay their players.

The standard of play had risen so much that during January and February 1884 four North Enders were selected to play for Lancashire: W. Smalley, F. Dewhurst, W. Joy and C. Duckworth. Preston lost only two of 18 games played away from Deepdale and in Jack Belger they had a goalscorer supreme. He scored 42 goals in just 48 games. New boundaries were opened up as the club ventured farther afield to play against more established clubs including Bolton Wanderers and West Bromwich Albion. And gone were the days of being thumped by Blackburn Rovers as North End beat them 3–2 at Deepdale after gaining a hard fought goalless draw away from home against them. A crowd of 3,987 assembled to see Sam Thomson's debut at Deepdale against the Sheffield based side, Lockwood Brothers. He scored four goals in a 9–0 win. Then an improved crowd of 5,236 saw PNE beat a North of England select eleven 5–0 on 23 April 1884, with North End playing a six-man forward line. The season had started on 1 September 1883 and stretched right through until 23 June 1884, when Preston beat the reserve eleven 3–1 with another healthy crowd of 2,101 people being entertained.

With Preston North End's name on the tongues of the football world in Britain, due to the furore surrounding their expulsion from the FA Cup competition, and the much higher level of performance in 1883–84, the club was able to arrange a much better and attractive fixture list for the 1884–85 season. It was amazing to see just how far

Preston North End had come in a very short space of time. Fewer than 4,000 spectators watched North End beat Padiham 10–0 during August 1884, but on the opening day of November the visit of Third Lanark from Scotland drew a crowd of 7,153. Jack Belger, having scored 14 goals in just 17 games, then had the misfortune to break his leg against Great Lever in December. The injury meant that Preston found a successful partnership by pairing Jimmy Ross with Sam Thomson and the celebrated Corinthians side were beaten 3–1 in their first game together in attack. On New Year's day, even Glasgow Rangers came down to challenge the up-and-coming North End team, but again Preston won 3–1, in front of 5,238 fans. During this season the club were to play other top teams for the first time. Notts County, Sheffield Wednesday and Wolverhampton Wanderers all came to play the new rising team from Preston and all went away with their tails between their legs. Then, at the end of April 1885 the famous Aston Villa club challenged Preston, home and away, and just to emphasise the enormous improvement of the Lancashire side their lads rose to the challenge to win 7–2 at Deepdale and 5–1 on Villa's home patch, results that would have been unthinkable just 18 months earlier. By this time Preston had England goalkeeper Billy Rose signed up, replacing local lad Billy Joy. At the other end the goals flowed with Jimmy Ross, Sam Thomson and Jack Gordon each scoring more than 30 apiece. Two home games attracted attendances of over 10,000, with 12,450 watching the match against Bolton and 11,394 against the Corinthians.

When the 1885–86 season began North End's reputation had grown beyond measure. With success breeding success it seemed that everyone wanted to pit their wits against Preston's new-found style of play. Crowds were still fluctuating as people came to terms with the success of the team. A gate of 10,631 assembled at Deepdale to see Preston beat Bolton 5–0, but then only 1,656 saw the 11–3 demolition of Astley Bridge in the FA Cup just three days later. The next game, against Fishwick Ramblers, was watched by 1,996 spectators, and they saw another 11 goals scored. These relatively poor gates may have had some influence on the committee arranging more games away from home than at home. This was the first time this had happened and at one point 12 games out of 16 were played away from Deepdale. Another reason was that everyone wanted to see Preston play and the club's appeal was stretching right across the country as they remained undefeated for the first 54 games, not losing until they played Accrington as late as 26 April 1886. And remember that 14–1 defeat against Darwen in 1880? Now, just six years

later, North End had improved so much that when they met again Preston won 16–0! A team called Earlstown Wanderers fared even worse, losing 19–0 to the rampant Lancastrian side. Even a Lancashire Players Select XI were well beaten as they failed to cope with the excellent free-flowing, free-scoring North Enders. They lost 10–1, with Sam Thomson scoring five of the goals. There were other incredible results, too. Notts County lost 8–2, Nottingham Forest 7–0, WBA 7–0 and Burnley were hammered twice, 8–3 and 9–1! Could the word 'Invincibles' have been first muttered this season, one wonders? Out of 65 games played, 59 were won, with the team scoring a staggering 318 goals along the way. Only 60 were conceded and even with 26 goalscorers untraced Jimmy Ross had a recorded 65 goals, with Johnny Goodall scoring 54, Sam Thomson 48 and Fred Dewhurst 41. It was awesome stuff. The only blot on an otherwise perfect season was expulsion from the FA Cup … again! This time it was because of a registration foul up over George Drummond. It is probably fair to say that North End's dominance in the football world would have seen them through to an FA Cup win had it not been for this poor administration error. There was also some suspicion that the FA were still angry with North End over their stance on professionalism.

Preston's affinity with Scotland was now growing in stature and the 1886–87 season began with the club making a quick tour north of the border before the playing season started. The tour saw Preston play three games in three days: fit or what? Only twelve players were used as North End beat Dundee Strathmore 8–3, Arbroath 6–2, but then lost to Third Lanark 4–2. Within a month Preston journeyed back to Scotland to fulfil an away fixture with the crack Scottish team, Queens Park. They returned to Deepdale with a 6–1 win under their belts. The lads followed this win with an emphatic 6–1 away win over the Rovers at Blackburn, having already beaten them at home by the same score. Revenge is sweet, especially when they followed this up by knocking Rovers out of the Lancashire Cup the very next week by 7–1! Once again double-figure scores were fairly common for this squad of players, as they trounced Notts County 14–0, Loveclough in the Lancashire Cup 12–0, Bolton Wanderers 12–1, Witton 12–0 in the Lancashire Cup semi-final, and just for good measure the FA Cup winners Aston Villa 11–1! Jimmy Ross, nicknamed the 'Little Demon', lead the way in those games with 17 of the goals. Thirty-one goals were registered on the way to lifting the Lancashire Cup where Preston had to play Bolton, at Bolton, in the final. At the

PRESTON 1886

DRAWN AND
PUBLISHED BY
WILLIAM BROWN
CHROMO LITHOGRAPHER, ARTISTIC PRINTER &c
PRESTON.

N. J. ROSS

W. C. ROSE.

R. H. HOWARTH.

D. RUSSELL.

W. SUDELL ESQ.

S. A. ROBERTSON.

J. GRAHAM.

J. GORDON.

S. THOMPSON.

J. GOODALL.

P. P.

G. DRUMMOND.

NORTH END FOOTBALL CLUB

FIRST TEAM.

F. DEWHURST.

FROM PHOTOGRAPHS BY H. WOOTTON, 125 ELLEN ST PRESTON.

end of October 1886, Arthur Wharton, generally recognised as the first black player in football, appeared in goal for North End when they beat Queens Park 3–0 in Glasgow in an FA Cup-tie. Although he played in all that season's FA Cup-ties, including the losing semi-final, he was not first choice custodian; that title fell to Billy Rose who clocked up 44 appearances that year. To emphasise the depth of the squad, on 16 April 1887 North End beat Halliwell away by 7–1. Nothing out of the ordinary in that, one might think, but on that very same afternoon Preston had no fewer than five players representing Lancashire against a United Ulster side. Although the season finished with a 5–0 victory away at Everton on 28 May 1887, another game was played during the summer break, away at Blackpool against a Lancashire XI who were defeated 6–2.

What a season 1887–88 turned out to be! A record 42 successive victories were totalled after North End lost their opening game by 2–1 against Hibernians. James Trainer made his debut in goal for Preston in that game, and he was to be the final piece in the jigsaw of what proved an all-conquering team. Soon Preston North End were the most complete footballing outfit the world had ever seen. As in the previous season three games were played in three days while on a mini-tour of Scotland. Dundee Strathmore were this time beaten 16–2 with Johnny Goodall scoring 9 of the goals. Unbelievably, Preston had been 1–0 down at one stage in this game! Glasgow Rangers were then beaten 8–1, Burnley 7–2 and Derby County 8–0 before Preston then played what was to turn out to be an historic game. It was an FA Cup-tie against Hyde and Preston ran out winners, as every schoolboy knew, by 26 goals to nil. Nine different players were on the scoresheet that day as Preston logged up the biggest win in history, and a record that still stands today. The following week another North End record was set as Lancashire chose nine North End players to represent the Red Rose county. The Lancashire FA had arranged two games on the same afternoon, just as North End had done on a couple of occasions two years previously. Five of the Lilywhites travelled to play Birmingham County while the other four went up to Scotland to play against Dumbartonshire. The desire to see North End play was phenomenal and the committee were forced to arrange a record 70 games as clubs queued up to challenge the unofficial champions of English football. On 26 November 1887 as North End were beating Everton 6–0 in the FA Cup, the club's reserve team was breaking new ground by visiting Ireland, beating Belfast Distillery 3–1. While on the subject of the

reserve team, Heart of Midlothian ventured south to Lancashire on New Year's Day and North End's reserves took them on and beat them 4–1. The first team at the time were in Southport training for the forthcoming epic FA Cup match against Aston Villa. Ironically, Preston's first defeat of the season was in the FA Cup final itself, when they lost 2–1 to WBA. It would seem that no thought was given to resting the players in those days as in one spell Preston again visited Scotland, this time playing five games in just six days. The next day, on the way home, they popped into Workington to play yet another game! One can only presume that the lads received appearance money; certainly the club did as they exploited the Preston North End roadshow to the full.

But the football world had to look out, as the best was yet to come. These pioneering footballers had played a staggering 200 games in just three seasons, scoring over 930 goals in that time. They really were invincible and twelve months later the 'Old Invincibles' nickname was to be carved permanently into Preston North End's history. The rise of the club was spellbinding enough, but the speed at which it was achieved, from nothing to League Champions and FA Cup double winners in just ten glorious years, was nothing short of miraculous.

Major William Sudell, Preston North End chairman and manager when the club first rose to fame.

Major William Sudell

A man with a dream

In 1849 William Sudell was born in Preston, and little did anyone know at the time just what an impact the man would have on the Lancashire town. As a youth he managed to find a job working in the offices of one of the many local cotton mills, Messrs Goodair's Peel Hall Mill, situated close to what is now Deepdale. The young Sudell was apparently adept with figures, earning a reputation for his lightning calculating skills. Not surprisingly he soon rose to the position of manager and was quickly regarded as something of an authority on mill management. In August 1867, by way of recreation, Sudell decided to join the local North End cricket club. It was to prove a life changing decision for him.

Sudell was a player for both the cricket team and later the rugby team, but it was mainly for his managerial prowess that he was propelled onto the committee, becoming chairman soon after the club had leased the field at Deepdale in 1875. When association football came along, Sudell quickly saw the potential and, ably assisted by other sports-minded businessmen, he was instrumental in laying the foundations of the proud town football team that is still going strong to this day. Sudell had a good eye for spotting raw talent and was a quick learner himself, soon realising that a mix of local talent and imported Scottish experienced players was the way forward. He did play a few matches himself early on, but was quick to spot that for the club to move forward they had to find a better quality of player.

William Sudell was the first person to admit to paying players for their services and was at the forefront of the legalisation of professionalism. In a celebrated case he was summoned to the FA to answer charges against his club that North End were breaking the strict rules against paying players. He never denied the charges and stoically made a stance to force the FA into a re-think. Soon professionalism was legalised and Sudell had his way.

By now Sudell was known as 'Major Sudell', brought about by the rank he achieved in his connections with the Rifle Corps of the local volunteer movement, another of his many involvements. And he was already a much sought after personality within the town. He was a genuine sportsman at heart: sincere, generous and very much in demand locally. He was vice-president of the Preston Bicycle Club and the Preston Swimming Club as well as being linked with an array of local junior football and cricket teams. He was later to be a representative of the FA Council and a vice-president of the Lancashire Football Association. He also had a stubborn and determined streak and many times he fell out with the Lancashire FA in those early footballing days. Eventually his organisational skills were noticed by the FA hierarchy, and Sudell was elected treasurer of the newly formed Football League in 1888. The Major's main concern, however, was still his beloved Preston North End, and through the 1880s he assembled a terrific squad of players that was to take the club to the top of the football tree. He ran the club as a virtual dictator through two League Championships and an FA Cup win, and was involved until 1893 when the club became a limited company. Sadly, after that Sudell's life took a downward turn and he was charged with embezzlement of funds from his cotton mill. It is inexplicable why he did this, but he was found guilty and was given a three-year prison sentence. The shame must have been hard for this previously well respected man to take. After his release Sudell had a short spell living in Morecambe, but he soon decided to emigrate with his family to South Africa. Perhaps the shame proved too hard to bear for him. It did not take him too long to carve his niche in South Africa and at the time of his death in 1911, he had been working as a member of the *South African News* editorial staff in Cape Town. Sudell's son, also named William, was later sports editor for the *Cape Argus* newspaper for 36 years.

The sad event in Major William Sudell's later life in no way detracts from the enormous contribution he made to the formation of Preston North End Football Club. If he could see the club as it is today then there would be no prouder man. He had a dream, back in those Victorian days, to make Preston the best team in the land. He brought in the best players and finally achieved that dream when North End were crowned the first League Champions in 1889. Sudell's players really were the Invincibles.

"A Book for the Fans, by the Fans"

SEASON 1888–1889

It was certainly a red letter day for Preston North End Football Club on September 8 1888. That was the day that they played their very first game in the very first Football League season. Preston, and the other eleven clubs in the newly formed competition, began what was to become the greatest sporting challenge of them all. Burnley were the first visitors to Deepdale and they were duly despatched with their tail between their legs and a 5–2 thrashing behind them. It was to set the trend for the season. Five more consecutive wins followed with the 7–0 demolition of Stoke being the highlight. Goals flowed freely with Jimmy Ross scoring ten in those first six games and the team notching an incredible 25 in the same period. The players were all superb, from Jimmy Trainer in goal to George Drummond at outside-left, and really, the other clubs could not live with this high class team. Seven times Preston scored five or more goals in a game, whilst in 13 of the 22 league games they kept a clean sheet. The only blips on an otherwise perfect season were draws against Accrington, Aston Villa, Burnley and Blackburn. All the other games were won to give North End a deserved Championship title, a title they had clinched long before the last game at Aston Villa on 9 February, 1889. Accrington did manage to achieve one remarkable feat in their home game. They stopped Preston scoring, the only team to do it. When the league campaign finished the FA Cup began and

Preston swept through the opposition in that competition as well. In the semi-final they beat WBA, at Bramall Lane, Sheffield and then, in the final they thrashed the Wolves 3–0. That game was played at the world famous cricket ground, the Oval, home of Surrey County Cricket Club. So, North End had won the league without losing a game and the cup without conceding a goal. Invincible records set up by an invincible team. 85 goals in just 27 league and cup games showed just how prolific the front men were and John Goodall topped scored with 22 goals. Jimmy Ross was just behind him on 21. That only told part of the story but it was indeed the key to the success.

DEBUTANTS: (18) Fred Dewhurst, George Drummond, John (Jack) Edwards, Archie Goodall, John Goodall, John (Jack) Gordon, Johnny Graham, William Graham, Bob Holmes, Bob Howarth, Jock Inglis, Dr Robert Mills-Roberts, Alex (Sandy) Robertson, Jimmy Ross, David Russell, Sam Thomson, Jimmy Trainer and Richard Whittle. (NB It is important to note that all of these players had actually played for North End in their pre-Football League days, but for the purposes of this book their appearances during this season were classed as their official first team debuts.)

LAST GAMES: (6) Edwards, Goodall A. L., Goodall J., Graham W., Mills-Roberts and Whittle.

PNE FA Cup winners. Left to right (players only): *Back row*: G. Drummond, R. Howarth, D. Russell, R. Holmes, J. Graham, Dr R. H. Mills-Roberts. *Front row*: J. Gordon, J. Ross, J. Goodall, F. Dewhurst, S. Thomson.

League position in Football League: Champions – P22 W18 D4 L0 F74 A15 Pts 40
Home: W10 D1 L0 F39 A7   Away: W8 D3 L0 F35 A8

Match Report: Late Start but Burnley Hit by North End's quick One-Two – 1 September 1880
Preston 5 Burnley 2

The opening game of the Football League's first ever season was blessed with fine, sunny weather for this very historic occasion. Mind you, it was nearly 3.50 p.m. before the match commenced due to the late arrival of the visitors. Six thousand patient fans lined the Deepdale enclosure anticipating a keenly fought contest, even though Burnley had only won one of the previous 15 games played between the two clubs. The visitors won the toss and elected to kick-off, but straight from the onset Fred Dewhurst won the ball, dribbled his way through a static defence and sent a shot whistling past the post. Bob Holmes repelled the initial Burnley thrust and from his long clearance John Goodall and Jimmy Ross set up Dewhurst who scored North End's first ever league goal after just two minutes play. Within sixty seconds Jack Gordon had secured the second goal, using the bright sunlight to his advantage with a high shot over the Burnley rearguard. The visitors were under real pressure and they were fortunate not to go further behind as Sandy Robertson and Dewhurst both went close. Eventually, Burnley clawed themselves back into the reckoning after 21 minutes as Gallacher scored from close range after good work by Keenan. Within minutes Holmes had to concede a rare corner which came to nothing as Burnley chased an equaliser. Soon after though one of Gordon's accurate crosses was headed home by Dewhurst but the goal was disallowed, much to the disappointment of the crowd. A free-kick had already been awarded by the referee for an infringement off the ball. (One wonders if playing the advantage rule had not been thought of at that time). Burnley began the second half brightly, but Preston's 'little demon' Jimmy Ross soon showed what he could do best, score at ease. He struck North End's third and fourth goals, both courtesy of Dewhurst passes, as gaps appeared within the opposition defensive line. Burnley then fell even further behind when Dewhurst himself, playing a true captain's role, made the score 5–1. With a minute to go the visitors, who seemed in no way discouraged by the scoreline, mounted a final attack which resulted in centre-forward Poland scoring their second goal. The result had meant that Preston had got off to a flying start, and little did they know that they would remain unbeaten in this inaugural Championship plus the FA Cup and therefore go into the record books forever as the first 'double winners'.

League appearances (22 games)

Dewhurst F. 16, Drummond G. 12, Edwards J. B. 4, Goodall A. L. 2, Goodall J. 21, Gordon J. B. 20, Graham J. 22, Graham W. 5, Holmes R. 22, Howarth R. H. 18, Inglis J. 1, Dr Mills-Roberts R. H. 2, Robertson A. S. 21, Ross J. D. 21, Russell D. K. 18, Thomson S. 16, Trainer J. 20, Whittle R. 1.

Goalscorers: 74 League–11 Cup – (Total 85)

Goodall J. 20–2 (22), Ross 19–2 (21), Dewhurst 12–1 (13), Gordon 10–1 (11), Thomson 3–3 (6), Edwards 3–0 (3), Robertson 3–0 (3), Goodall A. L. 1–0 (1), Drummond 1–0 (1), Inglis 1–0 (1), Whittle 1–0 (1), Russell 0–1 (1), Holmes 0–1 (1).

FA Cup appearances (5 games)

Mills-Roberts 5, Howarth 5, Holmes 5, Robertson 1, Drummond 4, Russell 5, Graham J. 5, Gordon 5, Ross 5, Goodall J. 5, Dewhurst 5, Thomson 5.

Season 1888–89: Football League	P	W	D	L	F	A	Pts
1 PRESTON	**22**	**18**	**4**	**0**	**74**	**15**	**40**
2 Aston Villa	22	12	5	5	61	43	29
3 Wolves	22	12	4	6	50	37	28
4 Blackburn	22	10	6	6	66	45	26
5 Bolton	22	10	2	10	63	59	22
6 WBA	22	10	2	10	40	46	22
7 Accrington	22	6	8	8	48	48	20
8 Everton	22	9	2	11	35	46	20
9 Burney	22	7	3	12	42	62	17
10 Derby	22	7	2	13	41	60	16
11 Notts County	22	5	2	15	39	73	12
12 Stoke	22	4	4	14	26	51	12

Bob Howarth, Preston North End 'Old Invincible'. He played for PNE and for England.

Ever presents: (2) Johnny Graham and Bob Holmes.
FA Cup: Winners. **Chairman:** Major William Sudell
Manager: Management Committee. **Hat-tricks:** (4) Gordon, J. Ross (4 goals vs. Stoke), and John Goodall (2).
Leading scorer: 22 goals John Goodall (20 League 2 Cup).
Players used: 18.

AUTHORS' UNOFFICIAL PLAYER OF THE SEASON: The Whole Team.

Trivia Facts:

Three of the North End players were selected for their countries in Internationals during the 1888–89 season. Jimmy Trainer was picked for Wales against England whilst Fred Dewhurst and John Goodall appeared for England in the same match. The game was played at Stoke and England won 4–1 with both the English North Enders scoring a goal against their clubmate. John Goodall went on to play in the match against Scotland later in the season, a match England lost 3–2. That game was played at The Kennington Oval just 13 days after Preston's FA Cup Final victory at the same ground.

Preston's Chairman, Major William Sudell, was a hugely influential man in football at the time. So much so that the League made him their first Honorary Treasurer.

Many publications give the first ever Football League goal as the first one scored by Preston, but the kick-off in their game was delayed 50 minutes so the other games had already completed one half before North End's game had kicked off.

The points scoring system devised for the new league did not come into effect until the November, two months after the season started.

Date 1888-9	Opponents	Comp	h or a	Score	Att.	1	2	3	4	5	6	7	8	9	10	11
Sep 8	Burnley	Div 1	h	5-2		Trainer	Howarth	Holmes	Robertson	Graham W.	Graham J.	Gordon (1)	Ross J. (2)	Goodall J.	Dewhurst (2)	Drummond
Sep 15	Wolverhampton	Div 1	a	4-0		Trainer	Drummond	Holmes	Robertson	Graham W.	Graham J.	Gordon (1)	Ross J. (1)	Goodall J. (1)	Goodall A. (1)	Thomson
Sep 22	Bolton Wanderers	Div 1	h	3-1		Trainer	Howarth	Holmes	Robertson	Russell	Graham J.	Gordon (2)	Ross J.	Thomson	Dewhurst	Drummond (1)
Sep 29	Derby County	Div 1	a	3-2		Trainer	Howarth	Holmes	Robertson (1)	Graham W.	Graham J.	Gordon	Ross J. (2)	Goodall J.	Goodall A.	Drummond
Oct 6	Stoke	Div 1	h	7-0		Trainer	Whittle (1)	Holmes	Robertson	Russell	Graham J.	Gordon	Ross J. (4)	Goodall J. (1)	Dewhurst (1)	Edwards (1)
Oct 13	W.B.A.	Div 1	h	3-0		Trainer	Drummond	Holmes	Robertson	Russell	Graham J.	Gordon	Ross J.	Goodall J.	Dewhurst	Drummond
Oct 20	Accrington	Div 1	a	0-0		Trainer	Howarth	Holmes	Robertson	Russell	Graham J.	Gordon	Ross J.	Goodall J.	Dewhurst	Drummond
Oct 27	Wolverhampton	Div 1	h	5-2		Trainer	Howarth	Holmes	Robertson	Russell	Graham J.	Gordon (1)	Ross J. (1)	Goodall J. (3)	Thomson	Edwards
Nov 3	Notts County	Div 1	h	7-0		Trainer	Howarth	Holmes	Robertson	Russell	Graham J.	Gordon (3)	Ross J. (1)	Goodall J. (3)	Thomson	Drummond
Nov 10	Aston Villa	Div 1	h	1-1		Trainer	Howarth	Holmes	Robertson	Russell	Graham J.	Edwards	Ross J.	Goodall J.	Dewhurst	Drummond
Nov 12	Stoke	Div 1	a	3-0		Trainer	Robertson (1)	Holmes	Graham W.	Russell	Graham J.	Thomson (1)	Ross J. (1)	Goodall J.	Dewhurst (1)	Thomson
Nov 17	Accrington	Div 1	h	2-0		Trainer	Howarth	Holmes	Robertson	Russell	Graham J.	Gordon (1)	Ross J.	Goodall J. (1)	Dewhurst (1)	Thomson
Nov 24	Bolton Wanderers	Div 1	a	5-2		Trainer	Howarth	Holmes	Robertson (1)	Graham W.	Graham J.	Gordon	Ross J. (2)	Goodall J. (2)	Dewhurst (2)	Thomson
Dec 8	Derby County	Div 1	h	5-0		Trainer	Howarth	Holmes	Robertson	Russell	Graham J.	Gordon	Inglis (1)	Goodall J. (2)	Dewhurst	Thomson (1)
Dec 15	Burnley	Div 1	a	2-2		Mills-Roberts	Howarth	Holmes	Robertson	Russell	Graham J.	Gordon	Ross J. (1)	Goodall J.	Dewhurst (1)	Drummond
Dec 22	Everton	Div 1	h	3-0		Trainer	Howarth	Holmes	Robertson	Russell	Graham J.	Gordon (1)	Ross J. (2)	Goodall J. (2)	Dewhurst	Thomson
Dec 26	W.B.A.	Div 1	a	5-0		Trainer	Howarth	Holmes	Robertson	Russell	Graham J.	Gordon	Ross J. (2)	Goodall J. (1)	Dewhurst	Thomson
Dec 29	Blackburn Rovers	Div 1	h	1-0		Trainer	Howarth	Holmes	Robertson	Russell	Graham J.	Gordon	Ross J.	Goodall J. (1)	Dewhurst	Thomson
Jan 5	Notts County	Div 1	h	4-1		Trainer	Howarth	Holmes	Robertson	Russell	Graham J.	Gordon	Ross J.	Goodall J. (2)	Thomson	Edwards (2)
Jan 12	Blackburn Rovers	Div 1	a	2-2		Trainer	Howarth	Holmes	Robertson	Russell	Graham J.	Gordon	Ross J.	Goodall J.	Dewhurst (1)	Thomson (1)
Jan 19	Everton	Div 1	a	2-0		Trainer	Howarth	Holmes	Robertson	Russell	Graham J.	Gordon	Drummond	Goodall J. (1)	Ross J. (1)	Thomson (1)
Feb 2	Bootle Rd 1	FAC	a	3-0		Mills-Roberts	Howarth	Holmes	Robertson	Russell	Graham J.	Gordon (1)	Ross J.	Goodall J. (1)	Dewhurst	Thomson (1)
Feb 9	Aston Villa	Div 1	a	2-0		Mills-Roberts	Howarth	Holmes	Drummond	Russell	Graham J.	Gordon	Ross J.	Goodall J.	Dewhurst (2)	Thomson
Feb 16	Grimsby Rd 2	FAC	a	2-0		Mills-Roberts	Howarth	Holmes	Drummond	Russell	Graham J.	Gordon	Ross J. (1)	Goodall J. (1)	Dewhurst	Thomson
Mar 2	Birmingham St. George's Rd 3	FAC	h	2-0		Mills-Roberts	Howarth	Holmes (1)	Drummond	Russell	Graham J.	Gordon	Ross J.	Goodall J.	Dewhurst	Thomson (1)
Mar 16	W.B.A. Semi-F.	FAC	N	1-0 *	22688	Mills-Roberts	Howarth	Holmes	Drummond	Russell (1)	Graham J.	Gordon	Ross J.	Goodall J.	Dewhurst	Thomson
Mar 30	Wolverhampton Final	FAC	N	3-0 +		Mills-Roberts	Howarth	Holmes	Drummond	Russell	Graham J.	Gordon	Ross J. (1)	Goodall J.	Dewhurst (1)	Thomson (1)
	* Played at Bramall Lane, Sheffield															
	+ Played at The Oval															

SEASON 1889–1890

When you have won it once there is only one thing left to do. Win it again! And that is exactly what Preston North End did in the league's second season. This time though they did not have everything quite as much their own way and their first ever league defeat came in only their second game of the campaign. Stoke had been walloped 10–0 in the opening game so whether some complacency crept in to Preston's play remains unclear, but Aston Villa were the side who broke the club's unbeaten sequence. In fact the Midlands was to become a bit of a graveyard to North End during the season as three of the four defeats came against Midland's teams. But that is the negative side of what was once again a very positive season. The ability to score goals was again the key to success with Preston very prolific in this department. Nick Ross and his brother Jimmy were brought together from the start of the action and they formed a lethal partnership up front. In the first five games they scored 19 goals between them out of the team's total of 27. The club only failed to score in one game during the whole programme of league matches and apart from the Ross boys there were other outstanding contributions. James Trainer and Jack Gordon played in every game and achieved a high level of consistency. Bob Howarth and David Russell, who both missed just the one game, played very well and George Drummond showed some great form on the left-wing, not only creating countless chances for others but also chipping in with 13 goals himself. But the star was undoubtedly Nick Ross. He had rejoined the club from Everton, scored a hat-trick on his league debut for PNE before going on to hit four others which included a four goal haul in the 5–0 win over Derby at Deepdale. The biggest disappointment of the season came after Preston lost their grip on the FA Cup. They went out to local rivals Bolton Wanderers in the third round, 3–2 at home. It was a bitter pill for the fans but they took great consolation from the second consecutive league title. Everton had pushed North End all the way but the race was ended when a last day win over Notts County sealed the championship for the Lilywhites. One thing that remained clear after the dust settled was how important the 5–1 win over Everton on their own ground had been in the November. It gave the club the two point cushion that in the end was to prove decisive.

DEBUTANTS: (7) Frederick Gray, C. Heaton, William Hendry, William Johnstone, Bob Kelso, C. A. Pauls and Nick Ross

LAST GAMES: (9) Graham, Inglis, Russell, Thomson, Gray, Heaton, Johnstone, Pauls and Robertson.

> **League position in Division One: Champions – P22 W15 D3 L4 F71 A30 Pts 33**
> **Home: W8 D1 L2 F41 A12 Away: W7 D2 L2 F30 A18**

League appearances (22 games)

Dewhurst F. 6, Drummond G. 18, Gordon J. B. 22, Graham J. 17, Gray F. J. S. 1, Heaton C. 2, Hendry W. H. 1, Holmes R. 18, Howarth R. H. 21, Inglis J. 2, Johnstone W. 2, Kelso R. 20, Pauls C. A. 3, Robertson A. S. 7, Ross J. D. 21, Ross N. J. 20, Russell D. K. 21, Thomson S. 18, Trainer J. 22

Goalscorers: 71 League–12 Cup – (Total 83)

Ross N. J. 22–2 (24), Ross J. D. 19–2 (21), Drummond 10–3 (13), Thomson 7–1 (8), Gordon 5–1 (6), Russell 4–0 (4), Gillespie 0–2 (2), Inglis 1–0 (1), Heaton 1–0 (1), Gray 1–0 (1), Pauls 0–1 (1), Own Goals 1–0 (1) (Haworth, Accrington)

FA Cup appearances (3 games)

Trainer 3, Howarth 3, Holmes 3, Kelso 3, Russell 2, N. Ross 3, Robertson 1, Drummond 3, Gordon 3, J. Ross 3, Thomson 3, Gillespie 1, Gray 1, Pauls 1.

Ever presents:
(2) Gordon and Trainer
FA Cup: Third Round
Hat-tricks: (7) N. Ross (5) (Including 1 x 4 goals *vs.* Derby), J. Ross (1) and Drummond (1) in the FA Cup.
Manager:
Management Committee
Chairman:
Major William Sudell
Leading scorer:
23 goals – Nick Ross (22 League 1 Cup)
Players used: 19

AUTHORS' UNOFFICIAL PLAYER OF THE SEASON:
Nick Ross

One of the original 'Old Invincibles', Jimmy Ross, later in his career played for Burnley. Jimmy was a top-class goalscorer, 1889–90.

Match report: Silence of the Lambs – 21 Sept 1889 Aston Villa 5 Preston 3.

Preston North End, still unbeaten in league football, arrived in Birmingham full of confidence on the back of their opening day 10–0 thrashing of Stoke. Johnny Graham won the toss and decided to let Villa face the sun. Straight from the kick-off it was flowing end to end football with both goalkeepers being kept busy. After 20 minutes play Russell fouled in front of goal (pre penalty days) and from the resultant free kick Cowan registered Villa's first goal from Hunter's pass. North End responded well and won a couple of corners, but Warner excelled in goal for Villa. An equaliser soon arrived however when Drummond and Jimmy Ross set up an opportunity for Nick Ross who duly scored. But within two minutes an error by Bob Holmes let in Dickson and Gray. Dickson's attempt was well saved by Trainer but Gray, following up, made the score 2–1 to Villa with half an hour played. North End once again surged forward and had plenty of the play but they fell for the sucker punch just prior to half-time when Brown, amid tremendous cheers made it 3–1. The pattern of the game stayed the same at the start of the second half and once again play flowed from end to end. Open football was played by two very good teams with counter attacks in abundance. From one of these Dickson centred for Allen to make it 4–1. North End, in what was for them a very unusual position, became disorganised and it ended with another rush on their goal and Cowan adding a fifth goal for Villa. With the game seemingly won Villa eased off but the Ross brothers, playing for pride, combined for Jimmy Ross to score two consolation goals for Preston. Both went in amid a deafening silence. *The Daily News* commented that 'The inexplicable result, for the time being, ought to have a stimulating and beneficial effect on football. The absolute supremacy of one club is not altogether a good thing and now that Aston Villa have lowered their colours, other clubs will no doubt go onto the field against Preston with greater hope!'

STAT FACTS:
Best home run without defeat: 4 games
Best away run without defeat: 7 games
Longest run unbeaten: 7 games
Longest run without a win: 2 games

Season 1889–90: Football League

	P	W	D	L	F	A	Pts
1 PRESTON	22	15	3	4	71	30	33
2 Everton	22	14	3	5	65	40	31
3 Blackburn	22	12	3	7	78	41	27
4 Wolves	22	10	5	7	51	38	25
5 WBA	22	11	3	8	47	50	25
6 Accrington	22	9	6	7	53	56	24
7 Derby	22	9	3	10	43	55	21
8 Aston Villa	22	7	5	10	43	51	19
9 Bolton	22	9	1	12	54	65	19
10 Notts County	22	6	5	11	43	51	17
11 Burnley	22	4	5	13	36	65	13
12 Stoke	22	3	4	15	27	69	10

Date 1889-90	Opponents	Comp	h or a	Score	Att.	1	2	3	4	5	6	7	8	9	10	11		
Sep 14	Stoke	Div 1	h	10-0		Trainer	Howarth	Holmes	Kelso	Russell (1)	Graham	Gordon	J.Ross (2)	N.Ross (3)	Thomson (2)	Drummond (2)		
Sep 21	Aston Villa	Div 1	a	3-5		Trainer	Howarth	Holmes	Kelso	Russell	Graham	Gordon	J.Ross (2)	N.Ross (1)	Thomson	Drummond		
Sep 28	Burnley	Div 1	a	3-0		Trainer	Howarth	Holmes	Robertson	Kelso	Graham	Gordon	Inglis	N.Ross (3)	Thomson	Drummond		
Oct 5	WBA	Div 1	h	5-0		Trainer	Howarth	Holmes	Kelso	Russell	Graham	Gordon	J.Ross (3)	N.Ross (1)	Inglis (1)	Drummond		
Oct 12	Bolton Wanderers	Div 1	a	6-2		Trainer	Howarth	Holmes	Kelso	Russell	Graham	Gordon (1)	J.Ross (1)	N.Ross (3)	Thomson	Drummond (1)		
Oct 19	Derby County	Div 1	a	1-2		Trainer	Kelso	Holmes	Graham	Russell	Robertson	Gordon	J.Ross (1)	N.Ross	Thomson	Drummond		
Oct 26	Wolverhampton W	Div 1	h	0-2		Trainer	Howarth	Holmes	Kelso	Russell	Graham	Gordon	J.Ross	Thomson	Dewhurst	Drummond		
Nov 2	Blackburn Rovers	Div 1	a	4-3		Trainer	Howarth	Holmes	Kelso	Russell	Graham	Gordon	J.Ross (1)	N.Ross (1)	Dewhurst	Drummond (2)		
Nov 9	Accrington	Div 1	h	3-1		Trainer	Howarth	Holmes	Kelso	Russell	Graham	Gordon (1)	J.Ross	N.Ross (1)	Thomson	Drummond (1)		
Nov 11	Stoke	Div 1	a	2-1		Trainer	Howarth	Holmes	Kelso	Robertson	Russell	Gordon (1)	J.Ross	N.Ross	Thomson (1)	Drummond		
Nov 16	Everton	Div 1	a	5-1		Trainer	Howarth	N. Ross	Kelso	Russell (2)	Graham	Gordon (1)	J.Ross (1)	Thomson (1)	Dewhurst	Drummond		
Nov 23	Bolton Wanderers	Div 1	h	3-1		Trainer	Howarth	Holmes	Robertson	Russell (1)	Graham	Gordon	J.Ross (1)	N.Ross	Thomson	Drummond (1)		
Nov 30	Burnley	Div 1	h	6-0		Trainer	Howarth	Holmes	Robertson	Russell	Graham	Gordon (1)	J.Ross (2)	N.Ross (2)	Thomson	Gray (1)		
Dec 7	Blackburn Rovers	Div 1	h	1-1		Trainer	Howarth	N.Ross	Kelso	Russell	Graham	Gordon	J.Ross (1)	Thomson	Dewhurst	Heaton		
Dec 21	Everton	Div 1	h	1-2		Trainer	Howarth	Holmes	Kelso	Russell	Graham	Gordon	J.Ross	Thomson	Dewhurst	Drummond (1)		
Dec 25	Aston Villa	Div 1	h	3-2		Trainer	Howarth	Holmes	Kelso	Russell	Graham	Gordon	J.Ross	N.Ross (3)	Johnstone	Drummond		
Dec 26	WBA	Div 1	a	2-2		Trainer	Howarth	Holmes	Kelso	Russell	Graham	Gordon	J.Ross (2)	N.Ross	Johnstone	Drummond		
Jan 4	Wolverhampton W	Div 1	a	1-0		Trainer	Howarth	Holmes	Kelso	Russell	Robertson	Gordon	J.Ross	Drummond	Heaton (1)	Drummond		
Jan 11	Derby County	Div 1	h	5-0		Trainer	Howarth	Holmes	Kelso	Russell	Robertson	Gordon	J.Ross	N.Ross (4)	Thomson	Drummond (1)		
Jan 18	Newton Heath	Rd 1 FAC	h	6-1		Trainer	Howarth	Holmes	Kelso	Russell	Robertson	Gordon (1)	J.Ross (1)	N.Ross (1)	Thomson	Drummond (3)		
Feb 1	Lincoln City	Rd 2 FAC	h	4-0		Trainer	Howarth	Holmes	Kelso	N.Ross (1)	Drummond	Gordon	J.Ross (1)	Thomson	Gillespie (2)	Gray		
Feb 15	Bolton Wanderers	Rd 3 FAC	h	2-3		Trainer	Howarth	Holmes	Kelso	Russell	Drummond	Gordon	J.Ross	N.Ross	Thomson (1)	Pauls (1)		
Mar 1	Notts County	Div 1	h	4-3		Trainer	Howarth	N.Ross	Kelso	Russell	Holmes	Gordon	J.Ross (1)	Thomson (2)	Pauls	Drummond (1)		
Mar 15	Accrington	Div 1	a	2-2		Trainer	Howarth	N.Ross	Kelso	Russell	Holmes	Gordon	J.Ross (1)	Thomson	Dewhurst	Pauls	1 o.g.	(Haworth)
Mar 27	Notts County	Div 1	a	1-0		Trainer	Howarth	N.Ross	Kelso	Russell	Graham	Gordon	J.Ross	Hendry	Thomson (1)	Pauls		

SEASON 1890–1891

Everton gained their revenge over Preston with their first Championship win in 1891. This time they pipped North End by two points which was ironic, especially as the Deepdale club did the league double over the Liverpool side. In actual fact this was a much closer title race all round as only four points separated the first five clubs. Preston were having a few problems on and off the field but the missing ingredient in Preston's play was goals. In the first two league seasons they scored 74 and 71 goals but this year only 44 were managed. The advent of the transfer fee was having an effect on most clubs and Preston, a club who had always attracted players simply because of their giant status in the game, were probably having as much difficulty as most in coming to terms with the new idea. New players were being tracked and approached but the standard of player coming in did not always meet the criteria needed for such a high standard of play in the Football League. Some of the stars from previous years were also finding life difficult. The Ross brothers had very different seasons with Nick playing most of the season at left-back whilst Jimmy only played in just over half the games due to injury. As a result they scored only one and five goals respectively and Hugh Gallacher ended as top scorer with just six goals. Ten new players were tried and amazingly five of them scored on their debuts for the club. Jimmy Trainer had another consistent season in goal and Bob Holmes gave him great support in defence. George Drummond also played well whilst of the new players, Gallacher and Billy Stewart were the pick. Preston's Deepdale record was excellent with only one game lost, (although, annoyingly to Blackburn, who later achieved the double over their arch rivals), but away from home Preston had problems, losing six games. Funnily enough they never drew one game away from home and one or two of those points lost may have made all the difference. The FA Cup brought more disappointment as Preston were knocked out in the first round by Stoke, who had been suspended from the league at the time. It was a heavy defeat too, by 3–0, and that was unusual in a season where Preston had far and away the best defensive record in the league games. Only 23 goals were conceded, just five at Deepdale, and incredibly six of those came in one disastrous match at Burnley in the March. It was a strange result in a season when Preston were struggling to replace the Old Invincibles as those players gradually moved on. Having said that it was still a magnificent achievement for North End, even despite their obvious difficulties, to push Everton all the way.

DEBUTANTS: (10) James Brandon, William Campbell, Bernard Crossan, Sammy Dobson, John Drummond, Hugh Gallacher, William McKenna, Thomas Metcalf, Harry Raeside and William Stewart.

LAST GAMES (10) Hendry, Kelso, Brandon, Campbell, Crossan, Dobson, Drummond J., Metcalf, Raeside and Dewhurst F.

Ever presents:
(2) Bob Holmes and Jimmy Trainer
FA Cup: First Round
Hat-tricks: None
Manager:
Management Committee
Chairman:
Major William Sudell
Leading scorer: 6 goals – Hugh Gallacher (all league)
Players used: 20
AUTHORS' UNOFFICIAL PLAYER OF THE SEASON:
Bob Holmes

STAT FACTS:
Best home run without defeat: 8 games
Best away run without defeat: 2 games
Longest run unbeaten: 6 games
Longest run without a win: 4 games

Trivia Facts:
Jock Ewart, who was to make 35 appearances for North End between 1928 and 1930, was born on the 14 February 1891.

In the 1890–91 Lancashire Cup Preston had a bye in the first round and then beat Newton Heath at Deepdale 3–1 in the next round. This took them to a semi-final, (after only one game!), which was played at Blackburn against Darwen. North End lost 2–1. The four goals came from Gordon, Jimmy Ross, Crossan and Gallacher.

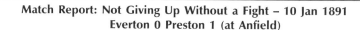

Match Report: Not Giving Up Without a Fight – 10 Jan 1891
Everton 0 Preston 1 (at Anfield)

Prior to this encounter, Everton were league leaders, having gained 29 points from 20 games. North End, on the other hand, only had 16 points, but to date they had played just 14 games leaving them six games in hand over the Toffees. Preston were not surrendering their title easily and a tough game was envisaged. So, on a hard ground covered with fine cinders and sawdust, Preston kicked off and before the ball had travelled 20 yards the first foul had been committed. The start was full of fast and direct football with Jack Gordon being particularly prominent. William Campbell, after a long run from the half-way line, shot low and hard but saw his effort narrowly miss Jardine's post. After 15 minutes the referee had to stop the game as he spotted one of the Everton players wearing 'illegal footwear'. Whenever Everton got near James Trainer's goal they came across their former player, Nick Ross, and he was in a 'thou shall not pass' frame of mind. After 25 minutes play Bob Holmes's long kick found Hugh Gallacher and his headed pass was perfect for Barney Crossan to score the opening goal on what was his league debut. As the minutes ticked by it was North End who were controlling the game, George Drummond feeding his forwards well from the half-back position. As was normal it was all out attack from both teams but Everton's forwards were struggling against the strong defence of the Champions. During the second half the Everton players were seemingly rougher in their approach and most of the referee's decisions went against them. Their best effort came midway through the half, with Geary sending a splendid long shot past the angle of crossbar and post. Many of the 15,000 spectators thought that he had equalised but when Trainer took the resultant goal kick the groans of the home fans were heard all around the ground. North End continued to defend well and proved the stronger of the two sides, holding on to their lead until the final whistle. It was a vital win but alas, in the end, Preston were pipped to the title by Everton. It was a case of points in the bag being better than games in hand, and how often that has been proved over the years.

James Trainer,
PNE 'Old Invincible'
and 'Prince of Goalkeepers'.
Capped for Wales while in North End Reserves, Trainer played in some of the Rawcliffe Charity Cup games.

League appearances: (22 games)

Brandon J. 8, Campbell W. C. 4, Crossan B. 7, Dewhurst F. 2, Dobson S. 8, Drummond G. 21, Drummond J. 11, Gallacher H. 16, Gordon J.B. 18, Hendry W.H. 14, Holmes R. 22, Howarth R. H. 6, Kelso R. 18, McKenna W. 8, Metcalf T. 1, Raeside H. 2, Ross N. J. 21, Ross J. D. 13, Stewart W. S. 20, Trainer J. 22

FA Cup appearances (1 game)

Trainer, Holmes, Ross N., Drummond G., Hendry, Stewart, Gordon, McKenna, Campbell, Drummond J. and Gallacher all one each.

Goalscorers: 44 League only.

Gallacher 6, Ross J. 5, Dobson 5, Gordon 5, Campbell 4, Drummond G. 4, Drummond J. 4, Brandon 3, Crossan 3, McKenna 2, Metcalf 1, Dewhurst 1, Ross N. 1.

Season 1890–91: Football League

	P	W	D	L	F	A	Pts
1 Everton	22	14	1	7	63	29	29
2 PRESTON	22	12	3	7	44	23	27
3 Notts County	22	11	4	7	52	35	26
4 Wolves	22	12	2	8	39	50	26
5 Bolton	22	12	1	9	47	34	25
6 Blackburn	22	11	2	9	52	43	24
7 Sunderland	22	10	5	7	51	31	23*
8 Burney	22	9	3	10	52	63	21
9 Aston Villa	22	7	4	11	45	58	18
10 Accrington	22	6	4	12	28	50	16
11 Derby	22	7	1	14	47	81	15
12 WBA	22	5	2	15	34	57	12

*Two points deducted for fielding Ned Doig against WBA on 20 September 1890 before the League had approved his registration from Arbroath.

Trivia Facts

On 29 November 1890 PNE, playing at Wolverhampton, had their dressing room visited by a thief. Eight North End players had possessions stolen including Bob Holmes, sixpence halfpenny (3p), Jack Gordon, a halfpenny and his pipe, Nick Ross, half an ounce of tobacco and Geordie Drummond who lost one pack of cards and a small gold locket. The thief left his sandwich though!

Jimmy Trainer and Nick Ross played for a Football League eleven against a Football Alliance side on April 20 1891.

League position in Division One: Runners-up – P22 W12 D3 L7 F44 A23 Pts 27
Home: W7 D3 L1 F30 A5 Away: W5 D0 L6 F14 A18

Date 1890-91	Opponents	Comp	h or a	Score	Att.	1	2	3	4	5	6	7	8	9	10	11
Sep 13	WBA	Div 1	h	3-0		Trainer	Holmes	N.Ross	Kelso	Hendry	Stewart	Gordon	J.Ross	Brandon (1)	J.Drummond (1)	G.Drummond (1)
Sep 20	Derby County	Div 1	a	3-1		Trainer	Howarth	N.Ross	Kelso	Hendry	Holmes	Gordon	J.Ross (1)	Brandon	Dobson (1)	G.Drummond (1)
Sep 27	Bolton W	Div 1	h	1-0		Trainer	Howarth	N.Ross	Kelso	Stewart	Holmes	Gordon (1)	J.Ross	Gallacher	Brandon	G.Drummond
Oct 4	Blackburn Rovers	Div 1	h	1-2		Trainer	Holmes	N.Ross	Kelso	Hendry	Stewart	Gordon	J.Ross	Gallacher (1)	Brandon	G.Drummond
Oct 11	Accrington	Div 1	a	3-1		Trainer	Holmes	N.Ross	Kelso	Hendry	Stewart	Gordon	J.Ross	Brandon (2)	Gallacher (1)	G.Drummond
Oct 18	Wolverhampton W	Div 1	h	5-1		Trainer	Holmes	N.Ross	Kelso	Hendry	Stewart	Gordon (1)	J.Ross (1)	Brandon	Dobson (2)	J.Drummond (1)
Oct 25	Blackburn Rovers	Div 1	a	0-1		Trainer	Howarth	N.Ross	Kelso	Holmes	Hendry	Gordon	J.Ross	J.Drummond	Dobson	G.Drummond
Nov 1	Accrington	Div 1	h	1-1		Trainer	Holmes	N.Ross	Kelso	Hendry	Stewart	Gordon	Brandon	G.Drummond	Dobson (1)	J.Drummond
Nov 8	Notts County	Div 1	h	0-0		Trainer	Holmes	N.Ross	Kelso	Hendry	Stewart	Gordon	McKenna	G.Drummond	Gallacher	J.Drummond
Nov 15	Bolton W	Div 1	a	0-1		Trainer	Howarth	N.Ross	Kelso	Holmes	Stewart	Gordon	McKenna	G.Drummond	J.Drummond	Gallacher
Nov 22	Everton	Div 1	h	2-0		Trainer	Holmes	N.Ross	Kelso	Hendry	Stewart	Gordon	Dobson	G.Drummond (1)	J.Drummond	Gallacher (1)
Nov 29	Wolverhampton W	Div 1	a	0-2		Trainer	Holmes	N.Ross	Kelso	Hendry	Stewart	Gordon	Dobson	G.Drummond	J.Drummond	Gallacher
Dec 6	Notts County	Div 1	a	1-2		Trainer	Holmes	N.Ross	G.Drummond	Hendry	Stewart	Gordon	Dobson	Brandon	J.Drummond	Gallacher (1)
Dec 20	Derby County	Div 1	h	6-0		Trainer	Holmes	N.Ross	G.Drummond	Hendry	Stewart	Gordon (1)	Dobson (1)	McKenna (1)	J.Drummond (2)	Gallacher (1)
Jan 10	Everton	Div 1	a	1-0		Trainer	Holmes	N.Ross	G.Drummond	Hendry	Stewart	Gordon	J.Drummond	Campbell	Crossan (1)	Gallacher
Jan 17	Stoke Rd 1	FAC	a	0-3		Trainer	Holmes	N.Ross	G.Drummond	Hendry	Stewart	Gordon	McKenna	Campbell	J.Drummond	Gallacher
Jan 24	Aston Villa	Div 1	h	4-1		Trainer	Howarth	Holmes	G.Drummond	Hendry	Stewart	Metcalf (1)	McKenna	Campbell (1)	Crossan (2)	Gallacher (1)
Feb 5	Burnley	Div 1	h	7-0		Trainer	Holmes	N.Ross (1)	Kelso	G.Drummond	Stewart	Gordon (1)	J.Ross (2)	Campbell (2)	Crossan	Gallacher (1)
Feb 7	WBA	Div 1	a	3-1		Trainer	Holmes	N.Ross	Kelso	G.Drummond	Stewart	Gordon (1)	J.Ross (1)	Campbell (1)	Crossan	McKenna
Feb 21	Sunderland	Div 1	h	0-0		Trainer	Holmes	N.Ross	Kelso	G.Drummond	Stewart	Gordon	J.Ross	McKenna	Crossan	Gallacher
Mar 7	Burnley	Div 1	a	2-6		Trainer	Howorth	Holmes	Kelso	G.Drummond (1)	Stewart	N.Ross	J.Ross	Dewhurst (1)	Crossan	Gallacher
Mar 9	Aston Villa	Div 1	a	1-0		Trainer	Holmes	N.Ross	Kelso	G.Drummond	Stewart	McKenna (1)	J.Ross	Raeside	Crossan	Gallacher
Mar 14	Sunderland	Div 1	a	0-3		Trainer	Holmes	N.Ross	Kelso	G.Drummond	Stewart	McKenna	J.Ross	Raeside	Dewhurst	Gallacher

SEASON 1891–1892

Preston again finished runners-up in this, the fourth league championship, but in this season it was a three horse race between Sunderland, North End and Bolton for the title. Home wins against each were cancelled out by heavy defeats at both Roker Park and Burnden Park and in the end it came down to the number of goals scored. Two extra clubs meant four extra games but once again Preston had the best defensive record in the league and only Sunderland and Aston Villa hit more than their 61 goals. Jimmy Ross found his goal touch again and George Drummond also scored his fair share including one marvellous four goal haul in a 6–0 home win over Notts County. Preston began the season badly, losing four of their opening six games. Again there was a distinct lack of drawn matches, only one in fact, but after that opening and from the October, Preston put together a run of 15 games where 14 were won and the other was drawn. Ironically the important game at Sunderland came at the end of that run. At the time Preston were six points in front of the Wearsiders although Sunderland had three games in hand, so it was a vital game. But the 4–1 win for the champions elect all but ended Preston's hopes as they were to lose two more games whilst Sunderland won those extra games they had to play. Jimmy Trainer continued his superb consistency in goal and played in all the games. Three other players were ever present. Moses Sanders, a local boy who was built like a house, was a tower of strength at centre-half, Hugh Gallacher who played at

outside-left and Jimmy Ross who ended up leading scorer with 18 league and cup goals. In the FA Cup Preston beat a team called Middlesbrough Ironopolis in round one, and then beat Middlesbrough in round two. Unfortunately their involvement in the competition ended in the next round when they were beaten by Nottingham Forest. Meanwhile in the league Sunderland gradually pulled away from the rest and won the title by a clear five points in the end. Their phenomenal 93 goals had meant that they were too powerful for the other teams. For Preston though there were plenty of good individual displays and Billy Stewart, Bob Holmes and Jack Gordon all gave excellent service whilst Frank Becton looked promising when he played.

DEBUTANTS: (10) Frank Becton, William Greer, John Holmes, Tinsley Lindley, Frank Norris, Bob Roberts, Moses Sanders, James Sharp, J. S. Taylor and Thomas Towie.

LAST GAMES: (6) McKenna, Lindley, Norris, Roberts, Taylor and Towie.

Bob Holmes in his England kit.

League position in Division One: Runners-up – P26 W18 D1 L7 F61 A31 Pts 37
Home: W12 D0 L1 F42 A8 Away: W6 D1 L6 F19 A23

Becton F. 10, Drummond G. 23, Gallacher H. 26, Gordon J. B. 25, Greer W. H. 1, Holmes J. 1, Holmes R. 25, Howarth R. H. 2, Lindley T. 1, McKenna W. 3, Norris F. 3, Roberts R. 5, Ross J. D. 26, Ross N. J. 16, Sanders M. 26, Sharp J. 19, Stewart W. S. 25, Taylor J. S. 1, Towie T. 22, Trainer J. 26.

FA Cup appearances (3 games*.)

Trainer 3, Holmes R. 3, Ross N. 3, Sharp 3, Sanders 3, Stewart 3, Gordon 3, Ross J. 3, Becton 3, Towie 3 and Gallacher 3.

*The FA Cup game against Middlesbrough Ironopolis on January 16 was completed but later declared void. For the purposes of this book the appearances and goals are not included as the match was expunged from the official records of the club.

Goalscorers: 61 League–8 Cup (Total 69)

Ross J. 16–2 (18), Drummond 12–0 (12), Towie 9–1 (10), Becton 5–2 (7), Gordon 6 (2pens)–0 (6), Gallacher 3–1 (4), Stewart 2–1 (3), Sanders 2–0 (2), Sharp 1–1 (2), Ross N. 1–0 (1), Taylor 1–0 (1), Greer 1–0 (1), Own Goals 2–0 (2) (Jones of Bolton and Underwood of Stoke)

Match report: Farcical Football – 12 Dec. 1891 Preston 6 Notts County 0

Nobody would have guessed before the start of this league match just what a farce it would turn out to be. Two players sent off, one returning later to score four goals, and then Notts County ending the game with only five players on the pitch. With only around 500 spectators on the Deepdale enclosure at the start, snow was on the pitch and still falling as Notts County kicked off, uphill and against the bitter, biting wind. After a quarter of an hour's play Preston took the lead with a goal by Nick Ross. Then, after 30 minutes the trouble began as Osborn deliberately fouled George Drummond and then punched him. It resulted in both players being sent off and the referee telling them to finish their fighting off the pitch, adding that they could come back on when it was done. The indignant pair took him to his word and indulged in further rough play, to the great edification of the crowd. Drummond did come back onto the pitch but Osborn refused. Within five minutes of play resuming Drummond actually scored amid much ill feeling on the pitch. The adrenalin was obviously pumping in Drummond though as he bagged another goal before half-time. Straight after the break North End thought they had scored a fourth goal but the ball stuck in the snow just before it reached the goalline. Jimmy Ross and Drummond were now running riot against County's ten men, obviously adapting to the conditions better than their still aggrieved opponents. It reached the stage where County were continually penned into their own goal area. Hugh Gallacher, Jack Gordon and William Stewart all had good chances to further the score but failed to take them. On 75 minutes Drummond scored his hat-trick goal from yet another corner. At this stage it was reported that 'someone went onto the field and spoke to the Notts players, five of whom left the field'. The referee however ordered that the game should continue in what was by now farcical circumstances. Toone was top class in goal for County but was inevitably beaten again by Drummond. It was now a complete farce with the four remaining outfield players of County trying to play North End offside! However Jimmy Ross ran clean through to score the game's sixth and final goal. As a footnote one of the Notts County players who stayed on was called Harry B. Daft!

Date 1891-2	Opponents	Comp	h or a	Score	Att.	1	2	3	4	5	6	7	8	9	10	11		
Sep 5	Notts County	Div 1	a	0-2		Trainer	R.Holmes	Drummond	Sharp	Sanders	Stewart	Gordon	J.Ross	Towie	McKenna	Gallacher		
Sep 7	Burnley	Div 1	a	0-2		Trainer	R.Holmes	Drummond	Sharp	Sanders	Stewart	Gordon	J.Ross	Towie	McKenna	Gallacher		
Sep 12	Sunderland	Div 1	h	3-1		Trainer	R.Holmes	N.Ross	Sharp	Sanders	Stewart	Gordon (1)	J.Ross	Towie (1)	Drummond (1)	Gallacher		
Sep 19	Aston Villa	Div 1	h	0-1		Trainer	Howarth	R.Holmes	Sharp	Sanders	Stewart	Gordon	J.Ross	Towie	Drummond	Gallacher		
Sep 21	Burnley	Div 1	h	5-1		Trainer	Howarth	R.Holmes	McKenna	Sanders (1)	Stewart (1)	Gordon (1)	J.Ross	Towie (1)	Drummond (1)	Gallacher		
Sep 26	Bolton W	Div 1	a	0-3		Trainer	R.Holmes	Norris	Sharp	Sanders	Stewart	Gordon	J.Ross	Towie	Drummond	Gallacher		
Oct 3	Wolverhampton W	Div 1	a	2-0		Trainer	R.Holmes	Norris	Sharp	Sanders	Stewart	Gordon	J.Ross (1)	Towie	Drummond	Gallacher		
Oct 10	Everton	Div 1	a	1-1		Trainer	R.Holmes	N.Ross	Sharp	Sanders	Stewart	Gordon	J.Ross	Drummond	Towie (1)	Gallacher		
Oct 24	Blackburn R	Div 1	a	4-2		Trainer	R.Holmes	N.Ross	Sharp	Sanders	Stewart	Gordon (1p)	J.Ross (1)	Towie (1)	Drummond (1)	Gallacher		
Oct 31	Everton	Div 1	h	4-0		Trainer	R.Holmes	N.Ross	Sharp	Sanders	Stewart	Gordon	J.Ross (1)	Drummond (1)	Towie (1)	Gallacher		
Nov 7	Stoke	Div 1	h	1-0		Trainer	R.Holmes	N.Ross	Sharp	Sanders	Stewart	Gordon	J.Ross (1)	Drummond	Towie	Gallacher		
Nov 14	Blackburn R	Div 1	h	3-2		Trainer	R.Holmes	N.Ross	Sharp	Sanders	Stewart	Gordon	J.Ross (2)	Drummond (1)	Towie	Gallacher		
Nov 21	WBA	Div 1	a	2-1		Trainer	R.Holmes	Drummond	Sharp	Sanders	Stewart	Gordon	J.Ross (2)	Towie	Becton	Gallacher		
Nov 28	Bolton W	Div 1	h	4-0		Trainer	R.Holmes	Drummond	Sharp	Sanders	Stewart	Gordon (1p)	J.Ross (1)	Becton (1)	Towie	Gallacher	1 o.g.	(Jones)
Dec 5	Derby County	Div 1	a	2-1		Trainer	R.Holmes	Drummond	Sharp (1)	Sanders	Stewart	Gordon	J.Ross	Becton (1)	Towie	Gallacher		
Dec 12	Notts County	Div 1	h	6-0		Trainer	R.Holmes	N.Ross (1)	Sharp	Sanders	Stewart	Gordon	J.Ross (1)	Drummond (4)	Towie	Gallacher		
Dec 25	Stoke	Div 1	h	3-2		Trainer	R.Holmes	N.Ross	Sharp	Sanders (1)	Stewart (1)	Gordon	J.Ross	Drummond	Towie	Gallacher	1 o.g.	(Underwood)
Jan 1	Darwen	Div 1	a	4-0		Trainer	R.Holmes	N.Ross	Sharp	Sanders	Stewart	Gordon (1)	J.Ross	Drummond (1)	Towie (1)	Gallacher (1)		
Jan 2	Accrington	Div 1	a	3-1		Trainer	R.Holmes	N.Ross	Sharp	Sanders	Stewart	Gordon	J.Ross (2)	Drummond	Towie (1)	Gallacher		
Jan 9	WBA	Div 1	h	1-0		Trainer	R.Holmes	N.Ross	Sharp	Sanders	Stewart	Gordon	J.Ross	Becton	Towie	Gallacher (1)		
Jan 23	Middlbro Ironopolis Rd1	FAC	h	6-0		Trainer	R.Holmes	N.Ross	Sharp (1)	Sanders	Stewart (1)	Gordon	J.Ross (1)	Becton (2)	Towie (1)	Gallacher		
Jan 30	Middlesbrough Rd 2	FAC	a	2-1		Trainer	R.Holmes	N.Ross	Sharp	Sanders	Stewart	Gordon	J.Ross (1)	Becton	Towie	Gallacher (1)		
Feb 13	Nottm Forest Rd 3	FAC	a	0-2		Trainer	R.Holmes	N.Ross	Sharp	Sanders	Stewart	Gordon	J.Ross	Becton	Towie	Gallacher		
Mar 5	Derby County	Div 1	h	3-0		Trainer	R.Holmes	N.Ross	J.Holmes	Sanders	Stewart	Becton (1)	J.Ross (1)	Taylor (1)	Gallacher			
Mar 12	Sunderland	Div 1	a	1-4		Trainer	R.Holmes	N.Ross	Roberts	Sanders	Stewart	Gordon	J.Ross (1)	Lindley	Gallacher			
Apr 2	Wolverhampton W	Div 1	a	0-3		Trainer	N.Ross	Norris	Drummond	Sanders	Roberts	Gordon	Towie	J.Ross	Becton	Gallacher		
Apr 15	Accrington	Div 1	h	4-1		Trainer	R.Holmes	N.Ross	Roberts	Sanders	Stewart	Gordon	J.Ross	Drummond (1)	Becton (2)	Gallacher (1)		
Apr 16	Aston Villa	Div 1	h	1-3		Trainer	R.Holmes	N.Ross	Sharp	Stewart	Sanders	Gordon	J.Ross	Drummond (1)	Becton	Gallacher		
Apr 18	Darwen	Div 1	h	4-0		Trainer	R.Holmes	Drummond	Stewart	Sanders	Roberts	Greer (1)	Becton	J.Ross (2)	Towie (1)	Gallacher		

Season 1891–92 Football League

		P	W	D	L	F	A	Pts
1	Sunderland	26	21	0	5	93	36	42
2	PRESTON	26	18	1	7	61	31	37
3	Bolton	26	17	2	7	51	37	36
4	Aston Villa	26	15	0	11	89	56	30
5	Everton	26	12	4	10	49	49	28
6	Wolves	26	11	4	11	59	46	26
7	Burney	26	11	4	11	49	45	26
8	Notts County	26	11	4	11	55	51	26
9	Blackburn	26	10	6	10	58	65	26
10	Derby	26	10	4	12	46	52	24
11	Accrington	26	8	4	14	40	78	20
12	WBA	26	6	6	14	51	58	18
13	Stoke	26	5	4	17	38	61	14
14	Darwen	26	4	3	19	38	112	11

SEASON 1892–1893

With the league extended to two divisions and the first division increased to 16 clubs, it meant that winning the league was to be a far more difficult proposition. Relegation now came into the equation although Preston were never in any danger of that. In fact, they again did very well and for the third year running they finished as runners-up. This time though Sunderland ran away with the title, winning by eleven clear points and scoring 100 goals in the process. Preston could not compete with that but they did have the perfect start to the season. Five straight wins and nine wins out of their first eleven games. Frank Becton, who had progressed through the reserves, looked good in his opening matches and carried on the promise he had shown the previous season. He hit four hat-tricks and that included a four goal haul against Notts County at Deepdale. Jimmy Trainer continued his prime form in goal and Bob Holmes and Moses Sanders rarely let their performances drop below the high standards they had set themselves. Other players came in and David Russell was a particular success at centre-forward and scored regularly to repay the faith shown by the Preston management. However, the real excitement of the season came in the FA Cup. Twenty-two goals were scored in the first three rounds which took Preston to

a semi-final clash with old rivals Everton. How the club did not make the final remained a complete mystery. The tie went to three games and North End played some magnificent football in all three games. But they could not make their superiority show with goals and Everton held them in the first two games. The second replay was played at Ewood Park and observers of the tie were full of praise for the Lilywhite's performance. They pulverised Everton but could not score the goals they deserved. In the end Everton caught them with a sucker punch and won the tie 2–1, completely against the run of play. That left Preston with a seven game run-in to the end of the league season. Unfortunately they could only win two of those games and finished the campaign with defeats against Wolves and Derby. Still, those points were enough to keep them one ahead of Everton, which gave North End some consolation for the cup defeat, and it also secured the runners-up spot. Two Championships and three runners-up spots in the first five years for Preston, an enviable record.

DEBUTANTS: (4) John Cowan, Hugh Maguire, Richard Thornber and David Russell (No2).

LAST GAMES: (3) Gallacher, Stewart and Thornber.

League appearances (30 games)

Becton F. 29, Cowan J. 26, Drummond G. 19, Gallacher H. 13, Gordon J. B. 16, Greer W. H. 29, Holmes J. 11, Holmes R. 28, Maguire H. 3, Ross J. D. 25, Ross N. J. 28, Russell D. 18, Sanders M. 28, Stewart W. S. 24, Thornber R. 3, Trainer J. 30

FA Cup appearances (7 games)

Trainer 5, Holmes R. 7, Ross N. 6, Greer 5, Sanders 7, Holmes J. 1, Gordon 7, Ross J. 7, Russell 6, Becton 7, Drummond 7, Cowan 6, Stewart 6.

Goalscorers: 57 League–25 Cup–(Total 82)

Becton 15–8 (23), Russell 14–3 (17), Ross 8–4 (12), Drummond 6–1 (7), Cowan 1–4 (5), Gordon 0–5 (5), Sanders 3–0 (3), Gallacher 3–0 (3), Stewart 2–0 (2), Greer 2–0 (2), Ross N. 1–0 (1) Own Goals 2–0 (2) (Hillman (Burnley) and Gardiner, (Bolton).

Left to right (players only): *Back row:* Greer, Sanders, Holmes, Trainer, N. J. Ross, Stewart. *Front row:* Gordon, Becton, J. D. Ross, Cowan, Drummond. This photograph was taken on 17 September 1892 at Home *vs.* Nottingham Forest, Preston won 1–0 (Sanders).

Match Report: North End Repel Fightback – 8 April 1893 Bootle *vs.* Preston (at Anfield) Lancs Cup Semi-final

Such was the interest in the Lancashire Cup in 1893 that a crowd of around 7,000 were present for this Saturday afternoon fixture. A re-arranged league game against Wolves was put back to the following Monday afternoon and only around 500 spectators took the trouble to attend. In the game with Bootle, Preston were firm favourites having beaten Everton in the previous round whereas Bootle had disposed of Liverpool. Bootle won the toss and in the initial stages of the contest both sides indulged in the long ball game which was not North End's usual practice. Once Preston started to string a few passes together it opened Bootle up and Frank Becton took one from Jimmy Ross to open the scoring. Within minutes George Drummond hit the upright, but not to be denied, North End then struck again, Becton again the marksman. Bootle seldom had the opportunity to venture over the half-way line as it was one-way traffic as North End took numerous pot shots at their opponent's goal. Before half-time arrived Jimmy Ross had made it 3–0 and from a fast right wing centre by Jack Gordon, Hutchinson was unfortunate to concede an own goal. The defender's misery continued after the break as he was quickly penalised for a foul on Drummond. From Geordie's free-kick Jimmy Ross made it 5–0 but in the process twisted his knee and retired hurt. Bootle could do no better against the ten men and went 6–0 down on the hour, John Cowan doing the damage. Five minutes later Clarkin rounded Jimmy Ross and centred for Brandon to pull a goal back. With Preston easing up and Bootle taking heart from their goal they then added a second amid great cheering, Gallagher scoring. This fresh approach by Bootle brought them even more reward soon afterwards. Grierson's shot hit the post but Jimmy Trainer could only watch as Montgomery reacted the quickest to make the score 6–3. Three goals in just five minutes! With the boot on the other foot so to speak Bootle again moved forward with some neat passing and Brandon beat Trainer again. 6–4 and now 4 in 7 minutes. At this stage Preston put up the shutters and they eventually held on to win but it was not without a flutter or two. 6–0 to 6–4, some comeback.

STAT FACTS:
Best home run without defeat: 9 games
Best away run without defeat: 2 games
Longest run unbeaten: 5 games
Longest run without a win: 3 games

Ever presents:
(1) Jimmy Trainer
FA Cup:
Semi-final second replay
Hat-tricks: (7) J. Ross (2, 1 Lg. 1 FAC), Russell (1), Becton (4, 2 Lg. incl. a 4 *vs.* Notts Co., and 2 FAC)
Manager:
Management Committee
Chairman:
Major William Sudell
Leading scorer: 23 goals – Frank Becton (15 League 8 Cup)
Players used: 16

AUTHORS' UNOFFICIAL
PLAYER OF THE
SEASON: Frank Becton

Trivia Fact:
Preston won the Lancashire Cup in 1892–93, but it was not without complications. In the March they beat Everton 3–0 at Deepdale but although the match was finished it was later declared void due to 'persistent crowd encroachment'. In the replay Preston won 5–1. They then beat Bootle 6–4 in the semi-final at Anfield before beating Bolton 2–0 in the Final which was played at Ewood.

Season 1892–93: First Division

	P	W	D	L	F	A	Pts
1 Sunderland	30	22	4	4	100	36	48
2 PRESTON	**30**	**17**	**3**	**10**	**57**	**39**	**37**
3 Everton	30	16	4	10	74	51	36
4 Aston Villa	30	16	3	11	73	62	35
5 Bolton	30	13	6	11	56	55	32
6 Burnley	30	13	4	13	51	44	30
7 Stoke	30	12	5	13	58	48	29
8 WBA	30	12	5	13	58	69	29
9 Blackburn	30	8	13	9	47	56	29
10 Nottingham Forest	30	10	8	12	48	52	28
11 Wolves	30	12	4	14	47	68	28
12 Wednesday	30	12	3	15	55	65	27
13 Derby	30	9	9	12	52	64	21
14 Notts County	30	10	4	16	53	61	24
15 Accrington	30	6	11	13	57	81	23
16 Newton Heath	30	6	6	18	50	85	18

League position in Division One: Runners-up – P30 W17 D3 L10 F57 A39 Pts 37
Home: W11 D2 L2 F34 A10   Away: W6 D1 L8 F23 A29

Match Report: County Battered by Becton – 31 March 1893 Preston 4 Notts County 0

This, the return league game between the two teams, was watched by approximately 6,000 spectators. The Notts County team arrived without their goalkeeper, Toone, who had missed his train, so they had to play with ten men. Hendry made an excellent substitute for Toone though, especially in the early stages when he repelled shots from Becton and Drummond splendidly. The visitors were pinned back for most of the time as Preston made the extra man count and when they did manage an attack Jack Ross nullified their futile attempts. With North End stretching County and using the width of the Deepdale enclosure to their advantage, Cowan received the ball and raced away, crossing the ball when he spotted Becton rushing up. Becton gratefully snapped up his chance by shooting past Hendry. The stand-in goalkeeper then saved shots from Cowan, Drummond and Ross, and the game was one-way traffic, the ball seldom being in the North End half. Becton doubled his and Preston's tally on 42 minutes when he latched onto a deflection off the full-back's legs. At this stage, with half-time looming, Oswald brought a save out of Trainer, County's first meaningful effort. After the break Hendry was again kept busy as he continued his creditable performance between the posts. North End kept up the pressure and Greer's shot just skimmed the upright. Eventually the keeper was beaten again with Becton once more doing the damage with a crisp, rising shot. Becton, seemingly not happy with a hat-trick, then went on to emulate Drummond's feat of the previous season by scoring a fourth goal against Notts County.

Date 1892-3	Opponents	Comp	h or a	Score	Att.	1	2	3	4	5	6	7	8	9	10	11		
Sep 3	Bolton W.	Div 1	h	2-1		Trainer	R.Holmes	N.Ross	Thornber	Sanders	Stewart	Greer	Becton (1)	J.Ross	Drummond (1)	Gallacher		
Sep 10	Derby County	Div 1	a	2-1		Trainer	R.Holmes	N.Ross	Greer	Sanders	Stewart	Cowan	Becton (1)	J.Ross	Drummond (1)	Gallacher		
Sep 12	Sheffield Wed.	Div 1	h	4-1		Trainer	R.Holmes	N.Ross	Greer	Sanders	Stewart	Cowan (1)	Becton (2)	J.Ross (1)	Drummond	Gallacher		
Sep 17	Nottm Forest	Div 1	h	1-0		Trainer	R.Holmes	N.Ross	Greer	Sanders (1)	Stewart	Gordon	Becton	J.Ross	Cowan	Drummond		
Sep 24	Nottm Forest	Div 1	a	2-1		Trainer	R.Holmes	N.Ross	Greer (1)	Sanders	Stewart	Cowan	Becton	J.Ross	Drummond (1)	Gallacher		
Oct 1	Notts County	Div 1	a	1-3		Trainer	R.Holmes	N.Ross (1)	Drummond	Sanders	Stewart	Gordon	J.Ross	Russell	Cowan	Becton		
Oct 8	Blackburn R.	Div 1	h	2-1		Trainer	R.Holmes	N.Ross	Greer	Sanders	Stewart (1)	Cowan	J.Ross	Russell	Drummond (1)	Gallacher		
Oct 15	Burnley	Div 1	h	2-0		Trainer	R.Holmes	N.Ross	Greer	Sanders	Stewart	Gordon	J.Ross	Russell (1)	Becton	Cowan	1 o.g.	(Hillman)
Oct 22	Aston Villa	Div 1	h	4-1		Trainer	R.Holmes	N.Ross	Greer	Sanders	Stewart	Cowan	J.Ross (1)	Russell (3)	Becton	Gallacher		
Oct 29	Blackburn R.	Div 1	a	0-0		Trainer	R.Holmes	N.Ross	Greer	Sanders	Stewart	Cowan	J.Ross	Russell	Becton	Becton		
Nov 5	Accrington	Div 1	h	2-1		Trainer	R.Holmes	N.Ross	Greer	Sanders	J.Holmes	Cowan	J.Ross	Russell	Becton	Gallacher (2)		
Nov 14	Stoke	Div 1	a	1-2		Trainer	R.Holmes	N.Ross	Greer	Sanders	J.Ross	Gordon	Cowan	Russell (1)	Becton	Gallacher		
Nov 19	Bolton W.	Div 1	h	4-2		Trainer	R.Holmes	N.Ross	Greer	Sanders	Thornber	Cowan	J.Ross (1)	Russell (1)	Becton (1)	Gallacher	1 o.g.	(Gardiner)
Nov 26	Aston Villa	Div 1	a	1-3		Trainer	R.Holmes	N.Ross	Greer	Sanders	Drummond	Cowan	J.Ross	Russell	Becton (1)	Gallacher		
Dec 3	Everton	Div 1	h	5-0		Trainer	R.Holmes	N.Ross	Greer	Sanders (1)	Drummond	Cowan	J.Ross (1)	Russell (2)	Becton (1)	Gordon		
Dec 10	WBA	Div 1	a	1-0		Trainer	R.Holmes	N.Ross	Greer	Sanders	Stewart	Cowan	J.Ross	Russell	Becton (1)	Gordon		
Dec 17	Sunderland	Div 1	a	0-2		Trainer	R.Holmes	N.Ross	Greer	Sanders	Stewart	Cowan	J.Ross	Russell	Becton	Gordon		
Dec 26	Newton Heath	Div 1	h	2-1		Trainer	R.Holmes	N.Ross	Greer	Sanders	Stewart	Cowan	J.Ross	Russell (2)	Becton	Gordon		
Dec 31	Stoke	Div 1	h	2-1		Trainer	R.Holmes	N.Ross	Greer	J.Holmes	Stewart	Gordon	J.Ross (1)	Russell (1)	Becton	Gallacher		
Jan 7	Sunderland	Div 1	h	1-2		Trainer	R.Holmes	N.Ross	Greer	Sanders	Stewart	Drummond	J.Ross	Russell	Becton	Gallacher (1)		
Jan 14	Sheff. Wed.	Div 1	a	5-0		Trainer	R.Holmes	N.Ross	Greer	Sanders	J.Holmes	Gordon	J.Ross (3)	Russell (2)	Becton	Drummond		
Jan 21	Burton Swifts Rd 1	FAC	h	9-2		Trainer	R.Holmes	N.Ross	Greer	Sanders	J.Holmes	Gordon (2)	J.Ross (3)	Russell	Becton (3)	Drummond (1)		
Feb 4	Accrington Rd 2	FAC	a	4-1		Trainer	R.Holmes	Drummond	Greer	Sanders	Stewart	Gordon	J.Ross	Russell	Becton (2)	Cowan (2)		
Feb 11	Everton	Div 1	h	0-6		Trainer	R.Holmes	Drummond	Greer	Sanders	Stewart	Gordon	J.Ross	Russell	Becton	Cowan		
Feb 18	Middlboro Ironopolis Rd 3	FAC	a	2-2*		Drummond	R.Holmes	N.Ross	Greer	Sanders	Stewart	Gordon (1)	J.Ross	Russell (1)	Becton	Cowan		
Feb 25	Middlboro Ironopolis Rd 3	FAC	h	7-0		Drummond	R.Holmes	N.Ross	Greer	Sanders	Stewart	Gordon	J.Ross (1)	Russell (2)	Becton (3)	Cowan (1)		
Mar 4	Everton * Semi-final	FAC	n	2-2		Trainer	R.Holmes	N.Ross	Greer	Sanders	Stewart	Gordon (1)	J.Ross	Drummond	Becton	Cowan (1)		
Mar 16	Everton * Semi-final	FAC	n	0-0		Trainer	R.Holmes	N.Ross	Drummond	Sanders	Stewart	Gordon	J.Ross	Russell	Becton	Cowan		
Mar 18	Burnley	Div 1	a	2-4		Trainer	R.Holmes	N.Ross	Greer	J.Holmes	Stewart	Gordon	Drummond (1)	Russell (1)	Becton	Cowan		
Mar 20	Everton + Semi-final	FAC	n	1-2		Trainer	R.Holmes	N.Ross	Drummond	Sanders	Stewart	Gordon (1)	J.Ross	Russell	Becton	Cowan		
Mar 31	Notts County	Div 1	h	4-0		Trainer	R.Holmes	N.Ross	J.Holmes	Sanders	Stewart	Cowan	Greer	Drummond	Becton (4)	J.Ross		
Apr 1	Newton Heath	Div 1	a	1-2		Trainer	Greer	N.Ross	Thornber	J.Holmes	Stewart (1)	Cowan	Becton	Drummond	Sanders	J.Ross		
Apr 3	Accrington	Div 1	h	0-0		Trainer	Maguire	N.Ross	J.Holmes	Sanders	Stewart	J.Ross	Greer	Drummond	Becton	Cowan		
Apr 10	Wolverhampton W.	Div 1	h	4-0		Trainer	R.Holmes	N.Ross	J.Holmes	Sanders	Stewart	Gordon	Greer	Drummond (1)	Becton (3)	Cowan		
Apr 13	WBA	Div 1	h	1-1		Trainer	R.Holmes	N.Ross	J.Holmes	Sanders	Stewart	Gordon	Greer (1)	Drummond	Becton	Cowan		
Apr 15	Wolverhampton W.	Div 1	a	1-2		Trainer	Maguire	N.Ross	J.Holmes	R.Holmes	Stewart	Gordon	Greer	Sanders (1)	Becton	Cowan		
Apr 17	Derby County	Div 1	h	0-1		Trainer	Maguire	R.Holmes	J.Holmes	Sanders	Stewart	Gordon	Greer	Drummond	Becton	Cowan		
	* First two semis at Bramall Lane, Sheffield			* a.e.t.														
	+ At Ewood Park, Blackburn																	

11

SEASON 1893–1894

This was very much a landmark season in Preston North End's history. For some time the dictatorial Major Sudell had suffered from poor health and his personal and business life had taken a turn for the worse. As a result the club members began to turn on him and at a stormy meeting in July 1893 North End were formed into a Limited Company with a new Board of Directors. The Major was not only ousted as Chairman of PNE but in 1895 he was actually charged with embezzling his company's funds. This resulted in an eventual three year jail sentence after which he was to emigrate to South Africa where he died in 1911. It was a very sad end for a man who had dedicated his life to North End and had been one of the most influential Chairmen the game had ever seen, before or since. With this background of events it came as no surprise that events on the field in the 1893–4 season also took a downward turn. New Chairman, William Ord, found that the Invincibles era was well and truly over and efforts were made to try and recruit new players. No fewer than 15 made their debuts in the new campaign with a good percentage being found in Scottish football, the traditional supplier of good Preston footballers. Twenty year old Johnny Cunningham came from Glasgow where he had played for both Rangers and Celtic and he quickly settled into a variety of forward positions. Jimmy McCann also boosted the forward power but a traumatic season was then to strike another blow when it was learned that Nick Ross had contracted tuberculosis. His health became so bad that he disappeared from the team early in the November. Other injuries stretched the playing resources to breaking point and at one stage

John Barton was in the side, and he was the team trainer! After Nick Ross dropped out of the line-up Preston had an awful run of results, winning just once in 16 games. However there was to be one memorable moment in the FA Cup when Reading visited Deepdale on 27 January 1894. Ironically Nick Ross played, a swan song if ever there was one, because Preston rattled in 18 goals without reply. Jimmy Ross hit six goals, Frank Becton and John Cowan four apiece whilst 'Trainer' Barton scored three. It was to be Nick Ross's last ever appearance at home although he did play again the following week at Darwen. Sadly his health was to deteriorate over the next few months and in the August of 1894 it was announced that he had died. So. in one season, for various reasons, Preston had lost probably the two most influential football men in the country at the time. All this sadness was to culminate in Preston, who had had a poor season, having to figure in a relegation 'Test Match' against Notts County to try to avoid the drop. Thankfully a convincing 4–0 win saved Preston's bacon.

DEBUTANTS: (15) Aloysius Ball, John Barton, E.A. Connor, John Cunningham, Charles Dickson, Hugh Dunn, Adam Henderson, James McCann, Henry Miller, George Nidd, Archibald Pinnell, R. Frederick Poole, James Roy, E. David Smith and Robert Stormont.

LAST GAMES: (16) J. D. Ross, N. J. Ross, J. Holmes, J. Cowan, Maguire, Ball, Barton, Connor, Dickson, McCann, Miller, Nidd, Pinnell, Poole, Roy and Stormont.

League appearances (30 games)

Ball A. 5, Barton J. 2, Becton F. 26, Connor E. A. 1, Cowan J. 29, Cunningham J. 16, Dickson C. 3, Drummond G. 24, Dunn H. 5, Gordon J. B. 6, Greer W. H. 30, Henderson A. 2, Holmes J. 8, Holmes R. 27, McCann J. 6, Maguire H. 1, Miller H. 2, Nidd G. F. 3, Pinnell A. 1, Poole R. F. 2, Ross J. D. 24, Ross N. J. 10, Roy J. 1, Sanders M. 29, Sharp J. 26, Smith E. D. 2, Stormont R. 9, Trainer J. 30.

FA Cup appearances: (2 games)

Trainer 2, Holmes R. 2, Ross N. 1, Drummond 2, Greer 2, Sanders 2, Sharp 1, Barton 1, Gordon 1, Cowan 2, Cunningham 2, Ross J. 2, Becton 2.

Goalscorers: 44 League–20 Cup–(Total 64)

Ross J. 18 (4 pens)–6 (24), Becton 6–6 (12), Cowan 7–4 (11), Sanders 3–1 (4), Barton 0–3 (3), Drummond 2–0 (2), Greer 2–0 (2), McCann 1–0 (1), Sharp 1–0 (1), Cunningham 1–0 (1), Gordon 1–0 (1), Smith 1–0 (1), Dickson 1–0 (1).

> **League position in Division One: 14th – P30 W10 D3 L17 F44 A56 Pts 23**
> **Home: W7 D1 L7 F25 A24 Away: W3 D2 L10 F19 A32***

> * N.B.Escaped relegation only by winning Test Match *vs.* Notts County

Date 1893-4	Opponents	Comp	h or a	Score	Att.	1	2	3	4	5	6	7	8	9	10	11
Sep 2	Derby County	Div 1	h	1-0		Trainer	R.Holmes	N.Ross	Greer	Sanders	J.Holmes	Gordon	J.Ross	Drummond	Becton (1)	Cowan
Sep 9	Burnley	Div 1	a	1-4		Trainer	R.Holmes	N.Ross	Greer	Sanders	Sharp	Drummond	Cunningham	J.Ross (1p)	Becton	Cowan
Sep 16	Sunderland	Div 1	a	1-2		Trainer	R.Holmes	N.Ross	Greer	Sanders	Sharp	Drummond	Cunningham	J.Ross (1)	Becton	Cowan
Sep 23	Darwen	Div 1	h	4-1		Trainer	R.Holmes	N.Ross	J.Holmes	Sanders	Sharp	Drummond	Cunningham	J.Ross (3)	Greer (1)	Cowan
Sep 30	Bolton W.	Div 1	a	3-0		Trainer	R.Holmes	N.Ross	Greer	Sanders (1)	Sharp	Drummond	Cunningham	J.Ross	Becton (1)	Cowan (1)
Oct 7	Blackburn R.	Div 1	a	0-1		Trainer	R.Holmes	N.Ross	Sharp	Greer	Sanders	J.Holmes	Cunningham	Drummond	Becton	Cowan
Oct 14	Burnley	Div 1	h	1-2		Trainer	R.Holmes	N.Ross	Sharp	Greer	J.Holmes	Cunningham	McCann (1)	Sanders	Becton	Cowan
Oct 28	Everton	Div 1	h	3-2		Trainer	R.Holmes	N.Ross	Sharp	Greer	J.Holmes	Cunningham (1)	McCann	Sanders (1)	Becton (1)	Cowan
Nov 4	Bolton W.	Div 1	h	1-0		Trainer	R.Holmes	N.Ross	Sharp	Greer	Sanders	Cunningham	McCann	Stormont	Becton	Cowan (1)
Nov 11	Blackburn R.	Div 1	h	0-1		Trainer	R.Holmes	Drummond	Sharp	Greer	Sanders	Cunningham	McCann	J.Ross	Becton	Cowan
Nov 13	Stoke	Div 1	a	1-2		Trainer	R.Holmes	Drummond	Sharp	Greer	Sanders	Cunningham	McCann	J.Ross (1p)	Becton	Cowan
Nov 20	Sheffield Utd.	Div 1	a	1-1		Trainer	R.Holmes	Sanders	Sharp	Greer	J.Holmes	Drummond	J.Ross	Stormont	Becton	Cowan (1)
Nov 25	Aston Villa	Div 1	h	0-2		Trainer	R.Holmes	Sanders	Sharp	Greer	J.Holmes	Barton	Drummond	Stormont	Becton	Cowan
Dec 2	Nottm. Forest	Div 1	h	0-2		Trainer	R.Holmes	Sanders	Sharp	Greer	Drummond	McCann	J.Ross	Stormont	Becton	Cowan
Dec 4	WBA	Div 1	a	0-2		Trainer	R.Holmes	Sanders	Sharp	Greer	Drummond	J.Ross	Poole	Stormont	Becton	Cowan
Dec 9	Wolverhampton W.	Div 1	h	0-0		Trainer	R.Holmes	Sanders	Sharp	Greer	Ball	J.Ross	Poole	Stormont	Becton	Drummond
Dec 16	Wolverhampton W.	Div 1	h	1-3		Trainer	R.Holmes	Sanders	Sharp	Greer	Ball	J.Ross (1)	Stormont	Drummond	Becton	Cowan
Dec 23	Newton Heath	Div 1	h	2-0		Trainer	R.Holmes	Sanders	Sharp (1)	Greer	Ball	Gordon	Cowan	J.Ross (1)	Becton	Drummond
Dec 25	Stoke	Div 1	h	3-3		Trainer	R.Holmes	Sanders	Sharp	Greer	Ball	Gordon	Cowan (1)	J.Ross (2)	Becton	Drummond
Jan 1	Sunderland	Div 1	a	3-6		Trainer	R.Holmes	Maguire	Sharp	Greer (1)	Sanders	Gordon	Cowan (1)	J.Ross (1p)	Cunningham	Drummond
Jan 6	Derby County	Div 1	a	1-2		Trainer	R.Holmes	Sanders	Sharp	Greer	Drummond	Gordon (1)	Cunningham	J.Ross	Becton	Cowan
Jan 13	Everton	Div 1	a	2-4		Trainer	R.Holmes	Sanders	Sharp	Greer	Drummond	Cunningham	Cowan (1)	J.Ross (1p)	Becton	Gordon
Jan 18	Aston Villa	Div 1	h	2-5		Trainer	R.Holmes	Drummond	J.Holmes	Greer	Ball	Cowan (1)	Connor	Sanders	Becton (1)	Cunningham
Jan 27	Reading Rd 1	FAC	h	18-0		Trainer	R.Holmes	N.Ross	Greer	Sanders (1)	Drummond	Barton (3)	Cowan (4)	J.Ross (6)	Becton (4)	Cunningham
Feb 3	Darwen	Div 1	a	1-2		Trainer	R.Holmes	N.Ross	Greer	Sanders	Drummond	Barton	Cowan	J.Ross (1)	Becton	Cunningham
Feb 6	Sheffield Wed.	Div 1	a	0-3		Trainer	R.Holmes	Drummond	Greer	Sanders	Stormont	Pinnell	Cowan	J.Ross	Becton	Cunningham
Feb 10	Liverpool Rd 2	FAC		2-3		Trainer	R.Holmes	Drummond	Greer	Sanders	Sharp	Gordon	Cunningham	J.Ross	Becton (2)	Cowan
Mar 3	WBA	Div 1	h	3-1		Trainer	Dunn	Nidd	Sharp	Greer	Stormont	Cowan	J.Ross (3)	Roy	Becton	Dickson
Mar 24	Nottm. Forest	Div 1	a	2-4		Trainer	Dunn	Nidd	Sharp	Greer	Sanders	Cowan	J.Ross (1)	Miller	Smith (1)	Henderson
Mar 26	Sheffield Wed.	Div 1	h	1-0		Trainer	Dunn	Nidd	Sharp	Greer	Sanders (1)	Cowan	J.Ross	Miller	Becton	Henderson
Apr 7	Sheffield Utd.	Div 1	h	3-0		Trainer	Dunn	R.Holmes	Sharp	Greer	Sanders	Cowan	J.Ross	Becton (2)	Drummond	Dickson
Apr 14	Newton Heath	Div 1	a	3-1		Trainer	Dunn	R.Holmes	Sharp	Greer	Sanders	Cowan	J.Ross (1)	Smith	Drummond (1)	Dickson (1)
Apr 28	Notts County (Test Match)	Play-off match	n	4-0		Pinnell	Dunn	R.Holmes	Sharp	Greer	Sanders	Cowan	J.Ross (1)	Drummond (1)	Cunningham (1)	Henderson (1)

Match Report: After the Lord Mayor's Show – 3 Feb 1894 Darwen 2 Preston 1

Just a week after Preston's famous 18–0 win over Reading in the FA Cup they met Darwen in a vital league game. Both sides were in the bottom three positions of the league prior to this crucial four pointer. The first two chances created by Preston fell to their trainer, Jack Barton, who was standing in for the injured Jack Gordon. Barton had scored three against the amateurs of Reading but this time Darwen's defence was a different proposition. It was described as 'sound to the core' and proved difficult to penetrate as both John Cunningham and Jimmy Ross found out. Darwen soaked up all Preston's early pressure before one of their own breakaways forced William Greer to concede a corner. McKennie took the kick well, using the wind to his advantage. The ball fell for McKnight who tried a shot at goal and Moses Sanders, in an attempt to block it only succeeded in heading into his own goal. The North End players objected as they had felt that Jimmy Trainer had been impeded but the goal stood. Preston then fought back with John Cowan's effort skimming past a post and then Ross's shot hit the upright. After 35 minutes Cowan broke away once more and passed to Ross who had quickly regained his footing after being 'grassed'. He was skilful enough to get his shot successfully on target and equalise, much to the annoyance of the home fans in the 3,000 crowd. It was his 19th goal of the season. Darwen then counter attacked and for some time play was all around Trainer's goal. Maxwell, the home centre-forward, missed a sitter from underneath the crossbar. The second-half was a poor spectacle for a the paying public as the game was peppered with niggling fouls and unsportsmanlike tactics. After 61 minutes Darwen crowded Trainer's box and Sutherland, given too much time and space, steadied himself before scoring what proved to be the winning goal. North End were rocky in defence with Jack Ross out of sorts. In fact it was to be his last game for Preston as he was ill with the early symptoms of tuberculosis. Darwen's tactics were dour, kicking the ball as far out of touch as possible, wasting time as the North End players had to retrieve the ball themselves. Preston had no luck at all in this fixture as Jimmy Ross even had a goal disallowed when given offside, from a throw-in! This defeat came at a bad time for the visitors, it was their sixth game without a win. Eventually only a win in the end of season Test Match against Notts County kept Preston in Division One.

Season 1893–94: First Division

		P	W	D	L	F	A	Pts
		P	W	B	L	F	A	Pts
1	Aston Villa	30	19	6	5	84	42	44
2	Sunderland	30	17	4	9	72	44	38
3	Derby	30	16	4	10	73	62	36
4	Blackburn	30	16	2	12	69	53	34
5	Burnley	30	15	4	11	61	51	34
6	Everton	30	15	4	11	90	57	33
7	Nottingham Forest	30	14	4	12	57	48	32
8	WBA	30	14	4	12	66	59	32
9	Wolves	30	14	3	13	52	63	31
10	Sheffield United	30	13	5	12	47	61	31
11	Stoke	30	13	3	14	65	79	29
12	Wednesday	30	9	8	13	48	57	26
13	Botton	30	10	4	16	38	52	24
14	**PRESTON**	**30**	**10**	**3**	**17**	**44**	**56**	**23**
15	Darwen	30	7	5	18	37	83	19
16	Newton Heath	30	6	2	22	36	72	14

Ever presents: (2) Billy Greer and Jimmy Trainer
FA Cup: Second Round
Hat-tricks: (6) Jimmy Ross 2 league plus one six goal haul in FAC. Cowan and Becton (4 goals each in FAC) and Barton (3 goals in FAC).
Manager: Management Committee
Chairman: Mr W. E. Ord J. P.
Leading scorer: 24 goals – Jimmy Ross (18 League 6 Cup)
Players used: 28

AUTHORS' UNOFFICIAL PLAYER OF THE SEASON:
Billy Greer

Trivia Fact:

Did you know that Jack Barton the team trainer-cum-groundsman was the Barton who played and scored three goals in the 18–0 FA Cup win against Reading?

SEASON 1894–1895

Only four teams had won the League Championship so far and those four clubs were to continue their dominance by finishing in the top four places in season 1894–5. Unfortunately for the Preston fans it was North End who were destined to be the fourth club, finishing twelve points behind Champions Sunderland and also well behind Everton and Aston Villa. Those teams were a class apart from the rest, although from Preston's point of view, it is interesting to note that only the home game against Sunderland produced a win from the matches played against the sides above them. All the other five games were lost. Defensively Preston were sound with Jimmy Trainer, Bob Holmes, James Sharp, Moses Sanders, Hugh Dunn and Billy Greer all showing consistent form. Sanders, especially was a rock in defence and he also tried to support his forwards when possible. The fans loved his wholehearted approach to every game. In goal, Trainer was in danger of being taken for granted such was his regular fine games. His talent was obvious and he was one player Preston could ill afford to lose. Despite these excellent individual performances North End's main problem during this season seemed to be their ability to lose against struggling sides at vital times, which upset any rhythm the club tried to sustain. Just when the fans thought they were building a good run a sloppy defeat would cause a hiccup. In attack the goals were spread around the forward line with three players managing to reach double figures, but none of the players could sustain their goalscoring to post a big total. Frank Becton, David Smith and Adam Henderson all had bursts of scoring and the team only failed to score on four occasions. One of those matches came in the FA Cup where Preston were unfortunate to be drawn away to Sunderland in the second round. A 2–0 win at Luton in round one was cancelled out by a defeat at Roker Park by the same score. To be fair, after the cup disappointment, Preston put together a good run in the league and lost only one of the seven games they played up until the end of the season. And in that spell they also scored freely too. They hit 24 goals in those seven games including a 5–0 win against WBA at Deepdale and a 5–2 win at Liverpool. New signing Robert Barr had an amazing start to his Preston career. He scored on his debut and made it two goals in five. Then he embarked on a run where he scored in each of his next five games making it 7 goals in ten appearances. Sadly that form did not continue and he only managed one more in the other 18 games he played. It is strange how those sort of sequences frequently pepper the Preston records down the years.

DEBUTANTS: (6) Richard Allan, Robert Barr, Robert Blyth, William Orr, John (Jackie) Pierce and Alex Tait

LAST GAMES: (2) Gordon and Allan.

League appearances (30 games)

Allan R. 2, Barr R. 28, Becton F. 22, Blyth R. 13, Cunningham J. 12, Drummond G. 13, Dunn H. 27, Gordon J. B. 6, Greer W. H. 21, Henderson A. 26, Holmes R. 29, Howarth R. H. 2, Orr W. 10, Pierce J. 1, Sanders M. 29, Sharp J. 28, Smith E. D. 28, Tait A. 3, Trainer J. 30.

FA Cup appearances (2 games)

Trainer 2, Dunn 2, Holmes 2, Orr 1, Sharp 1, Greer 2, Sanders 2, Henderson 2, Barr 2, Smith 2, Becton 2, Drummond 2.

Goalscorers: 62 League–2 Cup–(Total 64)

Smith 12–0 (12), Henderson 11–1 (12), Becton 11–0 (11), Barr 9–0 (9), Cunningham 5–0 (5), Sanders 3 (1pen)–1(pen) (4), Pierce 2–0 (2), Orr 2–0 (2), Blyth 2–0 (2), Allan 1–0 (1), Greer 1–0 (1), Sharp 1–0 (1). Own goals 2–0 (2) (McQueen, Liverpool–Collins, Nottm Forest)

League position in Division One: 4th – P30 W15 D5 L10 F62 A46 Pts 35
Home: W9 D3 L3 F32 A14   Away: W6 D2 L7 F30 A32

Match Report: Moses, North End's Man Mountain – 30 Mar 1895
Preston 2 Everton 0 Lancs Cup Final

Everton were going to be formidable opponents for North End in this Cup Final as they were the current holders of the trophy and also, in second place in the League Championship battle. Everton had beaten Liverpool in the semi-final whereas Preston had trounced Accrington 6–1. It was cold and showery at Ewood Park, Blackburn, the neutral ground chosen for the venue. It was the 16th final for the handsome Challenge Cup of the Lancashire Football Association. Boyle won the toss for Everton and his team showed signs early on as to how tough a fixture it was to be. Fortunately for Preston, on this occasion Everton's finishing was below par although their approach play was good to watch. The senior North End players, Jimmy Trainer, Bob Holmes and Moses Sanders, all past cup winners, were in fine fettle as they weathered the storm so to speak. On one occasion William Orr did force his way through an Everton defence, which included two former North Enders, Kelso and Stewart, only to see his shot rattle the crossbar. Luckily for Preston though the ball rebounded perfectly for David Smith to head the opening goal of the final in the 30th minute. It made North End look more confident and aggressive. Trainer, only just back in action after injury, was illegally charged and knocked off his feet by both Millward and Geary. A free-kick was given. Half-time arrived with Preston still holding their lead. After the interval the wind dropped considerably but Everton's shooting was still wayward. John Cunningham thought he had doubled the lead but Robert Barr was given offside. At this stage Preston were well on top and Everton's defence was severely tested. Kelso gave away a needless free-kick for handball when he should have let the ball go out of play. From the resultant kick, in the 53rd minute, Cunningham's shot rebounded to Orr who then hit a tremendous shot at goal which beat Cain all ends up. 2–0 to the PNE! Everton could not penetrate the North End rearguard after that. The Preston players were quicker to the ball and Sanders was running the midfield. The best Everton could offer was when Stewart hit a shot which grazed Trainer's crossbar. It was not Everton's day. In fact Orr nearly made it 3–0 but his confident 30 yard effort went narrowly wide of the mark. Footnote: The Lancashire FA had increased prices by 6d for this final so a smaller gate than expected (8,000) saw the game.

Season 1894–95: First Division

	P	W	D	L	F	A	Pts
1 Sunderland	30	21	5	4	80	37	47
2 Everton	30	18	6	6	82	50	42
3 Aston Villa	30	17	5	8	82	43	39
4 PRESTON	**30**	**15**	**5**	**10**	**62**	**46**	**35**
5 Blackburn	30	11	10	9	59	49	32
6 Sheffield United	30	14	4	12	57	55	32
7 Nottingham Forest	30	13	5	12	50	56	31
8 Wednesday	30	12	4	14	50	55	28
9 Burney	30	11	4	15	44	56	26
10 Bolton	30	9	7	14	61	62	25
11 Wolves	30	9	7	14	43	63	25
12 Small Heath	30	9	7	14	50	74	25
13 WBA	30	10	4	16	51	66	24
14 Stoke	30	9	6	15	50	67	24
15 Derby	30	7	9	14	45	68	23
16 Liverpool	30	7	8	15	51	70	22

Some Future Players born during 1894–5: Simpson Bainbridge, William Greatorex, John Marshall and John Tatton.

Ever presents: (1) Jimmy Trainer

FA Cup: Second Round

Hat-tricks: (1) Frank Becton

Manager: Management Committee

Chairman: Mr W. E. Ord J. P.

Players used: 19

Leading scorer: 12 goals – David Smith and Adam Henderson (Smith all league, Henderson 11 + 1 cup)

AUTHORS' UNOFFICIAL PLAYER OF THE SEASON:
Jimmy Trainer

Date 1894-5	Opponents	Comp	h or a	Score	Att.	1	2	3	4	5	6	7	8	9	10	11		
Sep 1	Wolverhampton W.	Div 1	a	3-1		Trainer	Dunn	Holmes	Sharp	Greer	Sanders	Blyth	Barr (1)	Smith (1)	Becton (1)	Drummond		
Sep 3	Sheffield Wed.	Div 1	a	1-3		Trainer	Dunn	Holmes	Sharp	Greer	Sanders	Allan (1)	Barr	Smith	Becton	Drummond		
Sep 8	Sheffield Utd.	Div 1	h	2-1		Trainer	Dunn	Holmes	Sharp	Greer (1)	Sanders	Allan	Barr (1)	Smith	Becton	Cunningham		
Sep 15	Bolton W.	Div 1	a	2-1		Trainer	Dunn	Holmes	Sharp	Greer	Sanders	Blyth	Barr	Smith (1)	Becton (1)	Henderson		
Sep 22	Small Heath	Div 1	h	0-1		Trainer	Howarth	Holmes	Dunn	Greer	Sanders	Blyth	Barr	Smith	Cunningham	Henderson		
Sep 29	Small Heath	Div 1	a	4-4		Trainer	Dunn	Holmes	Sharp	Greer	Sanders	Blyth	Barr (1)	Smith	Becton (1)	Henderson (2)		
Oct 4	Nottm. Forest	Div 1	a	2-0		Trainer	Dunn	Holmes	Sharp	Greer	Sanders	Blyth	Barr (1)	Smith	Becton	Henderson	1 o.g.	(Collins)
Oct 6	Blackburn R.	Div 1	h	1-1		Trainer	Dunn	Holmes	Sharp	Greer	Sanders	Blyth	Barr (1)	Smith	Becton	Henderson		
Oct 13	Sheffield Utd.	Div 1	h	1-0		Trainer	Dunn	Holmes	Sharp	Orr	Sanders	Blyth	Barr (1)	Becton	Cunningham	Henderson		
Oct 20	Wolverhampton W.	Div 1	h	2-0		Trainer	Dunn	Holmes	Sharp	Greer	Sanders	Gordon	Barr (1)	Smith	Becton (1)	Henderson		
Oct 27	Blackburn R.	Div 1	a	1-1		Trainer	Dunn	Holmes	Sharp	Greer	Sanders	Gordon	Barr	Smith	Becton (1)	Henderson		
Nov 10	Aston Villa	Div 1	a	1-1		Trainer	Dunn	Holmes	Sharp	Greer	Sanders	Gordon	Barr	Smith (1)	Becton	Henderson		
Nov 12	Stoke	Div 1	a	1-2		Trainer	Dunn	Holmes	Sharp	Greer	Sanders	Gordon	Barr	Smith	Becton	Henderson (1)		
Nov 17	Derby County	Div 1	h	3-2		Trainer	Dunn	Holmes	Sharp	Orr	Sanders (1p)	Gordon	Barr	Smith (2)	Becton	Henderson		
Nov 24	Derby County	Div 1	a	1-2		Trainer	Dunn	Holmes	Sharp	Orr	Sanders	Gordon	Blyth	Smith	Becton	Henderson (1)		
Dec 1	Bolton W.	Div 1	h	2-2		Trainer	Dunn	Holmes	Sharp	Greer	Orr	Barr (1)	Cunningham	Smith	Becton (1)	Henderson		
Dec 8	Burnley	Div 1	a	1-2		Trainer	Dunn	Holmes	Sharp	Greer	Sanders	Cunningham	Barr	Smith	Becton	Henderson (1)		
Dec 15	Everton	Div 1	h	1-2		Trainer	Dunn	Holmes	Sharp	Greer	Sanders	Drummond	Barr	Smith	Becton	Henderson (1)		
Dec 25	Stoke	Div 1	h	3-0		Trainer	Dunn	Holmes	Sharp	Greer	Sanders	Drummond	Barr	Smith	Becton (2)	Henderson (1)		
Dec 29	Sunderland	Div 1	h	1-0		Trainer	Dunn	Holmes	Sharp	Greer	Sanders	Drummond	Barr	Smith (1)	Becton	Henderson		
Jan 1	Sunderland	Div 1	a	0-2		Trainer	Dunn	Holmes	Sharp	Greer	Sanders	Drummond	Barr	Smith	Becton	Henderson		
Jan 5	WBA	Div 1	a	5-4		Trainer	Dunn	Holmes	Sharp	Greer	Sanders	Blyth (1)	Barr	Smith (1)	Becton (3)	Drummond		
Jan 12	Aston Villa	Div 1	h	0-1		Trainer	Dunn	Holmes	Sharp	Greer	Sanders	Henderson	Barr	Smith	Becton	Drummond		
Jan 26	Burnley	Div 1	h	4-0		Trainer	Dunn	Holmes	Sharp (1)	Greer	Sanders (1)	Henderson	Barr	Smith	Cunningham (2)	Drummond		
Feb 2	Luton Town	Rd 1 FAC	a	2-0	4000	Trainer	Dunn	Holmes	Orr	Greer	Sanders (1p)	Henderson (1)	Barr	Smith	Becton	Drummond		
Feb 16	Sunderland	Rd 2 FAC	a	0-2	15000	Trainer	Dunn	Holmes	Sharp	Greer	Sanders	Henderson	Barr	Smith	Becton	Drummond		
Feb 23	Everton	Div 1	a	2-4		Trainer	Howarth	Holmes	Sharp	Sanders	Orr	Henderson (1)	Barr	Smith (1)	Cunningham	Drummond		
Feb 26	WBA	Div 1	h	5-0		Trainer	Dunn	Holmes	Sharp	Sanders	Orr (1)	Henderson (1)	Barr	Smith (2)	Cunningham (1)	Drummond		
Mar 23	Nottm. Forest	Div 1	h	3-1		Trainer	Tait	Holmes	Sharp	Sanders	Orr (1)	Henderson	Barr	Drummond	Cunningham (1)	Blyth (1)		
Apr 12	Liverpool	Div 1	h	2-2		Trainer	Dunn	Holmes	Sharp	Sanders (1)	Orr	Henderson	Barr	Smith	Cunningham	Blyth	1 o.g.	(McQueen)
Apr 13	Sheffield Wed.	Div 1	h	3-1		Trainer	Dunn	Tait	Drummond	Sanders	Orr	Henderson (1)	Barr (1)	Smith (1)	Cunningham	Blyth		
Apr 20	Liverpool	Div 1	a	5-2		Trainer	Tait	Holmes	Sharp	Sanders	Orr	Henderson (1)	Pierce (2)	Smith (1)	Cunningham (1)	Blyth		

SEASON 1895–1896

Never in any danger of winning the league and never any chance of being relegated meant that the 1895–6 year passed Preston North End by without too much excitement. They began their season with a visit to current champions Sunderland and they suffered a heavy 4–1 defeat. That set the tone for the away form and only three wins were eventually recorded. Luckily the home form was excellent and they even beat Aston Villa in a 4–3 thriller just before Christmas. Villa were to go on and win the title. New players continued to arrive at Deepdale and they included James Stevenson who was signed from Dumbarton to take over the centre-forward role. Goals were badly needed because apart from the five games when the team scored four or more they then struggled throughout the rest of the season and in 20 games they scored one or less. Defensively North End were again pretty solid with Alex Tait, James Sharp and Moses Sanders in good form. Sanders, in fact, had a spell where he was switched to the centre-forward position whilst Billy Greer moved into the centre-half slot. Sanders was switched back though after Stevenson arrived. Bob Blyth had a good season but in an era where players rarely strayed from their natural position, it was strange to note that the left-winger often played at inside-right. Injuries took their toll on Preston's squad and with the club committed to the usual heavy programme of friendlies, (even the reserves played ten),

it meant that the playing resources were stretched to the limit. When research is made into a season like this and studies are made of the line-ups, it would be very helpful if you could turn back the clock and see just why certain things happened. For example, why did Alex Tait play right-back and Bob Holmes play left-back for the first half of the season, before, suddenly, the two of them switched positions for the second half of the campaign? Mind you, it did not seem to affect Holmes who once again had an outstanding year. Strong, effective and a master at organising those around him, Holmes enhanced his already considerable reputation. In the FA Cup Preston were unluckily drawn away to the mighty Sunderland. The score was the same as for the league game as North End had no answer to their power. Funnily enough though the Wearsiders then went out to the eventual winners of the trophy, Sheffield Wednesday. So, very much a season for Preston that saw the winds of change blowing steadily down the corridors of Deepdale.

DEBUTANTS: (9) William Brown, Thomas Eccleston, William Eccleston, William Joy, George Lonsdale, James Smith, Thomas Smith (No. 1), James Stevenson and John Wright.

LAST GAMES: (7) Sharp, Barr, Brown, Joy, Lonsdale, Smith J. and Wright.

Left to right: *Back row:* J. Smith, M. Sanders, H. Dunn, J. Trainer, R. Howarth, A. Henderson. *Middle row:* W. Eccleston, J. Sharp (Captain), G. Drummond *Front row:* J. Pierce, J. Cunningham

League position in Division One: 9th – P30 W11 D6 L13 F44 A48 Pts 28
Home: W8 D5 L2 F31 A18 Away: W3 D1 L11 F13 A30

Match Report: League Leaders Come to Town – 7 Dec 1895 Preston 4 Aston Villa 3

With Preston struggling the public expected a defeat against the league leaders Aston Villa. But the club was looking for a big crowd to swell the dwindling coffers. As it was only around 7,000 ventured out as a howling blizzard prevailed. Not for the first time North End experimented with a different permutation up front. Moses Sanders who had played at centre-half and wing-half was tried at centre-forward. Within four minutes of the start Sanders had applied the finishing touch to a pass from Cunningham. No sooner had the kick-off restarted the game but Preston regained possession and attacked as one, (don't forget there were five forwards in those days). Henderson cleverly dodged around Reynolds before launching a precise centre straight to the feet of Sanders. The big man, to his own satisfaction and to the intense delight of the still cheering fans he promptly banged the leather sphere into the net. With such blood stirring excitement the fans were oblivious to the foul weather, it is strange how it always seems warmer when you are winning. Villa were not to be denied though and they showed their mettle with some great passing and skill on the ball. Joy was more than a match though and kept Villa at bay with some good work in goal. Midway through the first-half Tom Smith showed a clean pair of heels to the Villa defence, setting up a chance for Cunningham to make it 3–0. The visitors did pull a goal back before the break with

a deflected free-kick by Welford and after the interval they came out fighting, forcing two early corners. But immediately Preston countered. Cunningham's fierce shot was not held and Henderson moved sharply to crash home the rebound. Villa were stunned and pulled out all the stops to rescue the game. Joy made save after save before he was finally beaten by Campbell's lob. With eight minutes to go the same player pulled another goal back but Preston held on for a well deserved victory and two precious points.

Left to right: *Back row:* Tait, Trainer, Holmes. *Middle row:* Mr Houghton (Director), Sharp, Sanders, Orr, J. Barton (Trainer). *Front row:* Henderson, Pierce, W. Brown, Cunningham, Blythe. Photograph taken on 19 October 1895 Preston *vs.* Burnley.

League appearances (30 games)

Barr R. 1, Blyth R. 30, Brown W. 1, Cunningham J. 19, Drummond G. 5, Dunn H. 5, Eccleston T. 2, Eccleston W. 3, Greer W. H. 20, Henderson A. 23, Holmes R. 30, Joy W. J. 9, Lonsdale G. 2, Orr W. 27, Pierce J. 19, Sanders M. 29, Sharp J. 20, Smith E. D. 3, Smith J. 5, Smith T. (No. 1) 19, Stevenson J. 12, Tait A. 25, Trainer J. 19, Wright J. 2.

FA Cup appearances (1 game)

Joy, Holmes, Tait, Sharp, Sanders, Orr, Smith T., Blyth, Stevenson, Cunningham, Henderson one each.

Goalscorers: 44 League–1 Cup–(Total 45)

Pierce 8–0 (8), Sanders 6 (1pen)–0 (6), Blyth 5–0 (5), Smith T. 5–0 (5), Henderson 5–0 (5), Stevenson 4–0 (4), Cunningham 2–1 (3), Lonsdale 1–0 (1), Smith E. D. 1–0 (1), Eccleston W. 1–0 (1), Drummond 1–0 (1), Greer 1–0 (1), Holmes 1–0 (1), Orr 1–0 (1), Own goals 2–0 (2).

Trivia Facts:

In the game at Small Heath on 23 November 1895, John Wright, playing in goal, sustained a broken wrist. In the days long before substitutes were even thought of, right-back Alex Tait went in goal to replace him and Preston played on with ten men. Wright never played for the first team again.

Players today complain about having too many games. It was just as well that they weren't around in the late nineteenth century, because during this season alone Preston played 32 friendlies, in addition to their 31 league and cup games. Even the reserves played ten friendlies, including one glamorous fixture at Rock Ferry, Birkenhead against the Lancashire and North Western Railway Locos! And it was on Christmas Day! For the record North End won 4–0.

James Trainer won another Welsh International cap in the March when he played against Scotland. It was his 13th appearance, unlucky too, as Wales lost 4–1 in Glasgow.

PNE Reserves, with help from George Drummond, won the league Championship of the Lancashire Combination.

Date 1895-6	Opponents		Comp	h or a	Score	Att.	1	2	3	4	5	6	7	8	9	10	11		
Sep 2	Sunderland		Div 1	a	1-4		Trainer	Dunn	Holmes	Sharp	Sanders	Orr	Henderson (1)	Barr	D.Smith	Cunningham	Blyth		
Sep 7	Wolverhampton W.		Div 1	h	4-3		Trainer	Tait	Holmes	Sharp	Sanders	Orr	Henderson	Pierce (2)	D.Smith (1)	J.Smith	Blyth (1)		
Sep 14	WBA		Div 1	a	2-1		Wright	Tait	Holmes	Sharp	Sanders	Orr	Henderson	Pierce (1)	D.Smith	Drummond (1)	Blyth		
Sep 28	Burnley		Div 1	a	0-1		Trainer	Dunn	Holmes	Sharp	Sanders	Orr	Henderson	Pierce	J.Smith	Drummond	Blyth		
Sep 30	Sheffield Utd.		Div 1	a	1-2		Trainer	Dunn	Holmes	Greer	Sanders	Orr	Henderson	Pierce (1)	Lonsdale	Drummond	Blyth		
Oct 5	Small Heath		Div 1	h	3-2		Trainer	Tait	Holmes	Greer	Sanders	Orr	Henderson	Pierce (2)	Lonsdale (1)	Drummond	Blyth		
Oct 12	Blackburn R.		Div 1	a	0-3		Trainer	Dunn	Holmes	Sharp	Sanders	Orr	Henderson	Pierce	Drummond	Cunningham	Blyth		
Oct 19	Burnley		Div 1	h	1-1		Trainer	Tait	Holmes (1)	Sharp	Sanders	Orr	Henderson	Pierce	W.Brown	Cunningham	Blyth		
Oct 26	Nottm. Forest		Div 1	a	1-0		Trainer	Tait	Holmes	Sharp	Greer	Orr	W.Eccleston	Pierce (1)	Sanders	Cunningham	Blyth		
Nov 2	Blackburn R.		Div 1	h	1-1		Trainer	Tait	Holmes	Sharp	Greer	Orr	T.Smith (1)	Pierce	Sanders	Cunningham	Blyth		
Nov 9	Bolton W.		Div 1	h	1-0		Trainer	Tait	Holmes	Sharp	Greer	Orr	T.Smith	Pierce	Sanders (1)	J.Smith	Blyth		
Nov 11	Burnley		Div 1	a	0-4		Trainer	Tait	Holmes	Sharp	Greer	Orr	T.Smith	Pierce	Sanders	J.Smith	Blyth		
Nov 23	Small Heath		Div 1	a	2-5		Wright	Tait	Holmes	Sharp	Greer	Orr	T.Smith (1)	Pierce	Sanders	Cunningham	Blyth	1 o.g.	
Nov 30	Sheffield Utd.		Div 1	h	4-3		Joy	Tait	Holmes	Sharp	Greer (1)	Orr	Henderson	W.Eccleston (1)	T.Smith	Cunningham	Blyth (2)		
Dec 7	Aston Villa		Div 1	h	4-3		Joy	Tait	Holmes	Sharp	Greer	Orr	T.Smith	Blyth	Sanders (2)	Cunningham (1)	Henderson (1)		
Dec 14	Bury		Div 1	a	2-1		Joy	Holmes	Tait	Sharp	Greer	Orr	T.Smith	Blyth	Sanders (1)	Cunningham (1)	Henderson (1)		
Dec 21	Wolverhampton W.		Div 1	a	1-2		Joy	Holmes	Tait	Sharp	Greer	Orr	T.Smith	Blyth	Sanders	Cunningham	Henderson (1)		
Dec 25	Stoke		Div 1	h	0-1		Joy	Holmes	Tait	Sharp	Greer	Orr	T.Smith	Blyth	Sanders	Cunningham	Henderson		
Jan 1	Sheffield Wed.		Div 1	a	1-1		Joy	Holmes	Tait	Sharp	Sanders	Orr	T.Smith	Blyth	Stevenson (1)	Cunningham	Henderson		
Jan 4	Sunderland		Div 1	h	4-1		Joy	Holmes	Tait	Sharp	Sanders (2,1p)	Orr	T.Smith	Blyth	Stevenson	Cunningham	Henderson (2)		
Jan 11	Aston Villa		Div 1	a	0-1		Joy	Holmes	Tait	Sharp	Sanders	Orr	J.Smith	Blyth	Stevenson	Cunningham	Henderson		
Jan 25	Everton		Div 1	h	1-1		Joy	Holmes	Tait	Sharp	Sanders	Orr	T.Smith	Blyth	Stevenson	Cunningham	Henderson	1 o.g.	
Feb 1	Sunderland	Rd 1	FAC	a	1-4	13700	Joy	Holmes	Tait	Sharp	Sanders	Orr	T.Smith	Blyth	Stevenson	Cunningham (1)	Henderson		
Feb 22	Nottm. Forest		Div 1	h	6-0		Trainer	Holmes	Tait	Greer	Sanders	Orr (1)	T.Smith (1)	Blyth (1)	Stevenson (2)	Pierce (1)	Henderson		
Mar 4	Derby County		Div 1	h	1-1		Trainer	Holmes	Tait	Greer	Sanders	T.Eccleston	W.Eccleston	Pierce	Stevenson	Cunningham	Blyth		
Mar 7	Everton		Div 1	a	2-3		Trainer	Holmes	Tait	Greer	Sanders	T.Eccleston	T.Smith	Pierce	Stevenson (1)	Cunningham	Blyth (1)		
Mar 14	Bolton W.		Div 1	a	0-1		Trainer	Holmes	Dunn	Greer	Sanders	Blyth	T.Smith	Pierce	Stevenson	Cunningham	Henderson		
Mar 28	Derby County		Div 1	h	1-0		Trainer	Holmes	Tait	Greer	Sanders	Orr	T.Smith (1)	Pierce	Stevenson	Blyth	Henderson		
Apr 3	WBA		Div 1	h	0-0		Trainer	Holmes	Tait	Greer	Sanders	Orr	T.Smith	Pierce	Stevenson	Blyth	Henderson		
Apr 4	Bury		Div 1	h	1-1		Trainer	Holmes	Tait	Greer	Sanders	Orr	T.Smith (1)	Pierce	Stevenson	Blyth	Henderson		
Apr 6	Sheffield Wed.		Div 1	h	0-1		Trainer	Holmes	Tait	Greer	Sanders	Orr	T.Smith	Blyth	Stevenson	Cunningham	Henderson		

Season 1895–96: First Division

		P	W	D	L	F	A	Pts
1	Aston Villa	30	20	5	5	78	45	45
2	Derby	30	17	7	6	68	35	41
3	Everton	30	16	7	7	66	43	39
4	Bolton	30	16	5	9	49	37	37
5	Sunderland	30	15	7	8	52	41	37
6	Stoke	30	15	0	15	56	47	30
7	Wednesday	30	12	5	13	44	53	29
8	Blackburn	30	12	5	13	40	50	29
9	**PRESTON**	**30**	**11**	**6**	**13**	**44**	**48**	**28**
10	Burnley	30	10	7	13	48	44	27
11	Bury	30	12	3	15	50	54	27
12	Sheffield United	30	10	6	14	40	50	26
13	Nottingham Forest	30	11	3	16	42	57	25
14	Wolves	30	10	1	19	61	65	21
15	Small Heath	30	8	4	18	39	79	20
16	WBA	30	6	7	17	30	59	19

Match Report: A Friendly Hangover – 23 November 1895 Small Heath 5 Preston 2

After a midweek 1–9 friendly thrashing at Millwall Athletic the North End team still seemed out of sorts when meeting Small Heath in the league at Coventry Road. And so it proved. The 'Heathens' won the toss resulting in North End kicking off against a blustery and bitterly cold wind. Wright, in Preston's goal, was called upon in the very first minute having to save a scorching shot from Wheldon. Eventually North End seemed to put their Millwall mauling behind them and they settled down for Pierce, Sanders, Cunningham and Sharp to all go close to scoring. Another shot from Sanders was saved but the rebound went straight to Smith who promptly ran the ball into the net after 20 minutes. This only acted as a booster to the 'Heathens' who then raised their game to put Wright under more pressure. North End steadied the ship though and should have increased their lead but both Pierce and Sanders were guilty of sloppy finishing. These misses proved fatal as Wheldon equalised on 35 minutes with a good goal. Holmes then conceded a corner and from it Wheldon missed a good opportunity to score again but a few minutes later the same player rectified his mistake to give Small Heath the lead. Unfortunately for Preston it was found at half-time that their goalkeeper had sustained a fractured wrist when he accidentally struck the knee of an opponent. It meant that North End had to play the second half with ten men with Tait taking over the mantle of goalkeeper. With the man advantage Small Heath made the running but ironically Preston then equalised with an own goal. In an era when the team went out to win and not just to avoid defeat, North End played with just one full-back but continued with five forwards! This tactic obviously failed them in this case though as Small Heath promptly rattled in three goals before the final whistle.

18

SEASON 1896–1897

Future PNE players born during 1896–97: Rowland Woodhouse, Alf Quantrill and Johnny Williamson.
Ever presents: (2) Bob Blyth and James Trainer
FA Cup: 3rd Rd 2nd Replay
Hat-tricks: None
Manager: Management Committee
Chairman: Mr W. E. Ord J. P.
Leading scorer: 13 goals – David Boyd (all League)
Players used: 19

AUTHORS' UNOFFICIAL
PLAYER OF THE SEASON:
Bob Blyth

STAT FACTS:
Best home run without defeat: 6 games
Best away run without defeat: 4 games
Longest run unbeaten: 6 games
Longest run without a win: 5 games

A much better season for the Lilywhites, a season where they finished fourth behind Aston Villa, Sheffield United and Derby County, but only two points behind the latter two teams. But for a poor run in the last five games they would surely have ended as runners-up. After an opening goalless draw at Bury, North End began to find the target. The, suddenly in decline Sunderland, were beaten 5–3 at Deepdale, where Tom Pratt scored twice on his home debut. Two matches later that score-line was repeated against Burnley. Pratt, Alex Brown and James Stevenson all looked in sharp form and although the defence struggled at times, at least Preston were able to find the net themselves. October saw a very satisfying league double over their arch rivals Blackburn, with a terrific 4–0 win at Ewood being particularly impressive. Bob Blyth had a fine season at wing-half, helping in defence and pushing forward in support of the attack at every opportunity. Tom Smith and Adam Henderson were lively wingers and David Boyd topped the scoring charts in his first year at Deepdale. Unfortunately Aston Villa were on course to emulate Preston's feat of 1888–9 by winning the double, only the second side to achieve it, and they were far too powerful to be caught in the championship. But North End were definitely pushing for the runners-up spot until they hit that disastrous last five matches. Having just beaten Everton 4–1 at the beginning of April, the subsequent trip to Nottingham Forest seemed little more than a formality. Alas, they were held to a 0–0 draw and suddenly the goals dried up. Not one goal was scored in those five games. Two more goalless draws followed before defeats at home to both Derby and Villa ended Preston's hopes. The key to Preston's fate however was their away record. Only beaten four times on their travels but only three wins recorded. So many 'if onlys' in this frustrating but interesting campaign. It was the same story in the FA Cup. Fine wins over Manchester City and Stoke gave them a third round tie with the mighty Aston Villa at Deepdale. A battling 1–1 draw led to an even more courageous 0–0 draw in the replay at Villa Park. The final outcome was settled at Bramall Lane, Sheffield where another superb effort pushed Villa all the way before they lost by the odd goal in five. Who knows, if Preston had won that game and picked up a few more away points then the fans might even have had another league and cup double to celebrate. And interesting to note this 'success' had come in a season when the amount of friendlies played was drastically reduced.

DEBUTANTS: (5) David Boyd, Alexander Brown, Alexander Findlay, Thomas Pratt and Harry Vickers.

LAST GAMES: (5) Greer, Cunningham, Orr, Findlay and Vickers

Match Report: North End Down But Not Out – 12 Sept 1896 Preston 5 Sunderland 3

Lightening flashed majestically over the Deepdale enclosure prior to the kick-off as Preston and Sunderland lined up, two teams who had fallen from high places in recent years. Sanders, the captain, led the home side who included Bob Blyth at half-back. Blyth was normally a winger but his pace was even more effective at half-back. There were some lively skirmishes in the opening period of the game in front of around 8,000 people gathered in the rain. Many of those fans thought that Brown had scored but his effort had only brushed the side netting. Out of the first 25 minutes Preston held possession for all but five of those, attacking almost without intermission. But suddenly, from a breakaway, Gillespie sped past Tait and beat Trainer with a splendid shot. The goal came right out of the blue. Although disappointed there was no time for North End to rest and mourn. Eventually Orr slid a pass through to Henderson who in turn fed Brown. The youngster shot low and hard but his effort unluckily hit the post but fortunately for Preston the ball rebounded to Pratt who equalised. A few minutes later Blyth received an injury to his knee and had to leave the field for treatment. Just prior to the interval he returned only to see Harvey snatch a second for Sunderland, once more against the run of play. The muddy conditions forced a stoppage early in the second-half as Hannah caught a large dollop of mud in his eye! With the ball very greasy and the pitch becoming heavier by the minute play had slowed considerably since the start. Smith should have equalised but as is often the case, the play then went up to the other end where Trainer sliced an attempted clearance to Hannah who gleefully scored a third for Sunderland. In reality Preston should have been winning 3–1, not losing 3–1. Sunderland's goal had been peppered with shots, but fate, bad luck, bad finishing, call it what you like, meant that the visitors' goal stayed intact. The pressure had to tell though and Brown eventually beat Dunlop to make it 3–2. With 20 minutes to go Pratt caught one just right to equalise. It was all Preston at this stage and from a free-kick Smith launched himself at the ball landing up in the net with the ball, 4–3. Now well on top Preston waltzed around the muddy pitch as if on air and Boyd finally finished Sunderland off with a fifth goal, finishing off a good move started by Sanders. It completed an amazing comeback by the Lilywhites.

League position in Division One: 4th – P30 W11 D12 L7 F55 A40 Pts 34
Home: W8 D4 L3 F35 A21 Away: W3 D8 L4 F20 A19

Date 1896-7	Opponents	Comp	h or a	Score	Att.	1	2	3	4	5	6	7	8	9	10	11		
Sep 5	Bury	Div 1	a	0-0		Trainer	Holmes	Tait	Blyth	Sanders	Orr	Smith	Pratt	Brown	Boyd	Henderson		
Sep 12	Sunderland	Div 1	h	5-3		Trainer	Holmes	Tait	Blyth	Sanders	Orr	Smith (1)	Pratt (2)	Brown (1)	Boyd (1)	Henderson		
Sep 19	WBA	Div 1	a	1-1		Trainer	Holmes	Tait	Blyth	Sanders	Orr	Smith	Pratt	Brown	Boyd	Henderson (1)		
Sep 26	Burnley	Div 1	h	5-3		Trainer	Holmes	Tait	Blyth	Sanders	Orr	Findlay (1)	Pratt (2)	Brown (2)	Boyd	Henderson		
Oct 3	Bolton W.	Div 1	a	1-3		Trainer	Holmes	Tait	Blyth	Sanders	Orr	Findlay	Stevenson	Brown (1)	Boyd	Henderson		
Oct 10	Blackburn R.	Div 1	h	3-1		Trainer	Holmes	Tait	Blyth	Greer	Orr	Smith	Pratt	Stevenson (1)	Boyd (1)	Henderson (1)		
Oct 17	Burnley	Div 1	a	2-2		Trainer	Holmes	Tait	Blyth	Sanders	Orr	Smith	Pratt	Stevenson (2)	Boyd	Henderson		
Oct 24	Sheffield Utd.	Div 1	a	1-0		Trainer	Holmes	Tait	Blyth	Sanders	Orr	Smith	Pratt	Stevenson (1)	Boyd	Henderson		
Oct 31	Blackburn R.	Div 1	a	4-0		Trainer	Holmes	Tait	Blyth	Sanders	Orr	Smith	Pratt	Brown	Boyd (2)	Henderson (2)		
Nov 7	Nottm. Forest	Div 1	h	3-2		Trainer	Dunn	Tait	Blyth	Sanders	Orr	Smith	Pratt	Brown	Boyd (2)	Henderson		
Nov 9	Stoke	Div 1	h	1-2		Trainer	Holmes	Tait	Blyth	Sanders	Orr	Smith	Pratt	Brown	Boyd (1)	Henderson		
Nov 14	Liverpool	Div 1	h	1-1		Trainer	Holmes	Tait	Blyth	Sanders	Orr	Smith	Stevenson	Brown (1)	Boyd	Henderson		
Nov 21	Bolton W.	Div 1	h	2-3		Trainer	Holmes	Tait	Blyth	Sanders	Orr	Smith	Stevenson	Brown	Boyd (1)	Henderson (1)		
Nov 28	Stoke	Div 1	h	3-0		Trainer	Holmes	Dunn	Blyth	Sanders	Orr	Smith	Pratt	Brown (1)	Boyd (1)	Henderson (1)		
Dec 19	Wolverhampton W.	Div 1	a	1-1		Trainer	Holmes	Dunn	Blyth	Sanders	Orr	Smith	Stevenson (1)	Brown	Pratt	Cunningham		
Dec 26	Bury	Div 1	h	2-2		Trainer	Holmes	Dunn	Blyth	Sanders	Orr	Smith	Stevenson	Brown	Cunningham	Pratt (2)		
Jan 1	Sunderland	Div 1	a	1-1		Trainer	Holmes	Dunn	Blyth	Sanders	Orr	Smith	Stevenson (1)	Brown	Cunningham	Pratt		
Jan 2	Sheffield Wed.	Div 1	a	0-1		Trainer	Holmes	Dunn	Blyth	Sanders	Orr	Smith	Stevenson	Pierce	Cunningham	Pratt		
Jan 16	Wolverhampton W.	Div 1	h	4-0		Trainer	Holmes	Dunn	Blyth	Sanders	Orr	Smith	Pratt	Stevenson (1)	Boyd (2)	Henderson (1)		
Jan 30	Manchester City Rd 1	FAC	h	6-0	5000	Trainer	Holmes	Dunn	Blyth	Greer	Orr (2)	Smith	Pratt	Stevenson (2)	Boyd (1)	Henderson (1)		
Feb 6	Everton	Div 1	h	4-3		Trainer	Holmes	Dunn	Blyth	Greer	Orr	Smith (1)	Pratt (1)	Stevenson	Boyd	Henderson (1)		
Feb 13	Stoke Rd 2	FAC	h	2-1	7000	Trainer	Holmes	Dunn	Blyth	Greer	Orr	Smith (1)	Pratt	Stevenson (1)	Boyd	Henderson		
Feb 20	Sheffield Wed.	Div 1	h	2-2		Trainer	Holmes	Dunn	Blyth	Greer	Orr	Smith	Pierce	Stevenson	Boyd (1)	Henderson	1 o.g.	
Feb 22	Aston Villa	Div 1	a	1-3		Trainer	Holmes	Dunn	Blyth	Sanders	Orr	Smith	Eccleston (1)	Stevenson	Boyd	Henderson		
Feb 27	Aston Villa Rd 3	FAC	h	1-1	14000	Trainer	Holmes	Dunn	Blyth	Sanders	Orr	Smith	Pratt	Stevenson (1)	Boyd	Henderson		
Mar 3	Aston Villa Replay	FAC	a	0-0 *	12000	Trainer	Tait	Dunn	Blyth	Sanders	Orr	Smith	Pratt	Stevenson	Boyd	Henderson		
Mar 10	Aston Villa + 2nd Replay	FAC	n	2-3	25000	Trainer	Holmes	Dunn	Blyth	Sanders (1)	Orr	Smith	Pratt	Stevenson (1)	Boyd	Henderson		
Mar 13	Sheffield Utd.	Div 1	a	2-0		Trainer	Holmes	Dunn	Blyth	Sanders	Orr	Smith	Eccleston (1)	Pratt	Boyd (1)	Henderson		
Mar 27	Derby County	Div 1	a	2-2		Trainer	Holmes	Dunn	Blyth	Pratt	Orr	Smith	Eccleston	Brown (1)	Boyd	Henderson (1)		
Apr 3	Everton	Div 1	h	4-1		Trainer	Holmes	Dunn	Blyth	Greer	Sanders (2)	Smith	Eccleston	Brown	Boyd	Henderson (2)		
Apr 8	Nottm. Forest	Div 1	a	0-0		Trainer	Holmes	Dunn	Blyth	Greer	Sanders	Smith	Eccleston	Brown	Boyd	Henderson		
Apr 10	Liverpool	Div 1	a	0-0		Trainer	Holmes	Dunn	Blyth	Greer	Sanders	Smith	Pratt	Brown	Boyd	Henderson		
Apr 16	WBA	Div 1	h	0-0		Trainer	Holmes	Dunn	Blyth	Sanders	Vickers	Smith	Pratt	Brown	Boyd	Henderson		
Apr 19	Derby County	Div 1	h	0-2		Trainer	Holmes	Tait	Blyth	Sanders	Orr	Smith	Eccleston	Pratt	Boyd	Henderson		
Apr 26	Aston Villa	Div 1	a	0-1		Trainer	Tait	Dunn	Blyth	Sanders	Holmes	Eccleston	Pierce	Brown	Boyd	Henderson		

* A.E.T.
+ At Bramall Lane, Sheffield

Season 1896–97: First Division

		P	W	D	L	F	A	Pts
1	Aston Villa	30	21	5	4	73	38	47
2	Sheffield United	30	13	10	7	42	29	36
3	Derby	30	16	4	10	70	50	36
4	**PRESTON**	**30**	**11**	**12**	**7**	**55**	**40**	**34**
5	Liverpool	30	12	9	9	46	38	33
6	Wednesday	30	10	11	9	42	37	31
7	Everton	30	14	3	13	62	57	31
8	Bolton	30	12	6	12	40	43	30
9	Bury	30	10	10	10	39	44	30
10	Wolves	30	11	6	13	45	41	28
11	Nottingham Forest	30	9	8	13	44	49	26
12	WBA	30	10	6	14	33	56	26
13	Stoke	30	11	3	16	48	59	25
14	Blackburn	30	11	3	16	35	62	25
15	Sunderland	30	7	9	14	34	47	23
16	Burney	30	6	7	17	43	61	19

League appearances (30 games)

Blyth R. 30, Boyd D. 26, Brown A. 20, Cunningham J. 4, Dunn H. 17, Eccleston W. 7, Findlay A. 2, Greer W. H. 6, Henderson A. 26, Holmes R. 29, Orr W. 25, Pierce J. 3, Pratt T. 22, Sanders M. 26, Smith T. (No 1) 27, Stevenson J. 14, Tait A. 15, Trainer J. 30, Vickers H. 1

FA Cup appearances (5 games)

Trainer 5, Holmes 4, Tait 1, Dunn 5, Blyth 5, Greer 2, Sanders 3, Orr 5, Smith 5, Pratt 5, Stevenson 5, Boyd 5 and Henderson 5.

Goalscorers: 55 League–11 Cup–(Total 66)

Boyd 13–1 (14), Henderson 12–1 (13), Stevenson 7–5 (12), Brown 7–0 (7), Pratt 7–0 (7), Smith 3–1 (4), Sanders 2–1 (3), Eccleston 2–0 (2), Orr 0–2 (2), Findlay 1–0 (1) Own goals 1–0 (1)

Trivia Facts:

James Trainer won a further three caps for Wales during the season, playing against all the other home countries.

On 8 April 1897 neither the referee nor linesmen turned up due to bad weather conditions!

Trivia Facts:

Alex Findlay was the 24th North Ender to score on his league debut.

North End travelled to Workington on the 9 January 1897 to take on Cumberland County in a friendly. They returned home with a 12–0 win under their belts.

SEASON 1897–1898

Some future players born during the 1897–8 season: Stanley Davies, Tommy Roberts, James 'Fred' Mitchell, Charles Bosbury and William Whitehead
Ever presents: None
FA Cup: First Round
Hat-tricks: None
Manager: Management Committee
Chairman: Mr W. E. Ord J. P.
Leading scorer: 11 goals – Alex Brown (all league)
Players used: 26

AUTHORS' UNOFFICIAL PLAYER OF THE SEASON: Moses Sanders

After the excitement of the previous year, the 1897–8 season came as a bitter disappointment. A disastrous away record, (you will notice when reading this book, how often that statement is made!), where only five points out of thirty were gained, was the root cause of North End's problems. Only one win, at bottom of the table Stoke, and only once did Preston score more than one goal in an away match. In fact, goalscoring was a problem all season with the last five goalless games from the previous season campaign to six with an opening day 3–0 beating at Molineux against the Wolves. The goal-keeping position also saw a significant change during 1897–8. Jimmy Trainer, who had given such magnificent service throughout his Deepdale career, finally played his last game for the club. On 5 March a new man took over the number one jersey (except that there were no numbers in those days). He kept a clean sheet and stayed between the posts for the next 14 years. His name was Peter McBride. The rest of the team was less clearcut however and no fewer than 26 players were used in the side, and that showed just how desperate the management were at times during the year. Twelve new men came in but apart from McBride only Laurence Halsall, John Hunter and Henry Matthews made significant contributions. Alex Brown did well at centre-forward, indeed, he ended the season on a high by scoring in each of the last five games and topping the goal charts, just pipping James Stevenson. But a team cannot expect to win a championship when it fails to score in 9 of the 30 matches as Preston did. Sheffield United, a rising power in the game, won the title and they did the double over North End, whilst Sunderland were back to their best form to finish runners-up, even though Preston had beaten them in the Deepdale clash. An FA Cup run was again over before it had begun for North End and it was somewhat of a surprise defeat. Drawn at home to Second division Newcastle they were expected to win, but promotion chasing Newcastle pulled off a shock by winning 2–1. Ironically United did eventually win promotion despite missing out after the Test matches. The reason for this was that for the 1898–9 season the league was again increased in number. Meanwhile, the Preston fans had to be content with 12th position, but they were not happy and had noticed that one or two of the senior players were becoming restless and also that the players being brought in were generally not up to the standards the club had set for themselves. It was a worrying trend that was to continue.

DEBUTANTS: (12) Thomas Becton, James Blessington, Laurence Halsall, Robert Hargreaves, George Henderson, John Hunter (No 1), Peter McBride, Colin McLatchie, M. Henry Matthews, James May, Thomas Smith (No 2) and Daniel Whittle.

LAST GAMES: (6) Boyd, Becton T., Henderson G., Matthews, May and Trainer.

League appearances (30 games)

Becton T. 4, Blessington J. 5, Blyth R. 17, Boyd D. 11, Brown A. 20, Drummond G. 3, Dunn H. 26, Eccleston W. 14, Halsall L. 17, Hargreaves R. 8, Henderson G. 2, Holmes R. 28, Hunter J. 15, McBride P. 6, McLatchie C. 7, Matthews M. H. 18, May J. 3, Pierce J. 12, Pratt T. 18, Sanders M. 28, Smith T. (No. 1) 7, Smith T. (No. 2) 4, Stevenson J. 25, Tait A. 7, Trainer J. 24, Whittle D. 1.

FA Cup (1 game)

Trainer, Holmes, Tait, Blyth, Sanders, Matthews, Smith T. (No. 2), Pratt, Brown, Stevenson and Halsall all one appearance each.

Goalscorers: 35 League–1 Cup–(Total 36)

Brown 11–0 (11), Stevenson 10–0 (10), Pratt 4–0 (4), Eccleston 3–0 (3), Halsall 2–0 (2), Pierce 1–0 (1), McLatchie 1–0 (1), Boyd 1–0 (1), Blyth 1(pen)–0 (1), Own goals 1–1 (2) (Sharp of Aston Villa in the league and White of Newcastle in the cup)

Trivia Facts:

The 35 goals that Preston scored during 1897–98 is the lowest total they have ever produced for a completed Football League season.

Hugh Dunn was made captain for the 1897–98 season, but North End were also captained by James Stevenson and Bob Blyth during that season. And Bob Holmes played for an England XI against Scotland in a Players Union International. Whatever happened to that fixture?!

Jack Barton, the famous 'trainer who played for the first team', left the club to join Wigan County as trainer in the pre-season of 1897–98. The man who followed him into the job at Deepdale was Joe Thornber.

How many of you have heard of a football magazine called the *Golden Penny*? Well, on 20 November 1897 a picture of both the North End team and the ground was featured in that week's issue.

In the April of 1898 Tom Pratt and James Stevenson went out on loan to Newtown FC. It was not quite as strange as it may seem as Preston's season had finished by that time.

There were two Tom Smiths playing for North End during this season and they were both right wingers. No wonder there was some confusion for the statisticians of the day. Not to mention today!

League position in Division One: 12th – P30 W8 D8 L14 F35 A43 Pts 24
Home: W7 D5 L3 F26 A15 Away: W1 D3 L11 F9 A28

Match Report: Brown, PNE's Saviour –
9 April 1898. Preston 5 Derby 0

Never in the history of the game had there been a Saturday where so much importance fell on the results of so many clubs. No fewer than five clubs were grouped on 22 points at the bottom of the league, including Preston. A few of the others had a game in hand of North End so a win for them, and if possible a good win, was imperative. Their final opponents were Derby County who had to play the FA Cup Final the following Saturday. With relegation threatening North End were really up for the game and were soon thundering shots in on Fryer's goal. Blyth, Holmes, Tait and Pratt all had good efforts cleared early on. After 18 minutes Hargreaves was tripped, a penalty being awarded only after the referee had consulted both linesmen! Preston had had a lean time with penalties and had not scored from one for two years, so it was Blyth who as captain decided to take the responsibility on himself for this crucial spot-kick. Despite some unsporting behaviour from Fryer in goal, Blyth duly scored. Hunter, outstanding in defence, ventured forward after 31 minutes and centred for Brown to head home, much to the jubilation of players and fans alike. Brown was suddenly hailed a saviour! He certainly was 11 minutes later after he waltzed around his marker to make the score 3–0 with only three minutes of the half remaining. There was no let up as North End made a storming start to the second half having a goal disallowed two minutes into the half. Preston were playing with great belief and within 5 minutes they made it 4–0. McLatchie shot hard at Fryer who mishandled only to see Pratt dancing into the unguarded net with the ball. All the North End fans' birthdays had come at once as their team was winning hands down. The goal of the game was yet to come. After an hour's play Pierce battled for the ball in a scramble. The little fellow wriggled free from one tackle after another with the ball at his feet. Then, quick as a flash, he released his shooting foot and Fryer, not knowing anything until he saw his net vibrating as if hit by a hurricane. 5–0 to the PNE! The other results also went Preston's way and they were able to look forward to another season in the top flight. Footnote: Derby lost the Final to Nottingham Forest 3–1.

Season 1897–98: First Division

	P	W	D	L	F	A	Pts
1 Sheffield United	30	17	8	5	56	31	42
2 Sunderland	30	16	5	9	43	30	37
3 Wolves	30	14	7	9	57	41	35
4 Everton	30	13	9	8	48	39	35
5 Wednesday	30	15	3	12	51	42	33
6 Aston Villa	30	14	5	11	61	51	33
7 WBA	30	11	10	9	44	45	32
8 Nottingham Forest	30	11	9	10	47	49	31
9 Liverpool	30	11	6	13	48	45	28
10 Derby	30	11	6	13	57	61	28
11 Bolton	30	11	4	15	28	41	26
12 PRESTON	**30**	**8**	**8**	**14**	**35**	**43**	**24**
13 Notts County	30	8	8	14	36	46	24
14 Bury	30	8	8	14	39	51	24
15 Blackburn	30	7	10	13	39	54	24
16 Stoke	30	8	8	14	35	55	24

Trivia Fact:

Tommy Smith (No. 1) was from Maryport Rugby Union Club whereas Tommy Smith (No. 2) was from Ashton-in-Makerfield.

Date 1897-8	Opponents	Comp	h or a	Score	Att.	1	2	3	4	5	6	7	8	9	10	11		
Sep 1	Wolverhampton W.	Div 1	a	0-3		Trainer	Tait	Dunn	Henderson	Sanders	Holmes	T.Smith *	Pratt	Stevenson	Boyd	McLatchie		
Sep 4	Sheffield Utd.	Div 1	h	1-3		Trainer	Holmes	Dunn	Pratt	Sanders	Drummond	T.Smith *	Hargreaves	Stevenson	Boyd (1)	McLatchie		
Sep 11	Liverpool	Div 1	a	0-0		Trainer	Holmes	Dunn	Pratt	Sanders	Drummond	T.Smith *	Hargreaves	Stevenson	Boyd	McLatchie		
Sep 18	Sunderland	Div 1	h	2-0		Trainer	Holmes	Dunn	Pratt	Sanders	Drummond	T.Smith *	Hargreaves	Stevenson (2)	Boyd	Eccleston		
Sep 25	Bolton W.	Div 1	a	0-1		Trainer	Holmes	Dunn	Pratt	Sanders	Matthews	Eccleston	Hargreaves	Stevenson	Boyd	Becton		
Oct 2	Liverpool	Div 1	h	1-1		Trainer	Holmes	Dunn	Pratt	Sanders	Matthews	Eccleston (1)	Hargreaves	Stevenson	Boyd	Becton		
Oct 7	Notts County	Div 1	a	1-1		Trainer	Holmes	Dunn	Hunter	Sanders	Matthews	Eccleston	Hargreaves	Stevenson (1)	Boyd	Becton		
Oct 9	Blackburn R.	Div 1	a	0-1		Trainer	Holmes	Dunn	Hunter	Sanders	Matthews	T.Smith *	Eccleston	Stevenson	Boyd	Becton		
Oct 16	Bolton W.	Div 1	h	0-0		Trainer	Holmes	Dunn	Hunter	Sanders	Matthews	Eccleston	Pratt	Stevenson	Hargreaves	Whittle		
Oct 23	Sheffield Utd.	Div 1	h	1-2		Trainer	Holmes	Tait	Hunter	Sanders	Matthews	Eccleston (1)	Stevenson	Brown	Pierce	Boyd		
Oct 30	Blackburn R.	Div 1	h	1-4		Trainer	Holmes	Dunn	Hunter	Sanders	Matthews	Eccleston	Stevenson	Brown (1)	Boyd	Halsall		
Nov 6	Aston Villa	Div 1	h	3-1		Trainer	Holmes	Dunn	Hunter	Sanders	Matthews	Eccleston	Stevenson	Brown (1)	Pierce	Halsall (1)	1 o.g.	(Sharp)
Nov 8	Stoke	Div 1	a	2-1		Trainer	Holmes	Dunn	Hunter	Sanders	Matthews	Eccleston (1)	Stevenson	Brown (1)	Pierce	Halsall		
Nov 13	Nottm. Forest	Div 1	a	1-4		Trainer	Holmes	Dunn	Blyth	Sanders	Matthews	Eccleston	Stevenson	Brown	Pierce	Halsall (1)		
Nov 20	Everton	Div 1	h	1-1		Trainer	Holmes	Dunn	Blyth	Sanders	Matthews	Eccleston	Stevenson (1)	Brown	Pierce	Halsall		
Nov 27	Wolverhampton W.	Div 1	h	1-2		Trainer	Holmes	Dunn	Blyth	Hunter	Matthews	T.Smith *	Stevenson	Brown (1)	Pierce	Halsall		
Dec 11	Sheffield Wed.	Div 1	a	1-2		Trainer	Holmes	Dunn	Blyth	Sanders	Matthews	T.Smith +	Pratt	Brown	Stevenson (1)	Halsall		
Dec 18	Sheffield Wed.	Div 1	h	2-0		Trainer	Holmes	Dunn	Blyth	Sanders	Matthews	T.Smith +	Pratt (1)	Brown	Stevenson (1)	Halsall		
Dec 25	Nottm. Forest	Div 1	h	3-0		Trainer	Holmes	Dunn	Blyth	Sanders	Matthews	T.Smith +	Pratt (1)	Brown (1)	Stevenson (1)	Halsall		
Jan 1	Sunderland	Div 1	a	0-1		Trainer	Holmes	Dunn	Blyth	Sanders	Matthews	Eccleston	Pratt	Brown	Stevenson	Halsall		
Jan 8	Bury	Div 1	a	2-1		Trainer	Holmes	Dunn	Blyth	Sanders	Matthews	Eccleston	Pratt	Brown	Stevenson (2)	Halsall		
Jan 15	WBA	Div 1	a	1-3		Trainer	Holmes	Dunn	Blyth	Sanders	Matthews	T.Smith +	Pratt	Brown	Stevenson (1)	Halsall		
Jan 29	**Newcastle Utd. Rd 1**	**FAC**	**h**	**1-2**	**3,000**	**Trainer**	**Holmes**	**Tait**	**Blyth**	**Sanders**	**Matthews**	**T.Smith +**	**Pratt**	**Brown**	**Stevenson**	**Halsall**	**1 o.g.**	**(White)**
Feb 5	Aston Villa	Div 1	a	0-4		Trainer	Holmes	Tait	Blyth	Stevenson	Henderson	Halsall	Pratt	Brown	Pierce	McLatchie		
Feb 12	Bury	Div 1	a	0-1		Trainer	Holmes	Dunn	Hunter	Sanders	Blyth	T.Smith *	Stevenson	Brown	Boyd	Halsall		
Mar 5	Stoke	Div 1	h	0-0		McBride	Holmes	Dunn	Blyth	Sanders	Hunter	May	Blessington	Stevenson	Pratt	Halsall		
Mar 12	Derby County	Div 1	a	1-3		McBride	Holmes	Dunn	Hunter	Sanders	Blyth	May	Blessington	Brown (1)	Pierce	Halsall		
Mar 21	Everton	Div 1	a	1-1		McBride	Tait	Dunn	Hunter	Sanders	Blyth	May	Blessington	Brown (1)	Pierce	Halsall		
Mar 31	WBA	Div 1	h	1-1		McBride	Tait	Dunn	Hunter	Sanders	Blyth	Pratt	Blessington	Brown (1)	Pierce	McLatchie		
Apr 8	Notts County	Div 1	h	3-1		McBride	Tait	Holmes	Hunter	Sanders	Blyth	Pratt (1)	Blessington	Brown (1)	Pierce	McLatchie (1)		
Apr 9	Derby County	Div 1	h	5-0		McBride	Tait	Holmes	Hunter	Sanders	Blyth (1p)	Pratt (1)	Hargreaves	Brown (2)	Pierce (1)	McLatchie		
												* T.Smith No.1 + T.Smith No.2						

22

SEASON 1898–1899

This was a very significant season, not only in Preston's history, but also in the history of football in this country. It was the first season when automatic promotion and relegation was introduced between the two divisions, which were also increased to 18 teams in each. For Preston it was a real struggle for them to avoid those last two positions before they finally gained enough points to save themselves. Most of their matches were closely fought with often just one goal separating the sides. However the club had an appalling away record and they never won once on an opponents ground. Thankfully, at Deepdale, it was a different story. At the back Peter McBride established his place in goal but several of the stalwart defenders of the previous few seasons were in and out of the side. Most noticeably Moses Sanders and Bob Holmes who did not make the same impact on the games as they had done in their earlier seasons with the club. Up front it was very much trial and error. Tommy Pratt was always a lively forward and he had his best goalscoring year, but generally the attack failed to find the necessary penetration needed. William Eccleston was an effective right-half and Alex Brown led the line well when he played. Brown scored in each of his first three games but when he was given an extended run in the team he struggled, although he did manage to score in all three of the FA Cup ties played. That competition also brought disappointment to a poor season. North End went out after a second round replay against fellow relegation candidates,

Sheffield United. But there was one special moment in North End's first round match, against Grimsby at Deepdale, as Pratt hit four goals in the 7–0 drubbing of the Mariners. Believe it or not but he also missed a penalty in this game. Other players had satisfactory seasons with Peter McIntyre, Patrick Murray and left-winger Laurence Halsall the pick. But with only two wins from their first 15 league games Preston were always playing 'catch up' and as a result it put too much pressure on the players. They could never put together a decent unbeaten run and it badly affected the confidence in the team. The best result of the season, and one that helped more than most to keep them in the division, came with a 2–0 home win over the eventual Champions, Aston Villa. Murray and Brown scored the vital goals. In the end though Preston had to be thankful for the failings of others before they guaranteed First Division football for another season. There was also much sadness amongst the Preston fans as they had to say goodbye to a number of former greats who reached the end of their Deepdale careers during this season.

DEBUTANTS: (6) James Chalmers, Joseph Elliott, Andrew Gara, James Green, Peter McIntyre and Patrick Murray.

LAST GAMES: (12) Drummond G., Howarth, J. Hunter (No.1), Sanders, Russell, Blyth R., Tait, Brown A., Blessington, Hargreaves, McLatchie and Chalmers.

Match Report: The Late Late Show –
15 Apr 1899 Blackburn Rovers 2 Preston 2

The visit of Preston North End to Ewood Park, Blackburn had always been of great interest locally but on this day Preston were going there fighting for their First Division survival. Favoured with dry weather, albeit with a cold wind blowing, only around 6,000 ardent followers were present at the start of the game. Russell won the toss and took advantage of the wind's direction. No sooner had the Rovers kicked off than North End gained possession, breaking away down the left hand side. Halsall latched onto the ball and lost no time in getting a shot in which cannoned off Branston for the first Preston corner. Halsall wasted that and Blackburn then attacked. Their first chance came after Bob Holmes misjudged a tackle, letting in Booth, Rover's captain, who squandered his golden opportunity. In one skirmish Thompson, the young home goalkeeper, headed the ball to safety, at the same time flooring Gara, the busy Preston forward. Eventually the first goal arrived courtesy of Russell who had initially gone up for a corner. In a lively melee in front of the Blackburn goal the ball was thumped against an upright. It rebounded to Russell who stretched to head the ball home. The home side took control after that and deservedly equalised with an overhead kick by Hirst on 43 minutes. Rain fell during the break and made conditions tricky but the game became dull as Preston used a 'play it safe' policy, defenders being on top. But with 15 minutes to go Mellor born Fred Blackburn put the Rovers ahead when he scored with a wind assisted beauty. North End struggled on, until, with only five minutes left they gained another corner from which Booth failed to clear giving Murray the chance to equalise, much to the delight of the rain soaked Preston fans. The point gained was priceless, as coupled with the defeats of Bolton and Sheffield Wednesday, at Bury and Newcastle respectively, Preston were thankful that they had staved off relegation for yet another season. But, alas, the inevitable was in the not too distant future.

League position in Division One: 15th – P34 W10 D9 L15 F44 A47 Pts 29
Home: W10 D4 L3 F29 A14 Away: W0 D5 L12 F15 A33

Some future players born during this season: Fred Marquis, Freddie Fox and James Phizacklea

Ever presents: (1) Peter McBride

FA Cup: Second Round Replay

Hat-tricks: (1) Tom Pratt who actually hit four goals in the cup-tie with Grimsby.

Manager: Management Committee

Chairman: Mr W. E. Ord J. P.

Leading scorer: 17 goals – Tom Pratt (13 League 4 Cup)

Players used: 25

AUTHORS' UNOFFICIAL PLAYER OF THE SEASON: Tom Pratt

Season 1898–99: First Division

		P	W	D	L	F	A	Pts
1	Aston Villa	34	19	7	8	76	40	45
2	Liverpool	34	19	5	10	49	33	43
3	Burney	34	15	9	10	45	47	39
4	Everton	34	15	8	11	48	41	38
5	Notts County	34	12	13	9	47	51	37
6	Blackburn	34	14	8	12	60	52	36
7	Sunderland	34	15	6	13	41	41	36
8	Wolves	34	14	7	13	54	48	35
9	Derby	34	12	11	11	62	57	35
10	Bury	34	14	7	13	48	49	35
11	Nottingham Forest	34	11	11	12	42	42	33
12	Stoke	34	13	7	14	47	52	33
13	Newcastle	34	11	8	15	49	48	30
14	WBA	34	12	6	16	42	57	30
15	**PRESTON**	**34**	**10**	**9**	**15**	**44**	**47**	**29**
16	Sheffield United	34	9	11	14	45	51	29
17	Bolton	34	9	7	18	37	51	25
18	Wednesday	34	8	8	18	32	61	24

League appearances: (34 games)

Blessington J. 10, Blyth R. 24, Brown A. 23, Chalmers J. 10, Drummond G. 1, Dunn H. 22, Eccleston W. 30, Elliott J. 1, Gara A. 7, Green J. 1, Halsall L. 28, Hargreaves R. 3, Holmes R. 19, Howarth R. H. 1, Hunter J. 1, McBride P. 34, McIntyre P. 22, McLatchie C. 2, Murray P. 31, Pierce J. 2, Pratt T. 31, Russell D. 26, Sanders M. 15, Tait A. 26, Whittle D. 4.

FA Cup appearances: (3 games)

McBride 3, Dunn 3, Holmes 3, Eccleston 3, Russell 3, Blyth 3, Murray 3, Pratt 3, Brown 3, Chalmers 3 and Halsall 3.

Goalscorers: 44 League–10 Cup–(Total 54)

Pratt 13 (2 pens)–4 (17), Brown 7–4 (11), Murray 7–0 (7), Halsall 4–1 (5), Russell 3 (1pen)–0 (3), Gara 3–0 (3), Chalmers 2–1 (3), McIntyre 2–0 (2), Blessington 1–0 (1), Sanders 1–0 (1), McLatchie 1–0 (1).

Date 1898-9	Opponents	Comp	h or a	Score	Att.	1	2	3	4	5	6	7	8	9	10	11
Sep 3	Sunderland	Div 1	h	2-3		McBride	Tait	Dunn	Blyth	Russell	Sanders	McIntyre	Blessington	Brown (1)	Pierce	McLatchie (1)
Sep 5	Burnley	Div 1	a	1-3		McBride	Tait	Dunn	Blyth	Russell	Elliott	McIntyre	Pratt	Brown (1)	Pierce	McLatchie
Sep 10	Wolverhampton W.	Div 1	a	0-0		McBride	Dunn	Tait	Eccleston	Russell	Blyth	Murray	Pratt	Whittle	Hargreaves	Halsall
Sep 17	Everton	Div 1	h	0-0		McBride	Dunn	Tait	Eccleston	Russell	Blyth	Murray	Pratt	Whittle	Hargreaves	Halsall
Sep 19	Sheffield Wed.	Div 1	a	1-2		McBride	Dunn	Tait	Eccleston	Russell	Blyth	Murray (1)	Pratt	Whittle	Drummond	Halsall
Sep 24	Notts County	Div 1	a	0-1		McBride	Dunn	Tait	Eccleston	Russell	Blyth	McIntyre	Pratt	Whittle	Hargreaves	Halsall
Oct 1	Stoke	Div 1	h	4-2		McBride	Dunn	Tait	Eccleston	Russell	Blyth	McIntyre	Blessington	Pratt (1)	Murray (1)	Halsall (2)
Oct 6	Nottm. Forest	Div 1	h	2-2		McBride	Dunn	Tait	Eccleston	Russell	Blyth	McIntyre	Blessington (1)	Pratt	Murray (1)	Halsall
Oct 8	Aston Villa	Div 1	a	2-4		McBride	Dunn	Tait	Eccleston	Russell	Blyth	McIntyre (1)	Blessington	Brown (1)	Murray	Halsall
Oct 15	Burnley	Div 1	h	1-1		McBride	Dunn	Tait	Eccleston	Russell (1p)	Blyth	McIntyre	Blessington	Pratt	Murray	Halsall
Oct 22	Sheffield Utd.	Div 1	a	1-1		McBride	Dunn	Tait	Eccleston	Sanders	Blyth	McIntyre	Pratt (1)	Russell	Murray	Halsall
Oct 29	Newcastle Utd.	Div 1	h	1-0		McBride	Dunn	Tait	Eccleston	Sanders	Blyth	McIntyre	Pratt (1)	Russell	Murray	Halsall
Nov 5	Bury	Div 1	a	1-3		McBride	Dunn	Tait	Eccleston	Russell	Blyth	McIntyre	Blessington	Pratt (1)	Murray	Chalmers
Nov 12	Liverpool	Div 1	a	1-3		McBride	Dunn	Tait	Eccleston	Russell	Blyth	McIntyre	Blessington	Pratt	Murray	Chalmers (1)
Nov 14	Stoke	Div 1	a	1-2		McBride	Dunn	Holmes	Eccleston	Sanders	Blyth	McIntyre	Pratt (1)	Brown	Murray	Chalmers
Nov 19	Nottm. Forest	Div 1	h	1-0		McBride	Dunn	Holmes	Hunter	Sanders	Blyth	McIntyre	Pratt (1)	Brown	Murray	Chalmers
Nov 26	Bolton W.	Div 1	a	2-2		McBride	Dunn	Holmes	McIntyre	Sanders	Blyth	Murray	Pratt	Brown (2)	Chalmers	Halsall
Dec 3	Derby County	Div 1	h	3-1		McBride	Dunn	Holmes	Eccleston	Sanders	Blyth	Murray (1)	Pratt (1p)	Brown	Chalmers (1)	Halsall
Dec 10	WBA	Div 1	a	0-2		McBride	Dunn	Holmes	Eccleston	Sanders	Blyth	Murray	Pratt	Brown	Chalmers	Halsall
Dec 17	Blackburn R.	Div 1	h	1-1		McBride	Dunn	Holmes	Eccleston	Sanders	Blyth	Murray	Pratt (1)	Brown	Chalmers	Halsall
Dec 26	Bury	Div 1	h	3-1		McBride	Holmes	Tait	Eccleston	Sanders	Russell (1)	Blessington	Pratt (1)	Brown	Murray	Halsall (1)
Dec 31	Sunderland	Div 1	a	0-1		McBride	Holmes	Tait	Eccleston	Sanders	Russell	Blyth	Blessington	Pratt	Brown	Murray	Halsall
Jan 7	Wolverhampton W.	Div 1	h	2-1		McBride	Holmes	Tait	Eccleston	Sanders	Russell	Green	Pratt (1p)	Brown	Murray (1)	Halsall
Jan 14	Everton	Div 1	a	0-2		McBride	Dunn	Holmes	Eccleston	Sanders	Russell	McIntyre	Pratt	Brown	Murray	Halsall
Jan 28	Grimsby Town	Rd 1 FAC	h	7-0	4517	McBride	Dunn	Holmes	Eccleston	Russell	Blyth	Murray	Pratt (4)	Brown (2)	Chalmers (1)	Halsall
Feb 4	Aston Villa	Div 1	h	2-0		McBride	Dunn	Holmes	Eccleston	Russell	Blyth	Murray (1)	Pratt	Brown (1)	Chalmers	Halsall
Feb 11	Sheffield Utd.	Rd 2 FAC	h	2-2	12000	McBride	Dunn	Holmes	Eccleston	Russell	Blyth	Murray	Pratt	Brown (1)	Chalmers	Halsall (1)
Feb 16	Sheffield Utd. Replay	FAC	a	1-2	17847	McBride	Dunn	Holmes	Eccleston	Russell	Blyth	Murray	Pratt	Brown (1)	Chalmers	Halsall
Feb 18	Sheffield Utd.	Div 1	h	1-0		McBride	Holmes	Tait	Eccleston	Sanders	Russell	Blessington	Pratt	Brown	Murray	Halsall (1)
Feb 25	Newcastle Utd.	Div 1	a	1-2		McBride	Holmes	Tait	Eccleston	Sanders (1)	McIntyre	Murray	Pratt	Brown	Chalmers	Halsall
Mar 11	Liverpool	Div 1	h	1-2		McBride	Holmes	Tait	Eccleston	Russell	Blyth	Murray	Pratt (1)	Brown	Gara	Halsall
Mar 20	Notts Coutny	Div 1	h	0-1		McBride	Howarth	Tait	Eccleston	Russell	McIntyre (1)	Murray	Pratt	Brown (1)	Gara	Halsall
Apr 1	Derby County	Div 1	a	0-1		McBride	Holmes	Tait	Eccleston	Russell	McIntyre	Murray	Pratt	Brown	Gara	Halsall
Apr 8	WBA	Div 1	h	4-0		McBride	Holmes	Tait	Eccleston	Russell	McIntyre	Murray	Pratt (2)	Brown	Gara (2)	Halsall
Apr 15	Blackburn R.	Div 1	a	2-2		McBride	Holmes	Tait	Eccleston	Russell (1)	McIntyre	Murray (1)	Pratt	Brown	Gara	Halsall
Apr 22	Sheffield Wed.	Div 1	h	1-1		McBride	Holmes	Tait	Eccleston	Russell	McIntyre	Murray	Pratt	Brown	Gara (1)	Halsall
Apr 29	Bolton W.	Div 1	h	0-0		McBride	Holmes	Tait	Eccleston	Sanders	McIntyre	Blyth	Murray	Brown	Gara	Halsall

Trivia Fact:

Although in relegation trouble and with just four league games remaining the North End Club strangely took a short trip to Ireland to play a couple of friendlies. They beat Glentoran 5–0 but lost 1–2 against Distillery.

SEASON 1899–1900

Some future players born during the season 1899–1900: James Green (No.2), Tommy Green, Albert Shears, John Gilchrist, Harry Hirst and David Morris
Ever presents: (2) Hugh Dunn and Peter McBride
Hat-tricks: (2) Pierce and Henderson one each
Manager:
Management Committee
FA Cup: Third Round Replay
Chairman:
Mr W. E. Ord J. P.
Leading scorer: 13 goals – Adam Henderson (12 League 1 Cup)
Players used: 24

AUTHORS' UNOFFICIAL
PLAYER OF THE SEASON:
Hugh Dunn

This was another year of struggle for the club and a season where goalscoring was a real problem for North End. A very poor start to the league campaign saw just three wins before Christmas and it was not to be until the last three vital games that the club won six crucial points which proved enough to save them from the very real possibility of relegation. In between it was a case of either very good or very bad. In one spell of nine games, seven ended goalless, thus emphasising the problem Preston had in attack. As far as individuals went Adam Henderson, who had returned to Preston after spells at Celtic and Gravesend, was the only player to reach a goal tally in double figures, although strangely 12 of his 13 league and cup goals came after the turn of the year. In defence Peter McBride and Hugh Dunn played very well and Joe Elliott was a fine left-half. Nine new players were brought in although of those only James Atherton and Richard Orrell managed double figures in appearances. It was interesting to note that Sheffield United, who had finished level on points with North End in the previous season, had this year pushed Aston Villa all the way for the title. That showed that they had worked hard to make changes to improve their standing in the game. Sadly, at Preston, this was not the case and the club was now feeling the full force from their own lack of initiative. They were certainly a team now made up of a few star players plus several others who were just not good enough for First Division football, and a few who were destined to become one game wonders. In the FA Cup Preston did at least manage to battle through to the third round. A home win over Southern League Tottenham Hotspur was followed by a superb morale boosting victory over Blackburn Rovers. Henderson scored the winner in the tie at Deepdale against our near neighbours. In the next round though Preston were held to a goalless draw, also at home, by Nottingham Forest, before losing by a single goal at Nottingham in the replay. After that disappointment Preston were left with eleven league games to try and salvage their season. Two wins at Deepdale and two defeats on their travels left April being one of the most crucial months in their history. It began disastrously with four defeats on the trot. For the Preston fans it looked all over but a spirited rally brought a vital win at fellow strugglers Burnley, followed by a victory at home against the Wolves. That left the club needing to win their last game to be sure of staying up and would you believe it but the opposition was to be Blackburn of all people. In the end goals from Tommy Eccleston and Harold Stansfield gave Preston a 2–0 victory and they pipped Burnley by just one point sending their Turf Moor neighbours down. Phew!

DEBUTANTS: (9) James Atherton, Richard Banks, Matthew Brunton, Thomas Hodgson, Richard Orrell, Harold Parker, Benjamin Sanderson, George Smith and Harold Stansfield.

LAST GAMES: (9) Eccleston W., Halsall, Whittle, Green, Murray, Atherton, Banks, Brunton and Stansfield.

STAT FACTS:
Best home run without defeat: 6 games
Best away run without defeat: 1 game
Longest run unbeaten: 3 games
Longest run without a win: 7 games

Trivia Fact:

Preston won the Lancashire Cup on 17 March 1900, beating Burnley 1–0 in the final. They had beaten Blackpool in a replay in the semi.

Match Report: Rovers Lose Dog-Fight – 17 Feb. 1900. Preston 1 Blackburn 0, FA Cup

How ironic that Preston and Blackburn, best of rivals over the years, had to wait until the new millennium before they faced each other in an FA Cup-tie. The players and spectators were blessed with sunny conditions for this second round tie. Preston had beaten Spurs in the previous round whilst Rovers had taken three games to dispose of Portsmouth. Dunn won the toss and elected to play 'downhill'. Although fewer than 14,000 people were spread around the Deepdale enclosure, both sides had plenty of support which helped create an electric atmosphere. An early chance fell to Henderson who used his speed to advantage but his shot went agonisingly inches wide of the post. Play was quickly transferred to the other end but Rovers found McBride in an uncharitable mood. Whittaker and Dewhurst for Blackburn and Gara for Preston all squandered golden chances to open the scoring, the huge occasion seemingly getting the better of them. On another foraging Rover's attack Hurst beat Dunn, his shot actually deceiving McBride, but luckily for North End it hit the upright and flew to safety. A little later Pierce was next to show his skills but he sent his effort into the waitng hands of Knowles, who unbeknown to anyone at the time, was playing his last first team game for Rovers. The reason for the goalless first half was probably a combination of good goalkeeping, poor finishing and nerves. On resuming North End were first to attack. Murray tricked Crompton and with a swiftly taken shot at goal he nearly opened the scoring. Knowles, now under extreme pressure from Gara and company, only just managed to clear his lines at the cost of yet another corner. The game was still fairly even though and a draw looked odds on, so much so that some spectators even started to leave the ground. Then out of the blue, with just seven minutes to go, Henderson, out on the extreme left, eluded Brandon and sent in a lightening shot on the run. Knowles was left grasping fresh air, and the North End players and fans celebrated their successful strike. Preston doggedly defended their lead as Blackburn tried in vain to equalise.

League position in Division One: 16th – P34 W12 D4 L18 F38 A48 Pts 28
Home: W9 D3 L5 F28 A20   Away: W3 D1 L13 F10 A28

League appearances (34 games)

Atherton J. 13, Banks R. 4, Brunton M. 8, Dunn H. 34,
Eccleston T. 16, Eccleston W. 18, Elliott J. 32,
Gara A. 19, Green J. 5, Halsall L. 9, Henderson A. 27,
Hodgson T. 2, Holmes R. 18, McBride P. 34,
McIntyre P. 33, Murray P. 20, Orrell R. 15, Parker H. 1,
Pierce J. 19, Sanderson B. S. 1, Smith G. 9,
Stansfield H. 4, Stevenson J. 28, Whittle D. 5.

FA Cup appearances (4 games)

McBride 4, Dunn 4, Orrell 4, Eccleston T. 1,
Eccleston W. 3, McIntyre 4, Elliott 4, Murray 4, Gara 4,
Stevenson 4, Pierce 4 and Henderson 4.

Goalscorers: 38 League–2 Cup–(Total 40)

Henderson 12 (2pens)–1 (13), Gara 6–0 (6),
Stevenson 5–1 (6), Pierce 4–0 (4), Murray 2–0 (2),
Brunton 2–0 (2), McIntyre 2–0 (2), Elliott 1–0 (1),
Eccleston T. 1–0 (1), Stansfield 1–0 (1),
Own goals 2–0 (2) Baddley (Wolves) and Livesey
(Newcastle).

Season 1899–1900: First Division

		P	W	D	L	F	A	Pts
1	Aston Villa	34	22	6	6	77	35	50
2	Sheffield United	34	18	12	4	63	33	48
3	Sunderland	34	19	3	12	50	35	41
4	Wolves	34	15	9	10	48	37	39
5	Newcastle	34	13	10	11	53	43	36
6	Derby	34	14	8	12	45	43	36
7	Man City	34	13	8	13	50	44	34
8	Nottingham Forest	34	13	8	13	56	55	34
9	Stoke	34	10	10	14	37	45	34
10	Liverpool	34	14	5	15	49	45	33
11	Everton	34	13	7	14	47	49	33
12	Bury	34	13	6	15	40	44	32
13	WBA	34	11	8	15	43	51	30
14	Blackburn	34	13	4	17	49	61	30
15	Notts County	34	9	11	14	46	60	29
16	**PRESTON**	**34**	**12**	**4**	**18**	**38**	**48**	**28**
17	Burnley	34	11	5	18	34	54	27
18	Glossop NE	34	4	10	20	31	74	18

Date 1899-1900	Opponents		Comp	h or a	Score	Att.	1	2	3	4	5	6	7	8	9	10	11		
Sep 2	Nottm. Forest		Div 1	a	1-3		McBride	Holmes	Dunn	W.Eccleston	McIntyre	T.Eccleston	Henderson	Murray	Brunton (1)	Gara	Halsall		
Sep 9	Glossop N.E.		Div 1	h	1-0		McBride	Dunn	Holmes	W.Eccleston	McIntyre	T.Eccleston	Henderson	Murray	Brunton (1)	Gara	Halsall		
Sep 16	Stoke		Div 1	a	1-3		McBride	Dunn	Holmes	W.Eccleston	McIntyre (1)	Elliott	Green	Smith	Brunton	Gara	Halsall		
Sep 23	Sunderland		Div 1	h	0-1		McBride	Dunn	Holmes	W.Eccleston	McIntyre	Elliott	Stansfield	Murray	Brunton	Gara	Halsall		
Sep 30	WBA		Div 1	a	0-1		McBride	Dunn	Holmes	W.Eccleston	McIntyre	Elliott	Stansfield	Murray	Banks	Gara	Halsall		
Oct 7	Everton		Div 1	h	1-1		McBride	Dunn	Holmes	W.Eccleston	McIntyre	Elliott	Murray	Banks	Stevenson (1)	Gara	Halsall		
Oct 14	Blackburn R.		Div 1	a	0-3		McBride	Dunn	Holmes	W.Eccleston	McIntyre	Elliott	Murray	Banks	Stevenson	Gara	Halsall		
Oct 21	Derby County		Div 1	h	0-0		McBride	Dunn	Holmes	W.Eccleston	McIntyre	Elliott	Murray	Brunton	Stevenson	Gara	Halsall		
Oct 28	Bury		Div 1	a	0-2		McBride	Dunn	Holmes	W.Eccleston	McIntyre	Elliott	Green	Brunton	Stevenson	Murray	Halsall		
Nov 4	Notts County		Div 1	h	4-3		McBride	Dunn	Orrell	W.Eccleston	McIntyre	Elliott	Green	Brunton	Stevenson	Pierce (3)	Henderson (1)		
Nov 11	Man. City		Div 1	a	1-3		McBride	Dunn	Holmes	W.Eccleston	Hodgson	Elliott (1)	Green	Brunton	Stevenson	Pierce	Henderson		
Nov 18	Sheffield Utd.		Div 1	h	0-1		McBride	Dunn	Holmes	W.Eccleston	McIntyre	Elliott	Green	Stansfield	Stevenson	Pierce	Henderson		
Nov 25	Newcastle Utd.		Div 1	h	0-0		McBride	Dunn	Holmes	W.Eccleston	McIntyre	Elliott	Atherton	Murray	Stevenson	Pierce	Henderson		
Dec 2	Aston Villa		Div 1	a	0-5		McBride	Dunn	Holmes	W.Eccleston	McIntyre	Elliott	Atherton	Murray	Stevenson	Pierce	Henderson		
Dec 9	Liverpool		Div 1	a	0-1		McBride	Dunn	Holmes	W.Eccleston	McIntyre	Elliott	Atherton	Banks	Gara	Pierce	Henderson		
Dec 16	Burnley		Div 1	h	1-1		McBride	Dunn	Holmes	Hodgson	McIntyre (1)	Elliott	Atherton	Gara	Stevenson	Pierce	Henderson		
Dec 23	Wolverhampton W.		Div 1	a	3-1		McBride	Dunn	Orrell	T.Eccleston	McIntyre	Elliott	Atherton	Gara (1)	Stevenson (1)	Pierce	Henderson	1 o.g.	(Baddley)
Dec 30	Nottm. Forest		Div 1	h	3-0		McBride	Dunn	Orrell	T.Eccleston	McIntyre	Elliott	Atherton	Gara (2)	Stevenson (1)	Pierce	Henderson		
Jan 1	Everton		Div 1	a	0-1		McBride	Dunn	Orrell	T.Eccleston	McIntyre	Elliott	Atherton	Gara	Stevenson	Pierce	Henderson		
Jan 6	Glossop N.E.		Div 1	a	2-0		McBride	Dunn	Orrell	T.Eccleston	McIntyre	Elliott	Atherton	Gara (1)	Stevenson	Pierce	Henderson (1)		
Jan 13	Stoke		Div 1	h	3-0		McBride	Dunn	Orrell	T.Eccleston	McIntyre	Elliott	Atherton	Gara	Stevenson	Pierce (1)	Henderson (2)		
Jan 20	Sunderland		Div 1	a	0-1		McBride	Dunn	Orrell	T.Eccleston	McIntyre	Elliott	Atherton	Gara	Stevenson	Pierce	Henderson		
Jan 27	**Tottenham H.**	**Rd 1**	**FAC**	**h**	**1-0**	**7000**	**McBride**	**Dunn**	**Orrell**	**T.Eccleston**	**McIntyre**	**Elliott**	**Murray**	**Gara**	**Stevenson (1)**	**Pierce**	**Henderson**		
Feb 3	WBA		Div 1	h	5-2		McBride	Dunn	Orrell	T.Eccleston	McIntyre	Elliott	Atherton	Gara (2)	Stevenson	Pierce	Henderson (3)		
Feb 17	**Blackburn R.**	**Rd 2**	**FAC**	**h**	**1-0**	**13462**	**McBride**	**Dunn**	**Orrell**	**W.Eccleston**	**McIntyre**	**Elliott**	**Murray**	**Gara**	**Stevenson**	**Pierce**	**Henderson (1)**		
Feb 24	**Nottm. Forest**	**Rd 3**	**FAC**	**h**	**0-0**	**10000**	**McBride**	**Dunn**	**Orrell**	**W.Eccleston**	**McIntyre**	**Elliott**	**Murray**	**Gara**	**Stevenson**	**Pierce**	**Henderson**		
Feb 28	**Nottm. Forest ***	**Replay**	**FAC**	**a**	**0-1**	**9000**	**McBride**	**Dunn**	**Orrell**	**W.Eccleston**	**McIntyre**	**Elliott**	**Murray**	**Gara**	**Stevenson**	**Pierce**	**Henderson**		
Mar 3	Bury		Div 1	h	1-0		McBride	Dunn	Orrell	W.Eccleston	McIntyre	Elliott	Murray	Gara	Stevenson	Pierce	Henderson (1)		
Mar 10	Notts County		Div 1	a	0-3		McBride	Dunn	Orrell	W.Eccleston	McIntyre	Elliott	Atherton	Gara	Stevenson	Murray	Henderson		
Mar 24	Sheffield Utd.		Div 1	a	0-1		McBride	Dunn	Orrell	T.Eccleston	McIntyre	Elliott	Atherton	Smith	Stevenson	Whittle	Henderson		
Mar 31	Newcastle Utd.		Div 1	h	4-1		McBride	Dunn	Orrell	T.Eccleston	McIntyre	Elliott	Murray (1)	Smith	Stevenson (1)	Whittle	Henderson (1)	1 o.g.	(Livesey)
Apr 4	Derby County		Div 1	a	0-2		McBride	Dunn	Orrell	T.Eccleston	McIntyre	Elliott	Murray	Smith	Stevenson	Whittle	Henderson		
Apr 7	Aston Villa		Div 1	h	1-3		McBride	Dunn	Orrell	Sanderson	McIntyre	Elliott	Murray	Smith	Stevenson	Whittle	Henderson (1)		
Apr 14	Liverpool		Div 1	h	1-3		McBride	Dunn	Orrell	T.Eccleston	McIntyre	Elliott	Murray	Smith	Stevenson	Whittle	Henderson (1p)		
Apr 16	Man. City		Div 1	h	0-2		McBride	Dunn	Parker	T.Eccleston	McIntyre	Elliott	Murray	Smith	Stevenson	Pierce	Henderson		
Apr 21	Burnley		Div 1	a	1-0		McBride	Dunn	Holmes	W.Eccleston	McIntyre	Elliott	Murray (1)	Smith	Stevenson	Pierce	Henderson		
Apr 28	Wolverhampton W.		Div 1	h	2-0		McBride	Dunn	Holmes	T.Eccleston	McIntyre	Elliott	Murray	Smith	Stevenson (1)	Pierce	Henderson (1p)		
Apr 30	Blackburn R.		Div 1	h	2-0		McBride	Dunn	Holmes	T.Eccleston (1)	McIntyre	Elliott	Murray	Stansfield (1)	Stevenson	Pierce	Henderson		
	* Played at Trent Bridge																		

After three seasons of continual struggle the inevitable finally hit the club when they were relegated at the end of this dismal year of action. For once the defence failed to stem the tide and Preston let in more goals than ever before, 75, and that total was not to be beaten for another 25 years. Even the great Peter McBride missed some games and his replacements, Ralph James, Sidney Woodhouse and Thomas Wilkie did little better behind a shaky and mistake ridden back line. North End badly missed the organisational ability of Bob Holmes and the newcomers to the defence were not always up to the standard required in the first division. To be fair, McBride played brilliantly on several occasions to keep scores respectable and his talents were recognised by Scotland's selectors, although this was to have dire consequences on his club. Playing in a Scottish trial match in the March, McBride injured a shoulder and had to miss Preston's last five games. Whether it actually made a difference was arguable but there was no doubt he was North End's most influential player at the time. In attack Tom Pratt appeared in all but one of the games and did well whilst Andrew Gara scored 11 goals in his 25 outings. Frank Becton, who had left the club but returned for this season, also helped boost the forward power and it was ironic that the club scored more goals than in any of the previous three poor seasons. But it was the inability to defend which caused the club so much heartache. Other individuals contributed useful seasons with George Tod and Peter McIntyre

prominent but unfortunately too many other players showed poor form and North End were a million miles away from the days of the Invincibles. The FA Cup brought little respite. A creditable draw 1–1 against powerful Southern League outfit Tottenham Hotspur on their own ground brought the Londoners back to Deepdale for a replay. But here all that good work was undone when Preston were soundly beaten. That result left Preston with a desperate fight to stave off relegation, but on the last day of the season, whilst they were being beaten 3–2 at home by WBA who were bottom of the table, their nearest rivals Stoke were pulling off a shock win at Notts County. It sent Preston down for the first time. The realisation of the enormity of the situation did not hit the club immediately but it did emphasise, what we all know too well now, that no club was immune to relegation. The Preston Directors were shell shocked and tried to vote in new legislation to increase the size of the league, alas, and quite rightly, to no avail. The pride at the club had never been so low.

DEBUTANTS: (9) John Beaver, Ellis Green, Ralph James, John McMahon, Gerald Montgomery, Joseph Rogers, George Tod, Thomas Wilkie and Sidney Woodhouse.

LAST GAMES: (15) Parker, Dunn, Becton F., Henderson, Pierce, Eccleston T., Stevenson, Wilkie, Smith T. (No2), McIntyre, Montgomery, Woodhouse, Hodgson, Smith G. and James.

League appearances (34 games)

Beaver J. 1, Becton F. 26, Dunn H. 28, Eccleston T. 8, Elliott J. 26, Gara A. 25, Green E. 21, Henderson A. 15, Hodgson T. 2, Holmes R. 4, James R. 3, McBride P. 26, McMahon J. 21, McIntyre P. 32, Montgomery G. 4, Orrell R. 13, Parker H. 2, Pierce J. 18, Pratt T. 33, Rogers J. 10, Sanderson B. S. 1, Smith G. 19, Smith T. (No 2) 2, Stevenson J. 3, Tod G. 26, Wilkie T. 3, Woodhouse S. H. 2.

FA Cup appearances (2 games)

McBride, Dunn, McMahon, Elliott, McIntyre, Tod, Parker, Gara, Pratt, Becton and Green all 2 each.

Goalscorers: 49 League–3 Cup–(Total 52)

Gara 11 (1pen)–0 (11), Becton 9–1 (10), Pratt 8–1 (9), Green 5–0 (5), Rogers 3–0 (3), Tod 3–0 (3), Elliott 2–0 (2), Eccleston 1–0 (1), McIntyre 1–0 (1), Henderson 1–0 (1), Pierce 1–0 (1), Smith G. 1–0 (1), McMahon 0–1 (1). Own goals 3–0 (3) Fleming (2) of Wolves and Raisbeck of Liverpool.

Some future players born during the season 1900–1: Billy Mercer, John Holland, Bobby Crawford, William Wade, Tony Carr, Sidney Chandler, Andy McCluggage and George Stephenson

Ever presents: None		**FA Cup:** First round
Manager: Management Committee		**Chairman:** Mr W. E. Ord J. P
Hat-tricks: None		**Leading scorer:** 11 goals Andrew Gara (All League)
Players used: 27		

AUTHORS' UNOFFICIAL PLAYER OF THE SEASON: Tom Pratt

League position in Division One: 17th (Relegated) – P34 W9 D7 L18 F49 A75 Pts 25
Home: W6 D4 L7 F29 A30   Away: W3 D3 L11 F20 A45

Match Report: Down and Out – 15 Apr 1901
Preston 2 West Bromwich Albion 3

Bottom of the league West Brom, with three games in hand, had the slenderest possible chance of escaping relegation whereas Preston, playing their last game of the season, required nothing less than a win. Hence the two teams fought like trojans in trying to hold onto their First Division status, not to mention avoiding the title of wooden spoonists! North End began with six forwards in a 2–2–6 formation but soon realised this was not working and they switched to a more familiar 2–3–5 style with Pratt moving back. Albion also tried six forwards but with only one full-back a ploy which constantly caught Preston offside. No more than 1,000 were present at the start of this crucial evening kick-off. Leading the line for the Throstles was Stevenson who had started the season with North End. Gara made gallant attempts to open the scoring, at one stage beating three opponents, but his skills failed to break through. West Brom then had a goal disallowed for an infringement on rookie goalkeeper Wilkie and Preston were finding it difficult to get into their stride. But six minutes from the interval they did manage to score against the run of play. Frank Becton in his last league game, dribbled through the opposition's defence and from just three yards out gave Reader no chance to save. After the break West Brom came at Preston with a renewed vigour and four minutes into the half Walker equalised. George Tod, moving forward, brought the best out of Reader twice in quick succession and then on 76 minutes Gara raced around Adams to set up Rogers who gleefully scored. It was nearly three shortly afterwards as Adams almost put through his own goal, but then Albion hit back after weathering the storm, to put Wilkie under great pressure. It culminated in another equaliser, this time from Pickering. With a couple of minutes left and Albion straining every sinew they forced a corner. From the kick by Walker, Perry was left with a chance to give his side what proved to be the winner. It left Preston crestfallen but their relegation only commanded the third paragraph on the local paper's sports page.

Season 1900–1: First Division

	P	W	D	L	F	A	Pts
1 Liverpool	34	19	7	8	59	35	45
2 Sunderland	34	15	13	6	57	26	43
3 Notts County	34	18	4	12	54	46	40
4 Nottingham Forest	34	16	7	11	53	36	39
5 Bury	34	16	7	11	53	37	39
6 Newcastle	34	14	10	10	42	37	38
7 Everton	34	16	5	13	55	42	37
8 Wednesday	34	13	10	11	52	42	36
9 Blackburn	34	12	9	13	39	47	33
10 Bolton	34	13	7	14	39	55	33
11 Man City	34	13	6	15	48	58	32
12 Derby	34	12	7	15	55	42	31
13 Wolves	34	9	13	12	39	55	31
14 Sheffield United	34	12	7	15	35	52	31
15 Aston Villa	34	10	10	14	45	51	30
16 Stoke	34	11	5	18	46	57	27
17 PRESTON	**34**	**9**	**7**	**18**	**49**	**75**	**25**
18 WBA	34	7	8	19	35	62	22

Date 1900-1	Opponents	Comp	h or a	Score	Att.	1	2	3	4	5	6	7	8	9	10	11		
Sep 1	Everton	Div 1	h	1-2		McBride	Dunn	Holmes	Eccleston	McIntyre	Elliott	T.Smith (No2)	Pratt	Stevenson	Gara	Henderson (1)		
Sep 3	Aston Villa	Div 1	a	0-4		McBride	Dunn	Holmes	Eccleston	McIntyre	Elliott	T.Smith (No2)	Pratt	Stevenson	Gara	Henderson		
Sep 8	Sunderland	Div 1	a	1-3		McBride	Dunn	Holmes	Eccleston	McIntyre	Elliott	G.Smith	Gara	Pratt (1)	Pierce	Henderson		
Sep 15	Derby County	Div 1	h	3-2		McBride	Dunn	Holmes	Eccleston (1)	McIntyre	Elliott	G.Smith	Gara (1)	Pratt (1)	Pierce	Henderson		
Sep 22	Bolton W.	Div 1	a	1-1		McBride	Dunn	Tod	Eccleston	McIntyre	Elliott	G.Smith	Gara (1)	Pratt	Pierce	Henderson		
Sep 29	Notts County	Div 1	h	0-1		McBride	Dunn	Orrell	Eccleston	McIntyre	Elliott	G.Smith	Gara	Pratt	Becton	Henderson		
Oct 4	Nottm. Forest	Div 1	a	1-4		McBride	Dunn	Orrell	Eccleston	McIntyre	Elliott	G.Smith (1)	Becton	Pratt	Pierce	Henderson		
Oct 6	Sheffield Wed.	Div 1	a	1-0		McBride	Dunn	Orrell	Eccleston	McIntyre	Elliott	G.Smith	Becton	Pratt (1)	Pierce	Henderson		
Oct 13	Wolverhampton W.	Div 1	a	2-2		James	Dunn	Orrell	Elliott	McIntyre	Tod	G.Smith	Becton	Pratt	Pierce	Henderson	2 o.g's	(Fleming)
Oct 20	Aston Villa	Div 1	h	0-2		James	Dunn	Orrell	Stevenson	McIntyre	Tod	G.Smith	Becton	Pratt	Pierce	Henderson		
Oct 27	Liverpool	Div 1	a	2-3		James	Dunn	Orrell	Elliott	McIntyre	Tod	G.Smith	Becton	Pratt	Pierce (1)	Green	1 o.g.	(Raisbeck)
Nov 3	Newcastle	Div 1	h	0-1		McBride	Parker	Orrell	Hodgson	McIntyre	Tod	G.Smith	Becton	Pratt	Pierce	Henderson		
Nov 10	Sheffield Utd.	Div 1	a	1-2		McBride	McIntyre	Orrell	Gara	Hodgson	Tod	G.Smith	Becton (1)	Pratt	Pierce	Henderson		
Nov 17	Manchester City	Div 1	h	0-4		McBride	McMahon	Orrell	Gara	McIntyre	Tod	G.Smith	Becton	Pratt	Pierce	Green		
Nov 24	Bury	Div 1	a	1-2		McBride	Dunn	McMahon	Elliott (1)	McIntyre	Tod	Beaver	Gara	Pratt	Becton	Green		
Dec 1	Nottm. Forest	Div 1	h	1-1		McBride	Dunn	McMahon	Elliott	McIntyre	Tod	G.Smith	Gara (1)	Pratt	Becton	Green		
Dec 8	Blackburn R.	Div 1	h	4-1		McBride	Dunn	McMahon	Elliott	McIntyre	Tod (1)	G.Smith	Gara (1)	Pratt (1)	Becton (1)	Green		
Dec 22	WBA	Div 1	h	1-0		McBride	Dunn	McMahon	Elliott	McIntyre (1)	Tod	G.Smith	Gara	Pratt	Becton	Green		
Dec 25	Stoke	Div 1	h	4-2		McBride	Dunn	McMahon	Elliott	McIntyre	Tod	G.Smith	Gara (1)	Pratt (2)	Becton (1)	Green		
Dec 26	Stoke	Div 1	a	0-5		McBride	Dunn	McMahon	Elliott	McIntyre	Tod	Henderson	Gara	Pratt	Becton	Green		
Dec 29	Everton	Div 1	a	1-4		McBride	Dunn	McMahon	Orrell	McIntyre	Tod	Henderson	Pierce	Pratt	Becton (1)	Green		
Jan 1	Blackburn R.	Div 1	a	1-3		McBride	Dunn	McMahon	Sanderson	Montgomery	Tod (1)	G.Smith	Gara	Pratt	Becton	Green		
Jan 5	Sunderland	Div 1	h	1-1		McBride	Dunn	McMahon	Montgomery	McIntyre	Tod	Parker	Gara	Pratt	Becton	Green (1)		
Jan 12	Derby County	Div 1	a	0-0		McBride	Dunn	McMahon	Elliott	McIntyre	Tod	G.Smith	Gara	Pratt	Becton	Green		
Feb 9	**Tottenham H.** Rd 1	**FAC**	**a**	**1-1**	**17000**	**McBride**	**Dunn**	**McMahon (1)**	**Elliott**	**McIntyre**	**Tod**	**Parker**	**Gara**	**Pratt**	**Becton**	**Green**		
Feb 13	**Tottenham H.** Replay	**FAC**	**h**	**2-4**		**McBride**	**Dunn**	**McMahon**	**Elliott**	**McIntyre**	**Tod**	**Parker**	**Gara**	**Pratt (1)**	**Becton (1)**	**Green**		
Feb 16	Wolverhampton W.	Div 1	h	1-1		McBride	Dunn	McMahon	Elliott	Montgomery	Tod	Rogers	Gara (1)	Pratt	Becton	Green		
Feb 23	Manchester City	Div 1	a	1-3		McBride	Dunn	McMahon	Elliott	McIntyre	Tod	Rogers	G.Smith	Pratt	Gara (1)	Green		
Mar 2	Liverpool	Div 1	h	2-2		McBride	Dunn	McMahon	Elliott	McIntyre	Tod	Rogers	Pratt	Gara	Becton (2)	Green		
Mar 9	Newcastle	Div 1	a	5-3		McBride	Dunn	McMahon	Elliott	McIntyre	Tod (1)	Rogers (1)	Pratt (1)	Gara (1)	Becton	Green (1)		
Mar 16	Sheffield Utd.	Div 1	h	3-1		McBride	Dunn	McMahon	Elliott	McIntyre	Tod	Rogers	Pratt	Gara (2)	Pierce	Green (1)		
Mar 23	Bolton W.	Div 1	h	1-3		Woodhouse	Dunn	McMahon	Elliott	McIntyre	Tod	Rogers	Pratt	Gara (1p)	Pierce	Green		
Mar 27	Notts County	Div 1	a	1-6		Woodhouse	Dunn	McMahon	Elliott	Montgomery	McIntyre	Rogers	Becton (1)	Gara	Pierce	Green		
Mar 30	Bury	Div 1	h	3-1		Wilkie	McMahon	Orrell	Elliott (1)	McIntyre	Tod	Rogers	Pratt (1)	Becton	Pierce	Green (1)		
Apr 5	Sheffield Wed.	Div 1	h	3-2		Wilkie	McMahon	Orrell	Elliott	McIntyre	Tod	Rogers (1)	Pratt	Becton (1)	Pierce	Green (1)		
Apr 15	WBA	Div 1	h	2-3		Wilkie	McMahon	Orrell	Pratt	McIntyre	Tod	Rogers (1)	Gara	Becton (1)	Pierce	Green		

SEASON 1901–1902

Preston's first ever season in Division Two of the Football League certainly brought home to the club the problems that they would now be facing, both in playing and financial terms. Having to visit places like Burton, Gainsborough and Glossop came as quite a culture shock, although to be fair, after an opening day defeat at WBA, Preston soon came to grips with the job in hand. There had been a huge turn over in players and 13 new ones came in although they all worked hard. Harry Wilcox proved an excellent signing at inside-forward. He scored regularly and laid on his fair share for the likes of Richard Pegg, Tom Pratt and Joe Rogers. After that opening defeat Preston put together a run of six consecutive wins without conceding a goal and the confidence, as a result, began to grow. At home, especially, the form was excellent and for the first time ever the team hit 50 goals in a season at Deepdale. Away from Deepdale though, as ever, the results were a little more patchy. The lesser clubs were usually beaten quite comfortably but against the better sides in the division Preston sometimes struggled. That had a real effect on Preston's championship hopes which always seemed to be just out of reach. Eventual Champions, WBA put together an outstanding season as did runners-up Middlesbrough and significantly both did the double over North End. Still, there were many positive things to come out of the season, with the attack scoring much more freely than of late and with the defence much tighter. Peter McBride, Richard Orrell and John McMahon were outstanding at the back. One game broke new records for the club as on the Saturday after Christmas Preston walloped Lincoln 8–0 at Deepdale and that was the fifth win in another impressive run of six wins on the trot. January then saw an FA Cup-tie with Manchester City. The tie was very closely fought and eventually went to three games and two lots of extra-time before it was finally settled. Unfortunately it was City who came out on top in that second replay and that was a rare piece of joy for the Manchester side who ended the season being relegated from the top division. Annoyingly for the fans Preston's season ended on a disappointing note as they suffered three consecutive defeats in their last three games. However they had gained enough points to hold on to third place, pipping Woolwich Arsenal on goal average. One ironic twist came in the last game of the season as Preston lost 2–1 … at Lincoln!

DEBUTANTS: (13) Frederick Fenton, Edward Forshaw, Michael Good, Frederick Griffiths, Rabbi Howell, Robert Jack, James Melia, Frank Pearson, Richard Pegg, George Spence, Bert Tickle, Joseph Walton and Harry Wilcox.

LAST GAMES: (11) Elliott, Gara, Green, Rogers, Forshaw, Good, Griffiths, Jack, Melia, Pegg, Spence.

League appearances (34 games)

Beaver J. 7, Elliott J. 21, Fenton F. 6, Forshaw E. 2, Gara A. 15, Good M. H. S. 24, Green E. 5, Griffiths F. J. 10, Howell R. 26, Jack R. 22, McBride P. 24, McMahon J. 32, Melia J. 2, Orrell R. 32, Pearson F. 5, Pegg R. 15, Pratt T. 21, Rogers J. 29, Spence G. 19, Tickle B. 2, Tod G. 17, Walton J. 7, Wilcox H. M. 31.

FA Cup appearances (3 games)

McBride 3, McMahon 3, Orrell 3, Howell 2, Beaver 1, Good 3, Elliott 2, Tod 1, Rogers 3, Wilcox 3, Pegg 2, Pratt 1, Spence 2, Gara 1 and Jack 3.

Goalscorers: 71 League–3 Cup–(Total 74)

Wilcox 14 (6pens)–0 (14), Pegg 9–0 (9), Pratt 8–1 (9), Rogers 8–1 (9), Gara 7–1 (8), Spence 7–0 (7), Jack 6–0 (6), Green 3–0 (3), Good 2–0 (2), Walton 2–0 (2), Pearson 2–0 (2), Elliott 1–0 (1), Howell 1–0 (1). Own goals 1–0 (1) (Kifford of WBA).

STAT FACTS:
Best home run without defeat: 10 games Best away run without defeat: 6 games
Longest run unbeaten: 8 games Longest run without a win: 4 games

League position in Division Two: 3rd – P34 W18 D6 L10 F71 A32 Pts 42
Home: W12 D3 L2 F50 A11 Away: W6 D3 L8 F21 A21

Match Report: Rogers the Dodger – Feb 22 1902 Preston 5 Chesterfield 0

The re-arranged league game, abandoned at half-time in the November through fog, with Preston leading 2–0, was this time played in much better conditions. A rapid bombardment of Chesterfield's goal came straight from the kick-off, all the home forwards looking very lively. One incident which brought laughter from the 3,000 crowd, was when Thorpe, the visitors' full-back, mis-kicked near the halfway line and saw the ball end up back with his own keeper. Thorpe was in the action again on 15 minutes, being tricked by Rogers who centred for Pratt. His goalbound header was saved but not held and Spence nipped in to open the score. Within two minutes the lead was doubled, Rogers scoring with a thunderous shot on the run. Not long after this double success Rogers again beat Thorpe but instead of passing the easy ball inside to Pratt he opted to go for glory himself but shot wildly over the top. At length, play was held up as a collie dog joined in the fun. Meanwhile Chesterfield could make little headway resulting in McBride and McMahon having a quiet afternoon. Although 2–0 up, North End squandered some good openings until Jack, the left winger, played a neat one-two with Spence and scored the game's third goal before half-time. The second half began as the first had ended, with the action around Maybank, the visitors' goalkeeper. Jack, Spence and Pratt all went close to adding to the total. Rogers, being well fed by Rabbi Howell, was proving something of a handful for poor Thorpe, who along with Banner, endangered their own team with some weak defensive kicking. The visitors kept the score down until the 70th minute when good, short passing between Jack, Spence and Pratt enabled the latter to beat Maybank at close quarters. A sarcastic cheer went up when Chesterfield scored direct from an indirect free-kick, the 'goal' being rightly disallowed. On 88 minutes one of the visiting defenders fisted the ball away with Maybank well beaten. Up stepped Wilcox to score from the resultant penalty to make it 5–0 to the PNE. It was interesting to note that all five forwards had scored in a league game for the first time ever. (Gara was missing, as he was away scoring for Ireland.).

Season 1901–2: Second Division

	P	W	D	L	F	A	Pts
1 WBA	34	25	5	4	82	29	55
2 Middlesbrough	34	23	5	6	90	24	51
3 PRESTON	**34**	**18**	**6**	**10**	**71**	**32**	**42**
4 Woolwich A	34	18	6	10	50	26	42
5 Lincoln	34	14	13	7	45	35	41
6 Bristol City	34	17	6	11	52	35	40
7 Doncaster	34	13	8	13	49	58	34
8 Glossop NE	34	10	12	12	36	40	32
9 Burnley	34	10	10	14	41	45	30
10 Burton United	34	11	8	15	46	54	30
11 Barnsley	34	12	6	16	51	63	30
12 Burslem PV	34	10	9	15	43	59	29
13 Blackpool	34	11	7	16	40	56	29
14 Leicester Fosse	34	12	5	17	38	56	29
15 Newton Heath	34	11	6	17	38	53	28
16 Chesterfield	34	11	6	17	47	68	28
17 Stockport	34	8	7	19	36	72	23
18 Gainsborough	34	4	11	19	30	80	19

Date 1901-2	Opponents	Comp	h or a	Score	Att.	1	2	3	4	5	6	7	8	9	10	11		
Sep 7	WBA	Div 2	a	1-3		McBride	Melia	Orrell	Howell	Good	Elliott	Rogers	Pratt	Gara	Spence	Green (1)		
Sep 14	Woolwich Arsenal	Div 2	h	2-0		McBride	McMahon	Orrell	Howell	Good	Elliott	Rogers	Pratt (1)	Gara (1)	Spence	Green		
Sep 21	Barnsley	Div 2	a	4-0		McBride	McMahon	Orrell	Howell	Good	Elliott	Rogers	Pratt	Gara (3)	Spence (1)	Green		
Sep 28	Leicester Fosse	Div 2	h	5-0		McBride	McMahon	Orrell	Howell	Good	Elliott	Rogers (1)	Wilcox (2p)	Gara	Spence	Green (2)		
Oct 5	Burton United	Div 2	h	1-0		McBride	McMahon	Orrell	Howell	Good	Tickle	Rogers	Wilcox (1)	Gara	Spence	Jack		
Oct 12	Burnley	Div 2	a	3-0		McBride	McMahon	Orrell	Howell	Good	Elliott	Rogers (2)	Wilcox (1p)	Gara	Pratt	Jack		
Oct 19	Burslem Port Vale	Div 2	h	2-0		McBride	McMahon	Orrell	Howell	Good	Elliott	Rogers	Wilcox	Gara (1)	Pratt (1)	Jack		
Oct 26	Chesterfield	Div 2	a	0-2		McBride	Melia	Orrell	Howell	Good	Elliott	Rogers	Wilcox	Gara	Pratt	Jack		
Nov 9	Middlesbrough	Div 2	a	1-2		McBride	McMahon	Orrell	Howell	Good	Elliott (1)	Rogers	Wilcox	Gara	Pratt	Green		
Nov 23	Blackpool	Div 2	h	4-1		McBride	McMahon	Orrell	Howell	Good	Elliott	Rogers	Wilcox	Gara (2)	Pratt (1)	Jack (1)		
Nov 30	Bristol City	Div 2	h	0-0		McBride	McMahon	Orrell	Howell	Good	Tickle	Rogers	Wilcox	Gara	Pratt	Jack		
Dec 7	Newton Heath	Div 2	h	5-1		McBride	McMahon	Orrell	Howell	Good (1)	Elliott	Rogers (2)	Wilcox	Pegg (1)	Spence	Jack (1)		
Dec 14	Barnsley	Div 2	h	4-0		McBride	McMahon	Orrell	Howell	Good (1)	Elliott	Rogers	Wilcox (1)	Pegg	Spence (1)	Jack (1)		
Dec 21	Doncaster R.	Div 2	h	3-0		McBride	McMahon	Orrell	Howell	Tod	Elliott	Rogers (1)	Wilcox	Pegg	Spence (2)	Jack		
Dec 25	Gainsborough	Div 2	h	4-1		McBride	McMahon	Orrell	Howell	Good	Tod	Rogers	Wilcox (2)	Pegg (2)	Spence	Jack		
Dec 28	Lincoln City	Div 2	h	8-0		McBride	McMahon	Orrell	Howell (1)	Pratt	Tod	Rogers (1)	Wilcox	Pegg (3)	Spence (2)	Jack (1)		
Jan 1	Newton Heath	Div 2	a	2-0		McBride	McMahon	Orrell	Howell	Pratt	Tod	Rogers	Wilcox	Pegg (1)	Spence	Jack (1)		
Jan 4	WBA	Div 2	h	1-2		McBride	McMahon	Orrell	Howell	Pratt	Tod	Rogers	Wilcox	Pegg	Spence	Jack	1 o.g.	(Kifford)
Jan 11	Woolwich Arsenal	Div 2	a	0-0		McBride	McMahon	Orrell	Howell	Elliott	Tod	Rogers	Wilcox	Pegg	Spence	Jack		
Jan 25	**Manchester City Rd 1**	**FAC**		**1-1**	**11000**	**McBride**	**McMahon**	**Orrell**	**Howell**	**Good**	**Elliott**	**Rogers (1)**	**Wilcox**	**Pegg**	**Spence**	**Jack**		
Jan 29	**Manchester City Replay**	**FAC**	**h**	**0-0 ***	**6000**	**McBride**	**McMahon**	**Orrell**	**Howell**	**Good**	**Elliott**	**Rogers**	**Wilcox**	**Pegg**	**Spence**	**Jack**		
Feb 1	Burton United	Div 2	a	1-1		McBride	McMahon	Pratt	Gara	Good	Tod	Rogers	Wilcox	Pegg (1)	Spence	Jack		
Feb 3	**Manchester C. 2nd Replaay**	**FAC**	**h**	**2-4 ***	**5,447**	**McBride**	**McMahon**	**Orrell**	**Beaver**	**Good**	**Tod**	**Rogers**	**Wilcox**	**Pratt (1)**	**Gara (1)**	**Jack**		
Feb 15	Burslem Port Vale	Div 2	a	0-0		McBride	McMahon	Pratt	Howell	Good	Tod	Rogers	Wilcox	Gara	Spence	Jack		
Feb 22	Chesterfield	Div 2	h	5-0		McBride	McMahon	Orrell	Howell	Good	Elliott	Rogers (1)	Wilcox (1p)	Pratt (1)	Spence (1)	Jack (1)		
Mar 1	Gainsborough	Div 2	a	1-0		McBride	McMahon	Orrell	Elliott	Good	Tod	Rogers	Wilcox	Pratt (1)	Spence	Jack		
Mar 8	Middlesbrough	Div 2	h	0-3		McBride	McMahon	Orrell	Howell	Good	Elliott	Rogers	Wilcox	Pratt	Gara	Jack		
Mar 15	Bristol City	Div 2	a	0-2		Griffiths	McMahon	Orrell	Beaver	Good	Elliott	Rogers	Wilcox	Pegg	Gara	Spence		
Mar 22	Blackpool	Div 2	h	1-1		Griffiths	McMahon	Orrell	Howell	Elliott	Tod	Beaver	Wilcox (1)	Pegg	Spence	Fenton		
Mar 28	Glossop NE	Div 2	h	2-2		Griffiths	McMahon	Orrell	Howell	Good	Elliott	Rogers	Wilcox (2, 1p)	Pegg	Pratt	Fenton		
Mar 29	Stockport	Div 2	h	4-0		Griffiths	McMahon	Orrell	Beaver	Tod	Elliott	Rogers	Wilcox (1)	Walton	Pratt (3)	Jack		
Mar 31	Leicester Fosse	Div 2	a	0-1		Griffiths	McMahon	Orrell	Howell	Tod	Elliott	Rogers	Wilcox	Walton	Pratt	Jack		
Apr 5	Stockport	Div 2	a	2-0		Griffiths	McMahon	Orrell	Beaver	Forshaw	Tod	Wilcox (1)	Walton (1)	Pegg	Pearson	Fenton		
Apr 7	Burnley	Div 2	h	3-1		Griffiths	McMahon	Orrell	Beaver	Forshaw	Tod	Wilcox	Walton (1)	Pegg (1)	Pearson (1)	Fenton		
Apr 12	Glossop NE	Div 2	a	1-3		Griffiths	McMahon	Orrell	Beaver	Good	Tod	Wilcox (1p)	Walton	Pegg	Pearson	Fenton		
Apr 19	Doncaster R.	Div 2	a	0-4		Griffiths	McMahon	Orrell	Beaver	Good	Tod	Wilcox	Walton	Pratt	Pearson	Fenton		
Apr 26	Lincoln City	Div 2	a	0-0		Griffiths	McMahon	Orrell	Howell	Good	Tod	Rogers	Wilcox	Walton	Pearson (1)	Jack		
				* aet														

SEASON 1902–1903

STAT FACTS:
Best home run without defeat: 8 games
Best away run without defeat: 3 games
Longest run unbeaten: 6 games
Longest run without a win: 3 games

Preston were losing vital revenue by being out of the top division and their finances were being stretched to the limit as they embarked on their fifteenth league campaign. The club were becoming desperate to climb out of the second division and hopes were high for promotion after their good showing of the previous year. But, alas, it did not work out that way and the North End management would have to have another serious rethink before the 1903–4 season began. Too many games were lost in this, their second year in the lower league, and their away form again left a lot to be desired. At least Deepdale was still proving to be something of a fortress and most visitors went home without too much reward. Scoring goals away from home proved very difficult and it was hard to explain just why the attack could score freely at home but not on other grounds. Frank Pearson played well and, with Percy Smith, made an effective inside-forward partnership. Harry Wilcox was another lively raider and all three players scored regularly enough to reach double figures. However, apart from that trio, Tom Pratt was the next highest scorer and he only managed three. At the other end though Preston had Peter McBride and the goalkeeper was again in prime form, showing outstanding consistency. He was well supported by Richard Orrell and John Hunter whilst George Tod had his best season so far. On Boxing Day one team selection had a touch of sentimentality about

it. Bob Holmes, stalwart of so many years, was selected at right-back for what was his 300th league game. It was not to be a particularly happy game for him as Manchester City won the game 2–0. It was a significant moment in Preston's history though as not only was it the last appearance by Holmes but also the last by one of the Old Invincibles. It was a sad day. Meanwhile, when the FA Cup began Preston had a tricky draw in round one, away at leading amateur side, Bishop Auckland. A convincing 3–1 win though saw them through and a home tie with Manchester City beckoned. Another good display, and another 3–1 win which left the fans with just a slight hope of a decent cup run. Sadly that feeling crashed around their ears in the next round as North End were thrashed 4–1 at Millwall. At least there was the satisfaction of a rally in the remaining league games and they were to only lose once in the last eight games which pushed them up to a respectable seventh place. Most clubs would have settled for that but Preston were not happy and more changes would have to be made before a serious challenge on promotion could be made.

DEBUTANTS: (8) Dicky Bond, Richard Bourne, Joseph Derbyshire, John Hunter (No2), James Shorrock, Percy Smith, John Warner and Herbert Danson (FAC).

LAST GAMES: (9) Pratt, Sanderson, Beaver, McMahon, Fenton, Pearson, Walton, Shorrock and Holmes.

League appearances (34 games)

Beaver J. 13, Bond R. 11, Bourne R. 5, Derbyshire J. E. 20, Fenton F. 14, Holmes R. 1, Howell R. 30, Hunter J. (No. 2) 33, McBride P. 34, McMahon J. 12, Orrell R. 33, Pearson F. 27, Pratt T. 19, Sanderson B. S. 4, Shorrock J. 1, Smith P. J. 28, Tickle B. 1, Tod G. 34, Walton J. 18, Warner J. 2, Wilcox H. M. 34.

FA Cup appearances (3 games)

McBride 3, McMahon 1, Derbyshire 2, Orrell 3, Howell 3, Hunter 3, Tod 3, Bond 3, Smith 3, Wilcox 3, Pratt 1, Pearson 3, Beaver 1 and Danson 1.

Goalscorers: 56 League–7 Cup–(Total 63)

Pearson 15–3 (18), Smith 16–1 (17), Wilcox 13 (5pens)–1 (16), Pratt 3–0 (3), Bond 2–1 (3), Walton 2–0 (2), Beaver 2–0 (2), Hunter 1–1 (2), Tod 1–0 (1). Own Goals 1–0 (1) (Wynne of Burnley)

Some future players born during the season 1902–3 include: Joe Craven, George Prout, Norman Wharton, Jasper Kerr and George Wolf

Ever presents: (3) Peter McBride, George Tod and Harry Wilcox **Manager:** Management Committee
FA Cup: Third round
Hat-tricks: (1) Percy Smith
Players used: 21

Chairman: Mr W. E. Ord J. P.
Leading scorer: 18 goals – Frank Pearson (15 League 3 Cup)
AUTHORS' UNOFFICIAL PLAYER OF THE SEASON: George Tod

League position in Division Two: 7th – P34 W13 D10 L11 F56 A40 Pts 36
Home: W10 D5 L2 F39 A12 Away: W3 D5 L9 F17 A28

Match Report: Enter Tricky Dicky – 13 Dec. 1902 Bishop Auckland 1 Preston 3 FA Cup

It was generally conceded that Preston's cup-tie at crack amateur side Bishop Auckland was going to be anything but easy as the North Eastern side boasted a terrific home record. But Preston's away performances were good at the time so they had high hopes themselves. Fenton and Walton had to drop out at the last minutes for different reasons, Fenton with injury and Walton because his mother had died suddenly. Walton's absence paved the way for tricky Dicky Bond to make his debut. Pratt, falling ill overnight, decided to play but was well out of sorts. The 'Bishops' came out fighting and actually took the lead in front of a record 5,000 crowd. Pratt, too ill to continue, left the proceedings, but the ten men soon pushed forward and Bond broke away and raced downfield before sending in a fierce daisy cutter which the goalkeeper fumbled. It gave Wilcox the chance to snap up the equaliser. It was just reward for the scorer who was holding up the attack well despite losing his partner Pratt. Just prior to the interval Bond swung the game North End's way. He sent in another rocket shot which the goalkeeper again failed to hold, dropping it like a hot potato, and then seeing the ball roll agonisingly slowly over the line. Where Atkinson, the goalkeeper had failed rather ignominiously McBride, at the other end, was excelling. Well supported by McMahon and Orrell Preston's defence had got over the early shock. Wilcox went close early in the second half and at this stage it looked as though the Bishops were going to be overrun. Bond was too quick for them and also himself at times, as he repeatedly strayed offside. Bishop Auckland never gave up but could not find another way past McBride and near the end Pearson made the game safe with a third goal for Preston leaving the home side content with a good performance which brought in a big crowd and takings of £200-0-6d. Preston's experience saw them through a typical cup-tie of football that was not very pretty, had little cohesion, but was full of tough tackling and commitment. The prize was a place in the first round proper.

Trivia Facts:

A financial crisis hit Deepdale at this time and among local efforts to raise funds for the club was a Bazaar to be held in the Public Hall on 4, 5, 6 and 7 February 1903. The object of the bazaar was 'to clear off existing debts and raise sufficient funds to enable the Committee to place the club in the high position it formerly occupied.'

Unusually, two players made their first team debuts in FA Cup ties. They were Dickie Bond, who made his debut at Bishop Auckland, and Herbert Danson, who first appeared at Millwall. The latter was not to make his league debut for another two years.

Season 1902–3: Second Division

	P	W	D	L	F	A	Pts
1 Man City	34	25	4	5	95	29	54
2 Small Heath	34	24	3	7	74	36	51
3 Woowich A	34	20	8	6	66	30	48
4 Bristol City	34	17	8	9	59	38	42
5 Man United	34	15	8	11	53	38	38
6 Chesterfield	34	14	9	11	67	40	37
7 PRESTON	**34**	**13**	**10**	**11**	**56**	**40**	**36**
8 Barnsley	34	13	8	13	55	51	34
9 Burslem PV	34	13	8	13	51	62	34
10 Lincoln	34	12	6	16	46	53	30
11 Glossop NE	34	11	7	16	43	58	29
12 Gainsborough	34	11	7	16	41	59	29
13 Burton United	34	11	7	16	39	59	29
14 Blackpool	34	9	10	15	44	59	28
15 Leicester Fosse	34	10	8	16	41	65	28
16 Doncaster	34	9	7	18	35	72	25
17 Stockport	34	7	6	21	39	74	20
18 Burney	34	6	8	20	30	77	20

Date 1902-3	Opponents	Comp	h or a	Score	Att.	1	2	3	4	5	6	7	8	9	10	11		
Sep 6	Woolwich Arsenal	Div 2	h	2-2		McBride	McMahon	Orrell	Sanderson	Hunter	Tod	Smith	Wilcox (2)	Walton	Pearson	Fenton		
Sep 8	Burslem Port Vale	Div 2	a	0-0		McBride	McMahon	Orrell	Sanderson	Hunter	Tod	Smith	Wilcox	Walton	Pearson	Fenton		
Sep 13	Doncaster Rovers	Div 2	a	2-1		McBride	McMahon	Orrell	Sanderson	Hunter	Tod	Beaver	Smith (1)	Wilcox	Pearson (1)	Fenton		
Sep 20	Lincoln City	Div 2	h	0-1		McBride	McMahon	Orrell	Howell	Hunter	Tod	Smith	Wilcox	Walton	Pearson	Fenton		
Sep 27	Small Heath	Div 2	h	1-3		McBride	McMahon	Orrell	Howell	Hunter	Tod	Beaver	Wilcox (1p)	Walton	Smith	Fenton		
Oct 4	Leicester Fosse	Div 2	h	2-0		McBride	McMahon	Orrell	Sanderson	Hunter	Tod	Walton	Smith	Wilcox (1)	Pearson (1)	Fenton		
Oct 11	Manchester City	Div 2	a	0-1		McBride	McMahon	Orrell	Howell	Hunter	Tod	Walton	Smith	Wilcox	Pearson	Fenton		
Oct 18	Burnley	Div 2	h	5-0		McBride	McMahon	Orrell	Howell	Hunter	Tod	Smith	Wilcox (1p)	Walton (2)	Pratt (1)	Fenton	1 o.g. (Wynne)	
Oct 25	Chesterfield	Div 2	a	2-4		McBride	McMahon	Orrell	Howell	Hunter	Tod	Walton	Smith	Wilcox (1p)	Pratt (1)	Fenton		
Nov 8	Barnsley	Div 2	h	3-0		McBride	McMahon	Orrell	Howell	Tod	Tickle	Walton	Smith (2)	Wilcox (1)	Pratt	Fenton		
Nov 22	Burton Utd.	Div 2	h	1-1		McBride	Derbyshire	Orrell	Howell	Hunter	Tod	Walton	Smith (1)	Wilcox	Pratt	Fenton		
Nov 29	Bristol City	Div 2	a	1-2		McBride	McMahon	Orrell	Howell	Hunter	Tod	Walton	Smith	Wilcox	Pratt	Shorrock		
Dec 6	Glossop N.E.	Div 2	a	0-0		McBride	McMahon	Orrell	Howell	Hunter	Tod	Walton	Smith	Wilcox	Pratt	Pearson		
Dec 13	Bishop Auckland Int. Rd	FAC	a	3-1	5000	McBride	McMahon	Orrell	Howell	Hunter	Tod	Bond (1)	Smith	Wilcox (1)	Pratt	Pearson (1)		
Dec 20	Stockport County	Div 2	h	6-1		McBride	Warner	Orrell	Howell	Hunter	Tod (1)	Bond (1)	Smith (1)	Wilcox (1)	Pearson (2)	Fenton		
Dec 26	Manchester City	Div 2	h	0-2		McBride	Holmes	Orrell	Howell	Hunter	Tod	Bond	Smith	Wilcox	Pratt	Fenton		
Dec 27	Blackpool	Div 2	h	2-2		McBride	Derbyshire	Orrell	Howell	Hunter	Tod	Bond	Smith	Wilcox (1)	Pratt	Pearson (1)		
Jan 3	Woolwich Arsenal	Div 2	a	1-3		McBride	Derbyshire	Orrell	Howell	Hunter (1)	Tod	Bond	Wilcox	Pratt	Pearson	Smith		
Jan 10	Doncaster Rovers	Div 2	h	5-0		McBride	Derbyshire	Orrell	Howell	Hunter	Tod	Bond	Wilcox (1)	Smith (1)	Pearson (2)	Beaver (1)		
Jan 17	Lincoln City	Div 2	a	3-2		McBride	Derbyshire	Orrell	Howell	Hunter	Tod	Bond	Wilcox	Smith (2)	Pearson (1)	Beaver		
Jan 24	Small Heath	Div 2	h	2-1		McBride	Derbyshire	Orrell	Howell	Hunter	Tod	Bond	Wilcox (1p)	Smith (1)	Pearson	Beaver		
Jan 31	Leicester Fosse	Div 2	a	1-1		McBride	Derbyshire	Orrell	Howell	Hunter	Tod	Bond (1)	Wilcox	Smith	Pearson	Beaver		
Feb 7	**Manchester City Rd 1**	**FAC**	h	**3-1**	8000	**McBride**	**Derbyshire**	**Orrell**	**Howell**	**Hunter (1)**	**Tod**	**Bond**	**Wilcox**	**Smith (1)**	**Pearson (1)**	**Beaver**		
Feb 14	Burnley	Div 2	a	1-1		McBride	Derbyshire	Orrell	Howell	Hunter	Tod	Bond	Wilcox	Smith (1)	Pearson	Fenton		
Feb 21	**Millwall Rd 2**	**FAC**	a	**1-4**	10000	**McBride**	**Derbyshire**	**Orrell**	**Howell**	**Hunter**	**Tod**	**Bond**	**Wilcox**	**Smith**	**Pearson (1)**	**Danson**		
Feb 28	Burslem Port Vale	Div 2	h	5-1		McBride	Derbyshire	Orrell	Howell	Hunter	Tod	Bond	Wilcox	Smith (3)	Pearson (2)	Beaver		
Mar 7	Barnsley	Div 2	a	0-3		McBride	Derbyshire	Orrell	Howell	Hunter	Tod	Walton	Wilcox	Walton	Pearson	Beaver		
Mar 14	Gainsborough	Div 2	h	0-1		McBride	Derbyshire	Orrell	Howell	Hunter	Tod	Walton	Wilcox	Pratt	Pearson	Beaver		
Mar 21	Burton Utd.	Div 2	a	1-2		McBride	Derbyshire	Orrell	Howell	Hunter	Tod	Walton	Wilcox	Pratt	Pearson (1)	Beaver		
Mar 28	Bristol City	Div 2	h	1-0		McBride	Derbyshire	Orrell	Howell	Hunter	Tod	Walton	Wilcox (1p)	Pratt	Pearson	Beaver		
Mar 30	Manchester Utd.	Div 2	a	1-0		McBride	Derbyshire	Warner	Howell	Hunter	Tod	Walton	Wilcox	Pratt	Pearson	Beaver (1)		
Apr 4	Glossop N.E.	Div 2	a	0-1		McBride	Derbyshire	Orrell	Howell	Hunter	Tod	Walton	Wilcox	Pratt	Pearson	Beaver		
Apr 10	Blackpool	Div 2	a	3-1		McBride	Derbyshire	Orrell	Howell	Hunter	Tod	Wilcox	Pratt	Smith (1)	Pearson (2)	Boume		
Apr 11	Manchester Utd.	Div 2	h	3-1		McBride	Derbyshire	Orrell	Howell	Hunter	Tod	Wilcox	Pratt (1)	Smith	Pearson (2)	Boume		
Apr 13	Gainsborough	Div 2	a	0-0		McBride	Derbyshire	Orrell	Howell	Hunter	Tod	Wilcox	Pratt	Smith	Pearson	Boume		
Apr 18	Stockport County	Div 2	a	1-1		McBride	Derbyshire	Orrell	Howell	Hunter	Tod	Wilcox	Pratt	Smith (1)	Pearson	Boume		
Apr 20	Chesterfield	Div 2	h	1-1		McBride	Derbyshire	Orrell	Howell	Hunter	Tod	Wilcox (1)	Pratt	Smith	Pearson	Boume		

SEASON 1903–1904

STAT FACTS:
Best home run without defeat: 17 games
Best away run without defeat: 6 games
Longest run unbeaten: 13 games
Longest run without a win: 3 games

At last! After a lean period the Preston fans had a season to savour as their team recorded their first Second Division Championship and their first promotion back to the top flight. A magnificent start to the campaign set the ball rolling as after twelve games North End's record read: Played 12 Won 11 Drawn 1. It was not until December 19 that they were to lose their first game. New signings John Bell and James McLean made a big difference to the side but it was the superb form of Percy Smith at centre-forward which made the greatest impact. The other important factor was the improved form of other players such as Joe Derbyshire, John Hunter, Richard Bourne and Harry Wilcox. With Peter McBride and Richard Orrell continuing with their outstanding play the side was very settled and virtually picked itself. This in turn led to a greater confidence building up and a defensive stability which over the season was only bettered by the Woolwich Arsenal. Not surprisingly, both games between the sides ended goalless. McBride had a particularly fine season in goal, keeping 14 clean sheets, including one spell of five on the trot, and he deservedly received a Benefit match in the September, a just reward for some outstanding service. As for Percy Smith's goalscoring exploits, the beauty of that came in the fact that he scored regularly for the whole season. With Wilcox also scoring a good total it meant that Preston had at last found a potent strike force. The scorelines were in general steady rather than spectacular but most of the record breaking 20 wins were clearcut. In the FA Cup Preston reached the second round where they received a warning of possible things to come. They were well beaten by first division side Middlesbrough, by 3–0, and it did emphasise the sort of standard they would have to reach should they gain promotion. Back in the league the run-in was nail-biting as Preston, Woolwich Arsenal and Manchester United battled for the coveted title. In the end it came down to the last game of the season and would you believe it, the opposition in this most crucial of games was, of all people, Blackpool. The tangerines had struggled throughout the season but they would have dearly loved to have put the spoke into Preston's hopes. But the Deepdale lads were having none of it and duly won the game thanks to Percy Smith's 26th goal of the season. The match was destined for local folklore. Fifty points achieved, another record total, and, more importantly, a one point gap established over the Arsenal.

DEBUTANTS: (7) John Bell, Billy Lyon, James McLean, David Maher, Tommy Rodway, Herbert Taylor and James Wilson.

LAST GAMES: (4) Smith T. (No. 1), Howell, Tickle and Warner.

Photograph taken after winning the Second Division Championship, but without the silverware.

League appearances (34 games)

Bell J. 32, Bond R. 12, Bourne R. A. 33, Derbyshire J. E. 34, Howell R. 4, Hunter J. 31, Lyon W. J. 6, McBride P. 30, McLean J. 33, Maher D. 14, Orrell R. 24, Rodway T. 1, Smith P. J. 33, Smith T. (No. 1) 8, Taylor H. 4, Tickle B. 3, Tod G. 31, Warner J. 9, Wilcox H. M. 28, Wilson J. 4.

FA Cup appearances (3 games)

McBride 3, Derbyshire 3, Orrell 3, McLean 3, Hunter 3, Tod 3, Bond 2, Maher 1, Wilcox 3, Smith P. J. 3, Bell 3 and Bourne 3.

Goalscorers: 62 League–3 Cup–(Total 65)

Smith P. J. 26–0 (26), Wilcox 15 (4pens)–2 (17), Bell 10–1 (11), Bourne 3–0 (3), Smith T. 3–0 (1), Maher 2–0 (2), McLean 2–0 (2), Bond 1–0 (1).

Match Report: And the Band Played On ... – 30 Apr 1904 Preston 1 Blackpool 0

Monday 25 April 1904 was a very important day in the history of PNE, even though the team never kicked a ball that day. Woolwich Arsenal, top of the Second Division, had to beat Burslem Port Vale at home to win the Championship, but they could only manage a 0–0 draw. That result, coupled with Bolton taking a point off third-placed Manchester United, not only meant that Preston were gauranteed promotion, but also that the club could win the title themselves if they could beat local arch rivals Blackpool at Deepdale the following Saturday. To have a championship absolutely dependent on a single match, on the last day of the season, was a unique situation and obviously aroused intense interest. The selection of the eleven to face Blackpool was a task which required considerable deliberation and was decided by the Directors who met on the Thursday evening prior to the game. One additional element of interest was the selection of Tommy Rodway, the full-back, who had only been signed during that week: obviously no transfer deadlines in those days. Although Preston had beaten Blackpool 3–0 earlier in the season this was a one-off – nerves and all that – with a trophy and medals at stake. North End were photographed before the game as the St Vincent's Boys Band played. From the kick-off Preston were cautious and took time to settle, probably suffering from over-anxiety, and they did not show their true form. But after 35 minutes the team were showing signs that they were coming to terms with the occasion, McLean and Bond looking particularly sharp down the right wing. In one move they brought Wilson into the play and he, in turn, fed Bell who, strongly but fairly, shouldered his marker off before deftly passing the ball to Percy Smith who duly scored with a superbly struck shot which whistled in from over 20 yards. The 8,000 crowd applauded wildly as with this one moment of skill and opportunism the Championship was won as it turned out to be the only goal of the game. At the final whistle fireworks were let off and the band played as Bell, the captain, and Smith, the goalscorer, were carried off shoulder high towards the dressing rooms by exhuberant fans who had spilled onto the pitch. 'Never before in the history of the Club has such enthusiasm been witnessed at Deepdale as was evident at the close of the game', was how the local paper of the day saw it. The Club received the Championship Shield at a Football League meeting one month later and it was announced that a profit of £510 15s 0d. had been made on this successful season.

Season 1903–4: Second Division

	P	W	D	L	F	A	Pts
1 PRESTON	34	20	10	4	62	24	50
2 Woolwich A	34	21	7	6	91	22	49
3 Man United	34	20	8	6	65	33	48
4 Bristol City	34	18	6	10	73	41	42
5 Burnley	34	15	9	10	50	55	39
6 Grimsby	34	14	8	12	50	49	36
7 Bolton	34	12	10	12	59	41	34
8 Barnsley	34	11	10	13	38	57	32
9 Gainsborough	34	14	3	17	53	60	31
10 Bradford City	34	12	7	15	45	59	31
11 Chesterfield	34	11	8	15	37	45	30
12 Lincoln	34	11	8	15	41	58	30
13 Burslem PV	34	10	9	15	54	52	29
14 Burton United	34	11	7	16	45	61	29
15 Blackpool	34	11	5	18	40	67	27
16 Stockport	34	8	11	15	40	72	27
17 Glossop NE	34	10	6	18	57	64	26
18 Leicester Fosse	34	6	10	18	42	82	22

Trivia Fact:

On 6 November 1903 Preston were supposed to play at Burton but the match was postponed because of thick fog. But the strange twist to this story came as the match had to be called off by the linesman because the referee did not show up!

Date 1903-4	Opponents	Comp	h or a	Score	Att.	1	2	3	4	5	6	7	8	9	10	11
Sep 5	Stockport County	Div 2	a	5-1		McBride	Derbyshire	Orrell	Howell	Hunter	Tod	McLean (1)	Wilcox (2,1p)	P.J.Smith (2)	Bell	Bourne
Sep 12	Chesterfield	Div 2	h	2-1		McBride	Derbyshire	Orrell	Howell	Hunter	Tod	McLean	Wilcox (1)	P.J.Smith (1)	Bell	Bourne
Sep 19	Bolton W.	Div 2	a	2-0		McBride	Derbyshire	Orrell	Howell	Hunter	Tod	McLean	Wilcox	P.J.Smith	Bell (1)	Bourne (1)
Sep 26	Burnley	Div 2	h	2-0		McBride	Derbyshire	Orrell	Howell	Hunter	Tod	McLean	Wilcox (1p)	P.J.Smith (1)	Bell	Bourne
Oct 3	Burslem Port Vale	Div 2	a	3-1		McBride	Derbyshire	Orrell	Tickle	Hunter	Tod	McLean	Wilcox (1p)	P.J.Smith (2)	Bell	Bourne
Oct 10	Grimsby	Div 2	a	1-1		McBride	Derbyshire	Orrell	Tickle	Hunter	Tod	McLean	Wilcox	P.J.Smith (1)	Bell	Bourne
Oct 17	Leicester Fosse	Div 2	h	4-3		McBride	Derbyshire	Orrell	Tickle	Hunter	Tod	Bond	Wilcox (2)	P.J.Smith	Bell (2)	Bourne
Oct 24	Blackpool	Div 2	a	3-0		McBride	Derbyshire	Orrell	McLean	Hunter	Tod	Bond (1)	Wilcox	P.J.Smith (2)	Bell	Maher
Oct 31	Grimsby	Div 2	h	2-0		McBride	Derbyshire	Orrell	McLean	Hunter	Tod	Bond	Wilcox	P.J.Smith	Bell (2)	Bourne
Nov 14	Bristol City	Div 2	h	3-0		McBride	Derbyshire	Orrell	McLean	Hunter	Tod	Bond	Wilcox (2)	P.J.Smith (1)	Bell	Bourne
Nov 21	Manchester Utd.	Div 2	a	2-0		McBride	Derbyshire	Orrell	McLean	Hunter	Tod	Bond	Wilcox (1p)	P.J.Smith (1)	Bell	Bourne
Nov 28	Glossop N.E.	Div 2	h	3-0		McBride	Derbyshire	Orrell	McLean	Hunter	Tod	Bond	Wilcox (1)	P.J.Smith (1)	Bell	Bourne (1)
Dec 5	Bradford City	Div 2	a	1-1		McBride	Derbyshire	Orrell	McLean	Hunter	Tod	Bond	Wilcox (1)	P.J.Smith	Bell	Bourne
Dec 12	Darwen Intermed. Rd	FAC	h	2-1	10000	McBride	Derbyshire	Orrell	McLean	Hunter	Tod	Bond	Wilcox (1)	P.J.Smith	Bell (1)	Bourne
Dec 19	Barnsley	Div 2	a	0-1		Taylor	Derbyshire	Orrell	McLean	Hunter	Tod	Bond	Wilcox	P.J.Smith	Bell	Bourne
Dec 25	Gainsborough	Div 2	h	2-0		McBride	Derbyshire	Warner	McLean	Hunter	Tod	Maher	Wilcox	P.J.Smith (2)	Bell	Bourne
Dec 26	Lincoln	Div 2	h	2-1		McBride	Derbyshire	Orrell	McLean	Hunter	Tod	Maher	Wilcox (2)	P.J.Smith	Bell	Bourne
Dec 28	Burton Utd.	Div 2	a	0-0		McBride	Derbyshire	Warner	McLean	Hunter	Tod	Bond	Wilcox	P.J.Smith	Bell	Bourne
Jan 2	Stockport County	Div 2	h	1-1		McBride	Derbyshire	Orrell	McLean	Hunter	Tod	Maher (1)	Wilcox	P.J.Smith	Bell	Bourne
Jan 9	Chesterfield	Div 2	h	1-0		McBride	Derbyshire	Orrell	McLean	Hunter	Tod	Maher	Wilcox	P.J.Smith (1)	Bell	Bourne
Jan 16	Bolton W.	Div 2	h	3-1		McBride	Derbyshire	Orrell	McLean	Hunter	Tod	Maher	Wilcox	P.J.Smith (2)	Bell (1)	Bourne
Jan 23	Burnley	Div 2	a	1-2		McBride	Derbyshire	Orrell	McLean	Hunter	Tod	Maher	Wilcox	P.J.Smith (1)	Bell	Bourne
Jan 30	Burslem Port Vale	Div 2	a	1-0		McBride	Derbyshire	Orrell	McLean	Hunter	Tod	bond	Wilcox	P.J.Smith (1)	Bell	Bourne
Feb 6	Grimsby Rd 1	FAC	h	1-0	9500	McBride	Derbyshire	Orrell	McLean	Hunter	Tod	Bond	Wilcox (1)	P.J.Smith	Bell	Bourne
Feb 13	Leicester Fosse	Div 2	a	4-1		McBride	Derbyshire	Orrell	McLean	Hunter	Tod	Maher	Wilcox	P.J.Smith (3)	Bell (1)	Bourne
Feb 20	Middlesbrough Rd 2	FAC	h	0-3	15924	McBride	Derbyshire	Orrell	McLean	Hunter	Tod	Maher	Wilcox	P.J.Smith	Bell	Bourne
Feb 27	Gainsborough	Div 2	a	0-2		McBride	Derbyshire	Orrell	McLean	Hunter	Tod	Maher	Wilcox	P.J.Smith	Bell	Bourne
Mar 5	Burton Utd.	Div 2	h	4-0		McBride	Derbyshire	Orrell	McLean	Hunter	Tod	T. Smith (2)	Wilcox (1)	P.J.Smith (1)	Bell	Bourne
Mar 12	Bristol City	Div 2	a	1-3		McBride	Derbyshire	Orrell	McLean	Hunter	Tod	T. Smith	Maher	P.J.Smith (1)	Bell	Bourne
Mar 19	Manchester Utd.	Div 2	h	1-1		McBride	Derbyshire	Warner	McLean	Hunter	Tod	T. Smith	Wilcox	P.J.Smith	Bell (1)	Bourne
Mar 26	Glossop N.E.	Div 2	a	2-2		McBride	Derbyshire	Warner	McLean (1)	Hunter	Tod	T. Smith	Maher	P.J.Smith	Bell (1)	Bourne
Apr 1	Woolwich Arsenal	Div 2	a	0-0		McBride	Derbyshire	Warner	McLean	Tod	Lyon	T. Smith	Maher	P.J.Smith	Bell	Bourne
Apr 2	Bradford City	Div 2	h	4-0		McBride	Derbyshire	Warner	McLean	Tod	Lyon	T. Smith (1)	Maher (1)	P.J.Smith	Bell (1)	Bourne (1)
Apr 9	Woolwich Arsenal	Div 2	h	0-0		Taylor	Derbyshire	Warner	McLean	Tod	Lyon	T. Smith	Maher	P.J.Smith	Wilson	Bourne
Apr 16	Barnsley	Div 2	h	1-1		McBride	Derbyshire	Warner	McLean	Hunter	Tod	T. Smith	Wilcox	P.J.Smith (1)	Wilson	Bourne
Apr 23	Lincoln	Div 2	a	0-0		Taylor	Derbyshire	Orrell	McLean	Hunter	Lyon	Bond	Wilcox	Wilson	Bell	Bourne
Apr 30	Blackpool	Div 2	h	1-0		Taylor	Derbyshire	Rodway	McLean	Hunter	Lyon	Bond	Wilson	P.J.Smith (1)	Bell	Bourne

Some future players born during the season 1903–4: John Bradford, James Dickie, Edward Gerrard, Tom Scott, Bill Tremelling, Dick Rowley and John Pears
Ever presents: (1) Joe Derbyshire
FA Cup: Second Round
Hat-tricks: (1) Percy Smith
Manager: Management Committee
Chairman: Mr W. E. Ord J. P.
Leading scorer: 26 goals – Percy Smith (all League)
Players used: 20

AUTHORS UNOFFICIAL PLAYER OF THE SEASON: Percy Smith

League position in Division Two: Champions – P34 W20 D10 L4 F62 A24 Pts 50
Home: W13 D4 L0 F38 A10 Away: W7 D6 L4 F24 A14

SEASON 1904–1905

The first season back in the top division for three years and a consolidating mid-table position was attained after an interesting campaign. Defensively, North End were once again very solid with Peter McBride having another magnificent season. Only the Champions and runners-up conceded less goals than Preston, but in attack the Lilywhites found goals hard to come by. Percy Smith again topped the scoring charts but this time he was not quite so prolific as he actually only scored in nine matches and in two of those he hit hat-tricks. He needed support to relieve the pressure on him to score but alas it was not forthcoming with only Dickie Bond able to chip in with a decent total. Three of his goals had also come in a hat-trick and not until the penultimate game of the season against Sheffield United. Preston started the season well for a change and lost only once in the first seven matches. But then they were beaten 6–1 at Manchester City and it came as something of a shock. In the December and January Preston had an awful period, losing seven out of ten with only one win to show for their efforts. However, they then rallied and in the last nine games they lost only once and let in only three goals. So it was a year of good and bad runs and a search to try and find the consistency they needed to make a challenge on the honours. Joe Derbyshire, John Hunter, Billy Lyon and James McLean could all be pleased with their form whilst Tommy Rodway and James Wilson gave good support. It was another good team effort although McBride enhanced his growing reputation with every game and was without doubt the star of the side. In the FA Cup Preston made a fight of each game and there was plenty of excitement. A 2–0 win at Derby County in the first round was achieved before Bristol City, who went on to win the Second Division, were beaten 1–0 after a goalless draw in Bristol. North End then had a really tough draw in the third round with current League Champions Sheffield Wednesday visiting Deepdale. Preston battled well but were held to a 1–1 draw. In the replay, unfortunately, they were well beaten and another cup run was over. In the remaining league games Preston did well. McBride continued his great form and let in just one goal in the last seven games. Indeed Preston finished on a high with three straight wins. In many ways it had been a good season for the club and the promise shown augered well for 1905–6. It remained to be seen whether North End could build on it.

DEBUTANTS: (5) Albert Brown, John Catterall, Daniel McKie, Thomas Rodger and James Turnbull.

LAST GAMES: (4) Wilcox, Bourne, McKie and Rodger.

League appearances (34 games)

Bell J. 14, Bond R. 30, Bourne R. A. 24, Brown A. 17, Catterall J. 4, Derbyshire J. E. 27, Hunter J. 31, Lyon W. J. 32, McBride P. 34, McKie D. 3, McLean J. 33, Maher D. 5, Orrell R. 14, Rodger T. 5, Rodway T. 27, Smith P. J. 32, Tod G. 6, Turnbull J. M. 8, Wilcox H. M. 6, Wilson J. 22.

FA Cup appearances (5 games)

McBride 5, Derbyshire 5, Rodway 5, McLean 5, Hunter 5, Lyon 5, Bond 5, Wilson 1, Brown 1, Wilcox 1, Maher 2, Smith 5, Bell 5 and Bourne 5.

Goalscorers: 42 League–4 Cup–(Total 46)

Smith 14–0 (14), Bond 8–2 (10), Brown 6 (2 pens)–0 (6), Wilson 4–0 (4), Bell 3–1 (4), Bourne 3–1 (4), McKie 2–0 (2), Hunter 1–0 (1), Rodger 1–0 (1).

After three seasons absence North End's first game back in the top flight was away at mighty Aston Villa on a Thursday evening with a 5.30 kick-off. The 10,000 spectators who were present at the start gave Preston a rousing reception as they stepped on to the pitch. It was a warm welcome back. But no harder task could have been envisaged, as the visitors had lost their last ten games played on Villa's ground. Brown, on his debut, kicked off for Preston. The game in the early stages was 'capitally contested' as the *Lancashire Daily Post* quaintly put it, with Lyon's keen tackling and Rodway's strong clearances being worthy of mention. As the game progressed the Villains enjoyed the lion's share of possession though every inch was earnestly contested. Villa's finishing was indifferent, to put it mildly, with McBride not being tested anything like as often as the crowd would have liked. Left-winger Lockett caused Derbyshire a few problems, but there always seemed to be another white shirt on hand to help. Quite pleasingly Preston still hung on to the 0–0 scoreline at half-time. The crowd had now swelled to around 16,000 and on the hour mark they saw Preston take the lead. Lyon won the ball and put the left-wing in possession and Bourne, taking advantage of a defensive error, slipped smartly away to deliver the ball right into the danger area. Brown, in anticipation, had dashed up to hinder the goalkeeper who could only manage to push the ball away weakly only to see Brown pounce again to score a debut goal. Ten minutes later the proud-to-be-back Prestononians staggered friend and foe alike by adding a second goal through Smith. Within two minutes Villa pulled a goal back after Rodway had fouled Bache in the area. The aptly named Brawn confidently scored from the resulting penalty, but North End held on for a deserved victory. Preston's superior teamwork had won the points and they had attacked with more purpose and devilment. The rock on which many Villa attacks were broken was the terrier-like half back line, well marshalled by Lyon who had covered every blade of grass with vigour. It was a long day for the Preston party as they only arrived back at Preston railway station at 2.30 a.m., but at least they were in good spirits.

Left to right:
Back row: G. Drummond (Trainer), Tod, McBride, Rodway, Hunter, W. E. Bahr (Secretary).
Middle row: Wilcox, Smith, Brown, Wilson, Derbyshire.
Front row: Bond, McLean, Bourne, Lyon.

Some future players born during the season 1904–5 include: James Devlin, George Shaw, Jack Nelson, David Galloway and John Jennings
Ever presents: (1) Peter McBride
Hat-tricks: (3) Smith 2 and Bond 1
FA Cup: Third Round Replay
Manager: Management Committee
Chairman: Mr W. E. Ord J. P.
Leading scorer: 14 goals – Percy Smith (all League)
Players used: 20
AUTHORS' UNOFFICIAL PLAYER OF THE SEASON: Peter McBride

Trivia Fact:
Part of the transfer deal that brought Jimmy Wilson to Deepdale was that North End had to visit St Mirren to play a friendly. Ironically, North End won 1–0 with a goal scored by Wilson himself against his former club.

Season 1904–5: First Division

		P	W	D	L	F	A	Pts
1	Newcastle	34	23	2	9	72	33	48
2	Everton	34	21	5	8	63	36	47
3	Man City	34	20	6	8	66	37	46
4	Aston Villa	34	19	4	11	63	43	42
5	Sunderland	34	16	8	10	60	44	40
6	Sheffield United	34	19	2	13	64	56	40
7	Small Heath	34	17	5	12	54	38	39
8	**PRESTON**	**34**	**13**	**10**	**11**	**42**	**37**	**36**
9	Wednesday	34	14	5	15	61	57	33
10	Woolwich A	34	12	9	13	36	40	33
11	Derby	34	12	8	14	37	48	32
12	Stoke	34	13	4	17	40	58	30
13	Blackburn	34	11	5	18	40	51	27
14	Wolves	34	11	4	19	47	73	26
15	Middlesbrough	34	9	8	17	36	56	26
16	Nottingham Forest	34	9	7	18	40	61	25
17	Bury	34	10	4	20	47	67	24
18	Notts County	34	5	8	21	36	69	18

League position in Division One: 8th – P34 W13 D10 L11 F42 A37 Pts 36
Home: W9 D5 L3 F28 A13   Away: W4 D5 L8 F14 A24

Date 1904-5	Opponents	Comp	h or a	Score	Att.	1	2	3	4	5	6	7	8	9	10	11
Sep 1	Aston Villa	Div 1	a	2-1		McBride	Derbyshire	Rodway	McLean	Hunter	Lyon	Bell	Smith (1)	Brown (1)	Wilson	Boume
Sep 3	Sunderland	Div 1	h	3-1		McBride	Derbyshire	Rodway	McLean	Hunter	Lyon	Bell	Smith (3)	Brown	Wilson	Boume
Sep 10	Woolwich Arsenal	Div 1	a	0-0		McBride	Derbyshire	Rodway	McLean	Hunter	Lyon	Bond	Smith	Brown	Wilson	Boume
Sep 17	Derby County	Div 1	h	2-0		McBride	Derbyshire	Rodway	McLean	Hunter	Lyon	Bond	Smith (1)	Brown	Wilson (1)	Boume
Sep 24	Everton	Div 1	a	0-1		McBride	Derbyshire	Rodway	McLean	Hunter	Lyon	Bell	Smith	Brown	Wilson	Boume
Oct 1	Small Heath	Div 1	a	2-2		McBride	Derbyshire	Rodway	McLean	Hunter	Lyon	Bond	Smith (2)	Brown	Wilson	Boume
Oct 6	Nottm. Forest	Div 1	a	1-0		McBride	Derbyshire	Rodway	McLean	Hunter	Lyon	Bond	Smith	Brown (1)	Wilson	Boume
Oct 8	Manchester City	Div 1	a	1-6		McBride	Derbyshire	Rodway	McLean	Hunter	Lyon	Bond	Smith	Brown (1)	Wilson	Boume
Oct 15	Notts County	Div 1	h	3-1		McBride	Derbyshire	Orrell	McLean	Hunter	Lyon	Bond	McKie	Brown (2p)	Wilson (1)	Boume
Oct 22	Sheffield Utd.	Div 1	a	0-1		McBride	Derbyshire	Orrell	McLean	Hunter	Lyon	Bond	Smith	Wilcox	Wilson	Boume
Oct 29	Newcastle Utd.	Div 1	h	1-0		McBride	Derbyshire	Orrell	McLean	Hunter	Lyon	Bond	Smith	Wilcox	Wilson (1)	Boume
Nov 5	Stoke	Div 1	a	1-1		McBride	Derbyshire	Orrell	Tod	Hunter	Lyon	Bond	Smith	Brown	Wilson	Boume (1)
Nov 12	Middlesbrough	Div 1	a	1-1		McBride	Derbyshire	Orrell	McLean	Hunter	Lyon	Bond (1)	Smith	Wilcox	Wilson	Boume
Nov 19	Wolverhampton W.	Div 1	h	2-2		McBride	Derbyshire	Orrell	McLean	Hunter	Lyon	Bond	Smith	Brown	Wilson (1)	Boume (1)
Nov 26	Bury	Div 1	h	1-0		McBride	Derbyshire	Rodway	McLean	Hunter	Lyon	Bond	Smith	Brown	Wilson	Boume (1)
Dec 3	Aston Villa	Div 1	h	2-3		McBride	Derbyshire	Rodway	McLean	Hunter	Lyon	Bond (2)	Smith	Brown	Wilson	Boume
Dec 10	Blackburn Rovers	Div 1	a	1-1		McBride	Orrell	Rodway	McLean	Hunter	Lyon	Bond	Smith	Bell (1)	Wilson	Boume
Dec 17	Nottm. Forest	Div 1	h	0-1		McBride	Rodway	Orrell	McLean	Hunter	Lyon	Bond	Smith	Bell	Wilson	Boume
Dec 26	Manchester City	Div 1	h	0-1		McBride	Rodway	Orrell	McLean	Hunter	Tod	Bond	Smith	Brown	Bell	Boume
Dec 31	Sunderland	Div 1	a	2-3		McBride	Rodway	Orrell	McLean	Hunter	Lyon	Bond (1)	Smith (1)	Wilcox	Bell	Catterall
Jan 2	Sheffield Wed.	Div 1	a	0-2		McBride	Rodway	Orrell	McLean	Hunter	Lyon	Bond	Smith	Wilcox	Bell	Catterall
Jan 7	Woolwich Arsenal	Div 1	h	3-0		McBride	Rodway	Orrell	McLean	Hunter (1)	Lyon	Bond (1)	Smith	Tumbull	Bell (1)	Boume
Jan 14	Derby County	Div 1	a	1-3		McBride	Rodway	Orrell	McLean	Hunter	Lyon	Bond	Smith	Tumbull	Bell (1)	Boume
Jan 21	Everton	Div 1	h	1-1		McBride	Derbyshire	Rodway	McLean	Hunter	Lyon	Bond	Smith (1)	Tumbull	Bell	Catterall
Jan 28	Small Heath	Div 1	h	0-2		McBride	Derbyshire	Rodway	McLean	Hunter	Lyon	Bond	Smith	Tumbull	Bell	Boume
Feb 4	Derby County Rd 1	FAC	a	2-0	14080	McBride	Derbyshire	Rodway	McLean	Hunter	Lyon	Bond (1)	Wilson	Smith	Bell (1)	Bourne
Feb 11	Notts County	Div 1		3-1		McBride	Derbyshire	Rodway	McLean	Hunter	Lyon	Bond	Wilson	Smith (3)	Bell	Boume
Feb 18	Bristol City Rd 2	FAC	a	0-0	19371	McBride	Derbyshire	Rodway	McLean	Hunter	Lyon	Bond	Brown	Smith	Bell	Bourne
Feb 23	Bristol City Replay	FAC	h	1-0	14000	McBride	Derbyshire	Rodway	McLean	Hunter	Lyon	Bond	Wilcox	Smith	Bell	Bourne (1)
Feb 25	Newcastle Utd.	Div 1	a	0-1		McBride	Derbyshire	Orrell	McLean	Hunter	Tod	Rodger	Wilcox	Smith	Bell	Catterall
Mar 4	Sheffield Wed. Rd 3	FAC	h	1-1	11000	McBride	Derbyshire	Rodway	McLean	Hunter	Lyon	Bond (1)	Maher	Smith	Bell	Bourne
Mar 9	Sheffield Wed. Replay	FAC	a	0-3	24898	McBride	Derbyshire	Rodway	McLean	Hunter	Lyon	Bond	Maher	Smith	Bell	Bourne
Mar 11	Middlesbrough	Div 1	h	2-0		McBride	Derbyshire	Rodway	McLean	Hunter	Lyon	Bond	Maher	Smith	Bell	McKie (2)
Mar 18	Wolverhampton W.	Div 1	a	0-0		McBride	Derbyshire	Rodway	McLean	Tod	Lyon	Bond	Maher	Smith	Tumbull	McKie
Mar 25	Bury	Div 1	a	0-0		McBride	Derbyshire	Rodway	McLean	Hunter	Lyon	Bond	Maher	Smith	Tumbull	Boume
Apr 8	Blackburn Rovers	Div 1	h	0-0		McBride	Derbyshire	Rodway	McLean	Hunter	Lyon	Bond	Maher	Smith	Tumbull	Rodger
Apr 10	Stoke	Div 1	h	2-1		McBride	Derbyshire	Rodway	McLean	Hunter	Lyon	Bond	Maher	Brown (1)	Tumbull	Rodger (1)
Apr 21	Sheffield Utd.	Div 1	h	4-0		McBride	Derbyshire	Rodway	McLean	Tod	Lyon	Bond (3)	Smith (1)	Brown	Wilson	Rodger
Apr 22	Sheffield Wed.	Div 1	h	1-0		McBride	Derbyshire	Rodway	McLean	Tod	Lyon	Bond	Smith (1)	Brown	Wilson	Rodger

Match Report: McKie's Double in Quagmire –
11 March 1905 Preston 2 Middlesbrough 0

Middlesbrough stayed over at Lytham the night before this game so as to be fresh and ready for the match. Bad weather before the start made the pitch a quagmire and a strong wind made good football very difficult. Bell won the toss and played towards the Barracks end. Preston put in early pressure and after Smith had missed a great chance they continued to press forward. Good passing and hard work gave the home side the edge and Williamson, the Boro keeper was kept busy. After 13 minutes the deadlock was broken when Lyon initiated a goalmouth scramble with his tenacity and eventually McKie prodded the ball into the net. A fine dribble by Common almost brought an equaliser but he just failed although a further reminder of the danger from Middlesbrough came when Jones put in a superb long range shot which McBride saved in splendid style. The sun was shining brightly by now into the Boro players' faces. Bell sustained an injury and had to play at outside-left to shield the injury. Soon afterwards though he was forced to go off and North End continued with ten men. Before half-time McBride did wonderfully well to stop a long range shot by Thackerey and Preston had done very well to still hold their lead at the break. After the interval, and still without Bell, Preston almost scored again when McKie's shot was blocked by the referee, of all people! Middlesbrough fought hard but Preston's defence was very determined with Derbyshire prominent and Hunter a rock at the heart of the team. With 20 minutes to go a shot by Lyon was not held by the visitors' keeper and McKie was again on hand to knock in the rebound. Preston were forced back for the rest of the game but the Boro lacked finish and it was Preston who came closest to scoring again when Maher's header missed the target in the last seconds of the game.

SEASON 1905–1906

Preston had their best season for years in the 1905–6 campaign and finished deserved runners-up behind Liverpool in a championship that for the first time had 20 teams competing. Liverpool, who were also Second Division Champions in the 1904–5 season, were the outstanding team again and ended four points clear of the Deepdale club. The three points that they took from Preston had contributed to that gap. It is incredible to think that North End did so well and yet had the most awful start to the season, winning just one game in their first seven fixtures. However, they also put together some useful unbeaten runs to accumulate their points. There was not an abundance of goals in the North End matches as generally each game was tight, with Preston's defence very strong. In attack Dickie Bond was the star and he scored some excellent goals from his right-wing position. Percy Smith and John Bell also reached double figures but gone were the days when the Lilywhites would hit six, seven or even more goals in a match. At the back Joe Derbyshire, James McLean, Tommy Rodway and John Hunter all performed admirably, and always there was the magnificent Peter McBride, a master in the art of goalkeeping. December was an especially good month for the club, winning three and drawing three of their six games. It looked as though their good form would coincide nicely with the start of the FA Cup. But Preston were drawn away at Birmingham, a city which was often a graveyard for North End's hopes. And so it proved as the Midland side put an end to a cup run before it had started. So, Preston then had to concentrate on the league and to be fair they made a great effort in trying to catch Liverpool. The crunch match came on March 24 1906 when Liverpool visited Deepdale.

Preston had to win but despite a goal from Herbert Danson the Merseysiders kept their heads and eventually cleverly won the match with two goals of their own. Two further defeats in the April virtually ended any chance Preston might still have had of taking the title. Goals had been the key throughout the season and although North End had by far and away the best defensive record in the division, only Derby County scored fewer than they did. Preston drew thirteen games, a high total, and if only one more goal in each of those games would have given them an emphatic league title. If only …

DEBUTANTS: (6) Herbert Ashton, William Blyth, Lawrence Cook, Percy Hartley, Arthur Lockett and Harry Pearson.

LAST GAMES: (5) Orrell, Maher, Brown, Turnbull and Blyth.

Left to right: *Back row:* G. Drummond (Trainer), Derbyshire, McBride, Rodway, Hunter, W. E. Bahr (Secretary). *Middle row:* Bond, Smith, Brown, Wilson, Lockett. *Front row:* McLean, Lyon.

League appearances (38 games)

Ashton H. 2, Bell J. 30, Blyth W. J. 1, Bond R. 33, Brown A. 5, Cook L. 3, Danson H. 8, Derbyshire J. E. 26, Hartley P. W. 1, Hunter J. 37, Lockett A. 32, Lyon W. J. 33, McBride P. 36, McLean J. 35, Maher D. 5, Orrell R. 9, Pearson H. 1, Rodway T. 37, Smith P. J. 35, Taylor H. 2, Tod G. 8, Turnbull J. M. 5, Wilson J. 34.

FA Cup appearances (1 game)

McBride, Derbyshire, Rodway, McLean, Hunter, Lyon, Bond, Wilson, Smith, Bell and Lockett, all one appearance each.

Goalscorers: 54 League only

Bond 17 (4 pens), Bell 10, Smith 10, Lockett 4, Wilson 3, Lyon 2, Danson 2, Brown 1, Hunter 1, Derbyshire 1 (pen), Rodway 1. Own Goals 2 (Morris of Derby and Leake of Aston Villa)

League position in Division One: Runners-up – P38 W17 D13 L8 F54 A39 Pts 47
Home: W12 D5 L2 F36 A15   Away: W5 D8 L6 F18 A24

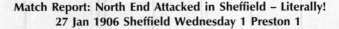

Match Report: North End Attacked in Sheffield – Literally!
27 Jan 1906 Sheffield Wednesday 1 Preston 1

Around 15,000 spectators attended this run of the mill league game although it turned out to be anything but that. The contest was full of pace, vigour and crunching tackles. Feelings on and off the pitch were running high, especially in the latter stages as North End strove for an equaliser. It came eleven miuntes from the end from the penalty spot after Lyall was adjudged to have fouled Brown. Dickie Bond kept his cool, and successfully converted the kick, much to the annoyance of the home crowd who already seemed to be in an angry mood. Preston held on and immediately after the final whistle, 'Perseus', the Lancashire Daily Post's well respected journalist, took a hansom cab back into the City centre to hand in his final wire at the Post Office. He then went to the Royal Hotel to await the team's return. When North End's players eventually turned up the party informed the ace reporter about an attack which had been made upon the team after they had left the ground. The players claimed that they had been pelted with mud and other missiles including stones, pieces of brick, a closed pen-knife and a potato! Lyon had sustained a nasty head injury and was still bleeding as he entered the hotel foyer. Passengers in passing tramcars, presumably Wednesday fans, had spat at the party on their journey back to the hotel. The players were eventually escorted by a couple of mounted police. The police apparently had to usher the referee and linesmen away from the ground hastily. Their decisions had incensed the crowd. Little Dickie Bond, already unpopular even before his penalty success, escaped unscathed, hidden as best as possible by his teammates. The whole episode was investigated at a private FA meeting a couple of weeks after the match. North End were represented by vice-chairman Tom Houghton, Bell, the captain, Percy Smith and Drummond, the trainer. The commission took five hours to come to these decisions: A) Match not played in the proper spirit. B) Officials lack of control, C) Mr Houghton's improper conduct after the match and D) PNE players conducted themselves in a vulgar manner to spectators after the match, (allegedly gesticulating through the dressing room windows). Both sets of players and officials were censured. Mr Houghton was suspended for one month and Sheffield Wednesday's ground was closed for 14 days. The commission found it impossible to identify which North End players had misconducted themselves so they fined each man who played that day one pound each.

Dickie Bond in his England shirt and cap.

Future players born during the 1905–6 season include: Herbert Hamilton, John Kendall and Gavin Nisbet.
Ever presents: None
FA Cup: First Round
Manager: Management Committee
Chairman: Mr W. E. Ord J. P
Hat-tricks: None
Leading scorer: 17 goals Dickie Bond (all League)
Players used: 23
AUTHORS' UNOFFICIAL PLAYER OF THE SEASON: Dickie Bond

STAT FACTS:
Best home run without defeat: 12 games
Best away run without defeat: 7 games
Longest run unbeaten: 9 games
Longest run without a win: 5 games

Trivia Facts:

Both Dickie Bond and Tommy Rodway played for the North vs South at Elland Road, Leeds 22.1.06 in an international trial match.

Two days after the season had finished North End were playing out a 3–3 draw in Belfast against Cliftonville. Danson, Maher & Bond scored Preston's goals.

Season 1905–6: First Division

	P	W	D	L	F	A	Pts
1 Liverpool	38	23	5	10	79	46	51
2 PRESTON	**38**	**17**	**13**	**8**	**54**	**39**	**47**
3 Wednesday	38	18	8	12	63	52	44
4 Newcastle	38	18	7	13	74	48	43
5 Man City	38	19	5	14	73	54	43
6 Bolton	38	17	7	14	81	67	41
7 Birmingham	38	17	7	14	65	59	41
8 Aston Villa	38	17	6	15	72	56	40
9 Blackburn	38	16	8	14	54	52	40
10 Stoke	38	16	7	15	54	55	39
11 Everton	38	15	7	16	70	66	37
12 Woolwich A	38	15	7	16	62	64	37
13 Sheffield United	38	15	6	17	57	62	36
14 Sunderland	38	15	5	18	61	70	35
15 Derby	38	14	7	17	39	58	35
16 Notts County	38	11	12	15	55	71	34
17 Bury	38	11	10	17	57	74	32
18 Middlesbrough	38	10	11	17	56	71	31
19 Nottingham Forest	38	13	5	20	58	79	31
20 Wolves	38	8	7	23	58	99	23

Date 1905-6	Opponents	Comp	h or a	Score	Att.	1	2	3	4	5	6	7	8	9	10	11		
Sep 2	Birmingham	Div 1	a	1-1		McBride	Derbyshire	Rodway	McLean	Hunter	Lyon	Bond	Smith	Brown (1)	Wilson	Lockett		
Sep 4	Nottm. Forest	Div 1	h	3-1		McBride	Derbyshire	Rodway	McLean	Hunter	Lyon	Bond (2)	Smith (1)	Brown	Wilson	Lockett		
Sep 9	Everton	Div 1	h	1-1		McBride	Derbyshire	Rodway	McLean	Hunter	Lyon	Bond (1)	Smith	Brown	Wilson	Lockett		
Sep 16	Derby County	Div 1	a	0-3		McBride	Derbyshire	Rodway	McLean	Hunter	Lyon	Bond	Smith	Brown	Wilson	Lockett		
Sep 18	Woolwich Arsenal	Div 1	a	2-2		McBride	Derbyshire	Rodway	McLean	Hunter	Lyon	Bond (1)	Bell	Smith (1)	Wilson	Lockett		
Sep 23	Sheffield Wed.	Div 1	h	0-1		McBride	Derbyshire	Rodway	McLean	Hunter	Lyon	Bond	Smith	Turnbull	Wilson	Lockett		
Sep 30	Nottm. Forest	Div 1	a	0-1		McBride	Derbyshire	Rodway	McLean	Hunter	Tod	Bond	Wilson	Turnbull	Bell	Lockett		
Oct 7	Manchester City	Div 1	h	2-0		McBride	Derbyshire	Rodway	McLean	Hunter	Tod	Bond (1)	Wilson	Smith	Bell	Lockett (1)		
Oct 14	Bury	Div 1	a	1-1		McBride	Derbyshire	Rodway	McLean	Hunter	Lyon	Bond	Wilson	Smith	Bell (1)	Lockett		
Oct 21	Middlesbrough	Div 1	h	2-1		McBride	Derbyshire	Rodway	McLean	Hunter	Lyon	Bond	Wilson (1)	Smith (1)	Bell	Lockett		
Oct 28	Wolverhampton W.	Div 1	h	3-2		McBride	Derbyshire	Rodway	McLean	Hunter	Tod	Bond (2)	Wilson	Smith (1)	Bell	Lockett		
Nov 4	Newcastle Utd.	Div 1	h	0-1		McBride	Derbyshire	Rodway	McLean	Hunter	Lyon	Bond	Wilson	Smith	Bell	Lockett		
Nov 11	Aston Villa	Div 1	h	2-0		McBride	Derbyshire	Rodway	McLean	Hunter	Lyon (1)	Bond (1)	Wilson	Smith	Bell	Lockett		
Nov 18	Liverpool	Div 1	a	1-1		McBride	Orrell	Rodway	Tod	Hunter	Lyon	Bond (1)	Wilson	Smith	Bell	Lockett		
Nov 25	Sheffield Utd.	Div 1	a	1-1		McBride	Orrell	Rodway	McLean	Hunter	Lyon	Bond (1)	Wilson	Smith	Bell	Lockett		
Dec 2	Notts County	Div 1	a	2-2		McBride	Derbyshire	Rodway	McLean	Hunter	Lyon	Bond	Wilson	Smith	Bell (1)	Lockett (1)		
Dec 9	Stoke	Div 1	h	2-0		McBride	Derbyshire	Rodway	McLean	Hunter	Tod	Bond (1)	Wilson	Smith (1)	Bell	Lockett		
Dec 16	Bolton W.	Div 1	a	2-1		McBride	Derbyshire	Rodway	McLean	Hunter	Tod	Bond	Wilson	Smith (1)	Bell (1)	Lockett		
Dec 23	Woolwich Arsenal	Div 1	h	2-2		Taylor	Derbyshire	Rodway	McLean	Hunter	Lyon	Bond (2p)	Wilson	Smith	Bell	Lockett		
Dec 25	Sunderland	Div 1	h	1-1		McBride	Derbyshire	Rodway	McLean	Hunter (1)	Lyon	Bond	Wilson	Brown	Bell	Lockett		
Dec 30	Birmingham	Div 1	h	3-0		McBride	Derbyshire	Rodway	McLean	Hunter	Lyon	Bond (1p)	Wilson (1)	Smith	Bell (1)	Lockett		
Jan 6	Everton	Div 1	a	0-1		McBride	Derbyshire	Rodway	McLean	Tod	Lyon	Bond	Maher	Smith	Turnbull	Lockett		
Jan 13	**Birmingham** Rd 1	**FAC**	**a**	**0-1**	**17000**	**McBride**	**Derbyshire**	**Rodway**	**McLean**	**Hunter**	**Lyon**	**Bond**	**Wilson**	**Smith**	**Bell**	**Lockett**		
Jan 20	Derby County	Div 1	h	3-1		McBride	Derbyshire	Rodway	McLean	Hunter	Lyon	Bond (1)	Maher	Smith	Bell	Lockett (1)	1 o.g.	(Morris)
Jan 27	Sheffield Wed.	Div 1	a	1-1		McBride	Derbyshire	Rodway	McLean	Hunter	Lyon	Bond (1p)	Maher	Smith	Bell	Lockett		
Feb 3	Blackburn Rovers	Div 1	h	2-1		McBride	Derbyshire	Rodway	McLean	Hunter	Lyon	Bond	Wilson	Smith	Bell (2)	Lockett		
Feb 10	Manchester City	Div 1	a	0-0		McBride	Manchester	Rodway	McLean	Hunter	Lyon	Bond	Wilson	Smith	Bell	Danson		
Feb 17	Bury	Div 1	h	1-0		McBride	Derbyshire(1p)	Rodway	McLean	Hunter	Lyon	Maher	Wilson	Smith	Bell	Lockett		
Mar 3	Wolverhampton W.	Div 1	a	3-2		McBride	Derbyshire	Rodway	McLean	Hunter	Lyon	Bond (1)	Wilson	Smith (1)	Bell (1)	Lockett		
Mar 14	Middlesbrough	Div 1	a	2-1		McBride	Orrell	Rodway	McLean	Hunter	Lyon	Bond	Maher	Smith (1)	Bell (1)	Lockett		
Mar 17	Aston Villa	Div 1	a	1-0		McBride	Orrell	Rodway	McLean	Hunter	Lyon	Bond	Wilson	Smith	Bell	Lockett	1 o.g.	(Leake)
Mar 24	Liverpool	Div 1	h	1-2		McBride	Orrell	Rodway	McLean	Hunter	Lyon	Danson (1)	Wilson	Smith	Bell	Lockett		
Mar 31	Sheffield Utd.	Div 1	a	0-0		McBride	Tod	Rodway	McLean	Hunter	Lyon	Bond	Wilson	Smith	Turnbull	Lockett		
Apr 7	Notts County	Div 1	h	4-1		Taylor	Cook	Rodway (1)	McLean	Hunter	Lyon	Danson (1)	Wilson	Smith (1)	Bell	Lockett (1)		
Apr 13	Blackburn Rovers	Div 1	a	2-1		McBride	Orrell	Rodway	McLean	Hunter	Lyon	Bond	Wilson	Smith (1)	Bell (1)	Danson		
Apr 14	Stoke	Div 1	a	0-3		McBride	Orrell	Rodway	McLean	Hunter	Lyon	Bond	Wilson	Smith	Bell	Danson		
Apr 16	Sunderland	Div 1	a	0-2		McBride	Cook	Orrell	Blyth	Hunter	Lyon	Bond	Wilson	Smith	Turnbull	Danson		
Apr 21	Bolton W.	Div 1	h	3-0		McBride	Cook	Rodway	Hartley	Hunter	Lyon (1)	Ashton	Wilson (1)	Pearson	Bell (1)	Danson		
Apr 26	Newcastle Utd.	Div 1	h	0-0		McBride	Orrell	Rodway	McLean	Hunter	Lyon	Ashton	Wilson	Smith	Bell	Danson		

SEASON 1906–1907

After the euphoria of the previous season's success, Preston came down to earth with a bump in the 1906–7 campaign. It was very much a home and away season, great at home, abysmal away from Deepdale. Only one game was won on their travels and they suffered some emphatic defeats along the way, including a 6–1 thrashing at Liverpool. They also equalled their own record for the least number of away goals scored, which was nine. Ironically Preston were to finish one place above the current champions as Liverpool also struggled for much of the season, but it was only thanks to North End's excellent home record which included an unbeaten ten match run. Player wise there were far too many changes to the side and a new record of 30 players were used, although it was interesting to note that seven of those players made just one appearance. One of those one game wonders was a certain Joe McCall, who made an undistinguished debut in a 3–0 defeat at home to the Woolwich Arsenal. John Hunter and James Wilson did perform consistently well and Peter McBride continued to show his usual composure in goal. New signing, Charles Dawson did fairly well in a shot-shy attack and Percy Smith also played some good games. With McBride, Hunter and Smith playing well, at least the heart of the side was settled, although the team as a whole saw too many changes to aid continuity. The truth was that too many players were just not good enough for this very tough

division. The FA Cup brought little relief from the mounting pressure as Preston went down 1–0 at Notts County in a disappointing clash. That goal was the only one between the sides in three games between the sides that year. Also in January came the tragic news that Harold Goodburn, who had just made it into the first team, was taken ill and sadly died of pleuro-pneumonia shortly afterwards. It was a moment when any football news seemed irrelevant and it was not to be the last time that such a tragedy was to hit the club. Understandably, the remainder of the season petered out somewhat with Preston finding it difficult to lift themselves out of their depression. In fact they were to win only four of their last fifteen games. It was as well for them that they had picked up points in the first half of the season because after Christmas all that they showed was relegation form. A season that had begun with such optimism had ended in acute disappointment and sadness.

DEBUTANTS: (12) George Barlow, Martin Becton, William Butler, Charles Dawson, Joe McCall, George Farrington, Harold Goodburn, William Lavery, William Roberts, William Sanderson, Harry Stringfellow and John Winchester.

LAST GAMES: (9) Tod, Ashton, Cook, Hartley, Pearson, Butler, Farrington, Goodburn and Roberts.

P. Smith scored North End's 1,000th League goal.

Only two of North End's future players are known to have been born during the 1906–7 season. They were George Smithies and Harry Lowe.

Ever presents: None   **FA Cup:** First Round
Hat-tricks: None
Manager: Management Committee
Chairman: Mr W. E. Ord J. P.
Leading scorer: 11 goals – Charles Dawson (all League)
Players used: 30

AUTHORS' UNOFFICIAL PLAYER OF THE SEASON:
John Hunter

In November 1906 Preston were ordered to pay Brynn Central £7 10s. 0d. for the transfer of William Lavery and they were also fined one guinea as a punishment for an illegal approach to the player.

Harry Stringfellow was secured from Wigan Town as an emergency signing. Billy Lyon was suspended and his deputy, Percy Hartley, was injured. Stringfellow then stood in for Hartley but was then injured himself. He had joined Wigan from Leeds City only a few days before joining Preston. As a result North End had to pay Leeds £40 for his registration. All this had come within a fortnight of the new season starting. To cap it all North End were also fined one guinea for not re-registering Hartley.

Preston had two amateurs make their debut in the 1906–7 season. George Barlow from Wigan Grammar School Old Boys and then John Winchester who was a school teacher on the Fylde.

For the opening game of this season new turnstiles were fitted and ready for use. 11,009 people went through them. On March 9 1907, Percy Smith scored Preston's 1,000th league goal, and finally, Harry Stringfellow was an expert cueist and, at billiards, beat John Hunter who was regarded as the best billiards player on the books.

Match Report: Toffees Prove Sticky Test – 8 September 1906
Everton 1 Preston 0

With the absence of Derbyshire (injured), Lyon (suspended) and Hartley (injured), Preston went to Goodison at a distinct disadvantage against the current cup holders and early league leaders. The experienced Harry Stringfellow, only recently signed because of Preston's injury situation, stood in for Hartley who, ironically, was himself standing in for Lyon. The two captains, Bell and Taylor, both ex Dumbarton players, tossed up with Bell losing and North End having to face the bright sun. The game's first worthwhile chance fell to Everton's centre-forward Young who disappointed the home crowd by booting his effort high and wide when in a good position. In their next attack, a scrambled affair, a foul by George Tod gave away a penalty. It was a decision which angered the North End players. Inside-left Settle took the spot-kick but McBride brilliantly saved his effort. (McBride also saved a Settle penalty at Deepdale in the return game.) Soon afterwards Settle left the field with a hand injury although the teams were evened up a few minutes later as Rodway received an injury and had to be helped off by the trainer. After 20 minutes the Toffees were awarded a goal. From a shot by Hardman there was a scrimmage in the goalmouth, the ball being swiftly cleared. But the referee, Mr Pollitt from Manchester, new on the referee's list this season, signalled a goal saying that the ball had already crossed the line. McBride appealed for a foul on himself as well as claiming that the ball had not crossed the line. Free-kicks became frequent as tempers frayed and the game became scrappy with numerous stoppages for offside. Having said that Bond, on one occasion, beat three defenders before setting up a Smith shot which was well saved by Scott, the Everton keeper. Rodway, having injured his knee, and Settle, having broken a finger in two places, sat out the second half. Lockett dropped back into defence to fill in for Rodway. The game progressed in a mediocre way and although the players did not lack effort they certainly lacked the skill. Whenever Preston did manage to construct an attack it was usually through Bond or Wilson. Bond had a couple of late chances to equalise but his finishing, although on target, was woeful. As a postscipt, it was interesting to note that George Tod, at the same time as he was playing in this match, was also having a benefit game played for him at Deepdale against Everton's reserves. Over 5,000 watched that game.

Peter McBride. Top class goalkeeper for Preston North End and Scotland.

Season 1906–7: First Division

	P	W	D	L	F	A	Pts
1 Newcastle	38	22	7	9	74	46	51
2 Bristol City	38	20	8	10	66	47	48
3 Everton	38	20	5	13	70	46	45
4 Sheffield United	38	17	11	10	57	55	45
5 Aston Villa	38	19	6	13	78	52	44
6 Bolton	38	18	8	12	59	47	44
7 Woolwich A	38	20	4	14	66	59	44
8 Man United	38	17	8	13	53	56	42
9 Birmingham	38	15	8	15	52	52	38
10 Sunderland	38	14	9	15	65	66	37
11 Middlesbrough	38	15	6	17	56	63	36
12 Blackburn	38	14	7	17	56	59	35
13 Wednesday	38	12	11	15	49	60	35
14 PRESTON	**38**	**14**	**7**	**17**	**44**	**57**	**35**
15 Liverpool	38	13	7	18	64	65	33
16 Bury	38	13	6	19	58	68	32
17 Man City	38	10	12	16	53	77	32
18 Notts County	38	8	15	15	46	50	31
19 Derby	38	9	9	20	41	59	27
20 Stoke	38	8	10	20	41	64	26

PRESTON NORTH END FOOTBALL TEAM 1906-7.

MR. T. HOUGHTON, MR. C. PARKER, Secretary. J. DERBYSHIRE, P. McBRIDE, T. RODWAY, W. J. JOY, Director. G. DRUMMOND,
(Director) R. BOND, J. McLEAN, J. WILSON, P. J. SMITH, J. BELL, Captain. J. HUNTER, (Trainer.)
G. TODD, H. STRINGFELLOW, H. DANSON, A. LOCKETT.

BY ARTHUR WINTER.

League appearances (38 games)

Ashton H. 2, Barlow G. H. 1, Becton M. 16, Bell J. 26, Bond R. 15, Butler W. 3, Cook L. 1, Danson H. 27, Dawson C. 24, Derbyshire J. E. 1, Farrington G. 2, Goodburn H. 2, Hartley P. W. 2, Hunter J. 37, Lavery W. 14, Lockett A. 23, Lyon W. J. 27, McBride P. 34, McCall J. 1, McLean J. 28, Pearson H. 1, Roberts W. 2, Rodway T. 30, Sanderson W. 1, Smith P. J. 31, Stringfellow H. 19, Taylor H. 4, Tod G. 9, Wilson J. 34, Winchester J. 1.

FA Cup (1 game)

McBride, Lavery, Rodway, McLean, Hunter, Lyon, Bond, Wilson, Dawson, Bell and Danson all one each.

Goalscorers: 44 League only

Dawson 11, Smith 8, Wilson 7, Danson 4 (2 pens), Bond 3 (2 pens), Becton 2, Bell 1, Barlow 1, Stringfellow 1, Hunter 1, McLean 1, Lockett 1 (pen), Rodway 1 (pen), Lyon 1. Own goal 1 (Cottle of Bristol City).

Postcard from this era.

North End v Rovers. A good return by Crompton.

League position in Division One: 14th – P38 W14 D7 L17 F44 A57 Pts 35
Home: W13 D4 L2 F35 A19   Away: W1 D3 L15 F9 A38

Date 1906-7	Opponents	Comp	h or a	Score	Att.	1	2	3	4	5	6	7	8	9	10	11		
Sep 1	Birmingham	Div 1	h	2-0		McBride	Tod	Rodway	McLean	Hunter	Hartley	Bond	Wilson (1)	Smith	Bell (1)	Lockett		
Sep 8	Everton	Div 1	a	0-1		McBride	Tod	Rodway	McLean	Hunter	Stringfellow	Bond	Wilson	Smith	Bell	Lockett		
Sep 15	Woolwich Arsenal	Div 1	h	0-3		McBride	Tod	McCall	McLean	Hunter	Hartley	Bond	Wilson	Smith	Bell	Lockett		
Sep 22	Sheffield Wed.	Div 1	a	1-2		McBride	Tod	Lockett	McLean	Hunter	Stringfellow	Bond	Wilson	Smith (1)	Bell	Danson		
Sep 29	Bury	Div 1	h	3-2		McBride	Tod	Lockett	McLean	Hunter (1)	Stringfellow	Bond	Wilson	Smith (2)	Bell	Danson		
Oct 6	Manchester City	Div 1	a	1-1		McBride	Tod	Lockett	McLean	Hunter	Stringfellow	Bond (1)	Wilson	Smith	Bell	Danson		
Oct 13	Middlesbrough	Div 1	h	4-2		McBride	Tod	Lockett	McLean (1)	Hunter	Stringfellow (1)	Bond (1p)	Smith	Dawson (1)	Bell	Danson		
Oct 20	Derby County	Div 1	a	0-3		McBride	Tod	Lockett	McLean	Hunter	Stringfellow	Bond	Smith	Dawson	Bell	Danson		
Oct 27	Newcastle Utd.	Div 1	a	1-2		McBride	Butler	Rodway	McLean	Hunter	Stringfellow	Bond	Wilson	Smith	Bell	Danson (1)		
Nov 3	Aston Villa	Div 1	h	2-0		McBride	Butler	Rodway	McLean	Hunter	Stringfellow	Bond	Wilson	Dawson (2)	Bell	Danson		
Nov 10	Liverpool	Div 1	a	1-6		Taylor	Butler	Rodway	Stringfellow	Hunter	Lyon	McLean	Wilson	Dawson	Bell	Lockett (1p)		
Nov 17	Bristol City	Div 1	h	3-1		Taylor	Lavery	Rodway	McLean	Hunter	Lyon	Dawson	Wilson (2)	Smith	Bell	Danson	1 o.g.	(Cottle)
Nov 24	Notts County	Div 1	a	0-0		McBride	Lavery	Rodway	McLean	Hunter	Lyon	Dawson	Wilson	Smith	Bell	Danson		
Dec 1	Sheffield Utd.	Div 1	h	2-1		McBride	Lavery	Rodway	McLean	Hunter	Lyon	Dawson (1)	Wilson	Smith (1)	Bell	Danson		
Dec 8	Bolton W.	Div 1	h	3-1		McBride	Lavery	Rodway	McLean	Hunter	Lyon	Dawson (1)	Wilson	Smith (2)	Bell	Danson		
Dec 15	Manchester Utd.	Div 1	a	2-0		McBride	Lavery	Rodway	McLean	Hunter	Lyon	Dawson	Wilson (2)	Smith	Bell	Danson		
Dec 22	Stoke City	Div 1	a	2-0		McBride	Lavery	Rodway	McLean	Hunter	Lyon	Bond (1p)	Wilson	Smith	Dawson (1)	Danson		
Dec 24	Aston Villa	Div 1	a	0-3		Taylor	Lavery	Rodway	McLean	Hunter	Lyon	Goodburn	Wilson	Smith	Dawson	Danson		
Dec 26	Blackburn Rovers	Div 1	h	1-0		McBride	Lavery	Rodway	McLean	Hunter	Lyon	Bond	Wilson (1)	Smith	Dawson	Danson		
Dec 29	Birmingham	Div 1	a	0-3		McBride	Lavery	Rodway	McLean	Hunter	Lyon	Goodburn	Wilson	Smith	Dawson	Danson		
Jan 1	Blackburn Rovers	Div 1	a	1-1		McBride	Lavery	Rodway	McLean	Hunter	Lyon	Becton	Wilson	Smith	Dawson	Danson (1)		
Jan 2	Bolton W.	Div 1	a	0-3		McBride	Lavery	Rodway	McLean	Hunter	Stringfellow	Becton	Wilson	Smith	Roberts	Lockett		
Jan 5	Everton	Div 1	h	1-1		McBride	Lavery	Rodway	McLean	Hunter	Lyon	Becton (1)	Wilson	Pearson	Bell	Danson		
Jan 12	Notts County Rd 1	FAC	a	0-1	16000	McBride	Lavery	Rodway	McLean	Hunter	Lyon	Bond	Wilson	Dawson	Bell	Danson		
Jan 19	Woolwich Arsenal	Div 1	a	0-1		McBride	Lavery	Rodway	Stringfellow	Hunter	Lyon	Becton	Wilson	Dawson	Bell	Danson		
Jan 26	Sheffield Wed.	Div 1	h	1-0		McBride	Lockett	Rodway	Stringfellow	Hunter	Lyon (1)	Becton	Wilson	Farrington	Dawson	Danson		
Feb 2	Sheffield Utd.	Div 1	a	1-3		McBride	Lockett	Rodway	Stringfellow	Tod	Lyon	Becton	Wilson	Smith	Dawson (1)	Danson		
Feb 9	Manchester City	Div 1	h	1-3		McBride	Lavery	Lockett	Stringfellow	Hunter	Lyon	Dawson	Wilson	Smith	Bell	Danson (1p)		
Feb 13	Sunderland	Div 1	a	0-1		McBride	Lockett	Rodway	Stringfellow	Hunter	Lyon	Dawson	Wilson	Smith	Becton	Danson		
Feb 16	Middlesbrough	Div 1	a	1-2		Taylor	Lockett	Rodway	Stringfellow	Hunter	Lyon	Dawson	Wilson	Smith	Becton	Danson (1p)		
Feb 23	Manchester Utd.	Div 1	h	0-3		McBride	Cook	Rodway	McLean	Hunter	Lyon	Dawson	Wilson	Becton	Smith	Lockett		
Mar 2	Newcastle Utd.	Div 1	h	2-2		McBride	Lockett	Rodway	Stringfellow	Hunter	Lyon	Bond	Becton	Smith	Dawson (2)	Danson		
Mar 9	Derby County	Div 1	h	1-0		McBride	Lockett	Winchester	Wilson	Hunter	Lyon	Bond	Becton	Smith (1)	Dawson	Danson		
Mar 16	Liverpool	Div 1	h	3-1		McBride	Lockett	Rodway (1p)	Stringfellow	Hunter	Lyon	Becton	Wilson	Smith (1)	Bell	Barlow (1)		
Mar 23	Bristol City	Div 1	a	0-1		McBride	Lockett	Rodway	Stringfellow	Hunter	Lyon	Becton	Wilson	Smith	Bell	Danson		
Mar 29	Sunderland	Div 1	h	2-0		McBride	Lockett	Rodway	McLean	Hunter	Lyon	Becton (1)	Wilson (1)	Smith	Bell	Roberts		
Mar 30	Notts County	Div 1	h	0-0		McBride	Lockett	Rodway	McLean	Hunter	Lyon	Becton	Wilson	Smith	Bell	Ashton		
Apr 1	Bury	Div 1	a	0-2		McBride	Derbyshire	Rodway	McLean	Hunter	Lyon	Becton	Wilson	Smith	Bell	Ashton		
Apr 27	Stoke City	Div 1	h	2-2		McBride	Lockett	Rodway	McLean	Hunter	Lyon	Bond	Dawson (2)	Farrington	Bell	Sanderson		

SEASON 1907–1908

Another year of mid-table obscurity for North End and another season of continual team changes. Only James McLean, Peter McBride, Billy Lyon, Tommy Rodway and Percy Smith could be regarded as automatic choices as the Preston management struggled desperately with the balance and quality of the team. The club made their usual poor start and took six games to record their first win, their away form was very poor and it was a case of *deja vu* for the fans. At Deepdale Preston were a different side and made it much harder for the opposition. It was certainly the home points won that again kept their heads above the relegation places. Percy Smith was the main attacker but he lacked support and showed his frustration on more than one occasion. Dicky Bond, too, was beginning to feel the pressure of always having to be on top form. Unfortunately some of the other players were not of the highest standard and their limited ability showed up at this level. Losing John Hunter around Christmas time gave the defence problems although it was still pretty strong with the likes of McBride, Rodway, McLean and Lyon working tirelessly in the North End cause. Only three teams bettered Preston's 53 goals against and that was to help determine their finishing position as, incredibly, six clubs were to finish on 36 points. On the other hand only two clubs scored fewer than Preston. The FA Cup also brought acute disappointment although it was not without some drama. North End had been drawn away at Brighton and Hove Albion, then in the Southern League. A goal by Winchester gave Preston a draw and the replay was played at Deepdale the following Thursday. It seemed odds on a home win but Brighton played well and were leading 2–1 with the match 22 minutes into extra-time. Incredibly, the referee then decided to abandon the game due to the poor light. needless to say the Brighton team were none too pleased. Maybe the powers that be took some pity on them because the second replay, the following Monday was played at Stamford Bridge, home of Chelsea. Perhaps poetic justice was done as in this game Brighton won 1–0 to deservedly go through to the next round. For the remainder of the season Preston struggled in the league, and especially found life difficult in front of goal. In one sequence they went five consecutive games without scoring. How the Invincibles would have frowned at that situation! In the end North End were to finish the season as they had begun it with another batch of winless games. It left their fans to face another summer of discontent.

DEBUTANTS: (7) John Carlin, John Donaldson, Charles Gillibrand, Edward Holdsworth, Charles McFadyen, William McLaughlin and Charles Williamson.

LAST GAMES: (9) Hunter, Bell, Lockett, Becton M., Stringfellow, Donaldson, Gillibrand, McLaughlin and Williamson.

> **League position in Division One: 12th – P38 W12 D12 L14 F47 A53 Pts 36**
> **Home: W9 D7 L3 F33 A18 Away: W3 D5 L11 F14 A35**

Ever presents: None
FA Cup: First round replay
Hat-tricks: None
Manager: Management Committee
Chairman: Mr W. E. Ord J. P.
Leading scorer: 12 goals – Percy Smith (all League)
Players used: 27

League appearances (38 games)

Barlow G. H. 9, Becton M. 7, Bell J. 7, Bond R. 18, Carlin J. 25, Danson H. 18, Dawson C. 24, Derbyshire J. E. 16, Donaldson J. 1, Gillibrand C. S. 3, Holdsworth E. 1, Hunter J. 17, Lockett A. 9, Lyon W. J. 36, McBride P. 35, McCall J. 6, McFadyen C. 13, McLaughlin W. J. 1, McLean J. 33, Rodway T. 37, Sanderson W. 12, Smith P. J. 34, Stringfellow H. 20, Taylor H. 3, Williamson C. W. 1, Wilson J. 27, Winchester J. 5.

FA Cup appearances (2 games)

McBride 2, Winchester 1, Lockett 1, Rodway 2, McLean 2, Stringfellow 2, Lyon 2, Bond 2, Wilson 2, Gillibrand 1, Smith 1, Danson 2, Sanderson 1, Dawson 1.

Goalscorers: 47 League–1 Cup–(Total 48)

Smith 12–0 (12), Wilson 7–0 (7), Dawson 6–0 (6), Derbyshire 5 (5 pens)–0 (5), Carlin 4–0 (4), Lyon 2–0 (2), Gillibrand 2–0 (2), Bell 1–0 (1), Bond 1 (pen)–0 (1), McLean 1–0 (1), Barlow 1–0 (1), Sanderson 1–0 (1), Hunter 1–0 (1), Stringfellow 1–0 (1), Becton 1–0 (1), Danson 1–0 (1), Winchester 0–1 (1).

Trivia Facts:

In 1907 footballs were quite expensive as they cost between 4s.11d and 12s.6d.

G.H. Barlow was selected as outside left for the England Amateurs vs. Holland Amateurs in a match played at Darlington on 21 December 1907.

At a Lancashire FA meeting in December 1907, Martin Becton was suspended for one week for kicking an opponent in a reserve game. A linesman from Fulwood, Mr W. Douglas, was suspended for three weeks for running on to the pitch and questioning the referee's decision!

In April 1908, ex Old Invincible, Bob Holmes, then trainer at Blackburn, was appointed trainer to the England Amateur International team to play in Belgium and Germany over Easter 1908.

In 1908 Blackpool Police beat Preston Police 3–0 but lost the return at Deepdale by 7–0. Peter McBride and Billy Lyon played for the Anglo Scots vs. Home Scots on 23 Mar 1908. McBride kept a clean sheet as the Anglos won 3–0. Meanwhile, Tommy Rodway played for the North vs. the South on 27 January 1908.

STAT FACTS:

Best home run without defeat: 9 games
Best away run without defeat: 3 games
Longest run unbeaten: 7 games
Longest run without a win: 6 games

Match Report: Hunter's Day – One Way and Another – 23 Nov. 1907
Liverpool 1 Preston 2

Having beaten Liverpool at Anfield in the Lancashire Cup semi-final a couple of weeks earlier, North End were in a confident mood to repeat their success in this league game. A strong wind was blowing making it very difficult to control the ball, although the wind varied in strength and direction, helping Preston in both halves. After a fairly even start the game's first goal came eighteen minutes into the first-half. John Carlin, showing a clean pair of heels to a couple of defenders, was upended by an outstretched limb, and he fell into the penalty area. The referee adjudged that the foul had been committed just outside the area. Jack Hunter was entrusted with the free-kick and in 1907 defenders had to be a minimum of six yards away from the kicker. Several Liverpool players were encroaching though as Hunter spied an opening. He hit the ball low and hard, the ball scarcely leaving the ground, as it found its way through a forest of legs to enter the net just inside the post. It was very appropriate that the popular centre-half should register his first league goal of the season on the very day that a benefit game was simultaneously being played on his behalf at Deepdale between Preston reserves and Liverpool reserves. How ironic too, that both Carlin and Hunter had joined Preston from Liverpool. Six minutes later ex Evertonian Harry Strigfellow made it 2–0. Barlow, out on the extreme left, sent over a swinging centre. Hardy, the goalkeeper, met it with his two fists and punched the ball over 20 yards clear. But as it was dropping Stringfellow met it on the volley and it flew straight and true into the net. It was out of the blue and unexpected as half backs usually controlled the ball first before passing it to a forward! Liverpool responded within five minutes. Their right wing broke away with Hewitt finding himself in acres of room. He waltzed around McBride, which was no mean feat, and shot towards goal and despite Winchester's brave attempt to save the ball found the net. North End rode their luck somewhat for the remainder of the game but with determination and tenacity came home with the two points.

Trivia Facts:

Prior to the new season starting George Drummond received by post, from a friend in Scotland, a parcel of white heather, which was regarded as something of a good luck charm. North End won one of their first seven games!

Joe Derbyshire was to be employed on the ground-staff at Old Trafford for the 1908 cricket season. He was a fast, right-arm, bowler who played regularly in the Bolton league.

Season 1907–8: First Division

	P	W	D	L	F	A	Pts
1 Man United	38	23	6	9	81	48	52
2 Aston Villa	38	17	9	12	77	59	43
3 Man City	38	16	11	11	62	54	43
4 Newcastle	38	15	12	11	65	54	42
5 Wednesday	38	19	4	15	73	64	42
6 Middlesbrough	38	17	7	14	54	45	41
7 Bury	38	14	11	13	58	61	39
8 Liverpool	38	16	6	16	68	61	38
9 Nottingham Forest	38	13	11	14	59	62	37
10 Bristol City	38	12	12	14	58	61	36
11 Everton	38	15	6	17	58	64	36
12 PRESTON	38	12	12	14	47	53	36
13 Chelsea	38	14	8	16	53	62	36
14 Blackburn*	38	12	12	14	51	63	36
15 Woowich A*	38	12	12	14	51	63	36
16 Sunderland	38	16	3	19	78	75	35
17 Sheffield United	38	12	11	15	52	58	35
18 Notts County	38	13	8	17	39	51	34
19 Bolton	38	14	5	19	52	58	33
20 Birmingham	38	9	12	17	40	60	30

*equal

Date 1907-8	Opponents	Comp	h or a	Score	Att.	1	2	3	4	5	6	7	8	9	10	11
Sep 2	Sheffield Wed.	Div 1	h	1-1		McBride	Lockett	Rodway	McLean	Hunter	Lyon (1)	Bond	Wilson	Smith	Dawson	Danson
Sep 7	Birmingham	Div 1	a	0-2		McBride	Lockett	Rodway	McLean	Stringfellow	Lyon	Bond	Carlin	Smith	Dawson	Danson
Sep 9	Everton	Div 1	a	1-2		Taylor	Lockett	Rodway	McLean	Hunter	Lyon	Bond	Carlin	Smith (1)	Dawson	Danson
Sep 14	Everton	Div 1	h	2-2		McBride	Derbyshire (1p)	Rodway	McLean (1)	Hunter	Lyon	Dawson	Carlin	Smith	Wilson	Sanderson
Sep 21	Sunderland	Div 1	a	1-4		McBride	Derbyshire	Rodway	McLean	Hunter	Lyon	Bond	Carlin	Smith	Wilson	Sanderson (1)
Sep 28	Woolwich Arsenal	Div 1	h	3-0		McBride	Derbyshire	Rodway	McLean	Hunter	Lyon	Sanderson	Carlin (2)	Smith	Bell (1)	Barlow
Oct 5	Sheffield Wed.	Div 1	a	0-1		McBride	Derbyshire	Rodway	McLean	Hunter	Lyon	Sanderson	Carlin	Smith	Bell	Barlow
Oct 12	Bristol City	Div 1	h	3-0		McBride	Derbyshire (1p)	Rodway	McLean	Hunter	Lyon	Sanderson	Carlin	Smith (1)	Bell	Barlow (1)
Oct 19	Notts County	Div 1	a	1-0		McBride	Derbyshire	Rodway	McLean	Hunter	Lyon	Danson	Carlin	Smith	Dawson (1)	Sanderson
Oct 26	Manchester City	Div 1	h	2-4		McBride	Derbyshire (1p)	Rodway	McLean	Hunter	Lyon	Danson	Carlin (1)	Smith	Dawson	Barlow
Nov 2	Newcastle Utd.	Div 1	h	2-0		McBride	Derbyshire (1p)	Rodway	McLean	Hunter	Lyon	Lockett	Carlin	Smith (1)	Bell	Barlow
Nov 9	Bury	Div 1	a	1-5		McBride	Derbyshire	Winchester	McLean	Hunter	Lyon	Lockett	McLaughlin	Wilson (1)	Bell	Barlow
Nov 16	Aston Villa	Div 1	h	3-0		McBride	Derbyshire	Rodway	Stringfellow	Hunter	Lyon	Lockett	Carlin (1)	Smith (1)	Wilson (1)	Barlow
Nov 23	Liverpool	Div 1	h	2-1		McBride	Winchester	Rodway	Stringfellow (1)	Hunter (1)	Lyon	Lockett	Carlin	Wilson	Bell	Barlow
Nov 30	Middlesbrough	Div 1	h	1-1		McBride	Derbyshire	Rodway	McLean	Hunter	Lyon	Dawson	Carlin	Smith (1)	Wilson	Danson
Dec 7	Sheffield Utd.	Div 1	a	0-2		McBride	Winchester	Rodway	Stringfellow	Hunter	Lyon	Dawson	Carlin	Smith	Wilson	Danson
Dec 14	Chelsea	Div 1	h	2-4		McBride	Lockett	Rodway	McCall	Hunter	Lyon	Williamson	Carlin	Smith (1)	Wilson (1)	Barlow
Dec 21	Nottm. Forest	Div 1	a	2-2		McBride	Derbyshire	Rodway	McLean	Hunter	Lyon	Becton (1)	Carlin	Smith (1)	Wilson	Danson
Dec 25	Bolton W.	Div 1	h	2-0		McBride	Derbyshire	Rodway	McLean	Stringfellow	Lyon	Becton	Carlin	Smith (2)	Wilson	Danson
Dec 26	Blackburn Rovers	Div 1	h	1-1		McBride	Derbyshire (1p)	Rodway	McLean	Stringfellow	Lyon	Becton	Dawson	Smith	Wilson	Danson
Dec 28	Manchester Utd.	Div 1	h	0-0		McBride	Winchester	Rodway	McLean	Stringfellow	Lyon	Becton	Dawson	Smith	Wilson	Sanderson
Jan 1	Blackburn Rovers	Div 1	a	1-1		McBride	Derbyshire	Rodway	McLean	Stringfellow	Lyon	Bond	Becton	Smith (1)	Wilson	Sanderson
Jan 2	Bolton W.	Div 1	a	0-2		McBride	Derbyshire	Rodway	McLean	Stringfellow	Donaldson	Becton	Dawson	Smith	Wilson	Danson
Jan 4	Birmingham	Div 1	h	1-1		McBride	Winchester	Rodway	McLean	Stringfellow	Lyon	Bond	Dawson (1)	Smith	Bell	Sanderson
Jan 11	**Brighton Rd 1**	**FAC**	**a**	**1-1**	**7500**	**McBride**	**Winchester (1)**	**Rodway**	**McLean**	**Stringfellow**	**Lyon**	**Bond**	**Wilson**	**Smith**	**Danson**	**Sanderson**
Jan 16	**Brighton Replay**	**FAC**	**h**	**1-2+**	**7000**	**McBride**	**Winchester**	**Rodway**	**McLean**	**Stringfellow**	**Lyon**	**Bond (1)**	**Gillibrand**	**Smith**	**Wilson**	**Danson**
Jan 18	Sunderland	Div 1	h	3-2		McBride	McFadyen	Rodway	McLean	Stringfellow	Lyon	Bond	Wilson	Gillibrand (1)	Danson (1)	Dawson (1)
Jan 20	**Brighton * 2nd Replay**	**FAC**	**n**	**0-1**	**18788**	**McBride**	**Lockett**	**Rodway**	**McLean**	**Stringfellow**	**Lyon**	**Bond**	**Wilson**	**Gillibrand**	**Danson**	**Dawson**
Jan 25	Woolwich Arsenal	Div 1	a	1-1		McBride	Lockett	Rodway	McLean	McCall	Lyon	Gillibrand	Becton	Smith	Wilson	Dawson (1)
Feb 8	Bristol City	Div 1	a	3-1		McBride	McFadyen	Rodway	McLean	Stringfellow	Lyon	Gillibrand (1)	Wilson (1)	Smith (1)	Danson	Dawson
Feb 15	Notts County	Div 1	h	1-0		McBride	McFadyen	Rodway	McLean	Stringfellow	Lyon	Bond	Wilson	Smith (1)	Danson	Dawson
Mar 7	Bury	Div 1	h	3-1		McBride	McFadyen	Rodway	McLean	Stringfellow	Lyon	Bond	Carlin	Smith	Wilson (2)	Dawson (1)
Mar 11	Newcastle Utd.	Div 1	a	0-0		McBride	McFadyen	Rodway	McLean	Stringfellow	Lyon	Bond	Carlin	Smith	Wilson	Dawson
Mar 14	Aston Villa	Div 1	a	0-3		McBride	McFadyen	Rodway	McLean	McCall	Stringfellow	Bond	Carlin	Smith	Wilson	Dawson
Mar 21	Liverpool	Div 1	a	3-0		McBride	McFadyen	Rodway	McLean	Stringfellow	Lyon	Bond (1p)	Carlin	Smith	Wilson (1)	Dawson (1)
Mar 28	Middlesbrough	Div 1	h	0-1		McBride	McFadyen	Rodway	McLean	Stringfellow	Lyon	Bond	Carlin	Smith	Wilson	Dawson
Apr 4	Sheffield Utd.	Div 1	h	0-0		Taylor	McFadyen	Rodway	Holdsworth	Stringfellow	Lyon	Bond	Wilson	Smith	Danson	Dawson
Apr 6	Manchester City	Div 1	a	0-5		McBride	McFadyen	Rodway	McLean	Stringfellow	Lyon	Bond	Dawson	Wilson	Danson	Sanderson
Apr 11	Chelsea	Div 1	h	0-0		Taylor	McFadyen	Rodway	McLean	McCall	Lyon	Bond	Carlin	Smith	Danson	Sanderson
Apr 18	Nottm. Forest	Div 1	h	0-1		McBride	McFadyen	Rodway	McLean	McCall	Lyon	Bond	Carlin	Smith	Danson	Sanderson
Apr 25	Manchester Utd.	Div 1	a	1-2		McBride	McFadyen	Rodway	McLean	McCall	Lyon (1)	Bond	Carlin	Smith	Wilson	Dawson
	+ Abandoned. a.e.t. (112 mins)															
	* Played at Stamford Bridge															

Left to right: *Back row:* Drummond (Trainer), T. Houghton (Director), Wilson, Derbyshire, McBride, Rodway, Lyon, C. Parker (Secretary), W. E. Ord (Chairman) *Middle row:* Dawson, Sanderson, Bond, Smith, Bell, Barlow, Hunter. *Front row:* Carlin, McLean, Lockett.

SEASON 1908–1909

The Preston fans were becoming used to approaching the new season with optimism only to find another serving of the same mid-table diet of ordinary football from their favourites. The 1908–9 season was another such menu and in many ways it mirrored the previous two years. The only consolation was that the mid-table position was achieved in the First Division and at least the fans had the chance to see all of the top players of the day visit Deepdale. Even though there were fewer players used this season the Preston line-up was chopped and changed many times with the same team rarely playing two games running. The North End attack was still goal shy but it was easy to see what their game was based on as only Champions Newcastle conceded less goals. Much of this good defensive play was down to the evergreen Peter McBride who consistently displayed his considerable skills in goal. Tommy Rodway and Billy Lyon were the other mainstays of the Preston defence whilst Joe McCall established a regular place in the side during the season. Up front only James Wilson reached double figures with Charles Dawson, Herbert Danson and Percy Smith scoring six apiece. Smith, in fact, played a number of games at centre-half to help out and did well until McCall took over. Preston made another indifferent start to the season, although a 6–0 hammering of Chelsea which featured

a Dawson hat-trick was a highlight, and too many points were lost to make a realistic challenge on the title. Only four wins from their first fifteen games was not what the club wanted but the form was quite good over Christmas and it augered well for the forthcoming FA Cup. The fans were hoping that perhaps North End could progress in that competition. A North Eastern side provided the opposition when the draw was made. Middlesbrough came to Deepdale but were beaten by Lyon's penalty in a 1–0 win. However the big talking point during the match came after the sending off of Dickie Bond. It is believed that he was the first North Ender ever to be sent off in an FA Cup tie. Any hopes of a decent cup run were dashed though when another side from the North East, Sunderland, came to Deepdale and won 2–1 in the next round. That was four seasons running that Preston had failed to make it past the second round. It also left North End with a long run-in of league games and after a mixed bag of results it finally left them in tenth position.

DEBUTANTS: (7) Thomas Chadwick, James Henderson, William Hodgson, William Main, John Platt, Richard Smith and Arthur Winterhalder

LAST GAMES: (7) Bond R., Derbyshire, Lavery, Carlin, Chadwick, Henderson and Smith R.

Trivia Facts:

When Preston played Blackburn on New Year's Day 1909 one player did not please the North End management. Eddie Holdsworth did not make it on to the field of play until five minutes after the kick-off and the club fined him one guinea for his trouble. Had he been celebrating the turn of the year too much, one wonders?

In November 1908 the well known Preston tailors, Messrs T. C. Palmer of 3 Fishergate, Preston, were offering a very good deal to the men of the town. They were giving away distinctive badges with 'Do it now, North End!' in dark blue and also two white streamers to anyone who bought one of their suits or overcoats.

George Barlow, who was still registered with North End, played for the Northern Nomads side against Blackburn Rovers Reserves in early September 1908. The following week he signed for Everton.

Preston Schoolboys drew 1–1 with Blackburn Schoolboys at Deepdale on 29 October 1908 in front of over 5,000 spectators.

In 1909 George Tod, ex-North Ender, was running the Heart of Oak Hotel in Adelphi Street, Preston. Home brewed ales being a speciality!

Left to right: *Back row*: C. Parker (Secretary), F. Paley (ass. trainer), H. Stringfellow, J. Derbyshire, H. Taylor, P. McBride, W. Hughes, Mr Croft (Director), Mr Holt (Director). *Third Row*: Mr Joy (Director), Mr Houghton (Director, J. Winchester, J. Wilson, T. Rodway, T. Chadwick, C. Dawson, J. Carlin, G. Drummond (Trainer), Mr Woodhouse (Director) *Second Row*: T. Worthington, J. McLean, P. J. Smith, W. Sanderson, A. Winterhalder, J. Henderson, J. McCall, E. Holdsworth, R. Bond, C. McFadyen. *Front row*: A. Booth, W. Main, W Lavery, J. Platt, W. J. Lyon, W. G. Daniels, A. Bond, H. Danson

Some future players born during the 1908–9 season include: Vince Farrall, Frank Gallimore, Herbert Hales and Harry Holdcroft

Ever presents: None   FA Cup: Second Round   Hat-tricks: (1) Dawson   Manager: Management Committee
Chairman: Mr W. E. Ord J. P.   Leading scorer: 11 goals – James Wilson (All League)   Players used 25

AUTHORS' UNOFFICIAL PLAYER OF THE SEASON: Billy Lyon

League position in Division One: 10th – P38 W13 D11 L14 F48 A44 Pts 37
Home: W8 D7 L4 F29 A17   Away: W5 D4 L10 F19 A27

Match Report: Six Goals for Sixpence –
7 Sept. 1908 Preston 6 Chelsea 0

Preston North End began the 1908–9 season as they had ended the previous campaign, finding it extremely difficult to score goals. Seven of the last nine league games of the 1907–8 season had been goalless for North End as had the first two games of the current term. So, with a team full of changes, some positional, Preston took the field on a dry September Monday evening for this encounter with Chelsea. A feeble showing on the previous Saturday against Manchester United had caused the changes in the side and this time it certainly worked. Great displays from new recruits Platt and Winterhalder, both making their debuts, was the feature of the game. Platt was perfect in his role as leader of the attack. Strong, fearless and tricky, he fed both wingers with confidence as well as bringing the best out of Dawson. Winterhalder not only justified his selection but was indeed the best wing forward on view this evening. Playing alongside his new team mates, his prowess surprised even the most sanguine of his admirers. He centred accurately and dribbled in a manner that would have done credit to Dickie Bond in his prime. Winterhalder was the instigator of the moves that registered three of the goals. Dawson made a first rate partner to the two debutants and had a fine game himself, scoring a superb second-half hat-trick. Platt had scored the first two goals in the first half and with a little more luck could have doubled his tally as he hit the crossbar and also missed a sitter. He was a real thorn to the Chelsea defenders, buzzing around the centre like an angry wasp. After the break with Chelsea's concentration already in tatters, the Preston forwards laid siege on the visitors' goal. This visually destroyed the Pensioners costly artists. The team from the capital city could not live with the pace and determination of this North End side and too many of the Chelsea stars were unwilling to do the fetching and carrying, unlike penalty scorer Billy Lyon who was superb at the heart of North End's midfield. He found a good ally in young Joe McCall who always made himself available and quickly recovered when and if he was beaten. Chadwick and McFadyen tended to wander a little but one presumes that they too wanted a bit of the goal action. Such football had not been seen at Deepdale for many a season, and all this for just sixpence admission.

League appearances (38 games)

Bond R. 29, Carlin J. 7, Chadwick T. 9, Danson H. 30, Dawson C. 15, Derbyshire J. E. 2, Henderson J. 7, Hodgson W.H. 1, Holdsworth E. 25, Lavery W. 8, Lyon W. J. 34, McBride P. 37, McCall J. 23, McFadyen C. 19, McLean J. 7, Main W. 6, Platt J. 12, Rodway T. 30, Sanderson W. 24, Smith P. J. 30, Smith R. 6, Taylor H. 1, Wilson J. 32, Winchester J. 17, Winterhalder A. 7.

FA Cup appearances (2 games)

McBride 2, Winchester 2, Rodway 1, McFadyen 1, Holdsworth 2, Smith P. J. 2, Lyon 2, Bond 1, Carlin 1, Wilson 2, Smith R. 1, Dawson 1, Danson 2, Sanderson 2.

Goalscorers: 48 League–2 Cup–(Total 50)

Wilson 11–0 (11), Dawson 6–1 (7), Danson 6–0 (6), Smith P. J. 6–0 (6), Sanderson 5–0 (5), Platt 4–0 (4), Lyon 3 (3 pens)–1 (pen) (4), Bond 2–0 (2), Derbyshire 2 (2 pens)–0 (2), Carlin 1–0 (1), Smith R. 1–0 (1), Own goals 1–0 (1) (Bartlett of Sheffield Wednesday).

Season 1908–9: First Division

	P	W	D	L	F	A	Pts
1 Newcastle	38	24	5	9	65	41	53
2 Everton	38	18	10	10	82	57	46
3 Sunderland	38	21	2	15	78	63	44
4 Blackburn	38	14	13	11	61	50	41
5 Wednesday	38	17	6	15	67	61	40
6 Woolwich A	38	14	10	14	52	49	38
7 Aston Villa	38	14	10	14	58	56	38
8 Bristol City	38	13	12	13	45	58	38
9 Middlesbrough	38	14	9	15	59	53	37
10 PRESTON	38	13	11	14	48	44	37
11 Chelsea	38	14	9	15	56	61	37
12 Sheffield United	38	14	9	15	51	59	37
13 Man United	38	15	7	16	58	68	37
14 Nottingham Forest	38	14	8	16	66	57	36
15 Notts County	38	14	8	16	51	48	36
16 Liverpool	38	15	6	17	57	65	36
17 Bury	38	14	8	16	63	77	36
18 Bradford City	38	12	10	16	47	47	34
19 Man City	38	15	4	19	67	69	34
20 Leicester Fosse	38	8	9	21	54	102	25

Match Report: McBride Saves the Day –
1 January 1909 Blackburn 1 Preston 1

Severe weather conditions during the week had caused the Blackburn club considerable anxiety, both on and off the pitch. They had to employ a 30 man gang to clear snow and ice off both the field and the terraces. Five football specials travelled the short rail journey from Preston with hundreds of fans apparently covering the distance on foot. Inside the ground one umbrella sporting the North End colours quickly had its' whiteness spoiled under a barrage of mucky snowballs thrown by the home fans. Holdsworth, who was travelling to Ewood from Southport, caused the Preston officials some concern by arriving late. The match was ten minutes old before he joined his teammates! Within five minutes of his arrival Preston took the lead with a Dickie Bond special, a shot fired high into the net. It was his first goal of the season. The Rovers then rallied in style but Holdsworth and Rodway defended admirably. When McBride was called into action he dealt with the situation competently, but even he could not prevent Blackburn equalising at the end of 24 minutes. From a corner conceded by Rodway, Cameron completely misjudged his attempt at goal, but fortunately for the Blackburn team the ball travelled straight into the path of Kyle who easily netted with a swiftly struck shot. Rovers were the livelier of the two teams but Preston held their own in the somewhat difficult playing conditions. McBride bravely saved the day when he smothered the greasy ball in a goalmouth rush, but was injured in the process. During the melee punches were seen to be thrown and soon after McBride had recovered Aitkenhead was brought down by Holdsworth. The referee at once signalled a penalty but Crompton's drive from the spot was brilliantly saved by McBride and the Preston fans showed their enthusiastic relief. After the half-time break Blackburn looked the more likely to score a winner but McBride was not to be beaten again, his display proving that he was one of the top class goalkeepers of his day. All things considered a draw was a fair result.

STAT FACTS:
Best home run without defeat: 6 games
Best away run without defeat: 4 games
Longest run unbeaten: 9 games
Longest run without a win: 4 games

Date 1908-9	Opponents	Comp	h or a	Score	Att.	1	2	3	4	5	6	7	8	9	10	11		
Sep 1	Chelsea	Div 1	a	0-0		McBride	McFadyen	Rodway	McLean	Chadwick	Lyon	Bond	Carlin	P.J.Smith	Wilson	Danson		
Sep 5	Manchester Utd.	Div 1	h	0-3		McBride	McFadyen	Rodway	McLean	Chadwick	Lyon	Bond	Carlin	P.J.Smith	Wilson	Danson		
Sep 7	Chelsea	Div 1	h	6-0		McBride	McFadyen	Rodway	Chadwick	McCall	Lyon (1p)	Winterhalder	Wilson	Platt (2)	Dawson (3)	Danson		
Sep 12	Everton	Div 1	h	1-0		McBride	McFadyen	Rodway	Chadwick	McCall	Lyon	Winterhalder	Wilson	Platt (1)	Dawson	Danson		
Sep 19	Leicester Fosse	Div 1	h	0-1		McBride	McFadyen	Rodway	McLean	McCall	Lyon	Winterhalder	Wilson	Platt	Dawson	Danson		
Sep 26	Woolwich Arsenal	Div 1	a	0-1		McBride	McFadyen	Rodway	Holdsworth	McCall	Lyon	Bond	Wilson	Platt	Dawson	Danson		
Oct 3	Notts County	Div 1	h	0-0		McBride	McFadyen	Rodway	Holdsworth	Chadwick	Lyon	Bond	Platt	P.J.Smith	Dawson	Danson		
Oct 10	Newcastle Utd.	Div 1	a	0-2		McBride	McFadyen	Rodway	Holdsworth	Chadwick	Lyon	Bond	Platt	P.J.Smith	Dawson	Sanderson		
Oct 17	Bristol City	Div 1	h	2-1		McBride	Lavery	Rodway	Chadwick	McCall	Lyon	Main	Carlin	P.J.Smith	Dawson	Sanderson (2)		
Oct 24	Sheffield Wed.	Div 1	a	0-1		McBride	Lavery	Rodway	McLean	McCall	Lyon	Main	Wilson	P.J.Smith	Dawson	Sanderson		
Oct 31	Middlesbrough	Div 1	a	2-4		McBride	Lavery	Rodway	McLean	McCall	Lyon	Main	Carlin (1)	P.J.Smith	Danson	Sanderson (1)		
Nov 7	Manchester City	Div 1	h	3-0		McBride	Lavery	Rodway	Henderson	McCall	Lyon	Bond	Wilson (1)	Platt	Danson (2)	Sanderson		
Nov 14	Liverpool	Div 1	a	1-2		McBride	Lavery	Rodway	Henderson	McCall	Lyon	Bond	Wilson	Platt	Danson (1)	Sanderson		
Nov 21	Bury	Div 1	h	0-2		McBride	Lavery	Rodway	Henderson	McCall	Lyon	Bond	Wilson	Platt	Danson	Sanderson		
Nov 28	Sheffield Utd.	Div 1	a	1-2		McBride	Lavery	Rodway	Holdsworth	Chadwick	Lyon	Main	Wilson (1)	P.J.Smith	Winterhalder	Danson		
Dec 5	Aston Villa	Div 1	h	3-2		McBride	Winchester	Rodway	Holdsworth	Chadwick	Lyon	Bond	Wilson (1)	P.J.Smith (1)	Dawson (1)	Danson		
Dec 12	Nottm. Forest	Div 1	a	1-1		McBride	Winchester	Rodway	Holdsworth	McCall	Lyon	Bond	Wilson	P.J.Smith	Dawson (1)	Danson		
Dec 19	Sunderland	Div 1	h	1-0		McBride	Winchester	Rodway	Holdsworth	P.J.Smith	Henderson	Bond	Wilson (1)	R.Smith	Dawson	Danson		
Dec 26	Blackburn Rovers	Div 1	h	2-0		McBride	Winchester	Rodway	Holdsworth	P.J.Smith	Lyon	Bond	Wilson (1)	R.Smith (1)	Dawson	Sanderson		
Jan 1	Blackburn Rovers	Div 1	a	1-1		McBride	Winchester	Rodway	Holdsworth	P.J.Smith	Lyon	Bond (1)	Wilson	R.Smith	Dawson	Sanderson		
Jan 2	Manchester Utd.	Div 1	a	2-0		Taylor	Winchester	Rodway	Holdsworth	P.J.Smith	Lyon (1p)	Bond	Wilson	Dawson (1)	Danson	Sanderson		
Jan 9	Everton	Div 1	h	3-3		McBride	Winchester	Rodway	Holdsworth	P.J.Smith	Lyon	Bond (1)	Wilson (1)	Dawson	Danson (1)	Sanderson		
Jan 16	Middlesbrough Rd 1	FAC	h	1-0	11700	McBride	Winchester	Rodway	Holdsworth	P.J.Smith	Lyon (1p)	Bond	Wilson	R.Smith	Danson	Sanderson		
Jan 23	Leicester Fosse	Div 1	a	0-0		McBride	Winchester	Rodway	Holdsworth	P.J.Smith	Lyon	Bond	Wilson	R.Smith	Danson	Sanderson		
Jan 30	Woolwich Arsenal	Div 1	h	0-0		McBride	Winchester	Rodway	Holdsworth	P.J.Smith	Lyon	Main	Wilson	R.Smith	Danson	Sanderson		
Feb 6	Sunderland Rd 2	FAC	a	1-2	21000	McBride	Winchester	McFadyen	Holdsworth	P.J.Smith	Lyon	Carlin	Wilson	Dawson (1)	Danson	Sanderson		
Feb 13	Newcastle Utd.	Div 1	h	0-1		McBride	McFadyen	Derbyshire	Holdsworth	P.J.Smith	Henderson	Main	Wilson	Winterhalder	Danson	Sanderson		
Feb 27	Sheffield Wed.	Div 1	h	4-1		McBride	McFadyen	Derbyshire	Holdsworth	McCall	Lyon	Bond	Wilson (1)	P.J.Smith (1)	Danson (1)	Sanderson	1 o.g.	(Bartlett)
Mar 6	Middlesbrough	Div 1	h	1-1		McBride	Winchester	McFadyen	Holdsworth	McCall	Lyon	Bond	Wilson (1)	Platt	Hodgson	Sanderson		
Mar 10	Notts County	Div 1	a	0-1		McBride	Lavery	McFadyen	Holdsworth	McCall	Lyon	Bond	Wilson	P.J.Smith	Carlin	Sanderson		
Mar 13	Manchester City	Div 1	a	1-4		McBride	Winchester	McFadyen	Holdsworth	P.J.Smith	Henderson	Bond	Wilson (1)	R.Smith	Carlin	Winterhalder		
Mar 17	Bristol City	Div 1	h	3-2		McBride	Derbyshire (2p)	McFadyen	Holdsworth	McCall	Henderson	Bond	Wilson	P.J.Smith (1)	Danson	Winterhalder		
Mar 20	Liverpool	Div 1	h	2-0		McBride	Winchester	Rodway	Holdsworth	McCall	Lyon	Bond	Carlin	P.J.Smith (1)	Danson (1)	Sanderson		
Mar 27	Bury	Div 1	a	1-0		McBride	Winchester	Rodway	Holdsworth	McCall	Lyon	Bond	Wilson	P.J.Smith	Danson	Sanderson (1)		
Apr 3	Sheffield Utd.	Div 1	h	1-1		McBride	Winchester	Rodway	Holdsworth	McCall	Lyon (1p)	Bond	Wilson	P.J.Smith	Danson	Sanderson		
Apr 9	Bradford City	Div 1	h	0-0		McBride	McFadyen	Rodway	Holdsworth	McCall	Lyon	Bond	Wilson	P.J.Smith	Danson	Sanderson		
Apr 10	Aston Villa	Div 1	a	4-2		McBride	Winchester	McFadyen	McLean	McCall	Lyon	Bond	Wilson (1)	P.J.Smith (2)	Danson	Sanderson (1)		
Apr 12	Bradford City	Div 1	a	0-2		McBride	Winchester	McFadyen	Holdsworth	McCall	Lyon	Bond	Wilson	Platt	Danson			
Apr 17	Nottm. Forest	Div 1	h	1-1		McBride	McFadyen	Rodway	Holdsworth	McCall	Lyon	Bond	Wilson (1)	P.J.Smith	Danson	Sanderson		
Apr 24	Sunderland	Div 1	a	1-2		McBride	McFadyen	Rodway	McLean	McCall	Lyon	Bond	Platt (1)	P.J.Smith	Danson	Sanderson		

Preston North End 1908–09.

Trivia Facts:

Dickie Bond was sent off at Deepdale against Middlesbrough on 16 January 1909. Consequently he missed 3 games, none of which was won.

Tommy Rodway once again played in the international trial match North vs South, but he never played for England.

North End's former captain, John Bell, received a benefit game from the Club on 14 September 1908 when PNE played Blackburn Rovers in a friendly match.

SEASON 1909–1910

The Preston management, players and fans alike were all desperate for an improvement when the 1909–10 season began on September 1 1909. So what happened? The team started the campaign with six matches without a win! Yet again the club were left with a huge points gap to close before they had even moved out of first gear. It was to be a season when the attack functioned a little better with David McLean making a big difference, coming into the side and scoring regularly after his debut against Notts County. The Scottish centre-forward proved an excellent signing from Celtic and was often Preston's star man. At the back however there was not the same solidness as in previous seasons, although Peter McBride, Tommy Rodway and Billy Lyon held their good form. Percy Smith was switched to the defence and played most of his games at the back whilst other new signings, James Bannister and Arthur Mounteney prompted well from their inside-forward positions. However, the bulk of the good North End play came

at Deepdale, as once again the away form was inexcusably bad. At home they were fine and few of the opposing teams went away with a result. This made the poor away form even more mysterious with just five points gained from their nineteen games. It was just not good enough and it was all so very frustrating. It seemed that the team hit a mental block as soon as they moved away from Preston soil. In one sequence of results Preston won eight home games on the trot. At the same time though they managed just one point from the eight away games. In the end it was not until the last away game of the season, at Woolwich Arsenal, that they at last managed a win. Strangely enough the FA Cup tie with Coventry came in the middle of that run but this time it was the home form which let them down as non-league Coventry ran out surprise 2–1 winners at Deepdale. The mysteries of football were never more plainly illustrated. There were plenty of good individual performances through the season, Charles McFadyen and Arthur Winterhalder were two players who had some impressive games, but the consistency was lacking. After the cup-tie the season continued in the same vein, win at home, lose away, but thankfully the side picked up enough points to finish in a safe mid-table position. It was obvious to everyone though that further changes would have to be made to the team to try and cure their away day blues. It is interesting to note that even if only half of the away points Preston lost had been won then a top six spot would have been theirs.

Postcard from this era.

DEBUTANTS: (9) Charles Arthurs, George Baker, James Bannister, David Galbraith, David McLean, Arthur Mounteney, Gresham Parnell, George Roche and William Spence.

LAST GAMES: (10) Smith P.J., Catterall, Dawson, Sanderson, Winchester, Hodgson, Main, Arthurs, Parnell and Roche.

League position in Division One: 12th – P38 W15 D5 L18 F52 A58 Pts 35
Home: W14 D2 L3 F36 A13   Away: W1 D3 L15 F16 A45

League appearances (38 games)

Arthurs C. H. 8, Baker G. 1, Bannister J. 29, Catterall J. 2, Danson H. 24, Dawson C. 4, Galbraith D. 3, Hodgson W. H. 2, Holdsworth E. 16, Lyon W. J. 33, McBride P. 36, McCall J. 24, McFadyen C. 24, McLean D. 27, McLean J. 14, Main W. 6, Mounteney A. 31, Parnell G. F. 15, Platt J. 16, Roche G. 3, Rodway T. 37, Sanderson W. 8, Smith P. J. 17, Spence W. E. 1, Taylor H. 2, Wilson J. 4, Winchester J. 14, Winterhalder A. 17.

FA Cup appearances (1 game)

McBride, McFadyen, Rodway, Holdsworth, McCall, Lyon, Platt, Bannister, McLean D., Mounteney and Winterhalder all one each.

Goalscorers: 52 League–1 Cup–(Total 53)

McLean D. 18–1 (pen) (19), Danson 6–0 (6), Mounteney 6–0 (6), Bannister 5–0 (5), Winterhalder 4–0 (4), Platt 3–0 (3), Rodway 2 (2 pens)–0 (2), Smith 2–0 (2), McCall 1–0 (1), Catterall 1–0 (1), Arthurs 1–0 (1), Spence 1–0 (1), Parnell 1–0 (1). Own Goals 1–0 (1) (Shaw of Woolwich Arsenal)

Season 1909–10: First Division

		P	W	D	L	F	A	Pts
1	Aston Villa	38	23	7	8	84	42	53
2	Liverpool	38	21	6	11	78	57	48
3	Blackburn	38	18	9	11	73	55	45
4	Newcastle	38	19	7	12	70	56	45
5	Man United	38	19	7	12	69	61	45
6	Sheffield United	38	16	10	12	62	41	42
7	Bradford City	38	17	8	13	64	47	42
8	Sunderland	38	18	5	15	66	51	41
9	Notts County	38	15	10	13	67	59	40
10	Everton	38	16	8	14	51	56	40
11	Wednesday	38	15	9	14	60	63	39
12	**PRESTON**	**38**	**15**	**5**	**18**	**52**	**58**	**35**
13	Bury	38	12	9	17	62	66	33
14	Nottingham Forest	38	11	11	16	54	72	33
15	Tottenham	38	11	10	17	53	69	32
16	Bristol City	38	12	8	18	45	60	32
17	Middlesbrough	38	11	9	18	56	73	31
18	Woolwich A	38	11	9	18	37	67	31
19	Chelsea	38	11	7	20	47	70	29
20	Bolton	38	9	6	23	44	71	24

Future players born during the 1909–10 season include: Frank Moss and Joe Brain
Ever presents: None   FA Cup: First Round   Hat-tricks: None
Manager: Management Committee   Chairman: Mr W. E. Ord J. P.
Leading scorer: 19 goals – David McLean (18 League 1 Cup)   Players used: 28

AUTHORS' UNOFFICIAL PLAYER OF THE SEASON: David McLean

Left to right: Back row: Arthur Mounteney, Hubert Taylor, Peter McBride, Tom Rodway. *Third Row:* E. Holdsworth, Jimmy Wilson, Percy Smith, David McLean, C. H. Arthurs, J. E. Derbyshire, Joe McCall. *Second Row:* Charlie McFadyen, W. Sanderson, Jack Platt, Billy Lyon, Willy Main, John Catterall, H. (Chippy) Danson.

**Match Report: Gunners Blown Away –
23 April 1910 Woolwich
Arsenal 1 Preston 3**

North End arrived at Plumstead to play against the Arsenal in their last away game of the season having not won any of the previous 18 games on their travels. Few people expected Arsenal to be defeated by Preston especially as the Gunners had enjoyed a strong mini revival of late which had ended any possibility of relegation for the Londoners. Nigh on 10,000 were present to see the Lancashire visitors get off to a flying start. It took just three minutes for Preston to open the scoring through a clever piece of play from David McLean. He wormed his way through an unsuspecting defence after latching on to a mis-kick by Lawrence. The second goal of the game followed seven minutes later. Once again it was the white shirted Northerners celebrating as the Gunners conceded a sloppy own goal, caused through a ridiculous misunderstanding between Shaw and the goalkeeper McDonald. From a Charlie McFadyen clearance, Shaw, under pressure from Bannister, was passing back to McDonald, but the goalkeeper slipped and watched the ball roll agonisingly slowly over the line, much to the delight of the North End players. Apart from their goals Preston had taken the game to the Arsenal and they thoroughly deserved their lead. Preston's half back line played a prominent part in shaping the course of the game with Joe McCall having an outstanding game and completely out-shining the ponderous Arsenal half backs. McLean also impressed and he led the line cleverly, distributing his passes with marked judgement. After the break there was a new fire in the Arsenal play, Shaw trying to redeem his earlier error by bringing the best out of McBride with a well taken free-kick which brought a full length save out of the keeper. Eventually Arsenal reduced the arrears with a penalty expertly taken by Ducat after Baker, making his debut, was adjudged to have handled. But just as the odds favoured the home side Preston hit back when Danson, put through by McLean, scored with a well directed shot. Although Arsenal had other chances to score in the latter stages good goalkeeping and poor finishing kept the score at 3–1 to Preston. It was a good show by the Lilywhites and they produced some intelligent and thrustful football. The two points were a just reward for their efforts.

Front row: Jimmy McLean, A. Winterhalder, W. Lavery, C. Dawson, Jimmy Bannister, J. Winchester

STAT FACTS:
Best home run without defeat: 10 games
Best away run without defeat: 1 game
Longest run unbeaten: 3 games
Longest run without a win: 6 games

Date 1909-10	Opponents	Comp	h or a	Score	Att.	1	2	3	4	5	6	7	8	9	10	11		
Sep 1	Nottm. Forest	Div 1	h	0-1		McBride	McFadyen	Rodway	Holdsworth	Smith	Lyon	Dawson	Platt	Mounteney	Danson	Sanderson		
Sep 4	Sunderland	Div 1	a	1-2		McBride	McFadyen	Rodway	Holdsworth	Smith	Lyon	Parnell	Platt	Mounteney	Dawson	Danson (1)		
Sep 11	Everton	Div 1	h	0-1		McBride	McFadyen	Rodway	Holdsworth	Smith	Lyon	Parnell	Platt	Mounteney	Dawson	Danson		
Sep 18	Manchester Utd.	Div 1	a	1-1		McBride	McFadyen	Rodway	Holdsworth	McCall	Lyon	Arthurs	Platt (1)	Dawson	Hodgson	Danson		
Sep 25	Bradford City	Div 1	h	2-2		McBride	McFadyen	Rodway	Holdsworth	Smith	Lyon	Winterhalder (1)	Platt	Mounteney (1)	Hodgson	Danson		
Oct 2	Sheffield Wed.	Div 1	a	1-4		McBride	McFadyen	Rodway	Arthurs	McCall	Lyon	Winterhalder	Platt	Smith (1)	Mounteney	Danson		
Oct 9	Bristol City	Div 1	h	3-0		McBride	McFadyen	Rodway	Holdsworth	Smith (1)	Lyon	Winterhalder	Platt (1)	Mounteney (1)	Danson	Sanderson		
Oct 16	Bury	Div 1	a	1-3		McBride	McFadyen	Rodway	Holdsworth	Smith	Lyon	Winterhalder	Platt	Mounteney	Catterall (1)	Danson		
Oct 27	Chelsea	Div 1	a	0-2		McBride	McFadyen	Rodway	J. McLean	Smith	Lyon	Winterhalder	Platt	Mounteney	Catterall	Danson		
Oct 30	Middlesbrough	Div 1	h	1-0		McBride	Winchester	Rodway	Holdsworth	Smith	Lyon	Winterhalder (1)	Bannister	Mounteney	Wilson	Danson		
Nov 6	Notts County	Div 1	a	1-3		McBride	Winchester	Rodway	Smith	McCall	Lyon	Winterhalder	Bannister	D. McLean (1)	Wilson	Sanderson		
Nov 13	Newcastle Utd.	Div 1	h	4-0		McBride	Winchester	Rodway	Holdsworth	McCall	Lyon	Main	Bannister (2)	D. McLean (2)	Mounteney	Danson		
Nov 20	Liverpool	Div 1	a	0-2		McBride	Winchester	Rodway	J. McLean	McCall	Lyon	Main	Bannister	D. McLean	Mounteney	Winterhalder		
Nov 22	Tottenham H.	Div 1	a	4-1		McBride	McFadyen	Rodway (1p)	Arthurs	McCall	Lyon	Main	Bannister	D. McLean (1)	Mounteney (1)	Winterhalder (1)		
Nov 27	Aston Villa	Div 1	h	1-0		McBride	Winchester	Rodway	Arthurs	Smith	Lyon	Main	Bannister	D. McLean (1)	Wilson	Winterhalder		
Dec 4	Sheffield Utd.	Div 1	a	1-5		McBride	Winchester	Rodway	Arthurs	McCall	Lyon	Main	Bannister	D. McLean	Mounteney	Danson (1)		
Dec 11	Woolwich Arsenal	Div 1	h	3-4		McBride	Winchester	Rodway	Arthurs	Smith	Lyon	Parnell	Bannister	D. McLean (2)	Mounteney (1)	Danson		
Dec 18	Bolton W.	Div 1	a	1-3		McBride	Winchester	Rodway	Holdsworth	Wilson	Arthurs (1)	Parnell	Bannister	D. McLean	Mounteney	Sanderson		
Dec 25	Blackburn Rovers	Div 1	h	2-2		McBride	Winchester	Rodway	Holdsworth	Smith	Lyon	Platt (1)	Bannister	D. McLean (1)	Mounteney	Sanderson		
Dec 27	Blackburn Rovers	Div 1	a	3-2		McBride	Winchester	Rodway (1p)	Holdsworth	Smith	Lyon	Platt	Bannister (1)	D. McLean (1)	Mounteney	Sanderson		
Jan 3	Newcastle Utd.	Div 1	a	2-5		McBride	Winchester	Rodway	Holdsworth	Smith	Lyon	Platt	Bannister	D. McLean (2)	Mounteney	Sanderson		
Jan 8	Sunderland	Div 1	h	1-0		McBride	Winchester	Rodway	Holdsworth	McCall	Lyon	Platt	Bannister	D. McLean	Mounteney (1)	Winterhalder		
Jan 10	Chelsea	Div 1	h	2-0		McBride	McFadyen	Rodway	Holdsworth	McCall	Arthurs	Main	Bannister (1)	D. McLean (1)	Mounteney	Sanderson		
Jan 15	Coventry Rd 1	FAC	h	1-2	8000	McBride	McFadyen	Rodway	Holdsworth	McCall	Lyon	Platt	Bannister	D. McLean (1p)	Mounteney	Winterhalder		
Jan 22	Everton	Div 1	a	1-2		McBride	McFadyen	Rodway	Holdsworth	McCall (1)	Lyon	Platt	Bannister	D. McLean	Mounteney	Danson		
Feb 5	Manchester Utd.	Div 1	h	1-0		McBride	Winchester	Rodway	J. McLean	McCall	Roche	Galbraith	Bannister	D. McLean (1)	Mounteney	Winterhalder		
Feb 12	Sheffield Wed.	Div 1	h	1-0		McBride	McFadyen	Rodway	J. McLean	McCall	Roche	Galbraith	Bannister	D. McLean	Mounteney	Winterhalder (1)		
Feb 19	Bristol City	Div 1	a	0-2		McBride	McFadyen	Rodway	J. McLean	McCall	Roche	Galbraith	Bannister	D. McLean	Mounteney	Winterhalder		
Feb 26	Bury	Div 1	h	2-1		Taylor	McFadyen	Rodway	Smith	McCall	Lyon	Parnell	Bannister (1)	D. McLean (1)	Platt	Winterhalder		
Mar 5	Tottenham H.	Div 1	a	1-2		McBride	McFadyen	Rodway	Smith	McCall	Lyon	Parnell (1)	Bannister	D. McLean	Mounteney	Danson		
Mar 12	Middlesbrough	Div 1	a	0-1		McBride	McFadyen	Rodway	J. McLean	McCall	Lyon	Parnell	Bannister	D. McLean	Mounteney	Danson		
Mar 19	Notts County	Div 1	h	4-0		McBride	McFadyen	Rodway	J. McLean	McCall	Lyon	Parnell	Bannister	D. McLean (1)	Mounteney (1)	Danson (2)		
Mar 25	Nottm. Forest	Div 1	a	0-0		McBride	McFadyen	Rodway	J. McLean	McCall	Lyon	Parnell	Bannister	D. McLean	Mounteney	Danson		
Mar 29	Bradford City	Div 1	a	0-2		Taylor	McFadyen	Rodway	J. McLean	McCall	Lyon	Parnell	Bannister	D. McLean	Mounteney	Danson		
Apr 2	Liverpool	Div 1	h	2-0		McBride	McFadyen	Rodway	J. McLean	McCall	Lyon	Parnell	Bannister	D. McLean (1)	Mounteney	Danson (1)		
Apr 9	Aston Villa	Div 1	a	0-3		McBride	Winchester	Rodway	J. McLean	McCall	Lyon	Parnell	Bannister	D. McLean	Mounteney	Danson		
Apr 16	Sheffield Utd.	Div 1	h	1-1		McBride	McFadyen	Rodway	J. McLean	McCall	Lyon	Parnell	Bannister	D. McLean (1)	Danson	Winterhalder		
Apr 23	Woolwich Arsenal	Div 1	a	3-1		McBride	McFadyen	Baker	J. McLean	McCall	Lyon	Parnell	Bannister	D. McLean (1)	Platt	Danson (1)	1 o.g.	(Shaw)
Apr 30	Bolton W.	Div 1	h	1-0		McBride	McFadyen	Rodway	J. McLean	McCall	Lyon	Parnell	Bannister	Winterhalder	Spence (1)	Danson		

SEASON 1910–1911

The ironies of football often have a habit of making their mark on any club history and for the 1910–11 season Preston were affected by a huge irony. After several years of struggling with their results away from Deepdale they finally managed a big improvement in this campaign. But, and it had to happen, this time their home form let them down badly. Avoiding defeat in over half their away fixtures was certainly a triumph bearing in mind their results in the immediate past seasons. A big player turnover reflected the management's determination to change the fortunes of the club, with twelve coming in and thirteen playing their last games. North End were again blighted by an inability to score, only 40 in their 38 games. Funnily enough though the whole league saw a big decrease in goals scored as defences grew meaner and wiser. Mind you, only Notts County scored fewer than North End. David McLean was still the main forward but he was not nearly as prolific, this time scoring only seven goals, the same as James Bannister, and they shared the lead in the goals chart. Individually, as ever, there were some good performances, with Peter McBride, William Wareing, John Thompson and Charles McFadyen having some excellent games, but as a unit Preston struggled to find both rhythm and balance for long spells. Their customary bad start did not help. Why was it that Preston always seemed to need five or six games before they registered a win? Was it their pre-season build up that was causing the problem, one wonders? After all, paddling in the sea at Blackpool and fell walking over Longridge Hills did not seem the ideal preparation. Eddie Holdsworth worked hard in the midfield trying to prompt the attack and Arthur Winterhalder had some lively games on the wing. Herbert Danson had a fine spell around February but all of these good performances were rarely sustained as Preston struggled to string the results together. In the FA Cup two trips to London were required. Brentford were beaten in the first round but West Ham proved far too strong in the second so once again the Preston fans were denied a decent cup challenge. After that inglorious exit it was back to the league and again Preston served up their usual mixed bag of results. The low point came when they were thrashed 5–0 at Manchester United. In the end enough points were won to stave off any thoughts of relegation but in reality the mid-table position was all North End deserved.

DEBUTANTS: (12) David Anderson, Harry Best, Frederick Broadhurst, Albert Chester, Thomas Dickinson, John English, John Hall, Lauchlan McLean, William Robertson, John Thompson, Robert Thompson and William Wareing.

LAST GAMES: (13) Lyon, McLean J., Wilson, Platt, Galbraith, McLean D., Mounteney, Spence, Best, Chester, Dickinson, McLean L. and Robertson.

51

Future players born during the 1910–11 season include: George Bargh, Jimmy Milne and Frank Beresford

Ever presents: None

FA Cup: Second Round

Hat-tricks: None

Manager: Management Committee

Chairman: Mr W. E. Ord J. P.

Players used: 30

Leading scorers: 7 League goals each – David McLean and James Bannister

AUTHORS' UNOFFICIAL PLAYER OF THE SEASON: William Wareing

Trivia Facts:

North End had 3 McLeans, 2 Robertsons, 2 Jacksons, 2 Thompsons and 2 Walfords on their books this season.

The 3–3 draw with Notts County in October 1910 was memorable for the fact that the one and only Joe McCall was sent off!

On Saturday 1 October 1910 Arthur Mounteney was summoned before the Preston Court for being drunk in a charge of a child under seven. However the Bench dismissed the case owing to a lack of corroborative evidence. Mounteney then played at Deepdale that afternoon against Newcastle.

'Chippy' Danson put in a transfer request in November 1911, as he said that he had had a verbal promise of a Benefit game, but it had not materialised. He left the club at the end of the season.

League appearances (38 games)

Anderson D. R. 1, Baker G. 8, Bannister J. 30, Best H. O. 4, Broadhurst F. 2, Chester A. 2, Danson H. 24, Dickinson T. S. 1, English J. 3, Galbraith D. 1, Hall J. 9, Holdsworth E. 33, Lyon W. J. 9, McBride P. 35, McCall J. 32, McFadyen C. 33, McLean D. 22, McLean J. 2, McLean L. 1, Mounteney A. 21, Platt J. 2, Robertson W. 2, Rodway T. 30, Spence W. E. 1, Taylor H. 3, Thompson J. W. 34, Thompson R. 1, Wareing W. 37, Wilson J. 5, Winterhalder A. 30.

FA Cup appearances (2 games)

McBride 2, McFadyen 2, Rodway 2, Holdsworth 2, McCall 2, Wareing 2, Thompson J. 2, Bannister 2, McLean D. 2, Danson 1, Mounteney 1, Winterhalder 2.

Goalscorers: 40 League–1 Cup (Total 41)

McLean D. 7–0 (7), Bannister 7–0 (7), Mounteney 5–0 (5), Thompson J. 5–0 (5), Danson 4–0 (4), Rodway 2 (2 pens)–1 (pen) (3), Hall 2–0 (2), Wareing 2–0 (2), McCall 2–0 (2), Winterhalder 2–0 (2), Anderson 1–0 (1), Chester 1–0 (1).

Season 1910–11: First Division

		P	W	D	L	F	A	Pts
1	Man United	38	22	8	8	72	40	52
2	Aston Villa	38	22	7	9	69	41	51
3	Sunderland	38	15	15	8	67	48	45
4	Everton	38	19	7	12	50	36	45
5	Bradford City	38	20	5	13	51	42	45
6	Wednesday	38	17	8	13	47	48	42
7	Oldham	38	16	9	13	44	41	41
8	Newcastle	38	15	10	13	61	43	40
9	Sheffield United	38	15	8	15	49	43	38
10	Woolwich A	38	13	12	13	41	49	38
11	Notts County	38	14	10	14	37	45	38
12	Blackburn	38	13	11	14	62	54	37
13	Liverpool	38	15	7	16	53	53	37
14	PRESTON	38	12	11	15	40	49	35
15	Tottenham	38	13	6	19	52	63	32
16	Middlesbrough	38	11	10	17	49	63	32
17	Man City	38	9	13	16	43	58	31
18	Bury	38	9	11	18	43	71	29
19	Bristol City	38	11	5	22	43	66	27
20	Nottingham Forest	38	9	7	22	55	75	25

STAT FACTS:

Best home run without defeat: 6 games

Best away run without defeat: 4 games

Longest run unbeaten: 5 games

Longest run without a win: 5 games

Match Report: McCall off as North End Fight to the end – 29 Oct. 1910 Notts County 3 Preston 3

Having beaten Nottingham Forest earlier in the month Preston returned to Robin Hood's City to see if they could also topple their neighbours across the Trent, Notts County. It took 36 minutes before the fans saw a goal but it was worth waiting for as it was a peach, a real gem.

It began with a beautifully executed run down the Preston right by Thompson and Bannister. They worked the ball well having been fed by McLean who followed the speedy pair moving down the centre of the field. When the return ball came in McLean took it in his stride to hit a terrific rising shot which gave Iremonger no chance to save. Within a minute Mounteney nearly doubled the goal tally but his header shaved the outside of a post. But Preston were not to be denied and four minutes into the second half they did score a second goal after Winterhalder was put through by McLean, having an eventful afternoon. Winterhalder worked his way through a static defence to score with relative ease and put Preston on course for an almost certain two points, or so they thought. Ten minutes after this goal all hell let loose as suddenly County produced a burst of three goals in just eleven minutes to completely turn the game around. Their first came from a free-kick after the Magpies had actually appealed for a penalty, as they thought that McFadyen had handled inside the penalty area. The free-kick was turned wide for Watersall to cross into the danger area. Although one forward miscued, Matthews followed up to score. On the hour Watersall himself scored the equaliser from a corner with North End at sixes and sevens. Cantrell, tricking McFadyen cleverly, then scored a third goal, but immediately was involved in a nasty skirmish with McCall. It was so serious that the referee had no option but to send both players off the field. To stop County going further ahead, McBride had to dive full length to nullify Emberson's attempt. But Preston's character shone through as they eventually fought back to equalise with a splendid goal by McLean after 84 minutes. In the end County had only themselves to blame for not winning as, once in front, they held the upper hand, but indifferent shooting let them down. McCall, usually such a good tempered and scrupulously fair player, was crestfallen by his dismissal. His actions could only suggest that he had been considerably provoked into his part in the fisticuffs. No excuses though and he was suspended for two weeks whilst Cantrell got four!

Trivia Facts:

No fewer than 15 players played five games or less during the season. The continuous team changing could not have been a confidence booster to the team.

The three McLeans who appeared in the first team were not related.

James McLean was granted a benefit match by the Club. North End beat Blackburn Rovers on 26 September in a friendly so low key that no decent match report is available.

League position in Division One: 14th – P38 W12 D11 L15 F40 A49 Pts 35
Home: W8 D5 L6 F25 A19 Away: W4 D6 L9 F15 A30

Date 1910-11	Opponents	Comp	h or a	Score	Att.	1	2	3	4	5	6	7	8	9	10	11
Sep 1	Nottm. Forest	Div 1	h	0-2		McBride	McFadyen	Rodway	Holdsworth	McCall	Lyon	J. Thompson	Mounteney	D. McLean	L. McLean	Robertson
Sep 3	Manchester City	Div 1	h	1-1		McBride	McFadyen	Rodway	Holdsworth	Wareing	Lyon	J. Thompson	Bannister (1)	D. McLean	Mounteney	Danson
Sep 10	Everton	Div 1	a	0-2		McBride	McFadyen	Rodway	J. McLean	Wareing	Lyon	J. Thompson	Bannister	D. McLean	Mounteney	Winterhalder
Sep 17	Sheffield Wed.	Div 1	h	1-3		McBride	McFadyen	Rodway	Holdsworth	Wareing	Wilson	J. Thompson	Spence	Platt	Mounteney (1)	Robertson
Sep 24	Bristol City	Div 1	a	0-0		McBride	McFadyen	Rodway	Wareing	McCall	Lyon	J. Thompson	Bannister	D. McLean	Mounteney	Danson
Oct 1	Newcastle Utd.	Div 1	h	2-1		McBride	McFadyen	Baker	Holdsworth	McCall	Wareing	J. Thompson (1)	Bannister	D. McLean (1)	Mounteney	Danson
Oct 6	Nottm. Forest	Div 1	a	3-1		McBride	McFadyen	Baker	Holdsworth	McCall	Wareing	J. Thompson (1)	Bannister (1)	D. McLean (1)	Mounteney	Winterhalder
Oct 8	Tottenham H.	Div 1	a	1-1		McBride	McFadyen	Baker	Holdsworth	McCall	Wareing	J. Thompson (1)	Bannister	D. McLean	Mounteney	Winterhalder
Oct 15	Middlesbrough	Div 1	h	1-1		McBride	McFadyen	Baker	Holdsworth	McCall	Wareing	J. Thompson	Bannister	D. McLean (1)	Mounteney	Winterhalder
Oct 22	Oldham Ath.	Div 1	a	1-2		McBride	McFadyen	Baker	Holdsworth	McCall	Wareing (1)	J. Thompson	Bannister	D. McLean	Mounteney	Winterhalder
Oct 29	Notts County	Div 1	h	3-3		McBride	McFadyen	Baker	Holdsworth	McCall	Wareing	J. Thompson	Bannister	D. McLean (2)	Mounteney	Winterhalder (1)
Nov 5	Manchester Utd.	Div 1	h	0-2		Taylor	McFadyen	Baker	Holdsworth	McCall	Wareing	J. Thompson	Bannister	D. McLean	Wilson	Winterhalder
Nov 12	Liverpool	Div 1	a	0-3		McBride	McFadyen	Baker	Wareing	Wilson	Lyon	J. Thompson	Bannister	Winterhalder	Mounteney	Galbraith
Nov 19	Bury	Div 1	h	2-0		McBride	McFadyen	Rodway (1p)	Holdsworth	Wareing	Lyon	J. Thompson	Bannister	D. McLean	Wilson	Winterhalder (1)
Nov 26	Sheffield Utd.	Div 1	a	0-5		McBride	McFadyen	Rodway	Holdsworth	McCall	Wareing	J. Thompson	Platt	D. McLean	Wilson	Winterhalder
Dec 3	Aston Villa	Div 1	h	0-1		McBride	McFadyen	Rodway	Holdsworth	McCall	Lyon	Dickinson	J. Thompson	D. McLean	Wareing	Winterhalder
Dec 10	Sunderland	Div 1	a	1-1		McBride	McFadyen	Rodway	Holdsworth	McCall	Wareing	J. Thompson	Bannister	D. McLean	Danson (1)	Winterhalder
Dec 17	Woolwich Arsenal	Div 1	h	4-1		McBride	McFadyen	Rodway (1p)	Holdsworth	McCall (1)	Wareing (1)	J. Thompson (1)	Bannister	D. McLean	Danson	Winterhalder
Dec 24	Bradford City	Div 1	a	0-1		McBride	McFadyen	Rodway	Holdsworth	McCall	Wareing	J. Thompson	Bannister	D. McLean	Danson	Winterhalder
Dec 26	Blackburn Rovers	Div 1	h	0-0		McBride	McFadyen	Rodway	Holdsworth	McCall	Wareing	J. Thompson	Bannister	Winterhalder	Mounteney	Danson
Dec 31	Manchester City	Div 1	a	2-0		McBride	McFadyen	Rodway	Holdsworth	McCall	Wareing	J. Thompson	Bannister (1)	D. McLean (1)	Danson	Winterhalder
Jan 2	Blackburn Rovers	Div 1	a	1-0		McBride	English	Rodway	Holdsworth	McCall	Wareing	J. Thompson (1)	Bannister	D. McLean	Danson	Winterhalder
Jan 3	Newcastle Utd.	Div 1	h	1-1		McBride	English	Rodway	J. McLean	Wareing	Lyon	J. Thompson	Bannister	D. McLean	Mounteney (1)	Winterhalder
Jan 7	Everton	Div 1	h	0-2		McBride	English	Rodway	Holdsworth	McCall	Wareing	J. Thompson	Bannister	D. McLean	Mounteney	Winterhalder
Jan 14	Brentford Rd 1	FAC	a	1-0	15000	McBride	McFadyen	Rodway (1p)	Holdsworth	McCall	Wareing	J. Thompson	Bannister	D. McLean	Danson	Winterhalder
Jan 21	Sheffield Wed.	Div 1	a	0-0		McBride	McFadyen	Rodway	Holdsworth	McCall	Wareing	J. Thompson	Bannister	Mounteney	Danson	Winterhalder
Jan 28	Bristol City	Div 1	h	4-0		McBride	McFadyen	Rodway	Holdsworth	McCall (1)	Wareing	J. Thompson	Bannister (2)	Mounteney (1)	Danson	Winterhalder
Feb 4	West Ham Utd. Rd 2	FAC	a	0-3	12500	McBride	McFadyen	Rodway	Holdsworth	McCall	Wareing	J. Thompson	Bannister	D. McLean	Mounteney	Winterhalder
Feb 11	Tottenham H.	Div 1	h	2-0		McBride	Broadhurst	Rodway	Holdsworth	McCall	Wareing	J. Thompson	Bannister	D. McLean (1)	Danson (1)	Winterhalder
Feb 18	Middlesbrough	Div 1	a	0-2		McBride	McFadyen	Rodway	Holdsworth	McCall	Wareing	Hall	Bannister	Mounteney	Danson	Winterhalder
Feb 25	Oldham Ath.	Div 1	h	1-1		Taylor	Broadhurst	Rodway	Holdsworth	McCall	Wareing	Hall	J. Thompson	Best	Danson (1)	Winterhalder
Mar 4	Notts County	Div 1	a	2-0		Taylor	McFadyen	Rodway	Holdsworth	McCall	Wareing	Hall (1)	J. Thompson	Best	Danson (1)	Winterhalder
Mar 11	Manchester Utd.	Div 1	a	0-5		McBride	McFadyen	Rodway	Holdsworth	McCall	Wareing	Hall	J. Thompson	Best	Danson	Winterhalder
Mar 18	Liverpool	Div 1	h	2-1		McBride	McFadyen	Rodway	Lyon	McCall	Wareing	Hall	Bannister (2)	Mounteney	Danson	Winterhalder
Mar 25	Bury	Div 1	a	0-1		McBride	McFadyen	Rodway	Holdsworth	McCall	Wareing	Hall	J. Thompson	Winterhalder	Bannister	Danson
Apr 1	Sheffield Utd.	Div 1	h	1-1		McBride	McFadyen	Rodway	Holdsworth	McCall	Wareing	Hall (1)	Bannister	Best	Danson	Winterhalder
Apr 8	Aston Villa	Div 1	a	2-0		McBride	McFadyen	Rodway	Holdsworth	McCall	Wareing	Hall	Bannister	Mounteney (2)	Danson	J. Thompson
Apr 15	Sunderland	Div 1	h	0-2		McBride	McFadyen	Rodway	Holdsworth	McCall	Wareing	J. Thompson	Bannister	Mounteney	Danson	Winterhalder
Apr 22	Woolwich Arsenal	Div 1	a	0-2		McBride	McFadyen	Rodway	Holdsworth	McCall	Wareing	J. Thompson	Bannister	Mounteney	Chester	Danson
Apr 29	Bradford City	Div 1	h	2-0		McBride	McFadyen	Rodway	Holdsworth	McCall	Wareing	Hall	Anderson (1)	R. Thompson	Chester (1)	Danson

SEASON 1911–1912

The warning signs that had been so much in evidence over the previous seasons went unheeded by the Preston management and the outcome was felt in full at the end of the 1911–12 season as, just like the Titanic, Preston went down! Relegation had almost been inevitable throughout the year although it was a close run thing as the threat of Division Two beckoned for a second spell. More new players were brought to the club with three making their debut on the opening day. Somewhat surprisingly Preston won their first game, but then a very poor run of results followed and North End were again playing catch-up. For the game against Notts County on October the 14, the selectors left out the legendary Peter McBride. It was a move met with raised eyebrows but Preston were desperate to stop the rot and drastic situations sometimes required drastic measures. Ironically Preston won that game but two matches later a 6–2 defeat at Spurs provoked questions from the fans. But despite playing behind a shaky defence Herbert Taylor played well in goal and revelled in his first chance of a regular place in the side. In attack though Preston were woeful and found scoring goals a nightmare. William Kirby was an exception though and the centre-forward had a good season, despite not receiving too much by way of support. In one spell during February and March Preston went five games without a goal and it was all very frustrating for the fans. Benjamin Green did his best but generally the midfield was weak and chances were not being created. Tommy Rodway, Eddie Holdsworth, Joe McCall and William Wareing strove manfully to keep Preston in with a chance of staying up. There was hope, as the league was tight with several other clubs in danger of the drop along with Preston. Indeed, at one point only three points separated North End from Sheffield United who eventually finished in 14th position. A single goal defeat knocked Preston out of the FA Cup, Manchester City winning at Deepdale, so it was yet another ignominious exit from the world's premier cup competition. After that game it was back to the league battle. A good 4–1 win at home to Aston Villa gave cause for some optimism, the win coming the day before that fateful Titanic ship disaster. But a week later Preston also went down, as a home defeat by Middlesbrough left them clinging to the wreckage of relegation. Even the return of McBride for the last game could not save the club, it needed more than McBride as the writing had been on the wall for some time. In the end Preston were relegated with Bury.

DEBUTANTS: (11) Sydney Beaumont, Herbert Bradley, Thomas Galloway, Benjamin Green, James Johnston, William Kirby, Charles McKellar, James McKnight, John Morley, Percy Toone, Robert Turner.

LAST GAMES: (13) McBride, Danson, Winterhalder, Bannister, Anderson, English, Thompson J.W., Hall, Beaumont, Bradley, Johnston, McKellar, Turner.

The keen rivalry between Preston North End and Blackburn Rovers, which still exists fervently today, was also evident in 1911 by a magnificent crowd which filled Deepdale on Boxing Day to watch the two sides battle it out for local supremacy. The crowd numbered around 22,000 at the start with thousands still clogging the Deepdale road. They were all in festive mood and consequently very noisy, especially as North End had beaten the league leaders, Newcastle, three days earlier. Blackburn themselves were well up the table whereas Preston were in the lower half of the league. A keen, hard fought battle ensued, a real derby match, with Rovers once again finding it hard to beat their arch rivals. In fact they had not beaten North End since New Year's Day 1901. Very early appeals for a penalty rang out as Kirby went down after a challenge by Crompton, but they fell on deaf ears as referee Mr Hargreaves waved play-on. Danson then put pressure on the Rovers defence but his shot hit the side netting. From the resultant goalkick Johnson, who was making his league debut, gained possession and promptly centred into the Blackburn goalmouth. Ashcroft got his hands to the ball but it squirmed out of his grasp and quick as a flash Green rushed the ball into the net. However, North End's joy was short lived as within six minutes Rovers equalised. Rodway, caught in two minds, lost the ball and watched in horror as Simpson curled the ball around Taylor and into the home net. It was probably meant as a centre but it had the desired result. 1–1 and still the fans were queing outside trying to get in. Midway through the half Bradshaw went close for Blackburn, robbed of a goal by a last ditch clearance by Wareing. Wareing was also instrumental in setting up a great opportunity for Kirby, but he put his effort a yard wide. After 25 minutes, following a cross from Simpson, Clennel gave Rovers the lead, which they deserved. Just prior to half-time both teams had an enforced breather as the trainer came on to deal with an injury to ex-North Ender Percy Smith. Three minutes after the break Thompson equalised for the home side with a well struck drive following a cross from Kirby. Play was as fast and exciting as one could imagine at this point of the game, both teams going hell for leather for the winner. Green actually got the ball in Blackburn's net but the goal was ruled out for offside. The match was played in an excellent spirit throughout and in the end both sets of fans went home happy. Four photographs of this game were printed in the following day's *Lancashire Daily Post*.

Two Future Players were known to be born during this season and they were Harry Jones and Tom Crawley

Ever presents: (1) William Kirby
Hat-tricks: None
Chairman: Mr W. E. Ord J. P.
Leading scorer: 14 goals – William Kirby (all league)

FA Cup: First Round
Manager: Management Committee
Players used: 28

AUTHORS' UNOFFICIAL PLAYER OF THE SEASON: William Kirby

League appearances (38 games)

Anderson D. R. 8, Baker G. 14, Bannister J. 6, Beaumont S. 1, Bradley H. 2, Broadhurst F. 1, Danson H. 25, English J. 3, Galloway T. 15, Green B. H. 36, Hall J. 9, Holdsworth E. 35, Johnston J. 3, Kirby W. 38, McBride P. 7, McCall J. 27, McFadyen C. 21, McKellar C. 2, McKnight J. 9, Morley J. B. 10, Rodway T. 37, Taylor H. 27, Thompson J. W. 24, Thompson R. 11, Toone P. E. S. 4, Turner R. F. 8, Wareing W. 33, Winterhalder A. 2.

FA Cup appearances (1 game)

Taylor, McFadyen, Rodway, Galloway, McCall, Wareing, Holdsworth, Thompson J. W., Green, Kirby and Danson all one each.

Goalscorers: 40 League only

Kirby 14 (2pens), Green 10, Thompson J. W. 4, Thompson R. 2, Rodway 2 (both pens), McKnight 2, Anderson 2, McFadyen 1, Hall 1, McCall 1, Morley 1.

Season 1911–12: First Division

		P	W	D	L	F	A	Pts
1	Blackburn	38	20	9	9	60	43	49
2	Everton	38	20	6	12	46	42	46
3	Newcastle	38	18	8	12	64	50	44
4	Bolton	38	20	3	15	54	43	43
5	Wednesday	38	16	9	13	69	49	41
6	Aston Villa	38	17	7	14	76	63	41
7	Middlesbrough	38	16	8	14	56	45	40
8	Sunderland	38	14	11	13	58	51	39
9	WBA	38	15	9	14	43	47	39
10	Woowich A	38	15	8	15	55	59	38
11	Bradford City	38	15	8	15	46	50	38
12	Tottenham	38	14	9	15	53	53	37
13	Man United	38	13	11	14	45	60	37
14	Sheffield United	38	13	10	15	63	56	36
15	Man City	38	13	9	16	56	58	35
16	Notts County	38	14	7	17	46	63	35
17	Liverpool	38	12	10	16	49	55	34
18	Oldham	38	12	10	16	46	54	34
19	**PRESTON**	38	13	7	18	40	57	33
20	Bury	38	6	9	23	32	59	21

STAT FACTS:
Best home run without defeat: 5 games   Best away run without defeat: 2 games   Longest run unbeaten: 5 games
Longest run without a win: 5 games

League position in Division One: 19th (Relegated) – P38 W13 D7 L18 F40 A57 Pts 33
Home: W8 D4 L7 F26 A25   Away: W5 D3 L11 F14 A32

Date 1911-12	Opponents	Comp	h or a	Score	Att.	1	2	3	4	5	6	7	8	9	10	11
Sep 2	Sheffield Wed.	Div 1	a	1-0		McBride	McFadyen	Rodway	Holdsworth	McCall	Wareing	Hall	Bannister	Kirby	Green (1)	Turner
Sep 9	Oldham Ath.	Div 1	h	0-1		McBride	McFadyen	Rodway	Holdsworth	McCall	Wareing	Hall	Bannister	Kirby	Green	Turner
Sep 16	Bury	Div 1	a	0-0		McBride	McFadyen	Rodway	Holdsworth	McCall	Wareing	Hall	Bannister	Kirby	Green	Turner
Sep 23	Bolton W.	Div 1	h	1-2		McBride	McFadyen	Rodway	Holdsworth	McCall	Wareing	J. Thompson	Green	R. Thompson (1)	Kirby	Danson
Sep 30	Middlesbrough	Div 1	a	2-4		McBride	English	Rodway	Holdsworth	McCall	Wareing	J. Thompson (1)	Green	R. Thompson	Kirby (1)	Danson
Oct 7	Bradford City	Div 1	h	2-2		McBride	English	Rodway	Holdsworth	McCall	Wareing	J. Thompson	Green (1)	R. Thompson	Kirby (1)	Danson
Oct 14	Notts County	Div 1	a	2-1		Taylor	McFadyen	Rodway	Holdsworth	McCall	Wareing	J. Thompson (1)	Bannister	Kirby (1)	Green	Danson
Oct 21	Woolwich Arsenal	Div 1	h	0-1		Taylor	Broadhurst	Rodway	Holdsworth	McCall	Wareing	J. Thompson	Bannister	Kirby	Green	Danson
Oct 28	Tottenham H.	Div 1	a	2-6		Taylor	English	Rodway	Holdsworth	McCall	Wareing	J. Thompson	Green	R. Thompson	Kirby (2)	Danson
Nov 4	Manchester City	Div 1	h	2-1		Taylor	McFadyen (1)	Rodway	Holdsworth	Galloway	Wareing	J. Thompson (1)	Green	Anderson	Kirby	Danson
Nov 11	Manchester Utd.	Div 1	a	0-0		Taylor	Baker	Rodway	Holdsworth	Galloway	Wareing	J. Thompson	Green	Anderson	Kirby	Turner
Nov 18	Everton	Div 1	h	2-1		Taylor	Baker	Rodway (1p)	Holdsworth	Galloway	Wareing	J. Thompson	Green (1)	Anderson	Kirby	Bradley
Nov 25	Liverpool	Div 1	a	1-0		Taylor	Baker	Rodway	Holdsworth	Galloway	Wareing	J. Thompson	Green (1)	Anderson	Kirby	Bradley
Dec 2	WBA	Div 1	h	1-1		Taylor	Baker	Rodway	Holdsworth	Galloway	Wareing	J. Thompson	Green (1)	Anderson	Kirby	Danson
Dec 9	Aston Villa	Div 1	a	0-1		Taylor	Baker	Rodway	Holdsworth	Galloway	Wareing	J. Thompson	Green	R. Thompson	Kirby	Danson
Dec 16	Sunderland	Div 1	a	0-3		Taylor	Baker	Rodway	Holdsworth	Galloway	Wareing	J. Thompson	Green	Anderson	Kirby	Danson
Dec 23	Newcastle Utd.	Div 1	h	2-1		Taylor	Baker	Rodway	Bannister	Galloway	Wareing	Holdsworth	J. Thompson	Green	Kirby (2)	Danson
Dec 26	Blackburn Rovers	Div 1	h	2-2		Taylor	Baker	Rodway	Johnston	Galloway	Wareing	Hall	J. Thompson (1)	Green (1)	Kirby	Danson
Dec 28	Sheffield Utd.	Div 1	a	2-4		Toone	McFadyen	Baker	Johnston	McCall	Galloway	Hall	Anderson (2)	Green	Kirby	Danson
Dec 30	Sheffield Wed.	Div 1	h	2-3		Toone	McFadyen	Rodway (1p)	Holdsworth	Galloway	Wareing	Hall	J. Thompson	Green	Kirby (1)	Danson
Jan 1	Blackburn Rovers	Div 1	a	0-3		Toone	Baker	Rodway	Holdsworth	McCall	Galloway	Hall	J. Thompson	Green	Kirby	Danson
Jan 6	Oldham Ath.	Div 1	a	0-1		Toone	McFadyen	Rodway	Beaumont	Galloway	Johnston	Hall	J. Thompson	Green	Kirby	Danson
Jan 13	Manchester City Rd 1	FAC	h	0-1	12000	Taylor	McFadyen	Rodway	Galloway	McCall	Wareing	Holdsworth	J. Thompson	Green	Kirby	Danson
Jan 20	Bury	Div 1	a	1-0		Toone	McFadyen	Rodway	Holdsworth	McCall	Wareing	Hall (1)	J. Thompson	Green	Kirby	Winterhalder
Jan 27	Bolton W.	Div 1	a	0-3		Taylor	McFadyen	Rodway	Holdsworth	McCall	Wareing	J. Thompson	Green	R. Thompson	Kirby	Winterhalder
Feb 10	Bradford City	Div 1	a	1-0		Taylor	McFadyen	Rodway	Holdsworth	McCall (1)	Wareing	J. Thompson	Green	R. Thompson	Kirby	Danson
Feb 17	Notts County	Div 1	h	2-1		Taylor	McFadyen	Rodway	Holdsworth	McCall	Wareing	J. Thompson	Green	R. Thompson (1)	Kirby (1p)	Danson
Feb 24	Newcastle Utd.	Div 1	a	0-1		Taylor	McFadyen	Rodway	Holdsworth	McCall	Wareing	J. Thompson	Green	R. Thompson	Kirby	Danson
Mar 2	Tottenham H.	Div 1	h	1-1		Taylor	McFadyen	Rodway	Holdsworth	McCall	Wareing	J. Thompson	Green	R. Thompson	McKnight	Kirby
Mar 9	Manchester City	Div 1	a	0-0		Taylor	McFadyen	Rodway	Holdsworth	McCall	Wareing	Morley	Green	Kirby	McKnight	Danson
Mar 16	Manchester Utd.	Div 1	h	0-0		Taylor	McFadyen	Rodway	Holdsworth	McCall	Wareing	Morley	Green	McKellar	Kirby	Danson
Mar 23	Everton	Div 1	a	0-1		Taylor	McFadyen	Rodway	Holdsworth	McCall	Wareing	Morley	Anderson	McKellar	Kirby	Danson
Mar 30	Liverpool	Div 1	h	2-1		Taylor	McFadyen	Rodway	Holdsworth	McCall	Wareing	Morley	McKnight (1)	R. Thompson	Kirby (1p)	Danson
Apr 5	Sheffield Utd.	Div 1	h	3-0		Taylor	McFadyen	Rodway	Holdsworth	McCall	Wareing	Morley	McKnight (1)	Green	Kirby (2)	Danson
Apr 8	Woolwich Arsenal	Div 1	a	1-4		Taylor	McFadyen	Rodway	Holdsworth	McCall	Wareing	Morley	McKnight	Green (1)	Kirby	Danson
Apr 9	WBA	Div 1	a	2-0		Taylor	Baker	Rodway	Holdsworth	McCall	Galloway	Morley	McKnight	Green (1)	Kirby (1)	Turner
Apr 13	Aston Villa	Div 1	h	4-1		Taylor	Baker	Rodway	Holdsworth	McCall	Galloway	Morley (1)	McKnight	Green (2)	Kirby (1)	Turner
Apr 20	Sunderland	Div 1	h	0-3		Taylor	Baker	Rodway	Holdsworth	McCall	Wareing	Morley	McKnight	Green	Kirby	Turner
Apr 22	Middlesbrough	Div 1	h	0-3		McBride	Baker	Rodway	Holdsworth	McCall	Wareing	Morley	McKnight	Green	Kirby	Turner

SEASON 1912–1913

The poor start to season 1912–13 gave no indication to the campaign that the Preston fans were to enjoy. This time the relegation suffered the year before was met with a positive response and a terrific comeback which saw Preston end as Division Two Champions. Only four games were lost throughout the season, a superb record, and one run of 15 unbeaten matches set North End up for the title. If there had been a Manager of the Month award given in 1912, then the Preston representative would have won it in the December as the club won six out of six and even stretched it to 11 out of 12 through January and February 1913. The differences were seen throughout the team but in attack Preston were far more dangerous than of late with Ben Green scoring regularly and new signings Joe Halliwell and Alf Common contributing very well in the second half of the season. At the back the defenders were much more secure and gave little away. The positions were settled with Charlie McFadyen, Tommy Rodway, Eddie Holdsworth, Joe McCall and another new signing, George Dawson, showing consistently good form. The goals for and against were the best since their last Division Two Championship season. Apart from a shock 5–1 defeat at Leeds City, Preston played some superb football from week to week and they were safely in a promotion spot well before the end of the season. The only real disappointment of an exciting year came in the FA Cup. Once again Preston made yet another woeful exit. This time they were visiting non league Plymouth Argyle and a crowd of nearly 15,000 saw the home side pull off a famous first round victory. One odd and interesting fact came with Preston scoring from no fewer than eight penalties during the season, a very high total. The Deepdale form was excellent with only Clapton Orient taking two points from North End. With thirteen games won at home it formed a perfect platform from which Preston made their challenge on the title. The whole team gave 100% effort with McFadyen and Holdsworth definitely the pick of the side. The signing of Alf Common certainly stirred the emotions of the Preston public. Common had, famously, been the first ever £1,000 transfer, and the Preston management showed considerable foresight, as not only did it create huge interest but it also lifted the other members of the team to know that players of his quality were being brought in. It certainly paid off.

DEBUTANTS: (7) Alf Common, George Dawson, William Gerrish, Joe Halliwell, William Luke, John Marshall (No. 1), William Swarbrick.

LAST GAMES: (9) Baker, Thompson, Wareing, Galloway, Kirby, McKnight, Toone, Gerrish, and Luke.

Match report: Derby Day Blues ... For Blackpool –
26 April 1913. Preston 2 Blackpool 1

What a scenario! North End, already assured of the Championship, having to play their last game of the season at home against near neighbours Blackpool, who had been relegated Preston and Burnley had been in a neck and neck tussle for the title and had Burnley won their game in hand at home to Barnsley the previous Wednesday then the game with Blackpool would have had an entirely different flavour as the Championship would have hinged on the result. As it was, the occasion, from a football point of view, was robbed of its importance. Therefore it was to the credit of the players that the game did not degenerate into a mere perfunctory fulfilment of an end of season fixture. Considering that there was the whole depth of the division between the clubs Blackpool did not discredit themselves, probably more to do with local pride but also in the fact that had they gained a point then they would not have been the wooden spoonists. North End played well within themselves during the first half despite defending against a stiff breeze. Blackpool's best chance of the half did not come until right on half time after McFadyen mis-kicked due to the strong wind and was only rescued by Rodway's timely clearance. The half had been devoid of goal action but if any supporter had taken too long over their half-time hot Bovril drink then they could well have missed the exciting start to the second half. Two minutes after the restart with the wind now behind them, Preston quickly found their shooting range as Halliwell's rousing shot bulged the back of the Blackpool net. McCall had begun the movement with a neat pass out to Barlow who whipped the ball into the centre with pace. Both Halliwell and Marshall raced for the same ball but Halliwell reached it first to give Fiske no chance in goal. Six minutes later Marshall himself got on the scoresheet. Morley set up the opportunity for him and from fully 25 yards Marshall unleashed a powerful rocket of a shot which Fiske never had an earthly of saving. It was sheer golden marksmanship, worthy of winning a Championship, never mind a derby match. Although Charles pulled one back for Blackpool it was celebration time at Deepdale once again, for the supporters would not go home until their team showed their faces to take the merited applause with modesty. After a couple of short speeches from the Chairman and from Holdsworth, the captain, Deepdale was left to its summer slumbers.

One Future Player who was born during this season, 5 May to be exact, was Sid Rawlings who was the son of another North Ender, Archie Rawlings

Ever presents: (2) Holdsworth and McFadyen   Hat-tricks: (1) Morley
Manager: Management Committee   FA Cup: First Round
Chairman: Mr W. E. Ord J. P.   Players used: 23
Leading scorer: 13 goals – Ben Green (all league)

AUTHORS' UNOFFICIAL PLAYER OF THE SEASON: Charlie McFadyen

League appearances: (38 games)

Baker G. 1, Barlow G. H. 28, Broadhurst F. 1, Common A. 21, Dawson G. 26, Galloway T. 9, Gerrish W. W. 3, Green B.H. 30, Halliwell J.A. 22, Holdsworth E. 38, Kirby W. 17, Luke W. 8, McCall J. 33, McFadyen C. 38, McKnight J. 3, Marshall J. (No. 1) 16, Morley J. B. 35, Rodway T. 36, Swarbrick W. 1, Taylor H. 28, Thompson R. 5, Toone P. E. S. 10, Wareing W. 9.

FA Cup appearances: (1 game)

Taylor, McFadyen, Rodway, Holdsworth, McCall, Johnston, Morley, Green, Luke, Common and Barlow.

Goalscorers: 56 League only

Green 13, Halliwell 10, Morley 8, Kirby 8 (4pens), Common 7 (3 pens), Marshall 2, Luke 2, Holdsworth 2, Barlow 1, Dawson 1, McCall 1, Rodway 1 (pen).

Trivia Facts:

On 10 April 1913 Preston paraded a special mascot around the pitch before the Burnley game at Deepdale. It was a live domesticated fox which was owned by Mr Sam Heath of the Stanley Arms, Preston.

The North End undertook a continental tour during May 1913 taking the following fourteen players: Taylor, McFadyen, Rodway, Holdsworth, Green, Dawson, Morley, Marshall, Halliwell, Pinch, Swarbrick, Broadhurst, Luke and Vickers. In the second game, against The Hague, Vickers the reserve goalkeeper came on as an outfield substitute for Dawson (injured ankle) and scored the third goal.

Photographs of North End's game *vs.* Blackpool in April 1913, were published in the *Lancashire Daily Post* and it showed advertisement hoardings around the pitch advertising the *Daily Mail*, Bovril and OXO.

Season 1912–13: Second Division

	P	W	D	L	F	A	Pts
1 PRESTON	38	19	15	4	56	33	53
2 Burnley	38	21	8	9	88	53	50
3 Birmingham	38	18	10	10	59	44	46
4 Barnsley	38	19	7	12	57	47	45
5 Huddersfield	38	17	9	12	66	40	43
6 Leeds City	38	15	10	13	10	64	40
7 Grimsby	38	15	10	13	51	50	40
8 Lincoln	38	15	10	13	50	52	40
9 Fulham	38	17	5	16	65	55	39
10 Wolves	38	14	10	14	56	54	38
11 Bury	38	15	8	15	53	57	38
12 Hull	38	15	6	17	60	56	36
13 Bradford PA	38	14	8	16	60	60	36
14 Clapton Orient	38	10	14	14	34	47	34
15 Leicester Fosse	38	13	7	18	50	65	33
16 Bristol City	38	9	15	14	46	72	33
17 Nottingham Forest	38	12	8	18	58	59	32
18 Glossop NE	38	12	8	18	49	68	32
19 Stockport	38	8	10	20	56	78	26
20 Blackpool	38	9	8	21	39	69	26

Trivia Facts:

Seven different centre-forwards were used during the season.

Alf Common who signed for PNE just before Christmas 1912 was the first £1,000 transfer fee earlier in his career.

League position in Division Two: Champions – P38 W19 D15 L4 F56 A33 Pts 53
Home: W13 D5 L1 F34 A12   Away: W6 D10 L3 F22 A21

Date 1912-13	Opponents	Comp	h or a	Score	Att.	1	2	3	4	5	6	7	8	9	10	11
Sep 2	Stockport County	Div 2	h	1-1		Toone	McFadyen	Rodway	Holdsworth	McCall	Wareing	Luke	Marshall	Gerrish	Kirby (1p)	Morley
Sep 7	Clapton Orient	Div 2	h	0-1		Toone	McFadyen	Rodway	Holdsworth	McCall	Wareing	Luke	McKnight	Thompson	Kirby	Morley
Sep 14	Lincoln	Div 2	a	0-0		Toone	McFadyen	Rodway	Holdsworth	McCall	Wareing	Luke	Marshall	Thompson	Kirby	Morley
Sep 16	Burnley	Div 2	a	2-2		Toone	McFadyen	Rodway	Holdsworth	McCall	Wareing	Morley	Marshall	Thompson	Green (2)	Kirby
Sep 21	Nottm. Forest	Div 2	h	1-1		Toone	McFadyen	Rodway	Holdsworth	McCall	Wareing	Morley	McKnight	Thompson	Green (1)	Kirby
Sep 28	Bristol City	Div 2	a	1-1		Toone	McFadyen	Rodway	Holdsworth	McCall	Galloway	Morley (1)	Green	Wareing	Gerrish	Kirby
Oct 5	Birmingham	Div 2	h	1-0		Toone	McFadyen	Rodway	Holdsworth	McCall	Galloway	Morley	Green (1)	Wareing	Gerrish	Kirby
Oct 12	Huddersfield	Div 2	a	1-1		Taylor	McFadyen	Rodway	Holdsworth	McCall	Wareing	Morley	Marshall	Green (1)	Kirby	McKnight
Oct 19	Leeds City	Div 2	h	3-2		Taylor	McFadyen	Rodway	Holdsworth	McCall	Wareing	Morley (1)	Green	Marshall	Kirby (2)	Barlow
Oct 26	Grimsby Town	Div 2	a	0-0		Taylor	McFadyen	Rodway	Holdsworth	McCall	Galloway	Morley	Green	Marshall	Thompson	Barlow
Nov 2	Bury	Div 2	h	2-0		Taylor	McFadyen	Rodway	Holdsworth	McCall	Galloway	Morley	Green (1)	Halliwell	Kirby (1p)	Barlow
Nov 9	Fulham	Div 2	a	1-3		Taylor	McFadyen	Baker	Holdsworth	McCall	Galloway	Morley	Green	Halliwell	Kirby (1)	Barlow
Nov 16	Barnsley	Div 2	h	4-0		Taylor	McFadyen	Rodway	Holdsworth	McCall	Dawson	Morley (1)	Green (1)	Halliwell (1)	Kirby (1p)	Barlow
Nov 23	Bradford P.A.	Div 2	a	0-0		Taylor	McFadyen	Rodway	Holdsworth	McCall	Dawson	Morley	Green	Halliwell	Kirby	Barlow
Nov 30	Wolverhampton W.	Div 2	h	1-1		Taylor	McFadyen	Rodway	Holdsworth	McCall	Dawson	Morley	Green (1)	Halliwell	Marshall	Barlow
Dec 7	Leicester Fosse	Div 2	a	3-0		Taylor	McFadyen	Rodway	Holdsworth	McCall	Dawson	Morley	Green (1)	Halliwell (2)	Kirby	Barlow
Dec 14	Bradford P.A.	Div 2	h	4-2		Taylor	McFadyen	Rodway	Holdsworth	McCall	Dawson	Morley	Green (1)	Marshall (1)	Kirby (2,1p)	Barlow
Dec 21	Blackpool	Div 2	a	1-0		Taylor	McFadyen	Rodway (1p)	Holdsworth	McCall	Dawson	Morley	Green	Halliwell	Common	Barlow
Dec 25	Glossop North End	Div 2	h	2-0		Taylor	McFadyen	Rodway	Holdsworth	McCall	Dawson	Morley (1)	Common (1)	Marshall	Kirby	Barlow
Dec 26	Hull City	Div 2	h	1-0		Taylor	McFadyen	Rodway	Holdsworth	Galloway	Dawson	Morley	Marshall	Halliwell (1)	Common	Barlow
Dec 28	Clapton Orient	Div 2	a	2-1		Taylor	McFadyen	Rodway	Holdsworth	Galloway	Dawson	Morley	Marshall	Luke (1)	Common (1)	Kirby
Jan 1	Glossop North End	Div 2	a	3-2		Taylor	McFadyen	Rodway	Holdsworth	Galloway	Dawson	Morley (3)	Marshall	Luke	Common	Barlow
Jan 4	Lincoln	Div 2	h	0-0		Taylor	McFadyen	Rodway	Holdsworth	Galloway	Dawson	Morley	Green	Marshall	Common	Barlow
Jan 11	**Plymouth Rd 1**	**FAC**	**a**	**0-2**	**14316**	**Taylor**	**McFadyen**	**Rodway**	**Holdsworth**	**McCall**	**Johnston**	**Morley**	**Green**	**Luke**	**Common**	**Barlow**
Jan 25	Bristol City	Div 2	h	5-1		Taylor	McFadyen	Rodway	Holdsworth	McCall	Dawson	Morley (1)	Green (1)	Halliwell (1)	Common (2,1p)	Barlow
Feb 5	Nottm. Forest	Div 2	a	2-0		Taylor	McFadyen	Rodway	Holdsworth	McCall	Dawson	Morley	Green (1)	Halliwell (1)	Common	Barlow
Feb 8	Birmingham	Div 2	a	1-0		Taylor	McFadyen	Rodway	Holdsworth	McCall	Dawson	Morley	Green	Halliwell (1)	Common	Barlow
Feb 15	Huddersfield	Div 2	h	2-1		Taylor	McFadyen	Rodway	Holdsworth	McCall	Dawson	Morley	Green (1)	Halliwell	Common (1p)	Barlow
Feb 22	Leeds City	Div 2	a	1-5		Taylor	McFadyen	Rodway	Holdsworth (1)	McCall	Dawson	Morley	Green	Halliwell	Common	Barlow
Mar 1	Grimsby Town	Div 2	h	2-0		Taylor	McFadyen	Rodway	Holdsworth	McCall	Dawson	Morley	Green	Halliwell (1)	Common (1p)	Barlow
Mar 8	Bury	Div 2	a	0-0		Taylor	McFadyen	Broadhurst	Holdsworth	McCall	Dawson	Morley	Green	Halliwell	Common	Barlow
Mar 15	Fulham	Div 2	h	1-0		Taylor	McFadyen	Rodway	Holdsworth	McCall	Dawson	Morley	Green	Halliwell	Common	Barlow (1)
Mar 22	Barnsley	Div 2	a	1-1		Taylor	McFadyen	Rodway	Holdsworth	McCall	Dawson (1)	Morley	Green	Halliwell	Common	Barlow
Mar 24	Hull City	Div 2	a	2-2		Taylor	McFadyen	Rodway	Holdsworth	McCall (1)	Dawson	Morley	Green	Halliwell (1)	Common	Barlow
Apr 5	Wolverhampton W.	Div 2	a	0-2		Taylor	McFadyen	Rodway	Holdsworth	Green	Dawson	Morley	Marshall	Halliwell	Common	Barlow
Apr 10	Burnley	Div 2	h	1-1		Toone	McFadyen	Rodway	Holdsworth	McCall	Dawson	Luke (1)	Green	Halliwell	Common	Barlow
Apr 12	Leicester Fosse	Div 2	h	1-0		Toone	McFadyen	Rodway	Holdsworth (1)	McCall	Dawson	Luke	Green	Halliwell	Common	Swarbrick
Apr 19	Stockport County	Div 2	a	1-1		Toone	McFadyen	Rodway	Holdsworth	McCall	Dawson	Luke	Green	Halliwell	Common (1)	Barlow
Apr 26	Blackpool	Div 2	h	2-1		Taylor	McFadyen	Rodway	Holdsworth	McCall	Dawson	Morley	Marshall (1)	Halliwell (1)	Common	Barlow

**Match Report: Morley's Hat-trick at the Devil's Elbow –
1 January 1913. Glossop 2 Preston 3**

North End brought in the New Year by visiting the curious little Glossop ground in the Lee of the Devil's Elbow. But with the local mills in full work on the day, a fair proportion of the small gate hailed from Preston as a football special train had been laid on. Glossop's goalkeeper was Causer who later joined Preston. After a slow start Preston forced the game for a while and their fans thought they had taken the lead but Marshall's bundled effort was disallowed as the referee had adjudged that he had handled the ball into the net. As if! In fact the mark of the ball was clearly seen on Marshall's white shirt. The playing surface was more like a ploughed field than a football pitch, but the conditions were the same for both teams so they had to get on with it. After 22 minutes Glossop's centre-half, Bowden, pushed the ball up field to his forwards. McFadyen completely lost the ball in flight leaving Hodgkinson a clear run at goal. Trying to centre for his colleagues running in he clumsily sliced the ball which then fortuitously sailed over Taylor's head and into the Preston net. A strange goal but they all count. The visitors pressed forward but bottom of the league, Glossop held onto their lead until the half-time break. Preston then equalised straight after the break when Morley scored. Taking an angled pass he appeared to lose control but he regained his posture to drive a fast oblique shot over Causer and underneath the crossbar. Preston's joy was shortlived though as Cooper, Glossop's young right-winger, regained the lead for his team. Determined not to be defeated Preston then equalised for a second time with Morley again the marksman. Although it was a scrambled effort, squeezing the ball just inside the post, he at least showed some enterprise. The winning goal also deservedly fell to Morley as he controlled Common's breast-high pass, hooked the ball over Causer and then ran round him to successfully finish the move off. It had been a tremendous second half from the Lilywhites and by Morley in particular. The hat-trick hero was carried off the pitch shoulder-high by enthusiastic Preston fans. The result put them on top of the league for the first time this season.

SEASON 1913–1914

Preston began to acquire a reputation as a yo-yo side during this period in their history. After the euphoria of their Championship and promotion triumph the year before, the realities suddenly hit them hard as they struggled to adapt to the top division again in 1913–14. Once again there was a huge turnaround of players coming and going as the Preston management searched for, not only players who would be good enough but also the right blend and balance. The summer of 1913 had seen Preston prepare well and the club was eager to make a good start when the season opened. In fact they made an awful start! It was not until the tenth game of the new campaign that they registered their first win, 2–1 over Burnley. But this was immediately followed by four straight defeats and the club was always paddling upstream against a fierce current after that. Goals were hard to come by, a fact recognised by the committee as they sought to change things around. To this end they moved Fred Osborn, signed from Leicester Fosse in the summer, to the centre-forward berth. Earlier he had played at inside-forward and had failed to score. But in his second game at centre-forward he scored a hat-trick and went on to become very prolific after the turn of the year. Not many players had gone 12 games without scoring and then notched a hat-trick in the first game he did score in! And to add to the strange facts he then scored another hat-trick in his first FA Cup-tie. If Osborn was the success story of the season then other players struggled to come to terms with Division One. Charlie McFadyen lost his consistency, and ultimately his place in the team, and Eddie Holdsworth missed games due to injury. The lack of a settled half-back line caused problems all year, an ironic fact, as that had

been the backbone of their success in 1912–13. Christmas 1913 was a nightmare for all Preston fans as Blackburn Rovers thrashed North End twice, on both Christmas Day and Boxing Day. Rovers were on their way to a Championship which they had dominated. In the FA Cup North End had a short run but it came to an end in a third round defeat at Sunderland. That was a disappointment but at least the Deepdale club made more of a fight of it in their league games after the New Year. They registered some good wins but alas the awful start had left a big points gap to overcome and although a spirited attempt was made it proved too great a task. In the end they finished four points adrift of Sheffield Wednesday, a team that, ironically, Preston had beaten 5–0 at Deepdale. So, another relegation season and with war clouds also gathering across Europe it was indeed a gloomy time for everyone. With Preston relegated and Blackburn Champions it could not have been worse for all true North Enders.

DEBUTANTS: (13) John Bond, Thomas Broome, John Ford, William Henderson (No1), Walter Holbem, Charles Jones, James Kennedy, James Macauley, Fred Osborn, Charles Pinch, Frank Shanley, Alf Toward, Simeon Vickers

LAST GAMES: (13) Taylor, McFadyen, Common, Halliwell, Marshall J. (No1), Swarbrick, Johnston, Kennedy, Pinch, Shanley, Vickers, Green and Bond.

Three Future Players are known to have been born during the 1913–14 season. They were Jimmy Dougal, Len Gallimore and the one and only Bill Shankly who was born on 2 September 1913

Ever presents: None	**FA Cup:** Third Round
Manager: Management Committee	**Chairman:** Mr W. E. Ord J. P.
Hat-tricks: (3) Osborn, 2 league 1 FAC	**Players used:** 28

Leading scorer: 26 goals – Fred Osborn (22 League 4 Cup)

AUTHORS' UNOFFICIAL PLAYER OF THE SEASON: Fred Osborn

STAT FACTS:
Best home run without defeat: 7 games
Best away run without defeat: 1 game
Longest run unbeaten: 3 games
Longest run without a win: 9 games

Trivia Fact:

It was not a happy Christmas for Charlie McFadyen as he unluckily broke a leg in the Christmas Day game against Blackburn at Ewood.

Joe McCall, PNE and England Centre-half.

JOE McCALL.
England and North End Centre-half.
Born at Kirkham. Joined North End in Season 1905-6.
Signed professional form July 20th, 1906. 328 League appearances.
Internationals—v. Scotland, 1913, 1914, 1920; v. Scotland (two Victory
Internationals), 1919; v. Wales, 1913; v. Ireland, 1920-21.
Inter-League—v. Ireland, 1919; v. Scotland, 1920.
Trial Matches, 1914 (2), 1920 (2). Professionals v. Amateurs, 1914.
First Benefit (with Holdsworth) v. Bristol City, Jan. 25th, 1913.
Second Benefit, December 11th, 1920 v. Oldham Athletic.

Match Report: A Win at Last – 25 Oct 1913 Preston 2 Burnley 1

With confidence at a very low ebb due to Preston not winning any of their first nine games back in the First Division, they could not have made a worse start than in this derby game with Burnley. The dependable Rodway had cried off with an ankle injury giving Broadhurst only his fifth appearance in four seasons, and Henderson was pressed into his league baptism through Dawson's indisposition. Within the first 90 seconds Burnley had twice broken through North End's patched up defence only to be whistled offside. Their third attempt however proved to be more successful as Freeman and Nesbitt found the Preston rearguard all at sea. Joe McCall raced back to stop a goalbound shot on the line but, in falling, his clearance was below strength and picked up by Hodgson and the ex Chorley player promptly put the ball into the Preston net. Taylor had no chance and was picking the ball out of his net with only two minutes gone. Broadhurst had to deal with two further rushes down the right-hand side before North End developed their first attack. Preston began to settle after this poor start with Barlow in particular looking to open up the Burnley defence. He engineered some nice openings only to see the front trio squander the chances. From a scrappy tussle in front of Dawson, the Burnley keeper, the ball was delivered up to Freeman who raced down the centre of the field with his pursuers in tow. Broadhurst and McFadyen closed in on him as he hit a good shot just wide. All three players collided with McFadyen coming off worse as he twisted his knee badly. All this and only 15 minutes played. McFadyen went out to the right wing limping on one leg as Alf Common dropped back into the full-back role. But North End overcame their problems and worked hard although the splendid endeavours of Barlow were still being wasted by his colleagues. Eventually though Preston equalised. McCall was instrumental in the goal on 35 minutes as he took possession in midfield before pushing forward his powerful run piercing the Burnley defence. His great defence splitting pass found Toward, who controlled it, turned, and shot all in one swift movement. It was a great goal. 28,000 people saw Burnley begin the second half in determined fashion but Preston again wrestled the initiative from them. A draw still looked the best bet though until McCall suddenly found Barlow in an excellent position with just seven minutes left. This time Barlow, the amateur, had a go himself and surprised Dawson in the Burnley goal with a well hit shot. For once the Preston fans were able to go home happy, although their team still floundered at the foot of the table. But at least they had a rare win to cheer.

Left to right: *Back row:* McFadyen, Holdsworth, Taylor, McCall, Henderson, Dawson, Broadhurst.
Front row: Morley, Common, Osborn, Macauley, G. H. Barlow

Season 1913–14: First Division

	P	W	D	L	F	A	Pts
1 Blackburn	38	20	11	7	78	42	51
2 Aston Villa	38	19	6	13	65	50	44
3 Oldham	38	17	9	12	55	45	43
4 Middlesbrough	38	19	5	14	77	60	43
5 WBA	38	15	13	10	46	42	43
6 Bolton	38	16	10	12	65	52	42
7 Sunderland	38	17	6	15	63	52	40
8 Chelsea	38	16	7	15	46	55	39
9 Bradford City	38	12	14	12	40	40	38
10 Sheffield United	38	16	5	17	63	60	37
11 Newcastle	38	13	11	14	39	48	37
12 Burnley	38	12	12	14	61	53	36
13 Man City	38	14	8	16	51	53	36
14 Man United	38	15	6	17	52	62	36
15 Everton	38	12	11	15	46	55	35
16 Liverpool	38	14	7	17	46	62	35
17 Tottenham	38	12	10	16	50	62	34
18 Wednesday	38	13	8	17	53	70	34
19 PRESTON	**38**	**12**	**6**	**20**	**52**	**69**	**30**
20 Derby	38	8	11	19	55	71	27

League appearances (38 games)

Barlow G. H. 34, Bond J. 1, Broadhurst F. 25, Broome T. A. 15, Common A. 14, Dawson G. 27, Ford J. 18, Green B. H. 7, Halliwell J. A. 4, Henderson W. (No. 1) 8, Holbem W. 8, Holdsworth E. 27, Johnston J. 7, Jones C. E. 2, Kennedy J. 3, McCall J. 29, McFadyen C. 16, Macauley J. L. 22, Marshall J. (No. 1) 10, Morley J. B. 21, Osborn F. 35, Pinch C. E. 3, Rodway T. 25, Shanley F. 1, Swarbrick W. 3, Taylor H. 34, Toward A. N. 18, Vickers S. 1.

FA Cup appearances (3 games)

Taylor 3, Broadhurst 3, Rodway 1, Holbem 2, Holdsworth 3, McCall 1, Toward 2, Dawson 3, Ford 3, Marshall 3, Osborn 3, Macauley 3, Barlow 3.

Goalscorers: 52 League–6 Cup–(Total 58)

Osborn 22 (3 pens)–4 (2 pens) (26), Macauley 7–0 (7), Toward 4–0 (4), Barlow 3–1 (4), Marshall 2–1 (3), Common 2–0 (2), Ford 2–0 (2), McCall 2–0 (2), Morley 2–0 (2), Swarbrick 2–0 (2), Dawson 1–0 (1), Henderson 1–0 (1), Kennedy 1–0 (1), Bond 1–0 (1).

League position in Division One: 19th (Relegated) – P38 W12 D6 L20 F52 A69 Pts 30
Home: W9 D4 L6 F39 A31   Away: W3 D2 L14 F13 A38

Date 1913-14	Opponents	Comp	h or a	Score	Att.	1	2	3	4	5	6	7	8	9	10	11
Sep 1	Sunderland	Div 1	h	2-2		Taylor	McFadyen	Rodway	Holdsworth	McCall (1)	Dawson	Morley	Green	Halliwell	Common (1)	Barlow
Sep 6	Everton	Div 1	a	0-2		Taylor	McFadyen	Rodway	Holdsworth	McCall	Dawson	Morley	Green	Halliwell	Osborn	Barlow
Sep 13	WBA	Div 1	h	0-2		Taylor	McFadyen	Rodway	Johnston	McCall	Dawson	Morley	Green	Halliwell	Common	Barlow
Sep 17	Bradford City	Div 1	a	0-0		Taylor	McFadyen	Rodway	Holdsworth	McCall	Dawson	Morley	Common	Green	Osborn	Barlow
Sep 20	Sheffield Wed.	Div 1	a	1-2		Taylor	McFadyen	Rodway	Johnston	McCall	Dawson	Morley (1)	Common	Green	Osborn	Barlow
Sep 27	Bolton W.	Div 1	h	1-1		Taylor	McFadyen	Rodway	Johnston	McCall (1)	Dawson	Morley	Common	Marshall	Osborn	Barlow
Oct 4	Chelsea	Div 1	a	0-2		Taylor	McFadyen	Rodway	Johnston	McCall	Dawson	Morley	Common	Marshall	Osborn	Barlow
Oct 11	Oldham Ath.	Div 1	h	0-1		Taylor	McFadyen	Rodway	Holdsworth	McCall	Dawson	Morley	Common	Toward	Osborn	Barlow
Oct 18	Manchester Utd.	Div 1	a	0-3		Taylor	McFadyen	Rodway	Johnston	McCall	Dawson	Marshall	Green	Toward	Osborn	Barlow
Oct 25	Burnley	Div 1	h	2-1		Taylor	McFadyen	Broadhurst	Johnston	McCall	Henderson	Morley	Common	Toward (1)	Osborn	Barlow (1)
Nov 1	Tottenham H.	Div 1	h	1-2		Taylor	McFadyen	Broadhurst	Holdsworth	McCall	Henderson	Morley	Common (1)	Toward	Osborn	Barlow
Nov 8	Newcastle Utd.	Div 1	a	0-2		Taylor	Broadhurst	Rodway	Johnston	McCall	Henderson	Morley	Common	Toward	Osborn	Dawson
Nov 15	Liverpool	Div 1	h	0-1		Taylor	Broadhurst	Rodway	Holdsworth	McCall	Henderson	Morley	Osborn	Toward	Macauley	Swarbrick
Nov 22	Aston Villa	Div 1	a	0-3		Taylor	McFadyen	Broadhurst	Holdsworth	McCall	Henderson	Morley	Common	Osborn	Macauley	Barlow
Nov 29	Middlesbrough	Div 1	h	4-1		Vickers	McFadyen	Rodway	Holdsworth	McCall	Henderson (1)	Ford	Common	Osborn (3)	Macauley	Barlow
Dec 6	Sheffield Utd.	Div 1	a	0-2		Taylor	McFadyen	Rodway	Dawson	McCall	Henderson	Ford	Green	Halliwell	Osborn	Barlow
Dec 13	Derby County	Div 1	h	2-0		Shanley	McFadyen	Rodway	Holdsworth	McCall	Dawson	Ford	Common	Osborn	Macauley (2)	Barlow
Dec 20	Manchester City	Div 1	a	1-1		Taylor	Broadhurst	Rodway	Holdsworth	McCall	Dawson	Ford	Common	Osborn (1)	Macauley	Barlow
Dec 25	Blackburn Rovers	Div 1	a	0-5		Taylor	McFadyen	Rodway	Holdsworth	McCall	Dawson	Morley	Osborn	Toward	Macauley	Barlow
Dec 26	Blackburn Rovers	Div 1	h	1-5		Taylor	Broadhurst	Rodway	Holdsworth	McCall	Dawson	Ford	Marshall	Broome	Osborn	Barlow (1)
Dec 27	Everton	Div 1	h	1-0		Taylor	Broadhurst	Rodway	Holdsworth	McCall	Henderson	Morley (1)	Marshall	Broome	Osborn	Barlow
Jan 1	Sunderland	Div 1	a	1-3		Taylor	Broadhurst	Rodway	Holdsworth	McCall	Pinch	Morley	Marshall	Broome	Osborn (1)	Barlow
Jan 3	WBA	Div 1	a	0-1		Taylor	Broadhurst	Holbem	Holdsworth	McCall	Pinch	Morley	Osborn	Broome	Macauley	Barlow
Jan 10	Bristol Rovers Rd 1	FAC	h	5-2	13500	Taylor	Broadhurst	Rodway	Holdsworth	McCall	Dawson	Ford	Marshall (1)	Osborn (3,2p)	Macauley	Barlow (1)
Jan 17	Sheffield Wed.	Div 1	h	5-0		Taylor	Broadhurst	Holbem	Holdsworth	McCall	Broome	Ford	Marshall (1)	Osborn (3)	Macauley	Barlow (1)
Jan 24	Bolton W.	Div 1	a	3-0		Taylor	Broadhurst	Holbem	Holdsworth	Toward	Broome	Ford (2)	Marshall	Osborn (1)	Macauley	Barlow
Jan 31	Glossop North End Rd 2	FAC	a	1-0	10731	Taylor	Broadhurst	Holbem	Holdsworth	Toward	Dawson	Ford	Marshall	Osborn (1)	Macauley	Barlow
Feb 7	Chelsea	Div 1	h	3-3		Taylor	Broadhurst	Holbem	Holdsworth	Toward	Broome	Ford	Marshall (1)	Osborn (2,1p)	Macauley	Barlow
Feb 14	Oldham Ath.	Div 1	a	0-1		Taylor	Broadhurst	Holbem	Holdsworth	McCall	Dawson	Ford	Marshall	Osborn	Macauley	Barlow
Feb 21	Sunderland Rd 3	FAC	a	0-2	34448	Taylor	Broadhurst	Holbem	Holdsworth	Toward	Dawson	Ford	Marshall	Osborn	Macauley	Barlow
Feb 28	Burnley	Div 1	a	4-3		Taylor	Broadhurst	Rodway	Holdsworth	Broome	Dawson	Ford	Toward (1)	Osborn (2)	Macauley (1)	Barlow
Mar 5	Manchester Utd.	Div 1	h	4-2		Taylor	Broadhurst	Rodway	Holdsworth	Toward	Dawson	Ford	Morley	Osborn (2)	Macauley	Swarbrick (2)
Mar 7	Tottenham H.	Div 1	a	0-1		Taylor	Toward	Broadhurst	Holdsworth	Broome	Dawson	Ford	Morley	Osborn	Macauley	Barlow
Mar 14	Newcastle Utd.	Div 1	h	4-1		Taylor	Toward	Broadhurst	Broome	McCall	Dawson	Ford	Morley	Osborn (2)	Macauley (2)	Barlow
Mar 21	Liverpool	Div 1	a	1-3		Taylor	Broadhurst	Holbem	Holdsworth	McCall	Dawson	Ford	Morley	Osborn (1)	Macauley	Swarbrick
Apr 1	Aston Villa	Div 1	h	3-2		Taylor	Broadhurst	Rodway	Broome	McCall	Dawson	Ford	Toward	Osborn (2,1p)	Macauley (1)	Barlow
Apr 4	Middlesbrough	Div 1	a	1-4		Taylor	Broadhurst	Rodway	Broome	Toward	Dawson	Ford	Kennedy (1)	Osborn	Macauley	Barlow
Apr 10	Bradford City	Div 1	h	2-1		Taylor	Broadhurst	Rodway	Holdsworth	McCall	Dawson	Kennedy	Toward (1)	Osborn (1p)	Macauley	Barlow
Apr 11	Sheffield Utd.	Div 1	a	2-4		Taylor	Broadhurst	Rodway	Holdsworth	Broome	Dawson	Ford	Kennedy	Toward (1)	Macauley (1)	Barlow
Apr 18	Derby County	Div 1	a	1-0		Jones	Broadhurst	Holbem	Holdsworth	Toward	Dawson	Ford	Broome	Osborn	Macauley	Barlow
Apr 25	Manchester City	Div 1	h	2-2		Jones	Broadhurst	Holbem	Holdsworth	Pinch	Dawson (1)	Bond (1)	Broome	Osborn	Macauley	Barlow

Match Report: Turf Moor Thriller – 28 February 1914 Burnley 3 Preston 4

The referee, Mr Fletcher of Bury, did not have a good afternoon in this local derby, making frequent mistakes at crucial stages of the game. (So, what's new?). This seven goal thriller began with North End taking the lead through Macauley with a hotly disputed goal. Dawson, the Burnley keeper, chased the referee all the way to the centre-circle, vehemently claiming that Macauley had brought the ball under control with his hand before shooting past him. Obviously the referee missed that one! Burnley then equalised with a penalty from Boyle, again hotly disputed, because the way it was achieved angered Preston's players and fans alike. The ball had been intentionally played against the defender's hand in such a manner that the poor fellow could not get out of the way. One all, and tempers frayed. The home side then took the lead from a free-kick given by the referee, his interpretation of Rodway's well timed tackle not being the same as everyone else's view of the incident. Boyle was not complaining as he stroked home his second goal from the kick. Mosscrop increased Burnley's lead but with North End seemingly down and out the visitors then conjured up a remarkable fightback, much to Burnley's dismay. Osborn pulled one goal back with a hooked volley from Ford's centre and from yet another free-kick Osborn equalised. The winning goal had to come about in suspect circumstances and so it proved. In a crowded active goalmouth, Burnley's defender, Taylor, was 'accidentally' injured and was lying prostrate on the ground. The referee did not spot anything wrong as North End's Toward powered home the winner. It was only when the referee had indicated the goal that he noticed the injured player. It had not been a game for the faint hearted and North End's victory had been the direct outcome of hard work, team spirit and fine opportunism. What a pity they did not have a system to play to.

SEASON 1914–1915

This was the last season of organised Football League action before the enforced shutdown caused by the outbreak of what became known as The Great War. Preston North End again proved that they were too good for Division Two as their relegation of the previous season was immediately reversed into a promotion spot as runners-up to Derby County. The club continued their yo-yo existence and the season was very similar to the 1912–13 term. With a tremendous home record and twenty wins in all paving the way for their success, Preston played some excellent football and as in all the previous 26 seasons of league football there were many outstanding individual performances. Joe McCall had his best season to date and the goalscoring duo of Fred Osborn and James Macauley proved a fine partnership. Eddie Holdsworth was back to his best at wing-half and Fred Broadhurst brought some stability to the right-back position. As you read this season by season account of Preston's league history you will notice just how important a good start has been for the club. In this 1914–15 season North End lost just one of their first eight games and although the away form was again patchy they did improve their play away from Deepdale after Christmas. There was one superb run between February and April which produced a new club record of ten consecutive victories. As far as Preston's title aspirations went, it was probably decided at the festive holiday in December. A home defeat by Champions elect Derby, and only one point from two games with lowly Lincoln cost the Lilywhites dearly. In the final outcome those results were crucial especially as Preston lost the title by losing 2–0 at Derby on the last day of the season. If North End had won that game they would have pipped Derby, but, alas, it was not to be. As in many Preston seasons, 'If only' was a phrase much used by the club's followers. Other players served the club well through this campaign with Tommy Broome, George Dawson and Walter Holbem making telling contributions. At the turn of the year Charlie Jones became the regular keeper and played very well indeed, sustaining his form right through to the end of the season. Fred Osborn was again top scorer and once again he had some devastating spells of scoring. In one

particular run he hit nine goals in six games around February. The FA Cup did not live up to expectations as Preston fell at the first hurdle, going out to Manchester City after a replay. That early exit did help their league form and the players put in 100% effort to try to win promotion again. The effort was duly rewarded and it was nice to know that the club went into the uncertainties of some difficult war years in the knowledge that when normality was restored the club would be returning to Division One again.

DEBUTANTS: (9) Anthony Alstead, John Barbour, William Clifton, George Dexter, Wilfred Gillow, Duncan Grant, William Hayes, Hugh Kelly, Sydney Newton.

LAST GAMES: (13) Barbour, Barlow, Dexter, Ford, Grant, Hayes, Holbem, Kelly, Macauley, Morley, Newton, Rodway and Toward.

1. D. C. Grant 2. John Barbour 3. G. H. Barlow
4. C. E. Jones 5. W. Hayes 6. J. McGuire 7. G. Dexter
8. Hugh Kelly

Ever presents: None
FA Cup: First Round Replay
Hat-tricks: None Players used: 24
Manager: Management Committee
Chairman: Mr W. E. Ord J. P.
Leading scorer: 17 goals – Fred Osborn (all league)
AUTHORS' UNOFFICIAL PLAYER OF THE SEASON:
Joe McCall

League position in Division Two: Runners-up – P38 W20 D10 L8 F61 A42 Pts 50
Home: W14 D4 L1 F41 A16 Away: W6 D6 L7 F20 A26

Match Report: Wet, Wet, Wet – 3 Apr 1915 Preston 2 Leeds City 0

For this league game against the soon to be disbanded Leeds City club, the Deepdale pitch was a quagmire with more water on it than grass! Even so, ninety minutes of aggressive, competitve football was witnessed as both teams tried hard to put on a good Easter show. Many of the games early moves were obviously spoilt by the awful conditions as the players, quite literally, tried to find their feet. Leeds had the better early chances and should have scored, but stout defending by Rodway and Broadhurst kept the Yorkshiremen at bay. It was North End who eventually opened the scoring after 18 minutes. Morley was fouled twenty yards out and a free-kick was awarded. Up strode McCall from the back and it was well within his capabilities to hit one from this range and so it proved as he let fly. McQuillan, the Leeds right-back, made a big effort to block the shot but it had been struck with perfection and the net bulged, much to the delight of the holiday crowd. After the goal North End kept their foot on the accelerator, so to speak, and soon afterwards they were awarded a penalty for a foul on Dawson. Toward placed the ball where he thought the penalty spot was and succeeded in scoring with his shot. However, the referee, Mr Eccles from Darwen, had spotted an infringement and ordered the kick to be retaken. This time Toward's shot struck the upright and the ball was scrambled clear by the Leeds' defenders. This encouraged the visitors and they fought hard for an equaliser, but the Preston half-back line stood firm and they were much too powerful for the City forwards. Both Morley and Ford were crudely injured during the course of the first-half by desperate challenges, but the referee gave them the benefit of the doubt due to the conditions and the offenders escaped lightly. Mind you, Jackson had to be lectured for kicking out at Macauley just before half-time. After the resumption both sides made a go of it regardless of the discomfort of continuous mud baths! Towards the end of the contest, Morley, whose knee had been injured in the first half, changed places with Ford and drifted out wide. North End reaped their just rewards with just two minutes remaining. Rodway, who had excelled in the atrocious conditions, lobbed a long ball into the goalmouth for the struggling Morley to painfully thump a shot against the goalkeeper's body. The ever alert Macauley reacted quickly and latched onto the rebound to crash the ball into the net and clinch what was to prove vital points in Preston's quest for promotion and First Division football.

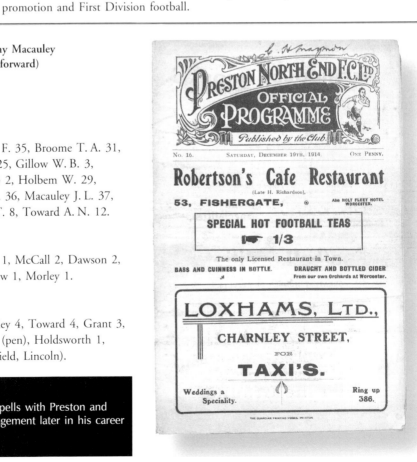

Jimmy Macauley
(inside forward)

League appearances (38 games)

Alstead A. 3, Barbour J. 12, Barlow G. H. 17, Broadhurst F. 35, Broome T. A. 31, Clifton W. 1, Dawson G. 26, Dexter G. 1, Ford J. 25, Gillow W. B. 3, D. C. Grant 9, Hayes W. 10, Henderson W. (No 1) 2, Holbem W. 29, Holdsworth E. 35, Jones C. E. 20, Kelly H. 4, McCall J. 36, Macauley J. L. 37, Morley J. B. 28, Newton S. 8, Osborn F. 26, Rodway T. 8, Toward A. N. 12.

FA Cup appearances (2 games)

Jones 2, Broadhurst 2, Holbem 2, Holdsworth 1, Toward 1, McCall 2, Dawson 2, Ford 2, Osborn 2, Broome 2, Macauley 2, Barlow 1, Morley 1.

Goalscorers: 61 League only

Osborn 17 (2 pens), Macauley 16, McCall 5 (1 pen), Morley 4, Toward 4, Grant 3, Ford 2, Barbour 2, Barlow 1, Broome 1, Broadhurst 1 (pen), Holdsworth 1, Dawson 1, Gillow 1, Kelly 1, Own Goal 1 (Wield, Lincoln).

Trivia Fact:

Wilfred B. Gillow had two spells with Lancaster Town two spells with Preston and two spells with Grimsby Town. He turned his hand to management later in his career and spent ten years as manager of Middlesbrough.

PNE at Blackpool's Norbreak Hydro Hotel. Trainer Jack Barton at the front, Joe McCall at the end.

Season 1914–15: Second Division

	P	W	D	L	F	A	Pts
1 Derby	38	23	7	8	71	33	53
2 PRESTON	**38**	**20**	**10**	**8**	**61**	**42**	**50**
3 Barnsley	38	22	3	13	51	51	47
4 Wolves	38	19	7	12	77	52	45
5 Arsenal	38	19	5	14	69	41	43
6 Birmingham	38	17	9	12	62	39	43
7 Hull	38	19	5	14	65	54	43
8 Huddersfield	38	17	8	13	61	42	42
9 Clapton Orient	38	16	9	13	50	48	41
10 Blackpool	38	17	5	16	58	57	39
11 Bury	38	15	8	15	61	56	38
12 Fulham	38	15	7	16	53	47	37
13 Bristol City	38	15	7	16	62	56	37
14 Stockport	38	15	7	16	54	60	37
15 Leeds City	38	14	4	20	65	64	32
16 Lincoln	38	11	9	18	46	65	31
17 Grimsby	38	11	9	18	48	76	31
18 Nottingham Forest	38	10	9	19	43	77	29
19 Leicester Fosse	38	10	4	24	47	88	24
20 Glossop NE	38	6	6	26	31	87	18

Date 1914-15	Opponents	Comp	h or a	Score	Att.	1	2	3	4	5	6	7	8	9	10	11		
Sep 1	Grimsby Town	Div 2	a	2-2		Newton	Broadhurst	Holbem	Holdsworth	McCall	Dawson	Morley	Barbour	Toward	Macauley (1)	Kelly (1)		
Sep 5	Huddersfield	Div 2	h	1-1		Hayes	Broadhurst	Holbem	Holdsworth	McCall	Dawson	Morley	Barbour	Toward (1)	Macauley	Kelly		
Sep 7	Grimsby Town	Div 2	h	3-0		Hayes	Dexter	Broadhurst	Holdsworth	McCall (2,1p)	Henderson	Morley	Barbour	Broome	Macauley (1)	Kelly		
Sep 12	Bristol City	Div 2	a	0-4		Hayes	Broadhurst	Holbem	Holdsworth	McCall	Henderson	Morley	Toward	Osborn	Macauley	Broome		
Sep 19	Bury	Div 2	h	2-0		Hayes	Broadhurst	Holbem	Holdsworth	McCall	Dawson	Morley	Broome	Osborn (1)	Macauley (1)	Barlow		
Sep 26	Blackpool	Div 2	a	2-0		Hayes	Broadhurst	Holbem	Holdsworth	McCall	Dawson	Ford	Broome	Osborn	Macauley (1)	Barlow (1)		
Oct 3	Nottm. Forest	Div 2	a	1-1		Hayes	Broadhurst	Rodway	Holdsworth	McCall	Dawson	Ford	Grant	Osborn (1)	Macauley	Barlow		
Oct 10	Leicester Fosse	Div 2	h	1-0		Hayes	Broadhurst	Holbem	Broome	McCall	Dawson	Ford	Morley	Osborn (1)	Macauley	Barlow		
Oct 17	Barnsley	Div 2	a	1-2		Hayes	Broadhurst	Holbem	Holdsworth	McCall	Dawson	Ford	Morley	Osborn (1)	Macauley	Barlow		
Oct 24	Glossop North End	Div 2	a	1-0		Hayes	Broadhurst	Holbem	Holdsworth	McCall	Broome	Morley	Barbour	Osborn	Macauley (1)	Barlow		
Oct 31	Wolverhampton W.	Div 2	a	0-2		Hayes	Broadhurst	Holbem	Holdsworth	McCall	Broome	Morley	Barbour	Osborn	Macauley	Barlow		
Nov 7	Fulham	Div 2	h	2-1		Jones	Rodway	Holbem	Holdsworth	McCall	Dawson	Ford	Morley	Osborn	Macauley (2)	Barlow		
Nov 14	Stockport County	Div 2	a	1-2		Jones	Broadhurst	Holbem	Holdsworth	Broome	Dawson	Ford	Barbour	Osborn (1)	Macauley	Barlow		
Nov 21	Hull City	Div 2	h	2-1		Newton	Broadhurst (1p)	Holbem	Holdsworth	McCall	Broome	Morley	Barbour	Grant (1)	Macauley	Barlow		
Nov 28	Leeds City	Div 2	h	0-0		Newton	Broadhurst	Holbem	Holdsworth	McCall	Broome	Morley	Barbour	Grant	Macauley	Barlow		
Dec 5	Clapton Orient	Div 2	h	2-2		Newton	Broadhurst	Holbem	Holdsworth	McCall (1)	Broome	Morley	Barbour (1)	Grant	Macauley	Barlow		
Dec 12	Arsenal	Div 2	a	2-1		Newton	Broadhurst	Holbem	Holdsworth	McCall (1)	Broome	Barbour	Toward	Grant (1)	Macauley	Barlow		
Dec 19	Derby County	Div 2	h	1-3		Newton	Broadhurst	Holbem	Holdsworth	McCall	Broome	Barbour	Toward	Grant (1)	Macauley	Barlow		
Dec 25	Lincoln City	Div 2	a	1-3		Newton	Broadhurst	Holbem	Holdsworth	McCall	Broome	Ford	Gillow	Grant	Macauley	Barlow	1 o.g.	(Wield)
Dec 26	Lincoln City	Div 2	h	0-0		Jones	Broadhurst	Rodway	Holbem	Toward	McCall	Broome	Ford	Gillow	Osborn	Macauley	Kelly	
Jan 2	Huddersfield	Div 2	a	1-3		Jones	Rodway	Holbem	Toward	McCall	Broome	Ford	Gillow (1)	Osborn	Macauley	Morley		
Jan 9	**Manchester City Rd 1**	**FAC**	**h**	**0-0**	**14326**	**Jones**	**Broadhurst**	**Holbem**	**Holdsworth**	**McCall**	**Dawson**	**Ford**	**Osborn**	**Broome**	**Macauley**	**Barlow**		
Jan 13	**Manchester City Replay**	**FAC**	**a**	**0-3**	**19985**	**Jones**	**Broadhurst**	**Holbem**	**Toward**	**McCall**	**Dawson**	**Ford**	**Osborn**	**Broome**	**Macauley**	**Morley**		
Jan 23	Bury	Div 2	a	0-0		Newton	Broadhurst	Alstead	Holdsworth	McCall	Dawson	Ford	Osborn	Grant	Macauley	Morley		
Jan 30	Blackpool	Div 2	h	1-0		Jones	Broadhurst	Alstead	Holdsworth	McCall	Dawson	Ford	Barbour (1)	Osborn	Broome	Morley		
Feb 6	Nottm. Forest	Div 2	h	2-2		Jones	Broadhurst	Alstead	Holdsworth	McCall	Dawson	Ford	Osborn (2,1p)	Grant	Macauley	Barlow		
Feb 11	Bristol City	Div 2	h	4-1		Jones	Broadhurst	Holbem	Holdsworth	McCall	Broome	Ford	Morley (1)	Osborn (1)	Macauley (2)	Dawson		
Feb 13	Leicester Fosse	Div 2	a	3-2		Jones	Broadhurst	Holbem	Holdsworth	Toward (1)	Broome	Ford	Morley	Osborn (1)	Macauley (1)	Dawson		
Feb 20	Barnsley	Div 2	h	5-2		Jones	Broadhurst	Holbem	Holdsworth	McCall	Broome	Ford (1)	Morley (1)	Osborn (2,1p)	Macauley	Dawson (1)		
Feb 27	Glossop North End	Div 2	a	1-0		Jones	Broadhurst	Holbem	Holdsworth	McCall	Broome	Ford	Morley	Osborn (1)	Macauley	Dawson		
Mar 6	Wolverhampton W.	Div 2	h	5-3		Jones	Broadhurst	Holbem	Holdsworth (1)	McCall	Broome	Ford	Morley (1)	Osborn (2)	Macauley (1)	Dawson		
Mar 13	Fulham	Div 2	a	2-0		Jones	Broadhurst	Holbem	Holdsworth	McCall	Broome	Ford (1)	Morley	Osborn	Macauley (1)	Dawson		
Mar 20	Stockport County	Div 2	h	2-0		Jones	Broadhurst	Holbem	Holdsworth	McCall	Broome	Ford	Morley	Osborn (1)	Macauley (1)	Dawson		
Mar 27	Hull City	Div 2	a	1-0		Jones	Broadhurst	Holbem	Holdsworth	McCall	Broome (1)	Ford	Morley	Toward	Macauley	Dawson		
Apr 2	Birmingham	Div 2	h	2-0		Jones	Broadhurst	Holbem	Holdsworth	McCall	Broome	Ford	Morley	Toward (2)	Macauley	Dawson		
Apr 3	Leeds City	Div 2	h	2-0		Jones	Broadhurst	Rodway	Holdsworth	McCall (1)	Broome	Ford	Morley	Toward	Macauley (1)	Dawson		
Apr 5	Birmingham	Div 2	a	1-1		Jones	Broadhurst	Rodway	Holdsworth	McCall	Broome	Ford	Osborn (1)	Toward	Macauley	Dawson		
Apr 10	Clapton Orient	Div 2	a	1-1		Jones	Broadhurst	Rodway	Holdsworth	McCall	Broome	Clifton	Morley	Osborn	Macauley (1)	Dawson		
Apr 17	Arsenal	Div 2	h	3-0		Jones	Broadhurst	Rodway	Holdsworth	McCall	Broome	Ford	Morley (1)	Osborn (1)	Macauley (1)	Dawson		
Apr 24	Derby County	Div 2	a	0-2		Jones	Broadhurst	Holbem	Holdsworth	McCall	Broome	Ford	Morley	Osborn	Macauley	Dawson		

The First World War Years, 1915–1919

Football did not completely evaporate whilst the Great War was on and the Football Association decided that, in an effort to lift the spirits of those left at home, there should be a certain amount of organised football still played. On 19 July 1915 the FA drew up a set of rules which included: 'That Associations, Leagues and Clubs be allowed to arrange matches without Cups, Medals or other awards to suit local conditions, provided that they do not interfere with the work of those engaged in war-work.' Another rule stated that matches were 'only to be played on Saturday afternoons, and on early closing and other recognised holidays.' More importantly it was stated that, 'No remuneration be paid to players, nor shall there be any registration of players.' This meant that players could be obtained from virtually anywhere, and in Preston's case there were many lads who played just one game, and many others who were 'guesting' from other clubs. They also had an advantage of having Fulwood Barracks close at hand. Many soldiers were stationed there and several were called upon.

There were some strange results during these war-time games, to be expected when realising the make-up of the team in some matches. They suffered some heavy defeats, the worst being at Manchester City on 26 February 1916 and again at Liverpool on September 1918 when the result both times was 8–0! Other teams also suffered through a lack of quality players available though and Preston's best win came at home to Bolton on 11 March 1916 when the result was 6–0.

Trivia Facts:

143 different players played for North End in those 144 games and that included 11 different goalkeepers. Of those 143 players, 56 had just one single appearance and 14 players scored just one single goal. PNE used 'guests' from 43 different football clubs plus one from Wigan Rugby Club, one from Broughton Rangers Rugby Club and also a Yorkshire County Cricketer!

The Yorkshire cricketer who played for North End was Roy Kilner, a left-hand batsman and bowler. After the war his cricket career with Yorkshire won him 9 England Test caps.

There was an admission charge of sixpence for these war-time games but there was a concession for soldiers and sailors in uniform. They were let in at half the price. Meanwhile, at the AGM of the Football Player's Union of 1915 it was reported that many members had failed to fulfil their obligations since the reduction of wages had come into force. Paying their subs was probably the least of their worries as Britain went to war. By November 1915 North End were experiencing some difficulty in team building and had requisitioned more players than any other club in either division of the league. A total of 38 men were used but the club still only scored six goals in 18 hours of toiling. One interesting incident saw the Preston Secretary, a Mr Lees, receive a postcard during December 1915 from two North End fans who were Prisoners of War in Germany. Besides asking about the fortunes of the club they also requested foodstuffs and any other useful articles. Over the Christmas period of 1915 North End played a fund raising friendly against munition workers who included six players with North End connections.

Bert Gilboy, a pre-war North End reject, was playing for Crystal Palace vs. Reading on September 30 1916 and scored such a fine goal that one of the linesmen forgot himself and ran on to the pitch to pat him on the back.

Fred Osborn, the first North Ender to enlist, was wounded on November 10 1918 after three years in France.

Sandy Robertson, a former 'Old Invincible', who had lied about his age to see action, was injured on the war front and brought back to England. He had been hit with a piece of shrapnel which had lodged in the bottom of his right lung and unfortunately it had to stay there. He later called it his 'war medal' as he recovered in a Tooting military hospital.

Walter Holbem was arrested on September 29 1916 for being an absentee under the Military Services Act and after being fined was then handed over to the Army authorities.

Dickie Bond, who was a P.O.W. at Menden, Westphalia, Germany, wrote in a letter to his wife that former North Ender Percy Hartley was also in the same camp. He also said that he was learning to knit and that the weather was nice.

North Enders, John Barbour and John Ford were killed in the early stages of the war as were North End reserve team players Tom Saul and Michael Swarbrick. Ex North Ender William Gerrish was another fatality and Benjamin Green was reported as wounded and missing in June 1917.

Arthur Mounteney played for the Footballer's Battalion XI during the war.

Match Report: A Win At Last –
27 November 1915 Preston 3 Manchester City 2

After a three month wait North End succeeded in encompassing their first victory of the season when least expected. The win came about with the introduction of two 'guest' inside-forwards capable of playing real football. The effect it had on the team was tremendous. Preston born Fazackerley, who had been released by North End, had developed in the USA and since his return from America he had fulfilled his potential playing for Accrington Stanley, Hull City and Sheffield United. His strength, pace and versatility gave Preston an added dimension that had previously been woefully lacking. Not all the improvements however, were due to Fazackerley's inclusion, as the other inside-forward, Williams, a guest from Notts County, played skilfully as well as thoughtfully. Goals from Broome (2),and Fazackerley proved sufficient to beat City for whom McIlwraith scored an own goal.

Match Report: Muted Christmas Derby Win –
26 December 1916 Preston 3 Blackburn 1

Although this match was played on Boxing Day, the absence of the usual keen excitement and colour, due to the hostilities, was noted, as thoughts were obviously elsewhere. The opening skirmishes of the game though produced some decent football with the ground just sufficiently holding to give the players a chance to control the ball. Preston's goalkeeper Taylor was injured very early on in the game and play had to be held up for awhile, but he continued after treatment amid sympathetic applause. Blackburn included Smith, Morris and Swarbrick in their squad, all of whom had represented North End in the past. At length, after 27 minutes play, North End took a deserved lead through Edmondson. Fazackerley started the move, passing out to Barlow who, after beating Crompton, sent over a glorious cross which McIvor could not hold. Edmondson pounced to head home. Preston continued to play in dashing fashion, their football being full of pace and vigour, but they did not at this stage capitalise on their possession. They were punished just prior to the interval when Orr equalised for the Rovers after receiving an accurate pass from Latheron. The second half produced a sensational start as play had only been running for 30 seconds when Barlow collected a pass from Dawson out wide on the wing. The move further involved Fazackerley and Edmondson, with the latter beating McIvor again with another firm header. The Rover's keeper should really have caught the ball but he must have had one eye on Fazackerley who was rushing in on him. Nine minutes later they forged further ahead when Edmondson again collected a pass from Fazackerley to give Preston a fully deserved 3–1 lead which they held on to.

Mr J. I. Taylor, very influential member of the boardroom for many years.

Match Report: North End Come From Behind –
6 October 1917 Oldham 1 Preston 3

A meagre crowd braved a bitterly cold wind on an otherwise fine afternoon to see this Lancashire derby match. North End were first to show with Fazackerley prominent in the early stages. Oldham tried to surge forward when they could but the Preston defence were generally too smart for them. Preston's best play stemmed from their two wingers, Clifton and Barlow who were in good form. It looked as though the visitors had the edge but just at that moment, and against the run of play, Oldham took the lead. 26 minutes of the match had gone when Ousley scored with a fast swerving shot which beat Foot in the Preston goal. Handley had the chance to equalise but sent his effort over the bar when goalkeeper Robinson was completely beaten. At length Preston finally found the target to equalise. Clifton was the goalscorer as he breasted the ball over the line following a scramble. To rub salt into the Latics' wounds Preston took the lead right on the stroke of half-time. This time a 25 yard screamer from Fazackerley beat the keeper and also just beat the referee's whistle for the break. The second half was evenly contested although early on Fazackerley hit the post and Handley then missed a sitter which would have really finished the game. As it was Oldham fought back and pressed forward. Foot made some good saves and his defenders also responded with some good play and gradually the threat of an equaliser petered out. With 12 minutes to go Barlow finished Oldham off with a good goal to seal victory.

THE WAR.

FOOTBALL AND RECRUITING.

PROPOSALS ACCEPTED BY THE WAR OFFICE

Whereby the Sport of Association Football may, in the present great National Emergency, assist in obtaining recruits for the Army.

The Football Association, speaking for all its Members, heartily desires to assist the Authorities, and places its whole organisation and influence at the service of the War Office.

Clubs to be requested to place their Grounds at the disposal of the War Office on days, other than Match Days, for use as Drill Grounds, or as the Service may require.

Where football matches are played arrangements to be made for well-known public men to address the players and spectators, urging men who are physically fit, and otherwise able, to at once enlist. Where practicable Recruiting Stations to be on or adjacent to the Grounds.

The County Football Association, or Club on whose ground the matches are to be played, to arrange details with the District Recruiting Officer, and for these to be made known to the Players and Spectators by posters to be published on the ground, and in the Programme of the Club, and through the Press.

It is hoped that where special matches are arranged to encourage enlistment, the whole of the net gate receipts will be given to a War Relief Fund.

42, RUSSELL SQUARE,
LONDON, W.C.
8th September, 1914.

Letter from the FA regarding The War and football

1915–16 Principal Tournament – Lancashire Section
P26 W4 D2 L20 F23 A 67

Appearances (with Guest source where known): Alstead A. 1, Barbour J. 1, Barlow G.H. 15, Broadhurst F. 9, Brodie A. (Doncaster Rovers) 2, Broome T.A. 19, Carlisle R. (South Liverpool) 1, Chorlton C. (Bury) 1, Clay G. (Exeter City) 13, Clifton W. 8, Crabtree J.J. (Blackburn Rovers) 1, Dempsey A. 3, Edwards E. (Bury) 1, Ellis G. (Accrington) 1, Fazackerley S.N. (Sheffield United) 2, Ford J. 7, Gillow C.R. 1, Gillow W.B. 20, Gornall F. 1, Hayes W. 17, Halliwell J. (Barnsley) 4, Henderson W. 2, Hosker J. 9, Hurst B. (Swansea) 2, Ives C.B. (QPR) 15, Johnson J. 2, Kennedy J. 1, Lee H. (Fulham) 7, Lyon W.J. 3, Macauley J.L. 3, Mawdsley R. 2, McCall J. 21, McIlwraigth F. (Barrow) 9, Morley J.B. 7, Morris R. (Blackburn Rovers) 2, Osborn F. 1, Platt J. 1, Rodway T. 1, Sloan P.R. 1, Smith James (Fulham) 1, Smith John (Reading) 2, Smith P.J. (Blackburn Rovers) 19, Stevens H. 1, Tattum B. (Golbourne) 4, Thompson A. 1, Threlfall T. 13, Timmins B.W. (Aston Villa) 1, Speak G. (West Ham) 15, Williams D. (Notts County) 6, Wilson G. (Gt. Harwood) 6.
A total of 50 players used.

1915–16 Subsidiary Tournament – Lancashire Section (Northern Group)
P10 W4 D2 L4 F22 A19

Aitkenhead W.C. (Blackburn R) 1, Barlow G.H. 8, Broadhurst F. 6, Broome T.A. 6, Clay G. (Exeter City) 1, Clifton W. 3, Dempsey A. 1, Ford J. 3, Gillow W.B. 10, Gimblett G.S. (Bolton) 1, Hayes W. 3, Hosker J. 10, Jackson J. (Leeds City) 2, Joyce T. 1, Kirkman A. 1, Lee H. (Fulham) 3, Lord J. 1, McCall J. 10, Morris R. (Blackburn R) 9, Speak G. (West Ham) 7, Smith Joseph (Bolton) 1, Smith John (Reading) 1, Smith P.J. (Blackburn R) 8, Threlfall T. 4, Vizard E (Bolton) 1, Williams D. (Notts Co.) 2, Wilson G. (Gt. Harwood) 6.
A total of 27 players used.

1915–16 Goalscorers 23 Principal – 22 Subsidiary (Total 45 goals).

Morris 0–8(1p) (8), McCall 2–4(3p) (6), Broome 4–0 (4), Hosker 2–2 (4), Williams 3–1 (4), Smith P.J. 0–4 (4), Barlow 2–1 (3), Clay 2–1 (3), Fazackerley 2(1p)–0 (2), Lee 2–0 (2), Gillow W.B. 1–0 (1), Halliwell 1–0 (1), Macauley 1–0 (1), Speak 1–0 (1), Ford 0–1 (1).

1916–17 Principal Tournament – Lancashire Section
P30 W8 D7 L15 F47 A65

Appearances: Banks F. 1, Barlow G.H. 26, Barnes H. (Man City) 1, Broad T. (Man City) 20, Broadhurst F. 15, Clayton P. 13, Clifton W. 5, Dawson G. 2, Dempsey A. 1, Dixon F. 2, Edmondson J. (Leeds City) 24, Fazackerley S.N. (Sheffield United) 6, Foot G. (Bury) 2, Gimblett G.S. (Bolton) 1, Goddard J. (Exeter) 1, Green J. 4, Henderson W. 1, Hobson J. (Sunderland) 1, Holdsworth E. 23, Hosker J. 25, Jackson J. (Leeds City) 25, Johnson J. 1, Kellock W. (Burnley) 1, Litherland T. 1, Lord J. 1, Mawdsley R. 1, McCall J. 28, Meyler E. 2, Molyneux J. (Chelsea) 1, Morley J.B. 3, Smith N. 1, Smith P.J. (Blackburn R) 1, Speak G. (West Ham) 23, Swarbrick A. 14, Taylor H. (Millwall) 24, Threlfall T. 23, Troughear W. (Sunderland) 1, Thompson A. 2, Wilcock H. 3.
A total of 39 players used.

1916–17 Subsidiary Tournament – Lancashire Section (Northern Group)
P6 W2 D2 L2 F8 A7

Barlow G.H. 4, Broad T. (Man City) 3, Broadhurst F. 1, Caldwell (Oldham) 1, Clifton W. 1, Dawson G. 2, Edmondson J. (Leeds City) 6, Fazackerley S.N. (Sheffield U) 5, Foot G. (Bury) 4, Gillow W.B. 1, Goddard J. (Exeter) 2, Holdsworth E. 6, Hosker J. 2, Jackson J. (Leeds City) 5, McCall J. 6, Meyler E. 3, Speak G. (West Ham) 2, Swarbrick A. 4, Taylor H. (Millwall) 2, Threlfall T. 5.
A total of 20 players used.

1916–17 Goalscorers 47 Principal – 8 Subsidiary (Total 55)

Edmondson 21(4p)–6 (27), Hosker 8–0 (8), Jackson 5–0 (5), Barlow 2–0 (2), Clayton 2–0 (2), Barnes 1–0 (1), Broad 1–0 (1), Clifton 1–0 (1), Holdsworth 1–0 (1), McCall 1–0 (1), Morley 1–0 (1), Speak 1–0 (1), Fazackerley 0–1 (1), Meyler 0–1 (1), Own Goals 2–0 (2)
(Wareing of Burnley and Wareing of Everton).

1917–18 Principal Tournament – Lancashire Section
P30 W12 D3 L15 F38 A53

Appearances: Atkinson A. 1, Bannister J. 5, Barlow G.H. 25, Barnes J. (Broughton Rangers, Rugby) 23, Bibby A. 1, Broad T. (Man City) 1, Broadhurst F. 1, Causer A.H. (Glossop) 19, Clarkson W. (Padiham) 1, Clay J. (Exeter) 2, Clifton W. 26, Cook H. 1, Cook W. (Oldham) 11, Edmondson J. (Leeds City) 4, Fay J. (Southport) 2, Fazackerley S.N. (Sheff.Utd.) 8, Foot G. (Bury) 9, Foster J. 2, Gillow W.B. 2, Gimblett G.S. (Bolton) 1, Goddard J. (Exeter) 21, Green J. 1, Gutridge C. 3, Handley G. (Chesterfield) 2, Hodgkiss J. (Bolton) 2, Holdsworth E. 21, Hosker J. 16, Jackson J. (Leeds City) 12, Johnson J. 1, Kilner R. (Yorkshire CCC) 2, Lavery G.C. (Clapton Orient) 8, Lees J.W. (Northwich Victoria) 16, McCall J. 3, McGuire J. (Chorley) 6, Malkin W. (Clapton Orient) 1, Meyler E. 5, Miller J. (Coventry) 1, Munro J.B. (Queens Park) 2, Orr J. (Blackburn R) 2, Potter J. 1, Rimmer J. (South Liverpool) 8, Robertson W. 2, Sergeant W. 1, Smith J. (Reading) 2, Smith P.J. (Blackburn R) 5, Strickland R.E. 1, Swarbrick A. 10, Tattum B. (Golbourne) 2, Taylor J. 1, Threlfall T. 25, Wilkinson F. 1, Wright J.H. 1.

A total of 52 players used.

1917–18 Subsidiary Tournament – Lancashire Section (Northern Group)
P6 W4 D1 L1 F10 A8

Atkinson A. 3, Bannister J. 2, Barlow G.H. 6, Barnes J. (Broughton Rangers, Rugby) 3, Causer A.H. (Glossop) 6, Clifton W. 6, Gillow W.B. 1, Goddard J. (Exeter) 5, Green J. 1, Gregson J.R. (Kirkham) 1, Holdsworth E. 6, Hosker J. 5, Kilner R. (Yorkshire CCC) 3, Lavery G.C. (Clapton Orient) 6, Lees J.W. (Northwich Victoria) 2, McGuire J. (Chorley) 4, Meyler E. 1, Strickland R.E. 1, Swarbrick A. 1, Threlfall T. 3.

A total of 20 players used.

1917–18 Goalscorers 38 Principal – 10 Subsidiary (Total 48)

Clifton 5–5 (10), Fazackerley 5(2p)–0 (5), Lavery 5–0 (5), Edmondson 4(1p)–0 (4), Jackson 3–0 (3), Barlow 2–1 (3), Hosker 2–1 (3), Meyler 2–0 (2), Bannister 1–1 (2), Barnes 1–1 (2), Holdsworth 1–1 (2), Cook W. 1–0 (1), Fay 1–0 (1), Lees 1–0 (1), McCall 1–0 (1), Sergeant 1–0 (1), Smith P.J. 1–0 (1), Swarbrick 1–0 (1).

1918–19 Principal Tournament – Lancashire Section
P30 W12 D6 L12 F41 A51

Appearances: Abbot J. (Man. City) 1, Alstead A. 1, Ashton E. 1, Bond R. (Bradford City) 1, Broadhurst F. 11, Broome T. A. 15, Carlisle R. (South Liverpool) 1, Causer A. H. 30, Charnley W. 3, Clifton W. 25, Connor E. (Bury) 5, Cook F. 1, Danson H. 1, Davies H. (Chorley) 2, Davies S. (Rochdale) 1, Dawson J. E. (Fleetwood) 1, Dawson W. (Millwall) 6, Eastham J. 2, Edmondson J. (Leeds City) 1, Edwards E. (Chorley) 11, Ellis W. 1, Gillow W. B. 8, Goddard J. (Exeter) 21, Green J. 1, Halliwell J. (Barnsley) 8, Harrison W. (West Ham) 2, Heaton J. (Wigan Rugby Club) 1, Henderson W. 2, Hilton F. A (Southport) 6, Holdsworth E. 30, Holmes J. W. (Port Vale) 1, Hosker J. 26, Howard P.S. 1, Kehoe W. 1, Kilner R. (Yorkshire CCC) 10, Lavery G.C. (Clapton Orient) 3, McCall J. 8, McFadyen C. (Everton) 1, McGuire J. (Chorley) 18, Meyler E. 2, Morley J. B. 2, Morris R. (Blackburn R) 10, Nesbitt W. (Burnley) 1, Osborn F. 1, Oustrey P. 1, Pendlebury J. 1, Ray P. (Blackpool) 1, Roberts W. T. (Southport) 1, Robinson B. (Broughton Rangers Rugby Club) 15, Smith A. (Rochdale) 1, Smith J. (Reading) 2, Speak G. (West Ham) 8, Swarbrick A. 5, Swarbrick M. 1, Threlfall T. 4, Turner H. 1, Wilkinson W. S. 1, Woodhouse R. T. (Lancaster City) 2, Yates J. (Millwall) 1.

A total of 59 players used.

1918–19 Subsidiary Tournament – Lancashire Section (Northern Group)
P6 W3 D1 L2 F6 A7

Alstead A. 1, Bond R. (Bradford City) 1, Broadhurst F. 5, Broome T. A. 5, Carlisle R. (South Liverpool) 1, Causer A.H. 6, Clifton W. 5, Davies S. (Rochdale) 1, Edmondson J. (Leeds City) 2, Ellis W. 1, Gillow W.B. 3, Goddard J. (Exeter) 1, Grant D.C. 1, Green J. 1, Halliwell J. (Barnsley) 4, Henderson W. 1, Hilton F. A. (Southport) 1, Holdsworth E. 4, Hosker J. 3, McCall J. 4, Roberts W. T. (Southport) 1, Schofield G. (Southport) 1, Speak G. 6, Swarbrick M. 1, Woodhouse R. T. (Lancaster City) 3, Yates J. (Millwall) 3.

A total of 26 players used.

1918–19 Goalscorers 41 Principal – 6 Subsidiary (Total 47)

Hosker 7–0 (7), Halliwell 5–2 (7), Clifton 5–0 (5), Hilton 5–0 (5), Morris 4–0 (4), Holdsworth 3–0 (3), Dawson W. 2–0 (2), Gillow 2–0 (2), Woodhouse 1–1 (2), Broome 1–0 (1), Ellis 1–0 (1), Heaton 1–0 (1), McCall 1(1p)–0 (1), Roberts 1–0 (1), Robinson 1–0 (1), Turner 1–0 (1), Edmondson 0–1 (1), Grant 0–1 (1), Green 0–1 (1).

SEASON 1919–1920

The horrors of the Great War, the memory of which would leave such a lasting impression on so many, had at last come to an end, and during the summer of 1919 football clubs up and down the country were trying hard to put together teams in time for the restart of the Football League competition. This was the first seaon of 42 games and although football had been played regularly during the war enthusiasm for the game was understandably muted but if ever the people needed the sport to lift their spirits, it was now. At Preston the club was frantically assembling a playing staff under the direction of the Secretary/Manager, Vincent Hayes who had been appointed in the previous March. In actual fact, as it turned out, Mr Hayes had little control over team affairs as behind the scenes a powerful committee was making all the important decisions. No fewer than 24 players were to make their debut for North End during this first post-war season and this huge change in personnel had a bad affect on the club's form. At the end of the day Preston were lucky to escape relegation. Only two draws in the first six games meant that Preston were off to their customary poor start. But one superb signing was made in the shape of Tommy Roberts who was signed from Leicester Fosse for a £500 fee after having made his mark playing for Southport Vulcan. It was to be probably the best £500 the club had ever spent. His 29 league and cup goals certainly made sure that Preston kept their Division One status. The diminutive Rowland Woodhouse was another who shone throughout this difficult campaign. The defence

was built around the magnificent Joe McCall, one of the few players who had played before the war, and the England international had an excellent year. There were some tough local derbies during the season with the FA Cup-tie against Blackpool giving the fans the most satisfaction. There were other notable results including several doubles, and a 5–2 home win over Sunderland gave much pleasure. Roberts' scoring was spread across the season with one spell of ten games producing eleven goals. In the end though Preston's fate came down to a nailbiting climax. In their last game at Everton the Lilywhites needed a result to avoid the drop. The home side looked certain to win when they were awarded a penalty, but their captain, Dickie Downs, fired his shot into the crowd. Ten minutes later the trusty left foot of Roberts put Preston into a lead they held on to and relegation was averted.

DEBUTANTS: (24) Simpson Bainbridge, Arthur Causer, George Daniel, Stanley Davies, George Foot, Ralph Goodwin, William Greatorex, James Green, William Halligan, John Hosker, Frank Jefferis, Edward Kerr, John Knight, John Lees, John Marshall, Billy Mercer, James Miller, Peter Quinn, Tommy Roberts, George Speak, John Tatton, Thomas Threlfall, Fred Whalley and Rowland Woodhouse.

LAST GAMES: (18) Alstead, Bainbridge, Broome, Clifton, Daniel, Foot, Gillow, Goodwin, Halligan, Henderson, Holdsworth, Jones, Kerr, Miller, Osborn, Tatton, Threlfall and Whalley.

League appearances (42 games)

Alstead A. 11, Bainbridge S. 14, Broadhurst F. 33, Broome T. A. 19, Causer A. H. 17, Clifton W. 3, Daniel G. 12, Davies S. 11, Dawson G. 35, Foot G. 5, Gillow W. B. 4, Goodwin R. 7, Greatorex W. H. A. 17, Green J. 4, Halligan W. 16, Henderson W. 1, Holdsworth E. 12, Hosker J. 10, Jefferis F. 12, Jones C. E. 12, Kerr E. J. 2, Knight J. H. 1, Lees J. W. 20, McCall J. 32, Marshall J. (No. 2) 4, Mercer W. 2, Miller J. 15, Osborn F. 7, Quinn P. 11, Roberts W. T. 35, Speak G. 13, Tatton J. H. 18, Threlfall T. 2, Whalley F. H. 8, Woodhouse R. T. 37.

FA Cup appearances (3 games)

Jones 3, Greatorex 3, Broadhurst 3, Lees 3, McCall 3, Dawson 3, Bainbridge 3, Miller 2, Woodhouse 3, Roberts 3, Daniel 1, Davies 2, Green 1.

Goalscorers: 57 League–5 Cup–(Total 62)

Roberts 26–3 (29), Woodhouse 9–1 (10), Davies 4–0 (4), Jefferis 4–0 (4), Hosker 2–0 (2), Broadhurst 2 (2 pens)–0 (2), Halligan 2–0 (2), Bainbridge 1–1 (2), Broome 1(pen)–0 (1), Daniel 1–0 (1), McCall 1–0 (1), Miller 1–0 (1), Osborn 1–0 (1), Quinn 1–0 (1), Tatton 1–0 (1)

Future Players born between August 1919 and July 1920: Willie McIntosh, Tommy Bogan and Jimmy Wharton
Ever presents: None
FA Cup: Third round
Manager/Secretary: Vincent Hayes
Hat-tricks: None
Chairman: Mr W. E. Ord J. P.
Leading scorer: 29 goals – Tommy Roberts (26 League 3 Cup)
Players used: 35

AUTHORS' UNOFFICIAL PLAYER OF THE SEASON: Tommy Roberts

League position in Division One: 19th – P42 W14 D10 L18 F57 A73 Pts 38
Home: W9 D6 L6 F35 A27 Away: W5 D4 L12 F22 A46

Match Report: Weary Wearsiders Easter Blues – 3 Apr 1920 Preston 5 Sunderland 2

Although the Easter weather was rather tempestuous, and the pitch terribly heavy, 16,000 spectators took time out to be present at the start. Within a couple of minutes of kicking off, North End's goalkeeper, Causer, was put under great pressure by an awful back pass from Greatorex. Jefferis, once he had found his feet, then put a great ball through to Roberts who smacked a well hit right-footed cross shot at Scott, the Sunderland keeper. He was caught by surprise but recovered sufficiently to turn the ball onto the crossbar and away to safety. That was the start of Scott's afternoon but certainly not the end. After eight minutes play a fine pass by Dawson set Miller off down the right-wing. England tried to bring him down but Miller evaded his lunge to deliver a fast cross shot which poor Scott could only divert into the path of Woodhouse who promptly made no mistake in putting North End 1–0 up. The Wearsiders back line successfully played the offside game, too often for the irate Preston fans. Woodhouse and Roberts were playing well together and it came as no surprise when, after 24 minutes, Preston went further ahead. Roberts, taking a ball from midfield, swerved over to his right and as his marker slipped he homed in on goal and scored with a beautiful oblique shot. The cheering had hardly died down when Jefferis sent Roberts away again. He, in turn, fed Quinn who was unmarked. The winger ran on for about ten yards before shooting a high ball beyond the reach of the helpless Scott. Towards half-time Sunderland had a little more of the game but Buchan's shooting was woeful although he did see a header hit the Preston crossbar. Five minutes after the break Sunderland should have pulled a goal back as, with Causer on the floor, Buchan saw McCall successfully slide back to clear off the goalline. Inside-right Crossley had to leave the pitch for treatment and whilst he was gone Preston increased their lead with another Roberts hot-shot. As the game progressed the leather ball became very heavy and in heading out yet another of Quinn's centres Hobson stunned himself. On 65 minutes Preston went nap as Quinn and Woodhouse ran through the visitors weary defence before playing the ball back to McCall who scored his first goal of the season via the underside of the crossbar. Preston then eased off and it enabled Sunderland to pull back a couple of goals through Crossley and Travers, but it was much too little, too late.

Season 1919–20: First Division

	P	W	D	L	F	A	Pts
1 WBA	42	28	4	10	104	47	60
2 Burnley	42	21	9	12	65	59	51
3 Chelsea	42	22	5	15	56	51	49
4 Liverpool	42	19	10	13	59	44	48
5 Sunderland	42	22	4	16	72	59	48
6 Bolton	42	19	9	14	72	65	47
7 Man City	42	18	9	15	71	62	45
8 Newcastle	42	17	9	16	44	39	43
9 Aston Villa	42	18	6	18	75	73	42
10 Arsenal	42	15	12	15	56	58	42
11 Bradford PA	42	15	12	15	60	63	42
12 Man United	42	13	14	15	54	50	40
13 Middlesbrough	42	15	10	17	61	65	40
14 Sheffield United	42	16	8	18	59	69	40
15 Bradford City	42	14	11	17	54	63	39
16 Everton	42	12	14	16	69	68	38
17 Oldham	42	15	8	19	49	52	38
18 Derby	42	13	12	17	47	57	38
19 PRESTON	42	14	10	18	57	73	38
20 Blackburn	42	13	11	18	64	77	37
21 Notts County	42	12	12	18	56	74	36
22 Wednesday	42	7	9	26	28	64	23

Date 1919-20	Opponents	Comp	h or a	Score	Att.	1	2	3	4	5	6	7	8	9	10	11
Aug 30	Blackburn Rovers	Div 1	a	0-4		Causer	Broadhurst	Speak	Holdsworth	McCall	Henderson	Tatton	Davies	Osbom	Halligan	Dawson
Sep 1	Bradford City	Div 1	h	1-5		Causer	Goodwin	Broadhurst	Holdsworth	McCall	Broome	Tatton	Davies (1)	Osbom	Halligan	Daniel
Sep 6	Blackburn Rovers	Div 1	h	0-0		Causer	Goodwin	Speak	Gillow	Broome	Dawson	Tatton	Davies	Roberts	Halligan	Daniel
Sep 10	Bradford City	Div 1	a	2-2		Causer	Goodwin	Speak	Gillow	Broome	Dawson	Tatton	Woodhouse (1)	Roberts (1)	Halligan	Daniel
Sep 13	Manchester Utd	Div 1	a	2-3		Causer	Goodwin	Speak	Gillow	Broome (1p)	Dawson	Tatton	Woodhouse (1)	Roberts	Davies	Daniel
Sep 20	Manchester Utd	Div 1	h	1-5		Causer	Broadhurst	Speak	Gillow	Broome	Dawson	Tatton	Woodhouse	Roberts (1)	Halligan	Daniel
Sep 27	Oldham Ath	Div 1	a	2-1		Whalley	Broadhurst	Alstead	Holdsworth	McCall	Dawson	Tatton	Woodhouse (1)	Roberts (1)	Hosker	Daniel
Oct 4	Oldham Ath	Div 1	a	1-4		Whalley	Broadhurst	Alstead	Holdsworth	McCall	Broome	Tatton	Woodhouse	Roberts	Hosker (1)	Daniel
Oct 11	Aston Villa	Div 1	h	3-0		Whalley	Broadhurst (1p)	Alstead	Broome	McCall	Dawson	Tatton (1)	Woodhouse	Roberts (1)	Hosker	Daniel
Oct 18	Aston Villa	Div 1	a	4-2		Whalley	Broadhurst	Alstead	Broome	McCall	Dawson	Tatton	Woodhouse (1)	Roberts (2)	Hosker (1)	Halligan
Oct 25	Newcastle Utd	Div 1	h	2-3		Whalley	Broadhurst	Alstead	Broome	McCall	Dawson	Tatton	Woodhouse	Roberts (2)	Hosker	Bainbridge
Nov 1	Newcastle Utd	Div 1	a	0-1		Whalley	Broadhurst	Alstead	Broome	McCall	Dawson	Tatton	Woodhouse	Roberts	Halligan	Bainbridge
Nov 8	Chelsea	Div 1	h	3-1		Whalley	Broadhurst (1p)	Alstead	Broome	McCall	Dawson	Tatton	Woodhouse	Roberts (2)	Halligan	Bainbridge
Nov 15	Chelsea	Div 1	a	0-4		Whalley	Broadhurst	Alstead	Broome	McCall	Dawson	Tatton	Woodhouse	Roberts	Halligan	Bainbridge
Nov 22	Liverpool	Div 1	h	2-1		Causer	Broadhurst	Alstead	Holdsworth	McCall	Broome	Tatton	Woodhouse	Osbom (1)	Halligan (1)	Bainbridge
Nov 29	Liverpool	Div 1	a	2-1		Causer	Broadhurst	Alstead	Holdsworth	McCall	Broome	Bainbridge (1)	Woodhouse	Osbom	Halligan (1)	Hosker
Dec 6	Bradford Pk. Av.	Div 1	h	0-3		Causer	Goodwin	Alstead	Holdsworth	McCall	Broome	Tatton	Woodhouse	Osbom	Halligan	Hosker
Dec 13	Bradford Pk. Av.	Div 1	a	3-3		Foot	Goodwin	Broadhurst	Lees	Broome	Dawson	Bainbridge	Woodhouse	Roberts (1)	Davies (2)	Kerr
Dec 20	Burnley	Div 1	h	0-1		Foot	Goodwin	Broadhurst	Lees	Broome	Dawson	Bainbridge	Woodhouse	Roberts	Davies	Halligan
Dec 25	Bolton W.	Div 1	a	1-4		Foot	Speak	Broadhurst	Holdsworth	McCall	Dawson	Bainbridge	Woodhouse (1)	Roberts	Davies	Kerr
Dec 26	Bolton W.	Div 1	h	1-1		Foot	Broome	Broadhurst	Holdsworth	McCall	Mercer	Bainbridge	Woodhouse	Roberts (1)	Davies	Daniel
Dec 27	Burnley	Div 1	a	1-1		Foot	Greatorex	Broadhurst	Broome	McCall	Mercer	Bainbridge	Woodhouse	Osbom	Halligan	Daniel (1)
Jan 1	Sheffield Utd	Div 1	a	1-2		Jones	Broadhurst	Threlfall	Broome	McCall	Dawson	Tatton	Osbom	Davies (1)	Halligan	Daniel
Jan 3	Middlesbrough	Div 1	h	1-4		Jones	Broadhurst	Threlfall	Holdsworth	McCall	Dawson	Tatton	Woodhouse (1)	Roberts	Halligan	Daniel
Jan 10	Stockport County Rd 1	FAC	h	3-1	16657	Jones	Greatorex	Broadhurst	Lees	McCall	Dawson	Bainbridge (1)	Woodhouse (1)	Roberts (1)	Daniel	Green
Jan 17	Middlesbrough	Div 1	h	3-1		Jones	Greatorex	Broadhurst	Lees	McCall	Dawson	Miller	Jefferis (1)	Roberts (2)	Woodhouse	Bainbridge
Jan 24	Notts County	Div 1	a	2-1		Jones	Greatorex	Broadhurst	Lees	McCall	Dawson	Miller	Jefferis	Roberts (2)	Woodhouse	Bainbridge
Jan 31	Blackpool Rd 2	FAC	h	2-1	23153	Jones	Greatorex	Broadhurst	Lees	McCall	Dawson	Miller	Woodhouse	Roberts (2)	Davies	Bainbridge
Feb 7	Sheffield Wed	Div 1	a	1-0		Jones	Greatorex	Broadhurst	Lees	McCall	Dawson	Miller (1)	Jefferis	Roberts	Woodhouse	Green
Feb 14	Sheffield Wed	Div 1	h	3-0		Jones	Greatorex	Broadhurst	Lees	McCall	Dawson	Miller	Jefferis (1)	Roberts (1)	Woodhouse (1)	Green
Feb 21	Bradford City Rd 3	FAC	h	0-3	29380	Jones	Greatorex	Broadhurst	Lees	McCall	Dawson	Miller	Woodhouse	Roberts	Davies	Bainbridge
Feb 28	Manchester City	Div 1	h	1-1		Jones	Greatorex	Broadhurst	Lees	Marshall	Dawson	Miller	Jefferis	Roberts (1)	Woodhouse	Green
Mar 4	Notts County	Div 1	h	2-0		Jones	Greatorex	Speak	Lees	Marshall	Dawson	Miller	Hosker	Roberts (1)	Woodhouse (1)	Green
Mar 6	Derby County	Div 1	h	1-1		Jones	Greatorex	Speak	Lees	McCall	Dawson	Miller	Davies	Roberts (1)	Woodhouse	Knight
Mar 13	Derby County	Div 1	a	0-2		Jones	Greatorex	Speak	Lees	McCall	Dawson	Clifton	Hosker	Roberts	Woodhouse	Quinn
Mar 17	Manchester City	Div 1	a	0-1		Jones	Greatorex	Speak	Lees	McCall	Dawson	Clifton	Hosker	Roberts	Woodhouse	Quinn
Mar 20	WBA	Div 1	h	0-1		Causer	Greatorex	Speak	Lees	Marshall	Dawson	Miller	Woodhouse	Roberts	Davies	Quinn
Mar 27	WBA	Div 1	a	1-4		Jones	Broadhurst	Speak	Lees	McCall	Dawson	Miller	Holdsworth	Roberts (1)	Bainbridge	Quinn
Apr 2	Sheffield Utd	Div 1	h	2-0		Causer	Greatorex	Broadhurst	Lees	McCall	Dawson	Miller	Jefferis	Roberts (2)	Woodhouse	Quinn
Apr 3	Sunderland	Div 1	h	5-2		Causer	Greatorex	Broadhurst	Lees	McCall (1)	Dawson	Miller	Jefferis	Roberts (2)	Woodhouse (1)	Quinn (1)
Apr 10	Sunderland	Div 1	a	0-1		Causer	Greatorex	Broadhurst	Lees	McCall	Marshall	Miller	Jefferis	Roberts	Woodhouse	Quinn
Apr 17	Arsenal	Div 1	h	1-1		Causer	Greatorex	Broadhurst	Lees	McCall	Dawson	Miller	Jefferis (1)	Roberts	Woodhouse	Quinn
Apr 24	Arsenal	Div 1	a	0-0		Causer	Greatorex	Broadhurst	Lees	McCall	Dawson	Miller	Jefferis	Roberts	Woodhouse	Quinn
Apr 26	Everton	Div 1	h	1-1		Causer	Greatorex	Broadhurst	Lees	McCall	Dawson	Miller	Jefferis (1)	Roberts	Woodhouse	Quinn
May 1	Everton	Div 1	a	1-0		Causer	Broadhurst	Speak	Lees	McCall	Dawson	Clifton	Jefferis	Roberts (1)	Woodhouse	Quinn

SEASON 1920–1921

That first season after the war was to prove a yardstick for what was to come over the next decade and this 1920–1 campaign once again proved a very difficult one for North End. Thankfully, Tommy Roberts, despite his temperamental difficulties with the management off the field, was still very prolific on it. He continued to bang in the goals freely and during the season notched up three hat-tricks, two of which came in the FA Cup. The famous old cup tournament was to be something of a relief for the club's fans away from the disappointments of the league games and North End so nearly reached the final. Another player who won the hearts of the supporters this year was undoubtedly Archie Rawlings, who was signed from Dundee. A quick and nimble winger, he added much to the Preston attack. He was sharp to see an opening and was a fine crosser of the ball, the perfect foil for Roberts. Frank Jefferis and Billy Mercer also had very good seasons and both proved to be superb players. However, there was certainly a mixed bag of results in the league. Lost 1–0, won 2–0, lost 6–0, won 6–1, indeed, the only consistency was in the inconsistency of it all! The double over Tottenham in the November was well received but was later to prove very ironic. At Christmas Preston did well against local rivals Blackburn, drawing at Ewood on Christmas Day before recording a superb 4–2 win at Deepdale two days later. Rowland Woodhouse was the hero as he hit a brilliant hat-trick. Generally though the league games were a big let down and it was the FA Cup which generated the real excitement. Preston fought their way to the semi-final which was played at Hillsborough. They were paired against Tottenham, a side that they had already beaten twice in the league. But this time the Londoners took revenge. Preston were never in it and the 2–1 scoreline did not reflect the superiority of the Spurs. There was huge disappointment felt around the town after the result and when the season ended without a win in their last six games it once again condemned the fans to a summer of pessimism rather than optimism.

DEBUTANTS: (13) Harry Croft, Sandy Doolan, Tom Duxbury, John Elliott, Tommy Green, Tommy Hamilton, John Holland, Fred Marquis, James Mitchell, Archie Rawlings, Bernard Starkey, George Waddell, George Wilcock.

LAST GAMES: (10) Davies, Dawson, Green J, Green T, Greatorex, Hosker, Knight, Lees, Sharkey, Wilcock.

Preston North End players and staff at the Cenotaph in Whitehall, London, after the very first Armistance Day Rememberance 11 November 1920.

League appearances (42 games)

Broadhurst F. 8, Causer A. H. 26, Croft H. 1, Davies S. 13, Dawson G. 9, Doolan A. 31, Duxbury T. 4, Elliott J. W. 4, Green J. 3, Green T. 1, Greatorex W. 7, Hamilton T. 14, Holland J. 4, Hosker J. 2, Jefferis F. 34, Knight J. H. 2, Lees J. W. 11, McCall J. 33, Marquis F. 2, Marshall J. (No2) 7, Mercer W. 31, Mitchell J. F. 5, Quinn P. 35, Rawlings A. 42, Roberts W. T. 35, Sharkey B. J. 1, Speak G. 24, Waddell G. 32, Wilcock G. H. 7, Woodhouse R. T. 34.

FA Cup appearances (6 games)

Mitchell 2, Causer 4, Doolan 6, Speak 6, Waddell 6, McCall 6, Mercer 6, Rawlings 6, Jefferis 6, Roberts 6, Woodhouse 3, Holland 2, Quinn 6, Knight 1.

Goalscorers: 61 League–11 Cup–(Total 72)

Roberts 18–7 (25), Woodhouse 16–1 (17), Davies 7–0 (7), Rawlings 6–1 (pen) (7), Jefferis 5–2 (7), Quinn 5–0 (5), Waddell 2–0 (2), McCall 1–0 (1). Own Goals 1 (Atkin of Derby)–0 (1)

Future Players born between August 1920 and July 1921: William Nuttall, Willie McClure, Bill Scott and Jimmy Gooch

Ever presents: (1) A. Rawlings   FA Cup: Semi-final
Manager/Secretary: Vincent Hayes   Chairman: Meyrick Hollins
Hat-tricks: (4) Roberts 3*, (1 lge 2 FAC) Woodhouse 1.
Leading scorer: 25 goals – Tommy Roberts (18 lge 7 Cup)
Players used: 30

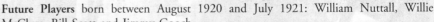

AUTHORS' UNOFFICIAL PLAYER OF THE SEASON: Archie Rawlings

STAT FACTS:
Best home run without defeat: 4 games
Best away run without defeat: 3 games
Longest run unbeaten: 4 games
Longest run without a win: 6 games

League position in Division One: 16th – P42 W15 D9 L18 F61 A65 Pts 39
Home: W10 D4 L7 F38 A25   Away: W5 D5 L11 F23 A40

Match Report: Roberts, the Master Goalscorer – 28 Mar 1921 Bradford Park Avenue 1 Preston 3

For this Easter Monday fixture Preston were unchanged for their third game in four days, having scored three goals in each of the previous two and looking to extend that run. The match was played in driving rain and high winds and Bradford began with the wind in their favour. As a result of this the Preston defenders struggled to clear their lines and came under heavy pressure. But the handicap that the elements put them under North End still managed to construct some attacking moves and Rawlings and Quinn stretched the Yorkshiremen's defence whenever possible. One run by Rawlings ended with the tall winger providing Tommy Roberts with a scoring chance, but the centre-forward, in great form of late, kicked fresh air as the wind blew the ball out of his reach. This was a prelude to an exciting siege on the Preston goal as McLean won a corner from Hamilton. Two consecutive shots were blocked by the Preston defenders before Beauchop was given offside just as the ball travelled over the goalline after hitting Causer's foot. After that let-off Preston quickly moved upfield as Jefferis brought Rawlings into play again. His centre

A. RAWLINGS.

Archie Rawlings capped by England at the end of the season.

found Roberts who knocked it on to Woodhouse. The Lilywhite's inside-left made no mistake with a low shot which Scattergood, Bradford's last line of defence, failed to save. Within four minutes though Bradford drew level as Bauchop skipped around Hamilton who slipped on the muddy surface in attempting to tackle. The winger centred and McLean beat Causer at the second attempt. The fortunes of the game continued to ebb and flow in a thrilling manner considering the conditions. Sandy Doolan was temporarily knocked out in a heavy collision with McCandless, and eleven minutes from the break Preston had a stroke of luck. McLean had struck the ball at Doolan, who was still dazed, and the referee gave Bradford a penalty for handball, a very harsh decision by all accounts. However, Turnbull's spot-kick flew straight at Causer and the goalkeeper was able to smother the ball at the second attempt. After the break it was Preston's turn for the wind advantage, Hamilton's clearance showing how severe the wind was when, from his own penalty box he kicked the heavy ball the length of the field. On 55 minutes Jefferis once again set Rawlings away down the right and as two home defenders converged on him he crossed perfectly for Roberts to smash another of what had now become legendary rocket shots. The final goal came from Woodhouse who capitalised on the keeper's fumble of yet another Roberts hot-shot. Roberts had ended the Easter period with 6 goals from 3 games in 4 days.

Season 1920–21: First Division

	P	W	D	L	F	A	Pts
1 Burney	42	23	13	6	79	36	59
2 Man City	42	24	6	12	70	50	54
3 Bolton	42	19	14	9	77	53	52
4 Liverpool	42	18	15	9	63	35	51
5 Newcastle	42	20	10	12	66	45	50
6 Tottenham	42	19	9	14	70	48	47
7 Everton	42	17	13	12	66	55	47
8 Middlesbrough	42	17	12	13	53	53	46
9 Arsenal	42	15	14	13	59	63	44
10 Aston Villa	42	18	7	17	63	70	43
11 Blackburn	42	13	15	14	57	59	41
12 Sunderland	42	14	13	15	57	60	41
13 Man United	42	15	10	17	64	68	40
14 WBA	42	13	14	15	54	58	40
15 Bradford City	42	12	15	15	61	63	39
16 PRESTON	**42**	**15**	**9**	**18**	**61**	**65**	**39**
17 Huddersfield	42	15	9	18	42	49	39
18 Chelsea	42	13	13	16	48	58	39
19 Oldham	42	9	15	18	49	86	33
20 Sheffield United	42	6	18	18	42	68	30
21 Derby	42	5	16	21	32	58	26
22 Bradford PA	42	8	8	26	43	76	24

Trivia Facts:

G. H. Barlow died on 3 March 1921 at Birkdale, Southport. Tragically his mother and brother had both died within a fortnight prior to his death. All three had died of septic pneumonia.

Many players suffered a reaction to the horrors of the Great War and one of Preston's was a typical example. Although Stanley Davies played after the war, he was quickly discarded as his own long and arduous military campaign caught up with him. His personal courage had earned him the Mons Medal, Military Medal and the prestigious Croix de Guerre.

Rowland Woodhouse was in the wars on a couple of occasions during the season. In the Villa Park dressing rooms on 9 October 1920 he cut his ankle on a broken bottle. On his return after injury, a reserve game at Stockport, he received a blow on the mouth and had to walk to Stockport Infirmary in his football attire to have three stitches inserted in the wound.

There was a wonderful story of two chaps from London who were arrested at Deepdale for pickpocketing at the cup-tie with Hull. When searched, one had just over £20 in his pockets, a huge amount in those days, while the other had 6s.11d.! Obviously he was not as good at it! They were refused bail because the Grand National was on and the police feared they would go to Aintree and rifle pockets there. So they were eventually charged and given three months' hard labour. The twist in the story was that one was 75 years of age and the other was 73!

Preston North End May 1921 (Whitehaven, Cumberland) taken on end of season trip to the Lake District.

Date 1920-1	Opponents	Comp	h or a	Score	Att.	1	2	3	4	5	6	7	8	9	10	11		
Aug 28	Huddersfield	Div 1	h	0-1		Wilcock	Greatorex	Speak	Lees	McCall	Dawson	Rawlings	Jefferis	Roberts	Woodhouse	Quinn		
Aug 30	Middlesbrough	Div 1	a	0-0		Wilcock	Doolan	Speak	Lees	McCall	Dawson	Rawlings	Jefferis	Roberts	Woodhouse	Quinn		
Sep 4	Huddersfield	Div 1	a	0-1		Wilcock	Doolan	Speak	Lees	McCall	Mercer	Rawlings	Jefferis	Davies	Woodhouse	Quinn		
Sep 6	Middlesbrough	Div 1	h	2-0		Wilcock	Doolan	Speak	Lees	McCall	Mercer	Rawlings (1)	Jefferis	Davies (1)	Woodhouse	Quinn		
Sep 11	Newcastle Utd.	Div 1	a	2-4		Wilcock	Doolan	Speak	Lees	McCall	Mercer	Rawlings	Jefferis	Davies (1)	Woodhouse (1)	Quinn		
Sep 18	Newcastle Utd.	Div 1	h	3-2		Wilcock	Doolan	Speak	Lees	McCall	Waddell	Rawlings	Jefferis	Roberts (1)	Woodhouse (2)	Quinn		
Sep 25	Liverpool	Div 1	a	0-6		Wilcock	Doolan	Speak	Lees	McCall	Waddell	Rawlings	Jefferis	Roberts	Woodhouse	J. Green		
Oct 2	Liverpool	Div 1	h	2-3		Causer	Doolan	Speak	Marshall	McCall	Waddell	Rawlings	Jefferis	Roberts (2)	Woodhouse	Quinn		
Oct 9	Aston Villa	Div 1	a	0-1		Causer	Greatorex	Speak	Waddell	McCall	Dawson	Rawlings	Jefferis	Roberts	Woodhouse	Quinn		
Oct 16	Aston Villa	Div 1	h	6-1		Causer	Greatorex	Speak	Waddell	McCall	Dawson	Rawlings (2)	Jefferis	Roberts (2)	Davies (1)	Quinn (1)		
Oct 23	Manchester Utd	Div 1	a	0-1		Causer	Greatorex	Speak	Lees	Waddell	Dawson	Rawlings	Jefferis	Roberts	Davies	Quinn		
Oct 30	Manchester Utd	Div 1	h	0-0		Causer	Greatorex	Speak	Waddell	McCall	Dawson	Rawlings	Jefferis	Roberts	Davies	Quinn		
Nov 6	Chelsea	Div 1	a	1-1		Causer	Doolan	Speak	Lees	McCall	Dawson	Rawlings	Jefferis	Roberts	Davies	Quinn (1)		
Nov 13	Chelsea	Div 1	h	0-1		Causer	Doolan	Speak	Lees	Waddell	Dawson	Rawlings	Jefferis	Roberts	Davies	Quinn		
Nov 20	Tottenham H	Div 1	a	2-1		Causer	Doolan	Speak	Waddell	Marshall	Mercer	Rawlings	Jefferis (1)	Davies (1)	Woodhouse	Quinn		
Nov 27	Tottenham H	Div 1	h	4-1		Causer	Doolan	Speak	Waddell	Marshall	Mercer	Rawlings	Jefferis (2)	Davies (1)	Woodhouse (1)	Quinn		
Dec 4	Oldham Ath	Div 1	a	2-0		Causer	Doolan	Speak	Waddell	Marshall	Mercer	Rawlings	Jefferis	Davies (2)	Woodhouse	Quinn		
Dec 11	Oldham Ath	Div 1	h	4-0		Causer	Doolan	Speak	Waddell	McCall	Mercer	Rawlings (1)	Jefferis	Roberts	Woodhouse (2)	Quinn (1)		
Dec 18	Burnley	Div 1	a	0-2		Causer	Doolan	Speak	Waddell	McCall	Mercer	Rawlings	Jefferis	Davies	Woodhouse	Quinn		
Dec 25	Blackburn Rovers	Div 1	a	2-2		Mitchell	Doolan	Speak	Waddell	McCall	Mercer	Rawlings	Jefferis	Roberts (1)	Woodhouse	Quinn (1)		
Dec 27	Blackburn Rovers	Div 1	h	4-2		Mitchell	Greatorex	Speak	Waddell	McCall	Mercer	Rawlings	Jefferis	Roberts	Woodhouse (3)	Quinn (1)		
Jan 1	Burnley	Div 1	h	0-3		Mitchell	Greatorex	Speak	Waddell	McCall	Mercer	Rawlings	Davies	Roberts	Woodhouse	Quinn		
Jan 8	Bolton W. Rd 1	FAC	h	2-0	24000	Mitchell	Doolan	Reaps	Waddell	McCall	Mercer	Rawlings (1p)	Jefferis	Roberts (1)	Woodhouse	Quinn		
Jan 15	Derby County	Div 1	h	2-1		Mitchell	Doolan	Broadhurst	Waddell	McCall	Mercer	Rawlings	Jefferis (1)	Roberts (1)	Woodhouse	Quinn		
Jan 22	Derby County	Div 1	a	1-1		Causer	Doolan	Broadhurst	Waddell	McCall	Mercer	Rawlings	Jefferis	Roberts	Holland	Quinn	1 o.g.	(Atkin)
Jan 29	Watford Rd 2	FAC	h	4-1	22000	Mitchell	Doolan	Speak	Waddell	McCall	Mercer	Rawlings	Jefferis	Roberts (3)	Woodhouse (1)	Quinn		
Feb 5	Sheffield Utd	Div 1	a	0-1		Causer	Doolan	Speak	Waddell	McCall	Mercer	Rawlings	Jefferis	Roberts	Woodhouse	Quinn		
Feb 7	Sheffield Utd	Div 1	h	2-0		Causer	Doolan	Broadhurst	Waddell	Marshall	Mercer	Rawlings (1)	Jefferis	Roberts (1)	Woodhouse	Quinn		
Feb 12	Bolton W.	Div 1	h	1-2		Mitchell	Doolan	Speak	Waddell	McCall	Mercer	Rawlings	Sharkey	Roberts	Woodhouse (1)	Quinn		
Feb 19	Luton Town Rd 3	FAC	a	3-2	17754	Causer	Doolan	Speak	Waddell	McCall	Mercer	Rawlings	Jefferis	Roberts (3)	Holland	Quinn		
Feb 26	Arsenal	Div 1	h	0-1		Causer	Hamilton	Broadhurst	Waddell	Marshall	Mercer	Rawlings	Jefferis	Roberts	Woodhouse	J. Green		
Mar 5	Hull City Rd 4	FAC	a	0-0	27000	Causer	Doolan	Speak	Waddell	McCall	Mercer	Rawlings	Jefferis	Roberts	Woodhouse	Quinn		
Mar 10	Hull City Replay	FAC	h	1-0	32853	Causer	Doolan	Speak	Waddell	McCall	Mercer	Rawlings	Jefferis (1)	Roberts	Holland	Quinn		
Mar 12	Manchester City	Div 1	h	0-1		Causer	Hamilton	Broadhurst	Lees	Marshall	Mercer	Rawlings	Marquis	Roberts	Holland	Quinn		
Mar 19	Tottenham H * Semi-fin.	FAC	N	1-2	44663	Causer	Doolan	Speak	Waddell	McCall	Mercer	Rawlings	Jefferis (1)	Roberts	Quinn	Knight		
Mar 25	Bradford Pk. Av.	Div 1	a	3-3		Causer	Hamilton	Doolan	Waddell	McCall	Mercer	Rawlings (1)	Jefferis	Roberts (2)	Woodhouse	Quinn		
Mar 26	WBA	Div 1	a	3-0		Causer	Hamilton	Doolan	Waddell	McCall	Mercer	Rawlings	Jefferis	Roberts (3)	Woodhouse	Quinn		
Mar 28	Bradford Pk. Av.	Div 1	h	3-1		Causer	Hamilton	Doolan	Waddell	McCall	Mercer	Rawlings	Jefferis	Roberts (1)	Woodhouse (2)	Quinn		
Apr 2	WBA	Div 1	h	2-1		Causer	Hamilton	Doolan	Waddell (1)	McCall	Mercer	Rawlings	Jefferis	Roberts (1)	Woodhouse	Quinn		
Apr 4	Bolton W.	Div 1	a	0-3		Causer	Hamilton	Broadhurst	Duxbury	Waddell	Mercer	Rawlings	Marquis	Roberts	J. Green	Quinn		
Apr 9	Everton	Div 1	a	1-0		Causer	Hamilton	Doolan	Waddell	McCall	Mercer	Rawlings	Jefferis	Roberts	Woodhouse (1)	Quinn		
Apr 16	Everton	Div 1	h	1-0		Causer	Hamilton	Doolan	Duxbury	McCall	Mercer	Rawlings	Jefferis	Roberts	Woodhouse (1)	Knight		
Apr 20	Manchester City	Div 1	a	1-5		Causer	Hamilton	Doolan	Waddell	McCall	Mercer	Rawlings	Jefferis	Roberts (1)	Woodhouse	Croft		
Apr 23	Sunderland	Div 1	a	2-2		Elliott	Hamilton	Doolan	Waddell	McCall	Mercer	Rawlings	Holland	Roberts (1)	Woodhouse (1)	Knight		
Apr 25	Arsenal	Div 1	a	1-2		Elliott	Hamilton	Doolan	Duxbury	McCall	Mercer	Rawlings	Holland	Roberts	Woodhouse	Waddell (1)		
Apr 30	Sunderland	Div 1	h	1-1		Elliott	Hamilton	Doolan	Duxbury	McCall (1)	Mercer	Rawlings	Hosker	Roberts	Woodhouse	Quinn		
May 2	Bradford City	Div 1	a	2-6		Elliott	Hamilton	Doolan	Dawson	McCall	Mercer	Rawlings	Woodhouse (1)	Roberts (1)	Hosker	Quinn		
May 7	Bradford City	Div 1	h	1-1		Causer	Broadhurst	Speak	Waddell	McCall	Mercer	Rawlings	Jefferis (1)	Roberts	Woodhouse	T. Green		
	* Match played at Hillsborough, Sheffield																	

Match Report: Rawlings Reaps Revenge – 7 February 1921 Preston 2 Sheffield United 0

Having lost 1–0 at Sheffield two days earlier, this return fixture at Deepdale saw North End determined to do better. Joe McCall missed the match because of a call up to an International trial game played at Tottenham and that, coupled with the fact that the game had been rearranged for a Monday afternoon, kept the crowd down to below average. The early play was in North End's favour and Jefferis set up Roberts for a chance, but visiting keeper Blackwell saved brilliantly with a two-fisted punch. It took Preston just five minutes to take the lead though as the early pressure paid off. Marshall passed the ball forward and both Woodhouse and Roberts went to meet it. They arrived together but defender Furniss blocked Woodhouse only to leave Roberts with a clear run at goal. A fast rising shot to the goalkeeper's right and Preston were one up. United fought back for awhile but their finishing was poor and gradually Preston won back control. Marshall hit the angle of bar and post with a long range shot and Woodhouse saw a clever effort well saved by Blackwell. Marshall's fine work in breaking up United's attacks played a big part in the home side's continued dominance after the break. But whilst it was only 1–0 Sheffield were still in the match and Causer had to be alert in Preston's goal on more than one occasion. The visitors were a pacey side with their wingers proving elusive and they almost equalised when three shots were blocked in quick succession by the determined home defenders. The Preston forwards always looked better in front of the United goal however and good work by Quinn and Woodhouse gave Roberts another chance which this time he missed. Preston were not to be denied though and Rawlings, who had played well throughout, scored a late goal from a Jefferis pass to seal the victory and thus gain revenge for the defeat in Sheffield.

Huddersfield, who Preston faced in the FA Cup Final, must have fancied their chances at Stamford Bridge because the week before the final, in a league game at Huddersfield, they thrashed North End 6–0! At the time the Yorkshire club was managed by a gentleman called Herbert Chapman who later went on to become arguably the greatest club manager of all time, especially with his success at Arsenal.

During this season Preston set up an unenviable record. Their away form has often been poor over the years but in 1921–22 they went thirteen consecutive away games without scoring a goal. Also during this season only seven different players scored a goal, which is the lowest amount for a season in North End's history.

Tommy Roberts played for the Football League against the Irish League at Bolton in October 1922 and he scored two goals. Meanwhile George Speak and Joe Irving represented the Central League against the North Eastern League on 15 October 1921 in another representative match.

John Holland and Billy Mercer both played locally with Roebuck Schoolboy teams under the tuition of Jack Winchester, the former North End full-back.

Injuries played a big part in the fortunes of Preston North End during the 1921–22 season. In fact, at one point the injuries were so bad that the management decided that it would be in the best interests of the club to concentrate on the FA Cup rather than the league games. This policy was to have some success as North End this time reached the final. But whether the fans were entirely happy with this arrangement was never fully clear and they were certainly not happy with another below average league campaign. In one incredible spell Preston went 13 consecutive away games without a goal, a record. The run was finally ended in the very last away game when George Sapsford scored both goals in a 2–0 win at Birmingham. Needless to say the away record was dreadful with only seven points gained out of the 38 they totalled. Thankfully it was quite the reverse situation at Deepdale in the home games. Only two matches were lost there. The fans were beginning to ask some serious questions though as it was fairly obvious that some senior players were by now coming to the end of their careers. Even the great Joe McCall came under fire following some poor displays. This all lead to the club bringing in some new players towards the end of the season in an effort to build something better for 1922–23. But in 1922 the Cup again proved to be North End's salvation. Fine wins over Wolves and Newcastle was followed by a really gutsy display at Barnsley, where Preston withstood terrific pressure to force a draw. A good win in the replay gave them a tie at Arsenal and it looked curtains. But again they defended well at Highbury in the first game before winning the replay. And so to Hillsborough again and a repeat of the previous year's semi-final against Spurs. The Southerners again took the lead but this time Preston fought back well and equalised through Archie Rawlings before the irrepressible Tommy Roberts settled the issue with a winning goal. Unfortunately that was the high spot of the season as the final itself proved a huge anti-climax. A very poor game was settled by a very dubious penalty. The Preston players protested that the foul was committed outside the area, but the referee was adamant and that was that. The one consolation came in the signing of a Scot called Bobby Crawford. He was to go on to be one of Preston's all time greats.

DEBUTANTS: (11) Jimmy Branston, Bobby Crawford, James Ferris, Freddie Fox, Joseph Irving, Nicholas Latham, Alf Quantrill, George Sapsford, Albert Shears, Johnny Williamson, Wilfred Yates.

LAST GAMES: (11) Broadhurst, Causer, Croft, Elliott, Fox, Holland, Irving, Latham, Mitchell, Shears, Waddell. (George Waddell was to return to Preston in the 1930s as an assistant trainer.)

PRESENTED WITH "BOYS' MAGAZINE".

PRESTON NORTH END F.C. 1921-22
BACK ROW: (left to right) Rawlings, Doolan, Elliott, Hamilton.
MIDDLE ROW: Roberts, Jeffries, Woodhouse, Quinn. BOTTOM ROW: Waddell, Marshall, Mercer.

STAT FACTS:
Best home run without defeat: 11 games
Best away run without defeat: 1 game
Longest run unbeaten: 3 games
Longest run without a win: 10 games

League position in Division One: 16th – P42 W13 D12 L17 F42 A65 Pts 38
Home: W12 D7 L2 F33 A20 Away: W1 D5 L15 F9 A45

Match Report: North End, Back Down to Earth – 1 May 1922 Preston 2 Birmingham 2

After losing in the Cup Final the previous Saturday, Preston North End arrived back in town via Platform 5 of the local railway station on May Day at 3.30 p.m. They were greeted by an outburst of cheering from the enthusiastic crowd who had gathered despite the rain. The team then boarded a waiting open motor charabanc decorated with the club colours, whilst the club officials elected to travel in a covered vehicle. The route to Deepdale was crowded as the party made their way to the ground in readiness for that evening's game with Birmingham, the club who had forgot to send in their entry for that season's cup competition! With some of the North End fans still in London and others *en route*, most of them broke after a weekend of drowning their sorrows, the low attendance of 10, 537 witnessed the last home game of the season. Preston lined up with their cup final team except for Yates who had come in for Doolan who was nursing a mouth abscess. North End found themselves a goal down after just five minutes. Foxall, the left-winger, swung over a deep early centre which Yates headed smartly away but Crosbie, Birmingham's inside-right, was lurking 25 yards out and he did not hesitate and fired in as good a shot as you are likely to see and it beat Fred Mitchell all ends up. Both Roberts, twice, and Jefferis hit the visitors woodwork in retaliation but as at Stamford Bridge in the final North End had little luck, or so it seemed. Woodhouse eventually equalised after 30 minutes following a corner, the ball passing through a crowded goalmouth giving Dan Tremelling no chance to see it, never mind stop it. Early in the second half Jefferis crowned a good all round display with a shot that the goalkeeper did not even bother to move for as he knew he was well beaten. The Midland side improved after conceding that goal and Foxall went close on a couple of occasions. Ten minutes from time Quinn missed an open goal which proved costly because Birmingham then equalised with the very last kick of the game. Mitchell, the bespectacled goalkeeper, was standing on the edge of his six yard box watching the game progress when Crosbie spotted him off his line. His shot was judged to perfection as it passed over Mitchell's outstretched reach and dipped just below the crossbar. Apparently there had been more football played in the first five minutes of this game than there had in the whole of the disappointing cup final.

Match Report: Blades Cut Down – 26 November 1921 Preston 3 Sheffield United 0

Although it was extremely cold in Preston the weather was so fine that many people were tempted out of their dwellings to take in this game with Sheffield United. North End had Causer in goal due to Mitchell sustaining a jarred thumb in their previous game. Preston proved the quicker of the two sides on a freely sanded pitch and they were unlucky not to take early advantage of their superiority. Woodhouse latched onto a long pass from Hamilton but both he and Rodway were unable to control the ball on the lively surface and the chance went begging. Within a minute however the jeering fans were cheering, as from another of Woodhouse's astute moves a chance opened up for Jefferis who ventured forward a few yards before striking the ball into the net. North End were making all the running but further chances again went astray. Having said that they full deserved their 1–0 half-time lead. Preston started the second half as they had the first, in great form. They created three good opportunities in quick succession, two of them falling for Roberts, but all were missed. However, the harassed United defence were not fated to escape lightly and after 48 minutes Roberts headed cleanly past Gough in the visitors' goal. Sheffield made futile efforts at a comeback but Joe McCall's men held the line well. On 56 minutes the match was settled when Roberts repeated his feat of heading past Gough for his second goal and Preston's third. But for inaccurate finishing, Preston could and should have scored a hatful, but 3–0 was emphatic enough and thoroughly deserved.

Future Players born between August 1921 and July 1922: William Hannah, Jack Hindle, Andy McLaren, Paddy Waters, David Gray, **Tom Finney**, William Jessop, Willie Forbes, Jimmy Garth and Charlie Wayman

Ever presents: (1) Tommy Roberts
Hat-tricks: (1) Roberts
Manager/Secretary: Vincent Hayes
FA Cup: Runners-up
Chairmen: Mr W. E. Ord J. P. and then Sir Meyrick Hollins
Leading scorer: 25 goals – Tommy Roberts (18 league 7 Cup)
Players used: 31

AUTHORS' UNOFFICIAL PLAYER OF THE SEASON: Frank Jefferis

League appearances (42 games)

Branston J. H. 12, Broadhurst F. 2, Causer A. H. 3, Crawford R. 6, Croft H. 1, Doolan A. 30, Duxbury T. 27, Elliott J. W. 8, Ferris J. 8, Fox F. S. 3, Hamilton T. 37, Holland J. 2, Irving J. 15, Jefferis F. 27, Latham N. 1, McCall J. 28, Marquis F. 4, Marshall J. (No2) 6, Mercer W. 16, Mitchell J. F. 16, Quantrill A. E. 5, Quinn P. 34, Rawlings A. 40, Roberts W. T. 42, Sapsford G. D. 1, Shears A. E. 2, Speak G. 10, Waddell G. 19, Williamson J. 14, Woodhouse R. T. 37, Yates W. J. 6.

FA Cup appearances (8 games)

Mitchell 6, Causer 2, Hamilton 8, Doolan 8, Duxbury 8, McCall 5, Marshall 3, Mercer 1, Irving 1, Williamson 7, Rawlings 8, Jefferis 8, Roberts 8, Woodhouse 8, Quinn 7.

Goalscorers: 42 League–15 Cup–(Total 57)

Roberts 18–7 (25), Woodhouse 12–3 (15), Jefferis 3–2 (5), Rawlings 2(1p)–3(1p) (5), Quinn 4–0 (4), Sapsford 2–0 (2), McCall 1–0 (1)

Season 1921–22: First Division

		P	W	D	L	F	A	Pts
1	Liverpool	42	22	13	7	63	36	57
2	Tottenham	42	21	9	12	65	39	51
3	Burnley	42	22	5	15	72	54	49
4	Cardiff	42	19	10	13	61	53	48
5	Aston Villa	42	22	3	11	74	55	47
6	Bolton	42	20	7	15	68	59	47
7	Newcastle	42	18	10	14	59	45	46
8	Middlesbrough	42	16	14	12	79	69	46
9	Chelsea	42	17	12	13	40	43	46
10	Man City	42	18	9	15	65	70	45
11	Sheffield United	42	15	10	17	59	54	40
12	Sunderland	42	16	8	18	60	62	40
13	WBA	42	15	10	17	51	63	40
14	Huddersfield	42	15	9	18	53	54	39
15	Blackburn	42	13	12	17	54	57	38
16	**PRESTON**	**42**	**13**	**12**	**17**	**42**	**65**	**38**
17	Arsenal	42	15	7	20	47	56	37
18	Birmingham	42	15	7	20	48	60	37
19	Oldham	42	13	11	18	38	50	37
20	Everton	42	12	12	18	57	55	36
21	Bradford City	42	11	10	21	48	72	32
22	Man United	42	8	12	22	41	73	28

Date 1921-2	Opponents	Comp	h or a	Score	Att.	1	2	3	4	5	6	7	8	9	10	11
Aug 27	Bolton W.	Div 1	h	2-2		Elliott	Hamilton	Doolan	Waddell	McCall	Mercer	Rawlings	Jefferis	Roberts (2)	Woodhouse	Quantrill
Aug 29	Arsenal	Div 1	h	3-2		Elliott	Hamilton	Doolan	Waddell	McCall (1)	Mercer	Rawlings	Jefferis	Roberts (1)	Woodhouse (1)	Quantrill
Sep 3	Bolton W.	Div 1	a	3-1		Elliott	Hamilton	Doolan	Waddell	McCall	Mercer	Rawlings	Jefferis	Roberts (3)	Woodhouse	Quinn
Sep 5	Arsenal	Div 1	a	0-1		Elliott	Hamilton	Doolan	Waddell	McCall	Mercer	Rawlings	Jefferis	Roberts	Woodhouse	Quinn
Sep 10	Aston Villa	Div 1	h	1-0	24320	Elliott	Hamilton	Doolan	Waddell	McCall	Mercer	Rawlings	Jefferis	Roberts	Woodhouse (1)	Quinn
Sep 17	Aston Villa	Div 1	a	0-2		Elliott	Hamilton	Doolan	Waddell	Marshall	Mercer	Rawlings	Jefferis	Roberts	Woodhouse	Quinn
Sep 24	Manchester Utd	Div 1	h	3-2	21115	Elliott	Hamilton	Doolan	Waddell	Marshall	Mercer	Rawlings	Jefferis	Roberts (2)	Woodhouse (1)	Quinn
Oct 1	Manchester Utd	Div 1	a	1-1		Fox	Hamilton	Doolan	Duxbury	McCall	Mercer	Rawlings (1)	Jefferis	Roberts	Woodhouse	Quinn
Oct 8	Liverpool	Div 1	h	1-1	20661	Fox	Hamilton	Doolan	Duxbury	McCall	Mercer	Rawlings (1p)	Jefferis	Roberts	Woodhouse	Quinn
Oct 15	Liverpool	Div 1	a	0-4		Fox	Hamilton	Doolan	Duxbury	McCall	Mercer	Rawlings	Jefferis	Roberts	Woodhouse	Quinn
Oct 22	Newcastle Utd	Div 1	h	2-0	12680	Mitchell	Hamilton	Doolan	Duxbury	McCall	Mercer	Rawlings	Williamson	Roberts (1)	Woodhouse	Quinn (1)
Oct 29	Newcastle Utd	Div 1	a	1-3		Mitchell	Hamilton	Doolan	Duxbury	McCall	Irving	Rawlings	Williamson	Roberts	Woodhouse (1)	Quinn
Nov 5	Burnley	Div 1	a	3-3		Mitchell	Hamilton	Doolan	Duxbury	McCall	Irving	Rawlings	Williamson	Roberts	Woodhouse (3)	Quinn
Nov 12	Burnley	Div 1	h	2-1	34144	Mitchell	Hamilton	Doolan	Duxbury	McCall	Mercer	Rawlings	Marquis	Roberts (1)	Woodhouse (1)	Quinn
Nov 19	Sheffield Utd	Div 1	h	0-3		Mitchell	Hamilton	Doolan	Duxbury	McCall	Irving	Rawlings	Williamson	Roberts	Woodhouse	Quinn
Nov 26	Sheffield Utd	Div 1	a	3-0	17765	Causer	Hamilton	Doolan	Duxbury	McCall	Irving	Rawlings	Jefferis (1)	Roberts (2)	Woodhouse	Quinn
Dec 3	Chelsea	Div 1	a	0-0		Mitchell	Hamilton	Doolan	Duxbury	McCall	Irving	Rawlings	Jefferis	Roberts	Woodhouse	Quinn
Dec 10	Chelsea	Div 1	h	2-0	17851	Mitchell	Hamilton	Doolan	Duxbury	McCall	Irving	Rawlings	Jefferis	Roberts (1)	Woodhouse	Quinn (1)
Dec 17	Bradford City	Div 1	a	0-1		Mitchell	Hamilton	Doolan	Duxbury	McCall	Mercer	Rawlings	Jefferis	Roberts	Woodhouse	Quinn
Dec 24	Bradford City	Div 1	h	2-1	18831	Mitchell	Hamilton	Doolan	Waddell	McCall	Irving	Rawlings	Jefferis	Roberts (1)	Woodhouse	Quinn (1)
Dec 26	Blackburn Rovers	Div 1	h	0-3		Mitchell	Hamilton	Doolan	Waddell	McCall	Irving	Rawlings	Jefferis	Roberts	Woodhouse	Quinn
Dec 27	Blackburn Rovers	Div 1	a	2-1	34340	Mitchell	Broadhurst	Speak	Duxbury	McCall	Mercer	Rawlings	Jefferis	Roberts (1)	Woodhouse (1)	Irving
Dec 31	Tottenham H	Div 1	a	0-5		Mitchell	Broadhurst	Speak	Duxbury	Marshall	Mercer	Rawlings	Latham	Roberts	Woodhouse	Irving
Jan 7	Wolverhampton W Rd 1	FAC	h	3-0	23408	Mitchell	Hamilton	Doolan	Duxbury	McCall	Mercer	Rawlings	Jefferis (1)	Roberts (2)	Woodhouse	Williamson
Jan 14	Tottenham H	Div 1	h	1-2	15698	Mitchell	Hamilton	Doolan	Duxbury	McCall	Waddell	Rawlings	Jefferis	Roberts (1)	Woodhouse	Quinn
Jan 21	Oldham Ath	Div 1	a	0-2		Mitchell	Hamilton	Doolan	Duxbury	McCall	Waddell	Rawlings	Jefferis	Roberts	Woodhouse	Quinn
Jan 28	Newcastle Utd Rd 2	FAC	h	3-1	28416	Mitchell	Hamilton	Doolan	Duxbury	McCall	Irving	Rawlings (1)	Jefferis	Roberts (1)	Woodhouse (1)	Quinn
Feb 4	Cardiff City	Div 1	a	0-3		Mitchell	Yates	Doolan	Waddell	Marshall	Irving	Rawlings	Jefferis	Roberts	Woodhouse	Quinn
Feb 9	Oldham Ath	Div 1	h	0-0	10734	Causer	Hamilton	Doolan	Crawford	Marshall	Williamson	Rawlings	Jefferis	Roberts	Woodhouse	Quinn
Feb 11	Cardiff City	Div 1	h	1-0	19447	Causer	Hamilton	Doolan	Duxbury	Marshall	Williamson	Rawlings	Roberts	Shears	Woodhouse (1)	Quinn
Feb 18	Barnsley Rd 3	FAC	a	1-1	36881	Causer	Hamilton	Doolan	Duxbury	Marshall	Williamson	Rawlings (1p)	Jefferis	Roberts	Woodhouse	Quinn
Feb 23	Barnsley Replay	FAC	h	3-0	31795	Causer	Hamilton	Doolan	Duxbury	Marshall	Williamson	Rawlings	Jefferis	Roberts (1)	Woodhouse (2)	Quinn
Feb 25	WBA	Div 1	h	0-3	17311	Elliott	Yates	Speak	Duxbury	Hamilton	Irving	Rawlings	Shears	Roberts	Croft	Quinn
Mar 4	Arsenal Rd 4	FAC	a	1-1	37517	Mitchell	Hamilton	Doolan	Duxbury	Marshall	Williamson	Rawlings	Jefferis (1)	Roberts	Woodhouse	Quinn
Mar 8	Arsenal Replay	FAC	h	2-1*	30414	Mitchell	Hamilton	Doolan	Duxbury	McCall	Williamson	Rawlings	Jefferis	Roberts (2)	Woodhouse	Quinn
Mar 11	Manchester City	Div 1	h	1-0	18079	Branston	Hamilton	Speak	Duxbury	Waddell	Crawford	Rawlings	Holland	Roberts	Woodhouse (1)	Irving
Mar 18	Everton	Div 1	h	1-0	17811	Branston	Hamilton	Speak	Duxbury	Waddell	Irving	Rawlings	Jefferis	Roberts (1)	Woodhouse	Quinn
Mar 25	Tottenham H * Semi-F	FAC	N	2-1	50095	Mitchell	Hamilton	Doolan	Duxbury	McCall	Williamson	Rawlings (1)	Jefferis	Roberts (1)	Woodhouse	Quinn
Mar 29	WBA	Div 1	a	0-2		Branston	Speak	Doolan	Duxbury	Waddell	Williamson	Holland	Ferris	Roberts	Woodhouse	Quinn
Apr 1	Sunderland	Div 1	h	1-1	19945	Branston	Yates	Speak	Duxbury	McCall	Williamson	Quantrill	Jefferis	Roberts (1)	Woodhouse	Quinn
Apr 5	Manchester City	Div 1	a	0-2		Branston	Hamilton	Speak	Duxbury	Waddell	Irving	Rawlings	Jefferis	Roberts	Ferris	Quantrill
Apr 8	Sunderland	Div 1	a	0-1		Branston	Hamilton	Doolan	Crawford	Waddell	Williamson	Rawlings	Marquis	Roberts	Woodhouse	Ferris
Apr 10	Everton	Div 1	a	0-0		Branston	Hamilton	Doolan	Crawford	McCall	Irving	Rawlings	Ferris	Roberts	Woodhouse	Quinn
Apr 14	Middlesbrough	Div 1	h	1-1	21290	Branston	Hamilton	Speak	Duxbury	McCall	Williamson	Rawlings	Jefferis (1)	Roberts	Woodhouse	Quinn
Apr 15	Huddersfield	Div 1	h	1-1	21695	Branston	Hamilton	Speak	Duxbury	McCall	Waddell	Rawlings	Jefferis	Roberts	Ferris	Quinn (1)
Apr 17	Middlesbrough	Div 1	a	0-1		Branston	Hamilton	Yates	Crawford	Waddell	Williamson	Rawlings	Marquis	Roberts	Ferris	Quinn
Apr 22	Huddersfield	Div 1	a	0-6		Branston	Hamilton	Doolan	Crawford	Mercer	Williamson	Rawlings	Marquis	Roberts	Ferris	Quantrill
Apr 29	Huddersfield ** Final	FAC	N	0-1	53710	Mitchell	Hamilton	Doolan	Duxbury	McCall	Williamson	Rawlings	Jefferis	Roberts	Woodhouse	Quinn
May 1	Birmingham	Div 1	h	2-2	10537	Mitchell	Hamilton	Yates	Duxbury	McCall	Williamson	Rawlings	Jefferis (1)	Roberts	Woodhouse (1)	Quinn
May 6	Birmingham	Div 1	a	2-0		Branston	Hamilton	Yates	Duxbury	McCall	Ferris	Rawlings	Woodhouse	Roberts	Sapsford (2)	Quinn
* Played @ Hillsborough ** Played @ Stamford Bridge			* AET													

T. HAMILTON.

A. E. QUANTRILL

TOM HAMILTON IN ACTION

75

SEASON 1922–1923

Continuing the theme of difficult post-war seasons, 1922–23 was certainly no exception and this time there was no good cup run to offer relief. The playing strength was stretched to the limit as injuries and transfers took their toll and with little money available for team building it was to prove another long, hard winter. It was not until around December time that changes were made. Peter Quinn left to join Bury and Preston signed two Scots, Alex, 'Sandy' Laird and John Gilchrist. Both the new players had good pedigrees but time would prove them both to be poor buys. Gilchrist was a Scottish International signed from Celtic for the huge sum of £4,500 and Laird was signed from Rangers. They both played throughout the second half of the season but neither created much of an impression. Once again it was left to the superb contribution of Tommy Roberts to rescue Preston from mediocrity. His goalscoring in the league did more than anyone to keep the club away from relegation worries. The other area of concern was the goalkeeping position but during this season Jimmy Branston made the number one spot his own and a series of fine and consistent performances was most pleasing to management and fans alike. He performed admirably. Bobby Crawford also had a good season and Archie Rawlings continued to show his fleet-footed skills on the right wing. The home form was good but away from Deepdale only one win was achieved and that was just not good enough. The season had begun well, with a 3–1 win over Bolton, but this was followed by a spell of one win in the next eleven games. The one saving grace was that there were other sides in the division who were worse than Preston. As the season wore on it was obvious that changes would have to be made and in the February Vincent Hayes resigned his position and the club appointed Jimmy Lawrence as their new manager with Walter Atkinson taking on the Secretary's role.

Lawrence, the former Newcastle player, who, even now, still holds the record appearance total for that club, had to make some early decisions as several players were beginning to show signs of their age. Even Joe McCall struggled through a poor year. The FA Cup draw gave non-league Welsh side Aberdare a dream home tie but after a hard won victory there Preston then went out to Charlton in round two. In the league Preston finished 16th for the second year running with Roberts again being the main asset.

DEBUTANTS: (3) John Gilchrist, Alex 'Sandy' Laird and John Storey.

LAST GAMES: (5) Doolan, Jefferis, Quinn, Speak and Storey.

PNE photographed before game versus Everton, May 1923. Drew 2–2. Photo shows newly built Spion Kop with no roof on. Left to right: *Back row:* J. Barton (trainer), Gilchrist, Hamilton, Branston, Yates, Marshall, Crawford. *Front row:* Rawlings, Woodhouse, Roberts, Laird, Quantrill.

League appearances (42 games)

Branston J. H. 42, Crawford R. 28, Doolan A. 16, Duxbury T. 12, Ferris J. 24, Gilchrist J. W. 17, Hamilton T. 38, Jefferis F. 6, Laird A. 17, McCall J. 14, Marquis F. 3, Marshall J. (No2) 28, Mercer W. 20, Quantrill A. E. 28, Quinn P. 7, Rawlings A. 38, Roberts W. T. 39, Sapsford G. D. 14, Speak G. 18, Storey J. H. 1, Williamson J. 9, Woodhouse R. T. 32, Yates W. J. 11

FA Cup appearances (2 games)

Branston 2, Hamilton 2, Speak 1, Doolan 1, Laird 2, Marshall 1, McCall 1, Crawford 2, Rawlings 2, Ferris 2, Jefferis 1, Roberts 2, Woodhouse 2, Quantrill 1

Goalscorers: 60 League–3 Cup–(Total 63)

Roberts 28–1 (29), Ferris 7–0 (7), Rawlings 6–1(pen) (7), Woodhouse 5–1 (6), Quantrill 5–0 (5), Marquis 3–0 (3), Sapsford 3–0 (3), Laird 2–0 (2), Duxbury 1–0 (1)

League position in Division One: 16th – P42 W13 D11 L18 F60 A64 Pts 37
Home: W12 D3 L6 F41 A26   Away: W1 D8 L12 F19 A38

Match Report: New Season, Great Expectations – 26 Aug. 1922. Preston 3 Bolton 1

Two minutes after the captains had tossed the coin Bolton had struck the first blow through Flood who hit a good shot in off the post. If you will pardon the pun, it seemed that the floodgates would open. The Wanderers proved to be very impressive visitors during the first 25 minutes of this match at Deepdale, as they opened the new season in a style which suggested that they were able to sweep through their opponents at will. They showed good strength, plenty of ideas and were full of running. North End, on the other hand, had looked lethargic, showing poor ball control and seemed to have entered the game void of a system or game plan. The ball was played in the air too much which suited Bolton who had a few players over six foot. But as the game progressed North End gradually mastered the ball on the ground, the only way that they could overcome the physical advantage of the Bolton side. After their initial burst it was amazing to see how Bolton suddenly lost their form and folded in front of your eyes. Had David Jack scored a second goal when given the opportunity for Bolton, then preston may have folded. As it was Branston made a brave save in smothering the ball at the forward's feet. It was the signal for Preston to come back and when Tommy Roberts equalised with a fierce shot which nearly took the net off its fixings the home side were back in the match. The goal was so special that the local newspaper deemed it noteworthy enough to feature it in cartoon form. By now the contest was proving a pulsating struggle. Relative newcomer George Sapsford left two defenders leaden footed to outjump them and score with a firm, well directed header. Woodhouse, probably the shortest player on view, benefitted by playing the ball along the ground to feet, and to prove the point he scored Preston's third goal after evading his much taller marker with good footwork. Sapsford's effectiveness was increased when he settled in on the same wavelength as Quinn, which meant that the whole North End forward line knitted together as one. One individual battle that caught the eye was the keen tussle between Hamilton and Vizard. Hamilton, the Scotsman, eventually harnessing the skills of the wily Welsh wizard. The crowd was 27,500.

Trivia Facts:

It was certainly a red letter day for Preston's captain Tommy Hamilton at Birmingham on 10 March 1923. He was sent off! Strangely he was not suspended and played in all the remaining games that season.

Did you know that on 5 May and 21 July 1923 Boxing Exhibitions were held at Deepdale? Attendances of 1,287 and 845 respectively were recorded.

The FA Cup-tie at Aberdare netted the home side the grand total of £678–6s–3d at the gate. Meanwhile the receipts at Charlton in round two amounted to £1,402 11s. 0d.

Tommy Roberts played for the Football League vs. Irish League in October 1922 and, of course, scored two goals. Will Scott arrived as Trainer at Deepdale in June 1923 from South Shields and one that got away was a reserve team player called Albert McInroy who left to join Sunderland before going on to play for England! We also had a player on our books called W.Titt, but that's another story!

Police Sports Day 1922.
Cost of the Spion Kop, without the roof, was £19,551.
That seasons wages bill was £14,236.

Future Players born between August 1922 and July 1923: William Corbett, Ken Horton, Jim Davie, Jack Knight, William Brown, Ian Wilson, Peter Corr and Reg Simpson
Ever presents: (1) Jim Branston
FA Cup: Round Two
Manager: Vincent Hayes (Resigned Feb 1923) – James Lawrence (Appointed Feb 1923)
Chairman: Sir Meyrick Hollins
Hat-tricks: (2) Marquis and Roberts, one each.
Leading scorer: 29 goals – Tommy Roberts (28 League 1 Cup)
Players used: 23
AUTHORS' UNOFFICIAL PLAYER OF THE SEASON: Tommy Roberts

Season 1922–23: First Division

	P	W	D	L	F	A	Pts
1 Liverpool	42	26	8	8	70	31	60
2 Sunderland	42	22	10	10	72	54	54
3 Huddersfield	42	21	11	10	60	32	53
4 Newcastle	42	18	12	12	45	37	48
5 Everton	42	20	7	15	63	59	41
6 Aston Villa	42	18	10	14	64	51	46
7 WBA	42	17	11	14	58	49	45
8 Man City	42	17	11	14	50	49	45
9 Cardiff	42	18	7	17	73	59	43
10 Sheffield United	42	16	10	16	68	64	42
11 Arsenal	42	16	10	16	61	62	42
12 Tottenham	42	17	7	18	50	50	41
13 Bolton	42	14	12	16	50	58	40
14 Blackburn	42	14	12	16	47	52	40
15 Burnley	42	16	6	20	58	59	38
16 PRESTON	42	13	11	18	60	64	37
17 Birmingham	42	13	11	18	41	57	37
18 Middlesbrough	42	13	10	19	57	63	36
19 Chelsea	42	9	18	15	45	53	35
20 Nottingham Forest	42	13	8	21	41	70	34
21 Stoke	42	10	10	22	47	67	30
22 Oldham	42	10	10	22	35	65	30

STAT FACTS:

Best home run without defeat: 5 games – Best away run without defeat: 2 games – Longest run unbeaten: 4 games – Longest run without a win: 6 games Best known home attendance: 34,076 vs. Liverpool 9.9.22

Date 1922-3	Opponents		Comp	h or a	Score	Att.	1	2	3	4	5	6	7	8	9	10	11
Aug 26	Bolton W.		Div 1	h	3-1	27557	Branston	Hamilton	Doolan	Duxbury	McCall	Mercer	Rawlings	Woodhouse (1)	Roberts (1)	Sapsford (1)	Quinn
Aug 28	WBA		Div 1	a	2-2		Branston	Hamilton	Doolan	Duxbury	McCall	Mercer	Rawlings (1)	Woodhouse	Roberts (1)	Sapsford	Quinn
Sep 2	Bolton W.		Div 1	a	1-1		Branston	Hamilton	Doolan	Duxbury	McCall	Mercer	Rawlings	Woodhouse	Roberts (1)	Sapsford	Quinn
Sep 4	WBA		Div 1	h	0-0	22067	Branston	Hamilton	Doolan	Duxbury	McCall	Mercer	Rawlings	Woodhouse	Roberts	Sapsford	Quinn
Sep 9	Liverpool		Div 1	h	1-3	34076	Branston	Hamilton	Speak	Duxbury	McCall	Ferris	Rawlings	Woodhouse	Roberts	Sapsford	Quantrill (1)
Sep 16	Liverpool		Div 1	a	2-5		Branston	Hamilton	Doolan	Duxbury	McCall	Ferris	Rawlings	Jefferis	Roberts (1)	Sapsford	Quantrill (1)
Sep 23	Newcastle Utd		Div 1	a	1-3		Branston	Hamilton	Doolan	Crawford	McCall	Mercer	Rawlings (1)	Jefferis	Roberts	Woodhouse	Quantrill
Sep 30	Newcastle Utd		Div 1	h	1-0	17695	Branston	Hamilton	Doolan	Crawford	McCall	Mercer	Rawlings	Jefferis	Roberts (1)	Sapsford	Quantrill
Oct 7	Nottm Forest		Div 1	a	0-3		Branston	Hamilton	Doolan	Crawford	Marshall	Mercer	Rawlings	Woodhouse	Roberts	Sapsford	Quantrill
Oct 14	Nottm Forest		Div 1	h	2-2	16136	Branston	Hamilton	Doolan	Crawford	Marshall	Mercer	Rawlings	Jefferis	Roberts (1)	Ferris (1)	Quantrill
Oct 21	Manchester City		Div 1	h	0-2	15656	Branston	Hamilton	Yates	Crawford	Marshall	Mercer	Rawlings	Jefferis	Roberts	Ferris	Quantrill
Oct 28	Manchester City		Div 1	a	1-2		Branston	Hamilton	Yates	Williamson	Marshall	Mercer	Quantrill	Woodhouse (1)	Roberts	Sapsford	Ferris
Nov 4	Chelsea		Div 1	h	2-0	14928	Branston	Hamilton	Yates	Williamson	Marshall	Mercer	Quantrill	Woodhouse	Roberts (1)	Ferris (1)	Quinn
Nov 11	Chelsea		Div 1	a	1-0		Branston	Hamilton	Yates	Williamson	Marshall	Mercer	Quantrill	Woodhouse (1)	Roberts	Ferris	Quinn
Nov 18	Middlesbrough		Div 1	h	1-2	18137	Branston	Hamilton	Yates	Williamson	Marshall	Mercer	Quantrill	Woodhouse	Roberts	Ferris (1)	Quinn
Nov 25	Middlesbrough		Div 1	a	1-1		Branston	Hamilton	Yates	Duxbury	Marshall	Crawford	Rawlings (1)	Woodhouse	Roberts	Ferris	Quantrill
Dec 2	Oldham Ath		Div 1	h	5-1	12950	Branston	Hamilton	Yates	Duxbury	Marshall	Williamson	Rawlings	Woodhouse	Roberts (2)	Ferris (1)	Quantrill (2)
Dec 9	Oldham Ath		Div 1	a	1-2		Branston	Hamilton	Yates	Duxbury (1)	Marshall	Williamson	Rawlings	Woodhouse	Roberts	Ferris	Quantrill
Dec 16	Sheffield Utd		Div 1	a	2-2		Branston	Hamilton	Yates	Duxbury	Marshall	Mercer	Rawlings	Ferris (1)	Roberts	Sapsford (1)	Quantrill
Dec 23	Sheffield Utd		Div 1	h	2-3	11764	Branston	Hamilton	Storey	Duxbury	Marshall	Mercer	Rawlings	Ferris	Roberts (2)	Sapsford	Quantrill
Dec 25	Blackburn Rovers		Div 1	a	1-1		Branston	Hamilton	Doolan	Laird	Marshall	Crawford	Rawlings	Ferris	Roberts	Sapsford (1)	Quantrill
Dec 26	Blackburn Rovers		Div 1	h	1-0	32959	Branston	Hamilton	Doolan	Laird	McCall	Crawford	Rawlings	Ferris (1)	Roberts	Sapsford	Quantrill
Dec 30	Aston Villa		Div 1	a	0-1		Branston	Doolan	Speak	Laird	Marshall	Crawford	Rawlings	Ferris	Marquis	Sapsford	Quantrill
Jan 6	Aston Villa		Div 1	h	3-2	17124	Branston	Hamilton	Speak	Laird	Marshall	Crawford	Rawlings	Ferris	Marquis (3)	Woodhouse	Quantrill
Jan 13	Aberdare	Rd 1	FAC	a	3-1	13000	Branston	Hamilton	Speak	Laird	Marshall	Crawford	Rawlings (1p)	Ferris	Roberts (1)	Woodhouse (1)	Quantrill
Jan 20	Burnley		Div 1	a	0-2		Branston	Hamilton	Speak	Duxbury	McCall	Crawford	Rawlings	Jefferis	Marquis	Woodhouse	Ferris
Jan 27	Burnley		Div 1	h	3-1	21234	Branston	Hamilton	Speak	Gilchrist	McCall	Crawford	Rawlings	Laird	Roberts (2)	Ferris	Quantrill (1)
Feb 3	Charlton Ath	Rd 2	FAC	a	0-2	21464	Branston	Hamilton	Doolan	Laird	McCall	Crawford	Rawlings	Jefferis	Roberts	Woodhouse	Ferris
Feb 8	Stoke City		Div 1	h	4-2	6153	Branston	Doolan	Speak	Gilchrist	Marshall	Crawford	Rawlings	Laird (1)	Roberts (3)	Woodhouse	Williamson
Feb 10	Stoke City		Div 1	a	2-4		Branston	Doolan	Speak	Gilchrist	Marshall	Crawford	Rawlings	Ferris (1)	Roberts (1)	Woodhouse	Williamson
Feb 17	Huddersfield		Div 1	a	1-0	17356	Branston	Doolan	Speak	Gilchrist	Marshall	Crawford	Rawlings	Ferris	Roberts (1)	Woodhouse	Quantrill
Mar 3	Birmingham		Div 1	h	2-3	13105	Branston	Hamilton	Doolan	Gilchrist	Marshall	Crawford	Rawlings	Laird	Roberts (2)	Woodhouse	Williamson
Mar 10	Birmingham		Div 1	a	0-1		Branston	Hamilton	Speak	Gilchrist	Marshall	Crawford	Rawlings	Laird	Roberts	Ferris	Woodhouse
Mar 17	Sunderland		Div 1	a	2-2		Branston	Hamilton	Speak	Gilchrist	McCall	Crawford	Rawlings	Woodhouse (1)	Roberts (1)	Ferris	Quantrill
Mar 21	Huddersfield		Div 1	a	0-2		Branston	Hamilton	Speak	Gilchrist	Marshall	Crawford	Rawlings	Woodhouse	Roberts	Ferris	Quantrill
Mar 24	Sunderland		Div 1	h	2-0	19708	Branston	Hamilton	Speak	Gilchrist	McCall	Crawford	Rawlings	Woodhouse	Roberts (1)	Laird (1)	Mercer
Mar 30	Tottenham H		Div 1	h	1-1		Branston	Hamilton	Speak	Gilchrist	McCall	Crawford	Rawlings	Woodhouse	Roberts (1)	Laird	Mercer
Mar 31	Cardiff City		Div 1	a	0-1		Branston	Hamilton	Yates	Gilchrist	Marshall	Crawford	Rawlings	Woodhouse	Roberts	Laird	Mercer
Apr 2	Tottenham H		Div 1	a	2-0	20114	Branston	Hamilton	Speak	Gilchrist	Marshall	Crawford	Rawlings (1)	Woodhouse (1)	Roberts	Laird	Mercer
Apr 7	Cardiff City		Div 1	h	3-0	15648	Branston	Hamilton	Speak	Gilchrist	Marshall	Crawford	Rawlings (1)	Woodhouse	Roberts (2)	Laird	Quantrill
Apr 14	Arsenal		Div 1	a	1-1		Branston	Hamilton	Speak	Gilchrist	Marshall	Crawford	Rawlings	Woodhouse	Roberts (1)	Laird	Quantrill
Apr 21	Arsenal		Div 1	h	1-2		Branston	Hamilton	Speak	Gilchrist	Marshall	Crawford	Rawlings	Woodhouse	Roberts (1)	Laird	Quantrill
Apr 28	Everton		Div 1	a	0-1		Branston	Hamilton	Speak	Gilchrist	Marshall	Crawford	Rawlings	Woodhouse	Roberts	Laird	Mercer
May 5	Everton		Div 1	h	2-2	12504	Branston	Hamilton	Yates	Gilchrist	Marshall	Crawford	Rawlings (1)	Woodhouse	Roberts (1)	Laird	Quantrill

---

Match Report: Bravery Wins Reward –
8 February 1923 Preston 4 Stoke 2

Stoke made the trip to Deepdale for this Thursday afternoon game with the prospect of having to pay a big sum in compensation to North End for the enforced postponement of their original league fixture from the previous Saturday, due to cup commitments. Because of poor weather, and the game being played during 'working hours' only 6,153 spectators attended the match. But those who could not attend missed a thrilling game, played out on a ground that was waterlogged in parts. Stoke may have lost the toss but their forwards were soon into their stride and but for brave goalkeeping by Branston they would surely have scored. It was the home side however who took the lead when centre-forward Roberts scored after five minutes. The ball had been pushed through to Woodhouse who beat the offside trap only for his effort to hit the post. Fortunately the rebound fell just right for Roberts who pushed the ball into an empty net. Branston again came to North End's rescue when he saved twice from good Stoke efforts, and when he was beaten the upright kept the lead intact. Preston quickly took the game in hand after this incident as Roberts, after a clever run by Laird, poached another goal on 29 minutes. North End held this two goal cushion until the break. The game then restarted in sensational fashion as Preston increased their lead in the very first minute when Laird scored following a pass from Gilchrist. Stoke responded and a scrambled goal six minutes later gave them hope. But almost immediately North End struck the Stoke crossbar with a shot from Rawlings … With just over an hour played Stoke scored again, through Broad, after a good run by the 42 year old Brittleton. This unexpected upset had a good effect on the Preston team as they then raised their game. Roberts received a head injury and had to leave the field for treatment and whilst he was absent Branston got himself into a bit of a pickle (!) as he was also injured stopping a Stoke equaliser. The closing stages were evenly contested as Roberts returned to the action, and a few minutes after finding his feet again playing out on the right wing, he then returned to his normal position and promptly scored Preston's fourth goal with a brave header. Fortune favours the brave they say and Branston and Roberts would certainly agree with that.

SEASON 1923–1924

Bobby Crawford and Tommy Roberts both remained ever present in the 1923–4 season which was testament to their fine form throughout another frustratingly poor year. The team, having just had two seasons where the home form had been very good and the away form abyssmal, tried hard to redress the balance. But this time, although indeed improving the away results, they then went and lost too many at Deepdale! Goalscoring was the main problem, not with Roberts who scored 26 of the 52 league goals, but with the rest of the side. Almost conclusive evidence is available that if Roberts didn't score then neither did Preston. In the 23 games he did not score in there were 13 where the team drew a blank. But one excellent signing did help the attack. George Harrison, an outside-left, was signed from Everton and the ex-England International quickly showed his paces for Preston. A goalscorer and a penalty expert to boot, in fact his first goal for the club was a penalty. This was the last season where the fixtures paired teams together, home and away, two weeks running and one of North End's best victories came when Burnley were beaten 5–0 at home, a week after losing 1–0 at Turf Moor. James Ferris scored a fine hat-trick in that 5–0 win, amazing when you think that he only scored one other goal

all season! Only one double was achieved, vs. Middlesbrough, whilst five teams beat Preston home and away, including Blackburn on Christmas Day and Boxing Day. Not a happy Christmas for Preston fans this particular year. Poor Jimmy Lawrence struggled to keep things going. With little money and a mood of depression sweeping the club he was at least hoping for a decent cup run. Alas this was not to be either as Preston suffered a first round exit at the hands of Everton. On top of that stalwarts Alf Quantrill and Archie Rawlings, two former England Internationals, played their last games for the club so it was gloom and despondency all round as Preston headed for the summer of 1924. The one bright spot was Roberts and not only was his goalscoring exploits recognised by the Preston fans but also by the England selectors. He won two caps during the season and needless to say he scored in both games.

DEBUTANTS: (8) Alf Duggins, James Forrest, George Harrison, Francis O'Rawe, George Prout, Harold Reay, Leslie Scott and William Wade.

LAST GAMES: (11) Duggins, Duxbury, Ferris, Gilchrist, Laird, Marshall, O'Rawe, Quantrill, Rawlings, Reay and Scott.

Future Players born between August 1923 and July 1924: Willie Dougall, Willie Robertson, Albert Dainty and Angus Morrison
Hat-tricks: (1) James Ferris
Ever presents: (2) Bobby Crawford and Tommy Roberts
FA Cup: Round One
Manager: Jimmy Lawrence
Chairman: Sir Meyrick Hollins
Leading scorer: 26 goals – Tommy Roberts (all league)
Players used: 26
AUTHORS' UNOFFICIAL PLAYER OF THE SEASON: Bobby Crawford

League appearances (42 games)

Branston J. H. 22, Crawford R. 42, Duggins A. E. 2, Duxbury T. 8, Ferris J. 21, Forrest J. 2, Gilchrist J. W. 2, Hamilton T. 36, Harrison G. 24, Laird A. 11, McCall J. 32, Marquis F. 17, Marshall J. (No2) 7, Mercer W. 30, O'Rawe F. 4, Prout G. W. 18, Quantrill A. E. 31, Rawlings A. 27, Reay H. 1, Roberts W. T. 42, Sapsford G. D. 7, Scott L. 2, Wade W. A. 8, Williamson J. 1, Woodhouse R. T. 25, Yates W. J. 40.

FA Cup Appeaarances (1 game)

Branston, Hamilton, Yates, Mercer, Marshall, Crawford, Woodhouse, Rawlings, Roberts, Ferris and Harrison all one each.

Goalscorers: 52 League–1 Cup–(Total 53)

Roberts 26–0 (26), Harrison 6(3p)–0 (6), Ferris 4–0 (4), Marquis 4–0 (4), Rawlings 3–1 (4), Sapsford 2–0 (2), Quantrill 2–0 (2), Laird 2–0 (2), Woodhouse 2–0 (2), Crawford 1–0 (1).

League position in Division One: 18th – P42 W12 D10 L20 F52 A67 Pts 34
Home: W8 D4 L9 F34 A27 Away: W4 D6 L11 F18 A40

Match Report: Ferris Triple Topples Burnley – Jan 5 1924 Preston 5 Burnley 0

Both teams entered this contest desperate for a win, Burnley because they had not won away since the previous March and Preston because they had lost a total of 14 points at home since the start of the season. It was Preston who started with gusto, going close a couple of times in the early stages through Ferris and Roberts. The home forwards were more mobile than their visitors and their domination paid off after 14 minutes. Rawlings did the spadework with a delightful dribble, but to the surprise of the crowd, his low centre was mis-kicked by Roberts even though he was unmarked. The ball, however, travelled straight to Ferris who scored with a shot just inside the left-hand post. Midway through the half North End's sprightly long passing game nearly brought them a second goal as the right-wing pair combined cleverly to set up Roberts, but his effort was hooked wide of the far post with Dawson, the goalkeeper, well beaten. On the half hour the Burnley goal had three thrilling escapes in the space of five minutes. Ferris and Roberts were again involved and all this adventurous play was much to the liking of the appreciative crowd. They cheered a second goal when Roberts eventually scored, this time with a header. The Burnley defenders were put under extreme pressure by the eager Preston players and were forced into many errors. With three minutes to go before the interval they were completely overrun. Goal number three came via Ferris who scored from another centre from Rawlings and within a minute Preston went 4–0 up as the crowd went wild. This time it was Roberts who was the marksman, scoring with a shot that went just under the crossbar. The second half was quiet by comparison as the Burnley players tightened up their marking. The damgae for them though had already been done as Branston in the Preston goal stood virtually as a spectator with just back passes and long range shots to field. Harrison received an injury on the hour mark and had to leave the field for treatment. Whilst he was away Preston scored their fifth goal, Ferris bagging his hat-trick to complete a fine afternoon. It was to be the highlight of his career.

PNE Reserves 1923–24.
Left to right. *Back row:* Smith, Wade, Branston, Mercer, Hirst, Gerrard, Doherty (trainer). *Front row:* Lovatt, Ratcliffe, Henderson, Miller, Dickie.

Season 1923–24: First Division

	P	W	D	L	F	A	Pts
1 Huddersfield	42	23	11	8	60	33	57
2 Cardiff	42	22	13	7	61	34	57
3 Sunderland	42	22	9	11	71	54	53
4 Bolton	42	18	14	10	68	34	50
5 Sheffield United	42	19	12	11	69	49	50
6 Aston Villa	42	18	13	11	52	37	49
7 Everton	42	18	13	11	62	53	49
8 Blackburn	42	17	11	14	54	50	45
9 Newcastle	42	17	10	15	60	54	44
10 Notts County	42	14	14	14	44	49	42
11 Man City	42	15	12	15	54	71	42
12 Liverpool	42	15	11	16	49	48	41
13 West Ham	42	13	15	14	40	43	41
14 Birmingham	42	13	13	16	41	49	39
15 Tottenham	42	12	14	16	50	56	38
16 WBA	42	12	14	16	51	62	38
17 Burnley	42	12	12	18	55	60	36
18 PRESTON	**42**	**12**	**10**	**20**	**52**	**67**	**34**
19 Arsenal	42	12	9	21	40	63	33
20 Nottingham Forest	42	10	12	20	42	64	32
21 Chelsea	42	9	14	19	31	53	22
22 Middlesbrough	42	7	8	27	37	60	22

Match Report: Liverpool Dish Out Lesson –
17 September 1923 Liverpool 7 Preston 3 Lancs Cup

This was the third meeting in just nine days between these two sides with Liverpool already having done the double over their West Lancashire opponents in the league. Preston reluctantly made five defensive changes for this game, bringing in reserves to replace their main defenders who all had knocks and sprains. Only around 1,000 spectators saw Preston, captained by Branston, kick off. Liverpool took the lead as early as the fifth minute through Walsh, following good work by Hopkins. This delighted their fans and three minutes later they doubled their lead when Walsh converted a square pass from Forshaw. Preston fought back and Roberts struck an opportunist goal in the 13th minute to bring the visitors back into the game. It was an all action match as Preston clawed themselves level when Woodhouse scored with a 25 yard shot. Roberts and Woodhouse were combining well in this North End rally but it was the experienced Liverpool wingers, up against the young Preston full-backs, Wade and O'Rawe, who turned the game. Liverpool stepped up a gear and Chambers scored two goals from close range inside a minute as preston's defence flagged. The Reds inside-left then completed his hat-trick five minutes later when Hopkin laid the ball back to him to take in his stride. Not to be outdone the home centre-forward, Walsh, also scored a third goal before the half-time interval. Liverpool were the current League Champions, and it showed! Although North End made a couple of token raids in the second half there was really only one team in it and it was not the Lilywhites on this occasion. Another consolation goal was scored by Roberts but in the end Liverpool ran out easy winners with all the goals being scored in a 63 minute spell.

Date 1923-4	Opponents	Comp	h or a	Score	Att.	1	2	3	4	5	6	7	8	9	10	11
Aug 25	Tottenham H	Div 1	a	0-2		Branston	Hamilton	Yates	Gilchrist	McCall	Crawford	Rawlings	Woodhouse	Roberts	Sapsford	Quantrill
Aug 27	Huddersfield	Div 1	h	1-3	18331	Branston	Hamilton	Yates	Gilchrist	Mercer	Crawford	Rawlings	Woodhouse	Roberts	Sapsford (1)	Quantrill
Sep 1	Tottenham H	Div 1	h	2-2	17034	Branston	Hamilton	Yates	Duxbury	Marshall	Crawford	Rawlings	Laird	Roberts (1)	Sapsford	Quantrill (1)
Sep 4	Huddersfield	Div 1	a	0-4		Branston	Hamilton	Yates	Duxbury	Marshall	Crawford	Rawlings	Marquis	Roberts	Laird	Quantrill
Sep 8	Liverpool	Div 1	h	0-1	18397	Branston	Hamilton	Yates	Duxbury	Marshall	Crawford	Rawlings	Laird	Roberts	Ferris	Quantrill
Sep 15	Liverpool	Div 1	a	1-3		Branston	Hamilton	Yates	Duxbury	Marshall	Crawford	Rawlings	Laird (1)	Roberts	Woodhouse	Reay
Sep 22	Aston Villa	Div 1	h	2-2	17906	Branston	Hamilton	Yates	Duxbury	McCall	Crawford	Rawlings	Laird	Roberts (2)	Sapsford	Quantrill
Sep 29	Aston Villa	Div 1	a	1-5		Branston	Hamilton	Yates	Duxbury	McCall	Crawford	Rawlings	Laird (1)	Roberts	Sapsford	Quantrill
Oct 6	Sheffield Utd	Div 1	h	1-1	13534	Branston	Wade	Yates	Duxbury	McCall	Crawford	Rawlings	Laird	Roberts (1)	Woodhouse	Quantrill
Oct 13	Sheffield Utd	Div 1	a	0-4		Branston	Wade	Yates	Duxbury	McCall	Crawford	Rawlings	O'Rawe	Roberts	Woodhouse	Quantrill
Oct 20	Cardiff City	Div 1	a	1-1		Branston	Hamilton	Yates	Mercer	McCall	Crawford	Rawlings	O'Rawe	Roberts (1)	Woodhouse	Quantrill
Oct 27	Cardiff City	Div 1	h	3-1	20887	Branston	Hamilton	Yates	Mercer	McCall	Crawford	Rawlings	Ferris	Roberts (2)	Woodhouse (1)	Quantrill
Nov 3	Sunderland	Div 1	a	1-2		Branston	Hamilton	Yates	Mercer	McCall	Crawford	Rawlings (1)	Ferris	Roberts	Woodhouse	Quantrill
Nov 10	Sunderland	Div 1	h	1-2	19708	Branston	Hamilton	Yates	Laird	McCall	Crawford	Rawlings	Ferris	Roberts (1)	Woodhouse	Quantrill
Nov 17	Newcastle Utd	Div 1	h	1-2	12500	Branston	Hamilton	Yates	Mercer	McCall	Crawford	Rawlings	Ferris	Roberts (1)	Laird	Quantrill
Nov 24	Newcastle Utd	Div 1	a	1-3		Scott	Hamilton	Yates	Mercer	Marshall	Crawford	Rawlings	Woodhouse	Roberts (1)	Laird	Quantrill
Dec 1	Chelsea	Div 1	h	1-1	15049	Scott	Hamilton	Yates	Mercer	McCall	Crawford	Rawlings	Marquis	Roberts	Woodhouse	Quantrill (1)
Dec 8	Chelsea	Div 1	a	2-1		Branston	Hamilton	Yates	Mercer	McCall	Crawford (1)	Quantrill	Rawlings (1)	Roberts	Ferris	Harrison
Dec 15	Middlesbrough	Div 1	h	4-0	15919	Branston	Hamilton	Yates	Marshall	McCall	Crawford	Quantrill	Rawlings (1)	Roberts (2)	Ferris	Harrison (1p)
Dec 22	Middlesbrough	Div 1	a	2-1		Branston	Hamilton	Yates	Mercer	McCall	Crawford	Quantrill	Rawlings	Roberts (1)	Ferris	Harrison (1)
Dec 25	Blackburn Rovers	Div 1	a	0-2		Branston	Hamilton	Yates	Mercer	Marshall	Crawford	Quantrill	Rawlings	Roberts	Ferris	Harrison
Dec 26	Blackburn Rovers	Div 1	h	0-1	32977	Branston	Hamilton	Yates	Mercer	McCall	Crawford	Quantrill	Rawlings	Roberts	Ferris	Harrison
Dec 29	Burnley	Div 1	a	0-1		Branston	Wade	Hamilton	Mercer	McCall	Crawford	Quantrill	Laird	Roberts	Ferris	Harrison
Jan 5	Burnley	Div 1	h	5-0	15564	Branston	Hamilton	Yates	Mercer	McCall	Crawford	Woodhouse	Rawlings	Roberts (2)	Ferris (3)	Harrison
Jan 12	**Everton** Rd 1	**FAC**	**a**	**1-3**	**33100**	**Branston**	**Hamilton**	**Yates**	**Mercer**	**Marshall**	**Crawford**	**Woodhouse**	**Rawlings (1)**	**Roberts**	**Ferris**	**Harrison**
Jan 19	Notts County	Div 1	a	0-0		Prout	Hamilton	Yates	Mercer	O'Rawe	Crawford	Quantrill	Rawlings	Roberts	Ferris	Harrison
Jan 26	Notts County	Div 1	h	2-1	14397	Prout	Hamilton	Yates	Mercer	O'Rawe	Crawford	Quantrill	Rawlings	Roberts (2)	Ferris	Harrison
Feb 2	Nottm Forest	Div 1	h	3-1	13691	Prout	Hamilton	Yates	Mercer	McCall	Crawford	Quantrill	Marquis	Roberts (2)	Ferris (1)	Harrison
Feb 6	Everton	Div 1	a	1-1		Prout	Hamilton	Yates	Mercer	McCall	Crawford	Rawlings	Marquis (1)	Roberts	Ferris	Harrison
Feb 9	Everton	Div 1	h	0-1	15074	Prout	Hamilton	Yates	Mercer	McCall	Crawford	Rawlings	Marquis	Roberts	Ferris	Harrison
Feb 16	WBA	Div 1	a	2-1		Prout	Hamilton	Yates	Mercer	McCall	Crawford	Quantrill	Marquis	Roberts (1)	Woodhouse (1)	Harrison
Mar 1	Birmingham	Div 1	a	0-2		Prout	Hamilton	Yates	Mercer	Forrest	Crawford	Quantrill	Marquis	Roberts	Woodhouse	Harrison
Mar 8	Birmingham	Div 1	h	1-0	15812	Prout	Wade	Yates	Mercer	McCall	Crawford	Quantrill	Marquis	Roberts	Woodhouse	Harrison (1)
Mar 15	Manchester City	Div 1	h	4-1	17117	Prout	Hamilton	Yates	Mercer	McCall	Crawford	Quantrill	Marquis (2)	Roberts (2)	Woodhouse	Harrison
Mar 19	WBA	Div 1	h	1-2	8222	Prout	Hamilton	Yates	Mercer	McCall	Crawford	Quantrill	Marquis	Roberts (1)	Woodhouse	Harrison
Mar 22	Manchester City	Div 1	a	2-2		Prout	Hamilton	Yates	Mercer	McCall	Crawford	Woodhouse	Marquis	Roberts (1)	Ferris	Harrison (1p)
Mar 29	Bolton W.	Div 1	h	0-2	18244	Prout	Hamilton	Yates	Mercer	McCall	Crawford	Woodhouse	Forrest	Roberts	Ferris	Harrison
Apr 5	Bolton W.	Div 1	a	0-0		Prout	Hamilton	Yates	Williamson	McCall	Crawford	Woodhouse	Marquis	Roberts	Duggins	Harrison
Apr 12	West Ham Utd	Div 1	a	1-3		Prout	Hamilton	Yates	Mercer	McCall	Crawford	Woodhouse	Marquis (1)	Roberts	Duggins	Harrison
Apr 19	West Ham Utd	Div 1	h	2-1	16002	Prout	Wade	Yates	Mercer	McCall	Crawford	Woodhouse	Marquis	Roberts	Ferris	Harrison (2) 1p
Apr 21	Nottm Forest	Div 1	a	1-1		Prout	Wade	Yates	Mercer	McCall	Crawford	Woodhouse	Marquis	Roberts (1)	Ferris	Harrison
Apr 26	Arsenal	Div 1	h	0-2	14029	Prout	Wade	Hamilton	Mercer	McCall	Crawford	Woodhouse	Marquis	Roberts	Sapsford	Harrison
May 3	Arsenal	Div 1	a	2-1		Prout	Wade	Yates	Mercer	McCall	Crawford	Woodhouse	Marquis	Roberts (1)	Sapsford (1)	Quantrill

SEASON 1924–1925

The writing had been on the wall for almost all of the post-war seasons so far and this time nothing could prevent relegation becoming a reality as Preston struggled from day one. Twenty-six defeats told its own story. The first five games were all lost, the first four without a goal being scored, the horror story just went from bad to worse. The manager chopped and changed the line-up in a vain effort to find the right formula but it was a hopeless task. And one of the saddest days in the club's illustrious history came on 31 January 1925 when the great Joe McCall made his last appearance in the famous white shirt, an FA Cup-tie at West Bromwich Albion. The former England player had amassed 370 league and 25 cup-tie appearances for the club, either side of the war. It was now pretty obvious that the bulk of the playing staff were just not good enough, although some did perform admirably. Notably George Harrison, William Aitken and Rowland Woodhouse. All three worked tirelessly to stem the tide. Probably the root of Preston's problems was the early season transfer of the ever reliable Tommy Roberts to Burnley. With him gone the goals dried up and it was left to Woodhouse to take on the goalscoring mantle. He tried his best and he even led the goal charts at the end of the season. He also provided one of the season's few highlights when he scored a superb hat-trick in the 4–1 home FA Cup win over Manchester City. But at the other end goalkeeper Jimmy Branston understandably lost form and in the end he shared the goalkeeping position with George Prout. The club's dreadful run up to Christmas was relieved by a Yuletide treble, a great double over arch rivals Blackburn and another win over West Ham. But this was a false dawn and when 1924 turned into 1925 the gloom returned as Preston suffered five straight defeats. Defeat at WBA ended any hopes of some relief from the cup and only four wins after Christmas finally put paid to North End's Division One status. On April 23 the beleaguered Jimmy Lawrence resigned as manager and the following month Preston appointed Frank Richards, formerly at Birmingham, as the new man in charge. Lawrence, meanwhile, went to a coaching job in Germany.

DEBUTANTS: (13) William Aitken, Horace Barnes, George Cook, William Henderson, Joe Hetherington, Thomas Hicks, Harry Hirst, Harry Miller, John Paterson, James Phizacklea, Francis Pickering, Charles Thompson and Thomas Woodward.

LAST GAMES: (11) Henderson, Hetherington, Hirst, McCall, Marquis, Mercer, Miller, Paterson, Pickering, Thompson and Yates.

Future Players born between August 1925 and July 1925: Gordon Kalie, **Willie Cunningham**, Malcolm Newlands, **Joe Walton** and Harry Mattinson

Ever presents: None	
Hat-tricks: (1) Woodhouse (FAC)	FA Cup: Second Round
	Chairman: Sir Meyrick Hollins
Manager: Jimmy Lawrence (Resigned April 1925) Frank Richards (Appointed May 1925)	
Leading scorer: 9 goals – Rowland Woodhouse (6 League 3 Cup)	
Players used: 28	

AUTHORS' UNOFFICIAL PLAYER OF THE SEASON: William Aitken

League appearances (42 games)

Aitken W. J. 41, Barnes H. 26, Branston J. H. 17, Cook G. 13, Crawford R. 25, Forrest J. 31, Hamilton T. 18, Harrison G. 38, Henderson W. (No2) 9, Hetherington J. 5, Hicks T. G. 2, Hirst H. 2, McCall J. 20, Marquis F. 9, Mercer W. 14, Miller J. H. 5, Paterson J. 17, Phizacklea J. R. 15, Pickering F. O. 1, Prout G. W. 25, Roberts W. T. 6, Sapsford G. D. 12, Thompson C. H. 1, Wade W. A. 30, Williamson J. 25, Woodhouse R. T. 34, Woodward T. 15, Yates W. J. 6.

FA Cup appearances (2 games)

Branston 2, Wade 2, Cook 2, Forrest 2, McCall 2, Williamson 2, Aitken 2, Paterson 2, Woodhouse 2, Barnes 2, Harrison 2.

Goalscorers: 37 League–4 FAC–(Total 41)

Woodhouse 6–3 (9), Harrison 8(3p)–0 (8), Barnes 8(1p)–0 (8), Aitken 6–0 (6), Roberts 2–0 (2), Marquis 2–0 (2), Williamson 2–0 (2), Sapsford 2–0 (2), Henderson 1–0 (1), Paterson 0–1 (1).

League position in Division One: 21st (Relegated) – P42 W10 D6 L26 F37 A74 Pts 26
Home: W8 D2 L11 F29 A35 Away: W2 D4 L15 F8 A39

Match Report: City's Defensive Wall Demolished –
10 Jan 1925 FA Cup First Round Preston 4 Man.City 1

For the sixth time in their history North End and Manchester City were paired together in the first round of the FA Cup. Preston had Barnes playing against his old club whereas Mitchell, North End's 1922 Cup Final goalkeeper was now with City. The Deepdale enclosure presented a typical cup-tie atmosphere as City, the slight favourites, won the toss. Both teams raided their opponent's territory vigorously but without creating any clear cut chances. The best so far fell to Barnes but his well struck shot cannoned off the full-back for a fruitless corner. For a short period Preston held the upper hand but their movements fell down in the penalty area. Barnes eventually paved the way for a grand opening goal after 24 minutes. He spoon-fed the ball out to Aitken on the right-wing where he, at the second attempt, crossed accurately into the path of Woodhouse, who headed the ball beyond Mitchell's reach. The visitors came more into the match at this tense stage but they found Cook in fine defensive form and North End were able to soak up this pressure before striking again themselves on 37 minutes. Having received the ball from the right-wing Barnes refused to be shaken off by Woosnam and Pringle and though forced back twice he then manoeuvred brilliantly to create an opening for Woodhouse who successfully drove home a first time shot to make it 2–0 at half-time. Within five minutes of the restart Barnes, on top form, dribbled between two defenders before once again supplying the perfect pass to Woodhouse. The Leyland born forward skilfully controlled the ball before completing North End's first hat-trick of the season. Before the cheering had died down the lead was increased by Paterson who lobbed in a shot-cum-centre, seeing it successfully fall beyond Mitchell and in off the far post. City retaliated in desperation and on three occasions they seemed destined to score but Branston saved brilliantly with impressive one handed saves. The game continued to ebb and flow and City notched a deserved consolation goal before the end. At the final whistle though they trooped off very dejectedly and were a well beaten side, much to the delight of the North End team and their fans.

Joe McCall. Towards the end of his career.

Match Report: Five On The Trot –
15 September 1924 Preston 1 Cardiff 3

Having started the season with four defeats without even a goal being scored, Preston looked for an improvement and the management made several team changes for this Monday match. Alas, though there was some better play the result again went against North End. The match was only six minutes old when the lively Gill broke well for Cardiff. The clever inside-forward centred and Len Davies scored easily. At least Preston then had the satisfaction of scoring their first goal of the season when Roberts headed in a right-wing centre for an equaliser. Before the fans had stopped clapping though Cardiff regained the lead. This time a free-kick on the edge of the box was awarded and Clennell's shot was deflected past the unfortunate Prout in Preston's goal. Amongst the Preston team changes was the inclusion of a young reserve player called Pickering. He was normally an outside-left but for this game he was asked to play on the opposite wing. It meant that the youngster was far from happy in this unaccutomed role and it affected his play, having to use his weaker foot. For all that the boy looked a capital footballer and with greater experience he will make good. Aitken's busyness, especially in the first half, added a bit more zest to North End's front line and Woodhouse looked good until he tired in the last half hour. In the second half Preston did everything except press home their territorial advantage. Cardiff comfortably held the best North End could offer despite McCall's magnificent promptings from the back. The villainous weather which blighted the match kept the crowd down to around 12,000 and the final irony came with just four minutes left. Having had so much of the play Preston fell to the sucker punch. A rare Cardiff attack left Clennell unmarked in the inside-right position and he had the easiest of tasks to make it 3–1.

Date 1924-5	Opponents	Comp	h or a	Score	Att.	1	2	3	4	5	6	7	8	9	10	11
Aug 30	West Ham Utd	Div 1	a	0-1		Prout	Wade	Yates	Mercer	McCall	Crawford	Aitken	Hetherington	Roberts	Miller	Harrison
Sep 3	Sunderland	Div 1	a	0-2		Prout	Wade	Yates	Mercer	McCall	Crawford	Aitken	Miller	Roberts	Sapsford	Harrison
Sep 6	Burnley	Div 1	h	0-2	21139	Prout	Wade	Hicks	Mercer	McCall	Crawford	Aitken	Miller	Roberts	Sapsford	Harrison
Sep 13	Leeds Utd	Div 1	h	0-4		Prout	Wade	Hicks	Mercer	McCall	Crawford	Aitken	Woodhouse	Roberts	Miller	Harrison
Sep 15	Cardiff City	Div 1	h	1-3	11309	Prout	Wade	Forrest	Mercer	McCall	Crawford	Pickering	Aitken	Roberts (1)	Woodhouse	Harrison
Sep 20	Birmingham	Div 1	h	1-0	17264	Prout	Wade	Hamilton	Mercer	McCall	Williamson	Aitken	Woodhouse	Roberts (1)	Crawford	Harrison
Sep 27	WBA	Div 1	a	1-1		Prout	Wade	Hamilton	Mercer	McCall	Williamson	Aitken	Woodhouse	Marquis (1)	Crawford	Harrison
Oct 4	Tottenham H	Div 1	h	0-3	21403	Prout	Wade	Hamilton	Mercer	McCall	Williamson	Aitken	Woodhouse	Marquis	Crawford	Harrison
Oct 11	Bolton W.	Div 1	a	1-6		Prout	Wade	Hamilton	Mercer	Forrest	Williamson (1)	Aitken	Woodhouse	Marquis	Crawford	Harrison
Oct 18	Notts County	Div 1	h	0-1	16810	Branston	Wade	Hamilton	Mercer	McCall	Crawford	Aitken	Woodhouse	Hetherington	Paterson	Harrison
Oct 25	Sheffield Utd	Div 1	a	0-3		Branston	Hamilton	Yates	Williamson	McCall	Crawford	Woodhouse	Aitken	Paterson	Miller	Harrison
Nov 1	Newcastle Utd	Div 1	h	0-1	12347	Branston	Hamilton	Yates	Mercer	McCall	Crawford	Woodhouse	Aitken	Paterson	Williamson	Harrison
Nov 8	Liverpool	Div 1	a	1-3		Branston	Hamilton	Yates	Mercer	McCall	Crawford	Aitken	Williamson	Paterson	Williamson	Harrison (1)
Nov 15	Nottm Forest	Div 1	h	3-1	17524	Branston	Cook	Hamilton	Mercer	McCall	Crawford	Aitken (1)	Marquis (1)	Barnes (1)	Paterson	Harrison
Nov 20	Sunderland	Div 1	h	1-2	10760	Branston	Hamilton	Cook	Forrest	McCall	Crawford	Aitken	Marquis	Paterson	Barnes (1)	Harrison
Nov 22	Bury	Div 1	a	1-1		Prout	Wade	Cook	Hirst	Forrest	Crawford	Aitken	Paterson	Woodhouse	Barnes (1)	Harrison
Nov 29	Manchester City	Div 1	h	2-3	19705	Prout	Wade	Yates	Mercer	Forrest	Crawford	Aitken	Paterson	Woodhouse (1)	Barnes	Harrison (1)
Dec 6	Arsenal	Div 1	a	0-4		Prout	Wade	Cook	Hirst	Forrest	Thompson	Aitken	Hetherington	Woodhouse	Barnes	Harrison
Dec 13	Aston Villa	Div 1	h	3-2	9122	Branston	Wade	Cook	Forrest	McCall	Williamson (1)	Aitken (1)	Paterson	Woodhouse (1)	Barnes	Sapsford
Dec 20	Huddersfield	Div 1	h	0-1		Branston	Wade	Cook	Forrest	McCall	Williamson	Aitken	Paterson	Woodhouse	Barnes	Harrison
Dec 25	Blackburn Rovers	Div 1	a	1-0		Branston	Wade	Cook	Forrest	McCall	Williamson	Aitken	Paterson	Woodhouse	Barnes (1)	Harrison
Dec 26	Blackburn Rovers	Div 1	h	3-2	33246	Branston	Wade	Cook	Forrest	McCall	Williamson	Aitken (1)	Paterson	Woodhouse (1)	Barnes (1)	Harrison
Dec 27	West Ham Utd	Div 1	h	3-2	14070	Branston	Wade	Cook	Forrest	McCall	Williamson	Aitken	Hetherington	Woodhouse	Barnes (1)	Harrison (2)
Jan 3	Burnley	Div 1	a	0-1		Branston	Wade	Cook	Forrest	McCall	Williamson	Aitken	Hetherington	Woodhouse	Barnes	Harrison
Jan 10	Manchester City Rd 1	FAC	h	4-1	24644	Branston	Wade	Cook	Forrest	McCall	Williamson	Aitken	Paterson (1)	Woodhouse (3)	Barnes	Harrison
Jan 17	Leeds Utd	Div 1	h	1-4	16212	Branston	Wade	Cook	Forrest	McCall	Williamson	Aitken (1)	Paterson	Woodhouse	Barnes	Harrison
Jan 24	Birmingham	Div 1	a	0-3		Branston	Wade	Cook	Forrest	Forrest	Williamson	Aitken	Paterson	Woodhouse	Barnes	Harrison
Jan 31	WBA Rd 2	FAC	a	0-2	39752	Branston	Wade	Cook	Forrest	McCall	Williamson	Aitken	Paterson	Woodhouse	Barnes	Harrison
Feb 7	Tottenham H	Div 1	h	0-2		Branston	Wade	Cook	Crawford	Forrest	Williamson	Aitken	Paterson	Henderson	Barnes	Harrison
Feb 12	WBA	Div 1	h	1-2	7171	Branston	Wade	Phizacklea	Woodward	Forrest	Crawford	Aitken	Paterson	Henderson	Barnes	Harrison (1p)
Feb 14	Bolton W.	Div 1	h	1-0	19253	Prout	Wade	Phizacklea	Woodward	Forrest	Crawford	Aitken	Woodhouse (1)	Henderson	Barnes	Harrison
Feb 28	Sheffield Utd	Div 1	h	0-1	15709	Prout	Wade	Phizacklea	Woodward	Forrest	Crawford	Aitken	Woodhouse	Henderson	Barnes	Harrison
Mar 7	Newcastle Utd	Div 1	a	1-3		Prout	Wade	Phizacklea	Woodward	Forrest	Williamson	Aitken	Woodhouse (1)	Henderson	Barnes	Harrison
Mar 14	Liverpool	Div 1	h	4-0	11556	Prout	Wade	Phizacklea	Woodward	Forrest	Williamson	Aitken (1)	Woodhouse	Barnes (1)	Sapsford (2)	Harrison
Mar 21	Nottm Forest	Div 1	a	1-0		Prout	Wade	Phizacklea	Woodward	Forrest	Williamson	Aitken	Woodhouse	Barnes	Sapsford	Harrison (1)
Mar 28	Bury	Div 1	h	1-1	19812	Prout	Wade	Phizacklea	Woodward	Forrest	Williamson	Aitken	Woodhouse	Barnes	Sapsford	Harrison (1p)
Apr 1	Notts County	Div 1	a	0-1		Prout	Wade	Phizacklea	Hamilton	Forrest	Williamson	Aitken	Woodward	Woodhouse	Barnes	Harrison
Apr 4	Manchester City	Div 1	a	1-2		Prout	Hamilton	Phizacklea	Woodward	Forrest	Williamson	Aitken	Woodhouse (1)	Henderson	Barnes	Sapsford
Apr 10	Everton	Div 1	h	1-1	18016	Prout	Hamilton	Phizacklea	Woodward	Forrest	Williamson	Aitken	Woodhouse	Henderson (1)	Barnes	Harrison
Apr 11	Arsenal	Div 1	h	2-0	9982	Prout	Hamilton	Phizacklea	Woodward	Forrest	Williamson	Aitken (1)	Woodhouse	Henderson	Sapsford	Harrison (1p)
Apr 13	Everton	Div 1	a	0-0		Prout	Hamilton	Phizacklea	Woodward	Forrest	Crawford	Aitken	Woodhouse	Henderson	Sapsford	Harrison
Apr 18	Aston Villa	Div 1	a	0-1		Prout	Hamilton	Phizacklea	Woodward	Forrest	Crawford	Aitken	Woodhouse	Marquis	Sapsford	Harrison
Apr 25	Huddersfield	Div 1	h	1-4	12634	Prout	Hamilton	Phizacklea	Woodward	Forrest	Crawford	Woodhouse	Paterson	Marquis	Barnes (1p)	Sapsford
May 2	Cardiff City	Div 1	a	0-0		Branston	Hamilton	Phizacklea	Woodward	Forrest	Williamson	Aitken	Woodhouse	Marquis	Barnes	Sapsford

**HORACE BARNES
PRESTON NORTH END**

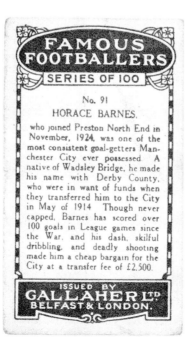

FAMOUS FOOTBALLERS

SERIES OF 100

No. 91

HORACE BARNES,

who joined Preston North End in November, 1924, was one of the most consistent goal-getters Manchester City ever possessed. A native of Wadsley Bridge, he made his name with Derby County, who were in want of funds when they transferred him to the City in May of 1914. Though never capped, Barnes has scored over 100 goals in League games since the War, and his dash, skilful dribbling, and deadly shooting made him a cheap bargain for the City at a transfer fee of £2,500.

ISSUED BY
GALLAHER LTD
BELFAST & LONDON.

Season 1924–25: First Division

	P	W	D	L	F	A	Pts
1 Huddersfield	42	21	16	5	69	28	58
2 WBA	42	23	10	9	58	34	56
3 Bolton	42	22	11	9	76	34	55
4 Liverpool	42	20	10	12	63	55	50
5 Bury	42	17	15	10	54	51	49
6 Newcastle	42	16	16	10	61	42	48
7 Sunderland	42	19	10	13	64	51	48
8 Birmingham	42	11	12	13	49	53	46
9 Notts County	42	16	13	13	42	31	45
10 Man City	42	17	9	16	76	68	43
11 Cardiff	42	16	11	15	56	51	43
12 Tottenham	42	15	12	15	52	43	42
13 West Ham	42	15	12	15	62	60	42
14 Sheffield United	42	13	13	16	55	63	39
15 Aston Villa	42	13	13	16	58	71	39
16 Blackburn	42	11	13	18	53	66	35
17 Everton	42	12	11	19	40	60	35
18 Leeds	42	11	12	19	46	59	34
19 Burnley	42	11	12	19	46	75	34
20 Arsenal	42	14	5	23	46	58	33
21 PRESTON	42	10	6	26	37	74	26
22 Nottingham Forest	42	6	12	24	29	65	24

SEASON 1925-1926

Alex James was a caracaturists dream subject.

Preston began their first season in Division Two under new management, Frank Richards, and with a determined ambition to return to the top flight as soon as possible. It was their first season in this division since the last pre-war season, 1914–15. Richards brought in former Aston Villa and England International Harry Hampton as coach but the season started as it was to go on, with a defeat away and a win at home. At Deepdale North End were almost invincible but away from home they were dreadful. Only two defeats at home but only one win, at Stoke, on their travels, told the story. The management tried everything to stem the tide of away defeats but all to no avail. In one away run eleven consecutive games were lost and it was a mystery to everyone as to why the club were so poor, especially as the home form was sensational. It was the travelling fans who were tearing their hair out the most. But there were still many positive aspects to take from the season, not least in the fact that Preston signed a little Scot called Alex James from Raith Rovers. The soon-to-be-a-genius footballer cost £3,250 and further money was also made available in the December to sign centre-half Dave Morris, also from Raith, to try and improve the defending, especially away from home. This spending, and the willingness by the club to at least try

to make changes did appease the fans somewhat. At Deepdale they could have no complaints as they saw some superb football, with plenty of goals. Willie Russell, signed in the summer of 1924, played very well up front and as the season wore on he struck up a fine partnership with James. The year also saw a large turnover of players as 17 made their debuts and 20 played their last games and left for pastures new. This emphasised the efforts by the management to bring in new blood but at the end of the day a mid-table position was a bitter disappointment for the fans. In the FA Cup hopes were high after Preston held First Division Blackburn at Ewood in the first round. But in the replay at Deepdale Preston were well beaten. How ironic that was, to play well away and then be beaten at home!

DEBUTANTS: (17) Charles Bosbury, John Bradford, Joe Craven, David Daniel, Tom Devlin, James Dickie, Cecil Eastwood, Edward Gerrard, David Gibson, Thomas Gillespie, Walter Jackson, Alex James, David McEachran, David Morris, William Russell, Charles Walsh, Norman Wharton.

LAST GAMES: (19) Aitken, Barnes, Bosbury, Bradford, Cook, Daniel, Dickie, Eastwood, Forrest, Gerrard, Gibson, McEachran, Phizacklea, Prout, Sapsford, Walsh, Williamson, Woodhouse, Woodward.

League appearances (42 games)

Aitken W. J. 15, Barnes H. 13, Bosbury C. E. 2, Bradford J. W. 1, Branston J. H. 32, Cook G. 10, Craven J. 1, Crawford R. 35, Daniel D. 1, Devlin T. 5, Dickie J. 3, Eastwood C. M. 20, Forrest J. 18, Gerrard E. 10, Gibson D. 13, Gillespie T. B. 19, Hamilton T. 27, Harrison G. 38, Hicks T. G. 5, Jackson W. 24, James A. W. 34, McEachran D. 1, Morris D. 20, Phizacklea J. R. 7, Prout G. W. 3, Russell W. F. 40, Sapsford G. D. 2, Wade W. A. 22, Walsh C. 4, Wharton C. N. 7, Williamson J. 14, Woodhouse R. T. 7, Woodward T. 9.

FA Cup appearances (2 games)

Branston 2, Wade 2, Gibson 2, Eastwood 2, Morris 2, Crawford 2, Jackson 2, Bosbury 1, Russell 2, Woodward 1, James 2, Harrison 2.

Goalscorers: 71 League–2 Cup–(Total 73)

James 14–0 (14), Russell 12–0 (12), Jackson 10–2 (12), Harrison 10 (6 pens)–0 (10), Barnes 8–0 (8), Aitken 5–0 (5), Eastwood 2–0 (2), Woodhouse 2–0 (2), Gillespie 2–0 (2), Woodward 1–0 (1), Craven 1–0 (1), Devlin 1–0 (1), Morris 1–0 (1), Dickie 1–0 (1), Own goals 1–0 (1) (Oakes of Port Vale)

David Morris Scottish International. Brought stability to North End's central defence.

STAT FACTS:
Best home run without defeat: 10 games
Best away run without defeat: 3 games
Longest run unbeaten: 5 games
Longest run without a win: 3 games
Best home attendance: 34,577 vs. Blackburn FAC 14.1.26
Worst home attendance: 6,020 vs. Fulham 25.3.26
Best away attendance: 41,088 vs. Blackburn FAC 9.1.26
Worst away attendance: 3,607 vs. Barnsley 19.12.25
Aggregate and Average home attendance: 308,800 – 14,705
Aggregate and Average away attendance: 301,231 – 14,344

League position in Division Two: 12th – P42 W18 D7 L17 F71 A84 Pts 43
Home: W17 D2 L2 F54 A28   Away: W1 D5 L15 F17 A56

Match Report: Rough and Tumble –
25 March 1926 Preston 2 Fulham 1

This rearranged midweek league game, postponed from 20 February because of Fulham's involvement in the FA Cup, was watched by only 6,020 spectators, the lowest league gate at Deepdale for years. Mind you, it was a Thursday afternoon kick-off! North End made a fair start with Alex James being involved in all the clever football produced. The Lilywhites nearly opened the scoring on eleven minutes when, after a couple of near misses by Jackson and James, the ball was knocked back by Gerrard to Wade who was a couple of yards inside his own half. Seeing the keeper off guard he let fly from fully 50 yards, only narrowly missing the target. Within a minute Gerrard's over-hit backpass bounced off keeper Branston as he failed to hold the ball and it rebounded to the incoming winger Linfoot. He hit the ball really hard but it hit Branston and flew clear. The goalkeeper knew nothing of his fortuitous save as he was badly injured in the process. He had to be assisted from the field and went to hospital for a precautionary check-up. Meanwhile North End's skipper David Morris took over in goal and instantly saw Wade collide with an opponent. Wade also had to leave the field for treatment leaving Preston with just nine men on the pitch. Even so the home side enjoyed most of the possession and the attacking play, but were still relieved to see Wade return after about ten minutes. At this point Morris went back to his defensive duties and Gerrard went in goal, holding out until half-time. After the interval Fulham were unlucky not to score as Linfoot hit the post with Gerrard floundering. With 52 minutes gone Morris was temporarily knocked out, he should have stayed in goal! Fulham tested Gerrard with a couple of high balls in quick succession but the stand-in custodian fisted both efforts away, albeit not very far. Preston eventually took the lead in the 64th minute through James, who side-stepped his marker before scoring. Fulham equalised 12 minutes later but little Dickie then hit Preston's winner after good work by James. Gerrard's lively and sometimes amusing style as the makeshift goalkeeper entertained the small Deepdale crowd.

Gallaher's Cigarettes.

*ALEC JAMES
PRESTON NORTH END*

Alex James scored 8 goals in his first 9 games for Preston North End.

Trivia Facts:

Alex James was capped by Scotland after just seven games in the white shirt of PNE.

There was a strange quirk to the signing of Alex James. The club was fined 10 guineas for an irregularity in relation to the transfer form for the little Scot. His registration arrived three days AFTER his debut for the club at Middlesbrough. So, not only were North End thrashed 5–1 at Ayresome Park but they were also fined for the privilege!

The two points gained against Fulham on March 25 1926 gave Preston a total of 1,200 since their league existence began.

A financial loss of £10,390 was made on the 1925–26 season, with £12,468 being spent on transfer fees.

Future Players born between August 1925 and July 1926: Joe Dunn, Jimmy Baxter, Len Kane, Joe Marston, Eddy Brown and Willie Hall

Ever presents: None
Hat-tricks: (1) Jackson
Chairman: Sir Meyrick Hollins

FA Cup: 1st Round replay
Manager: Frank Richards
Players used: 33

Leading scorer: 14 goals – Alex James (all league)

AUTHORS' UNOFFICIAL PLAYER OF THE SEASON: Alex James

Season 1925–26: Second Division

	P	W	D	L	F	A	Pts
1 Wednesday	42	27	6	9	88	48	60
2 Derby	42	25	7	10	77	42	57
3 Chelsea	42	19	14	9	76	49	52
4 Wolves	42	21	7	14	84	60	49
5 Swansea	42	19	11	12	77	57	49
6 Blackpool	42	17	11	14	76	69	45
7 Oldham	42	18	8	16	74	62	44
8 Port Vale	42	19	6	17	79	69	44
9 South Shields	42	18	8	16	14	55	44
10 Middlesbrough	42	21	2	19	77	68	44
11 Portsmouth	42	17	10	15	79	74	44
12 PRESTON	**42**	**18**	**7**	**17**	**71**	**84**	**43**
13 Hull	42	16	9	17	63	61	41
14 Southampton	42	15	8	19	63	63	38
15 Darlington	42	14	10	18	72	77	38
16 Bradford City	42	13	10	19	47	66	36
17 Nottingham Forest	42	14	8	20	51	73	36
18 Barnsley	42	12	12	18	58	84	36
19 Fulham	42	11	12	19	46	77	34
20 Clapton Orient	42	12	9	21	50	65	33
21 Stoke	42	12	8	22	54	77	32
22 Stockport	42	8	9	25	51	97	25

Tom Devlin. Scored on his North End debut *vs.* Oldham Athletic. It was his only goal for PNE. Devlin signed from Birmingham and soon moved on to Liverpool.

*Sincerely Your[s]
T. Devlin.*

Date 1925-6	Opponents	Comp	h or a	Score	Att.	1	2	3	4	5	6	7	8	9	10	11		
Aug 29	Wolverhampton W	Div 2	a	0-3	25273	Branston	Hamilton	Phizacklea	Woodward	Eastwood	Crawford	Aitken	Russell	Sapsford	Barnes	Harrison		
Aug 31	Portsmouth	Div 2	h	3-2	14065	Branston	Hamilton	Phizacklea	Woodward	Eastwood (1)	Crawford	Aitken	Russell	Daniel	Barnes (2)	Harrison		
Sep 5	Swansea	Div 2	h	4-2	15131	Branston	Hamilton	Phizacklea	Williamson	Eastwood	Crawford	Aitken	Russell	Woodhouse (2)	Barnes (2)	Harrison		
Sep 9	Darlington	Div 2	a	1-1	11285	Branston	Hamilton	Cook	Williamson	Forrest	Crawford	Aitken	Russell (1)	Woodhouse	Barnes	Harrison		
Sep 12	Sheffield Wed	Div 2	a	1-5	24967	Branston	Hamilton	Cook	Williamson	Forrest	Eastwood	Aitken (1)	Russell	Woodhouse	Barnes	Harrison		
Sep 14	Middlesbrough	Div 2	h	1-0	13075	Branston	Hamilton	Cook	Williamson	Eastwood	Crawford	Aitken	Russell	Barnes	Sapsford	Harrison (1p)		
Sep 19	Stoke City	Div 2	h	2-0	10791	Branston	Hamilton	Cook	Williamson	Forrest	Eastwood	Aitken	Russell (1)	Woodward (1)	Barnes	Harrison		
Sep 23	Middlesbrough	Div 2	a	1-5	14252	Branston	Hamilton	Cook	Williamson	Eastwood	Forrest	Aitken	Russell (1)	Woodward	James	Harrison		
Sep 26	Oldham Ath	Div 2	a	2-3	15260	Branston	Hamilton	Cook	Williamson	Eastwood	Crawford	Woodhouse	Russell	Barnes (1)	James (1)	Harrison		
Sep 30	Portsmouth	Div 2	a	2-5	11814	Branston	Hamilton	Cook	Walsh	Eastwood	Crawford	Woodhouse	Russell	Barnes (1)	James (1)	Harrison		
Oct 3	Stockport County	Div 2	h	5-3	14925	Branston	Wade	Hamilton	Williamson	Eastwood	Crawford	Woodhouse	Russell (1)	Barnes (2)	James (1)	Harrison (1p)		
Oct 10	Fulham	Div 2	a	1-2	19890	Branston	Hamilton	Phizacklea	Williamson	Eastwood	Walsh	Aitken	Russell	Barnes	James (1)	Harrison		
Oct 17	Hull City	Div 2	h	4-0	17542	Branston	Hamilton	Phizacklea	Williamson	Eastwood	Walsh	Aitken (1)	Russell	Jackson	James (2)	Harrison (1)		
Oct 24	Chelsea	Div 2	a	0-5	40539	Branston	Hamilton	Phizacklea	Williamson	Eastwood	Walsh	Aitken	Russell	Jackson	James	Harrison		
Oct 31	Southampton	Div 2	a	2-2	13707	Branston	Hamilton	Phizacklea	Williamson	Eastwood	Crawford	Aitken	Russell (1)	Jackson	Barnes	Harrison (1p)		
Nov 7	Blackpool	Div 2	a	1-3	10207	Branston	Hamilton	Cook	Woodward	Eastwood	Barnes	Williamson	Russell	Jackson	James (1)	Harrison		
Nov 14	Port Vale	Div 2	h	4-0	17681	Branston	Wade	Hamilton	Woodward	Eastwood	Crawford	Gillespie	Russell (1)	Jackson (1)	James (1)	Harrison	1 o.g.	(Oakes)
Nov 21	Bradford City	Div 2	a	0-2	14021	Branston	Hamilton	Cook	Woodward	Forrest	Crawford	Gillespie	Russell	Jackson	James	Harrison		
Nov 28	Derby County	Div 2	h	2-1	19461	Branston	Hamilton	Hicks	Forrest	Eastwood (1)	Crawford	Gillespie	Russell	Jackson (1)	James	Harrison		
Dec 5	Nottm Forest	Div 2	a	0-4	6648	Branston	Hamilton	Hicks	Forrest	Eastwood	Crawford	Gillespie	Russell	Jackson	James	Harrison		
Dec 12	Clapton Orient	Div 2	h	4-1	14080	Branston	Wade	Hicks	Forrest	Eastwood	Crawford	Gillespie	Russell	Jackson (3)	James	Harrison (1p)		
Dec 19	Barnsley	Div 2	a	0-2	3607	Prout	Wade	Hicks	Forrest	Eastwood	Crawford	Gillespie	Bradford	Jackson	James	Harrison		
Dec 26	South Shields	Div 2	h	0-4	29886	Prout	Hamilton	Gibson	Forrest	Morris	Crawford	Gillespie	Russell	Jackson	Woodward	Harrison		
Jan 2	Wolverhampton W	Div 2	h	1-0	13482	Branston	Wade	Gibson	Gerrard	Morris	Crawford	Bosbury	Craven (1)	Jackson	James	Dickie		
Jan 9	Blackburn Rovers Rd 3	FAC	a	1-1	41088	Branston	Wade	Gibson	Eastwood	Morris	Crawford	Jackson (1)	Russell	Woodward	James	Harrison		
Jan 14	Blackburn Rovers Replay	FAC	h	1-4	34577	Branston	Wade	Gibson	Eastwood	Morris	Crawford	Bosbury	Russell	Jackson (1)	James	Harrison		
Jan 16	Swansea	Div 2	a	1-4	18180	Branston	Wade	Gibson	Gerrard	Morris	Crawford	Bosbury	Russell	Woodward	James	Harrison (1)		
Jan 23	Sheffield Wed	Div 2	h	0-3	12047	Branston	Wade	Gibson	Gerrard	Morris	Crawford	Woodhouse	Russell	Jackson	James	Harrison		
Feb 6	Oldham Ath	Div 2	h	2-1	13611	Branston	Wade	Gibson	Gerrard	Morris	Crawford	Jackson	Russell (1)	Devlin (1)	James	Harrison		
Feb 13	Stockport County	Div 2	a	1-1	9556	Branston	Wade	Gibson	Gerrard	Morris (1)	Crawford	Gillespie	Russell	Jackson	James	Harrison		
Feb 22	Stoke City	Div 2	a	3-1	7423	Branston	Wade	Gibson	Gerrard	Morris	Crawford	Gillespie	Russell (1)	Jackson (1)	James	Harrison (1)		
Feb 27	Hull City	Div 2	a	1-1	8953	Branston	Wade	Gibson	Gerrard	Morris	Crawford	Gillespie	Russell	Jackson (1)	James	Harrison		
Mar 6	Chelsea	Div 2	h	3-1	16463	Branston	Wade	Gibson	Gerrard	Morris	Crawford	Gillespie	Russell	Jackson (2)	James (1)	Harrison		
Mar 13	Southampton	Div 2	a	0-2	8342	Branston	Wade	Gibson	Williamson	Morris	Crawford	Gillespie	Russell	Jackson	James	Harrison		
Mar 20	Blackpool	Div 2	h	6-4	20048	Branston	Wade	Gibson	Gerrard	Morris	Crawford	Gillespie (1)	Russell (1)	Jackson (1)	James (1)	Harrison (2,1p)		
Mar 25	Fulham	Div 2	h	2-1	6020	Branston	Wade	Gibson	Gerrard	Morris	Crawford	Gillespie	Russell	Jackson	James (1)	Dickie (1)		
Mar 27	Port Vale	Div 2	a	0-3	13531	Prout	Hamilton	Hicks	Forrest	Morris	Crawford	Gillespie	Russell	Jackson	James	Dickie		
Apr 2	Darlington	Div 2	h	0-0	17554	Wharton	Wade	Hamilton	Forrest	Morris	Crawford	Jackson	Russell	James	Devlin	McEachran		
Apr 3	Bradford City	Div 2	h	3-1	13784	Wharton	Wade	Hamilton	Forrest	Morris	Crawford	Jackson	Devlin	James (1)	Russell (1)	Harrison (1p)		
Apr 5	South Shields	Div 2	a	1-1	6708	Wharton	Wade	Cook	Forrest	Morris	Crawford	Jackson	Devlin	James (1)	Russell	Harrison		
Apr 10	Derby County	Div 2	a	0-2	17141	Wharton	Wade	Gibson	Forrest	Morris	Crawford	Gillespie	Devlin	James	Russell	Harrison		
Apr 17	Nottm Forest	Div 2	h	2-0	8450	Wharton	Wade	Hamilton	Forrest	Morris	Crawford	Gillespie	Russell	Aitken (2)	James	Harrison		
Apr 24	Clapton Orient	Div 2	a	1-1	13634	Wharton	Wade	Hamilton	Forrest	Morris	Crawford	Gillespie	Russell (1)	Aitken	James	Harrison		
May 1	Barnsley	Div 2	h	4-2	6997	Wharton	Wade	Hamilton	Forrest	Morris	Crawford	Gillespie (1)	Russell (1)	Aitken (1)	James (1)	Harrison		

SEASON 1926–1927

A definite improvement! That is the simple way to sum up the 1926–27 season and but for a few too many away defeats and a couple of crucial incidents then promotion may well have been achieved. As it was Preston had to be content with sixth position but along the way there more than a few plusses to be gained. Bobby Crawford and Tommy Roberts were outstanding throughout with Roberts once again enjoying some prolific goalscoring. He scored in each of the first five games, he actually totalled eight goals in those matches, and but for an injury which kept him out of the last eleven games he could have gone on to create a new record total for the club. In fact Tommy's injury probably cost Preston promotion. It came after the 3–0 defeat at Barnsley as he was travelling home across the Pennines. He was involved in a motor accident which left him with a broken leg. This coincided with a slump in form as North End lost seven of the last ten games, one of which was a 7–0 hammering at Nottingham Forest. Meanwhile, Alex James continued to add to his growing reputation with some brilliantly inventive displays and George Harrison also shone brightly on the left-wing in partnership with the little genius. At the back Dave Morris brought some much needed stability but it was still a far from watertight North End defence. Despite what was by far their best post-war season so far, Preston still conceded goals galore. Apart from the seven at Forest there were three other occasions when five goals were let in and two other games saw four goals past their keeper. The final for and against goals figures showed

that for the Preston fan who liked his football producing goals it was heaven! The FA Cup began well with Roberts scoring all the goals in a 4–2 win at Lincoln City but the run was abruptly ended at Deepdale in the next round by Middlesbrough, who also won the Division two title. It was annoying to think that North End had beaten them in the league game at Ayresome Park and held them to a draw at home. To be fair though Preston won only one other game against the sides who eventually finished above them in the table, at the same time losing the other seven. An important statistic of a nearly season. On the 20 May 1927 Manager Frank Richards decided to resign after two years in charge and five days later the club appointed Alex Gibson from Kilmarnock as his replacement.

DEBUTANTS: (10) Ken Cameron, Tony Carr, Sidney Chandler, George Grierson, Jasper Kerr, Norman Robson, George Shaw, William Whitehead, Frank Williams, Matthew Young.

LAST GAMES: (9) Branston, Devlin, Hicks, Jackson, Shaw, Wharton, Whitehead, Williams, Young.

Future Players born between August 1926 and July 1927: George Thompson and Harry Anders
Ever presents: (1) Bobby Crawford
Hat-tricks: (1) Roberts, 4 goals at Lincoln FAC
Manager: Frank Richards
Chairman: Sir Meyrick Hollins
FA Cup: Second Round **Players used:** 24
Leading scorer: 30 goals – Tommy Roberts (26 League 4 Cup)
AUTHORS' UNOFFICIAL PLAYER OF THE SEASON:
Tommy Roberts

League appearances (42 games)

Branston J. H. 4, Cameron K. 8, Carr A. G. 32, Chandler S. E. 41, Craven J. 2, Crawford R. 42, Devlin T. 3, Grierson G. 2, Hamilton T. 28, Harrison G. 38, Hicks T. G. 2, Jackson W. 21, James A. W. 39, Kerr J. 13, Morris D. 41, Roberts W. T. 30, Robson N. 9, Russell W. F. 40, Shaw G. 3, Wade W. A. 41, Wharton C. N. 6, Whitehead W. T. 3, Williams F. H. 8, Young M. S. 6.

FA Cup appearances (2 games)

Carr 2, Wade 2, Hamilton 1, Hicks 1, Russell 2, Morris 2, Crawford 2, Williams 1, Chandler 2, Whitehead 1, Roberts 2, James 2, Harrison 2.

Goalscorers: 74 League–4 Cup–(Total 78)

Roberts 26–4 (30), Chandler 11–0 (11), James 11(1p)–0 (11), Harrison 5(1p)–0 (5), Russell 5–0 (5), Robson 5–0 (5), Jackson 3–0 (3), Morris 2–0 (2), Crawford 1–0 (1), Whitehead 1–0 (1), Cameron 1–0 (1), Young 1–0 (1), Own goals 2–0 (2) (Shaw of Wolves and Smith of Middlesbrough)

PRESTON NORTH END
FOOTBALL CLUB, 1926-27.

Photo by H. Bamber, Preston.

Back Row, Left to Right—T. Hamilton, W. Whitehead, J. Ratcliffe, J. Branston, N. Wharton, B. Middleton, G. Cook, T. Gerrard.
Second Row, Left to Right—Geo. Waddell (Coach), W. Scott (Trainer), K. Cameron, T. Roberts, R. Fleming, W. Wade, M. Young, F. Lewis, E. Barrowclough, H. Jones, R. H. Taylor (Asst. Sec.), R. Garratt (Asst. Trainer).
Third Row, Left to Right—A. Small, N. Robson, J. Craven, A. James, T. Hicks, T Devlin, S. Chandler, G. Harrison.
Front Row, Left to Right—D. Morris, W. Jackson, R. Crawford, G. Grierson, P. Hulse, W. Fisher, W. Russell.

Match Report: Another Christmas Cracker – 27 Dec. 1926
Preston 4 South Shields 0

Burly George Harrison was prominent in all the early attacking moves but was not involved in the game's opening goal after just eight minutes play. Hamilton, Preston's right-back beat his opponent to the ball and instead of the usual punt upfield he dribbled along the touchline before putting over a delightful centre which Harrison would have been proud of. The unexpected cross led to confusion in the goalmouth from which Chandler snapped up a good half chance to give North End the early lead. South Shields' centre-forward, Parker, who had scored against Preston on Christmas Day, received a nasty accidental knock from Hamilton and had to leave the action for a short time. While he was absent North End squandered a great chance to go two up as Roberts' shot was well saved by goalkeeper McKenna. The visitors fought back proudly and most of the action was in North End's goalmouth. Having said that, Preston did go 2–0 up four minutes after the interval from Harrison's deep centre. Roberts misjudged the flight of the ball but Young, up against ex-North Ender Phizacklea, followed up and bustled both the ball and the goalkeeper towards goal. McKenna actually scooped the ball out but the officials had signalled a goal. It was to be the only goal Young scored for Preston. Over 30,000 were crammed into the Deepdale enclosure and they ten saw Hunter actually receive a booking for fouling the elusive James during the second half as North End won a series of corners. From an attempted clearance from the fourth corner James dribbled into the danger area only to see his shot cannon off an opponent. The ball fell for Chandler and he successfully scored his second goal of the game. The valiant goalkeeper McKenna had his work cut out and had to be on his toes as the game progressed. He even had to go off with slight concussion for a short while and although he returned to a heroes welcome he could not prevent James from scoring Preston's fourth goal. The result was some compensation for Preston as it avenged the 4–0 defeat South Shields inflicted on them twelve months earlier.

David Morris. Scottish International and Preston's captain.

Season 1926–27: Second Division

		P	W	D	L	F	A	Pts
1	Middlesbrough	42	27	8	7	122	60	62
2	Portsmouth	42	23	8	11	87	49	54
3	Man City	42	22	10	10	108	61	54
4	Chelsea	42	20	12	10	62	52	52
5	Nottingham Forest	42	18	14	10	80	55	50
6	**PRESTON**	**42**	**20**	**9**	**13**	**74**	**72**	**49**
7	Hull	42	20	7	15	63	52	47
8	Port Vale	42	16	13	13	88	78	45
9	Blackpool	42	18	8	16	95	80	44
10	Oldham	42	19	6	17	74	84	44
11	Barnsley	42	17	9	16	88	87	43
12	Swansea	42	16	11	15	68	72	43
13	Southampton	42	15	12	15	60	62	42
14	Reading	42	16	8	18	64	72	40
15	Wolves	42	14	7	21	73	75	35
16	Notts County	42	15	5	22	70	96	35
17	Grimsby	42	11	12	19	74	91	34
18	Fulham	42	13	8	21	58	92	34
19	South Shields	42	11	11	20	71	96	33
20	Clapton Orient	42	12	7	23	60	96	31
21	Darlington	42	12	6	24	79	98	30
22	Bradford City	42	7	9	26	50	88	23

STAT FACTS:
Best home run without defeat: 9 games
Best away run without defeat: 7 games
Longest run unbeaten: 8 games
Longest run without win: 4 games
Best home attendance:
34,778 *vs.* Middlesbrough FAC 29.1.27
Worst home attendance:
11766 *vs.* Oldham 5.3.27
Best away attendance:
49,343 *vs.* Man. City 23.4.27
Worst away attendance:
7,996 *vs.* Darlington 11.12.26
Aggregate and average home attendance: 360,204 – 17,153
Aggregate and average away attendance: 337,754 – 16,083

League position in Division Two: 6th – P42 W20 D9 L13 F74 A72 Pts 49
Home: W14 D4 L3 F54 A29 Away: W6 D5 L10 F20 A43

Match Report: Ten Men Tame The Wolves – 13 September 1926 Wolves 1 Preston 2

A very eventful match took place at the Molineux Stadium which saw North End put up a remarkable defensive performance, after everything had conspired against them. As early as the third minute a freak accident saw Morris injured. Apparently the laced part of the ball had hit him in the eye and caused a small blood clot to form impairing his sight temporarily. He went straight to the local Infirmary and had some treatment, he was later well enough to watch most of the second half from the stands. This all meant that North End had to play for 87 minutes with ten men. Alex James was moved to centre-half and Russell switched to a semi forward cum half back position (midfield!). Understandably the Wolves took the initiative and created several chances. Phillipson missed a sitter and Wharton had to be on his toes in goal. In the 23rd minute the home side took the lead following a break down the left. Scott converted the centre after Wharton had failed to hold the ball at the near post. Wolves had their tails up at this stage and Scott went close on two more occasions. Wharton raced out of his goal to kick clear from Lees and Wade cleared off the line when Wharton was beaten again. Gradually though, with James getting to grips with his new role, Preston stood firm. On 31 minutes the recovery was continued as, amazingly, Preston equalised. Jackson charged the keeper causing him to drop the ball. Jackson regained possession and then squared the ball inside for Roberts to guide it into the net with a deft touch. Six minutes later Preston scored what proved to be the winner. Good work by James, Roberts and Harrison ended with a lobbed pass which was met by Jackson's shot. Shaw, facing his own goal tried to clear but only succeeded in diverting the ball past his own goalkeeper. The second half saw Preston's rearguard desperately hold on to this hard earned lead and by a mixture of fine defending and no little amount of luck they managed it. Wharton's last minute magnificent save deservedly giving North End the two points.

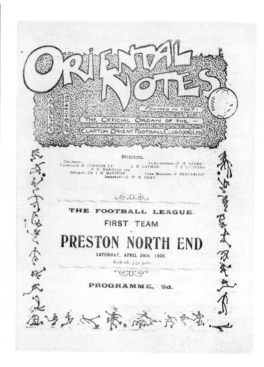

Date 1926-7	Opponents	Comp	h or a	Score	Att.	1	2	3	4	5	6	7	8	9	10	11		
Aug 28	Clapton Orient	Div 2	h	2-2	19674	Branston	Wade	Hamilton	Chandler	Morris	Crawford	Jackson	Russell	Roberts (1)	James (1)	Harrison		
Aug 30	Notts County	Div 2	h	4-1	15353	Branston	Wade	Hamilton	Chandler	Morris (1)	Crawford	Jackson	Russell (1)	Roberts (2)	James	Harrison		
Sep 4	Middlesbrough	Div 2	a	2-0	13496	Branston	Wade	Hamilton	Chandler	Morris	Crawford	Jackson	Devlin	Roberts (2)	James	Harrison		
Sep 11	Port Vale	Div 2	h	4-4	19133	Branston	Wade	Hamilton	Chandler	Morris	Crawford	Jackson (1)	Russell	Roberts (2)	James	Harrison (1)		
Sep 13	Wolverhampton W	Div 2	a	2-1	8266	Wharton	Wade	Hamilton	Chandler	Morris	Crawford	Jackson	Russell	Roberts (1)	James	Harrison	1 o.g.	(Shaw)
Sep 18	Southampton	Div 2	h	1-1	11600	Wharton	Wade	Hamilton	Chandler (1)	Craven	Crawford	Jackson	Russell	Roberts	James	Harrison		
Sep 25	Bradford City	Div 2	h	3-2	15809	Wharton	Wade	Hamilton	Chandler	Morris	Crawford	Jackson	Russell	Roberts (1)	James (2)	Harrison		
Sep 27	Wolverhampton W	Div 2	h	2-0	13676	Wharton	Wade	Hamilton	Chandler	Morris	Crawford	Devlin	Russell (1)	Roberts	James (1p)	Shaw		
Oct 2	Chelsea	Div 2	a	1-2	32398	Wharton	Wade	Hamilton	Chandler	Morris	Crawford	Devlin	Russell	Roberts (1)	James	Harrison		
Oct 9	Grimsby Town	Div 2	h	3-2	12424	Wharton	Wade	Hamilton	Chandler	Morris	Crawford	Jackson	Russell (1)	Whitehead (1)	James (1)	Harrison		
Oct 16	Oldham Ath	Div 2	a	1-5	20669	Carr	Wade	Hamilton	Chandler	Morris	Crawford	Jackson (1)	Russell	Roberts	James	Harrison		
Oct 23	Fulham	Div 2	h	2-2	17365	Carr	Wade	Hamilton	Chandler	Morris	Crawford (1)	Jackson	Russell	Roberts	James	Harrison (1)		
Oct 30	Blackpool	Div 2	a	3-2	16542	Carr	Wade	Hamilton	Russell	Morris	Crawford	Jackson	Chandler (2)	Roberts (1)	James	Harrison		
Nov 6	Reading	Div 2	h	3-1	13770	Carr	Wade	Hamilton	Russell	Morris	Crawford	Williams	Chandler (2)	Roberts (1)	James	Harrison		
Nov 13	Swansea	Div 2	a	0-0	17199	Carr	Wade	Hamilton	Russell	Morris	Crawford	Williams	Chandler	Roberts	James	Harrison		
Nov 20	Nottm Forest	Div 2	a	1-0	16014	Carr	Wade	Hamilton	Russell	Morris	Crawford	Williams	Chandler	Roberts	James (1)	Harrison		
Dec 4	Manchester City	Div 2	h	2-4	24556	Carr	Hamilton	Hicks	Russell	Morris	Crawford	Whitehead	Chandler	Roberts (2)	James	Williams		
Dec 11	Darlington	Div 2	a	1-0	7996	Carr	Wade	Hamilton	Russell (1)	Morris	Crawford	Cameron	Chandler	Roberts	James	Williams		
Dec 18	Portsmouth	Div 2	h	1-2	15901	Carr	Wade	Hamilton	Russell	Morris	Crawford	Young	Cameron	Roberts	James (1)	Harrison		
Dec 25	South Shields	Div 2	a	1-1	9238	Carr	Wade	Hamilton	Russell	Morris	Crawford	Young	Chandler (2)	Roberts (1)	James	Harrison		
Dec 27	South Shields	Div 2	h	4-0	30684	Carr	Wade	Hamilton	Russell	Morris	Crawford	Young (1)	Chandler	Roberts	James (1)	Harrison		
Jan 1	Notts County	Div 2	a	1-1	10006	Carr	Wade	Hamilton	Russell	Morris	Crawford	Jackson	Chandler	Roberts (1)	James	Harrison		
Jan 8	**Lincoln City Rd 3**	**FAC**	**a**	**4-2**	**6700**	**Carr**	**Wade**	**Hamilton**	**Russell**	**Morris**	**Crawford**	**Williams**	**Chandler**	**Roberts (4)**	**James**	**Harrison**		
Jan 15	Clapton Orient	Div 2	a	1-1	14051	Carr	Wade	Hamilton	Russell	Morris	Crawford	Williams	Chandler	Roberts (1)	James	Harrison		
Jan 22	Middlesbrough	Div 2	h	2-2	20419	Carr	Wade	Hamilton	Russell	Morris	Crawford	Williams	Chandler	Roberts	James (1)	Harrison	1 o.g.	(Smith)
Jan 29	**Middlesbrough Rd 4**	**FAC**	**h**	**0-3**	**34778**	**Carr**	**Wade**	**Hicks**	**Russell**	**Morris**	**Crawford**	**Chandler**	**Whitehead**	**Roberts**	**James**	**Harrison**		
Feb 5	Southampton	Div 2	h	1-0	14452	Carr	Wade	Hicks	Crawford	Morris	Grierson	Young	Chandler	Roberts (1)	James	Williams		
Feb 12	Bradford City	Div 2	a	1-0	12694	Carr	Wade	Hamilton	Chandler	Morris	Crawford	Roberts (1)	Russell	Whitehead	James	Harrison		
Feb 19	Darlington	Div 2	h	4-1	15029	Carr	Wade	Hamilton	Russell	Morris	Crawford	Jackson	Chandler (1)	Roberts (2)	James	Harrison (1)		
Feb 26	Grimsby Town	Div 2	a	2-5	15183	Carr	Wade	Hamilton	Russell	Morris	Crawford	Jackson	Chandler	Roberts (2)	James	Harrison		
Mar 5	Oldham Ath	Div 2	h	5-2	11766	Carr	Wade	Hamilton	Russell	Morris	Crawford	Jackson	Chandler (1)	Roberts (2)	James	Harrison (2,1p)		
Mar 12	Fulham	Div 2	a	1-0	16154	Carr	Wade	Kerr	Russell	Morris	Crawford	Jackson	Chandler	Roberts	James	Harrison		
Mar 14	Barnsley	Div 2	a	0-3	11074	Carr	Wade	Kerr	Russell	Morris	Crawford	Jackson	Chandler	Roberts	James	Harrison		
Mar 19	Blackpool	Div 2	h	4-1	24349	Carr	Wade	Kerr	Russell (1)	Morris	Crawford	Jackson (1)	James	Chandler (1)	Cameron (1)	Harrison		
Mar 21	Chelsea	Div 2	h	0-2	14995	Carr	Wade	Kerr	Russell	Morris	Crawford	Jackson	James	Chandler	Cameron	Harrison		
Mar 28	Port Vale	Div 2	a	0-2	8388	Carr	Wade	Kerr	Crawford	Morris	Grierson	Chandler	Russell	Robson	James	Harrison		
Apr 2	Swansea	Div 2	h	4-0	13672	Carr	Wade	Kerr	Russell	Morris (1)	Crawford	Jackson	Chandler	Robson (2)	James (1)	Harrison		
Apr 9	Nottm Forest	Div 2	h	0-7	13946	Carr	Wade	Kerr	Russell	Morris	Crawford	Jackson	Chandler	Robson	James	Harrison		
Apr 15	Hull City	Div 2	h	1-0	17177	Carr	Wade	Kerr	Russell	Morris	Crawford	Young	Chandler	Robson	James (1)	Harrison		
Apr 16	Barnsley	Div 2	h	2-1	16022	Carr	Wade	Kerr	Russell	Morris	Crawford	Craven	Chandler (1)	Robson (1)	James	Harrison		
Apr 18	Hull City	Div 2	a	1-3	12881	Carr	Wade	Kerr	Russell	Morris	Crawford	Chandler	Cameron	Robson (1)	James	Harrison		
Apr 23	Manchester City	Div 2	a	0-1	49343	Carr	Wade	Kerr	Russell	Morris	Crawford	Young	Chandler	Robson	Cameron	Harrison		
Apr 27	Reading	Div 2	a	0-3	9905	Carr	Wade	Kerr	Russell	Morris	Crawford	Shaw	Chandler	Robson	Cameron	Harrison		
May 7	Portsmouth	Div 2	a	1-5	26815	Carr	Wade	Kerr	Russell	Morris	Crawford	Shaw	Chandler	Robson (1)	Cameron	Harrison		

There was an upbeat air around Deepdale in the summer of 1927 as the club looked forward to a new season with a determination to build on the previous campaign. Unfortunately the season was again to ultimately end in disappointment but North End were to get even closer to their promotion goal. And one thing is for certain, the goalscorers certainly did their job as, for the first time ever, the club achieved a magnificent century of league goals. At home, especially, the goals flew in from all angles and in one amazing spell 28 were scored in just seven games, and one of those games was a nil! Five players reached double figures with Norman Robson leading the way on 19 goals, one in front of Alex James who once again made an outstanding contribution. Also prominent were big Dave Morris, Bobby Crawford, as dependable as ever and Tommy Hamilton who was ever present and superbly consistent. One of the keys to the goalscoring came from the two wingers Alex Reid and George Harrison. Their trickery created a host of chances for the other forwards and they weighed in with several goals themselves too. Preston's average crowd held up well in spite of acute difficulties in the national economy and for the FA Cup-tie with Everton a new Deepdale ground

record was set up of 37,788. Alas, the Merseysiders were far too good for North End and another cup run was over before it had begun. Meanwhile, in the league, Preston were in with a real chance and even as late as the Easter they were still challenging. But a 6–2 thrashing at Notts County struck them a mortal blow and three more consecutive defeats ended their hopes for another year. Some consolation did come though in the last game of the season. Preston travelled to Grimsby with a total of 94 goals to their credit. It was probably not in the fans' thoughts to imagine that they might make the 100. But in true fairy tale fashion Preston did indeed score six goals with the 100th goal being scored by George Harrison. The 6–4 win gave the club fourth position in the division and the fans were left with the feeling of so near and yet so far.

DEBUTANTS: (10) Herbert Hamilton, John Kendall, James Metcalf, Frank Moss, Guy Nisbet, George Parry, William Pilkington, Alex Reid, Albert Smith, Frank Ward.

LAST GAMES: (5) Carr, Kendall, Metcalf, Pilkington and Roberts.

Left to right:
Back row: Wade, Carr, Kerr, Cameron, Mr J. I. Taylor, Robson.
Front row: Chandler, Russell, Morris, Crawford, James.

League appearances (42 games)

Cameron K. 4, Carr A. G. 27, Chandler S. E. 19, Crawford R. 41, Hamilton H. 6, Hamilton T. 42, Harrison G. 41, James A. W. 38, Kendall J. 2, Metcalf J. 16, Morris D. 42, Moss F. 13, Nisbet G. 3, Parry G. 1, Pilkington W. 1, Reid A. M. 33, Roberts W. T. 25, Robson N. 22, Russell W. F. 25, Smith A. C. 8, Wade W. A. 27, Ward F. 26.

FA Cup appearances (1 game)

Carr, Wade, Hamilton T., Ward, Morris, Crawford, Reid, Russell, Roberts, James and Harrison all one each.

Goalscorers: 100 League–No FA Cup–(Total 100)

Robson 19, James 18, Harrison 15 (3p), Roberts 13, Reid 13, Russell 9, Cameron 4, Morris 4, Crawford 1, Nisbet 1, Parry 1. Own goals 2 (Oakes of Port Vale, Hampson of South Shields)

Future Players born between August 1927 and July 1928: John Garvie and Frank O'Farrell
Ever presents: (2) Tommy Hamilton and Dave Morris
FA Cup: Round One
Manager: Alex Gibson
Chairman: Sir Meyrick Hollins
Hat-tricks: (4) Roberts, Robson, Harrison and Cameron, one each.
Leading scorer: 19 goals – Norman Robson (all league)
Players used: 22

AUTHORS' UNOFFICIAL PLAYER OF THE SEASON: George Harrison

North End take a break from training.
Left to right: *Back row*: Alex Reid, William Wade, James Jnr, David Morris, George Harrison, Tony Carr, Tommy Roberts, Syd Chandler.
Front row: Tommy Hamilton, Alex James, Frank Ward, Norman Robson, Willie Russell.

Trivia Facts:

There was a unique happening in the 7–2 win over South Shields in February 1928. All five forwards managed to get their names on the scoresheet.

Tommy Roberts was injured in a car crash and had to miss eight games in January and February. He broke his left arm.

Alex James played for Scotland in their famous 5–1 win over England at Wembley in March 1928, and he scored two of the goals. It was the Scottish team later dubbed: 'The Wembley Wizards'.

League position in Division Two: 4th – P42 W22 D9 L11 F100 A66 Pts 53
Home: W15 D3 L3 F62 A24 Away: W7 D6 L8 F38 A42

Match Report: End of Season Ten Goal Bash – 5 May 1928 Grimsby 4 Preston 6

Preston North End's last league game of the season should probably have produced a draw as North End had not won a game for a month and Grimsby had failed to win at home on twelve occasions. Preston made the journey to Blundell Park without the services of Alex James or Willie Russell, their positions being taken by Norman Robson and Kenny Cameron. The visitors had the sun in their eyes at the kick-off but it was not detrimental to their approach play as the five man attack, well supported by the midfield, took a firm grip on the game from the early stages. A defence splitting pass through the heart of Grimsby's defence sent Cameron away, and as Jacobson advanced to tackle him the inside-right coolly lobbed the ball over the head of the oncoming full-back, rounded him, and resisting the challenge from another defender, then beat Read with a superb drive into the far corner of the net. Within minutes Preston had doubled their lead as Ward switched play quickly to his left. Robson's instant control enabled him to set up Cameron who scored his second goal of the afternoon, via the underside of the crossbar. Only 15 minutes played and 2–0 up. Any half chances that Grimsby did create fell to Joe Robson who looked dangerous, but generally the two Hamiltons at the rear of the North End defence made life difficult for the Mariners. Grimsby, already under the cosh, lost their full-back Harris through injury and while he was off the field Norman Robson broke clear to score Preston's third goal. Harris returned after ten minutes but was a virtual passenger on the wing, and he failed to appear at all after the interval. Roberts made a swift break on resuming but his shot deflected straight to Cameron who made no mistake with a first time drive to record his third and preston's fourth goal. The visitors were in complete control and there was no let up in their quest for more goals which duly arrived through Ward and Harrison. All three second half goals had come in an eight minute spell and it was the first time Preston had scored six away from home since 1889! Grimsby's ten men fought for some pride in a frantic finish as Joe Robson snatched an unbelievable three minute hat-trick with just five minutes to go. With North End's defence all at sea, Bestall claimed a fourth goal for Grimsby in the last minute. It all left the previously dominant North End relieved to hear the final whistle.

Alex James. PNE and Scotland. Top-class inside forward who was transferred to Arsenal.

Date 1927-8	Opponents	Comp	h or a	Score	Att.	1	2	3	4	5	6	7	8	9	10	11		
Aug 27	Fulham	Div 2	a	2-2	25655	Carr	Wade	T.Hamilton	Metcalf	Morris	Crawford	Reid	Russell	Roberts (1)	James	Harrison (1p)		
Aug 29	Hull City	Div 2	h	4-2	22138	Carr	Wade	T.Hamilton	Metcalf	Morris (1)	Crawford	Reid	Russell	Roberts	James	Harrison (3)		
Sep 3	Barnsley	Div 2	h	1-2	20736	Carr	Wade	T.Hamilton	Metcalf	Morris (1)	Crawford	Reid	Russell	Roberts	James	Harrison		
Sep 5	Hull City	Div 2	a	0-0	8915	Carr	Wade	T.Hamilton	Metcalf	Morris	Crawford	Smith	Russell	Roberts	James	Harrison		
Sep 10	Wolverhampton W	Div 2	h	3-2	17124	Carr	Wade	T.Hamilton	Metcalf	Morris	Crawford	Pilkington	Robson (2)	Roberts	James	Harrison (1)		
Sep 17	Port Vale	Div 2	h	4-0	18463	Carr	Wade	T.Hamilton	Metcalf	Morris	Crawford	Reid	Robson	Roberts (2)	James	Harrison (1)	1 o.g.	(Oakes)
Sep 24	South Shields	Div 2	a	3-2	6338	Carr	Wade	T.Hamilton	Metcalf	Morris	Crawford	Reid	Robson	Roberts (2)	James (1)	Harrison		
Oct 1	Leeds Utd	Div 2	h	5-1	17394	Carr	Wade	T.Hamilton	Metcalf	Morris	Crawford	Reid (1)	Russell (1)	Roberts	James (2)	Harrison (1)		
Oct 8	Nottm Forest	Div 2	a	1-3	17056	Carr	Wade	T.Hamilton	Metcalf	Morris	Crawford (1)	Reid	Russell	Roberts	James	Harrison		
Oct 15	Manchester City	Div 2	h	1-0	31095	Carr	Wade	T.Hamilton	Metcalf	Morris	Crawford	Reid (1)	Russell	Roberts	James	Harrison		
Oct 22	Clapton Orient	Div 2	a	1-1	10533	Kendall	Wade	T.Hamilton	Metcalf	Morris	Crawford	Reid	Russell	Robson	James (1)	Harrison		
Oct 29	Chelsea	Div 2	h	0-3	23555	Kendall	Wade	T.Hamilton	Metcalf	Morris	Crawford	Reid	Russell	Robson	James	Harrison		
Nov 5	Blackpool	Div 2	a	1-4	10789	Carr	Wade	T.Hamilton	Metcalf	Morris	Crawford	Reid (1)	Russell	Roberts	James	Harrison		
Nov 12	WBA	Div 2	h	3-3	15943	Carr	Wade	T.Hamilton	Ward	Morris	Crawford	Reid (1)	Cameron	Roberts (1)	James (1)	Harrison		
Nov 19	Bristol City	Div 2	a	3-1	9932	Carr	Wade	T.Hamilton	Ward	Morris	Crawford	Reid (1)	Chandler	Roberts (1)	James	Harrison (1)		
Nov 26	Notts County	Div 2	h	4-0	16361	Carr	Wade	T.Hamilton	Ward	Morris	Crawford	Reid	Chandler	Roberts (3)	James	Harrison (1)		
Dec 3	Southampton	Div 2	a	0-0	10383	Carr	Wade	T.Hamilton	Ward	Morris	Crawford	Reid	Chandler	Roberts	James	Harrison		
Dec 10	Stoke City	Div 2	h	2-0	15690	Carr	Wade	T.Hamilton	Ward	Morris (1)	Crawford	Reid (1)	Chandler	Roberts	James	Harrison		
Dec 17	Oldham Ath	Div 2	a	0-0	18366	Carr	Wade	T.Hamilton	Ward	Morris	Crawford	Reid	Chandler	Roberts	James	Harrison		
Dec 24	Grimsby Town	Div 2	h	3-0	12881	Carr	Wade	T.Hamilton	Ward	Morris	Crawford	Reid	Chandler	Roberts (1)	James (1)	Harrison (1)		
Dec 26	Swansea	Div 2	h	4-2	26761	Carr	Wade	T.Hamilton	Ward	Morris	Crawford	Reid (1)	Chandler	Roberts (1)	James (2)	Harrison		
Dec 27	Swansea	Div 2	a	1-0	15264	Carr	Wade	T.Hamilton	Ward	Morris	Crawford	Reid (1)	Chandler	Robson	James	Harrison		
Dec 31	Fulham	Div 2	h	1-0	15149	Carr	Wade	T.Hamilton	Ward	Morris	Crawford	Reid	Russell	Roberts	James (1)	Harrison		
Jan 7	Barnsley	Div 2	a	1-2	7967	Carr	Wade	T.Hamilton	Ward	Morris	Crawford	Reid (1)	Chandler	Roberts	James	Harrison		
Jan 14	Everton Rd 1	FAC	h	0-3	37788	Carr	Wade	T.Hamilton	Ward	Morris	Crawford	Reid	Russell	Roberts	James	Harrison		
Jan 21	Wolverhampton W	Div 2	a	5-4	14466	Carr	Wade	T.Hamilton	Metcalf	Morris	Crawford	Reid	Nisbet	Robson (3)	James (2)	Harrison		
Feb 4	South Shields	Div 2	h	7-2	10738	Carr	Wade	T.Hamilton	Metcalf	Morris	Crawford	Reid (1)	Nisbet	Robson (2)	James (1)	Harrison (1)	1 o.g.	(Hampson)
Feb 6	Port Vale	Div 2	a	0-2	9492	Carr	Wade	T.Hamilton	Ward	Morris	Crawford	Reid	Nisbet	Robson	James	Harrison		
Feb 11	Leeds Utd	Div 2	a	4-2	24216	H.Hamilton	T.Hamilton	Chandler	Morris	Ward	Reid (1)	Russell (1)	Robson (2)	James	Harrison			
Feb 25	Manchester City	Div 2	a	2-2	59500	Carr	Ward	T.Hamilton	Chandler	Morris	Crawford	Reid	Russell (1)	Robson	James (1)	Harrison		
Mar 3	Clapton Orient	Div 2	h	0-0	19225	Moss	Ward	T.Hamilton	Chandler	Morris	Crawford	Reid	Russell	Robson	James	Harrison		
Mar 5	Nottm Forest	Div 2	h	5-0	9969	Moss	Ward	T.Hamilton	Chandler	Morris (1)	Crawford	Reid (1)	Russell	Robson (1)	James	Harrison (2, 1p)		
Mar 10	Chelsea	Div 2	a	1-2	47780	Moss	Ward	T.Hamilton	Chandler	Morris	Crawford	Smith	Russell	Robson	James (1)	Harrison		
Mar 17	Blackpool	Div 2	h	2-1	22948	Moss	Ward	T.Hamilton	Chandler	Morris	Crawford	Smith	Russell	Roberts (1)	James (1)	Harrison		
Mar 24	WBA	Div 2	a	4-2	24067	Moss	Ward	T.Hamilton	Chandler	Morris	Crawford	Smith	Russell	Robson (2)	James (1)	Harrison (1p)		
Mar 31	Bristol City	Div 2	h	5-1	15022	Moss	Ward	T.Hamilton	Chandler	Morris	Crawford	Smith	Russell (2)	Robson (2)	Cameron (1)	Harrison		
Apr 6	Reading	Div 2	h	4-0	24579	Moss	Ward	T.Hamilton	Chandler	Morris	Crawford	Smith	Russell (1)	Robson (2)	James (1)	Harrison		
Apr 7	Notts County	Div 2	a	2-6	16226	Moss	Ward	T.Hamilton	Chandler	Morris	Crawford	Smith	Russell	Robson (1)	James (1)	Harrison		
Apr 9	Reading	Div 2	a	1-2	16661	Moss	H.Hamilton	T.Hamilton	Ward	Morris	Crawford	Smith	Russell (1)	Robson	James	Harrison		
Apr 14	Southampton	Div 2	h	1-2	13354	Moss	H.Hamilton	T.Hamilton	Metcalf	Morris	Crawford	Reid	Russell (1)	Robson	James	Harrison		
Apr 21	Stoke City	Div 2	a	2-3	11403	Moss	H.Hamilton	T.Hamilton	Metcalf	Morris	Crawford	Reid	Russell	Roberts	Cameron	Parry (1)		
Apr 28	Oldham Ath	Div 2	h	1-1	8374	Moss	H.Hamilton	T.Hamilton	Ward	Morris	Crawford	Reid	Russell	Roberts	Robson (1)	Harrison		
May 5	Grimsby Town	Div 2	a	6-4	8747	Moss	H.Hamilton	T.Hamilton	Ward	Morris	Crawford	Reid (1)	Cameron (3)	Roberts	Robson (1)	Harrison (1)		

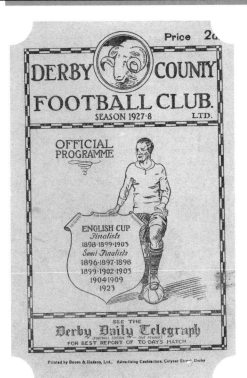

DERBY COUNTY FOOTBALL CLUB.
SEASON 1927-8 LTD.

Price 2d

OFFICIAL PROGRAMME

ENGLISH CUP
Finalists
1898·1899·1903
Semi-Finalists
1896·1897·1898
1899·1902·1903
1904·1909
1923

SEE THE
Derby Daily Telegraph
(FOOTBALL EDITION — ONE PENNY)
FOR BEST REPORT OF TO-DAY'S MATCH

Printed by Bacon & Hudson, Ltd., Advertising Contractors, Colyear Street, Derby

Season 1927–28: Second Division

	P	W	D	L	F	A	Pts
1 Man City	42	25	9	8	100	59	59
2 Leeds	42	25	7	10	98	49	57
3 Chelsea	42	23	8	11	75	45	54
4 PRESTON	42	22	9	11	100	66	53
5 Stoke	42	22	8	12	78	59	52
6 Swansea	42	18	12	12	75	63	48
7 Oldham	42	19	8	15	75	51	46
8 WBA	42	17	12	13	90	70	46
9 Port Vale	42	18	8	16	68	57	44
10 Nottingham Forest	42	15	10	17	83	84	40
11 Grimsby	42	14	12	16	69	83	40
12 Bristol City	42	15	9	18	76	79	39
13 Hull	42	12	15	15	41	54	39
14 Barnsley	42	14	11	17	65	85	39
15 Notts County	42	13	12	17	68	74	38
16 Wolves	42	13	10	19	63	91	36
17 Southampton	42	14	7	21	68	77	35
18 Reading	42	11	13	18	53	75	35
19 Blackpool	42	13	8	21	83	101	34
20 Clapton Orient	42	11	12	19	55	85	34
21 Fulham	42	13	7	22	68	89	33
22 South Shields	42	7	9	26	56	111	23

Yours Sincerely,
N. Robson

SEASON 1928–1929

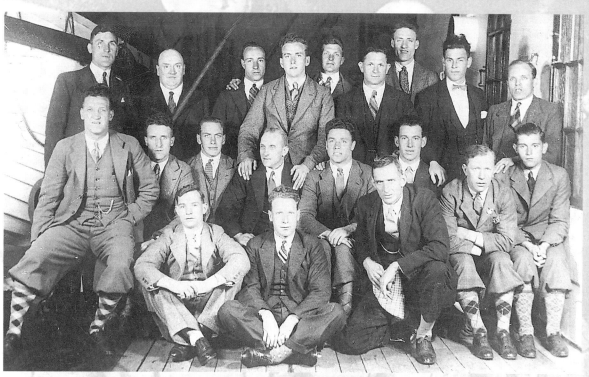

North End squad which went on tour of USA and Canada.

Trivia Facts:

On reading about all the facts and figures of these players of the 1920s it is difficult to conjure up a mental picture, but occasionally the written words of the time did offer some help. For instance, when Jock Ewart joined the club a local writer described him as 'long, lean and laconic'!

The end of season trip to America was an unbelievable experience for all those that went. It had been originally planned with the thought that Alex James would be with the party. Unfortunately for the organisers James's future away from Preston had already been decided and he didn't go to the States. This caused a furore when the ship carrying the party arrived in New York harbour as it was really James that everyone wanted to see. Nevertheless the tour went ahead and the games ranged from total farce to exhibition football in front of small crowds of mostly ex-patriots from England. There are lots of stories from the tour including the one about a visit to the famous Madison Square Gardens where the Preston players were introduced in typically brash American way as, 'The Preston North End Soccer Team, The Champions of the World!' And all this happened at midnight on the day of the first game. Apparently they entered the vast arena to a deathly silence!

After the promotion near misses of the previous two years, this season came as an acute disappointment to all concerned with the club. The biggest let down for the fans was that the away form was again the reason for Preston's poor showing. At Deepdale the record was good, opening up with four straight wins and 18 goals, but this was soon offset by some abyssmal performances on their travels. To find an explanation for this wayward form was not easy. The team line-up was reasonably settled, especially in defence, but the difference in goals scored, 58 at home and only 20 away, seems to indicate that a different system was used in the style of play. Individually though, there were some good performances. Bobby Crawford again showed remarkable consistency as did Dave Morris. Tommy Hamilton and Jasper Kerr played very well at full-back and George Harrison had another productive season on the left-wing. Inside-forward seemed to be the problem area as the number eight and ten were chopped and changed throughout the year. Even Alex James had a mixed season combining some magical displays with some indifferent ones. This could probably be partly explained by events off the field. At one point the Preston Directors refused James permission to play for Scotland in a crucial club versus country row. The mercurial James

did not openly protest but there was no doubt that he was very upset over the decision and it must have affected his form. It came as no surprise when, at the end of the season, the much-loved Scot was transferred. Arsenal were the lucky club who obtained his services for the ridiculously low fee of £8,750. It was indeed a very sad day for the North End fans when the little man left the field against Stoke on May 4 1928, his last appearance in the famous white shirt. On a brighter note, two players managed to hit four goals in a match, Harrison against Grimsby Town and Alex Reid against Port Vale, both games were at Deepdale. Two other players, Norman Robson and Alex 'Sandy' Hair scored hat-tricks, and again they were both at home, thus emphasising that there seemed to be no problem with the form at Deepdale. There was to be no relief from an FA Cup run as Preston crashed out to Third Division Watford, away from home, of course. That was the final straw for the frustrated Preston public from yet another sorry season.

DEBUTANTS: (4) George Bargh, John (Jock) Ewart, Alex (Sandy) Hair, John (Jack) Nelson.

LAST GAMES: (6) Cameron, Chandler, Hamilton T., Moss, Wade, James.

League position in Division Two: 13th – P42 W15 D9 L18 F78 A79 Pts 39
Home: W12 D6 L3 F58 A27 Away: W3 D3 L15 F20 A52

Match Report: James and Robson Run Riot as Biscuitmen Crumble – 27 Aug 1928 Preston 7 Reading 0

Reading were so out-manoeuvred, so swept off their feet, that instead of lamenting on the loss of seven goals they might well have congratulated themselves that it was not a repeat of the 18–0 defeat that they had suffered at Deepdale 34 years previously. They were unlucky to run up against a North End side on an evening when they could have beaten any team in the land. It was one of those games. Not only was the understanding from back to front perfect, but the movements were carried out with pace and ball control which left the Biscuitmen positively bewildered. Rain fell throughout the game and that suited North End as at this time they played some of their best football on a wet pitch. The real master of the conditions though was wee Alex James who, on one dazzling run, all but finished with a goal after waltzing past four hapless defenders. Once the North End players had found their feet and penetrated the Reading defence the goals flowed freely. So much so that three were scored in the last nne minutes of the first half and three more were scored in the first nine minutes of the second half. Six goals in just eighteen minutes. The opening goal after 35 minutes was the outcome of a triangular movement between Crawford, Harrison and Robson with the latter finishing the move coolly. Seven minutes later Robson had doubled his tally with a glancing header. Shell-shocked Reading then conceded a bad goal before the break when a long, hopeful shot from Ward found its target. The second half had hardly started when Russell headed home a fourth goal from Harrison's centre. The 11,000 crowd had not stopped cheering throughout and Reid then made it 5–0 with a long free-kick which deceived everyone as it found the top corner of the net. Robson raced clear for number six and his own hat-trick after cleverly beating the goalkeeper and finally James himself scored with an easy tap-in as Duckworth could only parry Robson's goalbound shot. Reading were absolutely overwhelmed and demoralised.

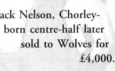

Jack Nelson, Chorley-born centre-half later sold to Wolves for £4,000.

STAT FACTS:
Best home run without defeat: 7 games
Best away run without defeat: 2 games
Longest run unbeaten: 5 games
Longest run without a win: 8 games
Best home attendance: 26,706 vs. Hull 26.12.28
Worst home attendance: 6,449 vs. Stoke 4.5.29
Best away attendance: 33,285 vs. Chelsea 10.11.28
Worst away attendance: 5,213 vs. Nottm Forest 13.4.29
Aggregate and average home gate: 319,421 – 15,211
Aggregate and average away gate: 325,965 – 15,522

League appearances (42 games)

Bargh G. W. 11, Cameron K. 12, Chandler S. E. 5, Craven J. 1, Crawford R. 42, Ewart J. 31, Hair A. 31, Hamilton H. 12, Hamilton T. 27, Harrison G. 41, James A. W. 36, Kerr J. 30, Morris D. 38, Moss F. 11, Nelson J. H. 4, Nisbet G. 6, Parry G. 2, Reid A. M. 41, Robson N. 8, Russell W. F. 8, Smith A. C. 15, Wade W. A. 11, Ward F. 39.

FA Cup appearances (1 game)

Moss, Hamilton T, Kerr, Ward, Morris, Crawford, Reid, Smith, Hair, James and Harrison 1 each.

Goalscorers: 78 League only (Total 78)

Hair 19, Harrison 16 (7 pens), Reid 13, James 10, Russell 6, Robson 5, Smith 3, Bargh 2, Ward 2, Chandler 1, Nisbet 1.

Future Players born between August 1928 and July 1929: Tommy Docherty, Bob Wilson, Tommy Thompson, Keith Mitton, Tommy Lawrenson, Derek Lewis and Bobby Foster
Hat-tricks: (4) Robson, Hair, Harrison (4 goals inc. 2 penalties) and Reid (also 4 goals).
Ever presents: (1) Bobby Crawford   **FA Cup:** Round One
Manager: Alex Gibson   **Players used:** 23   **Chairman:** Sir Meyrick Hollins
Leading scorer: 19 goals – Alex Hair (all league)
AUTHORS' UNOFFICIAL PLAYER OF THE SEASON: Bobby Crawford

Season 1928–29: Second Division

	P	W	D	L	F	A	Pts
1 Middlesbrough	42	22	11	9	92	57	55
2 Grimsby	42	24	5	13	82	61	53
3 Bradford PA	42	22	4	16	88	70	48
4 Southampton	42	17	14	11	74	60	48
5 Notts County	42	19	9	14	78	65	47
6 Stoke	42	17	12	13	74	51	46
7 WBA	42	19	8	15	80	79	45
8 Blackpool	42	19	7	16	92	76	45
9 Chelsea	42	17	10	15	64	65	44
10 Tottenham	42	17	9	16	75	81	43
11 Nottingham Forest	42	15	12	15	71	70	42
12 Hull	42	13	14	15	58	63	40
13 PRESTON	**42**	**15**	**9**	**18**	**78**	**79**	**39**
14 Millwall	42	16	7	19	71	86	39
15 Reading	42	15	9	18	63	86	39
16 Barnsley	42	16	6	20	69	66	38
17 Wolves	42	15	7	20	77	81	37
18 Oldham	42	16	5	21	54	75	37
19 Swansea	42	13	10	19	62	75	36
20 Bristol City	42	13	10	19	58	72	36
21 Port Vale	42	15	4	23	71	86	34
22 Clapton Orient	42	12	8	22	45	72	32

Date 1928-9	Opponents	Comp	h or a	Score	Att.	1	2	3	4	5	6	7	8	9	10	11
Aug 25	Blackpool	Div 2	h	3-1	23567	Ewart	Wade	T.Hamilton	Ward	Morris	Crawford	Reid	Russell (2)	Robson (1)	James	Harrison
Aug 27	Reading	Div 2	h	7-0	11211	Ewart	Wade	T.Hamilton	Ward (1)	Morris	Crawford	Reid (1)	Russell (1)	Robson (3)	James (1)	Harrison
Sep 1	Middlesbrough	Div 2	a	3-2	25280	Ewart	Wade	T.Hamilton	Ward	Nelson	Crawford	Reid (2)	Russell	Robson	James	Harrison (1p)
Sep 5	Reading	Div 2	a	0-0	11618	Ewart	Wade	T.Hamilton	Ward	Nelson	Crawford	Reid	Russell	Robson	James	Harrison
Sep 8	Oldham Ath	Div 2	h	3-2	16935	Ewart	Wade	T.Hamilton	Ward	Nelson	Crawford	Reid (1)	Russell (2)	Robson	James	Harrison
Sep 15	Southampton	Div 2	a	0-4	16744	Ewart	Wade	T.Hamilton	Ward	Morris	Crawford	Reid	Cameron	Smith	James	Harrison
Sep 22	Wolverhampton W	Div 2	h	5-1	16886	Ewart	Wade	T.Hamilton	Ward	Morris	Crawford	Reid (2)	Cameron	Smith (2)	James	Harrison (1)
Sep 29	Notts County	Div 2	a	1-0	19380	Ewart	Wade	T.Hamilton	Ward	Morris	Crawford	Reid (1)	Cameron	Smith	James	Harrison
Oct 6	Millwall	Div 2	h	3-4	18556	Ewart	Wade	T.Hamilton	Chandler	Morris	Crawford	Reid	Cameron	Ward (1)	James (1)	Harrison (1)
Oct 13	Port Vale	Div 2	a	2-3	12098	Ewart	Ward	T.Hamilton	Chandler	Morris	Crawford	Reid	Cameron	Robson (1)	James	Harrison (1)
Oct 20	Swansea Town	Div 2	h	2-2	14484	Ewart	H.Hamilton	T.Hamilton	Ward	Morris	Crawford	Reid (1)	Chandler (1)	Smith	James	Harrison
Oct 27	Bradford P.A.	Div 2	a	2-7	20558	Ewart	H.Hamilton	T.Hamilton	Ward	Morris	Crawford	Reid	Chandler	Hair (1)	James	Harrison (1)
Nov 3	Grimsby Town	Div 2	h	5-2	18827	Ewart	T.Hamilton	Kerr	Ward	Morris	Crawford	Reid	Chandler	Hair (1)	James	Harrison (4,2p)
Nov 10	Chelsea	Div 2	a	1-2	33285	Ewart	T.Hamilton	Kerr	Ward	Morris	Crawford	Reid (1)	Cameron	Hair	James	Harrison
Nov 17	Clapton Orient	Div 2	h	5-2	14052	Moss	T.Hamilton	Kerr	Ward	Morris	Crawford	Reid	Cameron	Hair (3)	James	Harrison (2,1p)
Nov 24	WBA	Div 2	a	1-1	12460	Moss	T.Hamilton	Kerr	Ward	Morris	Crawford	Reid	Cameron	Hair	Bargh	Harrison (1p)
Dec 1	Nottm Forest	Div 2	h	3-2	16220	Moss	T.Hamilton	Kerr	Ward	Morris	Crawford	Reid	Cameron	Hair (1)	James (2)	Harrison
Dec 8	Bristol City	Div 2	a	0-1	15747	Moss	T.Hamilton	Kerr	Ward	Morris	Crawford	Reid	Cameron	Hair	James	Harrison
Dec 15	Barnsley	Div 2	h	2-1	12413	Moss	T.Hamilton	Kerr	Ward	Morris	Crawford	Reid	Nisbet (1)	Hair (1)	James	Harrison
Dec 22	Stoke City	Div 2	a	1-1	10989	Moss	T.Hamilton	Kerr	Ward	Morris	Crawford	Reid	James	Hair (1)	Cameron	Harrison
Dec 25	Hull City	Div 2	a	1-5	17254	Moss	T.Hamilton	Kerr	Ward	Morris	Crawford	Reid	Smith (1)	Hair	James	Harrison
Dec 26	Hull City	Div 2	h	1-0	26706	Moss	T.Hamilton	Kerr	Ward	Morris	Crawford	Reid	Smith	Hair (1)	James	Harrison
Dec 29	Blackpool	Div 2	a	2-3	16339	Moss	T.Hamilton	Kerr	Ward	Morris	Crawford	Reid	Smith	Hair (1)	James	Harrison (1)
Jan 5	Middlesbrough	Div 2	h	0-0	17734	Moss	T.Hamilton	Kerr	Ward	Morris	Crawford	Reid	Smith	Hair	Cameron	Harrison
Jan 12	**Watford** Rd 1	**FAC**	**a**	**0-1**	**18344**	**Moss**	**T.Hamilton**	**Kerr**	**Ward**	**Morris**	**Crawford**	**Reid**	**Smith**	**Hair**	**James**	**Harrison**
Jan 19	Oldham Ath	Div 2	a	1-2	17212	Moss	T.Hamilton	Kerr	Ward	Morris	Crawford	Reid	Robson	Hair	Bargh (1)	Harrison
Jan 26	Southampton	Div 2	h	0-1	11623	Ewart	H.Hamilton	Kerr	Ward	Morris	Crawford	Reid	Robson	Hair	Bargh	Harrison
Feb 2	Wolverhampton W	Div 2	a	2-1	8461	Ewart	H.Hamilton	Kerr	Ward	Morris	Crawford	Reid	Smith	Hair (1)	James (1)	Harrison
Feb 9	Notts County	Div 2	h	0-1	15666	Ewart	H.Hamilton	Kerr	Ward	Morris	Crawford	Reid	Smith	Hair	James	Harrison
Feb 16	Millwall	Div 2	a	1-3	14255	Ewart	H.Hamilton	Kerr	Ward	Morris	Crawford	Smith	Reid	Hair	James	Harrison
Feb 23	Port Vale	Div 2	h	7-1	9356	Ewart	H.Hamilton	Kerr	Ward	Morris	Crawford	Smith	Reid (4)	Hair (2)	Bargh (1)	Harrison
Mar 2	Swansea Town	Div 2	a	0-5	13313	Ewart	T.Hamilton	Kerr	Ward	Morris	Crawford	Smith	Reid	Hair	James	Harrison
Mar 9	Bradford P.A.	Div 2	h	2-0	13912	Ewart	Wade	Kerr	Ward	Morris	Crawford	Reid	James	Hair (2)	Bargh	Harrison
Mar 16	Grimsby Town	Div 2	a	0-1	13268	Ewart	H.Hamilton	Kerr	Ward	Morris	Crawford	Reid	James	Hair	Bargh	Harrison
Mar 23	Chelsea	Div 2	h	3-0	14415	Ewart	H.Hamilton	Kerr	Ward	Morris	Crawford	Reid	James (1)	Hair (1)	Bargh	Harrison (1)
Mar 29	Tottenham H	Div 2	h	2-2	19216	Ewart	H.Hamilton	Kerr	Ward	Morris	Crawford	Reid	James (1)	Hair (1)	Bargh	Harrison
Mar 30	Clapton Orient	Div 2	a	0-1	9711	Ewart	H.Hamilton	Kerr	Ward	Morris	Crawford	Reid	James	Hair	Bargh	Harrison
Apr 1	Tottenham H	Div 2	a	0-2	23125	Ewart	H.Hamilton	Kerr	Ward	Morris	Crawford	Reid	Bargh	Hair	James	Harrison
Apr 6	WBA	Div 2	h	1-1	10609	Ewart	Ward	Kerr	Nisbet	Nelson	Crawford	Smith	Reid	Hair	James (1)	Harrison
Apr 13	Nottm Forest	Div 2	a	1-4	5213	Ewart	Ward	Kerr	Nisbet	Morris	Crawford	Reid	Bargh	Hair	Parry	Harrison (1p)
Apr 20	Bristol City	Div 2	h	2-2	10926	Ewart	Wade	Kerr	Nisbet	Morris	Crawford	Reid	Russell	Hair	James (1)	Harrison (1p)
Apr 27	Barnsley	Div 2	a	1-4	9655	Ewart	T.Hamilton	Kerr	Nisbet	Morris	Crawford	Reid	Russell	Hair (1)	James	Harrison
May 4	Stoke City	Div 2	h	2-2	6449	Ewart	Morris	Kerr	Nisbet	Craven	Crawford	Smith	Russell (1)	Parry	James	Hair (1)

R.M.S. *Olympic*, passing the Royal Yacht Squadron, Cowes.
This was the vessel that took PNE across the Atlantic for their USA and Canada tour.

Pennant presented to Bobby Crawford in Chicago

The very real threat of relegation to the Third Division hung over Preston for much of the 1929–30 season. Opening the campaign with five straight defeats gave the club the worst possible start and only a late run of results prevented the unthinkable from happening. Manager, Alex Gibson used a lot of players, some of whom proved not to be of the highest standard, and the side, especially up front, struggled for the necessary cohesion. Only Bobby Crawford played in all the games as once again the Scot showed how wonderfully consistent he had become. In fact, at one point the manager even tried Crawford as a makeshift centre-forward and the player rewarded him by scoring two goals in his first game and four goals in his second! Generally though goalscoring was a problem. George Smithies, a former England Amateur International, was signed to try and boost this area, but with Alex James now gone and George Harrison's form fading, the team created far fewer chances. A new goalkeeper was signed, Des Fawcett, but the fans, quite unfairly, gave him plenty of stick. He wasn't the only player to suffer as the frustrations of the Preston public boiled over. The average crowd dropped dramatically, which compounded the Board's anguish at the situation. Their only hope was that the club could salvage something from a good cup run but alas this was not to be as an early exit at Portsmouth failed to relieve the club's financial burdens and the players spirits. In the league there was an incredible game against Blackpool at Deepdale in the October. Over 21,000 people saw the Tangerines win 6–4 in a thriller, one of six games where Preston conceded four or more goals in a match. It was the City of Nottingham that proved the final salvation for North End's mini revival. At Easter a double over Notts County and a vital win at Forest gave Preston six precious points which were enough to stave off that relegation threat. The final league position was more than anything Preston could have hoped for. Crawford, Fawcett, Alex Reid, Jasper Kerr and Frank Ward were the pick of an otherwise ordinary team.

DEBUTANTS: (9) Des Fawcett, James Foster, Fred Heaton, Alfred Horne, James McClelland, Alex Sherry, George Smithies, David Steele and Albert Wilson.

LAST GAMES: (8) Ewart, Foster, Grierson, Hair, Morris, Parry, Robson and Steele.

Future Players born between August 1929 and July 1930: Ken Waterhouse, Sammy Baird and Dennis Hatsell

Ever presents: (1) Bobby Crawford   **Hat-tricks:** (1) Crawford   **Manager:** Alex Gibson

FA Cup: Third Round   **Chairman:** Sir Meyrick Hollins (4 goals *vs.* Stoke)   **Players used:** 27

Leading scorer: 10 goals – George Smithies and James McClelland (All league)

AUTHORS' UNOFFICIAL PLAYER OF THE SEASON: Bobby Crawford

League appearances (42 games)

Bargh G. W. 23, Craven J. 33, Crawford R. 42, Ewart J. 4, Fawcett D. H. 37, Foster J. 1, Grierson G. 3, Hair A. 14, Hamilton H. 2, Harrison G. 22, Heaton F. 2, Horne A. 28, Kerr J. 35, McClelland J. 25, Morris D. 5, Nelson J. H. 8, Nisbet G. 21, Parry G. 1, Reid A. M. 39, Robson N. 2, Russell W. F. 13, Sherry A. P. 4, Smith A. C. 9, Smithies G. H. 18, Steele D. M. 29, Ward F. 40, Wilson A. 2.

FA Cup appearances (1 game)

Fawcett, Ward, Kerr, Steele, Craven, Crawford, Reid, McClelland, Robson, Bargh, and Horne one each.

Goalscorers: 65 League only (Total 65)

Smithies 10, McClelland 10 (1 pen), Crawford 7, Reid 7, Harrison 6 (3pens), Bargh 6, Horne 4, Hair 3, Smith 3, Nisbet 2, Russell 2, Steele 2, Robson 1, Own goals 2 (Tootill of Wolves and Harkus of Southampton)

STAT FACTS:

Best home run without defeat: 5 games   Best away run without defeat: 4 games   Longest run unbeaten: 4 games

Longest run without a win: 6 games   Best Home attendance: 27,070 *vs.* Bury 26.12.29

Worst home attendance: 5,163 *vs.* Cardiff 9.9.29   Best away attendance: 28,852 *vs.* Portsmouth FAC 11.1.30

Worst away attendance: 5,767 *vs.* N. Forest 19.4.30   Aggregate and average home attendance: 239,723 – 11,415

Aggregate and average away attendance: 282,701 – 13,462

League position in Division Two: 16th – P42 W13 D11 L18 F65 A80 Pts 37
Home: W7 D7 L7 F42 A36   Away: W6 D4 L11 F23 A44

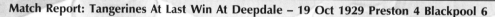

Match Report: Tangerines At Last Win At Deepdale – 19 Oct 1929 Preston 4 Blackpool 6

With seven defeats in the first ten league games North End entered this game parading new signing John McClelland at centre-forward. Even so, Blackpool, who had never won at Deepdale, were match favourites with future North Enders Wolf and Tremelling in their line-up. It was an even start to the game as each side battled for the crucial first opening. After ten minutes play Preston's Russell made the breakthrough when he headed in Harrison's pin-point cross. This goal only served to stimulate the visitors into action and it came as no surprise when they equalised through Lauderdale seven minutes later. Blackpool continued to look the more likely side to succeed in a game full of pace, Lauderdale and Hampson causing plenty of problems for North End's back line. After 35 minutes a hectic spell of scoring was witnessed as Blackpool, on chances created, deservedly took the lead when Hampson, after winning a race with Nelson, met Tremelling's through pass to steer the ball wide of Jock Ewart. The goal visibly lifted the Blackpool team and they immediately won the ball back and pressed forward again, catching the Preston rearguard

unprepared. The attack left Downes with the easy task of putting the ball past Ewart as it dropped invitingly for him. These were two painful blows for Preston but they struck back and in the very next attack they added to the hectic scoring after Grant fouled new boy McClelland in the box. Harrison placed the ball on the penalty spot and duly finished with his customary accuracy and venom. Although these goals were scored in a four minute spell it was not the end to the scoring as Hampson scored with another easy header before half-time. Preston came out fighting after the break and made the score 3–4 when Steele beat Wolf from long range on 57 minutes. After this the 21,000 crowd saw something like the North End of old and Wolf had to be at his best to keep out efforts from Harrison and Reid. As it happened Blackpool then scored another two goals, this time against the run of play. Downes scored number five and Hampson made it 6–3 after a penalty given away by Kerr's foul on Hampson. No-one in the crowd could grumble about value for money or lack of excitement and there was still one more twist as Horne forced his way through to score a fourth goal for North End two minutes from time.

Left to right: *Back row:* Nisbet, Ward, Fawcett, Kerr, Craven. *Front row:* Steele, Reid, Smith, Crawford (Captain), Bargh, Harrison.

Season 1929–30: Second Division

		P	W	D	L	F	A	Pts
1	Blackpool	42	27	4	11	98	67	58
2	Chelsea	42	22	11	9	74	46	55
3	Oldham	42	21	11	10	90	51	53
4	Bradford PA	42	19	12	11	91	70	50
5	Bury	42	22	5	15	78	67	49
5	WBA	42	21	5	16	105	73	47
7	Southampton	42	17	11	14	77	76	45
8	Cardiff	42	18	8	16	61	59	44
9	Wolves	42	16	9	17	77	79	41
10	Nottingham Forest	42	13	15	14	55	69	41
11	Stoke	42	16	8	18	74	72	40
12	Tottenham	42	15	9	18	59	61	39
13	Charlton	42	14	11	17	59	63	39
14	Millwall	42	12	15	15	57	73	39
15	Swansea	42	14	9	19	57	61	37
16	**PRESTON**	**42**	**13**	**11**	**18**	**65**	**80**	**37**
17	Barnsley	42	14	8	20	56	71	36
18	Bradford City	42	12	12	18	60	77	36
19	Reading	42	12	11	19	54	67	35
20	Bristol City	42	13	9	20	61	83	35
21	Hull	42	14	7	21	51	78	35
22	Notts County	42	9	15	18	54	70	33

Date 1929-30	Opponents	Comp	h or a	Score	Att.	1	2	3	4	5	6	7	8	9	10	11		
Aug 31	Reading	Div 2	a	0-2	18346	Fawcett	Ward	Morris	Steele	Nelson	Crawford	Reid	Russell	Hair	Bargh	Harrison		
Sep 2	Cardiff City	Div 2	a	0-2	13510	Fawcett	Ward	Morris	Steele	Nelson	Crawford	Reid	Russell	Hair	Bargh	Harrison		
Sep 7	Charlton Ath	Div 2	h	0-3	10386	Fawcett	Ward	Morris	Steele	Nelson	Crawford	Reid	Russell	Hair	Bargh	Harrison		
Sep 9	Cardiff City	Div 2	h	2-3	5963	Fawcett	Ward	Kerr	Steele	Morris	Crawford	Smith	Nisbet	Reid (1)	Robson (1)	Parry		
Sep 14	Hull City	Div 2	a	0-2	10232	Fawcett	Ward	Kerr	Steele	Morris	Crawford	Reid	Russell	Robson	Hair	Smith		
Sep 18	Bristol City	Div 2	a	2-2	11129	Fawcett	Ward	Sherry	Craven	Nelson	Grierson	Reid	Steele	Crawford (2)	Hair	Harrison		
Sep 21	Stoke City	Div 2	h	5-1	8104	Fawcett	Ward	Sherry	Steele	Nelson	Grierson	Reid	Home	Crawford (4)	Hair (1)	Smith		
Sep 28	Wolverhampton W	Div 2	a	0-4	16779	Ewart	Ward	Sherry	Steele	Nelson	Grierson	Reid	Home	Crawford	Hair	Smith		
Oct 5	Bradford City	Div 2	h	2-2	10226	Ewart	Ward	Sherry	Steele	Nelson	Nisbet	Heaton	Home (2)	Wilson	Crawford	Reid		
Oct 12	Swansea Town	Div 2	a	4-4	14636	Ewart	Ward	Kerr	Nisbet	Craven	Crawford	Reid	Russell	Wilson	Home	Harrison		
Oct 19	Blackpool	Div 2	h	4-6	21185	Ewart	Ward	Kerr	Steele (1)	Nelson	Crawford	Reid	Russell (1)	McClelland	Home (1)	Harrison (1p)		
Oct 26	Barnsley	Div 2	a	0-0	6076	Fawcett	Ward	Kerr	Steele	Craven	Crawford	Reid	Home	McClelland	Bargh	Harrison		
Nov 2	Bradford P.A.	Div 2	h	4-1	10333	Fawcett	Ward	Kerr	Steele	Craven	Crawford	Reid (1)	McClelland (1p)	Smithies (1)	Bargh (1)	Home		
Nov 9	WBA	Div 2	a	0-2	15759	Fawcett	Ward	Kerr	Steele	Craven	Crawford	Reid	McClelland	Smithies	Bargh	Home		
Nov 16	Tottenham H	Div 2	h	4-0	10687	Fawcett	Ward	Kerr	Steele	Craven	Crawford	Reid	McClelland (1)	Smithies	Bargh	Home (1)		
Nov 23	Southampton	Div 2	a	2-1	9889	Fawcett	Ward	Kerr	Steele	Craven	Crawford	Reid	McClelland (1)	Smithies (1)	Bargh	Home		
Nov 30	Millwall	Div 2	h	3-1	8829	Fawcett	Ward	Kerr	Steele	Craven	Crawford	Reid	McClelland (1)	Smithies (2)	Bargh	Home		
Dec 7	Oldham Ath	Div 2	a	2-0	8094	Fawcett	Ward	Kerr	Steele	Craven	Crawford	Reid	McClelland (1)	Smithies	Bargh (1)	Home		
Dec 14	Nottm Forest	Div 2	h	1-2	11566	Fawcett	Ward	Kerr	Steele	Craven	Crawford	Reid	McClelland	Smithies (1)	Bargh	Home		
Dec 21	Chelsea	Div 2	a	0-5	12769	Fawcett	Ward	Kerr	Steele	Craven	Crawford	Reid	McClelland	Smithies	Bargh	Home		
Dec 25	Bury	Div 2	a	2-1	13762	Fawcett	Ward	Kerr	Nisbet	Craven	Crawford	Reid	McClelland	Smithies (2)	Bargh	Home		
Dec 26	Bury	Div 2	h	1-1	27070	Fawcett	Ward	Kerr	Nisbet	Craven	Crawford	Reid (1)	McClelland	Smithies	Bargh	Home		
Dec 28	Reading	Div 2	h	2-1	10328	Fawcett	Ward	Kerr	Nisbet	Craven	Crawford	Reid	McClelland (2)	Smithies	Bargh	Home		
Jan 4	Charlton Ath	Div 2	a	1-1	17291	Fawcett	Ward	Kerr	Nisbet (1)	Craven	Crawford	Reid	McClelland	Smithies	Home	Harrison		
Jan 11	**Portsmouth**	**Rd 3 FAC**	**a**	**0-2**	**28852**	**Fawcett**	**Ward**	**Kerr**	**Steele**	**Craven**	**Crawford**	**Reid**	**McClelland**	**Robson**	**Bargh**	**Horne**		
Jan 18	Hull City	Div 2	h	1-2	13330	Fawcett	Ward	Kerr	Steele	Craven	Crawford	Reid	McClelland	Smithies (1)	Bargh	Home		
Jan 25	Stoke City	Div 2	a	3-2	10325	Fawcett	Ward	Kerr	Nisbet	Craven	Crawford	Home	McClelland (1)	Smithies	Hair (1)	Harrison (1)		
Feb 1	Wolverhampton W	Div 2	h	1-1	11000	Fawcett	Ward	Kerr	Nisbet	Craven	Crawford	Heaton	Russell	McClelland	Hair	Harrison	1 og	(Tootill)
Feb 8	Bradford City	Div 2	a	1-1	16738	Fawcett	Ward	Kerr	Nisbet	Craven	Crawford	Reid	Russell	McClelland (1)	Hair	Home		
Feb 15	Swansea Town	Div 2	h	0-0	9032	Fawcett	Ward	Kerr	Nisbet	Craven	Crawford	Reid	McClelland	Steele	Hair	Home		
Feb 22	Blackpool	Div 2	a	1-5	15347	Foster	Ward	Kerr	Nisbet	Craven	Crawford	Home	McClelland	Hair (1)	Steele	Harrison		
Mar 1	Barnsley	Div 2	h	3-1	9901	Fawcett	H.Hamilton	Kerr	Nisbet	Craven	Crawford	Reid	Russell (1)	Smithies	McClelland (1)	Harrison (1p)		
Mar 8	Bradford P.A.	Div 2	a	2-5	14396	Fawcett	Ward	Kerr	Nisbet	Craven	Crawford	Reid (2)	Russell	Home	McClelland	Harrison		
Mar 15	WBA	Div 2	h	2-2	7080	Fawcett	H.Hamilton	Kerr	Nisbet	Craven	Crawford (1)	Reid	Russell	Home	McClelland	Harrison (1p)		
Mar 22	Tottenham H	Div 2	a	0-1	27108	Fawcett	Ward	Kerr	Steele	Craven	Crawford	Reid	Home	Smithies	Hair	Harrison		
Mar 29	Southampton	Div 2	h	1-1	7958	Fawcett	Ward	Kerr	Steele	Craven	Crawford	Reid	Home	Smithies	Hair	Harrison	1 og	(Harkus)
Apr 5	Millwall	Div 2	a	0-2	14746	Fawcett	Ward	Kerr	Nisbet	Craven	Crawford	Reid	Russell	Smithies	Bargh	Harrison		
Apr 12	Oldham Ath	Div 2	h	0-3	15612	Fawcett	Ward	Kerr	Steele	Craven	Crawford	Reid	Russell	McClelland	Bargh	Harrison		
Apr 18	Notts County	Div 2	h	3-1	10592	Fawcett	Ward	Kerr	Nisbet (1)	Craven	Crawford	Reid	Steele	Smith (1)	McClelland	Harrison (1)		
Apr 19	Nottm Forest	Div 2	a	4-2	5767	Fawcett	Ward	Kerr	Nisbet	Craven	Crawford	Reid (1)	Steele	Smith (1)	Bargh (1)	Harrison (1)		
Apr 22	Notts County	Div 2	a	3-0	10002	Fawcett	Ward	Kerr	Nisbet	Craven	Crawford	Reid (1)	Steele	Smith (1)	Bargh (1)	Home		
Apr 26	Chelsea	Div 2	h	1-2	13475	Fawcett	Ward	Kerr	Nisbet	Craven	Crawford	Reid	Steele	Smith	Bargh (1)	Harrison		
May 3	Bristol City	Div 2	h	2-2	7066	Fawcett	Ward	Kerr	Nisbet	Craven	Crawford	Reid	Steele (1)	Smith	Bargh (1)	Harrison		

SEASON 1930–1931

Preston actually made some progress this season, which came as some relief for the fans after a dismal time of late. The side scored plenty of goals, especially at home, but defensively there were still far too many gaps left to be exploited and as a result no consistent unbeaten runs could be put together. For a couple of years the North End team had had a problem with the goalkeeping position. This time they signed John Hampton from Derby and once again the Deepdale crowd did not exactly take him to their hearts and showed little patience with him. To the goalkeeper's credit he performed well and he was never as bad as the crowd indicated. There was a better consistency about the North End line-up with Hampton, Frank Ward, Jasper Kerr, Gavin Nisbet, Bobby Crawford, Alex Reid and George Harrison all being regulars throughout the season. Crawford, especially, continued his run of appearances with a series of superb performances which emphasised his amazing consistency. Needless to say he was ever present. The club also made a significant signing during the season by bringing in Billy Tremelling. The short, stocky player joined Preston from Blackpool, as a forward, it was not until two years later that he was to make his mark as an outstanding defender. The 1930–31 season had begun and ended with unbeaten runs but in between there was a real mixed bag of results which frustrated players, management and fans alike. The highlight came just before Christmas when they hammered Cardiff by 7–0 at Deepdale. That was Tremelling's two goal debut although George Bargh stole the honours from the game with a hat-trick. Bargh and Tom Scott shared the leading goalscorer's position and both enjoyed short bursts of regular scoring, but significantly though, not many goals came from the centre-forward position, and that was something that the

management was acutely aware of. In the FA Cup it was again exit at the first attempt, against Spurs at White Hart Lane. This was particularly annoying as Preston had taken three points from the London club in the league. The final outcome of this acute disappointment came when manager, Alex Gibson resigned to make way for a new man, Lincoln Hyde. It was that sort of season though, some progress made but such a lot of work still to do before that elusive promotion could be achieved.

DEBUTANTS: (6) Vincent Farrell, John Hampton, Edward Owens, Tom Scott, Eli Thornborough, Billy Tremelling.

LAST GAMES: (9) Craven, Hamilton H., Hampton, Harrison, McClelland, Russell, Smith, Smithies, Wilson.

Left to right (players only): *Back row:* Ward Kerr, Hampton, Nisbet, Craven, Crawford. *Front row:* Reid, Bargh, Owens, McClelland, Harrison.

Future Players born between August 1930 and July 1931: Doug Holden, Peter Higham and Eric Jones
Ever presents: (1) Bobby Crawford
FA Cup: Third Round
Hat-tricks: (4) Bargh, Scott, McClelland (4 goals *vs.* Reading), and Farrell.
Managers: Alex Gibson (until January 27 1931) and then Lincoln Hyde
Leading scorer: 14 goals each – George Bargh and Tom Scott (all league)
Chairman: Sir Meyrick Hollins
Players used: 24
AUTHORS' UNOFFICIAL PLAYER OF THE SEASON:
Alex Reid

STAT FACTS:
Best home run without defeat: 7 games
Best away run without defeat: 4 games
Longest run unbeaten: 9 games
Longest run without win: 7 games
Best home attendance: 28,682 *vs.* Burnley 26.12.30
Worst home attendance: 6,135 *vs.* Bristol City 25.4.31
Best away attendance: 36,650 *vs.* Spurs FAC 10.1.31
Worst away attendance: 3,657 *vs.* Barnsley 7.3.31
Aggregate and average home attendance: 266,747 – 12,702
Aggregate and average away attendance: 297,942 – 14,188

League position in Division Two: 7th – P42 W17 D11 L14 F83 A64 Pts 45
Home: W12 D5 L4 F55 A31 Away: W5 D6 L10 F28 A33

Match Report: Goal Feast Served Up At The Den – 4 Oct 1930 Millwall 5 Preston 7

Having tasted defeat just once since the opening day of the season, scoring an amazing 24 goals in their eight games, North End travelled south to The Den with confidence seemingly sky high. But to beat Millwall on their own ground was never an easy task, and if you came away with a result you had probably earned it. Winning the toss meant little difference for there was hardly any wind blowing as Millwall set off at a fair pace, forcing three corners in two minutes and looking likely to score at any moment. Kerr and Crawford kept their heads in the heat of battle though and soon Preston settled down and got into their stride, playing a more open game than Millwall, bringing in their wingers at every opportunity. In fact it was one of the wide men who carved out the opening goal after 17 minutes, Reid heading across goal for Scott to strike with confidence. Millwall then made a series of attacks in reply, eventually equalising after 25 minutes through Poxton. However, the undismayed visitors regained the lead within 30 seconds. Scott scored a second goal, this time from a neat pass by Owens. It looked at this stage that the Lions roar was no more than a purr as North End held the upper hand with Harrison prominent, well supported by Crawford and McClelland. In defence, too, Preston were steady, Ward especially distinguishing himself. A great move on 40 minutes put North End even further ahead as McClelland and Harrison combined to give Reid the opportunity to score. Only two minutes later Millwall hit back again when Cock's shot proved too hot for Hampton to handle. Millwall restarted after the break with all guns blazing and hammered away at Preston's defence. As so often happens the team under pressure, in this case Preston, then broke away to score again as Owens made it 4–2 to the visitors. Reid then relieved the pressure even more by scoring a fifth goal with a daisy cutter that ripped into the far corner. Millwall were down, but not yet out, and Forsyth headed another goal on 65 minutes to make it 3–5. There was no lack of thrills or goalmouth action as Scott walked the ball in for Preston's sixth goal, the third goal in just six minutes of this extraordinary match. Owens then coolly finished another move for a seventh goal for Preston but still the action was not finished and as the visitors relaxed Millwall came back with a strong finish to hit two more goals themselves through Cock and Poxton in the final five minutes.

Alex Sherry, left-back, signed from Denny Hibs.

League appearances (42 games)

Bargh G. W. 20, Craven J. 28, Crawford R. 42, Farrell V. 11, Fawcett D. H. 5, Hamilton H. 4, Hampton J. W. 37, Harrison G. 32, Horne A. 6, Kerr J. 33, McClelland J. 28, Nelson J. H. 13, Nisbet G. 36, Owens E. 11, Reid A. M. 41, Russell W. F. 7, Scott T. 25, Sherry A. P. 8, Smith A. C. 7, Smithies G. H. 2, Thornborough E. H. 1, Tremelling W. 18, Ward F. 39, Wilson A. 8.

FA Cup (1 game)

Hampton, Hamilton, Ward, Nisbet, Craven, Crawford, Reid, Bargh, Tremelling, McClelland and Harrison all 1 each.

Goalscorers: 83 League–1 Cup–(Total 84)

Bargh 14–0 (14), Scott 14–0 (14), Reid 13–0 (13), McClelland 12–0 (12), Tremelling 6–1 (7), Harrison 6 (2pens)–0 (6), Farrell 5–0 (5), Owens 4–0 (4), Smith 4–0 (4), Crawford 2–0 (2), Nisbet 1–0 (1), Russell 1–0 (1), Wilson 1–0 (1).

Trivia Facts:

Preston reached the semi-final of the Lancashire Cup in 1930–31. They beat Barrow 3–2 at Deepdale in round two, their first game, in front of a crowd of 1,447. Nisbet, Russell and McClelland were the goalscorers. In the next round they beat New Brighton at home, 5–1 with Bargh 2, Sherry and Farrell 2, scoring. For that game 842 people turned out. In the semi-final though they were beaten at Liverpool, 4–2. Scott and McClelland scored for Preston. In each game the line-up was virtually the same as for a league game which emphasised the importance of that competition in years gone by.

The second goal conceded against Reading in the 3–3 draw at Deepdale was the 2,000th league goal conceded by Preston.

Albert Wilson, signed from Dundee Violet, scored three goals in his first game at Deepdale in a pre-season practice match, Whites vs. Stripes. Three weeks later he scored six for PNE Reserves in a 9–4 win over Everton reserves, but managed just one league goal in his two year stay at the club.

Season 1930–31: Second Division

	P	W	D	L	F	A	Pts
1 Everton	42	28	5	9	121	66	61
2 WBA	42	22	10	10	83	49	54
3 Tottenham	42	22	7	13	88	55	51
4 Wolves	42	21	5	16	84	67	47
5 Port Vale	42	21	5	16	67	61	47
6 Bradford PA	42	18	10	14	97	66	46
7 PRESTON	42	17	11	14	83	64	45
8 Burnley	42	17	11	14	81	77	45
9 Southampton	42	19	6	17	74	62	44
10 Bradford City	42	17	10	15	61	63	44
11 Stoke	42	17	10	15	64	71	44
12 Oldham	42	16	10	16	61	72	42
13 Bury	42	19	3	20	75	82	41
14 Millwall	42	16	7	19	71	80	39
15 Charlton	42	15	9	18	59	86	39
16 Bristol City	42	15	8	19	54	82	38
17 Nottingham Forest	42	14	9	19	80	85	37
18 Plymouth	42	14	8	20	76	84	36
19 Barnsley	42	13	9	20	59	79	35
20 Swansea	42	12	10	20	51	74	34
21 Reading	42	12	6	24	72	96	30
22 Cardiff	42	8	9	25	47	87	25

Date 1930-1	Opponents	Comp	h or a	Score	Att.	1	2	3	4	5	6	7	8	9	10	11
Aug 30	Southampton	Div 2	h	5-0	8945	Hampton	Ward	Kerr	Nisbet	Craven	Crawford	Reid (1)	Scott (2)	Smith (1)	McClelland	Harrison (1)
Sep 3	Everton	Div 2	a	1-2	29908	Hampton	Ward	Kerr	Nisbet	Craven	Crawford	Reid	Scott	Smith	McClelland	Harrison (1)
Sep 6	Reading	Div 2	a	4-1	10740	Hampton	Ward	Kerr	Nisbet	Craven	Crawford	Smith	Scott	Wilson	McClelland (4)	Harrison
Sep 8	Tottenham H	Div 2	h	2-1	17031	Hampton	Ward	Kerr	Nisbet	Craven	Crawford	Reid	Scott (1)	Smith (1)	McClelland	Harrison
Sep 13	Wolverhampton W	Div 2	h	5-4	15386	Hampton	Ward	Kerr	Nisbet	Craven	Crawford	Reid (2)	Scott (1)	Smith (1)	McClelland (1)	Harrison
Sep 15	Tottenham H	Div 2	a	0-0	18793	Hampton	Ward	Kerr	Nisbet	Craven	Crawford	Reid	Scott	Owens	McClelland	Harrison
Sep 20	Bradford P.A.	Div 2	a	2-2	16466	Hampton	Ward	Kerr	Nisbet	Craven	Crawford	Reid (1)	Scott (1)	Owens	McClelland	Harrison
Sep 27	Stoke City	Div 2	h	5-1	15530	Hampton	Ward	Kerr	Nisbet	Craven	Crawford	Reid (1)	Scott (1)	Owens (1)	McClelland (1)	Harrison (1p)
Oct 4	Millwall	Div 2	a	7-5	14674	Hampton	Ward	Kerr	Nisbet	Craven	Crawford	Reid (2)	Scott (3)	Owens (2)	McClelland	Harrison
Oct 11	Oldham Ath	Div 2	h	1-0	20203	Hampton	Ward	Kerr	Nisbet	Craven	Crawford	Reid (1)	Scott	Owens	McClelland	Harrison
Oct 18	Plymouth Arg	Div 2	h	2-1	17434	Hampton	Ward	Kerr	Nisbet	Craven	Crawford	Reid (1)	Scott	Owens (1)	McClelland	Harrison
Oct 25	Bury	Div 2	a	0-3	17456	Hampton	Ward	Kerr	Nisbet	Craven	Crawford	Reid	Scott	Owens	McClelland	Harrison
Nov 1	Barnsley	Div 2	h	1-1	12726	Hampton	Ward	Kerr	Nisbet	Craven	Crawford	Reid	Scott	Owens	McClelland	Harrison (1p)
Nov 8	Charlton Ath	Div 2	a	3-1	10098	Hampton	Ward	Kerr	Nisbet	Craven	Crawford	Reid	Bargh	Russell (1)	McClelland (1)	Farrell (1)
Nov 15	WBA	Div 2	h	2-3	15550	Hampton	Ward	Kerr	Nisbet (1)	Craven	Crawford	Reid	Bargh (1)	Russell	McClelland	Farrell
Nov 22	Port Vale	Div 2	a	0-1	10086	Hampton	Ward	Kerr	Nisbet	Craven	Crawford	Reid	Bargh	Owens	McClelland	Harrison
Nov 29	Bradford City	Div 2	h	4-2	11868	Hampton	Ward	Kerr	Nisbet	Craven	Crawford	Reid	Bargh (1)	Owens	McClelland (2)	Harrison (1)
Dec 6	Swansea Town	Div 2	a	1-2	9906	Hampton	Ward	Kerr	Nisbet	Craven	Crawford	Reid	Bargh	Smith (1)	McClelland	Harrison
Dec 13	Cardiff City	Div 2	h	7-0	13457	Hampton	Ward	Kerr	Nisbet	Craven	Crawford	Reid	Bargh (3)	Tremelling (2)	McClelland (2)	Harrison
Dec 20	Bristol City	Div 2	a	1-1	11169	Hampton	Ward	Kerr	Nisbet	Craven	Crawford	Reid (1)	Bargh	Tremelling	McClelland	Harrison
Dec 25	Burnley	Div 2	a	0-1	31000	Hampton	Ward	Kerr	Nisbet	Craven	Crawford	Reid	Bargh	Tremelling	McClelland	Harrison
Dec 26	Burnley	Div 2	h	2-0	28682	Hampton	Ward	Kerr	Nisbet	Craven	Crawford	Reid	Bargh (1)	Tremelling	McClelland (1)	Harrison
Dec 27	Southampton	Div 2	a	1-2	11518	Hampton	Ward	Kerr	Nisbet	Craven	Crawford	Reid	Bargh (1)	Tremelling	McClelland	Harrison
Jan 3	Reading	Div 2	h	3-3	11716	Hampton	Ward	Kerr	Nisbet	Craven	Crawford	Reid	Bargh (2)	Tremelling (1)	McClelland	Harrison
Jan 10	Tottenham H Rd 3	FAC	a	1-3	36650	Hampton	Hamilton	Ward	Nisbet	Craven	Crawford	Reid	Bargh	Tremelling (1)	McClelland	Harrison
Jan 17	Wolverhampton W	Div 2	a	0-2	18217	Fawcett	Hamilton	Ward	Nisbet	Craven	Crawford	Reid	Bargh	Tremelling	McClelland	Harrison
Jan 29	Bradford P.A.	Div 2	h	1-1	7001	Fawcett	Hamilton	Ward	Nisbet	Craven	Crawford	Reid	Bargh (1)	Tremelling	McClelland	Harrison
Feb 2	Stoke City	Div 2	a	1-3	4959	Hampton	Hamilton	Kerr	Nisbet	Craven	Crawford (1)	Reid	Bargh	Smith	Tremelling	Harrison
Feb 7	Millwall	Div 2	h	1-3	9951	Hampton	Hamilton	Kerr	Tremelling	Craven	Crawford	Reid	Bargh	Nisbet	McClelland	Harrison (1)
Feb 14	Oldham Ath	Div 2	a	0-2	10337	Hampton	Ward	Sherry	Nisbet	Nelson	Crawford	Reid	Home	Wilson	McClelland	Farrell
Feb 21	Plymouth Arg	Div 2	a	2-1	16382	Hampton	Ward	Sherry	Nisbet	Nelson	Crawford	Reid (1)	Bargh	Wilson (1)	Scott	Farrell
Feb 28	Bury	Div 2	h	3-0	7332	Hampton	Ward	Sherry	Nisbet	Nelson	Crawford	Reid	Bargh (1)	Wilson	Scott (2)	Farrell
Mar 7	Barnsley	Div 2	a	1-1	3657	Fawcett	Ward	Sherry	Nisbet	Nelson	Crawford	Reid	Bargh	Wilson	Scott	Farrell (1)
Mar 17	Charlton Ath	Div 2	h	4-1	9474	Fawcett	Ward	Sherry	Nisbet	Nelson	Crawford	Reid	Scott (1)	Wilson	Tremelling	Farrell (3)
Mar 21	WBA	Div 2	a	0-2	20952	Hampton	Ward	Sherry	Nisbet	Nelson	Crawford	Reid	Scott	Wilson	Tremelling	Farrell
Mar 28	Port Vale	Div 2	h	1-3	7696	Hampton	Ward	Sherry	Nisbet	Nelson	Crawford	Reid	Scott	Wilson	Tremelling (1)	Farrell
Apr 3	Nottm Forest	Div 2	h	2-4	13496	Hampton	Ward	Sherry	Thornborough	Tremelling	Crawford	Reid (1)	Scott (1)	Owens	Farrell	Harrison
Apr 4	Bradford City	Div 2	a	0-0	14329	Hampton	Ward	Kerr	Russell	Nelson	Crawford	Reid	Scott	Tremelling	Home	Harrison
Apr 6	Nottm Forest	Div 2	a	4-1	13213	Hampton	Ward	Kerr	Russell	Nelson	Crawford	Reid (1)	Scott (1)	Tremelling (2)	Home	Harrison
Apr 11	Swansea Town	Div 2	h	0-0	7697	Hampton	Ward	Kerr	Russell	Nelson	Crawford	Reid	Scott	Tremelling	Home	Harrison
Apr 18	Cardiff City	Div 2	a	0-0	4082	Hampton	Ward	Kerr	Russell	Nelson	Crawford	Reid	Scott	Tremelling	Home	Harrison
Apr 25	Bristol City	Div 2	h	2-2	6135	Hampton	Ward	Kerr	Russell	Nelson	Crawford (1)	Reid	Bargh (1)	Smithies	Home	Harrison
May 2	Everton	Div 2	h	2-1	9437	Hampton	Ward	Kerr	Nisbet	Nelson	Crawford	Reid	Bargh (2)	Smithies	Scott	Farrell

Alex Reid

Gavin Nisbet

Frank Ward

SEASON 1931–1932

Another struggling season for the North End and the club only staved off relegation by making two crucial signings around Christmas 1931. Only three wins in the first fifteen league games meant that Preston were languishing in the depths of the division by the November. In one incredible sequence the results read like this, lost 4–1, lost 4–1, lost 4–1, drew 1–1 and lost 4–1! The Directors, to their credit, recognised that drastic measures were needed and acting mainly under the guidance of Mr J. I. Taylor the club brought in two vital signings. Both Dick Rowley and Ted Harper were signed from Tottenham Hotspur and immediately the goal power of the team was increased. Harper, especially, was a revelation, and the former Blackburn player scored in five of his first six games and managed no fewer than three hat-tricks in the second half of the season. At last, the club had found a centre-forward who knew where the goal was! Rowley, too, added more to the side and in game at Notts County, where he deputised for Harper, he scored four goals. At the other end the defence had had a torrid time before Christmas and it was desperately upsetting to see the splendid Jasper Kerr suffer a nasty fracture to his left leg in the home game against Notts County. As it happened he was destined never to play for North End again after the injury. However, with goals coming more freely after Harper's arrival the spirits were lifted and the defenders tightened up their game. Bobby Crawford was again ever present and the

testimony to his consistency knew no bounds. However, it was Harper who made the greatest impact. Not the most gifted of footballers, Harper's role was simply to score goals, and this he did to perfection. The revival after his transfer lifted the spirits of even the most depressed of the Preston followers. Other players to show good form included Jack Nelson, George Bargh and Herbert Hales. It was hoped that the FA Cup might produce some excitement and for awhile it did. In the third round, First Division Bolton were held at home, but in the replay Preston went one better and scored a remarkable 5–2 victory. In the next round Wolves were beaten at Deepdale, before almost 45,000 people saw North End lose in the next tie at Huddersfield. Just for a moment it looked as though it might be another big Cup year but, alas, the competition ended as the league campaign did, in disappointment. Just before that tie at Huddersfield the club took a new direction when manager Lincoln Hyde resigned and a four man committee took over the running of team affairs. It was a move that proved very interesting.

DEBUTANTS: (9) Frank Gallimore, Herbert Hales, Ted Harper, Billy Hough, George Hughes, Andy McCluggage, Dick Rowley, Henry (Harry) Simmons, George Wolf.

LAST GAMES: (11) Fawcett, Gillespie, Heaton, Horne, Hughes, Kerr, McCluggage, Scott, Sherry, Simmons, Thornborough.

Date 1931-2	Opponents	Comp	h or a	Score	Att.	1	2	3	4	5	6	7	8	9	10	11			
Aug 29	Oldham Ath	Div 2	a	2-2	12153	Fawcett	Ward (1)	Sherry	Nisbet	Nelson	Crawford (1p)	Reid	Bargh	Simmons	Home	Hales			
Aug 31	Tottenham H	Div 2	a	0-4	22104	Fawcett	Ward	Sherry	Nisbet	Nelson	Crawford	Reid	Bargh	Simmons	Home	Hales			
Sep 5	Southampton	Div 2	h	2-1	11052	Wolf	Ward	Kerr	Nisbet	Nelson	Crawford (1)	Reid	Bargh	Simmons (1)	Hough	Hales			
Sep 7	Nottm Forest	Div 2	h	1-1	10201	Wolf	Ward	Kerr	Nisbet	Nelson	Crawford (1)	Reid	Bargh	Simmons	Hough	Hales			
Sep 12	Stoke City	Div 2	a	1-4	8985	Wolf	Ward	Kerr	Thornborough	Nelson	Crawford (1)	Reid	Scott	Owens	Bargh	Home			
Sep 16	Nottm Forest	Div 2	a	2-2	6481	Wolf	Ward	Kerr	Thornborough	Nelson	Crawford	Heaton	Bargh	Owens (1)	Scott (1)	Hales			
Sep 19	Charlton Ath	Div 2	h	3-2	10704	Wolf	Ward	Gallimore	Thornborough	Nelson	Crawford (1p)	Heaton	Bargh (1)	Simmons	Scott (1)	Hales			
Sep 26	Wolverhampton W	Div 2	a	2-3	20606	Wolf	Ward	Gallimore	Thornborough	Nelson (1)	Crawford	Heaton	Bargh	Owens (1)	Scott	Hales			
Oct 3	Bradford P.A.	Div 2	h	1-0	10240	Wolf	Ward	Gallimore	Thornborough	Nelson	Crawford	Heaton(1)	Bargh	Owens	Scott	Hales			
Oct 10	Manchester United	Div 2	a	2-3	8496	Wolf	Ward	Gallimore	Thornborough	Nelson	Crawford	Heaton	Bargh (1)	Owens	Scott (1)	Hales			
Oct 17	Bury	Div 2	a	1-4	10162	Wolf	Ward	Gallimore	Hough	Nelson	Crawford	Reid	Bargh	Owens (1)	Home	Hales			
Oct 24	Port Vale	Div 2	h	1-4	8936	Hughes	Ward	Gallimore	Thornborough	Nelson	Hough	Reid	Bargh (1)	Owens	Crawford	Hales			
Oct 31	Millwall	Div 2	a	1-4	15586	Hughes	Ward	Kerr	Hough	Nelson	Crawford	Heaton	Bargh	Tremelling (1)	Scott	Farrell			
Nov 7	Bristol City	Div 2	h	1-1	6621	Hughes	Ward	Kerr	Hough	Nelson	Crawford	Heaton	Bargh	Tremelling (1)	Scott	Farrell			
Nov 14	Leeds United	Div 2	a	1-4	15439	Hughes	Gallimore	Kerr	Ward	Tremelling	Crawford	Heaton	Reid	Gillespie	Bargh (1)	Farrell			
Nov 21	Swansea Town	Div 2	h	1-0	6410	Hughes	Gallimore	Kerr	Hough	Tremelling	Crawford	Heaton	Bargh	Simmons	Reid (1)	Hales			
Nov 28	Barnsley	Div 2	a	2-4	5549	Hughes	Gallimore	Kerr	Hough	Tremelling	Crawford	Heaton	Bargh	Simmons (2)	Reid	Hales			
Dec 5	Notts County	Div 2	h	0-0	6320	Hughes	Gallimore	Kerr	Hough	Tremelling	Crawford	Heaton	Bargh	Simmons	Reid	Hales			
Dec 12	Plymouth Arg	Div 2	a	1-2	20867	Hughes	Gallimore	Ward	Hough	Nelson	Crawford	Reid	Rowley	Harper (1)	Bargh	Hales			
Dec 19	Bradford City	Div 2	h	5-2	9231	Hughes	Gallimore	Ward	Hough	Nelson	Crawford	Reid (2)	Rowley	Harper (2)	Bargh	Hales (1)			
Dec 25	Burnley	Div 2	a	2-2	18105	Hughes	McCluggage	Ward	Nisbet	Nelson	Crawford	Reid	Rowley (2)	Harper	Bargh	Hales			
Dec 26	Burnley	Div 2	h	2-1	27677	Hughes	McCluggage	Ward	Nisbet	Nelson (1)	Crawford	Reid	Rowley	Harper (1)	Bargh	Hales			
Jan 2	Oldham Ath	Div 2	h	2-3	8528	Wolf	McCluggage	Ward	Nisbet	Nelson	Crawford	Reid	Rowley	Harper (1)	Bargh	Hales (1)			
Jan 9	Bolton W. Rd 3	FAC	h	0-0	29052	Wolf	Gallimore	Ward	Nisbet	Nelson	Crawford	Reid	Rowley	Harper	Bargh	Hales			
Jan 13	Bolton W. Replay	FAC	a	5-2	32862	Wolf	Gallimore	Ward	Nisbet	Nelson	Crawford (1)	Reid	Rowley	Harper (1)	Bargh (1)	Hales	2og	(Griffiths) +	(Wagstaffe)
Jan 16	Southampton	Div 2	a	3-3	8050	Wolf	Gallimore	Ward	Nisbet	Nelson	Crawford	Reid	Rowley	Harper (3)	Bargh	Hales			
Jan 23	Wolverhampton W Rd 4	FAC	h	2-0	39840	Wolf	Gallimore	Ward	Nisbet	Nelson	Crawford	Reid	Rowley (1)	Harper (1)	Bargh	Hales			
Jan 30	Charlton Ath	Div 2	a	1-2	8506	Wolf	Gallimore	Ward	Nisbet	Nelson	Crawford	Reid	Rowley	Harper	Bargh (1)	Hales			
Feb 6	Wolverhampton W	Div 2	h	4-2	12748	Wolf	Gallimore	Ward	Nisbet	Nelson	Crawford	Reid	Rowley	Harper (3,1p)	Bargh	Hales (1)			
Feb 13	Huddersfield Rd 5	FAC	a	0-4	44291	Wolf	Gallimore	Ward	Nisbet	Nelson	Crawford	Reid	Rowley	Harper	Bargh	Hales			
Feb 17	Bradford P.A.	Div 2	h	5-1	7617	Wolf	Gallimore	Ward	Nisbet	Nelson	Crawford	Reid (1)	Rowley (1)	Harper (2)	Gillespie (1)	Hales			
Feb 20	Manchester United	Div 2	h	0-0	13353	Wolf	Gallimore	Ward	Nisbet	Nelson	Crawford	Reid	Rowley	Harper	Gillespie	Hales			
Feb 25	Stoke City	Div 2	h	2-0	7086	Wolf	Gallimore	Ward	Nisbet	Nelson	Crawford	Reid	Rowley	Harper (2)	Bargh	Hales			
Feb 29	Bury	Div 2	h	0-2	5028	Wolf	Gallimore	Ward	Nisbet	Nelson	Crawford	Reid	Rowley	Harper	Bargh	Hales			
Mar 5	Port Vale	Div 2	a	1-0	8132	Wolf	Gallimore	Ward	Thornborough	Nelson	Crawford	Reid	Rowley	Harper	Gillespie	Hales (1)			
Mar 12	Millwall	Div 2	h	2-0	8552	Wolf	Gallimore	Ward	Thornborough	Nelson	Crawford	Reid	Rowley	Harper (1)	Scott (1)	Hales			
Mar 19	Bristol City	Div 2	a	2-4	5473	Wolf	Gallimore	Ward	Thornborough	Nelson	Crawford	Reid	Rowley	Harper (1)	Scott (1)	Hales			
Mar 25	Chesterfield	Div 2	h	2-2	10167	Wolf	Gallimore	Ward	Thornborough	Nelson	Crawford	Reid	Bargh (1)	Harper (1)	Rowley	Hales			
Mar 26	Leeds United	Div 2	h	2-0	12151	Wolf	Gallimore	Ward	Thornborough	Nelson	Crawford	Reid	Bargh	Harper (1)	Rowley	Hales			
Mar 28	Chesterfield	Div 2	a	1-3	13502	Wolf	Gallimore	Ward	Thornborough	Nelson	Crawford	Reid	Bargh	Harper (1)	Rowley	Hales			
Apr 2	Swansea Town	Div 2	a	3-0	9584	Wolf	Gallimore	Ward	Thornborough	Nelson	Crawford	Home (1)	Bargh	Harper (1)	Scott (1)	Hales			
Apr 9	Barnsley	Div 2	h	1-2	7034	Wolf	Gallimore	Ward	Thornborough	Nelson	Crawford	Home	Bargh	Rowley (4)	Scott	Hales			
Apr 16	Notts County	Div 2	a	4-1	5872	Wolf	Gallimore	Ward	Thornborough	Nelson	Crawford	Reid	Bargh	Rowley (4)	Scott	Hales			
Apr 23	Plymouth Arg	Div 2	h	5-2	5051	Wolf	Gallimore	Ward	Thornborough	Nelson	Crawford	Rowley	Bargh (1)	Harper (3)	Scott (1)	Hales			
Apr 30	Bradford City	Div 2	a	1-0	8963	Wolf	Gallimore	Ward	Thornborough	Nelson	Crawford	Reid	Rowley	Harper	Scott (1)	Hales			
May 7	Tottenham H	Div 2	h	2-0	5900	Wolf	Gallimore	Ward	Thornborough	Nelson	Crawford	Reid	Rowley	Harper	Scott (1)	Hales (1)			

Match Report: Trotters Trounced – 13 Jan 1932 Bolton 2 Preston 5 FA Cup Replay

Nearly 33,000 spectators attended this mid-week afternoon FA Cup replay to see which of these two old Lancashire rivals would win the right to play Wolverhampton Wanderers in round four. North End won the toss and gave a good account of their attacking intentions straight from the kick-off, with Bargh, Hales and Harper all showing early promise. The visitors bright start was quickly dimmed though as First Division Bolton took a sixth minute lead. Cook evaded Gallimore's challenge and judged his centre so well that Gibson just had to steer his header out of Wolf's reach to score. Wolf was beaten again a few minutes later but Taylor saw his attempt pass the wrong side of the goalpost. Preston were playing their football a little too close and, realising this fact, they began to play a more open style. The result was a concerted assault on the Trotters goal which meant that Jones in the home goal really had to earn his keep. Griffiths, playing a very effective role as stopper, did tremendously well to nullify efforts from Reid and Harper, whilst Jones had to save smartly from Bargh. With 36 minutes gone Preston's right-wing broke away and centred into the danger area. Bargh dummied, enabling Crawford to hit a pile-driving shot past Jones for the equaliser. It was a fitting climax to a splendid rally when Preston, two minutes from the interval, took the lead. Hales and Bargh had a hand in the own goal which Griffiths conceded when he deflected Bargh's shot with his head, wrong footing his own keeper. North End were too aggressive for the Trotters and it had disturbed the Bolton game plan, especially when Harper increased Preston's lead after 62 minutes with a neat header from Bargh's pass. The Deepdale side continued to play effective football, outplaying their rivals in every department. Jones, in quick succession, saved remarkably well from Rowley, Bargh and Reid, as all their efforts were on target. In a rare Bolton counter attack on 71 minutes, Blackmore wheeled around Nelson to sweep a long shot into the far corner of the net. Undaunted, Second Division Preston, cut through the Wanderer's defence a few minutes later and it culminated in Bargh, who had had a fine afternoon, scoring a superb individual goal after demonstrating his fine dribbling skills. Six minutes from time Wagstaffe, in trying to prevent Hales from scoring, did the job for him as he deceived his goalkeeper with an overhit backpass. Bolton finished somewhat disorganised and very well beaten.

Left to right: *Back row*: W. Scott (trainer), Gallimore, Rowley, Nelson, Crawford, Mr W. Pilkington (LEP). *Front row*: Wolf, Ward, Reid, Harper, Nisbet, Bargh, Hales.

Dick Rowley, Ted Harper and Andy McCluggage. Three December signings.

		P	W	D	L	F	A	Pts
1	Wolves	42	24	8	10	115	49	56
2	Leeds	42	22	10	10	78	54	54
3	Stoke	42	19	14	9	69	48	52
4	Plymouth	42	20	9	13	100	66	49
5	Bury	42	21	7	14	70	58	49
6	Bradford PA	42	21	7	14	72	63	49
7	Bradford City	42	16	13	13	80	61	45
8	Tottenham	42	16	11	15	87	78	43
9	Millwall	42	17	9	16	61	61	43
10	Charlton	42	17	9	16	61	66	43
11	Nottingham Forest	42	16	10	16	77	72	42
12	Man United	42	17	8	17	71	72	42
13	**PRESTON**	**42**	**16**	**10**	**16**	**75**	**77**	**42**
14	Southampton	42	17	7	18	66	77	41
15	Swansea	42	16	7	19	73	75	39
16	Notts County	42	13	12	17	75	75	38
17	Chesterfield	42	13	11	18	64	86	37
18	Oldham	42	13	10	19	62	84	36
19	Burnley	42	13	9	20	59	87	35
20	Port Vale	42	13	7	22	58	89	33
21	Barnsley	42	12	9	21	55	91	33
22	Bristol City	42	6	11	25	39	78	23

League appearances: (42 games)

Bargh G. W. 35, Crawford R. 42, Farrell V. 3, Fawcett D. H. 2, Gallimore F. 31, Gillespie T. B. 4, Hales H. 38, Harper E. C. 23, Heaton F. 11, Horne A. 6, Hough W. 11, Hughes G. 11, Kerr J. 10, McCluggage A. 3, Nelson J. H. 38, Nisbet G. 14, Owens E. 7, Reid A. M. 32, Rowley R. W. M. 22, Scott T. 16, Sherry A. P. 2, Simmons H. R. 8, Thornborough E. H. 19, Tremelling W. 6, Ward F. 39, Wolf G. 29.

FA Cup appearances (4 games)

Wolf 4, Gallimore 4, Ward 4, Nisbet 4, Nelson 4, Crawford 4, Reid 4, Rowley 4, Harper 4, Bargh 4, and Hales 4.

Goalscorers: 75 League–7 Cup–(Total 82)

Harper 24(1pen)–2 (26), Scott 9–0 (9), Bargh 7–1 (8), Rowley 7–1 (8), Crawford 5(2 pens)–1 (6), Hales 5–0 (5), Reid 4–0 (4), Owens 3–0 (3), Simmons 3–0 (3), Nelson 2–0 (2), Tremelling 2–0 (2), Gillespie 1–0 (1), Ward 1–0 (1), Horne 1–0 (1), Heaton 1–0 (1), Own Goals 0–2 (2)*. *Griffiths and Wagstaffe of Bolton.

William Tremelling signed from Blackpool and was to stabilise North End's defence and Captain the team.

OGDEN'S CIGARETTES

W. TREMELLING
(PRESTON NORTH END)

Future Players born between August 1931 and July 1932: None
Ever presents: (1) Bobby Crawford
FA Cup: Fifth Round
Manager: Lincoln Hyde, (Resigned February 9th 1932) and then a four man Committee took over.
Leading scorer: 26 goals – Ted Harper (24 league 2 Cup)
Players used: 26
AUTHORS UNOFFICIAL PLAYER OF THE SEASON: Ted Harper

STAT FACTS:
Best home run without defeat: 5 games
Best away run without defeat: 3 games
Longest run unbeaten: 4 games
Longest run without a win: 6 games
Best home attendance: 39,840 *vs.* Wolves FAC 23.1.32
Worst home attendance: 5,028 *vs.* Bury 29.2.32
Best away attendance: 44,291 *vs.* Huddersfield FAC 13.2.32
Worst away attendance: 5,473 *vs.* Bristol City 19.3.32
Aggregate and average home attendances: 202,990 – 9,666
Aggregate and average away attendances: 240,232 – 11,440

Trivia Fact:

From 1919 to 1978 there is only one year which failed to produce at least one player who went on to play for North End. The year was 1932. The best years so far were 1964 and 1969 when 16 future players were produced.

The four man committee that took over team affairs in February 1932 included the unforgettable Nathaniel Buck. 'Nat' Buck went on to become one of North End's most influential figures for many years to come and during his time at the club held the post of Chairman and later Club President until his death in March 1974.

When Dick Rowley and Ted Harper were signed from Spurs, the London club's manager at the time was none other than Percy Smith, the former North End player.

George Bargh was a versatile sportsman and once won a billiards handicap tournament at Garstang Liberal Club, beating off the challenge of 31 other entrants.

Jasper Kerr broke his left leg during the goalless draw with Notts County on 5 December 1931 at Deepdale.

League position in Division Two: 13th – P42 W16 D10 L16 F75 A77 Pts 42
Home: W11 D6 L4 F37 A25 Away: W5 D4 L12 F38 A52

SEASON 1932–1933

The ups and downs of a football club were never more in evidence than in the 1932–33 campaign. Preston again struggled to come to terms with life in Division Two as big wins were offset by heavy defeats and goals flowed freely at each end. It did, however, culminate in a wonderful season for ace marksman Ted Harper. The centre-forward notched a staggering 37 league goals which created a record which still stands today. Included in those goals were two four goal hauls, against Burnley and Lincoln, both at Deepdale, and two other hat-tricks. They, too, were at Deepdale, against West Ham and Manchester United. The longest the sharp-shooter went without a goal was just three games and all through the season he was consistently on target. Defensively though, Preston struggled to find a rhythm. Goalkeeping was a problem for a while, although this was somewhat remedied around Christmas time when Harry Holdcroft was signed from Everton. There was an immediate improvement in the goals conceded and the goalkeeper was ably supported by the excellent Frank Gallimore and Bill Tremelling. Gallimore's consistency was terrific and he was ever present at right-back. The club, now being run by a four man committee, brought several other new players into Deepdale and there were notable contributions from Arthur Fitton, Harry Lowe and a Scot from Dundee United called Jimmy Milne. But perhaps the most surprising and controversial

decision of the management was to allow the transfer of Bobby Crawford to Blackpool after he had missed just one game in six seasons. The fans saw plenty of goals, with the home games averaging four apiece, and there was a sensational 5–5 draw at Grimsby, sandwiched between a 6–2 defeat by Spurs at Deepdale and a 4–1 home win over West Ham. 23 goals in just three games! The big disappointment of the year came with yet another failure in the FA Cup. This time Preston went down 2–1 at Birmingham in the Third round, that's four seasons out of five where the club had failed to progress beyond the first hurdle. Gavin Nisbet and Bob Kelly had also shown some good form during the year, but despite all of these excellent individual performances, as a team, Preston North End were not quite there. Having said that the season belonged to the incredible Ted Harper. His contribution was, and is, phenomenal and guaranteed his deserved place in Preston folklore.

DEBUTANTS: (12) George Akers, William Broadbent, George (Arthur) Fitton, David Galloway, Harry Jones, Bob Kelly, Harry Lowe, Jimmy Milne, John Mustard, Robert Nisbet, Richard Twist and Harry Holdcroft.

LAST GAMES: (13) Akers, Broadbent, Crawford, Farrell, Hales, Jones, Mustard, Nisbet R., Nelson, Reid, Twist, Ward and Wolf.

Trivia Facts:

Ted Harper's 37 league goals is a record for the club, but in that 1932–33 season that was not the total of the goals he scored. He scored six more in the Lancashire Cup, including a five-goal haul against Everton, and he also hit five in friendlies. So, in all the great man hit 48 goals in his unforgettable year.

Bob Kelly was one of Preston's most obvious 'short term' signings because when he signed from Huddersfield in July 1932 he was already 39 years old! It was of course the twilight of Bob's brilliant career. In his time with Burnley, Sunderland and Huddersfield he won 14 England caps, a Championship medal whilst at Burnley and three FA Cup runners-up medals with Huddersfield. Mind you, his Preston career was in no way the end of his football days. In fact Bob was still playing in his fifties. After his stay at Deepdale he became player-manager at Carlisle, and then later managed Stockport County.

On 4 March 1933 Deepdale suffered a fire at the ground with the Town End being destroyed.

David Galloway, a 5' 5" inside-forward signed from Aberdeen, was described by a contemporary journalist as a 'rare box of tricks'.

Left to right: *Back row*: G. Nisbet, Gallimore, Holdcroft, Tremelling, Lowe, Milne. *Front row*: Kelly, Bargh, Harper, Rowley, Fitton.

League position in Division Two: 9th – P42 W16 D10 L16 F74 A70 Pts 42
Home: W12 D2 L7 F53 A36   Away: W4 D8 L9 F21 A34

Match Report: A Tale of Two Halves – 15 Oct 1932 Grimsby Town 5 Preston 5

After conceding six goals against Spurs, North End made a couple of changes for the encounter at Cleethorpes against Grimsby Town. Bill Tremelling appeared at centre-half in place of the unfit Nelson, whilst Hales resumed on the left-wing after a fortnight in the reserve team. To say that Preston got off to a bad start would be the understatement of the century! Grimsby's six foot centre-forward, Glover, rocked North End by scoring FOUR times in the first 13 minutes. His first goal came after just two minutes as Tremelling and Wolf got themselves into a right tangle leaving Glover with a free header. Goalkeeper Wolf, then presented Glover with another gift goal only three minutes later as he tried to collect from a melee which had developed some yards in front of him. Unfortunately he failed to gather the ball and Glover had another easy task to score. North End thought they had overcome the worst as Read, Grimsby's keeper, had to be on top form to deny Hales on three seperate occasions, but then Tremelling and Wolf once again combined erroneously to gift Glover yet another goal and the forward had a hat-trick in just ten minutes. This time Glover had nipped in to capitalise on a back pass which Wolf did not reach. So, in three attacks Grimsby had scored three times. Unbelievably, Glover helped himself to a fourth goal after 13 minutes, this time giving Wolf no chance to save. Shell-shocked is probably a phrase most suited to sum up the mood of the Preston team at this stage of the game. They had not played badly and in fact had probably had more of the possession during the game. Although 4–0 up Grimsby's goalkeeper had had more work to do than Wolf and after 20 minutes he was finally beaten by a shot from Hales as Preston came back. The visitors had improved beyond recognition as the first half concluded and after the break, with nothing to lose and led by the lively Hales, responded to the challenge manfully, forcing the home defenders into errors. This enterprising play paid off as in the 56th minute Harper scored his tenth goal of the season. Grimsby retaliated and a shot struck the crossbar. If that had gone in the game would have been all over but as it was Preston then hit two goals in rapid fashion, through the veteran Kelly and the impressive Hales, to equalise. Hales also hit the crossbar as Preston went for the winner although it was Grimsby who scored next when Dyson scored a fifth for them. That looked like the winning goal but North End had the last laugh as Mustard struck another equaliser to make it a memorable 5–5 draw.

Frank Gallimore

League appearances (42 games)

Akers G. 1, Bargh G. W. 21, Broadbent W. H. 2, Crawford R. 5, Farrell V. 2,
Fitton G. A. 19, Gallimore F. 42, Galloway D. W. 20, Hales H. 19, Harper E. C. 41,
Holdcroft G. H. 23, Hough W. 13, Jones H. J. 1, Kelly R. 40, Lowe H. 19,
Milne J. L. 20, Mustard J. 15, Nelson J. H. 8, Nisbet G. 40, Nisbet R. 2, Reid A. M. 7,
Rowley R. W. M. 24, Tremelling W. 34, Twist R. 3, Ward F. 25,
Wolf G. 16.

FA Cup appearances (1 game)

Holdcroft, Gallimore, Lowe, Nisbet, Tremelling, Milne, Bargh, Kelly, Harper, Rowley,
Fitton, all 1 each.

Goalscorers: 74 League–1 Cup

Harper 37(3 pens)–0 (37), Kelly 9(3 pens)–0 (9), Fitton 7–0 (7), Rowley 5–1 (6),
Hales 5–0 (5), Mustard 5–0 (5), Bargh 3–0 (3), Jones 1–0 (1), Nisbet G. 1–0 (1).
Own Goals 1–0 (1) (Bradshaw of Bury).

Future Players born between August 1932 and July 1933: Fred Else, Les Dagger and Ray Evans
Ever presents: (1) Frank Gallimore
FA Cup: Third Round
Hat-tricks: (4) All by Ted Harper (Includes 2 x 4 goals)
Chairman: Sir Meyrick Hollins
Leading scorer: 37 goals – Ted Harper (all league)
Players used: 26

AUTHORS' UNOFFICIAL PLAYER OF THE SEASON: Ted Harper

Season 1932–33: Second Division

		P	W	D	L	F	A	Pts
1	Stoke	42	25	6	11	78	39	56
2	Tottenham	42	20	15	7	96	51	55
3	Fulham	42	20	10	12	78	65	50
4	Bury	42	20	9	13	84	59	49
5	Nottingham Forest	42	17	15	10	67	59	49
6	Man United	42	15	13	14	71	68	43
7	Millwall	42	16	11	15	59	57	43
8	Bradford PA	42	17	8	17	77	71	42
9	PRESTON	42	16	10	16	74	70	42
10	Swansea	42	19	4	19	50	54	42
11	Bradford City	42	14	13	15	65	61	41
12	Southampton	42	18	5	19	66	66	41
13	Grimsby	42	14	13	15	79	84	41
14	Plymouth	42	16	9	17	63	67	41
15	Notts County	42	15	10	17	67	78	40
16	Oldham	42	15	8	19	67	80	38
17	Port Vale	42	14	10	18	66	79	38
18	Lincoln	42	12	13	17	72	87	37
19	Burnley	42	11	14	17	67	79	36
20	West Ham	42	13	9	20	75	93	35
21	Chesterfield	42	12	10	20	61	84	34
22	Charlton	42	12	7	23	60	91	31

Date 1932-3	Opponents	Comp	h or a	Score	Att.	1	2	3	4	5	6	7	8	9	10	11		
Aug 27	Bradford Pk. Av.	Div 2	h	2-3	15343	Wolf	Gallimore	Ward	G. Nisbet	Nelson	Crawford	Reid	Kelly	Harper (2)	Rowley	Hales		
Aug 29	Burnley	Div 2	h	6-1	12732	Wolf	Gallimore	R. Nisbet	G. Nisbet	Nelson	Crawford	Mustard	Kelly (1)	Harper (4)	Bargh	Hales (1)		
Sep 3	Plymouth Arg	Div 2	a	0-5	13318	Wolf	Gallimore	R. Nisbet	G. Nisbet	Nelson	Crawford	Mustard	Kelly	Harper	Bargh	Galloway		
Sep 5	Burnley	Div 2	a	0-4	14271	Wolf	Gallimore	Ward	G. Nisbet	Nelson	Crawford	Mustard	Kelly	Harper	Galloway	Hales		
Sep 10	Nottm Forest	Div 2	h	2-1	9338	Wolf	Gallimore	Ward	G. Nisbet	Tremelling	Crawford	Mustard	Kelly	Harper (2)	Galloway	Hales		
Sep 17	Charlton Ath.	Div 2	h	1-0	14350	Wolf	Gallimore	Ward	G. Nisbet	Nelson	Hough	Mustard (1)	Bargh	Harper	Galloway	Hales		
Sep 24	Stoke City	Div 2	h	1-3	11777	Wolf	Gallimore	Ward	G. Nisbet	Nelson	Hough	Mustard (1)	Bargh	Harper	Galloway	Hales		
Oct 1	Manchester Utd.	Div 2	a	0-0	20800	Wolf	Gallimore	Ward	G. Nisbet	Nelson	Hough	Mustard	Kelly	Harper	Galloway	Farrell		
Oct 8	Tottenham H.	Div 2	h	2-6	6368	Wolf	Gallimore	Ward	G. Nisbet	Nelson	Hough	Mustard (1)	Kelly	Harper (1)	Galloway	Farrell		
Oct 15	Grimsby Town	Div 2	a	5-5	8166	Wolf	Gallimore	Ward	G. Nisbet	Tremelling	Hough	Mustard (1)	Kelly (1)	Harper (1)	Galloway	Hales (2)		
Oct 22	West Ham Utd	Div 2	a	4-1	8525	Wolf	Gallimore	Ward	G. Nisbet	Tremelling	Hough	Mustard	Kelly (1)	Harper (3)	Galloway	Hales		
Oct 29	Lincoln City	Div 2	a	1-2	9207	Twist	Gallimore	Ward	Broadbent	Tremelling	Milne	Mustard	Kelly	Harper	Galloway	Hales (1)		
Nov 5	Bury	Div 2	h	1-3	13011	Twist	Gallimore	Ward	Broadbent	Tremelling	Milne	Reid	Kelly	Harper (1p)	Galloway	Hales		
Nov 12	Chesterfield	Div 2	a	3-4	9772	Twist	Gallimore	Ward	G. Nisbet	Tremelling	Hough	Reid	Kelly (2)	Harper (1)	Galloway	Hales		
Nov 19	Notts County	Div 2	h	3-0	7298	Wolf	Gallimore	Ward	G. Nisbet	Tremelling	Hough	Reid	Kelly (1)	Harper (2)	Galloway	Hales		
Nov 26	Port Vale	Div 2	h	1-0	6938	Wolf	Gallimore	Ward	G. Nisbet	Tremelling	Hough	Reid	Kelly	Harper	Galloway	Hales (1)		
Dec 3	Millwall	Div 2	h	0-1	7698	Wolf	Gallimore	Ward	G. Nisbet	Tremelling	Hough	Mustard	Kelly	Harper	Galloway	Hales		
Dec 10	Swansea Town	Div 2	a	1-3	6628	Wolf	Gallimore	Ward	G. Nisbet	Tremelling	Hough	Reid	Kelly	Harper (1)	Galloway	Hales		
Dec 17	Bradford City	Div 2	h	1-4	7347	Wolf	Gallimore	Ward	G. Nisbet	Tremelling	Hough	Reid	Kelly	Harper (1p)	Galloway	Hales		
Dec 24	Southampton	Div 2	a	0-1	9569	Holdcroft	Gallimore	Lowe	G. Nisbet	Tremelling	Ward	Bargh	Kelly	Harper	Rowley	Fitton		
Dec 26	Oldham Ath	Div 2	h	2-2	18816	Holdcroft	Gallimore	Lowe	G. Nisbet (1)	Tremelling	Ward	Bargh	Kelly	Harper	Rowley (1)	Fitton		
Dec 27	Oldham Ath	Div 2	a	2-0	10910	Holdcroft	Gallimore	Lowe	G. Nisbet	Tremelling	Ward	Mustard	Kelly	Harper (1)	Rowley	Fitton (1)		
Dec 31	Bradford Pk. Av.	Div 2	a	0-2	8699	Holdcroft	Gallimore	Lowe	G. Nisbet	Tremelling	Ward	Mustard	Kelly	Harper	Rowley	Fitton		
Jan 7	Plymouth Arg	Div 2	h	3-0	8730	Holdcroft	Gallimore	Lowe	G. Nisbet	Tremelling	Milne	Bargh (1)	Kelly	Harper (1)	Rowley (1)	Hales		
Jan 14	**Birmingham Rd 3**	**FAC**	**a**	**1-2**	**29497**	**Holdcroft**	**Gallimore**	**Lowe**	**G. Nisbet**	**Tremelling**	**Milne**	**Bargh**	**Kelly**	**Harper**	**Rowley (1)**	**Fitton**		
Jan 21	Nottm Forest	Div 2	a	1-2	7333	Holdcroft	Gallimore	Lowe	G. Nisbet	Tremelling	Hough	Kelly	Galloway	Harper	Rowley (1)	Fitton		
Jan 28	Charlton Ath	Div 2	h	4-2	6057	Holdcroft	Gallimore	Lowe	G. Nisbet	Tremelling	Milne	Mustard (1)	Kelly (1p)	Jones (1)	Rowley	Fitton (1)		
Feb 4	Stoke City	Div 2	a	1-1	12903	Holdcroft	Gallimore	Lowe	G. Nisbet	Tremelling	Milne	Kelly	Bargh	Harper (1)	Rowley	Fitton		
Feb 11	Manchester Utd	Div 2	h	3-3	15622	Holdcroft	Gallimore	Lowe	G. Nisbet	Tremelling	Milne	Kelly	Bargh	Harper (3,1p)	Rowley	Fitton		
Feb 18	Tottenham H.	Div 2	a	1-1	41209	Holdcroft	Gallimore	Lowe	G. Nisbet	Tremelling	Milne	Kelly	Bargh	Harper (1)	Rowley	Fitton		
Mar 2	Grimsby Town	Div 2	h	4-2	7449	Holdcroft	Gallimore	Lowe	G. Nisbet	Tremelling	Milne	Kelly (1p)	Bargh (1)	Harper (1)	Rowley	Fitton (1)		
Mar 6	West Ham Utd	Div 2	h	1-1	8648	Holdcroft	Gallimore	Lowe	G. Nisbet	Tremelling	Milne	Kelly	Bargh (1)	Harper	Rowley	Fitton		
Mar 11	Lincoln City	Div 2	h	5-0	11244	Holdcroft	Gallimore	Lowe	G. Nisbet	Tremelling	Milne	Kelly	Bargh	Harper (4)	Rowley	Fitton (1)		
Mar 18	Bury	Div 2	a	2-1	10502	Holdcroft	Gallimore	Lowe	G. Nisbet	Tremelling	Milne	Kelly	Bargh	Harper	Rowley	Fitton (1)	1 o.g.	(Bradshaw)
Mar 25	Chesterfield	Div 2	h	2-0	10245	Holdcroft	Gallimore	Lowe	G. Nisbet	Tremelling	Milne	Kelly	Bargh	Harper (2)	Rowley	Fitton		
Apr 1	Notts County	Div 2	a	0-0	9346	Holdcroft	Gallimore	Lowe	G. Nisbet	Tremelling	Milne	Kelly	Bargh	Harper	Rowley	Fitton		
Apr 8	Port Vale	Div 2	a	3-1	9490	Holdcroft	Gallimore	Lowe	G. Nisbet	Tremelling	Milne	Kelly	Bargh	Harper	Rowley	Fitton (1)		
Apr 14	Fulham	Div 2	a	0-1	21305	Holdcroft	Gallimore	Ward	G. Nisbet	Tremelling	Milne	Kelly	Bargh	Harper	Rowley	Fitton		
Apr 15	Millwall	Div 2	h	1-1	11449	Holdcroft	Gallimore	Ward	G. Nisbet	Tremelling	Milne	Kelly	Bargh	Harper (1)	Rowley	Akers		
Apr 17	Fulham	Div 2	h	1-2	14276	Holdcroft	Gallimore	Ward	G. Nisbet	Tremelling	Milne	Kelly (1p)	Bargh	Harper	Rowley	Hales		
Apr 22	Swansea Town	Div 2	h	1-0	8067	Holdcroft	Gallimore	Ward	G. Nisbet	Tremelling	Milne	Kelly	Bargh	Harper (1)	Rowley	Hales		
Apr 29	Bradford City	Div 2	a	0-0	4830	Holdcroft	Gallimore	Lowe	G. Nisbet	Tremelling	Milne	Kelly	Rowley	Harper	Galloway	Fitton		
May 6	Southampton	Div 2	h	3-1	5199	Holdcroft	Gallimore	Lowe	G. Nisbet	Tremelling	Milne	Kelly	Rowley (2)	Harper	Galloway	Fitton (1)		

STAT FACTS:

Best home run without defeat: 8 games
Best away run without defeat: 5 games
Longest run unbeaten: 11 games
Longest run without a win: 5 games
Best home attendance: 18,816 *vs.* Oldham 26.12.32
Worst home attendance: 5,199 *vs.* Southampton 6.5.33
Best away attendance: 41,209 *vs.* Spurs 18.2.33
Worst away attendance: 4,830 *vs.* Bradford City 29.4.33
Aggregate and average home attendance: 214,632 – 10,221
Aggregate and average away attendance: 260,153 – 12,388

Preston North End Football Club.

CHARITY MATCH
at Deepdale
SATURDAY, MAY 13th, 1933

TEAMS FOR TO-DAY.

PRESTON NORTH END
(COLOURS : WHITE SHIRTS, BLUE KNICKERS)

1
Holdcroft

2   3
Gallimore   Lowe

4   5   6
Nisbet   Tremelling   Milne

7   8   9   10   11
Kelly   Bargh   Harper   Rowley   Fitton

12   13   14   15   16
Cameron   James   Robson   McClelland   Mustard

17   18   19
Crawford   Craven   Reid

20   21
Ward   Owens

22
Moss

EX-NORTH END PLAYERS
(COLOURS : BLUE SHIRTS, WHITE KNICKERS)

REFEREE - W. F. BUNNELL (Preston)

LINESMEN :
Red Stripe - J. H. HARGREAVES   Blue Stripe - H. W. HUNT

SEASON 1933-1934

At last, promotion is achieved! After nine seasons of Division Two football, a concerted effort by all gave Preston the runners-up spot, seven points behind Champions Grimsby but a crucial one point ahead of both Bolton and Brentford. Although 13 games were lost, an unusually high number for a promoted side, the club also won 23, and this was the key to their success. Two signings made a big impact. One was an effervescent Scot named William Shankly. This tigerish wing-half added some much needed bite to the midfield and it was no coincidence that on his debut North End won 5-0. The other important signing was centre-forward Jack Palethorpe who was transferred from Stoke in the January and made a vital difference to the goals for column in the second half of the season. He scored 14 goals in that period and many of those goals won Preston the points. Harry Holdcroft, Harry Lowe, Bill Tremelling, Jimmy Milne and George Stephenson also made excellent contributions and even the loss of Ted Harper was overcome. Harper had been transferred to Blackburn in the September after the Ewood Park side had made Preston an offer that was too good to turn down. Harper had done his job to perfection and even in this promotion season he played his part. But understandable, with Harper gone, Preston's goal tally dropped and in fact their total for the season was lower than any of the top seven clubs.

Significantly though, their defensive record was the best in the division. With two opening victories against local rivals Blackpool and Burnley the season had got off to a flying start, and twelve goals were scored in the first four games. However, after the game at West Ham on September 23, promotion seemed but a distant dream. Preston were, if you will pardon the pun, hammered 6-0! A further run of six games without a win were played before a crucial 3-0 win at home to Swansea kick-started the season again. It all culminated in a tremendous final surge when six wins out of their last seven games edged out Bolton and Brentford for that coveted runners-up position. Even the FA Cup brought some excitement and a new record Deepdale attendance of 40,177 was drawn for the fifth round match against Northampton. Unfortunately North End were beaten in the next round but the consolation came for the fans when the return ticket to Division One was booked at The Dell, Southampton.

DEBUTANTS: (15) John Bell, Frank Beresford, Joseph Brain, Edward Common, Jimmy Dougal, Len Gallimore, John Pears, Jack Palethorpe, Thomas Pritchard, Sid Rawlings, Bill Shankly, George Stephenson, John Torbet and Frank Wilson.

LAST GAMES: (11) Brain, Common, Galloway, Harper, Owens, Pritchard, Rawlings, Rowley, Stephenson, Torbet and Wilson.

North End party pictured at Southampton docks on the morning prior to winning promotion back to Division One

League position in Division Two: Runners-up – P42 W23 D6 L13 F71 A52 Pts 52
Home: W15 D3 L3 F47 A20 Away: W8 D3 L10 F24 A32

Match Report: Shankly's Impressive Debut – 9 Dec 1933 Preston 5 Hull City 0

Less than 9,000 people were present as a young Bill Shankly stepped up onto the big stage to make his PNE debut against the Tigers of Hull City. North End dictated the game from the kick-off and it therefore came as no surprise when they took an early third minute lead. Jimmy Milne started the move, feeding Fitton, who narrowly beat his marker to the ball before crossing to Stephenson who, in turn, forced the ball over the goalline, despite the attentions of the goalkeeper, Maddison. For some apparent reason the ball seemed difficult to control and this obviously contributed to the poor standard of play. At this point the heady days of First Division football seemed miles away. However, as the game progressed Shankly grew in confidence. He was a positive player, never negative, and halfway through the first period he won a challenge, pushed the ball past a defender into space. As none of his teammates bothered to chase his pass he sped after it himself, retrieving possession and then crossing for Fitton who drove home the chance. Sheer opportunism! North End went three up two minutes later when Fitton's accurate crossball was misjudged by the Hull centre-half leaving Kelly with the relatively simple task of lobbing the ball over the goalkeeper and just under the crossbar. Milne nearly added to the scoreline but at the final momenthe caught the ball with his shin instead of his foot, resulting in the ball passing tamely wide of the target. Although Stephenson and Rowley missed sitters as Preston continued to dominate, Rowley then made amends by scoring with a powerful shot which beat Maddison all ends up, making it a half to remember for young Shankly as Preston led 4–0 at the interval. Shankly had not been overawed by the occasion, proving his selection justified, and he was involved in the game as much as his more experienced colleagues. Preston continued to control the match and Stephenson, Rowley, Rawlings and Kelly all should have done better when presented with good chances. The game, which was peppered with niggling little fouls, was controlled by the Preston midfield players who proved to be more than a match for the Tigers. Twelve minutes from the end Stephenson finished off Hull's futile challenge as he legitimately barged the goalkeeper, forcing him to drop the ball at the Preston player's feet for Stephenson to slot the ball into the net.

— • PRESTON NORTH END – SECOND DIVISION RUNNERS UP 1933-4 • —

BACK: Guy NISBET; Frank GALLIMORE; Billy HOUGH; Harry HOLDCROFT; Harry LOWE; Jimmy MILNE; Bill SCOTT (trainer)
R.H   R.B   R.B   GOAL   L.B   L.H   "Mr Cheerful!"

FRONT: Jimmy DOUGAL; George BARGH; Bob KELLY; Bill TREMELLING; Willie SHANKLY; Jack PALETHORPE; Arthur FITTON
O.R.   I.R   I.R   C.H & Captain   R.H   C.F   O.L

SEATED: Frank BERESFORD, AND Johnny BELL
inside left   inside left

League appearances (42 games)

Bargh G. W. 9, Bell J. G. 13, Beresford F. E. 14, Brain J. 7, Common E. 1,
Dougal J. 10, Fitton G. A. 24, Gallimore F. 21, Gallimore L. 4, Galloway D. W. 11,
Harper E. C. 11, Holdcroft G. H. 42, Hough W. 19, Kelly R. 27, Lowe H. 42,
Milne J. L. 38, Nisbet G. 17, Owens E. 1, Palethorpe J. T. 18, Pears J. 7,
Pritchard T. F. 1, Rawlings J. S. D. 12, Rowley R. W. M. 5, Shankly W. 25,
Stephenson G. T. 25, Torbet J. 11, Tremelling W. 41, Wilson F. 6.

FA Cup appearances: (4 games)

Holdcroft 4, Gallimore F. 2, Hough 2, Lowe 4, Shankly 4, Tremelling 4, Milne 4,
Rawlings 1, Bargh 1, Dougal 2, Kelly 4, Rowley 2, Stephenson 3, Palethorpe 2, Bell 1,
Fitton 4.

Goalscorers: 71 League–7 Cup–(Total 78)

Stephenson 16–0 (16), Palethorpe 11–3 (14), Kelly 7(1 pen)–2 (9), Fitton 6–1 (7),
Harper 6–0 (6), Bargh 4–0 (4), Bell 4–0 (4), Torbet 4(1 pen)–0 (4),
Beresford 2–0 (2), Brain 2–0 (2), Dougal 2–0 (2), Pears 2–0 (2),
Rowley 2–0 (2), Galloway 1–0 (1), Milne 1–0 (1), Wilson 1–0 (1). Own Goals 0–1
(1) (McGuire Northampton).

Season 1933–34: Second Division

		P	W	D	L	F	A	Pts
1	Grimsby	42	27	5	10	103	59	59
2	**PRESTON**	**42**	**23**	**6**	**13**	**71**	**52**	**52**
3	Bolton	42	21	9	12	79	55	51
4	Brentford	42	22	7	13	85	60	51
5	Bradford PA	42	23	3	16	86	67	49
6	Bradford City	42	20	6	16	73	67	46
7	West Ham	42	17	11	14	78	70	45
8	Port Vale	42	19	7	16	60	55	45
9	Oldham	42	17	10	15	72	60	44
10	Plymouth	42	15	13	14	69	70	43
11	Blackpool	42	15	13	14	62	64	43
12	Bury	42	17	9	16	70	73	43
13	Burnley	42	18	6	18	60	72	42
14	Southampton	42	15	8	19	54	58	38
15	Hull	42	13	12	17	52	68	38
16	Fulham	42	15	7	20	48	67	37
17	Nottingham Forest	42	13	9	20	73	74	35
18	Notts County	42	12	11	19	53	62	35
19	Swansea	42	10	15	17	51	60	35
20	Man United	42	14	6	22	59	85	34
21	Millwall	42	11	11	20	39	68	33
22	Lincoln	42	9	8	25	44	75	25

Future Players born between August 1933 and July 1934: Sammy Taylor and Jim Knowles
Ever presents: (2) Holdcroft and Lowe.
FA Cup: Sixth Round
Chairman: Sir Meyrick Hollins
Hat-tricks: (3) Stephenson, Bargh and Palethorpe (in the FA Cup)
Manager: A four man Committee
Leading scorer: 16 goals – George Stephenson (all league)
Players used: 28

AUTHORS' UNOFFICIAL PLAYER OF THE YEAR:
Harry Holdcroft

Date 1933-4	Opponents	Comp	h or a	Score	Att.	1	2	3	4	5	6	7	8	9	10	11		
Aug 26	Blackpool	Div 2	a	2-1	28771	Holdcroft	F.Gallimore	Lowe	Nisbet	Tremelling	Milne	Kelly	Galloway	Harper (1)	Stephenson	Torbet (1p)		
Aug 28	Burnley	Div 2	h	3-2	18950	Holdcroft	F.Gallimore	Lowe	Nisbet	Tremelling	Milne (1)	Kelly	Galloway (1)	Harper	Stephenson (1)	Torbet		
Sep 2	Bradford P.A.	Div 2	h	3-1	16488	Holdcroft	F.Gallimore	Lowe	Nisbet	Tremelling	Milne	Wilson	Galloway	Harper (2)	Stephenson (1)	Torbet		
Sep 4	Burnley	Div 2	a	4-1	13543	Holdcroft	F.Gallimore	Lowe	Nisbet	Tremelling	Milne	Wilson (1)	Galloway	Harper	Stephenson (2)	Torbet (1)		
Sep 9	Grimsby Town	Div 2	a	0-3	13025	Holdcroft	F.Gallimore	Lowe	Nisbet	Tremelling	Milne	Wilson	Galloway	Harper	Stephenson	Torbet		
Sep 16	Nottm Forest	Div 2	h	4-0	14281	Holdcroft	F.Gallimore	Lowe	Nisbet	Tremelling	Milne	Kelly	Galloway	Harper (2)	Stephenson	Torbet (2)		
Sep 23	West Ham Utd	Div 2	a	0-6	15738	Holdcroft	F.Gallimore	Lowe	Nisbet	Tremelling	Milne	Wilson	Galloway	Harper	Stephenson	Torbet		
Sep 30	Plymouth Arg	Div 2	h	1-1	13814	Holdcroft	F.Gallimore	Lowe	Nisbet	Tremelling	Milne	Wilson	Kelly	Harper (1)	Galloway	Torbet		
Oct 7	Manchester Utd	Div 2	a	0-1	22303	Holdcroft	F.Gallimore	Lowe	Nisbet	Tremelling	Milne	Wilson	Stephenson	Harper	Bargh	Torbet		
Oct 14	Bolton W.	Div 2	h	1-1	20054	Holdcroft	F.Gallimore	Lowe	Nisbet	Tremelling	Milne	Stephenson	Bargh	Harper	Galloway	Fitton (1)		
Oct 21	Bradford City	Div 2	a	0-1	13113	Holdcroft	F.Gallimore	Lowe	Nisbet	Tremelling	Milne	Stephenson	Rowley	Harper	Galloway	Fitton		
Oct 28	Port Vale	Div 2	h	0-0	14160	Holdcroft	F.Gallimore	Lowe	Nisbet	Tremelling	Milne	Rawlings	Kelly	Brain	Stephenson	Fitton		
Nov 4	Notts County	Div 2	a	2-2	11445	Holdcroft	F.Gallimore	Lowe	Nisbet	Tremelling	Milne	Rawlings	Kelly (1)	Brain (1)	Stephenson	Fitton		
Nov 11	Swansea Town	Div 2	h	3-0	11837	Holdcroft	F.Gallimore	Lowe	Nisbet	Tremelling	Milne	Rawlings	Kelly	Brain (1)	Stephenson (2)	Fitton		
Nov 18	Millwall	Div 2	a	1-1	10801	Holdcroft	F.Gallimore	Lowe	Nisbet	Tremelling	Milne	Rawlings	Kelly (1)	Brain	Stephenson	Fitton		
Nov 25	Lincoln City	Div 2	h	2-1	10335	Holdcroft	Hough	Lowe	Nisbet	Tremelling	Milne	Rawlings	Kelly (1p)	Brain	Stephenson (1)	Torbet		
Dec 2	Bury	Div 2	a	1-2	9229	Holdcroft	Hough	Lowe	Nisbet	Tremelling	Milne	Rawlings	Kelly	Brain	Stephenson (1)	Fitton		
Dec 9	Hull City	Div 2	h	5-0	8869	Holdcroft	Hough	Lowe	Shankly	Tremelling	Milne	Rawlings	Kelly (1)	Stephenson (2)	Rowley (1)	Fitton (1)		
Dec 16	Fulham	Div 2	a	0-1	11467	Holdcroft	Hough	Lowe	Shankly	Tremelling	Milne	Rawlings	Kelly	Stephenson	Rowley	Fitton		
Dec 23	Southampton	Div 2	h	3-1	9280	Holdcroft	Hough	Lowe	Shankly	Tremelling	Milne	Rawlings	Kelly	Stephenson (3)	Rowley	Fitton		
Dec 25	Brentford	Div 2	a	2-3	20662	Holdcroft	Common	Lowe	Shankly	Tremelling	Milne	Bargh	Stephenson	Brain	Rowley (1)	Fitton (1)		
Dec 26	Brentford	Div 2	h	3-2	24451	Holdcroft	F.Gallimore	Lowe	Shankly	Tremelling	Milne	Rawlings	Kelly	Stephenson (2)	Bell (1)	Fitton		
Dec 30	Blackpool	Div 2	h	3-0	23361	Holdcroft	F.Gallimore	Lowe	Shankly	Tremelling	Milne	Rawlings	Kelly (2)	Stephenson	Bell	Fitton (1)		
Jan 6	Bradford P.A.	Div 2	a	1-2	10655	Holdcroft	F.Gallimore	Lowe	Shankly	Tremelling	Milne	Rawlings	Kelly	Stephenson	Bell	Fitton (1)		
Jan 13	Leeds Utd Rd 3	FAC	a	1-0	29158	Holdcroft	F.Gallimore	Lowe	Shankly	Tremelling	Milne	Rawlings	Kelly (1)	Rowley	Bell	Fitton		
Jan 20	Grimsby Town	Div 2	h	1-2	24312	Holdcroft	F.Gallimore	Lowe	Shankly	Tremelling	Milne	Bargh	Kelly	Stephenson	Rowley	Fitton (1)		
Jan 27	Workington Rd 4	FAC	h	2-1	15321	Holdcroft	F.Gallimore	Lowe	Shankly	Tremelling	Milne	Bargh	Kelly (1)	Stephenson	Rowley	Fitton (1)		
Feb 3	West Ham Utd	Div 2	a	3-1	14419	Holdcroft	F.Gallimore	Lowe	Shankly	Tremelling	Milne	Dougal	Kelly	Palethorpe (2)	Stephenson (1)	Fitton		
Feb 7	Nottm Forest	Div 2	a	3-2	5271	Holdcroft	F.Gallimore	Lowe	Shankly	Tremelling	Milne	Dougal (1)	Kelly	Palethorpe (2)	Stephenson	Fitton		
Feb 10	Plymouth Arg	Div 2	a	0-0	15429	Holdcroft	Hough	Lowe	Shankly	Tremelling	Milne	Dougal	Kelly	Palethorpe	Galloway	Fitton		
Feb 17	Northampton Rd 5	FAC	h	4-0	40177	Holdcroft	Hough	Lowe	Shankly	Tremelling	Milne	Dougal	Kelly	Palethorpe (3)	Stephenson	Fitton	1o.g.	(McGuire)
Feb 21	Manchester Utd	Div 2	h	3-2	9173	Holdcroft	Hough	Lowe	Shankly	Tremelling	Pritchard	Dougal (1)	Kelly (1)	Palethorpe (1)	Beresford	Fitton		
Feb 24	Bolton W.	Div 2	a	2-0	27435	Holdcroft	Hough	Lowe	Shankly	Tremelling	Milne	Dougal	Beresford	Palethorpe (1)	Bargh (1)	Fitton		
Mar 3	Leicester City Rd 6	FAC	h	0-1	38766	Holdcroft	Hough	Lowe	Shankly	Tremelling	Milne	Dougal	Kelly	Palethorpe	Stephenson	Fitton		
Mar 7	Bradford City	Div 2	h	0-1	7920	Holdcroft	Hough	Lowe	Shankly	L.Gallimore	Milne	Dougal	Beresford	Palethorpe	Bargh	Fitton		
Mar 10	Port Vale	Div 2	a	0-2	12972	Holdcroft	Owens	Lowe	Shankly	Tremelling	Milne	Kelly	Beresford	Palethorpe	Bell	Torbet		
Mar 17	Notts County	Div 2	h	2-0	10797	Holdcroft	Hough	Lowe	Shankly	Tremelling	Milne	Kelly	Beresford	Palethorpe (1)	Bell (1)	Pears		
Mar 24	Swansea Town	Div 2	a	2-1	5968	Holdcroft	Hough	Lowe	Shankly	Tremelling	Milne	Kelly	Beresford (1)	Palethorpe (1)	Bell	Pears (1)		
Mar 30	Oldham Ath	Div 2	a	1-3	17406	Holdcroft	Hough	Lowe	Shankly	Tremelling	L.Gallimore	Kelly	Beresford	Palethorpe (1)	Bell	Pears		
Mar 31	Millwall	Div 2	h	4-2	15577	Holdcroft	Hough	Lowe	Shankly	Tremelling	L.Gallimore	Kelly	Beresford	Palethorpe	Bargh (3)	Pears (1)		
Apr 2	Oldham Ath	Div 2	h	1-0	17864	Holdcroft	Hough	Lowe	Shankly	Tremelling	L.Gallimore	Bargh	Beresford	Palethorpe (1)	Bell (1)	Pears		
Apr 7	Lincoln City	Div 2	a	1-0	5185	Holdcroft	Hough	Lowe	Shankly	Tremelling	Milne	Kelly	Beresford	Palethorpe (1)	Bell	Pears		
Apr 14	Bury	Div 2	h	0-3	16105	Holdcroft	Hough	Lowe	Shankly	Tremelling	Milne	Dougal	Beresford	Palethorpe	Bell	Pears		
Apr 21	Hull City	Div 2	a	1-0	8218	Holdcroft	Hough	Lowe	Shankly	Tremelling	Milne	Dougal	Beresford	Palethorpe (1)	Bell	Fitton		
Apr 28	Fulham	Div 2	h	2-0	12499	Holdcroft	Hough	Lowe	Shankly	Tremelling	Milne	Dougal	Beresford (1)	Palethorpe	Bell	Fitton (1)		
May 5	Southampton	Div 2	a	1-0	8374	Holdcroft	Hough	Lowe	Shankly	Tremelling	Milne	Dougal	Beresford	Palethorpe (1)	Bargh	Fitton		

111

SEASON 1934–1935

Preston produced a satisfactory season of consolodation in their first campaign back in the top flight for ten years. A new centre-forward was brought in when James 'Bud' Maxwell was signed from Kilmarnock. He immediately began to score goals and North End got off to an excellent start, losing just one of their first eight games. The October though was a bad month and the fans had to wait until after Christmas to see the results begin to even out again. In fact, the Christmas games proved to be hugely exciting as Preston battled against the mighty Arsenal in front of nearly 80,000 people over the two matches. Preston actually did remarkably well to gain revenge on Boxing Day for their Christmas Day defeat at Highbury. The 2–1 win at Deepdale against the team who were destined for the Championship was the high point of the season. It was also the springboard for an excellent FA Cup run which took North End to the quarter-finals. Bill Shankly, Harry Lowe, Bill Tremelling and Harry Holdcroft all had super seasons as did the lively Maxwell. The average home gate, up by around 6,000, reflected, not only the more attractive opposition, but also the extra interest of the Preston public. Having said that the fans had to endure some bad defeats along the way, with the defence caving in on more than one occasion. The away record,

particularly, was a little disappointing. After Christmas though the defence tightened up which was reflected in the twelve clean sheets achieved from the January. Maxwell hit two splendid hat-tricks and without his goals Preston would have struggled. It was significant that only two sides, the relegated Leicester and Spurs, scored fewer than North End, whilst conversely only four clubs conceded less. The Sixth round FA Cup defeat at the Hawthorns was a bitter disappointment to all at the club especially as the game against West Bromwich Albion was the only one Preston were to lose in a 15 match league and cup unbeaten run. It was pretty obvious that the aim of the management was to re-establish the team into the First Division again and this they achieved with a creditable 11th position. Two other signings during the season were to also prove excellent deals. Bob Batey, a half-back from Carlisle and Andy Beattie, who made his debut on the left-wing in the last game of the season.

DEBUTANTS: (8) Bob Batey, Andy Beattie, Albert Butterworth, Ted Critchley, John Friar, Jack Hetherington, James (Bud) Maxwell, Les Vernon.

LAST GAMES: (9) Bargh, Bell, Beresford F., Critchley, Fitton, Kelly, Nisbet G., Palethorpe and Pears.

Trivia Fact:

Another 'legend' appeared at Deepdale when one of England's greatest entertainers, Gracie Fields, kicked off at a charity pre-season friendly. The Lancashire lass from Rochdale was warmly greeted.

Left to right: *Back row*; Shankly, Gallimore, Hough, W. Pilkington (LEP), Holdcroft, Lowe, T. Higginson (*Daily Telegraph*), Milne.
Front row: Critchley, Beresford, Maxwell, Kelly, Pears, Tremelling.

STAT FACTS:

Best home run without defeat: 10 games
Best away run without defeat: 3 games
Longest run unbeaten: 9 games
Longest run without a win: 7 games
Best home attendance: 39,411 vs. Arsenal 26.12.34
Worst home attendance: 10,160 vs. Portsmouth 6.3.35
Best away attendance: 56,227 vs. WBA FAC 2.3.35
Worst away attendance: 6,572 vs. Middlesbrough 3.11.34
Aggregate and average home attendance: 440,910 – 20,996
Aggregate and average away attendance: 424,757 – 20,226

Match Report: Heroics from Holdcroft in Tense Thriller – 19 Jan 1935
Huddersfield Town 3 Preston 4

Inconsistent Huddersfield had lost their last three home games but made a tremendous start in this Roses battle with Preston. The Yorkshire side took the lead well within the first minute before most of the North Enders had even touched the ball. Harry Holdcroft had to be both active and daring in denying the Terriers further goals, foiling Luke on a couple of occasions. North End slowly settled down, eventually clawing their way back into the game in style. With 14 minutes played Batey ventured forward to distribute a good ball into the penalty area. Maxwell reacted the sharpest and duly beat Hesford with a snapshot from close range. This success spurred the Lancastrians into playing with great self-belief, and within minutes of their equaliser they then took the lead. Friar tricked Campbell with some clever footwork before slipping a nice pass to Bell who had run into space. Taking aim Bell hit the ball first time to score with a superb left-foot shot. Having taken an early lead and now finding themselves behind, Huddersfield then fought back and could have equalised but for Holdcroft saving spectacularly from Lythgoe. As the Town pressed forward the North End defence, as a unit, broke up some lively attacking moves. It had a demoralising effect on the home team and fans alike. Preston, when in possession, played neat football, moving the ball about freely, so much so that they forged further ahead on 28 minutes. Maxwell was the scorer again as he slammed the ball well out of Hesford's reach. The two goal margin was not held for long though as Lythgoe keenly anticipated a poorly directed backpass meant for Holdcroft and scored at will. The game continued to be closely contested, both sides of the interval, and Lythgoe proved to be the thorn in Preston's side as he brought the best out of Holdcroft on more than one occasion. In a frantic finish Bell hit a post before Maxwell bagged his third goal of the afternoon to make it 4–2. The final goal fell to the dangerous Lythgoe who hit a glorious shot past Holdcroft as the game entered its tense stirring finale.

League appearances (42 games)

Bargh G. W. 23, Batey N. R. 22, Beattie A. 1, Bell J. G. 7, Beresford F. E. 22, Butterworth A. 2, Critchley E. 11, Dougal J. 21, Fitton G. A. 19, Friar J. 23, Gallimore F. 21, Hetherington J. A. 9, Holdcroft G.H. 42, Hough W. 21, Kelly R. 11, Lowe H. 42, Maxwell J. M. 41, Milne J. L. 24, Nisbet G. 2, Palethorpe J. T. 6, Pears J. 11, Shankly W. 42, Tremelling W. 36, Vernon J. L. 3.

FA Cup appearances (6 games)

Holdcroft 6, Gallimore 6, Lowe 6, Shankly 6, Tremelling 6, Batey 6, Friar 6, Dougal 5, Kelly 1, Maxwell 5, Vernon 1, Bell 6, Fitton 3, Hetherington 3.

Goalscorers: 62 League–8 Cup–(Total 70)

Maxwell 23–3 (26), Friar 8–1 (9), Bargh 6–0 (6), Fitton 5–1 (6), Palethorpe 4–0 (4), Dougal 3–1 (4), Beresford 2–0 (2), Tremelling 2–0 (2), Pears 2–0 (2), Hetherington 1–1 (2), Critchley 1–0 (1), Kelly 1–0 (1), Bell 1–0 (1), Own Goals 3–1 (4)

Future Players born between August 1934 and July 1935: Eddie Lewis, Derek Mayers, Ray Charnley and Les Campbell
Ever presents: (3) Harry Holdcroft, Harry Lowe and Bill Shankly
FA Cup: Sixth Round
Hat-tricks: (2) Both by Bud Maxwell
Chairman: Sir Meyrick Hollins
Manager: A Committee
Leading scorer: 26 goals – Bud Maxwell (23 League 3 Cup)
Players used: 24
AUTHORS' UNOFFICIAL PLAYER OF THE SEASON: Bill Shankly

Left to right:
Back row: Shankly, F. Gallimore, Holdcroft, Lowe, Tremelling, Batey, Hetherington.
Front row: Friar, Kelly, Dougal, Maxwell, Bell, Beresford, Fitton.

League position in Division One: 11th – P42 W15 D12 L15 F62 A67 Pts 42
Home: W11 D5 L5 F33 A22   Away: W4 D7 L10 F29 A45

Date 1934-5	Opponents	Comp	h or a	Score	Att.	1	2	3	4	5	6	7	8	9	10	11		
Aug 25	Grimsby Town	Div 1	h	1-0	26805	Holdcroft	Hough	Lowe	Shankly	Tremelling	Milne	Critchley	Beresford	Maxwell	Bargh (1)	Pears		
Aug 27	Tottenham H	Div 1	a	2-1	24961	Holdcroft	Hough	Lowe	Shankly	Tremelling	Milne	Critchley	Beresford	Maxwell	Bargh (1)	Pears (1)		
Sep 1	Everton	Div 1	a	1-4	37792	Holdcroft	Hough	Lowe	Shankly	Tremelling	Milne	Critchley	Beresford	Maxwell (1)	Bargh	Pears		
Sep 3	Tottenham H	Div 1	h	1-0	25936	Holdcroft	Hough	Lowe	Shankly	Tremelling	Milne	Critchley	Beresford	Maxwell (1)	Bargh	Pears		
Sep 8	Huddersfield	Div 1	h	2-0	27727	Holdcroft	Hough	Lowe	Shankly	Tremelling	Milne	Critchley (1)	Beresford	Maxwell	Kelly	Pears (1)		
Sep 15	Wolverhampton W	Div 1	a	2-2	26523	Holdcroft	Hough	Lowe	Shankly	Tremelling	Milne	Critchley	Beresford	Maxwell (1)	Kelly (1)	Pears		
Sep 22	Chelsea	Div 1	h	2-0	18332	Holdcroft	Hough	Lowe	Shankly	Tremelling	Milne	Critchley	Beresford	Maxwell (1)	Kelly	Pears	1o.g.	(McAuley)
Sep 29	Aston Villa	Div 1	a	2-4	23781	Holdcroft	Hough	Lowe	Shankly	Tremelling	Milne	Critchley	Beresford (1)	Maxwell (1)	Kelly	Pears		
Oct 6	Derby County	Div 1	h	0-1	24037	Holdcroft	Hough	Lowe	Shankly	Tremelling	Milne	Critchley	Beresford	Maxwell	Kelly	Pears		
Oct 13	Leicester City	Div 1	a	0-0	19652	Holdcroft	Hough	Lowe	Shankly	Tremelling	Milne	Critchley	Beresford	Maxwell	Kelly	Pears		
Oct 20	Portsmouth	Div 1	a	0-4	15110	Holdcroft	Hough	Lowe	Shankly	Tremelling	Milne	Critchley	Beresford	Maxwell	Kelly	Pears		
Oct 27	Liverpool	Div 1	h	2-2	18573	Holdcroft	Hough	Lowe	Shankly	Tremelling	Milne	Bargh (1)	Beresford	Maxwell (1)	Bell	Fitton		
Nov 3	Middlesbrough	Div 1	a	3-3	6572	Holdcroft	Hough	Lowe	Shankly	Tremelling	Milne	Bargh (2)	Beresford	Palethorpe (1)	Bell	Maxwell		
Nov 10	Blackburn Rovers	Div 1	h	3-1	32306	Holdcroft	Hough	Lowe	Shankly	Tremelling	Milne	Bargh	Butterworth	Palethorpe (1)	Beresford	Maxwell (2)		
Nov 17	Sheffield Wed.	Div 1	a	1-2	14648	Holdcroft	Hough	Lowe	Shankly	Batey	Milne	Bargh	Vernon	Palethorpe	Beresford (1)	Maxwell		
Nov 24	Birmingham	Div 1	h	0-1	17655	Holdcroft	Hough	Lowe	Shankly	Batey	Milne	Bargh	Vernon	Palethorpe	Beresford	Maxwell		
Dec 1	Stoke City	Div 1	a	1-3	21452	Holdcroft	Hough	Lowe	Shankly	Batey	Milne	Bargh	Beresford	Palethorpe (1)	Dougal	Maxwell		
Dec 8	Manchester City	Div 1	h	2-4	22683	Holdcroft	Hough	Lowe	Shankly	Batey	Milne	Bargh	Beresford	Palethorpe (1)	Dougal	Maxwell (1)		
Dec 15	Leeds Utd	Div 1	a	3-3	13342	Holdcroft	Hough	Lowe	Shankly	Batey	Milne	Friar (1)	Beresford	Maxwell (1)	Dougal	Fitton (1)		
Dec 22	WBA	Div 1	h	1-2	16764	Holdcroft	Hough	Lowe	Shankly	Batey	Milne	Friar	Beresford	Maxwell	Dougal	Fitton (1)		
Dec 25	Arsenal	Div 1	a	3-5	40201	Holdcroft	Hough	Lowe	Shankly	Tremelling	Milne	Friar (1)	Kelly	Maxwell (2)	Bargh	Fitton		
Dec 26	Arsenal	Div 1	h	2-1	39411	Holdcroft	Gallimore	Lowe	Shankly	Tremelling	Milne	Friar	Kelly	Maxwell (1)	Bargh	Fitton (1)		
Dec 29	Grimsby Town	Div 1	a	1-3	10007	Holdcroft	Gallimore	Lowe	Shankly	Tremelling	Nisbet	Friar (1)	Kelly	Maxwell	Bargh	Fitton		
Jan 5	Everton	Div 1	h	2-2	22675	Holdcroft	Gallimore	Lowe	Shankly	Tremelling	Nisbet	Friar (2)	Kelly	Maxwell	Bargh	Fitton		
Jan 12	Barnsley Rd 3	FAC	h	0-0	21170	Holdcroft	Gallimore	Lowe	Shankly	Tremelling	Batey	Friar	Dougal	Maxwell	Bell	Fitton		
Jan 16	Barnsley Replay	FAC	a	1-0	22089	Holdcroft	Gallimore	Lowe	Shankly	Tremelling	Batey	Friar	Kelly	Maxwell (1)	Bell	Fitton		
Jan 19	Huddersfield	Div 1	a	4-3	10986	Holdcroft	Gallimore	Lowe	Shankly	Tremelling	Batey	Friar	Dougal	Maxwell (3)	Bell (1)	Hetherington		
Jan 26	Swindon Town Rd 4	FAC	a	2-0	24480	Holdcroft	Gallimore	Lowe	Shankly	Tremelling	Batey	Friar (1)	Dougal	Maxwell	Bell	Hetherington (1)		
Jan 28	Wolverhampton W	Div 1	h	2-1	10277	Holdcroft	Gallimore	Lowe	Shankly	Tremelling	Milne	Friar	Dougal	Maxwell (1)	Hetherington	Fitton	1o.g.	(Smalley)
Feb 2	Chelsea	Div 1	a	0-0	31994	Holdcroft	Gallimore	Lowe	Shankly	Tremelling	Batey	Friar	Dougal	Maxwell	Hetherington	Fitton		
Feb 9	Aston Villa	Div 1	h	0-0	22536	Holdcroft	Gallimore	Lowe	Shankly	Tremelling	Batey	Friar	Dougal	Maxwell	Bell	Hetherington		
Feb 16	Bristol City Rd 5	FAC	a	0-0	43335	Holdcroft	Gallimore	Lowe	Shankly	Tremelling	Batey	Friar	Dougal	Maxwell	Bell	Hetnerington		
Feb 23	Leicester City	Div 1	h	2-0	18276	Holdcroft	Gallimore	Lowe	Shankly	Tremelling	Batey	Friar (1)	Dougal	Maxwell (1)	Bell	Hetherington		
Feb 25	Bristol City Replay	FAC	h	5-0	19589	Holdcroft	Gallimore	Lowe	Shankly	Tremelling	Batey	Friar	Dougal (1)	Maxwell (2)	Bell	Fitton (1)	1o.g.	(Hughes)
Mar 2	WBA Rd 6	FAC	a	0-1	56227	Holdcroft	Gallimore	Lowe	Shankly	Tremelling	Batey	Friar	Dougal	Vernon	Bell	Hetherington		
Mar 6	Portsmouth	Div 1	h	1-1	10160	Holdcroft	Gallimore	Lowe	Shankly	Tremelling (1)	Batey	Friar	Dougal	Maxwell	Bell	Hetherington		
Mar 9	Liverpool	Div 1	a	0-0	23063	Holdcroft	Gallimore	Lowe	Shankly	Tremelling	Batey	Friar	Beresford	Vernon	Hetherington	Fitton		
Mar 16	Middlesbrough	Div 1	h	2-0	15555	Holdcroft	Gallimore	Lowe	Shankly	Tremelling	Batey	Friar	Dougal	Maxwell	Hetherington (1)	Fitton (1)		
Mar 23	Blackburn Rovers	Div 1	a	0-1	14661	Holdcroft	Gallimore	Lowe	Shankly	Tremelling	Batey	Friar	Dougal	Maxwell	Hetherington	Fitton		
Mar 30	Sheffield Wed.	Div 1	h	2-1	17656	Holdcroft	Gallimore	Lowe	Shankly	Tremelling	Batey	Friar	Dougal (1)	Maxwell (1)	Bargh	Fitton		
Apr 6	Birmingham	Div 1	a	0-3	15773	Holdcroft	Gallimore	Lowe	Shankly	Tremelling	Batey	Friar	Beresford	Maxwell	Bargh	Dougal		
Apr 10	Derby County	Div 1	a	3-0	8394	Holdcroft	Gallimore	Lowe	Shankly	Tremelling	Batey	Friar (1)	Dougal (1)	Maxwell	Bargh	Fitton	1o.g.	(Collin)
Apr 13	Stoke City	Div 1	h	5-2	15625	Holdcroft	Gallimore	Lowe	Shankly	Tremelling (1)	Batey	Friar (1)	Dougal	Maxwell (3)	Bargh	Fitton		
Apr 19	Sunderland	Div 1	a	1-3	32170	Holdcroft	Gallimore	Lowe	Shankly	Tremelling	Batey	Friar	Dougal	Maxwell	Bargh	Fitton (1)		
Apr 20	Manchester City	Div 1	a	2-1	23255	Holdcroft	Gallimore	Lowe	Shankly	Tremelling	Batey	Friar	Dougal (1)	Maxwell (1)	Bargh	Fitton		
Apr 22	Sunderland	Div 1	h	1-1	26163	Holdcroft	Gallimore	Lowe	Shankly	Tremelling	Batey	Friar	Dougal	Maxwell	Bargh (1)	Fitton		
Apr 27	Leeds Utd.	Div 1	h	0-2	11758	Holdcroft	Gallimore	Lowe	Shankly	Tremelling	Batey	Friar	Dougal	Maxwell	Bargh	Fitton		
May 4	WBA	Div 1	a	0-0	10420	Holdcroft	Gallimore	Lowe	Shankly	Tremelling	Milne	Butterworth	Dougal	Maxwell	Bell	Beattie		

Gracie Fields with North End's captain Bill Tremelling. Pre-season charity match.
She was performing at Blackpool for the season.

Season 1934–35: First Division

	P	W	D	L	F	A	Pts
1 Arsenal	42	23	12	7	115	46	58
2 Sunderland	42	19	16	7	90	51	54
3 Sheffield Wednesday	42	18	13	11	70	64	49
4 Man City	42	20	8	14	82	67	48
5 Grimsby	42	17	11	14	78	60	45
6 Derby	42	18	9	15	81	66	45
7 Liverpool	42	19	7	16	85	88	45
8 Everton	42	16	12	14	89	88	44
9 WBA	42	17	10	15	83	83	44
10 Stoke	42	18	6	18	71	70	42
11 PRESTON	42	15	12	15	62	67	42
12 Chelsea	42	16	9	17	73	82	41
13 Aston Villa	42	14	13	15	74	88	41
14 Portsmouth	42	15	10	17	71	72	40
15 Blackburn	42	14	11	17	66	78	39
16 Huddersfield	42	14	10	18	76	71	38
17 Wolves	42	15	8	19	88	94	38
18 Leeds	42	13	12	17	75	92	38
19 Birmingham	42	13	10	19	63	81	36
20 Middlesbrough	42	10	14	18	70	91	34
21 Leicester	42	12	9	21	61	86	33
22 Tottenham	42	10	10	22	54	93	30

SEASON 1935–1936

had made two super signings when the O'Donnell brothers, Hugh and Frank joined the club. The two Scots had both signed from Glasgow Celtic, both were forwards and both were quickly into their stride, scoring regularly. Actually the team was very much settled, selection wise, especially in defence where only two changes were made all year. This was reflected in the 12 clean sheets that North End kept at Deepdale. It also made it even more puzzling as to why the team had such wretched away results. Up front, meanwhile, after the initial trial and error, that too remained pretty settled. But the stars were in defence where Harry Holdcroft had a great season in goal. Frank Gallimore and Harry Lowe at full-back also showed outstanding form and Bill Tremelling was a rock at the

First eleven and reserve eleven photographed before a pre-season practice match in aid of Hospital Charities in 1935. Bill Shankly is on the front row in the centre.

F. O'DONNELL

Oh, what might have been! If Preston North End had managed even an average away record during the 1935–6 season then the club could so easily have been amongst the honours. Unbelievably, they lost eight of their first nine away games although luckily, for their home fans, the form at Deepdale was better and the club managed six home wins during the same period. It left the fans with mixed feelings as they were reasonably happy with what was on offer but they knew that there was little chance of winning the Championship with such an awful sequence of away results. The best time of the season came during the February and March when only one game was lost and it was then that the fans began to suspect the chance of a title challenge, albeit slight. Unfortunately though there was far too much ground to make up and in the end a comfortable seventh spot in the league was their only reward. Earlier, in the summer of 1935, Preston

heart of the side. In the April the latter received a well earned Benefit match and nearly 6,000 saw Blackpool thrashed 5–1 in Tremelling's honour. Another excellent signing was Frank Beresford who made a big impact at inside-forward. In the FA Cup a terrific win at Everton was followed in round four by a home draw against Second Division side Sheffield United. This disappointingly ended in a goalless draw and in the replay North End's misery was completed by a 2–0 defeat. The only consolation for the Preston fans at the end of the season came when they saw Blackburn relegated!

DEBUTANTS: (4) Thomas Crawley, Frank O'Donnell, Hugh O'Donnell and Joseph Beresford.

LAST GAMES: (4) Butterworth, Crawley, Friar and Hetherington.

League appearances (42 games)

Batey N. R. 4, Beresford J. 36, Butterworth A. 12, Crawley T. 2, Dougal J. 32, Friar J. 3, Gallimore F. 42, Hetherington J. A. 6, Holdcroft G. H. 42, Lowe H. 42, Maxwell J. M. 37, Milne J. L. 39, O'Donnell F. 39, O'Donnell H. 39, Shankly W. 41, Tremelling W. 42, Vernon J. L. 4.

FA Cup appearances (3 games)

Holdcroft 3, Gallimore 3, Lowe 3, Shankly 3, Tremelling 3, Milne 3, Dougal 3, Beresford 3, Maxwell 3, O'Donnell F. 3, O'Donnell H. 3.

Goalscorers: 67 League–3 Cup–(Total 70)

Maxwell 17–2 (19), O'Donnell H. 15 (1pen)–0 (15), O'Donnell F. 13–1 (14), Dougal 9–0 (9), Beresford 4–0 (4), Butterworth 4–0 (4), Hetherington 2–0 (2), Shankly 1–0 (1), Milne 1–0 (1), Vernon 1–0 (1)

League position in Division One: 7th – P42 W18 D8 L16 F67 A64 Pts 44
Home: W15 D3 L3 F44 A18   Away: W3 D5 L13 F23 A46

Match Report: League Leaders Lose at Deepdale – 29 Feb 1936 Preston 3 Sunderland 2

Sunderland, the league leaders, arrived in town the night before the game and stayed at the Park Hotel. Both sides were more than capable of putting the ball about on their day so the heavy pitch did not really suit either team. Although North End gave their visitors due respect for their top of the table spot, they were by no means overawed and in fact the free-scoring Sunderland forwards were given little chance by a competant North End defence. Bill Shankly's power was felt by his colleague Beresford as the latter was knocked out cold for a few moments after Shankly's clearance struck him. He felt the full force of the heavy leather ball. North End actually put the visitors under considerable pressure and were unlucky to see a Maxwell goal disallowed owing to an earlier infringement by Frank O'Donnell. Jimmy Dougal, too, was proving to be a thorn in Sunderland's side, although his finishing was haphazard after creating good openings. The visitors were struggling to subdue the North End spearhead and Middleton, in goal, was kept busy as the game progressed. Holdcroft, meanwhile, was rarely in the action. Although having most of the possession Preston could not turn their supremacy into goals and, as is often the case, it was Sunderland who stunned the crowd with a breakaway goal. On 35 minutes Gallacher played a one-two with Connor before eluding Gallimore and shooting wide of Holdcroft. They held the lead for just ten minutes as Dougal atoned for earlier misdemeanours by latching onto a Beresford pass to equalise. Sunderland's half-time pep talk did them a power of good as they reappeared more aggressive after the break. They hit the woodwork twice but Preston were also fighting hard and it was ebb and flow, cut and thrust, a good energetic start to the second half. With 63 minutes played Maxwell won an aerial challenge against Morrison, followed up, and beat Middleton with one of the linesmen waving his flag. After a brief consultation between the officials the referee signalled a goal. Preston's joy was shortlived however as Gurney equalised within a minute, snapping up a ricochet off Holdcroft's body. Preston almost regained the lead but Milne's shot unluckily hit the post, whilst Frank O'Donnell hit the crossbar. Perseverance did pay off in the end though as with just four minutes to go North End collected their due rewards when Maxwell finished with great aplomb, a move started by Shankly and Beresford. It had been a good game with Preston's win well merited.

"Bud" Maxwell leading goalscorer.

Trivia Facts:

Tommy Muirhead, the former Scottish international who was appointed manager in April 1936, had almost signed for PNE as a player in 1925.

Preston were drawn away to Accrington Stanley in the Lancashire Cup in the 1935–36 competition but their opponents asked for the game to be played at Deepdale. North End won 4–1 but then went out in the next round against Rossendale United in a match played at Rawtensall.

On 24 August 1935, at a pre-season practice match involving first team and reserve players, Preston officially opened their new Pavilion stand. It incorporated new dressing rooms, a Board room and the club's offices.

The match with Bolton on 13 April 1936 at Deepdale brought up the 1,600th league game for North End. Meanwhile, the fourth goal in the 4–0 home win over Huddersfield on 28 December 1935 was the 2,500th league goal scored by North End.

Frank and Hugh, the O'Donnell brothers. They scored twenty-eight goals between them in their first season in England.

Future Players born between August 1935 and July 1936: John O'Neill, Ken Heyes, Alfie Biggs, Alec Farrall, Tony Singleton, Dave Sneddon and **Alan Kelly Senior**
Ever presents: (4) Gallimore, Holdcroft, Lowe and Tremelling.
FA Cup: Fourth Round Replay
Hat-tricks: None
Chairman: Sir Meyrick Hollins
Manager: The Committee until April 21 1936 when Tommy Muirhead was appointed to the post of Secretary/Manager.
Leading scorer: 19 goals – Bud Maxwell (17 League 2 Cup)
Players used: 17
AUTHORS' UNOFFICIAL PLAYER OF THE SEASON: Frank Gallimore

STAT FACTS:
Best home run without defeat: 8 games
Best away run without defeat: 6 games
Longest run unbeaten: 12 games
Longest run without a win: 4 games
Best home attendance: 35,368 *vs.* Sheff. Utd FAC 25.2.36
Worst home attendance: 9,910 *vs.* Stoke 19.2.36
Best away attendance: 42,126 *vs.* Arsenal 26.10.35
Worst away attendance: 9,172 *vs.* Grimsby 7.3.36
Aggregate and average home attendance: 409,737 – 19,511
Aggregate and average away attendance: 482,188 – 22,961

Season 1935–36: First Division

	P	W	D	L	F	A	Pts
1 Sunderland	42	25	6	11	109	74	56
2 Derby	42	18	12	12	61	52	48
3 Huddersfield	42	18	12	12	59	56	48
4 Stoke	42	20	7	15	57	57	47
5 Brentford	42	17	12	13	81	60	46
6 Arsenal	42	15	15	12	78	48	45
7 PRESTON	42	18	8	16	67	64	44
8 Chelsea	42	15	13	14	65	72	43
9 Man City	42	17	8	17	68	60	42
10 Portsmouth	42	17	8	17	54	67	42
11 Leeds	42	15	11	16	66	64	41
12 Birmingham	42	15	11	16	61	63	41
13 Bolton	42	14	13	15	67	76	41
14 Middlesbrough	42	15	10	17	84	70	40
15 Wolves	42	15	10	17	77	76	40
16 Everton	42	13	13	16	89	89	39
17 Grimsby	42	17	5	20	65	73	39
18 WBA	42	16	6	20	89	88	38
19 Liverpool	42	13	12	17	60	64	38
20 Sheffield Wednesday	42	13	12	17	63	77	38
21 Aston Villa	42	13	9	20	81	110	35
22 Blackburn	42	12	9	21	55	96	33

Date 1935-6	Opponents		Comp	h or a	Score	Att.	1	2	3	4	5	6	7	8	9	10	11
Aug 31	Huddersfield		Div 1	a	0-1	17974	Holdcroft	Gallimore	Lowe	Shankly	Tremelling	Batey	Friar	Vemon	Maxwell	F.O'Donnell	H.O'Donnell
Sep 2	Derby County		Div 1	h	1-0	28362	Holdcroft	Gallimore	Lowe	Shankly	Tremelling	Batey	Friar	Hetherington (1)	Maxwell	F.O'Donnell	H.O'Donnell
Sep 7	Middlesbrough		Div 1	h	0-5	22196	Holdcroft	Gallimore	Lowe	Shankly	Tremelling	Batey	Friar	Dougal	Maxwell	F.O'Donnell	H.O'Donnell
Sep 11	Derby County		Div 1	a	0-2	21299	Holdcroft	Gallimore	Lowe	Shankly	Tremelling	Milne	Butterworth	Dougal	F.O'Donnell	Hetherington	H.O'Donnell
Sep 14	Aston Villa		Div 1	a	1-5	31501	Holdcroft	Gallimore	Lowe	Shankly	Tremelling	Milne	Dougal	Butterworth (1)	F.O'Donnell	Hetherington	H.O'Donnell
Sep 18	Everton		Div 1	h	2-2	18805	Holdcroft	Gallimore	Lowe	Shankly	Tremelling	Milne	Dougal (1)	Butterworth	Crawley	F.O'Donnell	Hetherington (1)
Sep 21	Wolverhampton W		Div 1	h	2-0	17022	Holdcroft	Gallimore	Lowe	Shankly	Tremelling	Milne	Dougal	Butterworth (1)	Crawley	F.O'Donnell (1)	Hetherington
Sep 28	Sheffield Wed.		Div 1	a	0-1	16546	Holdcroft	Gallimore	Lowe	Shankly	Tremelling	Milne	Dougal	Beresford	Maxwell	F.O'Donnell	Hetherington
Oct 5	Portsmouth		Div 1	h	1-1	15855	Holdcroft	Gallimore	Lowe	Batey	Tremelling	Milne	Butterworth	Beresford	Maxwell	F.O'Donnell (1)	Hetherington
Oct 12	Stoke City		Div 1	a	1-2	21980	Holdcroft	Gallimore	Lowe	Shankly	Tremelling	Milne	Butterworth	Beresford	Dougal (1)	F.O'Donnell	H.O'Donnell
Oct 19	Manchester City		Div 1	h	4-0	14946	Holdcroft	Gallimore	Lowe	Shankly	Tremelling	Milne	Butterworth	Beresford	Maxwell	F.O'Donnell (2)	H.O'Donnell (2)
Oct 26	Arsenal		Div 1	a	1-2	42126	Holdcroft	Gallimore	Lowe	Shankly	Tremelling	Milne	Butterworth	Beresford	Maxwell (1)	F.O'Donnell	H.O'Donnell
Nov 2	Birmingham		Div 1	a	3-1	16232	Holdcroft	Gallimore	Lowe	Shankly	Tremelling	Milne	Butterworth	Beresford (1)	Maxwell	F.O'Donnell (1)	H.O'Donnell (1)
Nov 9	Sunderland		Div 1	a	2-4	16739	Holdcroft	Gallimore	Lowe	Shankly	Tremelling	Milne	Butterworth	Beresford (1)	Maxwell	F.O'Donnell (1)	H.O'Donnell
Nov 16	WBA		Div 1	h	3-0	19070	Holdcroft	Gallimore	Lowe	Shankly	Tremelling	Milne	Butterworth	Beresford	Maxwell (1)	F.O'Donnell (2)	H.O'Donnell
Nov 23	Blackburn Rovers		Div 1	a	1-1	33016	Holdcroft	Gallimore	Lowe	Shankly	Tremelling	Milne	Butterworth	Beresford	Maxwell	F.O'Donnell (1)	H.O'Donnell
Nov 30	Grimsby Town		Div 1	h	1-0	17103	Holdcroft	Gallimore	Lowe	Shankly	Tremelling	Milne	Dougal	Beresford	Maxwell (1)	F.O'Donnell	H.O'Donnell
Dec 7	Liverpool		Div 1	a	1-2	24415	Holdcroft	Gallimore	Lowe	Shankly	Tremelling	Milne	Dougal	Beresford	Maxwell (1)	F.O'Donnell	H.O'Donnell
Dec 14	Chelsea		Div 1	h	2-0	16178	Holdcroft	Gallimore	Lowe	Shankly	Tremelling	Milne	Dougal (1)	Beresford	Maxwell	F.O'Donnell	H.O'Donnell (1)
Dec 21	Leeds Utd		Div 1	a	1-0	17749	Holdcroft	Gallimore	Lowe	Shankly	Tremelling	Milne	Dougal	Beresford	Maxwell (1)	F.O'Donnell	H.O'Donnell
Dec 25	Brentford		Div 1	a	2-5	21474	Holdcroft	Gallimore	Lowe	Shankly (1)	Tremelling	Milne	Dougal	Beresford	Maxwell (1)	F.O'Donnell	H.O'Donnell
Dec 26	Brentford		Div 1	h	2-4	22937	Holdcroft	Gallimore	Lowe	Shankly	Tremelling	Milne	Butterworth (1)	Beresford	Maxwell (1)	F.O'Donnell	H.O'Donnell
Dec 28	Huddersfield		Div 1	h	4-0	21487	Holdcroft	Gallimore	Lowe	Shankly	Tremelling	Milne (1)	Dougal	Beresford	Maxwell (2)	F.O'Donnell (1)	H.O'Donnell
Jan 4	Middlesbrough		Div 1	a	0-2	17245	Holdcroft	Gallimore	Lowe	Shankly	Tremelling	Milne	Dougal	Beresford	Maxwell	F.O'Donnell	H.O'Donnell
Jan 11	Everton	Rd 3	FAC	a	3-1	41642	Holdcroft	Gallimore	Lowe	Shankly	Tremelling	Milne	Dougal	Beresford	Maxwell (2)	F.O'Donnell (1)	H.O'Donnell
Jan 18	Aston Villa		Div 1	h	3-0	23178	Holdcroft	Gallimore	Lowe	Shankly	Tremelling	Milne	Dougal (1)	Beresford	Maxwell (1)	F.O'Donnell	H.O'Donnell (1)
Jan 25	Sheffield Utd	Rd 4	FAC	h	0-0	35368	Holdcroft	Gallimore	Lowe	Shankly	Tremelling	Milne	Dougal	Beresford	Maxwell	F.O'Donnell	H.O'Donnell
Jan 30	Sheffield Utd	Replay	FAC	a	0-2	34529	Holdcroft	Gallimore	Lowe	Shankly	Tremelling	Milne	Dougal	Beresford	Maxwell	F.O'Donnell	H.O'Donnell
Feb 1	Sheffield Wed.		Div 1	h	0-1	15828	Holdcroft	Gallimore	Lowe	Shankly	Tremelling	Milne	Dougal	Beresford	Maxwell	F.O'Donnell	H.O'Donnell
Feb 8	Portsmouth		Div 1	a	1-1	15116	Holdcroft	Gallimore	Lowe	Shankly	Tremelling	Milne	Dougal	Beresford	Maxwell	F.O'Donnell	H.O'Donnell (1)
Feb 19	Stoke City		Div 1	h	1-1	9910	Holdcroft	Gallimore	Lowe	Shankly	Tremelling	Milne	Dougal	Beresford	Maxwell	F.O'Donnell	H.O'Donnell (1)
Feb 22	Manchester City		Div 1	a	3-1	41415	Holdcroft	Gallimore	Lowe	Shankly	Tremelling	Milne	Dougal	Beresford	Maxwell (1)	F.O'Donnell (1)	H.O'Donnell (1)
Feb 29	Sunderland		Div 1	h	3-2	18718	Holdcroft	Gallimore	Lowe	Shankly	Tremelling	Milne	Dougal (1)	Beresford	Maxwell (2)	F.O'Donnell	H.O'Donnell
Mar 7	Grimsby Town		Div 1	a	0-0	9172	Holdcroft	Gallimore	Lowe	Shankly	Tremelling	Milne	Dougal	Beresford	Maxwell	F.O'Donnell	H.O'Donnell
Mar 14	Arsenal		Div 1	h	1-0	30039	Holdcroft	Gallimore	Lowe	Shankly	Tremelling	Milne	Dougal	Beresford	Maxwell	F.O'Donnell	H.O'Donnell (1)
Mar 21	WBA		Div 1	a	4-2	19665	Holdcroft	Gallimore	Lowe	Shankly	Tremelling	Milne	Dougal (1)	Beresford (1)	Maxwell (1)	F.O'Donnell	H.O'Donnell (1)
Mar 28	Blackburn Rovers		Div 1	h	2-0	24921	Holdcroft	Gallimore	Lowe	Shankly	Tremelling	Milne	Dougal	Beresford	Maxwell	F.O'Donnell (1)	H.O'Donnell
Apr 4	Birmingham		Div 1	h	0-0	15811	Holdcroft	Gallimore	Lowe	Shankly	Tremelling	Milne	Dougal	Beresford	Maxwell	F.O'Donnell	H.O'Donnell
Apr 10	Bolton W.		Div 1	a	1-1	35992	Holdcroft	Gallimore	Lowe	Shankly	Tremelling	Milne	Dougal	Beresford	Maxwell	Vemon	H.O'Donnell (1)
Apr 11	Liverpool		Div 1	h	3-1	20027	Holdcroft	Gallimore	Lowe	Shankly	Tremelling	Milne	Dougal (1)	Beresford	Maxwell (1)	Vemon (1)	H.O'Donnell
Apr 13	Bolton W.		Div 1	h	1-0	25996	Holdcroft	Gallimore	Lowe	Shankly	Tremelling	Milne	Dougal	Beresford	Maxwell (1)	Vemon	H.O'Donnell
Apr 18	Chelsea		Div 1	a	2-5	26274	Holdcroft	Gallimore	Lowe	Shankly	Tremelling	Milne	Dougal	Beresford	Maxwell (1)	F.O'Donnell	H.O'Donnell (1)
Apr 20	Wolverhampton W		Div 1	a	2-4	15544	Holdcroft	Gallimore	Lowe	Shankly	Tremelling	Milne	Dougal	Beresford	Maxwell	F.O'Donnell	H.O'Donnell (2)
Apr 25	Leeds Utd		Div 1	h	5-0	10927	Holdcroft	Gallimore	Lowe	Shankly	Tremelling	Milne	Dougal (1)	Beresford (1)	Maxwell	F.O'Donnell (2)	H.O'Donnell (1p)
May 2	Everton		Div 1	a	0-5	21135	Holdcroft	Gallimore	Lowe	Shankly	Tremelling	Milne	Dougal	Beresford	Maxwell	F.O'Donnell	H.O'Donnell

Plenty of gripping action and a first appearance at Wembley Stadium for the FA Cup final captivated the Preston North End fans in this, the club's 45th league campaign. The new Manager, Tommy Muirhead, had a funny start to his time in charge. Without a win in the first five games, Preston then recorded five on the trot! The inconsistency of the previous year was again in evidence and it was to continue throughout most of this year too and squashed any thoughts that the club had for making a challenge on the league title. One big problem came in the regular defensive lapses which resulted in some heavy defeats. Indeed, in one 5–0 thrashing Preston received at Wolves, Frank O'Donnell must have lost his patience because he was sent off. One of the few pre-war sendings off of a Preston player recorded. The eventual champions, Manchester City, hit nine goals in their two wins over Preston and the games on Christmas Day and Boxing Day produced four goal hauls and two wins for Arsenal and Huddersfield respectively. But there were many fine individual performances for the Deepdale club with Frank O'Donnell, despite his blemish at Molineux, the pick of the side. He had a terrific season and hit 27 league and cup goals. His 11 in the cup included two fine hat-tricks against Stoke and Exeter and the Buckhaven born striker went on to score in every round including the final. Other players who figured prominently were Frank's brother Hugh, Jimmy Milne, Harry Holdcroft, Jack Beresford and John Jennings. Bill Shankly's form dipped however and this is possibly one reason for some poor defending. Preston did make a significant signing though, when another Scot joined the club. His name was Tom Smith and he was signed from Kilmarnock. In the league Preston rarely looked like relegation candidates and in fact as the season went on their form improved to the extent that they lost just two of their last eleven games. In what was probably the most amazing game for years Preston fought out a pulsating match at Grimsby and although they eventually lost 6–4 it was one for the memory bank. Most of the real excitement though came in the cup run and losing the final was to be especially disappointing. Leading 1–0 and totally in control at half-time they allowed Sunderland to come back strongly after the break. So strongly in fact that they scored three times and took the trophy to Wearside.

DEBUTANTS: (7) James Atherton, John Batey, James Briscoe, Michael Burns, William Fagan, Jack Jennings and Tom Smith.

LAST GAMES: (7) Atherton, Batey J., Briscoe, Gallimore L., Hough, Jennings and Vernon.

League appearances (42 games)

Atherton J. 4, Batey J.C. 9, Batey N.R. 11, Beattie A. 18, Beresford J. 35, Briscoe J.E.R. 5, Burns M. 7, Dougal J. 30, Fagan W. 29, Gallimore F. 10, Gallimore L. 5, Holdcroft G.H. 35, Hough W. 5, Jennings J. 19, Lowe H. 27, Maxwell J.M. 26, Milne J.L. 35, O'Donnell F. 39, O'Donnell H. 38, Shankly W. 29, Smith T.M. 9, Tremelling W. 30, Vernon J.L. 7.

FA Cup appearances (6 games)

Holdcroft 2, Burns 4, Gallimore F. 4, Beattie 3, Jennings 1, Lowe 4, Shankly 6, Tremelling 6, Milne 6, Dougal 6, Beresford 6, O'Donnell F. 6, Fagan 6, O'Donnell H. 6.

Goalscorers: 56 League–20 Cup–(Total 76).

O'Donnell F. 16–11 (27), Maxwell 12–0 (12), O'Donnell H. 7–2 (9), Beresford 6–2 (8), Dougal 3–4 (7), Fagan 6 (2 Pens)–0 (6), Milne 2–0 (2), Atherton 1–0 (1), Jennings 1(pen)–0 (1) Tremelling 1(pen)–0 (1), Vernon 1–0 (1). Own goals 0–1 (1) (Turner of Stoke)

Future Players born between August 1936 and July 1937: John Wylie, John Donnelly, Alex Alston, Gil Lambert and Gordon Milne
Ever presents: None
FA Cup: Runners-up
Chairman: Sir Meyrick Hollins
Hat-tricks: (3) Maxwell and O'Donnell F. (2), both in the FA Cup.
Leading scorer: 27 goals – Frank O'Donnell (16 league 11 Cup)
Manager: Tommy Muirhead
Players used: 23
AUTHORS' UNOFFICIAL PLAYER OF THE SEASON:
Frank O'Donnell

STAT FACTS:
Best home run without defeat: 7 games
Best away run without defeat: 4 games
Longest run unbeaten: 6 games
Longest run without a win: 6 games
Best home attendance: 26,936 vs. Exeter FAC 20.2.37
Worst home attendance: 8,675 vs. Everton 14.4.37
Best away attendance: 93,495 at Wembley vs. Sunderland FAC
Worst away attendance: 9,052 vs. WBA 22.3.37
Aggregate and average home attendance: 378,935 – 18,045
Aggregate and average away attendance: 474,718 – 22,606

Date 1936-7	Opponents	Comp	h or a	Score	Att.	1	2	3	4	5	6	7	8	9	10	11		
Aug 29	Huddersfield Town	Div 1	h	1-1	22596	Holdcroft	Hough	Lowe	Shankly	Tremelling (1p)	Milne	Dougal	Beresford	Maxwell	F O'Donnell	H O'Donnell		
Aug 31	Bolton W.	Div 1	h	1-2	23449	Holdcroft	Hough	Lowe	Shankly	Tremelling	Milne	Dougal	Beresford	Maxwell	F O'Donnell (1)	H O'Donnell		
Sep 5	Sunderland	Div 1	a	0-3	31383	Holdcroft	Hough	Lowe	Shankly	R Batey	Milne	Briscoe	Beresford	Maxwell	F O'Donnell	H O'Donnell		
Sep 7	Bolton W.	Div 1	a	0-0	17622	Holdcroft	Hough	Lowe	Shankly	R Batey	Milne	Briscoe	Beresford	Maxwell	F O'Donnell	H O'Donnell		
Sep 12	Wolverhampton W	Div 1	h	1-3	12697	Holdcroft	Hough	Lowe	Shankly	Tremelling	R Batey	Briscoe	Beresford	Vernon	F O'Donnell (1)	H O'Donnell		
Sep 19	Derby County	Div 1	a	2-1	22173	Holdcroft	J Batey	Lowe	Beattie	Tremelling	Milne	Beresford	F O'Donnell	Maxwell (2)	Dougal	H O'Donnell		
Sep 26	Manchester Utd	Div 1	h	3-1	24149	Holdcroft	Jennings	Lowe	Beattie	Tremelling	Milne (1)	Beresford	F O'Donnell	Maxwell	Dougal (2)	H O'Donnell		
Oct 3	Sheffield Wed	Div 1	a	1-0	18090	Holdcroft	Jennings	Lowe	Beattie	Tremelling	Milne	Beresford	F O'Donnell	Maxwell	Dougal	H O'Donnell (1)		
Oct 10	Chelsea	Div 1	h	1-0	20040	Holdcroft	Jennings	Lowe	Beattie	Tremelling	Milne	Beresford	F O'Donnell (1)	Maxwell	Dougal	H O'Donnell		
Oct 17	Stoke City	Div 1	a	2-0	19716	Burns	Jennings	Lowe	Beattie	Tremelling	Milne	Fagan	F O'Donnell	Maxwell (1)	Dougal	H O'Donnell (1)		
Oct 24	Charlton Ath	Div 1	h	0-0	22730	Holdcroft	Jennings	Lowe	Beattie	Tremelling	Milne	Fagan	F O'Donnell	Maxwell	Dougal	H O'Donnell		
Oct 31	Grimsby Town	Div 1	a	4-6	12341	Holdcroft	Jennings	Lowe	Beattie	Tremelling	Milne (1)	Fagan	Beresford	Maxwell (1)	F O'Donnell (2)	H O'Donnell		
Nov 7	Liverpool	Div 1	h	3-1	16887	Holdcroft	Jennings	Lowe	Beattie	Tremelling	Milne	Fagan (1p)	Beresford (1)	Maxwell	F O'Donnell	H O'Donnell (1)		
Nov 14	Leeds Utd	Div 1	a	0-1	15651	Holdcroft	Jennings	Lowe	Shankly	Tremelling	Milne	Fagan	Beresford	Maxwell	F O'Donnell	H O'Donnell		
Nov 21	Birmingham	Div 1	h	2-2	16892	Holdcroft	Jennings	Lowe	Shankly	Tremelling	Milne	Fagan (1)	Beresford	Maxwell (1)	F O'Donnell	H O'Donnell		
Nov 28	Middlesbrough	Div 1	a	1-2	20308	Holdcroft	Jennings	Lowe	Shankly	Tremelling	Milne	Fagan	Beresford	Maxwell	F O'Donnell	H O'Donnell (1)		
Dec 5	WBA	Div 1	h	3-2	12000	Holdcroft	Jennings	L Gallimore	Shankly	Tremelling	Milne	Fagan	Beresford	Maxwell (3)	F O'Donnell	H O'Donnell		
Dec 12	Manchester City	Div 1	a	1-4	20093	Holdcroft	Jennings	Lowe	Shankly	Tremelling	Milne	Dougal	Beresford	Maxwell (1)	F O'Donnell	H O'Donnell		
Dec 19	Portsmouth	Div 1	h	1-1	16005	Holdcroft	Jennings (1p)	L Gallimore	Beattie	Smith	Milne	Dougal	Beresford	Maxwell	F O'Donnell	H O'Donnell		
Dec 25	Arsenal	Div 1	a	1-4	42781	Holdcroft	Jennings	Lowe	Vernon	Smith	Milne	Dougal	Beresford	Maxwell (1)	F O'Donnell	H O'Donnell		
Dec 26	Huddersfield Town	Div 1	a	2-4	33899	Holdcroft	Jennings	Lowe	Vernon	Tremelling	Milne	Dougal	Beresford	Maxwell	F O'Donnell (2)	H O'Donnell		
Dec 28	Arsenal	Div 1	h	1-3	25787	Holdcroft	Jennings	Lowe	Vernon	Smith	Milne	Dougal	Beresford	Maxwell	F O'Donnell (1)	H O'Donnell		
Jan 1	Everton	Div 1	a	2-2	28824	Holdcroft	F Gallimore	L Gallimore	Shankly	Tremelling	Milne	Dougal	Atherton	F O'Donnell (2)	Beresford	Fagan		
Jan 2	Sunderland	Div 1	h	2-0	20360	Holdcroft	F Gallimore	L Gallimore	Shankly	Tremelling	Milne	Dougal	Atherton (1)	F O'Donnell	Beresford (1)	Fagan		
Jan 9	Wolverhampton W	Div 1	a	0-5	20024	Holdcroft	F Gallimore	L Gallimore	Shankly	Tremelling	Milne	Briscoe	Atherton	F O'Donnell	Beresford	Fagan		
Jan 16	Newcastle Utd Rd 3	FAC	h	2-0	25387	Holdcroft	F Gallimore	Lowe	Shankly	Tremelling	Milne	Dougal	Beresford (1)	F O'Donnell (1)	Fagan	H O'Donnell		
Jan 23	Derby County	Div 1	h	5-2	15433	Holdcroft	F Gallimore	Lowe	Shankly	Tremelling	Milne	Dougal	Beresford (2)	F O'Donnell (1)	Fagan	H O'Donnell (2)		
Jan 30	Stoke City Rd 4	FAC	h	5-1	23866	Burns	F Gallimore	Lowe	Shankly	Tremelling	Milne	Dougal (1)	Beresford	F O'Donnell (3)	Fagan	H O'Donnell	1o.g.	(Turner)
Feb 3	Manchester Utd	Div 1	a	1-1	13225	Burns	F Gallimore	Lowe	Shankly	Tremelling	Milne	Dougal	Beresford	F O'Donnell	Fagan (1)	H O'Donnell		
Feb 6	Sheffield Wed	Div 1	h	1-1	17316	Burns	F Gallimore	Lowe	Shankly	Tremelling	Milne	Dougal	Beresford	F O'Donnell	Fagan (1p)	H O'Donnell		
Feb 13	Chelsea	Div 1	a	0-0	27465	Burns	Beattie	Lowe	Shankly	Tremelling	Milne	Dougal	Beresford	F O'Donnell	Fagan	H O'Donnell		
Feb 20	Exeter City Rd 5	FAC	h	5-3	26936	Burns	Beattie	Lowe	Shankly	Tremelling	Milne	Dougal	Beresford (1)	F O'Donnell (3)	Fagan	H O'Donnell (1)		
Feb 24	Stoke City	Div 1	h	0-1	8784	Holdcroft	Beattie	Lowe	Shankly	Tremelling	Milne	Dougal	Beresford	F O'Donnell	Fagan	H O'Donnell		
Feb 27	Charlton Ath	Div 1	a	1-3	25702	Holdcroft	Beattie	Lowe	Shankly	Smith	Milne	Dougal	Atherton	F O'Donnell	Fagan (1)	H O'Donnell		
Mar 6	Tottenham H Rd 6	FAC	a	3-1	71913	Holdcroft	Jennings	Lowe	Shankly	Tremelling	Milne	Dougal (1)	Beresford	F O'Donnell (1)	Fagan	H O'Donnell (1)		
Mar 10	Grimsby Town	Div 1	h	3-2	9557	Holdcroft	Jennings	Lowe	Shankly	Tremelling	Milne	Dougal	Beresford	F O'Donnell (2)	Fagan (1)	H O'Donnell		
Mar 13	Liverpool	Div 1	a	1-1	24375	Holdcroft	Beattie	J Batey	Shankly	Smith	Milne	Dougal	Fagan	F O'Donnell (1)	Maxwell	H O'Donnell		
Mar 20	Leeds Utd	Div 1	h	1-0	18050	Holdcroft	Jennings	J Batey	Shankly	Tremelling	R Batey	Dougal	Beresford	F O'Donnell (1)	Fagan	H O'Donnell		
Mar 22	WBA	Div 1	a	0-0	9052	Holdcroft	Beattie	J Batey	Shankly	Tremelling	R Batey	Dougal	Beresford	F O'Donnell	Fagan	H O'Donnell		
Mar 26	Brentford	Div 1	a	1-1	31069	Holdcroft	Beattie	J Batey	Shankly	Smith	R Batey	Dougal	Beresford	F O'Donnell	Fagan	Maxwell (1)		
Mar 27	Birmingham	Div 1	a	0-1	26350	Holdcroft	Jennings	J Batey	Shankly	Smith	R Batey	Dougal	Fagan	F O'Donnell	Maxwell	H O'Donnell		
Mar 29	Brentford	Div 1	h	1-1	26782	Holdcroft	Beattie	J Batey	Shankly	Tremelling	R Batey	Dougal	Beresford (1)	F O'Donnell	Fagan	H O'Donnell		
Apr 3	Middlesbrough	Div 1	h	2-0	18942	Holdcroft	F Gallimore	Beattie	Shankly	Smith	R Batey	Maxwell (1)	Beresford	F O'Donnell (1)	Fagan	H O'Donnell		
Apr 10	WBA + Semi-final	FAC	N	4-1	42636	Burns	F Gallimore	Beattie	Shankly	Tremelling	Milne	Dougal (2)	Beresford	F O'Donnell (2)	Fagan	H O'Donnell		
Apr 14	Everton	Div 1	a	1-0	8675	Burns	F Gallimore	J Batey	Shankly	R Batey	Milne	Dougal	Vernon	Maxwell	Fagan	H O'Donnell (1)		
Apr 17	Manchester City	Div 1	h	2-5	21804	Burns	F Gallimore	J Batey	Shankly	Tremelling	Milne	Briscoe	Dougal (1)	Vernon (1)	Fagan	H O'Donnell		
Apr 24	Portsmouth	Div 1	a	1-0	14575	Burns	F Gallimore	Beattie	R Batey	Smith	Milne	Dougal	Beresford (1)	Vernon	Fagan	H O'Donnell		
May 1	Sunderland * Cup Final	FAC	N	1-3	93495	Burns	F Gallimore	Beattie	Shankly	Tremelling	Milne	Dougal	Beresford	F O'Donnell (1)	Fagan	H O'Donnell		

+ Played at Highbury
* Played at Wembley

All Scottish forward line. Fagan, F. O'Donnell, Maxwell, Dougal and H. O'Donnell.

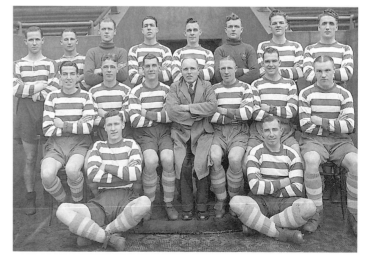

Left to right: *Back row*: Vernon, Beattie, Holdcroft, F. O'Donnell, Lowe, Burns, Milne, Dougal. *Middle row*: H. O'Donnell, Maxwell, Tremelling, Scott, Jennings, Gallimore, Shankly. *Front row*: Fagan, Beresford

League position in Division One: 14th – P42 W14 D13 L15 F56 A67 Pts 41
Home: W10 D6 L5 F35 A28 Away: W4 D7 L10 F21 A39

William Tremelling, cup-final captain.

Match Report: Underdogs Unlucky – 20 Feb 1937
Preston 5 Exeter City 3 FA Cup Fifth Round

Those fans who turned out in squally weather conditions expecting to see Exeter City receive a hiding from their illustrious opponents, were in for quite a shock as the Southerners had the audacity to steal a first minute lead. Andy Beattie, caught cold, hesitated over a challenge as Owen slipped past him and shot at goal as Shankly endeavoured to narrow the angle. The shot hit Shankly's foot, curled into the air and dropped under the crossbar with Burns beaten. A sorry start indeed for North End. The pitch was quickly churned up into a mud heap on which Preston were vastly more uncomfortable than their unfancied opponents, who were naturally inspired by their early success. The underdogs continued to be on top for the first 15 minutes before Preston eventually put their game together. Exeter rode their luck, especially in the latter stages of the first-half, and something had to give, and it did, in a dramatic last five minute period before the interval. An inch perfect centre by Fagan was prodded on by Beresford to Frank O'Donnell who brushed past Chesters, the goalkeeper, before slotting the ball agonisingly wide of his reach.

Within two minutes a delightful clean-cut goal was obtained once again by Frank O'Donnell, who read Dougal's fine pass perfectly to score. The second-half started just as dramatically with Exeter equalising with less than a minute played. Milne's error let in Smith but there was still Burns to beat. Unquestionably, Burns should have saved his shot but allowed it to squirm out of his grasp and over the line just as Williams gleefully slammed it into the net just to make sure. Chesters then had an inspired period as North End hammered away at his goal. He made fine saves from Dougal and Hugh O'Donnell. With the game still all square Exeter had thoughts of a giant killing act and on the hour Smith waltzed beyond Lowe and put in a shot which in all honesty should not have gone into the net. Burns, this time, went to ground too soon and obviously mistimed the pace of the ball as it bobbed over his outstretched arm towards the net. In the subsequent scramble Owen followed up to make sure it did not stick in the muddy goalmouth. The North End forwards found the conditions a severe handicap but contributed to their undoing by trying to do too much with the ball. However, much to their relief North End equalised after 70 minutes with a well directed header from Hugh O'Donnell, and then, five minutes later, regained the lead through Hugh's brother Frank. Burns was again beaten but luckily for Preston Williams was given offside. Then, on 87 minutes, North End eventually killed the tie off with a great strike by Beresford, which finally finished the minnows from cream tea land. It had been a very close call for the First Division side.

Jimmy Milne "Mr Preston North End".

North End in action *vs.* Leeds Utd 25 April 1936.

Season 1936–37: First Division

		P	W	D	L	F	A	Pts
1	Man City	42	22	13	7	107	61	57
2	Charlton	42	21	12	9	58	49	54
3	Arsenal	42	18	16	8	80	49	52
4	Derby	42	21	7	14	96	90	49
5	Wolves	42	21	5	16	84	67	47
6	Brentford	42	18	10	14	82	78	46
7	Middlesbrough	42	19	8	15	74	71	46
8	Sunderland	42	19	6	17	89	87	44
9	Portsmouth	42	17	10	15	62	66	44
10	Stoke	42	15	12	15	72	57	42
11	Birmingham	42	13	15	14	64	60	41
12	Grimsby	42	17	7	18	86	81	41
13	Chelsea	42	14	13	15	52	55	41
14	**PRESTON**	**42**	**14**	**13**	**15**	**56**	**67**	**41**
15	Huddersfield	42	12	15	15	62	64	39
16	WBA	42	16	6	20	77	98	38
17	Everton	42	14	9	19	81	78	37
18	Liverpool	42	12	11	19	62	84	35
19	Leeds	42	15	4	23	60	80	34
20	Bolton	42	10	14	18	43	66	34
21	Man United	42	10	12	20	55	78	32
22	Sheffield Wednesday	42	9	12	21	53	69	30

SEASON 1937-1938

Arguably, after their two Championships of the 1880s, this was Preston North End's finest ever season. A terrific league campaign was backed up by a glorious return to Wembley in the FA Cup final where, this time, the triumph of winning the trophy was savoured by the whole population of the Lancashire town. The summer of 1937 had begun with a shock for the club as manager Tommy Muirhead resigned. This could have been devastating as the Scot had done a superb job in the short time he had been at Preston. The Committee then made a brave decision to run the side without a manager and it was a decision that was to prove absolutely right. To cap it all they also made some super signings to boost the strength of the team. Exciting players were brought in with Bobby Beattie, Jimmy McIntosh, Dick Watmough and George Mutch adding some real quality to the play. But the success of the season could be pinpointed at the magnificent defence where Tom Smith had an outstanding season. It was reflected in the fact that the goals against column was the lowest since the war. However, a glance at the league table will also highlight just where the club lost the chance to overhaul Arsenal and Wolves above them. Preston had no fewer than 17 draws, their highest ever total of draws to date, and if only one extra goal had been scored in just three of those games then Preston would have won the league. Four players reached double figures in the goalscoring chart and George Mutch more than justified the £5,000

fee that Preston paid Manchester United for the Scot. Indeed, it was his hat-trick in the third round of the FA Cup that set Preston on their way to the eventual triumph over Huddersfield. And it was fitting that it was Mutch who scored the decisive goal at Wembley, an unbelievably nerve racking penalty in the dying seconds of extra-time. In the league Preston took three points off the runners-up, Wolves, but significantly lost both games against the Champions, Arsenal. It was the London side's fifth title of the 1930s. The Preston crowds reflected the club's success and nearly 500,000 watched the league games. On the field there were many fine performances. Harry Holdcroft was very consistent in goal, Andy Beattie superb at full-back, Billy Shankly was back to his best at wing-half and Jimmy Dougal and Bobby Beattie proved real handfuls for the opposing defences. A great season for Preston, FA Cup winners and third in Division One. The only sad aspect was that two players appeared for the last time in the white shirt during the year with Frank O'Donnell and Bill Tremelling moving on to pastures new after giving great service to the club.

DEBUTANTS: (7) Bobby Beattie, Archie Garrett, George Lowrie, Jimmy McIntosh, George Mutch, George Summerbee and Dick Watmough.

LAST GAMES: (8) Beresford, Burns, Fagan, Garrett, Lowrie, O'Donnell F., Tremelling and Watmough.

Future Players born between August 1937 and July 1938: Ian Davidson, Bobby Charlton, Jim Smith and Mike Lynne
Ever presents: None **FA Cup:** Winners **Chairman:** Sir Meyrick Hollins
Hat-tricks: (2) Maxwell and Mutch in the FA Cup. **Leading scorer:** 18 goals – George Mutch (12 League 6 Cup)
Manager: The Committee **Players used:** 23
AUTHORS' UNOFFICIAL PLAYER OF THE SEASON: George Mutch

League appearances (42 games)

Batey N. R. 14, Beattie A. 41, Beattie R. 31, Beresford J. 5, Burns M. 5, Dougal J. 32, Fagan W. 6, Gallimore F. 32, Garrett A. C. 2, Holdcroft G. H. 37, Lowe H. 9, Lowrie G. 5, McIntosh J. M. 4, Maxwell J. M. 24, Milne J. L. 36, Mutch G. 32, O'Donnell F. 14, O'Donnell H. 35, Shankly W. 41, Smith T. M. 34, Summerbee G. M. 1, Tremelling W. 2, Watmough R. 20.

FA Cup appearances (6 games)

Holdcroft 6, Gallimore 6, Beattie A. 6, Shankly 6, Smith 6, Milne 5, Watmough 6, Mutch 6, Dougal 5, Batey 1, Maxwell 1, Beattie R. 6, O'Donnell H. 6.

Goalscorers: 64 League–12 Cup–(Total 76)

Mutch 12 (2pens)–6 (1pen) (18), Dougal 14–1 (15), Beattie R. 9–2 (11), Maxwell 8–0 (8), O'Donnell H. 5–3 (8), O'Donnell F. 7–0 (7), Watmough 4–0 (4), Milne 2–0 (2), Garrett 2–0 (2), Shankly 1–0 (1).

League position in Division One: 3rd – P42 W16 D17 L9 F64 A44 Pts 49
Home: W9 D9 L3 F34 A21 Away: W7 D8 L6 F30 A23

FA CUP Final
1938

Above: George Mutch's penalty kick entering the net to give PNE a 1–0 win in the FA Cup

Right: In match action.

Bottom Right: The Flag-market in Preston scene of North End's homecoming

ENTER AT TURNSTILES
(See Plan on back)

PRESS GALLERY
North Grand Stand

Press Box No.
22

EMPIRE STADIUM, WEMBLEY

THE FOOTBALL ASSOCIATION
CUP COMPETITION

FINAL TIE

SATURDAY, APRIL 30th, 1938
Kick-off 3 p.m.

Admit to
Press Gallery

(Entrance by private
staircase from North
Stand Gallery)

COMPLIMENTARY

SECRETARY,
The Football Association

THIS PORTION TO BE RETAINED
(See Conditions on back)

Right: Tom Smith being escorted off the pitch with the FA Cup.

Above [clockwise]: Bill Shankly being introduced to The King — Hugh O'Donnell being introduced to The King — Tom Smith with the FA Cup supported by Bill Shankly and Andy Beattie.

Left: Tom Smith proudly showing off the FA Cup to the people of Preston.

Right: Joyous scenes from Wembley with Bill Shankly (next to the policeman) clutching his coverted winners medal.

Far Right: Bill Shankly, Andy Beattie, Tom Smith, Frank Gallimore proudly show off the FA Cup.

Match Report: North End's Skilful Scots – 30 Oct 1937 Everton 3 Preston 5

The best team seen at Goodison Park for years was the general verdict of the fans after Preston's brilliant display against Everton. Seldom had such a superb exhibition of forward play been witnessed before. There was not one weak link in North End's attack and but for a brilliant performance by Sagar in the home goal then Everton's defeat would have been worse. The Everton defeders could not cope with the all Scottish Preston forward line. Having said that, Everton had begun the game aggressively and had the audacity to score first. After just six minutes play, following a free-kick, Tommy Lawton, Bell and Burns all challenged for the ball. It should have been goalkeeper Burns's ball but it squirmed out of his grasp leaving Bell with the simple task of toe-poking it over the line. Four minutes later Preston equalised with a penalty after Bobbie Beattie had been fouled by Cook. Mutch took the kick and duly scored with a low shot. Very soon Everton regained the lead through Lawton, again after a gift from Burns who failed to hold the slippery ball. North End fought back with great determination but Sagar denied them several times, so Everton led 2–1 at the break. North End came back fighting as they launched a series of attacks giving the spectators value for money. It was plain to see that an equaliser was imminent and it arrived nine minutes into the second half. Beattie, the finest player on view, was again the organising force. He and Hugh O'Donnell combined in an inter-passing move which O'Donnell skilfully finished off.

The home team rallied and within a few minutes Lawton had headed Everton back in front for the third time. But once more Preston equalised as their spirit shone through. It was four minutes later when O'Donnell evaded his marker again to centre to the far poat where Jimmy Dougal met the ball with a low diving header. By now Preston were all over their Lancashire neighbours and their clever approach play bewildered the home defenders. On 67 minutes they forged ahead with a picture goal. Rapid passing between Mutch, Maxwell and Beattie caught the defence in a tangle and Beattie was able to shoot home his first goal for North End. To make the scoring and victory complete Mutch then converted his second penalty.

Bill Shankly.

CHURCHMAN'S CIGARETTES

A. BEATTIE (PRESTON NORTH END)

STAT FACTS:
Best home run without defeat: 10 games
Best away run without defeat: 6 games
Longest run unbeaten: 6 games
Longest run without a win: 5 games
Best home attendance: 42,684 vs. Arsenal 23.4.38 (New ground record)
Worst home attendance: 9,150 vs. Leicester 9.3.38
Best away attendance: 93,497 vs. Huddersfield Cup Final at Wembley
Worst away attendance: 6,719 vs. Huddersfield 16.3.38
Aggregate and average home attendance: 476,085 – 22,671
Aggregate and average away attendance: 571,884 – 27,232

Season 1937–38: First Division

	P	W	D	L	F	A	Pts
1 Arsenal	42	21	10	11	77	44	52
2 Wolves	42	20	11	11	72	49	51
3 PRESTON	42	16	17	9	64	44	49
4 Charlton	42	16	14	12	65	51	46
5 Middlesbrough	42	19	8	15	72	65	46
6 Brentford	42	18	9	15	69	59	45
7 Bolton	42	15	15	12	64	60	45
8 Sunderland	42	14	16	12	55	57	44
9 Leeds	42	14	15	13	64	69	43
10 Chelsea	42	14	13	15	65	65	41
11 Liverpool	42	15	11	16	65	71	41
12 Blackpool	42	16	8	18	61	66	40
13 Derby	42	15	10	17	66	87	40
14 Everton	42	16	7	19	79	75	39
15 Huddersfield	42	17	5	20	55	63	39
16 Leicester	42	14	11	17	54	75	39
17 Stoke	42	13	12	17	58	59	38
18 Birmingham	42	10	18	14	58	62	38
19 Portsmouth	42	13	12	17	62	68	38
20 Grimsby	42	13	12	17	51	68	38
21 Man City	42	14	8	20	80	77	36
22 WBA	42	14	8	20	74	91	36

Date 1937-8	Opponents	Comp	h or a	Score	Att.	1	2	3	4	5	6	7	8	9	10	11
Aug 28	Grimsby Town	Div 1	h	4-1	22098	Holdcroft	A Beattie	Lowe	Shankly	Smith	Milne	Dougal (2)	Beresford	F O'Donnell (1)	Fagan	H O'Donnell (1)
Sep 1	Brentford	Div 1	a	1-2	21228	Holdcroft	A Beattie	Lowe	Shankly	Smith	Milne	Dougal (1)	Beresford	F O'Donnell	Fagan	H O'Donnell
Sep 4	Leeds Utd	Div 1	a	0-0	22513	Holdcroft	A Beattie	Lowe	Shankly	Smith	Milne	Dougal	Beresford	F O'Donnell	Fagan	H O'Donnell
Sep 6	Brentford	Div 1	h	1-1	21746	Holdcroft	A Beattie	Lowe	Shankly	Smith	Milne	Dougal (1)	Beresford	F O'Donnell	Fagan	H O'Donnell
Sep 11	Liverpool	Div 1	h	4-1	22370	Holdcroft	A Beattie	Lowe	Shankly	Smith	Milne	Dougal	Fagan	Maxwell (3)	F O'Donnell	H O'Donnell (1)
Sep 13	Charlton Ath	Div 1	h	0-1	18032	Holdcroft	A Beattie	Lowe	Shankly	Smith	Milne	Dougal	Fagan	Maxwell	F O'Donnell	H O'Donnell
Sep 18	WBA	Div 1	a	1-1	23537	Holdcroft	Gallimore	A Beattie	Shankly	Smith	Milne	Dougal	Beresford	Maxwell	F O'Donnell	H O'Donnell (1)
Sep 25	Birmingham	Div 1	h	2-1	25066	Holdcroft	Gallimore	A Beattie	Shankly	Smith	Milne	Dougal (1)	Mutch	Maxwell (1)	F O'Donnell	H O'Donnell
Oct 2	Middlesbrough	Div 1	a	1-2	25050	Holdcroft	Gallimore	A Beattie	Shankly	Smith	Milne	Dougal	Mutch	Maxwell (1)	F O'Donnell	H O'Donnell
Oct 9	Stoke City	Div 1	h	2-1	26402	Burns	Gallimore	A Beattie	Shankly	Smith	Milne	Dougal	Mutch	F O'Donnell (2)	R Beattie	Maxwell
Oct 16	Bolton W.	Div 1	a	4-1	37911	Burns	Gallimore	A Beattie	Shankly	Tremelling	Milne	Dougal	Mutch (1)	F O'Donnell (2)	R Beattie	Maxwell (1)
Oct 23	Huddersfield	Div 1	h	1-1	16483	Burns	Gallimore	A Beattie	Shankly	Tremelling	Milne	Dougal	Mutch	F O'Donnell (1)	R Beattie	Maxwell
Oct 30	Everton	Div 1	a	5-3	26250	Burns	Gallimore	A Beattie	Shankly	Batey	Milne	Dougal (1)	Mutch (2 pens)	Maxwell	R Beattie (1)	H O'Donnell (1)
Nov 6	Manchester City	Div 1	h	2-2	33107	Burns	Gallimore	A Beattie	Shankly	Batey	Milne	Dougal	Mutch (1)	Maxwell	R Beattie (1)	H O'Donnell
Nov 13	Leicester City	Div 1	a	0-1	19968	Holdcroft	Gallimore	A Beattie	Shankly	Batey	Milne	Dougal	Mutch	Maxwell	R Beattie	H O'Donnell
Nov 20	Blackpool	Div 1	h	2-0	30815	Holdcroft	Gallimore	A Beattie	Shankly	Smith	Milne	Maxwell	Mutch (1)	F O'Donnell (1)	R Beattie	H O'Donnell
Nov 27	Derby County	Div 1	a	1-1	14294	Holdcroft	Gallimore	A Beattie	Shankly	Smith	Milne	Dougal (1)	Mutch	F O'Donnell	R Beattie	H O'Donnell
Dec 4	Wolverhampton W	Div 1	h	2-0	15746	Holdcroft	Gallimore	A Beattie	Shankly	Smith	Milne (1)	Dougal (1)	Mutch	Maxwell	R Beattie	H O'Donnell
Dec 11	Arsenal	Div 1	a	0-2	35679	Holdcroft	Gallimore	A Beattie	Shankly	Smith	Milne	Dougal	Mutch	Maxwell	R Beattie	H O'Donnell
Dec 18	Sunderland	Div 1	h	0-0	18296	Holdcroft	Gallimore	A Beattie	Shankly	Smith	Milne	Dougal	Mutch	Maxwell	R Beattie	H O'Donnell
Dec 25	Portsmouth	Div 1	a	2-3	25909	Holdcroft	Gallimore	A Beattie	Shankly	Smith	Milne	Watmough (2)	Mutch	Dougal	R Beattie	Maxwell
Dec 27	Portsmouth	Div 1	h	1-1	31951	Holdcroft	Gallimore	A Beattie	Shankly	Smith	Milne	Watmough	Mutch	Maxwell	R Beattie (1)	H O'Donnell
Jan 1	Grimsby Town	Div 1	a	1-1	9427	Holdcroft	Gallimore	A Beattie	Shankly	Smith	Milne	Watmough	Mutch (1)	Dougal	R Beattie	H O'Donnell
Jan 8	**West Ham Utd Rd 3**	**FAC**	**h**	**3-0**	**30198**	**Holdcroft**	**Gallimore**	**A Beattie**	**Shankly**	**Smith**	**Milne**	**Watmough**	**Mutch (3)**	**Dougal**	**R Beattie**	**H O'Donnell**
Jan 15	Leeds Utd	Div 1	h	3-1	14032	Holdcroft	Gallimore	A Beattie	Shankly	Batey	Milne (1)	Watmough	Mutch (1)	Dougal	R Beattie (1)	H O'Donnell
Jan 22	**Leicester City Rd 4**	**FAC**	**h**	**2-0**		**Holdcroft**	**Gallimore**	**A Beattie**	**Shankly**	**Smith**	**Milne**	**Watmough**	**Mutch (1)**	**Dougal**	**R Beattie**	**H O'Donnell (1)**
Jan 29	WBA	Div 1	a	1-1	16299	Holdcroft	Gallimore	A Beattie	Shankly	Smith	Milne	Watmough	Mutch (1)	Dougal	R Beattie	H O'Donnell
Feb 2	Liverpool	Div 1	a	2-2	16852	Holdcroft	Gallimore	A Beattie	Shankly (1)	Smith	Milne	Watmough	Mutch	Dougal	Maxwell (1)	H O'Donnell
Feb 5	Birmingham	Div 1	a	2-0	24908	Holdcroft	Gallimore	A Beattie	Shankly	Smith	Batey	Watmough	Mutch	Dougal (2)	Garrett	H O'Donnell
Feb 12	**Arsenal Rd 5**	**FAC**	**a**	**1-0**	**72121**	**Holdcroft**	**Gallimore**	**A Beattie**	**Shankly**	**Smith**	**Milne**	**Watmough**	**Mutch**	**Dougal (1)**	**R Beattie**	**H O'Donnell**
Feb 16	Middlesbrough	Div 1	h	0-2	13416	Holdcroft	Gallimore	A Beattie	Shankly	Smith	Batey	Watmough	Mutch	Dougal	R Beattie	McIntosh
Feb 19	Stoke City	Div 1	a	1-1	30636	Holdcroft	Batey	A Beattie	Shankly	Smith	Milne	Watmough	Lowrie	Dougal	R Beattie (1)	H O'Donnell
Feb 26	Bolton W.	Div 1	h	2-2	29335	Holdcroft	Batey	A Beattie	Shankly	Smith	Milne	Watmough	Mutch (2)	Dougal	R Beattie	H O'Donnell
Mar 5	**Brentford Rd 6**	**FAC**	**a**	**3-0**	**39626**	**Holdcroft**	**Gallimore**	**A Beattie**	**Shankly**	**Smith**	**Milne**	**Watmough**	**Mutch**	**Dougal**	**R Beattie (2)**	**H O'Donnell (1)**
Mar 9	Leicester City	Div 1	a	0-0	9150	Holdcroft	Lowe	A Beattie	Shankly	Batey	Milne	Watmough	Mutch	Dougal	R Beattie	Maxwell
Mar 12	Everton	Div 1	h	2-1	23618	Holdcroft	Gallimore	A Beattie	Shankly	Smith	Milne	Watmough	Mutch	Dougal (1)	R Beattie	Maxwell (1)
Mar 16	Huddersfield	Div 1	a	3-1	6719	Holdcroft	Lowe	A Beattie	Shankly	Smith	Batey	Watmough	Mutch	Dougal (1)	R Beattie (2)	Maxwell
Mar 19	Manchester City	Div 1	a	2-1	54911	Holdcroft	Gallimore	A Beattie	Shankly	Smith	Milne	Watmough	Mutch	Dougal (2)	R Beattie	H O'Donnell
Mar 26	**Aston Villa + Semi-final**	**FAC**	**N**	**2-1**	**55129**	**Holdcroft**	**Gallimore**	**A Beattie**	**Shankly**	**Smith**	**Milne**	**Watmough**	**Mutch**	**Dougal**	**R Beattie**	**H O'Donnell (1)**
Apr 2	Blackpool	Div 1	a	0-1	26112	Holdcroft	Gallimore	A Beattie	Shankly	Smith	Milne	Watmough	Mutch	Maxwell	R Beattie	H O'Donnell
Apr 9	Derby County	Div 1	h	4-1	13343	Holdcroft	Gallimore	Lowe	Summerbee	Batey	Milne	Watmough	Garrett (2)	Maxwell	R Beattie (2)	H O'Donnell
Apr 15	Chelsea	Div 1	a	2-0	54735	Holdcroft	Gallimore	A Beattie	Shankly	Smith	Milne	Watmough (1)	Mutch (1)	Maxwell	R Beattie	H O'Donnell
Apr 16	Wolverhampton W	Div 1	a	0-0	42885	Holdcroft	Gallimore	A Beattie	Shankly	Smith	Batey	Lowrie	Mutch	McIntosh	R Beattie	H O'Donnell
Apr 18	Chelsea	Div 1	h	0-0	32096	Holdcroft	Gallimore	A Beattie	Shankly	Smith	Milne	Lowrie	Mutch	McIntosh	R Beattie	H O'Donnell
Apr 23	Arsenal	Div 1	h	1-3	42684	Holdcroft	Gallimore	A Beattie	Shankly	Smith	Milne	Watmough	Lowrie	Mutch	R Beattie	H O'Donnell (1)
Apr 30	**Huddersfield * Cup Final**	**FAC**	**N**	**1-0**	**93497**	**Holdcroft**	**Gallimore**	**A Beattie**	**Shankly**	**Smith**	**Batey**	**Watmough**	**Mutch (1p)**	**Maxwell**	**R Beattie**	**H O'Donnell**
May 4	Sunderland	Div 1	a	2-0	22307	Holdcroft	Gallimore	A Beattie	Shankly	Smith	Batey	Watmough (1)	Mutch (1)	McIntosh	R Beattie	H O'Donnell
May 7	Charlton Ath	Div 1	a	0-0	30053	Holdcroft	Gallimore	A Beattie	Shankly	Smith	Batey	Watmough	Lowrie	Maxwell	R Beattie	H O'Donnell

+ Played at Bramall Lane Sheffield
* Played at Wembley

PNE with the FA Cup, 1938.

SEASON 1938–1939

The continental tour of Europe that North End undertook at the end of the 1937–8 season took more of a toll than it was at first realised. In fact it was not properly realised until the 1938–9 season was in full swing. The big problems were injuries to two key players. Tom Smith was the most significant loss as his leg injury meant that he made just one appearance during the year. This was a bitter blow as he was the player that the club could least afford to lose. The other player sadly missed was Dick Watmough who actually missed the whole season. As a result of all this Preston had an indifferent campaign. True, the home record could not be faulted, but the away record was as bad as the home record was good and that put paid to any hopes Preston had of the championship. However there were some fine performances from individuals and Harry Holdcroft, Frank Gallimore, Bobby Beattie and George Mutch were all ever present. In fact it was a season where team changes were kept to a minimum but alas, it was that away record that let them down. When you look at the results it was difficult to pin down exactly where it went wrong. Goals were scored fairly freely and the defence generally played well. However there were times when goals were let in at vital times and maybe that was the key. The replacement for Watmough, Terry McGibbons, signed from Ayr United, had all the right credentials but alas, his transfer did not work out and it was soon evident that Preston would have to go back into the transfer market. This they did and they brought in Frank White from Birmingham. He did better and the second half of the season improved as a result. Of their 14 defeats only four came after the turn of the year. With the FA Cup also starting around this upsurge in form the Preston fans had high hopes for another good cup run. The club's recent love affair with the competition did continue for awhile but came to a surprising and disappointing end at Portsmouth in the sixth round. Though they did at least have the satisfaction of going out to the eventual winners. In the league though Preston had to be content with a mid-table position. Jimmy Dougal topped scored and was always a threat to opposing defenders and other players who could be pleased with their contributions were Bill Shankly, Bob Batey, Jimmy Milne and Andy Beattie. But it was that sort of season, full of excellent performances but always with just that little something missing. Sadly, this was to be the last chance for fans to watch top class soccer for awhile as in the September of 1939 the Second World War broke out and league football was to end for seven years. It also meant the premature end to the careers of the players who featured in this and the previous few seasons.

DEBUTANTS: (5) Jackie Cox, Terry McGibbons, Alex Millar, Frank White and David Willacy.

LAST GAMES: (15) Batey R., Cox, Gallimore F., Holdcroft, Lowe, McGibbons, McIntosh, Maxwell, Millar, Milne, O,Donnell H., Smith T., Summerbee, White and Willacy.

Jimmy Dougal, leading goalscorer.

George Mutch in action at Deepdale against Liverpool

Trivia Facts:

This is one of the saddest pieces of trivia in this book as it records the fact that David Willacy was to be the only player who had appeared in the Preston first team who died during the Second World War. He was tragically killed in a motor bike accident.

The team that lost in the FA Charity Shield match against Arsenal was: Holdcroft; Gallimore, Beattie A; Shankly, Batey, Milne; McGibbons, Mutch, Dougal, Beattie R. and Maxwell. Bobby Beattie scored Preston's goal.

League position in Division One: 9th – P42 W16 D12 L14 F63 A59 Pts 44
Home: W13 D7 L1 F44 A19 Away: W3 D5 L13 F19 A40

Match Report: Minnows Succumb to Cup Holders – 7 Jan 1939
Runcorn 2 Preston 4 FA Cup Third round

As FA Cup holders Preston's first defence of the trophy was a very tricky visit to Cheshire League side Runcorn. To add to the difficulty, snow was laying in the county. The town had gone cup-tie crazy with local enthusiasts making sure that the tie went ahead on schedule by moving up to nine inches of snow from the pitch in the early hours of the morning. Runcorn, in their blue and white quarters, ran out to a tumultuous roar, their fans out to enjoy the occasion whatever the outcome. At the onset only one press photographer positioned himself behind North End's goal, all the others expecting the action to be around Williams in the home goal. The pitch, as expected, cut up quickly which encouraged the long ball game, the type of football Runcorn were happy to play. After 20 minutes play the non-leaguers sent their fans wild with delight by taking the lead. The move developed out on the left wing. Gallimore failed to clear whilst being harrassed and the ball was delivered into the goalmouth where Fletcher touched it on to the unmarked Mason who scored. Make no mistake, this was a shock to North End's

Left to right: *Back row:* Gallimore, Shankly, Holdcroft, Batey, Milne, A. Beattie. *Front row:* White, Mutch, Dougal, R. Beattie, McIntosh.

system, but to their credit they responded in the best possible way by scoring themselves, Runcorn's lead lasting just two minutes. Shankly took a free-kick and delivered it to the incoming Milne who duly headed the equaliser. Ten minutes later Williams kept Runcorn in the tie with a brilliant double save from Mutch and Bobbie Beattie. The kick and rush style adopted by North End due to the wet conditions paid dividends just prior to the half-time break when Mutch chased a long ball leaving Lightfoot leaden-footed before slipping the ball past Williams for a great solo effort. Preston dominated the early stages of the second half as Shankly and Gallimore dealt with Runcorn's aggressive play by dishing out some of the same. On 69 minutes North End conceded a corner which proved fatal as Mason headed powerfully past Holdcroft. North End then came through a trying period of play but as Runcorn tired on the heavy ground Preston won a corner in the 80th minute which was to lead to another goal. McIntosh's kick was cleared, only as far as Mutch who lobbed a high ball into the danger area where Milne once again found time and space to head home. North End ventured forward yet again and after some clever right-wing play Bobbie Beattie converted a square pass from Mutch, scoring from point blank range. This double success knocked the heart out of tiny Runcorn who had battled bravely against their famous cup opponents.

H. ODonnell, J. Dougal, R. Beattie and H. Holdcroft caught in relaxed mood.

League appearances (42 games)

Batey N. R. 39, Beattie A. 40, Beattie R. 42, Cox J. 5, Dougal J. 40, Gallimore F. 42, Holdcroft G. H. 42, Lowe H. 1, McGibbons T. 22, McIntosh J. M. 23, Maxwell J. M. 1, Millar A. 2, Milne J. L. 38, Mutch G. 42, O'Donnell H. 20, Shankly W. 40, Smith T. M. 1, Summerbee G. M. 2, White F. R. H. 19, Willacy D. L. 1.

FA Cup appearances (4 games)

Holdcroft 4, Gallimore 4, Beattie A. 4, Shankly 4, Batey 4, Milne 4, McIntosh 4, White 3, Mutch 4, Dougal 4, Beattie R. 4, O'Donnell H. 1.

Goalscorers: 63 League–8 Cup–(Total 71)

Dougal 19–0 (19), Mutch 10 (1pen)–2 (12), White 10 (1pen)–2 (1pen) (12), Beattie R. 9–2 (11), Milne 3–2 (5), Beattie A. 4 (3pens)–0 (4), McIntosh 3–0 (3), McGibbons 2–0 (2), O'Donnell 2–0 (2), Cox 1–0 (1).

STAT FACTS:
Best home run without defeat: 12 games
Best away run without defeat: 3 games
Longest run unbeaten: 7 games
Longest run without a win: 7 games
Best home attendance: 38,240 vs. Bolton 27.12.38
Worst home attendance: 13,029 vs. Stoke 15.2.39
Best away attendance: 62,327 vs. Newcastle FAC 11.2.39
Worst away attendance: 8,916 vs. Huddersfield 17.12.38
Aggregate and average home attendance: 452,206 – 21,537
Aggregate and average away attendance: 502,696 – 23,938

Season 1938–39: First Division

	P	W	D	L	F	A	Pts
1 Everton	42	27	5	10	88	52	59
2 Wolves	42	22	11	9	88	39	55
3 Charlton	42	22	6	14	75	59	50
4 Middlesbrough	42	20	9	13	93	74	49
5 Arsenal	42	19	9	14	55	41	47
6 Derby	42	19	8	15	66	55	46
7 Stoke	42	17	12	13	11	68	46
8 Bolton	42	15	15	12	67	58	45
9 PRESTON	42	16	12	14	63	59	44
10 Grimsby	42	16	11	15	61	69	43
11 Liverpool	42	14	14	14	62	63	42
12 Aston Villa	42	15	11	16	71	60	41
13 Leeds	42	16	9	17	59	67	41
14 Man United	42	11	16	15	57	65	38
15 Blackpool	42	12	14	16	56	68	38
16 Sunderland	42	13	12	17	54	67	38
11 Portsmouth	42	12	13	17	47	70	37
18 Brentford	42	14	8	20	53	74	36
19 Huddersfield	42	12	11	19	58	64	35
20 Chelsea	42	12	9	21	64	80	33
21 Birmingham	42	12	8	22	62	84	32
22 Leicester	42	9	11	22	48	82	29

Future Players who were born between August 1938 and
July 1939: Garbutt Richardson, Alex Smith and
Derek Temple
Ever presents: (4) Holdcroft, Gallimore, Beattie R.
and Mutch.
Chairman: Mr J. I. Taylor
Hat-tricks: None
FA Cup: Sixth round
Manager: The Committee
Leading scorer: 19 goals – Jimmy Dougal (all League)
Players used: 20

AUTHORS' UNOFFICIAL PLAYER OF THE SEASON:
Jimmy Dougal

Date 1938-9	Opponents	Comp	h or a	Score	Att.	1	2	3	4	5	6	7	8	9	10	11
Aug 27	Leeds Utd	Div 1	a	1-2	19258	Holdcroft	Gallimore	A Beattie	Shankly	Batey	Milne	McGibbons	Mutch	Dougal	R Beattie	O'Donnell (1)
Aug 31	Chelsea	Div 1	a	1-3	24821	Holdcroft	Gallimore	A Beattie	Shankly	Summerbee	Milne	McGibbons	Mutch	Dougal (1)	R Beattie	O'Donnell
Sep 3	Liverpool	Div 1	h	1-0	22340	Holdcroft	Gallimore	A Beattie	Shankly	Batey	Milne	McGibbons	Mutch	Dougal	R Beattie (1)	O'Donnell
Sep 5	Charlton Ath	Div 1	h	2-0	21963	Holdcroft	Gallimore	A Beattie	Shankly	Batey	Milne	McGibbons	Mutch (1p)	Dougal	R Beattie	O'Donnell (1)
Sep 10	Leicester City	Div 1	a	1-2	17507	Holdcroft	Gallimore	A Beattie	Shankly	Batey	Cox	McGibbons	Mutch (1)	Dougal	R Beattie	O'Donnell
Sep 17	Middlesbrough	Div 1	h	3-1	23746	Holdcroft	Gallimore	A Beattie	Shankly	Batey	Cox (1)	McGibbons	Mutch	Dougal (2)	R Beattie	O'Donnell
Sep 24	Birmingham	Div 1	a	3-1	26221	Holdcroft	Gallimore	A Beattie (1p)	Shankly	Batey	Milne	McGibbons	Mutch (1)	Dougal	R Beattie (1)	O'Donnell
Oct 1	Manchester Utd	Div 1	h	1-1	25964	Holdcroft	Gallimore	A Beattie	Shankly	Batey	Milne (1)	McGibbons	Mutch	Dougal	R Beattie	O'Donnell
Oct 8	Stoke City	Div 1	a	1-3	20930	Holdcroft	Gallimore	Lowe	Cox	Batey	Milne	McGibbons	Mutch	Dougal (1)	R Beattie	O'Donnell
Oct 15	Portsmouth	Div 1	h	2-2	19471	Holdcroft	Gallimore	A Beattie	Shankly	Batey	Milne	McGibbons	Mutch	Dougal	R Beattie (2)	O'Donnell
Oct 22	Arsenal	Div 1	a	0-1	40296	Holdcroft	Gallimore	A Beattie	Shankly	Batey	Milne	McGibbons	Mutch	Dougal	R Beattie	O'Donnell
Oct 29	Blackpool	Div 1	h	1-1	29443	Holdcroft	Gallimore	A Beattie	Shankly	Batey	Milne (1)	McGibbons	Mutch	Dougal	R Beattie	O'Donnell
Nov 5	Derby County	Div 1	a	0-2	33293	Holdcroft	Gallimore	A Beattie	Shankly	Batey	Milne	McGibbons	Mutch	Dougal	R Beattie	O'Donnell
Nov 12	Grimsby Town	Div 1	h	1-1	15506	Holdcroft	Gallimore	A Beattie (1p)	Shankly	Batey	Milne	McGibbons	Mutch	Dougal	R Beattie	O'Donnell
Nov 19	Sunderland	Div 1	a	2-1	20184	Holdcroft	Gallimore	A Beattie	Shankly	Batey	Milne	McGibbons (1)	Mutch	Dougal	R Beattie (1)	O'Donnell
Nov 26	Aston Villa	Div 1	h	3-2	21002	Holdcroft	Gallimore	A Beattie	Shankly	Batey	Milne	McGibbons (1)	Mutch	Dougal (2)	R Beattie	O'Donnell
Dec 3	Wolverhampton W	Div 1	a	0-3	26320	Holdcroft	Gallimore	A Beattie	Shankly	Batey	Milne	McGibbons	Mutch	Dougal	R Beattie	O'Donnell
Dec 10	Everton	Div 1	h	0-1	26549	Holdcroft	Gallimore	A Beattie	Shankly	Batey	Milne	McGibbons	Mutch	Dougal	R Beattie	O'Donnell
Dec 17	Huddersfield	Div 1	a	0-3	8916	Holdcroft	Gallimore	A Beattie	Shankly	Batey	Milne	McGibbons	Mutch	Dougal	R Beattie	O'Donnell
Dec 24	Leeds Utd	Div 1	h	2-0	18424	Holdcroft	Gallimore	A Beattie	Shankly	Batey	Milne	White	Mutch	Dougal (1)	R Beattie	McIntosh (1)
Dec 27	Bolton W.	Div 1	h	2-2	38240	Holdcroft	Gallimore	A Beattie	Shankly	Batey	Milne	White (1)	Mutch	Dougal	R Beattie(1)	McIntosh
Dec 31	Liverpool	Div 1	a	1-4	30453	Holdcroft	Gallimore	A Beattie	Shankly	Millar	Cox	Dougal	Mutch (1)	McGibbons	R Beattie	McIntosh
Jan 7	**Runcorn Rd 3**	**FAC**	**a**	**4-2**	**10111**	**Holdcroft**	**Gallimore**	**A Beattie**	**Shankly**	**Batey**	**Milne (2)**	**McIntosh**	**Mutch (1)**	**Dougal**	**R Beattie (1)**	**O'Donnell (1)**
Jan 14	Leicester City	Div 1	h	2-1	15724	Holdcroft	Gallimore	A Beattie	Shankly	Batey	Milne	McIntosh	Mutch	Dougal	R Beattie (1)	McIntosh
Jan 21	**Aston Villa Rd 4**	**FAC**	**h**	**2-0**	**37548**	**Holdcroft**	**Gallimore**	**A Beattie**	**Shankly**	**Batey**	**Milne**	**White (2,1p)**	**Mutch**	**Dougal**	**R Beattie**	**McIntosh**
Jan 25	Middlesbrough	Div 1	a	2-2	9262	Holdcroft	Gallimore	A Beattie	Shankly	Batey	Millar	White (2)	Mutch	Dougal	R Beattie	McIntosh
Jan 28	Birmingham	Div 1	h	5-0	18477	Holdcroft	Gallimore	A Beattie	Shankly	Batey	Milne	White (1)	Mutch (1)	Dougal (2)	R Beattie (1)	McIntosh
Feb 4	Manchester Utd	Div 1	a	1-1	41061	Holdcroft	Gallimore	A Beattie	Shankly	Batey	Milne	White	Mutch	Dougal	R Beattie	McIntosh (1)
Feb 11	**Newcastle Utd Rd 5**	**FAC**	**a**	**2-1**	**62327**	**Holdcroft**	**Gallimore**	**A Beattie**	**Shankly**	**Batey**	**Milne**	**White**	**Mutch (1)**	**Dougal**	**R Beattie (1)**	**McIntosh**
Feb 15	Stoke City	Div 1	h	1-1	13029	Holdcroft	Gallimore	A Beattie	Shankly	Batey	Milne	White	Mutch	Dougal (1)	R Beattie	McIntosh
Feb 18	Portsmouth	Div 1	a	0-0	24699	Holdcroft	Gallimore	A Beattie	Shankly	Batey	Milne	White	Mutch	Dougal	R Beattie	McIntosh
Feb 25	Arsenal	Div 1	h	2-1	29678	Holdcroft	Gallimore	A Beattie	Shankly	Batey	Milne	White (1)	Mutch	Dougal (1)	R Beattie	McIntosh
Mar 4	**Portsmouth Rd 6**	**FAC**	**a**	**0-1**	**44237**	**Holdcroft**	**Gallimore**	**A Beattie**	**Shankly**	**Batey**	**Milne**	**White**	**Mutch**	**Dougal**	**R Beattie**	**McIntosh**
Mar 8	Blackpool	Div 1	a	1-2	10680	Holdcroft	Gallimore	A Beattie	Shankly	Smith	Milne	White (1)	Mutch	Dougal	R Beattie	McIntosh
Mar 11	Derby County	Div 1	h	4-1	14691	Holdcroft	Gallimore	A Beattie (1)	Shankly	Batey	Milne	White (1)	Mutch (1)	Dougal (1)	R Beattie	McIntosh
Mar 18	Grimsby Town	Div 1	h	1-1	10600	Holdcroft	Gallimore	A Beattie	Shankly	Batey	Milne	White	Mutch	Dougal (1)	R Beattie	McIntosh
Mar 25	Sunderland	Div 1	h	2-1	17130	Holdcroft	Gallimore	A Beattie	Shankly	Batey	Milne	White	Mutch (1)	Dougal (1)	R Beattie	McIntosh
Apr 1	Aston Villa	Div 1	a	0-3	41894	Holdcroft	Gallimore	A Beattie	Shankly	Batey	Milne	White	Mutch	Dougal	R Beattie	McIntosh
Apr 7	Brentford	Div 1	a	1-3	30780	Holdcroft	Gallimore	A Beattie	Shankly	Batey	Milne	White (1p)	Mutch	Dougal	R Beattie	McIntosh
Apr 8	Wolverhampton W	Div 1	h	4-2	31243	Holdcroft	Gallimore	A Beattie	Shankly	Batey	Milne	White	Mutch	Dougal (2)	R Beattie (1)	McIntosh
Apr 10	Brentford	Div 1	h	2-0	22350	Holdcroft	Gallimore	A Beattie	Shankly	Batey	Milne	White	Mutch	Dougal (1)	R Beattie	McIntosh (1)
Apr 15	Everton	Div 1	a	0-0	31987	Holdcroft	Gallimore	A Beattie	Cox	Batey	Milne	White	Mutch	Maxwell	R Beattie	McIntosh
Apr 22	Huddersfield	Div 1	h	3-0	13903	Holdcroft	Gallimore	A Beattie (1p)	Shankly	Batey	Milne	McGibbons	Mutch	Dougal (2)	R Beattie	McIntosh
Apr 26	Bolton W.	Div 1	a	2-0	15353	Holdcroft	Gallimore	A Beattie	Shankly	Batey	Milne (1)	McGibbons	Mutch (1)	Dougal	R Beattie	McIntosh
Apr 29	Chelsea	Div 1	h	1-1	13333	Holdcroft	Gallimore	A Beattie	Shankly	Batey	Milne	White	Mutch (1)	Dougal	R Beattie	McIntosh
May 6	Charlton Ath	Div 1	a	1-3	18181	Holdcroft	Gallimore	Summerbee	Shankly	Batey	Milne	Willacy	Mutch	White (1)	R Beattie	McIntosh

The Second World War Years, 1939–1946

In the summer of 1939 the government of the country was eager to allay fears of the impending war and for all intents and purposes the build up to the 1939–40 season was much as in previous years. However, only three league games had been completed when the dreaded news of war being declared was broadcast to the nation on Sunday September 3 1939. The league programme was immediately abandoned with the three games being expunged from the record books. Not surprisingly the country was thrown into turmoil. It was agreed to play some football though and by October 21 1939 Preston were playing in one of ten mini regional

Bobbie Beattie PNE's Scottish International seen shaking hands with the First Lord of the Admiralty at Wembley in the 1941 Football League Cup Final.

leagues. They had already played seven friendlies, none of which were lost. For the following season only two regional divisions were created with North End topping the Northern Division and Crystal Palace topping the Southern Division. Preston also won the League War Cup Final, beating Arsenal 2–1 at Ewood Park, Blackburn after a 1–1 draw at Wembley. Season 1941–42 saw PNE competing in the North Division again, but the season was split into two separate championships, the first one ending on Christmas Day 1941. After the end of that season the Club was then shut down for the next two years as Deepdale was taken over by the Military and used as a Disposal Centre, a reception for Prisoners of War. During the 1944–45

season Preston again took part in the North Division which was again a two separate championship format. That season also saw the restart of the FA Cup competition after a five year suspension. The matches were played on a two-legged basis. By this time football had almost returned to some normality as only Hull and New Brighton of the Third Division North, did not participate during that 1945–46 season. It was all still unofficial but Preston competed in a normal size North Division. However they did not do particularly well as many local youngsters were given a chance to play. It was the club's policy not to use the 'guest player' scheme whenever possible as several members of the Board believed that the scheme had been misused during the war years. North End's final game during this enforced period was on May 4 1946 when they lost 0–1 at Grimsby Town.

War-time League Cup-Winners, beat Arsenal 2–1 after a 1–1 draw. Left to right: *Back row:* Mr Scott (trainer), Shankly, Gallimore, Fairbrother, Beattie, Mansley. *Front row:* Dougal, Finney, McLaren, Smith, R. Beattie, H. O'Donnell, Scott.

PNE 1944–45
Left to right: Back row: Smith, Hamilton, Robertson, Fairbrother, Watson, Milne.
Front row: Horton, Mutch, Dougal, Strachan, Wharton.

Those three league games played prior to the abandonment of the league programme saw Preston draw 0–0 at home to both Leeds and Sheffield United and lose 2–0 at Grimsby. At the time of the suspension of action the club was fourth from bottom of Division One with no goals and just two points. The team selected had remained the same in all three games. It was: Holdcroft, Gallimore, Williams, Shankly, Milne, Batey, Mutch, White, Hunter, Beattie R. and Wharton. Six years later, in the 1945–46 season, a year before the official resumption of League football, the FA Cup was played for again. This time the records were accepted as official and therefore these games are recorded in this book. For the purposes of this North End history though we have recorded the first team debuts of those players involved in these cup-ties as the 1946–47 season, when they made their official league bow. However, there was one player who did not make a first team debut either before or after the war. Jack Livesey left the club to join Bury when the war was over and although he subsequently had other claims to fame he never again played for PNE.

Trivia Facts:

Jimmy Dougal made 154 wartime appearances for North End, scoring 96 goals. He also scored for Scotland against England at Hampden Park, Glasgow on 11 May 1940. And did you know that during the war years Tom Finney guested for Newcastle, Bolton and Southampton.

At a PNE Extraordinary General Meeting of Shareholders called in March 1946, only one shareholder attended. The meeting lasted just two and a half minutes.

No programmes or teamsheets were printed for home games during 1944–45 and 1945–46.

Goalkeeper Ken Groves saved a penalty in his only appearance of the 1939–40 season, standing in for Harry Holdcroft in the game at Burnley. Preston still lost 0–1.

1939–40 Preston's biggest win was 10–1 away at Accrington Stanley. As well as the 22 'league' games North End played no fewer than 20 friendlies. Bill Shankly represented Scotland against England.

1940–41 The biggest win was 12–1 against Tranmere Rovers. Preston played nine of their home games at nearby Leyland Motors ground. Andy McLaren scored all six goals against Liverpool in a 6–1 win and during the season both Andy Beattie and Bill Shankly represented Scotland.

1941–42 The biggest win during this season was 7–0 against Oldham Athletic. North End's David L. Willacy and Percival Thomas Taylor were killed during the year. Andy Beattie, Bill Shankly and Tom Smith all played for Scotland against England on April 18 1942 in a 5–4 win for the Scots.

1944–45 The biggest gate at Deepdale was 10,780 against Blackpool. North End's Juniors were champions of the YMCA league having won 26 of their 28 games, scoring 168 goals in the process. In the first team North End used 40 different players.

1945–46 The biggest win during this season was an 8–2 victory over Leeds United when George Mutch played at full-back for Preston. The club had 15 players still serving overseas including Andy Beattie, Bobbie Beattie, Tom Finney and Andy McLaren. A further 22 players were in the Services in Britain.

Harry Holdcroft XI which played at Leyland Motors included North Enders Willie Robertson, Lou Bradford, Jackie Wharton and George Mutch

Preston North End's wartime statistics

1939–40 North West Division – 12 teams (Ten Regional Divisions)

P22 W15 D2 L5 F63 A27 Pts 32 – Finished 2nd in Division

1939–40 Football League War Cup

Played Everton, home and away, lost 1–3 at Everton and drew 2–2 at Deepdale. Appearances: Batey R. 2, Beattie A. 2, Beattie R. 2, Dougal J. 2, Fairbrother J. 1, Gallimore F. 2, Holdcroft G.H. 1, Hunter J.B. 2, Mutch G. 2, Rookes P.W. (Portsmouth) 1, Shankly W. 2, Smith T.M. 1, Wharton J.E. 2.

1939–40 Goalscorers 63 North West Division – 3 War Cup (Total 66)

Dougal 13–3 (16), O'Donnell F. 15–0 (15), Beattie R. 10–0 (10), Wharton 5–0 (5), Batey 4–0 (4), Mutch 4–0 (4), Standing 4–0 (4), McIntosh 2–0 (2), Milne 2–0 (2), O'Donnell H. 2–0 (2), Bargh 1–0 (1) Own Goals 1–0 (1)

1940–41 North Division – 36 teams
(Just two divisions, one in the North and one in the South)

P29 W18 D7 L4 F81 A37 Goal average 2.187

Due to the logistical complexity of playing the games during these difficult times the 36 teams did not complete the same amount of fixtures. For example Bolton only played 16 games whilst Bury played 38 and North End completed 29. It was therefore decided to settle the title by goal average and North End were crowned as Champions. Crystal Palace won the Southern Division. Ever-present in the Preston side this season was an up and coming 18 year old called Tom Finney.

1940–41 Football League War Cup – PNE were the winners, so a League and Cup double.

12 games, based on a two-legged home and away fixture: P12 W9 D3 L0 F42 A11 Appearances: Beattie A. 4, Beattie R. 8, Dougal J. 12, Fairbrother J. 12, Finney T. 12, Gallimore F. 12, Jessop W. 6, Mansley V.C. 10, McLaren A. 12, O'Donnell H. (Blackpool) 7, Scott W. 10, Shankly W. 12, Smith T.M. 12, Taylor P.T. 2, Wharton J.E. 1.

1940–41 Goalscorers 81 North Divison – 42 War Cup (Total 123)

Dougal 26–6 (32), McLaren 18–13 (31), Finney 6–6 (12), Mutch 11(2p)–0 (11), Beattie R. 4–5 (9), O'Donnell 2–4 (6), Shankly 3(3p)–4(4p) (7), Wharton 3–1 (4), Jessop 2–2 (4), Hough 2–0 (2), Mansley 2–0 (2), Owens 2–0 (2), Taylor 0–1 (1).

League appearances (1939–40)

Bargh G.W. (Chesterfield) 2, Batey N.R. 21, Beattie A. 3, Beattie R. 22, Dougal J. 17, Fairbrother J. 2, Finch R. 1, Gallimore F. 19, Groves K. 1, Holdcroft G.H. 19, Iceton O.L. 2, Maxwell J.M. (Barnsley) 1, McIntosh J.M. 9, Milne J.L. 4, Mutch G. 12, O'Donnell F. (Aston Villa) 14, O'Donnell H. (Blackpool) 13, Rawlings J.S.D. (Millwall) 2, Rookes P.W. (Portsmouth) 8, Scott W. 2, Shankly W. 20, Smith T.M. 18, Standing J.S. 2, Summerbee G.M. 2, Wharton J.E. 14, White F.R.H. 1, Williams E. 11.
A total of 27 players used.

1941 Football League War Cup

Feb 15	A	Bury	4–4	Finney 2, Beattie R., McLaren
Feb 22	H	Bury	2–1	Beattie R., Jessop
Mar 1	A	Bolton W.	4–1	Finney 2, Dougal, Jessop
Mar 8	H	Bolton W.	2–0	McLaren, Taylor
Mar 15	H	Tranmere	12–1	McLaren 5, O'Donnell 4, Finney, Wharton, Dougal
Mar 22	A	Tranmere	8–1	Dougal 3, McLaren 2, Shankly 2 (both pens.), Finney
Mar 29	A	Man City	2–1	Beattie R., Dougal
Apr 5	H	Man City	3–0	McLaren 3
Apr 19	H	Newcastle	2–0	Shankly 2 (both pens.)
Apr 26	A	Newcastle	0–0	
May 10	N	Arsenal	1–1	McLaren
May 31	N	Arsenal	2–1	Beattie R. 2

The first game of the final was played at Wembley Stadium and the replay was at Ewood Park, Blackburn.

Appearances (1940–41)

Beattie A. 1, Beattie R. 7, Dougal J. 28, Fairbrother J. 15, Finch R. 15, Finney T. 29, Gallimore F. 26, Gore E. 1, Holdcroft G.H. 14, Horton J.K. 2, Hough T. 5, Jessop W. 19, Mansley V.C. 27, McLaren A. 27, McPhee J. 1, Mutch G. 17, Nuttall W. 1, O'Donnell H. (Blackpool) 3, Owens J. 3, Robertson W.J.T. 2, Scott W. 28, Seed T. 2, Shankly W. 13, Smith T.M. 26, Taylor P.T. 2, Wharton J.E. 5.

1941–42 North Division (First Competition, up to and including December 25 1941)

P18 W13 D1 L4 F58 A18 Pts 27 – Finished 3rd out of 38 teams

Appearances: Batey N.R. 6, Beattie A. 10, Beattie R. 3, Bradford L. 2, Dougal J. 17, Fairbrother J. 17, Finch R. 1, Finney T. 17, Gallimore F. 8, Gore E. 1, Holdcroft G.H. 1, Horton J.K. 8, Jessop W. 1, Mansley V.C. 9, McLaren A. 18, Mutch G. 14, Robertson W.J.T. 1, Scott W. 18, Shankly W. 10, Smith T.M. 18, Wharton J.E. 18.

1941–42 North Division Inc. League War Cup (Second Competition from Dec 27 to May 30)

P19 W6 D 7 L6 F41 A30 Pts 19 – Finished 12th out of 22 teams

Appearances: Beattie A. 7+1 sub*, Beattie R. 1, Beardwood G. 2, Bradford L. 15, Bremner G.H. (Motherwell) 8, Bright R. (Burnley) 1, Dougal J. 17, Fairbrother J. 15, Finney T. 16, Gallimore F. 5, Gardner T. (Burnley) 1, Gooch J.A.G. 3, Holdcroft G.H. 1, Horton J.K. 5, Iddon H. 1, Mansley V.C. 4, McDougal L. 1, McIntosh J.M. 2, McLaren A. 19, Mutch G. 18, Robertson W.J.T. 2, Scott W. 14, Seed T. 1, Shankly W. 15, Smith T.M. 14, Snowden R. (Burnley) 1, Taylor P.T. 1, Wharton J.E. 17, White F.R.H. 2.
*Beattie A. came on as a second half substitute for McDougal at Newcastle on March 21 1942.

1941–42 Goalscorers 58 (First Comp.) – 41 (Second Comp.) (Total 99)

Dougal 18(1p)–5 (23), Wharton 12–9 (21), McLaren 11–7 (18), Mutch 9–7(1p) (16), Finney 4–2 (6), Shankly 0–4(2p) (4), Beattie R. 1–3 (4), Gore 1–0 (1), Horton 1–0 (1), Beardwood 0–1 (1), Bremner 0–1 (1), Taylor 0–1 (1). Own Goals 1–1 (2), Eaves (Oldham) and Ancell (Blackburn).

Preston North End did not compete in any organised football during the 1942–3 and 1943–4 seasons due to their ground being shut down for use as a POW detention centre.

1944–45 North Division (First competition up to and including December 23 1944)

P18 W7 D4 L7 F26 A28 Pts 18 Finished 31st out of 54 teams.

Appearances: Bond A. 7, Bradford L. 16, Bryant A. 1, Dougal J. 17, Fairbrother J. 2, Hamilton W. 18, Holdcroft G.H. 16, Horton J.K. 4, Iddon H. 2, Kiely T.E. 1, Livesey J. 5, McIntosh J.M. 11, Milne J.L. 14, Mutch G. 17, Robertson W.J.T. 17, Seddon H. 2, Smith T.M. 16, Squires A. 1, Strachan D. 1, Watson W.T. 13, Wharton J.E. 18.
A total of 21 players used.

1944–45 North Division Incl. League War Cup (Second Competition from Dec 26 to May 26)

P25 W9 D4 L12 F41 A56 Pts 34 Finished 29th out of 54 teams.

Appearances: Anders H. 4, Attwell R. (West Ham) 1, Bond A. 8, Boyes W. (Everton) 1, Bradford L. 11, Bradshaw G.F. (Bury) 1, Cater R. (West Ham) 11, Dainty A. 2, Darley J. 2, Dougal J. 11, Dunn R. (West Ham) 12, Fairbrother J. 7, Griffiths G. (Bury) 1, Griffiths W. (Bury), 1, Groves K. 1, Hamilton W. 12, Hesketh A. 5, Horton J.K. 2, Hough T. 2, Iceton O.L. 2, Iddon H. 7, Kiely T.E. 1, Livesey J. 11, McIntosh J.M. 12, Milne J.L. 9, Mutch G. 5, Robertson W.J.T. 23, Scott W. 21, Seddon H. 5, Simpson R. 8, Smith T.M. 16, Squires A. 1, Strachan D. 8, Urquhart W. (Clyde) 2, Walmsley J. 11, Watson W.T. 11, Wharton J.E. 25, Willingham C.K. (Huddersfield) 1.
A total of 38 players used.

1944–45 Goalscorers 26 First Comp. – 41 Second Comp. (Total 67)

Dougal 8–5 (13), McIntosh 5–7 (12), Mutch 5(2p)–3(1p) (8), Dunn 0–6 (6), Wharton 0–5(1p) (5), Livesey 1–4 (5), Strachan 0–4 (4), Bond 3(2p)–0 (3), Iddon 0–3 (3), Seddon 1–1 (2), Horton 1–0 (1), Watson 1–0 (1), Dainty 0–1 (1), Hough 0–1 (1), Robertson 0–1 (1).

1945–46 North Division

P42 W14 D6 L22 F70 A77 Pts 34 Finished 19th out of 22 teams.

Appearances: Anders H. 15, Anders J. 1, Batey N.R. 8, Beattie A. 25, Beattie R. 15, Bradford L. 2, Brown W.F. 2, Dougal J. 35, Fairbrother J. 37, Finney T. 5, Groves K. 1, Hamilton W. 35, Holdcroft G.H. 1, Horton J.K. 13, Hunter J.B. 1, Iceton O.L. 2, Iddon H. 12, Livesey J. 12, Mansley V.C. 2, McIntosh J.M. 42, Mutch G. 42, Robertson W.J.T. 1, Scott W. 23, Shankly W. 14, Simpson R. 20, Squires A. 1, Summerbee G.M. 28, Walmsley J. 3, Watson W.T. 15, Wharton J.E. 30, Williams E. 19.
A total of 31 players used.

1945–46 FA Cup official competition re-started, see grid below.

P6 W2 D2 L2 F8 A 12

Appearances: Anders H. 1, Beattie A. 6, Dougal J. 6, Fairbrother J. 6, Hamilton W. 6, Livesey J. 5, McIntosh J.M. 6, Mutch G. 6, Scott W. 3, Shankly W. 6, Summerbee G.M. 1, Watson W.T. 2, Wharton J.E. 6, Williams E. 6.

1945–46 Goalscorers 70 North Division – 8 FAC (Total 78)

Mutch 18(5p)–0 (18), McIntosh 14–2 (16), Dougal 12–0 (12), Iddon 7–0 (7), Wharton 4–1 (5), Beattie R. 5–0 (5), Shankly 2(2p)–2(1p) (4), Finney 4(2p)–0 (4), Livesey 1–2 (3), Anders H. 1–0 (1),
Own goals 2–1 (3) – Charlesworth of Grimsby, Hobson of Chesterfield in the league, and Humphreys of Everton in the FA Cup.

Trivia Facts:

During the 1940–1 season North End's average 'home' gate when playing at nearby Leyland was 1,864. But once they went back to Deepdale the average attendance in the league games went up to 5,973. For the League War Cup matches the average shot up to 10,770. The lowest gate was at Leyland against Bury with just 323 turning up, but the best at Deepdale was 17,432 for the visit of Newcastle in the cup competition.

Quite a few players came to Preston as a guest player during these years but it also worked the other way round too. George Summerbee played for Portsmouth, Bill Shankly for Northampton, Cardiff and (ironically as it turned out) Liverpool. George Mutch played for Everton, Liverpool and Manchester City, Frank White turned out for Wrexham and Chester, Bob Batey for Liverpool and Newcastle, Tom Smith for Manchester United, Andy McLaren for Blackburn and Bristol City and Bobbie Beattie for Blackpool, Notts County and Everton.

A number of friendlies were also played during these war years and these included a match away to Glasgow Rangers on September 1 1941 (Lost 1–3), away to Queen of the South on January 1 1941 (won 3–0), away at Leeds United on March 25 1944 (lost 1–2), and a special match against Blackpool, played at Whitehaven on May 1 1946. The Blackpool match was in aid of the Bolton Wanderers Disaster Fund and was drawn 2–2.

Date 1945-6	Opponents FA Cup only	Comp	h or a	Score	Att.	1	2	3	4	5	6	7	8	9	10	11
Jan 5	Everton (1 o.g. +)	FAC	h	2-1	25,361	Fairbrother	Beattie	Scott	Shankly	Williams	Hamilton	Dougal	Mutch	Livesey (1)	Wharton	McIntosh
Jan 9	Everton	FAC	a	2-2*	35,461	Fairbrother	Beattie	Scott	Shankly (1p)	Williams	Hamilton	Dougal	Mutch	Livesey	Wharton	McIntosh (1)
Jan 26	Man. Utd. *	FAC	a	0-1	36,237	Fairbrother	Beattie	Scott	Shankly	Williams	Hamilton	Dougal	Mutch	Livesey	Wharton	McIntosh
Jan 30	Man. Utd.	FAC	h	3-1*	24,845	Fairbrother	Beattie	Scott	Watson	Shankly (1)	Hamilton	Livesey (1)	Mutch	Dougal	Wharton	McIntosh (1)
Feb 9	Charlton Ath.	FAC	h	1-1	39,303	Fairbrother	Beattie	Summerbee	Shankly	Williams	Hamilton	Livesey	Mutch	Dougal	Wharton (1)	McIntosh
Feb 13	Charlton Ath.	FAC	a	0-6	50,000	Fairbrother	Beattie	Watson	Shankly	Williams	Hamilton	Anders	Mutch	Dougal	Wharton	McIntosh
	* Played at Maine Road			*a.e.t.												
	+ Own Goal by Humphreys															

SEASON 1946–1947

Left to right: *Back row:* A. Beattie, Shankly, Fairbrother, Watson, Williams, Scott. *Front row:* Finney, Mutch, McIntosh, R. Beattie, Dougal.

After six years of war and all the sadness and tragedy that it had brought to the British public, it was such a relief for everyone to see the resumption of top class football. Preston were in Division One of the Football League and began the campaign with a home game against Leeds United. Four players were in the starting line-up who had played league football for the club before the war, Andy Beattie, Billy Shankly, Jimmy Dougal and Bobbie Beattie. Seven others were making their full league debut although most eyes it would seem were on a pale faced local boy called Tom Finney. Already a star, thanks to his war-time appearances for Preston and the many exciting things that had already been written about him, this was the first chance to see him in full league action. He was not to disappoint as he scored one of the goals against Leeds in a 3–2 win. Willie McIntosh also scored a debut goal before going on to score a hat-trick in each of his third and

fourth appearance in the famous white shirt. It was just the start the new centre-forward wanted and he continued to score regularly throughout the season. Another pre-war survivor, George Mutch, managed just six more games before he moved on and it was sad for the fans to see him go. The crowds during this season were incredible. Starved for so long of top class football, the public took every opportunity to see the games' top players. And everyone wanted to see Finney. However, overall the season was one of fluctuating fortunes for North End, with big wins being offset by heavy defeats, although the crowds could have no complaints about the entertainment value or the goals scored. Unfortunately, because they conceded so many goals, Preston were never in with a realistic chance of honours. In the FA Cup though there was some excitement generated as the club went through to the sixth round before finally losing to the eventual winners of the trophy, Charlton Athletic. A run of just three wins from the last thirteen league games was bitterly disappointing and a final position of seventh in the league was all the fans had to show. Individually, as ever, there were some excellent displays with Jack Fairbrother, Bill Scott, Bill Shankly, Andy Beattie, Willie McIntosh and of course Tom Finney all playing very well.

DEBUTANTS: (20) Jack Fairbrother, Bill Scott, Ken Horton, Willie Watson, Tom Finney, Willie McIntosh, Emlyn Williams, Willie Hamilton, Jackie Wharton, Jimmy Gooch, Willie Jessop, Jimmy Garth, Willie Robertson, Andy McLaren, Albert Dainty, Willie Nuttall, Peter Corr, Ian Wilson, Reg Simpson and Willie Brown.

LAST GAMES: (12) Jack Fairbrother, Willie Watson, Jimmy Dougal, Andy Beattie, Jackie Wharton, George Mutch, Willie Hamilton, Willie Jessop, Albert Dainty, Willie Nuttall, Peter Corr and Reg Simpson.

Future Players born between August 1946 and July 1947: Gerry Stewart, David Bright, Brian Greenhalgh, Archie Gemmill, Barrie Mitchell and George Lyall

Ever presents: (1) Bill Scott **Players used:** 25

FA Cup: Sixth Round

Hat-tricks: (2) both by Willie McIntosh

Manager: Selection Committee led by J. I. Taylor

Leading scorer: 32 goals – Willie McIntosh (27 league 5 cup)

Chairman: J. I. Taylor

AUTHORS' UNOFFICIAL PLAYER OF THE SEASON: Tom Finney

League position in Division One: 7th – P42 W18 D11 L13 F76 A74 Pts 47
Home: W10 D7 L4 F45 A27 Away: W8 D4 L9 F31 A47

Match Report: The Arrival of Tom Finney –
31Aug 1946 Preston 3 Leeds United 2

The turnstiles clicked merrily at Deepdale for the start of the big kick-off in League football after seven long years of ersatz variety. Chief interests in North End's team were the long awaited arrival of Tom Finney after his demobilisation from the army, the debut of new signing McIntosh from St Johnstone and the experiment of playing Shankly at centre-half. Andy Beattie won the toss. Leeds, a well built, upstanding side, opened briskly with plenty of vigour and bustle to cause an alarm or two to the fans stood behind the Town End goal. They need not have been so anxious as after just four minutes play Preston gave the crowd a real tonic with a well executed goal, scored by debutant McIntosh. Leeds were left bewildered by the speed and accuracy of a perfect forward move in which Finney, found unmarked by Horton, slipped a deadly accurate pass inside for McIntosh to take it in his stride and score with an excellent shot across goal well out of Hodgson's reach. Play was subsequently tame for a while, until that is, the 18th minute when Preston scored again. The move again had class written all over it and Finney, the schemer and scorer alike, showed that beyond any doubt he was going to be a tremendous asset for North End. (An understatement or what!). One solo effort, greeted with storming applause, saw him take Milburn to the line and with a quick turn and flick he sent his opponent stumbling and reeling off balance as he created a clear opening for himself. Leeds then caught Preston out after 25 minutes when their left-wing, set up by ex-North Ender Bob Batey, put Grainger through with a clear path to goal, the resultant shot was straight and true, much to Fairbrother's disgust. With Finney's trickery an advantage Preston did enough in the second half to gain what was their first league win since beating Bolton on April 26 1939. Jimmy Dougal, the pre-war Scottish International, notched Preston's third goal in the 75th minute and the points were virtually safe. Bobbie Beattie brought three splendid saves out of Hodgson before the game's final goal, a soft one, fell to Grainger of Leeds. The season was now underway and the local reporter noted that twelve North End corners were futile, the game had 45 throw-ins, ten offside decisions and the goalkeepers had to make 21 saves.

Andy Beattie Scottish International.

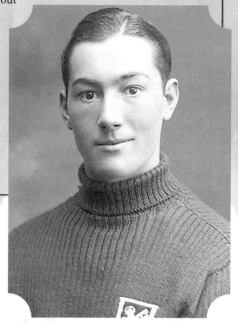

Jack Fairbrother, transferred to Newcastle United.

STAT FACTS:

Best home run without defeat: 8 games – Best away run without defeat: 6 games
Longest run unbeaten: 11 games – Longest run without a win: 4 games
Best home attendance: 40,167 *vs.* Chelsea, Boxing Day 1946
Worst home attendance: 15,911 *vs.* Middlesbrough 29.1.47
Best away attendance: 56,340 *vs.* Charlton 1.3.47
Worst away attendance: 16,686 *vs.* Sheffield United 24.5.47
Aggregate and average home attendance: 559,619 – 26,648
Aggregate and average away attendance: 694,146 – 33,054

League appearances (42 games):

Beattie A. 25, Beattie R. 37, Brown W. F. 8, Corr P. J. 3, Dainty A. 1, Dougal J. 5, Fairbrother J. 41, Finney T. 32, Garth J. 21, Gooch J. A. G. 1, Hamilton W. 37, Horton J. K. 10, Jessop W. 4, McIntosh W. D. 40, McLaren A. 14, Mutch G. 6, Nuttall W. 2, Robertson W. J. T. 1, Scott W. J. 42, Shankly W. 41, Simpson R. 4, Watson W. T. 15, Wharton J. E. 25, Williams E. 33, Wilson J. G. 14.

FA Cup appearances (4 games):

Fairbrother 4, A Beattie 2, Scott 4, Shankly 4, Finney 3, McIntosh 4, R Beattie 3, Wharton 4, Hamilton 4, Williams 4, Garth 1, McLaren 4, Nuttall 1, Wilson 1, Simpson 1.

Goalscorers: 76 league–11 FA Cup–(Total 87)

McIntosh 27–5 (32), Finney 7(1pen)–2 (1 pen) (9), Garth 8–0 (8), Beattie R. 7–1 (8),
Wharton 7–0 (7), McLaren 5–1 (6), Wilson 5–1 (6), Shankly 5 (3 pens)–0 (5),
Mutch 2–0 (2), Dainty 1–0 (1), Dougal 1–0 (1), Hamilton 0–1 (1).
Own Goals 1–0 (1) (Lowe, A. Villa).

Season 1946–47: First Division

		P	W	D	L	F	A	Pts
1	Liverpool	42	25	7	10	84	52	57
2	Man United	42	22	12	8	95	54	56
3	Wolves	42	25	6	11	98	56	56
4	Stoke	42	24	7	11	90	53	55
5	Blackpool	42	22	6	14	71	70	50
6	Sheffield United	42	21	7	14	89	75	49
7	PRESTON	42	18	11	13	76	74	47
8	Aston Villa	42	18	9	15	67	53	45
9	Sunderland	42	18	8	16	65	66	44
10	Everton	42	17	9	16	62	67	43
11	Middlesbrough	42	17	8	17	73	68	42
12	Portsmouth	42	16	9	17	66	60	41
13	Arsenal	42	16	9	17	72	70	41
14	Derby	42	18	5	19	73	79	41
15	Chelsea	42	16	7	19	69	84	39
16	Grimsby	42	13	12	17	61	82	38
17	Blackburn	42	14	8	20	45	53	36
18	Bolton	42	13	8	21	57	69	34
19	Charlton	42	11	12	19	57	71	34
20	Huddersfield	42	13	7	22	53	79	33
21	Brentford	42	9	7	26	45	88	25
22	Leeds	42	6	6	30	45	90	18

Date 1946-7	Opponents	Comp	h or a	Score	Att.	1	2	3	4	5	6	7	8	9	10	11		
Aug 31	Leeds Utd	Div 1	h	3-2	25311	Fairbrother	A Beattie	Scott	Horton	Shankly	Watson	Finney (1)	McIntosh (1)	Dougal (1)	R Beattie	Wharton		
Sep 4	Sheffield Utd	Div 1	h	1-2	25529	Fairbrother	A Beattie	Scott	Shankly	Williams	Watson	Finney	Mutch	McIntosh	R Beattie (1)	Wharton		
Sep 7	Grimsby Town	Div 1	a	3-2	18571	Fairbrother	A Beattie	Scott	Shankly	Williams	Watson	Finney	Mutch	McIntosh (3)	R Beattie	Dougal		
Sep 14	Charlton Ath	Div 1	h	5-1	26206	Fairbrother	A Beattie	Scott	Shankly	Williams	Watson	Finney	Mutch (2)	McIntosh (3)	R Beattie	Dougal		
Sep 16	Bolton W	Div 1	h	0-4	32536	Fairbrother	A Beattie	Scott	Shankly	Williams	Watson	Finney	Mutch	McIntosh	R Beattie	Dougal		
Sep 21	Middlesbrough	Div 1	a	0-2	40317	Fairbrother	A Beattie	Scott	Shankly	Hamilton	Watson	Finney	R Beattie	McIntosh	Mutch	Jessop		
Sep 28	Stoke City	Div 1	h	1-3	22787	Fairbrother	A Beattie	Scott	Shankly (1p)	Hamilton	Watson	Dougal	Mutch	McIntosh	Wharton	Jessop		
Oct 5	Manchester Utd	Div 1	a	1-1	55562	Fairbrother	A Beattie	Scott	Shankly	Williams	Hamilton	Finney	Horton	McIntosh (1)	R Beattie	Wharton		
Oct 12	Blackpool	Div 1	h	2-0	34488	Fairbrother	A Beattie	Scott	Shankly	Williams	Hamilton	Finney	Horton	McIntosh (1)	R Beattie (1)	Wharton		
Oct 19	Brentford	Div 1	a	3-2	25303	Fairbrother	A Beattie	Scott	Shankly (1p)	Williams	Hamilton	Finney	Horton	McIntosh (1)	R Beattie (1)	Wharton		
Oct 26	Aston Villa	Div 1	h	3-1	27778	Fairbrother	Robertson	Scott	Shankly	Williams	Hamilton	Finney	Horton	McIntosh	R Beattie	Wharton (2)	1 o.g.	(Lowe)
Nov 2	Derby County	Div 1	a	2-2	28251	Fairbrother	A Beattie	Scott	Shankly	Williams	Hamilton	Finney (1)	Garth	McIntosh (1)	R Beattie	Wharton		
Nov 9	Arsenal	Div 1	h	2-1	29084	Fairbrother	A Beattie	Scott	Shankly	Williams	Hamilton	Finney	Garth (1)	McIntosh (1)	R Beattie	Wharton		
Nov 16	Huddersfield	Div 1	a	0-3	17773	Fairbrother	A Beattie	Scott	Shankly	Williams	Hamilton	Finney	Garth	McIntosh	R Beattie	Wharton		
Nov 23	Wolverhampton W	Div 1	h	2-2	30293	Gooch	A Beattie	Scott	Shankly	Williams	Hamilton	Finney	Garth	McIntosh (1)	R Beattie	Wharton (1)		
Nov 30	Sunderland	Div 1	a	2-0	31621	Fairbrother	A Beattie	Scott	Shankly (1)	Williams	Hamilton	Wharton	Garth	McIntosh (1)	R Beattie	Jessop		
Dec 7	Blackburn R.	Div 1	h	4-0	32238	Fairbrother	A Beattie	Scott	Shankly	Williams	Hamilton	Finney (1)	Garth	McIntosh (2)	R Beattie (1)	Wharton		
Dec 14	Portsmouth	Div 1	a	4-4	24702	Fairbrother	A Beattie	Scott	Horton	Williams	Hamilton	Finney	Garth (1)	McIntosh (1)	R Beattie (1)	Wharton (1)		
Dec 21	Everton	Div 1	h	2-1	23334	Fairbrother	A Beattie	Scott	Shankly	Williams	Hamilton	Finney (1p)	Garth	McIntosh	R Beattie (1)	Wharton		
Dec 25	Chelsea	Div 1	a	2-1	37126	Fairbrother	A Beattie	Scott	Shankly	Williams	Hamilton	Finney (1)	Garth	McIntosh	R Beattie	Wharton (1)		
Dec 26	Chelsea	Div 1	h	1-1	40167	Fairbrother	A Beattie	Scott	Shankly	Williams	Hamilton	Finney	Garth (1)	McIntosh	R Beattie	Wharton		
Dec 28	Leeds Utd.	Div 1	a	3-0	33433	Fairbrother	A Beattie	Scott	Shankly	Williams	Hamilton	Finney (1)	Garth (1)	McLaren	R Beattie	Wharton (1)		
Jan 1	Bolton W	Div 1	a	2-1	47040	Fairbrother	A Beattie	Scott	Shankly	Williams	Hamilton	Finney	Garth	McIntosh	R Beattie (1)	Wharton (1)		
Jan 4	Grimsby Town	Div 1	h	3-0	27262	Fairbrother	A Beattie	Scott	Shankly	Williams	Hamilton	Finney	McLaren (1)	Dainty (1)	R Beattie	Wharton (1)		
Jan 11	**Northampton** Rd 3	**FAC**	**a**	**2-1**	**16858**	**Fairbrother**	**A Beattie**	**Scott**	**Shankly**	**Williams**	**Hamilton**	**Finney**	**McLaren (1)**	**McIntosh (1)**	**R Beattie**	**Wharton**		
Jan 18	Charlton Ath	Div 1	a	0-0	39032	Fairbrother	A Beattie	Scott	Shankly	Williams	Hamilton	Finney	Garth	McIntosh	R Beattie	Wharton		
Jan 25	**Barnsley** Rd 4	**FAC**	**h**	**6-0**	**39738**	**Fairbrother**	**A Beattie**	**Scott**	**Shankly**	**Williams**	**Hamilton (1)**	**Finney (2, 1p)**	**McLaren**	**McIntosh (2)**	**R Beattie (1)**	**Wharton**		
Jan 29	Middlesbrough	Div 1	a	0-1	15911	Fairbrother	Nuttall	Scott	Shankly	Williams	Hamilton	Finney	McLaren	McIntosh	R Beattie	Wharton		
Feb 1	Stoke City	Div 1	a	0-5	32753	Fairbrother	Nuttall	Scott	Shankly	Williams	Hamilton	Finney	McLaren	McIntosh	R Beattie	Wharton		
Feb 15	Blackpool	Div 1	a	0-4	28907	Fairbrother	A Beattie	Scott	Shankly	Williams	Hamilton	Finney	McLaren	McIntosh	R Beattie	Wharton		
Feb 20	**Sheffield Wed** Rd 5	**FAC**	**a**	**2-0**	**50277**	**Fairbrother**	**Simpson**	**Scott**	**Shankly**	**Williams**	**Hamilton**	**Wharton**	**McLaren**	**McIntosh (1)**	**Garth**	**Wilson (1)**		
Feb 22	Brentford	Div 1	h	5-2	25591	Fairbrother	Simpson	Scott	Shankly	Williams	Hamilton	Wharton	McLaren (1)	McIntosh (2)	Garth (1)	Wilson (1)		
Mar 1	**Charlton Ath** Rd 6	**FAC**	**a**	**1-2**	**56340**	**Fairbrother**	**Nuttall**	**Scott**	**Shankly**	**Williams**	**Hamilton**	**Finney**	**McLaren**	**McIntosh (1)**	**R Beattie**	**Wharton**		
Mar 15	Arsenal	Div 1	a	1-4	45775	Fairbrother	Simpson	Scott	Shankly	Williams	Hamilton	Finney	McLaren	McIntosh	Garth	Wilson (1)		
Mar 22	Huddersfield	Div 1	h	6-2	25460	Fairbrother	Simpson	Scott	Shankly (1p)	Williams	Hamilton	Finney	McLaren (1)	McIntosh (2)	Garth (1)	Wilson (1)		
Mar 29	Wolverhampton W	Div 1	a	1-4	37561	Fairbrother	Simpson	Scott	Shankly	Brown	Hamilton	Finney	McLaren	McIntosh (1)	Garth	Wilson		
Apr 4	Liverpool	Div 1	h	0-0	32542	Fairbrother	Watson	Scott	Shankly	Brown	Hamilton	Finney	McLaren	McIntosh	R Beattie	Wilson		
Apr 5	Sunderland	Div 1	h	2-2	19650	Fairbrother	Watson	Scott	Shankly (1)	Brown	Hamilton	Horton	McLaren (1)	McIntosh	R Beattie	Wilson		
Apr 7	Liverpool	Div 1	a	0-3	46477	Fairbrother	Watson	Scott	Shankly	Brown	Hamilton	Horton	McIntosh	Jessop	R Beattie	Wilson		
Apr 12	Blackburn R.	Div 1	a	2-1	34688	Fairbrother	Watson	Scott	Shankly	Brown	Hamilton	Finney (1)	Garth	McIntosh	R Beattie	Wilson (1)		
Apr 19	Portsmouth	Div 1	h	1-1	22530	Fairbrother	Watson	Scott	Shankly	Brown	Hamilton	Horton	McLaren (1)	McIntosh	R Beattie	Wilson		
Apr 26	Everton	Div 1	a	0-2	26371	Fairbrother	Watson	Scott	Shankly	Williams	Hamilton	Horton	McLaren	McIntosh	R Beattie	Wilson		
May 10	Manchester Utd	Div 1	h	1-1	23278	Fairbrother	Watson	Scott	Shankly	Williams	Hamilton	Finney	McLaren (1)	McIntosh	R Beattie	Wilson		
May 17	Aston Villa	Div 1	a	2-4	26197	Fairbrother	Watson	Scott	Shankly	Williams	Hamilton	Corr	Garth	McIntosh (1)	R Beattie	Wilson (1)		
May 24	Sheffield Utd	Div 1	a	3-2	16686	Fairbrother	Brown	Scott	Shankly	Williams	Hamilton	Corr	Garth (1)	McIntosh (2)	R Beattie	Wilson		
May 26	Derby County	Div 1	h	1-1	17644	Fairbrother	Brown	Scott	Shankly	Williams	Hamilton	Corr	Garth (1)	McIntosh	R Beattie	Wilson		

SEASON 1947-1948

Once again a failure to prevent goals going past their goalkeeper cost Preston dearly in a season where they again finished in seventh position in Division One, the same as the previous year. Amazingly they actually conceded more goals than they scored, although to be fair, the last result of the season did tip the balance somewhat. And that match was a disaster! A 7–0 home thrashing by Preston's deadliest rivals, Blackpool, of all people. That defeat, still the record against Preston to this day, caused years of anguish to all true North Enders. The fact that it also happened at Deepdale made it even more distressing. Earlier though, the season had begun in fine fashion with Preston winning nine of their first eleven games. But that form could not be sustained and North End's challenge gradually petered out. The crowds though were phenomenal with huge attendances watching Preston wherever they went. In one game, a cup-tie at Maine Road against Manchester United, over 74,000 people crammed into the stadium. Several new players made their league bow with Harry Anders, Paddy Waters, Joe Walton and David Gray being the most notable. Gray, signed from Glasgow Rangers in the summer, looked an excellent full-back and Walton, although only making a few appearances, was destined for a long stay at the club. Spare a thought for poor Anders though. He had the unenviable task of filling in for Tom Finney when the great man was unavailable. Sadly, the crowd, who often only came to see Tom, would boo loudly if Harry's name was announced and that was unfair on Anders who was a good player in his own right. But the crowd were appeased somewhat by some superb football served up at Deepdale. Some great

games, including the incredible 7–4 win over Derby, which is still talked about today, was just a sample of the action on view. Andy McLaren and Willie McIntosh struck up a fine partnership and there were fine seasons for Bill Scott, Bill Shankly, Ken Horton and the superstar, Finney. It was interesting to note that Shanks scored six times from the penalty spot during the campaign. Meanwhile, despite being drawn away in each round, Preston had another exciting run in the FA Cup. The ultimate defeat against Manchester United in the sixth round was bitterly disappointing, although once again North End went out to the eventual winners. Mind you, the summer of 1948 was ruined, not by the cup defeat, but by that awful result against Blackpool. I doubt whether many Preston fans took their holiday on the Golden Mile that year!

DEBUTANTS: (11) Alf Calverley, Harry Anders, Willie McLure, Harry Jackson, Paddy Waters, Jack Hindle, Willie Hall, Joe Walton, Willie Hannah, Willie Dougall and David Gray.

LAST GAMES: (8) David Gray, Emlyn Williams, Willie Hall, Jimmy Garth, Willie McLure, Jack Hindle, Ian Wilson and Alf Calverley.

Andy McLaren

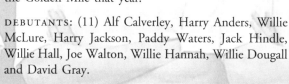

Future Players born between August 1947 and May 1948: Gerry Ingram, John Brown, John Blackley
Ever presents: None   **Players used:** 24   **Hat-tricks:** None   **Manager:** Selection Committee led by J. I. Taylor
Chairman: J. I. Taylor   **FA Cup:** Sixth Round   **Leading scorer:** 18 goals – Andy McLaren (17 league 1 cup)
AUTHORS UNOFFICIAL PLAYER OF THE SEASON: Andy McLaren

League appearances (42 games)

Anders H. 20, Beattie R. 30, Brown W. F. 1, Calverley A. 13, Dougall W. 10, Finney T. 33, Garth J. 2, Gooch J. A. G. 34, Gray D. 36, Hall W. F. 7, Hannah W. K. 11, Hindle J. 1, Horton J. K. 41, Jackson H. 12, McClure W. 12, McIntosh W. D. 34, McLaren A. 41, Robertson W. J. T. 6, Scott W. J. 31, Shankly W. 32, Walton J. 11, Waters P. M. 13, Williams E. 29, Wilson J. G. 2.

FA Cup appearances (4 games)

Gooch 3, Gray 4, Scott 4, Shankly 4, Williams 3, Horton 4, Finney 4, McLaren 4, McIntosh 4, Beattie 4, Anders 4, Waters 1, Hindle 1.

Goalscorers: 67 league–7 Cup–(Total 74)

McLaren 17–1 (18), McIntosh 14–3 (17), Finney 13 (1 pen)–1 (14), Shankly 6 (5 pens)–1 (1 pen) (7), Beattie 5–0 (5), Hannah 3–0 (3), Jackson 3–0 (3), McLure 2–0 (2), Walton 2 (2 pens)–0 (2), Wilson 1–0 (1), Anders 0–1 (1). Own goals 1–0 (1) (Jones, Everton)

Match Report: Eleven Goal Thriller – 6 Dec 1947 Preston 7 Derby County 4

The well behaved crowd which was assembled at Deepdale, could not, in their wildest dreams, have envisaged the game of football that they were about to witness. North End had just lost their last three games whereas Derby had been unbeaten in their last ten. The match quickly swept into a real crescendo of excitement as three goals were scored in six minutes, two of them from penalties. First Howe scored from the spot after a Raich Carter header had bounced up and struck Williams' arm as he was fending off Angus Morrison. With Preston off guard Morrison then ran between Shankly and Williams scoring with a shot in off the post for Derby's second goal. The Rams were now well on top and visually eased off slightly. North End took advantage of this and fought back strongly. Anders and McLaren were prominent in attack and after Anders had been fouled when cutting in from the wing, the referee, after consulting a linesman awarded Preston a penalty. Shankly confidently side-footed the spot-kick home. The game was now developing into the most exciting of the season as near misses and corners were in abundance. From one of these corners, taken by Finney, McLaren neatly headed home the equaliser. It came as no surprise though when Derby regained the lead after 32 minutes with a solo effort from Morrison. In spite of this further setback North End's endeavour could not be faulted and just before half-time a very determined Shankly stole in on the blind side to make it 3–3. It was difficult to imagine this hectic pace being maintained but it did as Finney turned on his silky skills, even though Preston could not gain the advantage. After some end to end play Derby took the lead yet again as Morrison completed his hat-trick. Within two minutes Finney had set up Bobbie Beattie to make it 4–4 as the thrills continued. The noisy crowd were by now ecstatic and they wondered just what else the game would conjure up. It was the first time this season that PNE had scored four goals and Derby had conceded four. Preston finished the stronger side as McIntosh on 75 minutes put Preston ahead for the first time and in a whirlwind finish McIntosh claimed his second goal as did McLaren who finished off a great move by Finney and in doing so also finished off Derby's challenge.

Bill Scott, Bill Shankly, Emlyn Williams, David Gray and Willie McIntosh stretching in the clubs gymnasium.

Left to right: *Back row*: Mr H. Ross (trainer), E. Williams, D. Gray, J. Gooch, Mr J. Metcalf (team supervisor), W. Scott, K. Horton, W. Brown.
Front row: T. Finney, A. McLaren, W. McIntosh, W. Shankly, R. Beattie, H. Anders.

Season 1947–48: First Division

	P	W	D	L	F	A	Pts
1 Arsenal	42	23	13	6	81	32	59
2 Man United	42	19	14	9	81	48	52
3 Burnley	42	20	12	10	56	43	52
4 Derby	42	19	12	11	77	57	50
5 Wolves	42	19	9	14	83	70	47
6 Aston Villa	42	19	9	14	65	57	47
7 PRESTON	42	20	7	15	67	68	47
8 Portsmouth	42	19	7	16	68	50	45
9 Blackpool	42	17	10	15	57	41	44
10 Man City	42	15	12	15	52	47	42
11 Liverpool	42	16	10	16	65	61	42
12 Sheffield United	42	16	10	16	65	70	42
13 Charlton	42	17	6	19	57	66	40
14 Everton	42	17	6	19	52	66	40
15 Stoke	42	14	10	18	41	55	38
16 Middlesbrough	42	14	9	19	71	73	37
17 Bolton	42	16	5	21	46	58	37
18 Chelsea	42	14	9	19	53	71	37
19 Huddersfield	42	12	12	18	51	60	36
20 Sunderland	42	13	10	19	56	67	36
21 Blackburn	42	11	10	21	54	72	32
22 Grimsby	42	8	6	28	45	111	22

STAT FACTS:

Best home run without defeat: 8 games – Best away run without defeat: 3 games
Longest run unbeaten: 7 games – Longest run without a win: 6 games
Best home attendance: 40,040 *vs.* Arsenal 13.9.47
Worst home attendance: 18,771 *vs.* Sheff.Utd. 7.4.48
Best away attendance: 74,243 *vs.* Manchester United at Maine Road
in the FA Cup 28.2.48
Worst away attendance: 17,915 *vs.* Grimsby 18.10.47
Aggregate and average home attendance: 637,403 – 30,352
Aggregate and average away attendance: 808,769 – 38,513

League position in Division One: 7th – P42 W20 D7 L15 F67 A68 Pts 47
Home: W13 D4 L4 F43 A35 Away: W7 D3 L11 F24 A33

Date 1947-8	Opponents	Comp	h or a	Score	Att.	1	2	3	4	5	6	7	8	9	10	11		
Aug 23	Liverpool	Div 1	a	1-3	49353	Gooch	Gray	Scott	Shankly	Williams	Horton	Finney	McLaren	McIntosh (1)	Beattie	Calverley		
Aug 25	Bolton W.	Div 1	h	1-0	33901	Gooch	Gray	Scott	Shankly	Williams	Horton	Finney	McLaren	McIntosh	Beattie (1)	Calverley		
Aug 30	Middlesbrough	Div 1	h	2-1	31326	Gooch	Gray	Scott	Shankly	Williams	Horton	Finney (1)	McLaren	McIntosh (1)	Beattie	Calverley		
Sep 1	Bolton W.	Div 1	a	2-1	31867	Gooch	Gray	Scott	Shankly	Williams	Horton	Finney	McLaren (1)	McIntosh (1)	Beattie	Calverley		
Sep 6	Charlton Ath.	Div 1	a	2-1	29633	Gooch	Gray	Robertson	Shankly	Williams	Horton	Finney	McLaren	McIntosh (2)	Beattie	Calverley		
Sep 8	Stoke City	Div 1	h	1-0	26814	Gooch	Gray	Robertson	Shankly	Williams	Horton	Finney	McLaren (1)	McIntosh	Beattie	Calverley		
Sep 13	Arsenal	Div 1	h	0-0	40040	Gooch	Gray	Scott	Shankly	Williams	Horton	Finney	McLaren	McIntosh	Beattie	Calverley		
Sep 17	Stoke City	Div 1	a	2-1	29243	Gooch	Gray	Scott	Shankly	Williams	Horton	Finney (1)	McLaren	McIntosh (1)	Beattie	Calverley		
Sep 20	Sheffield Utd.	Div 1	a	1-3	36458	Gooch	Gray	Scott	Shankly (1p)	Williams	Horton	Anders	Garth	McIntosh	Beattie	Calverley		
Sep 27	Manchester Utd.	Div 1	h	2-1	34372	Gooch	Gray	Scott	Shankly	Williams	Horton	Finney	McLaren (1)	McIntosh	Beattie (1)	Calverley		
Oct 4	Blackburn R.	Div 1	a	3-2	46874	Gooch	Gray	Scott	Shankly (1p)	Williams	Horton	Finney (1)	McLaren (1)	McIntosh	Beattie	Calverley		
Oct 11	Manchester City	Div 1	h	2-1	35947	Gooch	Gray	Scott	Shankly (1p)	Williams	Horton	Finney	McLaren (1)	McIntosh	Beattie	Calverley		
Oct 18	Grimsby Town	Div 1	a	1-1	17915	Gooch	Gray	Scott	Shankly	Williams	Horton	Anders	McLaren (1)	McIntosh	Beattie	Calverley		
Oct 25	Sunderland	Div 1	h	2-2	31595	Gooch	Gray	Scott	Shankly	Williams	Horton	Finney	McLaren	McIntosh (1)	Beattie (1)	Anders		
Nov 1	Aston Villa	Div 1	a	1-4	51362	Gooch	Gray	Scott	Shankly	Williams	Horton	Finney (1)	McLaren	McIntosh	Beattie	Anders		
Nov 8	Chelsea	Div 1	h	2-0	31986	Gooch	Gray	Scott	Shankly (1p)	Williams	Horton	Finney (1)	McLaren	McIntosh	Beattie	Anders		
Nov 15	Huddersfield T.	Div 1	a	0-1	27506	Gooch	Gray	Scott	Shankly	Williams	Horton	Finney	McLaren	McIntosh	Beattie	Anders		
Nov 22	Wolverhampton W.	Div 1	h	1-3	28099	Gooch	Gray	Scott	Shankly	Williams	Horton	Finney	McLaren	McIntosh (1)	Beattie	Anders		
Nov 29	Everton	Div 1	a	1-2	44884	Gooch	Gray	Robertson	Shankly	Williams	Horton	Finney (1)	Beattie	McIntosh	McLaren	Anders		
Dec 6	Derby County	Div 1	h	7-4	28924	Gooch	Gray	Robertson	Shankly (2,1p)	Williams	Horton	Finney	Beattie (1)	McIntosh (2)	McLaren (2)	Anders		
Dec 13	Blackpool	Div 1	a	1-0	29587	Gooch	Gray	Robertson	Shankly	Williams	Horton	Finney	Beattie	McIntosh (1)	McLaren	Anders		
Dec 20	Liverpool	Div 1	h	3-3	30452	Gooch	Gray	Robertson	Shankly	Williams	Horton	Finney	Beattie	McIntosh (2)	McLaren (1)	Anders		
Dec 25	Burnley	Div 1	h	0-1	44645	Gooch	Gray	Scott	Shankly	Williams	Horton	Anders	Beattie	McIntosh	McLaren	McClure		
Dec 26	Burnley	Div 1	h	3-2	39400	Gooch	Gray	Scott	Shankly	Williams	Horton	Finney	Garth	Jackson (1)	McLaren (2)	Anders		
Jan 3	Middlesbrough	Div 1	a	1-1	37375	Gooch	Gray	Scott	Shankly	Williams	Horton	Finney (1)	Beattie	Jackson	McLaren	Anders		
Jan 10	Millwall Rd 3	FAC	a	2-1	28418	Gooch	Gray	Scott	Shankly	Williams	Horton	Finney	Beattie	McIntosh	McLaren (1)	Anders (1)		
Jan 17	Charlton Ath.	Div 1	a	2-1	28096	Gooch	Gray	Scott	Shankly	Williams	Horton	Finney (2)	Beattie	McIntosh	McLaren	Anders		
Jan 24	Portsmouth Rd 4	FAC	a	3-1	41798	Gooch	Gray	Scott	Shankly (1p)	Williams	Horton	Finney (1)	Beattie	McIntosh (1)	McLaren	Anders		
Jan 31	Arsenal	Div 1	a	0-3	63162	Gooch	Gray	Scott	Shankly	Williams	Horton	Finney	Beattie	McIntosh	McLaren	Anders		
Feb 7	Manchester City Rd 5	FAC	a	1-0	67494	Gooch	Gray	Scott	Shankly	Williams	Horton	Finney	Beattie	McIntosh (1)	McLaren	Anders		
Feb 14	Manchester Utd.	Div 1	a	1-1	64902	Gooch	Gray	Scott	Shankly	Waters	Horton	Anders	Beattie	McIntosh	McLaren (1)	Jackson		
Feb 21	Blackburn R.	Div 1	h	2-1	31735	Gooch	Gray	Scott	Brown	Williams	Horton	Finney (1p)	Beattie	McIntosh	McLaren (1)	Jackson		
Feb 28	Manchester Utd. * Rd 6	FAC	a	1-4	74243	Hindle	Gray	Scott	Shankly	Waters	Horton	Finney	Beattie	McIntosh (1)	McLaren	Anders		
Mar 6	Grimsby Town	Div 1	h	2-1	25534	Hindle	Gray	Scott	Shankly	Waters	Horton	Finney	Beattie (1)	Jackson (1)	McLaren	Wilson		
Mar 13	Sunderland	Div 1	a	2-0	45920	Hall	Gray	Walton	Horton	Waters	Dougall	Finney	McLaren (1)	Jackson (1)	Hannah	McClure		
Mar 20	Aston Villa	Div 1	h	3-0	28001	Gooch	Gray	Walton	Horton	Waters	Dougall	Anders	McLaren (1)	Jackson	Hannah (1)	McClure (1)		
Mar 26	Portsmouth	Div 1	h	0-1	34913	Gooch	Gray	Walton	Shankly	Waters	Dougall	McIntosh	McLaren	Jackson	Hannah	McClure		
Mar 27	Chelsea	Div 1	a	0-2	55651	Hall	Gray	Walton	Horton	Waters	Dougall	McIntosh	McLaren	Jackson	Hannah	McClure		
Mar 29	Portsmouth	Div 1	a	1-2	31688	Hall	Gray	Walton	Horton	Waters	Dougall	Finney	McLaren (1)	Jackson	Hannah	McClure		
Apr 3	Huddersfield T.	Div 1	h	0-2	27648	Gooch	Walton	Scott	Horton	Waters	Shankly	Finney	McLaren	Jackson	Beattie	McClure		
Apr 7	Sheffield Utd.	Div 1	h	3-3	18771	Gooch	Walton (1p)	Scott	Horton	Waters	Dougall	Anders	McLaren (1)	McIntosh (1)	Hannah	McClure		
Apr 10	Wolverhampton W.	Div 1	a	2-4	29550	Gooch	Walton	Scott	Horton	Williams	Shankly	Anders	McLaren	McIntosh	Hannah (1)	Wilson (1)		
Apr 17	Everton	Div 1	h	3-0	25035	Hall	Walton (1p)	Scott	Horton	Waters	Dougall	Finney	McLaren	McIntosh	Hannah (1)	McClure (1)	1 o.g.	(Jones)
Apr 21	Manchester City	Div 1	a	3-0	20902	Hall	Walton	Scott	Horton	Waters	Dougall	Finney (2)	McLaren	McIntosh	Hannah	McClure		
Apr 24	Derby County	Div 1	a	1-2	19496	Hall	Gray	Scott	Horton	Waters	Dougall	Finney (1)	McLaren	McIntosh	Hannah	McClure		
May 1	Blackpool	Div 1	h	0-7	26610	Hall	Walton	Scott	Horton	Waters	Dougall	Finney	McLaren	Jackson	Hannah	McClure		
	* Played at Maine Rd																	

Braziers and straw used to prevent the pitch from icing up.

The first post-war relegation season and a very disappointing one indeed. Tom Finney was out of the side with injuries for long spells and as a result the whole team suffered. Confidence was missing as another influential player ended his playing days at Deepdale. Bill Shankly, one of North End's favourite sons left the club to join Carlisle. Sadly he went with a slightly bitter taste in his mouth as he felt he had been let down by the Preston management over his registration as a player which prevented him taking on a player/manager's role. Having said that, the loss of Shankly was only part of North End's problem. Most of the trouble stemmed from the side's defending, or lack of it, but there was also a period in mid season when the goals dried up at the other end as well. As always though there were some positive things to be taken from the season. The signing of Bobby Langton was a good one and the former Blackburn winger ended the year as top scorer. Joe Walton, Andy Beattie and Ken Horton all showed good form and Angus Morrison, another new signing, also impressed. The goalkeeping position was shared by Malcolm Newlands and Jimmy Gooch and both players had good and bad days. As a team though, Preston always struggled and there were several heavy defeats. The away form was particularly poor and when North End sold Andy McLaren to Burnley that was about as much as the fans could take. The one exception to their dismal away performances came with a 5–2 win at Newcastle, watched by 63,549. That crowd emphasised yet again the magnificent attendances across the country. This really was the boom era of the game and many of the legends of the game were cementing their names in history during this exciting time. Unfortunately Preston's fortunes plummeted during the season and the fans were looking to the FA Cup to bring some much needed cheer. But this brought little relief as the club were knocked out in the fourth round by Second Division Leicester City. The league form continued to cause concern and in the end Preston could muster just 33 points, level with Sheffield United and one below Huddersfield, who, ironically, Preston had achieved a league double over. So, relegation was the final outcome, and as in other relegation seasons, before and since, the phrase 'if only …' regularly springs to mind. All in all the fans endured a depressing year of soccer action at Deepdale.

DEBUTANTS: (10) William Corbett, Jim Davie, Bobby Langton, Malcolm Newlands, Tom Bogan, Angus Morrison, Eddy Brown, Jackie Knight, Len Kane, Harry Mattinson.

LAST GAMES: (7) Corbett, Bogan, McIntosh, Dougall, McLaren, Shankly and Jackson.

Future Players born between August 1948 and May 1949: Les Chapman, David Hughes, Francis Burns, Alan Tarbuck, Frank Worthington, Alan Gowling, Ricky Heppolette

Ever presents: None **FA Cup:** Fourth Round
Hat-tricks: (1) Bobbie Beattie **Manager:** Committee led by J. I. Taylor
Leading scorer: 12 goals – Bobby Langton (all league) **Chairman:** J. I. Taylor
Players used: 26 AUTHORS' UNOFFICIAL PLAYER OF THE SEASON: Joe Walton

League appearances (42 games)

Anders H. 15, Beattie R. 37, Bogan T. 11, Brown E. 7, Brown W. F. 28, Corbett W. R. 19, Davie J. G. 18, Dougall W. 12, Finney T. 24, Gooch J. A. G. 16, Hannah W. K. 3, Horton J. K. 27, Jackson H. 6, Kane L. R. 2, Knight J. 16, Langton R. 39, McIntosh W. D. 17, McLaren A. 14, Mattinson H. 2, Morrison A. C. 19, Newlands M. 26, Robertson W. J. T. 20, Scott W. J. 19, Shankly W. 6, Walton J. 38, Waters P. M. 21.

FA Cup appearances (2 games):

Walton 2, Horton 2, Finney 2, Beattie 2, Langton 2, Newlands 2, W Brown 2, Waters 2, Morrison 2, Knight 2, Robertson 2.

Goalscorers: 62 League–2 Cup–(Total 64)

Langton 12 (4 pens)–0 (12), Beattie 10–0 (10), Finney 7 (1 pen)–2 (1 pen) (9), Morrison 8–0 (8), McLaren 7–0 (7), McIntosh 5–0 (5), Knight 4–0 (4), Anders 2–0 (2), Brown E. 2–0 (2), Dougall 2–0 (2), Jackson 2–0 (2), Hannah 1–0 (1)

League position in Division One: 21st (Relegated) – P42 W11 D11 L20 F62 A75 Pts 33
Home: W8 D6 L7 F36 A36 Away: W3 D5 L13 F26 A39

Match Report: Class Tells in Away Romp –
28 Aug 1948 Newcastle 2 Preston 5

Newcastle's new £20,000 signing, George Lowrie, a pre-war ex-North Ender, was out injured for this early season contest. United won the toss and attacked down wind. As expected there was a lot of noise from the huge Tyneside crowd, but in the very early exchanges there was nothing really worth shouting about. Preston's defence had a shock after seven minutes when Donaldson evaded Corbett and beat Newlands with a fine strike. Undismayed North End crept back into the game with Bobbie Beattie showing his class in the art of using the ball to his advantage. He was even involved in the Preston equaliser on 13 minutes. Gaining possession of the ball he put over a deep backward centre from the bye-line to see McIntosh meet it and gleefully beat another ex-North Ender, Fairbrother, in the Newcastle goal. McLaren and Finney, a very useful partnership, started to trouble the home defence with Finney's control and crafty, deceptive movement especially appealing to the appreciative crowd. Preston were commanding the game and it was not too surprising when sustained pressure yielded a second goal. Finney dropped a corner kick menacingly into the danger area where McLaren, not the tallest of forwards, timed his run to perfection to glide a header wide of the goalkeeper. As Preston continued to press forward it became inevitable that United would concede another goal, which they did, on 42 minutes. Davie, Beattie and McIntosh toyed with United and when their defenders were drawn out of position McLaren slotted into the gap, received a pass and scored at will. Poor Newcastle's mighty crowd, exuberant at the start, but now disconsolate, must have longed for the same shrewd, purposeful, balanced touches in attack that they were seeing from a Preston vanguard inspired by Finney. On 55 minutes the lead was extended to three goals as Fairbrother could only parry McLaren's shot to McIntosh who was in the right place at the right time to score. United came back briefly to raise flagging spirits and pulled a goal back on 64 minutes through Stobbart. But the game's last goal fittingly fell to Preston and to Finney with 15 minutes remaining. Newcastle fans, spoonfed with good football in the past, appreciated the finer arts of the game which Preston dished out on this particular day.

Left to right: *Back row*: Horton, Walton, Newlands, Mr J. Metcalf (team supervisor), Scott, Garvie. *Front row*: Anders, McLaren, Jackson, Beattie, Langton, Corbett.

North End Squad at their hotel prior to the 4th round FA Cup tie at Leicester.

Season 1948–49: First Division

	P	W	D	L	F	A	Pts
1 Portsmouth	42	25	8	9	84	42	58
2 Man United	42	21	11	10	77	44	53
3 Derby	42	22	9	11	74	55	53
4 Newcastle	42	20	12	10	70	56	52
5 Arsenal	42	18	13	11	74	44	49
6 Wolves	42	17	12	13	79	66	46
7 Man City	42	15	15	12	47	51	45
8 Sunderland	42	13	17	12	49	58	43
9 Charlton	42	15	12	15	63	67	42
10 Aston Villa	42	16	10	16	60	76	42
11 Stoke	42	16	9	17	66	68	41
12 Liverpool	42	13	14	15	53	43	40
13 Chelsea	42	12	14	16	69	68	38
14 Bolton	42	14	10	18	59	68	38
15 Burnley	42	12	14	16	43	50	38
16 Blackpool	42	11	16	15	54	67	38
17 Birmingham	42	11	15	16	36	38	37
18 Everton	42	13	11	18	41	63	37
19 Middlesbrough	42	11	12	19	46	57	34
20 Huddersfield	42	12	10	20	40	69	34
21 PRESTON	**42**	**11**	**11**	**20**	**62**	**75**	**33**
22 Sheffield United	42	11	11	20	57	78	33

Date 1948-9	Opponents	Comp	h or a	Score	Att.	1	2	3	4	5	6	7	8	9	10	11
Aug 21	Portsmouth	Div 1	h	2-2	37062	Gooch	Walton	Scott	Horton	Corbett	Davie	Finney (1p)	Dougall (1)	McIntosh	Beattie	Langton
Aug 25	Manchester City	Div 1	a	2-3	39024	Gooch	Walton	Scott	Horton	Corbett	Davie	Finney	McLaren	Jackson (1)	Beattie	Langton (1)
Aug 28	Newcastle Utd	Div 1	a	5-2	63549	Newlands	Walton	Scott	Horton	Corbett	Davie	Finney (1)	McLaren (2)	Mcintosh (2)	Beattie	Langton
Sep 1	Manchester City	Div 1	h	1-3	38700	Newlands	Walton	Scott	Horton	Corbett	Davie	Finney	McLaren (1)	McIntosh	Beattie	Langton
Sep 4	Middlesbrough	Div 1	h	6-1	36468	Newlands	W Brown	Walton	Horton	Corbett	Davie	Finney	McLaren (1)	Jackson (1)	Beattie (3)	Langton (1)
Sep 6	Burnley	Div 1	a	0-1	35665	Newlands	W Brown	Walton	Horton	Corbett	Davie	Anders	McLaren	Jackson	Beattie	Langton
Sep 11	Birmingham City	Div 1	a	0-1	43499	Newlands	Walton	Scott	Horton	Corbett	Davie	Anders	McLaren	Jackson	Beattie	Langton
Sep 15	Burnley	Div 1	h	0-3	33032	Newlands	Walton	Scott	Horton	Corbett	Davie	Anders	McLaren	McIntosh	Beattie	Langton
Sep 18	Chelsea	Div 1	h	3-2	32164	Newlands	Walton	Scott	Horton	Waters	Davie	Finney	McLaren (1)	McIntosh (1)	Beattie (1)	Langton
Sep 25	Everton	Div 1	a	1-4	48674	Newlands	Walton	Scott	Horton	Waters	Davie	McIntosh	McLaren (1)	Jackson	Beattie	Anders
Oct 2	Blackpool	Div 1	h	1-3	38280	Newlands	Walton	Scott	Horton	Corbett	Davie	Bogan	McLaren	McIntosh (1)	Beattie	Langton
Oct 9	Derby County	Div 1	a	0-1	31195	Newlands	W Brown	Scott	Horton	Corbett	Davie	Anders	Bogan	McIntosh	McLaren	Langton
Oct 16	Arsenal	Div 1	h	1-1	31476	Newlands	W Brown	Scott	Horton	Corbett	Davie	Bogan	McLaren	McIntosh (1)	Beattie	Langton
Oct 23	Huddersfield T.	Div 1	a	2-0	20819	Newlands	W Brown	Scott	Shankly	Corbett	Horton	Bogan	McLaren (1)	McIntosh	Beattie (1)	Langton
Oct 30	Manchester Utd	Div 1	h	1-6	37372	Newlands	W Brown	Scott	Shankly	Corbett	Horton	Bogan	McLaren	McIntosh	Beattie (1)	Langton
Nov 6	Sheffield Utd	Div 1	a	2-3	38509	Newlands	Walton	Scott	Horton	Corbett	Davie	Finney	Beattie (1)	McIntosh	Hannah (1)	Langton
Nov 13	Aston Villa	Div 1	h	0-1	22289	Newlands	Walton	Scott	Horton	Corbett	Davie	Finney	Bogan	McIntosh	Beattie	Langton
Nov 20	Sunderland	Div 1	a	0-0	37683	Newlands	Walton	Scott	W.Brown	Corbett	Dougall	E.Brown	Beattie	McIntosh	Knight	Langton
Nov 27	Wolverhampton W	Div 1	h	1-1	30064	Newlands	Walton	Scott	W.Brown	Corbett	Dougall	McIntosh	Beattie	Morrison	Hannah	Langton (1)
Dec 4	Bolton W	Div 1	a	3-5	40140	Newlands	Walton	Scott	W.Brown	Corbett	Dougall	McIntosh	Knight (1)	Morrison (2)	Hannah	Langton
Dec 11	Liverpool	Div 1	h	3-2	29257	Newlands	Walton	Kane	Davie	Waters	Dougall	Bogan	E.Brown	Morrison (2)	Knight (1)	Langton
Dec 18	Portsmouth	Div 1	a	1-3	26545	Newlands	Walton	Kane	Davie	Waters	Dougall	E.Brown (1)	Knight	McIntosh	Jackson	Langton
Dec 25	Charlton Ath	Div 1	a	0-0	28119	Newlands	W Brown	Walton	Horton	Waters	Robertson	Bogan	Beattie	Morrison	Knight	Langton
Dec 27	Charlton Ath	Div 1	h	2-3	34708	Newlands	W Brown	Walton	Horton	Waters	Robertson	Bogan	Beattie	Morrison (2)	Knight	Langton
Jan 1	Newcastle Utd	Div 1	h	2-1	39428	Newlands	W Brown	Walton	Horton	Waters	Robertson	Finney	Beattie	Morrison	Knight	Langton (2)
Jan 8	**Mansfield Town** Rd 3	**FAC**	**h**	**2-1**	**32985**	**Newlands**	**W Brown**	**Walton**	**Horton**	**Waters**	**Robertson**	**Finney (2, 1p)**	**Beattie**	**Morrison**	**Knight**	**Langton**
Jan 15	Middlesbrough	Div 1	a	0-1	37702	Newlands	W Brown	Walton	Horton	Waters	Robertson	Finney	Beattie	Morrison	Knight	Anders
Jan 22	Birmingham City	Div 1	h	0-0	31894	Newlands	W Brown	Walton	Horton	Waters	Robertson	Finney	Morrison	E.Brown	Knight	Langton
Jan 29	**Leicester City** Rd 4	**FAC**	**a**	**0-2**	**37775**	**Newlands**	**W Brown**	**Walton**	**Horton**	**Waters**	**Robertson**	**Finney**	**Beattie**	**Morrison**	**Knight**	**Langton**
Feb 5	Chelsea	Div 1	a	3-5	41483	Gooch	Walton	Scott	Shankly	Corbett	Robertson	Anders (1)	Beattie	Morrison	Knight	Langton (2)
Feb 19	Everton	Div 1	h	3-1	35496	Gooch	W Brown	Walton	Horton	Waters	Robertson	Finney (1)	Beattie	Morrison (1)	Knight (1)	Langton
Feb 26	Blackpool	Div 1	a	2-2	27487	Gooch	W Brown	Walton	Horton	Waters	Robertson	Finney	Beattie (1)	Morrison	Knight	Langton (1)
Mar 5	Derby County	Div 1	h	0-0	22261	Gooch	W Brown	Walton	Shankly	Waters	Robertson	Finney	Beattie	Morrison	Knight	Anders
Mar 12	Arsenal	Div 1	a	0-0	54977	Gooch	W Brown	Walton	Shankly	Waters	Robertson	Finney	Beattie	Morrison	Knight	Langton
Mar 19	Sunderland	Div 1	h	1-3	34195	Gooch	W Brown	Walton	Shankly	Waters	Robertson	Finney	Beattie	Morrison	Knight	Langton (1p)
Apr 2	Sheffield Utd	Div 1	h	4-1	31404	Gooch	W Brown	Walton	Robertson	Waters	Dougall (1)	Bogan	Finney (1)	Morrison (1)	Beattie	Langton (1p)
Apr 9	Aston Villa	Div 1	a	0-2	37526	Gooch	W Brown	Walton	Robertson	Mattinson	Dougall	Bogan	Beattie	Morrison	Horton	Langton
Apr 15	Stoke City	Div 1	h	2-1	32548	Gooch	W Brown	Walton	Robertson	Mattinson	Dougall	Anders (1)	Beattie	Morrison	Finney (1)	Langton
Apr 16	Huddersfield T.	Div 1	h	2-0	36153	Gooch	W Brown	Walton	Horton	Waters	Robertson	Anders	Beattie (1)	Morrison	Finney	Langton (1p)
Apr 18	Stoke City	Div 1	a	0-2	22963	Gooch	W Brown	Walton	Horton	Waters	Robertson	Anders	Beattie	Morrison	Finney	Langton
Apr 23	Manchester Utd	Div 1	a	2-2	46086	Gooch	W Brown	Walton	Robertson	Waters	Dougall	Anders	Beattie	E.Brown (1)	Finney (1)	Langton
Apr 30	Bolton W	Div 1	h	1-1	33495	Gooch	W Brown	Walton	Robertson	Waters	Dougall	Anders	Beattie (1)	E.Brown	Finney	Langton
May 2	Wolverhampton W	Div 1	a	1-2	54425	Gooch	W Brown	Walton	Robertson	Waters	Dougall	Anders	Beattie	E.Brown	Knight	Langton (1p)
May 7	Liverpool	Div 1	a	2-0	31937	Newlands	W Brown	Walton	Robertson	Waters	Davie	Anders	Beattie	Langton	Knight (1)	Finney (1)

SEASON 1949–1950

This was North End's first season in the Second division since the 1933–34 season when they won promotion with Grimsby. Sadly it was another indifferent year for the club and promotion this time was never on. Too many games were lost and too few goals were scored. It was an altogether difficult year, with visits to some of football's far flung outposts, hard to accept for a generation of Preston fans brought up on top games at the top grounds. Some progress was made however, and the club brought in some excellent signings. The fans had their first view of Willie Cunningham and other quality players, Willie Forbes, Tommy Docherty and Eddie Quigley joined the Deepdale ranks. Bobby Langton did leave in the November and that was as a direct result of Preston's relegation. Tom Finney though continued to delight and the crowds flocked to see the Preston plumber wherever he played. He did not disappoint them and it was also very pleasing to see that he only missed five games all season. North End's home form was fairly good but away from home they were not as sharp and this contributed to the lack of a serious challenge on promotion. Some consolation came with an Easter double over local rivals Blackburn in front of a combined attendance of over 70,000. Apart from Finney, Paddy Waters had a solid season as did Joe Walton and Ken Horton, and Eddy Brown did well in attack, ending the season as leading scorer. And during September and October, Angus Morrison, then playing centre-forward, achieved an unusual feat as he scored in six consecutive league games. Unbelievably though he never managed another goal all season! This was the boom time of the English game as the crowds packed the stadia up and down the country and it became known as the Golden Age of Football. At Christmas 1949 for instance almost 40,000 watched Preston's game with Sheffield United at Deepdale on Boxing Day, whilst over 50,000 turned up at Bramall Lane for the return fixture the next day. Incredible. On the down side, once again it was a disappointing FA Cup campaign as North End again lost to a club from a lower division, this time Watford from Division Three after a replay at Deepdale. In the league, Preston failed to score in too many games and it cost Preston dearly, but at least they could be satisfied with a place in the top six … just!

DEBUTANTS: (6) Willie Cunningham, Fred Ramscar, Eddie Quigley, Tommy Docherty, Willie Forbes, John Garvie.

LAST GAMES: (8) Jim Davie, Bobby Langton, Jackie Knight, Len Kane, John Garvie, William Brown, Paddy Waters and Willie Hannah.

Future Players born between August 1949 and May 1950: Norman Lloyd, Alex Spark, Tommy Booth, John McMahon, Eric Potts.

Ever presents: None   FA Cup: Third Round Replay

Hat-tricks: None   Manager: Will Scott   Chairman: N. Buck Esq.

Leading scorer: 13 goals – Eddy Brown (12 league 1 FA Cup)   Players used: 25

AUTHORS' UNOFFICIAL PLAYER OF THE SEASON: Tom Finney

League appearances (42 games)

Anders H. 19, Beattie R. 14, Brown E. 24, Brown W. F. 3, Cunningham W. C. 30, Davie J. G. 10, Docherty T. H. 15, Finney T. 37, Forbes W. 16, Garvie J. 5, Gooch J. A. G. 23, Hannah W. K. 1, Horton J. K. 31, Kane L. R. 3, Knight J. 23, Langton R. 16, Mattinson H. 12, Morrison A. C. 23, Newlands M. 19, Quigley E. 20, Ramscar F. T. 14, Robertson W. T. J. 24, Scott W. J. 18, Walton J. 32, Waters P. M. 30.

FA Cup appearances (2 games)

Newlands 2, Walton 1, Horton 2, Waters 2, Finney 1, Knight 2, Cunningham 2, Robertson 1, E Brown 2, Ramscar 2, Quigley 2, Docherty 1, Forbes 2.

Goalscorers: 60 League–2 Cup–Total 62)

E Brown 12–1 (13), Finney 10 (2 pens)–1 (pen) (11), Morrison 9–0 (9), Horton 6–0 (6), Beattie 5–0 (5), Quigley 5–0 (5), Knight 3–0 (3), Ramscar 3–0 (3), Langton 2 (2 pens)–0 (2), Cunningham 1–0 (1), Anders 1–0 (1), *Own goals 3–0 (3)* (G. Mason, Coventry, Devlin, West Ham and Williams, Cardiff)

League position in Division Two: 6th – P42 W18 D9 L15 F60 A49 Pts 45
Home: W12 D5 L4 F37 A21 Away: W6 D4 L11 F23 A28

Below: Action against Coventry City 10 September, showing Garvie and Morrison ready to pounce.

Above: North End pictured using Whittingham Hospital's ground for training purposes. Angus Morrison prepares to kick-off.

Match Report: Finney's Friendly Hat-Trick – 11 Feb 1950 Dundee 2 Preston 6 (Friendly)

For this friendly match at Dens Park, Dundee, North End turned up with new Australian signing Joe Marston who watched the game from the stands. About 12,000 were present as the teams emerged onto the pitch with a score of schoolboy autograph hunters pursuing Tom Finney, only to be chased off by the police. Apart from back passes both goalkeepers, Newlands and Brown, were spectators during the first ten minutes. Preston were quicker at running into the open spaces to receive the ball but they didn't always part with it to their advantage. The Scots began to force the pace and after 14 minutes Dundee went in front as Paddy Waters, in attempting a backpass, beat his own goalkeeper. It was reported that at this stage right-winger Finney was the only forward to give Dundee any trouble. He beat the Canadian defender, Cowan, four times in as many seconds during one attack, only to shoot into the side-netting. The equaliser came on 24 minutes via Finney from the penalty spot after Cowie had fouled Eddy Brown. A second penalty was awarded soon afterwards when a shot from Court struck Joe Walton's arm. Preston protested in vain but Newlands saved Boyd's spot-kick in any case. Brown, who had been caught offside on numerous occasions successfully broke through on 39 minutes to give Preston a 2–1 half-time lead. Newlands was in fine form, saving low shots and cutting out high crosses as the Dundee pressure intensified. He was well guarded by Horton and Forbes. After an hour's play North End switched Brown and Finney around and almost immediately went close to scoring again. Brown dashed down the touchline and his cross was met by Robertson but Massie's last gasp clearance saved Dundee. Finney then showed his skills again on 68 minutes as he accepted a great pass from Robertson before dashing through to beat his marker and finish with a clinical shot. Within a minute Dundee pulled a goal back through Court but two goals in quick succession put Preston in command. Ramscar on 77 minutes and Finney, his third, seconds later made it 5–2. A late individual effort by Ramscar completed the scoring.

Season 1949–50: First Division

	P	W	D	L	F	A	Pts
1 Tottenham	42	27	7	8	81	35	61
2 Sheffield Wednesday	42	18	16	8	67	48	52
3 Sheffield United	42	19	14	9	68	49	52
4 Southampton	42	19	14	9	64	48	52
5 Leeds	42	17	13	12	54	45	47
6 PRESTON	42	18	9	15	60	49	45
7 Hull	42	17	11	14	64	72	45
8 Swansea	42	17	9	16	53	49	43
9 Brentford	42	15	13	14	44	49	43
10 Cardiff	42	16	10	16	41	44	42
11 Grimsby	42	16	8	18	74	73	40
12 Coventry	42	13	13	16	55	55	39
13 Barnsley	42	13	13	16	64	67	39
14 Chesterfield	42	15	9	18	43	47	39
15 Leicester	42	12	15	15	55	65	39
16 Blackburn	42	14	10	18	55	60	38
17 Luton	42	10	18	14	41	51	38
18 Bury	42	14	9	19	60	65	37
19 West Ham	42	12	12	18	53	61	36
20 QPR	42	11	12	19	40	57	34
21 Plymouth	42	8	16	18	44	65	32
22 Bradford PA	42	10	11	21	51	77	31

PRESTON NORTH END *v.* BLACKBURN ROVERS

at Deepdale, Easter Monday, April 10th, 1950

Photo.: *Lancashire Evening Post*

THE MAGNET.—Finney draws Eckersley, Horton and Holt

Date 1949-50	Opponents	Comp	h or a	Score	Att.	1	2	3	4	5	6	7	8	9	10	11		
Aug 20	Swansea Town	Div 2	a	1-2	26041	Newlands	W.Brown	Walton	Horton	Waters	Davie	Finney	Beattie	Morrison	Knight (1)	Langton		
Aug 24	Grimsby Town	Div 2	h	2-0	30935	Newlands	Walton	Cunningham	Horton	Waters	Davie	Finney (1)	Beattie	Morrison	Knight	Langton (1p)		
Aug 27	Leeds Utd.	Div 2	h	1-1	31378	Newlands	Walton	Cunningham	Horton	Waters	Davie	Anders	Finney (1)	Morrison	Knight	Langton		
Aug 31	Grimsby Town	Div 2	a	3-1	23421	Newlands	Walton	Cunningham	Robertson	Waters	Davie	Finney (1)	Garvie	Morrison (2)	Knight	Langton		
Sep 3	Southampton	Div 2	a	0-1	26317	Newlands	Walton	Cunningham	Robertson	Waters	Davie	Finney	Garvie	Morrison	Knight	Langton		
Sep 7	QPR	Div 2	a	0-0	20113	Gooch	Walton	Cunningham	Robertson	Waters	Davie	Finney	Garvie	Morrison	Knight	Langton		
Sep 10	Coventry City	Div 2	h	1-1	27384	Gooch	Walton	Cunningham	Robertson	Waters	Davie	Finney	Garvie	Morrison	Knight	Langton	1 og	(Mason)
Sep 14	QPR	Div 2	h	3-2	26515	Gooch	Walton	Cunningham	Robertson	Waters	Davie	Finney (1)	Horton (1)	Morrison (1)	Knight	Langton		
Sep 17	Luton Town	Div 2	a	1-1	20135	Gooch	Walton	Cunningham	W.Brown	Waters	Robertson	Finney	Horton	Morrison (1)	Knight	Langton		
Sep 24	Barnsley	Div 2	h	1-1	31633	Gooch	Walton	Cunningham	W.Brown	Waters	Robertson	Finney	Horton	Morrison (1)	Knight	Langton		
Oct 1	West Ham Utd.	Div 2	a	3-0	36653	Gooch	Walton	Cunningham	Davie	Waters	Robertson	Finney	Beattie (1)	Morrison (1)	Knight	Langton	1 og	(Devlin)
Oct 8	Brentford	Div 2	h	2-0	30178	Gooch	Walton	Cunningham	Davie	Waters	Robertson	Finney	Beattie	Morrison (1)	Knight	Langton (1p)		
Oct 15	Hull City	Div 2	a	2-4	46179	Gooch	Walton	Cunningham	Horton	Waters	Robertson	Garvie	Beattie	Morrison (2)	Knight	Langton		
Oct 22	Sheffield Wed.	Div 2	h	0-1	32569	Gooch	Walton	Cunningham	Horton	Waters	Robertson	Finney	Beattie	Morrison	Knight	Langton		
Oct 29	Plymouth Argyle	Div 2	a	0-1	29238	Gooch	Kane	Cunningham	Horton	Waters	Robertson	Finney	Beattie	E.Brown	Morrison	Langton		
Nov 5	Chesterfield	Div 2	h	0-0	29550	Gooch	Walton	Cunningham	Horton	Waters	Robertson	Finney	Ramscar	E.Brown	Knight	Langton		
Nov 12	Bradford P.A.	Div 2	h	2-1	14017	Gooch	Walton	Cunningham (1)	Horton	Waters	Robertson	Finney	Ramscar	E.Brown (1)	Knight	Morrison		
Nov 19	Leicester City	Div 2	h	2-1	28722	Gooch	Walton	Cunningham	Horton (1)	Waters	Robertson	Finney	Ramscar	Morrison	Knight (1)	Anders		
Nov 26	Bury	Div 2	a	1-1	30471	Gooch	Kane	Scott	Horton	Waters	Robertson	Finney	Ramscar	Morrison	Knight (1)	Anders		
Dec 3	Tottenham H.	Div 2	h	1-3	35501	Gooch	Kane	Scott	Horton	Waters	Robertson	Finney	Ramscar	E.Brown (1)	Knight	Morrison		
Dec 10	Cardiff City	Div 2	a	2-3	21922	Gooch	Walton	Cunningham	Horton	Waters	Robertson	Finney	Ramscar (2)	E.Brown	Knight	Anders		
Dec 17	Swansea Town	Div 2	h	2-1	28649	Gooch	Walton	Cunningham	Horton	Waters	Robertson	Finney (1)	Quigley	E.Brown (1)	Ramscar	Anders		
Dec 24	Leeds Utd.	Div 2	a	1-3	41303	Newlands	Walton	Cunningham	Horton	Waters	Robertson	Finney	Quigley (1)	E.Brown	Ramscar	Docherty		
Dec 26	Sheffield Utd.	Div 2	h	4-1	39878	Newlands	Walton	Cunningham	Horton	Waters	Robertson	Finney (1p)	Quigley (1)	E.Brown (2)	Ramscar	Docherty		
Dec 27	Sheffield Utd.	Div 2	a	0-1	50586	Newlands	Cunningham	Scott	Horton	Mattinson	Morrison	Finney	Quigley	E.Brown	Ramscar	Robertson		
Dec 31	Southampton	Div 2	h	0-3	33240	Newlands	Cunningham	Scott	Horton	Mattinson	Forbes	Finney	Quigley	E.Brown	Ramscar	Docherty		
Jan 7	Watford Rd 3	FAC	a	2-2	25087	Newlands	Robertson	Cunningham	Horton	Waters	Forbes	Finney (1p)	Quigley	E.Brown (1)	Ramscar	Knight		
Jan 11	Watford Replay	FAC	h	0-1	27386	Newlands	Walton	Cunningham	Horton	Waters	Forbes	Docherty	Quigley	E.Brown	Ramscar	Knight		
Jan 14	Coventry City	Div 2	a	0-0	21046	Newlands	Walton	Cunningham	Horton	Waters	Forbes	Docherty	Quigley	Morrison	Knight	Anders		
Jan 21	Luton Town	Div 2	h	0-1	23532	Newlands	Walton	Cunningham	Horton	Waters	Forbes	Finney	Ramscar	Morrison	Knight	Anders		
Feb 4	Barnsley	Div 2	a	1-0	23736	Newlands	Walton	Scott	Horton	Waters	Forbes	Finney	Quigley	E.Brown (1)	Beattie	Hannah		
Feb 18	West Ham Utd.	Div 2	h	2-1	26381	Newlands	Walton	Scott	Horton	Waters	Forbes	Finney	Quigley	E.Brown	Ramscar (1)	Anders		
Feb 25	Brentford	Div 2	a	0-1	25387	Newlands	Walton	Scott	Horton	Waters	Forbes	Finney	Quigley	E.Brown	Ramscar	Anders		
Mar 4	Hull City	Div 2	h	4-2	27745	Newlands	Walton	Scott	Docherty	Waters	Forbes	Finney (1)	Horton (2)	E.Brown (1)	Quigley	Anders		
Mar 11	Sheffield Wed.	Div 2	a	1-0	49222	Newlands	Walton	Scott	Docherty	Mattinson	Forbes	Finney (1)	Beattie	E.Brown	Quigley	Anders		
Mar 18	Plymouth Argyle	Div 2	h	0-0	20226	Newlands	Walton	Scott	Docherty	Mattinson	Forbes	Anders	Horton	E.Brown	Quigley	Robertson		
Mar 25	Chesterfield	Div 2	a	0-2	11230	Newlands	Walton	Scott	Docherty	Mattinson	Forbes	Knight	Horton	E.Brown	Quigley	Morrison		
Apr 1	Bury	Div 2	h	2-0	26445	Newlands	Walton	Scott	Docherty	Mattinson	Forbes	Finney	Horton (1)	E.Brown (1)	Quigley (1)	Anders		
Apr 7	Blackburn R.	Div 2	a	3-2	42891	Gooch	Walton	Scott	Docherty	Mattinson	Forbes	Finney	Beattie (1)	E.Brown (1)	Quigley	Anders		
Apr 8	Tottenham H.	Div 2	a	2-3	49710	Gooch	Cunningham	Scott	Docherty	Mattinson	Forbes	Finney (1p)	Horton	E.Brown	Quigley (1)	Anders		
Apr 10	Blackburn R.	Div 2	h	3-1	27925	Gooch	Cunningham	Scott	Docherty	Mattinson	Robertson	Finney	Beattie (2)	E.Brown	Quigley (1)	Anders		
Apr 15	Bradford P.A.	Div 2	h	3-0	19251	Gooch	Cunningham	Scott	Docherty	Mattinson	Forbes	Horton (1)	Beattie	E.Brown (2)	Quigley	Anders		
Apr 22	Leicester City	Div 2	a	0-1	29764	Gooch	Cunningham	Scott	Docherty	Mattinson	Forbes	Finney	Beattie	E.Brown	Quigley	Anders		
Apr 29	Cardiff City	Div 2	h	3-0	13799	Gooch	Cunningham	Scott	Docherty	Mattinson	Forbes	Finney (1)	Beattie	E.Brown	Quigley	Anders (1)	1 og	(Williams)

SEASON 1950–1951

Left to right: *Back row:*
J. Milne (Trainer),
Docherty, Newlands,
Mattinson, Forbes, Scott,
Waters, Mr Scott
(Manager). *Front row:*
Anders, Horton, Walton,
Wayman, Quigley, Morrison

A magnificent season winning the Division Two Championship and promotion back to Division One at the second attempt. However, there was little inkling of the excitement to come for the fans as Preston made a very poor start to the season. Just two wins in their first eight games and an away record that after ten games on opponents' grounds read P10 W2 D1 L7. But on Christmas Day a run was to begin that would set up a club record. Fourteen consecutive wins were registered as the team put together some superb performances, scoring goals seemingly at will. A goal ratio of 42 for and 10 against in this period showed the power of the Preston attack. The touch of masterstroke came with the signing by Will Scott of the Southampton centre-forward, Charlie Wayman. The pugnacious little striker had a superb season and was the perfect foil for the brilliant approach play Preston produced. In the end no fewer than 26 games were won and the goals flew in from all angles. So many players had outstanding seasons and it is difficult to select a player of the year. Tommy Docherty, Willie Forbes, Angus Morrison and Ken Horton were all magnificent and another player who joined the club at this time was Australian Joe Marston and he quickly won over the crowd once he established his position at centre-half. The crowds packed Deepdale to the rafters to see some magnificent football. And, of course, there was always the incomparable Tom Finney, who showed outstanding form, and his partnership on the right with Horton was devastating at times. With Bobbie Beattie and Morrison combining almost as effectively down the left it was no surprise that Wayman was fed an abundance of chances, the majority of which he put away. The fans were treated to some special performances, 5–1 *vs.* Swansea, 6–1 *vs.* Doncaster, 7–0 *vs.* Barnsley and 4–0 *vs.* Grimsby was just a sample of the action on offer. Wayman's four goal haul at QPR was another highlight and the hat-trick by Horton against Barnsley emphasised just what a fine year he had. It was not just about the attack though as the defenders played their part, with Willie Cunningham the pick at the back. A fourth round home defeat by Huddersfield in the FA Cup was disappointing but, in the time honoured tradition, it did allow Preston to concentrate on the league. The only other disappointing aspect of a super season came with the last game, away at Doncaster. Almost 30,000 turned up for what should have been a huge party to celebrate the winning of the Championship. Unfortunately the visitors forgot to play their part and lost 2–0! It was also interesting to note that only 18 players were used, a very low total and often symptomatic of success.

DEBUTANTS: (2) Charlie Wayman, Joe Marston

LAST GAMES: (2) Eddy Brown, Fred Ramscar

Future Players born between August 1950 and May 1951: Jim Arnold, Roger Davies, Ray Robinson, Alan Tinsley, Roy Tunks
Ever presents: (3) Tommy Docherty, Willie Forbes, Angus Morrison   **Players used:** 18
Hat-tricks: (3) Wayman (2), (4 goals *vs.* QPR) Horton.   **FA Cup:** Fourth Round   **Manager:** Will Scott
Leading scorer: 29 goals – Charlie Wayman (27 league 2 cup)   **Chairman:** N. Buck Esq.
AUTHORS' UNOFFICIAL PLAYER OF THE SEASON: Charlie Wayman

League position in Division Two: 1st (Champions) – P42 W26 D5 L11 F91 A49 Pts 57
Home: W16 D3 L2 F53 A18 Away: W10 D2 L9 F38 A31

Match Report: Quigley Double in Deepdale Defeat – 19 Aug 1950
Preston 2 Manchester City 4

North End put the town of Preston under a cloud of depression by losing their opening game of the season to Manchester City who were determined to bounce straight back to Division One after suffering relegation. The opening goal of the game came on nine minutes after some enterprising, but fluctuating play. A judicious pass by Docherty originated the move which was ended when Quigley was first to react to a pass from Anders. North End had not finished congratulating each other when City took advantage of some slack defending to equalise through Smith just thirty seconds later. Barely had the cheers died away when Gooch had to fling himself desperately at Hart's feet to avert a second goal. A crowd exceeding 36,000 saw a good game between well matched teams. Clarke, Oakes and Paul showed stylish touches whereas Smith was an active forager and Westcott a bustling leader. Walton, North End's captain, and Forbes were equal to City's forwards though and at the other end Brown tested Trautmann on more than one occasion. Both sides could have finished better but the season was young and players were not yet completely in tune. During the interval the crowd was entertained by a live brass band marching around the ground, a nice change after several years of broadcast music. Within thirty seconds of the restart North End restored their lead, again the marksman was Quigley. He resisted a tackle by Paul to shoot through after good approach work by Anders and Morrison. City then struck back more or less straight away, just as they had done in the first half, Westcott heading home from Oakes's corner as Gooch and Walton left the ball to each other. North End's defence was looking decidedly shaky under pressure as they showed on 56 minutes when they all stopped claiming offside whilst Smith ran on to shoot past Gooch. An anxious ten minute period followed as the visitors ran the game but Morrison gave Preston fans some hope of an equaliser with an excellent cross shot which unfortunately hit the far post. Preston were struggling now and became disheartened as their efforts continued to fail. Then, to cap it all, Clarke made it 2–4 late in the game.

Above: North End stop for a break on their bus trip to Scotland May 1951. Left to right: Paddy Waters, Joe Marston, Eddy Brown, Fred Ramscar, Willie Robertson, Malcolm Newlands, Willie Forbes, Jimmy Milne, Joe Walton, Tom Finney, Bill Scott, Angus Morrison, Ken Horton and Eddie Quigley.

Right: Pre-season jogging with Willie Robertson, Eddie Quigley, Ken Horton and Willie Forbes leading the way.

Trivia Facts:

Ken Horton's goal against Luton on October 7 1950 was North End's 3,000th league goal.

Preston set several records during 1950–51. Ten away wins was a new record, as was the season's total of 26 wins. The 14 wins in succession was not only a Preston record but it also equalled the Football League record. And finally, the 57 points was a new season's best.

STAT FACTS:

Best home run without defeat: 18 games
Best away run without defeat: 10 games
Longest run unbeaten: 20 games
Longest run without a win: 3 games
Best home attendance: 39,552 vs. Huddersfield FAC 21.1.51
Worst home attendance: 20,793 vs. Bury 23.8.50
Best away attendance: 44,612 vs. Blackburn 4.11.50
Worst away attendance: 15,568 vs. Chesterfield 11.9.50
Aggregate and average home attendance: 656,381 – 31,256
Aggregate and average away attendance: 594,055 – 28,288

League appearances (42 games)

Anders H. 6, Beattie R. 27, Brown E. 5, Cunningham W. C. 31, Docherty T. H. 42, Finney T. 34, Forbes W. 42, Gooch J. A. G. 27, Horton J. K. 37, Marston J. E. 19, Mattinson H. 28, Morrison A. C. 42, Newlands M. 15, Quigley E. 20, Ramscar F. T. 5, Scott W. J. 32, Walton J. 16, Wayman C. 34.

FA Cup appearances (2 games)

Gooch 2, Scott 2, Docherty 2, Mattinson 2, Forbes 2, Beattie 2, Morrison 2, Horton 2, Cunningham 2, Finney 2, Wayman 2.

Goalscorers: 91 League–3 Cup–(Total 94)

Wayman 27–2 (29), Horton 22–1 (23), Finney 13 (4 pens)–0 (13), Quigley 9–0 (9), Morrison 8–0 (8), Beattie 4–0 (4), Forbes 2–0 (2), Brown 2–0 (2), Ramscar 1–0 (1). Own Goals 3–0 (3) Kerfoot of Leeds, Lucas of Swansea and Bycroft of Doncaster.

Ken Horton.

Charlie Wayman.

Season 1950–51: Second Division

	P	W	D	L	F	A	Pts
1 PRESTON	42	26	5	11	91	49	57
2 Man City	42	19	14	9	89	61	52
3 Cardiff	42	17	16	9	53	45	50
4 Birmingham	42	20	9	13	64	53	49
5 Leeds	42	20	8	14	63	55	48
6 Blackbutn	42	19	8	15	65	66	46
7 Coventry	42	19	7	16	75	59	45
8 Sheffield United	42	16	12	14	72	62	44
9 Brentford	42	18	8	16	75	74	44
10 Hull	42	16	11	15	74	70	43
11 Doncaster	42	15	13	14	64	68	43
12 Southampton	42	15	13	14	66	73	43
13 West Ham	42	16	10	16	68	69	42
14 Leicester	42	15	11	16	68	58	41
15 Barnsley	42	15	10	17	74	68	40
16 QPR	42	15	10	17	71	82	40
17 Notts County	42	13	13	16	61	60	39
18 Swansea	42	16	4	22	54	77	36
19 Luton	42	9	14	19	57	70	32
20 Bury	42	12	8	22	60	86	32
21 Chesterfield	42	9	12	21	44	69	30
22 Grimsby	42	8	12	22	61	95	28

Date 1950-1	Opponents	Comp	h or a	Score	Att.	1	2	3	4	5	6	7	8	9	10	11		
Aug 19	Manchester City	Div 2	h	2-4	36294	Gooch	Walton	Scott	Docherty	Mattinson	Forbes	Anders	Beattie	Brown	Quigley (2)	Morrison		
Aug 23	Bury	Div 2	h	2-0	20793	Newlands	Walton	Scott	Docherty	Mattinson	Forbes	Horton	Beattie	Brown (1)	Quigley	Morrison (1)		
Aug 26	Coventry City	Div 2	a	0-1	24676	Newlands	Walton	Scott	Docherty	Mattinson	Forbes	Horton	Beattie	Brown	Quigley	Morrison		
Aug 30	Bury	Div 2	a	1-3	16558	Newlands	Walton	Cunningham	Docherty	Mattinson	Forbes	Horton	Ramscar	Brown (1)	Quigley	Morrison		
Sep 2	Cardiff City	Div 2	h	1-1	25900	Newlands	Cunningham	Walton	Docherty	Mattinson	Forbes	Horton	Ramscar	Brown	Quigley (1)	Morrison		
Sep 6	Chesterfield	Div 2	h	4-1	20896	Newlands	Cunningham	Walton	Docherty	Mattinson	Forbes	Finney	Horton (1)	Quigley (1)	Ramscar (1)	Morrison (1)		
Sep 9	Birmingham City	Div 2	h	0-1	32633	Newlands	Cunningham	Walton	Docherty	Mattinson	Forbes	Finney	Horton	Wayman	Quigley	Morrison		
Sep 11	Chesterfield	Div 2	a	0-2	15568	Newlands	Cunningham	Walton	Docherty	Mattinson	Forbes	Finney	Horton	Quigley	Ramscar	Morrison		
Sep 16	Grimsby Town	Div 2	h	2-0	26461	Newlands	Walton	Scott	Docherty	Mattinson	Forbes	Finney (1p)	Horton	Wayman	Quigley (1)	Morrison		
Sep 23	Notts County	Div 2	a	3-1	44277	Newlands	Walton	Scott	Docherty	Mattinson	Forbes	Finney	Horton	Wayman (1)	Quigley (1)	Morrison (1)		
Sep 30	Brentford	Div 2	h	4-2	29881	Newlands	Walton	Scott	Docherty	Mattinson	Forbes	Finney (1p)	Horton (1)	Wayman (2)	Quigley	Morrison		
Oct 7	Luton Town	Div 2	a	2-1	16637	Newlands	Walton	Scott	Docherty	Mattinson	Forbes	Anders	Horton (1)	Wayman (1)	Quigley	Morrison		
Oct 14	Leeds Utd.	Div 2	h	2-0	35578	Newlands	Walton	Scott	Docherty	Mattinson	Forbes	Finney	Horton	Wayman	Quigley (1)	Morrison	1 og	(Kerfoot)
Oct 21	Barnsley	Div 2	a	1-4	30081	Newlands	Marston	Walton	Docherty	Mattinson	Forbes	Finney	Horton (1)	Wayman	Quigley	Morrison		
Oct 28	Sheffield Utd.	Div 2	h	1-1	32628	Newlands	Marston	Walton	Docherty	Mattinson	Forbes	Finney (1p)	Quigley	Wayman	Horton	Morrison		
Nov 4	Blackburn R.	Div 2	a	1-2	44612	Newlands	Marston	Walton	Docherty	Mattinson	Forbes	Finney	Quigley (1)	Wayman	Morrison	Anders		
Nov 11	Southampton	Div 2	h	3-2	30939	Gooch	Marston	Cunningham	Docherty	Mattinson	Forbes	Finney	Quigley (1)	Wayman (2)	Morrison	Anders		
Nov 18	West Ham Utd.	Div 2	a	0-2	26360	Gooch	Marston	Cunningham	Docherty	Mattinson	Forbes	Finney	Quigley	Wayman	Ramscar	Morrison		
Nov 25	Swansea Town	Div 2	h	5-1	25898	Gooch	Cunningham	Scott	Docherty	Mattinson	Forbes	Finney (1p)	Horton (1)	Wayman (2)	Beattie	Morrison	1 og	(Lucas)
Dec 2	Hull City	Div 2	h	0-0	37269	Gooch	Cunningham	Scott	Docherty	Mattinson	Forbes	Finney	Horton	Wayman	Beattie	Morrison		
Dec 9	Doncaster R.	Div 2	h	6-1	27024	Gooch	Cunningham	Scott	Docherty	Mattinson	Forbes	Finney	Horton (2)	Wayman (2)	Beattie (1)	Morrison	1 og	(Bycroft)
Dec 16	Manchester City	Div 2	h	3-0	30512	Gooch	Cunningham	Scott	Docherty	Mattinson	Forbes	Finney (1)	Horton (1)	Wayman	Beattie	Morrison (1)		
Dec 23	Coventry City	Div 2	h	1-1	30031	Gooch	Cunningham	Scott	Docherty	Mattinson	Forbes	Finney	Horton (1)	Wayman	Beattie	Morrison		
Dec 25	QPR	Div 2	a	4-1	16881	Gooch	Cunningham	Scott	Docherty	Mattinson	Forbes	Finney	Horton	Wayman (4)	Beattie	Morrison		
Dec 26	QPR	Div 2	h	1-0	38993	Gooch	Cunningham	Scott	Docherty	Mattinson	Forbes	Finney	Horton	Wayman	Beattie	Morrison (1)		
Dec 30	Cardiff City	Div 2	h	2-0	26717	Gooch	Cunningham	Scott	Docherty	Mattinson	Forbes	Finney	Horton	Wayman (1)	Beattie	Morrison (1)		
Jan 6	**Leicester City Rd 3**	FAC	a	3-0	31078	Gooch	Cunningham	Scott	Docherty	Mattinson	Forbes	Finney	Horton (1)	Wayman (2)	Beattie	Morrison		
Jan 13	Birmingham City	Div 2	h	1-0	30622	Gooch	Cunningham	Scott	Docherty	Mattinson	Forbes	Finney	Horton	Wayman	Beattie (1)	Morrison		
Jan 20	Grimsby Town	Div 2	a	4-0	16836	Gooch	Cunningham	Scott	Docherty	Mattinson	Forbes	Finney	Horton	Wayman (3)	Beattie	Morrison		
Jan 27	**Huddersfield T. Rd 4**	FAC	h	0-2	39552	Gooch	Cunningham	Scott	Docherty	Mattinson	Forbes	Finney	Horton	Wayman	Beattie	Morrison		
Feb 3	Notts County	Div 2	h	3-1	35597	Gooch	Cunningham	Scott	Docherty	Marston	Forbes	Finney (1)	Horton	Wayman (1)	Beattie	Morrison (1)		
Feb 17	Brentford	Div 2	a	4-2	23434	Gooch	Cunningham	Scott	Docherty	Marston	Forbes	Finney (2)	Horton (2)	Wayman	Beattie	Morrison		
Feb 24	Luton Town	Div 2	h	1-0	31086	Gooch	Cunningham	Scott	Docherty	Marston	Forbes	Finney	Horton (1)	Wayman	Beattie	Morrison		
Mar 3	Leeds Utd.	Div 2	a	3-0	42114	Gooch	Cunningham	Scott	Docherty	Marston	Forbes	Finney (2)	Horton (1)	Wayman (1)	Beattie	Morrison		
Mar 10	Barnsley	Div 2	h	7-0	31184	Gooch	Cunningham	Scott	Docherty	Marston	Forbes	Finney	Horton (3)	Wayman (2)	Beattie	Morrison		
Mar 17	Sheffield Utd.	Div 2	a	3-2	31187	Gooch	Cunningham	Scott	Docherty	Marston	Forbes (1)	Finney	Horton (1)	Wayman (1)	Beattie	Morrison		
Mar 24	Blackburn R.	Div 2	h	3-0	39122	Gooch	Cunningham	Scott	Docherty	Marston	Forbes (1)	Finney	Horton	Wayman	Beattie (1)	Morrison		
Mar 26	Leicester City	Div 2	h	3-2	37581	Gooch	Cunningham	Scott	Docherty	Marston	Forbes	Finney (1)	Horton	Wayman (2)	Beattie	Morrison		
Mar 27	Leicester City	Div 2	a	3-2	37252	Gooch	Cunningham	Scott	Docherty	Marston	Forbes	Finney	Horton	Wayman	Beattie (1)	Morrison (1)		
Mar 31	Southampton	Div 2	a	3-3	27306	Gooch	Cunningham	Scott	Docherty	Marston	Forbes	Finney	Horton	Wayman	Beattie	Morrison		
Apr 7	West Ham Utd.	Div 2	h	0-1	32043	Gooch	Cunningham	Scott	Docherty	Marston	Forbes	Finney	Horton	Wayman	Beattie	Morrison		
Apr 14	Swansea Town	Div 2	a	1-2	23878	Gooch	Cunningham	Scott	Docherty	Marston	Forbes	Anders	Horton	Wayman (1)	Beattie	Morrison		
Apr 21	Hull City	Div 2	a	1-0	37827	Gooch	Cunningham	Scott	Docherty	Marston	Forbes	Finney (1)	Horton	Quigley	Beattie	Morrison		
Apr 26	Doncaster R.	Div 2	a	0-2	29327	Gooch	Cunningham	Scott	Docherty	Marston	Forbes	Anders	Quigley	Wayman	Beattie	Morrison		

SEASON 1951–1952

Promoted back to the First Division and a satisfactory season of consolidation for North End in the higher grade. The early part of the New Year unfortunately let them down somewhat as a run of 11 games without a win seriously affected their challenge on the Championship title. But apart from that the side acquitted itself well and produced some thrilling performances in front of packed stadia. A terrific September double over Blackpool was certainly a high spot with a superb 40,809 crowd attending the Deepdale clash. Two new players quickly settled into the side with Joe Dunn and Bobby Foster adding much to Preston's play. Charlie Wayman continued his fantastic scoring achievements and Angus Morrison also carried on his form from the previous season. In defence Willie Cunningham and Joe Marston were rock solid and Tommy Docherty was tigerish in midfield. Preston also had the mercurial Tom Finney. The wing wizard continued his apparently never ending superb form

and he was undoubtedly world class at this stage of his career. Preston were served well by all of these fine individual performers but as a whole the season was filled with 'if onlys'. Only the Champions and runners-up conceded less goals than Preston but the 12 draws were crucial in the final analysis and if North End could have turned a few of those into wins then they would have put more pressure on the leading teams. Ironically Preston beat eventual Champions, Manchester United on their own ground, and took three points off third place Arsenal. Generally though North End's results against the sides who finished above them reflected their final position in the table. There was more disappointment in the FA Cup as Preston failed to progress beyond the third round, this time losing to Bristol Rovers, a Division Three (South) team, at their Eastville Stadium. This competition had been poor for Preston since the war but this was one of their worst defeats. Still, in the league games there was plenty to applaud and Deepdale was bursting at the seams as the crowds flocked to see the pick of the country's footballers. In one great spell of three games Preston hit 13 goals as 4–2, 4–1 and 5–2 wins over Sunderland, Wolves and Huddersfield respectively, and the crowds could hardly complain about the lack of incident! On a sadder note the Preston fans said goodbye to Jimmy Gooch and Eddie Quigley who left for pastures new but overall it was a satisfying first season back in the top flight.

DEBUTANTS: (4) Bobby Foster, Gordon Kaile, Joe Dunn and Derek Lewis

LAST GAMES: (2) Jim Gooch and Eddie Quigley

Joe Dunn being welcomed to Deepdale by Mr Will Scott watched by Jimmy Milne.

STAT FACTS:

Best home run without defeat: 6 games
Best away run without defeat: 5 games
Longest run unbeaten: 6 games
Longest run without a win: 11 games
Best home attendance: 40,809 vs. Blackpool 5.9.51
Worst home attendance: 20,800 vs. Wolves 29.3.52
Best away attendance: 59,949 vs. Arsenal 16.2.52
Worst away attendance: 15,815 vs. Huddersfield 5.4.52
Aggregate and average home attendance: 691,646 – 32,935
Aggregate and average away attendance: 766,133 – 36,482

Future Players born between August 1951 and May 1952: Jeff Wealands, David Johnson, Barry Dunn.
Ever presents: (4) Willie Cunningham, Tommy Docherty, Joe Marston and Angus Morrison.
Hat-tricks: (1) Charlie Wayman
FA Cup: Third Round
Players used: 19
Leading scorer: 24 goals – Charlie Wayman (all league)
Manager: Will Scott
Chairman: N. Buck Esq.
AUTHORS' UNOFFICIAL PLAYER OF THE SEASON: Angus Morrison

Match Report: Wayman, Hat-Trick Hero – 16 Feb 1952 Arsenal 3 Preston 3

With six away wins already in the bag Preston travelled down to London with high hopes of returning with at least a draw, and what a draw it was. The Gunners took an early third minute lead through Lewis who headed home a perfectly placed cross by Cox. North End did not panic though despite this early reverse. Instead they began to play neat, constructive football which gave the Arsenal defenders the jitters. Having said that Arsenal were experts at the breakaway attack and after 13 minutes Lewis fed a great ball through to Roper who tricked Docherty and Cunningham with nimble footwork before beating an unsighted Gooch with a low shot just inside the post. Away from home and 2–0 down, but North End failed to capitulate and in fact persevered with their style and almost pulled a goal back on 20 minutes as Beattie's header beat Swindin but unluckily hit the crossbar. Persistance eventually paid off though and in the 24th minute Finney and Beattie between

them created an easy chance for Wayman who punished some slack marking with his 45th goal for Preston in just 65 games. At this stage Arsenal's defence was fully stretched and the appreciative crowd applauded North End's efforts. Yet another counter attack by Arsenal then brought another goal for the home side. Swift passing between Forbes and Logie set up another excellent goal from Lewis. But North End still refused to give up and retaliated quickly. Within a minute it was 3–2 as Wayman claimed his second goal following a free-kick taken by Finney. The second half was as lively as the first and although Preston had more of the possession it was the Arsenal who were more dangerous in front of goal. Another equaliser looked on the cards as Morrison's header hit the crossbar and just as you thought Preston's luck was out they finally managed a deserved equaliser. In the very last minute of the game Wayman intercepted an intended time-wasting backpass from Barnes to Swindin and he successfully gave his team a well deserved point with his hat-trick goal.

Top right: **North End party in their hotel prior to the FA Cup tie at Bristol Rovers 12 January 1952.**

Above: **Wayman (in blue shirt) attacking at Fulham 18 August 1951.**

Right: **Left to right:** *Back row:* **Cunningham, Gooch, Marston, Forbes, Scott.** *Front row:* **Quigley, Beattie, Finney, Wayman, Morrison.**

Season 1951–52: First Division

		P	W	D	L	F	A	Pts
1	Man United	42	23	11	8	95	52	57
2	Tottenham	42	22	9	11	76	51	53
3	Arsenal	42	21	11	10	80	61	53
4	Portsmouth	42	20	8	14	68	58	48
5	Bolton	42	19	10	13	65	61	48
6	Aston Villa	42	19	9	14	79	70	47
7	**PRESTON**	**42**	**17**	**12**	**13**	**74**	**54**	**46**
8	Newcastle	42	18	9	15	98	73	45
9	Blackpool	42	18	9	15	64	64	45
10	Chalton	42	17	10	15	68	63	44
11	Liverpool	42	12	19	11	57	61	43
12	Sunderland	42	15	12	15	70	61	42
13	WBA	42	14	13	15	74	77	41
14	Burnley	42	15	10	17	56	63	40
15	Man City	42	13	13	16	58	61	39
16	Wolves	42	12	14	16	73	73	38
17	Derby	42	15	7	20	63	80	37
18	Middlesbrough	42	15	6	21	64	88	36
19	Chelsea	42	14	8	20	52	72	36
20	Stoke	42	12	7	23	49	88	31
21	Huddersfield	42	10	8	24	49	82	28
22	Fulham	42	8	11	23	58	77	27

League appearances (42 games)

Anders H. 7, Beattie R. 33, Cunningham W. C. 42, Docherty T. H. 42, Dunn J. P. 13, Finney T. 33, Forbes W. 29, Foster R. J. 17, Gooch J. A. G. 34, Horton J. K. 15, Kaile G. W. 2, Lewis D. I. E. 8, Marston J. E. 42, Morrison A. C. 42, Newlands M. 8, Quigley E. 12, Scott W. J. 34, Walton J. 8, Wayman C. 41.

FA Cup appearances (1 game)

Gooch, Cunningham, Scott, Docherty, Marston, Forbes, Horton, Wayman, Beattie, Morrison and Kaile all one each.

Goalscorers: 74 League–No Cup Goals

Wayman 24, Finney 13 (1 pen), Morrison 12, Beattie 6, Horton 5, Forbes 3, Quigley 3, Foster 2, Lewis 2, Own Goals 4 (Crosland and Hayward of Blackpool, Lambert of Liverpool and Whittaker of Middlesbrough).

W. Forbes

Date 1951-2	Opponents	Comp	h or a	Score	Att.	1	2	3	4	5	6	7	8	9	10	11		
Aug 18	Fulham	Div 1	a	3-2	38330	Gooch	Cunningham	Scott	Docherty	Marston	Forbes	Finney	Horton (1)	Wayman (1)	Beattie (1)	Morrison		
Aug 22	Charlton Ath.	Div 1	h	3-0	36577	Gooch	Cunningham	Scott	Docherty	Marston	Forbes (1)	Anders	Horton	Wayman (2)	Beattie	Morrison		
Aug 25	Middlesbrough	Div 1	a	0-1	37389	Gooch	Cunningham	Scott	Docherty	Marston	Forbes	Anders	Horton	Wayman	Beattie	Morrison		
Aug 29	Charlton Ath.	Div 1	a	2-4	18573	Gooch	Cunningham	Scott	Docherty	Marston	Forbes (1)	Anders	Beattie	Wayman (1)	Quigley	Morrison		
Sep 1	WBA	Div 1	a	1-1	27526	Gooch	Cunningham	Scott	Docherty	Marston	Forbes	Finney (1)	Beattie	Wayman	Quigley	Morrison		
Sep 5	Blackpool	Div 1	h	3-1	40809	Gooch	Cunningham	Scott	Docherty	Marston	Forbes	Finney	Beattie (1)	Wayman	Quigley (1)	Morrison (1)		
Sep 8	Newcastle Utd.	Div 1	h	1-2	39452	Gooch	Cunningham	Scott	Docherty	Marston	Forbes	Finney	Beattie (1)	Wayman	Quigley	Morrison		
Sep 10	Blackpool	Div 1	a	3-0	36120	Gooch	Cunningham	Scott	Docherty	Marston	Forbes	Finney	Beattie	Wayman	Quigley (1)	Morrison	2 og	(Crosland) (Hayward)
Sep 15	Bolton W.	Div 1	a	1-1	46523	Gooch	Cunningham	Scott	Docherty	Marston	Forbes (1)	Finney	Beattie	Wayman	Quigley	Morrison		
Sep 22	Stoke City	Div 1	h	2-0	32144	Gooch	Cunningham	Scott	Docherty	Marston	Forbes	Finney (2)	Beattie	Wayman	Quigley	Morrison		
Sep 29	Manchester Utd.	Div 1	a	2-1	55267	Gooch	Cunningham	Scott	Docherty	Marston	Forbes	Finney	Beattie	Wayman (1)	Quigley (1)	Morrison		
Oct 6	Arsenal	Div 1	a	2-0	38321	Gooch	Cunningham	Scott	Docherty	Marston	Forbes	Finney	Beattie	Wayman	Quigley	Morrison (2)		
Oct 13	Manchester City	Div 1	h	0-1	57663	Gooch	Cunningham	Scott	Docherty	Marston	Forbes	Finney	Beattie	Wayman	Quigley	Morrison		
Oct 20	Derby County	Div 1	h	0-1	26829	Gooch	Cunningham	Scott	Docherty	Marston	Forbes	Anders	Beattie	Wayman	Quigley	Morrison		
Oct 27	Aston Villa	Div 1	a	2-3	40504	Gooch	Cunningham	Scott	Docherty	Marston	Forbes	Finney (1)	Beattie	Wayman (1)	Quigley	Morrison		
Nov 3	Sunderland	Div 1	a	4-2	28488	Gooch	Cunningham	Scott	Docherty	Marston	Forbes	Finney (1)	Horton	Wayman (1)	Beattie (2)	Morrison		
Nov 10	Wolverhampton W.	Div 1	a	4-1	37416	Gooch	Cunningham	Scott	Docherty	Marston	Forbes	Finney	Horton (2)	Wayman (2)	Beattie	Morrison		
Nov 17	Huddersfield T.	Div 1	h	5-2	31695	Gooch	Cunningham	Scott	Docherty	Marston	Forbes	Finney (1)	Horton (1)	Wayman (1)	Beattie (1)	Morrison (1)		
Nov 24	Chelsea	Div 1	h	0-0	43873	Gooch	Cunningham	Scott	Docherty	Marston	Forbes	Finney	Horton	Wayman	Beattie	Morrison		
Dec 1	Portsmouth	Div 1	h	2-2	31302	Gooch	Cunningham	Scott	Docherty	Marston	Forbes	Anders	Horton	Wayman (1)	Beattie	Morrison (1)		
Dec 8	Liverpool	Div 1	a	2-2	34722	Gooch	Cunningham	Scott	Docherty	Marston	Forbes	Anders	Horton	Wayman (1)	Beattie	Morrison	1 og	(Lambert)
Dec 15	Fulham	Div 1	h	0-1	25702	Gooch	Cunningham	Scott	Docherty	Marston	Forbes	Kaile	Horton	Wayman	Beattie	Morrison		
Dec 22	Middlesbrough	Div 1	h	5-2	16899	Gooch	Cunningham	Scott	Docherty	Marston	Forbes	Finney (2)	Horton (1)	Wayman (1)	Beattie	Morrison	1 og	(Whittaker)
Dec 25	Burnley	Div 1	a	2-0	36468	Gooch	Cunningham	Scott	Docherty	Marston	Forbes	Finney	Horton	Wayman (2)	Foster	Morrison		
Dec 29	WBA	Div 1	h	1-0	32814	Gooch	Cunningham	Scott	Docherty	Marston	Forbes	Finney	Horton	Wayman	Foster (1)	Morrison		
Jan 1	Burnley	Div 1	h	1-2	34097	Gooch	Cunningham	Scott	Docherty	Marston	Forbes	Finney (1)	Horton	Quigley	Beattie	Morrison		
Jan 5	Newcastle Utd.	Div 1	a	0-3	42410	Gooch	Cunningham	Scott	Docherty	Marston	Forbes	Kaile	Horton	Wayman	Beattie	Morrison		
Jan 12	Bristol Rovers Rd 3	FAC	a	0-2	30681	Gooch	Cunningham	Scott	Docherty	Marston	Forbes	Kaile	Horton	Wayman	Beattie	Morrison		
Jan 19	Bolton W.	Div 1	h	2-2	38646	Gooch	Cunningham	Scott	Docherty	Marston	Forbes	Finney (1)	Beattie	Wayman (1)	Foster	Morrison		
Jan 26	Stoke City	Div 1	a	0-0	24810	Gooch	Cunningham	Scott	Docherty	Marston	Forbes	Finney	Foster	Wayman	Beattie	Morrison		
Feb 9	Manchester Utd.	Div 1	h	1-2	38792	Gooch	Cunningham	Scott	Docherty	Marston	Dunn	Finney	Foster	Wayman (1)	Beattie	Morrison		
Feb 16	Arsenal	Div 1	h	3-3	59949	Gooch	Cunningham	Scott	Docherty	Marston	Dunn	Finney	Foster	Wayman (3)	Beattie	Morrison		
Feb 23	Tottenham H.	Div 1	a	0-1	49193	Gooch	Cunningham	Scott	Docherty	Marston	Dunn	Finney	Foster	Wayman	Beattie	Morrison		
Mar 1	Manchester City	Div 1	h	1-1	34353	Gooch	Cunningham	Scott	Docherty	Marston	Dunn	Finney	Lewis	Wayman	Foster	Morrison (1)		
Mar 8	Derby County	Div 1	a	3-4	22224	Gooch	Cunningham	Scott	Docherty	Marston	Dunn	Finney (1)	Lewis	Wayman	Foster (1)	Morrison (1)		
Mar 15	Aston Villa	Div 1	h	2-2	30192	Newlands	Cunningham	Walton	Docherty	Marston	Dunn	Finney	Lewis (1)	Wayman (1)	Foster	Morrison		
Mar 22	Sunderland	Div 1	h	0-0	34147	Newlands	Cunningham	Walton	Docherty	Marston	Dunn	Finney	Lewis	Wayman	Foster	Morrison		
Mar 29	Wolverhampton W.	Div 1	h	3-0	20800	Newlands	Cunningham	Walton	Docherty	Marston	Dunn	Finney (1)	Lewis	Wayman (1)	Foster	Morrison (1)		
Apr 5	Huddersfield T.	Div 1	a	0-2	15815	Newlands	Cunningham	Walton	Docherty	Marston	Dunn	Anders	Lewis	Wayman	Foster	Morrison		
Apr 12	Chelsea	Div 1	a	1-0	28081	Newlands	Cunningham	Walton	Docherty	Marston	Dunn	Finney	Lewis	Wayman	Foster	Morrison (1)		
Apr 14	Tottenham H.	Div 1	h	1-1	36525	Newlands	Cunningham	Walton	Docherty	Marston	Dunn	Finney	Beattie	Wayman	Foster	Morrison (1)		
Apr 19	Portsmouth	Div 1	a	2-1	27701	Newlands	Cunningham	Walton	Docherty	Marston	Dunn	Finney	Beattie	Lewis (1)	Foster	Morrison (1)		
Apr 26	Liverpool	Div 1	h	4-0	28638	Newlands	Cunningham	Walton	Docherty	Marston	Dunn	Finney (1p)	Beattie	Wayman (2)	Foster	Morrison (1)		

League position in Division One: 7th – P42 W17 D12 L13 F74 A54 Pts 46
Home: W10 D5 L6 F39 A22   Away: W7 D7 L7 F35 A32

SEASON 1952–1953

Marston, Foster and Wayman skipping rope training.

What a season! Runners-up to Arsenal in a nail biting climax to the First Division Championship with only the narrowest of goal average eventually separating the two sides. It was the nearest that Preston had come to winning the title since their win back in the 1889–90 season. Oh, for the dropped points early in the season! In the first 12 games North End managed just three wins and in that spell dropped thirteen vital points, just one of which would have won them that elusive third league championship. But even allowing for the acute disappointment of missing out on the honours there were so many other positive things that could be taken from the season. With Tom Finney and Charlie Wayman in top form and other brilliant contributions coming from Willie Cunningham, Tommy Docherty, Joe Marston and Angus Morrison, the side, with such a settled look about it, performed brilliantly. The year was full of thrills and spills galore for the fans as once again the stadia up and down the country were packed to capacity to see the great players on view. The Preston fans certainly saw plenty of goals and it was significant to note that several of North End's nine defeats were heavy ones, a crucial factor in the final analysis. The 5–0 home defeat by Manchester United was particularly damaging. But to dwell on the downside of the season would be churlish because the performances of some of the Preston players this season was definitely world class. The arrival of Jimmy Baxter, cousin of Willie Cunningham, added new guile to the already potent attack and all the forwards benefitted from his promptings. The form of Joe Marston was a revelation however and the big Australian impressed all the top judges in the game. In the FA Cup North End knocked out Wolves before going out to Spurs after a replay in round four. In the league though there was no stopping the Lilywhites. Inch by inch Preston edged there way towards the top and the exciting campaign reached an unbelievable climax with just the last games due to be played. Preston played on the Wednesday and beat Derby 1–0 thus leaving Arsenal, who played on the following Friday, knowing exactly what they had to do against Preston's near neighbours Burnley. The side from East Lancashire, after a poor first-half, certainly did their best but in the end a 3–2 win gave the Gunners the title. The Preston players and fans were devastated on hearing the news but this disappointment was put into perspective during the summer when events on the field were very much overshadowed by the untimely death of one of North End's most promising youngsters, Derek Lewis, who died following a brain haemorrhage in the summer of 1953. The whole of Preston mourned his passing. The one thing that is certain about the 1952–3 season and that is that the public certainly had their share of entertainment at North End games.

DEBUTANTS: (3) Jimmy Baxter, George Thompson and Bob Wilson

LAST GAMES: (5) Ken Horton, Willie Robertson, Harry Anders, Malcolm Newlands and Derek Lewis

Future Players born between August 1952 and May 1953: Ron Healey, Jimmy Mullen, Alex Bruce, Steve Uzelac
Ever presents: (3) Joe Marston, Charlie Wayman, Angus Morrison   **Players used:** 20   **Hat-tricks:** (2) Both by Wayman, 1 in league and 1 in cup.
FA Cup: Fourth Round replay   **Manager:** Will Scott up to March 1953, then Scott Symon took over.   **Chairman:** N. Buck Esq.
Leading scorer: 26 goals – Charlie Wayman (23 league 3 cup)
AUTHORS' UNOFFICIAL PLAYER OF THE SEASON: Tommy Docherty

League position in Division One: Runners-up – P42 W21 D12 L9 F85 A60 Pts 54
Home: W15 D3 L3 F46 A25 Away: W6 D9 L6 F39 A35

Match Report: Ding Dong Battle With Spurs – 21 Feb 1953
Tottenham Hotspur 4 Preston 4

Highly placed Preston North End were in the capital city to play against Spurs, who earlier in the month had knocked North End out of the FA Cup. Tottenham got off to a flying start in this tense game, going 2–0 up in the first eight minutes. After five minutes their Channel Islander centre-forward, Duquemin mis-hit an attempted hook shot which caught Preston's keeper Thompson in two minds and found the net. With the Preston defence still reeling from this soft goal Walters then made it 2–0 for Spurs. He took advantage of a smart pass by Bailey and shot on the run from a narrow angle. Thompson again must have been disappointed at letting that type of shot squeeze past him. North End then quickly composed themselves and rallied in style, playing methodical football. Finney reduced the arrears after 12 minutes with an excellent goal, coolly taken by a player on top of his form. Most of Preston's attacking moves pivoted around the outstanding Finney. The equaliser came about when Morrison broke away, only to see his shot, which had beaten Ditchburn all ends up, half cleared by a defender. Unfortunately for Tottenham the ball fell straight to the feet of Wayman and the centre-forward unhesitatingly put away the chance with unerring accuracy. Having done the hard work in getting back on level terms, Preston then almost threw it all away again as that man Duquemin scored a brace of goals in the last minute before half-time, against the run of play. It had been a frantic finish to the half and it was a bewildered North End team who trooped off at the break but ten minutes after the restart Morrison handed his colleagues a lifeline. The winger was left unmarked by the Spurs full-back Ramsey and received a pass from Wayman before drilling home a good shot into the far corner. Ditchburn was possibly unsighted but it gave North End the lift they needed. In the 74th minute they found another equaliser as Lewis darted in to finish off a smart move. Chances were made at both ends after that goal but on reflection both sides could be pleased with a point. It had been a thrilling match.

Left to right: Back row: Hepplewhite, Docherty, Cunningham, Thompson, Forbes, Marston, Anders. *Front row:* Finney, Lewis, Wayman, Baxter, Morrison, Scott

STAT FACTS:
Best home run without defeat: 11 games
Best away run without defeat: 4 games
Longest run unbeaten: 8 games
Longest run without a win: 4 games
Best home attendance: 39,741 *vs.* Burnley 6.4.53
Worst home attendance: 19,913 *vs.* Derby 13.12.52
Best away attendance: 54,397 *vs.* Man Utd 7.3.53
Worst away attendance: 22,173 *vs.* Bolton 25.3.53
Aggregate and average home attendance:
642,309 – 30,586
Aggregate and average away attendance:
799,036 – 38,049

Season 1952–53: First Division

		P	W	D	L	F	A	Pts
1	Arsenal	42	21	12	9	97	64	54
2	PRESTON	42	21	12	9	85	60	54
3	Wolves	42	19	13	10	86	63	51
4	WBA	42	21	8	13	66	60	50
5	Charlton	42	19	11	12	77	63	49
6	Burnley	42	18	12	12	67	52	48
7	Blackpool	42	19	9	14	71	70	47
8	Man United	42	18	10	14	69	72	46
9	Sunderland	42	15	13	14	68	82	43
10	Tottenham	42	15	11	16	78	69	41
11	Aston Villa	42	14	13	15	63	61	41
12	Cardiff	42	14	12	16	54	46	40
13	Middlesbrough	42	14	11	17	70	77	39
14	Bolton	42	15	9	18	61	68	39
15	Portsmouth	42	14	10	18	74	83	38
16	Newcastle	42	14	9	19	59	70	37
17	Liverpool	42	14	8	20	61	82	36
18	Sheffield Wednesday	42	12	11	19	62	72	35
19	Chelsea	42	12	11	19	56	66	35
20	Man City	42	14	7	21	72	87	35
21	Stoke	42	12	10	20	53	66	34
22	Derby	42	11	10	21	59	74	32

League appearances (42 games)

Anders H. 2, Beattie R. 12, Baxter J.C. 33, Cunningham W. C. 41, Docherty T. H. 41, Dunn J. P. 25, Finney T. 34, Forbes W. 17, Foster R. J. 11, Horton J. K. 5, Lewis D. I. E. 29, Marston J. E. 42, Morrison A. C. 42, Newlands M. 12, Robertson W. J. T. 1, Scott W. J. 28, Thompson G. H. 30, Walton J. 14, Wayman C. 42, Wilson J. R. 1.

FA Cup appearances (3 games)

Cunningham 3, Docherty 3, Marston 3, Finney 3, Wayman 3, Morrison 3, Baxter 3, Thompson 3, Forbes 3, Lewis 3, Scott 3.

Goalscorers: 85 League–7 Cup–(Total 92)

Wayman 23–3 (26), Finney 17 (5 pens)–2 (1 pen) (19), Lewis 12–2 (14), Morrison 13–0 (13), Baxter 7 (1 pen)–0 (7), Foster 4–0 (4), Horton 3–0 (3), Dunn 2–0 (2), Beattie 2–0 (2), Anders 1–0 (1). Own Goals 1–0 (1) (Westwood of Man. City)

Date 1952-3	Opponents	Comp	h or a	Score	Att.	1	2	3	4	5	6	7	8	9	10	11	
Aug 23	Liverpool	Div 1	h	1-1	34712	Newlands	Cunningham	Walton	Docherty	Marston	Dunn	Finney	Beattie	Wayman (1)	Foster	Morrison	
Aug 25	Blackpool	Div 1	a	1-1	36159	Newlands	Cunningham	Walton	Docherty	Marston	Dunn	Finney	Beattie	Wayman (1)	Foster	Morrison	
Aug 30	Middlesbrough	Div 1	a	1-1	36412	Newlands	Cunningham	Walton	Docherty	Marston	Dunn	Finney (1)	Beattie	Wayman	Foster	Morrison	
Sep 6	WBA	Div 1	h	1-0	34109	Newlands	Cunningham	Walton	Docherty	Marston	Dunn	Finney	Beattie	Wayman (1)	Foster	Morrison	
Sep 10	Stoke City	Div 1	h	3-0	26294	Newlands	Cunningham	Walton	Docherty	Marston	Dunn	Finney (2)	Horton (1)	Wayman	Beattie	Morrison	
Sep 13	Newcastle Utd.	Div 1	a	3-4	52020	Newlands	Cunningham	Walton	Docherty	Marston	Dunn (1)	Finney	Horton (1)	Wayman (1)	Beattie	Morrison	
Sep 15	Stoke City	Div 1	a	0-0	28436	Newlands	Cunningham	Walton	Docherty	Marston	Dunn	Finney	Horton	Wayman	Beattie	Morrison	
Sep 20	Cardiff City	Div 1	h	2-3	29337	Newlands	Cunningham	Walton	Docherty	Marston	Dunn (1)	Finney	Horton (1)	Wayman	Beattie	Morrison	
Sep 27	Sheffield Wed.	Div 1	a	1-1	47708	Newlands	Cunningham	Walton	Docherty	Marston	Dunn	Finney	Horton	Wayman (1)	Beattie	Morrison	
Oct 4	Tottenham H.	Div 1	h	1-0	28108	Newlands	Cunningham	Walton	Docherty	Marston	Dunn	Anders	Beattie	Wayman	Baxter	Morrison (1)	
Oct 11	Chelsea	Div 1	a	3-5	51426	Newlands	Cunningham	Walton	Docherty	Marston	Dunn	Finney	Beattie (2)	Wayman	Baxter	Morrison (1)	
Oct 18	Manchester Utd.	Div 1	h	0-5	33502	Newlands	Cunningham	Walton	Docherty	Marston	Dunn	Finney	Beattie	Wayman	Baxter	Morrison	
Oct 25	Portsmouth	Div 1	a	5-2	31865	Thompson	Cunningham	Walton	Docherty	Marston	Forbes	Finney (2)	Lewis (1)	Wayman (1)	Baxter (1)	Morrison	
Nov 1	Bolton W.	Div 1	h	2-2	37848	Thompson	Cunningham	Walton	Docherty	Marston	Forbes	Finney (1p)	Lewis	Wayman	Baxter	Morrison (1)	
Nov 8	Aston Villa	Div 1	a	0-1	41990	Thompson	Cunningham	Scott	Docherty	Marston	Forbes	Finney	Lewis	Wayman	Baxter	Morrison	
Nov 15	Sunderland	Div 1	h	3-2	28693	Thompson	Cunningham	Scott	Docherty	Marston	Forbes	Finney	Lewis (1)	Wayman	Baxter	Morrison (1)	
Nov 22	Wolverhampton W.	Div 1	a	2-0	32555	Thompson	Cunningham	Scott	Docherty	Marston	Forbes	Finney	Lewis	Wayman	Baxter (1)	Morrison (1)	
Nov 29	Charlton Ath.	Div 1	h	2-1	22573	Thompson	Cunningham	Scott	Docherty	Marston	Forbes	Finney (1)	Lewis	Wayman (1)	Baxter	Morrison	
Dec 13	Derby County	Div 1	h	3-0	19913	Thompson	Cunningham	Scott	Docherty	Marston	Forbes	Finney (1p)	Lewis (1)	Wayman	Baxter	Morrison (1)	
Dec 20	Liverpool	Div 1	a	2-2	27659	Thompson	Cunningham	Scott	Docherty	Marston	Forbes	Finney	Lewis	Wayman	Baxter (1)	Morrison (1)	
Dec 26	Manchester City	Div 1	h	6-2	37093	Thompson	Cunningham	Scott	Docherty	Marston	Forbes	Finney (1)	Lewis	Wayman (2)	Baxter (1)	Morrison (1)	1 og (Westwood)
Jan 1	Blackpool	Div 1	h	4-2	30696	Thompson	Cunningham	Scott	Docherty	Marston	Dunn	Finney (1)	Lewis	Wayman (1)	Baxter	Morrison (2)	
Jan 3	Middlesbrough	Div 1	h	3-0	29139	Thompson	Cunningham	Scott	Docherty	Marston	Dunn	Finney	Lewis	Wayman (3)	Baxter	Morrison	
Jan 10	**Wolverhampton W.** Rd 3	**FAC**	**h**	**5-2**	**31611**	**Thompson**	**Cunningham**	**Scott**	**Docherty**	**Marston**	**Forbes**	**Finney (1)**	**Lewis (1)**	**Wayman (3)**	**Baxter**	**Morrison**	
Jan 17	WBA	Div 1	h	1-2	44571	Thompson	Cunningham	Scott	Docherty	Marston	Forbes	Finney	Lewis (1)	Wayman	Baxter	Morrison	
Jan 24	Newcastle Utd.	Div 1	h	2-1	26394	Thompson	Cunningham	Scott	Docherty	Marston	Dunn	Anders (1)	Lewis (1)	Wayman	Baxter	Morrison	
Jan 31	**Tottenham H.** Rd 4	**FAC**	**h**	**2-2**	**35194**	**Thompson**	**Cunningham**	**Scott**	**Docherty**	**Marston**	**Forbes**	**Finney (1p)**	**Lewis (1)**	**Wayman**	**Baxter**	**Morrison**	
Feb 4	**Tottenham H.** Replay	**FAC**	**a**	**0-1**	**52559**	**Thompson**	**Cunningham**	**Scott**	**Docherty**	**Marston**	**Forbes**	**Finney**	**Lewis**	**Wayman**	**Baxter**	**Morrison**	
Feb 7	Cardiff City	Div 1	a	2-0	32445	Thompson	Cunningham	Scott	Docherty	Marston	Dunn	Finney (1p)	Lewis (1)	Wayman	Baxter	Morrison	
Feb 14	Sheffield Wed.	Div 1	h	1-0	28624	Thompson	Cunningham	Scott	Docherty	Marston	Forbes	Finney (1)	Lewis	Wayman	Baxter	Morrison	
Feb 21	Tottenham H.	Div 1	a	4-4	50070	Thompson	Cunningham	Scott	Docherty	Marston	Forbes	Finney (1)	Lewis (1)	Wayman (1)	Baxter	Morrison (1)	
Feb 28	Chelsea	Div 1	h	2-1	30501	Thompson	Cunningham	Scott	Docherty	Marston	Forbes	Finney	Lewis (2)	Wayman	Baxter	Morrison	
Mar 7	Manchester Utd.	Div 1	a	2-5	54397	Thompson	Cunningham	Scott	Docherty	Marston	Forbes	Finney	Lewis	Wayman (2)	Baxter	Morrison	
Mar 14	Portsmouth	Div 1	h	4-0	28322	Thompson	Wilson	Scott	Docherty	Marston	Dunn	Finney (1)	Lewis	Wayman (2)	Baxter (1)	Morrison	
Mar 19	Arsenal	Div 1	h	1-1	33597	Thompson	Cunningham	Scott	Docherty	Marston	Dunn	Finney (1)	Lewis	Wayman	Baxter	Morrison	
Mar 25	Bolton W.	Div 1	a	3-0	22173	Thompson	Cunningham	Scott	Docherty	Marston	Dunn	Foster (1)	Lewis (2)	Wayman	Baxter	Morrison	
Mar 28	Aston Villa	Div 1	h	1-3	21385	Thompson	Cunningham	Scott	Docherty	Marston	Dunn	Foster	Lewis	Wayman	Baxter	Morrison (1)	
Apr 3	Burnley	Div 1	a	2-2	41685	Thompson	Cunningham	Scott	Docherty	Marston	Forbes	Finney	Lewis	Wayman (1)	Baxter	Morrison (1)	
Apr 4	Sunderland	Div 1	a	2-2	29793	Thompson	Cunningham	Scott	Docherty	Marston	Robertson	Foster (1)	Lewis	Wayman	Baxter	Morrison (1)	
Apr 6	Burnley	Div 1	h	2-1	39741	Thompson	Cunningham	Scott	Docherty	Marston	Forbes	Foster (1)	Lewis	Wayman	Baxter (1p)	Morrison	
Apr 11	Wolverhampton W.	Div 1	h	1-1	35788	Thompson	Cunningham	Scott	Docherty	Marston	Dunn	Finney	Lewis	Wayman	Baxter (1)	Morrison	
Apr 18	Charlton Ath.	Div 1	a	1-2	29716	Thompson	Cunningham	Scott	Dunn	Marston	Forbes	Foster	Lewis	Wayman (1)	Baxter	Morrison	
Apr 22	Manchester City	Div 1	a	2-0	42863	Thompson	Cunningham	Scott	Docherty	Marston	Dunn	Finney	Lewis (1)	Wayman (1)	Baxter	Morrison	
Apr 25	Arsenal	Div 1	a	2-0	39537	Thompson	Cunningham	Scott	Docherty	Marston	Dunn	Finney (1p)	Lewis	Wayman (1)	Baxter	Morrison	
Apr 29	Derby County	Div 1	a	1-0	31496	Thompson	Cunningham	Scott	Docherty	Marston	Dunn	Finney (1p)	Foster	Wayman	Baxter	Morrison	

Jimmy Baxter and Joe Dunn.

SEASON 1953–1954

After achieving the dizzy heights of the runners-up spot the year before North End came down to earth somewhat with an indifferent and disappointing league season. However, this was offset by an exciting FA Cup run which took the club to Wembley and a final date with West Bromwich Albion. Alas, that too was to end in ultimate disappointment, with Preston pipped 3–2 on the big day. It was so disappointing that Tom Finney just failed to win a cup winner's medal and thus emulate his great pal Stanley Matthews, who had done it the year before. At least though, Tom had the satisfaction of winning the prestigious Footballer of the Year award from the Football Writers after an almost unanimous vote. That was some feat as Tom had been dogged by injuries all season and they were to keep him out of nearly half of the league games, and although he played in all the cup-ties he was not always 100% fit for those. The results in the league had the fans tearing their hair out in frustration as the scores went from the sublime to the ridiculous. North End had some fine wins, scoring four goals or more in no fewer than nine fixtures, but these results were always let down by equally bad performances and defeats. As always there were plenty of fine individual displays to enthuse over with Charlie Wayman, Jimmy Baxter and Joe Marston having particularly good seasons. George Thompson did well in goal and Bobby Foster showed an excellent knack of scoring some vital goals. The key to their league season though came in the fact that they lost 18 games, far too many and not good enough to make any sort of title challenge. Other players were to make their mark during the season and it was interesting to see the progress of Dennis Hatsell who certainly looked an exciting prospect. Goalscoring was never a problem but the disappointment came in that Preston managed to score 107 league and cup goals and yet still never won a trophy. The FA Cup semi-final win over Sheffield Wednesday at Maine Road, Manchester provided one of the best moments of the campaign as goals from Wayman and Baxter beat off the Yorkshire team's challenge and sent home the Preston fans, in a huge 75,000 crowd, deliriously happy at the thought of a Wembley trip. The final itself was a bitter pill to take though and by his own admission it was probably one of Finney's worst games in a Preston shirt. Overall disappointment, but much to remember, that is the summary of 1953–54.

DEBUTANTS: (8) Dennis Hatsell, Ray Evans, Keith Mitton, Les Campbell, Peter Higham, Ken Waterhouse, Eric Jones, Fred Else

LAST GAMES: (4) Bill Scott, Gordon Kaile, Keith Mitton, Bobbie Beattie.

North End had a young mascot, called Bobby Roe, for seven years during the 1950s, and he invariably led the team out at Deepdale games. But although he was at Wembley for the 1954 Cup Final, decked out in his replica strip, he was banned from leading the team out on the big day because the Queen Mother was in attendance. The beauty of Bobby's mascotship though was that he did not have to pay a penny for the privilege, unlike today's lucky lads.

Future Players born between August 1953 and May 1954: Stuart Baxter, Danny Cameron, Harry Wilson, Gordon Coleman, Gary Williams, Mike Elwiss.
Ever presents: (2) Joe Marston, Jimmy Baxter
Hat-tricks: (4) Foster, Baxter, Wayman and Hatsell   FA Cup: Runners-up
Players used: 25   Manager: Scott Symon   Chairman: N. Buck Esq.
Leading scorer: 32 goals – Charlie Wayman (25 league 7 cup)

AUTHORS' UNOFFICIAL PLAYER OF THE SEASON:
Charlie Wayman and Tom Finney (joint winners)

League appearances (42 League games)

Baxter J. C. 42, Beattie R. 1, Campbell L. G. 13, Cunningham W. C. 30, Docherty T. H. 26, Dunn J. P. 21, Else F. 1, Evans R. P. 3, Finney T. 23, Forbes W. 19, Foster R. J. 28, Hatsell D. 17, Higham P. 1, Jones E. 7, Kaile G. W. 5, Marston J. E. 42, Mattinson H. 27, Mitton G. K. 2, Morrison A. C. 35, Scott W. J. 4, Thompson G. H. 39, Walton J. 37, Waterhouse K. 1, Wayman C. 34, Wilson J. R. 4.

FA Cup appearances (8 games)

Thompson 8, Cunningham 7, Marston 8, Forbes 8, Finney 8, Foster 8, Wayman 8, Baxter 8, Morrison 8, Mattinson 1, Walton 8, Docherty 8.

Goalscorers: 87 League–20 Cup–(Total 107)

Wayman 25–7 (32), Baxter 15 (7 pens)–5 (20), Foster 15–1 (16), Finney 11–3 (14), Hatsell 11–0 (11), Morrison 7–4 (11), Forbes 1–0 (1), Kaile 1–0 (1), Evans 1–0 (1).

STAT FACTS:
Best home run without defeat: 5 games
Best away run without defeat: 3 games
Longest run unbeaten: 6 games
Longest run without a win: 3 games
Best home attendance: 39,553 vs. Bolton 26.9.53
Worst home attendance: 15,464 vs. Portsmouth 3.4.54
Best away attendance: 100,000 vs. WBA FA Cup Final at Wembley
Worst away attendance: 16,674 vs. Blackpool 30.3.54
Aggregate and average home attendance: 585,645 – 27,888
Aggregate and average away attendance: 730,230 – 34,773

League position in Division One: 11th – P42 W19 D5 L18 F87 A58 Pts 43
Home: W12 D2 L7 F43 A24 Away: W7 D3 L11 F44 A34

Match Report: Finney Finally Finishes Off Foxes – 22 Mar 1954 Leicester 1 Preston 3 FA Cup 6th Rd second replay

There was an ugly looking incident in the first minute of this FA Cup 6th round second replay at Hillsborough, Sheffield from a drop ball situation. Rowley, stood with Foster, rolled over, seemingly writhing with pain and looking as if he had been shot. But he made a miraculous recovery after referee Arthur Holland of Barnsley waved play on. It touched off partisan feelings, the Leicester fans being noisy with their cat-calls and booing. With no quarter given both sides started steadily with defences on top. In the 17th minute though Preston took the lead with a snap shot by Baxter, finishing off a move he had initially started with Morrison and Wayman. Inspired by this opening success Preston held the upper hand for some time but failed to capitalise on their openings. Finney was being closely man-marked by Jackson and Russell, with man-marking being the correct phrase! Despite this attention Finney still managed to produce goalworthy attempts and opportunities for his fellow forwards. During this period Cunningham, Docherty and Marston stood tall in a resolute defence as Preston continued to dominate. A chance then fell to Dryburgh who

Gordon Kaile and Joe Walton.

froze as Thompson flustered the youngster into shooting wide. Meanwhile, the Leicester goal escaped many raids, brought about by Finney's dazzling runs and Baxter's guile. But North End themselves had a narrow escape on 40 minutes when Docherty dispossessed Rowley with a crunching tackle but the ball was only half cleared and only a timely and brave save from Thompson saved the day after the resulting melee. Finney almost scored immediately after the restart but lost his footing at the crucial moment. With Leicester not playing as well as in the previous two ties Preston eventually and deservedly increased their lead. A freakish shot by Foster from a very acute angle found the net, and yes, he really meant to score! A hotly disputed goal by Rowley then brought Leicester back into the game on 67 minutes as the linesman's offside flag was overuled by the referee, much to North End's disgust. The Foxes were now having a purple patch but Marston and his troops rallied courageously as Preston defended well. As Leicester then tired Finney showed his match winning skills on 79 minutes with a header which finally gave his team a safe passage into the semi-final stage once again.

Season 1953–54: First Division							
	P	W	D	L	F	A	Pts
1 Wolves	42	25	7	10	96	56	57
2 WBA	42	22	9	11	86	63	53
3 Huddersfield	42	20	11	11	78	61	51
4 Man United	42	18	12	12	73	58	48
5 Bolton	42	18	12	12	75	60	48
6 Blackpool	42	19	10	13	80	69	48
7 Burney	42	21	4	17	78	67	46
8 Chelsea	42	16	12	14	74	68	44
9 Charlton	42	19	6	17	75	77	44
10 Cardiff	42	18	8	16	51	71	44
11 PRESTON	42	19	5	18	87	58	43
12 Arsenal	42	15	13	14	75	73	43
13 Aston Villa	42	16	9	17	70	68	41
14 Portsmouth	42	14	11	17	81	89	39
15 Newcastle	42	14	10	18	72	77	38
16 Tottenham	42	16	5	21	65	76	37
17 Man City	42	14	9	19	62	77	37
18 Sunderland	42	14	8	20	81	89	36
19 Sheffield Wednesday	42	15	6	21	70	91	36
20 Sheffield United	42	11	11	20	69	90	33
21 Middlesbrough	42	10	10	22	60	91	30
22 Liverpool	42	9	10	23	68	97	28

Left to right: Back row: Mattinson, Cunningham, Walton, Thompson, Docherty, Marston, Forbes.
Front row: J. Milne (trainer), Finney, Foster, Wayman, Mr J. S. Symon, Baxter, Morrison.

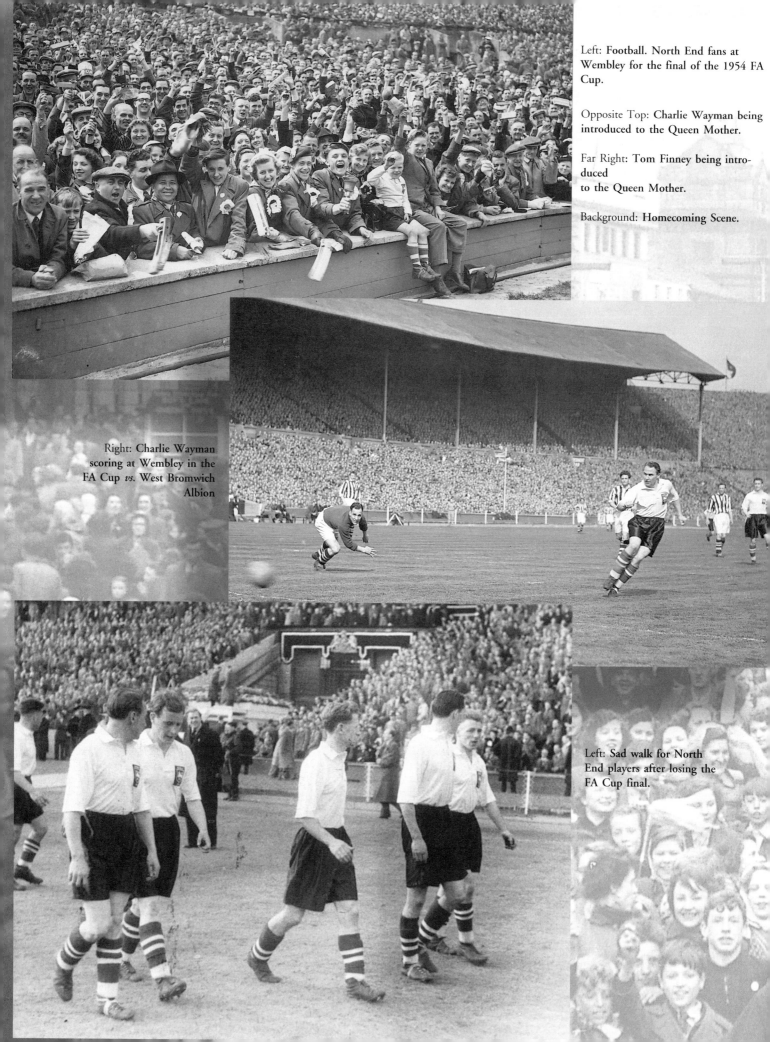

Left: Football. North End fans at Wembley for the final of the 1954 FA Cup.

Opposite Top: Charlie Wayman being introduced to the Queen Mother.

Far Right: Tom Finney being introduced to the Queen Mother.

Background: Homecoming Scene.

Right: Charlie Wayman scoring at Wembley in the FA Cup *vs.* West Bromwich Albion

Left: Sad walk for North End players after losing the FA Cup final.

THE FOOTBALL ASSOCIATION

Challenge Cup Competition—Season 1953-54

THE FINAL TIE

to be played at

THE EMPIRE STADIUM, WEMBLEY

SATURDAY, 1st MAY, 1954

Kick-off 3 p.m.

Admit Bearer to Stadium and to

THE ROYAL BOX

(ENTER AT STADIUM RESTAURANT)

Secretary.

WEST STANDING ENCLOSURE

ENTER AT TURNSTILES H
(See Plan and Conditions on back)

ENTRANCE 63

Empire Stadium, Wembley

THE FOOTBALL ASSOCIATION
CUP COMPETITION

FINAL TIE

SATURDAY, MAY 1st, 1954

Kick-off 3 p.m.

CHAIRMAN AND
MANAGING DIRECTOR
Wembley Stadium Limited

Price 3/6
(Including Tax)

THIS PORTION TO BE RETAINED
This Ticket is issued on the condition that it is not
re-sold for more than its face value.

1954
FA CUP Final

West Bromwich Albion 3
Preston North End 2

Date 1953-4	Opponents	Comp	h or a	Score	Att.	1	2	3	4	5	6	7	8	9	10	11
Aug 19	Huddersfield T.	Div 1	h	1-2	35925	Thompson	Cunningham	Scott	Dunn	Marston	Forbes	Finney	Foster (1)	Wayman	Baxter	Morrison
Aug 22	Middlesbrough	Div 1	a	4-0	32891	Thompson	Cunningham	Scott	Mattinson	Marston	Dunn	Finney	Foster (3)	Wayman (1)	Baxter	Morrison
Aug 26	Sheffield Wed.	Div 1	h	6-0	33118	Thompson	Cunningham	Scott	Mattinson	Marston	Dunn	Finney (1)	Foster (1)	Wayman (1)	Baxter (3)	Morrison
Aug 29	WBA	Div 1	h	0-2	30462	Thompson	Cunningham	Scott	Mattinson	Marston	Dunn	Finney	Foster	Wayman	Baxter	Morrison
Sep 2	Sheffield Wed.	Div 1	a	2-4	36976	Thompson	Cunningham	Wilson	Mattinson	Marston	Dunn	Finney (1)	Foster (1)	Wayman	Baxter	Kaile
Sep 5	Liverpool	Div 1	a	5-1	46928	Thompson	Wilson	Walton	Mattinson	Marston	Dunn	Finney (2)	Foster (1)	Wayman (1)	Baxter	Kaile (1)
Sep 9	Charlton Ath.	Div 1	h	2-0	28055	Thompson	Wilson	Walton	Mattinson	Marston	Dunn	Finney	Foster (1)	Wayman	Baxter (1)	Kaile
Sep 12	Newcastle Utd.	Div 1	h	2-2	36035	Thompson	Wilson	Walton	Mattinson	Marston	Dunn	Finney (1)	Foster	Wayman	Baxter (1p)	Kaile
Sep 17	Charlton Ath.	Div 1	a	1-2	18208	Thompson	Cunningham	Walton	Mattinson	Marston	Dunn	Finney (1)	Foster	Wayman	Baxter	Kaile
Sep 19	Manchester Utd.	Div 1	a	0-1	43003	Thompson	Cunningham	Walton	Mattinson	Marston	Dunn	Finney	Hatsell	Wayman	Baxter	Foster
Sep 26	Bolton W.	Div 1	h	3-1	39553	Thompson	Cunningham	Walton	Mattinson	Marston	Dunn	Finney	Hatsell (1)	Wayman (1)	Baxter (1p)	Morrison
Oct 3	Arsenal	Div 1	a	2-3	61807	Thompson	Cunningham	Walton	Mattinson	Marston	Dunn	Finney	Baxter	Hatsell (2)	Evans	Morrison
Oct 10	Cardiff City	Div 1	h	1-2	23500	Thompson	Cunningham	Walton	Mattinson	Marston	Dunn	Foster	Hatsell (1)	Wayman	Baxter	Morrison
Oct 17	Manchester City	Div 1	a	4-1	43295	Mitton	Cunningham	Walton	Mattinson	Marston	Dunn	Finney (1)	Hatsell (1)	Wayman (2)	Baxter	Morrison
Oct 24	Sunderland	Div 1	h	6-2	34466	Mitton	Cunningham	Walton	Mattinson	Marston	Dunn	Finney	Hatsell (1)	Wayman (3)	Baxter (1)	Morrison (1)
Oct 31	Wolverhampton W.	Div 1	a	0-1	34211	Thompson	Cunningham	Walton	Mattinson	Marston	Dunn	Campbell	Hatsell	Wayman	Baxter	Morrison
Nov 7	Blackpool	Div 1	h	2-3	31886	Thompson	Mattinson	Walton	Docherty	Marston	Dunn	Campbell	Beattie	Hatsell	Baxter (1)	Morrison (1)
Nov 14	Portsmouth	Div 1	a	3-1	30734	Thompson	Mattinson	Walton	Docherty	Marston	Dunn	Finney (1)	Evans	Higham	Baxter (1p)	Morrison (1)
Nov 21	Sheffield Utd.	Div 1	h	2-1	23703	Thompson	Mattinson	Walton	Docherty	Marston	Dunn	Campbell	Evans (1)	Wayman (1)	Baxter	Morrison
Nov 28	Chelsea	Div 1	a	0-1	40922	Thompson	Mattinson	Walton	Docherty	Marston	Dunn	Campbell	Hatsell	Wayman	Baxter	Morrison
Dec 5	Aston Villa	Div 1	h	1-1	20590	Thompson	Mattinson	Walton	Docherty	Marston	Forbes	Campbell	Hatsell (1)	Wayman	Baxter	Morrison
Dec 12	Huddersfield T.	Div 1	a	2-2	26972	Thompson	Mattinson	Walton	Docherty	Marston	Forbes	Campbell	Hatsell	Wayman (1)	Baxter	Morrison (1)
Dec 19	Middlesbrough	Div 1	h	1-0	18909	Thompson	Mattinson	Walton	Docherty	Marston	Forbes	Campbell	Hatsell	Wayman (1)	Baxter	Morrison
Dec 25	Burnley	Div 1	h	1-2	33398	Thompson	Mattinson	Walton	Docherty	Marston	Forbes	Campbell	Baxter	Wayman	Waterhouse	Morrison (1)
Dec 26	Burnley	Div 1	a	2-1	32416	Thompson	Cunningham	Walton	Docherty	Marston	Forbes	Jones	Foster	Wayman (2)	Baxter	Morrison
Jan 2	WBA	Div 1	a	2-3	20174	Thompson	Cunningham	Walton	Docherty	Marston	Forbes	Jones	Foster	Wayman (1)	Baxter	Morrison (1)
Jan 9	**Derby County** Rd 3	**FAC**	**a**	**2-0**	**25339**	**Thompson**	**Cunningham**	**Walton**	**Docherty**	**Marston**	**Forbes**	**Finney (1)**	**Foster**	**Wayman (1)**	**Baxter**	**Morrison**
Jan 16	Liverpool	Div 1	h	2-1	26128	Thompson	Cunningham	Walton	Docherty	Marston	Forbes	Campbell	Foster (1)	Wayman (1)	Baxter	Morrison
Jan 23	Newcastle Utd.	Div 1	a	4-0	40340	Thompson	Cunningham	Walton	Docherty	Marston	Forbes	Campbell	Foster (1)	Wayman (2)	Baxter (1)	Morrison
Jan 30	**Lincoln City** Rd 4	**FAC**	**a**	**2-0**	**23027**	**Thompson**	**Cunningham**	**Walton**	**Docherty**	**Marston**	**Forbes**	**Finney**	**Foster**	**Wayman (1)**	**Baxter (1)**	**Morrison**
Feb 6	Manchester Utd.	Div 1	h	1-3	30064	Thompson	Cunningham	Walton	Docherty	Marston	Forbes	Finney	Foster	Wayman	Baxter (1p)	Morrison
Feb 13	Bolton W.	Div 1	a	2-0	44639	Thompson	Cunningham	Walton	Docherty	Marston	Forbes	Finney (1)	Foster	Wayman	Baxter (1)	Morrison
Feb 20	**Ipswich Town** Rd 5	**FAC**	**h**	**6-1**	**34630**	**Thompson**	**Cunningham**	**Walton**	**Docherty**	**Marston**	**Forbes**	**Finney (1)**	**Foster**	**Wayman (2)**	**Baxter (2)**	**Morrison (1)**
Feb 24	Arsenal	Div 1	h	0-1	25633	Thompson	Cunningham	Walton	Docherty	Marston	Forbes	Finney	Foster	Wayman	Baxter	Morrison
Feb 27	Cardiff City	Div 1	a	1-2	30502	Thompson	Cunningham	Walton	Docherty	Marston	Forbes	Finney (1)	Foster	Wayman	Baxter	Morrison
Mar 6	Manchester City	Div 1	h	4-0	23669	Else	Cunningham	Walton	Docherty	Marston	Forbes	Finney (1)	Foster	Wayman (2)	Baxter (1p)	Morrison
Mar 13	**Leicester C.** Rd 6	**FAC**	**a**	**1-1**	**40065**	**Thompson**	**Cunningham**	**Walton**	**Docherty**	**Marston**	**Forbes**	**Finney**	**Foster**	**Wayman**	**Baxter**	**Morrison (1)**
Mar 17	**Leicester C.** Replay	**FAC ***	**h**	**2-2**	**38130**	**Thompson**	**Cunningham**	**Walton**	**Docherty**	**Marston**	**Forbes**	**Finney**	**Foster**	**Wayman (1)**	**Baxter**	**Morrison (1)**
Mar 20	Wolverhampton W.	Div 1	h	0-1	24376	Thompson	Cunningham	Walton	Docherty	Marston	Dunn	Campbell	Baxter	Hatsell	Jones	Morrison
Mar 22	**Leicester C. 2nd Replay +**	**FAC**	**n**	**3-1**	**44588**	**Thompson**	**Cunningham**	**Walton**	**Docherty**	**Marston**	**Forbes**	**Finney (1)**	**Foster (1)**	**Wayman**	**Baxter (1)**	**Morrison**
Mar 27	**Sheffield Wed. Semi-F. #**	**FAC**	**n**	**2-0**	**75213**	**Thompson**	**Mattinson**	**Walton**	**Docherty**	**Marston**	**Forbes**	**Finney**	**Foster**	**Wayman (1)**	**Baxter (1)**	**Morrison**
Mar 30	Blackpool	Div 1	a	2-4	16674	Thompson	Mattinson	Walton	Docherty	Marston	Forbes	Jones	Foster (1)	Wayman (1)	Baxter (1p)	Morrison
Apr 3	Portsmouth	Div 1	h	4-0	15464	Thompson	Cunningham	Walton	Docherty	Marston	Forbes	Jones	Foster (2)	Wayman (1)	Baxter	Morrison
Apr 7	Sunderland	Div 1	a	2-2	36143	Thompson	Cunningham	Walton	Docherty	Marston	Mattinson	Finney	Foster	Wayman (2)	Baxter	Morrison
Apr 10	Sheffield Utd.	Div 1	a	1-1	30712	Thompson	Cunningham	Walton	Docherty	Marston	Forbes	Finney	Foster	Hatsell (1)	Baxter	Morrison
Apr 16	Tottenham H.	Div 1	a	2-1	24521	Thompson	Cunningham	Walton	Docherty	Marston	Forbes (1)	Finney	Foster	Wayman (1)	Baxter	Morrison
Apr 17	Chelsea	Div 1	h	1-0	27172	Thompson	Cunningham	Walton	Docherty	Marston	Mattinson	Campbell	Foster (1)	Hatsell	Baxter	Jones
Apr 19	Tottenham H.	Div 1	h	6-2	30206	Thompson	Cunningham	Walton	Docherty	Marston	Mattinson	Campbell	Foster (1)	Hatsell (3)	Baxter (1p)	Morrison (1)
Apr 24	Aston Villa	Div 1	a	0-1	31495	Thompson	Cunningham	Walton	Docherty	Marston	Mattinson	Jones	Foster	Hatsell	Baxter	Morrison
May 1	**WBA Final ****	**FAC**	**n**	**2-3**	**100000**	**Thompson**	**Cunningham**	**Walton**	**Docherty**	**Marston**	**Forbes**	**Finney**	**Foster**	**Wayman (1)**	**Baxter**	**Morrison (1)**

+ at Hillsborough
# at Maine Road
** at Wembley

* AET

North End team arriving back in Preston after the 1954 Cup Final.

SEASON 1954–1955

Jimmy Baxter.

This was a very average season for North End, a season which produced little continuity and too many indifferent performances. When Preston won, they usually won well, but there were far too many defeats for the fans to endure. What was all the more disappointing was that it all came after a terrific start to the campaign when the club won nine points out of the first twelve. Scoring goals was never a problem but stopping them going in at the other end was and the defence, despite being quite settled player wise, did not always perform as they should have. Seven times Preston hit four goals or more and Cardiff were swamped as twelve goals went past their keeper in the two early games against the Welsh side. Charlie Wayman hit a hat-trick on the opening day and then scored two goals in the 7–1 thrashing of Cardiff at Deepdale but shortly after that game the ace goalscoring centre-forward was transferred to Middlesbrough in a shock move. Preston missed him and the fans took a while to come to terms with their loss. Manager Frank Hill decided that Dennis Hatsell would be an excellent replacement and he was proved correct as Hatsell scored regularly in his early appearances. The manager also made his one signing, bringing in Sammy Baird, a Scot with a fine pedigree, but he found it hard to settle into the English First Division and struggled as a result.

Preston's midfield was strong with Jimmy Baxter having another excellent season along with the powerful Tommy Docherty. Other players though, struggled for form and it led to many poor team performances. Tom Finney again suffered persistent injuries and the great man found it difficult to find any consistency as his season stopped and started. The fans were magnificent though, as up and down the country the crowds continued to flock to the games, with some attendances breathtaking. A massive 76,839, for instance, watched Preston's game at Goodison Park. They did however fall away a little as the season progressed which was hardly surprising given Preston's indifferent form. There was little relief in the FA Cup as that too brought disappointment. North End. beaten finalists the previous year, were knocked out early on, this time in a fourth round replay at Sunderland. At least local pride was restored as Preston did the double over Blackpool, with Baird scoring a rare goal in the 3–1 home win over the Seasiders.

DEBUTANTS: (2) Sammy Baird, Tommy Lawrenson

LAST GAMES: (6) Charlie Wayman, Joe Marston, Peter Higham, Eric Jones, Sammy Baird and Tommy Lawrenson

Tommy Lawrenson (father of Mark Lawrenson) photographed on his PNE debut at Tottenham.

Trivia Facts:

Dennis Hatsell played centre-forward for an FA xi vs. the RAF at Highbury on October 20.

One of North End's legendary former players, winger Dickie Bond, died on April 24 1955, in Preston. Known as, 'Tricky Dickie', he was a great favourite of the fans from 1902 to 1909 and he was also an England international.

Willie Cunningham missed seven league games through being injured playing for Scotland against England in April.

Preston lost 21 points at home, the worse record since 1924/5 when 24 points were lost.

STAT FACTS:
Best home run without defeat: 3 games
Best away run without defeat: 2 games
Longest run unbeaten: 4 games
Longest run without a win: 5 games
Best home attendance: 38,525 vs. Burnley 27.12.54
Worst home attendance: 13,328 vs. Man Utd 26.3.55
Best away attendance: 76,839 vs. Everton 28.8.54
Worst away attendance: 15,120 vs. Charlton 30.4.55
Aggregate and average home attendance: 559,123 – 26,625
Aggregate and average away attendance: 672,009 – 32,000

Trivia Fact:
PNE reserves, who had never, and have never, won the Central League title, were top of the table at the end of March 1955. Unfortunately they then lost six and drew two of their last eight games.

161

Sunderland, the league leaders, arrived at Deepdale in the knowledge that Preston had lost the previous five FA Cup games between the sides. The fans had queued from mid-morning for admission to what, on paper, looked to be one of the ties of the fourth round. Sunderland had over 6,000 noisy fans at the game decked out in red and white, many of them carrying either a football rattle or horn. As the game settled down the football improved with Finney and Shackleton catching the eyes of their respective fans. The first narrow escape came when Hatsell's glancing header beat Fraser, the visitors' goalkeeper, only to bounce to safety off the face of the crossbar. Elliott, Sunderland's left-winger, had several clashes with North End's sturdy full-back Cunningham as both teams battled for the lead. With 25 minutes played Finney skilfully evaded three opponents before setting up Foster who never made the best of his chance. However, Foster more than made amends a few minutes later when his perfectly placed pass enabled

Pictured changing their footwear are Joe Marston, Tommy Docherty and George Thompson.

Finney to shoot right-footed past Fraser. Sunderland looked disjointed but against the run of play they then equalised through Purdon four minutes after North End's goal. This success spurred on the visitors and three further assaults in quick succession were repelled by Walton, Morrison and Docherty. But a minute before the interval Chisholm scored a second goal for Sunderland to send their noisy following wild with delight. Preston responded after the restart by winning a number of corners. From one of these Morrison equalised as his shot found its way through a crowded goalmouth. Unfortunately the North End joy was short-lived as within two minutes Shackleton restored Sunderland's lead with a long shot over Thompson's head. Determination was a North End strong point though and they deservedly dug out another equaliser through the busy inside-forward Foster who bravely dived in where the boots were flying to gain his just reward. Both sides had served up splendid entertainment and had further chances to win, but in the end a draw was a fair result.

League appearances (42 League games)

Baird S. 15, Baxter J. C. 39, Campbell L. G. 11, Cunningham W. C. 24, Docherty T. H. 39, Dunn J. P. 3, Else F. 5, Evans R. P. 2, Finney T. 30, Forbes W. 38, Foster R. J. 28, Hatsell D. 17, Higham P. 14, Jones E. 6, Lawrenson T. 1, Marston J. E. 40, Mattinson H. 7, Morrison A. C. 33, Thompson G. H. 37, Walton J. 38, Waterhouse K. 8, Wayman C. 6, Wilson J. R. 21.

FA Cup appearances (3 games)

Thompson 3, Cunningham 3, Walton 3, Docherty 3, Marston 3, Forbes 3, Finney 3, Foster 2, Baxter 3, Morrison 3, Hatsell 2, Wilson 1, Evans 1.

Goalscorers: 83 League–6 Cup–(Total 89)

Baxter 17 (3 pens)–0 (17), Foster 13–0 (13), Hatsell 10–2 (12), Higham 10–0 (10), Morrison 8–1 (9), Finney 7 (1 pen)–2 (9), Wayman 6–0 (6), Docherty 3–0 (3), Waterhouse 3–0 (3), Baird 2–0 (2), Campbell 2–0 (2), Evans 1–0 (1), Forbes 0–1 (1), Own goals 1–0 (1) (Martin of Aston Villa)

Left to right: *Back row:* Docherty, Cunningham, Thompson, Forbes, Marston, Walton. *Front row:* Finney, Foster, Higham, Baxter, Morrison, Bobby Roe (mascot).

Season 1954-55: First Division

	P	W	D	L	F	A	Pts
1 Chelsea	42	20	12	10	81	57	52
2 Wolves	42	19	10	13	89	70	48
3 Portsmouth	42	18	12	12	74	62	48
4 Sunderland	42	15	18	9	64	54	48
5 Man United	42	20	7	15	84	74	47
6 Aston Villa	42	20	7	15	72	73	41
7 Man City	42	18	10	14	76	69	46
8 Newcastle	42	17	9	16	89	77	43
9 Arsenal	42	17	9	16	69	63	43
10 Burnley	42	17	9	16	51	48	43
11 Everton	42	16	10	16	62	68	42
12 Huddersfield	42	14	13	15	63	68	41
13 Sheffield United	42	17	7	18	70	86	41
14 PRESTON	42	16	8	18	83	64	40
15 Charlton	42	15	10	17	76	75	40
16 Tottenham	42	16	8	18	72	73	40
17 WBA	42	16	8	18	76	96	40
18 Bolton	42	13	13	16	62	69	39
19 Blackpool	42	14	10	18	60	64	38
20 Cardiff	42	13	11	18	62	76	37
21 Leicester	42	12	11	19	74	86	35
22 Sheffield Wednesday	42	8	10	24	63	100	26

Future Players born between August 1954 and May 1955: Mel Holden, Sammy McIlroy, Tony Morley, John Platt, Barry Siddall, Sam Allardyce, Peter Houghton, Jim Blyth, Graham Bell, Eric Snookes, Peter Sayer.
Ever presents: None
Hat-tricks: (3) Wayman, Higham and Waterhouse 1 each
FA Cup: Fourth Round replay
Players used: 23
Manager: Frank Hill
Chairman: N. Buck Esq.
Leading scorer: 17 goals – Jimmy Baxter (all league)
AUTHORS' UNOFFICIAL PLAYER OF THE SEASON: Jimmy Baxter

League position in Division One: 14th – P42 W16 D8 L18 F83 A64 Pts 40
Home: W8 D5 L8 F47 A33   Away: W8 D3 L10 F36 A31

Date 1954-5	Opponents	Comp	h or a	Score	Att.	1	2	3	4	5	6	7	8	9	10	11		
Aug 21	Manchester City	Div 1	h	5-0	33098	Thompson	Cunningham	Walton	Docherty	Marston	Forbes	Finney	Foster (1)	Wayman (3)	Baxter (1)	Morrison		
Aug 25	Cardiff City	Div 1	a	5-2	39448	Thompson	Cunningham	Walton	Docherty	Marston	Forbes	Finney (1)	Foster (1)	Hatsell (1)	Baxter (2, 1p)	Morrison		
Aug 28	Everton	Div 1	a	0-1	76839	Thompson	Cunningham	Walton	Docherty	Marston	Forbes	Finney	Foster	Hatsell	Baxter	Morrison		
Sep 1	Cardiff City	Div 1	h	7-1	29057	Thompson	Cunningham	Walton	Docherty	Marston	Forbes	Finney (1)	Foster (2)	Wayman (3)	Baxter (1)	Morrison (1)		
Sep 4	Newcastle Utd.	Div 1	h	3-3	35831	Thompson	Cunningham	Walton	Docherty	Marston	Forbes	Finney	Foster (1)	Wayman	Baxter (1)	Morrison (1)		
Sep 6	Chelsea	Div 1	h	1-0	35947	Thompson	Cunningham	Walton	Docherty	Marston	Forbes	Finney	Foster (1)	Wayman	Baxter	Morrison		
Sep 11	WBA	Div 1	a	0-2	40964	Thompson	Cunningham	Walton	Docherty	Marston	Forbes	Finney	Foster	Wayman	Baxter	Morrison		
Sep 15	Chelsea	Div 1	h	1-2	27549	Thompson	Cunningham	Walton	Docherty	Marston	Forbes	Finney	Foster	Wayman (1)	Baxter	Morrison		
Sep 18	Arsenal	Div 1	h	3-1	35812	Thompson	Cunningham	Walton	Docherty	Marston	Mattinson	Finney	Foster (1)	Hatsell (2)	Baird	Morrison		
Sep 25	Sheffield Utd.	Div 1	h	5-0	23325	Thompson	Cunningham	Walton	Docherty	Marston	Forbes	Finney (2)	Foster (1)	Hatsell (1)	Baird	Morrison (1)		
Oct 2	Portsmouth	Div 1	h	1-1	26846	Thompson	Cunningham	Walton	Docherty	Marston	Forbes	Campbell	Foster	Hatsell (1)	Baxter	Morrison		
Oct 9	Blackpool	Div 1	a	2-1	36264	Thompson	Cunningham	Walton	Docherty	Marston	Forbes	Jones	Foster (1)	Hatsell	Baxter (1)	Morrison		
Oct 16	Charlton Ath.	Div 1	a	1-2	26201	Thompson	Wilson	Walton	Waterhouse	Marston	Forbes	Finney	Foster	Hatsell (1)	Baxter	Morrison		
Oct 23	Tottenham H.	Div 1	a	1-3	42863	Thompson	Wilson	Walton	Docherty	Marston	Forbes	Finney (1p)	Foster	Hatsell	Baxter	Lawrenson		
Oct 30	Sheffield Wed.	Div 1	h	6-0	23401	Thompson	Wilson	Walton	Docherty	Marston	Forbes	Finney	Hatsell (1)	Higham (3)	Baxter	Morrison (2)		
Nov 6	Manchester Utd.	Div 1	a	1-2	31902	Thompson	Wilson	Walton	Dunn	Marston	Forbes	Finney	Hatsell	Higham	Baxter (1)	Morrison		
Nov 13	Wolverhampton W.	Div 1	h	3-3	27889	Thompson	Cunningham	Walton	Docherty	Marston	Forbes	Finney	Foster (1)	Higham (1)	Baxter (1p)	Morrison		
Nov 20	Aston Villa	Div 1	a	3-1	25187	Thompson	Cunningham	Walton	Docherty	Marston	Forbes	Finney	Foster	Higham (2)	Baxter	Morrison	1 og	(Martin)
Nov 27	Sunderland	Div 1	a	3-1	28353	Thompson	Cunningham	Walton	Docherty	Marston	Forbes	Finney (1)	Baird (1)	Higham	Baxter (1)	Morrison		
Dec 11	Huddersfield T.	Div 1	h	2-3	23765	Thompson	Cunningham	Walton	Docherty	Marston	Forbes	Finney	Baird	Higham	Baxter (2, 1p)	Morrison		
Dec 18	Manchester City	Div 1	a	1-3	26615	Thompson	Cunningham	Walton	Docherty	Marston	Forbes	Finney	Baird	Higham (1)	Baxter	Morrison		
Dec 25	Burnley	Div 1	a	2-2	29758	Thompson	Cunningham	Wilson	Docherty	Marston	Forbes	Finney	Hatsell (1)	Higham	Baxter	Jones		
Dec 27	Burnley	Div 1	h	0-1	38525	Thompson	Cunningham	Wilson	Docherty	Marston	Forbes	Finney	Hatsell	Higham	Baxter	Jones		
Jan 1	Everton	Div 1	h	0-0	33881	Thompson	Cunningham	Wilson	Docherty	Marston	Forbes	Finney	Hatsell	Higham	Baxter	Jones		
Jan 8	Fulham Rd 3	FAC	h	3-2	24766	**Thompson**	**Cunningham**	**Walton**	**Docherty**	**Marston**	**Forbes**	**Finney (1)**	**Foster**	**Hatsell (2)**	**Baxter**	**Morrison**		
Jan 22	WBA	Div 1	h	3-1	23481	Thompson	Cunningham	Walton	Docherty	Marston	Forbes	Finney	Foster	Hatsell (1)	Baxter	Morrison (2)		
Jan 29	Sunderland Rd 4	FAC	h	3-3	38215	**Thompson**	**Cunningham**	**Walton**	**Docherty**	**Marston**	**Forbes (1)**	**Finney (1)**	**Foster**	**Hatsell**	**Baxter**	**Morrison (1)**		
Feb 2	Sunderland Replay	FAC	a	0-2	57432	**Thompson**	**Cunningham**	**Wilson**	**Docherty**	**Marston**	**Forbes**	**Finney**	**Evans**	**Walton**	**Baxter**	**Morrison**		
Feb 5	Arsenal	Div 1	a	0-2	41218	Thompson	Cunningham	Walton	Docherty	Marston	Forbes	Campbell	Foster	Waterhouse	Baxter	Morrison		
Feb 12	Sheffield Utd.	Div 1	h	1-2	17600	Else	Wilson	Walton	Docherty	Marston	Forbes	Campbell (1)	Baxter	Hatsell	Baird	Morrison		
Feb 19	Portsmouth	Div 1	a	0-2	19823	Thompson	Wilson	Walton	Docherty	Marston	Forbes	Campbell	Baxter	Hatsell	Baird	Morrison		
Feb 26	Blackpool	Div 1	h	3-1	30853	Thompson	Wilson	Walton	Docherty	Marston	Forbes	Finney	Foster (2)	Baird (1)	Baxter	Morrison		
Mar 5	Huddersfield T.	Div 1	a	4-0	24929	Thompson	Wilson	Walton	Docherty (1)	Marston	Forbes	Finney	Foster (1)	Baird	Baxter (2)	Morrison		
Mar 9	Bolton W.	Div 1	a	1-2	19250	Thompson	Wilson	Walton	Docherty	Marston	Forbes	Finney (1)	Foster	Baird	Baxter	Morrison		
Mar 12	Tottenham H.	Div 1	h	1-0	24344	Thompson	Wilson	Walton	Docherty (1)	Marston	Forbes	Finney	Foster	Baird	Baxter	Morrison		
Mar 19	Sheffield Wed.	Div 1	a	0-2	20051	Thompson	Wilson	Walton	Docherty	Marston	Forbes	Campbell	Foster	Baird	Baxter	Morrison		
Mar 26	Manchester Utd.	Div 1	h	0-2	13328	Thompson	Cunningham	Walton	Docherty	Marston	Forbes	Campbell	Foster	Evans	Baxter	Morrison		
Apr 2	Wolverhampton W.	Div 1	a	1-1	28140	Thompson	Wilson	Walton	Waterhouse	Marston	Dunn	Finney	Foster	Baird	Baxter	Morrison (1)		
Apr 8	Leicester City	Div 1	h	2-4	18949	Thompson	Wilson	Walton	Docherty (1)	Marston	Forbes	Finney	Evans (1)	Hatsell	Baird	Morrison		
Apr 9	Bolton W.	Div 1	h	2-2	25213	Thompson	Wilson	Walton	Docherty	Mattinson	Forbes	Finney	Baxter (1)	Higham (1)	Baxter	Jones		
Apr 11	Leicester City	Div 1	a	1-0	33076	Else	Wilson	Walton	Mattinson	Marston	Forbes	Campbell (1)	Docherty	Waterhouse	Baxter	Jones		
Apr 16	Sunderland	Div 1	a	1-2	22609	Else	Wilson	Walton	Mattinson	Marston	Dunn	Campbell	Docherty	Waterhouse	Baxter (1)	Jones		
Apr 20	Newcastle Utd.	Div 1	a	3-3	38681	Else	Wilson	Walton	Docherty	Mattinson	Forbes	Campbell	Waterhouse	Higham (2)	Baxter (1)	Foster		
Apr 23	Aston Villa	Div 1	h	0-3	15147	Else	Wilson	Walton	Docherty	Mattinson	Marston	Campbell	Waterhouse	Higham	Baxter	Foster		
Apr 30	Charlton Ath.	Div 1	a	4-0	15120	Thompson	Mattinson	Wilson	Docherty	Marston	Forbes	Campbell	Waterhouse (3)	Higham	Baxter (1)	Foster		

SEASON 1955-1956

Trivia Fact:
On November 16 1955, the last of the Old Invincibles, Bob Holmes, died in Preston at the age of 88. It was a very sad day for the football club as he was the last link with the illustrious days of the Championship sides.

In November 1955 Harry Soulsby, an 18 year old from Mickley village in Northumberland, was invited down for a trial at Deepdale. But not wanting to let down his local side, Mickley Juniors, who had an important game, he asked if he could play for them first before travelling down to Preston to try and impress their coaching staff. Unfortunately for Harry, he broke a leg in the second half of his game for Mickley and he never arrived for his trial. One that got away perhaps.

Mr J. I. Taylor, the much respected and revered former North End Chairman died on September 22 1955 aged 79. He received 80 floral tributes and his coffin was carried by Jimmy Milne, Frank Hill, George Bargh, Tom Finney, Joe Walton and Harry Mattinson.

PNE youth players, Gordon Sheffield and Brian Parkinson were both chosen to represent the Lancashire FA Youth team in two games against Manchester and Liverpool Youth sides.

Anyone who thinks that North End were a force to be reckoned with in the 1950s usually forget about this season. The club finished just four up from the bottom of the table and only good runs at Christmas and Easter prevented further disaster. However, there were plenty of plusses from the year and it must be considered unusual for a club to struggle so much and yet still score more goals than they concede. Preston did develop an infuriating habit of following a good result with a bad one and the frustration amongst the fans was understandable. North End started the season well enough, winning four of their opening five games, their supporters at this time rubbing their hands in eager anticipation. An opening day 4–0 win at Everton saw Tommy Thompson, not only score, but also demonstrate just why his signing from Aston Villa was to be so important for the club. Over the season he played brilliantly and his partnership with Tom Finney blossomed from day one. In defence though Willie Cunningham missed much of the early part of the season through injury and his absence was sorely noticed, the wise head being missed in many a defensive situation. The form at Deepdale, usually so reliable, was very disappointing, and it was ironic, not to mention surprising, for Preston to win more points away from home than at home. Manager Frank Hill further strengthened the team when he signed Sammy Taylor and the Scottish winger soon made his mark, playing some excellent games. A terrific 6–2 win at Blackpool in the October went some way to avenging that infamous 7–0 home thrashing which Preston had endured back in 1947–48. But to emphasise North End's topsy turvy season the 5–0 defeat suffered at Newcastle on Christmas Eve was awful. Thankfully, a happy Christmas was rescued for the fans by a holiday double over Burnley and it had the supporters looking forward to the forthcoming FA Cup. Alas, a heavy third round defeat at West Ham ended any hopes of a decent run and it was back to the grind of the league matches. The remainder of the campaign was a struggle for Preston and in the end they finished just one point ahead of Huddersfield and Aston Villa and just three ahead of Sheffield United. Preston had won just one point in the six games against those three teams so, as it turned out, it was a very lucky escape from relegation and at the end of the season the club dispensed with the services of Frank Hill, appointing Cliff Britton to replace him.

DEBUTANTS: (3) Sammy Taylor, Eddie Lewis and Tommy Thompson

LAST GAMES: (2) Willie Forbes and George Thompson

League appearances (42 League games)

Baxter J. C. 29, Campbell L. G. 13, Cunningham W. C. 24, Docherty T. H. 41, Dunn J. P. 21, Else F. 8, Evans R. P. 9, Finney T. 32, Forbes W. 30, Foster R. J. 15, Hatsell D. 23, Lewis E. 11, Mattinson H. 27, Morrison A. C. 19, Taylor S. M. 15, Thompson G. H. 34, Thompson T. 42, Walton J. 39, Waterhouse K. 6, Wilson J. R. 24.

FA Cup appearances (1 game)

Thompson G., Walton, Docherty, Forbes, Dunn, Finney, Thompson T., Taylor, Baxter, Cunningham and Lewis, all one each.

Goalscorers: 73 League–2 Cup–(Total 75)

Thompson T. 23–1 (24), Finney 17 (5 pens)–1 (pen) (18), Hatsell 9–0 (9), Baxter 7 (1 pen)–0 (7), Foster 5–0 (5), Morrison 4–0 (4), Taylor 2–0 (2), Lewis 2–0 (2), Docherty 1–0 (1), Forbes 1–0 (1), Waterhouse 1–0 (1). Own goals 1–0 (1) Seith of Burnley.

STAT FACTS:
Best home run without defeat: 3 games
Best away run without defeat: 5 games
Longest run unbeaten: 6 games
Longest run without a win: 7 games
Best home attendance: 38,085 vs. Blackpool 10.3.56
Worst home attendance: 16,175 vs. Aston Villa 21.4.56
Best away attendance: 54,357 vs. Everton 20.8.55
Worst away attendance: 13,999 vs. Charlton 15.9.55
Aggregate and average home attendance: 517,793 – 24,657
Aggregate and average away attendance: 620,810 – 29,562

Future Players born between August 1955 and May 1956: Steve Taylor, Gary Hudson, Joe Hinnigan
Ever presents: (1) Tommy Thompson
Hat-tricks: None
FA Cup: Third Round
Players used: 20
Manager: Frank Hill
Chairman: N. Buck Esq.
Leading scorer: 24 goals – Tommy Thompson (23 league 1 cup)
AUTHORS' UNOFFICIAL PLAYER OF THE SEASON:
Tommy Thompson

Jimmy Baxter putting Manchester United's goalkeeper under pressure.

Former Manchester United players, Joe Walton and Eddie Lewis, were involved from the start of this game, Walton, the captain, winning the toss, and Lewis scoring the game's first goal after just eight minutes. It was his first goal at Deepdale as a North End player. Tommy Thompson made the goal possible with a sudden high dropping shot which Wood failed to collect cleanly. Lewis gratefully snapped up the loose ball to shock the league leaders. United, who had won on their last five visits to Preston, were stung into action with this early reverse and duly equalised within a couple of minutes through Whelan. He scored with a shot which demanded accuracy from such an acute angle. High flying United looked nimble and adroit in spite of the muddy surface which was not going to get any better. Dunn, and local boy, Evans, had a tough task trying to curtail the Red Devils' inside-forwards. Coleman was proving an aggressive, clever forager for the visitors but with Finney and Thompson in good form the so called top dogs were not having everything their own way. The Deepdale pitch resembled something of a quagmire after the interval as United now had to face the raw breeze and soaking rain. It was Finney's 300th league game for North End and the maestro stood up to the testing conditions remarkably well. Two minutes into the second half Preston regained the lead with a delightful goal by the consistant and ever-alert Thompson. His effort, hit unerringly with his right foot, beat Wood all ends up. North End had now gained the upper hand, pleasing their fans in the big crowd with their obvious all round improvement. Five minutes from time the well built Duncan Edwards fouled Thompson and from the resultant free-kick, taken by Cunningham, Foster out-thought Foulkes and darted in to flick the ball past Wood. It finally ended the challenge from the well drenched United although the Red Devils did eventually go on to win the Championship with an amazing eleven point gap over Blackpool and Wolves. It certainly emphasised what a good win this was for North End.

Willie Cunningham and Tommy Docherty.
Both captained Scotland.

Left to right: Back row: Mattinson, Lewis, G. Thompson, Wilson, Forbes.
Front row: Docherty, Finney, T. Thompson, Baxter, Taylor, Walton.

Season 1955–56: First Division

	P	W	D	L	F	A	Pts
1 Man United	42	25	10	7	83	51	60
2 Blackpool	42	20	9	13	86	62	49
3 Wolves	42	20	9	13	89	65	49
4 Man City	42	18	10	14	82	69	46
5 Arsenal	42	18	10	14	60	61	46
6 Birmingham	42	18	9	15	75	57	45
7 Burnley	42	18	8	16	64	54	44
8 Bolton	42	18	7	17	71	58	43
9 Sunderland	42	17	9	16	80	95	43
10 Luton	42	17	8	17	66	64	42
11 Newcastle	42	17	7	18	85	70	41
12 Portsmouth	42	16	9	17	78	85	41
13 WBA	42	18	5	19	58	70	41
14 Charlton	42	17	6	19	75	81	40
15 Everton	42	15	10	17	55	69	40
16 Chelsea	42	14	11	17	64	77	39
17 Cardiff	42	15	9	18	55	69	39
18 Tottenham	42	15	7	20	61	71	37
19 PRESTON	**42**	**14**	**8**	**20**	**73**	**72**	**36**
20 Aston Villa	42	11	13	18	52	69	35
21 Huddersfield	42	14	7	21	54	83	35
22 Sheffield United	42	12	9	21	63	77	33

Ray Evans

Tom Finney in his England strip

Les Campbell

League position in Division One: 19th – P42 W14 D8 L20 F73 A72 Pts 36
Home: W6 D5 L10 F32 A36   Away: W8 D3 L10 F41 A36

Date 1955-6	Opponents	Comp	h or a	Score	Att.	1	2	3	4	5	6	7	8	9	10	11		
Aug 20	Everton	Div 1	a	4-0	54357	G. Thompson	Wilson	Walton	Docherty	Mattinson	Forbes	Finney (2)	T. Thompson (1)	Hatsell	Foster	Morrison (1)		
Aug 24	Luton Town	Div 1	h	2-1	30770	G. Thompson	Wilson	Walton	Docherty	Mattinson	Forbes	Finney	T. Thompson (1)	Hatsell	Foster (1)	Morrison		
Aug 27	Newcastle Utd.	Div 1	h	4-3	29588	G. Thompson	Wilson	Walton	Docherty	Mattinson	Forbes	Taylor	T. Thompson (1)	Hatsell (1)	Foster (1)	Morrison (1)		
Aug 31	Luton Town	Div 1	a	1-2	24174	G. Thompson	Wilson	Walton	Docherty	Mattinson	Forbes	Taylor	T. Thompson (1)	Hatsell	Foster	Morrison		
Sep 3	Birmingham City	Div 1	a	3-0	47014	G. Thompson	Wilson	Walton	Docherty	Mattinson	Forbes	Finney (1)	T. Thompson	Foster (1)	Baxter (1)	Morrison		
Sep 7	Charlton Ath.	Div 1	h	2-2	28423	G. Thompson	Wilson	Walton	Docherty	Mattinson	Forbes	Finney (1)	T. Thompson (1)	Foster	Baxter	Morrison		
Sep 10	WBA	Div 1	h	0-1	28203	G. Thompson	Wilson	Walton	Docherty	Mattinson	Forbes	Taylor	T. Thompson	Foster	Baxter	Morrison		
Sep 15	Charlton Ath.	Div 1	a	1-2	13999	G. Thompson	Wilson	Walton	Docherty	Mattinson	Forbes	Taylor	T. Thompson	Foster	Baxter	Morrison (1)		
Sep 17	Manchester Utd.	Div 1	a	2-3	33362	G. Thompson	Wilson	Walton	Docherty	Mattinson	Forbes	Taylor (1)	T. Thompson	Waterhouse	Baxter (1)	Morrison		
Sep 24	Sheffield Utd.	Div 1	h	0-2	24475	G. Thompson	Wilson	Walton	Docherty	Mattinson	Waterhouse	Finney	T. Thompson	Hatsell	Baxter	Taylor		
Oct 1	Huddersfield T.	Div 1	a	2-2	23892	Else	Cunningham	Walton	Docherty	Mattinson	Dunn	Campbell	T. Thompson (1)	Hatsell	Baxter (1p)	Taylor		
Oct 8	Cardiff City	Div 1	h	1-2	19433	Else	Cunningham	Wilson	Docherty	Mattinson	Dunn	Finney (1p)	T. Thompson	Hatsell	Foster	Campbell		
Oct 15	Manchester City	Div 1	a	2-0	33187	G. Thompson	Cunningham	Wilson	Docherty	Mattinson	Dunn	Finney (1)	T. Thompson (1)	Hatsell	Baxter	Morrison		
Oct 22	Chelsea	Div 1	h	2-3	17799	G. Thompson	Cunningham	Wilson	Docherty	Mattinson	Dunn	Campbell	T.Thompson (2)	Hatsell	Baxter	Morrison		
Oct 29	Blackpool	Div 1	a	6-2	25692	G. Thompson	Cunningham	Walton	Docherty	Mattinson	Forbes	Finney (1)	T. Thompson (1)	Hatsell (2)	Baxter (1)	Morrison (1)		
Nov 5	Sunderland	Div 1	h	2-2	27688	G. Thompson	Cunningham	Walton	Docherty	Mattinson	Forbes	Finney (1p)	T. Thompson	Evans	Baxter (1)	Morrison		
Nov 12	Portsmouth	Div 1	a	2-0	27720	G. Thompson	Cunningham	Walton	Docherty	Mattinson	Forbes	Finney (1)	T. Thompson	Evans	Baxter (1)	Morrison		
Nov 19	Arsenal	Div 1	h	0-1	23033	G. Thompson	Cunningham	Walton	Docherty	Mattinson	Forbes	Finney	T. Thompson	Evans	Baxter	Taylor		
Nov 26	Bolton W.	Div 1	a	0-0	32630	G. Thompson	Wilson	Walton	Docherty	Mattinson	Forbes	Finney	T. Thompson	Hatsell	Baxter	Morrison		
Dec 3	Wolverhampton W.	Div 1	h	2-0	26423	G. Thompson	Wilson	Walton	Docherty	Mattinson	Forbes	Finney	T. Thompson (1)	Evans	Baxter	Taylor		
Dec 10	Aston Villa	Div 1	a	2-3	27814	G. Thompson	Wilson	Walton	Docherty	Mattinson	Forbes	Finney	T. Thompson (1)	Lewis (1)	Baxter	Taylor		
Dec 17	Everton	Div 1	h	0-1	21917	G. Thompson	Wilson	Walton	Docherty	Mattinson	Forbes	Finney	T. Thompson	Lewis	Baxter	Taylor		
Dec 24	Newcastle Utd.	Div 1	a	0-5	32976	G. Thompson	Wilson	Walton	Docherty	Dunn	Forbes	Finney	Baxter	Lewis	T Thompson	Taylor		
Dec 26	Burnley	Div 1	a	2-1	31006	G. Thompson	Wilson	Walton	Docherty	Dunn	Forbes	Finney	T. Thompson (1)	Lewis	Baxter	Taylor (1)		
Dec 27	Burnley	Div 1	h	4-2	29524	G. Thompson	Wilson	Walton	Docherty	Dunn	Mattinson	Finney (2, 1p)	T. Thompson (1)	Lewis	Evans	Taylor	1 og	(Seith)
Dec 31	Birmingham City	Div 1	h	1-1	25834	G. Thompson	Wilson	Walton	Docherty	Dunn	Forbes	Finney	T. Thompson (1)	Lewis	Baxter	Taylor		
Jan 7	**West Ham Utd.** Rd 3	**FAC**	**a**	**2-5**	**28854**	**G.Thompson**	**Cunningham**	**Walton**	**Docherty**	**Dunn**	**Forbes**	**Finney (1p)**	**T. Thompson (1)**	**Lewis**	**Baxter**	**Taylor**		
Jan 14	WBA	Div 1	a	2-3	22318	G. Thompson	Cunningham	Walton	Docherty	Dunn	Evans	Hatsell(1)	T. Thompson (1)	Lewis	Baxter	Foster		
Jan 21	Manchester Utd.	Div 1	h	3-1	28047	G. Thompson	Cunningham	Walton	Docherty	Dunn	Evans	Finney	T. Thompson (1)	Lewis (1)	Baxter	Foster (1)		
Feb 4	Sheffield Utd.	Div 1	a	1-3	20977	G. Thompson	Cunningham	Walton	Docherty (1)	Dunn	Mattinson	Finney	T. Thompson	Evans	Baxter	Foster		
Feb 11	Huddersfield T.	Div 1	h	1-2	17363	G. Thompson	Cunningham	Walton	Docherty	Dunn	Evans	Finney (1)	T. Thompson	Lewis	Baxter	Morrison		
Feb18	Cardiff City	Div 1	a	1-3	25300	G. Thompson	Cunningham	Walton	Docherty	Mattinson	Forbes	Finney	T. Thompson	Lewis	Foster (1)	Morrison		
Feb 25	Manchester City	Div 1	h	0-3	22464	G. Thompson	Cunningham	Walton	Docherty	Mattinson	Forbes	Finney	T. Thompson	Hatsell	Foster	Morrison		
Mar 6	Arsenal	Div 1	a	2-3	34617	G. Thompson	Cunningham	Walton	Docherty	Dunn	Forbes	Finney	T. Thompson	Hatsell (2)	Waterhouse	Campbell		
Mar 10	Blackpool	Div 1	h	3-3	38085	G. Thompson	Cunningham	Walton	Docherty	Dunn	Forbes	Finney (1p)	T. Thompson (1)	Hatsell	Waterhouse (1)	Campbell		
Mar 21	Sunderland	Div 1	a	2-2	20438	G. Thompson	Cunningham	Walton	Docherty	Dunn	Forbes	Finney (1)	T. Thompson (1)	Hatsell	Waterhouse	Campbell		
Mar 24	Portsmouth	Div 1	h	2-1	17016	G. Thompson	Cunningham	Walton	Docherty	Dunn	Forbes	Finney	T. Thompson (1)	Hatsell (1)	Waterhouse	Campbell		
Mar 30	Tottenham H.	Div 1	a	4-0	39441	Else	Cunningham	Walton	Docherty	Dunn	Forbes	Finney (2)	T. Thompson (2)	Hatsell	Baxter	Campbell		
Mar 31	Chelsea	Div 1	a	1-0	31450	Else	Cunningham	Walton	Docherty	Dunn	Wilson	Finney (1p)	T. Thompson	Hatsell	Baxter	Campbell		
Apr 2	Tottenham H.	Div 1	h	3-3	26699	Else	Cunningham	Walton	Docherty	Dunn	Forbes (1)	Finney	T. Thompson (1)	Hatsell (1)	Baxter	Campbell		
Apr 7	Bolton W.	Div 1	h	0-1	18834	Else	Cunningham	Walton	Docherty	Dunn	Wilson	Campbell	T. Thompson	Lewis	Hatsell	Foster		
Apr 14	Wolverhampton W.	Div 1	a	1-2	18446	Else	Cunningham	Walton	Wilson	Dunn	Forbes	Campbell	T. Thompson	Hatsell (1)	Baxter	Morrison		
Apr 21	Aston Villa	Div 1	h	0-1	16175	Else	Cunningham	Walton	Docherty	Dunn	Mattinson	Finney	T. Thompson	Hatsell	Baxter	Campbell		

SEASON 1956–1957

After opening with four straight defeats there was certainly no indication that Preston would enjoy an exciting season. But everything exploded into life after Cardiff had been thrashed 6–0 on 1 September at Deepdale. The club produced some superb football over the next few weeks and then, in December, embarked on a sixteen match unbeaten run. To the great delight of their fans the team not only played superbly at times but also scored lots of goals along the way. Tom Finney and Tommy Thompson were in blistering form throughout and they scored an incredible 57 league and cup goals between them. In three games alone the North End attack hit 19 goals as Cardiff, Sunderland and Portsmouth were all sent packing after heavy defeats. Meanwhile, at the back Preston did have their moments, such as a 4–0 defeat at Blackpool, but generally the defence played well and North End were able to sustain a challenge at the top. Fred Else was in good form and had an excellent season in goal, Willie Cunningham and Joe Walton were as good a full-back pairing in the division and Joe Dunn was a solid centre-half. The start of Preston's long unbeaten run had coincided with the signing of Frank O'Farrell, an Irishman bought from West Ham. Amazingly the wing-half only finished on the losing side twice in his 24 league and cup appearances. There were good contributions from other players too, most notably from Jimmy Baxter and Sammy Taylor. Finney's positional switch to the centre-forward berth proved a success for manager Cliff Britton and

Tom Finney. Football Writers' Footballer of the Year.

it also provided even more evidence, if indeed it was needed, of Finney's immense talent. It was to win him the Football Writer's Player of the Year Award for the second time, the first player to achieve that honour. Tommy Docherty gave Preston the crucial bite in midfield and with all these fine individual performances gelling together, it was not hard to understand why this Preston side was so highly rated. It looked for awhile that the FA Cup would provide the reward for all of this superb football. A terrific tie with Sheffield Wednesday ended with a convincing 5–1 win in a second replay at Goodison Park before Bristol Rovers were beaten in the fourth round. This brought Preston a mammoth home draw with the mighty Arsenal. In a thrill a minute tie the Gunners held Preston to a 3–3 draw. Over 61,000 people packed into Highbury for the replay where Arsenal won 2–1. After that Preston made a determined effort to catch the formidable Manchester United side, but in the end, with United Champions, Preston were even pipped to the runners-up spot by Tottenham Hotspur. It was so disappointing for the club to end up with nothing to show for such a fine season, and it was ironic that the home crowds were at their lowest since the war.

DEBUTANTS: (3) Gordon Milne, Les Dagger and Frank O'Farrell

LAST GAMES: (5) Angus Morrison, Bobby Foster, Ray Evans, Ken Waterhouse and Eddie Lewis

---

STAT FACTS:
Best home run without defeat: 19 games
Best away run without defeat: 9 games
Longest run unbeaten: 16 games
Longest run without win: 4 games
Best home attendance: 39,608 *vs.*
Arsenal FAC 16.2.57
Worst home attendance: 13,311 *vs.* Wolves 6.4.57
Best away attendance: 61,451 *vs.*
Arsenal FAC 19.2.57
Worst away attendance: 15,474 *vs.* Cardiff 29.12.56
Aggregate and average home attendance:
493,953 – 23,521
Aggregate and average away attendance:
624,009 – 29,715

Trivia Fact:
There were several representative appearances by North Enders in 1956–57, including Tom Finney and Tommy Thompson playing for an FA XI against the Army at Maine Road on November 7. The FA side won 7–3 with Finney scoring 2 and Thompson 3. Fred Else and Thompson played for England 'B' against Scotland 'B' and again 'Topper' scored. Meanwhile Finney, Thompson and Tommy Docherty played in the England *vs.* Scotland full international at Wembley in April 1957. On the same day Preston beat Wolves 1–0 without these three players.

League appearances (42 games)

Baxter J. C. 39, Campbell L. G. 13, Cunningham W. C. 41, Dagger J. L. 25, Docherty T. H. 37, Dunn J. P. 38, Else F. 42, Evans R. P. 19, Finney T. 34, Foster R. J. 2, Hatsell D. 10, Lewis E. 1, Mattinson H. 9, Milne G. 5, Morrison A. C. 6, O'Farrell F. 18, Taylor S. M. 37, Thompson T. 38, Walton J. 42, Waterhouse K. 5, Wilson J. R. 1.

FA Cup appearances (6 games)

Else 6, Cunningham 6, Walton 6, Docherty 6, Dunn 5, Mattinson 1, Finney 6, Thompson 5, Baxter 6, Taylor 6, Waterhouse 1, Dagger 6, O'Farrell 6.

Goalscorers: 84 League–15 Cup–(Total 99)

Thompson 26–3 (29), Finney 23 (6 pens)–5 (28), Taylor 12–3 (15), Baxter 9–1 (10), Hatsell 5–0 (5), Dagger 2–2 (4), Foster 2–0 (2), O'Farrell 1–1 (2), Waterhouse 1–0 (1), Own goals 3–0 (3) Malloy of Cardiff (1 in each game) and Miller of Burnley.

Future Players born between August 1956 and May 1957: David Jones, Roy Taylor, Mark Fielding, John Smith, Mick Baxter, David Brown, Dan O'Riordan
Ever presents: Fred Else, Joe Walton   **Chairman:** N. Buck Esq.
Manager: Cliff Britton   **Hat-tricks:** (2) Tommy Thompson, Sammy Taylor
FA Cup: Fifth Round Replay
Players used: 21   **Leading scorer:** 29 goals – Tommy Thompson (26 league 3 cup)
AUTHORS' UNOFFICIAL PLAYER OF THE SEASON: Tom Finney

Match Report: Shoot Out at the Valley – 8 Dec 1956 Charlton Athletic 3 Preston 4

The vast amphitheatre of the Charlton ground, capable of accomodating 80,000 spectators, was only sparsely populated as play began at 2.15p.m. due to the Valley Stadium not being equipped with floodlights. Within a couple of minutes Dunn knew he was going to be in for a busy afternoon as the Charlton centre-forward, Summers, was thwarted twice by the alert Else in Preston's goal. Eventually North End collected their thoughts and began to play well which resulted in them taking the lead on six minutes. Dagger broke away and his backward centre was seized upon by Baxter who lobbed the home goalkeeper, Marsh, from 18 yards out. But (as seemed normal in the 1950s) the equalising goal arrived within a minute, from the left foot of Summers, who had found himself momentarily unmarked. Unruffled by this sudden setback Preston responded in business like fashion, combining much better than Charlton, and thus proving themselves a superior footballing side. On 13 minutes Finney, with a choice pass, put Dagger clear. Before the winger could be tackled he shot and was visibly delighted to see the ball squirm through the keeper's hands and between his legs, thus registering his first goal for Preston. A fusilade of shots from Preston followed with Thompson and Taylor going particularly close. Charlton's spirit diminished as the half progressed, their defenders being preoccupied in trying to cope with the nippy, skilful North End forwards. It came as no surprise when Preston increased their lead on 38 minutes. Thompson's shot rebounded off a defender straight to Finney who scored from close range. North End then went 4–1 up on 54 minutes. Taylor forced Marsh to save bravely from 12 yards but he mishandled the ball which fell perfectly for Thompson to shoot into the empty net. It was so characteristic of his opportunism. Baxter was close to making it 5–1 as Marsh just saved with his fingertips. As Preston eased off Charlton came back with two late goals from Summers who thus collected a hat-trick. North End held out though to gain two valuable points and a win bonus from their trip to London.

Top: Arsenal's goalkeeper Kelsey, takes the ball off Sammy Taylor's foot, watched by Jimmy Baxter.

Left to right: *Back row:* Docherty, Cunningham, Dunn, Else, Walton, O'Farrell. *Front row:* Bobby Roe (Mascot), Dagger, Thompson, Finney, Baxter, Taylor.

Season 1956–57: First Division

	P	W	D	L	F	A	Pts
1 Man United	42	28	8	6	103	54	64
2 Tottenham	42	22	12	8	104	56	56
3 PRESTON	**42**	**23**	**10**	**9**	**84**	**56**	**56**
4 Blackpool	42	22	9	11	93	65	53
5 Arsenal	42	21	8	13	85	69	50
6 Wolves	42	20	8	14	94	70	48
7 Burnley	42	18	10	14	56	50	46
8 Leeds	42	15	14	13	72	63	44
9 Bolton	42	16	12	14	65	65	44
10 Aston Villa	42	14	15	13	65	55	43
11 WBA	42	14	14	14	59	61	42
12 Birmingham*	42	15	9	18	69	69	39
13 Chelsea*	42	13	13	16	73	73	39
14 Sheffield Wednesday	42	16	6	20	82	88	38
15 Everton	42	14	10	18	61	79	38
16 Luton	42	14	9	19	58	76	37
17 Newcastle	42	14	8	20	67	87	36
18 Man City	42	13	9	20	78	88	35
19 Portsmouth	42	10	13	19	62	92	33
20 Sunderland	42	12	8	22	67	88	32
21 Cardiff	42	10	9	23	53	88	29
22 Charlton	42	9	4	29	62	120	22

*Equal

League position in Division One: 3rd – P42 W23 D10 L9 F84 A56 Pts 56
Home: W15 D4 L2 F50 A19   Away: W8 D6 L7 F34 A37

Preston North End players at a pre-match get-together with Manager Cliff Britton.

Fred Else. Top-class goalkeeper who played for England 'B'.

Date 1956-7	Opponents	Comp	h or a	Score	Att.	1	2	3	4	5	6	7	8	9	10	11		
Aug 18	Tottenham H.	Div 1	h	1-4	22752	Else	Cunningham	Walton	Docherty	Dunn	Mattinson	Finney (1p)	Thompson	Hatsell	Baxter	Morrison		
Aug 20	Manchester Utd.	Div 1	h	1-3	32569	Else	Cunningham	Walton	Docherty	Dunn	Mattinson	Finney	Waterhouse (1)	Hatsell	Baxter	Taylor		
Aug 25	Chelsea	Div 1	a	0-1	21832	Else	Cunningham	Walton	Docherty	Dunn	Mattinson	Finney	Waterhouse	Lewis	Baxter	Taylor		
Aug 29	Manchester Utd.	Div 1	a	2-3	32515	Else	Cunningham	Walton	Docherty	Dunn	Mattinson	Campbell	Thompson	Finney (1p)	Baxter	Taylor (1)		
Sep 1	Cardiff City	Div 1	h	6-0	22102	Else	Cunningham	Walton	Docherty	Dunn	Evans	Campbell	Thompson (2)	Finney (2, 1p)	Baxter (1)	Taylor	1 og	(Malloy)
Sep 4	Arsenal	Div 1	a	2-1	40470	Else	Cunningham	Walton	Docherty	Dunn	Evans	Campbell	Thompson (1)	Finney	Baxter (1)	Taylor		
Sep 8	Birmingham City	Div 1	a	0-3	44458	Else	Cunningham	Walton	Docherty	Dunn	Evans	Campbell	Thompson	Finney	Baxter	Taylor		
Sep 10	Arsenal	Div 1	h	3-0	35510	Else	Cunningham	Walton	Docherty	Dunn	Evans	Campbell	Thompson (1)	Finney (2)	Baxter	Taylor		
Sep 15	WBA	Div 1	h	3-2	28380	Else	Cunningham	Walton	Docherty	Dunn	Evans	Campbell	Thompson (1)	Finney (1)	Baxter	Taylor (1)		
Sep 22	Portsmouth	Div 1	a	2-2	28197	Else	Cunningham	Walton	Milne	Dunn	Evans	Campbell	Thompson (1)	Finney (1)	Baxter	Taylor		
Sep 29	Newcastle Utd.	Div 1	h	1-0	29199	Else	Cunningham	Walton	Milne	Dunn	Evans	Campbell	Thompson (1)	Finney	Baxter	Taylor		
Oct 6	Everton	Div 1	h	0-0	21778	Else	Cunningham	Walton	Milne	Dunn	Evans	Campbell	Thompson	Hatsell	Baxter	Taylor		
Oct 13	Blackpool	Div 1	a	0-4	36006	Else	Cunningham	Walton	Docherty	Dunn	Evans	Campbell	Thompson	Hatsell	Baxter	Taylor		
Oct 20	Bolton W.	Div 1	h	2-2	26994	Else	Cunningham	Walton	Docherty	Dunn	Evans	Campbell	Thompson	Finney (1)	Baxter	Taylor (1)		
Oct 27	Leeds Utd.	Div 1	a	2-1	36571	Else	Wilson	Walton	Docherty	Dunn	Evans	Campbell	Thompson	Finney (1)	Baxter (1)	Taylor		
Nov 3	Sunderland	Div 1	h	6-0	26021	Else	Cunningham	Walton	Docherty	Dunn	Evans	Dagger	Thompson (3)	Finney (2, 1p)	Baxter	Taylor (1)		
Nov 10	Luton Town	Div 1	a	1-1	18721	Else	Cunningham	Walton	Docherty	Dunn	Evans	Dagger	Thompson	Finney	Baxter (1)	Taylor		
Nov 17	Aston Villa	Div 1	h	3-3	19270	Else	Cunningham	Walton	Docherty	Dunn	Evans	Dagger	Thompson (1)	Hatsell (2)	Baxter	Taylor		
Nov 24	Wolverhampton W.	Div 1	a	3-4	30254	Else	Cunningham	Walton	Docherty	Dunn	Evans	Dagger	Thompson	Finney (2)	Baxter (1)	Taylor		
Dec 1	Manchester City	Div 1	h	3-1	25433	Else	Cunningham	Walton	Docherty	Dunn	O'Farrell (1)	Dagger	Thompson (1)	Finney	Baxter	Taylor (1)		
Dec 8	Charlton Ath.	Div 1	a	4-3	15628	Else	Cunningham	Walton	Docherty	Dunn	O'Farrell	Dagger (1)	Thompson (1)	Finney (1)	Baxter (1)	Taylor		
Dec 15	Tottenham H.	Div 1	a	1-1	29748	Else	Cunningham	Walton	Docherty	Dunn	O'Farrell	Dagger	Thompson	Finney (1)	Baxter	Taylor		
Dec 25	Burnley	Div 1	a	2-2	23737	Else	Cunningham	Walton	Docherty	Dunn	O'Farrell	Dagger	Thompson (2)	Finney	Baxter	Taylor		
Dec 26	Burnley	Div 1	h	1-0	19265	Else	Cunningham	Walton	Docherty	Dunn	O'Farrell	Dagger	Thompson	Finney	Baxter	Morrison	1 og	(Malloy)
Dec 29	Cardiff City	Div 1	a	3-2	15474	Else	Cunningham	Walton	Docherty	Dunn	O'Farrell	Dagger	Thompson (2)	Finney	Baxter	Morrison	1 og	(Miller)
Jan 5	Sheffield Wed. Rd 3	FAC	h	0-0	28777	Else	Cunningham	Walton	Docherty	Dunn	O'Farrell	Dagger	Thompson	Finney	Baxter	Taylor		
Jan 9	Sheffield Wed. Replay	FAC	a	2-2*	60168	Else	Cunningham	Walton	Docherty	Dunn	O'Farrell	Dagger	Thompson	Finney (1)	Baxter	Taylor (1)		
Jan 12	Birmingham City	Div 1	h	1-0	19430	Else	Cunningham	Walton	Docherty	Mattinson	O'Farrell	Campbell	Thompson (1)	Hatsell	Baxter	Morrison		
Jan 14	Sheffield W. 2nd Rep. *	FAC	n	5-1	32108	Else	Cunningham	Walton	Docherty	Mattinson	O'Farrell (1)	Dagger	Thompson (2)	Finney	Baxter (1)	Taylor (1)		
Jan 19	WBA	Div 1	a	0-0	24168	Else	Cunningham	Walton	Docherty	Dunn	O'Farrell	Dagger	Thompson	Finney	Foster	Taylor		
Jan 26	Bristol Rovers Rd 4	FAC	a	4-1	32778	Else	Cunningham	Walton	Docherty	Dunn	O'Farrell	Dagger (1)	Thompson	Finney (2)	Baxter	Taylor (1)		
Feb 2	Portsmouth	Div 1	h	7-1	23512	Else	Cunningham	Walton	Docherty	Dunn	O'Farrell	Dagger	Thompson (1)	Finney (1)	Baxter (2)	Taylor (3)		
Feb 9	Newcastle Utd.	Div 1	a	2-1	43086	Else	Cunningham	Walton	Docherty	Dunn	O'Farrell	Dagger	Thompson (1)	Finney	Baxter	Taylor (1)		
Feb 16	Arsenal Rd 5	FAC	h	3-3	39608	Else	Cunningham	Walton	Docherty	Dunn	O'Farrell	Dagger	Thompson (1)	Finney (2)	Baxter	Taylor		
Feb 19	Arsenal Replay	FAC	a	1-2	61451	Else	Cunningham	Walton	Docherty	Dunn	O'Farrell	Dagger (1)	Waterhouse	Finney	Baxter	Taylor		
Feb 23	Leeds Utd.	Div 1	h	3-0	14036	Else	Cunningham	Walton	Docherty	Dunn	O'Farrell	Dagger	Waterhouse	Finney (1)	Foster (2)	Taylor		
Feb 27	Everton	Div 1	a	4-1	23345	Else	Cunningham	Walton	Docherty	Dunn	O'Farrell	Dagger	Thompson (2)	Finney (1)	Baxter	Taylor (1)		
Mar 2	Bolton W.	Div 1	a	3-2	37090	Else	Cunningham	Walton	Docherty	Dunn	O'Farrell	Dagger	Thompson	Finney (2p)	Baxter	Taylor (1)		
Mar 9	Charlton Ath.	Div 1	h	4-3	21482	Else	Cunningham	Walton	Milne	Dunn	Evans	Dagger (1)	Thompson (2)	Finney (1)	Baxter	Taylor		
Mar 16	Sunderland	Div 1	a	0-0	37907	Else	Cunningham	Walton	Docherty	Dunn	Evans	Dagger	Thompson	Finney	Baxter	Taylor		
Mar 23	Luton Town	Div 1	h	2-0	23361	Else	Cunningham	Walton	Docherty	Dunn	Evans	Dagger	Thompson (1)	Finney (1)	Baxter	Taylor		
Mar 30	Aston Villa	Div 1	a	0-2	33185	Else	Cunningham	Walton	Docherty	Dunn	Evans	Dagger	Thompson	Finney	Waterhouse	Taylor		
Apr 6	Wolverhampton W.	Div 1	h	1-0	13311	Else	Cunningham	Walton	Milne	Dunn	Mattinson	Taylor	Waterhouse	Hatsell	Baxter (1)	Morrison		
Apr 13	Manchester City	Div 1	a	2-0	31305	Else	Cunningham	Walton	Docherty	Dunn	O'Farrell	Dagger	Thompson	Hatsell (2)	Baxter	Morrison		
Apr 19	Sheffield Wed.	Div 1	h	1-0	20069	Else	Cunningham	Walton	Docherty	Dunn	O'Farrell	Dagger	Thompson	Finney	Baxter	Taylor (1)		
Apr 20	Blackpool	Div 1	h	0-0	35887	Else	Cunningham	Walton	Docherty	Mattinson	O'Farrell	Dagger	Thompson	Finney	Baxter	Taylor		
Apr 22	Sheffield Wed.	Div 1	a	1-3	20312	Else	Cunningham	Walton	Docherty	Mattinson	O'Farrell	Dagger	Thompson (1)	Hatsell	Baxter	Taylor		
Apr 27	Chelsea	Div 1	h	1-0	13592	Else	Cunningham	Walton	Docherty	Mattinson	O'Farrell	Dagger	Thompson	Hatsell (1)	Baxter	Taylor		
	* at Goodison Park			* AET														

SEASON 1957–1958

If the 1956–57 season was exciting then this year, arguably, saw the modern Preston North End at their peak. Certainly, this was the last of the great seasons and the one that the club, as it approaches the new millennium, is still trying to aspire to. Preston eventually had to be content with the runners-up position behind the great Wolverhampton Wanderers side led by England's Billy Wright. This time North End's challenge was never as close as their 1952–53 runners-up spot had been, the Wolves were too much of a dominant force for that, but many observers believe that this Preston side was a stronger one. The Lilywhites banged in goals from all angles and with Tommy Thompson and Tom Finney continuing their devastating partnership the side was a match for most. Only one major signing was made by Cliff Britton during the summer with Derek Mayers joining North End from Everton. He soon slotted into a very smooth running outfit, making a goalscoring debut and going on to make the number seven shirt his own. The team had rarely seen so few changes to the line-up in a season and no fewer than six players made 40 appearances or more. In defence Joe Walton and Willie Cunningham were models of consistency whilst Joe Dunn had another outstanding season at centre-half. With Tommy Docherty and Jimmy Baxter again in majestic form in midfield it was clear to see just why Preston were such a strong side. Some magnificent wins were recorded with

Sammy Taylor. goalscoring winger who scored two hat-tricks for North End.

several high scoring performances catching the eye. None more so than the 8–0 demolition of Birmingham at Deepdale in the February. Thompson scored a superb hat-trick in that match and those goals came during an incredible run for the number eight. The popular Geordie scored in eleven consecutive games, a new record for the club, and his total during that spell was, in fact, a staggering 17 goals. It was only right and proper that 'Topper', as he was known, should score the last goal against Arsenal in the final game. It brought Preston's league total to the magic 100. The Preston fans went wild as they realised the significance of the goal. If there was any disappointment about the season then it was only in the fact that the club again failed to win a trophy. The FA Cup was again put out of reach as an early exit, 3–0 at home to Bolton in the third round, ended the dream for another year. The only consolation from that came with the fact that Bolton went on to win the trophy. Overall though the season had been quite memorable with some of the best football ever seen at Deepdale played by North End.

DEBUTANTS: (4) Derek Mayers, Alec Farrell, Alex Alston and Jim Knowles

LAST GAMES: (2) Jim Knowles and Tommy Docherty

Tommy Thompson. His 34 league goals is a PNE record for the First Division

STAT FACTS:
Best home run without defeat: 11 games
Best away run without defeat: 5 games
Longest run unbeaten: 10 games
Longest run without a win: 3 games
Best home attendance:
39,066 vs. Man Utd 9.11.57
Worst home attendance:
17,944 vs. Chelsea 28.9.57
Best away attendance:
48,413 vs. Man Utd 5.4.58
Worst away attendance:
22,549 vs. Luton 22.2.58
Aggregate and average home attendance:
525,250 – 25,012
Aggregate and average away attendance:
677,090 – 32,242

Future Players born between August 1957 and May 1958: George Berry, John Lowey, Oshor Williams.
Ever presents: Willie Cunningham and Joe Walton
Hat-tricks: (3) Taylor 2, Thompson
FA Cup: Third Round   **Players used:** 18
Manager: Cliff Britton
Chairman: N. Buck Esq.
Leading scorer: 34 goals – Tommy Thompson (all league)
AUTHORS' UNOFFICIAL PLAYER OF THE SEASON:
Tommy Thompson

League position in Division One: Runners-up – P42 W26 D7 L9 F100 A51 Pts 59
Home: W18 D2 L1 F63 A14 Away: W8 D5 L8 F37 A37

Left to right: *Back row:* Waterhouse, Docherty, Cunningham, Else, Dunn, Walton, J. Milne (trainer).
Front row: Dagger, Thompson, Finney, Baxter, Taylor, O'Farrell

Match Report: Scots in Charitable Mood – 3 Aug 1957 Edinburgh Select XI 1 Preston 3

Preston North End joined the list of notable English clubs to travel north to help raise £74,000 on behalf of deserving charities. Not since 1951 had an English club won the Allison Trophy, which was at stake. The King's African Rifles, in Edinburgh for the forthcoming Military Tattoo, entertained the 40,000 Easter Road crowd prior to kick-off. The select eleven included six players from Hibernian and five from Hearts. The white shirts of Preston, the green and white of the Select side, a billiard table pitch and brilliant sunshine formed an ideal picture setting for this pre-season encounter. North End, fresh from a Scandinavian tour, looked good and the game opened with fast inter-passing from both sides. The play delighted the charitable crowd who applauded good play whether it came from the Scots or the visitors. A Baxter thunderbolt shot brought the best out of Leslie in the home goal whilst at the other end Harrower went close with another hot shot. The Scots then had a let-off when Finney, after gathering the ball on the wing, tricked both Muir and Plenderleith before setting up a chance for Taylor. Unfortunately for Preston Taylor's effort cleared the crossbar. A minute later, however, Dagger lashed home the first goal from just inside the penalty box giving Preston a deserved lead. The Scots retaliated which meant more work for Preston's Scots, Dunn, Cunningham and Docherty. Then came real grief for the Select side as Dagger, showing a real appetite for the game, dashed down the right wing and delivered a precision cross which Baxter successfully met with his head to put Preston two up. Goalkeeper Leslie was injured and Muir went in goal with a substitute coming on, Cumming of Hearts. Leslie then came back on and his side momentarily had 12 men, so the referee had to stop play to allow Cumming to leave the game after his short spell of action. After the break Leslie did not return, so Cumming was back on and this time went in goal! Confused?! Meanwhile, in the match, Thompson then scored a third for Preston whilst Dave Mackay, later to join Spurs, scored a consolation goal for the hosts with a fiercely taken free-kick.

League appearances (42 games)

Alston A. G. 2, Baxter J.C. 37, Cunningham W. C. 42, Dagger J. L. 10, Docherty T. H. 40, Dunn J. P. 37, Else F. 40, Farrall A. 6, Finney T. 34, Hatsell D. 10, Knowles J. 2, Mattinson H. 4, Mayers D. 34, Milne G. 5, O'Farrell F. 40, Taylor S. M. 36, Thompson T. 41, Walton J. 42.

FA Cup appearances (1 game)

Else, Cunningham, Walton, Docherty, Dunn, O'Farrell, Thompson, Finney, Baxter, Mayers, Hatsell, all one each.

Goalscorers: 100 League Goals

Thompson 34, Finney 26 (5 pens), Taylor 14 (1 pen), Mayers 12, Baxter 5 (1 pen), Hatsell 3, Docherty 1, Dagger 1, Farrall 1, Alston 1.
Own goals 2. (Stevens of Bolton and Ryden of Tottenham H.)

Trivia Facts:

North End did the double over eight teams during the season.

In his last game in North End's colours, Angus Morrison deputised as captain for Harry Mattinson in the reserve game with Liverpool at Deepdale. It was his first such honour during his long stay with the club. It came two weeks before his move to Millwall.

Season 1957–58: First Division

	P	W	D	L	F	A	Pts
1 Wolves	42	28	8	6	103	47	64
2 PRESTON	42	26	7	9	100	51	59
3 Tottenham	42	21	9	12	93	77	51
4 WBA	42	18	14	10	92	70	50
5 Man City	42	22	5	15	104	100	49
6 Burnley	42	21	5	16	80	74	47
7 Blackpool	42	19	6	17	80	67	44
8 Luton	42	19	6	17	69	63	44
9 Man United	42	16	11	15	85	75	43
10 Nottingham Forest	42	16	10	16	69	63	42
11 Chelsea	42	15	12	15	83	79	42
12 Arsenal	42	16	7	19	73	85	39
13 Birmingham	42	14	11	17	76	89	39
14 Aston Villa	42	16	7	19	73	86	39
15 Bolton	42	14	10	18	65	87	38
16 Everton	42	13	11	18	65	75	37
17 Leeds	42	14	9	19	51	63	37
18 Leicester	42	14	5	23	91	112	33
19 Newcastle	42	12	8	22	73	81	32
20 Portsmouth	42	12	8	22	73	88	32
21 Sunderland	42	10	12	20	54	97	32
22 Sheffield Wednesday	42	12	7	23	69	92	31

PNE *vs.* Tottenham Sept 14 1957. Else clears under pressure.

Date 1957-8	Opponents	Comp	h or a	Score	Att.	1	2	3	4	5	6	7	8	9	10	11		
Aug 24	Nottm. Forest	Div 1	a	1-2	33285	Else	Cunningham	Walton	Docherty	Dunn	O'Farrell	Dagger	Thompson	Finney	Baxter	Taylor (1)		
Aug 27	Burnley	Div 1	a	0-2	27804	Else	Cunningham	Walton	Docherty	Dunn	O'Farrell	Dagger	Thompson	Finney	Baxter	Taylor		
Aug 31	Portsmouth	Div 1	h	4-0	24422	Else	Cunningham	Walton	Docherty	Dunn	O'Farrell	Dagger	Thompson (2)	Finney (1)	Baxter (1)	Taylor		
Sep 4	Burnley	Div 1	h	2-1	31267	Else	Cunningham	Walton	Docherty	Dunn	O'Farrell	Dagger	Thompson (1)	Finney (1)	Baxter	Taylor		
Sep 7	WBA	Div 1	a	1-4	29768	Else	Cunningham	Walton	Docherty (1)	Dunn	O'Farrell	Dagger	Thompson	Finney	Baxter	Taylor		
Sep 11	Manchester City	Div 1	a	0-2	24439	Else	Cunningham	Walton	Docherty	Dunn	O'Farrell	Dagger	Thompson	Finney	Baxter	Taylor		
Sep 14	Tottenham H.	Div 1	h	3-1	23364	Else	Cunningham	Walton	Docherty	Dunn	O'Farrell	Mayers (1)	Thompson (2)	Finney	Baxter	Taylor		
Sep 18	Manchester City	Div 1	h	6-1	22034	Else	Cunningham	Walton	Docherty	Dunn	O'Farrell	Dagger (1)	Thompson (1)	Finney (2)	Baxter	Taylor (2)		
Sep 21	Birmingham City	Div 1	a	1-3	24894	Else	Cunningham	Walton	Milne	O'Farrell	Docherty	Dagger	Thompson (1)	Hatsell	Baxter	Taylor		
Sep 28	Chelsea	Div 1	a	5-2	17944	Else	Cunningham	Walton	Docherty	Dunn	O'Farrell	Mayers	Thompson (1)	Finney (1)	Baxter	Taylor (3, 1p)		
Oct 5	Newcastle Utd.	Div 1	a	2-0	36131	Else	Cunningham	Walton	Milne	Dunn	O'Farrell	Mayers	Thompson	Finney (1)	Baxter	Taylor (1)		
Oct 12	Luton Town	Div 1	h	1-0	25403	Else	Cunningham	Walton	Docherty	Dunn	O'Farrell	Dagger	Thompson	Finney (1p)	Baxter	Mayers		
Oct 19	Sunderland	Div 1	a	0-0	34676	Else	Cunningham	Walton	Docherty	Dunn	O'Farrell	Dagger	Farrall	Alston	Baxter	Mayers		
Oct 26	Everton	Div 1	h	3-1	31449	Else	Cunningham	Walton	Docherty	Dunn	O'Farrell	Mayers (2)	Thompson	Finney (1)	Baxter	Taylor		
Nov 2	Leeds Utd.	Div 1	h	3-2	23832	Else	Cunningham	Walton	Docherty	Dunn	O'Farrell	Mayers (1)	Thompson	Alston (1)	Baxter (1p)	Taylor		
Nov 9	Manchester Utd.	Div 1	h	1-1	39066	Else	Cunningham	Walton	Docherty	Dunn	O'Farrell	Mayers	Thompson	Finney (1)	Baxter	Taylor		
Nov 16	Leicester City	Div 1	h	3-1	27319	Else	Cunningham	Walton	Docherty	Mattinson	O'Farrell	Mayers	Thompson (1)	Finney (1)	Baxter	Taylor (1)		
Nov 23	Bolton W.	Div 1	h	3-0	28036	Else	Cunningham	Walton	Docherty	Dunn	O'Farrell	Mayers	Thompson (1)	Finney (1)	Baxter	Taylor	1 og	(Stevens)
Nov 30	Aston Villa	Div 1	a	2-2	25847	Else	Cunningham	Walton	Docherty	Dunn	O'Farrell	Mayers	Thompson (1)	Finney	Baxter	Taylor (1)		
Dec 7	Wolverhampton W.	Div 1	h	1-2	22771	Else	Cunningham	Walton	Docherty	Dunn	O'Farrell	Mayers	Thompson	Hatsell (1)	Baxter	Taylor		
Dec 14	Arsenal	Div 1	a	2-4	31840	Else	Cunningham	Walton	Docherty	Dunn	O'Farrell	Mayers (1)	Thompson (1)	Hatsell	Baxter	Taylor		
Dec 21	Nottm. Forest	Div 1	h	2-0	20945	Knowles	Cunningham	Walton	Docherty	Dunn	O'Farrell	Mayers (1)	Thompson (1)	Finney	Baxter	Taylor		
Dec 25	Sheffield Wed.	Div 1	a	4-4	25525	Knowles	Cunningham	Walton	Docherty	Dunn	O'Farrell	Mayers	Thompson (2)	Hatsell	Baxter	Finney (2)		
Dec 26	Sheffield Wed.	Div 1	h	3-0	28053	Else	Cunningham	Walton	Docherty	Dunn	O'Farrell	Mayers	Thompson (2)	Hatsell	Baxter	Finney (1)		
Dec 28	Portsmouth	Div 1	a	2-0	31735	Else	Cunningham	Walton	Docherty	Dunn	O'Farrell	Mayers (1)	Thompson (1)	Hatsell	Baxter	Taylor		
Jan 4	**Bolton W. Rd 3**	**FAC**	**h**	**0-3**	**32641**	**Else**	**Cunningham**	**Walton**	**Docherty**	**Dunn**	**O'Farrell**	**Mayers**	**Thompson**	**Hatsell**	**Baxter**	**Finney**		
Jan 11	WBA	Div 1	h	3-1	25262	Else	Cunningham	Walton	Docherty	Dunn	O'Farrell	Mayers	Thompson (1)	Finney (1p)	Farrall (1)	Taylor		
Jan 18	Tottenham H.	Div 1	a	3-3	43941	Else	Cunningham	Walton	Docherty	Dunn	O'Farrell	Mayers	Thompson (2)	Finney	Farrall	Taylor	1 og	(Ryden)
Feb 1	Birmingham City	Div 1	h	8-0	21511	Else	Cunningham	Walton	Docherty	Dunn	O'Farrell	Mayers	Thompson (3)	Finney (2)	Baxter	Taylor (3)		
Feb 8	Chelsea	Div 1	a	2-0	42704	Else	Cunningham	Walton	Docherty	Dunn	O'Farrell	Mayers (1)	Thompson (1)	Hatsell	Baxter	Finney (1)		
Feb 22	Luton Town	Div 1	a	3-1	22549	Else	Cunningham	Walton	Docherty	Dunn	Milne	Mayers	Thompson (1)	Finney (1p)	Baxter	Taylor (1)		
Mar 1	Sunderland	Div 1	h	3-0	23974	Else	Cunningham	Walton	Docherty	Mattinson	Milne	Mayers	Thompson (2)	Finney	Baxter (1)	Taylor		
Mar 8	Everton	Div 1	a	2-4	43291	Else	Cunningham	Walton	Docherty	Mattinson	O'Farrell	Mayers	Thompson	Finney (1p)	Baxter (1)	Taylor		
Mar 15	Leeds Utd.	Div 1	h	3-0	21353	Else	Cunningham	Walton	Docherty	Mattinson	O'Farrell	Mayers	Thompson (1)	Finney (2)	Baxter	Taylor		
Mar 19	Newcastle Utd.	Div 1	h	2-1	24787	Else	Cunningham	Walton	Docherty	Dunn	O'Farrell	Mayers	Thompson	Finney (2)	Baxter	Taylor		
Mar 29	Leicester City	Div 1	h	4-1	18392	Else	Cunningham	Walton	Docherty	Dunn	O'Farrell	Mayers (1)	Thompson (2)	Finney (1)	Baxter	Taylor		
Apr 4	Blackpool	Div 1	h	2-1	29029	Else	Cunningham	Walton	Docherty	Dunn	O'Farrell	Mayers (1)	Thompson	Finney	Baxter (1)	Taylor		
Apr 5	Manchester Utd.	Div 1	a	0-0	48413	Else	Cunningham	Walton	Docherty	Dunn	O'Farrell	Mayers	Thompson	Finney	Farrall	Taylor		
Apr 7	Blackpool	Div 1	a	2-1	32626	Else	Cunningham	Walton	Docherty	Dunn	O'Farrell	Mayers	Thompson (1)	Hatsell	Baxter	Taylor (1)		
Apr 12	Aston Villa	Div 1	h	1-1	21053	Else	Cunningham	Walton	Docherty	Dunn	O'Farrell	Mayers (1)	Thompson	Finney	Farrall	Taylor		
Apr 19	Wolverhampton W.	Div 1	a	0-2	46001	Else	Cunningham	Walton	Milne	Dunn	O'Farrell	Mayers	Thompson	Hatsell	Farrall	Taylor		
Apr 21	Bolton W.	Div 1	a	4-0	24067	Else	Cunningham	Walton	Docherty	Dunn	O'Farrell	Mayers	Thompson (1)	Hatsell (2)	Baxter	Finney (1p)		
Apr 26	Arsenal	Div 1	h	3-0	21538	Else	Cunningham	Walton	Docherty	Dunn	O'Farrell	Mayers (2)	Thompson (1)	Finney	Baxter	Taylor		

SEASON 1958–1959

Hopes were high at the start of the 1958–59 season, especially as in the previous two seasons Preston had been one of the top three teams in the country. But, alas, this year was to prove an anti-climax and the best the club could do was to occupy a mid-table position. Their games produced plenty of goalmouth incident, although not always at the right end, in fact, in no fewer than nine games Preston conceded four goals or more. This was surprising because little had changed in the defence although maybe the absence of the transferred Tommy Docherty had more of an effect than was at first realised. Other players continued to show good form though with Frank O'Farrell playing well at wing-half and Dennis Hatsell having his best season so far in attack. One of the big problems, although Hatsell was an excellent replacement, was that Tom Finney had another season dogged by injury. He was to play in only sixteen league games, some were missed through International call ups, and the continuity of the side seen over the previous two years was affected badly. Jimmy Baxter was another who only showed glimpses of his earlier play and Preston struggled as these key players found it difficult to sustain their best form. The early results were encouraging, without setting the world alight but gradually North End developed an infuriating habit of following a good result with a bad one. To illustrate this point Preston suffered a double Christmas defeat by Blackpool immediately after a terrific win at Highbury against the Arsenal. The fans became a little restless as

this sort of result sequence happened time and again. The supporters did find relief in an FA Cup run that so nearly brought glory and that coveted second chance for Finney to reach Wembley. Once again, as in the previous year, it was Bolton Wanderers who proved the stumbling block. Preston tried desperately to win through as the tie went to three epic ties before being settled in Bolton's favour in a second replay. Nearly 147,000 people watched the three games, some indication of the popularity of football in the 1950s. Some new players made their mark with Gordon Milne, son of the Preston stalwart of yesteryear, Jimmy Milne, showing great promise and John Wylie and John O'Neill making their debuts. But no player, before or since, made the impact that 16 year old goalkeeper John Barton made. The youngster was drafted in at the last moment for his league baptism at Highbury in the game just before Christmas against Arsenal. Barton, in front of his proud parents, played a blinder in a 2–1 win, making national headlines the next day. It will always remain one of the most cherished of the many memories recorded in this book and was one of the best highlights of this or any other season.

DEBUTANTS: (7) John Wylie, Gil Lambert, Jim Smith, John Barton, John O'Neill, Mike Lynn, Dave Sneddon

LAST GAMES: (3) Harry Mattinson, Jimmy Baxter, Mike Lynne

Future Players born between August 1958 and May 1959: John Thomas, Steve Elliott, Jon Clark, Mick Rathbone, Martin Hodge, Geoff Twentyman, Ian Cochrane, Vernon Allatt.

Ever presents: Willie Cunningham
Hat-tricks: None
Players used: 25
FA Cup: Fifth Round Second Replay
Manager: Cliff Britton
Chairman: N. Buck Esq.
Leading scorer: 21 goals – Tommy Thompson (19 league 2 cup)

AUTHORS' UNOFFICIAL PLAYER OF THE SEASON:
Willie Cunningham

League appearances (42 games)

Alston A. G. 7, Barton J. B. 3, Baxter J. C. 26, Campbell L. G. 6, Cunningham W. C. 42, Dagger J. L. 6, Dunn J. P. 33, Else F. 37, Farrall A. 11, Finney T. 16, Hatsell D. 35, Lambert J. G. 13, Lynne M. G. A. 2, Mattinson H. 8, Mayers D. 37, Milne G. 30, O'Farrell F. 33, O'Neill J. N. 2, Smith J. A. G. 18, Sneddon D. 1, Taylor S. M. 17, Thompson T. 34, Walton J. 36, Wilson J. R. 4, Wylie J. E. 5.

FA Cup appearances (6 games)

Else 3, Cunningham 6, Walton 6, Milne 3, Dunn 3, O'Farrell 3, Mayers 6, Thompson 5, Hatsell 4, Farrall 3, Lambert 4, Smith 6, Mattinson 3, Campbell 6, Lynne 3, Alston 2

Goalscorers: 70 League–12 Cup–(Total 82)

Thompson 19–2 (1 pen) (21), Hatsell 16 (1 pen) –2 (18), Mayers 7–1 (8), Finney 6–0 (6), Farrell 4 (1 pen)–3 (7), Baxter 5 (2 pens)–0 (5), Taylor 3–0 (3), Campbell 2–1 (3), Alston 2–0 (2), Smith 1–2 (3), Cunningham 1–0 (1), Walton 1–0 (1), Milne 1–0 (1), Lambert 1–0 (1), O'Farrell 0–1 (1). Own goals 1–0 (1) Whitehead of Newcastle.

League position in Division One: 12th – P42 W17 D7 L18 F70 A77 Pts 41
Home: W9 D3 L9 F40 A39   Away: W8 D4 L9 F30 A38

Frank O'Farrell. North End's Irish International wing-half.

Match Report: Gunners Hit by Dennis's Double – 20 Dec 1958 Arsenal 1 Preston 2

The interest in this important clash of championship contenders at Highbury was heightened by the introduction of two debutants by North End. John Barton, a 16 year old amateur goalkeeper, had to step up the ladder in a crisis to replace Fred Else who was under orders to rest due to slight concussion. Alan Kelly, the reserve keeper, was also unavailable injured with a fractured wrist. John O'Neill, a young Irishman, replaced the injured Joe Walton who thus ended a run of 134 consecutive league games. Gordon Milne returned to wing-half after representing the Army in Paris. When the teams appeared, Barton was immediately swamped by photographers as he entered his goal for kicking in practice. When the game began Barton was quickly given an early touch to calm his nerves, and to be fair this was some ordeal as he had not even appeared in a reserve game. After 14 minutes of play Preston swept downfield where Thompson, up against former North Ender Docherty, neatly put Hatsell into a clear scoring position. The Preston number nine made no mistake with an accurate low drive from an awkward angle. On this chilly day Preston had been given little chance of succeeding with their rather depleted side, Finney was also absent, but the early goal gave them great confidence. On the half hour mark O'Farrell accurately found Mayers with a long ball from the left and the winger centred to the head of Hatsell who once again took his chance excellently to put the Lancashire side two up. It was Hatsell's ninth goal against the Gunners. In defence Cunningham, the seasoned campaigner, was a tower of strength around the two North End debutants. Six minutes before the interval though Henderson pierced the defensive barrier and drove a powerful shot past the helpless Barton. Early in the second half Barton made a series of fine saves to keep his side in front. He dived full length to keep out Henderson before turning a fierce goalbound shot by Bloomfield around the post. He also fisted clear a dangerous inswinging corner before confidently catching Docherty's return header high above everyone else. Barton had an inspired second half and can be proud of his overall display against the Gunners.

Dennis Hatsell. Regular goalscorer with over 50 league goals to his credit.

Preston North End Reserve Team 1958–59.

STAT FACTS:
Best home run without defeat: 3 games
Best away run without defeat: 4 games
Longest run unbeaten: 5 games
Longest run without a win: 5 games
Best home attendance: 37,122 vs. Bolton FAC 18.2.59
Worst home attendance: 10,545 vs. Luton 6.4.59
Best away attendance: 58,692 vs. Bolton FAC 14.2.59
Worst away attendance: 15,790 vs. Portsmouth 4.4.59
Aggregate and average home attendance: 471,131 – 22,345
Aggregate and average away attendance: 638,405 – 30,400

Left to right: *Back row:* Wylie, Cunningham, Dunn, Else, Walton, O'Farrell.
Front row: Mayers, Thompson, Hatsell, Lambert, Finney.

Season 1958–59: First Division

		P	W	D	L	F	A	Pts
1	Wolves	42	28	5	9	110	49	61
2	Man United	42	24	7	11	103	66	55
3	Arsenal	42	21	8	13	88	68	50
4	Bolton	42	20	10	12	79	66	50
5	WBA	42	18	13	11	88	68	49
6	West Ham	42	21	6	15	85	70	48
7	Burney	42	19	10	13	81	70	48
8	Blackpool	42	18	11	13	66	49	47
9	Birmingham	42	20	6	16	84	68	46
10	Blackburn	42	17	10	15	76	70	44
11	Newcastle	42	17	7	18	80	80	41
12	PRESTON	42	17	7	18	70	77	41
13	Nottingham Forest	42	17	6	19	71	74	40
14	Chelsea	42	18	4	20	77	98	40
15	Leeds	42	15	9	18	51	74	39
16	Everton	42	17	4	21	71	87	38
17	Luton	42	12	13	17	68	71	37
18	Tottenham	42	13	10	19	85	95	36
19	Leicester	42	11	10	21	67	98	32
20	Man City	42	11	9	22	64	95	31
21	Aston Villa	42	11	8	23	58	87	30
22	Portsmouth	42	6	9	27	64	112	21

Date 1958-9	Opponents		Comp	h or a	Score	Att.	1	2	3	4	5	6	7	8	9	10	11		
Aug 23	Arsenal		Div 1	h	2-1	30588	Else	Cunningham	Walton	Milne	Dunn	O'Farrell	Mayers	Thompson (1)	Hatsell (1)	Baxter	Finney		
Aug 27	Everton		Div 1	a	4-1	52306	Else	Cunningham	Walton	Milne	Dunn	O'Farrell	Mayers	Farrall	Hatsell (2)	Baxter (1)	Finney (1)		
Aug 30	Manchester City		Div 1	a	1-1	42576	Else	Cunningham	Walton	Milne	Dunn	O'Farrell	Mayers	Thompson	Hatsell	Baxter	Finney (1)		
Sep 1	Everton		Div 1	h	3-1	28339	Else	Cunningham	Walton	Milne	Dunn	O'Farrell	Mayers (1)	Thompson	Hatsell (1)	Baxter (1)	Finney		
Sep 6	Leeds Utd.		Div 1	h	1-2	22765	Else	Cunningham	Walton	Milne	Dunn	Wylie	Mayers	Thompson	Hatsell	Baxter	Finney (1)		
Sep 13	WBA		Div 1	a	1-1	36402	Else	Cunningham	Walton	Milne	Dunn	O'Farrell	Mayers (1)	Thompson	Hatsell	Baxter	Finney		
Sep 17	Leicester City		Div 1	a	2-2	34513	Else	Cunningham	Walton	Milne	Dunn	O'Farrell	Mayers	Thompson (2)	Hatsell	Baxter	Finney		
Sep 20	Birmingham City		Div 1	h	3-0	24257	Else	Cunningham	Walton	Milne	Dunn	O'Farrell	Mayers (1)	Thompson (1)	Hatsell (1)	Lambert	Finney		
Sep 22	Leicester City		Div 1	h	3-1	25443	Else	Cunningham	Walton	Milne	Dunn	O'Farrell	Mayers	Thompson (1)	Hatsell	Lambert (1)	Finney (1)		
Sep 27	Luton Town		Div 1	a	1-4	23056	Else	Cunningham	Walton	Wylie	Dunn	O'Farrell	Mayers	Thompson	Hatsell (1)	Lambert	Finney		
Oct 4	Bolton W.		Div 1	h	0-0	28769	Else	Cunningham	Walton	Milne	Dunn	O'Farrell	Mayers	Thompson	Hatsell	Lambert	Taylor		
Oct 8	Manchester Utd.		Div 1	a	2-0	46163	Else	Cunningham	Walton	Milne	Dunn	O'Farrell	Mayers	Thompson (1)	Hatsell (1)	Baxter	Finney		
Oct 11	Blackburn R.		Div 1	a	1-4	39075	Else	Cunningham	Walton	Milne (1)	Dunn	O'Farrell	Mayers	Thompson	Hatsell	Baxter	Taylor		
Oct 18	Newcastle Utd.		Div 1	h	3-4	25709	Else	Cunningham	Walton	Milne	Dunn	O'Farrell	Mayers	Thompson	Hatsell (1)	Baxter	Finney (2)		
Oct 25	Nottm Forest		Div 1	a	1-0	33583	Else	Cunningham	Walton	Milne	Dunn	O'Farrell	Mayers	Thompson (1)	Hatsell	Baxter	Finney		
Nov 1	Chelsea		Div 1	h	2-0	21513	Else	Cunningham	Walton	Milne	Dunn	O'Farrell	Mayers	Thompson (1)	Hatsell	Farrall (1)	Lambert		
Nov 8	Wolverhampton W.		Div 1	a	0-2	35593	Else	Cunningham	Walton	Milne	Dunn	O'Farrell	Mayers	Thompson	Finney	Hatsell	Lambert		
Nov 15	Portsmouth		Div 1	h	3-1	16107	Else	Cunningham	Walton (1)	Milne	Dunn	O'Farrell	Mayers (1)	Thompson	Hatsell	Baxter	Lambert		
Nov 22	Aston Villa		Div 1	a	0-2	28060	Else	Cunningham	Walton	Milne	Dunn	O'Farrell	Mayers	Finney	Hatsell	Baxter	Lambert		
Nov 29	West Ham Utd.		Div 1	h	2-1	19438	Else	Cunningham	Walton	Milne	Dunn	O'Farrell	Mayers	Hatsell (2, 1p)	Finney	Baxter	Taylor		
Dec 6	Tottenham H.		Div 1	a	2-1	31806	Else	Cunningham	Walton	Milne	Dunn	O'Farrell	Mayers (1)	Farrall	Hatsell (1)	Baxter	Taylor		
Dec 13	Manchester Utd.		Div 1	h	3-4	26290	Else	Cunningham	Walton	O'Farrell	Dunn	Smith	Mayers	Thompson (1)	Hatsell (2)	Baxter	Taylor		
Dec 20	Arsenal		Div 1	a	2-1	32640	Barton	Cunningham	O'Neill	Milne	Dunn	O'Farrell	Mayers	Thompson	Hatsell (2)	Baxter	Finney		
Dec 25	Blackpool		Div 1	a	2-4	24411	Barton	Cunningham	Walton	Milne	Dunn	O'Farrell	Mayers	Thompson (2)	Hatsell	Baxter	Taylor		
Dec 26	Blackpool		Div 1	h	0-3	36435	Barton	Cunningham	Walton	Milne	Mattinson	O'Farrell	Mayers	Thompson	Hatsell	Baxter	Taylor		
Jan 3	Manchester City		Div 1	h	2-0	21268	Else	Cunningham	Walton	O'Farrell	Dunn	Smith	Campbell (1)	Farrall (1)	Hatsell	Lambert	Mayers		
Jan 10	Derby County	Rd 3	FAC	a	2-2	29237	Else	Cunningham	Walton	O'Farrell	Dunn	Smith	Campbell	Farrall (1)	Hatsell (1)	Lambert	Mayers		
Jan 17	Leeds Utd.		Div 1	a	3-1	22043	Else	Cunningham	Walton	O'Farrell	Dunn	Smith	Campbell	Thompson (1)	Hatsell	Farrall (1)	Mayers (1)		
Jan 19	Derby County	Replay	FAC	h	4-2*	29294	Lynne	Cunningham	Walton	O'Farrell	Dunn	Smith (1)	Campbell	Thompson (1)	Hatsell	Farrall (1)	Mayers (1)		
Jan 24	Bradford City	Rd 4	FAC	h	3-2	35716	Lynne	Cunningham	Walton	O'Farrell (1)	Dunn	Smith	Campbell	Thompson	Hatsell (1)	Farrall (1)	Mayers		
Jan 31	WBA		Div 1	h	2-4	23138	Lynne	Cunningham	Walton	O'Farrell	Dunn	Smith	Campbell	Thompson (1)	Hatsell	Farrall	Mayers (1)		
Feb 7	Birmingham City		Div 1	a	1-5	21233	Lynne	Cunningham (1)	Walton	Milne	Dunn	Smith	Campbell	Thompson	Hatsell	Farrall	Mayers		
Feb 14	Bolton W.	Rd 5	FAC	a	2-2	58692	Lynne	Cunningham	Walton	Milne	Mattinson	Smith	Campbell (1)	Thompson (1p)	Alston	Lambert	Mayers		
Feb 18	Bolton W.	Replay	FAC	h	1-1*	37122	Else	Cunningham	Walton	Milne	Mattinson	Smith (1)	Campbell	Thompson	Alston	Lambert	Mayers		
Feb 21	Bolton W.		Div 1	a	1-2	16472	Else	Cunningham	O'Neill	Milne	O'Farrell	Smith	Campbell (1)	Farrall	Alston	Lambert	Taylor		
Feb 23	Bolton W. *	2nd Replay	FAC	n	0-1	51090	Else	Cunningham	Walton	Milne	Mattinson	Smith	Campbell	Thompson	Hatsell	Lambert	Mayers		
Feb 28	Blackburn R.		Div 1	h	1-2	22700	Else	Cunningham	Walton	O'Farrell	Mattinson	Smith	Campbell	Thompson (1)	Hatsell	Milne	Mayers		
Mar 7	Newcastle Utd.		Div 1	h	2-1	31962	Else	Cunningham	Wilson	Milne	Dunn	Smith	Mayers	Baxter	Alston (1)	Lambert	Taylor	1 og	(Whitehead)
Mar 16	Nottm Forest		Div 1	h	3-5	15438	Else	Cunningham	Walton	Milne	Dunn	Smith	Mayers	Baxter (1p)	Alston (1)	Lambert	Taylor (1)		
Mar 21	Chelsea		Div 1	a	1-3	31270	Else	Cunningham	Walton	Milne	Dunn	Smith	Mayers	Baxter (1p)	Alston	Lambert	Taylor		
Mar 27	Burnley		Div 1	a	0-1	18322	Else	Cunningham	Wilson	Wylie	Dunn	Smith	Dagger	Thompson	Alston	Farrall	Mayers		
Mar 28	Wolverhampton W.		Div 1	h	1-2	22465	Else	Cunningham	Wilson	Wylie	Dunn	Smith	Dagger	Thompson	Alston	Farrall (1p)	Mayers		
Mar 30	Burnley		Div 1	h	0-4	17357	Else	Cunningham	Wilson	Wylie	Mattinson	Smith	Dagger	Thompson	Alston	Farrall	Mayers		
Apr 4	Portsmouth		Div 1	a	2-1	15790	Else	Cunningham	Walton	O'Farrell	Mattinson	Smith	Dagger	Thompson (1)	Hatsell	Baxter	Taylor (1)		
Apr 6	Luton Town		Div 1	h	0-0	10545	Else	Cunningham	Walton	O'Farrell	Mattinson	Smith	Dagger	Thompson	Hatsell	Baxter	Taylor		
Apr 11	Aston Villa		Div 1	h	4-2	12244	Else	Cunningham	Walton	Milne	Mattinson	Smith	Dagger	Thompson (2)	Hatsell (1)	Baxter	Taylor (1)		
Apr 18	West Ham Utd.		Div 1	a	1-1	21129	Else	Cunningham	Walton	O'Farrell	Mattinson	Smith	Mayers	Thompson	Hatsell	Baxter (1)	Taylor		
Apr 25	Tottenham H.		Div 1	a	2-2	20323	Else	Cunningham	Walton	O'Farrell	Mattinson	Smith (1)	Finney	Thompson (1)	Hatsell	Sneddon	Taylor		
	* played at Ewood Park				*AET														

SEASON 1959–1960

This season will always hold a special significance in the memory of all Preston North End supporters. It will forever be known as Tom Finney's last season. With injuries finally taking their toll, the great man decided that the game against Luton Town on April 30 1960 would be his last for the club. The season itself did produce an improvement on the previous year and there was no shortage of thrills and spills. Ironically Finney was to achieve something he had never done before as he ended the season as leading goalscorer. The goals were actually shared around the team but with David Sneddon, the natural successor to Jimmy Baxter, settling in well to his task as the main schemer, the chances were created in abundance. The Scottish player impressed everybody and his partnership with the lively Sammy Taylor on the left-wing was a key influence on the team. Newcomer Johnny Fullam also looked a good signing and with Gordon Milne continuing his good form the wing-half berths looked strong. Preston had a poor start to the season, not unusually, and won only one of the first six games. But soon the fans were watching some really exciting football and in one spell the club won seven matches on the trot. Unfortunately North End also lost some silly points and there was never a chance of a challenge on the title. Two particular games stood out as the matches with Chelsea created incredible excitement. Young goalscoring phenomenon, Jimmy Greaves was the Chelsea hitman, as he scored eight of the nine goals for the Londoners in a 4–4 draw and a 5–4 victory over North End. It would have been a fairy tale for the mercurial Finney to finish his career at Wembley in an FA Cup final and for a while it looked a distinct possibility. A terrific run was only ended at the sixth round stage, against Aston Villa. Finney's dream was over and he was destined never to win a cup

Alex Alston and Les Dagger. Two local lads who made over 150 league appearances between them as North Enders.

winner's medal. In the league games the second half of the season proved a disappointment as Preston struggled to find the necessary consistency. A double over Blackpool pleased the locals and a 4–0 win over Manchester United at Deepdale was another highlight. Finally though, the eyes of the football world focused on Deepdale on that day in April 1960. Luton just made up the numbers as Preston ran out comfortable winners by 2–0. At the end, many a grown man, and woman, had a tear in their eye as Finney said his goodbyes on a microphone in front of the packed stands. In many ways watching North End would never be the same again. The overwhelming sense of loss was to take a long time to recover from.

DEBUTANTS: (4) Johnny Fullam, Garbutt Richardson, Ken Heyes, Jimmy Humes.

LAST GAMES: (5) Tom Finney, Dennis Hatsell, Les Campbell, Alex Farrall, Ken Heyes.

League appearances (42 games)

Alston A. G. 10, Campbell L. G. 8, Cunningham W. C. 24, Dagger J. L. 14, Dunn J. P. 29, Else F. 42, Farrall A. 10, Finney T. 37, Fullam J. 12, Hatsell D. 3, Heyes K. 3, Humes J. 1, Lambert J. G. 3, Mayers D. 19, Milne G. 38, O'Farrell F. 10, Richardson G. 13, Smith J. A. G. 34, Sneddon D. 40, Taylor S. M. 34, Thompson T. 21, Walton J. 42, Wilson J. R. 15.

FA Cup appearances (6 games)

Else 6, Walton 6, Dunn 5, Smith 6, Mayers 2, Thompson 6, Finney 6, Sneddon 6, Taylor 6, Milne 6, Richardson 1, Wilson 6, Dagger 4.

Goalscorers: 79 League–14 Cup–(Total 93)

Finney 17 (2 pens)–4 (21), Thompson 12–2 (14), Sneddon 11–3 (14), Taylor 10–4 (14) Dagger 5–0 (5), Mayers 4–1 (5), Farrall 4 (1 pen)–0 (4), Smith 3–0 (3), Alston 3–0 (3), Milne 2–0 (2), Lambert 2–0 (2), Campbell 2–0 (2), Cunningham 1–0 (1), Walton 1–0 (1), O'Farrell 1–0 (1). Own goals 1–0 (1) Knapp of Leicester.

Future Players born between August 1959 and May 1960: John Kilner, John Anderson, Chris Sulley, Graham Houston.
Ever presents: Fred Else and Joe Walton
Hat-tricks: (1) Tommy Thompson
FA Cup: Sixth Round
Players used: 23
Manager: Cliff Britton
Chairman: N. Buck Esq.
Leading scorer: 21 goals – Tom Finney (17 league 4 cup)
AUTHORS' UNOFFICIAL PLAYER OF THE SEASON: David Sneddon

Match Report: Jimmy Greaves Goes Nap – 19 Dec 1959 Preston 4 Chelsea 5

When these two teams met at Stamford Bridge on the opening day of the season, 43,000 saw a 4–4 thriller, but due to the traditional pre-Christmas shopping rush, coupled with the raw, murky weather, only around 15,000 were present at the start of this game. As it was the table topping Preston faced a Chelsea side which had lost their last four games. The floodlights were switched on at the outset to relieve the gloom and Chelsea were immediately dangerous on the soft, rain soaked, but still well grassed Deepdale surface. Play was fast, even and entertaining with exciting incidents around both goals. Uncertainty in both defences gave the swift, assertive forward play every hope to succeed and the attacking play of both teams was a joy to watch. The man who caused most problems though was Jimmy Greaves the Chelsea inside-forward. He proved to be a thorn in Preston's side all afternoon. He opened the scoring after 14 minutes breaking through a flat, static North End defence before shooting home. Little more than a minute had elapsed, during which time Preston had already retaliated strongly, when Thompson ghosted in to a packed goalmouth to get his foot to a cross before the goalkeeper could smother it. A typical poacher's goal, well received by the crowd. North End kept the ball moving sweetly, they needed to, to beat Chelsea's quick markers, and after 21 minutes Sneddon gave Preston the lead from a pass by Thompson. It was a great goal, in as much as Sneddon was harassed whilst in possession and had the narrowest of angles to judge in order to find a gap wide of Matthews in the Chelsea goal. Unflappable Chelsea kept probing away using wingers Brabrook and Blunstone effectively. On the half hour mark Greaves showed his superb potential by scoring two goals in a three minute spell. His first was an excellent solo effort using his pace and ball control to leave Walton and Else floundering, and his second was down to his quick thinking. North End fought back without enjoying much luck, Finney going close four times before the break. Then on 52 minutes Chelsea increased their lead with Greaves again doing the damage. The talented Londoner made it five for himself and for Chelsea twelve minutes later before Preston began a stirring fightback. Unfortunately it arrived a bit too late but at least Thompson had the satisfaction of scoring two more goals to complete his own hat-trick before the end of this Christmas cracker.

Left to right: Back row: O'Farrell, Cunningham, Dunn, Else, Walton, Smith, O'Neill.
Front row: Mayers, Thompson, Finney, Hatsell, Sneddon, Taylor.

STAT FACTS:
Best home run without defeat: 5 games
Best away run without defeat: 7 games
Longest run unbeaten: 9 games
Longest run without a win: 11 games
Best home attendance: 35,352 vs. Stoke FAC 12.1.60
Worst home attendance: 15,007 vs. Fulham 2.4.60
Best away attendance: 69,732 vs. Aston Villa FAC 12.3.60
Worst away attendance: 17,174 vs. Luton 28.11.59
Aggregate and average home attendance:
515,602 – 24,552
Aggregate and average away attendance:
657,069 – 31,289

Trivia Facts:

The game at Spurs on Sept 19 1959 marked the 200th appearance in a North End league game for Joe Dunn and also the 100th Preston appearance for Frank O'Farrell. There were nearly 52,000 present to watch an eventful match in which Finney was taken to hospital with concussion and Gil Lambert ended up with a fractured ankle, an injury that kept him out for a year.

Former North End player of the 1920s, Tommy Hamilton, died on Christmas Day 1959.

Jim Smith played for the Army at right-half, centre-half and left-half in three games against The FA in Newcastle, The Navy at Aldershot and the Belgium Army in Brussels. Meanwhile, Gordon Milne played for an FA XI against the RAF at Norwich in October 1959.

The North End Youth team won the 'Martini' sponsored 5 Nations Junior Tournament in Geneva playing against teams from Italy, Switzerland and Austria.

Season 1959–60: First Division

		P	W	D	L	F	A	Pts
1	Burnley	42	24	7	11	85	61	55
2	Wolves	42	24	6	12	106	67	54
3	Tottenham	42	21	11	10	86	50	53
4	WBA	42	19	11	12	83	57	49
5	Sheffield Wednesday	42	19	11	12	80	59	49
6	Bohon	42	20	8	14	59	51	48
7	Man United	42	19	7	16	102	80	45
8	Newcastle	42	18	8	16	82	78	44
9	**PRESTON**	42	16	12	14	79	76	44
10	Fulham	42	17	10	15	73	80	44
11	Blackpool	42	15	10	17	59	71	40
12	Leicester	42	13	13	16	66	75	39
13	Arsenal	42	15	9	18	68	80	39
14	West Ham	42	16	6	20	75	91	38
15	Man City	42	17	3	22	78	84	37
16	Everton	42	13	11	18	73	78	37
17	Blackburn	42	16	5	21	60	70	37
18	Chelsea	42	14	9	19	76	91	37
19	Birmingham	42	13	10	19	63	80	36
20	Nottingham Forest	42	13	9	20	50	74	35
21	Leeds	42	12	10	20	65	92	34
22	Luton	42	9	12	21	50	73	30

League position in Division One: 9th – P42 W16 D12 L14 F79 A76 Pts 44
Home: W10 D6 L5 F43 A34   Away: W6 D6 L9 F36 A42

Sir Tom Finney

Above: Finney's League farewell at Deepdale *vs.* Luton Town 30 April 1960.

Right: Passing tips on to the PNE Youth Squad.

Below: Leading PNE out at the 1954 FA Cup final.

Right: Hanging up his boots, April 1960.

Above Tom in action against Arsenal, 24 February 1954, whilst the referee watches on.

Background: Tom Finney saying farewell to the fans, April 1960.

Tom Finney taking a corner in his last league game against Luton Town.

Tom Finney taking his boots off for the last time after the win against Luton Town. April 1960.

Date 1959-60	Opponents	Comp	h or a	Score	Att.	1	2	3	4	5	6	7	8	9	10	11		
Aug 22	Chelsea	Div 1	a	4-4	42891	Else	Cunningham	Walton	O'Farrell (1)	Dunn	Smith	Mayers (1)	Thompson (1)	Finney (1)	Sneddon	Taylor		
Aug 25	West Ham Utd.	Div 1	h	1-1	29489	Else	Cunningham	Walton	O'Farrell	Dunn	Smith	Mayers	Thompson (1)	Finney	Sneddon	Taylor		
Aug 29	WBA	Div 1	h	1-1	24876	Else	Cunningham	Walton	O'Farrell	Dunn	Smith	Mayers	Milne (1)	Finney	Sneddon	Taylor		
Aug 31	West Ham Utd.	Div 1	a	1-2	31916	Else	Cunningham	Walton	O'Farrell	Dunn	Smith (1)	Finney	Milne	Hatsell	Sneddon	Taylor		
Sep 5	Newcastle Utd.	Div 1	a	2-1	37683	Else	Cunningham	Walton	Fullam	Dunn	O'Farrell	Finney (1)	Milne (1)	Hatsell	Sneddon	Taylor		
Sep 8	Burnley	Div 1	a	1-2	29195	Else	Cunningham	Walton	Fullam	Dunn	O'Farrell	Finney	Milne	Hatsell	Sneddon (1)	Taylor		
Sep 12	Birmingham City	Div 1	h	3-2	18934	Else	Cunningham	Walton	Milne	Dunn	O'Farrell	Finney	Sneddon	Alston	Lambert (1)	Taylor (2)		
Sep 15	Burnley	Div 1	h	1-0	27299	Else	Cunningham	Walton	Milne	Dunn	O'Farrell	Finney (1)	Sneddon	Alston	Lambert	Taylor		
Sep 19	Tottenham H.	Div 1	a	1-5	51776	Else	Cunningham	Walton	Milne	Dunn	O'Farrell	Mayers	Sneddon	Alston	Lambert (1)	Taylor		
Sep 26	Manchester Utd.	Div 1	h	4-0	35016	Else	Cunningham	Walton	Milne	Dunn	Smith	Mayers	Farrall	Finney (2, 1p)	Sneddon (1)	Taylor (1)		
Oct 3	Blackburn R.	Div 1	a	4-1	41694	Else	Cunningham	Walton	Milne	Dunn	Smith	Mayers	Farrall (1)	Finney (1)	Sneddon (1)	Taylor (1)		
Oct 10	Manchester City	Div 1	h	1-5	32546	Else	Cunningham	Walton	Milne	Dunn	Smith	Campbell	Farrall	Finney (1)	Sneddon	Taylor		
Oct 17	Arsenal	Div 1	a	3-0	43941	Else	Cunningham	Walton (1)	Milne	Dunn	Smith	Alston (1)	Thompson	Finney	Sneddon (1)	Taylor		
Oct 24	Wolverhampton W.	Div 1	h	4-3	22612	Else	Cunningham	Walton	Milne	Richardson	Smith	Alston (1)	Thompson (1)	Finney (1p)	Sneddon	Taylor (1)		
Oct 31	Blackpool	Div 1	a	2-0	27796	Else	Cunningham	Walton	Milne	Richardson	Smith	Mayers	Thompson	Finney (1)	Sneddon	Taylor		
Nov 7	Nottm Forest	Div 1	h	1-0	21226	Else	Cunningham (1)	Walton	Milne	Dunn	O'Farrell	Mayers	Thompson	Finney	Sneddon	Taylor		
Nov 14	Fulham	Div 1	a	2-1	26432	Else	Cunningham	Walton	Milne	Dunn	Smith	Mayers (1)	Thompson	Finney	Sneddon	Taylor (1)		
Nov 21	Bolton W.	Div 1	h	1-0	28723	Else	Cunningham	Walton	Milne	Dunn	Smith	Mayers (1)	Thompson	Finney	Sneddon	Taylor		
Nov 28	Luton Town	Div 1	a	3-1	17174	Else	Cunningham	Walton	Milne	Dunn	Smith	Mayers (1)	Thompson (2)	Finney	Sneddon	Taylor		
Dec 5	Everton	Div 1	h	0-0	24463	Else	Cunningham	Walton	Milne	Richardson	Smith	Mayers	Thompson	Finney	Sneddon	Taylor		
Dec 12	Sheffield Wed.	Div 1	a	2-2	41633	Else	Cunningham	Walton	Milne	Richardson	Smith	Mayers	Thompson	Finney (2)	Sneddon	Taylor		
Dec 19	Chelsea	Div 1	h	4-5	15775	Else	Cunningham	Walton	Milne	Richardson	Smith	Mayers	Thompson (3)	Finney	Sneddon (1)	Taylor		
Dec 26	Leicester City	Div 1	a	2-2	32864	Else	Cunningham	Walton	Milne	Richardson	Smith	Mayers	Thompson (1)	Alston	Sneddon	Taylor (1)		
Dec 28	Leicester City	Div 1	h	1-1	23545	Else	Wilson	Walton	Milne	Richardson	Smith	Campbell	Thompson	Alston	Sneddon	Mayers	1 og	(Knapp)
Jan 2	WBA	Div 1	a	0-4	23917	Else	Wilson	Walton	Milne	Richardson	Smith	Mayers	Thompson	Finney	Sneddon	Taylor		
Jan 9	**Stoke City** Rd 3	FAC	a	1-1	38465	Else	**Wilson**	**Walton**	**Milne**	**Dunn**	**Smith**	**Mayers**	**Thompson**	**Finney**	**Sneddon (1)**	**Taylor**		
Jan 12	**Stoke City** Replay	FAC	h	3-1	35352	Else	**Wilson**	**Walton**	**Milne**	**Dunn**	**Smith**	**Mayers (1)**	**Thompson (1)**	**Finney (1)**	**Sneddon**	**Taylor**		
Jan 16	Newcastle Utd.	Div 1	h	1-2	24353	Else	Cunningham	Walton	Milne	Dunn	Smith	Mayers	Thompson	Finney (1)	Sneddon	Taylor		
Jan 23	Birmingham City	Div 1	a	1-2	24160	Else	Wilson	Walton	Milne	Dunn	Smith	Mayers	Thompson	Finney	Sneddon (1)	Taylor		
Jan 30	**Bristol Rovers** Rd 4	FAC	a	3-3	38472	Else	**Wilson**	**Walton**	**Milne**	**Dunn**	**Smith**	**Dagger**	**Thompson**	**Finney (1)**	**Sneddon (1)**	**Taylor (1)**		
Feb 2	**Bristol Rovers** Replay	FAC	h	5-1	33164	Else	**Wilson**	**Walton**	**Milne**	**Dunn**	**Smith**	**Dagger**	**Thompson (1)**	**Finney (2)**	**Sneddon**	**Taylor (2)**		
Feb 6	Tottenham H.	Div 1	h	1-1	33039	Else	Wilson	Walton	Milne	Dunn	Fullam	Dagger	Thompson (1)	Finney	Sneddon	Taylor		
Feb 13	Manchester Utd.	Div 1	a	1-1	44014	Else	Heyes	Walton	Milne	Dunn	Smith	Dagger	Thompson	Finney (1)	Sneddon	Taylor		
Feb 20	**Brighton** Rd 5	FAC	h	2-1	34543	Else	**Wilson**	**Walton**	**Milne**	**Dunn**	**Smith**	**Dagger**	**Thompson**	**Finney**	**Sneddon (1)**	**Taylor (1)**		
Feb 27	Everton	Div 1	a	0-4	50990	Else	Wilson	Walton	Milne	Dunn	Smith	Dagger	Thompson	Finney	Sneddon	Taylor		
Mar 1	Blackburn R.	Div 1	h	5-3	26781	Else	Heyes	Walton	Milne	Richardson	Smith (1)	Dagger (1)	Thompson (2)	Finney	Sneddon (1)	Taylor		
Mar 5	Arsenal	Div 1	h	0-3	23635	Else	Heyes	Walton	Milne	Richardson	Smith	Dagger	Farrall	Finney	Sneddon	Campbell		
Mar 12	**Aston Villa** Rd 6	FAC	a	0-2	69732	Else	**Wilson**	**Walton**	**Milne**	**Richardson**	**Smith**	**Dagger**	**Farrall**	**Finney**	**Sneddon**	**Taylor**		
Mar 16	Wolverhampton W.	Div 1	a	3-3	28760	Else	Wilson	Walton	Milne	Richardson	Fullam	Dagger (1)	Farrall (1)	Alston	Sneddon	Taylor (1)		
Mar 19	Sheffield Wed.	Div 1	h	3-4	16497	Else	Wilson	Walton	Milne	Richardson	Smith	Dagger	Farrall (2, 1p)	Alston	Sneddon	Taylor (1)		
Mar 26	Nottm Forest	Div 1	a	1-1	19855	Else	Wilson	Walton	Fullam	Richardson	Smith	Dagger	Farrall	Alston	Sneddon (1)	Humes		
Apr 2	Fulham	Div 1	h	4-1	15007	Else	Wilson	Walton	Fullam	Dunn	Smith	Dagger (1)	Farrall	Finney (2)	Sneddon (1)	Taylor		
Apr 9	Bolton W.	Div 1	a	1-2	30816	Else	Wilson	Walton	Fullam	Dunn	Smith	Dagger	Milne	Finney (1)	Sneddon	Campbell		
Apr 16	Blackpool	Div 1	h	4-1	26126	Else	Wilson	Walton	Fullam	Dunn	Smith	Dagger (1)	Milne	Finney (1)	Sneddon (1)	Campbell (1)		
Apr 18	Leeds Utd.	Div 1	h	1-1	15879	Else	Wilson	Walton	Fullam	Dunn	Smith	Dagger	Milne	Finney	Sneddon (1)	Campbell		
Apr 19	Leeds Utd.	Div 1	a	1-2	23764	Else	Wilson	Walton	Fullam	Dunn	Smith	Dagger	Milne	Finney	Farrall	Campbell (1)		
Apr 23	Manchester City	Div 1	a	1-2	29812	Else	Wilson	Walton	Fullam	Dunn	Smith	Dagger (1)	Milne	Finney	Farrall	Campbell		
Apr 30	Luton Town	Div 1	h	2-0	29781	Else	Wilson	Walton	Fullam	Dunn	Smith (1)	Finney	Milne	Alston (1)	Sneddon	Taylor		

SEASON 1960–1961

A sad, sad season for all followers of the club. Relegation from the First Division, ironically just a year after Tom Finney's retirement. The season began with three straight defeats and North End never really recovered. The big problem was a lack of goals, only 43 in the 42 league games, and in one spell Preston went six consecutive games without scoring. Ironically, it was a season when goals were scored all over the country, even Newcastle, who were relegated with North End, scored 86. The Preston total was far and away the lowest in the division and only Stoke scored less in the whole of the Football League. This year also saw the start of the new League Cup competition with Preston eventually going out in a third round replay against Aston Villa. There was some consolation in that Villa went on to become the first winners of the trophy. There was also little joy in the FA Cup with Accrington Stanley almost bringing acute embarrassment on the Lilywhites, holding on for a 1–1 draw at Deepdale. North End did win the replay, 4–0 at Peel Park, but they then went out to Swansea in round four. That game marked the debut, in goal, of Alan Kelly. The Irish goalkeeper, signed from Drumcondra, was destined to make his own special place in North End's history, but more of that later. Kelly was in good company in 1960–61 as all six players who made their debut during the season, unusually, went on to make many appearances for the club. There were no one game wonders who made their debut this season! The youngsters drafted into the team all did well with Alan Spavin, Tony Singleton, George Ross and especially Peter Thompson created an immediate

impact. Fred Else, Johnny Fullam, Alec Alston and Dave Sneddon also played their hearts out. Preston's league form continued to cause concern but after a dismal 5–1 thrashing at Sheffield Wednesday the players knuckled down and put together their best run of the campaign. Only one defeat in eight games followed and the fans were given just a glimmer of hope. Unfortunately it all came crashing down to earth at White Hart Lane as the all conquering Tottenham side walloped Preston 5–0. Poor Kelly had been in goal for both of those five goal maulings but luckily Manager Cliff Britton stayed faithful to the Irishman, obviously seeing some potential. The Easter period brought no improvement and the side had to win their last two league games to have any chance of staying up. Alas, defeat by Manchester United at Deepdale ended their hopes and despite a 1–1 draw in their last Division One game, at Bolton, the relegation was confirmed. The loss of Preston's First Division status had an immediate affect as several players moved on in the summer of 1961, most notably Fred Else, Sammy Taylor and Tommy Thompson. The main hope for the future lay in the promise shown by the members of the successful members of North End's Youth Cup final side.

DEBUTANTS: (6) Tony Singleton, Alan Spavin, Peter Thompson, David Wilson, George Ross, Alan Kelly

LAST GAMES: (12) Joe Walton, Joe Dunn, Fred Else, Sammy Taylor, Tommy Thompson, Gordon Milne, Les Dagger, Frank O'Farrell, Derek Mayers, Gil Lambert, Johnny Fullam and Garbutt Richardson.

Near miss at Chelsea as Tony Singleton heads clear watched by Willie Cunningham and Frank O'Farrell.

League position in Division One: 22nd (Relegated) – P42 W10 D10 L22 F43 A71 Pts 30
Home: W7 D6 L8 F28 A25   Away: W3 D4 L14 F15 A46

Left to right: *Back row:*
G. Ross, A. Singleton,
F. Else, J. Wylie, J. O'Neill.
Front row: A. Alston,
P. Thompson, F. O'Farrell
(Captain), D. Sneddon,
D. Mayers, J. Fullam.

**Match Report: New Blood Works Wonders –
30 Aug. 1960. Preston 2 Arsenal 0**

After three successive defeats North End made dramatic changes for this game with young players, Peter Thompson, Alan Spavin and Tony Singleton all coming in for their league debuts. The depression cloud around Preston due to the poor start to the season needed something to lift the gloom and bringing in some of the reserves was to have the desired result. Everyone appreciated the youthful spirit and zest put into a fast flowing, entertaining and evenly contested match. During the first half there were no fewer than 19 goal attempts and near misses but no goals to show for all the excitement. Just before the interval Singleton had a promising league baptism cut short by a jab in the ribs, severe enough to call for an X-Ray examination, resulting in him missing the whole of the second half. In his absence Smith moved across to centre-half and functioned so well that many observers believe this to be his best position. His height and long stride made him look commanding and he curbed and finally blotted out the threat of Herd, Arsenal's strong centre-forward. Behind Smith, Else again demonstrated why he is regarded as being in the top flight of goalkeepers with a superb display. Eventually the ten man Preston side took command and even outplayed their illustrious London visitors whose side was peppered with internationals. With 73 minutes played Kelsey, Arsenal's Welsh international goalie, fumbled a centre by Alston whilst under pressure from Peter Thompson, and Spavin was on hand to knock the ball over the line to score a debut goal. His unbounded delight was shared by his colleagues and the Deepdale crowd alike. Thus inspired, North End incredibly struck again within two minutes, through Alston, who rounded off some good approach play by the youngsters Thompson (P) and Spavin. The new players had really impressed and had proved with their confident displays that they would be around the football scene for some time to come.

League appearances (42 games)

Alston A. G. 37, Cunningham W. C. 31, Dagger J. L. 6, Dunn J. P. 4, Else F. 40, Fullam J. 37, Humes J. 1, Kelly J. A. 2, Lambert J. G. 6, Mayers D. 28, Milne G. 3, O'Farrell F. 17, O'Neill J. N. 36, Richardson G. 2, Ross G. 3, Singleton A. J. 37, Smith J. A. G. 10, Sneddon D. 37, Spavin A. 9, Taylor S. M. 10, Thompson P. 38, Thompson T. 13, Walton J. 6, Wilson D. C. 2, Wilson J. R. 8, Wylie J. E. 39.

FA Cup appearances (3 games)

Else 2, Fullam 2, Alston 3, Sneddon 3, Mayers 3, Wylie 3, Singleton 3, Thompson P. 3, Cunningham 2, O,Neill 3, Thompson T. 2, Taylor 1, Ross 1, O'Farrell 1, Kelly 1.

League Cup appearances (5 games)

Else 5, Wilson J. R. 1, Fullam 5, Dagger 1, Alston 3, Sneddon 5, Mayers 2, Wylie 5, Singleton 5, Thompson P. 5, Cunningham 4, O'Neill 5, Lambert 2, Thompson T. 4, Taylor 3.

Goalscorers: 43 League–6 FAC–12 LC–(Total 61)

Thompson P. 7–1–4 (12), Alston 9 (2 pens)–1–1 (11), Sneddon 5–1–3 (9), Fullam 6–0–0 (6), Thompson T. 2–2–2 (6), Mayers 3–1–0 (4), Smith 2–0–0 (2), Wylie 1–0–1 (2), Spavin 1–0–0 (1), Lambert 1–0–0 (1), Wilson D. C. 1–0–0 (1), Richardson 1–0–0 (1), Own goals 4–0–1 (5) Swan of Sheffield Wed., Woods (2) of Blackburn and Norman of Leicester. Walker of Peterborough in the League Cup.

Future Players born between August 1960 and May 1961: Mark Jones, John Kelly, Paul Lodge, Gary Buckley, Andy McAteer.
Hat-tricks: None
Ever presents: None
FA Cup: Fourth Round
League Cup: Third Round Replay
Players used: 26
Manager: Cliff Britton until April 1961 and then Jimmy Milne.
Chairman: N. Buck Esq.
Leading scorer: 12 goals – Peter Thompson (7 league, 1 FAC, 4 L Cup)
AUTHORS' UNOFFICIAL PLAYER OF THE SEASON: Fred Else

Fred Else in action.

Date 1960-1	Opponents	Comp	h or a	Score	Att.	1	2	3	4	5	6	7	8	9	10	11		
Aug 20	Newcastle Utd.	Div 1	h	2-3	17363	Else	R.Wilson	Walton	Fullam	Dunn	Smith	Dagger	Milne	Alston	Sneddon (2)	Mayers		
Aug 23	Arsenal	Div 1	a	0-1	31393	Else	R.Wilson	Walton	Fullam	Dunn	Smith	Dagger	Milne	Alston	Sneddon	Mayers		
Aug 27	Cardiff City	Div 1	a	0-2	27213	Else	R.Wilson	Walton	Fullam	Dunn	Smith	Dagger	Milne	Alston	Sneddon	Mayers		
Aug 30	Arsenal	Div 1	h	2-0	20104	Else	R.Wilson	Walton	Wylie	Singleton	Smith	Alston (1)	Sneddon	P.Thompson	Spavin (1)	Mayers		
Sep 3	WBA	Div 1	h	2-1	18476	Else	R.Wilson	Walton	Wylie	Smith	Fullam	Alston (1)	Sneddon	P.Thompson (1)	Spavin	Mayers		
Sep 6	Burnley	Div 1	a	0-5	19443	Else	R.Wilson	Walton	Wylie	Singleton	Smith	Alston	Sneddon	P.Thompson	Spavin	Mayers		
Sep 10	Birmingham City	Div 1	a	3-1	24435	Else	Cunningham	O'Neill	Fullam	Singleton	Wylie	Alston (2)	Sneddon	Smith (1)	Spavin	Lambert		
Sep 13	Burnley	Div 1	h	2-3	25604	Else	Cunningham	O'Neill	Fullam (1)	Singleton	Wylie	Alston	Sneddon	P.Thompson	Spavin	Lambert (1)		
Sep 17	Sheffield Wed.	Div 1	h	2-2	17499	Else	Cunningham	O'Neill	Fullam	Singleton	Wylie	Alston	Sneddon	Smith (1)	Spavin	P.Thompson	1 og	(Swan)
Sep 24	Fulham	Div 1	a	0-2	23770	Else	Cunningham	O'Neill	Fullam	Singleton	Wylie	P.Thompson	Sneddon	Smith	Spavin	Lambert		
Oct 1	Blackpool	Div 1	h	1-0	17445	Else	Cunningham	O'Neill	Fullam	Singleton	Wylie	Alston (1p)	T.Thompson	P.Thompson	Sneddon	Lambert		
Oct 8	Everton	Div 1	a	0-0	36717	Else	Cunningham	O'Neill	Fullam	Singleton	Wylie	Alston	Sneddon	P.Thompson	Spavin	Taylor		
Oct 11	Peterborough Utd. Rd 1	LC	h	4-1	12958	Else	Cunningham	O'Neill	Fullam	Singleton	Wylie	Alston	Sneddon (1)	P.Thompson (2)	Lambert	Taylor	1 og	(Walker)
Oct 15	Blackburn R.	Div 1	a	2-0	24229	Else	Cunningham	O'Neill	Fullam	Singleton	Wylie	Alston	T.Thompson	P.Thompson	Sneddon	Lambert	2 og	(Woods 2)
Oct 19	Gillingham Rd 2	LC	a	1-1	5735	Else	Cunningham	O'Neill	Fullam	Singleton	Wylie	Alston (1)	T.Thompson	P.Thompson	Sneddon	Lambert		
Oct 22	West Ham Utd.	Div 1	a	2-5	16295	Else	Cunningham	O'Neill	Fullam	Singleton	Wylie	Alston	T.Thompson (2)	P.Thompson	Sneddon	Taylor		
Oct 25	Gillingham Replay	LC	h	3-0	9218	Else	Cunningham	O'Neill	Fullam	Singleton	Wylie	Dagger	T.Thompson (1)	P.Thompson (1)	Sneddon (1)	Taylor		
Oct 29	Chelsea	Div 1	h	0-2	14174	Else	Cunningham	O'Neill	Fullam	Singleton	Wylie	Mayers	T.Thompson	Alston	Sneddon	Taylor		
Nov 4	Leicester City	Div 1	a	2-5	16920	Else	Cunningham	O'Neill	Fullam	Singleton	Wylie	Mayers (1)	T.Thompson	P.Thompson	Lambert	Taylor	1 og	(Norman)
Nov 12	Aston Villa	Div 1	h	1-1	11093	Else	Cunningham	O'Neill	Fullam	Singleton	Wylie	Mayers	T.Thompson	P.Thompson	Sneddon (1)	Taylor		
Nov 15	Aston Villa Rd 3	LC	h	3-3	7577	Else	Cunningham	O'Neill	Fullam	Singleton	Wylie (1)	Mayers	T.Thompson (1)	P.Thompson	Sneddon (1)	Taylor		
Nov 19	Wolverhampton W.	Div 1	a	0-3	23192	Else	R.Wilson	O'Neill	Fullam	Singleton	Wylie	Mayers	T.Thompson	P.Thompson	Sneddon	P.Thompson		
Nov 23	Aston Villa Replay	LC	a	1-3	20545	Else	R.Wilson	O'Neill	Fullam	Singleton	Wylie	Mayers	T.Thompson	Alston	Sneddon	P.Thompson (1)		
Dec 3	Manchester Utd.	Div 1	a	0-1	24698	Else	Cunningham	O'Neill	Fullam	Singleton	Wylie	Mayers	T.Thompson	Alston	Sneddon	P.Thompson		
Dec 10	Tottenham H.	Div 1	h	0-1	21657	Else	Cunningham	O'Neill	Fullam	Singleton	Wylie	Mayers	T.Thompson	Alston	Sneddon	P.Thompson		
Dec 17	Newcastle Utd.	Div 1	a	0-0	21514	Else	Cunningham	O'Neill	Fullam	Singleton	Wylie	Mayers	T.Thompson	Alston	Sneddon	P.Thompson		
Dec 24	Nottm Forest	Div 1	a	0-2	22799	Else	Cunningham	O'Neill	Fullam	Singleton	Wylie	Mayers	T.Thompson	Alston	Sneddon	P.Thompson		
Dec 26	Nottm Forest	Div 1	h	0-1	12705	Else	Ross	O'Neill	Fullam	Singleton	Wylie	Alston	D.Wilson	P.Thompson (1)	Spavin	Taylor		
Dec 31	Cardiff City	Div 1	h	1-1	11048	Else	Ross	O'Neill	Fullam	Singleton	Wylie	Alston	T.Thompson	P.Thompson (1)	Sneddon	Mayers		
Jan 7	Accrington St. Rd 3	FAC	h	1-1	20268	Else	Cunningham	O'Neill	Fullam	Singleton	Wylie	Alston	T.Thompson (1)	P.Thompson	Sneddon	Mayers		
Jan 9	Accrington St. Replay	FAC	a	4-0	14596	Else	Ross	O'Neill	Fullam	Singleton	Wylie	Alston	T.Thompson (1)	P.Thompson (1)	Sneddon (1)	Mayers (1)		
Jan 14	WBA	Div 1	h	1-3	19639	Else	Ross	O'Neill	Fullam	Singleton	Wylie	Alston	O'Farrell	P.Thompson (1)	Sneddon	Mayers		
Jan 21	Birmingham City	Div 1	h	2-3	7667	Else	Cunningham	O'Neill	O'Farrell	Singleton	Wylie	Mayers	P.Thompson	Alston (2)	Sneddon	Taylor		
Jan 28	Swansea Town Rd 4	FAC	a	1-2	22352	Kelly	Cunningham	O'Neill	Wylie	Singleton	O'Farrell	Mayers	P.Thompson	Alston (1)	Sneddon	Taylor		
Feb 4	Sheffield Wed.	Div 1	a	1-5	21156	Kelly	Cunningham	O'Neill	Wylie	Dunn	O'Farrell	Mayers (1)	Fullam	Alston	Sneddon (1)	P.Thompson		
Feb 11	Fulham	Div 1	h	2-0	8692	Else	Cunningham	O'Neill	Wylie	Singleton	O'Farrell	Mayers (1)	Fullam (1)	Alston	Sneddon (1)	P.Thompson		
Feb 18	Blackpool	Div 1	a	1-0	20541	Else	Cunningham	O'Neill	Wylie	Singleton	O'Farrell	Mayers (1)	Fullam	Alston	Sneddon	P.Thompson		
Feb 25	Everton	Div 1	h	1-0	17812	Else	R.Wilson	O'Neill	Wylie	Singleton	O'Farrell	Mayers	Fullam (1)	Alston	Sneddon	P.Thompson		
Mar 4	Blackburn R.	Div 1	h	0-1	23270	Else	Cunningham	O'Neill	Wylie	Singleton	O'Farrell	Mayers	Fullam	Alston	Sneddon	P.Thompson		
Mar 11	West Ham Utd.	Div 1	h	4-0	12084	Else	Cunningham	O'Neill	Wylie	Singleton	O'Farrell	Mayers	Fullam (1)	Alston (1)	Sneddon	P.Thompson (1)		
Mar 18	Chelsea	Div 1	a	1-1	22031	Else	Cunningham	O'Neill	Wylie	Singleton	O'Farrell	Mayers	Fullam	Alston	Sneddon	P.Thompson (1)		
Mar 25	Leicester City	Div 1	h	0-0	12619	Else	Cunningham	O'Neill	Wylie	Singleton	O'Farrell	Mayers	Fullam	Alston	Sneddon	P.Thompson		
Mar 31	Manchester City	Div 1	a	3-2	31164	Else	Cunningham	O'Neill	Wylie	Singleton	O'Farrell	Mayers	Fullam (1)	Alston (1p)	Sneddon (1)	P.Thompson		
Apr 1	Tottenham H.	Div 1	a	0-5	46325	Kelly	Cunningham	O'Neill	Wylie	Singleton	O'Farrell	Dagger	Fullam	Alston	Sneddon	P.Thompson		
Apr 3	Manchester City	Div 1	h	1-1	25358	Else	Cunningham	O'Neill	Wylie (1)	Singleton	O'Farrell	Dagger	Fullam	Alston	Sneddon	P.Thompson		
Apr 8	Wolverhampton W.	Div 1	h	1-2	18210	Else	Cunningham	O'Neill	Wylie	Singleton	O'Farrell	Mayers	Fullam	Alston	Sneddon	P.Thompson (1)		
Apr 15	Aston Villa	Div 1	a	0-1	24028	Else	Cunningham	O'Neill	Wylie	Singleton	O'Farrell	Dagger	Fullam	Alston	P.Thompson	Mayers		
Apr 18	Bolton W.	Div 1	a	0-0	17786	Else	Cunningham	O'Neill	Wylie	Singleton	O'Farrell	Alston	Fullam	Richardson	P.Thompson	Taylor		
Apr 22	Manchester Utd.	Div 1	h	2-4	21256	Else	Cunningham	O'Neill	Wylie	Singleton	O'Farrell	Alston	P.Thompson (1)	Richardson (1)	Sneddon	Taylor		
Apr 29	Bolton W.	Div 1	a	1-1	12637	Else	Cunningham	O'Neill	Wylie	Singleton	Smith	Humes	T.Thompson	Alston	P.Thompson	D.Wilson (1)		

Tom Finney Testimonial programme.

Season 1960–61: First Division

	P	W	D	L	F	A	Pts
1 Tottenham	42	31	4	7	115	55	66
2 Sheffield Wednesday	42	23	12	7	78	47	58
3 Wolves	42	25	7	10	103	75	57
4 Burney	42	22	7	13	102	77	51
5 Everton	42	22	6	14	87	69	50
6 Leicester	42	18	9	15	87	70	45
7 Man United	42	18	9	15	88	76	45
8 Blackburn	42	15	13	14	77	76	43
9 Aston Villa	42	17	9	16	78	77	43
10 WBA	42	18	5	19	67	71	41
11 Arsenal	42	15	11	16	77	85	41
12 Chelsea	42	15	7	20	98	100	37
13 Man City	42	13	11	18	79	90	37
14 Nottingham Forest	42	14	9	19	62	78	37
15 Cardiff	42	13	11	18	60	85	37
16 West Ham	42	13	10	19	77	88	36
17 Fulham	42	14	8	20	72	95	36
18 Bolton	42	12	11	19	58	73	35
19 Birmingham	42	14	6	22	62	84	34
20 Blackpool	42	12	9	21	68	73	33
21 Newcastle	42	11	10	21	86	109	32
22 PRESTON	**42**	**10**	**10**	**22**	**43**	**71**	**30**

SEASON 1961–1962

Two major signings were made by Jimmy Milne in the summer of 1961 as Preston prepared to meet the challenge of Division Two. Alfie Biggs, tall, blond, and a goalscoring inside-forward, was signed from Bristol Rovers, whilst highly rated wing-half Dave Barber came from Barnsley. The manager felt that these two players were all that were needed to back up the good young players already on the books. North End began the campaign badly though and won just one game out of their first eight. It was the start that the club dreaded and unfortunately it set the trend for the season. Away from home Preston struggled throughout the year and they found it difficult to come to terms with their task. Alan Kelly, as the one senior goalkeeper, established his place with some excellent performances although players around him found it difficult to find their form. In the October Preston went back into the transfer market and paid £20,000 to Manchester United for their powerful centre-forward Alex Dawson. Immediately he began to repay his fee as he scored on his debut, a 2–2 draw at Rotherham. It was noticeable how much he added to North End's attack. The results began to pick up and the season improved. The highlight, however, came in the New Year when the FA Cup started. Early wins over Watford and non-league Weymouth set up a tie with Liverpool who were running away with the Second Division. Preston played superbly as the tie went to three games before Peter Thompson finally settled it with a brilliant winning goal in the second replay at Old Trafford. The draw then brought the mighty Manchester United to Deepdale and Preston came so close to winning before eventually being beaten 2–1 in a replay. In between the cup-ties the league form dipped but after the cup run was over North End only lost three in the last eleven games. Thompson enhanced his growing reputation with a series of fine displays and Alan Spavin worked tirelessly at inside-forward. Biggs did his bit, passing 20 goals for the season and working well with Dawson, whilst George Ross and Tony Singleton played some storming games in defence. Some of the most brilliant performances though came from the veteran, Willie Cunningham. The craggy Scot's full-back play, especially in the cup-ties, was text book stuff and it was no coincidence that the only cup-tie Preston lost was the one he did not play in. Overall it had been a difficult season although some players made excellent progress in their careers.

DEBUTANTS: (4) Alfie Biggs, Dave Barber, Alex Dawson, Jack Gornall

LAST GAMES: (2) David Sneddon, Jimmy Humes

League appearances (42 games)

Alston A. G. 31, Barber D. E. 17, Barton J. B. 4, Biggs A. G. 39, Cunningham W. C. 29, Dawson A. D. 19, Gornall J. 1, Humes J. 16, Kelly J. A. 38, O'Neill J. N. 3, Ross G. 40, Singleton A. J. 40, Smith J. A. G. 31, Sneddon D. 13, Spavin A. 26, Thompson P. 42, Wilson D. C. 23, Wilson J. R. 12, Wylie J. E. 38.

FA Cup appearances (7 games)

Kelly 7, Cunningham 5, Wilson J. R. 1, Singleton 7, Wylie 7, Wilson D. C. 7, Biggs 7, P Thompson 7, Spavin 7, Ross 7, Smith 7, O'Neill 1, Dawson 7.

League Cup appearances (4 games)

Kelly 4, Cunningham 3, Barber 2, Singleton 4, Wylie 3, Alston 3, D Wilson 2, Biggs 3, Sneddon 1, Thompson 4, Humes 3, Ross 4, Spavin 2, Smith 3, O'Neill 1, Dawson 2.

Goalscorers: 55 League–7 FAC–6 LC–(Total 68)

Biggs 21–1–0 (22), Thompson 9–2–4 (15), Dawson 9 (2 pens)–2–0 (11), Alston 7–0–1 (8), Spavin 2–1–0 (3), Smith 2–1–0 (3), Wilson D. C. 1–0–1 (2), Barber 1–0–0 (1), Sneddon 1–0–(1), Humes 1–0–0 (1), Own goals 1–0–0 (1) Gutteridge of Walsall.

Future Players born between August 1961 and May 1962: Nigel Keen, Simon Westwell, Mike Farrelly, Peter Zelem, Willie Naughton, Gary Swann, Kelham O'Hanlon, David Thompson

Ever presents: (1) P Thompson   Hat-tricks: (2) both by Alfie Biggs
FA Cup: Sixth Round Replay   League Cup: Third Round Replay
Players used: 19   Manager: Jimmy Milne   Chairman: N. Buck Esq.
Leading scorer: 22 goals – Alfie Biggs (21 league 1 FAC)
AUTHORS' UNOFFICIAL PLAYER OF THE SEASON: Willie Cunningham

Alfie Biggs

Above: **Left to right:** *Back row:* Ross, Singleton, Wylie, Else, Kelly, Barber, O'Neill, Humes. *Front row:* D. Wilson, Spavin, Alston, R. Wilson, Cunningham, Thompson, Biggs, Sneddon.

Left: **North End players before taking on Blackburn Rovers at cricket.** Left to right: Peter Thompson, Fred Else, Alan Kelly, David Sneddon, George Ross, John O'Neill, Bob Wilson, Joe Jaques, Gavin Laing.

Below: **North End squad flying to Bristol in February 1962.**

Match Report: Liverpool Here We Come – 29 Jan 1962 Preston 2 Weymouth 0 FA Cup 4th Round

The first attempt at this fourth round fixture was abandoned after just 14 minutes due to the dense fog around Deepdale and Lancashire. Southern League side Weymouth, led by player/manager Frank O'Farrell, also had an aptly named centre-forward called Fogg! Unfortunately for Weymouth the majority of their 1,200 travelling fans who had been at the aborted game could not attend this re-run due to their work commitments. It came across that Weymouth's intentions from the start were to concentrate on spoiling tactics against acknowledged superior opponents, but they did do their fair share of attacking and to their credit they did not serve up the usual bruising kick and rush style usually associated with non-league battles in the FA Cup. Under O'Farrell's experienced leadership the well organised Southerners gave North End some anxious moments but without any real threat from the 'Terras' on the home goal. Preston had to fight hard for victory and Weymouth held out until three minutes before the interval when Alex Dawson finally broke the deadlock. Shepherd, a dockyard carpenter, had kicked a Spavin goalbound effort off the line only to see Dawson react the quickest to send a bullet header past 41 year old goalkeeper Bly, who managed a touch but could not stop it. A great sigh of relief went up around the stadium but the floodgates did not open as the fans expected. After the interval Preston strived to settle the issue quickly but Bly's heroics denied Dawson again with a superb save. However, six minutes into the half the excellent Bly was finally beaten again, with a goal worthy of settling any cup-tie. Peter Thompson's nimble feet took him past a couple of defenders before letting fly with an unstoppable shot which thrilled the crowd and sent a buzz around the ground as the realisation set in that the prospect of facing Liverpool in the next round was now a reality. The plucky Weymouth lads had done their best and O'Farrell was justifiably proud of his team

League position in Division Two: 10th – P42 W15 D10 L17 F55 A57 Pts 40
Home: W11 D4 L6 F34 A23   Away: W4 D6 L11 F21 A34

Date 1961-2	Opponents		Comp	h or a	Score	Att.	1	2	3	4	5	6	7	8	9	10	11		
Aug 19	Luton Town		Div 2	a	1-4	14109	Kelly	Cunningham	R.Wilson	Barber	Singleton	Wylie	Alston	D.Wilson	Biggs	Sneddon	Thompson (1)		
Aug 22	Swansea Town		Div 2	h	1-1	14570	Kelly	Cunningham	R.Wilson	Barber	Singleton	Wylie	Humes	Biggs	Alston (1)	D.Wilson	Thompson		
Aug 26	Newcastle Utd.		Div 2	h	0-1	14121	Kelly	Cunningham	Ross	Barber	Singleton	Wylie	Humes	Biggs	Alston	Spavin	Thompson		
Aug 29	Swansea Town		Div 2	a	2-1	18499	Kelly	Cunningham	Ross	Wylie	Singleton	Smith	Humes	Biggs	Alston (2)	Spavin	Thompson		
Sep 2	Middlesbrough		Div 2	a	0-1	16100	Kelly	Cunningham	Ross	Wylie	Singleton	Smith	Humes	Biggs	Alston	Spavin	Thompson		
Sep 9	Walsall		Div 2	h	2-3	12638	Kelly	Cunningham	Ross	Wylie	Singleton	Smith	Humes	Biggs (1)	Alston	Sneddon	Humes	1 og	(Gutteridge)
Sep 13	Aldershot	Rd 1	LC	h	3-1	6608	Kelly	Cunningham	Ross	Wylie	Singleton	Smith	Humes	Biggs	Alston (1)	Spavin	Thompson (2)		
Sep 16	Derby County		Div 2	a	2-3	13263	Kelly	Cunningham	Ross	Wylie	Singleton	Smith	Alston	Biggs	Thompson (2)	Sneddon	Humes		
Sep 20	Plymouth Arg.		Div 2	a	0-1	17174	Kelly	Cunningham	Ross	Wylie	Singleton	Smith	Alston	Biggs	Thompson	Sneddon	Humes		
Sep 23	Leyton Orient		Div 2	h	3-2	9969	Kelly	Ross	O'Neill	Wylie	Singleton	Smith	Humes (1)	Biggs (1)	Alston	Sneddon	Thompson (1)		
Sep 26	Plymouth Arg.		Div 2	h	1-1	11921	Kelly	Cunningham	Ross	Wylie	Singleton	Smith	Humes	Biggs	Alston	Sneddon	Thompson (1)		
Sep 30	Leeds Utd.		Div 2	a	2-1	9360	Kelly	Cunningham	Ross	Wylie	Singleton	Barber	Humes	D.Wilson	Alston	Sneddon	Thompson (2)		
Oct 5	Swindon Town	Rd 2	LC	h	3-1	8136	Kelly	Cunningham	Ross	Wylie	Singleton	Barber	Humes	D.Wilson (1)	Alston	Sneddon	Thompson (2)		
Oct 7	Bristol Rovers		Div 2	h	1-0	11331	Kelly	Cunningham	Ross	Wylie	Singleton	Barber	Humes	Biggs (1)	Alston	Sneddon	Thompson		
Oct 14	Stoke City		Div 2	a	1-1	8409	Kelly	Cunningham	Ross	Wylie	Singleton	Barber	Humes	Biggs (1)	Alston	Sneddon	Thompson		
Oct 18	Southampton		Div 2	h	0-0	14133	Kelly	Cunningham	Ross	Wylie	Singleton	Barber	Humes	Biggs	Alston	Sneddon	Thompson		
Oct 21	Sunderland		Div 2	a	0-1	17973	Kelly	Cunningham	Ross	Wylie	Singleton	Barber	Humes	Biggs	Alston	Sneddon	Thompson		
Oct 28	Rotherham Utd.		Div 2	a	2-2	10069	Kelly	Cunningham	Ross	Wylie	Singleton	Barber	Alston	D.Wilson (1)	Dawson (1)	Sneddon	Thompson		
Nov 4	Liverpool		Div 2	h	1-3	29243	Kelly	Cunningham	Ross	Wylie	Singleton	Barber	Alston	Biggs	Dawson	Sneddon (1)	Thompson		
Nov 11	Norwich City		Div 2	a	0-2	15494	Kelly	Cunningham	Ross	Wylie	Singleton	Barber	Alston	Biggs	Dawson	Sneddon	Thompson		
Nov 14	Rotherham Utd.	Rd 4	LC	h	0-0	7871	Kelly	Cunningham	Ross	Barber	Singleton	Smith	Alston	D.Wilson	Dawson	Biggs	Thompson		
Nov 18	Bury		Div 2	h	1-2	12438	Kelly	Cunningham	Ross	Barber	Singleton	Smith	Humes	D.Wilson	Dawson (1)	Biggs	Thompson		
Nov 25	Brighton		Div 2	a	0-0	13016	Kelly	Cunningham	Ross	Wylie	Singleton	Smith	Humes	Biggs	Dawson	Spavin	Thompson		
Nov 28	Rotherham Utd.	Replay	LC	a	0-3	10078	Kelly	Ross	O'Neill	Wylie	Singleton	Smith	Humes	Biggs	Dawson	Spavin	Thompson		
Dec 2	Scunthorpe		Div 2	h	4-1	8326	Kelly	Cunningham	Ross	Wylie	Singleton	Smith	D.Wilson	Biggs (3)	Dawson (1p)	Spavin	Thompson		
Dec 9	Charlton Ath.		Div 2	a	0-4	8699	Kelly	Cunningham	Ross	Wylie	Singleton	Smith	D.Wilson	Biggs	Dawson	Spavin	Thompson		
Dec 16	Luton Town		Div 2	h	2-0	8702	Kelly	Cunningham	Ross	Wylie	Singleton	Smith	D.Wilson	Biggs (2)	Dawson	Spavin	Thompson		
Dec 23	Newcastle Utd.		Div 2	a	2-0	18775	Kelly	Cunningham	Ross	Wylie	Singleton	Smith	D.Wilson	Biggs (1)	Dawson (1)	Spavin	Thompson		
Dec 26	Huddersfield T.		Div 2	h	1-0	15524	Kelly	Cunningham	Ross	Wylie	Singleton	Smith	D.Wilson	Biggs	Dawson (1)	Spavin	Thompson		
Jan 6	Watford	Rd 3	FAC	h	3-2	16518	Kelly	Ross	O'Neill	Wylie	Singleton	Smith (1)	D.Wilson	Biggs (1)	Dawson (1)	Spavin	Thompson		
Jan 13	Middlesbrough		Div 2	h	4-3	10912	Barton	Ross	O'Neill	Wylie	Singleton	Smith	D.Wilson	Biggs (1)	Dawson (2,1p)	Spavin	Thompson (1)		
Jan 20	Walsall		Div 2	a	1-2	10284	Kelly	Cunningham	Ross	Wylie	Singleton	Smith	D.Wilson	Biggs (1)	Dawson	Spavin	Thompson		
Jan 29	Weymouth	Rd 4	FAC	h	2-0	26026	Kelly	Cunningham	Ross	Wylie	Singleton	Smith	D.Wilson	Biggs	Dawson (1)	Spavin	Thompson (1)		
Feb 3	Derby County		Div 2	h	1-0	12125	Kelly	Cunningham	Ross	Wylie	Singleton	Smith	D.Wilson	Biggs	Alston	Spavin (1)	Thompson		
Feb 9	Leyton Orient		Div 2	a	2-0	18899	Kelly	Cunningham	Ross	Wylie	Singleton	Smith (1)	D.Wilson	Biggs	Alston	Spavin (1)	Thompson		
Feb 17	Liverpool	Rd 5	FAC	a	0-0	54967	Kelly	Cunningham	Ross	Wylie	Singleton	Smith	D.Wilson	Biggs	Dawson	Spavin	Thompson		
Feb 20	Liverpool	Replay	FAC	h	0-0*	37825	Kelly	Cunningham	Ross	Wylie	Singleton	Smith	D.Wilson	Biggs	Dawson	Spavin	Thompson		
Feb 24	Bristol Rovers		Div 2	a	1-2	10601	Kelly	Ross	O'Neill	Wylie	Singleton	Smith	D.Wilson	Biggs (1)	Dawson	Spavin	Thompson		
Feb 26	Liverpool	2nd Rep.*	FAC	n	1-0	43944	Kelly	Cunningham	Ross	Wylie	Singleton	Smith	D.Wilson	Biggs	Dawson	Spavin	Thompson (1)		
Mar 3	Stoke City		Div 2	h	1-2	19091	Kelly	Cunningham	Ross	Wylie	Singleton	Smith	D.Wilson	Biggs	Dawson	Spavin	Thompson (1)		
Mar 10	Manchester Utd.	Rd 6	FAC	h	0-0	37521	Kelly	Cunningham	Ross	Wylie	Singleton	Smith	D.Wilson	Biggs	Dawson	Spavin	Thompson		
Mar 14	Manchester Utd.	Replay	FAC	a	1-2	63468	Kelly	R.Wilson	Ross	Wylie	Singleton	Smith	D.Wilson	Biggs	Dawson	Spavin (1)	Thompson		
Mar 17	Rotherham		Div 2	h	2-0	12100	Kelly	R.Wilson	Ross	Wylie	Smith	Barber	D.Wilson	Biggs (2)	Alston	Spavin	Thompson		
Mar 21	Sunderland		Div 2	h	0-0	21714	Kelly	R.Wilson	Ross	Wylie	Singleton	Smith	D.Wilson	Biggs	Alston	Spavin	Thompson		
Mar 24	Liverpool		Div 2	a	1-4	39701	Kelly	R.Wilson	Ross	Wylie	Singleton	Smith	D.Wilson	Biggs	Alston (1)	Barber	Thompson		
Mar 30	Norwich City		Div 2	h	2-0	11015	Barton	R.Wilson	Ross	Wylie	Singleton	Smith	Alston (1)	Biggs	Dawson (1)	Spavin	Thompson		
Apr 2	Huddersfield T.		Div 2	a	2-2	5256	Barton	R.Wilson	Ross	Wylie	Singleton	Smith	Alston (1)	Biggs (1)	Dawson	Spavin	Thompson		
Apr 7	Bury		Div 2	a	1-2	8234	Kelly	R.Wilson	Ross	Wylie	Singleton	Smith	Alston	Biggs (1)	Dawson	Spavin	Thompson		
Apr 9	Leeds Utd.		Div 2	h	1-1	10492	Barton	Cunningham	Ross	Wylie	Singleton	Smith	Alston (1)	Biggs	Dawson	Spavin	Thompson		
Apr 14	Brighton		Div 2	h	3-1	9160	Kelly	R.Wilson	Ross	Wylie	Singleton	Smith	D.Wilson	Biggs (3)	Alston	Spavin	Thompson		
Apr 20	Scunthorpe		Div 2	a	1-2	11368	Kelly	R.Wilson	Ross	Barber	Gornall	Smith	D.Wilson	Biggs	Alston	Spavin	Thompson		
Apr 23	Southampton		Div 2	a	1-1	13292	Kelly	R.Wilson	Ross	Barber	Singleton	Smith (1)	D.Wilson	Biggs	Alston	Spavin	Thompson		
Apr 28	Charlton Ath.		Div 2	h	2-0	9458	Kelly	R.Wilson	Ross	Barber (1)	Singleton	Smith	D.Wilson	Thompson	Dawson (1)	Spavin	Alston		
	* Played at Old Trafford				*AET														

Peter Thompson

Trivia Facts:

When Preston entertained Stoke, Tommy Thompson was made captain for the day by the visitors. The referee, Ken Howley, must have been sick of seeing North End as it was the fourth time in a fortnight that he had handled the club. He had just controlled the three cup-ties with Liverpool.

When Preston played at Brighton there was a colour clash so North End borrowed a set of Brighton's gold and blue shirts.

In his debut at Luton, Alfie Biggs had two goals disallowed whilst at the other end, Luton's Alex Ashworth scored twice.

Season 1961–62: Second Division

		P	W	D	L	F	A	Pts
1	Liverpool	42	27	8	7	99	43	62
2	Leyton Orient	42	22	10	10	69	40	54
3	Sunderland	42	22	9	11	85	50	53
4	Scunthorpe	42	21	7	14	86	71	49
5	Plymouth	42	19	8	15	75	75	46
6	Southampton	42	18	9	15	77	62	45
7	Huddersfield	42	16	12	14	67	59	44
8	Stoke	42	17	8	17	55	57	42
9	Rotherham	42	16	9	17	70	76	41
10	PRESTON	42	15	10	17	55	57	40
11	Newcastle	42	15	9	18	64	58	39
12	Middlesbrough	42	16	7	19	76	72	39
13	Luton	42	17	5	20	69	71	39
14	Walsall	42	14	11	17	70	75	39
15	Charlton	42	15	9	18	69	75	39
16	Derby	42	14	11	17	68	75	39
17	Norwich	42	14	11	17	61	70	39
18	Bury	42	17	5	20	52	76	39
19	Leeds	42	12	12	18	50	61	36
20	Swansea	42	12	12	18	61	83	36
21	Bristol Rovers	42	13	7	22	53	81	33
22	Brighton	42	10	11	21	42	86	31

SEASON 1962–1963

An appalling away record led to Preston having a very poor season in 1962–63 the club winning just two games on their travels. Luckily for North End the form at Deepdale was much better, indeed, it was good enough to give them the necessary points to avoid the shame of a drop into Division Three. At times though that threat was a very real one. A lack of transfer activity in the summer of 1962 did not inspire optimism amongst the North End fans as only John Donnelly was brought in. It was not until the November that another new player was sought, by which time the situation was already showing signs of desperation. Only four wins had been achieved in those early months and a 7–1 thrashing at Plymouth in only the second game of the season had sent spirits tumbling. It was a mood the players found difficult to shake off. Alfie Biggs had returned to Bristol Rovers early in the campaign and Alex Dawson was left with little support up front. Goals were scarce although to be fair Dawson's form was good and he scored regularly. Before Christmas, with the outlook even bleaker, Preston made other signings as the veteran Bolton winger Doug Holden and Ian Davidson, a tall, gangly wing-half from Kilmarnock, were brought in to strengthen the squad. It gave all the players a boost and two good wins over Portsmouth and Leeds, both at Deepdale, further lifted the spirits in the camp. But on Boxing Day football across the country was thrown into turmoil by the weather! Heavy snow hit Britain hard and the winter of 1963 was to go down as one of the worst in history. North End managed just two games between January and March and football was at a standstill. One of those Preston games came in the FA Cup,

one of only two third round ties to be played, but Preston lost 4–1 to Sunderland so that was the end of that competition. When North End finally restarted their league programme their form was poor and manager Jimmy Milne again dipped into the transfer market, signing Nobby Lawton from Manchester United. He was to prove a good buy, although not immediately. North End continued to struggle and, infuriatingly for their fans, mixed an excellent performance with an awful one. Relegation was a distinct possibility especially as they gained just one point from six at Easter. But a late rally, in which star player Peter Thompson excelled, saw four wins in the last nine games, edging the team closer to safety. In the end they finished six points clear of the relegation positions with wins at Portsmouth and at home to Huddersfield being crucial in the final outcome. The season had to be extended to allow for all the earlier postponements and on May 6 1963 that great defender Willie Cunningham played his last game for the club. It was a sad day, but on the other hand a young lad made his first team bow called Howard Kendall and North End had high hopes of him.

DEBUTANTS: (6) Stan Lapot, John Donnelly, Doug Holden, Ian Davidson, Nobby Lawton, Howard Kendall.

LAST GAMES: (8) Cunningham, Wilson R., Alston, Thompson, Biggs, Gornall, O'Neill, Wylie.

League appearances (42 games)

Alston A. G. 15, Barber D. E. 15, Barton J. B. 2, Biggs A. G. 9, Cunningham W. C. 9, Davidson I. 16, Dawson A. D. 41, Donnelly J. 29, Gornall J. 3, Holden A. D. 23, Kelly J. A. 40, Kendall H. 2, Lapot S. 4, Lawton N. 15, O'Neill J. N. 9, Ross G. 39, Singleton A. J. 38, Smith J. A. G. 29, Spavin A. 32, Thompson P. 42, Wilson D. C. 39, Wilson J. R. 2, Wylie J. E. 9.

FA Cup appearances (1 game)

Kelly, Ross, Barber, Dawson, Spavin, Thompson, Donnelly, Alston, Singleton, Holden and Davidson, all one each.

League Cup appearances (4 games)

Kelly 3, Ross 4, Barber 2, Smith 2, D Wilson 4, Biggs 1, Dawson 4, Spavin 4, Thompson 4, Donnelly 4, O'Neill 3, Wylie 1, Alston 3, Singleton 3, Barton 1, Cunningham 1.

Goalscorers: 59 League–1 FAC–7 LC–(Total 67)

Dawson 22 (1 pen) 0–5 (27), Wilson D. C. 6–0–0 (6), Holden 5–1–0 (6), Spavin 5–0–0 (5), Alston 4–0–1 (5), Thompson 4–0–0 (4), Lawton 3–0–0 (3), Ross 2–0–0 (2), Smith 2–0–0 (2), Biggs 1–0–1 (2), Barber 1–0–0 (1), Donnelly 1–0–0 (1), Own goals 3–0–0 (3), Kelly of Luton, Nelson of Sunderland and Davies of Swansea.

Nobby Lawton and Alex Dawson.

Willie Cunningham and Alex Dawson finishing another lap around the pitch.

Future Players born between August 1962 and May 1963: Gary Brazil, Mark Leonard, Bob Atkins, Mark Walsh, Bob McNeill, Ian Bryson, Paul Birch, Trevor Matthewson, David Moyes, Gavin Nebbeling, Steve Senior, Ronnie Jepson.
Manager: Jimmy Milne **Chairman:** J. H. Ingham Esq.
Ever presents: (1) Peter Thompson
Hat-tricks: (1) Alex Dawson
FA Cup: 3rd Round **League Cup:** 4th Round
Players used: 23
Leading scorer: 27 goals – Alex Dawson
(22 league 5 League Cup)

AUTHORS' UNOFFICIAL PLAYER OF THE SEASON:
Peter Thompson

Match Report: Swans Hit for Six – 20 April 1963
Preston 6 Swansea Town 3

A win for Preston was of paramount importance in this fixture owing to their inability to win any of their last six fixtures, thus leaving themselves in deep trouble at the wrong end of the table. The shadow of relegation drew even darker when Morgan put the visitors ahead within the first minute. Cunningham, recalled to the defence, miscued a clearance straight to Reynolds, who then put the ball over to the unmarked inside-left, giving him an easy chance to beat Kelly. Fortunately North End equalised quickly through the dependable Dawson who, on six minutes, rounded off a strong, surging attack by applying his left foot to a low square pass from Thompson from 12 yards out. It gave Dwyer no chance to save. Heartened by their success Preston then pressured the red-shirted Swans who, by necessity, had to defend well to keep North End at bay. However, against the run of play, Swansea then regained the lead after 31 minutes. Defenders were caught in two minds when an Evans free-kick found Thomas who was unhindered as he calmly placed the ball wide of Kelly. The North End fans watched this grim turn of events in glum silence, but the turnaround about to be witnessed in the second half changed the mood of the spectators. Lawton was inspirational in the quest to overcome the deficit, prodding and probing with his usual tenacity. Swansea's Davies felt the power of Dawson's shooting as he headed clear a goalbound effort and he went down as if pole-axed having to leave the field to recover. Just as he returned he saw Ross's free-kick find the head of Smith who equalised in style. The comeback was now in full swing and the cheers had hardly died away when Davies, still under the influence of Dawson's shot, turned a Wilson centre past his own goalkeeper. Reacting positively to this overdue tonic Preston ventured forward at every opportunity, mainly through Lawton and Wilson. Lawton was rewarded on 65 minutes when he scored his first goal for the club. Thomas then pulled one back but that only stirred Preston into action again as Dawson headed two late goals, both made by Lawton, to bring their losing streak to an emphatic end.

Left to right: *Back row:* Donnelly, Ross, Wylie, Kelly, Singleton, Barber, Smith, R. Wilson. *Front row:* D. Wilson, Biggs, Dawson, Alston, Spavin, Thompson.

Trivia Facts:

In 22 year old Jack Gornall's first match of the season, at Stoke, he was up against a 48 year old Stanley Matthews and another veteran, Jackie Mudie, who gave the youngster a nightmare afternoon.

The balance sheet for 1962–63 showed a loss of £13,141. Only the FA Cup run made that figure respectable as £21,278 had been made on that. The wage bill was £43,892.

Nobby Lawton gave away a penalty on his debut for the club and the match at Derby was Jim Smith's 100th league game.

Date 1962-3	Opponents	Comp	h or a	Score	Att.	1	2	3	4	5	6	7	8	9	10	11		
Aug 18	Norwich City	Div 2	h	2-2	13363	Kelly	R.Wilson	Ross	Barber	Smith	Lapot	D.Wilson	Biggs	Dawson (1)	Spavin (1)	Thompson		
Aug 22	Plymouth Arg.	Div 2	a	1-7	21012	Kelly	R.Wilson	Ross	Barber	Smith	Lapot	D.Wilson	Biggs	Dawson (1)	Spavin	Thompson		
Aug 25	Walsall	Div 2	a	1-4	10259	Kelly	Donnelly	O'Neill	Barber	Smith	Wylie	Alston	Biggs	Dawson (1)	Spavin	Thompson		
Aug 28	Plymouth Arg.	Div 2	h	0-0	14248	Kelly	Donnelly	O'Neill	Wylie	Singleton	Smith	D.Wilson	Biggs	Dawson	Thompson	Alston		
Sep 1	Newcastle Utd.	Div 2	h	2-1	13884	Barton	Donnelly	O'Neill	Wylie	Singleton	Smith	D.Wilson (1)	Biggs	Dawson	Thompson	Alston (1)		
Sep 5	Luton Town	Div 2	a	2-0	6702	Kelly	Donnelly	Ross	Wylie	Singleton	Smith	D.Wilson (1)	Biggs (1)	Dawson	Thompson	Alston		
Sep 8	Derby County	Div 2	a	0-1	11482	Kelly	Donnelly	Ross	Wylie	Singleton	Smith	D.Wilson	Biggs	Dawson	Alston	Thompson		
Sep 11	Luton Town	Div 2	h	3-1	12216	Kelly	Donnelly	Ross	Wylie	Singleton	Smith	D.Wilson (1)	Alston	Dawson (1)	Spavin	Thompson	1 og	(Kelly)
Sep 15	Middlesbrough	Div 2	a	0-1	14070	Kelly	Donnelly	Ross	Wylie	Singleton	Smith	D.Wilson	Alston	Dawson	Spavin	Thompson		
Sep 22	Huddersfield T.	Div 2	a	0-1	17594	Kelly	Donnelly	Ross	Wylie	Singleton	Smith	D.Wilson	Biggs	Dawson	Spavin	Thompson		
Sep 24	Q.P.R. Rd 2	LC	a	2-1	11005	Kelly	Donnelly	Ross	Wylie	Singleton	Smith	D.Wilson	Biggs (1)	Dawson (1)	Spavin	Thompson		
Sep 29	Cardiff City	Div 2	h	2-6	11994	Kelly	Donnelly (1)	Ross	Wylie	Singleton	Smith	D.Wilson	Biggs	Dawson (1)	Spavin	Thompson		
Oct 6	Southampton	Div 2	a	0-1	16853	Kelly	Donnelly	O'Neill	Ross	Singleton	Smith	D.Wilson	Alston	Dawson	Spavin	Thompson		
Oct 13	Scunthorpe Utd.	Div 2	h	3-1	10107	Kelly	Donnelly	O'Neill	Ross	Singleton	Smith	D.Wilson	Alston (1)	Dawson (2, 1p)	Spavin	Thompson		
Oct 16	Northampton T. Rd 3	LC	a	1-1	12418	Kelly	Donnelly	O'Neill	Ross	Singleton	Barber	D.Wilson	Alston	Dawson (1)	Spavin	Thompson		
Oct 20	Bury	Div 2	a	0-0	13037	Kelly	Donnelly	O'Neill	Ross	Singleton	Barber	D.Wilson	Alston	Dawson	Spavin	Thompson		
Oct 27	Rotherham Utd.	Div 2	h	2-2	8863	Kelly	Donnelly	O'Neill	Ross	Singleton	Barber (1)	D.Wilson	Alston (1)	Dawson	Spavin	Thompson		
Oct 29	Northampton T. Replay	LC	h	2-1	7040	Barton	Cunningham	O'Neill	Donnelly	Singleton	Ross	D.Wilson	Alston (1)	Dawson (1)	Spavin	Thompson		
Nov 3	Charlton Ath.	Div 2	a	1-2	10971	Barton	Donnelly	O'Neill	Ross (1)	Singleton	Barber	D.Wilson	Alston	Dawson	Spavin	Thompson		
Nov 10	Stoke City	Div 2	h	1-1	14697	Kelly	Donnelly	O'Neill	Ross (1)	Singleton	Barber	D.Wilson	Alston	Dawson	Spavin	Thompson		
Nov 12	Aston Villa Rd 4	LC	a	2-6	16704	Kelly	Donnelly	O'Neill	Ross	Smith	Barber	D.Wilson	Alston	Dawson (2)	Spavin	Thompson		
Nov 17	Sunderland	Div 2	a	1-2	29976	Kelly	Donnelly	Ross	Barber	Singleton	Smith	Holden	D.Wilson	Dawson	Spavin	Thompson	1 og	(Nelson)
Nov 24	Leeds Utd.	Div 2	h	4-1	13145	Kelly	Donnelly	Ross	Barber	Singleton	Smith	D.Wilson	Thompson (1)	Dawson (2)	Spavin (1)	Holden		
Dec 1	Swansea Town	Div 2	a	1-1	7085	Kelly	Donnelly	Ross	Barber	Singleton	Davidson	D.Wilson	Thompson	Dawson	Spavin (1)	Holden		
Dec 8	Chelsea	Div 2	h	1-3	14487	Kelly	Donnelly	Ross	Barber	Singleton	Davidson	D.Wilson	Thompson (1)	Dawson	Spavin	Holden		
Dec 15	Norwich City	Div 2	a	1-1	11566	Kelly	Donnelly	Ross	Barber	Singleton	Davidson	Holden	Thompson	Dawson (1)	Spavin	Alston		
Dec 26	Portsmouth	Div 2	h	4-2	8742	Kelly	Donnelly	Ross	Barber	Singleton	Davidson	Holden (1)	Thompson	Dawson (1)	Spavin (1)	Alston (1)		
Jan 5	Sunderland Rd 3	FAC	h	1-4	25917	Kelly	Donnelly	Ross	Barber	Singleton	Davidson	Holden (1)	Thompson	Dawson	Spavin	Alston		
Feb 23	Southampton	Div 2	h	1-0	10073	Kelly	Donnelly	Ross	Barber	Singleton	Smith	D.Wilson	Thompson	Dawson	Spavin	Holden (1)		
Mar 9	Bury	Div 2	h	0-2	10598	Kelly	Donnelly	Ross	Barber	Singleton	Smith	D.Wilson	Thompson	Dawson	Spavin	Holden		
Mar 16	Rotherham Utd.	Div 2	a	1-3	7270	Kelly	Cunningham	Ross	Donnelly	Singleton	Smith	D.Wilson (1)	Thompson	Dawson	Spavin	Holden		
Mar 19	Walsall	Div 2	h	4-2	10705	Kelly	Cunningham	Ross	Lawton	Singleton	Smith (1)	D.Wilson	Thompson (1)	Dawson (1)	Spavin	Holden		
Mar 23	Charlton Ath.	Div 2	h	4-1	11131	Kelly	Cunningham	Ross	Lawton	Singleton	Smith	D.Wilson (1)	Thompson	Dawson (2)	Spavin (1)	Holden		
Mar 26	Scunthorpe Utd.	Div 2	a	1-4	7239	Kelly	Cunningham	Ross	Lawton	Singleton	Davidson	D.Wilson	Thompson	Dawson	Spavin	Holden (1)		
Mar 30	Stoke City	Div 2	a	0-3	21881	Kelly	Donnelly	Ross	Lawton	Gomall	Davidson	D.Wilson	Thompson	Dawson	Spavin	Holden		
Apr 6	Sunderland	Div 2	h	1-1	14015	Kelly	Donnelly	Ross	Davidson	Singleton	Smith	D.Wilson	Thompson	Dawson	Lawton	Holden (1)		
Apr 12	Grimsby Town	Div 2	a	0-2	14115	Kelly	Donnelly	Ross	Lawton	Singleton	Davidson	D.Wilson	Thompson	Dawson	Spavin	Holden		
Apr 13	Leeds Utd.	Div 2	a	1-4	16016	Kelly	Donnelly	Ross	Davidson	Singleton	Gomall	D.Wilson	Lawton	Dawson	Spavin	Thompson (1)		
Apr 15	Grimsby Town	Div 2	h	0-0	11487	Kelly	Donnelly	Ross	Davidson	Singleton	Gomall	D.Wilson	Lawton	Dawson	Spavin	Thompson		
Apr 20	Swansea Town	Div 2	h	6-3	7652	Kelly	Cunningham	Ross	Davidson	Singleton	Smith (1)	D.Wilson	Thompson	Dawson (3)	Lawton (1)	Holden	1 og	(Davies)
Apr 27	Chelsea	Div 2	a	0-2	23770	Kelly	Cunningham	Ross	Davidson	Singleton	Smith	D.Wilson	Thompson	Dawson	Lawton	Holden		
May 1	Portsmouth	Div 2	a	2-1	8599	Kelly	Cunningham	Ross	Davidson	Singleton	Smith	D.Wilson (1)	Thompson	Dawson (1)	Lawton	Holden		
May 4	Huddersfield T.	Div 2	h	2-0	11770	Kelly	Cunningham	Ross	Davidson	Singleton	Smith	D.Wilson	Thompson	Dawson (1)	Lawton	Holden		
May 6	Cardiff City	Div 2	a	1-1	8389	Kelly	Cunningham	Ross	Davidson	Singleton	Smith	D.Wilson	Thompson	Dawson	Lawton (1)	Holden		
May 11	Newcastle Utd.	Div 2	a	2-2	13552	Kelly	Ross	Smith	Davidson	Singleton	Kendall	D.Wilson	Thompson	Dawson (2)	Spavin	Holden		
May 15	Middlesbrough	Div 2	a	0-2	11553	Kelly	Ross	Smith	Kendall	Singleton	Lapot	D.Wilson	Lawton	Thompson	Spavin	Holden		
May 18	Derby County	Div 2	h	1-0	8323	Kelly	Ross	Smith	Lawton	Singleton	Lapot	D.Wilson	Thompson	Dawson (1)	Spavin	Holden		

League position in Division Two: 17th – P42 W13 D11 L18 F59 A74 Pts 37
Home: W11 D6 L4 F43 A30 Away: W2 D5 L14 F16 A44

STAT FACTS:
Best home run without defeat: 7 games
Best away run without defeat: 3 games
Longest run unbeaten: 4 games
Longest run without a win: 6 games
Best home attendance: 25,917 *vs.* Sunderland FAC 5.1.63
Worst home attendance: 7,040 *vs.* Northampton LC 29.10.62
Best away attendance: 29,976 *vs.* Sunderland 17.11.62
Worst away attendance: 6,702 *vs.* Luton 5.9.62
Aggregate and average home attendance: 245,570 – 11,694
Aggregate and average away attendance: 288,921 – 13,758

Season 1962–63: Second Division

	P	W	D	L	F	A	Pts
1 Stoke	42	20	13	9	73	50	53
2 Chelsea	42	24	4	14	81	42	52
3 Sunderland	42	20	12	10	84	55	52
4 Middlesbrough	42	20	9	13	86	85	49
5 Leeds	42	19	10	13	79	53	48
6 Huddersfield	42	17	14	11	63	50	48
7 Newcastle	42	18	11	13	79	59	47
8 Bury	42	18	11	13	51	47	47
9 Scunthorpe	42	16	12	14	57	59	44
10 Cardiff	42	18	7	17	83	73	43
11 Southampton	42	17	8	17	72	67	42
12 Plymouth	42	15	12	15	76	73	42
13 Norwich	42	17	8	17	80	79	42
14 Rotherham	42	17	6	19	67	74	40
15 Swansea	42	15	9	18	51	72	39
16 Portsmouth	42	13	11	18	63	79	37
17 PRESTON	**42**	**13**	**11**	**18**	**59**	**74**	**37**
18 Derby	42	12	12	18	61	72	36
19 Grimsby	42	11	13	18	55	66	35
20 Charlton	42	13	5	24	62	94	31
21 Walsall	42	11	9	22	53	89	31
22 Luton	42	11	7	24	61	84	29

189

SEASON 1963–1964

So near and yet so far, that was the verdict on the 1963–64 season, a season that promised so much and yet ended in bitter disappointment. After a sluggish start the side then produced a brilliant 5–4 win at Southampton. With Nobby Lawton's increasing influence playing a big part, North End then began to string together an impressive run of results to look likely promotion material. Manager Jimmy Milne was able to keep a fairly settled side and this was reflected in the improved form. This better play was especially noticable away from home where Preston picked up regular points for a change. Alex Dawson was in superb form from day one, scoring 13 goals in his first nine appearances, and he struck up an immediate partnership with new signing Alec Ashworth. Dawson's ability in the air was particularly effective. Other players showed excellent form too and both Dave Wilson and George Ross attracted the attention of the International selectors from England and Scotland. An early exit from the League Cup did not distract North End from their league form and for much of the season Preston battled it out with Sunderland and Leeds for the championship title. With another new signing Brian Godfrey stepping in when Dawson or Ashworth were injured, the potential for goals was immense. Lawton, Ian Davidson and Alan Spavin played splendidly in the midfield and at the back George Ross and Jim Smith were immaculate full-backs. Tony Singleton was a

tower of strength at centre-half and Alan Kelly showed his class in goal. Doug Holden was another whose influence on the side was immeasurable. The already exciting season reached new heights at the turn of the year as the club embarked on a run in the FA Cup which was to take them all the way to Wembley. Nottingham Forest, Bolton, Carlisle and Oxford were all beaten and Preston then faced Swansea Town in a Villa Park semi-final. With rain lashing down and the pitch a quagmire Preston showed all their strength and character. With the score 1–1, Singleton decided it was about time he scored his first ever goal for the club and he lashed the ball home from fully 30 yards out! The final was to come but first it was time to concentrate on the league. A disastrous 4–0 defeat at Sunderland hit Preston hard but six points out of six at Easter put them back into the promotion race. Unfortunately just one point from the next six cost them their chance and they had to be content with third place. That just left the Cup Final with West Ham. A magnificent game ended with an oh, so cruel injury time goal which gave the Hammers a 3–2 win after North End had earlier played superbly to lead 2–1. It was a sad end to a wonderful season.

DEBUTANTS: (4) Alec Ashworth, Kit Napier, Brian Godfrey, Frank Lee.

LAST GAMES: (2) Barber, Napier.

Left to right: *Back row:* Ross, Kendall, Singleton, Holden, Barton, Kelly, Smith, Davidson, Godfrey. *Front row:* Wilson, Ashworth, Dawson, Lawton, Spavin.

League position in Division Two: 3rd – P42 W23 D10 L9 F79 A54 Pts 56
Home: W13 D7 L1 F37 A14 Away: W10 D3 L8 F42 A40

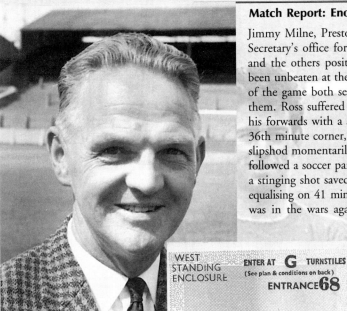

Above: Mr J. Milne, PNE Manager.

WEST STANDING ENCLOSURE

ENTER AT **G** TURNSTILES
(See plan & conditions on back)

ENTRANCE **68**

EMPIRE STADIUM, WEMBLEY
The Football Association
Cup Competition

FINAL TIE

SATURDAY, MAY 2nd, 1964
KICK-OFF 3 p.m.

Price 7/6   *Chairman, Wembley Stadium Limited*

THIS PORTION TO BE RETAINED
This ticket is issued on the condition that
it is not re-sold for more than its face value.

Match Report: Enough to Make a Saint Swear – 7 Sept. 1963 Southampton 4 Preston 5

Jimmy Milne, Preston's manager, apparently apologised when he called in at the Southampton's Secretary's office for having to make six changes to the printed programme, half due to injuries and the others positional. So, how would a re-organised team cope against the Saints who had been unbeaten at the Dell for 21 games? Well, Nobby Lawton won the toss and in the early stages of the game both sets of forwards were very active, anxious to put their midweek defeats behind them. Ross suffered an early knock but recovered well enough to play an attacking role, feeding his forwards with a stream of well placed passes. But it was the Saints who took the lead when a 36th minute corner, their eighth from the left, was headed in by Kirby. North End's play became slipshod momentarily, resulting from their obvious lack of cohesion, but as so often happens there followed a soccer paradox. From their worst moment Preston suddenly had their best. Wilson had a stinging shot saved by Reynolds and a quickly taken corner kick to Dawson ended with Lawton equalising on 41 minutes. Kelly, having already taken a nasty knock from Paine before the break was in the wars again soon after the interval, being involved in an incident with Kirby. Kelly cleared his lines before collapsing, clutching his head, thus holding up the game for several minutes whilst he was treated. Burnside then put the home team in front again on 57 minutes but their joy was shortlived as a smart move involving Holden, Lawton and Dawson resulted in the latter firing in a hard, rising shot from around the penalty spot. As the game progressed the gallant Kelly had to receive further treatment. It seemed as though North End had gained control of the game especially after Dawson put them ahead with just 12 minutes left. However, Southampton bounced back and the troublesome Kirby scored from yet another corner. The thrills were far from over though as in th 85th minute, Kendall collected the ball in midfield and scored at the end of a great solo run. Yet again the Saints came back and equalised with just three minutes remaining. O'Brien latching on to the ball after a shot hit the crossbar. Four-all, the unbeaten record still intact, or so Southampton thought. With time almost up Lawton scored what proved to be the winner just before the final whistle. Real crowd pleasing material! One blot on the game was a rare booking for Barber who argued about the third home goal.

League appearances (42 games)

Ashworth A. 31, Barber D.E. 5, Barton J.B. 2, Davidson I. 37, Dawson A.D. 41, Donnelly J. 9, Godfrey B.C. 11, Holden A.D. 39, Kelly J.A. 40, Kendall H. 9, Lawton N. 38, Lee F. 1, Napier C.R.A. 1, Ross G. 42, Singleton A.J. 42, Smith J.A.G. 33, Spavin A. 40, Wilson D.C. 41.

FA Cup appearances (8 Games)

Kelly 8, Ross 8, Smith 2, Lawton 8, Singleton 8, Davidson 7, Wilson 8, Ashworth 4, Dawson 8, Spavin 8, Holden 8, Kendall 5 Donnelly 2, Godfrey 4.

League Cup appearances (1 game)

Barton, Ross, Smith, Lawton, Singleton, Davidson, Wilson, Barber, Dawson, Spavin, Holden all one each.

Goalscorers: 79 League–12 FAC–(Total 91)

Dawson 30 (3 pens)–6 (1 pen) (36), Ashworth 14–0 (14), Wilson 11–0 (11), Lawton 6–1 (7), Holden 6–1 (7), Godfrey 5–1 (6), Spavin 4–1 (5), Kendall 1–1 (2), Davidson 1–0 (1), Singleton 0–1 (1), Own goals 1–0 (1) Kiernan of Northampton

Future Players born between August 1963 and May 1964: Wayne Foster, Dale Rudge, Paul Williams, Simon Farnworth, Phil Harrington, Colin Greenall, Mick Bennett, Chris Hunter, David Miller, Paul Wilkins, Matt Carmichael.

Ever presents: (2) George Ross and Tony Singleton.   **FA Cup:** Runners-up
Hat-tricks: (3) Alex Dawson, Alex Ashworth and Dave Wilson, one each.
Players used: 18   **League Cup:** 2nd Round   **Manager:** Jimmy Milne
Chairman: J.H. Ingham Esq. (died February 1964) then A. Harrison Esq. BEM
Leading scorer: 36 goals – Alex Dawson (30 league 6 FAC)

AUTHORS' UNOFFICIAL PLAYERS OF THE SEASON:
Nobby Lawton and Alex Dawson (Joint Winners)

Howard Kendall, who became a household name in soccer circles.

Date 1963-4	Opponents		Comp	h or a	Score * aet	Att.	1	2	3	4	5	6	7	8	9	10	11		
Aug 24	Leyton Orient		Div 2	a	2-2	12002	Kelly	Ross	Smith	Lawton (1)	Singleton	Davidson	Wilson	Ashworth	Dawson (1)	Spavin	Holden		
Aug 27	Charlton Ath.		Div 2	h	3-1	16695	Kelly	Ross	Smith	Lawton	Singleton	Davidson	Wilson (2)	Ashworth	Dawson (1)	Spavin	Holden		
Aug 31	Swansea Town		Div 2	h	3-3	14613	Kelly	Ross	Smith	Lawton	Singleton	Davidson	Wilson	Ashworth	Dawson (3, 1p)	Spavin	Holden		
Sep 3	Charlton Ath.		Div 2	a	0-3	10626	Kelly	Ross	Smith	Lawton	Singleton	Kendall	Napier	Wilson	Dawson	Spavin	Holden		
Sep 7	Southampton		Div 2	a	5-4	15925	Kelly	Ross	Donnelly	Kendall (1)	Singleton	Smith	Wilson	Lawton (2)	Dawson (2)	Barber	Holden		
Sep 9	Plymouth Arg.		Div 2	h	0-0	16131	Kelly	Ross	Donnelly	Kendall	Singleton	Smith	Wilson	Lawton	Dawson	Barber	Holden		
Sep 14	Middlesbrough		Div 2	h	2-2	15499	Kelly	Ross	Donnelly	Davidson	Singleton	Smith	Wilson	Lawton	Dawson (2)	Spavin	Holden		
Sep 18	Plymouth Arg.		Div 2	a	2-0	13274	Kelly	Ross	Smith	Lawton	Singleton	Davidson	Wilson	Ashworth	Dawson (2)	Spavin	Holden		
Sep 21	Newcastle Utd.		Div 2	a	4-2	29710	Kelly	Ross	Smith	Lawton	Singleton	Davidson	Wilson	Ashworth (2)	Dawson (2)	Spavin	Holden		
Sep 25	Newcastle Utd.	Rd 2	LC	a	0-3	14897	Barton	Ross	Smith	Lawton	Singleton	Davidson	Wilson	Barber	Dawson	Spavin	Holden		
Sep 28	Huddersfield T.		Div 2	h	2-1	15842	Kelly	Ross	Smith	Lawton	Singleton	Davidson	Wilson	Ashworth	Dawson (1)	Spavin (1)	Holden		
Oct 2	Norwich City		Div 2	a	1-2	16887	Kelly	Ross	Smith	Lawton	Singleton	Davidson	Wilson	Ashworth	Dawson	Spavin (1)	Holden		
Oct 5	Derby County		Div 2	a	2-1	14129	Barton	Ross	Smith	Lawton	Singleton	Davidson	Wilson	Ashworth (1)	Dawson	Spavin (1)	Holden		
Oct 12	Swindon Town		Div 2	h	1-0	21263	Kelly	Ross	Smith	Lawton	Singleton	Davidson	Wilson	Ashworth	Dawson	Spavin	Holden (1)		
Oct 19	Manchester City		Div 2	a	3-2	23153	Kelly	Ross	Smith	Lawton	Singleton	Davidson	Wilson	Ashworth (1)	Dawson (1)	Spavin	Holden (1)		
Oct 26	Scunthorpe Utd.		Div 2	h	1-0	15832	Kelly	Ross	Smith	Lawton	Singleton	Davidson	Wilson	Ashworth	Dawson (1)	Spavin	Holden		
Nov 2	Northampton T.		Div 2	a	3-0	13693	Kelly	Ross	Smith	Lawton	Singleton	Davidson	Wilson	Ashworth (1)	Dawson (1)	Spavin	Godfrey	1 og	(Kiernan)
Nov 9	Sunderland		Div 2	h	1-1	26579	Kelly	Ross	Smith	Lawton	Singleton	Davidson	Wilson	Ashworth	Dawson	Spavin	Holden		
Nov 16	Leeds Utd.		Div 2	a	1-1	33991	Kelly	Ross	Smith	Lawton	Singleton	Davidson	Wilson	Godfrey	Dawson	Spavin	Holden (1)		
Nov 23	Rotherham Utd.		Div 2	h	2-2	13883	Kelly	Ross	Smith	Lawton	Singleton	Davidson	Wilson	Ashworth (1)	Dawson (1)	Spavin	Holden		
Nov 30	Portsmouth		Div 2	a	2-1	18958	Kelly	Ross	Smith	Lawton	Singleton	Davidson	Wilson	Ashworth	Dawson (2)	Spavin	Holden		
Dec 7	Bury		Div 2	h	3-0	16374	Kelly	Ross	Smith	Lawton	Singleton	Davidson	Wilson	Ashworth (3)	Dawson	Spavin	Holden		
Dec 14	Leyton Orient		Div 2	h	0-0	13763	Kelly	Ross	Smith	Lawton	Singleton	Davidson	Wilson	Ashworth	Dawson	Spavin	Holden		
Dec 20	Swansea Town		Div 2	a	1-5	6773	Kelly	Ross	Smith	Lawton	Singleton	Davidson	Wilson (1)	Ashworth	Dawson	Spavin	Holden		
Dec 26	Cardiff City		Div 2	a	4-0	18682	Kelly	Ross	Smith	Lawton	Singleton	Davidson (1)	Wilson (3)	Ashworth	Dawson	Spavin	Holden		
Dec 28	Cardiff City		Div 2	h	4-0	19458	Kelly	Ross	Smith	Lawton (1)	Singleton	Davidson	Wilson	Ashworth	Dawson (2, 1p)	Spavin (1)	Holden		
Jan 4	Nottm Forest	Rd 3	FAC	a	0-0	26906	Kelly	Ross	Smith	Lawton	Singleton	Davidson	Wilson	Ashworth	Dawson	Spavin	Holden		
Jan 11	Southampton		Div 2	h	2-1	18453	Kelly	Ross	Smith	Lawton	Singleton	Davidson	Wilson	Ashworth (1)	Dawson (1)	Spavin	Holden		
Jan 13	Nottm Forest	Replay	FAC	h	1-0*	29374	Kelly	Ross	Davidson	Lawton	Singleton	Kendall (1)	Wilson	Ashworth	Dawson	Spavin	Holden		
Jan 18	Middlesbrough		Div 2	a	0-3	14985	Kelly	Ross	Davidson	Lawton	Singleton	Kendall	Wilson	Ashworth	Dawson	Spavin	Holden		
Jan 25	Bolton W.	Rd 4	FAC	a	2-2	39234	Kelly	Ross	Davidson	Lawton	Singleton	Kendall	Wilson	Godfrey	Dawson (2)	Spavin	Holden		
Jan 27	Bolton W.	Replay	FAC	h	2-1	38290	Kelly	Ross	Davidson	Lawton (1)	Singleton	Kendall	Wilson	Godfrey	Dawson (1)	Spavin	Holden		
Feb 1	Newcastle Utd.		Div 2	h	3-0	18982	Barton	Ross	Davidson	Lawton	Singleton	Kendall	Wilson	Godfrey (1)	Dawson (2)	Spavin	Holden		
Feb 8	Huddersfield T.		Div 2	a	2-2	15792	Kelly	Ross	Davidson	Lawton	Singleton	Kendall	Wilson	Godfrey (1)	Dawson	Spavin	Holden (1)		
Feb 15	Carlisle Utd.	Rd 5	FAC	h	1-0	36953	Kelly	Ross	Davidson	Lawton	Singleton	Kendall	Wilson	Godfrey	Dawson	Spavin (1)	Holden		
Feb 17	Derby County		Div 2	h	0-2	17675	Kelly	Ross	Donnelly	Lawton	Singleton	Kendall	Lee	Godfrey	Dawson	Spavin	Holden		
Feb 22	Swindon Town		Div 2	a	4-1	14998	Kelly	Ross	Donnelly	Lawton	Singleton	Davidson	Wilson (1)	Godfrey (1)	Dawson (2)	Spavin	Holden		
Feb 29	Oxford Utd.	Rd 6	FAC	a	2-1	22870	Kelly	Ross	Donnelly	Lawton	Singleton	Davidson	Wilson	Godfrey (1)	Dawson (1)	Spavin	Holden		
Mar 3	Leeds Utd.		Div 2	h	2-0	35612	Kelly	Ross	Donnelly	Lawton	Singleton	Davidson	Wilson (1)	Ashworth (1)	Dawson	Spavin	Holden		
Mar 7	Scunthorpe Utd.		Div 2	a	0-1	6492	Kelly	Ross	Donnelly	Lawton	Singleton	Davidson	Wilson	Ashworth	Dawson	Spavin	Holden		
Mar 14	Swansea Town	* Semi-F.	FAC	n	2-1	68000	Kelly	Ross	Donnelly	Lawton	Singleton (1)	Davidson	Wilson	Ashworth	Dawson (1p)	Spavin	Holden		
Mar 17	Norwich City		Div 2	h	3-0	20803	Kelly	Ross	Donnelly	Lawton (1)	Singleton	Davidson	Wilson (1)	Ashworth	Dawson (1)	Spavin	Holden		
Mar 21	Sunderland		Div 2	a	0-4	35420	Kelly	Ross	Donnelly	Lawton	Singleton	Davidson	Wilson	Ashworth	Dawson	Spavin	Holden		
Mar 27	Grimsby Town		Div 2	a	3-0	12138	Kelly	Ross	Smith	Lawton	Singleton	Davidson	Wilson	Godfrey (1)	Ashworth (1)	Spavin	Holden (1)		
Mar 28	Manchester City		Div 2	h	2-0	24796	Kelly	Ross	Smith	Barber	Singleton	Davidson	Wilson	Godfrey (1)	Dawson (1p)	Spavin	Holden		
Mar 30	Grimsby Town		Div 2	h	1-0	24125	Kelly	Ross	Smith	Barber	Singleton	Davidson	Wilson (1)	Ashworth	Dawson	Spavin	Godfrey		
Apr 4	Rotherham Utd.		Div 2	a	2-4	11803	Kelly	Ross	Smith	Barber	Singleton	Davidson	Wilson	Ashworth (2)	Dawson	Spavin	Godfrey		
Apr 11	Portsmouth		Div 2	h	0-0	15933	Kelly	Ross	Smith	Lawton	Singleton	Davidson	Wilson	Ashworth	Dawson	Spavin	Holden		
Apr 18	Bury		Div 2	a	1-2	11649	Kelly	Ross	Smith	Kendall	Singleton	Davidson	Wilson (1)	Godfrey	Dawson	Spavin	Holden		
Apr 25	Northampton T.		Div 2	h	2-1	12933	Kelly	Ross	Smith	Lawton (1)	Singleton	Kendall	Wilson	Ashworth	Dawson	Spavin	Holden (1)		
May 2	West Ham Utd. +	Final	FAC	n	2-3	100000	Kelly	Ross	Smith	Lawton	Singleton	Kendall	Wilson	Ashworth	Dawson (1)	Spavin	Holden (1)		
	* Played at Villa Park + Played at Wembley																		

Des O'Connor with Nobby Lawton, George Ross and their wives. Pictured after the 1964 FA Cup Final.

Season 1963–64: Second Division

		P	W	D	L	F	A	Pts
1	Leeds	42	24	15	3	71	34	63
2	Sunderland	42	25	11	6	81	31	61
3	**PRESTON**	42	23	10	9	79	54	56
4	Charlton	42	19	10	13	76	70	48
5	Southampton	42	19	9	14	100	73	47
6	Man City	42	18	10	14	84	66	46
7	Rotherham	42	19	7	16	90	78	45
8	Newcastle	42	20	5	17	74	69	45
9	Portsmouth	42	16	11	15	79	70	43
10	Middlesbrough	42	15	11	16	67	52	41
11	Northampton	42	16	9	17	58	60	41
12	Huddersfield	42	15	10	17	57	64	40
13	Derby	42	14	11	11	56	67	39
14	Swindon	42	14	10	18	57	69	38
15	Cardiff	42	14	10	18	56	81	38
16	Leyton Orient	42	13	10	19	54	72	36
17	Norwich	42	11	13	18	64	80	35
18	Bury	42	13	9	20	57	73	35
19	Swansea	42	12	9	21	63	74	33
20	Plymouth	42	8	16	18	45	67	32
21	Grimsby	42	9	14	19	47	75	32
22	Scunthorpe	42	10	10	22	52	82	30

After the glory of the previous season, expectations were high that North End could now go one better and regain their Division One status. In the event the new season was one of acute disappointment, although it must be said that from day one North End were hit by a series of injuries to key players. Alex Dawson was hurt during the first game and then Alec Ashworth received a very serious injury which ruled him out for the season after just five matches. Thankfully the emergence of Brian Godfrey saved the day and the Welsh striker scored five goals in his first three outings including a superb hat-trick in a magnificent 5–1 win at Ipswich. This was the high spot of the first half of the campaign, which in the main was a struggle for North End. Other players were also injured for long spells, notably Alan Kelly, Nobby Lawton and Doug Holden, and it made it very difficult for manager Jimmy Milne to find the continuity which had been so important the previous year. After Dawson's return the former Busby Babe struck up a fine understanding with Godfrey which brought back memories of the Tom Finney and Tommy Thompson partnership. Though Preston scored plenty of goals themselves the defence was not nearly as tight as in the previous season. The injuries took more of a toll in that area of the field. Howard Kendall took his brilliant Cup Final form into the new season though and he received rave notices wherever he performed.

And in Alan Spavin Preston had one of their best schemers since the days of Jimmy Baxter. 'Spav' had an outstanding year and was again watched by England representatives. In the cups a defeat at lowly Doncaster ended the League Cup hopes early whilst in the FA Cup Bolton gained revenge for their defeat 12 months earlier in a fourth round tie. After their cup exit Preston had to work hard in their league games. A graph of their results would show the topsy, turvy nature of their play, with a 6–1 win over Portsmouth and a 4–0 defeat at Swansea being typical. The away form again left a lot to be desired but nobody could fault Dawson's contribution, home or away. Three times he hit a hat-trick with one special effort at Charlton being memorable as he headed all three of his goals that day. New players, Bill Cranston, Ernie Hannigan and Bert Patrick, were all Scots, and all made promising early appearances, adding some depth to the squad. The Scottish influence in the team was very pronounced with nine first teamers and several reserves making their presence felt. Over the year though it was clear that North End had taken a backward step.

DEBUTANTS: (6) Ernie Hannigan, Mick Wearmouth, Bill Cranston, Tony Coleman, Bert Patrick, Willie Watt.

LAST GAMES: (3) Holden, Davidson, Coleman

League appearances (42 games)

Ashworth A. 5, Barton J. B. 25, Coleman A. G. 5, Cranston W. 14, Davidson I. 14, Dawson A. D. 36, Donnelly J. 7, Godfrey B. C. 37, Hannigan E. 11, Holden A. D. 28, Kelly J. A. 17, Kendall H. 29, Lapot S. 2, Lawton N. 24, Lee F. 4, Ross G. 32, Singleton A. J. 40, Smith J. A. G. 40, Spavin A. 42, Watt W. D. 4, Wearmouth M. 1, Wilson D. C. 36.

FA Cup appearances (2 games)

Ross 2, Smith 2, Singleton 2, Kendall 2, Wilson 2, Dawson 2, Spavin 1, Holden 2, Godfrey 2, Kelly 2, Davidson 2, Cranston 1.

League Cup appearances: (1 game)

Barton, Ross, Smith, Singleton, Kendall, Wilson, Dawson, Spavin, Holden, Godfrey, Donnelly one each.

Goalscorers: 76 League–4 FAC–(Total 80)

Dawson 26 (4 pens)–1 (27), Godfrey 25 (1 pen)–1 (26), Kendall 7–1 (8), Wilson 6–0 (6), Lawton 2–0 (2), Lee 2–0 (2), Spavin 2–0 (2), Holden 2–0 (2), Smith 1–0 (1), Coleman 1–0 (1), Own goals 2–1 (3), Webb of L. Orient, Dawson of Swindon in the league, Casey of Barnet in the FAC.

Future Players born between August 1964 and May 1965: Steve Saunders, Brian Chippendale, Tony Ellis, Neil Williams, Stuart Rimmer, Alex Jones, Simon Gibson, Andy Saville, Russ Wilcox, Kevin Gage, Warren Joyce, Glen Campbell, Tony Philliskirk, David Bleasdale, Ronnie Hildersley, Mike Stowell, Mark Patterson.

Ever presents: (1) Alan Spavin   **Hat-tricks:** (4) Brian Godfrey (1), Alex Dawson (3).   **FA Cup:** 4th Round
League Cup: 2nd Round   **Players used:** 23   **Manager:** Jimmy Milne
Leading scorer: 27 goals – Alex Dawson (26 league 1 FAC)   **Chairman:** A. Harrison Esq. B. E. M.

AUTHORS' UNOFFICIAL PLAYER OF THE SEASON: Alan Spavin

League position in Division Two: 12th – P42 W14 D13 L15 F76 A81 Pts 41
Home: W11 D8 L2 F46 A29   Away: W3 D5 L13 F30 A52

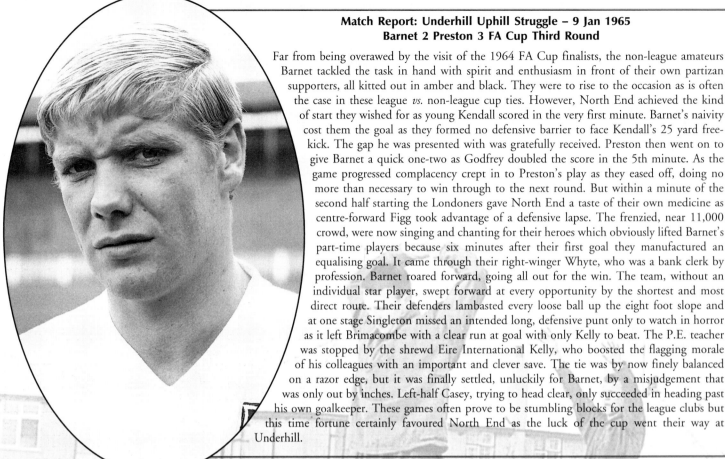

Match Report: Underhill Uphill Struggle – 9 Jan 1965
Barnet 2 Preston 3 FA Cup Third Round

Far from being overawed by the visit of the 1964 FA Cup finalists, the non-league amateurs Barnet tackled the task in hand with spirit and enthusiasm in front of their own partizan supporters, all kitted out in amber and black. They were to rise to the occasion as is often the case in these league *vs.* non-league cup ties. However, North End achieved the kind of start they wished for as young Kendall scored in the very first minute. Barnet's naivity cost them the goal as they formed no defensive barrier to face Kendall's 25 yard free-kick. The gap he was presented with was gratefully received. Preston then went on to give Barnet a quick one-two as Godfrey doubled the score in the 5th minute. As the game progressed complacency crept in to Preston's play as they eased off, doing no more than necessary to win through to the next round. But within a minute of the second half starting the Londoners gave North End a taste of their own medicine as centre-forward Figg took advantage of a defensive lapse. The frenzied, near 11,000 crowd, were now singing and chanting for their heroes which obviously lifted Barnet's part-time players because six minutes after their first goal they manufactured an equalising goal. It came through their right-winger Whyte, who was a bank clerk by profession. Barnet roared forward, going all out for the win. The team, without an individual star player, swept forward at every opportunity by the shortest and most direct route. Their defenders lambasted every loose ball up the eight foot slope and at one stage Singleton missed an intended long, defensive punt only to watch in horror as it left Brimacombe with a clear run at goal with only Kelly to beat. The P.E. teacher was stopped by the shrewd Eire International Kelly, who boosted the flagging morale of his colleagues with an important and clever save. The tie was by now finely balanced on a razor edge, but it was finally settled, unluckily for Barnet, by a misjudgement that was only out by inches. Left-half Casey, trying to head clear, only succeeded in heading past his own goalkeeper. These games often prove to be stumbling blocks for the league clubs but this time fortune certainly favoured North End as the luck of the cup went their way at Underhill.

Tony Coleman, went on to mature in to a good player later in his career.

STAT FACTS:
Best home run without defeat: 12 games
Best away run without defeat: 3 games
Longest run unbeaten: 7 games
Longest run without a win: 5 games
Best home attendance: 33,553 vs. Bolton FAC 30.1.65
Worst home attendance: 11,390 vs. C.Palace 5.12.64
Best away attendance: 34,219 vs. Newcastle 26.9.64
Worst away attendance: 8,021 vs. L.Orient 3.4.65
Aggregate and average home attendance: 327,850 – 15,612
Aggregate and average away attendance: 306,949 – 14,617

Season 1964–65: First Division

	P	W	D	L	F	A	Pts
1 Newcastle	42	24	9	9	81	45	57
2 Northampton	42	20	16	6	66	50	56
3 Bolton	42	20	10	12	80	58	50
4 Southampton	42	17	14	11	83	63	48
5 Ipswich	42	15	17	10	74	67	47
6 Norwich	42	20	7	15	61	57	47
7 Crystal Palace	42	16	13	13	55	51	45
8 Huddersfield	42	17	10	15	53	51	44
9 Derby	42	16	11	15	84	79	43
10 Coventry	42	17	9	16	72	70	43
11 Man City	42	16	9	17	63	62	41
12 **PRESTON**	42	14	13	15	76	81	41
13 Cardiff	42	13	14	15	64	57	40
14 Rotherham	42	14	12	16	70	69	40
15 Plymouth	42	16	8	18	63	79	40
16 Bury	42	14	10	18	60	66	38
11 Middlesbrough	42	13	9	20	70	76	35
18 Charlton	42	13	9	20	64	75	35
19 Leyton Orient	42	12	11	19	50	72	35
20 Portsmouth	42	12	10	20	56	77	34
21 Swindon	42	14	5	23	63	81	33
22 Swansea	42	11	10	21	62	84	32

Preparing for the cup tie with Bolton. Left to right: Holden, Wilson, Smith, Cranston, Kendall, Lawton, Dawson.

Date 1964-5	Opponents	Comp	h or a	Score	Att.	1	2	3	4	5	6	7	8	9	10	11		
Aug 22	Rotherham Utd.	Div 2	h	0-0	18038	Kelly	Ross	Smith	Lawton	Singleton	Kendall	Wilson	Ashworth	Dawson	Spavin	Holden		
Aug 26	Cardiff City	Div 2	a	3-3	15805	Kelly	Ross	Smith	Lawton	Singleton	Kendall (1)	Wilson	Godfrey (1)	Ashworth	Spavin (1)	Holden		
Aug 29	Ipswich Town	Div 2	a	5-1	12823	Barton	Ross	Donnelly	Lawton	Singleton	Kendall	Wilson (2)	Godfrey (3)	Ashworth	Spavin	Holden		
Aug 31	Cardiff City	Div 2	h	1-1	23303	Barton	Ross	Donnelly	Lawton	Singleton	Kendall	Hannigan	Wilson	Godfrey (1)	Spavin	Holden		
Sep 5	Plymouth Arg.	Div 2	h	1-3	18425	Barton	Ross	Donnelly	Lawton	Singleton	Smith	Wilson	Godfrey	Dawson	Spavin	Holden (1)		
Sep 12	Bolton W.	Div 2	a	1-5	18186	Kelly	Ross	Donnelly	Lawton	Singleton	Smith	Wilson	Godfrey (1)	Dawson	Spavin	Holden		
Sep 16	Southampton	Div 2	a	1-3	18719	Barton	Ross	Donnelly	Lawton	Singleton	Smith	Wilson	Godfrey	Dawson (1p)	Spavin	Hannigan		
Sep 19	Middlesbrough	Div 2	h	4-3	15726	Barton	Ross	Donnelly	Lawton	Singleton	Smith (1)	Wilson	Godfrey (2)	Dawson (1p)	Spavin	Holden		
Sep 23	Doncaster R. Rd 2	LC	a	0-1	13399	Barton	Ross	Donnelly	Kendall	Singleton	Smith	Wilson	Godfrey	Dawson	Spavin	Holden		
Sep 26	Newcastle Utd.	Div 2	a	2-5	34219	Barton	Donnelly	Smith	Lawton	Wearmouth	Kendall	Hannigan	Wilson (1)	Godfrey	Spavin	Lee (1)		
Oct 3	Northampton T.	Div 2	h	2-2	15953	Kelly	Ross	Smith	Lawton	Singleton	Kendall	Wilson	Godfrey (1)	Dawson (1)	Spavin	Holden		
Oct 7	Norwich City	Div 2	a	2-4	21822	Kelly	Ross	Smith	Lawton	Singleton	Kendall	Wilson	Godfrey (1)	Dawson (1)	Spavin	Holden		
Oct 10	Swansea Town	Div 2	h	2-2	15336	Kelly	Ross	Smith	Lawton (1)	Singleton	Kendall	Wilson	Godfrey	Dawson (1)	Spavin	Holden		
Oct 17	Derby County	Div 2	a	1-3	12609	Barton	Ross	Smith	Lawton	Singleton	Davidson	Wilson	Godfrey	Dawson	Spavin	Holden (1)		
Oct 24	Swindon Town	Div 2	a	2-1	13907	Barton	Ross	Smith	Lawton (1)	Singleton	Davidson	Hannigan	Godfrey (1)	Dawson	Spavin	Holden		
Oct 31	Portsmouth	Div 2	a	0-1	10547	Barton	Ross	Smith	Lawton	Singleton	Davidson	Wilson	Godfrey	Ashworth	Spavin	Holden		
Nov 2	Southampton	Div 2	h	0-0	15378	Barton	Ross	Smith	Lawton	Singleton	Davidson	Hannigan	Godfrey	Ashworth	Spavin	Holden		
Nov 7	Manchester City	Div 2	h	2-5	19367	Barton	Ross	Smith	Lawton	Singleton	Davidson	Wilson	Godfrey (2)	Dawson	Spavin	Holden		
Nov 14	Charlton Ath.	Div 2	a	3-2	8403	Barton	Ross	Smith	Kendall	Singleton	Davidson	Wilson	Godfrey	Dawson (3)	Spavin	Holden		
Nov 21	Leyton Orient	Div 2	h	3-0	14964	Barton	Ross	Smith	Kendall (1)	Singleton	Davidson	Wilson	Lawton	Dawson	Spavin (1)	Godfrey	1 og	(Webb)
Nov 27	Bury	Div 2	a	1-1	9896	Barton	Ross	Smith	Kendall	Singleton	Davidson	Wilson (1)	Godfrey	Dawson	Spavin	Lee		
Dec 5	Crystal Palace	Div 2	h	1-0	11390	Barton	Ross	Smith	Kendall	Singleton	Davidson	Wilson	Godfrey	Dawson	Spavin	Lee (1)		
Dec 12	Rotherham Utd.	Div 2	a	2-2	9579	Barton	Ross	Smith	Kendall	Singleton	Davidson	Hannigan	Godfrey (1)	Dawson (1)	Spavin	Lee		
Dec 19	Ipswich Town	Div 2	h	4-1	11835	Barton	Ross	Smith	Kendall	Singleton	Davidson	Wilson	Godfrey (2)	Dawson (2)	Spavin	Holden		
Dec 26	Coventry City	Div 2	h	3-2	22215	Barton	Ross	Smith	Kendall (2)	Singleton	Davidson	Wilson (1)	Godfrey	Dawson	Spavin	Holden		
Dec 28	Coventry City	Div 2	a	0-3	22681	Barton	Ross	Smith	Davidson	Singleton	Cranston	Wilson	Godfrey	Dawson	Spavin	Holden		
Jan 2	Plymouth Arg.	Div 2	a	1-0	13432	Kelly	Ross	Smith	Davidson	Cranston	Lapot	Wilson	Godfrey	Dawson (1)	Spavin	Holden		
Jan 9	Barnet Rd 3	FAC	a	3-2	10861	Kelly	Ross	Smith	Kendall (1)	Singleton	Davidson	Wilson	Godfrey (1)	Dawson	Spavin	Holden	1 og	(Casey)
Jan 16	Bolton W.	Div 2	h	2-2	19187	Kelly	Ross	Smith	Kendall (1)	Singleton	Cranston	Hannigan	Godfrey	Dawson (1p)	Spavin	Holden		
Jan 23	Middlesbrough	Div 2	a	1-1	12466	Kelly	Ross	Smith	Kendall	Singleton	Cranston	Wilson	Godfrey	Dawson (1)	Spavin	Holden		
Jan 30	Bolton W. Rd 4	FAC	h	1-2	33553	Kelly	Ross	Smith	Davidson	Singleton	Cranston	Wilson	Godfrey	Dawson (1)	Kendall	Holden		
Feb 6	Newcastle Utd.	Div 2	h	2-0	18961	Kelly	Ross	Smith	Lawton	Singleton	Kendall	Wilson	Godfrey (2)	Dawson	Spavin	Holden		
Feb 13	Northampton T.	Div 2	a	1-2	14010	Kelly	Ross	Smith	Lawton	Singleton	Kendall	Wilson	Godfrey (1)	Dawson	Spavin	Holden		
Feb 27	Derby County	Div 2	h	2-2	12983	Kelly	Ross	Smith	Lawton	Singleton	Kendall	Wilson	Godfrey (2, 1p)	Dawson	Spavin	Coleman		
Mar 13	Portsmouth	Div 2	h	6-1	12028	Kelly	Ross	Smith	Kendall (1)	Singleton	Cranston	Wilson (1)	Godfrey	Dawson (3)	Spavin	Coleman (1)		
Mar 17	Crystal Palace	Div 2	a	0-1	14976	Kelly	Patrick	Smith	Kendall	Singleton	Cranston	Wilson	Lapot	Dawson	Spavin	Coleman		
Mar 20	Manchester City	Div 2	a	3-4	12884	Kelly	Patrick	Smith	Kendall	Singleton	Cranston	Hannigan	Wilson	Dawson (3)	Spavin	Coleman		
Mar 23	Swansea Town	Div 2	a	0-4	8686	Barton	Patrick	Smith	Kendall	Singleton	Cranston	Hannigan	Holden	Dawson	Spavin	Coleman		
Mar 26	Charlton Ath.	Div 2	h	2-1	12391	Kelly	Patrick	Smith	Lawton	Singleton	Cranston	Hannigan	Wilson	Dawson (2, 1p)	Spavin	Holden		
Apr 3	Leyton Orient	Div 2	a	1-2	8021	Kelly	Patrick	Smith	Lawton	Singleton	Kendall	Wilson	Godfrey (1)	Dawson	Spavin	Holden		
Apr 10	Bury	Div 2	h	2-2	11510	Barton	Patrick	Smith	Lawton	Singleton	Kendall (1)	Wilson	Godfrey	Dawson (1)	Spavin	Watt		
Apr 17	Swindon Town	Div 2	a	2-2	14136	Kelly	Patrick	Smith	Kendall	Singleton	Cranston	Wilson	Godfrey	Dawson (1)	Spavin	Watt	1 og	(Dawson)
Apr 19	Huddersfield T.	Div 2	a	0-3	12261	Barton	Ross	Smith	Kendall	Singleton	Cranston	Wilson	Godfrey	Dawson	Spavin	Holden		
Apr 20	Huddersfield T.	Div 2	h	2-0	13256	Barton	Patrick	Smith	Kendall	Singleton	Cranston	Hannigan	Godfrey (2)	Dawson	Spavin	Watt		
Apr 24	Norwich City	Div 2	h	3-1	11900	Barton	Patrick	Smith	Kendall	Singleton	Cranston	Wilson	Godfrey (1)	Dawson (2)	Spavin	Watt		

Alan Spavin

Alex Dawson

Alec Ashworth

SEASON 1965–1966

Once again North End's league form proved very disappointing and their final position of 17th in Division Two upset many of their supporters who had been starved of success for several years. Early injuries to Alan Kelly and defender Jim Smith upset the rhythm of the side and the opening results were mixed. It was also obvious that Ray Veall, who had been signed in the summer as replacement for the veteran Doug Holden, was not the answer and he quickly moved on. Apart from Veall the activity in the transfer market was non-existent although Jimmy Milne was given little money to spend and so had little scope. The League Cup came and went, with a bad 4–0 defeat by Third Division Grimsby ending North End's interest, and several heavy league defeats followed. Alex Dawson began the season as he had ended the last by banging in the goals, 11 in his first twelve games. The poor form of the team then affected his output though with injuries also not helping the centre-forward. His replacement, a youngster from the reserves, Brian Greenhalgh, looked impressive when called upon and he hit a wonderful hat-trick in a 3–1 win at Bolton. Brian Godfrey also continued his good form and the consistent George Ross was on top of his game at right-back. Howard Kendall again showed what a great player he was going to be and the scouts from the big clubs were beginning to show great interest in the wing-half. But any transfer speculation was halted by the fact that Preston again embarked on a thrilling FA Cup run. A terrific win at Charlton set up their 'annual' tie with Bolton and this time it was Preston's turn to win, after a replay. The mighty Spurs came to Deepdale for the fifth round tie and a huge crowd saw a magnificent match which North End won 2–1 with goals by Dawson and Ernie Hannigan. There was another great Deepdale occasion in the sixth round and Manchester United could consider themselves very fortunate to survive with a draw. In the replay at Old Trafford, Tony Singleton decided it was about time he scored a second career goal, and bearing in mind that his only other goal had sent Preston to Wembley in 1964, it looked promising. Sadly, in the end, United proved just a little too strong and North End were out. It was difficult to lift the side after that defeat but relegation was still very much on the cards. Easter saw Preston gain just one point from six but the three remaining home games produced five points and that was enough to keep them in the division. The last day of the season was an unbelievable day in the club's history. Preston beat Cardiff 9–0! In a magnificent display Hannigan and Godfrey scored hat-tricks and Greenhalgh hit two. Unforgettable!

Brian Godfrey North End's Welsh International.

DEBUTANTS: (3) Ray Veall, Brian Greenhalgh, George Lyall.

LAST GAMES: (4) John Barton, Alec Ashworth, Willie Watt, Ray Veall.

League appearances (42 games) First season of substitutes

Ashworth A. 6 + 1, Barton J.B. 12, Cranston W. 13 + 1, Dawson A.D. 35, Donnelly J. 10 + 2, Godfrey B.C. 38 + 1, Greenhalgh B.A. 7, Hannigan E. 29, Kelly J.A. 30, Kendall H. 39, Lapot S. 6 + 1, Lawton N. 36, Lee F. 29 + 1, Lyall G. 2, Ross G. 42, Singleton A.J. 32 + 1, Smith J.A.G. 32, Spavin A. 35 + 2, Veall R.J. 10, Watt W.D. 3 + 1, Wearmouth M. 2, Wilson D.C. 14

FA Cup appearances (6 games)

Barton 3, Ross 6, Smith 6, Kendall 6, Singleton 6, Wilson 1, Godfrey 6, Dawson 5, Spavin 6, Lee 5, Lawton 6, Kelly 3, Hannigan 6, Greenhalgh 1.

League Cup appearances (3 games)

Ross 3, Kendall 3, Cranston 2, Wilson 2, Godfrey 3, Dawson 3, Spavin 2, Veall 1, Lee 1, Lawton 2, Kelly 3, Hannigan 1, Donnelly 3, Ashworth 2, Watt 1, Wearmouth 1.

Goalscorers: 62 League–11 FAC–2 LC–(Total 75)

Godfrey 17 (3 pens)–2 (pens)–1 (20), Dawson 14 –4–0 (18), Hannigan 11–3–0 (14), Greenhalgh 5–0–0 (5), Lawton 4–0–0 (4), Kendall 4–0–0 (4), Lee 3–1–0 (4), Lapot 2–0–0 (2), Wilson 1–0–0 (1), Spavin 1–0–0 (1), Singleton 0–1–0 (1), Ashworth 0–0–1 (1).

> **League position in Division Two: 17th – P42 W11 D15 L16 F62 A70 Pts 37**
> **Home: W7 D10 L4 F37 A23 Away: W4 D5 L12 F25 A47**

Above: **Bert Patrick, Alec Ashworth,** and **John Barton** doing pre-season jogging.

Right: Left to right:
Back row: Kendall, Lawton, Ross, Kelly, Barton, Singleton, Smith, Cranston.
Front row: Wilson, Godfrey, Dawson, Spavin, Ashworth, Veall.

Trivia Facts:

During the second half of the cup replay with Bolton it was noticed that Preston's full-backs, Ross and Smith, were both wearing number three shirts. At the same game one man died and a 75 year old Preston woman was hit by a bottle in unrelated incidents.

North End were on £8 win bonuses during 1965–66 with an added incentive of a stepped crowd bonus of up to a maximum of £22 for each player if and when the Deepdale attendance topped 38,000.

Match Report: Bolton Pay the Penalty – 14 Feb 1966
Preston 3 Bolton 2 FA Cup 4th Rd Replay

With the knowledge that a plum draw against Tottenham Hotspur awaited the winners, North End tackled this replay with added determination. They had seldom had to fight so hard for what was eventually a deserved reward. This game had everything that enthusiasts expect to see in a cup-tie, exciting incidents, tense escapes, fluctuations at a rapid pace, thrills, spills and goals. North End took a 12th minute lead to calm the nerves both on and off the pitch. Godfrey found Hannigan out wide on the right with a delightful pass and the nimble footed winger promptly slipped into a favourable position to deliver a first rate centre. It swerved past Napier, the tall defender, just as Dawson took off on a headlong dive to head low and expertly away from Hopkinson into the net, thus repeating his equally impressive goal at Burnden Park in the first tie. Preston, vulnerable after scoring, then had an escape when Francis Lee shot wide from a good position, before the chunky striker atoned for that miss a few minutes later when he latched onto a header from Hatton to score with reasonable ease. All square at the half way stage but the deadlock was unceremoniously broken within the first two minutes of the second half. Barton could only parry a wicked cross shot from Bolton's hot-shot centre-forward Wyn Davies, but the alert Welshman reacted the quickest to shoot gleefully into Preston's net.

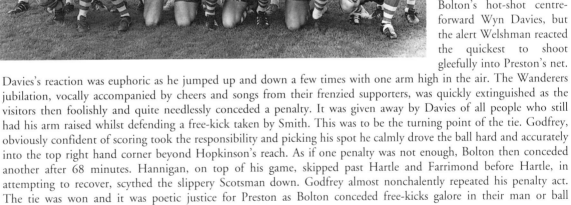

Davies's reaction was euphoric as he jumped up and down a few times with one arm high in the air. The Wanderers jubilation, vocally accompanied by cheers and songs from their frenzied supporters, was quickly extinguished as the visitors then foolishly and quite needlessly conceded a penalty. It was given away by Davies of all people who still had his arm raised whilst defending a free-kick taken by Smith. This was to be the turning point of the tie. Godfrey, obviously confident of scoring took the responsibility and picking his spot he calmly drove the ball hard and accurately into the top right hand corner beyond Hopkinson's reach. As if one penalty was not enough, Bolton then conceded another after 68 minutes. Hannigan, on top of his game, skipped past Hartle and Farrimond before Hartle, in attempting to recover, scythed the slippery Scotsman down. Godfrey almost nonchalently repeated his penalty act. The tie was won and it was poetic justice for Preston as Bolton conceded free-kicks galore in their man or ball defensive tactics.

Future Players born between August 1965 and May 1966: Peter Bulmer, Paul Cross, Shaun Reid, Neil Whalley, Paul Fitzpatrick, Paul Booth, Mike Conroy, Neil McDonald, Simon Jeffels, Brian Mooney, Paul Raynor, Simon Snow, Paul Welsh.

Ever presents: (1) George Ross   **FA Cup:** 6th Round Replay
Hat-tricks: (3) Brian Greenhalgh, Brian Godfrey and Ernie Hannigan
League Cup: 4th Round   **Players used:** 22   **Manager:** Jimmy Milne
Chairman: A. Harrison Esq. BEM
Leading scorer: 20 goals – Brian Godfrey
(17 league 1 FACup 2 League Cup)

AUTHORS' UNOFFICIAL PLAYER OF THE SEASON: George Ross

Date 1965-6	Opponents		Comp	h or a	Score	Att.	1	2	3	4	5	6	7	8	9	10	11	12 *Sub Used
Aug 21	Ipswich Town		Div 2	a	0-1	14548	Barton	Ross	Smith	Kendall	Singleton	Cranston	Wilson	Godfrey	Dawson	Spavin	Veall	Lee
Aug 23	Portsmouth		Div 2	h	4-1	17952	Barton	Ross	Smith	Lawton	Singleton	Kendall	Wilson (1)	Godfrey (2)	Dawson (1)	Spavin	Lee	Cranston
Aug 28	Birmingham City		Div 2	h	3-3	16397	Barton	Ross	Smith	Lawton	Singleton	Kendall	Wilson	Godfrey (1)	Dawson (2)	Spavin	Lee	Cranston
Sep 1	Portsmouth		Div 2	a	1-4	17630	Kelly	Ross	Smith	Lawton	Singleton	Kendall	Wilson *	Godfrey	Dawson (1)	Spavin	Veall	Lee *
Sep 4	Leyton Orient		Div 2	a	2-2	6529	Kelly	Ross	Smith *	Lawton	Singleton	Kendall	Hannigan	Godfrey	Dawson (2)	Spavin	Veall	Cranston *
Sep 8	Plymouth Arg.		Div 2	a	1-0	12741	Kelly	Ross	Donnelly	Lawton	Cranston	Kendall	Lee	Godfrey (1)	Dawson	Spavin	Veall	Singleton
Sep 11	Middlesbrough		Div 2	h	1-1	15024	Kelly	Ross	Donnelly	Lawton (1)	Cranston	Kendall	Lee	Godfrey	Dawson	Spavin	Veall	Singleton
Sep 13	Plymouth Arg.		Div 2	h	2-0	15924	Kelly	Ross	Donnelly	Lawton	Cranston	Kendall	Lee	Godfrey	Dawson (2)	Spavin	Veall	Singleton
Sep 18	Huddersfield T.		Div 2	a	1-2	18114	Kelly	Ross	Donnelly	Lawton *	Cranston	Kendall	Lee	Godfrey	Dawson (1)	Spavin	Veall	Singleton *
Sep 22	Plymouth Arg.	Rd 2	LC	h	1-0	10583	Kelly	Ross	Donnelly	Lawton	Cranston	Kendall	Wilson	Godfrey (1)	Dawson	Spavin	Veall	
Sep 25	Crystal Palace		Div 2	h	2-0	12665	Kelly	Ross	Donnelly	Lawton	Cranston	Kendall (1)	Wilson	Godfrey	Dawson (1)	Spavin	Veall	Hannigan
Oct 2	Carlisle Utd.		Div 2	a	2-0	14729	Kelly	Ross	Donnelly	Lawton	Cranston	Kendall	Wilson	Godfrey (1)	Dawson (1)	Spavin	Veall	Hannigan
Oct 9	Coventry City		Div 2	h	0-0	19672	Kelly	Ross	Donnelly	Lawton	Cranston	Kendall	Wilson	Godfrey	Dawson	Spavin	Veall *	Ashworth *
Oct 13	Huddersfield T.	Rd 3	LC	a	1-0	9774	Kelly	Ross	Donnelly	Lawton *	Cranston	Kendall	Wilson	Ashworth (1)	Dawson	Godfrey	Watt	Spavin *
Oct 16	Bristol City		Div 2	a	0-1	15583	Kelly	Ross	Donnelly	Lawton *	Cranston	Kendall	Wilson	Ashworth	Dawson	Godfrey	Watt	Spavin *
Oct 23	Manchester City		Div 2	h	0-3	25117	Kelly	Ross	Donnelly	Lawton	Cranston	Kendall	Wilson	Ashworth	Dawson	Godfrey	Watt	Hannigan
Oct 30	Rotherham Utd.		Div 2	a	3-6	8634	Kelly	Ross	Donnelly	Spavin (1)	Cranston	Kendall	Wilson	Godfrey (2)	Dawson	Hannigan	Watt *	Lapot *
Nov 3	Grimsby Town	Rd 4	LC	a	0-4	10443	Kelly	Ross	Donnelly	Spavin	Wearmouth	Kendall	Hannigan	Ashworth	Dawson	Godfrey	Lee	
Nov 6	Wolverhampton W.		Div 2	h	2-2	15940	Barton	Ross	Smith	Spavin	Singleton	Kendall (1)	Hannigan	Ashworth	Dawson	Lawton	Lee (1)	Patrick
Nov 13	Norwich City		Div 2	a	1-1	15024	Barton	Ross	Smith	Spavin	Singleton	Kendall	Hannigan	Godfrey (1)	Dawson	Lawton	Lee	Donnelly
Nov 20	Bury		Div 2	h	2-1	13139	Barton	Ross	Smith	Spavin	Singleton	Kendall (1)	Hannigan	Godfrey (1)	Dawson	Lawton	Lee	Lapot
Nov 27	Southampton		Div 2	a	2-5	14776	Barton	Ross	Smith	Lapot	Singleton	Kendall	Hannigan (1)	Godfrey	Dawson (1)	Lawton	Lee	Donnelly
Dec 4	Derby County		Div 2	h	2-0	10377	Barton	Ross	Smith	Wearmouth	Singleton	Lapot (1)	Hannigan (1)	Godfrey	Dawson	Lawton	Lee	Wilson
Dec 11	Cardiff City		Div 2	h	3-1	10754	Barton	Ross	Smith	Kendall	Singleton	Lapot (1)	Hannigan (1)	Wilson	Dawson * (1)	Lawton	Lee	Spavin *
Dec 18	Bristol City		Div 2	h	1-1	10766	Barton	Ross	Smith	Kendall (1)	Singleton	Lapot	Hannigan	Wilson	Greenhalgh	Spavin	Lee	Cranston
Jan 1	Coventry City		Div 2	a	1-5	26818	Barton	Ross	Smith	Kendall	Singleton	Lapot	Hannigan	Wilson	Dawson *	Spavin	Lee	Godfrey * (1)
Jan 8	Norwich City		Div 2	h	0-0	12346	Kelly	Ross	Smith	Lawton	Singleton	Kendall	Hannigan	Godfrey	Dawson	Spavin	Lee	Lapot
Jan 15	Manchester City		Div 2	a	0-0	26668	Kelly	Ross	Smith	Lawton	Singleton	Kendall	Hannigan	Godfrey	Greenhalgh	Spavin	Lee	Wearmouth
Jan 22	Charlton Ath.	Rd 3	FAC	h	3-2	13946	Kelly	Ross	Smith	Lawton	Singleton	Kendall	Hannigan (2)	Godfrey	Greenhalgh	Spavin	Lee (1)	
Jan 29	Ipswich Town		Div 2	h	0-1	11879	Kelly	Ross	Smith	Lawton	Singleton	Kendall	Hannigan	Godfrey	Dawson	Spavin	Lee	Wearmouth
Feb 5	Birmingham City		Div 2	a	1-1	14054	Kelly *	Ross	Smith	Lawton	Singleton	Kendall	Hannigan	Godfrey	Dawson	Spavin	Lee (1)	Donnelly *
Feb 12	Bolton W.	Rd 4	FAC	a	1-1	35632	Barton	Ross	Smith	Lawton	Singleton	Kendall	Hannigan	Godfrey	Dawson (1)	Spavin	Lee	
Feb 14	Bolton W. Replay		FAC	h	3-2	31579	Barton	Ross	Smith	Lawton	Singleton	Kendall	Hannigan	Godfrey (2p)	Dawson (1)	Spavin	Wilson	
Feb 19	Leyton Orient		Div 2	h	1-2	10640	Kelly	Ross	Smith	Wearmouth	Singleton	Kendall	Hannigan	Godfrey (1p)	Dawson	Spavin	Wilson	Lapot
Feb 26	Middlesbrough		Div 2	a	1-2	13229	Kelly	Ross	Smith	Lawton	Singleton	Cranston	Hannigan	Godfrey (1p)	Dawson	Spavin	Lee	Donnelly
Mar 5	Tottenham H.	Rd 5	FAC	h	2-1	36792	Kelly	Ross	Smith	Lawton	Singleton	Kendall	Hannigan (1)	Godfrey	Dawson (1)	Spavin	Lee	
Mar 12	Huddersfield T.		Div 2	h	1-1	17724	Kelly	Ross	Smith	Lawton	Singleton	Kendall	Hannigan	Godfrey	Greenhalgh	Spavin	Lee (1)	Wilson
Mar 16	Bolton W.		Div 2	h	3-1	13961	Kelly	Ross	Smith	Lawton	Singleton	Kendall	Hannigan	Godfrey	Greenhalgh (3)	Spavin	Lee	Wilson
Mar 19	Crystal Palace		Div 2	a	1-1	11786	Kelly	Ross	Smith	Lawton *	Singleton	Kendall	Hannigan (1)	Godfrey	Dawson	Spavin	Lee	Donnelly *
Mar 26	Manchester U.	Rd 6	FAC	h	1-1	37876	Kelly	Ross	Smith	Lawton	Singleton	Kendall	Hannigan	Godfrey	Dawson (1)	Spavin	Lee	
Mar 30	Manchester U. Replay		FAC	a	1-3	60433	Barton	Ross	Smith	Lawton	Singleton (1)	Kendall	Hannigan	Godfrey	Dawson	Spavin	Lee	
Apr 2	Wolverhampton W.		Div 2	a	0-3	13573	Barton	Ross	Smith	Lawton	Singleton	Kendall	Hannigan	Godfrey	Dawson	Spavin	Lee	Lapot
Apr 8	Charlton Ath.		Div 2	a	2-5	14490	Kelly	Ross	Smith	Cranston	Singleton	Kendall *	Hannigan	Lyall	Dawson (1)	Spavin	Godfrey (1)	Watt *
Apr 9	Rotherham Utd.		Div 2	h	1-1	10733	Kelly	Ross	Smith	Lawton (1)	Singleton	Lapot	Hannigan	Lyall	Dawson	Spavin	Godfrey	Donnelly
Apr 11	Charlton Ath.		Div 2	h	3-3	11945	Kelly	Ross	Smith	Lawton (1)	Singleton	Kendall	Hannigan (1)	Godfrey (1)	Dawson	Spavin	Lee	Lapot
Apr 16	Bury		Div 2	a	0-5	7029	Kelly	Ross	Smith	Lawton	Singleton	Kendall	Hannigan	Godfrey	Dawson	Spavin	Lee	Lapot
Apr 19	Bolton W.		Div 2	h	0-1	11231	Kelly	Ross	Smith	Lawton	Singleton	Kendall	Hannigan	Ashworth	Dawson	Spavin	Godfrey	Lapot
Apr 23	Southampton		Div 2	h	1-1	11227	Kelly	Ross	Smith	Lawton	Singleton	Kendall	Hannigan (1)	Ashworth	Dawson	Godfrey	Lee	Spavin
Apr 25	Carlisle Utd.		Div 2	h	2-1	13777	Kelly	Ross	Smith	Lawton	Singleton	Kendall	Hannigan (2)	Ashworth	Greenhalgh	Godfrey	Lee	Spavin
Apr 30	Derby County		Div 2	a	0-1	11188	Kelly	Ross	Smith	Lawton	Singleton	Kendall	Hannigan	Ashworth	Greenhalgh	Godfrey	Lee	Spavin
May 7	Cardiff City		Div 2	h	9-0	10018	Kelly	Ross	Smith	Lawton (1)	Singleton	Kendall	Hannigan (3)	Godfrey (3, 1p)	Greenhalgh (2)	Spavin	Lee	Ashworth

Frank Lee

Season 1965–66: Second Division

		P	W	D	L	F	A	Pts
1	Man City	42	22	15	5	76	44	59
2	Southampton	42	22	10	10	85	56	54
3	Coventry	42	20	13	9	73	53	53
4	Huddersfield	42	19	13	10	62	36	51
5	Bristol City	42	17	17	8	63	48	51
6	Wolves	42	20	10	12	87	61	50
7	Rotherham	42	16	14	12	75	74	46
8	Derby	42	16	11	15	71	68	43
9	Bolton	42	16	9	17	62	59	41
10	Birmingham	42	16	9	17	70	75	41
11	Crystal Palace	42	14	13	15	47	52	41
12	Portsmouth	42	16	8	18	74	78	40
13	Norwich	42	12	15	15	52	52	39
14	Carlisle	42	17	5	20	60	63	39
15	Ipswich	42	15	9	18	58	66	39
16	Charlton	42	12	14	16	61	70	38
17	PRESTON	42	11	15	16	62	70	37
18	Plymouth	42	12	13	17	54	63	37
19	Bury	42	14	7	21	62	76	35
20	Cardiff	42	12	10	20	71	91	34
21	Middlesbrough	42	10	13	19	58	86	33
22	Leyton Orient	42	5	13	24	38	80	23

Brian Greenhalgh

SEASON 1966–1967

If Preston North End had received a school report for the 1966–67 term it would have read, 'Slight improvement, could do better'. It was a season of major changes, both on and off the field, and a year tinged with some sadness as old favourites moved on. There was an amazing start to the campaign as North End won their first ten consecutive home games. Unfortunately, this was offset by the fact that they lost nine and drew one of their first ten away games! Ironically, as soon as they reversed the trend and lost their first home game, they then promptly went to Northampton and won 5–1! Preston never do things by half, that is for sure. The sadness came in the last appearances in North End shirts for Alex Dawson, John Donnelly and Howard Kendall. Dawson, The Black Prince, ended his stay with a slightly bitter taste in his mouth following a disagreement with the club. He was transferred to Brighton. His contribution to the club's illustrious history cannot be overstated and to this day he remains a crowd favourite. Donnelly left the professional game and eventually emigrated to South Africa, whilst Kendall finally made his expected big money move. It was a sign of the times that Preston fans were resigned to losing their greatest talent and they always knew that the young England Youth star would move on to better things. In retrospect, Everton's £60,000 fee was a paltry amount, but at the time Preston urgently needed some cash to finance some new signings. As the topsy turvy results continued the Board felt a change was required. In the November the Directors appointed a new manager in another Scot, Bobby Seith. The former Burnley player took over from Jimmy Milne, who in turn moved to a General Manager's role. The move was greeted with a mixed reaction but as with any new manager only time would tell if the choice was the right one. Meanwhile, on the field it was a question of consistency, or lack of it. Ernie Hannigan was the star player with a series of fine performances on the wing. The ever present Scottish player won many friends with his exciting wing trickery. In defence Alan Kelly and Tony Singleton were the pick with new signings Jim McNab and Jimmy Forrest creating an immediate impact, especially on their joint debut at home to Derby. The away form continued to hold Preston back and far too many goals were conceded away from Deepdale. In the cups Preston managed a brief run in the League Cup but fell at the first hurdle in the FA Cup, defeat at home to Aston Villa ending their involvement. It was significant that even though he left in the March, Dawson still ended the season as the club's leading scorer.

DEBUTANTS: (7) John Brown, Gerry Stewart, Jim McNab, Jim Forrest, David Hughes, John Ritchie, Paul Crossley

LAST GAMES: Dawson, Lapot, Donnelly, Kendall, Wearmouth.

League appearances (42 games)

Brown J.C. 1, Cranston W. 17 + 1, Crossley P. 1, Dawson A.D. 27, Donnelly J. 1, Forrest J. 8, Godfrey B.C. 33, Greenhalgh B.A. 8, Hannigan E. 42, Hughes D.R. 1, Kelly J.A. 40, Kendall H. 25, Lapot S. 3 + 2, Lawton N. 27, Lee F. 36 + 2, Lyall G. 6 + 2, McNab J. 5, Patrick B. 1, Ritchie J. 2, Ross G. 40, Singleton A.J. 36, Smith J.A.G. 40, Spavin A. 39 + 1, Stewart G. 1, Wearmouth M. 8, Wilson D.C. 14 + 1.

FA Cup appearances (1 game) First season of substitutes in cup competitions.

Kelly, Ross, Kendall, Singleton, Hannigan, Godfrey, Dawson, Spavin, Lee, Lawton and Lyall one each and Wilson 0 + 1.

League Cup (3 games)

Kelly 3, Ross 2, Smith 1, Kendall 2, Singleton 3, Hannigan 3, Godfrey 3, Dawson 3, Spavin 1, Lee 3, Wilson 3, Lawton 2, Cranston 2 + 1, Donnelly 1, Patrick 1.

Goalscorers: 65 League–3 LC (Total 68) (No FAC goals scored)

Dawson 13 (1 pen)–0 (13), Hannigan 12–0 (12), Lee 8–1 (9), Lawton 7–0 (7), Godfrey 5 (2 pens)–0 (5), Spavin 4–0 (4), Forrest 3–0 (3), Wilson 3–0 (3), Smith 2–0 (2), Greenhalgh 2–0 (2), Lyall 1–0 (1), Kendall 1–0 (1), Ross 1–0 (1), Cranston 0–1 (1), Own goals 3–1 (4) Richardson of Derby, Lindsay of Bury, Briggs of Bristol C., Mailey of Crewe in LC.

League position in Division Two: 13th – P42 W16 D7 L19 F65 A67 Pts 39
Home: W14 D3 L4 F44 A23 Away: W2 D4 L15 F21 A44

Match Report: Christmas Cracker as Bury are Buried – Dec 27 1966 Bury 3 Preston 4

Preston North End, having finally broken their away duck in the previous outing at Northampton, travelled the short journey to Gigg Lane hoping to dish up Christmas cheer for their band of merry followers. Ninety minutes of non-stop endeavour ensured that the return trip to Deepdale was a joyous occasion after a scintillating, thrill packed night match. It was the best North End away performance for well over twelve months in terms of attitude, industry and enthusiasm. After a bright opening start by both teams Preston duly handed over a Christmas present in the 19th minute. A lofted cross from Lowes looked harmless as both Kelly and Smith went up for the ball, but to the amazement of all present, the pair fell over each other and Aimson, as surprised as anyone, collected the ball and gratefully shot into the empty net. Bury came close to increasing their lead 15 minutes later but Ross was on hand to clear a shot off the line with Kelly beaten. North End then deservedly drew level on 37 minutes. Frank Lee took a free-kick out on the left which full-back Smith met perfectly to head into the top corner, recording his second goal in as many matches. Lee was also involved with Preston's second goal five minutes after the interval, racing onto a pass from Spavin before centring for Dawson to head in off the crossbar. However the lead lasted just seven minutes as Lowes, bursting down the right hand side, fed Aimson who completed a good move by shooting past Kelly. North End then piled on the pressure forcing Ramsbottom to save from Spavin, Dawson and Lawton, twice, before man-of-the-match Lee scored a superb solo goal in the 71st minute. He jinked past Colquhoun and Leech, cut inside and then shot hard and true past the bewildered goalkeeper who was going the wrong way when the ball entered the net. With just five minutes left the luckless goalkeeper was left stranded again as Ross joined in the fun, scoring with a thunderous shot from well outside the area. In a hectic finish Aimson completed his hat-trick from the penalty spot after Smith had brought down Lowes. Bury finished strongly but Preston held on for another rare, but deserved, away victory.

Ernie Hannigan, popular skilful winger who had an eye for goal.

Season 1966–67: Second Division	P	W	D	L	F	A	Pts
1 Coventry	42	23	13	6	74	43	59
2 Wolves	42	25	8	9	88	48	58
3 Carlisle	42	23	6	13	71	54	52
4 Blackburn	42	19	13	10	56	46	51
5 Ipswich	42	17	16	9	70	54	50
6 Huddersfield	42	20	9	13	58	46	49
7 Crystal Palace	42	19	10	13	61	55	48
8 Millwall	42	18	9	15	49	58	45
9 Bolton	42	14	14	14	64	58	42
10 Birmingham	42	16	8	18	70	66	40
11 Norwich	42	13	14	15	49	55	40
12 Hull	42	16	7	19	77	72	39
13 PRESTON	42	16	7	19	65	67	39
14 Portsmouth	42	13	13	16	59	70	39
15 Bristol City	42	12	14	16	56	62	38
16 Plymouth	42	14	9	19	59	58	37
17 Derby	42	12	12	18	68	72	36
18 Rotherham	42	13	10	19	61	70	36
19 Charlton	42	13	9	20	49	53	35
20 Cardiff	42	12	9	21	61	87	33
21 Northampton	42	12	6	24	47	84	30
22 Bury	42	11	6	25	45	83	28

Future Players born between August 1966 and May 1967: Robert Cooper, Aaron Callaghan, Andy Murphy, Ian Stevens, Stuart Cameron, Nigel Greenwood, Shane Beeby, Stuart Hicks.

Ever presents: (1) Ernie Hannigan

Hat-tricks: None

Players used: 26

FA Cup: 3rd Round

League Cup: 3rd Round Replay

Chairman: A. Harrison Esq. BEM

Manager: From August 1966, Jimmy Milne, then Bobby Seith took over in the November.

Leading scorer: 13 goals – Alex Dawson (all league)

AUTHORS' UNOFFICIAL PLAYER OF THE SEASON: Ernie Hannigan

Date 1966-7	Opponents	Comp	h or a	Score	Att.	1	2	3	4	5	6	7	8	9	10	11	12 * Sub Used		
Aug 20	Northampton T.	Div 2	h	2-1	12912	Kelly	Ross	Smith	Kendall	Singleton	Wearmouth	Hannigan	Godfrey (1p)	Dawson	Spavin	Lee (1)	Lapot		
Aug 27	Plymouth Arg.	Div 2	a	0-1	15493	Kelly	Ross	Smith	Kendall	Singleton	Wearmouth	Hannigan	Godfrey	Dawson	Spavin	Lee	Lapot		
Sep 3	Hull City	Div 2	h	4-2	14959	Kelly	Ross	Smith	Kendall	Singleton	Wearmouth	Hannigan	Godfrey (1)	Wilson (2)	Spavin	Lee (1)	Lawton		
Sep 7	Blackburn R.	Div 2	a	0-2	23529	Kelly	Ross	Smith	Kendall	Singleton	Wearmouth	Hannigan	Godfrey	Wilson	Spavin	Lee	Cranston		
Sep 10	Portsmouth	Div 2	h	2-2	11019	Kelly	Ross	Smith	Wearmouth	Singleton	Cranston	Hannigan	Godfrey	Wilson	Spavin	Lee	Donnelly		
Sep 14	Crewe Alex. Rd 2	LC	h	2-0	6397	Kelly	Ross	Donnelly	Lawton	Singleton	Kendall *	Wilson	Hannigan	Dawson	Godfrey	Lee (1)	Cranston *	1 og	(Mailey)
Sep 17	Birmingham City	Div 2	h	3-0	13577	Kelly	Ross	Smith	Lawton	Singleton	Cranston	Wilson	Hannigan (2)	Dawson	Godfrey * (1p)	Lee	Spavin *		
Sep 19	Millwall	Div 2	a	0-2	18640	Kelly	Ross	Smith	Lawton	Singleton	Kendall	Godfrey	Hannigan	Dawson	Spavin	Lee	Cranston		
Sep 24	Norwich City	Div 2	a	1-1	9280	Kelly	Ross	Smith	Lawton	Singleton	Kendall	Wilson	Hannigan (1)	Dawson	Godfrey	Lee	Cranston		
Sep 26	Blackburn R.	Div 2	h	3-0	24173	Kelly	Ross	Smith	Spavin (1)	Singleton	Cranston	Wilson	Hannigan	Dawson (1)	Godfrey	Lee (1)	Greenhalgh		
Oct 1	Coventry City	Div 2	h	3-2	13681	Kelly	Ross	Smith	Spavin	Singleton	Cranston	Wilson (1)	Hannigan	Dawson (1p)	Lawton	Lee (1)	Lapot		
Oct 4	Leeds Utd. Rd 3	LC	h	1-1	15049	Kelly	Ross	Kendall	Spavin	Singleton	Cranston (1)	Wilson	Hannigan	Dawson	Godfrey	Lee	Lawton		
Oct 8	Bolton W.	Div 2	a	2-4	20239	Brown	Kendall	Smith	Spavin	Singleton	Cranston	Wilson	Hannigan	Dawson (2)	Godfrey	Lee	Lawton		
Oct 12	Leeds Utd. Replay	LC	a	0-3	17221	Kelly	Patrick	Smith	Lawton	Singleton	Cranston	Wilson	Hannigan	Dawson	Godfrey	Lee	Spavin		
Oct 15	Charlton Ath.	Div 2	h	2-1	10666	Kelly	Ross	Smith	Lawton	Singleton	Cranston	Wilson	Hannigan	Dawson (1)	Spavin	Godfrey (1)	Donnelly		
Oct 22	Derby County	Div 2	a	1-5	18703	Kelly	Ross	Smith	Lawton	Cranston	Kendall	Wilson	Godfrey *	Dawson	Spavin	Hannigan	Lapot *	1 og	(Richardson)
Oct 24	Millwall	Div 2	h	2-1	12286	Kelly	Ross	Smith	Lawton	Cranston	Kendall	Wilson	Lyall (1)	Dawson (1)	Spavin	Hannigan	Lapot		
Oct 29	Crystal Palace	Div 2	h	1-0	13475	Kelly	Ross	Smith	Lawton	Singleton	Kendall	Wilson	Hannigan	Dawson	Spavin	Lee	Cranston		
Nov 5	Huddersfield T.	Div 2	a	0-1	13624	Kelly	Ross	Smith	Lawton	Singleton	Kendall	Hannigan	Godfrey	Dawson	Spavin	Lee *	Wilson *		
Nov 12	Cardiff City	Div 2	h	4-0	11283	Kelly	Ross	Smith	Lawton	Singleton	Kendall *	Hannigan (1)	Godfrey (1)	Dawson (1)	Spavin (1)	Lee	Cranston *		
Nov 19	Wolverhampton W.	Div 2	a	2-3	22733	Stewart	Ross	Smith	Lawton	Singleton	Cranston	Hannigan (1)	Godfrey	Dawson	Spavin	Lee (1)	Wilson		
Nov 26	Ipswich Town	Div 2	h	2-0	14122	Kelly	Ross	Smith	Lawton (1)	Singleton	Cranston	Hannigan	Godfrey	Dawson	Spavin (1)	Lee	Lyall		
Dec 3	Bristol City	Div 2	a	0-2	10804	Kelly	Ross	Smith	Lawton	Singleton	Kendall	Hannigan	Godfrey	Dawson	Spavin	Lee	Cranston		
Dec 10	Carlisle Utd.	Div 2	h	2-3	15569	Kelly	Ross	Smith	Lawton (1)	Singleton	Kendall (1)	Hannigan	Godfrey	Dawson	Spavin	Lee	Cranston		
Dec 17	Northampton T.	Div 2	a	5-1	10050	Kelly	Ross	Smith	Lawton (1)	Singleton	Kendall	Hannigan (2)	Godfrey	Dawson (1)	Spavin (1)	Lee (1)	Lyall		
Dec 24	Bury	Div 2	h	2-2	15522	Kelly	Ross	Smith (1)	Lawton	Singleton	Kendall	Hannigan	Godfrey *	Dawson	Spavin	Lee	Lyall *	1 og	(Lindsay)
Dec 27	Bury	Div 2	a	4-3	11267	Kelly	Ross (1)	Smith (1)	Lawton	Singleton	Kendall	Hannigan	Lyall	Dawson (1)	Spavin	Lee (1)	Crossley		
Dec 31	Plymouth Arg.	Div 2	a	2-0	14375	Kelly	Ross	Smith	Lawton (1)	Singleton	Kendall	Hannigan (1)	Godfrey	Dawson	Spavin	Lee	Lyall		
Jan 7	Hull City	Div 2	a	2-2	22047	Kelly	Ross	Smith	Lawton	Singleton	Kendall	Hannigan	Godfrey	Dawson (2)	Spavin	Lee	Lyall		
Jan 14	Portsmouth	Div 2	h	1-0	14419	Kelly	Ross	Smith *	Lawton	Singleton	Kendall	Hannigan	Godfrey	Dawson (1)	Spavin	Lee	Lyall *		
Jan 21	Birmingham City	Div 2	a	1-3	18486	Kelly	Ross	Kendall	Lawton (1)	Singleton	Cranston	Hannigan	Godfrey	Dawson	Spavin	Lee	Lyall		
Jan 28	Aston Villa Rd 3	FAC	h	0-1	26385	Kelly	Ross *	Kendall	Lawton	Singleton	Spavin	Hannigan	Godfrey	Dawson	Lyall	Lee	Wilson *		
Feb 4	Norwich City	Div 2	h	3-1	12807	Kelly	Patrick	Donnelly	Lawton (2)	Singleton	Kendall	Hannigan (1)	Godfrey	Dawson	Spavin	Wilson	Lee *		
Feb 11	Coventry City	Div 2	a	1-2	29047	Kelly	Ross	Smith	Lawton (1)	Singleton	Kendall	Hannigan	Godfrey	Greenhalgh	Spavin *	Wilson	Lee *		
Feb 25	Bolton W.	Div 2	h	1-3	16067	Kelly	Ross	Smith	Lawton	Cranston	Kendall	Hannigan	Godfrey	Greenhalgh (1)	Spavin	Lee	Crossley		
Mar 7	Crystal Palace	Div 2	a	0-1	19719	Kelly	Ross	Smith	Lawton	Cranston	Kendall	Hannigan	Greenhalgh	Dawson	Spavin	Lee	Cranston		
Mar 11	Charlton Ath.	Div 2	a	1-2	11840	Kelly	Ross	Smith	Lawton	Cranston	Lapot	Hannigan	Lyall	Greenhalgh	Spavin	Lee	Donnelly		
Mar 18	Derby County	Div 2	h	2-0	14985	Kelly	Ross	Smith	Lawton *	Singleton	McNab	Hannigan (1)	Greenhalgh	Forrest (1)	Spavin	Lee	Lapot *		
Mar 27	Rotherham Utd.	Div 2	a	1-2	8696	Kelly	Ross	Smith	Lapot	Singleton	McNab	Hannigan	Greenhalgh (1)	Forrest	Spavin	Lee	Godfrey		
Mar 28	Rotherham Utd.	Div 2	h	1-1	13797	Kelly	Ross	Smith	Lapot	Singleton	Wearmouth	Hannigan	Godfrey	Greenhalgh	Spavin	Lee (1)	Lyall		
Apr 1	Huddersfield T.	Div 2	h	1-2	14161	Kelly	Ross	Smith	Wearmouth	Singleton	McNab	Hannigan	Godfrey	Forrest (1)	Spavin	Lee	Greenhalgh		
Apr 8	Cardiff City	Div 2	a	0-4	9630	Kelly	Ross	Smith	Wearmouth	Singleton	McNab	Hannigan	Hughes	Forrest	Lyall	Lee	Greenhalgh		
Apr 15	Wolverhampton W.	Div 2	h	1-2	18791	Kelly	Ross	Smith	Cranston	Singleton	McNab *	Hannigan (1)	Lyall	Forrest	Spavin	Godfrey	Lee *		
Apr 22	Ipswich Town	Div 2	a	0-0	12758	Kelly	Ross	Smith	Spavin	Singleton	Cranston	Hannigan	Lyall	Forrest	Godfrey	Lee	Wearmouth		
Apr 29	Bristol City	Div 2	h	2-2	9431	Kelly	Ross	Ritchie	Spavin	Smith	Cranston	Hannigan	Greenhalgh	Forrest (1)	Godfrey	Lee	Singleton	1 og	(Briggs)
May 6	Carlisle Utd.	Div 2	a	1-1	9443	Kelly	Ross	Ritchie	Spavin	Smith	Cranston	Crossley	Hannigan	Forrest	Godfrey	Lee	Singleton		

George Ross in his Tartan with fellow Scotsmen.

SEASON 1967–1968

Only the failings of Rotherham United and Plymouth Argyle prevented Preston from crashing into Division Three as the club endured yet another dreadful season. It began badly with a home defeat by arch rivals Blackpool and it was not until a late rally around Easter that North End saved themselves. On the plus side it was pleasing to see the club buy some useful players and they were all to undoubtedly strengthen the team. Indeed, Archie Gemmill scored on his debut, as substitute at Norwich, Derek Temple hit both goals on his debut at Plymouth and Willie Irvine, signed from Burnley, hit a priceless hat-trick in only his third appearance. Apart from one crazy spell in the November the defence was generally sound, but at the other end the Preston attack struggled continuously. In almost half of the 42 league games North End failed to score, and it was obvious that this was the root of their problems. Ray Charnley, a proven goalscorer, was brought in from Blackpool and Irvine was signed just before the transfer deadline. Throughout the season though the chances were just not being made as the midfield players struggled to make an impact. Alan Kelly played some superb games in goal and John Ritchie had an excellent season at left-back and these two worked tirelessly at times to stem the tide. Manager Bobby Seith, who was able to make more signings in this season than any manager had been allowed to for years. His choice of player was pretty good though and bringing in midfielder, Ken Knighton from Wolves, was another good move. Gemmill showed obvious talent and another young Scot called George Lyall continued his progress. In the cups Preston made another poor showing. Defeat at the first hurdle in the League Cup, away at Oxford, where Jimmy Forrest scored his only goal of the season, kept up the dismal record Preston had in that particular competition. Then, in the New Year Preston faced two FA Cup-ties in London. In the third round, ironically just a week after a league defeat there, Preston travelled to Loftus Road for a match with QPR. For once the Preston fans had something to cheer as their team produced a thrilling and wholly unexpected win. In the fourth round it was a visit to Tottenham Hotspur and despite North End giving a good performance the Jimmy Greaves inspired London side eventually won through with ease. The remaining league games were a struggle but a win over Aston Villa triggered off some improved form and the best run of the season. A great 1–0 win at Blackburn on Easter Saturday was the highlight and gave the club a big boost. In the end Preston were four points clear of relegation but it had been a long, hard season and all too close for comfort.

DEBUTANTS: (8) Archie Gemmill, Derek Temple, Ray Charnley, Ken Knighton, Graham Hawkins, Willie Irvine, Ricky Heppolette, Alex Spark.

LAST GAMES: (8) Singleton, Lawton, Godfrey, Hannigan, Greenhalgh, Forrest, Crossley, Charnley.

Trivia Facts:

This was the first season that there was an official Player of the Season trophy. It was presented by the Supporters club and Alan Kelly was the first winner. The trophy is still awarded.

Australian, Joe Marston, the former North End favourite was back in England for six weeks watching training sessions at Preston, Manchester United, Liverpool, Everton, Blackpool and Chelsea. He had been appointed coach to Western Suburbs, an Australian second division team. He told the L.E.P. that his club actually made £50,000 profit on one-arm bandits and that the club were ploughing the money back into the training programme.

Walter Crook, North End's trainer, was severely censured, fined £10 and warned as to his future conduct after making an ungentlemanly comment to the referee at the PNE *vs.* Bolton game on 4 November 1967.

An advert in the Evening Post advertising for the vacant manager's job of the Moor Park Celtic's 'A' team, denied that the recently resigned manager of Chelsea, Mr Tommy Docherty, had applied for the job!

A 16 year old youth from Huddersfield was fined £2 for throwing a stone at North End's keeper Alan Kelly during their match with Preston on 28 October.

League appearances (42 games)

Charnley R.O. 23, Cranston W. 11 + 3, Crossley P. 2, Forrest J. 16 + 2, Gemmill A. 29 + 3, Godfrey B.C. 7, Greenhalgh B.A. 4, Hannigan E. 15, Hawkins G.N. 11, Heppolette R.A.W. 2 + 1, Hughes D.R. 2, Irvine W.J. 11, Kelly J.A. 41, Knighton K. 20, Lawton N. 4, Lee F. 19, Lyall G. 15 + 4, McNab J. 39, Patrick B. 23, Ritchie J. 32, Ross G. 27, Singleton A.J. 21, Smith J.A.G. 35, Spark A.M. 0 + 1, Spavin A. 20 + 1, Stewart G. 1, Temple D.W. 32.

FA Cup appearances (2 games)

Kelly 2, Ritchie 2, Smith 2, McNab 2, Lee 2, Lyall 2, Spavin 0 + 1, Gemmill 2, Cranston 2, Patrick 2, Temple 2, Charnley 2.

League Cup appearances (1 game)

Kelly, Ritchie, Smith, Singleton, McNab, Forrest, Lee, Spavin, Gemmill, Patrick, Crossley all 1 each.

Goalscorers: 43 League–4 FAC–1 LC–(Total 48)

Temple 8–0–0 (8), Charnley 4–3–0 (7), Gemmill 4–1–0 (5), Irvine 6 (1pen)–0–0 (6), Hannigan 5–0–0 (5), Lyall 4–0–0 (4), Ritchie 4 (2pens)–0–0 (4), Lee 3–0–0 (3), Greenhalgh 2–0–0 (2), Cranston 1–0–0 (1), McNab 1–0–0 (1), Forrest 0–0–1 (1), Own goals 1–0–0 (1) Webster of Derby.

League position in Division Two: 20th – P42 W12 D11 L19 F43 A65 Pts 35
Home: W8 D7 L6 F29 A24 Away: W4 D4 L13 F14 A41

Match Report: Preston Pay the Penalty – Nov 18 1967
Preston 3 Blackburn 5

Eight goal thrillers are great, especially in derby games, but when your goalkeeper is the star man after conceding five goals you know that not everything is right at the club. Over 20,000 turned up at Deepdale to savour the atmosphere generated and local pride as well as league points were at stake. The first half of the game was a quite placid affair with Blackburn, peppered with international players, gaining the upper hand. Blacklaw, Rover's goalkeeper, only had one worthwhile shot to save whereas Kelly was overworked by comparison. Both Gilliver and Hole forced Kelly to make thrilling saves before Hole gave the visitors the lead with a well struck thunderbolt. Valiant Kelly was beaten again after 29 minutes when Gilliver headed his first league goal since a leg operation twelve months previously. That gave Blackburn a deserved 2–0 lead at the interval. On the resumption Preston fought back gamely and during a hectic second half six more goals were scored. The lead was reduced early in the half by Lyall, one of five Scots in the North End side, but that man Hole restored Blackburn's two goal lead with yet another fierce drive. Lyall, prompting from midfield, pumped a long ball into the path of Lee, the left-winger beating his marker, Newton, before scoring his third goal of the season. 3–2 down and everything to fight for, until that is Darling quickly put Rovers two goals ahead again, all four goals coming in an 18 minutes spell. Irish international Kelly continued to excel, keeping the visitors at bay, if that's possible having already conceded four goals! If anyone left the ground early to beat the rush then they missed a most exciting finale. In the 89th minute Gemmill fouled Rodgers and Ferguson netted the resultant penalty. Then, before the final whistle sounded, Blacklaw brought down Temple for another penalty, this time for Preston, and Ritchie took the opportunity to fire home from the spot to make the score 3–5.

Future Players born between August 1967 and May 1968: Mark Rodgers, Ian Bogie, David Reeves, Julian Darby, Jeff Wrightson, Mickey Brown, Charlie Bishop, Gary Parkinson.
Ever presents: None
Hat-tricks: (1) Willie Irvine
Players used: 27
Manager: Bobby Seith
Chairman: A. Harrison Esq. BEM
FA Cup: Fourth Round
League Cup: Second Round
Leading scorer: 8 goals – Derek Temple (all League)

OFFICIAL PLAYER OF THE SEASON:
Alan Kelly

STAT FACTS:
Best home run without defeat: 5 games
Best away run without defeat: 3 games
Longest run unbeaten: 8 games
Longest run without a win: 10 games
Best home attendance: 21,603 *vs.* Blackpool 19.8.67
Worst home attendance: 9,938 *vs.* Portsmouth 11.5.68
Best away attendance: 47,088 *vs.* Spurs FAC 17.2.68
Worst away attendance: 7,357 *vs.* Crystal Palace 15.5.68 Aggregate and average home attendance: 315,894 – 15,042;Aggregate and average away attendance: 318,692 – 15,175

Alan Kelly and George Ross, North End's defensive stalwarts.

Date 1967-8	Opponents	Comp	h or a	Score	Att.	1	2	3	4	5	6	7	8	9	10	11	12 * Sub Used		
Aug 19	Blackpool	Div 2	h	0-2	21603	Kelly	Ross	Ritchie	Smith	Singleton	McNab	Hannigan	Lawton	Forrest	Godfrey	Lee	Lyall		
Aug 23	Norwich City	Div 2	a	3-1	18231	Kelly	Ross	Ritchie	Smith	Singleton	McNab *	Hannigan (2)	Lawton	Forrest	Spavin	Godfrey	Gemmill * (1)		
Aug 26	Charlton Ath.	Div 2	a	0-0	11612	Kelly	Ross	Ritchie	Smith	Singleton	McNab	Hannigan	Lawton	Forrest	Spavin	Godfrey	Gemmill		
Aug 28	Norwich City	Div 2	h	1-0	15036	Kelly	Ross	Ritchie	Smith	Singleton	McNab	Hannigan	Lawton	Greenhalgh (1)	Spavin	Godfrey	Gemmill		
Sep 2	Crystal Palace	Div 2	h	0-0	13313	Kelly	Ross	Ritchie	Smith	Singleton	McNab	Hannigan	Greenhalgh	Forrest	Spavin	Godfrey	Gemmill		
Sep 6	Portsmouth	Div 2	a	1-2	21435	Kelly	Ross	Ritchie	Smith	Singleton	McNab	Hannigan	Forrest	Greenhalgh (1)	Spavin	Godfrey	Cranston		
Sep 9	Aston Villa	Div 2	a	0-1	13285	Kelly	Ross	Ritchie	Smith	Singleton	McNab	Hannigan	Godfrey	Greenhalgh *	Spavin	Gemmill	Lyall *		
Sep 13	Oxford Utd. Rd 2	LC	a	1-2	9596	Kelly	Patrick	Ritchie	Smith	Singleton	McNab	Crossley	Gemmill	Forrest (1)	Spavin	Lee	Lyall		
Sep 16	QPR	Div 2	h	0-2	15791	Kelly	Ross	Ritchie	Smith	Singleton	McNab	Hannigan	Gemmill	Forrest	Cranston	Lee	Lyall		
Sep 23	Plymouth Arg.	Div 2	a	2-1	10889	Kelly	Ross	Patrick	Smith	Singleton	McNab	Hannigan	Gemmill	Forrest	Temple (2)	Lee	Lyall		
Sep 30	Cardiff City	Div 2	a	3-0	13735	Kelly	Patrick	Smith	Spavin	Singleton	McNab	Hannigan (2)	Temple	Forrest	Lyall (1)	Lee	Cranston		
Oct 7	Hull City	Div 2	h	3-2	14318	Kelly	Patrick	Smith	Spavin	Singleton	McNab *	Hannigan	Temple (1)	Forrest	Lyall	Lee (1)	Cranston * (1)		
Oct 14	Carlisle Utd.	Div 2	a	1-4	11228	Kelly	Patrick	Ritchie	Smith	Singleton	McNab	Hannigan	Temple	Forrest	Spavin	Lee (1)	Lyall		
Oct 21	Ipswich Town	Div 2	h	1-1	13740	Kelly	Patrick	Ritchie	Spavin	Singleton	McNab	Hannigan	Temple	Forrest	Gemmill (1)	Lee	Ross		
Oct 28	Huddersfield T.	Div 2	a	1-1	10834	Kelly	Ross	Ritchie	Smith	Singleton	McNab	Hannigan (1)	Gemmill	Temple	Spavin	Lee	Patrick		
Nov 4	Bolton W.	Div 2	h	1-1	19796	Kelly	Ross	Ritchie	Smith	Singleton	McNab	Hannigan	Gemmill	Temple (1)	Spavin	Lee	Patrick		
Nov 11	Birmingham City	Div 2	a	0-3	27664	Kelly	Ross	Ritchie	Smith	Singleton	McNab *	Crossley	Gemmill	Temple	Spavin	Lee	Forrest *		
Nov 18	Blackburn R.	Div 2	a	3-5	20039	Kelly	Ross	Ritchie (1p)	Smith	Singleton	Spavin	Forrest	Lyall (1)	Temple	Gemmill	Lee (1)	Crossley		
Nov 25	Middlesbrough	Div 2	h	0-5	14350	Kelly	Ross	Ritchie	Smith	Singleton	McNab	Lee *	Temple	Forrest	Spavin	Gemmill	Lyall *		
Dec 2	Bristol City	Div 2	a	0-1	10127	Kelly	Ross	Ritchie	Smith	Singleton	McNab	Lee	Spavin *	Forrest	Lyall	Temple	Gemmill *		
Dec 9	Millwall	Div 2	h	0-2	9736	Kelly	Ross	Ritchie	Smith *	Singleton	McNab	Lee	Spavin	Charnley	Lyall	Forrest	Gemmill *		
Dec 16	Blackpool	Div 2	a	1-4	16291	Kelly	Ross	Ritchie	Spavin	Singleton	McNab	Lee	Lyall	Charnley (1)	Gemmill	Temple	Cranston		
Dec 23	Charlton Ath.	Div 2	h	4-1	11203	Kelly	Ross	Ritchie	McNab	Cranston	Knighton	Lee	Lyall (1)	Charnley	Gemmill (2)	Temple (1)	Forrest		
Dec 26	Rotherham Utd.	Div 2	a	2-2	18008	Kelly	Ross *	Ritchie	McNab	Cranston	Knighton	Lee	Lyall (1)	Charnley	Gemmill	Temple (1)	Forrest *		
Dec 30	Rotherham Utd.	Div 2	h	0-1	12704	Kelly	Patrick	Ritchie	McNab *	Cranston	Knighton	Lee	Lyall	Charnley	Gemmill	Temple	Spark *		
Jan 20	QPR	Div 2	a	0-2	16633	Kelly	Patrick	Ritchie	Smith	Hawkins *	Knighton	Lyall	McNab	Charnley	Gemmill	Temple	Cranston *		
Jan 27	QPR Rd 3	FAC	a	3-1	18424	Kelly	Patrick	Ritchie	Smith	Cranston	McNab	Lee	Lyall	Charnley (2)	Gemmill (1)	Temple	Spark		
Feb 3	Plymouth Arg.	Div 2	h	2-0	13980	Kelly	Patrick	Ritchie	Smith	Cranston	McNab	Lyall	Knighton	Charnley (1)	Gemmill	Temple (1)	Lee		
Feb 10	Cardiff City	Div 2	h	2-2	12897	Kelly	Patrick	Ritchie	Smith	Cranston	McNab	Lyall	Knighton	Charnley	Gemmill	Temple	Lee		
Feb 17	Tottenham H. Rd 4	FAC	a	1-3	47088	Kelly	Patrick	Ritchie	Smith	Cranston	McNab	Lee	Lyall	Charnley (1)	Gemmill	Temple *	Spavin *		
Feb 24	Hull City	Div 2	a	1-1	14082	Kelly	Patrick	Ritchie	Smith	Cranston	McNab * (1)	Lyall	Knighton	Charnley	Gemmill	Hughes	Spavin *		
Mar 2	Carlisle Utd.	Div 2	h	0-2	13481	Kelly	Patrick	Ritchie	Smith	Cranston	Knighton	Temple *	Spavin	Charnley	Gemmill	Hughes	Lyall *		
Mar 16	Ipswich Town	Div 2	a	0-4	19558	Kelly	Patrick	Ritchie	Smith	Cranston	McNab	Forrest	Irvine	Charnley	Knighton	Temple	Spavin		
Mar 18	Aston Villa	Div 2	h	2-1	17043	Kelly	Patrick	Ritchie (1)	Smith	Cranston	McNab	Temple	Irvine (1)	Charnley	Spavin	Gemmill	Lyall		
Mar 23	Huddersfield T.	Div 2	h	3-1	13504	Kelly	Patrick	Ritchie	Smith	Cranston	Knighton	Temple	Irvine (3)	Charnley	McNab	Gemmill	Bright		
Mar 30	Bolton W.	Div 2	a	0-0	14664	Kelly	Patrick	Ross	Smith	Hawkins	Knighton	Temple	Irvine	Charnley	McNab	Gemmill	Lyall		
Apr 6	Birmingham City	Div 2	h	0-0	16876	Kelly	Patrick	Ross	Smith	Hawkins	Knighton	Temple	Irvine	Charnley	McNab	Gemmill	Lyall		
Apr 13	Blackburn R.	Div 2	h	1-0	20255	Kelly	Patrick	Ross	Smith	Hawkins	Knighton	Temple	Irvine (1p)	Charnley	McNab	Gemmill	Lyall		
Apr 15	Derby County	Div 2	a	2-1	17783	Kelly	Patrick	Ross	Smith	Hawkins	Knighton	Temple (1)	Irvine	Charnley	McNab	Gemmill	Lyall	1 og	(Webster)
Apr 16	Derby County	Div 2	h	1-1	17871	Kelly	Patrick	Ross	Smith *	Hawkins	Knighton	Temple	Irvine	Charnley (1)	McNab	Gemmill	Lyall *		
Apr 20	Middlesbrough	Div 2	a	0-0	15529	Kelly	Patrick	Ross	McNab	Hawkins	Knighton	Temple	Irvine	Charnley	Lyall *	Gemmill	Heppolette *		
Apr 27	Bristol City	Div 2	a	1-4	16935	Kelly	Patrick	Ross	Smith	Hawkins	Knighton	Temple	Irvine (1)	Charnley	McNab	Gemmill	Heppolette		
May 4	Millwall	Div 2	h	0-1	11445	Kelly	Patrick	Ritchie	McNab	Hawkins	Heppolette *	Crossley	Temple	Charnley	Knighton	Gemmill	Cranston *		
May 11	Portsmouth	Div 2	h	3-1	9938	Kelly	Patrick	Ritchie (2, 1p)	Smith	Hawkins	Heppolette	Temple	McNab	Charnley (1)	Knighton	Gemmill	Crossley		
May 15	Crystal Palace	Div 2	a	0-2	7357	Stewart	Ross	Ritchie	Smith	Hawkins	Knighton	Lee	Irvine	Charnley	Lyall	Temple	Hughes		

Jim McNab

Season 1967–68: Second Division

	P	W	D	L	F	A	Pts
1 Ipswich	42	22	15	5	79	44	59
2 QPR	42	25	8	9	67	36	58
3 Blackpool	42	24	10	8	71	43	58
4 Birmingham	42	19	14	9	83	51	52
5 Portsmouth	42	18	13	11	68	55	49
6 Middlesbrough	42	17	12	13	60	54	46
7 Millwall	42	14	17	11	62	50	45
8 Blackburn	42	16	11	15	56	49	43
9 Norwich	42	16	11	15	60	65	43
10 Carlisle	42	14	13	15	58	52	41
11 Crystal Palace	42	14	11	17	56	56	39
12 Bolton	42	13	13	16	60	63	39
13 Cardiff	42	13	12	17	60	66	38
14 Huddersfield	42	13	12	17	46	61	38
15 Charlton	42	12	13	17	63	68	37
16 Aston Villa	42	15	7	20	54	64	37
17 Hull	42	12	13	17	58	73	37
18 Derby	42	13	10	19	71	78	36
19 Bristol City	42	13	10	19	48	62	36
20 PRESTON	**42**	**12**	**11**	**19**	**43**	**65**	**35**
21 Rotherham	42	10	11	21	42	76	31
22 Plymouth	42	9	9	24	38	72	27

John Ritchie

SEASON 1968–1969

This was a strange year for the club, which although seeing a slight improvement in their league position, did not excite the fans very much at all. There were few thrills and goalscoring was a real problem from the opening day. Defensively Preston were very sound and conceded fewer goals than for a long time but the midfield created little and the forwards were starved of a decent service. Only 38 league goals were scored, an abysmal total, and but for Willie Irvine things would have been even worse. The former Burnley player began the season in sparkling form, scoring in 13 of the first 16 league and cup games. Unfortunately, in the main, when Irvine failed to score then so did Preston. In the September Gerry Ingram was signed from Blackpool and it did give the attack some extra height and weight, but the North End fans had to wait ten matches for Ingram to register his first goal and that was not what was required. The unproductive midfield was the area manager Bobby Seith worked on, trying all sorts of combinations to try to find the right balance. Individually Ken Knighton, Alan Spavin

Willie Irvine, PNE and Northern Ireland centre-forward

and Archie Gemmill were all good players but for some inexplicable reason they failed to work as a unit. Youngsters Alex Spark and Ricky Heppolette worked hard when they were drafted in and they made good progress but the chances were not being created. Collectively there was not the flair to break down the well organised tight defences of the division. Alan Kelly was in majestic form in goal though and Jim McNab and Graham Hawkins were towers of strength. Curiously it was difficult to fault any of the players individually and that made it all the more frustrating for the fans. The second half of the season saw Irvine's goals dry up and Preston hit just 16 goals in the 17 games played after the turn of the year. Luckily they only concede 17 in the same period so important points were picked up. The cups were also a disappointment. A narrow win over two legs against Oldham in the League Cup was hardly memorable and Preston were soon out of that competition after defeat at Crystal Palace in the next round. In the FA Cup a third round win over Nottingham Forest gave the fans one of the few highlights of a mediocre season and will be remembered for a wonderful goal by Derek Temple. The former Everton player ran the length of the field before shooting past the goalkeeper. In the next round Preston held Chelsea at home but then trailed 2–0 at Stamford Bridge before, amazingly, a floodlight failure caused the match to be abandoned. In the second replay Preston were leading until the 90th minute but Chelsea then scored twice to claim a dramatic win.

DEBUTANTS: (4) Gerry Ingram, David Bright, Norman Lloyd, Ray Robinson.

LAST GAMES: (4) Smith J., Knighton, Bright, Robinson.

Future Players born between August 1968 and July 1969: Alan Kelly Jnr, John Tinkler, Steve Wilkinson, Danny Ibbotson, Lee Bamber, Lee Fowler, Mike Flynn, Micky Norbury, Steve Harper, Andy Fensome, Neil Trebble, Stuart Pilling.

Ever presents: Ken Knighton   **Hat Tricks:** None
Players used: 24   **FA Cup:** Fourth Round Replay
Manager: Bobby Seith
Chairman: A. Harrison Esq. BEM then T. C. Nicholson JP FCIOB
League Cup: Second Round
Leading scorer: 20 goals – Willie Irvine (15 League 2 FAC 3 LC)

OFFICIAL PLAYER OF THE SEASON: Jim McNab

Match Report: Preston Pipped at the Post
3 Feb 1969 Chelsea 2 Preston 1
FA Cup 4th Round Replay

Over 44,00 spectators had witnessed the floodlight failure the previous week when Chelsea were 2–0 up, and the way they entered this rearranged cup-tie one would have thought that the Pensioners were under the impression that those two goals still counted. The well fancied Londoners paid the price for such a foolhardy attitude when North End, playing in all white, took a shock lead after 15 minutes play. A perfect Lee corner to the near post was touched on by Temple and in a flash Ingram had headed past an astonished Bonetti in goal. Preston, hard hit by injuries, had entered this replay minus McNab, Cranston and Irvine but welcomed the return of Hawkins. North End's playing resources were so stretched that several of the side had treatment for knocks and bruises at Arsenal's Highbury stadium only hours before the kick-off. Yet gallant goalkeeper Kelly hardly had to extend himself to make a worthwhile save in the first half. Chelsea changed up a gear, pushing Osgood up front from his midfield role as part of their second half survival bid. At times it was as if the old Eton Wall Game was played out in Kelly's goalmouth. Hawkins and Gemmill performed like inspired demons as Preston defended with grit and determination. They not only held on but nearly put Chelsea out of their misery, going close to scoring after 70 minutes. Gemmill strode through the middle, hitting a shot that came down off the underside of the bar, but unfortunately for Preston it bounced out to safety. If Lady Luck had smiled on Chelsea at that moment it certainly did again later. With 90 minutes played and the anxious Preston contingent whistling for time, a combined effort from Osgood and Webb resulted in the equalising goal, which just squeezed inside the post. With their spirits raised Chelsea's Birchenall had a 93rd minute shot which beat Kelly but would have drifted wide had it not been for Cooke lunging in to deflect the ball over the line for the winner. It was cruel on Preston who had made a valiant effort to overcome their First Division opponents. What a way for Chelsea's goalkeeper Bonetti to celebrate his 400th appearance for the Blues.

Season 1968–69: Second Division

	P	W	D	L	F	A	Pts
1 Derby	42	26	11	5	65	32	63
2 Crystal Palace	42	22	12	8	70	47	56
3 Charlton	42	18	14	10	61	52	50
4 Middlesbrough	42	19	11	12	58	49	49
5 Cardiff	42	20	7	15	67	54	47
6 Huddersfield	42	17	12	13	53	46	46
7 Birmingham	42	18	8	16	73	59	44
3 Blackpool	42	14	15	13	51	41	43
9 Sheffield United	42	16	11	15	61	50	43
10 Millwall	42	17	9	16	57	49	43
11 Hull	42	13	16	13	59	52	42
12 Carlisle	42	16	10	16	46	49	42
13 Norwich	42	15	10	17	53	56	40
14 PRESTON	42	12	15	15	38	44	39
15 Portsmouth	42	12	14	16	58	58	38
16 Bristol City	42	11	16	15	46	53	38
17 Bolton	42	12	14	16	55	67	38
18 Aston Villa	42	12	14	16	37	48	38
19 Blackburn	42	13	11	18	52	63	37
20 Oxford	42	12	9	21	34	55	33
21 Bury	42	11	8	23	51	80	30
22 Fulham	42	7	11	24	40	81	25

League appearances (42 games)

Bright D. 1, Cranston W. 9, Gemmill A. 18 + 4, Hawkins G. N. 35 + 3, Heppolette R. A. W. 17 + 1, Hughes D. R. 5 + 1, Ingram G. 32, Irvine W. J. 37, Kelly J. A. 41, Knighton K. 42, Lee F. 28 + 1, Lloyd N. W. M. 1, Lyall G. 5 + 3, McNab J. 31 + 1, Patrick B. 6, Ritchie J. 16, Robinson R. 2, Ross G. 39, Smith J. A. G. 12, Spark A. M. 14, Spavin A. 31, Stewart G. 1, Temple D. W. 22, Wilson D. C. 17 + 1.

FA Cup appearances (3 games)

Kelly 3, Ross 3, McNab 2, Spark 3, Hawkins 1, Cranston 2, Knighton 3, Heppolette 3, Temple 3, Spavin 1, Gemmill 1, Irvine 2, Ingram 3, Lee 3.

League Cup appearances (3 games)

Kelly 3, Patrick 2, Ross 1, Ritchie 3, Smith 3, McNab 1 + 1, Hawkins 3, Knighton 3, Wilson 3, Temple 2, Spavin 3, Gemmill 1, Lyall 1, Irvine 3, Lee 1.

Goalscorers: 38 League–4 FAC–3 LC–(Total 45)

Irvine 15–2 (1 pen)–3 (20), Ingram 6–1–0 (7), Lee 4–0–0 (4), Knighton 4–0–0 (4), Gemmill 3–0–0 (3), Temple 2–1–0 (3), Spavin 1–0–0 (1), Spark 1–0–0 (1), McNab 1–0–0 (1), Wilson 1–0–0 (1).

League position in Division Two: 14th – P42 W12 D15 L15 F38 A44 Pts 39
Home: W8 D8 L5 F23 A19   Away: W4 D7 L10 F15 A25

Date 1968-9	Opponents	Comp	h or a	Score	Att.	1	2	3	4	5	6	7	8	9	10	11	12 *Sub Used
Aug 10	Middlesbrough	Div 2	a	1-2	19014	Kelly	Patrick	Ritchie	Smith	Hawkins	Knighton	Wilson	Spavin	Irvine (1)	Lyall	Temple	Ross
Aug 14	Oldham Ath. Rd 1	LC	h	1-1	10543	Kelly	Patrick	Ritchie	Smith	Hawkins	Knighton	Wilson	Spavin	Irvine (1)	Lyall	Temple	McNab
Aug 17	Huddersfield T.	Div 2	h	1-0	12673	Kelly	Patrick	Ritchie	Smith	Hawkins *	Knighton	Wilson	Spavin	Irvine (1)	Gemmill	Temple	McNab *
Aug 21	Oldham Ath. Replay	LC	a	1-0	4434	Kelly	Patrick	Ritchie	Smith	Hawkins	Knighton	Wilson	Spavin	Irvine (1)	Gemmill *	Temple	McNab *
Aug 24	Cardiff City	Div 2	a	0-1	11344	Kelly	Patrick	Ritchie	Smith	Hawkins	McNab	Wilson	Spavin	Irvine	Knighton	Temple *	Lyall *
Aug 26	Portsmouth	Div 2	h	0-0	13828	Kelly	Ross	Ritchie	Smith	Hawkins	McNab	Wilson	Spavin	Irvine	Knighton	Lee	Lyall
Aug 31	Birmingham City	Div 2	h	4-1	14112	Kelly	Ross	Ritchie	Smith	Hawkins	McNab	Wilson	Spavin (1)	Irvine (1)	Knighton (1)	Lee (1)	Spark
Sep 4	Crystal Palace Rd 2	LC	a	1-3	12594	Kelly	Ross	Ritchie	Smith	Hawkins	McNab	Wilson	Spavin	Irvine (1)	Knighton	Lee	Smith
Sep 7	Bury	Div 2	a	1-0	10609	Kelly	Ross	Ritchie	McNab	Hawkins	Knighton	Wilson	Spavin	Irvine (1)	Ingram	Lee	Smith
Sep 14	Charlton Ath.	Div 2	h	1-1	13986	Kelly	Ross	Ritchie	McNab	Hawkins	Knighton	Wilson	Spavin	Irvine (1)	Ingram	Lee	Smith
Sep 16	Blackpool	Div 2	a	1-1	27975	Kelly	Ross	Ritchie	McNab	Hawkins	Knighton (1)	Wilson	Spavin	Irvine	Ingram	Lee	Smith
Sep 21	Crystal Palace	Div 2	a	2-1	13577	Kelly	Ross	Ritchie	McNab	Hawkins	Knighton	Wilson	Spavin	Irvine (2)	Ingram	Lee	Smith
Sep 28	Norwich City	Div 2	h	1-3	14778	Kelly	Ross	Ritchie	McNab	Hawkins	Knighton	Wilson	Spavin	Irvine (1)	Ingram	Lee	Smith
Sep 30	Carlisle Utd.	Div 2	h	2-2	14984	Kelly	Ross	Ritchie	McNab	Hawkins	Knighton	Wilson	Spavin	Irvine (1)	Ingram	Temple (1)	Smith
Oct 5	Blackburn R.	Div 2	h	1-1	20681	Kelly	Ross	Ritchie	Smith	Hawkins	Knighton	Wilson	Spavin	Irvine (1)	Ingram	Temple *	Gemmill *
Oct 9	Portsmouth	Div 2	a	1-1	20393	Kelly	Ross	Ritchie	Smith	Hawkins	Knighton	Wilson	Spavin	Irvine	Ingram	Temple	Gemmill *
Oct 12	Derby County	Div 2	a	0-1	27146	Kelly	Ross	Ritchie	Smith	Hawkins	Knighton	Wilson *	Spavin	Irvine	Ingram	Temple	Gemmill *
Oct 19	Hull City	Div 2	h	1-0	13823	Kelly	Ross	Ritchie *	Smith	Hawkins	Knighton	Temple	Spavin	Irvine	Ingram (1)	Gemmill	Lyall *
Oct 26	Millwall	Div 2	a	0-0	15827	Kelly	Ross	Smith	McNab	Hawkins	Knighton	Temple	Spavin	Ingram	Lyall	Gemmill	Spark
Nov 9	Aston Villa	Div 2	a	1-0	13374	Kelly	Ross	Smith	McNab	Hawkins	Knighton (1)	Temple	Spavin	Irvine	Ingram	Gemmill	Hughes *
Nov 16	Bristol City	Div 2	h	1-0	12325	Kelly	Ross	Ritchie	McNab	Hawkins	Knighton	Temple	Spavin *	Irvine	Ingram	Temple *	Lyall *
Nov 23	Sheffield Utd.	Div 2	a	0-4	15969	Kelly	Patrick	Ross	McNab	Hawkins	Knighton	Wilson	Gemmill	Irvine	Ingram	Wilson	Lee *
Nov 25	Fulham	Div 2	h	1-0	14730	Kelly	Patrick	Ross	McNab	Hawkins	Knighton	Hughes *	Lyall	Irvine	Ingram	Lee	Lee *
Nov 30	Bolton W.	Div 2	h	1-4	15242	Kelly	Ross	Smith	McNab	Hawkins	Knighton	Hughes	Irvine (1)	Ingram	Lyall	Gemmill	Lee
Dec 7	Oxford Utd.	Div 2	a	1-2	7005	Kelly	Ross	Bright	McNab	Hawkins	Knighton	Hughes	Lyall	Irvine	Ingram (1)	Lee	Gemmill
Dec 14	Derby County	Div 2	h	0-0	12648	Kelly	Ross	McNab *	Spark	Hawkins	Heppolette	Temple	Irvine	Ingram	Knighton	Lee	Gemmill *
Dec 20	Hull City	Div 2	a	1-1	15976	Kelly	Ross	McNab	Spark	Hawkins	Heppolette	Temple *	Irvine	Ingram (1)	Knighton	Lee	Gemmill
Dec 26	Blackburn R.	Div 2	a	0-1	21224	Kelly	Ross	McNab	Spark	Hawkins	Heppolette	Temple	Irvine	Ingram	Knighton	Lee	Gemmill
Jan 4	Nottm Forest Rd 3	FAC	h	3-0	20008	Kelly	Ross	McNab	Spark	Cranston	Heppolette	Temple (1)	Knighton	Irvine (2, 1p)	Ingram	Lee	Wilson
Jan 18	Aston Villa	Div 2	a	1-0	15252	Kelly	Ross	McNab (1)	Spark	Cranston	Heppolette	Temple	Knighton	Irvine	Ingram	Lee	Gemmill
Jan 25	Chelsea Rd 4	FAC	h	0-0	31875	Kelly	Ross	McNab	Spark	Cranston	Heppolette	Temple	Knighton	Irvine	Ingram	Lee	Gemmill
Feb 1	Bristol City	Div 2	a	1-2	13419	Kelly	Ross	McNab *	Spark	Cranston	Heppolette	Temple	Spavin	Ingram	Knighton	Lee (1)	Hawkins *
Feb 3	Chelsea Replay	FAC	a	1-2	36522	Kelly	Ross	Knighton	Spark	Hawkins	Heppolette	Temple	Spavin	Ingram (1)	Gemmill	Lee	Lloyd
Feb 22	Oxford Utd.	Div 2	h	2-1	10305	Kelly	Ross	McNab	Spark	Hawkins	Heppolette	Temple	Spavin	Ingram (1)	Knighton	Lee (1)	Gemmill
Feb 26	Fulham	Div 2	a	1-2	11726	Kelly	Ross	McNab	Spark (1)	Hawkins	Heppolette	Temple	Spavin	Ingram	Knighton	Lee	Hughes
Mar 1	Middlesbrough	Div 2	h	1-2	12520	Kelly	Ross	McNab	Spark	Hawkins	Heppolette	Spavin	Irvine	Ingram (1)	Knighton	Lee	Gemmill *
Mar 3	Millwall	Div 2	h	0-1	10884	Kelly	Ross	McNab	Spark	Hawkins	Heppolette *	Spavin	Irvine	Ingram	Knighton	Lee	Wilson
Mar 8	Huddersfield T.	Div 2	a	1-1	10281	Kelly	Ross	Knighton	Spark	McNab	Heppolette	Spavin	Irvine (1)	Ingram	Gemmill	Lee	Wilson
Mar 15	Cardiff City	Div 2	h	0-1	10752	Kelly	Ross	Knighton	Spark	McNab	Heppolette	Spavin	Irvine	Ingram	Gemmill	Lee	Hawkins
Mar 17	Sheffield Utd.	Div 2	h	2-2	8224	Kelly	Ross	Knighton *	Spark	McNab	Heppolette	Wilson (1)	Spavin	Irvine	Gemmill (1)	Lee	Wilson *
Mar 21	Birmingham City	Div 2	a	1-3	22020	Kelly	Ross	Knighton	Spark	McNab	Heppolette	Irvine *	Spavin	Irvine * (1)	Gemmill	Lee (1)	Hawkins *
Mar 29	Bury	Div 2	h	3-0	9467	Kelly	Ross	McNab	Spark *	Cranston	Knighton (1)	Spavin	Lloyd	Ingram (1)	Gemmill	Lee (1)	Heppolette *
Apr 5	Norwich City	Div 2	h	1-1	12169	Kelly	Ross	McNab *	Hawkins	Cranston	Knighton	Spavin	Irvine	Ingram	Gemmill (1)	Lee	Heppolette *
Apr 7	Carlisle Utd.	Div 2	a	0-1	7349	Kelly	Ross	Knighton	Hawkins	Cranston	Spavin	Heppolette	Temple	Irvine	Gemmill	Lee	Tinsley
Apr 8	Blackpool	Div 2	h	1-0	17233	Kelly	Ross	Knighton	Hawkins	Cranston	Heppolette	Temple (1)	Spavin	Irvine	Gemmill	Lee	Tinsley
Apr 12	Crystal Palace	Div 2	h	0-0	10245	Kelly	Ross	Patrick	Hawkins	Cranston	Knighton	Temple	Robinson	Irvine	Gemmill	Lee	Hughes
Apr 16	Bolton W.	Div 2	a	0-0	8028	Kelly	Ross	Knighton	Hawkins	Cranston	Heppolette	Hughes	Robinson	Irvine	Gemmill	Lee	Patrick
Apr 19	Charlton Ath.	Div 2	a	1-0	16362	Stewart	Ross	Knighton	Hawkins	Cranston	Heppolette	Hughes	Irvine (1)	Ingram	Gemmill	Lee	Patrick

SEASON 1969–1970

Preston North End's decline in the late 1960s came to a head in this, the last season of the decade, when the relegation that had threatened over the previous few years finally happened. For the first time in their history the club would have to play in the Third Division. One of North End's faithful fans summed the season up in a nutshell when he was reported to have said, 'Preston started badly, and fell away!'. Just two wins in their first 14 league and cup games was the dismal run up until the October and the team never recovered from this awful start. With no new players coming in to boost the squad in the summer of 1969, hopes were not optimistic amongst the supporters. Defensively North End weren't too bad, but up front and in midfield there was no fire and little fight. The Willie Irvine and Gerry Ingram partnership produced very little although the blame could not entirely be put on their shoulders. The midfield was sterile, lacking in imagination or flair and without the necessary guile to break down the strong Second Division defenders. Alan Spavin and Archie Gemmill worked hard but too many players had poor runs of form at the same time. Dave Wilson went right off

the boil, Derek Temple reached the end of his career and even George Ross and John Ritchie looked to be struggling at full-back, both losing their place in the side as the season progressed. Ricky Heppolette and Alex Spark were certainly learning their trade in the most difficult of circumstances although both youngsters showed talent and character. Two players who shone most consistently were Alan Kelly, in goal, and Bill Cranston at centre-half. The former Blackpool player showed such wholehearted committment in the 20 games he played that the fans elected him their player of a most depressing year. The cups brought no respite from the gloom. The League Cup came and went without so much as a goal and the FA Cup was over at the first hurdle despite Preston holding Derby to a 1–1 draw at Deepdale. In the league run-in a storming win over Charlton in mid-March gave the fans some hope but it proved to be a flash in the pan as in the seven games that remained after that Preston failed to register a single win. It meant an end to Second Division football for the Lilywhites for awhile and in 1970, after 70 Football League seasons, Preston were relegated to the Third Division. It was obvious that the club would have to undergo some radical changes to try and stem the rot. Those changes began with the sacking of Bobby Seith as manager.

DEBUTANTS: (2) Alan Tinsley, Clive Clark.

LAST GAMES: (4) Cranston, Stewart, Temple, Tinsley.

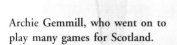

Archie Gemmill, who went on to play many games for Scotland.

STAT FACTS:
Best home run without defeat: 4 games
Best away run without defeat: 3 games
Longest run unbeaten: 6 games
Longest run without a win: 8 games
Best home attendance: 35,400 vs. Blackpool 13.4.70
Worst home attendance: 8,012 vs. Cardiff 20.4.70
Best away attendance: 25,432 vs. Derby Co. FAC 3.1.69
Worst away attendance: 7,474 vs. Hull 8.11.69
Aggregate and average home attendance: 285,002 – 13,572
Aggregate and average away attendance: 335,777 – 15,989

League position in Division Two: 22nd (Relegated) – P42 W8 D12 L22 F43 A63 Pts 28
Home: W7 D6 L8 F31 A28   Away: W1 D6 L14 F12 A35

Match Report: Tigers Claw Their Way Back – 21 Feb 1970 Preston 3 Hull City 3

Both sides were on edge in this relegation battle as whistle happy referee, Mr Jim Finney of Hereford, tried to control a niggly game which was littered with petty fouls. Although both sides were fearful of losing, the players still dished up an exciting six goal affair. Hull got off to a poor start in a comedy of errors type first half. Clark was the first to be spoken to for showing dissent at a decision against him, but the incident was quickly forgotten as North End took the lead after only four minutes play through Lloyd. The Hull defender, Greenwood, misjudged a clearance, leaving 19 year old Lloyd the chance to run on rounding goalkeeper McKechnie before slotting neatly home. The Tigers then had the lion's share of the game as they tried to level matters, but Greenwood shot woefully wide of the target with a volley as he tried to atone for his earlier error. Although Spavin and Gemmill kept probing away, the visitors conjured up an equaliser after 19 minutes as a low shot from Simpkin was luckily deflected through a ruck of defenders. On 34 minutes it was North End's turn to have a touch of luck as Hull's centre-half, Wilson conceded an own goal, sliding the ball past McKechnie whilst under pressure from Lloyd. This incident rekindled North End's appetite for the game and Gemmill covered the whole ground with his usual tenacity. Simpkin and Hawkins were both booked as the pressure mounted and both teams struggled for supremacy in the mud. Hull literally came out fighting in the second half, Clark being floored on numerous occasions and in their quest to avoid defeat Greenwood completed a miserable afternoon when he too was booked for a foul on Tinsley. Hull then equalised on the half hour mark through Chilton who immediately after his goal also hit the bar. After this let off Preston amazingly regained the lead with a 71st minute goal by Spark. But before the cheering had died away Hull's Wagstaffe, a tricky customer throughout, equalised yet again from a well taken opportunist goal. The point gained by Hull proved more vital for them than the one gained by North End at the final reckoning.

League appearances (42 games)

Clark C. 13, Cranston W. 16 + 1, Gemmill A. 39, Hawkins G. N. 41, Heppolette R. A. W. 39 + 1, Hughes D. R. 1, Ingram G. 18 + 1, Irvine W. J. 16 + 3, Kelly J. A. 41, Lee F. 19 + 4, Lloyd N. W. M. 12 + 1, Lyall G. 2 + 3, McNab J. 30, Patrick 11, Ritchie J. 32, Ross G. 31, Spark A. M. 14 + 1, Spavin A. 32, Stewart G. 1, Temple D. W. 21 + 1, Tinsley A. 8 + 1, Wilson D. C. 25.

FA Cup appearances (2 games)

Kelly 2, Ross 2, Ritchie 2, Heppolette 2, Cranston 2, McNab 2, Lyall 1, Spark 1, Spavin 2, Hawkins 2, Gemmill 2, Temple 2, Lloyd 0 + 1.

League Cup appearances (1 game)

Kelly, Ross, Ritchie, Heppolette, Cranston, Hawkins, Wilson, Irvine, Ingram, Gemmill, Lee, all one each.

Goalscorers: 43 League–2 FAC–(Total 45)

Gemmill 6–0 (6), Irvine 5 (1 pen)–0 (5), Lloyd 5–0 (5), Ingram 4–0 (4), Temple 4–0 (4), Hawkins 3 (1 pen)–1 (4), Heppolette 2–0 (2), Lee 2–0 (2), Clark 1–0 (1), Ritchie 1–0 (1), Wilson 1–0 (1), Spavin 1–0 (1), McNab 1–0 (1), Spark 1–0 (1), Tinsley 1–0 (1), Patrick 1–0 (1), Lyall 0–1 (1), Own goals 4–0 (4), Hockey of Birmingham, Trollope of Swindon, Smithson of Oxford and Wilson of Hull.

Future Players born between August 1969 and July 1970: Nigel Jemson, Barry Richardson, Graham Easter, Gary Walker, Deniol Graham, Steven Anderton, Lennie Johnrose, Dean Barrick, Mark Rankine, Darren Patterson, Steven Greaves, Steve Woods, Julian James, Jon Davidson, Liam Watson, Pat Scully.
Ever presents: None
Hat-tricks: None
FA Cup: Third Round Replay
League Cup: First Round
Manager: Bobby Seith
Chairman: T. C. Nicholson Esq. JP FCIOB
Players used: 22
Leading scorer: 6 goals – Archie Gemmill
(all League)

OFFICIAL PLAYER OF THE SEASON:
Bill Cranston

Season 1969–70: Second Division						
	P	W	D	L	F	A	Pts
1 Huddersfield	42	24	12	6	68	37	60
2 Blackpool	42	20	13	9	56	45	53
3 Leicester	42	19	13	10	64	50	51
4 Middlesbrough	42	20	10	12	55	45	50
5 Swindon	42	17	16	9	57	47	50
6 Sheffield United	42	22	5	15	73	38	49
7 Cardiff	42	18	13	11	61	41	49
3 Blackburn	42	20	7	15	54	50	47
9 QPR	42	17	11	14	66	57	45
10 Millwall	42	15	14	13	56	56	44
11 Norwich	42	16	11	15	49	46	43
12 Carlisle	42	14	13	15	58	56	41
13 Hull	42	15	11	16	72	70	41
14 Bristol City	42	13	13	16	54	50	39
15 Oxford	42	12	15	15	35	42	39
16 Bolton	42	12	12	18	54	61	36
17 Portsmouth	42	13	9	20	66	80	35
18 Birmingham	42	11	11	20	51	78	33
19 Watford	42	9	13	20	44	57	31
20 Charlton	42	7	17	18	35	76	31
21 Aston Villa	42	8	13	21	36	62	29
22 PRESTON	**42**	**8**	**12**	**22**	**43**	**63**	**28**

Derby County Football Club Ltd.
SEASON 1969—1970

F.A. CUP—3rd ROUND REPLAY
DERBY COUNTY
versus
PRESTON NORTH END
WEDNESDAY, 7th JANUARY, 1970
Kick-off 7.30 p.m.

OFFICIAL PROGRAMME
1/–

1969–70: Full playing and coaching staff.

Date 1969-70	Opponents	Comp	h or a	Score	Att.	1	2	3	4	5	6	7	8	9	10	11	12 *Sub Used		
Aug 9	Charlton Ath.	Div 2	a	1-2	13599	Kelly	Ross	Ritchie	Heppolette (1)	Cranston	Hawkins	Wilson	Irvine	Ingram	Gemmill	Lee	Lyall		
Aug 13	Bury Rd 1	LC	h	0-1	9021	Kelly	Ross	Ritchie	Heppolette	Cranston	Hawkins	Wilson	Irvine	Ingram	Gemmill	Lee	Lyall		
Aug 16	QPR	Div 2	a	0-0	11179	Kelly	Ross	Ritchie	Heppolette	Cranston	Hawkins	Hughes *	Lyall	Irvine	Gemmill	Wilson	Lee *		
Aug 19	Huddersfield T.	Div 2	a	2-3	13050	Kelly	Ross	Ritchie	Heppolette	Cranston	Hawkins	Wilson	Irvine (2, 1p)	Ingram	Gemmill	Lee	McNab		
Aug 23	Bolton W.	Div 2	a	0-2	14702	Kelly	Ross	Ritchie	Heppolette	Hawkins	McNab	Wilson	Irvine	Ingram	Gemmill	Lee	Cranston		
Aug 25	Watford	Div 2	h	3-0	10416	Kelly	Ross	Ritchie (1)	Heppolette	Hawkins	McNab	Wilson	Irvine (1)	Ingram (1)	Gemmill	Lee	Cranston		
Aug 30	Oxford Utd.	Div 2	a	0-1	10058	Kelly	Ross	Ritchie	Heppolette *	Hawkins	McNab	Wilson	Irvine	Ingram	Gemmill	Lee	Cranston *		
Sep 6	Bristol City	Div 2	h	0-0	13478	Kelly	Ross	Ritchie	Heppolette	Hawkins	McNab	Wilson	Irvine	Ingram	Gemmill	Lee	Lyall		
Sep 13	Blackburn R.	Div 2	h	0-0	17125	Kelly	Ross	Ritchie	Heppolette	Hawkins	McNab	Wilson	Irvine	Ingram	Spavin	Lee	Lyall		
Sep 15	Blackpool	Div 2	a	0-0	19708	Kelly	Ross	Ritchie	Heppolette	Hawkins	McNab	Wilson	Irvine	Ingram	Gemmill	Lee	Spavin		
Sep 20	Carlisle Utd.	Div 2	a	0-1	9782	Kelly	Ross	Ritchie	Heppolette	Hawkins	McNab	Wilson	Irvine	Ingram	Gemmill	Lee	Tinsley		
Sep 27	Sheffield Utd.	Div 2	h	2-1	11885	Kelly	Ross	Ritchie	Heppolette	Hawkins (1p)	McNab	Wilson (1)	Spavin	Tinsley	Gemmill	Temple	Lyall		
Oct 4	Aston Villa	Div 2	h	0-0	25421	Kelly	Ross	Ritchie	Heppolette	Hawkins	McNab	Wilson	Spavin	Tinsley *	Gemmill	Temple	Irvine *		
Oct 7	QPR	Div 2	h	0-0	21127	Kelly	Ross	Ritchie	Heppolette	Hawkins	McNab	Wilson	Spavin	Irvine	Gemmill	Temple	Ingram		
Oct 11	Leicester City	Div 2	h	2-1	14992	Kelly	Ross	Ritchie	Heppolette	Hawkins	McNab	Wilson	Spavin	Irvine	Gemmill (2)	Temple	Ingram		
Oct 18	Millwall	Div 2	h	1-1	12124	Kelly	Ross	Ritchie	Heppolette	Hawkins	McNab	Wilson	Spavin	Irvine	Gemmill (1)	Temple	Ingram		
Oct 25	Norwich City	Div 2	a	2-1	15566	Kelly	Ross	Ritchie	Heppolette	Hawkins	McNab	Wilson	Spavin (1)	Ingram (1)	Gemmill	Temple	Lyall		
Nov 1	Middlesbrough	Div 2	h	0-1	13075	Kelly	Ross	Ritchie	Heppolette	Hawkins	McNab	Wilson	Spavin	Ingram	Gemmill	Temple	Lyall		
Nov 8	Hull City	Div 2	a	1-3	7474	Kelly	Ross	Ritchie	Heppolette	Hawkins	McNab	Wilson	Ingram (1)	Ingram *	Gemmill	Temple *	Lyall *		
Nov 10	Huddersfield T.	Div 2	h	1-3	12795	Kelly	Ross	Ritchie	Heppolette	Hawkins	McNab	Wilson	Irvine	Ingram *	Gemmill (1)	Lyall	Lee *		
Nov 15	Birmingham City	Div 2	h	4-1	9692	Kelly	Ross	Ritchie	Heppolette	Hawkins	McNab	Wilson	Spavin	Irvine (2)	Gemmill	Lee (1)	Lyall *	1 og	(Hockey)
Nov 22	Cardiff City	Div 2	a	1-2	22678	Stewart	Ross	Ritchie	Heppolette *	Hawkins	McNab	Wilson	Spavin	Ingram (1)	Gemmill	Lee	Temple *		
Nov 29	Swindon Town	Div 2	h	3-1	9252	Kelly	Ross	Ritchie	Heppolette	Hawkins	McNab *	Wilson	Spavin	Ingram	Gemmill	Temple (2)	Lee *	1 og	(Trollope)
Dec 6	Portsmouth	Div 2	a	0-4	11121	Kelly	Ross	Ritchie	Heppolette	Hawkins	McNab	Wilson	Spavin	Ingram	Gemmill	Temple *	Lee *		
Dec 13	Blackburn R.	Div 2	a	2-4	16216	Kelly	Ross	Ritchie	Spark	Hawkins	Heppolette (1)	Wilson	Spavin	Ingram	Gemmill	Temple (1)	Lee		
Dec 26	Bolton W.	Div 2	h	1-3	23934	Kelly	Ross	Ritchie	Spark	Hawkins	McNab	Lee	Spavin	Temple	Gemmill (1)	Ingram	Spark		
Jan 3	Derby County Rd 3	FAC	h	1-1	21479	Kelly	Ross	Ritchie	Heppolette	Cranston	McNab	Lyall (1)	Spavin	Hawkins	Gemmill	Temple	Lee		
Jan 7	Derby County Replay	FAC	a	1-4	25432	Kelly	Ross	Ritchie	Heppolette	Cranston	McNab	Spark	Spavin	Hawkins (1)	Gemmill *	Temple	Lloyd *		
Jan 10	Carlisle Utd.	Div 2	a	3-1	9586	Kelly	Ross	Ritchie	Heppolette	Cranston	McNab (1)	Lee (1)	Spavin	Hawkins	Lloyd (1)	Temple	Tinsley		
Jan 17	Sheffield Utd.	Div 2	a	0-2	17143	Kelly	Ross	Ritchie	Heppolette	Cranston *	McNab	Lee	Spavin	Hawkins	Tinsley	Temple	Spark *		
Jan 24	Bristol City	Div 2	a	0-1	11045	Kelly	Ross	Ritchie	Heppolette	McNab	Spark	Lee	Spavin	Hawkins	Gemmill	Clark	Tinsley		
Jan 31	Aston Villa	Div 2	a	1-1	14182	Kelly	Ross	Ritchie	Heppolette	McNab	Spark	Tinsley	Spavin	Hawkins (1)	Gemmill	Clark *	Ingram *		
Feb 18	Oxford Utd.	Div 2	a	1-3	8897	Kelly	Ross	Ritchie	Spark	McNab	Heppolette	Spavin	Lloyd	Hawkins	Gemmill	Clark	Lyall	1 og	(Smithson)
Feb 21	Hull City	Div 2	h	3-3	10038	Kelly	Ross	Ritchie	Spark (1)	McNab	Hawkins	Clark	Spavin	Tinsley	Lloyd (1)	Gemmill	Lyall	1 og	(Wilson)
Feb 25	Leicester City	Div 2	a	0-3	21973	Kelly	Patrick	Ritchie	Spark	Cranston	Hawkins	Clark	Spavin	Tinsley	Lloyd	Gemmill	Heppolette		
Feb 28	Middlesbrough	Div 2	a	1-1	25050	Kelly	Patrick	Heppolette	Spark	Cranston	Hawkins	Lee	Spavin	Tinsley (1)	Gemmill	Clark *	Lyall *		
Mar 14	Swindon Town	Div 2	a	0-1	17668	Kelly	Patrick	Heppolette	Spark	Cranston	Hawkins	Lloyd	Spavin	Tinsley	Gemmill	Clark	Ingram		
Mar 16	Charlton Ath.	Div 2	h	4-1	14667	Kelly	Patrick	Heppolette	Spark	Cranston	Hawkins	Clark	Spavin	Temple (1)	Lloyd (2)	Gemmill (1)	McNab		
Mar 21	Portsmouth	Div 2	h	1-2	12461	Kelly	Patrick	Heppolette	Spark	Cranston	Hawkins	Clark *	Spavin	Temple	Lloyd *	Gemmill	Lee *		
Mar 28	Birmingham City	Div 2	a	0-1	16469	Kelly	Patrick	McNab *	Spark	Cranston	Hawkins	Clark	Spavin	Temple	Lloyd	Gemmill	Heppolette *		
Mar 30	Millwall	Div 2	a	1-2	9419	Kelly	Patrick	Heppolette	Spark	Cranston	Hawkins (1)	Clark	Spavin	Temple *	Lloyd	Gemmill	Lyall *		
Mar 31	Norwich City	Div 2	h	1-1	13084	Kelly	Patrick	Heppolette	Spark	Cranston	Hawkins	Clark	Spavin	Temple	Lloyd (1)	Gemmill	Lyall		
Apr 4	Watford	Div 2	a	0-0	15236	Kelly	Patrick	Heppolette	Spavin	Cranston	McNab	Lee	Lloyd	Temple	Gemmill	Clark *	Irvine *		
Apr 13	Blackpool	Div 2	h	0-3	35400	Kelly	Patrick	McNab	Hawkins	Cranston	Heppolette	Lee *	Spavin	Lloyd	Gemmill	Temple	Irvine *		
Apr 20	Cardiff City	Div 2	h	1-2	8012	Kelly	Patrick (1)	Heppolette	Spark	Cranston	McNab	Wilson	Spavin	Irvine *	Gemmill	Lee	Lloyd *		

Trivia Facts:

16 year old goalkeeper, Jim Blyth, was named 'Young Player of the Season'.

Preston received the Third Division Championship trophy from Bob Lord of the Football League in front of thousands on the balcony of the Harris Library. The crowd, amongst other things sang, 'Eee aye addio Sir Alan Ball!'

Alan Kelly was presented with a Connemara marble statuette by the Eire FA for winning more caps than any other goalkeeper.

BBC's Match of the Day cameras were at Bristol Rovers to see Preston's 0–0 draw. In the match viewers and fans were able to see Alan Ball's clever free-kick routine for the first time in which Preston built a wall in front of the Rovers wall. Although they didn't score it was the main talking point of the programme.

Keith Douglas, a 19 year old West Indian forward was coming to Deepdale on a four month trial and arrived at Preston Docks on the Geest Banana Boat which brought him from St Lucia. Chairman Tom Nicholson and Director Cyril Pilkington met him, Pilkington being the shipping manager of Geest Industries Ltd.

The radical change, so desperately sought at the end of the 1969–70 season came in the shape of new manager, Alan Ball, father of the Everton and England World Cup winning midfield star. In an amazing season, the genial Ball Senior took virtually the same players, as had been relegated, to the Third Division Championship, and promotion at the first attempt. No new players came in during the Summer of 1970, but the manager found the right blend and balance almost immediately and for once Preston began the campaign well and sustained their form. Goals were scored more freely with Gerry Ingram suddenly finding his shooting boots at last. The blond striker had a fine season with an early hat-trick against Reading giving him the confidence he needed. That was in the September and a month later Ball pulled off a marvellous signing, using some of the money from the sale of Archie Gemmill to Derby County. In came Bobby Ham from Bradford City and the little Yorkshireman was an instant hit, scoring on his debut at Plymouth and going on to form an excellent partnership with Ingram. Ham has to go down as one of Preston's best ever short term signings and he certainly played a big part in this promotion side. But this was a year of other consistent star performers. Alan Kelly was magnificent, George Ross back to his best, Jim McNab outstanding and Graham Hawkins, Alex Spark and Ricky Heppollette (pictured) playing very well too. But head and shoulders above all others was the brilliant Alan Spavin. The midfield player was adjudged Third Division Player of the Year and never was the award more merited. 'Spav' was also accorded the North End Player of the Year award and it was fitting that he should score two goals in the final game of the season at Deepdale in front of a near 30,000 crowd. After Preston had kept in the running with a series of good results they suddenly found life difficult around Easter. It enabled Fulham to take control and when the clubs met at Craven Cottage in the penultimate game Fulham could have taken the title with a draw. But North End showed all the skill and character that their manager had instilled into them from day one. In front of the BBC's Match of the Day cameras Preston earned a superb 1–0 win thanks to a great diving header by Heppollette. The Londoners were gutted as three days later Preston beat Rotherham 3–0 at Deepdale and the Championship belonged to North End. In the cups Preston had again disappointed but that could be forgiven as promotion was absolutely vital for the club. With 'The Gentry', as the travelling fans were christened, in full voice on that May evening everything at the club looked rosy again. How long that feeling would last was anybody's guess, but enjoying the moment was priority at this time.

DEBUTANTS: (3) John McMahon, Bobby Ham, John Bird.

LAST GAMES: (5) Lee, Patrick, Gemmill, Irvine, Lloyd.

League appearances (46 games)

Bird J. C. 7, Clark C. 33, Gemmill A. 7, Ham R. S. 30, Hawkins G. N. 46, Heppollette R. A. W. 38 + 2, Hughes D. R. 13 + 6, Ingram G. 39 + 1, Irvine W. J. 13 + 1, Kelly J. A. 46, Lee F. 6 + 2, Lloyd N. W. M. 4 + 1, Lyall G. 27, McMahon J. J. 11, McNab J. 39, Ross G. 43, Spark A. M. 42, Spavin A. 41, Wilson D. C. 21 + 6.

FA Cup appearances (2 games)

Kelly 2, Ross 1, Patrick 1, McMahon 1, McNab 1, Spark 2, Hawkins 2, Spavin 2, Wilson 1, Hughes 1, Ham 2, Ingram 2, Heppollette 2, Clark 2, Lyall 0 + 2.

League Cup appearances (3 games)

Kelly 3, Ross 3, McNab 2, Spark 3, Hawkins 3, Heppollette 3, Wilson 3, Irvine 3, Gemmill 2, Hughes 2, Ingram 3, Clark 0 + 1, Lee 0 + 1, Spavin 2, McMahon 1.

Goalscorers: 63 League–1 FAC–4 LC–(Total 68)

Ingram 22 (1 pen)–0–2 (24), Ham 11–0–0 (11), Heppollette 8–1–0 (9), Lyall 5–0–0 (5), Spavin 4–0–1 (5), Wilson 3–0–0 (3), Clark 4–0–0 (4), Irvine 1–0–1 (2), Spark 1–0–0 (1), McNab 1–0–0 (1), Lloyd 1–0–0 (1), Own goals 2–0–0 (2), Robertson of Doncaster and Crossley of Tranmere.

Preston's manager, Mr Alan Ball, with the Third Division Championship Trophy.

Match Report: Heads We Win! – 1 May 1971. Fulham 0 Preston 1

This game lived up to all its pre-match billing, being played in a cup final atmosphere in front of the Match of the Day cameras, with the Championship of the Third Division depending on the result. Fulham, the favourites who had been in pole position for 24 weeks of the season, only needed a draw, and with their record of 24 wins and 19 clean sheets, everyone south of Watford expected them to succeed. Both teams were given a tremendous reception as they came out with Preston looking colourful as the sun caught their red shirts for this May Day showdown. Fulham were first to show their attacking flair but Preston were far from being overawed as Hawkins showed when he headed inches over the crossbar from a Clark corner. The North End, after a composed start, then took the game to their hosts with Clark, Spavin, and Heppolette forcing the pace. Ross and Kelly were solid at the back with Ross even finding time and space to go on a couple of dangerous sorties down the right wing. The team reaped their just reward for this positive approach on 22 minutes after winning another corner on the right. Clark accurately placed the ball to the near post where the ball was flicked on. Heppolette anticipating the training ground move and ran unopposed into the space where the ball was dropping, and with a full length dive scored with a superb flying header. A goal that would be etched into the memory for many a long year. This strike stirred the Cottagers into action and for a lengthy period they tested the likes of Hawkins, Bird and McNab, but the visitors from Deepdale proved more than a match for their opponents. The division's best attack was being stifled by the division's meanest defence as the first half ended. Kelly showed his ability during the second half as Fulham mounted a 'nothing-to-lose' effort in an effort to equalise, which in turn would have given them the Championship. But Alan Ball's team were having none of it and against all the odds the Preston players pulled off a tremendous victory. The scenes of jubilation at the end were unforgettable as Ball hugged each one of his players in turn. Their night of glory then came three days later as a Deepdale victory over Rotherham clinched the Championship for North End and their ecstatic fans.

STAT FACTS:
Best home run without defeat: 23 games
Best away run without defeat: 6 games
Longest run unbeaten: 14 games
Longest run without a win: 7 games
Best home attendance: 28,224 vs. Rotherham 4.5.71
Worst home attendance: 7,957 vs. Bristol Rovers 29.8.70
Best away attendance: 26,139 vs. Aston Villa 19.9.70
Worst away attendance: 4,353 vs. Stockport LC 19.8.70
Aggregate and average home attendance: 316,485 – 13,760
Aggregate and average away attendance: 218,960 – 9,520

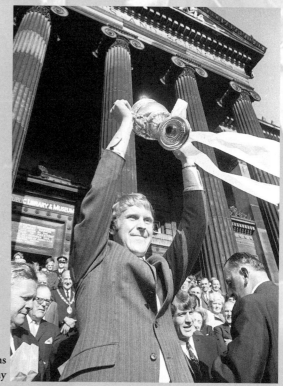

Graham Hawkins lifts the trophy

Future Players born between August 1970 and July 1971:
Richard Lucas, Andy Gill, Simon Davey, Paul Masefield, Adrian Hughes, Kurt Nogan, Tony Lormor, Martin James, Tim Allpress, Kevin Magee, Allan Johnson, Habib Sissoko

Ever presents: (2) Kelly, Hawkins   **Manager:** Alan Ball
Hat-tricks: (1) Ingram   **FA Cup:** First Round Replay
League Cup: Third Round   **Players used:** 20
Chairman: T. C. Nicholson Esq. JP FCIOB
Leading scorer: 24 goals – Gerry Ingram
(22 League 2 LC)
OFFICIAL PLAYER OF THE SEASON:
Alan Spavin

Date 1970-1	Opponents	Comp	h or a	Score	Att.	1	2	3	4	5	6	7	8	9	10	11	12 *Sub Used		
Aug 15	Halifax Town	Div 3	h	1-1	9646	Kelly	Ross	McNab	Spark	Hawkins	Heppolette (1)	Wilson	Lyall *	Irvine	Gemmill	Hughes	Ingram *		
Aug 19	Stockport Co. Rd 1	LC	a	1-0	4353	Kelly	Ross	McNab	Spark	Hawkins	Heppolette	Wilson	Gemmill	Ingram	Irvine (1)	Hughes	Lyall		
Aug 22	Torquay Utd.	Div 3	a	1-3	5908	Kelly	Ross	McNab	Spark	Hawkins	Heppolette	Hughes *	Gemmill	Ingram (1)	Irvine	Clark	Wilson *		
Aug 29	Bristol Rovers	Div 3	h	3-2	7957	Kelly	Ross	McNab	Spark	Hawkins	Heppolette	Hughes	Gemmill	Ingram (2)	Irvine (1)	Clark	Wilson		
Aug 31	Wrexham	Div 3	h	3-2	10653	Kelly	Ross	McNab	Spark (1)	Hawkins	Heppolette	Hughes	Gemmill	Ingram (2)	Irvine	Clark *	Wilson *		
Sep 5	Port Vale	Div 3	a	0-1	6954	Kelly	Ross	McNab	Spark	Hawkins	Heppolette	Hughes *	Gemmill	Ingram	Irvine	Clark	Wilson *		
Sep 9	Torquay Utd. Rd 2	LC	a	3-1	6339	Kelly	Ross	McNab	Spark	Hawkins	Heppolette *	Wilson	Irvine	Ingram (2)	Spavin (1)	Gemmill	Lee		
Sep 12	Reading	Div 3	h	4-1	9357	Kelly	Ross	McNab	Spark	Hawkins	Spavin	Wilson (1)	Gemmill	Ingram (3)	Irvine	Lee	Lyall		
Sep 19	Aston Villa	Div 3	a	0-2	26139	Kelly	Ross	McNab	Spark	Hawkins	Spavin	Wilson	Gemmill	Ingram	Irvine	Lee	Heppolette		
Sep 22	Bury	Div 3	a	1-0	5821	Kelly	Ross	McNab	Spark	Hawkins	Heppolette	Wilson	Spavin	Ingram (1)	Irvine	Hughes	Lee		
Sep 26	Fulham	Div 3	h	1-1	12103	Kelly	Ross	McNab (1)	Spark	Hawkins	Spavin	Wilson	Irvine	Ingram	Heppolette	Hughes	Lee		
Sep 30	Shrewsbury T.	Div 3	a	1-0	8026	Kelly	Ross	McNab	Spark	Hawkins	Spavin	Wilson	Lee	Ingram	Heppolette (1)	Hughes	Irvine		
Oct 3	Bradford City	Div 3	a	2-0	7259	Kelly	Ross	McNab	Spark	Hawkins	Spavin	Wilson (1)	Irvine	Ingram (1)	Heppolette	Hughes	Schofield		
Oct 6	WBA Rd 3	LC	h	0-1	18222	Kelly	Ross	McMahon	Spark	Hawkins	Spavin	Wilson	Irvine	Ingram *	Heppolette	Hughes	Clark *		
Oct 10	Mansfield Town	Div 3	h	2-1	12052	Kelly	Ross	McNab *	Spark	Hawkins	Spavin	Wilson	Lee	Irvine	Heppolette (2)	Hughes	Lloyd *		
Oct 17	Halifax Town	Div 3	a	0-1	5922	Kelly	Ross	McMahon	Spark	Hawkins	Spavin	Wilson	Lee	Ingram	Heppolette	Hughes *	Lee *		
Oct 19	Swansea City	Div 3	h	1-1	10328	Kelly	Ross	McMahon	Spark	Hawkins	Spavin	Wilson	Lloyd *	Ingram (1)	Heppolette	Clark	Irvine *		
Oct 24	Plymouth Arg.	Div 3	h	1-1	9628	Kelly	Ross	McMahon	Spark	Hawkins	Spavin	Wilson	Ham (1)	Ingram	Heppolette	Clark *	Lee *		
Oct 31	Brighton	Div 3	h	1-1	12567	Kelly	Ross	McMahon	Spark	Hawkins	Spavin	Wilson	Ham (1)	Ingram	Heppolette	Lee	Ll0yd		
Nov 6	Doncaster R.	Div 3	a	1-1	5300	Kelly	Ross	McMahon	Spark	Hawkins	Spavin	Wilson	Ham	Ingram	Lyall	Lee *	Hughes	1 og	(Robertson)
Nov 9	Barnsley	Div 3	h	3-1	11053	Kelly	Ross	McMahon	Spark	Hawkins	Spavin	Wilson	Ham (1)	Ingram (1)	Lyall (1)	Clark	Lee		
Nov 14	Rochdale	Div 3	h	3-1	13460	Kelly	Ross	McMahon	Spark	Hawkins	Spavin	Wilson * (1)	Ham (1)	Ingram	Lyall (1)	Clark	Heppolette *		
Nov 21	Chester Rd 1	FAC	h	1-1	15023	Kelly	Ross *	McMahon	Spark	Hawkins	Spavin	Wilson	Ham	Ingram	Heppolette (1)	Clark	Lyall *		
Nov 25	Chester Replay	FAC	a	0-1	11164	Kelly	Patrick	McNab	Spark	Hawkins	Spavin	Hughes	Ham	Ingram	Heppolette *	Clark	Lyall *		
Nov 28	Chesterfield	Div 3	a	0-0	10504	Kelly	Ross	McNab	Spark	Hawkins	Spavin	Wilson	Lyall	Ingram	Heppolette	Clark	Wilson		
Dec 5	Gillingham	Div 3	h	1-0	10274	Kelly	Ross	McNab	Spark	Hawkins	Spavin	Wilson	Ham (1)	Ingram	Lyall	Clark	Heppolette		
Dec 19	Torquay Utd.	Div 3	h	2-2	11637	Kelly	Ross	McNab	Spark	Hawkins	Spavin	Wilson	Ham *	Ingram (1)	Lyall (1)	Clark	Heppolette *		
Dec 26	Tranmere R.	Div 3	a	3-3	7130	Kelly	Ross	McNab	Spark	Hawkins	Spavin	Heppolette (1)	Irvine	Ingram	Lyall	Clark (1)	Hughes	1 og	(Crossley)
Jan 9	Shrewsbury T.	Div 3	h	2-0	11961	Kelly	McMahon	McNab	Spark	Hawkins	Spavin	Wilson	Ham	Ingram (2, 1p)	Lyall	Clark	Heppolette		
Jan 15	Swansea City	Div 3	a	2-2	12776	Kelly	Ross	McNab	Spark	Hawkins	Ham (1)	Heppolette	Ingram (1)	Lyall	Clark	Wilson		
Jan 27	Walsall	Div 3	a	1-0	6435	Kelly	Ross	McNab	Spark	Hawkins	Spavin	Ham	Heppolette	Ingram	Lyall (1)	Hughes	Wilson		
Jan 30	Chesterfield	Div 3	h	1-0	14020	Kelly	Ross	McNab	Spark	Hawkins	Spavin	Ham	Heppolette	Ingram (1)	Lyall	Hughes	Wilson		
Feb 6	Gillingham	Div 3	a	1-2	4798	Kelly	Ross	McNab	McMahon	Hawkins	Spavin	Ham	Heppolette	Ingram (1)	Lyall	Clark	Hughes		
Feb 13	Walsall	Div 3	h	1-0	11540	Kelly	Ross	McNab	Spark	Hawkins	Heppolette	Ham (1)	Ingram	Lyall *	Clark	Hughes *		
Feb 20	Barnsley	Div 3	a	1-0	6619	Kelly	McMahon	McNab	Spark	Hawkins	Heppolette	Ham (1)	Ingram	Lyall	Clark *	Hughes *		
Feb 27	Brighton	Div 3	a	0-0	9957	Kelly	McMahon	McNab	Spark	Hawkins	Heppolette	Ham	Ingram	Lyall	Clark	Hughes		
Mar 6	Plymouth Arg.	Div 3	a	1-0	12621	Kelly	Ross	McNab	Spark	Hawkins	Heppolette	Ham	Ingram	Lyall	Clark	Hughes		
Mar 8	Bury	Div 3	h	2-0	17136	Kelly	Ross	McNab	Spark	Hawkins	Spavin (1)	Heppolette	Ham	Ingram	Lyall	Clark (1)	Hughes		
Mar 13	Rochdale	Div 3	a	2-1	10249	Kelly	Ross	McNab	Spark	Hawkins	Spavin	Heppolette (1)	Ham	Ingram (1)	Lyall	Clark	Hughes		
Mar 16	Rotherham Utd.	Div 3	a	1-1	8291	Kelly	Ross	McNab	Spark	Hawkins	Spavin (1)	Heppolette	Ham	Ingram	Lyall	Clark	Hughes		
Mar 20	Doncaster R.	Div 3	h	4-0	14613	Kelly	Ross	McNab	Spark *	Hawkins	Spavin	Heppolette	Ham (1)	Ingram (1)	Lyall (1)	Clark (1)	Hughes *		
Mar 27	Port Vale	Div 3	h	1-0	16591	Kelly	Ross	McNab	Spark	Hawkins	Spavin	Heppolette	Ham	Ingram (1)	Lyall	Clark	Hughes		
Apr 3	Bristol Rovers	Div 3	a	0-0	10802	Kelly	Ross	McNab	Bird	Hawkins	Spavin	Heppolette	Ham	Ingram	Lyall	Clark	Hughes *		
Apr 10	Tranmere R.	Div 3	h	1-1	17382	Kelly	Ross	McNab	Bird	Hawkins	Spavin	Heppolette (1)	Ham	Ingram *	Lyall	Clark	Hughes *		
Apr 12	Reading	Div 3	a	0-1	7821	Kelly	Ross	McNab	Bird	Hawkins	Spavin *	Heppolette	Ham	Ingram	Lyall	Clark	Wilson *		
Apr 13	Bradford City	Div 3	h	1-1	18694	Kelly	Ross	McNab	Spark	Hawkins	Spavin	Heppolette	Ham (1)	Ingram	Lyall	Clark	Wilson *		
Apr 17	Mansfield Town	Div 3	a	1-3	7185	Kelly	Ross	McNab	Spark	Hawkins	Spavin	Heppolette	Ham *	Ingram (1)	Lyall	Clark	Wilson *		
Apr 24	Aston Villa	Div 3	h	0-0	22616	Kelly	Ross	McNab	Bird	Hawkins	Spavin	Heppolette	Wilson	Ham	Spark	Clark	Lloyd		
Apr 26	Wrexham	Div 3	a	1-1	9662	Kelly	Ross	McNab	Bird	Hawkins	Spavin	Heppolette	Wilson	Lloyd (1)	Spark	Clark	Lyall		
May 1	Fulham	Div 3	a	1-0	25774	Kelly	Ross	McNab	Bird	Hawkins	Spavin	Heppolette (1)	Ham	Lloyd	Spark	Clark	Wilson		
May 4	Rotherham Utd.	Div 3	h	3-0	28224	Kelly	Ross	McNab	Bird	Hawkins	Spavin (2)	Heppolette	Ham	Lloyd	Spark	Clark (1)	Wilson		

Season 1970–71: Third Division

		P	W	D	L	F	A	Pts
1	PRESTON	46	22	17	7	63	39	61
2	Fulham	46	24	12	10	68	41	60
3	Halifax	46	22	12	12	74	55	56
4	Aston Villa	46	19	15	12	54	46	53
5	Chesterfield	46	17	17	12	66	38	51
8	Bristol Rovers	46	19	13	14	69	50	51
7	Mansfield	46	18	15	13	64	62	51
8	Rotherham	46	17	16	13	64	60	50
9	Wrexham	46	18	13	15	72	65	49
10	Torquay	46	19	11	16	54	57	49
11	Swansea	46	15	16	15	59	56	46
12	Barnsley	46	17	11	18	49	52	45
13	Shrewsbury	46	16	13	17	58	62	45
14	Brighton	46	14	16	16	50	47	44
15	Plymouth	46	12	19	15	63	63	43
16	Rochdale	46	14	15	17	61	68	43
17	Port Vale	46	15	12	19	52	59	42
18	Tranmere	46	10	22	14	45	55	42
19	Bradford City	46	13	14	19	49	62	40
20	Walsall	46	14	11	21	51	57	39
21	Reading	46	14	11	21	48	85	39
22	Bury	46	12	13	21	52	60	37
23	Doncaster	46	13	9	24	45	66	35
24	Gillingham	46	10	13	23	42	67	33

Gerry Ingram.
Splendid season
from the
blond striker.

League position in Division Three: Champions – P46 W22 D17 L7 F63 A39 Pts 61
Home: W15 D8 L0 F42 A16   Away: W7 D9 L7 F21 A23

SEASON 1971–1972

The gulf in standard between the Third and Second division, even in 1971, was very noticeable and it was obvious from the outset that manager Alan Ball would have to bring in new players to meet the challenge. Hugh McIlmoyle, a much travelled and experienced striker, was brought in from Middlesbrough, but other than that Ball was too rely on the side which so gloriously won promotion. North End made a good start in the league and progressed in the League Cup, but as the weeks turned into months the quality of the division began to stretch Preston. Up to Christmas everything went reasonably well. Good crowds at Deepdale and some excellent results which included a very narrow defeat by Tottenham in a fourth round League Cup replay. The game went to extra-time before Spurs snatched victory. It had been Preston's best showing in that competition for a number of years. However, a New Year's Day defeat at Charlton heralded the start of a very poor run of results. Only a win over Bristol City in the FA Cup relieved the pressure, especially as that win gave Preston a glamour home tie with Manchester United. Over 37,000 people crammed into Deepdale for that match which despite a good battle was lost 2–0. After that game it was a case of dropping down the league like a stone as a series of defeats, some of them heavy, threatened North End with relegation again. Luckily the points accumulated before Christmas proved enough. The away form was awful and only one win away from Deepdale told its own story. The fans were not happy with that and suddenly Alan Ball was coming under pressure. Three new players were signed and Ball was never afraid to blood some of his youngsters coming up through the reserves. The Manchester City pair of David Connor and Neil Young looked costly signings but Alan Tarbuck from Chester quickly became a crowd favourite. As ever there were other notable individual performances, with John Bird, Alan Kelly, Alan Spavin and John McMahon doing particularly well. George Lyall began to blossom into a very good player and Graham Hawkins had another good season. Preston's problem seemed to be their inability to put together a lengthy unbeaten run, especially away from home, and also that players could not sustain their best form. There was no doubt that the poor run of results in the second half of the season were causing concern and it was the opinion of the fans that new signings were essential in the summer of 1971. Whether the Board could find the extra money to finance such deals was another matter altogether.

DEBUTANTS: (8) Hugh McIlmoyle, Alan Tarbuck, Alan Lamb, Dave Connor, Neil Young, Jim Blyth, Alex Bruce, Gary Williams.

LAST GAMES: (6) Lyall, Hughes, Ritchie, Ingram, Ham, Blyth.

League appearances (42 games)

Bird J.C. 42, Blyth J.A. 1, Brown J.C. 5, Bruce A.R. 1, Clark C. 19, Connor D.R. 14, Ham R.S. 13, Hawkins G.N. 38, Heppolette R.A.W. 36, Hughes D.R. 0 + 2, Ingram G. 18 + 1, Kelly J.A. 36, Lamb A.D. 7 + 2, Lyall G. 34 + 2, McIlmoyle H. 35, McMahon J.J. 32, McNab J. 25, Ritchie J. 12, Ross G. 3, Spark A.M. 19 + 8, Spavin A. 36, Tarbuck A.D. 19 + 4, Williams G.P. 1, Wilson D.C. 2 + 3, Young N.J. 14.

FA Cup appearances (2 games)

Kelly 2, McNab 2, Bird 2, Hawkins 1, Spavin 2, Heppolette 2, McIlmoyle 2, Spark 1, Clark 1, McMahon 2, Lyall 2, Ingram 2, Connor 1.

League Cup appearances (6 games)

Kelly 5, Brown 1, Ross 1, McNab 2, Bird 6, Hawkins 6, Spavin 6, Heppolette 6, Ham 4, McIlmoyle 6, Spark 2, Clark 5, Wilson 0 + 1, McMahon 4, Lyall 5, Ritchie 4, Ingram 3 + 1.

Goalscorers: 52 League–4 FAC–8 LC–(Total 64)

McIlmoyle 10 (2 pens)–0–3 (13), Tarbuck 10–0–0 (10), Ingram 8 (1 pen)–1–0 (9), Lyall 6 (1 pen)–1–1 (8), Clark 5–2–0 (7), Ham 4–0–1 (5), Young 3–0–0 (3), Spavin 1–0–2 (3), Heppolette 2–0–0 (2), Spark 1–0–0 (1), Bird 1–0–0 (1), Lamb 1–0–0 (1). Own goals 0–0–1 (1) Clarke of Barrow in LC.

Future Players born between August 1971 and July 1972: Matt Lambert, Ryan Kidd, Matt Jackson, Graeme Atkinson, Colin Taylor, Steve Holmes, Mark Sale, Neil Whitworth, Nathan Peel, Graham Alexander

Ever presents: (1) Bird   Players used: 25
Hat-tricks: None
FA Cup: Fourth Round
League Cup: Fourth Round Replay
Manager: Alan Ball
Chairman: T. C. Nicholson Esq. JP FCIOB
Leading scorer: 13 goals – Hugh McIlmoyle (10 League 3 LC)
OFFICIAL PLAYER OF THE SEASON: John McMahon

League position in Division Two: 18th – P42 W12 D12 L18 F52 A58 Pts 36
Home: W11 D4 L6 F32 A21   Away: W1 D8 L12 F20 A37

Match Report: Quick One-Two Puts Preston Through – Jan 15 1972 Preston 4 Bristol City 2 FA Cup 3rd Round

After passing late fitness tests Preston manager, Alan Ball, recalled the experienced Spavin and Ingram in place of Lamb and Tarbuck. The game's first anxious moment came in the 7th minute when Clark ran on to a Lyall through ball. Gibson, City's goalkeeper, ran out to meet the challenge and consequently handled the ball outside the area, conceding a free-kick. Spavin's effort was blocked by the red-shirted wall of defenders though. McMahon ventured forward a few minutes later and was on target with his shot which Gibson did well to reach at the expense of a corner. The midfield foraging of Heppolette, Spavin and Lyall seemed to be putting North End in the driving seat, but on 25 minutes, completely against the run of play, the visitors went ahead. Tainton, out on the right wing, flicked the ball square to Gow, who then sent over a cross to the far post. Lyall, in a good defensive position, somehow failed to clear, leaving Spiring the simple task of slotting the ball past Kelly into the far corner of the Preston net. Within ten minutes Lyall made amends for his error, volleying the ball past Gibson after Spavin had set him up, beating two opponents in the process. This equaliser brought a tremendous roar of approval from the North End fans. Preston's joy was short-lived however because City regained their lead in the 39th minute, following a corner taken by Tainton. Poor marking was responsible, for Wilson was virtually unchallenged as he headed past Kelly from ten yards. The half had been riddled with errors and there were no further goals before the break. In the second half both sides were guilty of poor finishing and it seemed that the Robins would proceed to the next round, until that is, North End hit them with a quick one-two late in the game. The considerable barracking from the crowd, probably justified, turned to cheers as in the 83rd minute Ingram equalised from close range from Heppolette's centre. Within a minute Preston took the lead when McIlmoyle latched onto a poor clearance and from his astute pass Clark forced the ball beyond Gibson, again from close range. The fans then went wild as Preston clinched the result with another goal from Clark, from Lyall's pass, this time in the 88th minute. At the final whistle the pitch was invaded by delirious schoolboys who mobbed their heroes off.

Left to right: Lyall, Jimmie Scott (chief scout), Lamb, Ross, Spark.

STAT FACTS:
Best home run without defeat: 6 games
Best away run without defeat: 4 games
Longest run unbeaten: 8 games
Longest run without a win: 7 games
Best home attendance: 37,025 vs. Man.Utd. FAC 5.2.72
Worst home attendance: 9,566 vs. Swindon 1.5.72
Best away attendance: 30,338 vs. Spurs LC 27.10.71
Worst away attendance: 4,319 vs. Barrow LC 18.8.71
Aggregate and average home attendance: 318,284 – 15,156
Aggregate and average away attendance: 286,901 – 13,662

Season 1971–72: Second Division

	P	W	D	L	F	A	Pts
1 Norwich	42	21	15	6	60	36	57
2 Birmingham	42	19	18	5	60	31	56
3 Millwall	42	19	17	6	64	46	55
4 QPR	42	20	14	8	57	28	54
5 Sunderland	42	17	16	9	67	57	50
6 Blackpool	42	20	7	15	70	50	47
7 Burnley	42	20	6	16	70	55	46
8 Bristol City	42	18	10	14	61	49	46
9 Middlesbrough	42	19	8	15	50	48	46
10 Carlisle	42	17	9	16	61	57	43
11 Swindon	42	15	12	15	47	47	42
12 Hull	42	14	10	18	49	53	38
13 Luton	42	10	18	14	43	48	38
14 Sheffield Wednesday	42	13	12	17	51	58	38
15 Oxford	42	12	14	16	43	55	38
16 Portsmouth	42	12	13	17	59	68	37
11 Orient	42	14	9	19	50	61	37
18 PRESTON	**42**	**12**	**12**	**18**	**52**	**58**	**36**
19 Cardiff	42	10	14	18	56	69	34
20 Fulham	42	12	10	20	45	68	34
21 Charlton	42	12	9	21	55	77	33
22 Watford	42	5	9	28	24	75	19

John Bird

Gary Williams

Ricky Heppolette

Date 1971-2	Opponents	Comp	h or a	Score *aet	Att.	1	2	3	4	5	6	7	8	9	10	11	12 *Sub Used		
Aug 14	Carlisle Utd.	Div 2	a	0-0	11063	Kelly	Ross	McNab	Bird	Hawkins	Spavin	Heppolette	Ham	McIlmoyle	Spark	Clark	Lyall		
Aug 18	Barrow Rd 1	LC	a	2-0	4319	Kelly	Ross *	McNab	Bird	Hawkins	Spavin	Heppolette	Ham (1)	McIlmoyle	Spark	Clark	Wilson *	1 og	(Clarke)
Aug 21	Fulham	Div 2	h	2-0	16425	Kelly	McMahon	McNab	Bird	Hawkins	Spavin	Heppolette	Ham	McIlmoyle (2)	Spark	Clark	Lyall		
Aug 28	Luton Town	Div 2	a	1-1	11772	Kelly	McMahon	McNab	Bird	Hawkins	Lyall	Heppolette (1)	Ham	McIlmoyle	Spark	Clark *	Wilson *		
Aug 30	Burnley	Div 2	h	1-3	27284	Kelly	McMahon	McNab	Bird	Hawkins	Spavin	Heppolette	Ham	McIlmoyle (1p)	Spark	Wilson	Lyall		
Sep 4	Oxford Utd.	Div 2	a	1-0	12891	Kelly	McMahon	McNab *	Bird	Hawkins	Spavin	Heppolette	Ham	McIlmoyle (1)	Spark	Wilson	Lyall *		
Sep 8	Tranmere R. Rd 2	LC	a	1-0	5873	Brown	Spark	Ritchie	Bird	Hawkins	Spavin	Heppolette	Ham	McIlmoyle (1)	Lyall	Clark	Ingram		
Sep 11	QPR	Div 2	a	1-2	13578	Brown	Spark	Ritchie	Bird	Hawkins	Spavin	Heppolette	Ham (1)	McIlmoyle	Lyall	Clark	Ingram		
Sep 18	Charlton Ath.	Div 2	h	2-1	13198	Brown	Spark	McNab	Bird	Hawkins	Spavin	Heppolette	Ham (1)	McIlmoyle	Lyall	Clark (1)	Ingram		
Sep 25	Sunderland	Div 2	a	3-4	13102	Brown	Spark	McNab	Bird	Hawkins	Spavin	Heppolette	Ham (1)	McIlmoyle (1p)	Lyall (1)	Clark	Ritchie		
Sep 28	Norwich City	Div 2	h	0-2	15644	Brown	McMahon	McNab	Bird	Hawkins	Spavin	Heppolette	Ham *	McIlmoyle	Lyall	Clark	Tarbuck *		
Oct 2	Cardiff City	Div 2	h	1-2	13511	Brown	McMahon	McNab	Bird	Hawkins	Spavin	Heppolette	Ham * (1)	McIlmoyle	Lyall	Clark	Ingram *		
Oct 6	Watford Rd 3	LC	a	1-1	8853	Kelly	McMahon	McNab	Bird	Hawkins	Spavin (1)	Heppolette	Ham *	McIlmoyle	Lyall	Clark	Ingram *		
Oct 9	Portsmouth	Div 2	a	1-1	12749	Kelly	McMahon	McNab *	Bird	Hawkins	Spavin	Heppolette	Ham	McIlmoyle (1)	Lyall	Ingram	Spark *		
Oct 11	Watford Replay	LC	h	2-1	12436	Kelly	McMahon	Ritchie	Bird	Hawkins	Spavin (1)	Heppolette	Ham	McIlmoyle (1)	Lyall	Ingram	Clark		
Oct 16	Carlisle Utd.	Div 2	h	3-0	15430	Kelly	McMahon	Ritchie	Bird	Hawkins	Spavin	Heppolette	Ham	McIlmoyle	Lyall (2)	Ingram (1)	Clark		
Oct 18	Orient	Div 2	a	2-3	7391	Kelly	McMahon	Ritchie	Bird	Hawkins	Spavin	Heppolette	Ham	McIlmoyle (1)	Lyall	Ingram (1)	Spark		
Oct 23	Birmingham City	Div 2	a	2-2	28956	Kelly	McMahon	Ritchie *	Bird	Hawkins	Spavin	Heppolette	Tarbuck (1)	McIlmoyle	Lyall	Ingram (1)	Spark *		
Oct 27	Tottenham H. Rd 4	LC	a	1-1	30338	Kelly	McMahon	Ritchie	Bird	Hawkins	Spavin	Heppolette	Clark	McIlmoyle	Lyall (1)	Ingram	Clark		
Oct 30	Hull City	Div 2	h	3-1	14413	Kelly	McMahon	Ritchie	Bird	Hawkins	Spavin	Heppolette	Clark (1)	McIlmoyle	Lyall	Ingram (2)	Spark		
Nov 6	Middlesbrough	Div 2	a	1-0	21907	Kelly	McMahon	Ritchie	Bird	Hawkins	Spavin	Heppolette	Tarbuck (1)	McIlmoyle	Lyall	Ingram	McNab		
Nov 8	Tottenham H. Replay	LC	h	1-2*	27239	Kelly	McMahon	Ritchie	Bird	Hawkins	Spavin	Heppolette	Clark	McIlmoyle (1)	Lyall	Ingram	Spark		
Nov 13	Sheffield Wed.	Div 2	h	1-0	16903	Kelly	McMahon	Ritchie	Bird	Hawkins *	Spavin	Heppolette (1)	Clark	McIlmoyle	Lyall	Ingram	Spark *		
Nov 20	Swindon Town	Div 2	a	1-1	10833	Kelly	McMahon	Ritchie	Bird	Hawkins	Spavin	Heppolette	Clark	McIlmoyle *	Lyall	Ingram (1)	Spark *		
Nov 27	Watford	Div 2	a	2-0	11318	Kelly	McMahon	Ritchie	Bird	Hawkins	Spavin	Heppolette *	Clark	Tarbuck (1)	Lyall	Ingram	Spark * (1)		
Dec 4	Blackpool	Div 2	a	1-1	18912	Kelly	McMahon	Ritchie	Bird	Hawkins	Spavin	Heppolette	Clark (1)	Tarbuck	Lyall	Ingram	Spark		
Dec 11	Millwall	Div 2	h	4-0	14097	Kelly	McMahon	Ritchie	Bird	Hawkins	Spavin	Spark	Clark (1)	Tarbuck (1)	Lyall (1)	Ingram (1p)	McNab		
Dec 18	Oxford Utd.	Div 2	h	0-2	7758	Kelly	McMahon	Ritchie	Bird	Hawkins	Spavin	Spark	Clark	Tarbuck	Lyall	Ingram	McNab		
Dec 27	Bristol City	Div 2	a	1-0	19738	Kelly	McMahon	McNab	Bird	Hawkins	Spavin *	Spark	Clark	McIlmoyle	Lyall (1)	Ingram	Tarbuck *		
Jan 1	Charlton Ath.	Div 2	a	1-2	8038	Kelly	McMahon	McNab	Bird	Hawkins	Lamb	Heppolette	Clark (1)	McIlmoyle	Lyall	Ingram	Tarbuck		
Jan 8	Luton Town	Div 2	h	0-1	12844	Kelly	McMahon	McNab	Bird	Hawkins	Lamb	Heppolette	Clark	McIlmoyle	Lyall	Tarbuck *	Wilson *		
Jan 15	Bristol City Rd 3	FAC	h	4-2	13619	Kelly	McMahon	McNab	Bird	Hawkins	Spavin	Heppolette	Clark (2)	McIlmoyle	Lyall (1)	Ingram (1)	Lamb		
Jan 22	Norwich City	Div 2	a	1-1	21390	Kelly	McMahon	McNab	Bird (1)	Hawkins *	Spavin	Heppolette	Clark	McIlmoyle	Lyall	Ingram	Lamb *		
Jan 29	Orient	Div 2	h	1-1	19692	Kelly	McMahon	Connor	Bird	McNab	Spavin	Heppolette	Lamb *	McIlmoyle	Lyall	Ingram	Tarbuck *		
Feb 5	Manchester Utd. Rd 4	FAC	h	0-2	37052	Kelly	McMahon	Connor	Bird	McNab	Spavin	Heppolette	Spark	McIlmoyle	Lyall	Ingram	Lamb		
Feb 12	Birmingham City	Div 2	h	0-0	17794	Kelly	McMahon	Connor	Bird	McNab	Spavin	Young	Spark	McIlmoyle	Lyall	Ingram	Tarbuck		
Feb 19	Hull City	Div 2	a	2-3	14313	Kelly	Connor	McNab	Spark	Bird	Spavin	Heppolette	Tarbuck (1)	Young (1)	Lyall *	Ingram	Lamb *		
Mar 4	Sheffield Wed.	Div 2	a	0-1	12162	Kelly	McMahon	Connor	Bird	Hawkins	Spavin	Heppolette	Tarbuck	McIlmoyle	Lyall	Young	Lamb		
Mar 11	Portsmouth	Div 2	h	4-0	10575	Kelly	Connor	McNab	Bird	Hawkins	Spavin	Heppolette	Young (1)	McIlmoyle (1)	Lyall (1p)	Tarbuck (1)	Lamb		
Mar 18	Fulham	Div 2	a	0-0	9071	Kelly	Connor	McNab	Bird	Hawkins	Spavin	Spark	Young	McIlmoyle	Lyall	Tarbuck	Lamb		
Mar 25	QPR	Div 2	h	1-1	12304	Kelly	Connor	McNab	Bird	Hawkins	Spavin	Heppolette *	Young	McIlmoyle	Lyall	Tarbuck (1)	Spark *		
Mar 29	Cardiff City	Div 2	a	2-5	13294	Kelly	Connor	McNab	Bird	Hawkins *	Spavin (1)	Heppolette	Tarbuck (1)	Young	Lyall	Spark	Hughes *		
Apr 1	Bristol City	Div 2	h	1-4	12962	Kelly	McMahon	Connor	Bird	McNab	Spavin	Heppolette	Young *	McIlmoyle	Lamb	Tarbuck (1)	Hughes *		
Apr 4	Sunderland	Div 2	h	1-3	13450	Kelly	McMahon	Connor	Bird	Hawkins	Spavin	Heppolette	Young (1)	McIlmoyle	Lyall	Tarbuck *	Spark *		
Apr 15	Watford	Div 2	h	0-1	5507	Kelly	McMahon	Connor	Bird	Hawkins	Spavin	Spark	Young	McIlmoyle	Lyall	Tarbuck	McNab		
Apr 17	Middlesbrough	Div 2	h	1-0	11388	Kelly	McMahon	McNab	Bird	Hawkins *	Spavin	Heppolette	Young	McIlmoyle (1)	Connor	Tarbuck	Lyall *		
Apr 22	Blackpool	Div 2	h	1-4	19819	Kelly	McMahon	McNab *	Bird	Hawkins	Spavin	Heppolette	Young	McIlmoyle (1)	Connor	Tarbuck	Spark *		
Apr 25	Burnley	Div 2	a	0-1	13020	Kelly	McMahon	Connor	Bird	Hawkins	Spark *	Heppolette	Lyall	McIlmoyle	Young	Lamb	Wilson *		
Apr 29	Millwall	Div 2	a	0-2	19123	Kelly	McMahon	Ross	Bird	Hawkins	Spark	Heppolette	Lyall	Tarbuck	Young	Lamb	Wilson		
May 1	Swindon Town	Div 2	h	2-2	9566	Blyth	McMahon	Ross	Bird	Hawkins	Spark	Heppolette *	Bruce	McIlmoyle	Lamb (1)	Williams	Tarbuck * (1)		

Once again, much to the disappointment of the fans, there were no new players signed during the summer break and Alan Ball went into the new season with the same squad which had struggled during 1971–72. The result of this lack of activity from the Board was another very poor year in which Preston only saved themselves from relegation with a last day draw at home to Burnley. The first five games saw just one goal scored by North End in four defeats and one draw, and also exit from the League Cup at the hands of lowly Workington from Division Four. On top of this Alan Lamb broke his leg in that game and on loan Roger Davies was recalled by Derby County after just two fruitless games. When Fulham visited Deepdale on September's opening day, North End were already in a desperate situation but two goals from Dave Wilson and another by Neil Young gave the club a 3–1 win and lifted everyone's spirits. It was also to trigger a run in which Preston went six games without conceding a goal picking up some very useful points along the way. But, and it has happened many times down the years, just when you think North End are on the verge of achieving something special they then do their best to spoil it all. From December to late April the club could do nothing right. A miserable Christmas, which saw Preston lose 6–1 at Carlisle on Boxing Day, was followed by an even bleaker New Year. The very poor run of results ended with the not unexpected news that Alan Ball was sacked leaving Frank Lord in temporary charge. It was a sad end for Ball who, in the

main, managed the club well. He lifted spirits when the club was at a very low ebb and raised the enthusiasm. In the end though it was results on the pitch which dictated what most Preston fans thought was inevitable at the time. Before Ball left, Preston had gone out of the FA Cup, losing to another lower league side, Grimsby. That was probably the last straw and it left North End with a long run in to salvage their league status. To record just one win after Christmas was an appalling state of affairs and quite frankly Preston deserved to be relegated. Luckily for them though the failings of other teams kept them in with a slim chance of survival. When it came to the last match Preston entertained Burnley, the Champions, and they needed to avoid defeat to save themselves. After a harrowing afternoon of nailbiting tension North End, thanks to an Alex Bruce goal, managed to earn a 1–1 draw and it was enough to keep them up. Jim McNab, John Bird, John McMahon, Graham Hawkins, and the very promising Bruce had been the pick of a poor side. One consolation from the season came in the blooding of some of the good crop of young players who had progressed through the junior ranks, Tony Morley looking the brightest star.

DEBUTANTS: (5) Roger Davies, Mel Holden, Tony Morley, Eric Snookes, Stuart Baxter.

LAST GAMES: (8) Cross, Heppolette, Clark, Ross, McIlmoyle, Tarbuck, Connor, Davies.

Future Players born between August 1972 and July 1973:
Lee Cartwright, Lee Ashcroft, Graham Lancashire, Craig Moylon, Terry Flemming, Greg Challender, David Eaves, David Christie, Jason Kerfoot, Gareth Ainsworth
Ever presents: None   **Hat-tricks:** None   **FA Cup:** Third Round Replay
League Cup: First Round   **Players used:** 24
Manager: Alan Ball until February 1973 then Frank Lord took over as Caretaker until the season's end.
Chairman: T. C. Nicholson Esq. JP FCIOB
Leading scorer: 13 goals – Alex Bruce (all League)
OFFICIAL PLAYER OF THE SEASON: Jim McNab

League appearances (42 games)

Baxter S. W. 2 + 1, Bird J. C. 41, Brown J. C. 12, Bruce A. R. 28 + 7, Clark C. 7 + 1, Connor D. R. 15, Davies R. 2, Hawkins G. N. 39, Heppolette R. A. W. 17, Holden M. G. 6 + 1, Kelly J. A. 30, Lamb A. D. 14, McIlmoyle H. 24 + 1, McMahon J. J. 36, McNab J. 30 + 1, Morley W. A. 2 + 2, Ross G. 3 + 2, Snookes E. 7, Spark A. M. 36 + 3, Spavin A. 24, Tarbuck A. D. 23 + 2, Williams G. P. 2, Wilson D. C. 33 + 2, Young N. J. 29.

FA Cup appearances (2 games)

Kelly 2, Ross 2, McNab 2, Bird 2, Hawkins 2, Connor 1, Spavin 1, Wilson 2, Spark 2, McIlmoyle 2, Tarbuck 2, Bruce 2.

League Cup appearances (1 game)

Kelly, McMahon, McNab, Bird, Hawkins, Lamb, Heppolette, Tarbuck, McIlmoyle, Young, Clark, 1 each, Connor 0 + 1.

Goalscorers: 37 League only

Bruce 13, Young 7 (3 pens), Tarbuck 6, Wilson 5, McNab 2, McMahon 1, Spark 1, Spavin 1, Holden 1.

League position in Division Two: 19th – P42 W11 D12 L19 F37 A64 Pts 34
Home: W6 D8 L7 F19 A25   Away: W5 D4 L12 F18 A39

Match Report: Deepdale Draw Endures Safety – 28 Apr 1973 Preston 1 Burnley 1

Burnley, the champions elect, arrived at Deepdale to find that the pitch had been narrowed. Some said it was to help curb the threat of Burnley's James down the flanks. As if a club of Preston's stature would do a trick like that! The on song Clarets only required a point to clinch the Second Division title, whereas North End desperately needed a point to be safe from relegation. Caretaker manager, Frank Lord, made one change for the home side by bringing in Connor at the expense of McIlmoyle who had not scored in 27 first team games, a very disappointing return from a striker with such experience. The Preston players sportingly lined up to welcome their East Lancashire rivals onto the pitch in recognition of them winning promotion. North End adopted a 4–4–2 formation at the start with just Lamb supporting Bruce up front. Burnley soon illustrated their attacking skills in front of a large and noisy following when Casper and James combined but Snookes cleared at the expense of a corner. North End survived a penalty appeal when Baxter appeared to handle the ball, but the referee waved play on. Preston were being pinned back and it seemed just a matter of time before the arrival of the first goal from a Burnley side, showing slick passing skills around the well grassed pitch. Then, amazingly, and against the run of play North End took the lead right on the stroke of half-time. The ball had been belted out of Preston's area only as far as Burnley's right-back Ingham, but he mis-headed the ball into the path of Lamb who gained possession and ran towards the penalty area before squaring a pass inside. Bruce was there and he nonchalantly beat Stevenson with a well struck shot. It was the first goal conceded by Burnley in six matches. In the second half Preston were soon back-pedalling as Burnley surged forward looking for the equaliser. The goal, inevitably perhaps, finally arrived on 54 minutes when Waldron volleyed a tremendous shot past Kelly's vain leap. Kelly equalled Preston's appearance record with this game and the keeper could thank Snookes and Connor, who both cleared off the line, for helping to keep his clean sheet and give Preston that oh, so vital point. The game ended with both sides content with the draw and at the end both sets of fans breathed a sigh of relief.

Season 1972–73: Second Division

	P	W	D	L	F	A	Pts
1 Burnley	42	24	14	4	72	35	62
2 QPR	42	24	13	5	81	31	61
3 Aston Villa	42	18	14	10	51	47	50
4 Middlesbrough	42	17	13	12	46	43	47
5 Bristol City	42	17	12	13	63	51	46
6 Sunderland	42	17	12	13	59	49	46
7 Blackpool	42	18	10	14	56	51	46
6 Oxford	42	19	7	16	52	43	45
7 Fulham	42	16	12	14	58	49	44
10 Sheffield Wednesday	42	17	10	15	59	55	44
11 Millwall	42	16	10	16	55	47	42
12 Luton	42	15	11	16	44	53	41
13 Hull	42	14	12	16	64	59	40
14 Nottingham Forest	42	14	12	16	47	52	40
15 Orient	42	12	12	18	49	53	36
16 Swindon	42	10	16	16	46	60	36
17 Portsmouth	42	12	11	19	42	59	35
18 Carlisle	42	11	12	19	50	52	34
19 PRESTON	42	11	12	19	37	64	34
20 Cardiff	42	11	11	20	43	58	33
21 Huddersfield	42	8	17	17	36	56	33
22 Brighton	42	8	13	21	46	83	29

Date 1972-3	Opponents	Comp	h or a	Score	Att.	1	2	3	4	5	6	7	8	9	10	11	12 * Sub. Used
Aug 12	Aston Villa	Div 2	h	0-1	17371	Kelly	McMahon	McNab	Bird	Hawkins	Connor	Young	Lamb	McIlmoyle	Williams	Heppolette	Spark
Aug 16	Workington T. Rd 1	LC	a	0-1	4055	Kelly	McMahon	McNab	Bird	Hawkins	Lamb *	Heppolette	Tarbuck	McIlmoyle	Young	Clark	Connor *
Aug 19	Luton Town	Div 2	a	0-1	11507	Kelly	McMahon	McNab	Bird	Hawkins	Connor *	Heppolette	Wilson	Tarbuck	Young	Clark	Spark *
Aug 26	QPR	Div 2	h	1-1	9242	Kelly	McMahon	McNab	Bird	Hawkins	Spark	Heppolette	Wilson	Davies	Young (1)	Clark	Tarbuck
Aug 29	Burnley	Div 2	h	0-2	13166	Kelly	McMahon	McNab	Bird	Hawkins	Spark	Heppolette	Young	Davies	Spavin	Clark *	Wilson *
Sep 2	Fulham	Div 2	a	3-1	7640	Kelly	McMahon	McNab	Bird	Hawkins	Spavin	Wilson (2)	Spark	Tarbuck	Young * (1)	Heppolette	Bruce *
Sep 9	Hull City	Div 2	h	1-0	8136	Kelly	McMahon	McNab	Bird	Hawkins	Spavin	Wilson	Spark	Tarbuck (1)	Young	Heppolette	Bruce
Sep 16	Portsmouth	Div 2	a	1-0	6965	Kelly	McMahon	McNab	Bird	Hawkins	Spavin	Wilson	Spark	Tarbuck (1)	Young	Heppolette	Ross
Sep 19	Middlesbrough	Div 2	a	0-0	9679	Kelly *	McMahon	McNab	Bird	Hawkins	Spavin	Wilson	Spark	Tarbuck	Young	Heppolette	Bruce *
Sep 23	Carlisle Utd.	Div 2	h	1-0	10957	Brown	McMahon	McNab	Bird	Hawkins	Spavin	Wilson	Spark	Tarbuck (1)	Young	Heppolette *	Bruce *
Sep 25	Orient	Div 2	h	1-0	10709	Brown	McMahon	McNab	Bird	Hawkins	Spavin	Wilson	Spark	Tarbuck	Young	Bruce	Heppolette
Sep 30	Oxford Utd.	Div 2	a	2-0	8850	Brown	McMahon	McNab	Bird	Hawkins	Spavin	Wilson (1)	Spark	Tarbuck	Young (1p)	Heppolette	Bruce
Oct 7	Sheffield Wed.	Div 2	h	1-1	15600	Kelly	McMahon	McNab *	Bird	Hawkins	Spavin	Wilson (1)	Spark	Tarbuck	Young	Heppolette	Bruce *
Oct 14	Swindon Town	Div 2	a	2-3	8198	Kelly	McMahon	McNab (1)	Spark	Hawkins	Spavin	Wilson	Bruce	Tarbuck (1)	Young	Heppolette	Ross
Oct 21	Millwall	Div 2	h	1-0	10010	Kelly	McMahon	McNab	Bird	Hawkins	Spavin (1)	Wilson	Spark	Tarbuck	Young *	Heppolette	Bruce *
Oct 28	Cardiff City	Div 2	a	0-3	12208	Kelly	McMahon	McNab	Bird	Hawkins	Spavin	Wilson	Spark	Tarbuck	Young *	Heppolette	Bruce *
Nov 3	Orient	Div 2	a	2-1	5661	Kelly	McMahon	McNab	Bird	Hawkins	Spavin	Wilson	Spark	Tarbuck *	Young (1)	Heppolette	Bruce * (1)
Nov 11	Middlesbrough	Div 2	h	0-1	10015	Kelly	McMahon	McNab	Spark	Bird	Spavin	Wilson	Bruce	Tarbuck	Young	Heppolette *	McIlmoyle *
Nov 18	Nottm Forest	Div 2	a	1-0	10382	Kelly	McMahon	McNab	Bird	Hawkins	Spavin	Wilson	Spark	McIlmoyle	Young	Bruce (1)	Clark
Nov 25	Brighton	Div 2	h	4-0	8005	Kelly	McMahon	McNab (1)	Bird	Hawkins	Spavin	Wilson	Spark	McIlmoyle	Young (1p)	Bruce (2)	Clark
Dec 2	Huddersfield T.	Div 2	h	0-0	6900	Kelly	McMahon	McNab *	Bird	Hawkins	Spavin	Wilson	Spark	McIlmoyle	Clark	Bruce	Tarbuck *
Dec 9	Blackpool	Div 2	a	0-3	18822	Kelly	McMahon	Spark	Bird	Hawkins	Spavin	Wilson	Heppolette	McIlmoyle	Young *	Bruce	Tarbuck *
Dec 16	Sunderland	Div 2	a	0-0	11529	Kelly	McMahon	Connor	Bird	Hawkins	Spavin	Wilson	Spark	McIlmoyle	Tarbuck	Bruce	Young
Dec 23	Bristol City	Div 2	h	3-3	7700	Kelly	McMahon (1)	Connor	Bird	Hawkins	Spavin	Wilson	Spark	McIlmoyle	Tarbuck (1)	Bruce (1)	McNab
Dec 26	Carlisle Utd.	Div 2	a	1-6	9939	Kelly	McMahon *	Connor	Bird	Hawkins	Spavin	Wilson	Spark	McIlmoyle	Tarbuck	Bruce (1)	McNab *
Dec 30	Luton Town	Div 2	a	2-0	9638	Kelly	McMahon	Connor	Bird	Hawkins	Connor	Wilson (1)	Spark	McIlmoyle	Tarbuck	Bruce (1)	Young
Jan 6	QPR	Div 2	a	0-3	10519	Kelly	Ross	McNab	Bird	Hawkins	Connor	Wilson *	Spark	McIlmoyle	Tarbuck	Bruce	Morley *
Jan 13	Grimsby Town Rd 3	FAC	a	0-0	16000	Kelly	Ross	McNab	Bird	Hawkins	Connor	Wilson	Spark	McIlmoyle	Tarbuck	Bruce	Spavin
Jan 15	Grimsby Town Replay	FAC	h	0-1	13175	Kelly	Ross	McNab	Bird	Hawkins	Spavin	Wilson	Spark	McIlmoyle	Tarbuck	Bruce	Connor
Jan 20	Fulham	Div 2	a	0-3	5759	Kelly	McMahon	McNab	Ross	Bird	Spavin	Tarbuck	Young	McIlmoyle	Connor *	Bruce	Wilson *
Jan 27	Hull City	Div 2	a	2-6	9120	Kelly	Ross	McMahon	McNab	Bird	Spavin	Tarbuck	Spark (1)	Holden	Bruce	Young (1)	Wilson
Feb 10	Portsmouth	Div 2	a	0-5	6230	Kelly	McMahon	McNab	Bird	Hawkins	Spavin	Tarbuck *	Young	McIlmoyle	Spark	Bruce	Clark *
Feb 17	Aston Villa	Div 2	a	1-1	27717	Brown	Hawkins	McNab	Bird	Spark	Lamb	Clark	Wilson	McIlmoyle	Connor	Bruce (1)	Spavin
Mar 3	Sheffield Wed.	Div 2	a	1-2	13427	Brown	Hawkins	Bird	McNab	Spark	Connor	Bruce	Lamb	McIlmoyle	Tarbuck (1)	Wilson	Ross
Mar 10	Swindon Town	Div 2	h	1-1	6468	Brown	Hawkins	Bird	McNab	Spark	Connor	Lamb	Bruce (1)	McIlmoyle	Clark	Wilson	Morley
Mar 17	Millwall	Div 2	a	1-4	8233	Brown	Connor	Bruce *	Bird	Spark	Wilson	Lamb	McIlmoyle	McNab	Clark	Hawkins	Holden * (1)
Mar 19	Sunderland	Div 2	h	1-3	7636	Brown	Connor	McNab *	Bird	Hawkins	Morley	Lamb	Bruce (1)	McIlmoyle	Holden	Wilson	Spark *
Mar 24	Cardiff City	Div 2	h	0-0	6889	Brown	Connor	McMahon	Bird	Hawkins	Morley	Lamb	Bruce	McIlmoyle	Holden	Wilson *	Spark *
Mar 31	Brighton	Div 2	a	0-2	12047	Brown	McMahon	Snookes	Bird	Hawkins	Bruce	Wilson	Lamb *	Holden	McIlmoyle	Williams	Ross *
Apr 7	Huddersfield T.	Div 2	a	0-0	7896	Kelly	McMahon	Snookes	Bird	Hawkins	Bruce	Lamb	Spark	Holden	McIlmoyle	Young	Morley
Apr 14	Blackpool	Div 2	h	0-2	12195	Kelly *	McMahon	Snookes	Bird	Hawkins	Bruce	Lamb	Spark	McIlmoyle	Holden	Young	Ross *
Apr 21	Nottm Forest	Div 2	h	2-1	7701	Brown	McMahon	Snookes	Bird	Hawkins	Bruce (1)	Lamb	Spark	McIlmoyle *	Wilson	Young (1p)	Morley *
Apr 23	Bristol City	Div 2	h	1-2	10799	Brown	McMahon	Snookes	Bird	Hawkins	Spark	Wilson *	Lamb	McIlmoyle	Bruce (1)	Young	S.Baxter *
Apr 24	Oxford Utd.	Div 2	a	0-1	7792	Kelly	McMahon	Snookes	Bird	S.Baxter	Spark	Lamb	Hawkins	McIlmoyle	Bruce	Young	Connor
Apr 28	Burnley	Div 2	h	1-1	21550	Kelly	McMahon	Snookes	Bird	Hawkins	S.Baxter	Connor	Bruce (1)	Lamb	Spark	Young	McIlmoyle

SEASON 1973–1974

Trivia Facts:

The referee, in what proved to be Alan Kelly's last first team game, was Jack Taylor, who later that season refereed the World Cup Final between Holland and West Germany.

When PNE reserves met Man. City reserves at Deepdale there was a big contrast in goalkeepers. Preston fielded a young trialist from Newton le Willows called Graham Cunneely whilst City had the experienced Joe Corrigan in goal. For the record Preston won 4–3.

When Bobby Charlton's Preston beat WBA 3–1 at Deepdale it put his side level on points at the top of the table with his brother Jack's Middlesbrough team. By the time the two brothers' teams met in the last game of the season at Preston, Jack was heading for promotion whilst Bobby's team were going down.

Ron Healey, brought in on loan from Manchester City as goalkeeper cover, made his debut at Middlesbrough. An early facial injury meant he had to go off for 15 minutes to be treated. Whilst he was gone David Sadler went in goal and was beaten by a John Bird own goal. Some teammate he turned out to be!.

In some publications it has been erroneously recorded that Mike Elwiss was Bobby Charlton's first signing. Prior to Elwiss's arrival Charlton had already signed his former Old Trafford team-mates Burns, Stiles and Sadler.

The news that football legend, Bobby Charlton had become manager of Preston North End during the summer break created a great deal of national interest in the club. The early days looked promising with North End for once making a close season signing. Francis Burns came in from Charlton's old club Manchester United and he made his debut in the opening game against Aston Villa at Villa Park, a traditional graveyard for North End's hopes. The 2–0 defeat set the trend for the early games but a 2–0 home win over Millwall then lifted the spirits. Tony Morley soon showed that he was a good player and the youngster quickly established a place in the side. Other young players also impressed, notably Mel Holden and John McMahon. The manager was unlucky to suffer a major blow on September 15 1973 when Preston's stalwart goalkeeper Alan Kelly received, what proved to be, a career ending injury. Kelly's last game was against Bristol City and though he worked hard to try and reach fitness again it was to no avail. It was terrible luck for both club and player. Initially the form was unaffected as Preston continued to play good football, indeed, by mid-October North End were second in the table and it looked good. Sadly the joy of being at the top end of the table for a change was short-lived as from that peak the club struggled desperately. Nobby Stiles and David Sadler, both former United colleagues of Charlton, were signed and they quickly settled in. Defensively though Preston were weak. With no Kelly in goal the defenders seemed to lack confidence and several heavy defeats were suffered as a result. The lack of confidence also hit the attack and in the 19 games after the turn of the year Preston only scored in seven of them, an appalling record and one that brought the threat of relegation. As the season went on the threat became an inevitability, although the signing of Mike Elwiss from

Doncaster did give cause for some optimism as the player quickly won the fans over with a two goal debut against Carlisle. But the fact that Alex Bruce, who had left the club for Newcastle in the February, still ended as top scorer really said it all. The cups brought no respite, North End going out of both competitions at the first hurdle. Francis Burns worked hard all year, John Brown did not let the side down in goal and John Bird never gave less than 100% effort. The big disappointment was the form of another Charlton signing, Ray Treacy. The player, transferred from Swindon, always seemed to score against Preston, but in his 21 appearances in the white shirt he could not manage a single goal. At the end of a miserable season the FA even deducted a point because Preston had fielded an ineligible player, David Carrick. It made no difference to their relegation. It was obvious that Bobby Charlton would have to do some serious re-thinking.

DEBUTANTS: (10) Francis Burns, Nobby Stiles, Gordon Coleman, David Sadler, David Carrick, Gary Hudson, Ron Healey, Ray Treacy, Mike Elwiss, John Smith.

LAST GAMES: (9) Wilson D., Kelly, McNab, Hawkins, Young, Snookes, Hudson, Healey, Carrick.

Future Players born between August 1973 and July 1974: Steve Finney, Simon Burton, Michael Jackson, David Flitcroft, Allan Smart, Sean Gregan, Teuvo Moilanen, Dominic Ludden
Ever presents: (2) Burns, McMahon
Hat-tricks: None
Manager: Bobby Charlton
Chairman: A. R. W. Jones JP FRICS
FA Cup: Third Round
League Cup: First Round
Players used: 27
Leading scorer: 9 goals – Alex Bruce (all League)
OFFICIAL PLAYER OF THE SEASON:
Francis Burns

Francis Burns. Former "Red Devil".

Match Report: John Brown's Bonus – 10 Feb 1974 Preston 2 Nottm. Forest 1

This game was the first league game ever to be played at Deepdale on a Sunday and despite protests from the Lord's Day Observance Society there was an increase of more than 3,000 spectators on the average of the last four home games. North End got off to a good start and could have had a couple of goals early in the match. As it was the visitors scored first, taking the lead against the run of play after 25 minutes. It was somewhat of a fluke, as a right wing corner taken by Richardson, was turned into his own goal by Burns as he leapt to challenge McKenzie at the near post. The situation looked bleak for a Preston side low on confidence. They had dominated most of the play with little reward. However the sun shone on the righteous as North End then equalised with another own goal. McMahon, venturing forward, hit a 30 yard shot, and in trying to clear, Richardson only managed to deflect the ball over Barron and into the gaping net. By comparison the second half was poor with the only noteworthy incidents being the bookings of McKenzie and Burns for arguing with the referee, Mr Yates of Redditch. The games finale was as dramatic as any seen at Deepdale for some time as North End took the lead with just three minutes left. Lamb's low centre from the right wing was met by Bird who guided the ball wide of Barron to score his first goal of the campaign. With just one minute remaining the referee awarded Forest a penalty at the town end, ruling that Sadler had fouled former Deepdale favourite Lyall. After a short delay whilst the Preston players protested vehemently, Jackson stepped up to take the the crucial kick, amid tremendous booing. The jeers turned to cheers as goalkeeper Brown became the hero of the hour, diving to his right to make a dramatic save, thus enabling Preston to keep both points and a well deserved win bonus for the first time in 1974. It was the second penalty Brown had saved in successive games, and both had been on a Sunday!

League appearances (42 games)

Baxter S. W. 24 + 3, Bird J. C. 28, Brown J. C. 30, Bruce A. R. 26, Burns F. 42, Carrick M. D. 0 + 2, Coleman G. M. 7, Elwiss M. W. 11, Hawkins G. N. 31 + 1, Healey R. 6, Holden M. G. 21 + 2, Hudson G. 1, Kelly J. A. 5, Lamb A. D. 19 + 1, McMahon J. J. 42, McNab J. 23, Morley W. A. 7 + 3, Sadler D. 27, Smith J. 1 + 2, Snookes E. 13, Spark A. M. 17 + 2, Spavin A. 4 + 2, Stiles N. P. 27, Treacy R. C. P. 19 + 1, Williams G. P. 6 + 5, Wilson D. C. 1, Young N. J. 24 + 1.

FA Cup appearances (1 game)

Brown, McMahon, Snookes, Sadler, Baxter, Stiles, Morley, Bruce, Holden, Burns, Treacy, 1 each and Bird 0 + 1.

League Cup appearances (2 games)

Kelly 2, McMahon 2, McNab 2, Spark 1, Baxter 2, Hawkins 2, Stiles 1, Morley 2, Spavin 2, Holden 2, Burns 2, Young 1, Bruce 1 and Lamb 0 + 1.

Goalscorers: 40 League–1 LC–(Total 41)

Bruce 9–0 (9), Young 7–1 (pen) (8), Elwiss 5–0 (5), Burns 4–0 (4), Holden 4–0 (4), Bird 2–0 (2), Williams 2–0 (2), Sadler 2–0 (2), McMahon 1–0 (1), Baxter 1–0 (1), Spark 1–0 (1), Stiles 1–0 (1), Own goals 1–0 (1) Richardson of Nottm. Forest

League position in Division Two: 21st (Relegated) – P42 W9 D14 L19 F40 A62 Pts 31*
Home: W7 D8 L6 F24 A23   Away: W2 D6 L13 F16 A39

(*One point deducted by the FA for fielding an ineligible player)

STAT FACTS:
Best home run without defeat: 7 games
Best away run without defeat: 3 games
Longest run unbeaten: 8 games
Longest run without a win: 11 games
Best home attendance: 21,747 vs. Sunderland 13.10.73
Worst home attendance: 7,650 vs. Orient 30.3.74
Best away attendance: 28,861 vs. Aston Villa 25.8.73
Worst away attendance: 6,750 vs. Oxford 17.11.73
Aggregate and average home attendance: 255,587 – 12,171
Aggregate and average away attendance: 288,079 – 13,718

Season 1973–74: Second Division

	P	W	D	L	F	A	Pts
1 Middlesbrough	42	27	11	4	77	30	65
2 Luton	42	19	12	11	64	51	50
3 Carlisle*	42	20	9	13	61	48	49
4 Orient	42	15	18	9	55	42	48
5 Blackpool	42	17	13	12	57	40	47
6 Sunderland	42	19	9	14	58	44	41
7 Nottingham Forest	42	15	15	12	57	43	45
8 WBA	42	14	16	12	48	45	44
9 Hull	42	13	17	12	46	47	43
10 Notts County	42	15	13	14	55	60	43
11 Bolton	42	15	12	15	44	40	42
12 Millwall	42	14	14	14	51	51	42
13 Fulham	42	16	10	16	39	43	42
14 Aston Villa	42	13	15	14	48	45	41
15 Portsmouth	42	14	12	16	45	62	40
16 Bristol City	42	14	10	18	47	54	38
17 Cardiff	42	10	16	16	49	62	36
18 Oxford	42	10	16	16	35	46	36
19 Sheffield Wednesday	42	12	11	19	51	63	35
20 Crystal Palace‡	42	11	12	19	43	56	34
21 PRESTON‡§	42	9	14	19	40	62	31
22 Swindon‡	42	7	11	24	36	72	25

* Three clubs promoted.
‡ Three clubs relegated.
§ PRESTON had one point deducted for fielding an ineligible player.

Date 1973-4	Opponents	Comp	h or a	Score *aet	Att.	1	2	3	4	5	6	7	8	9	10	11	12 * Sub. Used		
Aug 25	Aston Villa	Div 2	a	0-2	28861	Kelly	McMahon	McNab *	Spark	Hawkins	Burns	Morley	Spavin	Holden	Wilson	Young	S.Baxter *		
Aug 28	Bolton W. Rd 1	LC	a	1-1	17101	Kelly	McMahon	McNab	Spark	Hawkins	S.Baxter	Morley	Spavin	Holden *	Burns	Bruce (1)	Young *		
Sep 1	Swindon Town	Div 2	h	1-1	12034	Kelly	McMahon	McNab	Stiles	Hawkins	S.Baxter	Morley	Spavin	Holden	Burns	Bruce	Lamb		
Sep 3	Bolton W. Replay	LC	h	0-2*	18571	Kelly	McMahon	McNab	S.Baxter	Hawkins	Stiles	Morley	Spavin *	Holden	Burns	Bruce	Lamb *		
Sep 8	Hull City	Div 2	a	0-1	7009	Kelly	McMahon	McNab	S.Baxter	Hawkins	Stiles	Bird	Spavin *	Young	Burns	Bruce	Lamb *		
Sep 11	Millwall	Div 2	h	2-0	10325	Kelly	McMahon	McNab	S.Baxter	Hawkins	Stiles	Lamb	Bruce	Holden (1)	Burns (1)	Young	Morley		
Sep 15	Bristol City	Div 2	h	1-1	10790	Kelly	McMahon	McNab	S.Baxter	Hawkins	Stiles	Lamb	Bruce	Holden (1)	Burns *	Young	Morley *		
Sep 18	WBA	Div 2	a	2-0	11822	Brown	McMahon	McNab	S.Baxter	Hawkins	Stiles	Lamb	Bruce (1)	Holden (1)	Burns	Young	Snookes		
Sep 22	Nottm Forest	Div 2	a	1-1	12598	Brown	McMahon	McNab	S.Baxter	Hawkins	Stiles	Lamb	Bruce	Holden	Burns (1)	Young	Snookes		
Sep 29	Portsmouth	Div 2	h	2-1	10640	Brown	McMahon	McNab	S.Baxter (1)	Hawkins	Stiles	Lamb	Bruce (1)	Holden *	Burns	Young	Williams *		
Oct 1	WBA	Div 2	h	3-1	15419	Brown	McMahon (1)	McNab *	S.Baxter	Hawkins	Stiles	Spark	Bruce	Coleman	Burns	Young (2)	Williams *		
Oct 6	Fulham	Div 2	a	0-0	10520	Brown	McMahon	McNab	S.Baxter	Hawkins	Stiles	Spark	Bruce	Coleman	Burns	Young *	Williams *		
Oct 13	Sunderland	Div 2	h	4-0	21747	Brown	McMahon	McNab	Spark	Hawkins	Stiles	Bruce	Young (1p)	Coleman	Burns	Williams	Richmond		
Oct 20	Notts County	Div 2	a	1-2	12479	Brown	McMahon	McNab	S.Baxter	Hawkins	Stiles *	Bruce	Young	Coleman	Burns	Williams (1)	Spark *		
Oct 22	Millwall	Div 2	a	1-5	7625	Brown	McMahon	McNab	S.Baxter	Hawkins	Spark	Bruce	Coleman *	Young	Burns (1)	Williams	Morley *		
Oct 27	Cardiff City	Div 2	h	2-2	12050	Brown	McMahon	McNab	S.Baxter	Bird	Spark (1)	Bruce (1)	Coleman *	Holden	Burns	Young	Spavin *		
Nov 3	Orient	Div 2	a	2-2	12484	Brown	McMahon	Snookes	S.Baxter	Bird	Spark	Spavin	Bruce (2)	Holden	Burns	Young	Morley		
Nov 10	Blackpool	Div 2	h	1-3	21580	Brown	McMahon	Snookes	Spark	Hawkins	Stiles *	Sadler	Bruce (1)	Holden	Burns	Young	S.Baxter *		
Nov 17	Oxford Utd.	Div 2	a	1-1	6750	Brown	McMahon	Snookes	Bird	Hawkins *	Stiles	Spark	Sadler	Bruce (1)	Burns	Young	Carrick *		
Nov 24	Luton Town	Div 2	h	2-2	10279	Brown	McMahon	Snookes	Sadler	Bird	Stiles *	Lamb	Spark	Bruce	Burns	Young (2)	Carrick *		
Dec 8	Bolton W.	Div 2	h	2-1	14715	Hudson	McMahon	McNab	Sadler	Bird	Stiles	Lamb	Spark	Bruce (1)	Burns	Young (1)	S.Baxter		
Dec 11	Middlesbrough	Div 2	a	0-3	23980	Healey	McMahon	McNab *	Sadler	Bird	Stiles	Lamb	Treacy	Bruce	Burns	Young	Hawkins *		
Dec 15	Crystal Palace	Div 2	h	1-1	9121	Healey	McMahon	Snookes	Bird	Hawkins	Stiles *	Sadler (1)	Treacy	Bruce	Burns	Young	Williams *		
Dec 22	Portsmouth	Div 2	a	0-3	13957	Healey	McMahon	Snookes	Bird	Hawkins	Stiles	Sadler	Bruce	Holden	Burns	Young	Morley		
Dec 26	Carlisle Utd.	Div 2	h	0-1	11446	Healey	McMahon	Snookes	Bird	Hawkins	Stiles	Sadler	Bruce	Holden	Burns	Williams	Lamb		
Dec 29	Hull City	Div 2	h	2-0	10050	Healey	McMahon	Snookes	Bird	Hawkins	Sadler	Treacy	Bruce	Holden (2)	Burns	Williams	Morley		
Jan 1	Swindon Town	Div 2	a	1-1	8299	Healey	McMahon	Snookes	Bird	Hawkins	Sadler	Treacy	Bruce	Holden	Burns	Williams * (1)	S.Baxter *		
Jan 5	Fulham Rd 3	FAC	a	0-1	6937	Brown	McMahon	Snookes	Sadler	S.Baxter	Stiles *	Morley	Bruce	Holden	Burns	Treacy	Bird *		
Jan 12	Bristol City	Div 2	a	0-0	11450	Brown	McMahon	McNab	Sadler	S.Baxter	Bird	Treacy	Hawkins	Holden	Burns	Bruce	Spavin *		
Jan 19	Aston Villa	Div 2	h	0-0	10766	Brown	McMahon	McNab *	Sadler	S.Baxter	Bird	Treacy	Hawkins	Holden	Burns	Treacy	Kershaw		
Feb 3	Crystal Palace	Div 2	a	0-2	24575	Brown	McMahon	Snookes	Sadler	S.Baxter	Bird	Lamb	Hawkins	Holden	Burns	Treacy	Williams *		
Feb 10	Nottm Forest	Div 2	h	2-1	13486	Brown	McMahon	Snookes	Hawkins	S.Baxter	Bird (1)	Lamb	Sadler	Holden *	Burns	Treacy	Williams *	1 og	(Richardson)
Feb 16	Sunderland	Div 2	a	1-2	21129	Brown	McMahon	Snookes	Sadler	S.Baxter	Bird	Lamb	Stiles (1)	Holden	Burns	Treacy	Williams		
Feb 23	Fulham	Div 2	h	0-1	9412	Brown	McMahon	Snookes	Sadler	Bird	Lamb *	Stiles	Coleman	Burns	Treacy	Morley *			
Mar 2	Carlisle Utd.	Div 2	a	2-2	7671	Brown	McMahon	McNab	Sadler	S.Baxter	Stiles	Bird	Lamb	Elwiss (2)	Burns	Treacy	Carrick		
Mar 9	Cardiff City	Div 2	a	0-2	7216	Brown	McMahon	McNab	Sadler	S.Baxter	Morley	Bird	Lamb *	Elwiss	Burns	Treacy	Spark *		
Mar 16	Notts County	Div 2	h	0-2	8907	Brown	McMahon	McNab	Sadler	Hawkins *	Bird	Morley	Burns	Elwiss	Treacy	Young	Holden *		
Mar 23	Blackpool	Div 2	a	0-3	13243	Brown	McMahon	McNab *	Stiles	Sadler	Bird	Morley	Burns	Elwiss	Treacy	Young	Holden *		
Mar 30	Orient	Div 2	h	0-1	7650	Brown	McMahon	McNab	Stiles	Sadler	Bird	Lamb	Burns	Elwiss	Treacy	Young	Smith		
Apr 6	Luton Town	Div 2	a	2-4	11806	Brown	McMahon	Spark	Stiles	Hawkins	S.Baxter	Lamb	Burns (1)	Elwiss	Smith *	Sadler (1)	Treacy *		
Apr 12	Sheffield Wed.	Div 2	h	0-0	11286	Brown	McMahon	Spark	Stiles	Hawkins	Bird	Lamb	Burns	Elwiss	Holden *	Sadler	Smith *		
Apr 13	Oxford Utd.	Div 2	a	0-0	7707	Brown	McMahon	Spark	Lamb	Hawkins	Bird	Treacy	Burns	Elwiss	Holden *	Sadler	Smith *		
Apr 15	Sheffield Wed.	Div 2	a	0-1	17332	Brown	McMahon	Spark	Stiles	Hawkins	Bird	Lamb *	Burns	Elwiss	Treacy	Sadler	Smith *		
Apr 20	Bolton W.	Div 2	a	2-0	17273	Brown	McMahon	Spark	S.Baxter	Hawkins	Bird (1)	Morley	Burns	Elwiss (1)	Treacy	Sadler	Holden		
Apr 27	Middlesbrough	Div 2	h	2-4	16177	Brown	McMahon	Spark	S.Baxter	Hawkins	Bird	Morley	Burns	Elwiss (2)	Treacy	Sadler	Lamb		

221

SEASON 1974–1975

Bobby Charlton, player/manager

Preston again started the season under the national microscope as Bobby Charlton put his boots back on to take on a player/manager's role. The media interest was incredible as that familiar graceful run, dip of the shoulders and long range shooting was suddenly there for all to see again. The crowds, especially away from Deepdale, were much bigger than they might have been as the fans came out in force to have one last glimpse at one of the World's greatest footballers. Charlton did not let the fans down and one of the features of the season was to see again that famous shooting power. North End had a strange campaign though, starting well, but gradually falling away as the months progressed. A good win over Sunderland in the League Cup highlighted the early form but in the next round a bad defeat at Chester ended any hopes of a decent run. At least the team's youngsters showed just why Charlton had put so much faith in them. Tony Morley, Alan Lamb and Mel Holden continued to show good form throughout and towards the end of the season Charlton introduced further exciting players, Ricky Thomson, Mick Baxter, Steve Doyle and Mark Lawrenson into the first team. They all acquitted themselves well. The most impressive player though was Mike Elwiss and the fans loved his wholehearted approach to each game. Charlton also signed Roy Tunks, from Rotherham, as goalkeeper and certainly he added some consistency to that role. That was just what was needed in the absence of the still much missed Alan Kelly. Results were a little erratic for the club to make a serious threat on promotion. The home form was brilliant but away from home only three wins were registered. Goalscoring seemed to be impossible away from Deepdale as inexplicably the free-scoring home form deserted the players. In March Charlton again hung up his boots, this time for good, but his time in the team will always be remembered with affection and his skills certainly helped all these young stars take first team football in their stride. Before he retired as a player the FA Cup matches gave the fans some extra cheer, especially as one of the ties took Charlton back to his roots as Preston took on Bishop Auckland from his native Northumberland. After the cup run was ended by Carlisle, Preston then had to concentrate on the league games. March was a bad month, one win, two draws and three defeats. In fact few wins were registered during the run-in but at least a number of draws were forced, thus emphasising that North End were now a side that was at least difficult to beat.

DEBUTANTS: (7) Bobby Charlton, Mark Fielding, Roy Tunks, Steve Doyle, Ricky Thomson, Mick Baxter, Mark Lawrenson.

LAST GAMES: (5) John Brown, Holden, Stiles, Charlton, Fielding.

League appearances (46 games)

Baxter M. J. 1, Baxter S. W. 8 + 3, Bird J. C. 46, Brown J. C. 19, Burns F. 45, Charlton R. 38, Coleman G. M. 10 + 7, Doyle S. C. 12 + 1, Elwiss M. W. 43 + 1, Fielding M. J. 9, Holden M. G. 42, Lamb A. D. 25, Lawrenson M. T. 3, McMahon J. J. 25, Morley W. A. 44 + 1, Sadler D. 29, Smith J. 3 + 3, Spark A. M. 36, Stiles N. P. 17 + 2, Thomson R. B. 6 + 1, Treacy R. C. P. 8 + 2, Tunks R. W. 27, Williams G. P. 10.

FA Cup appearances (4 games)

Tunks 4, Fielding 4, Burns 4, Charlton 4, Doyle 4, Stiles 2, Bird 4, Sadler 4, Lamb 4, Morley 3 + 1, Elwiss 4, Holden 3 + 1.

League Cup appearances (3 games)

Brown 3, McMahon 2, Spark 3, Burns 3, Williams 1, Charlton 3, Bird 3, Sadler 3, Lamb 3, Morley 3, Elwiss 3, Holden 3.

Goalscorers: 63 League–8 FAC–3 LC–(Total 74)

Holden 17–4–1 (22), Elwiss 11–2–0 (13), Morley 10 (2 pens)–1–1 (12), Charlton 8 (2 pens)–1–1 (10), Bird 6–0–0 (6), Burns 3–0–0 (3), Coleman 2–0–0 (2), Lamb 1–0–0 (1), McMahon 1–0–0 (1), Smith 1–0–0 (1), Own goals 3–0–0 (3), Darling of Chesterfield, Tartt of Port Vale and Winstanley of Brighton.

League position in Division Three: 9th – P46 W19 D11 L16 F63 A56 Pts 49
Home: W16 D5 L2 F42 A19   Away: W3 D6 L14 F21 A37

Mel Holden and John Bird in the action at Halifax, 2 November 1974.

Match Report: Fireworks as Cherries Explode – 28 Sept. 1974 Preston 5 Bournemouth 2

If ever a spectator had value for money, then this was the game. Bournemouth, on their first ever visit to Deepdale, will not forget this meeting in a hurry, as after one incident, with an hour played, turned the match with the two teams level at 2–2. That in itself was something of a surprise as North End had previously kept seven clean sheets in 11 games whilst the visitors had only conceded one league goal so far. Bournemouth had taken a sixth minute lead, in the pouring rain, through left-winger Buttle. It was a shock for the fans as it was the first time Preston had been behind in a match at Deepdale this season. But with the likes of Elwiss, Lamb, Morley and Holden forcing their way forward it was just a matter of time before North End equalised. The goal duly came after 20 minutes when Lamb's long shot took a slight deflection past goalkeeper Baker. The gangly figure of Holden was causing problems for the Cherries as he revelled in the muddy conditions. He nearly scored in the 28th minute but when the ball wasn't cleared properly North End did find the net. Morley gained possession and from his left-wing cross Burns dived forward to head home. Although North End had now gained the upper hand it was the visitors who scored next, ten minutes from half-time, as Hague ran on to a pass from Howard and hit a great shot past the helpless Brown in Preston's goal. Charlton began the second half more involved than he had been in the first period and he tried a couple of shots, the type of which were his trademark in his Manchester United days. On 62 minutes Baker pulled Elwiss down just inside the penalty area and Mr. Hackney, the referee from Barnsley, awarded a penalty. Hague argued so much over the decision that he was promptly ordered off. Charlton waited patiently to take the spot-kick and scored with ease. As the Preston players lined up for the restart, Bournemouth's Rickard was seen arguing over both the penalty and the sending off and the referee sent him off too! Down to nine men, Bournemouth were then finished off with further goals from Elwiss and leading scorer Holden. A tough match with fortune favouring North End.

Season 1974–75: Third Division

	P	W	D	L	F	A	Pts
1 Blackburn	46	22	16	8	68	45	60
2 Plymouth	46	24	11	11	79	58	59
3 Charlton Athletic	46	22	11	13	76	61	55
4 Swindon	46	21	11	14	64	58	53
5 Crystal Palace	46	18	15	13	66	57	51
6 Port Vale	46	18	15	13	61	54	51
7 Peterborough	46	19	12	15	47	53	50
8 Walsall	46	18	13	15	67	52	49
9 PRESTON	46	19	11	16	63	56	49
10 Gillingham	46	17	14	15	65	80	48
11 Colchester	46	17	13	16	70	63	47
12 Hereford	46	16	14	16	64	66	46
13 Wrexham	46	15	15	16	65	55	45
14 Bury	46	16	12	18	53	50	44
15 Chesterfield	46	16	12	18	62	66	44
16 Grimsby	46	15	13	18	55	64	43
17 Halifax	46	13	17	16	49	65	43
18 Southend	46	13	16	17	46	51	42
19 Brighton	46	16	10	20	56	64	42
20 Aldershot	46	14	11	21	53	63	38*
21 Bournemouth	46	13	12	21	44	58	38
22 Tranmere	46	14	9	23	55	57	37
23 Watford	46	10	17	19	52	75	37
24 Huddersfield	46	11	10	25	47	76	32

* One point deducted for playing unregistered player.

STAT FACTS:

Best home run without defeat: 13 games
Best away run without defeat: 2 games
Longest run unbeaten: 6 games
Longest run without a win: 7 games
Best home attendance: 18,682 *vs.* Carlisle FAC 4.1.75
Worst home attendance: 5,819 *vs.* Watford 22.4.75
Best away attendance: 24,195 *vs.* Charlton 29.4.75
Worst away attendance: 4,878 *vs.* Halifax 2.11.74
Aggregate and average home attendance: 227,842 – 9,906
Aggregate and average away attendance: 262,227 – 11,401

Future Players born between August 1974 and July 1975:
Farrell Kibane, John Fowler, Mark Stallard, David Beckham, Craig Allardyce, Paul Sparrow, Colin Murdock, Paul McGregor.
Ever presents: John Bird
Hat-tricks: (1) Holden *vs.* Blyth (FAC)
Players used: 23
FA Cup: Third Round
League Cup: Third Round
Manager: Bobby Charlton (Player / Manager from August to March)
Chairman: A. R. W. Jones JP FRICS
Leading scorer: 22 goals – Mel Holden (17 League, 4 FAC, 1 LC)
OFFICAL PLAYER OF THE SEASON: Mike Elwiss

Trivia Fact:

Bobby Charlton's goal against Bury for Preston was the 200th league goal of his career.

Under Bobby Charlton, Nobby Stiles was manager of the reserves and chose his own teams. After one game at Blackpool where he named himself as substitute he returned to Deepdale with a nasty gash on his head. When Bobby asked what happened, Nobby explained that he had jumped up to leave the dugout and hit his head on the roof!

Left to right: *Back row:* Williams, Stiles, Brown, Treacy, Baxter. *Middle row:* Holden, Spark, McMahon, Sadler, Elwiss. *Front row:* Lamb, Coleman, Bird, Charlton, Burns, Morley.

Date 1974-5	Opponents	Comp	h or a	Score	Att.	1	2	3	4	5	6	7	8	9	10	11	12 * Sub. Used		
Aug 17	Plymouth Arg.	Div 3	h	1-0	11663	Brown	McMahon	Spark	Charlton	Bird	Sadler	Lamb	Morley (1)	Elwiss	Coleman *	Burns	Smith *		
Aug 20	Rochdale Rd 1	LC	h	1-0	7780	Brown	McMahon	Spark	Charlton	Bird	Sadler	Lamb	Morley	Elwiss	Holden (1)	Burns	Smith		
Aug 24	Watford	Div 3	a	2-3	8918	Brown	McMahon	Spark	Charlton	Bird	Sadler	Lamb	Morley	Elwiss (1)	Holden * (1)	Burns	S.Baxter *		
Aug 31	Walsall	Div 3	h	3-2	7446	Brown	McMahon	Spark	Charlton (1)	Bird	Sadler	Lamb	Morley (1)	Elwiss (1)	Holden	Burns	Smith		
Sep 3	Bury	Div 3	h	3-0	10404	Brown	McMahon	Spark	Charlton (1)	Bird	Sadler	Lamb	Morley	Elwiss	Holden (2)	Burns	Smith		
Sep 7	Aldershot	Div 3	a	2-1	6357	Brown	McMahon	Spark	Bums	Bird	S.Baxter	Lamb	Morley (1)	Elwiss	Holden (1)	Burns	Williams		
Sep 10	Sunderland Rd 2	LC	h	2-0	13279	Brown	McMahon	Spark	Burns	Bird	Sadler	Lamb	Morley (1)	Elwiss	Holden	Charlton (1)	Williams		
Sep 14	Blackbum R.	Div 3	h	0-0	18042	Brown	McMahon	Spark	Bums	Bird	Sadler	Lamb	Morley	Elwiss	Holden	Charlton	S.Baxter		
Sep 17	Charlton Ath.	Div 3	a	2-0	11869	Brown	McMahon	Spark	Bums	Bird	Sadler	Lamb	Morley (1)	Elwiss (1)	Holden	Charlton	Williams		
Sep 21	Peterborough Utd.	Div 3	h	0-0	13120	Brown	McMahon	Spark	Bums	Bird	Sadler	Lamb	Morley	Elwiss	Holden	Charlton	Smith		
Sep 24	Crystal Palace	Div 3	a	0-1	19680	Brown	McMahon	Spark	Bums	Bird	Sadler	Lamb	Morley	Elwiss	Holden	Charlton	Williams		
Sep 28	Bournemouth	Div 3	h	5-2	10421	Brown	McMahon	Spark	Bums (1)	Bird	Sadler	Lamb (1)	Morley	Elwiss (1)	Holden (1)	Charlton * (1p)	Coleman *		
Oct 1	Bury	Div 3	a	0-2	11914	Brown	Fielding	Spark	Bums	Bird	Sadler	Lamb	Morley	Elwiss	Holden	Charlton	Stiles		
Oct 5	Hereford Utd.	Div 3	a	2-2	11488	Brown	Spark	Bums	Charlton	Bird (1)	Sadler	Lamb	Morley	Elwiss	Holden (1)	Williams *	S.Baxter *		
Oct 9	Chester Rd 3	LC	a	0-1	11262	Brown	Spark	Bums	Charlton	Bird	Sadler	Lamb	Morley	Elwiss	Holden	Williams	Treacy		
Oct 12	Colchester Utd.	Div 3	a	0-2	10259	Brown	Fielding	Bums	Charlton	Bird	Sadler	Lamb	Morley	Elwiss	Holden	Williams *	Treacy *		
Oct 19	Brighton	Div 3	h	4-0	16413	Brown	Spark	Bums	Treacy	Bird	Sadler	Lamb	Morley (1)	Elwiss (1)	Holden (2)	Charlton	S.Baxter		
Oct 22	Gillingham	Div 3	h	1-0	9867	Brown	Spark	Bums	Treacy	Bird (1)	Sadler	Lamb	Morley	Elwiss	Holden	Charlton	S.Baxter		
Oct 26	Grimsby Town	Div 3	a	2-0	9934	Brown	Spark	Bums	Treacy	Bird	Sadler	Lamb	Morley (1)	Elwiss	Holden	Charlton (1p)	S.Baxter		
Nov 2	Halifax Town	Div 3	a	0-3	4878	Brown	Spark	Bums	Treacy	Bird	Sadler	Lamb	Morley *	Elwiss	Holden	Charlton	Stiles *		
Nov 6	Gillingham	Div 3	a	1-2	10494	Brown	Spark	Bums	Treacy	Bird	Sadler	Lamb	Morley	Elwiss (1)	Holden *	Charlton	Stiles *		
Nov 9	Southend Utd.	Div 3	a	1-4	8295	Brown	Spark	Bums	Treacy	Bird	Sadler	Lamb	Morley	Elwiss (1)	Holden	Charlton	Smith		
Nov 15	Tranmere R.	Div 3	a	1-3	6534	Tunks	S.Baxter	Spark	Doyle	Bird	Sadler *	Lamb	Morley	Elwiss	Holden (1)	Charlton	Treacy *		
Nov 23	Blyth Spartans Rd 1	FAC	a	1-1	8500	Tunks	Fielding	Burns	Doyle	Bird	Sadler	Lamb	Morley *	Elwiss	Stiles	Charlton	Holden * (1)		
Nov 26	Blyth Spartans Replay	FAC	h	5-1	10101	Tunks	Fielding	Burns	Doyle	Bird *	Sadler	Lamb	Stiles	Elwiss (2)	Holden (3)	Charlton	Morley *		
Nov 30	Huddersfield T.	Div 3	h	4-0	7958	Tunks	Fielding	Bums	Doyle	Bird	Sadler	Lamb	Stiles *	Elwiss (1)	Holden (2)	Charlton (1)	Morley *		
Dec 7	Wrexham	Div 3	a	1-1	8226	Tunks	Fielding	Bums	Doyle	Bird	Sadler	Lamb	Morley	Elwiss	Holden (1)	Charlton	Treacy		
Dec 14	Bishop Auckland Rd 2	FAC	a	2-0	6500	Tunks	Fielding	Bums	Doyle	Bird	Sadler	Lamb	Morley (1)	Elwiss	Holden	Charlton (1)	Treacy		
Dec 21	Port Vale	Div 3	h	1-0	8743	Tunks	Fielding	Bums	Stiles	Bird (1)	Sadler	Lamb	Morley	Elwiss	Holden	Charlton	R.Taylor		
Dec 26	Blackbum R.	Div 3	a	0-3	24005	Tunks	Fielding	Bums	Stiles	Bird	Sadler	Lamb	Morley	Elwiss	Holden	Charlton	Doyle		
Dec 28	Chesterfield	Div 3	a	2-1	9258	Tunks	Fielding	Bums	Stiles	Bird	Sadler	Lamb	Morley	Elwiss	Holden	Charlton (1)	Treacy	1 og	(Darling)
Jan 4	Carlisle Utd. Rd 3	FAC	h	0-1	18682	Tunks	Fielding	Burns	Doyle	Bird	Sadler	Lamb	Morley	Elwiss	Holden	Charlton	Treacy		
Jan 11	Wrexham	Div 3	h	3-1	9293	Tunks	McMahon	Bums	Stiles	Bird	Sadler	Spark	Morley (1p)	Elwiss (1)	Holden (1)	Charlton	Doyle		
Jan 18	Huddesfield T.	Div 3	a	1-0	7654	Tunks	McMahon	Bums	Stiles	Bird	Sadler	Spark	Morley	Elwiss	Holden (1)	Charlton	Treacy		
Feb 1	Southend Utd.	Div 3	h	1-1	9134	Tunks	McMahon	Bums	Stiles *	Bird	Sadler	Spark	Morley	Elwiss	Holden (1)	Charlton	Doyle *		
Feb 8	Halifax Town	Div 3	h	1-0	9786	Tunks	McMahon	Bums	Stiles	Bird	Sadler	Spark	Morley	Elwiss	Holden (1)	Charlton	R.Taylor		
Feb 15	Swindon Town	Div 3	a	0-1	11892	Tunks	McMahon	Bums	Stiles	Bird	Sadler *	Spark	Morley	Elwiss	Holden	Charlton	Coleman *		
Feb 18	Swindon Town	Div 3	h	2-0	11139	Tunks	McMahon	Bums	Stiles	Bird	Spark	Coleman	Morley (1)	Elwiss (1)	Holden	Charlton	Doyle		
Feb 22	Tranmere R.	Div 3	h	1-0	10798	Tunks	McMahon	Bums	Stiles	Bird	Spark	Coleman	Morley	Elwiss	Holden (1)	Charlton	S.Baxter		
Feb 28	Walsall	Div 3	a	0-2	10151	Tunks	McMahon	Bums	Stiles	Bird	Spark	Coleman	Morley *	Treacy	Holden	Charlton	S.Baxter *		
Mar 8	Crystal Palace	Div 3	h	1-1	12119	Tunks	McMahon	Bums	Stiles	Bird	Spark	S.Baxter	Morley	Coleman (1)	Holden	Charlton	Smith		
Mar 15	Bournemouth	Div 3	a	0-1	7337	Tunks	McMahon	Bums	Stiles	Bird	Spark	Doyle	Morley *	Elwiss	Holden	Charlton	Coleman *		
Mar 18	Plymouth Arg.	Div 3	a	1-2	22063	Tunks	McMahon	Bums	Stiles	Bird	Spark	S.Baxter *	Coleman	Elwiss	Holden	Charlton (1)	Smith *		
Mar 22	Aldershot	Div 3	h	3-1	7474	Tunks	McMahon (1)	Bums	Doyle	Bird (1)	Spark	Morley	Smith	Elwiss	Holden (1)	Charlton	S.Baxter		
Mar 29	Port Vale	Div 3	a	1-2	6583	Tunks	McMahon	Bums	Doyle	Bird	Spark	Morley	Smith	Elwiss	Holden *	Charlton	Coleman *	1 og	(Tartt)
Mar 31	Chesterfield	Div 3	h	0-0	8705	Tunks	McMahon	Williams	Doyle	Bird	Spark	Thomson	Bums	Elwiss	Holden	Morley	Smith		
Apr 1	Peterborough Utd.	Div 3	h	1-1	6507	Tunks	McMahon *	Williams	Stiles	Bird (1)	Spark	Thomson	Bums	Elwiss	Holden	Morley	Coleman *		
Apr 5	Grimsby Town	Div 3	a	1-2	6221	Tunks	Spark *	Williams	Stiles	Bird	M.Baxter	Thomson	Bums	Elwiss (1)	Coleman	Morley	Smith *		
Apr 12	Hereford Utd.	Div 3	h	2-2	6528	Tunks	Fielding	Williams	Doyle	Bird	Spark *	Thomson	Bums (1)	Elwiss	Holden	Morley (1p)	Coleman *		
Apr 19	Colchester Utd.	Div 3	h	2-2	5228	Tunks	Fielding	Williams	Doyle	Bird	S.Baxter	Thomson *	Bums	Elwiss	Smith (1)	Morley (1)	Coleman *		
Apr 22	Watford	Div 3	h	2-2	5819	Tunks	Lawrenson	Williams	Doyle	Bird (1)	S.Baxter	Thomson *	Bums (1)	Treacy	Coleman	Morley	Elwiss *		
Apr 26	Brighton	Div 3	a	1-0	6222	Tunks	Lawrenson	Williams	Doyle	Bird	S.Baxter	Coleman	Bums	Elwiss	Holden *	Morley	Thomson *	1 og	(Winstanley)
Apr 29	Charlton Ath.	Div 3	a	1-3	24195	Tunks	Lawrenson	Williams	Doyle	Bird	S.Baxter	Coleman (1)	Bums	Elwiss	Holden	Morley	Thomson		

SEASON 1975-1976

The 1975–76 season had hardly started when news from Deepdale rocked the football world. Bobby Charlton had resigned! The manager had objected to the Board's decision to sell centre-half John Bird to Newcastle in a part exchange deal which was to also bring Alex Bruce back to Preston. All this had happened after an opening day win over Colchester and a very good two legged win over Blackburn in the League Cup. Everything looked good at the club and even Ray Treacy, who had not scored in the 18 months he had been at Preston, suddenly found his form and scored four in the first five games. However, the upheavel caused by Charlton's departure had an immediate effect with defeats at Gillingham and Hull in the League Cup stunting the impressive start. It was not long before North End appointed former Everton boss Harry Catterick as the new manager and he soon signed Jimmy Brown from Aston Villa, and this strengthened the midfield. At home the form from the previous season was retained and gradually the away form improved as well, although there was still an erratic look about the results at times. Just when it looked as though the side would put together a decent unbeaten run, sloppy defeats would ruin all the hard work. Despite Bobby Charlton's objections the return of Bruce certainly pepped up the attack. The little Scot scored regularly and there were signs of a developing partnership with Mike Elwiss. Other players were in good form too with Roy Tunks, John McMahon and Gary Williams all enjoying very consistent seasons. The FA Cup proved a great disappointment as the club went out to non-league Scarborough on a snow covered pitch, and that after being two goals up. The New Year continued to reflect Preston's patchy form and at times it was frustrating for the supporters. Too many games were lost for the club to make a serious promotion challenge but there was certainly plenty of exciting football played by this very young team and the fans warmed to the effort that was being put into their game. The experienced David Sadler showed his considerable skills and both Mick Baxter and Mark Lawrenson benefitted from his presence. Those two young players, along with Steve Doyle and John Smith continued their exciting developement, and Gordon Coleman

Alex Spark

put in a lot of under-rated work. Not a bad season, but certainly further fine tuning was required before Preston could make a proper attempt at promotion.

DEBUTANTS: (5) Royston Taylor, Jimmy Brown, Tom Clarke, Michael Robinson, Danny Cameron.

LAST GAMES: (7) Spark, Bird, Morley, Baxter, Treacy, Taylor, Clarke.

League position in Division Three: 8th – P46 W19 D10 L17 F62 A57 Pts 48
Home: W15 D4 L4 F45 A23   Away: W4 D6 L13 F17 A34

Above: **Tony Morley**, went on to play for England.

Right: **Ray Treacy**, Irish International Striker.

Match Report: Preston Skid to Defeat – 13 Dec 1975
Scarborough 3 Preston 2 FA Cup 2nd Round

Top non-league sides away in the FA Cup can always be tricky, but when the pitch is covered in snow as well, and the date is the 13th, it can and often does become a lottery! Scarborough kicked off and nearly scored in the very first minute as Barmby saw his header beat Tunks but Burns was on hand to head off the line. The home team, cheered on by over 4,000 fans, had the lion's share of the play and they attacked at every opportunity. Both Coleman and Lawrenson were spoken to by the referee after committing fouls prior to Scarborough taking a 24th minute lead. A free-kick taken by Fountain was punched clear by Tunks but Harry A. Dunn shot straight back at goal where Ayre was on hand to deflect the ball into the net. The goal was just the tonic that Boro needed but it also served as a pick-me-up to Preston who equalised within three minutes. Burns slotted a precise pass into Smith's path and the young Scot duly obliged by clipping home his first goal of the season. Smith, preferred to Treacy or Bruce, then gave his team the lead ten minutes before the break. This time he made the goal from a half-chance in a goalmouth melee after Scarborough were slow to clear. As the home side tried to level before half-time Tunks saved well from Barmby and Woodall. Police had to go into the crowd to break up fights and two youths were led away. As the second half progressed ground conditions deteriorated as the top layer of snow froze over. Certain North End players showed great skill in staying on their feet especially Smith who, in one incident, turned on a sixpence before shooting narrowly wide. After 66 minutes Boro's manager Colin Appleton sent on an extra forward in place of a midfield player and four minutes later the gamble paid off. Woodall scored an equaliser and the tie was back in the balance. Chances were created and missed at both ends but with time almost up a last minute corner gave Marshall the chance to beat Tunks who dived in the snow in vain. The goal gave Scarborough a famous victory.

Future Players born between August 1975 and July 1976: Chris Holland, Jamie Squires, Michael Appleton, John Mullin.
Ever presents: (1) Mike Elwiss
FA Cup: Second Round
League Cup: Second Round
Players used: 23
Hat-tricks: None
Manager: Bobby Charlton (resigned August) then Harry Catterick
Chairman: A. R. W. Jones JP FRICS
Leading scorer: 16 goals – Mike Elwiss (15 League 1 FAC)

OFFICIAL PLAYER OF THE SEASON: **Gary Williams**

League appearances (46 games)

Baxter M. J. 16 + 1, Baxter S. W. 5, Bird J. C. 2, Brown J. K. 29, Bruce A. R. 38 + 2, Burns F. 27, Cameron D. 0 + 1, Clarke T. 3, Coleman G. M. 15 + 5, Doyle S. C. 24, Elwiss M. W. 46, Lamb A. D. 8, Lawrenson M. T. 24, McMahon J. J. 41, Morley W. A. 25, Robinson M. J. 1 + 1, Sadler D. 28 + 1, Spark A. M. 29 + 3, Smith J. 27 + 1, Taylor R. 3, Thomson R. B. 1 + 1, Treacy R. C. P. 27 + 1, Tunks R. W. 43, Williams G. P. 44.

FA Cup appearances (2 games)

Tunks 2, McMahon 2, Williams 2, Brown 1, Lawrenson 1, Sadler 2, Spark 2, Bruce 1, Coleman 1, Burns 2, Treacy 1, Smith 1 + 1, Elwiss 2, Morley 2.

League Cup appearances (3 games)

Tunks 3, McMahon 3, Williams 3, Bird 2, Spark 3, Lamb 3, Burns 3, Treacy 3, Elwiss 3, Morley 3, Baxter S. 3, Bruce 1.

Goalscorers: 62 League–4 FAC–4 LC–(Total 70)

Elwiss 15–1–0 (16), Bruce 15 (2 pens)–0–0 (15), Treacy 11–0–2 (13), Smith 7–2–0 (9), Morley 5 (2 pens)–1 (pen)–2 (8), Coleman 2–0–0 (2), McMahon 2–0–0 (2), Baxter M. 1–0–0 (1), Doyle 1–0–0 (1), Brown 1 (pen)–0–0 (1), Own goals 2–0–0 (2), Taylor of Swindon and Earls of Aldershot.

STAT FACTS:
Best home run without defeat: 7 games
Best away run without defeat: 3 games
Longest run unbeaten: 4 games
Longest run without a win: 6 games
Best home attendance: 11,503 vs. Blackburn LC 19.8.75
Worst home attendance: 4,621 vs. Chesterfield 9.3.76
Best away attendance: 22,213 vs. C.Palace 16.3.76
Worst away attendance: 2,657 vs. Colchester 3.4.76
Aggregate and average home attendance: 162,644 – 7,072
Aggregate and average away attendance: 160,668 – 6,985

Season 1975–76: Third Division

	P	W	D	L	F	A	Pts
1 Hereford	46	26	11	9	86	55	63
2 Cardiff	46	22	13	11	69	48	57
3 Millwall	46	20	16	10	54	43	56
4 Brighton	46	22	9	15	78	53	53
5 Crystal Palace	46	18	17	11	61	46	53
6 Wrexham	46	20	12	14	66	55	52
7 Walsall	46	18	14	14	74	61	50
8 PRESTON	**46**	**19**	**10**	**17**	**62**	**57**	**48**
9 Shrewsbury	46	19	10	17	61	59	48
10 Peterborough	46	15	18	13	63	63	48
11 Mansfield	46	16	15	15	58	52	47
12 Port Vale	46	15	16	15	55	54	46
13 Bury	46	14	16	16	51	46	44
14 Chesterfield	46	17	9	20	69	69	43
15 Gillingham	46	12	19	15	58	68	43
16 Rotherham	46	15	12	19	54	65	42
17 Chester	46	15	12	19	53	62	42
18 Grimsby	46	15	10	21	62	74	40
19 Swindon	46	16	8	22	62	75	40
20 Sheffield Wednesday	46	12	16	18	48	59	40
21 Aldershot	46	13	13	20	59	75	39
22 Colchester	46	12	14	20	41	65	38
23 Southend	46	12	13	21	65	75	37
24 Halifax	46	11	13	22	41	61	35

Date 1975-6	Opponents	Comp	h or a	Score	Att.	1	2	3	4	5	6	7	8	9	10	11	12 * Sub Used		
Aug 16	Colchester Utd.	Div 3	h	2-1	6324	Tunks	McMahon	Williams	Doyle	Bird	Spark	Lamb	Burns	Treacy (2)	Elwiss	Morley	S.Baxter		
Aug 19	Blackburn R. Rd 1 1L	LC	h	2-0	11503	Tunks	McMahon	Williams	S.Baxter	Bird	Spark	Lamb	Burns	Treacy (1)	Elwiss	Morley (1)	Coleman		
Aug 23	Port Vale	Div 3	a	1-1	4282	Tunks	McMahon	Williams	S.Baxter	Bird	Spark	Lamb	Burns	Treacy (1)	Elwiss	Morley	Coleman		
Aug 27	Blackburn R. Rd 1 2L	LC	a	0-0	14077	Tunks	McMahon	Williams	S.Baxter	Bird	Spark	Lamb	Burns	Treacy	Elwiss	Morley	Doyle		
Aug 30	Millwall	Div 3	h	2-1	7707	Tunks	McMahon	Williams	Doyle	S.Baxter	Spark	Lamb	Burns	Treacy (1)	Elwiss (1)	Morley	Bruce		
Sep 6	Gillingham	Div 3	a	0-1	5786	Tunks	McMahon	Williams	S.Baxter	Sadler	Spark	Doyle *	Burns	Treacy	Elwiss	Morley	Bruce *		
Sep 9	Hull City Rd 2	LC	a	2-4	5095	Tunks	McMahon	Williams	Lamb	S.Baxter	Spark	Bruce	Burns	Treacy (1)	Elwiss (1)	Morley (1)	Sadler		
Sep 13	Walsall	Div 3	h	3-1	7015	Tunks	McMahon	Williams	Lamb	S.Baxter	Spark	Bruce (1)	Burns	Treacy (1)	Elwiss (1)	Morley	Smith		
Sep 20	Aldershot	Div 3	h	1-1	3883	Tunks	McMahon	Williams	Lamb	S.Baxter	Spark	Bruce (1)	Burns	Treacy	Elwiss	Morley	Coleman		
Sep 22	Southend Utd.	Div 3	a	2-0	4583	Tunks	McMahon	Williams	Lamb *	M.Baxter	Spark	Bruce	Burns	Treacy	Elwiss	Morley (1)	Coleman * (1)		
Sep 27	Cardiff City	Div 3	h	3-1	8103	Tunks	McMahon	Williams	Coleman *	M.Baxter	Spark	Bruce	Burns	Treacy	Elwiss (1)	Morley (1p)	Sadler *		
Oct 4	Chesterfield	Div 3	a	0-3	4384	Tunks	Sadler	Williams	Taylor *	M.Baxter	Spark	Bruce	Burns	Treacy	Elwiss	Morley *	Thomson *		
Oct 11	Brighton	Div 3	a	0-1	14375	Tunks	Sadler	Williams	Brown	M.Baxter	Spark	Bruce	Burns	Treacy	Elwiss	Morley	Lawrenson		
Oct 18	Crystal Palace	Div 3	h	0-0	10971	Tunks	McMahon	Williams	Brown	M.Baxter	Spark	Bruce	Burns	Treacy	Elwiss	Morley	Lawrenson		
Oct 21	Peterborough Utd.	Div 3	h	2-1	9597	Tunks	McMahon	Williams	Brown	M.Baxter	Spark	Bruce (1)	Burns	Treacy (1)	Elwiss	Morley	Smith		
Oct 25	Mansfield Town	Div 3	a	1-0	6677	Tunks	McMahon	Williams	Brown	M.Baxter	Spark	Bruce	Burns	Treacy (1)	Elwiss (1)	Morley	Coleman *		
Nov 1	Hereford Utd.	Div 3	h	3-4	9682	Tunks	McMahon	Williams	Brown	M.Baxter (1)	Spark	Bruce *	Burns	Treacy (1)	Elwiss	Morley (1p)	Smith *		
Nov 4	Halifax Town	Div 3	a	1-2	3366	Tunks	McMahon	Williams	Brown	M.Baxter	Spark	Bruce	Burns	Treacy	Elwiss	Morley (1)	Sadler		
Nov 8	Swindon Town	Div 3	a	3-1	6332	Tunks	McMahon	Williams	Brown	Sadler	Spark	Bruce (1)	Burns	Treacy	Elwiss (1)	Morley	Thomson	1 og	(Taylor)
Nov 15	Bury	Div 3	h	0-0	11017	Tunks	McMahon	Williams	Brown	Sadler	Spark	Bruce	Burns	Treacy	Elwiss	Morley	Lawrenson		
Nov 22	Scunthorpe Utd. Rd 1	FAC	h	2-1	8119	Tunks	McMahon	Williams	Brown *	Sadler	Spark	Bruce	Burns	Treacy	Elwiss (1)	Morley (1p)	Smith *		
Nov 29	Grimsby Town	Div 3	a	0-0	4519	Tunks	McMahon	Williams	Brown	Sadler	Spark	Bruce	Burns	Treacy *	Elwiss	Morley	Coleman *		
Dec 6	Wrexham	Div 3	h	0-1	7438	Tunks	Lawrenson	Williams	Thomson	M.Baxter	Spark	Bruce	Burns	Treacy *	Elwiss	Morley	Coleman *		
Dec 13	Scarborough Rd 2	FAC	a	2-3	4100	Tunks	McMahon	Williams	Lawrenson	Sadler	Spark	Coleman	Burns	Smith (2)	Elwiss	Morley	Bruce		
Dec 20	Sheffield Wed.	Div 3	a	2-2	8553	Tunks	McMahon	Williams	M.Baxter	Sadler	Spark	Doyle	Burns	Smith	Elwiss	Morley	Bruce		
Dec 27	Chester	Div 3	h	0-3	8137	Clarke	McMahon	Williams	Lawrenson	Sadler	Spark	Doyle	Burns	Smith	Elwiss	Morley	Taylor		
Jan 10	Millwall	Div 3	a	0-2	6057	Clarke	McMahon *	Williams	Lawrenson	Sadler	Spark	Bruce	Burns	Smith	Elwiss	Morley	Coleman *		
Jan 13	Rotherham Utd.	Div 3	h	3-2	6289	Clarke	McMahon	Williams	Lawrenson	Sadler	Taylor *	Smith (1)	Burns	Treacy	Elwiss (1)	Morley (1)	Bruce *		
Jan 17	Aldershot	Div 3	a	1-0	6326	Tunks	McMahon	Williams	Taylor	Sadler	Spark	Smith	Burns	Treacy	Elwiss	Morley	Lawrenson	1 og	(Earls)
Jan 24	Walsall	Div 3	a	1-3	6721	Tunks	McMahon	Williams	Lawrenson	Sadler	Spark	Smith	Burns	Treacy (1)	Elwiss	Bruce	Doyle		
Jan 31	Peterborough Utd.	Div 3	a	0-2	7728	Tunks	McMahon	Williams	Brown	M.Baxter	Spark	Bruce	Burns	Smith	Elwiss	Morley	Lawrenson		
Feb 3	Shrewsbury T.	Div 3	h	0-2	4995	Tunks	Lawrenson	Williams	Brown	Sadler	Spark	Coleman	Burns *	Smith	Treacy	Bruce	Treacy *		
Feb 7	Halifax Town	Div 3	h	2-1	5480	Tunks	McMahon	Williams	Doyle (1)	Sadler	Spark	Brown	Smith	Treacy	Elwiss (1)	Bruce	Coleman		
Feb 14	Swindon Town	Div 3	h	4-2	5868	Tunks	McMahon	Williams	Doyle	Sadler	Lawrenson	Brown (1p)	Smith (1)	Treacy (1)	Elwiss	Bruce (1)	Coleman		
Feb 21	Bury	Div 3	a	0-2	7049	Tunks	McMahon	Williams	Doyle	Sadler	Lawrenson	Brown	Smith	Treacy	Elwiss	Bruce	Burns		
Feb 24	Southend Utd.	Div 3	h	5-1	5210	Tunks	McMahon	Williams	Doyle	Sadler	Lawrenson	Brown	Smith (2)	Treacy (1)	Elwiss (2)	Bruce	Coleman		
Feb 28	Mansfield Town	Div 3	h	0-2	6945	Tunks	McMahon	Williams	Doyle *	Sadler	Lawrenson	Brown	Smith	Treacy	Elwiss	Bruce	Coleman *		
Mar 9	Chesterfield	Div 3	h	3-1	4621	Tunks	McMahon	Williams	Doyle	Sadler	Lawrenson	Brown	Coleman	Smith	Elwiss (1)	Bruce (2)	Spark		
Mar 13	Brighton	Div 3	h	1-0	6720	Tunks	McMahon	Williams	Doyle	Sadler	Lawrenson	Brown	Coleman	Smith	Elwiss	Bruce (1p)	Spark		
Mar 16	Crystal Palace	Div 3	a	0-2	22213	Tunks	McMahon	Williams	Doyle	Sadler	Lawrenson	Brown	Coleman	Smith	Elwiss	Bruce	Spark		
Mar 20	Grimsby Town	Div 3	h	0-0	6586	Tunks	McMahon	Williams	Doyle	Sadler	Lawrenson	Brown	Coleman	Smith	Elwiss	Bruce	Spark		
Mar 27	Wrexham	Div 3	a	2-1	4906	Tunks	McMahon	Williams	Doyle	Sadler	Lawrenson *	Brown	Coleman	Smith (1)	Elwiss	Bruce (1)	Spark *		
Mar 30	Sheffield Wed.	Div 3	h	4-2	6899	Tunks	McMahon (1)	Williams	Doyle	Sadler	Lawrenson	Brown	Coleman	Smith	Elwiss (1)	Bruce (2)	Spark		
Apr 3	Colchester Utd.	Div 3	a	1-1	2657	Tunks	McMahon *	Williams	Doyle	Sadler	Lawrenson	Brown	Coleman	Smith	Elwiss (1)	Bruce	Spark *		
Apr 7	Cardiff City	Div 3	a	0-1	12447	Tunks	Coleman	Lawrenson	Doyle	Sadler	Spark	Brown	Robinson *	Smith	Elwiss	Bruce	M.Baxter *		
Apr 10	Gillingham	Div 3	h	4-0	6349	Tunks	McMahon * (1)	Williams	Doyle	M.Baxter	Lawrenson	Brown	Coleman	Smith (1)	Elwiss	Bruce (2, 1p)	Robinson		
Apr 17	Shrewsbury T.	Div 3	a	0-1	3547	Tunks	McMahon	Spark	Doyle	M.Baxter	Lawrenson	Brown	Coleman	Smith	Elwiss	Bruce	Robinson		
Apr 19	Chester	Div 3	h	0-0	6719	Tunks	McMahon	Williams	Doyle	M.Baxter	Lawrenson	Brown *	Coleman	Smith	Elwiss	Bruce	Robinson *		
Apr 20	Rotherham Utd.	Div 3	a	1-1	4874	Tunks	McMahon	Williams	Doyle	M.Baxter	Lawrenson	Lamb	Coleman (1)	Smith	Elwiss	Bruce	Cameron		
Apr 24	Port Vale	Div 3	h	3-0	5783	Tunks	McMahon	Williams	Doyle	M.Baxter	Lawrenson	Brown	Coleman	Smith	Elwiss (1)	Bruce (2)	Cameron		
Apr 28	Hereford Utd.	Div 3	a	1-3	7592	Tunks	McMahon	Williams	Doyle	Sadler	Lawrenson	Brown *	Lamb	Smith	Elwiss (1)	Bruce	Cameron *		

227

SEASON 1976–1977

The gradual improvement that Preston had shown over the previous two seasons was continued in the 1976–77 campaign and but for a very poor April then promotion might have been more than a dream. The progress was maintained with virtually the same squad of players, with the youngsters now playing some assured and confident football as their experience increased. One of the keys in this mini success story came in the potent strike force that North End had cultivated. Mike Elwiss and Alex Bruce formed the best forward partnership since Alex Dawson had partnered Brian Godfrey to such good effect ten years earlier. In one game, against Peterborough at Deepdale, Bruce scored a terrific hat-trick and Elwiss scored once in a 6–2 victory. In the midfield Francis Burns and Gordon Coleman worked tirelessly and they were well backed up by Steve Doyle or Jimmy Brown. John Smith's contribution should also not be undervalued and the inter-weaving of Smith, Elwiss and Bruce up front had defences stretched to the limit at times. In defence Mark Lawrenson was immaculate and his form had the scouts flocking to Deepdale. Mick Baxter also impressed and he eventually took over the centre-half role from David Sadler. With Roy Tunks showing the consistency so necessary in the goalkeeper role the team had a solid base. The all round strength of the side showed in their teamwork and swift inter-passing. It was very good to watch at times, but unfortunately North End were still vulnerable to an irritating defeat, usually by the odd goal, with each one a setback for manager Harry Catterick. Preston went out

of the League Cup at the first hurdle again and fared little better when the FA Cup started. Although it was a season when Preston won at Anfield, no, not against Liverpool, but against Crewe, in a first round second replay. Sadly, in the next round Preston went out meekly to Halifax Town, a side managed by none other than Alan Ball Senior. After the turn of the year Preston continued to play some sparkling football and in March won five out of their six games. But when April came the form went the other way as they could only manage two wins out of eight matches and that put paid to earlier thoughts of promotion. Overall though the season certainly gave cause for optimism as Preston had the nucleus of a very good side. With one or two astute signings they would definitely be a good bet for promotion. The increasing influence of coach Nobby Stiles was felt this season. The players thought very highly of him. Little did they know that they were soon to see his role change.

DEBUTANTS: (3) Alex Smith, Barrie Mitchell, Ian Cochrane.

LAST GAMES: (6) Lamb, Williams, Sadler, Lawrenson, Smith A., Mitchell.

Mike Elwiss in full flow watched by Steve Doyle.

League appearances (46 games)

Baxter M. J. 26, Brown J. K. 33, Burns F. 44, Bruce A. R. 46, Cameron D. 14 + 1, Cochrane I. 1, Coleman G. M. 44, Doyle S. C. 18 + 4, Elwiss M. W. 45, Lamb A. D. 3 + 1, Lawrenson M. T. 46, McMahon J. J. 31 + 1, Mitchell B. 7 + 4, Sadler D. 20, Smith A. 8, Smith J. 34 + 1, Thomson R. B. 4 + 3, Tunks R. W. 38, Williams G. P. 44.

FA Cup appearances (4 games)

Tunks 4, McMahon 4, Williams 2, Doyle 2, Sadler 4, Lawrenson 4, Brown 2, Coleman 4, Smith J. 4, Elwiss 4, Bruce 4, Burns 4, Mitchell 0 + 2, Cameron 2.

League Cup appearances (2 games)

Tunks 2, McMahon 2, Williams 2, Doyle 2, Sadler 2, Lawrenson 2, Coleman 2, Brown 2, Robinson 1, Smith J. 1, Elwiss 2, Bruce 2, Cameron 0 + 1, Mitchell 0 + 1.

Goalscorers: 64 League–6 FAC–2 LC–(Total 72)

Bruce 24 (1 pen)–2–0 (26), Elwiss 21–1–0 (22), Coleman 3–1–0 (4), Smith J. 3–0–1 (4), Brown 2–1–1 (4), Thomson 3–0–0 (3), Lawrenson 2–0–0 (2), Mitchell 2–0–0 (2), Sadler 1–1–0 (2), Burns 1–0–0 (1), Baxter 1–0–0 (1), Cochrane 1–0–0 (1).

Future Players born between August 1976 and July 1977: Tony Grant, Kevin Kilbane, Michael Holt, Darren Byfield, Jason Harris
Ever presents: (2) Mark Lawrenson and Alex Bruce
Hat-tricks: (1) Alex Bruce
FA Cup: Second Round
League Cup: First Round
Players used: 20
Manager: Harry Catterick
Chairman: A. R. W. Jones JP FRICS
Leading scorer: 26 goals – Alex Bruce (24 League 2 FAC)

OFFICIAL PLAYER OF THE SEASON:
Mark Lawrenson

League position in Division Three: 6th – P46 W21 D12 L13 F64 A43 Pts 54
Home: W15 D4 L4 F48 A21   Away: W6 D8 L9 F16 A22

Left to right: *Back row:* Tickle, Thomson, Baxter, Cameron, Lamb. *Middle row:* Brown, Doyle, Williams, Tunks, Smith (A), Lawrenson, Robinson, Elwiss. *Front row:* H. Hubbick (trainer), Bruce, Burns, McMahon Mr Catterick (manager), Sadler, Coleman, Smith (J), Stiles.

Match Report: Posh Paupers Pulverised – 12 October 1976 Preston 6 Peterborough 2

With PNE Chairman, Alan Jones, only saying the day before that, 'It was time for the big push to try to join the contenders for promotion', the North End team duly went out and recorded the club's biggest win for years. There is nothing better than witnessing an emphatic win at a floodlit night match, but unfortunately there were only 5,651 at the game. The wet conditions helped the forwards whereas it made turning difficult for the bigger defenders. Bruce started the ball rolling after just six minutes with a shot that the Posh goalkeeper, Steele, could not hold. It was a good start but the visitors quickly equalised through Moss. Bruce was then able to set up Mitchell for Preston's second goal and Bruce then claimed a third and his second just before the interval to put North End in a commanding position. That goal took a deflection and in some morning papers it was given as an own goal, but the club officially gave it to Brucey, and it was never in doubt in his mind! Substitute Smith replaced hamstring victim Mitchell for the second half and Preston were soon attacking again. On 65 minutes Bruce clinched the result with a superbly struck shot following an exchange of passes with Elwiss. There were no doubts about that goal! Twelve minutes later Elwiss himself made the scoresheet as he scored direct from a free-kick, just as he had in the last home game against York. Bruce, Elwiss, Smith, Brown, Williams, Coleman and Lawrenson all went close as Preston laid siege to the Peterborough goal. The Posh had no answer to it all. The rout continued when Smith headed past Steele from a Williams centre before the United substitute, Walker, who was on for Turner, headed a late consolation goal from a Doyle cross. It was too little, too late for the visitors though and they were a well beaten team at the end. Scouts from Leeds, Birmingham, Everton and Coventry were at the match and they saw Preston at their best.

Mark Lawrenson, now a television pundit after a top-class career, and Steve Doyle, North End's youngest ever player.

		P	W	D	L	F	A	Pts
1	Mansfield	46	28	8	10	78	33	64
2	Brighton	46	25	11	10	83	39	61
3	Crystal Palace	46	23	13	10	68	40	59
4	Rotherham	46	22	15	9	69	44	59
5	Wrexham	46	24	10	12	80	54	58
6	PRESTON	46	21	12	13	64	43	54
7	Bury	46	23	8	15	64	59	54
8	Sheffield Wednesday	46	22	9	15	65	55	53
9	Lincoln	46	25	14	13	77	70	52
10	Shrewsbury	46	18	11	17	65	59	47
11	Swindon	46	15	15	16	68	75	45
12	Gillingham	46	14	12	18	55	64	44
13	Chester	46	18	8	20	48	58	44
14	Tranmere	46	13	17	16	51	53	43
15	Walsall	46	13	15	18	57	65	41
16	Peterborough	46	13	15	18	55	65	41
17	Oxford	46	12	15	19	55	65	39
18	Chesterfield	46	14	10	22	56	64	38
19	Port Vale	46	11	16	19	47	71	38
20	Portsmouth	46	11	14	21	43	70	35
21	Reading	46	13	9	24	49	73	35
22	Northampton	46	13	8	25	60	75	34
23	Grimsby	46	12	9	25	45	69	33
24	York	46	10	12	24	50	89	32

STAT FACTS:

Best home run without defeat: 9 games
Best away run without defeat: 8 games
Longest run unbeaten: 10 games
Longest run without a win: 5 games
Best home attendance: 11,753 *vs.* Sheff.Wed. 29.3.77
Worst home attendance: 4,879 *vs.* Reading 23.4.77
Best away attendance: 21,338 *vs.* Brighton 5.2.77
Worst away attendance: 2,849 *vs.* Shrewsbury 14.5.77
Aggregate and average home attendance: 183,703 – 7,987
Aggregate and average away attendance: 167,585 – 7,286

Trivia Facts:

Southern Television covered the Reading *vs.* PNE match for their Sunday afternoon highlights programme.

Harry Catterick made a determined bid to bring Howard Kendall back to Deepdale at the end of the season. He arranged a player exchange deal involving Steve Doyle. In the end though the deal never materialised.

Gary Williams was sent off in the match at Gillingham.

Date 1976-7	Opponents	Comp.	h or a	Score *aet	Att.	1	2	3	4	5	6	7	8	9	10	11	12 *Sub Used
Aug 14	Bury Rd 1 1L	LC	a	1-2	5858	Tunks	McMahon	Williams	Doyle	Sadler	Lawrenson	Brown (1)	Coleman	Robinson *	Elwiss	Bruce	Cameron *
Aug 17	Bury Rd 2 2L	LC	h	1-1	7649	Tunks	McMahon	Williams	Doyle	Sadler	Lawrenson	Coleman *	Brown	J.Smith (1)	Elwiss	Bruce	Mitchell *
Aug 21	Mansfield Town	Div 3	a	1-3	5688	A.Smith	Cameron *	Williams	Doyle	Sadler	Lawrenson	Coleman	Lamb	J.Smith	Elwiss (1)	Bruce	Mitchell *
Aug 28	Brighton	Div 3	h	1-1	6265	Tunks	Coleman	Williams	Burns	Sadler	Lawrenson	Lamb	Brown	J.Smith *	Elwiss	Bruce	Mitchell * (1)
Sep 4	Oxford Utd.	Div 3	a	2-2	4580	Tunks	McMahon	Williams	Burns	Sadler	Lawrenson	Coleman	Brown	J.Smith *	Elwiss (2)	Bruce	Mitchell *
Sep 11	Chester	Div 3	a	0-0	4326	Tunks	McMahon	Williams	Burns	Sadler	Lawrenson	Coleman	Brown	J.Smith	Elwiss	Bruce	Doyle
Sep 14	Port Vale	Div 3	h	4-0	6592	Tunks	McMahon	Williams	Burns	Sadler	Lawrenson	Coleman (1)	Brown	J.Smith *	Elwiss (1)	Bruce (2, 1p)	Lamb *
Sep 18	Rotherham Utd.	Div 3	h	1-1	7812	Tunks	McMahon	Williams	Burns	Sadler	Lawrenson	Coleman	Brown	Lamb *	Elwiss	Bruce	Doyle *
Sep 25	Grimsby Town	Div 3	a	0-1	4100	Tunks	McMahon *	Williams	Burns	Baxter	Lawrenson	Doyle	Brown	Mitchell	Elwiss	Bruce	Cameron *
Oct 2	York City	Div 3	h	4-2	6380	Tunks	Coleman	Williams	Burns (1)	Baxter	Lawrenson	Doyle	Brown	Mitchell	Elwiss (2)	Bruce (1)	Thomson
Oct 8	Tranmere R.	Div 3	a	0-0	5005	Tunks	Coleman	Williams	Burns	Sadler	Lawrenson	Doyle	Brown	Mitchell	Elwiss	Bruce	Baxter
Oct 12	Peterborough Utd.	Div 3	h	6-2	5761	Tunks	Coleman	Williams	Burns	Sadler	Lawrenson	Doyle	Brown	Mitchell * (1)	Elwiss (1)	Bruce (3)	Smith * (1)
Oct 16	Crystal Palace	Div 3	h	2-1	10524	Tunks	McMahon	Williams	Burns	Sadler	Lawrenson	Coleman	Brown	J.Smith	Elwiss (2)	Bruce	Doyle
Oct 23	Bury	Div 3	a	2-3	8724	Tunks	McMahon	Williams	Burns	Sadler	Lawrenson	Coleman	Brown	J.Smith	Elwiss	Bruce (2)	Doyle
Oct 30	Gillingham	Div 3	a	1-1	5070	Tunks	McMahon	Williams	Burns	Sadler	Lawrenson	Coleman	Doyle	J.Smith	Elwiss	Bruce (1)	Baxter
Nov 1	Port Vale	Div 3	a	0-0	4686	Tunks	McMahon	Cameron	Burns	Baxter	Lawrenson	Coleman	Doyle	J.Smith	Elwiss	Bruce	Lamb
Nov 6	Northampton T.	Div 3	h	3-0	7306	Tunks	McMahon	Burns	Sadler	Lawrenson	Coleman (1)	Doyle	J.Smith	Elwiss (2)	Bruce	Cameron
Nov 13	Reading	Div 3	a	2-0	6816	Tunks	McMahon	Cameron	Burns	Sadler	Lawrenson	Coleman	Doyle	J.Smith	Elwiss (1)	Bruce (1)	Baxter
Nov 20	Crewe A. Rd 1	FAC	a	1-1	6373	Tunks	McMahon	Cameron	Burns	Sadler	Lawrenson	Coleman (1)	Doyle	J.Smith	Elwiss	Bruce	Mitchell
Nov 23	Crewe A. Replay	FAC	h	2-2*	10833	Tunks	McMahon	Cameron	Burns	Sadler	Lawrenson	Coleman	Doyle	J.Smith *	Elwiss	Bruce (2)	Mitchell *
Nov 27	Lincoln City	Div 3	a	3-0	7964	Tunks	McMahon	Williams	Burns	Sadler	Lawrenson	Coleman	Brown	J.Smith	Elwiss (1)	Bruce (2)	Doyle
Nov 29	Crewe A. 2nd Replay +	FAC	a	3-0	7334	Tunks	McMahon	Williams	Burns	Sadler (1)	Lawrenson	Coleman	Brown (1)	J.Smith	Elwiss (1)	Bruce	Doyle
Dec 4	Portsmouth	Div 3	a	0-0	9238	Tunks	McMahon	Williams	Burns	Sadler	Lawrenson	Coleman	Brown	J.Smith	Elwiss	Bruce	Doyle
Dec 14	Halifax Town Rd 2	FAC	a	0-1	5219	Tunks	McMahon	Williams	Burns	Sadler	Lawrenson	Coleman	Brown	J.Smith *	Elwiss	Bruce	Mitchell *
Dec 17	Shrewsbury T.	Div 3	h	2-1	7809	Tunks	McMahon	Burns	Sadler (1)	Lawrenson (1)	Coleman	Brown	J.Smith	Elwiss	Bruce	Doyle
Dec 27	Walsall	Div 3	a	1-0	8769	Tunks	McMahon	Williams	Burns	Baxter	Lawrenson	Coleman	Brown	J.Smith	Elwiss	Bruce (1)	Doyle
Jan 1	Northampton T.	Div 3	a	1-0	5024	Tunks	McMahon	Williams	Burns	Baxter	Lawrenson	Coleman	Brown	J.Smith	Elwiss	Bruce (1)	Baxter
Jan 15	Peterborough Utd.	Div 3	a	0-0	5308	Tunks	McMahon	Williams	Burns	Baxter	Lawrenson	Coleman	Brown	J.Smith	Elwiss	Bruce	Mitchell
Jan 22	Mansfield Town	Div 3	h	1-2	11110	Tunks	McMahon	Williams	Burns	Baxter	Lawrenson	Coleman	Brown	J.Smith	Elwiss (1)	Bruce	Mitchell
Jan 29	Chesterfield	Div 3	a	1-1	4992	Tunks	McMahon	Williams	Burns	Baxter	Lawrenson	Coleman	Brown	J.Smith	Elwiss	Bruce (1)	Doyle
Feb 5	Brighton	Div 3	a	0-2	21265	Tunks	McMahon	Williams	Burns	Baxter	Lawrenson	Cameron *	Brown	J.Smith	Elwiss	Bruce	Doyle *
Feb 8	Swindon Town	Div 3	h	2-0	9409	Tunks	McMahon	Williams	Burns	Baxter	Lawrenson	Coleman	Brown (1)	Mitchell	Elwiss	Bruce (1)	Doyle
Feb 12	Oxford Utd.	Div 3	h	2-1	9950	Tunks	McMahon	Williams	Burns	Baxter	Lawrenson	Coleman	Brown	Mitchell	Elwiss (1)	Bruce (1)	Doyle
Feb 19	Chester	Div 3	h	3-4	10101	Tunks	McMahon	Williams	Burns	Baxter	Lawrenson	Coleman	Brown	Mitchell	Elwiss (2)	Bruce (1)	Doyle
Feb 26	Rotherham Utd.	Div 3	a	0-2	8860	Tunks	McMahon	Williams	Burns	Baxter	Lawrenson	Coleman	Brown	J.Smith	Elwiss	Bruce	Mitchell
Mar 5	Grimsby Town	Div 3	h	2-1	7278	Tunks	McMahon	Williams	Burns *	Baxter	Lawrenson	Coleman	Brown (1)	J.Smith	Elwiss	Bruce (1)	Doyle *
Mar 12	York City	Div 3	a	2-0	3575	Tunks	Cameron	Williams	Burns	Baxter	Lawrenson	Coleman	Brown	J.Smith (1)	Elwiss (1)	Bruce *	Doyle *
Mar 15	Wrexham	Div 3	h	2-1	10491	Tunks	Cameron	Williams	Burns	Baxter	Lawrenson	Coleman	Brown	J.Smith	Elwiss	Bruce (2)	Doyle
Mar 19	Tranmere R.	Div 3	h	1-0	9100	Tunks	Cameron	Williams	Burns	Baxter	Lawrenson	Coleman (1)	Brown	J.Smith	Elwiss	Bruce	Doyle
Mar 22	Crystal Palace	Div 3	a	0-1	15225	Tunks	Cameron	Williams	Burns	Baxter	Lawrenson	Coleman	Brown	J.Smith	Elwiss	Bruce	Doyle
Mar 29	Sheffield Wed.	Div 3	h	4-1	11753	Tunks	Cameron	Williams	Burns	Sadler	Lawrenson (1)	Coleman	Brown	J.Smith (1)	Elwiss (1)	Bruce (1)	McMahon
Apr 2	Bury	Div 3	h	0-2	9793	A.Smith	McMahon	Williams	Burns	Sadler	Lawrenson	Coleman	Brown	J.Smith	Elwiss	Bruce	McMahon
Apr 9	Wrexham	Div 3	a	0-2	10545	A.Smith	Cameron *	Williams	Burns	Sadler	Lawrenson	Coleman	Brown	J.Smith	Elwiss	Bruce	McMahon *
Apr 11	Walsall	Div 3	h	0-1	7850	A.Smith	McMahon	Williams	Burns	Baxter	Lawrenson	Coleman	Doyle	J.Smith	Elwiss	Bruce	Mitchell
Apr 16	Sheffield Wed.	Div 3	a	0-1	13217	A.Smith	McMahon	Williams	Burns	Baxter	Lawrenson	Coleman	Doyle	J.Smith *	Elwiss	Bruce	Thomson *
Apr 19	Chesterfield	Div 3	h	2-2	5288	A.Smith	McMahon	Williams	Brown	Baxter (1)	Lawrenson	Coleman	Doyle	Thomson (1)	Elwiss	Bruce	Burns
Apr 23	Reading	Div 3	h	3-0	4872	A.Smith	McMahon	Williams	Burns	Baxter	Lawrenson	Coleman	Doyle	Thomson (2)	Elwiss	Bruce (1)	Smith
Apr 26	Gillingham	Div 3	h	1-0	4943	A.Smith	McMahon	Williams	Burns	Baxter	Lawrenson	Coleman	Doyle	Thomson	Elwiss (1)	Bruce	Mitchell
Apr 30	Lincoln City	Div 3	a	0-2	5357	Tunks	McMahon	Williams	Burns	Baxter	Lawrenson	Coleman	Doyle	Thomson *	Elwiss	Bruce	Mitchell *
May 3	Swindon Town	Div 3	a	0-0	4366	Tunks	Cameron	Williams	Burns	Baxter	Lawrenson	Coleman	Doyle	Thomson	Elwiss	Bruce	Thomson *
May 7	Portsmouth	Div 3	h	0-0	5352	Tunks	Cameron	Williams	Burns *	Baxter	Lawrenson	Coleman	Doyle	J.Smith	Elwiss	Bruce	Thomson *
May 14	Shrewsbury	Div 3	a	2-1	2849	Tunks	Cameron	Williams	Burns	Baxter	Lawrenson	Coleman	Doyle	J.Smith	Cochrane (1)	Bruce (1)	Thomson
	+ Second Replay at Anfield, Liverpool																

SEASON 1977–1978

Hopes were high amongst the North End fans at the start of the 1977–78 season. Although Preston had bowed to financial pressure and sold both Gary Williams and Mark Lawrenson to Brighton in the summer, the cash plus player deal meant that two new signings made the journey in the opposite direction. Harry Wilson and Graham Cross came in as straight replacements for the two talented youngsters. There were changes off the field as well as Harry Catterick stepped aside as manager leaving Nobby Stiles in charge with Alan Kelly as his number two. The club needed a good start and they made one. Once again the Mike Elwiss, Alex Bruce combination looked sharp and Preston were soon amongst the goals. Ricky Thomson, another youngster who had progressed through the junior sides, looked a real find as North End looked to better the previous season's sixth position. A second round defeat against Walsall in the League Cup and a hiccup in form up to the end of September was ended when Preston had a good win over Cambridge at Deepdale. Sean Haslegrave made his debut in that match and his presence strengthened the midfield. But one of the team's main improvements during this season came with their away form. It was much harder to beat North End on their travels this year and the number of draws on opponents' grounds reflected this. These results were vital and coupled with another excellent season of home form it meant that Preston had the platform to make a promotion challenge. Roy Tunks had another very consistent season in goal, John McMahon and Danny Cameron always gave 100% effort at full-back, with McMahon showing what a cultured footballer he had become. Mick Baxter had his best campaign yet and Gordon Coleman worked tirelessly, and with no little amount of skill. A great run by the team which began in the November and ran through to early March really added to the thoughts of promotion. Bruce, in particular, was in superb form, scoring all four goals in a 4–0 win over Colchester. An early exit from the FA Cup focussed all minds on the league battle and despite poor results in April it eventually came down to the last day of the season. Preston trailed Shrewsbury 2–1 at half-time and needed a result to put the pressure on Peterborough, North End's closest rivals. A precious equaliser by Bruce, his 30th goal of the season, and a defeat for Peterborough left North End two points ahead but with the Posh having one game left at Wrexham. A nerve racking afternoon was spent by the radio tuned in to news from Wales. It was all good as Peterborough could only manage a draw and Preston's third place was enough for Nobby Stiles to celebrate his first promotion.

DEBUTANTS: (4) Harry Wilson, Graham Cross, Sean Haslegrave, Steve Uzelac.

LAST GAMES: (1) Jimmy Brown

Future Players born between August 1977 and July 1978: Jonathon Macken, Paul McKenna, David Lucas, Craig Harrison, Andy Gray, Steve Basham.
Ever presents: (2) Roy Tunks and Mike Elwiss
Hat-tricks: (1) Alex Bruce (4 goals vs. Colchester)
FA Cup: Second Round
League Cup: Second Round
Players used: 18
Manager: Nobby Stiles
Chairman: A. R. W. Jones JP FRICS
Leading scorer: 30 goals – Alex Bruce
(27 League, 1 FAC, 2 LC)
OFFICIAL PLAYER OF THE SEASON:
Mike Elwiss

Alex Bruce and Graham Cross.

STAT FACTS:
Best home run without defeat: 10 games
Best away run without defeat: 4 games
Longest run unbeaten: 8 games
Longest run without a win: 6 games
Best home attendance: 16,078 vs. Shrewsbury 29.4.78
Worst home attendance: 5,319 vs. Cambridge 1.10.77
Best away attendance: 19,088 vs. Wrexham 8.4.78
Worst away attendance: 2,201 vs. Port Vale LC 23.8.77
Aggregate and average home attendance: 202,371 – 8,799
Aggregate and average away attendance: 163,769 – 7,120

Match Report: Brucey's Four Goal Blitz – 28 February 1978 Preston 4 Colchester 0

Colchester United, known as the Oystermen, did not go down as easily as this score suggests and in fact held North End to a goalless first half. The elusive Thomson caused their defence some problems and both Wignall and Foley were booked for fouling the talented Scot. United's goalkeeper Walker was peppered with shots from Thomson, Bruce, Elwiss and Burns but he managed to keep his goal intact for an hour before the deadlock was finally broken by a penalty decision. Elwiss put Bruce through but Durham referee, Peter Willis, had spotted that Dowman had handled in trying to prevent Bruce access to goal. The ever confident Bruce calmly sidefooted the ball into the net, sending Walker the wrong way. It was the ninth home game in succession that Bruce had scored. On 75 minutes great play involving Thomson, Elwiss and Bruce ended with the latter scoring a second goal with a powerful header after he cleverly lost his marker. Within three minutes super-striker Bruce was celebrating his hat-trick thanks to yet another penalty, and this time the credit went to the skills of Thomson who was illegally stopped in his tracks by Wignall. Having previously been cautioned Wignall's only punishment this time was to see Bruce put the penalty away, on the other side of Walker this time. The game's scoring was completed five minutes from time when goal hero Bruce crashed home a typical close range shot on the volley after the busy Thomson had just failed to reach another Elwiss centre. All Bruce's goals had come in a 25 minute spell and he was now on 82 goals for the club. Colchester's manager, Bobby Roberts said after the game that he, 'did not think that Preston would have scored if Bruce's first penalty had not been given. Naturally I am bitterly disappointed because we were the better team before that decision. We got a bit ragged before the end.' There was no comment from the home camp for Bruce's goals had done all the talking as Colchester became the 13th team to lose at Deepdale this season.

League appearances (46 games)

Baxter M. J. 45, Brown J. K. 2, Bruce A. R. 45, Burns F. 36 + 2, Cameron D. 40, Coleman G. M. 45, Cross G. F. 40, Doyle S. C. 25 + 7, Elwiss M. W. 46, Haslegrave S. M. 38, McMahon J. J. 30, Robinson M. J. 8 + 2, Smith J. 14 + 1, Spavin A. 1 + 4, Thomson R. B. 25 + 1, Tunks R. W. 46, Uzelac S. 2, Wilson H. 18.

FA Cup appearances (2 games)

Tunks 2, McMahon 2, Doyle 2, Baxter 2, Coleman 2, Smith 2, Elwiss 2, Bruce 2, Burns 2, Cameron 2, Spavin 0 + 1, Haslegrave 2.

League Cup appearances (5 games)

Tunks 5, McMahon 5, Wilson 5, Doyle 5, Baxter 5, Cross 5, Coleman 4, Brown 3, Smith 2, Elwiss 5, Bruce 5, Burns 3, Thomson 3 + 1.

Goalscorers: 63 League–3 FAC–5 LC–(Total 71)

Bruce 27 (5 pens)–1–2 (30), Elwiss 12–2–3 (17), Thomson 6–0–0 (6), Baxter 5–0–0 (5), Coleman 4–0–0 (4), Robinson 3–0–0 (3), Smith 3–0–0 (3), Doyle 1–0–0 (1), Cross 1–0–0 (1), McMahon 1–0–0 (1).

Ricky Thomson

League position in Division Three: 3th (Promoted) – P46 W20 D16 L10 F63 A38 Pts 56
Home: W16 D5 L2 F48 A19   Away: W4 D11 L8 F15 A19

Nobby Stiles (left) and Alan Kelly. Management Team.

Season 1977–78: Third Division

		P	W	D	L	F	A	Pts
1	Wrexham	46	23	15	8	78	45	61
2	Cambridge	46	23	12	11	72	51	58
3	**PRESTON**	**46**	**20**	**16**	**10**	**63**	**38**	**56**
4	Peterborough	46	20	16	10	47	33	56
5	Chester	46	16	22	8	59	56	54
6	Walsall	46	18	17	11	61	50	53
7	Gillingham	46	15	20	11	67	60	50
8	Colchester	45	15	18	13	55	44	48
9	Chesterfield	46	17	14	15	58	49	48
10	Swindon	46	16	16	14	67	60	48
11	Shrewsbury	46	16	15	15	63	57	47
12	Tranmere	46	16	15	15	57	52	47
13	Carlisle	46	14	19	13	59	59	47
14	Sheffield Wednesday	46	15	16	15	50	52	46
15	Bury	46	13	19	14	62	56	45
16	Lincoln	46	15	15	16	53	61	45
11	Exeter	46	15	14	17	49	59	44
18	Oxford	46	13	14	19	64	67	40
19	Plymouth	46	11	17	18	61	68	39
20	Rotherham	46	13	13	20	51	68	39
21	Port Vale	46	8	20	18	46	67	36
22	Bradford	46	12	10	24	56	86	34
23	Hereford	46	9	14	23	34	60	32
24	Portsmouth	46	7	17	22	31	75	31

Date 1977-8	Opponents	Comp	h or a	Score * aet	Att.	1	2	3	4	5	6	7	8	9	10	11	12 *Sub Used
Aug 13	Port Vale Rd 1 1L	LC	a	1-2	4530	Tunks	McMahon	Wilson	Doyle	Baxter	Cross	Coleman	Brown	Smith	Elwiss	Bruce (1)	Thomson
Aug 16	Port Vale Rd 1 2L	LC	h	2-1 *	5816	Tunks	McMahon	Wilson	Doyle	Baxter	Cross	Coleman	Brown	Smith *	Elwiss (2)	Bruce	Thomson *
Aug 20	Plymouth Arg.	Div 3	a	0-0	7154	Tunks	McMahon	Wilson	Doyle *	Baxter	Cross	Coleman	Brown	Thomson	Elwiss	Bruce	Burns *
Aug 23	Port Vale Replay *	LC	n	2-1	2201	Tunks	McMahon	Wilson	Doyle	Baxter	Cross	Burns	Brown	Thomson	Elwiss (1)	Bruce (1)	Smith
Aug 27	Rotherham Utd.	Div 3	a	3-2	5964	Tunks	McMahon	Wilson	Doyle (1)	Baxter	Cross	Burns	Brown	Thomson	Elwiss (1)	Bruce (1)	Coleman
Aug 30	Walsall Rd 2	LC	a	0-0	5445	Tunks	McMahon	Wilson	Doyle	Baxter	Cross	Coleman	Burns	Thomson	Elwiss	Bruce	Smith
Sep 3	Oxford Utd.	Div 3	a	0-1	4804	Tunks	Cameron	Wilson	Doyle	Baxter	Cross	Coleman	Burns	Thomson *	Elwiss	Bruce	Smith *
Sep 6	Walsall Replay	LC	h	0-1	7079	Tunks	McMahon	Wilson	Doyle	Baxter	Cross	Coleman	Burns	Thomson	Elwiss	Bruce	Smith
Sep 10	Carlisle Utd.	Div 3	a	1-3	5743	Tunks	McMahon	Wilson	Doyle	Baxter	Cross	Coleman	Burns	Thomson	Elwiss	Bruce (1)	Cochrane
Sep 13	Swindon Town	Div 3	h	1-1	6014	Tunks	McMahon	Wilson	Doyle	Baxter	Cross	Coleman	Burns *	Thomson	Elwiss	Bruce	Robinson * (1)
Sep 17	Hereford Utd.	Div 3	h	0-0	5447	Tunks	McMahon	Wilson	Doyle	Baxter	Cross	Coleman	Burns *	Robinson	Elwiss	Bruce	Thomson *
Sep 24	Colchester Utd.	Div 3	h	0-0	4978	Tunks	McMahon	Wilson	Doyle	Baxter	Cross	Coleman	Burns	Smith	Elwiss	Bruce	Robinson
Sep 27	Walsall	Div 3	a	0-0	5138	Tunks	Cameron	Wilson	Doyle	Baxter	Cross	Coleman	Burns	Smith	Elwiss	Bruce	Robinson
Oct 1	Cambridge Utd.	Div 3	h	2-0	5319	Tunks	Cameron	Wilson	Doyle	Baxter (1)	Cross	Coleman	Haslegrave	Smith	Elwiss	Bruce (1)	Burns
Oct 4	Sheffield Wed.	Div 3	h	2-1	7627	Tunks	Cameron	Wilson	Doyle	Baxter	Cross (1)	Coleman	Haslegrave	Smith	Elwiss (1)	Bruce	Robinson
Oct 8	Bradford City	Div 3	a	1-1	5815	Tunks	Cameron	Wilson	Doyle	Baxter	Cross	Coleman	Haslegrave	Smith (1)	Elwiss	Bruce	Burns
Oct 15	Gillingham	Div 3	h	2-0	7212	Tunks	Cameron	Wilson	Doyle	Baxter	Cross	Coleman	Haslegrave	Smith (1)	Elwiss (1)	Bruce *	Robinson *
Oct 22	Exeter City	Div 3	a	0-2	5444	Tunks	Cameron	Wilson	Doyle	Baxter	Cross	Coleman	Haslegrave	Smith	Elwiss	Thomson *	Burns *
Oct 25	Tranmere R.	Div 3	h	2-1	7906	Tunks	Cameron	Wilson	Doyle	Baxter (1)	Cross	Coleman	Haslegrave	Smith	Elwiss (1)	Bruce	Robinson
Oct 29	Chester	Div 3	h	2-1	7550	Tunks	Cameron	Wilson	Doyle	Baxter	Cross	Coleman	Haslegrave	Smith	Elwiss	Bruce (2)	Uzelac
Nov 5	Port Vale	Div 3	a			Tunks	Cameron	Wilson	Doyle	Baxter	Uzelac	Coleman	Haslegrave	Smith	Elwiss	Bruce	Burns
Nov 12	Wrexham	Div 3	h	1-3	10342	Tunks	Cameron	Wilson	Doyle	Baxter	Uzelac	Coleman	Haslegrave	Smith *	Elwiss	Bruce (1)	Spavin *
Nov 19	Lincoln City	Div 3	a	2-2	3924	Tunks	Cameron	Wilson *	Doyle	Baxter	Burns	Coleman	Haslegrave	Smith	Elwiss	Bruce (2)	Spavin *
Nov 26	**Lincoln City**	FAC	h	3-2	6965	Tunks	McMahon	Cameron	Doyle	Baxter	Burns	Coleman	Haslegrave	Smith	Elwiss (2)	Bruce (1)	Spavin
Dec 3	Portsmouth	Div 3	h	3-1	5936	Tunks	McMahon	Cameron	Doyle	Baxter	Burns	Coleman	Haslegrave	Smith (1)	Elwiss (1)	Bruce (1)	Robinson
Dec 10	Shrewsbury T.	Div 3	a	0-0	3764	Tunks	McMahon	Cameron	Doyle	Baxter	Burns	Coleman	Haslegrave	Smith	Elwiss	Bruce	Spavin
Dec 17	**Wrexham**	FAC	h	0-2	11134	Tunks	McMahon	Cameron	Doyle	Baxter	Burns	Coleman	Haslegrave *	Smith	Elwiss	Bruce	Spavin *
Dec 26	Bury	Div 3	h	4-0	10297	Tunks	McMahon	Cameron	Burns *	Baxter	Cross	Coleman (1)	Haslegrave	Thomson	Elwiss (1)	Bruce (2, 1p)	Spavin *
Dec 27	Chesterfield	Div 3	a	1-0	6484	Tunks	McMahon	Cameron	Burns	Baxter	Cross	Coleman	Haslegrave	Thomson	Elwiss	Bruce (1)	Spavin
Dec 31	Peterborough Utd.	Div 3	a	0-1	7134	Tunks	McMahon	Cameron	Burns	Baxter	Cross	Coleman	Haslegrave	Thomson	Elwiss	Bruce	Doyle
Jan 2	Port Vale	Div 3	h	2-0	10930	Tunks	McMahon	Cameron	Burns	Baxter	Cross	Coleman	Haslegrave	Thomson (1)	Elwiss	Bruce (1)	Spavin
Jan 6	Tranmere R.	Div 3	a	1-0	7254	Tunks	McMahon	Cameron	Burns	Baxter	Cross	Coleman	Haslegrave	Thomson (1)	Elwiss	Bruce	Doyle
Jan 14	Plymouth Arg.	Div 3	h	5-2	7065	Tunks	McMahon	Cameron	Burns	Baxter (1)	Cross *	Coleman (1)	Haslegrave	Thomson (1)	Elwiss (1)	Bruce (1)	Doyle *
Feb 4	Carlisle Utd.	Div 3	h	2-1	9095	Tunks	McMahon	Cameron	Burns	Baxter	Cross	Coleman	Haslegrave	Thomson	Elwiss	Bruce (2p)	Doyle
Feb 11	Hereford Utd.	Div 3	a	0-0	4791	Tunks	Coleman	Cameron	Burns	Baxter	Cross	Doyle	Haslegrave	Thomson	Elwiss	Bruce	Robinson
Feb 21	Oxford Utd.	Div 3	h	3-2	6189	Tunks	Coleman	Cameron	Burns	Baxter	Cross	Doyle	Haslegrave	Thomson (2)	Elwiss	Bruce (1)	Robinson
Feb 25	Cambridge Utd.	Div 3	a	1-1	5766	Tunks	Coleman	Cameron	Burns	Baxter	Cross	Doyle	Haslegrave	Thomson (1)	Elwiss	Bruce	Robinson
Feb 28	Colchester Utd.	Div 3	h	4-0	9225	Tunks	Coleman	Cameron	Burns	Baxter	Cross	Doyle	Haslegrave	Thomson	Elwiss	Bruce (4, 2p)	Robinson
Mar 4	Bradford City	Div 3	h	3-1	11920	Tunks	McMahon (1)	Cameron	Burns	Baxter	Cross	Doyle	Haslegrave	Thomson	Elwiss (2)	Bruce	Doyle
Mar 7	Swindon Town	Div 3	a	2-0	10211	Tunks	McMahon	Cameron	Burns	Baxter (1)	Cross	Coleman	Haslegrave	Thomson	Elwiss	Bruce (1)	Doyle
Mar 11	Gillingham	Div 3	a	1-2	9568	Tunks	McMahon	Cameron	Burns	Baxter	Cross	Coleman (1)	Haslegrave	Thomson	Elwiss	Bruce	Doyle
Mar 18	Exeter City	Div 3	h	0-0	9189	Tunks	McMahon	Cameron	Burns	Baxter	Cross	Coleman	Haslegrave	Thomson *	Elwiss	Bruce	Spavin *
Mar 24	Chester	Div 3	a	2-1	7864	Tunks	McMahon	Cameron	Burns	Baxter	Cross	Coleman	Haslegrave	Thomson	Elwiss (1)	Bruce (1)	Doyle
Mar 25	Chesterfield	Div 3	h	0-0	10922	Tunks	McMahon	Cameron	Burns	Baxter *	Cross	Coleman	Haslegrave	Thomson	Elwiss	Bruce	Doyle *
Mar 27	Bury	Div 3	a	1-1	9783	Tunks	McMahon	Cameron	Burns	Doyle	Coleman	Spavin	Haslegrave	Thomson (1)	Elwiss	Bruce	Cochrane
Apr 1	Peterborough Utd.	Div 3	h	0-1	9695	Tunks	McMahon	Cameron	Burns	Baxter	Cross	Coleman	Haslegrave	Thomson *	Elwiss	Bruce	Doyle *
Apr 4	Walsall	Div 3	h	1-0	11239	Tunks	McMahon	Cameron	Burns	Baxter	Cross	Coleman	Haslegrave	Robinson (1)	Elwiss	Bruce	Doyle
Apr 8	Wrexham	Div 3	a	0-0	19088	Tunks	McMahon	Cameron	Burns	Baxter	Cross	Coleman	Haslegrave	Robinson	Elwiss	Bruce	Doyle
Apr 15	Lincoln City	Div 3	h	4-0	11208	Tunks	McMahon	Cameron	Burns *	Baxter (1)	Cross	Coleman (1)	Haslegrave	Robinson (1)	Elwiss	Bruce (1)	Doyle *
Apr 18	Sheffield Wed.	Div 3	a	0-1	12426	Tunks	McMahon *	Cameron	Burns	Baxter	Cross	Coleman	Haslegrave	Robinson	Elwiss	Bruce	Doyle *
Apr 22	Portsmouth	Div 3	a	0-0	6866	Tunks	McMahon	Cameron	Burns	Baxter	Cross	Coleman	Haslegrave	Robinson	Elwiss (1)	Bruce (1)	Doyle
Apr 25	Rotherham Utd.	Div 3	a	1-2	5646	Tunks	McMahon	Cameron	Burns	Baxter	Cross *	Coleman	Haslegrave	Robinson	Elwiss	Bruce (1)	Doyle *
Apr 29	Shrewsbury T.	Div 3	h	2-2	16078	Tunks	McMahon	Cameron	Burns	Baxter	Cross	Coleman	Haslegrave	Robinson *	Elwiss (1)	Bruce (1)	Doyle *
	*Played at Stockport																

233

SEASON 1978-1979

Preston continued to make progress after their promotion and achieved their best season for several years finishing in a very creditable seventh position. With Mike Elwiss transferred, not unexpectedly to North End fans, who by now were used to seeing their best players sold on, manager Nobby Stiles brought in another youngster from the reserves, Mick Robinson, (later to be called Michael). The exciting and strong player thus became another who would go on and forge a partnership with the irrepressible Alex Bruce. Robinson had had a few games the previous season but this time he blossomed into a powerful and skilful striker. Progress in the League Cup and three unbeaten league games gave North End a lively start but after that things went slightly pear-shaped. Eric Potts was signed from Brighton and Stiles shuffled his players around trying to keep faith with his system of good passing football. What the club did lack through these weeks was a little luck, having said that, careless defensive errors were usually punished. Defeats against a Mike Elwiss inspired Crystal Palace, Fulham and West Ham highlighted this but after Cardiff were beaten 2–1 at Deepdale the side settled down again and a terrific run of results was then put together. Only one defeat followed in the next 19 games, although in one spell between February and March, Preston played six consecutive drawn games. At least that showed how difficult they were to beat and the never say die attitude

instilled in them by Stiles was very evident. Earlier an exciting 3–0 win over Derby County in the FA Cup thrilled a big Deepdale crowd and North End then gave Southampton a good game in the next round before eventually going out to a single goal by, ironically, Alan Ball Junior, son of the former North End manager. Bad weather hit football in the January and the Derby cup-tie was the only game Preston played in the month. This meant a late finish to the season, with the last league game being played at Millwall in late May. Only one game was lost in the last seven so the run-in kept the Preston fans happy. On the player front, Don O'Riordan, who had joined the club in the October had added some steel to the defence, whilst both Steve Elliott and Graham Bell were quality signings made around the transfer deadline. Brian Taylor was another excellent buy and he slotted in well at right-back. It was difficult to find fault with any of the players in this campaign and it was pleasing to say that the manager had done a superb job. For the second season running Roy Tunks had been ever-present in goal and his consistency had been a telling factor in a very good year.

DEBUTANTS: (6) John Kilner, Eric Potts, Don O'Riordan, Brian Taylor, Steve Elliott, Graham Bell.

LAST GAMES: (7) Spavin, McMahon, John Smith, Robinson, Cross, Uzelac, Kilner.

League appearances (42 games)

Baxter M. J. 37, Bell G. T. A. 10, Bruce A. R. 40, Burns F. 21, Cameron D. 36, Cochrane I. 2 + 2, Coleman G. M. 37, Cross G. F. 5, Doyle S. C. 25 + 4, Elliott S. B. 5 + 2, Haslegrave S. M. 41, McMahon J. J. 8, O'Riordan D. J. 32, Potts E. T. 25 + 4, Robinson M. J. 36, Smith J. 1 + 3, Spavin A. 2, Taylor B. J. 29 + 1, Thomson R. B. 13 + 4, Tunks R. W. 42, Uzelac S. 7, Wilson H. 8 + 4.

FA Cup appearances (2 games)

Tunks 2, Taylor 2, Cameron 2, Burns 2, Baxter 2, O'Riordan 2, Coleman 2, Haslegrave 2, Robinson 2, Potts 2, Bruce 2, Doyle 0 + 1.

League Cup appearances (3 games)

Tunks 2, Kilner J. 1, McMahon 2, Cameron 2, Doyle 3, Baxter 3, Cochrane 1, Cross 3, Haslegrave 3, Robinson 3, Thomson 3, Smith 1, Bruce 2 + 1, Coleman 1, Burns 1, Wilson 1, Potts 0 + 1, Spavin 1.

Goalscorers: 59 League–3 FAC–6 LC–(Total 68)

Bruce 21–2–3 (26), Robinson 13 (1 pen)–0–1 (14), Coleman 7–0–0 (7), Potts 5–0–0 (5), Baxter 4–0–1 (5), Thomson 4–0–1 (5), Doyle 2–0–0 (2), Haslegrave 1–0–0 (1), Bell 1–0–0 (1), Cochrane 1–0–0 (1), Burns 0–1–0 (1).

Future Players born between August 1978 and July 1979: Neil Clement   **Ever presents:** Roy Tunks
Hat-tricks: None   **Players used:** 23   **FA Cup:** Fourth Round
League Cup: Second Round   **Manager:** Nobby Stiles
Chairman: A. R. W. Jones JP FRICS   **Leading scorer:** 26 goals – Alex Bruce (21 League, 2 FAC, 3 LC)
OFFICIAL PLAYER OF THE SEASON: Mick Robinson

League position in Division Two: 7th – P42 W12 D18 L12 F59 A57 Pts 42
Home: W7 D11 L3 F36 A23   Away: W5 D7 L9 F23 A34

Match Report: Rovers Run Ragged – 22 Aug 1978 Preston 4 Blackburn 1

If ever a game was played which was to give fans a yardstick on which to measure their team's improvement, then this was it. A full-blooded local derby against a Blackburn Rovers side which finished fifth in the Second Division last season. North End's elevation to that division was seemingly a deserved promotion as the Rovers were torn apart with ease. Ironically the visitors took an early lead after just three minutes when Cameron accidentally handled just outside the penalty box. Parkes took the free-kick to Metcalfe who cannoned a rocket shot against the crossbar. Unfortunately for Preston the ball bounced nicely for Gregory to head over Tunks's head. From then on though it was one-way traffic the other way as North End knocked the ball around in pleasing fashion. The deserved equaliser arrived on 12 minutes when the inimitable Bruce started a move which ended successfully when Robinson, thundering in on the blind side, steered the moving ball past the Rover's goalkeeper Butcher. North End then took the initiative and ran Rovers ragged as Thomson, Haslegrave and Robinson all went close before the tireless Doyle put the home side ahead after 26 minutes. Once again Bruce was involved as he cut in from the left before setting up Doyle. The Welsh youngster, who always seemed to show maturity beyond his years, made no mistake to give his side a 2–1 half-time lead. Five minutes into the second half the North End fans went wild with excitement as their team scored again. Thomson seized onto an opening created by Hird's lack of control and sent the ever alert Bruce away on the right. There was no stopping his 25 yard angled drive which emphatically beat Butcher in off the far post. With Rovers in dire straits Preston's midfield controlled the show as they ventured forward in search of another goal and a certain two points. On 74 minutes that goal arrived. From Thomson's corner Burns forced Butcher to save but the ball fell to lethal predator Bruce who struck Butcher with his first attempt but did not fail when given a second chance.

Michael Robinson. Sold to Manchester City for £756,000.

Left to right: Back row: **Baxter, Doyle, Kilner, Tunks, Haslegrave, Wilson, McMahon.**
Middle row: **Smith, Burns, Bruce, Cross, Robinson, Uzelac, Spavin.** *Front row:* **G. Warr (Kitman), Cameron, Thomson, Stiles, Kelly, Cochrane, Coleman, H. Hubbick (trainer).**

	P	W	D	L	F	A	Pts
1 Crystal Palace	42	19	19	4	51	24	57
2 Brighton	42	23	10	9	72	39	56
3 Stoke	42	20	16	6	58	31	56
4 Sunderland	42	22	11	9	70	44	55
5 West Ham	42	18	14	10	70	39	50
6 Notts County	42	14	16	12	48	60	44
7 PRESTON	42	12	18	12	59	57	42
8 Newcastle	42	17	8	17	51	55	42
9 Cardiff	42	16	10	16	56	70	42
10 Fulham	42	13	15	14	50	47	41
11 Orient	42	15	10	17	51	51	40
12 Cambridge	42	12	16	14	44	52	40
13 Burnley	42	14	12	16	51	62	40
14 Oldham	42	13	13	16	52	61	39
15 Wrexham	42	12	14	16	45	42	38
16 Bristol Rovers	42	14	10	18	48	60	38
11 Leicester	42	10	17	15	43	52	37
18 Luton	42	13	10	19	60	57	36
19 Charlton	42	11	13	18	60	69	35
20 Sheffield United	42	11	12	19	52	69	34
21 Millwall	42	11	10	21	42	61	32
22 Blackburn	42	10	10	22	41	72	30

STAT FACTS:
Best home run without defeat: 14 games
Best away run without defeat: 6 games
Longest run unbeaten: 15 games
Longest run without a win: 11 games
Best home attendance: 20,727 *vs.* Southampton FAC 12.2.79
Worst home attendance: 6,841 *vs.* Huddersfield LC 12.8.78
Best away attendance: 23,579 *vs.* West Ham 4.11.78
Worst away attendance: 2,833 *vs.* Millwall 22.5.79
Aggregate and average home attendance: 254,387 – 12,114
Aggregate and average away attendance: 243,138 – 11,578

Date 1978-9	Opponents	Comp	h or a	Score	Att.	1	2	3	4	5	6	7	8	9	10	11	12 *Sub Used
Aug 12	Huddersfield Rd 1 1L	LC	h	3-0	6841	Tunks	McMahon	Cameron	Doyle	Baxter (1)	Cross	Cochrane *	Haslegrave	Robinson	Thomson	Smith	Bruce * (2)
Aug 15	Huddersfield Rd 1 2L	LC	a	2-2	3435	Kilner	McMahon	Cameron	Doyle	Baxter	Cross	Coleman	Haslegrave	Robinson	Thomson (1)	Bruce (1)	Burns
Aug 19	Cardiff City	Div 2	a	2-2	7812	Tunks	McMahon	Cameron	Doyle	Baxter	Cross	Bums	Haslegrave	Robinson	Thomson	Bruce (2)	Smith
Aug 22	Blackburn R.	Div 2	h	4-1	15412	Tunks	Cameron *	Wilson	Doyle (1)	Baxter	Cross	Bums	Haslegrave	Robinson (1)	Thomson	Bruce (2)	Smith *
Aug 26	Sheffield Utd.	Div 2	h	2-2	13208	Tunks	Haslegrave	Wilson	Doyle	Baxter	Cross	Bums	Spavin	Robinson (2)	Thomson *	Bruce	Potts *
Aug 29	QPR Rd 2	LC	h	1-3	14913	Tunks	Haslegrave	Wilson	Doyle	Baxter	Cross	Burns *	Spavin	Robinson (1)	Thomson	Bruce	Potts *
Sep 2	Sunderland	Div 2	a	1-3	16819	Tunks	Haslegrave	Wilson	Doyle	Baxter	Cross	Bums	Spavin *	Robinson (1)	Thomson	Bruce	Potts *
Sep 9	Millwall	Div 2	h	0-0	8926	Tunks	McMahon	Wilson	Bums	Baxter	Doyle	Potts	Haslegrave	Robinson	Thomson	Bruce	Smith *
Sep 16	Oldham Ath.	Div 2	a	0-2	8766	Tunks	McMahon	Wilson	Bums	Baxter	Doyle	Coleman	Haslegrave	Robinson *	Thomson	Bruce	Smith *
Sep 23	Stoke City	Div 2	h	0-1	14600	Tunks	McMahon *	Wilson	Bums	Baxter	Doyle	Coleman	Haslegrave	Smith	Potts	Bruce	Cochrane *
Sep 30	Brighton	Div 2	a	1-5	19217	Tunks	Cameron *	Wilson	Bums	Baxter	Cross	Coleman	Haslegrave	Robinson	Potts	Bruce	Cochrane * (1)
Oct 7	Cambridge Utd.	Div 2	a	0-1	5398	Tunks	Coleman	Wilson	Doyle	Baxter	Uzelac	Bums *	Haslegrave	Cochrane	Potts	Bruce	Thomson *
Oct 14	Crystal Palace	Div 2	h	2-3	10795	Tunks	McMahon	Cameron	Doyle	Baxter	O'Riordan	Coleman	Haslegrave (1)	Robinson	Thomson (1)	Bruce	Taylor
Oct 21	Fulham	Div 2	a	3-5	8719	Tunks	McMahon	Cameron	Doyle	Baxter (1)	O'Riordan *	Coleman (1)	Haslegrave	Robinson	Thomson	Bruce (1)	Taylor *
Oct 28	Burnley	Div 2	h	2-2	15014	Tunks	McMahon	Cameron	Doyle	Baxter	O'Riordan	Coleman	Haslegrave	Robinson	Thomson (1)	Bruce (1)	Taylor
Nov 4	West Ham Utd.	Div 2	a	1-3	23579	Tunks	McMahon	Cameron	Doyle	Baxter	O'Riordan	Coleman	Haslegrave	Robinson	Thomson (1)	Bruce	Taylor
Nov 11	Cardiff City	Div 2	h	2-1	9268	Tunks	Taylor	Cameron	Bums	Baxter	O'Riordan	Coleman	Haslegrave	Robinson (2)	Thomson	Bruce	Doyle
Nov 18	Sheffield Utd.	Div 2	a	1-0	14807	Tunks	Taylor	Cameron	Bums	Baxter	O'Riordan	Coleman	Haslegrave *	Robinson	Thomson	Bruce (1)	Doyle *
Nov 21	Sunderland	Div 2	h	3-1	13204	Tunks	Taylor	Cameron	Bums	Baxter	O'Riordan	Coleman	Haslegrave	Robinson (1)	Thomson * (1)	Bruce (1)	Doyle *
Nov 25	Orient	Div 2	a	0-2	4702	Tunks	Taylor *	Cameron	Bums	Baxter	O'Riordan	Coleman	Haslegrave	Robinson	Doyle	Bruce	Wilson *
Dec 9	Luton Town	Div 2	a	2-1	7036	Tunks	Taylor	Cameron	Bums	Baxter (1)	O'Riordan	Coleman	Haslegrave	Robinson (1p)	Potts	Bruce	Wilson
Dec 12	Charlton Ath.	Div 2	h	6-1	10385	Tunks	Taylor	Cameron	Bums	Baxter	O'Riordan	Coleman (1)	Haslegrave *	Robinson (1)	Potts (2)	Bruce (2)	Wilson *
Dec 16	Notts County	Div 2	h	1-1	10728	Tunks	Taylor	Cameron	Bums	Baxter (1)	O'Riordan	Coleman	Haslegrave	Robinson	Potts	Bruce	Doyle
Dec 23	Leicester City	Div 2	a	1-1	10481	Tunks	Taylor	Cameron	Bums	Baxter	O'Riordan	Coleman	Haslegrave	Robinson	Potts	Bruce (1)	Doyle
Dec 26	Wrexham	Div 2	h	2-1	17820	Tunks	Taylor	Cameron	Bums	Baxter	O'Riordan	Coleman	Haslegrave	Robinson	Potts (1)	Bruce (1)	Doyle
Dec 30	Bristol Rovers	Div 2	h	1-1	12660	Tunks	Taylor	Cameron	Bums	Baxter	O'Riordan	Coleman	Haslegrave	Robinson	Potts	Bruce (1)	Doyle
Jan 16	Derby County Rd 3	FAC	h	3-0	19901	Tunks	Taylor	Cameron	Burns (1)	Baxter	O'Riordan	Coleman	Haslegrave	Robinson	Potts	Bruce (2)	Doyle
Feb 10	Brighton	Div 2	h	1-0	11649	Tunks	Taylor	Cameron	Bums	Baxter	O'Riordan	Coleman	Haslegrave	Robinson	Potts	Bruce (1)	Doyle
Feb 12	Southampton Rd 4	FAC	h	0-1	20727	Tunks	Taylor	Cameron	Burns *	Baxter	O'Riordan	Coleman	Haslegrave	Robinson	Potts *	Bruce	Doyle *
Feb 24	Crystal Palace	Div 2	a	0-0	17592	Tunks	Taylor	Cameron	Bums *	Baxter	O'Riordan	Coleman	Haslegrave	Robinson	Potts	Bruce	Doyle *
Feb 28	Stoke City	Div 2	a	1-1	18177	Tunks	Taylor	Cameron	Doyle	Baxter	O'Riordan	Coleman	Haslegrave	Robinson	Potts	Bruce (1)	Smith
Mar 3	Fulham	Div 2	h	2-2	10890	Tunks	Taylor	Cameron	Doyle	Baxter	O'Riordan	Coleman	Haslegrave	Robinson	Potts (1)	Bruce (1)	Wilson
Mar 10	Burnley	Div 2	a	1-1	15175	Tunks	Taylor	Cameron	Doyle	Baxter	O'Riordan	Coleman	Haslegrave	Robinson	Potts	Bruce (1)	Wilson
Mar 17	West Ham Utd.	Div 2	h	0-0	15376	Tunks	Taylor	Cameron	Doyle *	Baxter	O'Riordan	Coleman	Haslegrave	Elliott	Potts	Bruce	Wilson *
Mar 20	Oldham Ath.	Div 2	h	1-1	12535	Tunks	Taylor *	Cameron	Doyle	Baxter	O'Riordan	Coleman (1)	Haslegrave	Elliott	Potts	Bruce	Wilson *
Mar 24	Blackburn R.	Div 2	a	1-0	17790	Tunks	Taylor	Cameron	Doyle	Baxter	O'Riordan	Coleman	Bell	Elliott	Potts	Bruce (1)	Cochrane
Mar 31	Orient	Div 2	h	1-1	9494	Tunks	Taylor	Cameron	Doyle *	Baxter	O'Riordan	Coleman (1)	Haslegrave	Cochrane	Potts	Bruce	Thomson *
Apr 4	Newcastle Utd.	Div 2	a	3-4	12157	Tunks	Taylor	Cameron	Bell	Baxter	O'Riordan	Coleman	Haslegrave	Robinson (2)	Potts *	Bruce (1)	Thomson *
Apr 7	Charlton Ath.	Div 2	a	1-1	5836	Tunks	Taylor	Cameron	Bell	Baxter	O'Riordan	Coleman	Haslegrave	Robinson	Potts	Bruce	Elliott
Apr 14	Wrexham	Div 2	a	1-2	13419	Tunks	Taylor	Cameron	Bell	Baxter	O'Riordan	Coleman	Haslegrave	Robinson (1)	Potts	Bruce *	Elliott *
Apr 16	Newcastle Utd.	Div 2	h	0-0	12966	Tunks	Taylor	Cameron	Bell	Uzelac	O'Riordan	Coleman	Haslegrave	Robinson	Potts *	Elliott	Doyle *
Apr 17	Leicester City	Div 2	h	4-0	10394	Tunks	Taylor	Cameron	Doyle	Uzelac	O'Riordan	Coleman (1)	Haslegrave	Robinson (1)	Bell	Bruce (2)	Thomson
Apr 21	Notts County	Div 2	a	0-0	7009	Tunks	Taylor	Cameron	Doyle	Uzelac	O'Riordan	Coleman	Haslegrave	Robinson *	Bell	Bruce	Potts *
Apr 24	Cambridge Utd.	Div 2	h	0-2	10136	Tunks	Taylor	Cameron	Doyle	Uzelac	O'Riordan	Coleman	Haslegrave *	Robinson	Bell	Bruce	Potts *
Apr 28	Luton Town	Div 2	a	2-2	8927	Tunks	Taylor	Cameron	Doyle (1)	Uzelac	O'Riordan	Coleman (1)	Haslegrave	Robinson	Bell	Bruce	Potts
May 5	Bristol Rovers	Div 2	a	1-0	5814	Tunks	Taylor *	Cameron	Doyle	Baxter (1)	O'Riordan	Coleman	Haslegrave	Robinson	Potts	Bruce	Elliott *
May 22	Millwall	Div 2	a	2-0	2833	Tunks	Taylor	Cameron	Bell (1)	Baxter	Uzelac	Coleman	Haslegrave	Robinson	Potts * (1)	Elliott	Thomson *

SEASON 1979–1980

After the promise shown in the previous year, hopes were high that Preston could make another improvement for the 1979–80 season. At the end of the day it was amazing that Preston could only manage to finish in tenth position, especially as they lost just 11 games all season. The problem was that North End could not stop drawing games. The record number of 18 set up in the previous campaign was beaten by one as 19 games finished level. How the Preston fans would have loved to have seen just one more goal per game in this particular season. With Michael Robinson (originally Mick) now transferred to Manchester City for Preston's record selling fee of £756,000, it was left to Steve Elliott to begin the season as partner to Alex Bruce. Elliott looked sharp but his goals dried up early on and Bruce, too, struggled to recapture his form of the past two years. But two goals for Bruce against Bristol Rovers in a 3–2 win brought both his and Preston's lean spell to an end. New signing, John Blackley, brought all his experience to the defence and Ricky Thomson, despite his injury worries, looked a real talent. Sadly, that talent was never allowed to blossom as, in the end, the injuries proved too much for the Scot. Graham Bell worked hard in midfield and another who had progressed through the junior ranks, Andy McAteer, held his place after his debut, playing some cultured football at left-back. Roy Tunks was again ever present and his form, although it should not have been, was taken for granted. Graham Houston and Willie Naughton also progressed to the first team from the reserves as Nobby Stiles showed that he would always give good young players their chance. The FA Cup gave Preston another attractive home third round tie but this time Ipswich, led by Chorley born Paul

Mariner, proved far too strong for the Lilywhites. As the league unfolded Preston did well in their last 15 games, losing only twice. Good football and some excellent performances but only five wins so progress up the league table was made difficult. It was good to see Mike Elwiss return for a loan spell towards the end of the season. The striker, dogged by injuries since leaving Preston, typically marked his return with both goals in a great 2–1 win at Leicester. The away record had been reasonable but at home the number of draws proved costly in the final analysis. Probably the saddest fact, was that Ricky Thomson's career was virtually ended by his injuries, although he did make a couple of appearances during 1980–81. It was a cruel blow for the young midfield player and the fans who saw him play will always wonder just how far his talents might have taken him too, had he been luckier.

DEBUTANTS: (6) John Blackley, John Anderson, Graham Houston, Paul McGee, Andy McAteer, Willie Naughton.

LAST GAMES: (3) Elwiss, Cochrane, Wilson H.

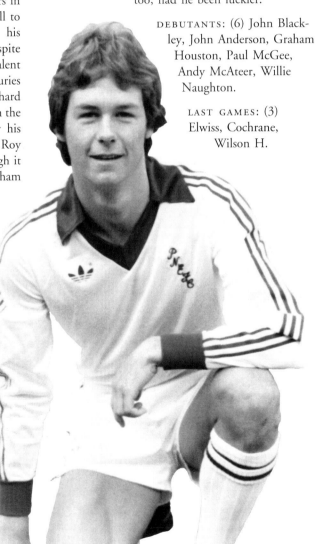

Ever presents: (2) Roy Tunks, Steve Elliott
Hat-tricks: None
Players used: 23
FA Cup: Third Round
League Cup: Second Round
N.B. Also competed in Anglo Scottish Cup
Manager: Nobby Stiles
Chairman: A. R. W. Jones JP FRICS
Leading scorer: 18 goals – Steve Elliott (16 League 2 ASC)

OFFICIAL PLAYER
OF THE SEASON:
Roy Tunks

Pictured: Steve Elliott

League position in Division Two: 10th – P42 W12 D19 L11 F56 A52 Pts 43
Home: W8 D10 L3 F30 A23   Away: W4 D9 L8 F26 A29

Match Report: Preston Plunder Point off Pirates – Mar 11 1980 Bristol Rovers 3 Preston 3

Preston travelled down to the Eastville Stadium without the services of the injured Doyle and Bruce although Burns returned after missing eight games. North End were the better of two poor teams in the first half as chances went begging at both ends. The visitors had done most of the attacking as the corner count of 12–2 in their favour proves, but no one could capitalise on those or the many dangerous crosses from McAteer and McGee. Elliott and Baxter did go close to opening the scoring as did Barrowclough and Mabbutt for the Rovers. Blackley, who played despite a thigh strain, received a knock on the same leg and had to be replaced by O'Riordan. The home side stepped up a gear and gained the upper hand as both Baxter and Burns were booked. Early in the second half Bristol took the lead when Williams hammered in a close range shot which gave Tunks no chance to save. The Rovers midfield took control for awhile and they forged further ahead after 62 minutes through Barrowclough, after Elliott had gone close to an equaliser just moments earlier. Barrowclough, who had been sent off in the earlier meeting between the two clubs, collected the ball near the half way line and outpaced McAteer before drawing Tunks and slotting the ball home for a 2–0 lead. Although behind Preston won their 16th corner in the 70th minute and this time Baxter met the ball to head a fine goal to put North End back in contention. The tempo had been lifted and exciting chances were both created and missed at each end. The equalising goal eventually came after 77 minutes as McGee scored with a well placed shot. Six minutes later Pulis forced the ball past Tunks following a scramble after another corner to regain the lead for Rovers, but Preston did not lose heart and they went all out for another goal which deservedly came with just three minutes left. Bristol's captain Aitken, under pressure from McGee, had the misfortune to lob the ball over his own goalkeeper to hand Preston a priceless point

Left to right: *Back row:* Taylor, McAteer, Litchfield, Tunks, Kilner, Cochrane, Coleman. *Middle row:* Houston, Bell, Wilson, Elliott, Baxter, Uzelac, Doyle, Blackley. *Front row:* Cameron, Potts, Haslegrave, A. Kelly (Ass. trainer), N. Stiles (Manager), Burns, Bruce, Thomson.

League appearances (42 games)

Anderson J.C.P. 5, Baxter M.J. 37, Bell G.T.A. 35 + 1, Blackley J.H. 27, Bruce A.R. 22 + 4, Burns F. 27, Cameron D. 17, Coleman G.M. 24 + 6, Doyle S.C. 14, Elliott S.B. 42, Elwiss M.W. 8 + 2, Haslegrave S.M. 24 + 1, Houston G.R. 0 + 1, McAteer A.W. 21, McGee P.G. 20 + 2, Naughton W.B.S. 2 + 1, O'Riordan D.J. 16 + 2, Potts E.T. 22 + 3, Taylor B.J. 34 + 1, Thomson R.B. 11 + 1, Tunks R.W. 42, Wilson H. 12.

FA Cup appearances (1 game)

Tunks, Taylor, McAteer, Doyle, Baxter, O'Riordan, Bell, Haslegrave, Elliott, McGee, and Bruce all 1 each.

League Cup appearances (2 games)

Tunks 2, Taylor 2, Wilson 2, Doyle 2, Baxter 2, Blackley 1, Bell 1, Haslegrave 1, Elliott 2, Potts 2, Thomson 1, Coleman 2, O'Riordan 1, Burns 0 + 1, Bruce 1 + 1.

Goalscorers: 56 League–1 LC–(Total 57)

Elliott 16 (2 pens)–0 (16), Bruce 10–0 (10), McGee 8–0 (8), Thomson 6–0 (6), Coleman 3–0 (3), Elwiss 3–0 (3), Bell 2–0 (2), Baxter 2–0 (2), Potts 1 (pen)–1 (2), Doyle 1–0 (1), Taylor 1–0 (1), Own goals 3–0 (3), Hindmarch of Sunderland, Aitken of Bristol Rovers and Keay of Shrewsbury

Season 1979–80: Second Division

		P	W	D	L	F	A	Pts
1	Leicester	42	21	13	8	58	38	55
2	Sunderland	42	21	12	9	69	42	54
3	Birmingham	42	21	11	10	58	38	53
4	Chelsea	42	23	7	12	66	52	53
5	QPR	42	18	13	11	75	53	49
6	Luton	42	16	17	9	66	45	49
7	West Ham	42	20	7	15	54	43	47
8	Cambridge	42	14	16	12	61	53	44
9	Newcastle	42	15	14	13	53	49	44
10	**PRESTON**	**42**	**12**	**19**	**11**	**56**	**52**	**43**
11	Oldham	42	16	11	15	49	53	43
12	Swansea	42	17	9	16	48	53	43
13	Shrewsbury	42	18	5	19	60	53	41
14	Orient	42	12	17	13	48	54	41
15	Cardiff	42	16	8	18	41	48	40
16	Wrexham	42	16	6	20	40	49	38
17	Notts County	42	11	15	16	51	52	37
18	Watford	42	12	13	17	39	46	37
19	Bristol Rovers	42	11	13	18	50	64	35
20	Fulham	42	11	7	24	42	74	29
21	Burnley	42	6	15	21	39	73	27
22	Charlton	42	6	10	26	39	78	22

Pictured: Eric Potts

Date 1979-80	Opponents	Comp	h or a	Score	Att.	1	2	3	4	5	6	7	8	9	10	11	12 *Sub Used		
Aug 18	Charlton Ath.	Div 2	a	3-0	6148	Tunks	Taylor	Wilson	Doyle	Baxter	Blackley	Bell (1)	Haslegrave	Elliott (1)	Potts	Thomson (1)	Coleman		
Aug 21	Newcastle Utd.	Div 2	h	1-0	12707	Tunks	Taylor	Wilson	Doyle	Baxter	Blackley	Bell	Haslegrave	Elliott	Potts (1p)	Thomson *	Coleman *		
Aug 25	Swansea City	Div 2	h	1-1	12116	Tunks	Taylor	Wilson	Doyle (1)	Baxter	Blackley	Bell	Coleman	Haslegrave	Elliott	Potts	Thomson	Bums		
Aug 28	Birmingham Rd 1 1L	LC	a	1-2	13887	Tunks	Taylor	Wilson	Doyle	Baxter	Blackley	Bell	Coleman *	Elliott	Potts (1)	Thomson	Bruce *		
Sep 1	Fulham	Div 2	a	0-1	7922	Tunks	Cameron	Wilson	Doyle	Baxter	Blackley *	Bell	Haslegrave	Elliott	Potts	Thomson	Coleman *		
Sep 4	Birmingham Rd 1 2L	LC	h	0-1	11043	Tunks	Taylor	Wilson	Doyle *	Baxter	O'Riordan	Coleman	Haslegrave	Elliott	Potts	Bruce	Burns *		
Sep 8	West Ham Utd.	Div 2	h	1-1	10460	Tunks	Taylor	Cameron	Doyle	Baxter	O'Riordan	Coleman (1)	Haslegrave	Elliott	Potts	Bruce	Thomson		
Sep 15	Oldham Ath.	Div 2	a	2-3	9849	Tunks	Taylor	Cameron	Doyle	Baxter	O'Riordan	Coleman	Haslegrave	Elliott	Potts *	Thomson (2)	Bruce *		
Sep 22	Bristol Rovers	Div 2	h	3-2	7555	Tunks	Taylor	Cameron	Bums	Baxter	Blackley	Coleman *	Haslegrave	Elliott (1)	Potts	Bruce (2)	Bell *		
Sep 29	Sunderland	Div 2	a	1-1	24599	Tunks	Taylor	Cameron	Bums	Baxter	Blackley	Bell	Haslegrave	Elliott (1)	Potts *	Bruce	Thomson *		
Oct 6	Birmingham C.	Div 2	h	0-0	10740	Tunks	Taylor	Cameron	Bums	Baxter	Blackley	Bell	Haslegrave	Elliott	Thomson	Bruce	Doyle		
Oct 10	Newcastle Utd.	Div 2	a	0-0	24985	Tunks	Taylor	Cameron	Bums	Baxter	Blackley	Bell	Haslegrave	Elliott	Thomson	Bruce	Doyle		
Oct 13	QPR	Div 2	a	1-1	14316	Tunks	Taylor	Cameron	Bums	Baxter	Blackley	Bell	Haslegrave	Elliott	Thomson (1)	Bruce	Doyle		
Oct 20	Burnley	Div 2	h	3-2	12300	Tunks	Taylor	Cameron	Bums	Baxter	Blackley	Bell	Haslegrave	Elliott *	Thomson (2)	Bruce (1)	Potts *		
Oct 27	Luton Town	Div 2	a	1-1	11648	Tunks	Taylor	Cameron *	Bums	Baxter	Blackley	Bell	Haslegrave	Elliott (1)	Thomson	Bruce	McGee *		
Nov 3	Charlton Ath.	Div 2	h	1-1	9950	Tunks	Taylor	Wilson	Bums	Baxter	Blackley	Bell	Haslegrave	Elliott (1)	Potts	Bruce	Doyle		
Nov 10	Notts County	Div 2	a	1-2	8602	Tunks	Taylor	Wilson	Bums	Baxter	Blackley	Bell	Haslegrave	Elliott	Potts	Bruce (1)	Doyle		
Nov 17	Leicester City	Div 2	h	1-1	9739	Tunks	Taylor	Wilson *	Bums	Baxter	O'Riordan	Bell	Haslegrave	Elliott	McGee	Bruce (1)	Potts *		
Nov 24	Orient	Div 2	h	2-2	7835	Tunks	Taylor	Wilson	Bums	Baxter	O'Riordan	Bell	Haslegrave	Elliott	Potts	Bruce (1)	McGee		
Dec 1	Chelsea	Div 2	a	0-2	21192	Tunks	Taylor	Wilson	Bums *	Baxter	O'Riordan	Bell	Haslegrave	Elliott	McGee	Bruce	Coleman *		
Dec 8	Cambridge Utd.	Div 2	h	2-2	7585	Tunks	Taylor	Wilson	Bums	Baxter	O'Riordan	Bell	Haslegrave	Elliott (1)	McGee *	Bruce (1)	Coleman *		
Dec 15	Cardiff City	Div 2	a	2-0	6419	Tunks	Taylor	Wilson	Bums	Baxter	O'Riordan	Bell	Haslegrave	Elliott	Coleman	Bruce (2)	McGee		
Dec 21	Watford	Div 2	h	1-2	8956	Tunks	Taylor	Wilson	Bums *	Baxter	O'Riordan	Bell	Haslegrave	Elliott (1p)	Coleman	Bruce	McGee *		
Dec 26	Shrewsbury T.	Div 2	h	3-0	8875	Tunks	Taylor	McAteer	Bums	Baxter	O'Riordan	Bell (1)	Coleman	Elliott (1)	Potts	Bruce (1)	McGee		
Dec 29	Swansea City	Div 2	a	0-1	11401	Tunks	Taylor	McAteer	Bums	Baxter	O'Riordan	Bell	Coleman	Elliott	Potts *	Bruce	Haslegrave *		
Jan 1	Wrexham	Div 2	a	0-2	14738	Tunks	Taylor	McAteer	Doyle	Baxter	O'Riordan	Bell	Haslegrave	Elliott	McGee *	Coleman	Naughton *		
Jan 5	Ipswich Town Rd 3	FAC	h	0-3	16986	Tunks	Taylor	McAteer	Doyle	Baxter	O'Riordan	Bell	Haslegrave	Elliott	McGee	Bruce	Cochrane		
Jan 12	Fulham	Div 2	h	3-2	7912	Tunks	Taylor	McAteer	Doyle	Anderson	O'Riordan	Bell	Haslegrave	Elliott (2, 1p)	McGee (1)	Bruce	Baxter		
Jan 19	West Ham Utd.	Div 2	a	0-2	17603	Tunks	Taylor	McAteer	Doyle	Anderson	O'Riordan	Bell	Haslegrave	Elliott	McGee *	Bruce	Coleman *		
Feb 2	Oldham Ath.	Div 2	h	0-1	8932	Tunks	Taylor	McAteer	Doyle	Anderson	O'Riordan	Bell	Haslegrave	Elliott	McGee *	Bruce	Coleman *		
Feb 16	Sunderland	Div 2	h	2-1	12165	Tunks	Taylor	McAteer	Doyle	Anderson	Blackley	Bell	Coleman (1)	Elliott	Naughton *	Bruce	O'Riordan *	1 og	(Hindmarch)
Feb 23	QPR	Div 2	h	1-0	10350	Tunks	Taylor *	McAteer	Doyle	Anderson	Blackley	Bell	Coleman	Elliott	Naughton	Bruce	Houston *		
Mar 1	Burnley	Div 2	a	1-1	10843	Tunks	Cameron	McAteer	Doyle	Baxter	Blackley	Bell	Coleman	Elliott	Potts	McGee (1)	Bums		
Mar 8	Luton Town	Div 2	h	1-1	7862	Tunks	Cameron	McAteer	Doyle *	Baxter	Blackley	Bell	Coleman	Elliott	Potts	McGee (1)	Taylor *		
Mar 11	Bristol Rovers	Div 2	a	3-3	6022	Tunks	Taylor	McAteer	Bums	Baxter (1)	Blackley *	Bell	Coleman	Elliott	Potts	McGee (1)	O'Riordan *	1 og	(Aitken)
Mar 15	Birmingham C.	Div 2	a	2-2	19548	Tunks	Taylor	McAteer	Bums	Baxter	O'Riordan	Bell	Coleman	Elliott (1)	Potts *	McGee (1)	Elwiss *		
Mar 22	Notts County	Div 2	h	2-0	7407	Tunks	Taylor (1)	McAteer	Bums	Baxter	Blackley	Bell	Coleman	Elliott	Potts *	McGee (1)	Elwiss *		
Mar 29	Leicester City	Div 2	a	2-1	15293	Tunks	Taylor	McAteer	Bums	Baxter	Blackley	Bell *	Coleman	Elliott	Elwiss (2)	McGee	Potts *		
Apr 1	Shrewsbury T.	Div 2	a	3-1	8602	Tunks	Taylor	McAteer	Bums	Baxter	Blackley	Potts	Coleman	Elliott (2)	Elwiss	McGee	O'Riordan *	1 og	(Keay)
Apr 5	Wrexham	Div 2	h	0-0	9739	Tunks	Taylor *	McAteer	Bums	Baxter	Blackley	Potts	Coleman	Elliott	Elwiss	McGee	Bruce *		
Apr 9	Watford	Div 2	a	0-0	11967	Tunks	Taylor	McAteer	Bums	Baxter	Blackley	Bell	Coleman	Elliott	Elwiss	McGee	Bruce		
Apr 12	Chelsea	Div 2	h	1-1	13069	Tunks	Cameron	McAteer	O'Riordan	Baxter (1)	Blackley	Bell	Coleman	Elliott	Elwiss	McGee	Bruce		
Apr 19	Orient	Div 2	a	2-2	4509	Tunks	Cameron	McAteer	Bums	Baxter	Blackley	Bell	Coleman	Elliott (1)	Elwiss	McGee (1)	Bruce *		
Apr 26	Cardiff City	Div 2	h	2-0	7481	Tunks	Cameron	McAteer	Bums	Baxter	Blackley	Bell	Coleman (1)	Elliott	Elwiss	McGee (1)	Bruce		
May 3	Cambridge Utd.	Div 2	a	2-3	5395	Tunks	Cameron	McAteer	Bums	Baxter	Blackley	Bell	Coleman	Elliott (1)	Elwiss (1)	McGee *	Bruce *		

Official Programme 5p

Preston
North End

FOURTH ROUND

STER UNITE

th February, 19

PRESTON NORTH END v CELTIC F.C.
official club sponsor
ASHWORTHS

PRE-SEASON FRIENDLY
Sunday 26th July 1998 Kick-off 3.00pm

NorthEnd

matchday magazine

ORIENT

CANON LEAGUE
DIVISION THREE

OFFICIAL MATCHDAY MAGAZINE
PRICE 50p

ZANUSS

ZANUSS

Canon
LEAGUE

PRESTON
NORTH
END

TUESDAY.

WALSALL

TUESDAY 30th AUGUST 1977
Kick off 7.30 p.m.

FOOTBALL LEAGUE CUP
Round Two

OFFICIAL PROGRAMME
Vol. 12 Issue 3
Price 15 pence

PRESTON

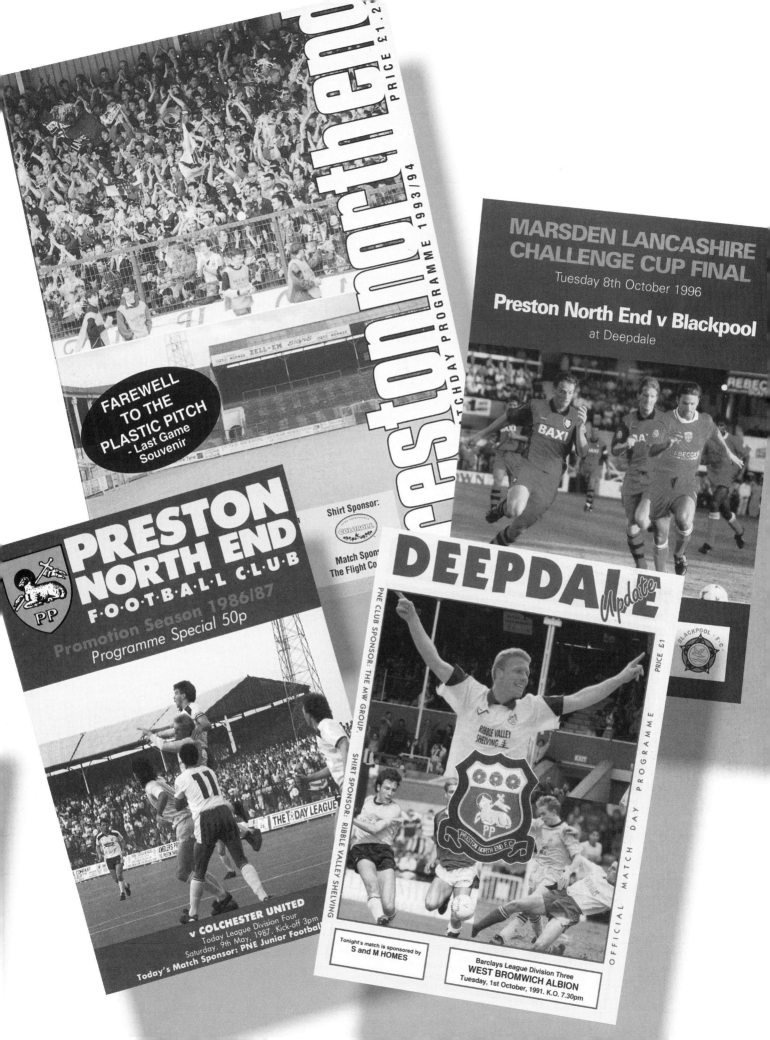

SEASON 1980–1981

After a few years of the promise of better things to come, North End succumbed to another bitterly disappointing season which ended with relegation back to the Third Division again. The club struggled from day one and it was easy to see where their main problem was in 1980–81. As in many seasons before the goalscoring proved a nightmare. The campaign opened with a pre-season tournament called the Anglo-Scottish Cup and there was a sign of things to come as Preston failed to score in any of their three games. In fact only two goals were scored in their first eight league and cup outings. To be fair the defence looked solid enough and Mick Baxter looked in sparkling form at centre-half. North End did progress in the League Cup as early wins gave them an attractive third round tie with WBA. It took three games to seperate these sides as Preston battled well. Eventually though a 2–1 win for the Albion after extra-time in the second replay ended the Lilywhite's interest. That game proved to be the high point of the season as from then on it was all downhill as Preston could only muster just seven more wins from 27 matches. Nobby Stiles shuffled his pack of players but North End's play was predictable and easily countered. Roy Tunks, as ever, played well in goal, whilst Gordon Coleman and Steve Elliott could be pleased with their contributions. Overall though the team rarely gelled as a unit and there were several players not playing to the necessary high standards required in

this tough division. The FA Cup saw a remarkable match at Deepdale as Bristol Rovers romped to a 4–0 interval lead. It looked all over, and was, although Preston almost made a draw as three second half goals so nearly saved the tie. A 5–0 thrashing at West Ham shortly afterwards was particularly damaging to their league hopes, although to their credit Preston bounced back by beating Watford in their next game, their first win in eleven. Despite some good performances, notably against Chelsea, when Peter Litchfield made a tremendous debut in goal, North End struggled to find the consistency they needed. In the end the outcome in the league came down to a last day fixtures scenario. Preston had to win at Derby County and then hope that Cardiff would lose at home to the Champions, West Ham. North End did their bit, with Alex Bruce scoring twice in a 2–1 win, but unfortunately Cardiff managed to hold the Hammers to a goalless draw and Preston were relegated. It was a bitter blow and it was to ultimately cost Nobby Stiles his job as manager. One could not help but feel sorry for the former Manchester United and England star as he had had little cash made available to him at crucial stages of his career as the Preston manager.

DEBUTANTS: (3) Peter Sayer, Simon Westwell, Peter Litchfield.

LAST GAMES: (7) Burns, Thomson, Cameron, Haslegrave, Potts.

League appearances (42 games)
Anderson J.C.P. 7 + 1, Baxter M.J. 42, Bell G.T.A. 34 + 1, Blackley J.H. 21 + 2, Bruce A.R. 29 + 2, Burns F. 29, Cameron D. 13, Coleman G.M. 36, Doyle S.C. 24 + 3, Elliott S.B. 32 + 3, Haslegrave S.M. 8 + 1, Houston G.R. 17, Litchfield P. 3, McAteer A.W. 20, McGee P.G. 32 + 2, Naughton W.B.S. 9 + 1, O'Riordan D.J. 19 + 2, Potts E.T. 3, Sayer P.A. 5 + 3, Taylor B.J. 20 + 2, Tunks R.W. 39, Westwell S. 20.

FA Cup appearances (1 game)
Tunks, Taylor, McAteer, Burns, Baxter, O'Riordan, Doyle, Coleman, Elliott, Bruce, Houston all 1 each and McGee 0 + 1.

League Cup appearances (6 games)
Tunks 6, Taylor 0 + 2, McAteer 5, Baxter 6, Blackley 3, Bell 5 + 1, Naughton 1, Elliott 4 + 1, McGee 6, Bruce 4, Burns 5, Houston 3, Cameron 3, Doyle 2 + 1, O'Riordan 3, Westwell 4, Sayer 0 + 1, Coleman 6.

Goalscorers: 41 League–3 FAC–6 LC–(Total 50)
Bruce 13–1–1 (15), Elliott 9 (2 pens)–0 0 (9), McGee 4–1–2 (7), Coleman 3–0–2 (5), Baxter 4–0–0 (4), Naughton 2–0–0 (2), Houston 1–1–0 (2), Bell 1–0–1 (2), Doyle 1–0–0 (1), Haslegrave 1–0–0 (1), Own goals 2–0–0 (2), Stevens of Cardiff and Taylor of Orient.

Ever presents: (1) Mick Baxter   **Hat-tricks:** None   **Players used:** 25
FA Cup: Third Round   **Manager:** Nobby Stiles   **Chairman:** A.R.W. Jones JP FRICS
League Cup: Third Round Second Replay – Also competed in Anglo Scottish Cup
Leading scorer: 15 goals – Alex Bruce (13 League 1 FAC 1 LC)

OFFICIAL PLAYER OF THE SEASON: Mick Baxter

Match Report: The Good News and the Bad News –
6 May 1981 Derby 1 Preston 2

The culmination of a couple of seasons which threatened relegation finally ended with the inevitable for Preston as this time their luck ran out, despite this win over Derby. This was Roy McFarland's last game for Derby and he was determined to go out with a bang. But Preston battled as hard as their fans expected given their precarious league position. In the first half Derby had much of the play but they wasted several opportunities. North End clung on and Taylor, Blackley and Baxter all played well in defence, but Preston's man of the match was undoubtedly Coleman, the versatile midfield player. He had been playing at full-back but was switched to the right wing for this game and gave a wholehearted performance, making both Preston goals. The breakthrough finally came after 71 minutes as Coleman put in a good cross, McFarland and Jones hesitated, and Bruce pounced to punish them for their mistake. The game was not a good one but the scoreline at least gave North End hope and they were hanging on for dear life. But with ten minutes to go Derby found an equaliser. Tunks missed a cross and Swindlehurst was able to head into an empty net. It looked curtains for the Preston lads but to their credit they kept plugging away and were rewarded with just two minutes to go. Jones repeated Tunks's error and dropped a cross from Coleman after Taylor's quick throw-in. Bruce again showed his predatory instincts and tucked away the chance with glee. Preston held on for the win but on their return to the dressing room they found that other results had gone against them and relegation could not be avoided after all.

Nobby Stiles in jovial mood.

STAT FACTS:
Best home run without defeat: 5 games
Best away run without defeat: 3 games
Longest run unbeaten: 5 games
Longest run without a win: 9 games
Best home attendance: 18,970 *vs.* Swansea 2.5.81
Worst home attendance: 4,748 *vs.* Wrexham 20.12.80
Best away attendance: 26,413 *vs.* West Ham 31.1.81
Worst away attendance: 4,228 *vs.* Cambridge 14.2.81
Aggregate and average home attendance: 159,746 – 7,607
Aggregate and average away attendance: 211,220 – 10,058

Alex Bruce.

Season 1980–81: Second Division

	P	W	D	L	F	A	Pts
1 West Ham	42	28	10	4	70	29	66
2 Notts County	42	18	17	7	49	38	53
3 Swansea	42	18	14	10	64	44	50
4 Blackburn	42	16	18	8	42	29	50
5 Luton	42	18	12	12	61	46	48
6 Derby	42	15	15	12	57	52	45
7 Grimsby	42	15	15	12	44	42	45
8 QPR	42	15	13	14	56	46	43
9 Watford	42	16	11	15	50	45	43
10 Sheffield Wednesday	42	17	8	17	53	51	42
11 Newcastle	42	14	14	14	30	45	42
12 Chelsea	42	14	12	16	46	41	40
13 Cambridge	42	17	6	17	53	65	40
14 Shrewsbury	42	11	17	14	46	47	39
15 Oldham	42	12	15	15	39	48	39
16 Wrexham	42	12	14	16	43	45	38
17 Orient	42	13	12	17	52	56	38
18 Bolton	42	14	10	18	61	66	38
19 Cardiff	42	12	12	18	44	60	36
20 PRESTON	**42**	**11**	**14**	**17**	**41**	**62**	**36**
21 Bristol City	42	7	16	19	29	51	30
22 Bristol Rovers	42	5	13	24	34	65	23

Trivia Fact:
Preston received a profit of £125,000 on commercial activities during the season and they also received £25,000 as their share from the television fees. Even allowing for that Preston North End made a record net loss of £344,000 on the season.

League position in Division Two: 20th (Relegated) – P42 W11 D14 L17 F41 A62 Pts 36
Home: W8 D7 L6 F28 A26 Away: W3 D7 L11 F13 A36

Gordon Coleman   **Mick Baxter**   **Danny Cameron**

Date 1980-1	Opponents	Comp	h or a	Score *aet	Att.	1	2	3	4	5	6	7	8	9	10	11	12 *Sub Used		
Aug 16	Bristol City	Div 2	h	1-1	6293	Tunks	Taylor	Cameron	Burns	Baxter	Blackley	Bell	Coleman	Elliott (1)	Potts	McGee	O'Riordan		
Aug 19	Grimsby Town	Div 2	a	0-0	10460	Tunks	Taylor *	Cameron	Burns	Baxter	Blackley	Bell	Coleman	Elliott	Potts	McGee	Doyle*		
Aug 23	West Ham Utd.	Div 2	h	0-0	9306	Tunks	Cameron	McAteer	Burns	Baxter	Blackley *	Bell	Coleman	Elliott	Potts	McGee	Doyle *		
Aug 26	Wigan Ath. Rd 1 1L	LC	h	1-0	8108	Tunks	Cameron	McAteer	Burns	Baxter	O'Riordan	Bell	Coleman	Elliott *	Houston	McGee (1)	Doyle *		
Aug 30	Sheffield Wed.	Div 2	a	0-3	16724	Tunks	Cameron	McAteer	Burns *	Baxter	O'Riordan	Bell	Coleman	Sayer	McGee		Doyle *		
Sep 3	Wigan Ath. Rd 1 2L	LC	a	2-1	9698	Tunks	Cameron	McAteer	Burns	Baxter	O'Riordan	Bell	Coleman (1)	Houston	McGee (1)	Bruce *	Elliott *		
Sep 6	Cambridge Utd.	Div 2	a	2-0	5516	Tunks	Cameron	McAteer	Burns	Baxter	O'Riordan	Bell	Coleman	McGee (2)	Houston	Bruce	Sayer		
Sep 13	Watford	Div 2	a	1-2	11275	Tunks	Cameron	McAteer	Burns	Baxter	O'Riordan	Bell	Coleman (1)	McGee	Sayer *	Bruce	Elliott *		
Sep 20	Chelsea	Div 2	a	1-1	13755	Tunks	Westwell	Cameron	Doyle	Baxter	O'Riordan	Bell	Coleman	Elliott (1)	McGee	Houston	Blackley		
Sep 23	Oxford Utd. Rd 2	LC	h	1-0	5722	Tunks	Westwell	Cameron	Doyle	Baxter	O'Riordan	Bell	Coleman (1)	Elliott *	McGee	Houston	Sayer *		
Sep 27	Shrewsbury T.	Div 2	h	0-0	6309	Tunks	Westwell *	McAteer	Doyle	Baxter	O'Riordan	Bell	Coleman	McGee	Sayer	Houston	Elliott *		
Oct 4	Orient	Div 2	a	0-4	4395	Tunks	Taylor	McAteer	Doyle	Baxter	O'Riordan	Sayer	Coleman	Elliott	McGee	Houston *	Blackley *		
Oct 7	Newcastle Utd.	Div 2	h	2-3	5301	Tunks	Taylor	Cameron	Burns	Baxter	Blackley	Doyle	Coleman (1)	Elliott	Bruce (1)	Houston *	McGee *		
Oct 11	Luton Town	Div 2	a	1-0	5620	Tunks	O'Riordan	Cameron	Burns	Baxter	Blackley	Doyle	Coleman	Elliott (1)	Bruce	McGee	Bell		
Oct 18	Wrexham	Div 2	h	1-0	5775	Tunks	O'Riordan	Cameron	Burns	Baxter	Blackley	Doyle	Coleman	Elliott	Bruce (1)	McGee	Bell		
Oct 21	Bolton W.	Div 2	a	1-2	10713	Tunks	O'Riordan	McAteer	Burns	Baxter	Blackley	Doyle	Bell	Elliott	Bruce (1)	McGee	Haslegrave		
Oct 25	Bristol Rovers	Div 2	h	0-0	5807	Tunks	Taylor	O'Riordan	Burns	Baxter	Blackley	Doyle *	Coleman	Elliott	Bruce	McGee	Haslegrave *		
Oct 29	WBA Rd 3	LC	h	0-0	17579	Tunks	Westwell	McAteer	Burns	Baxter	Blackley	Doyle *	Coleman	Elliott	Bruce	McGee	Bell *		
Nov 1	Oldham Ath.	Div 2	a	1-1	6739	Tunks	Westwell	McAteer	Burns	Baxter	Blackley	Bell	Coleman	Elliott *	Bruce (1)	McGee	O'Riordan *		
Nov 4	WBA Replay	LC	h	1-1 *	14420	Tunks	Westwell	McAteer	Burns	Baxter	Blackley	Bell (1)	Coleman	McGee	Naughton *	Bruce	Taylor *		
Nov 8	Cardiff City	Div 2	h	3-1	5458	Tunks	Westwell	McAteer	Burns	Baxter (1)	O'Riordan	Bell	Coleman	McGee	Naughton *	Bruce (1)	Taylor *	1 og	(Stevens)
Nov 12	WBA 2nd Replay	LC	a	1-2 *	15218	Tunks	Westwell	McAteer	Burns *	Baxter	Blackley	Bell	Coleman	Elliott	Bruce (1)	McGee	Taylor *		
Nov 15	Bristol City	Div 2	a	0-0	8042	Tunks	Westwell	McAteer	Burns	Baxter	Blackley	Bell	Coleman *	Elliott	Bruce	McGee	Taylor *		
Nov 22	QPR	Div 2	h	3-2	6725	Tunks	Westwell	McAteer	Burns	Baxter (1)	Blackley	Bell	Taylor	Elliott	Naughton (2)	McGee	Haslegrave		
Nov 28	Swansea City	Div 2	a	0-3	9115	Tunks	Westwell	Cameron	Burns	Baxter	Blackley	Bell	Taylor	Elliott	Bruce	McGee	Anderson		
Dec 2	Grimsby Town	Div 2	h	2-4	5289	Tunks	Westwell	Cameron	Burns	Baxter (1)	Blackley *	Bell	Taylor	Elliott (1p)	Bruce	McGee	Naughton *		
Dec 6	Derby County	Div 2	h	0-3	6118	Tunks	Westwell	Cameron *	Taylor	Baxter	Anderson	Bell	Doyle	Elliott	Bruce	McGee	Sayer *		
Dec 13	Luton Town	Div 2	h	2-4	7874	Tunks	Taylor	Westwell	Bell	Baxter	Anderson	Bell	Doyle	Elliott (1)	Bruce (1)	McGee *	Sayer *		
Dec 20	Wrexham	Div 2	h	1-1	4748	Tunks	Taylor	McAteer	Burns	Baxter	O'Riordan	Coleman	Doyle	Elliott (1)	Bruce	Houston	Bell		
Dec 26	Blackburn R.	Div 2	a	0-0	17738	Tunks	Taylor	McAteer	Burns	Baxter	O'Riordan	Coleman	Doyle	Elliott	Bruce	Houston	Bell		
Dec 27	Notts County	Div 2	h	2-2	6547	Tunks	Taylor	McAteer	Bell	Baxter (1)	O'Riordan	Coleman	Doyle	Elliott (1p)	Bruce *	Houston	McGee *		
Jan 3	Bristol Rovers Rd 3	FAC	h	3-4	6352	Tunks	Taylor	McAteer	Burns *	Baxter	O'Riordan	Doyle	Coleman	Elliott	Bruce (1)	Houston (1)	McGee * (1)		
Jan 10	QPR	Div 2	a	1-1	8415	Tunks	Westwell	McAteer	Bell (1)	Baxter	O'Riordan	Doyle	Coleman	Elliott	McGee	Houston	Bruce		
Jan 31	West Ham Utd.	Div 2	a	0-5	26413	Tunks	Westwell	McAteer	Bell	Baxter	O'Riordan	Doyle	Coleman	Elliott	McGee *	Houston	Sayer *		
Feb 7	Watford	Div 2	h	2-1	5162	Tunks	Westwell	McAteer	Bell	Baxter	O'Riordan	Doyle	Coleman (1)	Elliott	McGee (1)	Naughton	Bruce		
Feb 14	Cambridge Utd.	Div 2	h	0-1	4228	Tunks	Westwell	McAteer	Bell	Baxter	O'Riordan	Doyle	Coleman	Elliott	McGee	Naughton	Bruce		
Feb 21	Shrewsbury T.	Div 2	a	0-3	4660	Tunks	Westwell	McAteer	Bell	Baxter	O'Riordan	Doyle *	Coleman	Elliott	McGee	Naughton	Bruce *		
Feb 28	Chelsea	Div 2	h	1-0	8129	Litchfield	Westwell	Burns	Bell	Baxter	Anderson	Doyle	Coleman	Sayer *	McGee	Naughton	Bruce * (1)		
Mar 7	Orient	Div 2	h	3-0	5510	Litchfield	Westwell	Burns	Bell	Baxter	Anderson	Doyle (1)	Coleman	Bruce	McGee (1)	Naughton	Elliott	1 og	(Taylor)
Mar 14	Newcastle Utd.	Div 2	a	0-2	11946	Litchfield	Westwell	Burns	Bell	Baxter	Anderson	Doyle	Coleman	Bruce *	McGee	Naughton	Elliott *		
Mar 24	Bolton W.	Div 2	h	1-2	8505	Tunks	Westwell	Burns	Bell	Baxter	Anderson *	Doyle	Coleman	Bruce (1)	McGee	Naughton	Blackley *		
Mar 28	Bristol Rovers	Div 2	a	0-2	4427	Tunks	Westwell *	McAteer	Haslegrave	Baxter	Blackley	Doyle	Coleman	Elliott	Bruce	McGee	Bell *		
Apr 4	Oldham Ath.	Div 2	h	1-2	6154	Tunks	Taylor	Coleman	Haslegrave	Baxter	Blackley	Doyle	Bell	McGee	Houston	Bruce (1)	Burns		
Apr 11	Cardiff City	Div 2	a	3-1	4991	Tunks	Taylor	Coleman	Haslegrave (1)	Baxter	Blackley	Burns	Bell	Elliott (1)	Houston	Bruce (1)	Anderson		
Apr 14	Sheffield Wed.	Div 2	h	2-1	9537	Tunks	Taylor	Burns	Haslegrave	Baxter	Blackley	Coleman	Bell	Elliott (1)	Houston (1)	Bruce	Anderson		
Apr 18	Notts County	Div 2	a	0-0	8485	Tunks	Taylor	Burns	Haslegrave	Baxter	Blackley	Coleman	Bell	Elliott	Houston	Bruce	Anderson		
Apr 21	Blackburn R.	Div 2	h	0-0	18742	Tunks	Taylor	Burns	Haslegrave	Baxter	Blackley	Coleman	Bell	Elliott	Houston	Bruce	Anderson		
May 2	Swansea City	Div 2	h	1-3	18970	Tunks	Taylor	Burns *	Haslegrave	Baxter	Blackley	Coleman	Bell	Elliott	Houston	Bruce (1)	Anderson *		
May 6	Derby County	Div 2	a	2-1	15050	Tunks	Taylor	Anderson	Haslegrave	Baxter	Blackley	Coleman	Bell	Elliott	Houston	Bruce (2)	O'Riordan *		

SEASON 1981–1982

This season was regarded as the club's Centenary season although our research proves that it actually should have been the 1980–81 season as North End were playing regular football in 1880–81. The year should have been a memorable one and one of celebration, instead, it turned out to be a nightmare, with the club only saved from relegation by a late run of better results. The summer saw the arrival of Tommy Docherty, this time returning to Deepdale as manager. Docherty had performed admirably for the club as a player in the 1950s and in his own words his career had come 'full circle' as he prepared to meet the daunting challenge his old club was to face in the Third Division. Preston began poorly and immediately found it difficult to score goals. Jonathan Clark was brought in during the close season, but by October it was obvious that more new blood would be needed. As a result Docherty signed Tommy Booth, Gary Buckley, Barry Dunn and John Kelly, and they were quickly thrust into an ailing side. Things failed to improve, it was not just that Preston struggled to win games, but also that their poor style of play which kept the fans away in droves. Both the Cups had come and gone without success and after just 17 league games the Preston Directors decided to admit their mistake and sacked Docherty. All this, and it was only 4 December! Alan Kelly took over team affairs until, a week later, North End appointed Gordon Lee as their new manager. All this upheaval had a bad effect on the players, although John Kelly, Andy McAteer, Don O'Riordan and Steve Elliott all showed admirable skills, never giving less than 100% effort. Lee then brought in Martin Hodge on loan and the goalkeeper organised the back line well, thus giving Preston the platform to improve from. To their credit the team did play better, they could hardly have played worse, and the results in the New Year were much improved. Elliott and Alex Bruce worked well together and in a more settled side John Anderson and Steve Doyle also found their form. The defence was much tighter, the midfield worked hard and even up front the goals were easier to come by. Lee had certainly improved things noticeably. O'Riordan was the pick of the side and deservedly won the Player of the Year award. Overall though, it had been a traumatic season for the club. With the Docherty fiasco ruining any chance of a Centenary season to celebrate, Preston at least had the opportunity to build on Gordon Lee's impressive managerial start with the club.

DEBUTANTS: (10) Jonathan Clark, Mark Walsh, Jimmy Bell, Mike Farrelly, Tommy Booth, Gary Buckley, Barry Dunn, John Kelly, Jimmy Mullen, Martin Hodge.

LAST GAMES: (8) Doyle, Baxter M., Taylor, Blackley, Anderson, Bell J., Dunn, Mullen.

Jonathan Clark tries out his new kit after signing for PNE.

League appearances (46 games)

Anderson J. C. P. 35 + 3, Bell G. T. A. 22, Blackley J. H. 3, Booth T. A. 27, Bruce A. R. 46, Buckley G. 20 + 2, Clark J. 18, Coleman G. M. 15, Doyle S. C. 36, Dunn H. 8, Elliott S. B. 34 + 1, Farrelly M. J. 3 + 4, Hodge M. J. 28, Houston G. R. 9 + 9, Kelly J. 28 + 2, Litchfield P. 18, McAteer A. W. 41, McGee P. G. 10, Mullen J. 1, Naughton W. B. S. 31 + 2, O'Riordan D. J. 46, Sayer P. A. 1, Taylor B. J. 10 + 2, Walsh M. 4 + 6, Westwell S. 12.

FA Cup appearances (1 game) (All one each)

Litchfield, Clark, McAteer, Doyle, Anderson, O'Riordan, Houston, Buckley, Bruce, Naughton and Dunn.

League Cup appearances (4 games)

Litchfield 4, Coleman 4, Westwell 3, Clark 4, Anderson 2, McAteer 3, Naughton 1, Houston 1, O'Riordan 4, Bell G. 1, Booth 1, Blackley 1, Doyle 2, Walsh 1 + 1, Buckley 2, Bell J. 1, Elliott 1, Bruce 4, McGee 1, Farrelly 1 + 1, Dunn 2.

Goalscorers: 50 League–1 FAC–3 LC–(Total 54)

Bruce 18 (2 pens)–0–1 (19), Elliott 10 (2 pens)–0–0 (10), Kelly 5–0–0 (5) O'Riordan 4–0–0 (4), Naughton 3–0–1 (4), Doyle 3–1–0 (4), Buckley 2 (1 pen)–0–0 (2), Walsh 1–0–0 (1), Dunn 1–0–0 (1), McGee 1–0–0 (1), Bell G. 1–0–0 (1), Clark 0–0–1 (1), Own goals 1–0–0 (1), (Pountney of Southend.)

Match Report: Centenary Celebrations Fall Flat – 20 Oct 1981 Preston 1 Burnley 1

This game was chosen as the official Preston North End Centenary celebration match and manager Tommy Docherty was not even present. Mind you, he never missed much as the game proved to be a damp squib. The first half was instantly forgettable with few chances created at either end and the first goal took 58 minutes to arrive. The scoring shot came from O'Riordan although the ball struck Dunn on the way into the net. It was Preston's first goal in 430 minutes of football and their poor run was indicative of their performance in this game. The goal had come after a Kelly corner had been flicked on by Booth, but the fan's joy was shortlived. Only four minutes had elapsed when Burnley, who were also in their Centenary year, hit back with an equaliser. Good work by Scott and Hamilton set up Wharton and he scored with a good shot beyond Litchfield in the Preston goal. Doyle and McAteer were booked for Preston whilst Overson went into the referee's notebook for Burnley. Apart from that there was very little to report on a night when Preston's best crowd of the season should have had a lot more to cheer. Instead they were left with a feeling that if the squad was not improved and the players did not perform better then relegation would be a definite possibility. It was obvious that Docherty was struggling, the side was not creating chances, players were not good enough and the mood of the fans was deteriorating. Something had to be done.

Don O' Riordan

STAT FACTS:
Best home run without defeat: 4 games
Best away run without defeat: 6 games
Longest run unbeaten: 6 games
Longest run without a win: 10 games
Best home attendance: 7,815 vs. Carlisle 10.4.82
Worst home attendance: 4,171 vs. Brentford 5.12.81
Best away attendance: 13,871 vs. Burnley 11.5.82
Worst away attendance: 2,428 vs. Wimbledon 14.11.81
Aggregate and average home attendance: 126,373 – 5,494
Aggregate and average away attendance: 118,263 – 5,142

Ever presents: (2) Don O'Riordan, Alex Bruce   **Hat-tricks:** None
Players used: 27   **FA Cup:** First Round   **Chairman:** A. R. W. Jones JP FRICS
League Cup: Second Round – Also competed in the League Group Cup
Manager: Tommy Docherty until December, then Gordon Lee
Leading scorer: 19 goals – Alex Bruce (18 League 1 LC)

OFFICIAL PLAYER OF THE SEASON: Don O'Riordan

Brian Taylor

(*First season of three points for a win)

John Anderson

John Blackley

Season 1981–82: Third Division

	P	W	D	L	F	A	Pts
1 Burnley	46	21	17	8	66	49	80
2 Carlisle	46	23	11	12	65	50	80
3 Fulham	48	21	15	10	77	51	78
4 Lincoln	46	21	14	11	66	40	77
5 Oxford	46	19	14	13	63	49	71
8 Gillingham	48	20	11	15	64	56	71
7 Southend	46	18	15	13	63	51	69
8 Brentford	46	19	11	16	58	47	68
9 Milwall	46	18	13	15	62	62	67
10 Plymouth	46	18	11	17	64	56	65
11 Chesterfield	46	18	10	18	67	58	64
12 Reading	46	17	11	18	67	75	62
13 Portsmouth	46	14	19	13	56	51	61
14 PRESTON	**46**	**16**	**13**	**17**	**50**	**56**	**61**
15 Bristol Rovers*	46	18	9	19	58	65	61
16 Newport	46	14	16	16	54	54	58
17 Huddersfield	46	15	12	19	64	59	57
18 Exeter	46	16	9	21	71	84	57
19 Doncaster	46	13	17	16	55	68	56
20 Walsall	46	13	14	19	51	55	53
21 Wimbledon	46	14	11	21	61	75	53
22 Swindon	46	13	13	20	55	71	52
23 Bristol City	46	11	13	22	40	65	46
24 Chester	46	7	11	28	36	78	32

* Two points deducted by League.

Date 1981-2	Opponents	Comp	h or a	Score	Att.	1	2	3	4	5	6	7	8	9	10	11	12 *Sub Used		
Aug 29	Millwall	Div 3	a	1-2	4549	Litchfield	Taylor	Coleman	Clark	O'Riordan	Blackley	Walsh (1)	Houston	Bruce	Doyle	Naughton *	Elliott *		
Sep 1	Halifax Town Rd 1 1L	LC	a	2-1	2719	Litchfield	Westwell	Coleman	Clark (1)	O'Riordan	Blackley	Houston	Doyle	Elliott *	Bruce	Naughton (1)	Walsh *		
Sep 5	Portsmouth	Div 3	h	1-0	6124	Litchfield	Coleman	Westwell	Clark	O'Riordan	Blackley	Houston *	Doyle	McGee	Bruce (1)	Naughton	Walsh *		
Sep 12	Swindon Town	Div 3	a	0-4	5695	Litchfield	Taylor	Westwell	Clark	O'Riordan	Blackley	Houston	Doyle *	McGee	Bruce	Naughton	Walsh *		
Sep 15	Halifax Town Rd 1 2L	LC	h	0-0	4090	Litchfield	Westwell	McAteer	Clark	O'Riordan	Bell J.	Walsh	Bell G.	Bruce	Coleman	McGee	Naughton		
Sep 19	Gillingham	Div 3	a	1-1	4563	Litchfield	Coleman	McAteer	Clark	O'Riordan	Anderson	Walsh	Houston	Bruce (1p)	Elliott *	Naughton	Walsh *		
Sep 22	Huddersfield T.	Div 3	h	1-1	6497	Litchfield	Coleman	McAteer	Clark	O'Riordan	Anderson	Walsh	Houston	Bruce	Bell G.	Naughton * (1	Farrelly *		
Sep 26	Newport Co.	Div 3	a	1-1	5064	Litchfield	Coleman	McAteer	Clark	O'Riordan	Anderson	Houston	Doyle (1)	Bruce	Farrelly	Walsh	Hanson		
Sep 29	Doncaster R.	Div 3	a	0-1	7513	Litchfield	Coleman	McAteer	Clark	O'Riordan	Anderson	Walsh *	Doyle	Bruce	Farrelly	McGee	Houston *		
Oct 3	Bristol Rovers	Div 3	h	0-1	4964	Litchfield	Coleman	McAteer	Clark	O'Riordan	Anderson	Houston	Doyle *	Bruce	Farrelly	McGee	Walsh *		
Oct 6	Leicester C. Rd 2 1L	LC	h	1-0	5592	Litchfield	Coleman	McAteer	Clark	Booth	O'Riordan	Buckley	Anderson	Bruce (1)	Farrelly	Dunn	Houston		
Oct 10	Bristol City	Div 3	a	0-0	5389	Litchfield	Coleman	McAteer	Clark	Booth	O'Riordan	Kelly	Buckley	Bruce	Anderson *	Dunn	Farrelly *		
Oct 17	Reading	Div 3	h	0-0	5671	Litchfield	Coleman	McAteer	Clark	Booth	O'Riordan	Kelly	Buckley	Bruce	Anderson *	Dunn	Farrelly *		
Oct 20	Burnley	Div 3	a	1-1	7521	Litchfield	Coleman	McAteer	Clark	Booth	O'Riordan (1)	Kelly	Buckley	Bruce	Doyle *	Dunn	Taylor *		
Oct 24	Exeter City	Div 3	a	3-4	3642	Litchfield	Westwell	McAteer	Clark	Booth *	O'Riordan	Buckley	Coleman	Bruce (2, 1p)	Doyle (1)	Dunn	Anderson *		
Oct 28	Leicester C. Rd 2 2L	LC	a	0-4	7658	Litchfield	Westwell *	McAteer	Clark	Anderson	O'Riordan	Buckley	Coleman	Bruce	Doyle	Dunn	Farrelly *		
Oct 31	Southend Utd.	Div 3	h	1-0	4487	Litchfield	Coleman	McAteer	Clark	Anderson	O'Riordan	Kelly *	Buckley	Bruce	Doyle	Dunn	Farrelly *	1 og	(Pountney)
Nov 4	Lincoln City	Div 3	a	2-1	3683	Litchfield	Coleman	McAteer	Clark	Booth *	O'Riordan	Elliott (1)	Buckley (1)	Bruce	Doyle	Dunn	Anderson *		
Nov 7	Chester	Div 3	h	0-1	5185	Litchfield	Coleman *	McAteer	Clark	Anderson	O'Riordan	Buckley	Elliott	Bruce	Doyle	Dunn	Kelly *		
Nov 14	Wimbledon	Div 3	a	2-3	2428	Litchfield	Coleman *	McAteer	Clark	Anderson	O'Riordan	Buckley	Elliott	Bruce (1)	Doyle	Dunn (1)	Naughton *		
Nov 21	Chesterfield Rd 1	FAC	a	1-4	5435	Litchfield	Clark	McAteer	Doyle (1)	Anderson	O'Riordan	Houston	Buckley	Bruce	Naughton	Dunn	Walsh		
Nov 28	Oxford Utd.	Div 3	a	0-3	3798	Litchfield	Clark	McAteer	O'Riordan	Booth	Mullen	Houston	Bruce *	Elliott	Doyle	Naughton	Taylor *		
Dec 5	Brentford	Div 3	h	1-3	4171	Litchfield	Taylor	McAteer	O'Riordan	Booth	Doyle	Anderson	Clark	Bruce (1)	Elliott	Sayer	Naughton		
Jan 5	Chesterfield	Div 3	a	0-0	3969	Hodge	Taylor	McAteer	Bell G.	Booth	O'Riordan	Anderson *	Doyle	Elliott	Naughton	Bruce	Buckley *		
Jan 16	Plymouth Arg.	Div 3	h	1-0	4936	Hodge	Taylor	McAteer	Bell G.	Booth	O'Riordan	Anderson	Doyle	Elliott	Naughton	Bruce (1)	McGee		
Jan 23	Millwall	Div 3	h	1-0	5082	Hodge	Taylor	McAteer	Bell G.	Booth	O'Riordan	Anderson	Doyle	Elliott (1p)	Naughton	Bruce	Sayer		
Jan 30	Gillingham	Div 3	h	2-0	5379	Hodge	Taylor	McAteer	Bell G.	Booth	O'Riordan	Anderson *	Doyle	Elliott	Naughton (1)	Bruce (1)	Kelly *		
Feb 2	Carlisle Utd.	Div 3	a	0-1	5044	Hodge	Westwell	McAteer	Bell G. *	Booth	O'Riordan	Kelly	Doyle	Elliott	Naughton	Bruce	Houston *		
Feb 6	Swindon Town	Div 3	h	0-0	5616	Hodge	Westwell *	McAteer	Bell G.	Booth	O'Riordan	Kelly	Doyle	Elliott	Naughton	Bruce	Houston *		
Feb 9	Huddersfield T.	Div 3	a	3-2	6674	Hodge	Taylor	McAteer	Bell G.	Booth	O'Riordan	Kelly	Doyle	Elliott (1)	Naughton	Bruce (2)	Houston		
Feb 13	Bristol Rovers	Div 3	a	0-2	5003	Hodge	Anderson	McAteer	Bell G.	Booth	O'Riordan	Kelly	McGee	Elliott	Naughton *	Bruce	Buckley *		
Feb 20	Doncaster R.	Div 3	h	3-1	5830	Hodge	Taylor	McAteer	Bell G.	Anderson	O'Riordan	Kelly	McGee (1)	Elliott (1p)	Naughton	Bruce (1)	Buckley		
Feb 27	Bristol City	Div 3	h	1-3	6424	Hodge	Taylor *	McAteer	Bell G.	Booth	O'Riordan	Kelly (1)	McGee	Elliott	Naughton	Bruce	Anderson *		
Mar 6	Reading	Div 3	a	1-2	2655	Hodge	Anderson	McAteer	Bell G.	Booth *	O'Riordan	Kelly	McGee	Elliott (1)	Naughton	Bruce	Naughton *		
Mar 13	Exeter City	Div 3	h	1-0	4770	Hodge	Anderson	McAteer	Bell G.	Booth	O'Riordan	Kelly	McGee	Elliott (1)	Buckley	Bruce	Naughton		
Mar 16	Lincoln City	Div 3	h	1-1	4885	Hodge	Anderson	McAteer	Bell G.	Booth	O'Riordan (1)	Kelly	McGee	Elliott	Buckley	Bruce	Naughton		
Mar 19	Southend Utd.	Div 3	a	2-2	3915	Hodge	Anderson	Naughton	Bell G. *	Booth	O'Riordan	Kelly	Doyle	Elliott (1)	Buckley	Bruce (1)	Walsh *		
Mar 27	Chester	Div 3	a	1-0	2842	Hodge	Anderson	Naughton	McAteer	Booth	O'Riordan	Kelly	Doyle	Elliott (1)	Buckley	Bruce	Houston		
Apr 3	Wimbledon	Div 3	h	3-2	4964	Hodge	Anderson	McAteer	Naughton	Booth	O'Riordan (1)	Kelly	Doyle	Elliott	Buckley	Bruce (2)	Houston		
Apr 6	Portsmouth	Div 3	a	1-1	6712	Hodge	Anderson *	McAteer	Naughton	Booth	O'Riordan (1)	Kelly	Doyle	Elliott	Buckley	Bruce	Walsh *		
Apr 10	Carlisle Utd.	Div 3	h	0-1	7815	Hodge	Anderson	McAteer	Naughton	Booth	O'Riordan	Kelly	Doyle	Elliott	Buckley *	Bruce	Houston *		
Apr 13	Walsall	Div 3	a	3-0	3507	Hodge	Anderson	McAteer (1)	Naughton	Booth	O'Riordan	Kelly	Doyle	Elliott (1)	Buckley	Bruce (2)	Walsh		
Apr 17	Brentford	Div 3	a	0-0	5627	Hodge	Anderson	McAteer	Naughton	Booth	O'Riordan	Kelly	Doyle	Elliott	Buckley	Bruce	Walsh		
Apr 20	Fulham	Div 3	h	1-3	6009	Hodge	Anderson	McAteer	Naughton	Booth *	O'Riordan	Kelly	Doyle	Elliott	Buckley (1p)	Bruce	Houston *		
Apr 24	Oxford Utd.	Div 3	h	2-2	5516	Hodge	Anderson	McAteer	Naughton	Westwell	O'Riordan	Kelly (1)	Doyle (1)	Elliott	Buckley *	Bruce	Houston *		
Apr 27	Walsall	Div 3	h	1-0	4926	Hodge	Anderson	McAteer	Naughton	Westwell	O'Riordan	Kelly (1)	Doyle	Elliott *	Bell G.	Bruce	Houston *		
May 1	Plymouth Arg.	Div 3	a	3-0	3319	Hodge	Anderson	McAteer	Naughton	Westwell	O'Riordan	Kelly (1)	Doyle	Elliott (1)	Bell G. (1)	Bruce	Walsh		
May 4	Newport Co.	Div 3	a	2-1	4972	Hodge	Anderson	Naughton	Houston	Westwell	O'Riordan	Kelly (1)	Doyle	Elliott	Bell G.	Bruce (1)	Walsh		
May 8	Chesterfield	Div 3	h	2-0	5445	Hodge	Anderson	McAteer	Naughton (1)	Westwell	O'Riordan	Kelly	Doyle	Elliott	Bell G.	Bruce (1)	Houston		
May 11	Burnley	Div 3	h	0-2	13871	Hodge	Anderson	McAteer	Naughton	Westwell	O'Riordan	Kelly	Doyle	Elliott	Bell G. *	Bruce	Houston *		
May 15	Fulham	Div 3	a	0-3	7985	Hodge	Anderson	McAteer	Naughton	Westwell	O'Riordan	Kelly *	Doyle	Elliott	Bell G.	Bruce	Houston *		

247

SEASON 1982-1983

A new Chairman, Keith Leeming, was in place for the new season and August 1982 saw the start of another very difficult year for the Preston North End football club, but at least they started the campaign with a win. Steve Elliott was the opening day hero as he scored a terrific hat-trick against Millwall at Deepdale, the first opening day hat-trick since Charlie Wayman had scored three against Manchester City in 1954. (Nick Ross had been the only other player to do it, back in 1889). North End followed the win over Millwall with a victory at Walsall in the League Cup, or Milk Cup as it was now called. It looked an encouraging start but the club then embarked on a poor run that left them languishing at the bottom of the division. New signing, Alan Gowling added a little experience to the squad and it must be said that Preston did not enjoy the best of luck over the next few weeks. With only four wins in the first 20 league and cup games manager Gordon Lee was under pressure and he struggled to find the right blend. He was hampered by injuries to Gordon Coleman, Don O'Riordan, Peter Litchfield and Tommy Booth, and with such a small squad he could ill afford to lose such players. The goals dried up with only Elliott looking likely to score, and even Alex Bruce lost his form. The FA Cup did bring some relief as non-league minnows Shepshed Charterhouse came to Deepdale on a hiding to nothing. They put up a good

show before eventually going down 5-1, which gave Preston a super home draw against neighbours Blackpool. The league form continued to depress the fans though and relegation was already a distinct possibility. A win over Blackpool in the cup lifted everyone's spirits and it gave Preston's hard pressed fans something to look forward to in the new year as North End were drawn away to Leeds. The Yorkshire club won that match with ease though and it was not until mid-March before Preston found some better league form. In fact North End only lost one of their last 13 games and ended the season with three consecutive wins. The players had at last found their feet, coincidentally after goalkeeper Martin Hodge had returned for another loan spell. Andy McAteer and Willie Naughton had played well and new signing Joe Hinnigan slotted in perfectly to the problem right-back position. Booth also came back for the last third of the season and his presence also helped stabilise the defence. It was very frustrating though that Preston had taken so long to find their best form and Mr Leeming had been left in no doubt as to the difficulty of his job...

DEBUTANTS: (6) Alan Gowling, Jim Arnold, Glen Campbell, Paul Lodge, Joe Hinnigan, Chris Hunter.

LAST GAMES: (9) Bruce, Coleman, O'Riordan, Bell G., Westwell, Buckley, Hodge, Gowling, Arnold.

League appearances (46 games)

Arnold J.A. 6, Bell G.T.A. 39 + 1, Booth T.A. 15, Bruce A.R. 22 + 5, Buckley G. 7 + 5, Campbell A.G. 1, Clark J. 3, Coleman G.M. 15 + 3, Elliott S.B. 45, Farrelly M.J. 4 + 1, Gowling A. 37 + 3, Hinnigan J.P. 13, Hodge M.J. 16, Houston G.R. 15 + 5, Hunter C.P. 0 + 1, Kelly J. 23 + 6, Litchfield P. 23, Lodge P. 19, McAteer A.W. 44, Naughton W.B.S. 40 + 1, O'Riordan D.J. 40 + 1, Sayer P.A. 21, Walsh M. 27, Westwell S. 31.

FA Cup appearances (3 games)

Litchfield 3, McAteer 3, O'Riordan 3, Westwell 2, Walsh 2, Kelly 2, Bell 0 + 1, Elliott 3, Naughton 3, Bruce 1, Houston 3, Gowling 3, Coleman 2, Booth 1, Sayer 2.

League Cup appearances (4 games)

Litchfield 4, McAteer 4, O'Riordan 2, Westwell 4, Walsh 4, Kelly 4, Bell 4, Elliott 4, Naughton 4, Bruce 3, Houston 1, Gowling 3, Coleman 1, Farrelly 1, Clark 1.

Goalscorers: 60 League–7 FAC–4 LC–(Total 71)

Elliott 19 (2 pens)–2–2 (23), Bruce 7–0–1 (8), McAteer 5 (1 pen)–1–0 (6), Gowling 5–0 (5), O'Riordan 4–1–0 (5), Bell 4–0–0 (4), Hinnigan 3–0–0 (3), Kelly 2 (1 pen)–1 (pen)–0 (3), Coleman 1–2–0 (3), Houston 2–0–0 (2), Sayer 2–0–0 (2), Naughton 1–0–1 (2), Walsh 1–0–0 (1), Booth 1–0–0 (1), Westwell 1–0–0 (1), Own goals 2–0–0 (2), Humphries of Doncaster and Houston of Sheffield United

---

League position in Division Three: 16th – P46 W15 D13 L18 F60 A69 Pts 58
Home: W11 D10 L2 F35 A17   Away: W4 D3 L16 F25 A52

Match Report: Elliott Hat-Trick Sinks Lions –
28 Aug 1982 Preston 3 Millwall 2

It is not very often that Preston North End win on the opening day of the season but thanks to a terrific hat-trick by Elliott Millwall were sent back to London empty handed. In a game full of goal chances Preston played bright, attacking football from the start and took only seven minutes to take the lead. Bell's shot was not cleared and Coleman picked up possession only to be fouled by the Millwall goalkeeper for a clear penalty. Elliott duly despatched the spot-kick and Preston's somewhat nervous start was put behind them. Neal for Millwall and Elliott and McAteer for Preston all went close before Elliott scored his second goal on 31 minutes. O'Riordan shot, the keeper could not hold the ball and Elliott followed up. Other chances had gone begging, especially for Millwall but Preston had deserved their 2–0 half-time lead. Litchfield saved a penalty early in the second half as Chatterton shot weakly, but on 54 minutes the same player made amends by pulling a goal back. Six minutes later, after continuous end to end football, Elliott completed his hat-trick with a fine goal. Naughton had set up the chance with a fine pass which the North End striker thumped home. Again the play flowed to and fro with Preston creating the better chances whilst Millwall missed theirs. With seven minutes to go a mistake by O'Riordan let in Neal and Millwall pulled another goal back. Despite other chances at both ends being wasted and a few jangling nerves amongst the Preston fans the game ended in a home victory. It was deserved and Elliott proudly clutched the match ball.

Andy McAteer local-lad.

STAT FACTS:
Best home run without defeat: 16 games
Best away run without defeat: 2 games
Longest run unbeaten: 7 games
Longest run without a win: 8 games
Best home attendance: 14,148 *vs.* Blackpool FAC 11.12.82
Worst home attendance: 3,169 *vs.* Walsall MC 14.9.82
Best away attendance: 16,816 *vs.* Leeds FAC 8.1.83
Worst away attendance: 1,668 *vs.* Orient 18.12.82
Aggregate and average home attendance: 113,655 – 4,941
Aggregate and average away attendance: 108,906 – 4,735

Ever presents: None   Hat-tricks: (1) Steve Elliott   Players used: 24
FA Cup: Third Round   Milk Cup: (League Cup) Second Round
Manager: Gordon Lee   Chairman: K. W. Leeming Esq.
Leading scorer: 23 goals – Steve Elliott (19 League 2 FAC 2 MC)

OFFICIAL PLAYER OF THE SEASON: Steve Elliott

Season 1982–83: Third Division

		P	W	D	L	F	A	Pts
1	Portsmouth	46	27	10	9	74	41	91
2	Cardiff	46	25	11	10	76	50	86
3	Huddersfield	46	23	13	10	84	49	82
4	Newport	46	23	9	14	76	54	78
5	Oxford	46	22	12	12	71	53	78
6	Lincoln	46	23	7	16	77	51	76
8	Bristol Rovers	46	22	9	15	84	57	75
8	Plymouth	46	19	8	19	61	66	65
9	Brentford	46	18	10	18	88	77	64
10	Walsall	46	17	13	16	64	63	64
11	Sheffield United	46	19	7	20	62	64	64
12	Bradford City	46	16	13	17	68	69	61
13	Gillingham	46	16	13	17	58	59	61
14	Bournemouth	46	16	13	17	59	68	61
15	Southend	46	15	14	17	66	65	59
16	**PRESTON**	**46**	**15**	**13**	**18**	**60**	**69**	**58**
17	Millwall	46	14	13	19	64	78	55
13	Wigan	46	15	9	22	60	72	54
19	Exeter	46	14	12	20	81	104	54
20	Orient	46	15	9	22	64	88	54
21	Reading	46	12	17	17	63	80	53
22	Wrexham	46	12	15	19	57	76	51
23	Doncaster	48	9	11	26	57	97	38
24	Chesterfield	46	8	13	25	44	68	37

Far Left: Graham Bell.
Left: Mark Walsh

Date 1982-3	Opponents	Comp	h or a	Score	Att.	1	2	3	4	5	6	7	8	9	10	11	12 *Sub Used		
Aug 28	Millwall	Div 3	h	3-2	4498	Litchfield	Walsh	McAteer	O'Riordan	Westwell	Coleman	Kelly *	Bell	Elliott (3, 1p)	Naughton	Bruce	Houston *		
Aug 31	Walsall Rd 1 1L	MC	a	1-0	2490	Litchfield	Walsh	McAteer	O'Riordan	Westwell	Farrelly	Kelly	Bell	Elliott	Naughton (1)	Bruce	Houston		
Sep 4	Sheffield Utd.	Div 3	a	1-2	14527	Litchfield	Walsh	McAteer	O'Riordan	Westwell	Gowling	Kelly (1)	Bell	Elliott	Naughton	Bruce *	Houston *		
Sep 7	Walsall	Div 3	a	1-2	2060	Litchfield	Walsh	McAteer (1)	O'Riordan	Westwell	Gowling	Kelly	Bell	Elliott	Naughton	Bruce	Houston		
Sep 11	Oxford Utd.	Div 3	a	1-2	4607	Litchfield	Walsh	McAteer	O'Riordan	Westwell	Gowling	Kelly	Bell	Elliott	Naughton	Houston *	Bruce *		
Sep 14	Walsall Rd 1 2L	MC	h	1-1	3169	Litchfield	Walsh	McAteer	O'Riordan	Westwell	Gowling	Kelly	Bell	Elliott (1)	Naughton	Houston	Bruce		
Sep 18	Exeter City	Div 3	h	1-5	2310	Litchfield	Walsh	McAteer	O'Riordan	Westwell *	Gowling	Kelly	Bell	Elliott (1p)	Naughton	Houston	Coleman *		
Sep 25	Bristol Rovers	Div 3	h	2-2	3872	Litchfield	Walsh	McAteer	O'Riordan	Westwell	Gowling	Kelly	Bell (1)	Elliott (1)	Naughton *	Houston	Coleman *		
Sep 28	Wrexham	Div 3	h	3-0	3340	Litchfield	Walsh	McAteer	O'Riordan (1)	Westwell	Gowling	Kelly	Bell	Elliott (2)	Naughton	Houston	Coleman		
Oct 2	Reading	Div3	h	3-2	1943	Litchfield	Walsh	McAteer	Coleman	Westwell	Gowling	Kelly	Bell	Elliott (2)	Naughton	Houston *	Bruce * (1)		
Oct 6	Norwich City Rd 1 1L	MC	a	1-2	7273	Litchfield	Walsh	McAteer	Coleman	Westwell	Gowling	Kelly	Bell	Elliott	Naughton	Bruce (1)	Buckley		
Oct 9	Gillingham	Div 3	h	1-2	4390	Litchfield	Walsh *	McAteer	Coleman	Westwell	Gowling	Kelly	Bell	Elliott	Naughton	Bruce (1)	Buckley *		
Oct 16	Huddersfield T.	Div 3	h	0-0	5570	Arnold	Walsh	McAteer	Coleman *	Westwell	Gowling	Kelly	Bell	Elliott	Naughton	Bruce	Buckley *		
Oct 19	Newport Co.	Div 3	h	0-0	3759	Arnold	Walsh *	McAteer	Clark	Westwell	Gowling	Kelly	Bell	Elliott	Naughton	Bruce	Buckley *		
Oct 23	Portsmouth	Div3	a	1-3	10331	Arnold	Walsh *	McAteer	Clark	Westwell	Gowling	Kelly	Bell	Elliott	Naughton	Bruce (1)	Buckley *		
Oct 26	Norwich City Rd 2 2L	MC	h	1-2	6082	Litchfield	Walsh	McAteer	Clark	Westwell	Gowling	Kelly	Bell	Elliott (1)	Naughton	Bruce	Houston		
Oct 30	Bournemouth	Div 3	h	0-1	3583	Arnold	Walsh *	McAteer	Clark	Westwell	Gowling	Kelly	Bell	Elliott	Naughton	Bruce	O'Riordan *		
Nov 2	Brentford	Div 3	a	1-3	6142	Arnold	Westwell	McAteer *	O'Riordan	Walsh	Gowling	Kelly	Bell	Elliott (1)	Buckley	Bruce	Houston *		
Nov 6	Cardiff City	Div 3	a	1-3	5546	Arnold	Westwell	Naughton *	O'Riordan (1)	Coleman	Gowling	Kelly	Bell	Elliott	Buckley	Bruce	Houston *		
Nov 13	Chesterfield	Div3	a	1-1	3574	Campbell	Westwell	McAteer	O'Riordan	Coleman	Gowling	Kelly	Sayer	Elliott	Buckley *	Houston (1)	Naughton *		
Nov 20	Shepshed Chart. Rd 1	FAC	h	5-1	6200	Litchfield	Westwell	McAteer (1)	O'Riordan	Coleman (1)	Gowling	Kelly (1p)	Sayer	Elliott (2)	Naughton	Houston	Buckley		
Nov 27	Plymouth Arg.	Div 3	h	2-2	3648	Litchfield	Westwell	McAteer (1)	O'Riordan	Coleman	Gowling	Walsh	Sayer	Elliott (1)	Naughton	Houston	Bruce		
Dec 3	Southend Utd.	Div 3	a	3-2	3749	Litchfield	Westwell	McAteer	O'Riordan	Coleman	Gowling	Walsh (1)	Sayer	Elliott (1)	Naughton	Houston (1)	Booth		
Dec 11	Blackpool Rd 2	FAC	h	2-1	14148	Litchfield	Westwell	McAteer	O'Riordan (1)	Coleman (1)	Gowling	Walsh	Sayer	Elliott	Naughton	Houston	Booth		
Dec 17	Orient	Div 3	h	1-2	1668	Litchfield	Westwell	McAteer	O'Riordan	Coleman (1)	Gowling	Walsh	Sayer	Elliott	Naughton	Houston	Buckley *		
Dec 27	Bradford City	Div 3	h	0-0	7235	Litchfield	Westwell	McAteer	O'Riordan	Coleman *	Gowling	Walsh	Sayer	Elliott	Naughton	Houston	Bell *		
Dec 28	Doncaster R.	Div 3	a	0-2	3895	Litchfield	Westwell	McAteer	O'Riordan	Bell	Gowling	Walsh	Sayer *	Elliott	Kelly	Houston	Bruce *		
Jan 1	Wigan Ath.	Div3	a	4-1	7560	Litchfield	Kelly (1p)	McAteer (1)	O'Riordan	Coleman	Gowling	Walsh	Sayer	Elliott	Bruce (2)	Houston	Bell		
Jan 3	Lincoln City	Div 3	a	0-3	5891	Litchfield	Kelly	McAteer	O'Riordan	Coleman	Gowling	Walsh	Sayer	Elliott	Bruce	Houston	Bell		
Jan 8	Leeds Utd. Rd 3	FAC	a	0-3	16816	Litchfield	O'Riordan	McAteer	Kelly	Booth	Gowling	Walsh	Bruce	Elliott	Naughton	Houston *	Bell *		
Jan 15	Millwall	Div 3	a	0-1	2816	Litchfield	O'Riordan	McAteer	Gowling	Booth	Buckley	Kelly	Bruce	Bell	Naughton	Houston	Westwell		
Jan 22	Exeter City	Div 3	a	2-2	3769	Litchfield	Westwell	McAteer	Booth	Buckley	Kelly	Bruce (1)	Elliott (1)	Naughton	Bell	Gowling			
Jan 29	Oxford Utd.	Div 3	a	2-3	4441	Litchfield	Westwell	McAteer	Booth	Buckley	Kelly *	Gowling (1)	Elliott	Naughton (1)	Bell	Bruce *		
Feb 5	Wrexham	Div3	a	1-3	1930	Litchfield	Westwell	McAteer	Gowling	Buckley	Kelly *	Bruce	Elliott	Naughton	Bell (1)	Farrelly *		
Feb 15	Newport Co.	Div 3	a	0-3	2317	Litchfield	Farrelly	McAteer	O'Riordan	Westwell	Lodge	Walsh	Bruce *	Elliott	Naughton	Bell	Hunter *		
Feb 19	Gillingham	Div 3	a	0-0	3475	Litchfield	Farrelly	McAteer	O'Riordan	Westwell	Lodge	Walsh *	Bruce	Elliott	Naughton	Bell	Coleman *		
Feb 26	Huddersfield T.	Div 3	a	1-1	8562	Litchfield	Farrelly *	McAteer	O'Riordan (1)	Westwell	Lodge	Walsh	Bruce	Elliott	Naughton	Bell	Kelly *		
Mar 1	Brentford	Div3	h	3-0	3669	Hodge	Coleman *	McAteer	O'Riordan	Westwell (1)	Lodge	Walsh	Bruce	Elliott (1)	Naughton	Bell (1)	Gowling *		
Mar 5	Portsmouth	Div 3	h	0-0	5598	Hodge	Coleman	McAteer	O'Riordan	Westwell	Lodge	Walsh *	Bruce	Elliott	Naughton	Bell	Gowling *		
Mar 12	Bournemouth	Div 3	a	0-4	4407	Hodge	Coleman	McAteer	O'Riordan	Westwell	Lodge	Walsh *	Bruce	Elliott	Naughton	Bell	Kelly *		
Mar 19	Cardiff City	Div 3	a	2-1	4608	Hodge	Hinnigan	McAteer	O'Riordan	Westwell *	Lodge	Sayer	Bruce (1)	Elliott (1)	Naughton	Bell	Gowling *		
Mar 26	Chesterfield	Div3	a	1-1	2332	Hodge	Hinnigan	McAteer	O'Riordan (1)	Booth	Lodge	Sayer *	Gowling	Elliott	Naughton	Bell	Kelly *		
Mar 29	Walsall	Div 3	h	1-0	4013	Hodge	Hinnigan	McAteer	O'Riordan	Booth	Lodge	Sayer (1)	Gowling	Elliott	Naughton	Bell	Bruce		
Apr 2	Doncaster R.	Div 3	h	4-1	5287	Hodge	Hinnigan (1)	McAteer (1)	O'Riordan	Booth	Lodge	Sayer	Gowling	Elliott (1)	Naughton	Bell	Bruce	1 og	(Humphries)
Apr 4	Bradford City	Div 3	a	2-1	4357	Hodge	Hinnigan	McAteer (1p)	O'Riordan	Booth	Lodge	Sayer	Gowling (1)	Elliott	Naughton	Bell	Kelly		
Apr 8	Southend Utd.	Div 3	h	1-1	6286	Hodge	Hinnigan	McAteer	O'Riordan	Booth	Lodge	Sayer *	Gowling	Elliott	Naughton	Bell (1)	Bruce *		
Apr 12	Sheffield Utd.	Div 3	h	1-0	6302	Hodge	Farrelly	Hinnigan	O'Riordan	Booth	Lodge	Sayer	Gowling	Elliott	Naughton	Bell	Houston G.	1 og	(Houston S.)
Apr 16	Bristol Rovers	Div 3	a	2-3	5189	Hodge	Hinnigan (1)	McAteer *	O'Riordan	Booth	Lodge	Sayer	Gowling	Elliott (1)	Houston	Bell	Kelly *		
Apr 23	Orient	Div 3	h	2-1	5627	Hodge	Hinnigan (1)	McAteer	O'Riordan	Booth	Lodge	Sayer (1)	Gowling *	Elliott	Naughton	Bell	Houston *		
Apr 30	Plymouth Arg.	Div 3	a	1-1	2912	Hodge	Hinnigan	McAteer	O'Riordan	Booth (1)	Lodge	Sayer	Gowling *	Elliott	Naughton	Bell	Kelly *		
May 2	Lincoln City	Div 3	h	1-0	6523	Hodge	Hinnigan	McAteer	O'Riordan	Booth	Lodge	Sayer	Gowling (1)	Elliott	Naughton	Bell	Houston		
May 7	Reading	Div 3	a	2-0	7252	Hodge	Hinnigan	McAteer	O'Riordan	Booth	Lodge	Sayer	Gowling (1)	Elliott (1)	Naughton	Bell	Houston		
May 14	Wigan Ath.	Div3	a	1-0	7191	Hodge	Hinnigan	McAteer	O'Riordan	Booth	Lodge	Sayer	Gowling * (1)	Elliott	Naughton	Bell	Kelly *		

Peter Sayer

John Kelly

Gary Buckley

During the summer of 1983 Alex Bruce said goodbye to his magnificent Deepdale career and the initial worry amongst the fans was whether North End would be able to score the necessary goals to make a promotion challenge. The start to the campaign allayed those fears somewhat as Preston opened with seven unbeaten league and cup games. A home defeat against Oxford then led to a terrible run of eight consecutive league defeats and all the pre-season worries returned. A series of silly defensive errors undermined a lot of good play, much to the frustration of the increasingly under pressure manager, Gordon Lee. The away form was particularly poor. His new signings of David Jones, Geoff Twentyman and Peter Houghton made little difference although Preston did win a few more games during the November. But also during eleven days of that month North End went out of both cup competitions. A great win over Wolves in the Milk Cup gave North End a home tie with Sheffield Wednesday, which they lost 2–0. Eleven days later the visit to Scunthorpe in the FA Cup first round ended in another defeat and Preston's season was effectively over. After being beaten at Orient and then drawing at Bolton the Directors lost patience and decided to dispense with the services of Gordon Lee. Alan Kelly was again put in charge of the team and as often happens when a manager is sacked, Preston won their next two games

4–0 and 5–1! The second of those wins came, ironically, at Scunthorpe. The manager's position was not the only off the field problem. Shortly after Christmas the bombshell announcement came that Preston North End would cease to exist after the end of the season unless a rescue package of £250,000 was found. It was a bolt from the blue and although it was known that the finances of the club were poor, not many people were aware just what an awful state they were actually in. Thankfully many efforts were made to raise funds by everyone connected with the club, indeed, Alec Ashworth even auctioned his 1964 cup final shirt! Meanwhile Kelly was installed as manager, this time in a full-time capacity and the loyalty of the former Eire International knew no bounds towards his only professional club. On the field Preston continued to struggle but were able to win just enough points to stay out of trouble. Relegation was the last thing the club wanted at this stage of their history. The team was weak but Peter Litchfield, John Kelly and Steve Elliott at least showed that there was still some quality left at the club.

DEBUTANTS: (8) David Jones, George Telfer, David Bleasdale, Geoff Twentyman, Peter Houghton, Mark Jones, Andy Murphy, Stuart Cameron.

LAST GAMES: (8) Elliott, Sayer, Walsh, Lodge, Hinnigan, Bleasdale, Cameron, Telfer.

League appearances (46 games)

Bleasdale D. G. 4 + 1, Booth T. A. 31, Cameron S. J. 1, Clark J. 31, Elliott S. B. 44, Farrelly M. J. 31, Hinnigan J. P. 38 + 1, Houghton P. 31 + 2, Houston G. R. 23 + 18, Jones D. R. 37, Jones M. T. 4, Kelly J. 34, Litchfield P. 45, Lodge P. 17 + 2, McAteer A. W. 32 + 2, Murphy A. C. 4 + 1, Naughton W. B. S. 34 + 7, Sayer P. A. 15, Telfer G. A. 0 + 2, Twentyman G. 25 + 3, Walsh M. 25.

FA Cup appearances (1 game)

Litchfield, Hinnigan, McAteer, Jones D. Booth, Lodge, Kelly, Naughton, Elliott, Clark and Houghton all one each, Twentyman 0 + 1.

Milk Cup appearances (5 games)

Litchfield 5, Hinnigan 3, Clark 3, Farrelly 1, McAteer 5, Jones D. 5, Twentyman 3, Booth 4, Lodge 5, Walsh 2, Sayer 3 + 1, Kelly 3, Houston 4, Bleasdale 1, Naughton 3, Elliott 5.

Associate Members Cup appearances (3 games)

Litchfield 3, Hinnigan 3, Clark 1, Farrelly 2, McAteer 3, Jones D. 3, Booth 1, Twentyman 2 + 1, Walsh 2, Sayer 1 + 1, Kelly 2, Houston 1 + 2, Bleasdale 1, Naughton 3, Houghton 2 + 1, Murphy 0 + 1, Elliott 3.

Goalscorers: 66 League–5 LC–4 AMC–(Total 75) (No FA Cup goals)

Elliott 16 (2 Pens)–1–3 (20), Kelly 13 (1 pen)–1–0 (14), Houghton 9–0–0 (9), Hinnigan 5–2–0 (7), Clark 5 (2 pens)–0–0 (5), Naughton 3–1–1 (5), Sayer 4–0–0 (4), Houston 3–0–0 (3), Farrelly 2–0–0 (2), Twentyman 2–0–0 (2), Jones D. 1–0–0 (1), Walsh 1–0–0 (1), Booth 1–0–0 (1), Own goals 1–0–0 (1), Farnworth of Bolton.

League position in Division Three: 16th – P46 W15 D11 L20 F66 A66 Pts 56
Home: W12 D5 L6 F42 A27   Away: W3 D6 L14 F24 A39

Match Report: Stick to Cricket Both! – 12 Dec 1983
Scunthorpe 1 Preston 5

This was the match that Ian Botham should never have played in. Not only was it on the eve of the England cricket team's winter tour, but England's number one cricketer had a nightmare in this match against North End. The Preston lads followed up their 4–0 win over Port Vale in their previous game with a scintillating performance at Scunthorpe. The Elliott, Houghton partnership up front tore the home side apart and from the moment they took the lead there was little doubt about the outcome. Managerless Preston, being led by acting manager Alan Kelly, went in front on 37 minutes, a minute after Botham had been booked. Houghton collected the ball on the left and slipped it across to Elliott who drove his shot into the net. The 1–0 half-time lead was just about deserved but in the second half Preston totally took control. The second goal came five minutes after the break as Botham continued his nightmare by failing to control the ball. Houghton again gained possession and once more set up Elliott who put the ball into the net for his second goal. The game was effectively ended ten minutes later when home goalkeeper Noonan dropped a Naughton centre allowing Houghton to score. A superb shot on the run by Elliott in the 70th minute after a headed pass by Farrelly completed the number nine's hat-trick. With eight minutes to go John Kelly made it 5–0 after man of the match Houghton had yet again been the provider. Cammack scored a consolation goal for Scunthorpe with six minutes remaining but the Irons were left a well beaten side and Botham probably realised that he would be far better off playing cricket!

Graham Houston in action
vs. Oxford United,
1 October 1983.

Ever presents: None
Hat-tricks: (2) Both by Steve Elliott
Players used: 21
FA Cup: First Round
Milk Cup: Third Round – Preston also competed in the Associate Members Cup
Manager: Gordon Lee until December 1983, then Alan Kelly
Chairman: K. W. Leeming Esq
Leading scorer: 20 goals – Steve Elliott (16 League 1 MC 3 AMC)

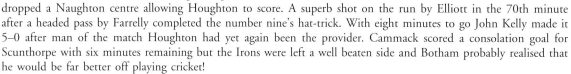

OFFICIAL PLAYER OF THE SEASON: Peter Litchfield

STAT FACTS:
Best home run without defeat: 10 games
Best away run without defeat: 2 games
Longest run unbeaten: 5 games
Longest run without a win: 12 games
Best home attendance: 11,060 *vs.* Sheffield Wed. MC 8.11.83
Worst home attendance: 3,144 *vs.* Orient 14.4.84
Best away attendance: 12,441 *vs.* Sheff. Utd. 10.9.83
Worst away attendance: 1,300 *vs.* Rochdale AMC 2.2.84
Aggregate and average home attendance: 104,714 – 4,553
Aggregate and average away attendance: 109,078 – 4,742

Peter Litchfield

Season 1983–84: Third Division

	P	W	D	L	F	A	Pts
1 Oxford	46	28	11	7	91	50	95
2 Wimbledon	46	26	9	11	97	76	87
3 Sheffield United	46	24	11	11	86	53	83
4 Hull	46	23	14	9	71	38	83
5 Bristol Rovers	46	22	13	11	68	54	79
6 Walsall	46	22	9	15	68	61	75
7 Bradford	46	20	11	15	73	65	71
8 Gillingham	46	20	10	16	74	69	70
9 Millwall	46	18	13	15	71	65	67
10 Bolton	46	18	10	18	56	60	64
11 Orient	46	18	9	19	71	81	63
12 Burnley	46	16	14	16	76	61	62
13 Newport	46	16	14	16	58	75	62
14 Lincoln	46	17	10	19	59	62	61
15 Wigan	46	16	13	17	46	56	61
16 PRESTON	46	15	11	20	66	66	56
17 Bournemouth	46	16	7	23	63	73	55
18 Rotherham	46	15	9	22	57	64	54
19 Plymouth	46	13	12	21	56	62	51
20 Brentford	46	11	16	19	69	79	49
21 Scunthorpe	46	9	19	18	54	73	46
22 Southend	46	10	14	22	55	76	44
23 Port Vale	46	11	10	25	51	83	43
24 Exeter	46	6	15	25	50	84	33

Left to right:
Back row: Booth, Naughton, Clark, Campbell, Litchfield, Farrelly, Hinnigan, G. Nulty (Ass. Manager).
Front row: McAteer, Houston, Kelly, Walsh, Gordon Lee (Manager), Sayer, Elliott, Bleasdale, Lodge.

Date 1983-4	Opponents	Comp	h or a	Score	Att.	1	2	3	4	5	6	7	8	9	10	11	12 *Sub Used		
Aug 27	Bournemouth	Div 3	a	1-0	4163	Litchfield	Hinnigan	McAteer	D.Jones	Booth	Lodge	Kelly	Sayer	Elliott	Naughton	Houston (1)	Farrelly		
Aug 30	Tranmere R. Rd 1 1L	MC	h	1-0	3210	Litchfield	Hinnigan	McAteer	D.Jones	Booth	Lodge	Kelly (1)	Sayer	Elliott	Naughton	Houston	Walsh		
Sep 3	Brentford	Div 3	h	3-3	3799	Litchfield	Hinnigan	McAteer *	D.Jones	Booth	Lodge	Kelly (2, 1p)	Sayer (1)	Elliott	Bleasdale	Houston	Telfer *		
Sep 6	Southend Utd.	Div 3	h	4-1	3967	Litchfield	Hinnigan	McAteer	D.Jones	Booth	Lodge	Kelly	Sayer (1)	Elliott (2)	Bleasdale	Houston *	Telfer *		
Sep 10	Sheffield Utd.	Div 3	a	1-1	12441	Litchfield	Clark	McAteer	D.Jones	Booth	Lodge	Kelly	Sayer (1)	Elliott	Bleasdale	Houston *	Naughton *		
Sep 12	Tranmere R. Rd 1 2L	MC	a	0-0	2986	Litchfield	Clark	McAteer	D.Jones	Booth	Lodge	Kelly	Sayer	Elliott	Bleasdale *	Houston	Naughton *		
Sep 17	Hull City	Div 3	h	0-0	6661	Litchfield	Clark	McAteer	D.Jones	Booth	Lodge	Kelly	Sayer	Elliott	Bleasdale *	Houston	Naughton *		
Sep 24	Plymouth Arg.	Div 3	a	0-1	3674	Litchfield	Clark	McAteer	D.Jones *	Booth	Lodge	Walsh	Sayer	Elliott	Naughton	Houston	Hinnigan *		
Sep 27	Newport Co.	Div 3	a	1-1	2542	Litchfield	Farrelly	Hinnigan	D.Jones	Booth	Lodge	Walsh	Sayer	Elliott (1p)	Naughton	Houston	Bleasdale		
Oct 1	Oxford Utd.	Div 3	h	1-2	4668	Litchfield	Hinnigan	McAteer	D.Jones	Booth *	Lodge	Walsh	Sayer (1)	Twentyman	Naughton	Houston	Bleasdale *		
Oct 4	Wolverhptn W. Rd 2 1L	MC	h	3-2	7790	Litchfield	Hinnigan (2)	McAteer	D.Jones	Twentyman	Lodge	Walsh	Sayer	Elliott	Naughton (1)	Houston	Clark		
Oct 8	Gillingham	Div 3	a	0-2	3725	Litchfield	Hinnigan	McAteer	D.Jones	Twentyman	Lodge	Clark	Sayer	Elliott *	Naughton *	Houghton	Houston *		
Oct 15	Wigan Ath.	Div 3	h	2-3	6622	Litchfield	Hinnigan (1)	McAteer	D.Jones	Twentyman	Lodge	Clark *	Sayer	Elliott (1p)	Naughton	Houghton	Houston *		
Oct 18	Wimbledon	Div 3	h	2-3	3517	Litchfield	Farrelly	McAteer	Twentyman	Booth	Lodge	Houston	Walsh *	Elliott (2)	Clark	Houghton	Naughton *		
Oct 21	Millwall	Div 3	a	0-1	5243	Litchfield	Farrelly *	McAteer	Twentyman	Booth	Lodge	Houston	Walsh	Elliott	Clark	Houghton	Twentyman *		
Oct 25	Wolverhptn W. Rd 2 2L	MC	a	1-0	8857	Litchfield	Farrelly	McAteer	D.Jones	Booth	Lodge	Houston	Walsh	Elliott (1)	Clark	Twentyman	Sayer		
Oct 29	Lincoln City	Div 3	a	1-2	4440	Litchfield	Farrelly	Hinnigan	D.Jones	Booth	Lodge	Houston	Walsh	Elliott	Clark (1)	Twentyman *	Naughton *		
Nov 1	Bristol Rovers	Div 3	a	1-3	5635	Litchfield	Farrelly (1)	Hinnigan	D.Jones	Booth	Lodge	Houston	Walsh	Elliott	Clark *	Houghton	Twentyman *		
Nov 5	Burnley	Div 3	a	1-2	7915	Litchfield	Farrelly	Hinnigan	D.Jones	Booth	Lodge	Kelly	Naughton	Elliott	Clark	Houghton (1) *	Houston		
Nov 8	Sheffield Wed. Rd 3	MC	h	0-2	11060	Litchfield	Hinnigan	McAteer	D.Jones	Booth	Lodge *	Kelly	Naughton	Elliott	Clark	Twentyman	Sayer *		
Nov 12	Rotherham Utd.	Div 3	h	1-0	3926	Litchfield	Hinnigan (1) *	McAteer	D.Jones	Booth	Lodge	Kelly	Naughton	Elliott	Clark	Houghton	Twentyman *		
Nov 19	Scunthorpe Utd. Rd 1	FAC	a	0-1	3484	Litchfield	Hinnigan	McAteer	D.Jones	Booth	Lodge	Kelly	Naughton	Elliott	Clark	Houghton *	Twentyman *		
Nov 26	Exeter City	Div 3	h	2-1	3474	Litchfield	Hinnigan	McAteer	D.Jones	Twentyman *	Lodge	Kelly (2)	Naughton	Elliott	Clark	Houghton	Houston *		
Dec 3	Orient	Div 3	a	1-2	2679	Litchfield	Hinnigan	McAteer	D.Jones (1)	Booth	Lodge	Walsh	Kelly	Naughton *	Elliott	Clark	Houston *		
Dec 17	Bolton W.	Div 3	a	2-2	6275	Litchfield	Hinnigan	McAteer	D.Jones	Booth	Farrelly *	Kelly	Walsh	Elliott	Naughton	Houghton (1)	Houston *	1 og	(Farnworth)
Dec 26	Port Vale	Div 3	h	4-0	5599	Litchfield	Hinnigan	McAteer	D.Jones	Booth	Farrelly	Kelly (1)	Walsh	Elliott (1)	Naughton	Houghton (2)	Houston		
Dec 27	Scunthorpe Utd.	Div 3	a	5-1	3986	Litchfield	Hinnigan	McAteer *	D.Jones	Booth	Farrelly	Kelly (1)	Walsh	Elliott (3)	Naughton	Houghton (1)	Houston *		
Dec 31	Walsall	Div 3	h	0-1	6204	Litchfield	Hinnigan	Clark	D.Jones	Booth	Farrelly *	Kelly	Walsh	Elliott	Naughton	Houghton	Houston *		
Jan 2	Bradford City	Div 3	a	2-3	6407	Litchfield	Clark	Hinnigan	D.Jones	Booth	Farrelly	Kelly (1)	Walsh	Elliott	Naughton (1)	Houghton	Houston		
Jan 14	Bournemouth	Div 3	h	2-0	3512	Litchfield	Clark (1p)	Hinnigan	D.Jones	Booth *	Farrelly	Kelly	Walsh	Elliott	Naughton	Houghton (1)	Houston *		
Jan 31	Sheffield Utd.	Div 3	h	2-2	5028	Litchfield	Clark	Hinnigan	D.Jones	Twentyman	Farrelly (1)	Kelly *	Walsh (1) *	Elliott	Naughton	Houghton	Houston *		
Feb 4	Oxford Utd.	Div 3	a	0-2	9105	Litchfield	Clark	Hinnigan	D.Jones	Twentyman	Farrelly	Kelly	Walsh *	Elliott	Naughton	Houghton	Houston *		
Feb 11	Plymouth Arg.	Div 3	h	2-1	4370	Litchfield	Clark	Hinnigan	D.Jones	Twentyman (1)	Farrelly	Kelly	Walsh	Elliott	Naughton (1)	Houghton *	McAteer *		
Feb 14	Bristol Rovers	Div 3	h	1-0	3719	Litchfield	Clark (1)	Hinnigan	D.Jones	Twentyman	Farrelly	Kelly	Walsh *	Elliott	Naughton	Houston	McAteer *		
Feb 18	Lincoln City	Div 3	h	1-2	2780	Litchfield	Hinnigan	McAteer	D.Jones	Twentyman	Clark	Farrelly *	Walsh	Elliott	Naughton	Houghton (1)	Lodge *		
Feb 22	Rochdale	AMC	a	3-0	1300	Litchfield	Hinnigan	McAteer	D.Jones	Twentyman	Clark	Bleasdale	Walsh	Elliott (3)	Naughton *	Farrelly +	Houston * Houghton +		
Feb 25	Millwall	Div 3	h	0-0	4109	Litchfield	Hinnigan	McAteer	Booth	Twentyman	Clark	Farrelly	Walsh *	Elliott	Naughton	Houghton	Houston *		
Mar 3	Wimbledon	Div 3	a	2-2	2524	Litchfield	Hinnigan (1)	McAteer	Booth (1) *	Twentyman	Clark	Farrelly	Kelly	Elliott	Naughton	Houghton	Houston *		
Mar 6	Burnley	Div 3	h	4-2	8812	Litchfield	Hinnigan (1)	McAteer	D.Jones	Twentyman	Clark	Kelly (1)	Farrelly	Elliott (1)	Naughton	Houghton (1) *	Houston *		
Mar 10	Rotherham Utd.	Div 3	a	1-0	3256	Litchfield	Hinnigan (1)	McAteer	D.Jones	Twentyman	Clark	Kelly	Farrelly *	Elliott	Naughton	Houghton	Houston *		
Mar 13	Doncaster R.	AMC	a	1-2	2098	Litchfield	Hinnigan	McAteer	D.Jones	Twentyman	Walsh *	Kelly	Houston +	Elliott	Naughton (1)	Houghton	Murphy * Sayer +		
Mar 17	Gillingham	Div 3	h	2-2	3874	Litchfield	Hinnigan	McAteer	D.Jones	Twentyman (1)	Walsh *	Kelly	Farrelly	Elliott (1)	Naughton	Houghton	Houston *		
Mar 20	Hull City	AMC	a	0-3	4377	Litchfield	Hinnigan	McAteer	D.Jones	Booth	Sayer	Kelly	Farrelly *	Elliott	Naughton	Houghton +	Houston * Twentyman +		
Mar 24	Wigan Ath.	Div 3	a	0-1	4470	Litchfield	Hinnigan	McAteer	D.Jones	Booth	Walsh	Kelly	Farrelly	Elliott	Naughton	Houghton *	Houston *		
Mar 30	Newport Co.	Div 3	h	2-0	3537	Litchfield	Hinnigan	McAteer	D.Jones	Booth	Walsh	Kelly (1)	Farrelly	Elliott (1)	Naughton	Sayer	Houston *		
Apr 3	Brentford	Div 3	a	1-4	3446	Litchfield	Hinnigan	McAteer	Twentyman	Booth	Sayer *	Kelly (1)	Walsh	Elliott	Naughton	Houston (1)	Houghton *		
Apr 6	Southend Utd.	Div 3	a	1-1	1826	Litchfield	Hinnigan	McAteer	Twentyman	Booth	Sayer *	Kelly (1)	Walsh	Elliott	Naughton	Houston	Houghton *		
Apr 10	Hull City	Div 3	a	0-3	8134	Litchfield	Hinnigan	McAteer	D.Jones	Twentyman	Walsh *	Kelly	Houghton	Elliott	Naughton	Houston	Lodge *		
Apr 14	Orient	Div 3	h	3-1	3144	Litchfield	M.Jones	McAteer	D.Jones	Booth	Clark	Kelly (1)	Murphy	Twentyman *	Naughton	Houghton (1)	Houston * (1)		
Apr 21	Port Vale	Div 3	a	1-1	3574	Litchfield	Hinnigan	McAteer	D.Jones *	Booth	Farrelly	Kelly	Murphy	Elliott	Houghton (1)	Houston	Naughton *		
Apr 24	Scunthorpe Utd.	Div 3	h	1-0	3413	Cameron	Farrelly	Hinnigan *	Twentyman	Booth	Clark	Kelly	Murphy	Elliott (1)	Houghton	Houston	Naughton *		
Apr 28	Exeter City	Div 3	a	1-2	2005	Litchfield	Farrelly	Hinnigan	Twentyman	Booth	Clark	Kelly	Murphy *	Elliott (1)	Houghton	Houston	Naughton *		
May 5	Bradford City	Div 3	h	1-2	3242	Litchfield	Farrelly	M.Jones	Hinnigan	Twentyman	Clark (1p)	Kelly	Sayer	Elliott	Houghton	Houston	Naughton		
May 7	Walsall	Div 3	a	1-2	3273	Litchfield	M.Jones	McAteer	Farrelly	Twentyman	Clark	Kelly (1)	Sayer	Elliott	Houghton	Houston	Murphy *		
May 12	Bolton W.	Div 3	h	2-1	5077	Litchfield	M.Jones	McAteer	Twentyman	Booth	Clark (1)	Farrelly	Houghton	Elliott (1)	Naughton	Houston	Murphy		

253

SEASON 1984–1985

Few things had improved as Preston's team took the field for the opening match of the 1984–5 season against Doncaster at Deepdale. Money for new players was unthinkable, although two free transfer signings, Paul Wilkins and Dale Rudge made their debuts in that first game. In fact, North End made a bright start to the new campaign and only lost once in the first seven league and cup games. But as so often in previous years, the hopes and expectations of something better to come turned out to be premature. In the next eleven outings Preston managed one draw and ten defeats, eight of them consecutively! It was an horrendous time for the fans, whose loyalty was stretched to the limit. Six goals were conceded at Plymouth and six more at Norwich in the Milk Cup, whilst four goals went in the Preston net at Lincoln, Bolton and Bradford City. Nothing that the manager, Alan Kelly could do seemed to stem the tide and confidence dropped to an all time low. The defence was leaking goals at will and the defenders seemed to have forgotten how to defend. The midfield looked lost and up front the players struggled to find the opponent's net. Nigel Greenwood was promoted from the reserves to try to improve things and David Johnson, the former Everton and England player was brought in from exile in the USA. Both players found the net occasionally and a 4–3 win over Bury in the FA Cup lifted the spirits. In the second round however Preston hit new depths of despair as non-league Telford United came to Deepdale and not only won 4–1, but out-thought, and

out-fought their league opponents. That result and the following poor run through Christmas proved the final straw for Kelly as he then resigned as manager. Tommy Booth took over in a temporary capacity but it made little difference to the team, and by the time they beat Cambridge at Deepdale in February, only 2,653 people paid to watch. Booth was then given the job full-time and he quickly persuaded Brian Kidd to become his assistant. Bob Atkins and Gary Brazil came in from Sheffield United, initially on loan, but results wise things went from bad to worse. There was a resigned inevitability about the final outcome to the season with Preston needing to beat Wigan at Deepdale in the penultimate games to have even the faintest chance of staying up. North End were hammered 5–2 and all was lost. Relegation and 100 league goals conceded. Typically, Preston then went to York for their last game and although the result did not matter they returned to Lancashire with a 1–0 win. Who would have thought that the name of Preston North End would ever appear in the Fourth Division? Now it was a reality.

DEBUTANTS: (12) Paul Wilkins, Dale Rudge, Nigel Greenwood, David Johnson, Terry Gray, Paul Welsh, Simon Gibson, Jeff Wealands, Gary Brazil, Bob Atkins, John Platt, Ian Stevens.

LAST GAMES: (14) McGee, Naughton, Litchfield, Farrelly, Booth, Kelly J., Campbell, Jones D., Hunter, Houghton, Murphy, Wilkins, Johnson, Wealands.

League appearances (46 games)

Atkins R. G. 13, Booth T. A. 11, Brazil G. N. 17, Campbell G. 17, Clark J. 39 + 1, Farrelly M. J. 39, Gibson S. J. 17, Gray T. I. 13, Greenwood N. P. 11 + 4, Houghton P. 22 + 2, Houston G. R. 26 + 5, Hunter C. P. 3 + 3, Johnson D. E. 20 + 4, Jones D. R. 13, Jones M. T. 35, Kelly J. 35 + 2, Litchfield P. 18, McAteer A. W. 33, McGee P. G. 2, Murphy A. C. 5, Naughton W. B. S. 31 + 2, Platt J. R. 7, Rudge D. A. 23 + 1, Stevens I. D. 3 + 1, Twentyman G. 44, Wealands J. A. 4, Welsh P. W. 2 + 1, Wilkins P. 3 + 3.

FA Cup appearances (2 games)

Litchfield 2, Jones M. 2, Jones D. 1, Farrelly 1, McAteer 2, Twentyman 2, Gray 2, Clark 2, Kelly 1, McGee 1, Hunter 0 + 1, Johnson 2, Naughton 2, Houston 2.

Milk Cup appearances (4 games)

Litchfield 4, Jones M. 3, Rudge 3, Jones D. 1, Farrelly 4, McAteer 2, Twentyman 4, Booth 3, Murphy 1, Clark 3, Kelly 4, Houghton 2 + 2, Greenwood 1, Wilkins 2 + 1, Naughton 4, Houston 3 + 1.

Freight Rover Trophy Appearances (2 games)

Campbell 2, Jones M. 1, Rudge 1, Jones D. 1, Farrelly 2, Atkins 1, McAteer 1, Gibson 1, Twentyman 2, Murphy 1, Clark 2, Kelly 1, Greenwood 0 + 1, Johnson 2, Naughton 2, Houston 1 + 1, Brazil 1.

Goalscorers: 51 League–5 FAC–9 MC–2 FRT–(Total 66)

Houghton 6–0–3–0 (9), Kelly 7 (1 pen)–0–1–0 (8), Houston 5–0–0–1 (6), Clark 5–0–0–0 (5), Greenwood 5–0–0–0 (5), Johnson 3 (1 pen)–2–0–0 (5), Gibson 3–0–0–1 (4), Wilkins 2–0–2–0 (4), Twentyman 2–0–2–0 (4), Brazil 3–0–0–0 (3), Farrelly 2–0–1–0 (3), Rudge 2–0–0–0 (2), McAteer 2 (1 pen)–0–0–0 (2), Naughton 1–1–0–0 (2), Jones M. 2–0–0–0 (2), Stevens 1–0–0–0 (1), Gray 0–1–0–0 (1), Hunter 0–1–0–0 (1)

Match Report: All This and Sir Francis Drake Too – 29 Sept. 1984 Plymouth 6 Preston 4

Paul Agnew's words in the opening paragraph of his match report summed up everyone's feelings about this incredible game. He wrote in the Post, 'Everyone stood around shaking their heads in what can only be described as stunned amazement.' For incident and drama this match could hardly have been bettered. Nothing much had happened in the first quarter hour but on that 15 minute mark Tynan headed Argyle in front. It took Preston until the 37th minute to equalise but when it came it was a beauty. Clark picked up the ball and moved forward before unleashing a superb 30 yard drive which beat Philp all ends up. Just before half-time John Kelly nipped in to take advantage of a defensive error and Preston led 2–1 at the break. Three minutes into the second half Clark scored another super goal, this time with a volley, and the match looked all over. It was anything but! In the 58th minute Hodges pulled another goal back and shortly after that came the turning point of the match. Clark, so far the hero, became the villain as he was sent off for arguing with the referee over a free-kick decision. Immediately Plymouth equalised with a fine goal by Coughlin and they then tried to turn the screw against the ten men. But Preston defended well and with five minutes to go they were given a great chance to take all three points. Naughton was fouled in the box and Kelly made no mistake with the spot-kick. The joy of the band of travelling North End fans was shortlived however as suddenly the game was turned on its head. Staniforth equalised after a rather dubious penalty was awarded to Argyle. The decision caused temperatures to rise and Booth became the second Preston player to receive his marching orders, again for dissent. This left the remaining players a mountain to climb. In the end it proved too much as Hodges and English scored late goals to secure the points.

Ever presents: None
Hat Tricks: None
Players used: 28
FA Cup: Second Round
Milk Cup: Second Round – Preston also entered the Freight Rover Trophy
Manager: Alan Kelly until February 1985, then Tommy Booth
Chairman: K. W. Leeming Esq.
Leading scorer: 9 goals – Peter Houghton (6 League 3 MC)
OFFICIAL PLAYER OF THE SEASON: Jonathan Clark

Season 1984–85: Third Division

	P	W	D	L	F	A	Pts
1 Bradford	48	28	10	8	77	45	94
2 Millwall	46	26	12	8	83	42	90
3 Hull City	46	25	12	9	88	49	87
4 Gillingham	46	25	8	13	80	62	83
5 Bristol City	48	24	9	13	74	47	81
6 Bristol Rovers	46	21	12	13	66	48	75
7 Derby	46	19	13	14	65	54	70
8 York	46	20	9	17	70	57	69
9 Reading	46	19	15	15	68	62	69
10 Bournemouth	46	19	11	16	57	46	68
11 Walsall	46	18	13	15	58	52	67
12 Rotherham	46	18	11	17	55	55	65
13 Brentford	46	16	14	16	62	64	62
14 Doncaster	46	17	8	21	72	74	59
15 Plymouth	46	15	14	17	62	65	59
16 Wigan	46	15	14	17	60	64	59
17 Bolton	46	16	6	24	69	75	54
18 Newport	46	13	13	20	55	67	52
19 Lincoln	46	11	18	17	50	51	51
20 Swansea	46	12	11	23	53	80	47
21 Burnley	46	11	13	22	60	73	46
22 Orient	46	11	13	22	51	76	46
23 PRESTON	46	13	7	26	51	100	46
24 Cambridge	46	4	9	33	37	95	21

Peter Houghton leaps up high as Geoff Twentyman looks on.

League position in Division Three: 23th (Relegated) – P46 W13 D7 L26 F51 A100 Pts 46
Home: W9 D5 L9 F33 A41 Away: W4 D2 L17 F18 A59

Ian Stevens

Dale Rudge

Peter Houghton

Date 1984-5	Opponents	Comp	h or a	Score * a.e.t.	Att.	1	2	3	4	5	6	7	8	9	10	11	12 *Sub Used	14
Aug 25	Doncaster R.	Div 3	h	2-0	3748	Litchfield	M.Jones	McAteer	Twentyman	Booth	Clark	Kelly	Rudge	Wilkins (1)	Naughton *	Houston (1)	Houghton *	
Aug 28	Tranmere R. Rd 1 1L	MC	a	3-2	2015	Litchfield	M.Jones	McAteer	Twentyman (1)	Booth	Farrelly (1)	Kelly (1)	Rudge	Wilkins *	Naughton	Houston	Houghton *	
Sep 1	Bristol R.	Div 3	a	0-3	5357	Litchfield	D.Jones *	McAteer	Twentyman	Booth	Farrelly	Kelly	Rudge	Wilkins	Naughton	Houston	Clark *	
Sep 4	Tranmere R. Rd 1 2L	MC	h	2-2 *	2557	Litchfield	Clark	McAteer *	Twentyman	Booth	Farrelly	Kelly	Rudge	Wilkins (1)	Naughton	Houston	Houghton * (1)	
Sep 8	Derby County	Div 3	h	2-1	5427	Litchfield	M.Jones	Rudge	Twentyman	Booth	Clark	Kelly (1)	Farrelly	Houghton (1)	Naughton	Houston	Greenwood	
Sep 15	Hull City	Div 3	a	2-1	7323	Litchfield	M.Jones (1)	Rudge	Twentyman	Booth	Clark (1)	Murphy	Farrelly	Houghton (1)	Naughton	Houston	Wilkins	
Sep 18	Cambridge Utd.	Div 3	a	3-0	2310	Litchfield	M.Jones *	Rudge	Twentyman	Booth	Clark	Murphy	Farrelly	Houghton (1)	Naughton	Houston (1)	Wilkins * (1)	
Sep 22	Rotherham Utd.	Div 3	h	0-3	5063	Litchfield	M.Jones	Rudge	Twentyman	Booth	Clark	Murphy *	Farrelly	Houghton	Naughton	Houston	Wilkins *	
Sep 25	Norwich City Rd 2 1L	MC	h	3-3	5361	Litchfield	M.Jones	Farrelly	Twentyman	Booth	Clark	Kelly	Murphy *	Houghton (2)	Naughton	Houston	Wilkins * (1)	
Sep 29	Plymouth Arg.	Div 3	a	4-6	4258	Litchfield	M.Jones	Rudge	Twentyman	Booth	Clark (2)	Kelly (2, 1p)	Farrelly	Houghton	Naughton	Houston	Wilkins	
Oct 2	Orient	Div 3	h	0-1	3704	Litchfield	D.Jones *	M.Jones	Twentyman	Booth	Clark	Kelly	Rudge	Houghton	Naughton	Houston	Wilkins *	
Oct 6	Lincoln City	Div 3	a	0-4	1906	Litchfield	M.Jones	Rudge	Twentyman	Booth *	Farrelly	Kelly	Murphy	Wilkins	Houghton	Houston	Greenwood *	
Oct 10	Norwich City Rd 2 2L	MC	a	1-6	13506	Litchfield	M.Jones	Rudge	D.Jones	Twentyman (1)	Clark	Kelly	Farrelly *	Greenwood	Houghton	Naughton	Houston *	
Oct 13	Reading	Div 3	h	0-2	3675	Litchfield	M.Jones	Rudge	D.Jones	Twentyman	Farrelly	Kelly	Greenwood	Johnson	Naughton	Houston	Hunter *	
Oct 20	Bolton W.	Div 3	a	0-4	5691	Litchfield	M.Jones	McAteer	D.Jones	Twentyman	Farrelly	Kelly	Houghton	Johnson	Naughton	Houston	Greenwood	
Oct 23	Bradford City	Div 3	h	1-4	3586	Litchfield	M.Jones	McAteer	D.Jones	Twentyman	Clark	Kelly	Farrelly	Johnson *	Naughton	Greenwood (1)	Houston *	
Oct 27	Bournemouth	Div 3	a	0-2	3509	Litchfield	M.Jones	McAteer	Farrelly	Twentyman	Clark	Kelly	Hunter	Greenwood *	Naughton	Houston	Houghton *	
Nov 3	Burnley	Div 3	h	3-3	4995	Litchfield	M.Jones	McAteer	Farrelly	Twentyman	Clark	Kelly (1)	Gray	Greenwood (2)	Naughton	Houston	Hunter	
Nov 6	Swansea City	Div 3	h	3-2	3205	Litchfield	M.Jones	McAteer *	Booth	Twentyman	Clark (1)	Kelly	Gray	Greenwood (1)	Naughton	Houston (1)	Hunter *	
Nov 10	Millwall	Div 3	h	0-3	5680	Litchfield	M.Jones	McAteer	Booth	Twentyman	Clark	Kelly	Gray	Greenwood	Naughton	Houston	Hunter	
Nov 17	Bury Rd 1	FAC	h	4-3	5013	Litchfield	M.Jones	McAteer	Farrelly	Twentyman	Clark	Kelly	Gray (1)	Johnson (2)	Naughton (1)	Houston	Greenwood	
Nov 24	Bristol City	Div 3	a	3-2	3912	Litchfield	M.Jones (1)	McAteer	D.Jones	Welsh	Clark	McGee	Gray	Johnson	Naughton (1)	Houston (1)	Farrelly	
Dec 1	Gillingham	Div 3	a	0-0	4055	Litchfield	M.Jones	McAteer	D.Jones	Welsh	Clark	McGee	Gray	Hunter	Naughton	Houston	Twentyman	
Dec 8	Telford Utd. Rd 2	FAC	h	1-4	6136	Litchfield	M.Jones	McAteer	D.Jones	Twentyman	Clark	McGee	Gray	Johnson	Naughton	Houston *	Hunter * (1)	
Dec 15	Brentford	Div 3	h	1-1	2809	Campbell	Farrelly	McAteer	Twentyman	Gibson (1)	Clark	Kelly	Gray	Johnson	Naughton	Hunter *	Greenwood *	
Dec 21	York City	Div 3	a	2-4	2864	Campbell	Farrelly	McAteer	Twentyman	Gibson	Clark	Kelly	Gray	Johnson (1p)	Naughton *	Greenwood	Rudge * (1)	
Dec 26	Walsall	Div 3	a	1-1	5856	Wealands	Farrelly	McAteer	Twentyman	Gibson *	Clark	Kelly	Gray	Johnson	Rudge	Greenwood (1)	Naughton *	
Dec 29	Wigan Ath.	Div 3	h	0-2	4503	Wealands	Farrelly	M.Jones	Gray	Twentyman	Clark	Kelly	Rudge	Johnson *	Naughton	Greenwood	Hunter *	
Jan 1	Newport Co.	Div 3	h	1-1	3375	Wealands	Farrelly	M.Jones	Gray	Twentyman	Clark	Kelly (1)	Rudge	Houghton	Naughton	Greenwood	Johnson	
Jan 12	Bristol R.	Div 3	h	2-2	3164	Farrelly	Farrelly	M.Jones	Twentyman (1)	Gray	Clark	Kelly	Rudge *	Greenwood	Naughton	Houghton	Johnson * (1)	
Feb 2	Plymouth Arg.	Div 3	h	1-2	3261	Campbell	Farrelly	McAteer	Twentyman	Gibson	Clark	Kelly (1)	Rudge	Johnson	Naughton	Houston *	Houston *	
Feb 5	Rochdale Rd1 1L	FRT	a	2-2	1093	Campbell	M.Jones	McAteer	Twentyman	Gibson (1)	Clark	Kelly	Farrelly	Johnson *	Naughton	Houston (1)	Greenwood *	Stevens
Feb 9	Rotherham Utd.	Div3	a	0-3	3645	Campbell	D.Jones	McAteer	Murphy	Twentyman	Clark	Kelly	Farrelly	Johnson	Naughton	Houston *	Greenwood *	
Feb 19	Rochdale Rd 2L	FRT	h	0-1	1853	Campbell	D.Jones	Rudge	Farrelly	Twentyman	Clark	Murphy	Brazil	Johnson	Naughton *	Atkins	Houston *	Greenwood
Feb 23	Burnley	Div 3	a	0-2	4740	Campbell	M.Jones	McAteer	Atkins	Gibson *	Clark	Kelly	Rudge	Twentyman	Johnson	Brazil	Naughton *	
Feb 26	Cambridge Utd.	Div 3	h	3-1	2653	Platt	M.Jones	McAteer	Atkins	Twentyman	Clark (1)	Farrelly (1)	Rudge	Naughton	Johnson (1)	Brazil (1)	Kelly *	
Mar 2	Bournemouth	Div 3	h	2-1	2991	Platt	M.Jones *	McAteer	Atkins	Twentyman	Clark	Farrelly (1)	Rudge	Naughton	Johnson (1)	Brazil	Kelly *	
Mar 6	Bradford City	Div 3	a	0-3	6345	Platt	Farrelly	McAteer	Atkins	Twentyman	Gibson	Kelly	Rudge	Naughton	Johnson	Brazil	Houston	
Mar 9	Bolton W.	Div 3	h	1-0	5581	Platt	Farrelly	McAteer	Farrelly	Twentyman	Gibson (1)	Kelly	Rudge	Naughton	Johnson *	Brazil	Houston *	
Mar 13	Derby Co.	Div 3	a	0-2	8248	Platt	M.Jones	McAteer	Gibson	Twentyman	Clark	Farrelly	Rudge	Naughton	Houston	Brazil	Greenwood	
Mar 16	Reading	Div 3	a	0-3	3053	Platt	M.Jones	McAteer	Gibson	Twentyman	Clark	Kelly	Rudge	Naughton	Johnson *	Farrelly	Houston *	
Mar 23	Lincoln City	Div 3	h	0-0	2926	Platt	M.Jones	McAteer	Gibson	Twentyman	Clark	Kelly	Houghton	Naughton	Johnson *	Farrelly	Stevens *	
Mar 26	Doncaster R.	Div 3	a	2-1	2784	Campbell	Farrelly	McAteer	Gibson	Twentyman	Clark	Kelly (1)	Rudge * (1)	Naughton	Stevens	Houston	Johnson *	
Mar 30	Swansea City	Div 3	a	1-4	2380	Campbell	Farrelly	McAteer	Gibson	Twentyman	Clark	Kelly	Atkins	Houston *	Stevens	Brazil (1)	Johnson *	
Apr 6	Walsall	Div 3	h	1-0	3776	Campbell	M.Jones	McAteer	Gibson	Atkins	Clark	Houghton (1)	Farrelly	Twentyman	Brazil	Houston	Stevens	
Apr 8	Newport Co.	Div 3	h	3-3	2119	Campbell	M.Jones	McAteer (1)	Gibson	Atkins	Clark	Houghton (1)	Farrelly	Twentyman (1)	Brazil	Houston	Stevens	
Apr 13	Millwall	Div 3	a	2-1	3855	Campbell	Farrelly	M.Jones	Gibson	Atkins	Clark	Kelly	Houghton	Twentyman	Brazil (1)	Houston (1)	Johnson	
Apr 20	Bristol City	Div 3	h	0-4	6937	Campbell	Farrelly	M.Jones	Gibson	Atkins	Clark	Kelly	Houghton *	Twentyman	Brazil	Houston	Johnson *	
Apr 23	Hull City	Div 3	h	1-4	4636	Campbell	M.Jones	McAteer	Gibson (1)	Atkins	Clark	Kelly	Farrelly	Twentyman	Brazil	Johnson *	Houston *	
Apr 27	Gillingham	Div 3	h	0-0	3190	Campbell	M.Jones	McAteer	D.Jones	Twentyman	Clark	Kelly	Gray	Houston *	Houghton	Brazil	Greenwood *	
Apr 30	Orient	Div 3	a	0-0	3162	Campbell	M.Jones	McAteer	D.Jones	Twentyman	Clark	Kelly	Gray	Houston	Gray	Brazil	Johnson	
May 4	Brentford	Div 3	a	1-3	3476	Campbell	Atkins	McAteer	D.Jones	Twentyman	Clark	Kelly	Farrelly	Houghton (1)	Johnson	Brazil	Gibson	
May 6	Wigan Ath.	Div 3	h	2-5	4875	Campbell	M.Jones	McAteer (1p)	D.Jones	Twentyman	Clark	Kelly	Farrelly	Houghton (1)	Atkins	Brazil	Johnson	
May 11	York City	Div 3	a	1-0	4523	Campbell	M.Jones	D.Jones	Atkins	Twentyman	Farrelly	Kelly	Stevens (1)	Houghton	Johnson *	Brazil	Welsh *	

SEASON 1985–1986

Trivia Facts:

A team from Bobby Robson's School of Excellence played against a North End youth side at Deepdale. North End lost 6–2 but a crowd of 300 people braved awful weather to watch the match.

Preston also competed in the Freight Rover Trophy.

North End's floodlights were condemned in October 1985 as unsafe and quickly had to be dismantled. They had been standing for 32 years having been erected in 1953. As a result no night games were played for five months and this caused the lowest recorded crowd for a league game at Deepdale, the 2,007 which saw the Scunthorpe match, played in the afternoon.

At the AGM it was announced that Preston would have a plastic pitch installed during the summer. But just to emphasise the many problems at the ground, the AGM venue had to be switched due to a burst water pipe causing severe flooding!

The 1985–6 team photo featured a female physio, Lynne Lea. It is understood that there was an abundance of groin injuries during the season! And did you know that both Bob Atkins and Simon Gibson were sent off at Colchester?

This was to be the season that Preston North End would begin the long road back from oblivion, or so it was thought. Instead, without question, it was to turn out to be the worst season in the club's long history so far. The early games saw mixed results and mixed performances but when Torquay were beaten 4–0 at Deepdale, it seemed that Preston had finally found their Fourth Division feet. The next game however, was a trip to Northampton and what followed shocked every true bloodied North End fan who was unlucky enough to be there. Preston were thrashed 6–0, and they were lucky to get nil!. It was an abysmal display and must rank amongst their worst ever. Only Nigel Greenwood escaped criticism on the night and a lot of soul searching had to be done by manager Tommy Booth, his assistant Brian Kidd and all the players. The situation led to Mick Martin being signed from Rotherham on a month's contract and he played well as North End recovered to win against Hereford. Generally though results did not improve much and a 6–3 home defeat against Chester brought home the reality of Preston's dreadful plight. Bob Atkins and Gary Brazil looked good and other players played well in individual games, but few showed any consistency and confidence has never reached such a low point. To make matters worse for the club, the floodlights were condemned by safety experts and the stands were in need of much urgent repair. Nothing was going right at all. Injuries hit the club to such an extent that local parks footballer Mel Tottoh was drafted into the side. Seeking some solace in the FA Cup proved pointless as another dreadful display saw North End lose 7–3 at Walsall in the first round. In the January Booth resigned as manager leaving Kidd in charge but humiliation followed humiliation despite several new faces being introduced. Unfortunately many of those players were little better than those already with the club and it was not until mid-March before anything like a decent run was put together. It coincided with Jonathan Clark becoming caretaker boss, replacing Kidd, and suddenly Preston managed five wins on the trot, finding scoring goals easier than they had for the previous seven months. But a home defeat against Orient and a thrashing at Colchester brought everyone back down to earth, virtually ending any thoughts of escaping from the bottom four. As it turned out only Torquay's failings saved Preston from the dreaded last position in the Football League, and that in itself was total humiliation for the first winners of the league. Having to apply for re-election was the final shame for this once proud club.

DEBUTANTS: (16) Nigel Keen, Wayne Foster, John Thomas, Mick Martin, Brian Chippendale, Mark Rodgers, Vernon Allatt, Bob McNeil, Shaun Reid, Robert Cooper, Alan Kelly Jnr., Phil Harrington, Andy Pilling, Danny Ibbotson, Mel Tottoh, Nigel Jemson.

LAST GAMES: (20) Houston, Twentyman, Jones M., Rudge, Gray, Welsh, Gibson, Pilling, Platt, Stevens, Keen, Foster, Ibbotson, Tottoh, Martin, Chippendale, Rodgers, Reid, Cooper, Harrington.

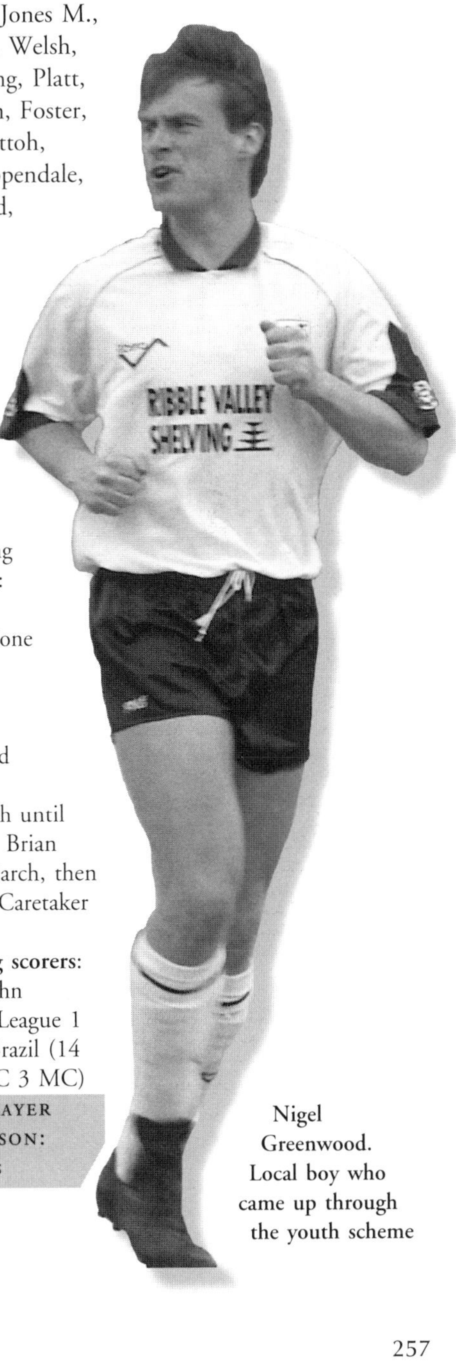

Players used: 30
Chairman: K. W. Leeming
Ever presents: None
Hat-tricks: None
FA Cup: First Round
Milk Cup: Second Round
Manager: Tommy Booth until January, then Brian Kidd until March, then Jon Clark as Caretaker until May 3.
Joint Leading scorers: 18 goals – John Thomas (17 League 1 FAC) Gary Brazil (14 League 1 FAC 3 MC)

OFFICIAL PLAYER OF THE SEASON: John Thomas

Nigel Greenwood. Local boy who came up through the youth scheme

STAT FACTS:
Best home run without defeat: 2 games
Best away run without defeat: 3 games
Longest run unbeaten: 5 games
Longest run without a win: 11 games
Best home attendance: 5,585 *vs.* Burnley 17.9.85
Worst home attendance: 768 *vs.* Bury FRT 29.1.86
Best away attendance: 11,537 *vs.* Norwich MC 9.10.85
Worst away attendance: 1,047 *vs.* Tranmere FRT 20.1.86
Aggregate and average home attendance: 80,502 – 3,500
Aggregate and average away attendance: 58,199 – 2,530

Left to right: *Back row*: Hubbick (Kit Man), Jones, Clark, Gibson, Campbell, Platt, Welsh, Greenwood, Atkins. *Middle row*: Cooke (Youth Coach), McAteer, Gray, Brazil, Rudge, Foster, Twentyman, Keen, Lea (Physiotherapist). *Front row*: Phillips, Ibbotson, Brown, Booth (Manager), Kidd (Asst Manager), Pilling, Thomas, Jemson.

Match Report: Doom and Gloom, A Load of Cobblers – 10 Sept. 1985
Northampton 6 Preston 0

In a season that ended with Preston North End Football Club having to go cap in hand to the League to seek re-election, this had to be the worst of many bad defeats. Preston, fresh from an excellent 4–0 win over Torquay, could do absolutely nothing right at all from the first whistle. Showing their old defensive frailties the visitors handed Northampton victory on a plate. As early as the first minute North End were a goal down. Benjamin was the scorer as he toe-poked the ball past a static defence. Eleven minutes later the same player scored again after nipping in behind Twentyman. Keen was then unlucky when his good effort bounced back off a post but it was a token chance as Northampton continued to dominate. With four minutes of the first half left Morley made it 3–0 and then the second half followed exactly the same pattern. A Clark own goal on 53 minutes compounded Preston's problems and then Hill scored the best goal of the match with a diving header in the 77th minute. By this time Preston looked totally bewildered and only Greenwood showed anything like good form. He worked very hard up front but alas, was fighting a losing battle. It came as little surprise when the home side's direct style brought another goal. It was Hill again as he ran through unchallenged to shoot past the shell-shocked Platt in the Preston goal. In many heavy defeats of the past it has usually been possible to find something to praise, but in this match at the three sided County Ground it was impossible. As someone once famously said, 'Preston started badly … and fell away!'

League appearances (46 games)

Allatt V. 17 + 2, Atkins R. G. 34, Brazil G. N. 43, Chippendale B. A. 5 + 1, Clark J. 6, Cooper R. C. 3 + 2, Foster W. P. 25 + 6, Gibson S. J. 25, Gray T. I. 27, Greenwood N. P. 25 + 5, Harrington P. 2, Ibbotson D. 1, Jemson N. B. 0 + 1, Jones M. T. 37, Keen N. 24, Kelly A. T. 13, Martin M. P. 35, McAteer A. W. 29, McNeil R. M. 19, Pilling A. J. 1, Platt J. R. 31, Reid S. 3, Rodgers M. 1, Rudge D. A. 23, Stevens I. D. 6 + 1, Tottoh M. D. 0 + 1, Twentyman G. 26, Welsh P. W. 11 + 6.

FA Cup appearances (1 game)

Platt, Twentyman, Jones, Atkins, Gibson, Martin, Rudge, Foster, Thomas, Allatt and Brazil all one each and Greenwood 0 + 1.

Milk Cup appearances (4 games)

Platt 4, Jones 4, McAteer 2, Atkins 4, Twentyman 4, Gray 2, Keen 3, Foster 3, Thomas 4, Rudge 2, Brazil 4, Greenwood 1 + 3, Clark 2, Welsh 2 Gibson 3.

Freight Rover Trophy Appearances (2 games)

Platt 2, Jones 1, Keen 1, McAteer 1, Atkins 2, Gray 1, Foster 1 + 1, Thomas 1, Rudge 1, Brazil 1, Greenwood 1, Welsh 2, Gibson 2, McNeil 1, Houston 2, Stevens 1, Allatt 1 + 1.

Goalscorers: 54 League–3 FAC–7 MC–2 FRT–(Total 66)

Thomas 17–1–0–0 (18), Brazil 14 (6 pens)–1–3 (1 pen)–0 (18), Greenwood 9–0–0–1 (10), Foster 3–0–1–0 (4), Allatt 3 (1 pen)–0–0–1 (pen) (4), Gibson 2–0–0–0 (2), Atkins 2–0–0–0 (2), Welsh 1–0–0–0 (1), Gray 1–0–0–0 (1), Stevens 1–0–0–0 (1), Jones 1–0–0–0 (1), Martin 0–1–0–0 (1), Keen 0–0–1–0 (1), Rudge 0–0–1–0 (1), Twentyman 0–0–1–0 (1).

Season 1985–86: Fourth Division

		P	W	D	L	F	A	Pts
1	Swindon	46	32	6	8	82	43	102
2	Chester	46	23	15	8	83	50	84
3	Mansfield	46	23	12	11	74	47	81
4	Port Vale	46	21	16	9	67	37	79
5	Orient	46	20	12	14	79	64	72
6	Colchester	46	19	13	14	88	63	70
7	Hartlepool	46	20	10	16	68	67	70
8	Northampton	46	18	10	18	79	58	64
9	Southend	46	18	10	18	69	67	64
10	Hereford	46	18	10	18	74	73	64
11	Stockport	46	17	13	16	63	71	64
12	Crewe	46	18	9	19	54	61	63
13	Wrexham	46	17	9	20	68	80	60
14	Burnley	46	16	11	19	60	65	59
15	Scunthorpe	46	15	14	19	50	55	59
16	Aldershot	46	17	7	22	66	74	58
17	Peterborough	46	13	17	16	52	64	56
18	Rochdale	46	14	13	19	57	77	55
19	Tranmere	46	15	9	22	74	73	54
20	Halifax	46	14	12	20	60	71	64
21	Exeter	46	13	15	18	47	59	54
22	Cambridge	46	15	9	22	65	80	54
23	**PRESTON**	**46**	**11**	**10**	**25**	**54**	**89**	**43**
24	Torquay	46	9	10	27	43	88	37

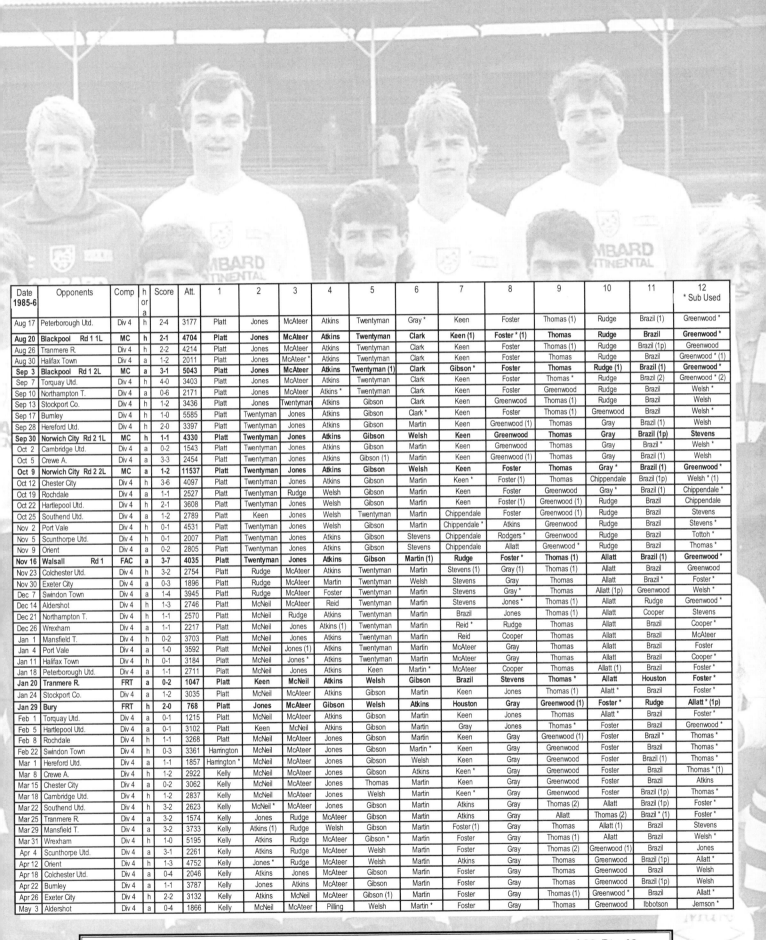

Date 1985-6	Opponents	Comp	h or a	Score	Att.	1	2	3	4	5	6	7	8	9	10	11	12 * Sub Used
Aug 17	Peterborough Utd.	Div 4	h	2-4	3177	Platt	Jones	McAteer	Atkins	Twentyman	Gray *	Keen	Foster	Thomas (1)	Rudge	Brazil (1)	Greenwood *
Aug 20	Blackpool Rd 1 1L	MC	h	2-1	4704	Platt	Jones	McAteer	Atkins	Twentyman	Clark	Keen (1)	Foster * (1)	Thomas	Rudge	Brazil	Greenwood *
Aug 26	Tranmere R.	Div 4	h	2-2	4214	Platt	Jones	McAteer	Atkins	Twentyman	Clark	Keen	Foster	Thomas (1)	Rudge	Brazil (1p)	Greenwood
Aug 30	Halifax Town	Div 4	a	1-2	2011	Platt	Jones	McAteer *	Atkins	Twentyman	Clark	Keen	Foster	Thomas	Rudge	Brazil	Greenwood * (1)
Sep 3	Blackpool Rd 1 2L	MC	h	3-1	5043	Platt	Jones	McAteer	Atkins	Twentyman (1)	Clark	Gibson *	Foster	Thomas	Rudge (1)	Brazil (1)	Greenwood *
Sep 7	Torquay Utd.	Div 4	h	4-0	3403	Platt	Jones	McAteer	Atkins	Twentyman	Clark	Keen	Foster	Thomas *	Rudge	Brazil (2)	Greenwood * (2)
Sep 10	Northampton T.	Div 4	a	0-6	2171	Platt	Jones	McAteer	Atkins *	Twentyman	Clark	Keen	Foster	Greenwood	Rudge	Brazil	Welsh *
Sep 13	Stockport Co.	Div 4	h	1-2	3436	Platt	Jones	Twentyman	Atkins	Gibson	Clark	Keen	Greenwood	Thomas (1)	Rudge	Brazil	Welsh
Sep 17	Burnley	Div 4	h	1-0	5585	Platt	Twentyman	Jones	Atkins	Gibson	Clark *	Keen	Foster	Thomas (1)	Greenwood	Brazil	Welsh
Sep 28	Hereford Utd.	Div 4	a	2-0	3397	Platt	Twentyman	Jones	Atkins	Gibson	Martin	Keen	Greenwood (1)	Thomas	Gray	Brazil (1)	Welsh
Sep 30	Norwich City Rd 2 1L	MC	h	1-1	4330	Platt	Twentyman	Jones	Atkins	Gibson	Welsh	Keen	Greenwood	Thomas	Gray	Brazil (1p)	Stevens
Oct 2	Cambridge Utd.	Div 4	a	0-2	1543	Platt	Twentyman	Jones	Atkins	Gibson	Martin	Keen	Greenwood	Thomas	Gray	Brazil *	Welsh *
Oct 5	Crewe A.	Div 4	a	3-3	2454	Platt	Twentyman	Jones	Atkins	Gibson (1)	Martin	Keen	Greenwood (1)	Thomas	Gray	Brazil (1)	Welsh
Oct 9	Norwich City Rd 2 2L	MC	a	1-2	11537	Platt	Twentyman	Jones	Atkins	Gibson	Welsh	Keen	Foster	Thomas	Gray *	Brazil (1)	Greenwood *
Oct 12	Chester City	Div 4	a	3-6	4097	Platt	Twentyman	Jones	Atkins	Gibson	Martin	Keen *	Foster (1)	Thomas	Chippendale	Brazil (1p)	Welsh * (1)
Oct 19	Rochdale	Div 4	a	1-1	2527	Platt	Twentyman	Rudge	Welsh	Gibson	Martin	Keen	Foster	Greenwood	Gray *	Brazil (1)	Chippendale
Oct 22	Hartlepool Utd.	Div 4	h	2-1	3608	Platt	Twentyman	Jones	Welsh	Gibson	Martin	Keen	Foster (1)	Greenwood (1)	Rudge	Brazil	Chippendale
Oct 25	Southend Utd.	Div 4	h	1-2	2789	Platt	Keen	Jones	Welsh	Twentyman	Martin	Chippendale *	Foster	Greenwood (1)	Rudge	Brazil	Stevens
Nov 2	Port Vale	Div 4	a	0-1	4531	Platt	Twentyman	Jones	Welsh	Gibson	Martin	Chippendale *	Atkins	Greenwood	Rudge	Brazil	Stevens *
Nov 5	Scunthorpe Utd.	Div 4	h	2-0	2007	Platt	Twentyman	Jones	Atkins	Gibson	Stevens	Chippendale	Rodgers *	Greenwood	Rudge	Brazil	Tottoh *
Nov 9	Orient	Div 4	a	0-2	2805	Platt	Twentyman	Jones	Atkins	Gibson	Stevens	Chippendale	Allatt	Greenwood *	Rudge	Brazil	Thomas *
Nov 16	Walsall Rd 1	FAC	a	3-7	4035	Platt	Twentyman	Jones	Atkins	Gibson	Martin (1)	Rudge	Foster *	Thomas (1)	Allatt	Brazil (1)	Greenwood *
Nov 23	Colchester Utd.	Div 4	h	3-2	2754	Platt	Rudge	McAteer	Atkins	Twentyman	Martin	Stevens (1)	Gray (1)	Thomas (1)	Allatt	Brazil	Greenwood
Nov 30	Exeter City	Div 4	a	0-3	1896	Platt	Rudge	McAteer	Martin	Twentyman	Welsh	Stevens	Gray	Thomas	Allatt	Brazil *	Foster *
Dec 7	Swindon Town	Div 4	a	1-4	3945	Platt	Rudge	McAteer	Foster	Twentyman	Martin	Stevens	Gray *	Thomas	Allatt (1p)	Greenwood	Welsh *
Dec 14	Aldershot	Div 4	h	1-3	2746	Platt	McNeil	McAteer	Reid	Twentyman	Martin	Stevens	Jones *	Thomas (1)	Allatt	Rudge	Greenwood *
Dec 21	Northampton T.	Div 4	h	1-1	2570	Platt	McNeil	Rudge	Atkins	Twentyman	Martin	Brazil	Jones	Thomas (1)	Allatt	Cooper	Stevens
Dec 26	Wrexham	Div 4	a	1-1	2217	Platt	McNeil	Jones	Atkins (1)	Twentyman	Martin	Reid *	Rudge	Thomas	Allatt	Brazil	Cooper *
Jan 1	Mansfield T.	Div 4	h	0-2	3703	Platt	McNeil	Jones	Atkins	Twentyman	Martin	Reid	Cooper	Thomas	Allatt	Brazil	McAteer
Jan 4	Port Vale	Div 4	h	1-0	3592	Platt	McNeil	Jones (1)	Atkins	Twentyman	Martin	McAteer	Gray	Thomas	Allatt	Brazil	Foster
Jan 11	Halifax Town	Div 4	h	0-1	3184	Platt	McNeil	Jones *	Atkins	Twentyman	Martin	McAteer	Gray	Thomas	Allatt	Brazil	Cooper *
Jan 18	Peterborough Utd.	Div 4	a	1-1	2711	Platt	McNeil	Jones	Atkins	Keen	Martin *	McAteer	Cooper	Thomas	Allatt (1)	Brazil	Foster *
Jan 20	Tranmere R.	FRT	a	0-2	1047	Platt	Keen	McNeil	Atkins	Welsh	Gibson	Brazil	Stevens	Thomas (1)	Allatt	Houston	Foster *
Jan 24	Stockport Co.	Div 4	a	1-2	3035	Platt	McNeil	McAteer	Atkins	Gibson	Martin	Keen	Jones	Thomas (1)	Allatt *	Brazil	Foster *
Jan 29	Bury	FRT	h	2-0	768	Platt	Jones	McAteer	Gibson	Welsh	Atkins	Houston	Gray	Greenwood (1)	Foster *	Rudge	Allatt * (1p)
Feb 1	Torquay Utd.	Div 4	h	0-1	1215	Platt	McNeil	McAteer	Atkins	Gibson	Martin	Keen	Jones	Thomas	Allatt *	Brazil	Foster *
Feb 5	Hartlepool Utd.	Div 4	a	0-1	3102	Platt	Keen	McNeil	Atkins	Gibson	Martin	Gray	Jones	Thomas *	Foster	Brazil	Greenwood *
Feb 8	Rochdale	Div 4	h	1-1	3268	Platt	McNeil	McAteer	Jones	Gibson	Martin	Keen	Gray	Greenwood (1)	Foster	Brazil *	Thomas *
Feb 22	Swindon Town	Div 4	a	0-3	3361	Harrington	McNeil	McAteer	Jones	Gibson	Martin *	Keen	Gray	Greenwood	Foster	Brazil	Thomas *
Mar 1	Hereford Utd.	Div 4	h	1-1	1857	Harrington *	McNeil	McAteer	Jones	Gibson	Welsh	Keen	Gray	Greenwood	Foster	Brazil (1)	Thomas *
Mar 8	Crewe A.	Div 4	h	1-2	2922	Kelly	McNeil	McAteer	Jones	Gibson	Atkins	Keen *	Gray	Greenwood	Foster	Brazil	Thomas * (1)
Mar 15	Chester City	Div 4	a	0-2	3062	Kelly	McNeil	McAteer	Jones	Thomas	Martin	Keen	Gray	Greenwood	Foster	Brazil	Atkins
Mar 18	Cambridge Utd.	Div 4	a	1-2	2837	Kelly	McNeil	McAteer	Jones	Welsh	Gibson	Keen *	Atkins	Greenwood	Foster	Brazil (1p)	Thomas *
Mar 22	Southend Utd.	Div 4	a	3-2	2623	Kelly	McNeil *	McAteer	Jones	Gibson	Martin	Atkins	Gray	Thomas (2)	Allatt	Brazil * (1)	Foster *
Mar 25	Tranmere R.	Div 4	h	3-2	1574	Kelly	Jones	Rudge	McAteer	Gibson	Martin	Atkins	Gray	Allatt	Thomas (2)	Brazil * (1)	Foster *
Mar 29	Mansfield T.	Div 4	a	3-2	3733	Kelly	Atkins (1)	Rudge	Welsh	Gibson	Martin	Foster (1)	Gray	Thomas	Allatt (1)	Brazil	Stevens
Mar 31	Wrexham	Div 4	h	1-0	5195	Kelly	Atkins	Rudge	McAteer	Gibson *	Martin	Foster	Gray	Thomas (1)	Allatt	Brazil	Welsh *
Apr 4	Scunthorpe Utd.	Div 4	a	3-1	2261	Kelly	Atkins	Rudge	McAteer	Welsh	Martin	Atkins	Gray	Thomas (2)	Greenwood (1)	Brazil (1p)	Jones
Apr 12	Orient	Div 4	h	1-3	4752	Kelly	Jones *	Rudge	McAteer	Welsh	Martin	Atkins	Gray	Thomas	Greenwood	Brazil (1p)	Allatt *
Apr 18	Colchester Utd.	Div 4	a	0-4	2046	Kelly	Atkins	Jones	McAteer	Gibson	Martin	Foster	Gray	Thomas	Greenwood	Brazil	Welsh
Apr 22	Burnley	Div 4	a	1-1	3787	Kelly	Jones	Atkins	McAteer	Gibson	Martin	Foster	Gray	Thomas	Greenwood	Brazil (1p)	Welsh
Apr 26	Exeter City	Div 4	h	2-2	3132	Kelly	Atkins	McNeil	McAteer	Gibson (1)	Martin	Foster	Gray	Thomas (1)	Greenwood *	Brazil	Allatt *
May 3	Aldershot	Div 4	a	0-4	1866	Kelly	McNeil	McAteer	Pilling	Welsh	Martin *	Foster	Gray	Thomas	Greenwood	Ibbotson	Jemson *

League position in Division Four: 23rd (Re-elected) – P46 W11 D10 L25 F54 A89 Pts 43
Home: W7 D4 L12 F32 A41 Away: W4 D6 L13 F22 A48

A new beginning! That was the message from North End during the summer of 1986 and in every sense the club was reborn and revitalised during the welcome break. How it was so desperately needed. So much had changed when the fans reported back to Deepdale in the August. A new pitch, not grass, but a synthetic surface laid by En-Tout-Cas, popularly called a plastic pitch. The Preston directors had taken this dramatic step purely on financial grounds, with the opportunity to pull in much needed funds for the club. Another momentus decision came with the appointment of the effervescent John McGrath as manager. At this point in time McGrath was just the sort of ebullient character that the club needed. New coaches Walter Joyce and Les Chapman joined him and several interesting signings were made. When the league games began there was a completely new spirit in the camp, unthinkable just a few weeks previously, and the team made a good start. A first round victory over Blackpool in the League Cup, now called the Littlewoods Cup, soon won the fans over and apart from one bad defeat at Scunthorpe, North End continued their improved form. John Thomas became the fan's favourite, scoring an early hat-tick against Halifax, and after scoring two goals in a great win at Burnley in the October, Gary Brazil partnered Thomas to great effect. The FA Cup saw the best run for years with huge interest

generated before a fourth round defeat at Newcastle ended the adventure. The league games then built into a crescendo of excitement as promotion grew ever nearer. The players all played well and the team spirit was testament to McGrath's influence. Alan Kelly (Junior), Michael Bennett, Bob Atkins, Alex Jones, Sam Allardyce and Oshor Williams all performed to a high level of consistency and Ronnie Hildersley and Les Chapman both played brilliantly in the midfield. Two other signings, Gary Swann and Frank Worthington added more class to the team with the latter giving several virtuoso performances to thrill the returning crowds. Even the fringe players did well when called upon and by the time Preston played at Orient at the end of April there were still five games to go. But the glory came on that day as a rare Chapman goal gave North End a 2–1 win and triggered mass celebrations as promotion was clinched. The only sad aspect was that Northampton pipped them for the Championship. Now that would have been the icing on the cake. The transformation had been remarkable and at last the Preston North End fans could hold their heads high again.

DEBUTANTS: (18) David Brown, Peter Bulmer, Les Chapman, Alex Jones, Sam Allardyce, Oshor Williams, Ronnie Hildersley, Mike Bennett, Steve Taylor, Gary Swann, Steve Saunders, Steve Wilkes, David Miller, Paul Williams, Frank Worthington, Peter Zelem, Shane Beeby, Paul Booth.

LAST GAMES: (10) Clark, Allatt, McNeil, Bulmer, Taylor, Saunders, Williams P., Zelem, Beeby, Booth.

John McGrath. PNE Manager.

Former North Ender Wayne Foster, freed in the summer of 1986, joined Hearts in Scotland and was soon playing European football for the Scots. He even scored in the 3–2 win over Dukla Prague.

Trivia Facts:

One of the most horrifying suggestions ever to come out of Deepdale reared its ugly head during this season. And that was the suggestion that Blackpool might share Deepdale. The troubled Tangerines were in dire financial straits and were looking to share with North End so they could stay afloat. Thankfully the idea never materialised. Well not yet anyway …

Deepdale faced a press invasion at a game late in the season. Sixteen newspapermen from eight countries visited Preston as part of a tour to investigate football hooliganism. The PFA had suggested they visit Preston. (Why, one wonders?)

The Deepdale plastic pitch played host to a floodlit cricket match for Lancashire and West Indies favourite Clive Lloyd's Benefit. Over 7,000 people turned out for this unique event.

Les Chapman's appearance at Swansea was of special significance to him because it meant that the veteran player was completing a marvellous record of having played on all 92 league grounds.

Ever presents: (1) Alex Jones
Hat-tricks: (3) all by John Thomas
Players used: 27
FA Cup: Fourth Round
Littlewoods Cup: Second Round – Also competed in the Freight Rover Trophy
Manager: John McGrath
Chairman: K. W. Leeming Esq.
Leading scorer: 28 goals – John Thomas (21 League 6 FAC 1 FRT)

OFFICIAL PLAYER OF THE SEASON:
Gary Brazil

Left to right: *Back row:* Oshor Williams, Andy McAteer, Bob Atkins, Paul Welsh, Alex Jones, David Brown, Sam Alladyce, Vernon Allatt, Shaun Allen, George Shepherd, Steve Saunders. *Front row:* Shane Beeby, Bob McNeil, Gary Brazil, Jonathan Clark, Les Chapman, John Thomas, Peter Bulmer, Ronnie Hildersley.

The full romance of the FA Cup was there for all to see as North End were drawn against near neighbours Chorley, from the Multipart League. After an exciting goalless draw at Ewood Park, where the match was held, Chorley came to Deepdale full of hope. A bumper crowd expected the Magpies to give Preston a tough match, but in truth, North End romped home. Creating a hatful of chances Preston hardly allowed Chorley a kick and from as early as the third minute it was one-way traffic. Clark's interception left Thomas running clear and the striker left goalkeeper Senior groping at thin air with a hard, low shot into the corner. Thomas added a second goal in almost identical fashion after 32 minutes. Other chances then came and went before Hildersley was fouled in the penalty area on 58 minutes. Thomas stepped up to ram home the penalty and complete a terrific hat-trick. A great goal on 66 minutes by Williams after a pass by Swann further added to Chorley's woes. The non-league side took their defeat with great dignity though and they won many friends with their whole-hearted efforts. Preston, meanwhile, were not quite finished, and Brazil, who had been outstanding throughout, scored a deserved goal from a pass by Thomas to make it 5–0. A header by Marsden which was saved by Brown was really all that Chorley could muster during the whole match. Thomas, Brazil, Williams, Hildersley and Swann all played well for North End and for once skill outgunned the traditional pride and passion of the underdogs.

GARRATT, SON & FLOWERDEW Ltd.
Sponsors of Preston North End F.C. 1986/87

STAT FACTS:
Best home run without defeat: 10 games
Best away run without defeat: 9 games
Longest run unbeaten: 16 games
Longest run without a win: 3 games
Best home attendance: 16,456 *vs.* Northampton 3.4.87
Worst home attendance: 2,301 *vs.* Crewe FRT 5.1.87
Best away attendance: 30,495 *vs.* Newcastle FAC 31.1.87
Worst away attendance: 1,125 *vs.* Chester FRT 16.12.86
Aggregate and average home attendance: 184,785 – 8,034
Aggregate and average away attendance: 85,247 – 3,706

League appearances (46 games)

Allardyce S. 37, Atkins R. G. 40 + 1, Bennett M. 41 + 1, Brazil G. N. 44 + 1, Brown D. J. 24, Bulmer P. 4, Chapman L. 35 + 1, Clark J. 10 + 2, Hildersley R. 33, Jemson N. B. 4, Jones A. 46, Kelly A. T. 22, McAteer A. W. 16, McNeil R. M. 24, Miller D. B. 15, Swann G. 29 + 1, Taylor S. J. 5, Thomas J. W. 35 + 3, Williams O. J. 29, Williams P. A. 1, Worthington F. S. 6 + 4, Zelem P. R. 6.

Trivia Fact:
John McGrath was named Manager of the Month for April 1987.

FA Cup appearances (5 games)

Brown 4, Kelly 1, Bennett 5, McNeil 2, Chapman 2, Miller 0 + 1, Clark 3, McAteer 1, Atkins 5, Hildersley 5, Jones 5, Allardyce 5, Williams O. 3, Brazil 5, Thomas 4 + 1, Swann 4, Jemson 1.

Littlewoods Cup appearances (4 games)

Brown 3, Kelly 1, Bulmer 3, Bennett 1, McNeil 1, Chapman 3, Clark 3, McAteer 4, Atkins 2, Hildersley 4, Jones 4, Allardyce 3, Williams O. 4, Brazil 4, Thomas 4, Saunders S. 0 + 1, Allatt V. 0 + 1.

Freight Rover Trophy Appearances (4 games)

Kelly 4, Bennett 4, McNeil 3, Chapman 4, Miller 2 + 1, Atkins 4, Hildersley 1, Jones 3 + 1, Allardyce 4, Williams P. 1, Brazil 3, Thomas 2, Swann 4, Jemson 2 + 1, Saunders 2, Beeby S. 0 + 1, Booth P. 0 + 1, Wilkes S. 1.

Goalscorers: 72 League–11 FAC–4 LC–5 FRT–(Total 92)

Thomas 21 (3 pens)–6 (2 pens)–0–1 (28), Brazil 18 (1 pen)–1–0–1 (20), Williams O. 10–2–2–0 (14), Swann 5–0–0–1 (6), Jemson 3–0–0–2 (5), Hildersley 2–1–1–0 (4), Worthington 3–0–0–0 (3), Allardyce 2–0–1–0 (3), Taylor 2–0–0–0 (2), Bennett 1–0–0–0 (1), Chapman 1–0–0–0 (1), McAteer 1–0–0–0 (1), Zelem 1–0–0–0 (1), Atkins 1–0–0–0 (1), Jones 1–0–0–0 (1).

League position in Division Four: Runners-up – P46 W26 D12 L8 F72 A47 Pts 90
Home: W16 D4 L3 F36 A18   Away: W10 D8 L5 F36 A29

Date 1986-7	Opponents	Comp	h or a	Score	Att.	1	2	3	4	5	6	7	8	9	10	11	12	14
Aug 23	Tranmere R.	Div 4	a	1-1	2108	Brown	Bulmer	McAteer	Chapman	Jones	Allardyce	O. Williams	Clark	Thomas (1)	Hildersley	Brazil	McNeil	
Aug 26	**Blackpool Rd 1 1L**	**LC**	**a**	**0-0**	**3929**	**Brown**	**Bulmer**	**McAteer**	**Chapman**	**Jones**	**Allardyce**	**O. Williams**	**Clark**	**Thomas**	**Hildersley**	**Brazil**	**McNeil**	**Saunders**
Aug 30	Swansea City	Div 4	h	2-1	4362	Brown	Bulmer	McAteer	Chapman	Jones	Allardyce	O. Williams (1)	Clark	Thomas (1)	Hildersley	Brazil	Atkins	
Sep 2	**Blackpool Rd 2 2L**	**LC**	**h**	**2-1**	**5914**	**Brown**	**Bulmer**	**McAteer**	**Chapman**	**Jones**	**Allardyce**	**O. Williams (1)**	**Clark**	**Thomas**	**Hildersley (1)**	**Brazil**	**Saunders**	**Atkins**
Sep 6	Lincoln City	Div 4	a	1-1	2305	Brown	Bulmer	Bennett	Chapman	Jones	Allardyce	O. Williams	Clark	Thomas (1)	Hildersley	Brazil	Atkins	
Sep 13	Hereford Utd.	Div 4	h	2-1	4707	Brown	Bulmer *	McAteer	Chapman	Jones	Allardyce	O. Williams (1)	Clark	Thomas (1p)	Hildersley	Brazil	Bennett *	
Sep 16	Halifax Town	Div 4	h	3-2	5259	Brown	Bennett	McAteer	Chapman	Jones	Allardyce	O. Williams	Clark	Thomas (3)	Hildersley	Brazil	Atkins	
Sep 19	Scunthorpe Utd.	Div 4	a	0-4	2689	Brown	Bennett	McAteer	Chapman *	Jones	Allardyce	O. Williams	Clark	Thomas	Hildersley	Brazil	Atkins *	
Sep 23	**West Ham Utd. Rd 2 1L**	**LC**	**h**	**1-1**	**13153**	**Brown**	**Bulmer**	**McAteer**	**Atkins**	**Jones**	**Allardyce (1)**	**O. Williams**	**Clark**	**Thomas**	**Hildersley**	**Brazil**	**Bennett**	**Chapman**
Sep 27	Torquay Utd.	Div 4	h	1-1	5053	Brown	Bennett	McAteer	Atkins	Jones	Allardyce (1)	O. Williams	Clark	Thomas	Hildersley	Brazil	Chapman	
Sep 30	Wolverhampton W.	Div 4	a	0-1	4409	Brown	Bennett	McAteer	Chapman	Jones	Allardyce	O. Williams	Clark *	Thomas	Hildersley	Atkins	Brazil *	
Oct 4	Burnley	Div 4	a	4-1	5865	Brown	McNeil	Bennett	Chapman	Jones	Atkins	O. Williams	McAteer	Thomas (2)	Hildersley	Brazil (2)	Allatt	
Oct 7	**West Ham Utd. Rd 2 2L**	**LC**	**a**	**1-4**	**12742**	**Kelly**	**McNeil**	**Bennett**	**Chapman +**	**Jones**	**Atkins**	**O. Williams (1)**	**McAteer**	**Thomas ***	**Hildersley**	**Brazil**	**Allatt ***	**Saunders +**
Oct 11	Cambridge Utd.	Div 4	h	1-0	5236	Kelly	McNeil	Bennett	Chapman	Jones	Atkins	O. Williams	McAteer	Thomas	Hildersley	Brazil (1)	Saunders	
Oct 18	Aldershot	Div 4	h	1-2	5241	Kelly	McNeil	Bennett	Hildersley *	Jones	Atkins	O. Williams	McAteer	Thomas (1p)	Taylor	Brazil	Clark *	
Oct 20	Stockport Co.	Div 4	a	3-1	2888	Kelly	McNeil	Bennett	Chapman	Jones	Atkins	O. Williams (2)	Brazil	Taylor (1)	McAteer	Hildersley	Clark	
Nov 1	Exeter City	Div 4	h	2-1	5818	Brown	Chapman	Bennett	Atkins	Jones	Allardyce	O. Williams (1)	Brazil	Taylor	McAteer (1)	Hildersley	Clark	
Nov 4	Cardiff City	Div 4	h	0-1	6616	Brown	Chapman *	Bennett	Atkins	Jones	Allardyce	O. Williams	Brazil	Taylor	McAteer	Hildersley	Clark *	
Nov 8	Northampton T.	Div 4	a	1-3	6537	Brown	McNeil	Bennett	Atkins	Jones	Allardyce	O. Williams	Thomas	Taylor (1)	McAteer	Hildersley	Clark	
Nov 15	**Bury Rd 1**	**FAC**	**h**	**5-1**	**7946**	**Brown**	**Clark**	**Bennett**	**Atkins**	**Jones (1)**	**Allardyce**	**O. Williams (1)**	**Brazil**	**Thomas (3,1p)**	**McAteer**	**Hildersley**	**Saunders**	**Chapman**
Nov 22	Southend Utd.	Div 4	h	2-0	6033	Brown	Clark	Bennett	Atkins	Jones	Allardyce	Chapman	Brazil	Thomas (1)	McAteer	Hildersley (1)	McNeil	
Nov 29	Peterborough Utd.	Div 4	a	1-2	3462	Brown	Clark	Bennett	Atkins	Jones	Allardyce	O. Williams (1)	Brazil	Thomas	McAteer *	Hildersley	Swann *	
Dec 6	**Chorley Rd 2 ***	**FAC**	**a**	**0-0**	**15153**	**Brown**	**Clark**	**Bennett**	**Atkins**	**Jones**	**Allardyce**	**O. Williams**	**Brazil**	**Thomas**	**Swann**	**Hildersley**	**McAteer**	**Chapman**
Dec 9	**Chorley Replay**	**FAC**	**h**	**5-0**	**16308**	**Brown**	**Clark**	**Bennett**	**Atkins**	**Jones**	**Allardyce**	**O. Williams (1)**	**Brazil (1)**	**Thomas (3,1p)**	**Swann**	**Hildersley**	**McAteer**	**Saunders**
Dec 13	Colchester Utd.	Div 4	a	2-0	2240	Brown	McNeil	Bennett	Atkins	Jones	Allardyce	O. Williams (1)	Brazil	Thomas	Swann	Hildersley (1)	Chapman	
Dec 16	**Chester**	**FRT**	**a**	**1-1**	**1125**	**Kelly**	**McNeil**	**Bennett**	**Atkins**	**Jones**	**Allardyce**	**Chapman ***	**Brazil +**	**Saunders**	**Swann**	**Hildersley**	**Beeby ***	**Jemson + (1)**
Dec 20	Orient	Div 4	h	1-0	5925	Brown	McNeil	Bennett	Atkins	Jones	Allardyce	O. Williams (1)	Swann	Thomas	Brazil	Hildersley	Chapman	
Dec 26	Crewe A.	Div 4	a	2-2	3784	Brown	McNeil	Bennett	Atkins (1)	Jones	Allardyce	O. Williams	Swann	Thomas (1)	Brazil	Hildersley	Chapman	
Dec 27	Hartlepool Utd.	Div 4	h	0-0	7782	Brown	McNeil	Bennett	Atkins	Jones	Allardyce	O. Williams	Swann	Thomas	Brazil	Hildersley	Chapman	
Jan 1	Wrexham	Div 4	h	1-0	9373	Brown	McNeil	Bennett	Atkins	Jones	Allardyce	Chapman	Swann	Thomas (1)	Brazil	Hildersley	Miller	
Jan 3	Southend Utd.	Div 4	a	2-1	4479	Brown	McNeil	Bennett (1)	Atkins	Jones	Allardyce	Chapman	Swann	Thomas	Brazil (1)	Hildersley	Miller	
Jan 5	**Crewe A. Prelim Rd**	**FRT**	**h**	**1-0**	**2301**	**Kelly**	**Wilkes**	**Bennett**	**Atkins**	**P. Williams**	**Allardyce**	**Chapman ***	**Miller**	**Jemson**	**Saunders +**	**Swann (1)**	**Booth ***	**Jones +**
Jan 10	**Middlesbrough Rd 3**	**FAC**	**a**	**1-0**	**15458**	**Brown**	**McNeil**	**Bennett**	**Atkins**	**Jones**	**Allardyce**	**Chapman**	**Swann**	**Thomas**	**Brazil**	**Hildersley (1)**	**O.Williams**	**Miller**
Jan 17	Swansea City	Div 4	a	1-1	7677	Brown	McNeil	Bennett	Atkins	Jones	Allardyce	Chapman	Swann	Jemson (1)	Brazil	Hildersley	P. Williams	
Jan 21	**Carlisle Utd. Rd 1**	**FRT**	**a**	**2-1**	**1400**	**Kelly**	**McNeil**	**Bennett**	**Atkins**	**Jones**	**Allardyce**	**Chapman**	**Swann**	**Thomas ***	**Brazil (1)**	**Jemson (1)**	**Miller ***	**P.Williams**
Jan 24	Lincoln City	Div 4	h	3-0	7821	Kelly	McNeil	Bennett	Atkins	Jones	Allardyce	Chapman	Swann (1)	Jemson (1)	Brazil (1)	Miller	Thomas	
Jan 31	**Newcastle Utd. Rd 4**	**FAC**	**a**	**0-2**	**30495**	**Kelly**	**McNeil**	**Bennett**	**Atkins**	**Jones**	**Allardyce**	**Chapman ***	**Swann**	**Jemson +**	**Brazil**	**Hildersley**	**Miller ***	**Thomas +**
Feb 7	Halifax T.	Div 4	a	3-1	2968	Kelly	McNeil	Bennett	Atkins	Jones	Allardyce	Chapman	Swann (1)	Jemson (1) *	Brazil (1)	Miller	Thomas *	
Feb 14	Scunthorpe Utd.	Div 4	h	2-1	7968	Kelly	McNeil	Bennett	Atkins	Jones	Allardyce (1)	Chapman	Swann	Jemson *	Brazil (1)	Miller	Thomas *	
Feb 17	**Wrexham Qtr. Final**	**FRT**	**a**	**1-2**	**2193**	**Kelly**	**McNeil**	**Bennett**	**Atkins**	**Jones**	**Allardyce**	**Chapman**	**Swann**	**Thomas (1)**	**Brazil**	**Miller**	**Jemson**	**Hildersley**
Feb 21	Torquay Utd.	Div 4	a	2-0	1871	Kelly	McNeil	Bennett	Atkins	Jones (1)	Allardyce	Chapman	Swann	Worthington	Brazil (1)	Miller	Thomas	
Feb 25	Hereford Utd.	Div 4	a	3-2	2628	Kelly	McNeil	Bennett	Atkins	Jones	Allardyce	Hildersley	Swann	Worthington (1)	Brazil (2)	Miller	Thomas	
Feb 28	Wolverhampton W.	Div 4	h	2-2	12592	Kelly	McNeil	Bennett	Atkins	Jones	Allardyce	Chapman	Swann (1)	Worthington (1)	Brazil	Hildersley	Miller	
Mar 4	Exeter City	Div 4	a	2-1	2801	Kelly	McNeil	Bennett	Atkins	Jones	Allardyce	Chapman	Swann	Worthington *	Brazil (1p)	Hildersley	Thomas * (1)	
Mar 14	Aldershot	Div 4	a	0-0	3496	Kelly	McNeil	Bennett	Atkins	Jones	Allardyce	Chapman	Swann	Thomas	Brazil	Hildersley	Worthington	
Mar 17	Stockport Co.	Div 4	h	3-0	7823	Kelly	McNeil	Bennett	Atkins	Jones	Allardyce *	Chapman	Swann (1)	Thomas (1)	Brazil	Hildersley	Worthington *(1)	
Mar 21	Cambridge Utd.	Div 4	a	0-2	2804	Kelly	McNeil *	Bennett	Atkins	Jones	P.Williams	Chapman	Swann	Thomas	Brazil	Hildersley	Worthington *	
Mar 28	Burnley	Div 4	h	2-1	10643	Kelly	McNeil	Bennett	Atkins	Jones	Zelem *	Chapman	Swann	Thomas (1)	Brazil	O. Williams (1)	Worthington *	
Apr 3	Northampton T.	Div 4	h	1-0	16456	Kelly	McNeil	Bennett	Atkins	Jones	Zelem	Chapman	Swann	Thomas	Brazil (1)	O. Williams	Worthington	
Apr 7	Rochdale	Div 4	a	2-0	4986	Kelly	Miller	Bennett	Atkins	Jones	Zelem (1)	Chapman	Swann	Thomas	Brazil (1)	O. Williams	Worthington	
Apr 11	Cardiff City	Div 4	a	1-1	2528	Kelly	Miller	Bennett	Atkins	Jones	Zelem	Chapman	Swann	Thomas (1)	Brazil	O. Williams	Worthington	
Apr 14	Rochdale	Div 4	h	2-4	10185	Kelly	Miller	Bennett	Atkins	Jones	Allardyce	Chapman *	Swann	Thomas (1)	Brazil (1)	O. Williams	Worthington *	
Apr 18	Wrexham	Div 4	a	1-1	4850	Kelly	Miller	Bennett	Atkins	Jones	Allardyce	Chapman	Swann	Thomas	Brazil	O. Williams (1)	Worthington	
Apr 20	Crewe A.	Div 4	h	2-1	11107	Kelly	Miller	Bennett	Atkins	Jones	Allardyce	Chapman	Swann	Thomas (1p)	Brazil (1)	O. Williams	Worthington	
Apr 25	Orient	Div 4	a	2-1	5255	Kelly	Miller	Bennett	Atkins	Jones	Allardyce	Chapman (1)	Swann	Thomas	Brazil (1)	O. Williams	Worthington	
Apr 28	Tranmere R.	Div 4	h	2-0	12109	Kelly	Miller	Bennett	Atkins	Jones	Allardyce	Chapman *	Swann	Thomas (1)	Brazil (1)	O. Williams	Worthington *	
May 2	Peterborough Utd.	Div 4	h	0-0	7919	Brown	Miller	Zelem	Atkins	Jones	Allardyce	Worthington	Swann	Thomas	Brazil	Hildersley	Chapman	
May 4	Hartlepool Utd.	Div 4	a	2-2	2617	Brown	Miller	Zelem	Atkins	Jones	Allardyce	Worthington *	Swann	Thomas (1)	Brazil (1)	Hildersley	Chapman *	
May 9	Colchester Utd.	Div 4	h	1-0	8757	Brown	Miller	Bennett	Atkins	Jones	Allardyce	Chapman	Swann (1)	Thomas	Brazil	Hildersley	O. Williams	

* Played at Ewood Park, Blackburn

Sam Allardyce

David Brown

Oshor Williams

Season 1986–87: Fourth Division

	P	W	D	L	F	A	Pts
1 Northampton	46	30	9	7	103	53	99
2 PRESTON	**46**	**26**	**12**	**8**	**72**	**47**	**90**
3 Southend	46	25	5	16	68	55	80
4 Wolves	46	24	7	15	69	50	79
5 Colchester	46	21	7	18	64	56	70
6 Aldershot	46	20	10	16	64	57	70
7 Orient	46	20	9	17	64	61	69
8 Scunthorpe	46	18	12	16	73	57	66
9 Wrexham	46	15	20	11	70	51	65
10 Peterborough	46	17	14	15	57	50	65
11 Cambridge	46	17	11	18	60	62	62
12 Swansea	46	17	11	18	56	61	62
13 Cardiff	46	15	16	15	48	50	61
14 Exeter	46	11	23	12	53	49	56
15 Halifax	46	15	10	21	59	74	55
18 Hereford	46	14	11	21	60	61	53
17 Crewe	46	13	14	19	70	72	53
18 Hartlepool	46	11	18	17	44	65	51
19 Stockport	46	13	12	21	40	69	51
20 Tranmere	46	11	17	18	54	72	50
21 Rochdale	46	11	17	18	54	73	50
22 Burnley	46	12	13	21	53	74	49
23 Torquay	46	10	18	18	56	72	48
24 Lincoln	46	12	12	22	45	65	48

SEASON 1987–1988

Consolidation in the higher division was manager John McGrath's number one priority as the new season began. A bad start came as a bit of a setback though and it took a while for North End to find their feet. Opening with four consecutive home defeats was not what was required but despite new players, Jim Branagan, John Lowey, Mick Rathbone and Jeff Wrightson coming in, the side still struggled. It was a case of only one win in the first 13 league and cup ties and the pressure was suddenly on for the manager who up to then could do no wrong. Two more players were brought in for the match with Port Vale at Deepdale in early October and Tony Ellis and Brian Mooney made all the difference. They were both quality players and perfectly suited to the plastic pitch. Mind you, when Port Vale went into a 2–0 lead it did not look too promising. But a storming comeback and a last minute winner from Ellis at last woke the club from its slumbers. Results gradually improved and progress was made in the Sherpa Van Trophy. Unfortunately Preston were still prone to defensive errors and some defeats, usually at home, could have been avoided. An FA Cup replay defeat at Mansfield also upset the fans. Around Christmas though, signs were there for an improved New Year and that is exactly how it turned out. A good win over Blackpool on Boxing Day set the ball rolling more in Preston's favour. Mooney looked a great buy, Gary Brazil did well in attack, and worked effectively with Ellis, whilst Nigel Jemson looked the best home grown talent for some time. Bob Atkins and Gary Swann were models of consistency, with Swann developing a wonderful knack of scoring vital goals at vital times from his midfield role. Warren Joyce added some extra bite in the middle and he played a big part in the remaining cup competition. Interest was maintained as Preston reached the two-legged Northern Final of the Sherpa Van Trophy to be played against Burnley for a place at Wembley. Alas, after a titanic battle with their old enemy from Turf Moor, Preston were beaten on aggregate, losing at Deepdale after a goalless draw at Burnley. The remaining league games saw more mixed results and significantly North End lost their last game at home. The theory that Preston would gain an advantage playing on their plastic pitch never held water during this season. In fact, it had been one of the worst ever seasons at Deepdale. Considering the poor start and all that had happened, the final league position was very creditable and at least it gave the manager a good base to build from.

DEBUTANTS: (10) Jim Branagan, Mick Rathbone, John Lowey, Jeff Wrightson, Simon Jeffels, Brian Mooney, Tony Ellis, Warren Joyce, Gary Walker, Adrian Hughes.

League appearances (46 games)

Allardyce S. 38 + 1, Atkins R. G. 45, Bennett M. 34, Branagan J. P. S. 3, Brazil G. N. 36, Brown D. J. 27, Chapman L. 15 + 2, Ellis A. J. 20 + 4, Hildersley R. 21 + 4, Hughes A. F. S. 1, Jeffels S. 1, Jemson N. B. 24 + 3, Jones A. 22, Joyce W. G. 21 + 1, Kelly A. T. 19, Lowey J. A. 4, Miller D. B. 23 + 5, Mooney B. J. 34, Rathbone M. J. 36, Swann G. 45 + 1, Wilkes S. B. 1 + 2, Williams O. J. 9 + 1, Worthington F. S. 4 + 8, Wrightson J. G. 23 + 2.

FA Cup appearances (2 games)

Kelly 2, Miller D. B. 0 + 1, Rathbone 2, Bennett 2, Atkins 2, Jones 2, Allardyce 2, Mooney 2, Swann 2, Jemson 1, Ellis 1, Brazil 2, Hildersley 2.

Littlewoods Cup (2 games)

Brown 2, Branagan 2, Miller 2, Rathbone 2, Bennett 1, Wrightson 0 + 1, Chapman 1, Atkins 2, Jones 1, Allardyce 2, Swann 2, Lowey 2, Worthington 0 + 2, Brazil 2, Hildersley 1.

Sherpa Van Trophy (7 games)

Kelly 1, Brown 6, Miller 5 + 1, Rathbone 4, Bennett 4, Wrightson 6, Joyce 4, Atkins 7, Jones 3, Allardyce 3, Williams 1 + 1, Mooney 6, Swann 7, Lowey 1, Jemson 3, Worthington 0 + 1, Ellis 5 + 1, Brazil 5, Hildersley 3, Walker G. 1, Chapman 2 + 1.

Goalscorers: 48 League–3 FAC–4 LC–13 SVT–(Total 68)

Brazil 14 (3 pens)–1–2–3 (20), Swann 12–0–0–2 (14), Jemson 5–1–0–3 (1 pen) (9), Ellis 4–0–0–2 (6), Mooney 3–0–0–1 (4), Atkins 1–1–0–2 (4), Williams 2–0–0–0 (2), Miller 2–0–0–0 (2), Jones 2–0–0–0 (2), Lowey 1–0–0–0 (1), Rathbone 1–0–0–0 (1), Hildersley 1–0–0–0 (1), Allardyce 0–0–1–0 (1), Own Goals 0–0–1–0 (1) (Hill of Bury LC)

LAST GAMES: (8) Chapman, Hildersley, Wilkes, Worthington, Branagan, Lowey, Jeffels, Walker.

Nigel Jemson. Local boy who went on to play in European cup football.

Match Report: Robbed at Roker – 28 Dec 1987 Sunderland 1 Preston 1

John McGrath's battlers came within a whisker of silencing the Roker Roar and toppling the Third Division leaders. Over 24,000 fans came to Sunderland for this game and most of them expected an easy home victory. How wrong they were. A superb rearguard action in the first half by the North End defence frustrated everything that Sunderland could muster and the home fans quickly became restless. Atkins, Allardyce, Jones and especially keeper Kelly, all played brilliantly. After the change round Preston had the wind at their backs and came into the game more as an attacking force. Mooney, doubtful to start the match right up until the kick-off, was the playmaker in the midfield for the visitors and his skills caught the eye. One chance he created set up Swann who should have done better than fire his shot wide, whilst Mooney also set up Ellis for another chance but goalkeeper Hesford produced an acrobatic save to thwart the North End striker. The crowd were beginning to sense Preston's increasing confidence and the visiting fans chant of, 'We're going to score in a minute', came true with 73 minutes on the clock. Brazil swung over a cross from the left, Swann nodded the ball back and Jones, up with the attack, slid in to squeeze a shot wide of Hesford. It looked odds on a Preston win at this stage but with just four minutes to go the referee awarded Sunderland a penalty after Kelly had clashed with substitute Gray. The challenge seemed innocuous and the Preston players protested furiously. But the decision stood and MacPhail scored from the spot-kick to rescue his side from a certain defeat.

Alex Jones,
Commanding
centre-half.

Ever presents: None
Hat-tricks: None
Players used: 25
FA Cup: First Round
Littlewoods Cup: First Round
Also reached Northern Final of Sherpa Van Trophy
Manager: John McGrath
Chairman: K. W. Leeming Esq.
Leading scorer: 20 goals – Gary Brazil
(14 League 1 FAC 2 LC 3 SVT)

OFFICIAL PLAYER OF THE SEASON:
Bob Atkins

Season 1987–88: Third Division

		P	W	D	L	F	A	Pts
1	Sunderland	46	27	12	7	92	48	93
2	Brighton & Hove A	46	23	15	8	69	47	84
3	Walsall	46	23	13	10	68	50	82
4	Notts County	46	23	12	11	82	49	81
5	Bristol City	46	21	12	13	77	62	75
6	Northampton Town	46	18	19	9	9	70	51
7	Wigan Athletic	46	20	12	14	70	61	72
8	Bristol Rovers	46	18	12	16	68	56	66
9	Fulham	46	19	9	18	69	60	66
10	Blackpool	46	17	14	15	71	62	65
11	Port Vale	46	18	11	17	58	56	65
12	Brentford	46	16	14	16	53	59	62
13	Gillingham	46	14	17	15	77	61	59
14	Bury	46	15	14	17	58	57	59
15	Chester City	46	14	16	16	51	62	58
16	**PRESTON**	46	15	13	18	48	59	58
17	Southend United	46	14	13	19	65	83	55
18	Chesterfield	46	15	10	21	41	70	55
19	Mansfield Town	46	14	12	20	48	59	54
20	Aldershot	46	15	8	23	64	74	53
21	Rotherham United	46	12	16	18	50	66	52
22	Grimsby Town	46	12	14	20	48	58	50
23	York City	46	8	9	29	48	91	33
24	Doncaster Rovers	46	8	9	29	40	84	33

Trivia Facts:

Alan Kelly Junior broke his right leg early in the season, and it happened in the most bizarre way. He had popped into town to buy a new pair of padded shorts and as he got out of his car in Friargate he was knocked down by a motorcycle. He also suffered head injuries in the accident and was very lucky not to have been more seriously hurt.

Which member of the North End staff once served in the Royal Navy on HMS *Illustrious*? It was Andy Jones, Preston's new full-time physio.

Preston made a profit of £80,000 on the year ending June 1987.

STAT FACTS:
Best home run without defeat: 11 games
Best away run without defeat: 4 games
Longest run unbeaten: 9 games
Longest run without a win: 7 games
Best home attendance: 17,592 *vs.* Burnley SVT 19.4.88
Worst home attendance: 1,968 *vs.* Stockport SVT 27.10.87
Best away attendance: 24,814 *vs.* Sunderland 28.12.87
Worst away attendance: 2,167 *vs.* Doncaster 4.4.88
Aggregate and average home attendance: 141,577 – 6,155
Aggregate and average away attendance: 122,965 – 5,346

League position in Division Three: 16th – P46 W15 D13 L18 F48 A59 Pts 58
Home: W10 D6 L7 F30 A23 Away: W5 D7 L11 F18 A36

Ronnie Hidersley

Mick Bennett

David Miller

Date 1987-8	Opponents	Comp	h or a	Score *aet	Att.	1	2	3	4	5	6	7	8	9	10	11	12	14	
Aug 15	Chesterfield	Div 3	h	0-1	6509	Kelly	Branagan	Rathbone	Atkins	Chapman	Allardyce	Miller *	Swann	Lowey	Brazil	Hidersley	Wrightson	Worthington *	
Aug 18	Bury Rd 1 1L	LC	a	2-2	2363	Brown	Branagan	Rathbone	Atkins	Chapman *	Allardyce (1)	Miller	Swann	Lowey	Brazil (1)	Hidersley	Worthington *	Wrightson	
Aug 22	Bristol City	Div 3	a	1-3	7655	Brown	Branagan +	Bennett	Atkins	Jones	Allardyce	Miller	Swann	Lowey	Brazil (1)	Rathbone *	Wrightson +	Worthington *	
Aug 25	Bury Rd 2 2L	LC	h	2-3*	4923	Brown	Branagan	Bennett	Atkins	Jones	Allardyce	Miller *	Swann	Lowey	Brazil (1)	Rathbone	Worthington *	Wrightson	1 og #
Aug 29	Wigan Ath.	Div 3	h	0-1	7057	Brown	Miller	Bennett	Atkins	Chapman *	Allardyce	Williams	Swann	Jemson	Brazil	Hidersley	Wrightson	Worthington *	
Sep 1	Southend Utd.	Div 3	h	2-1	2600	Brown	Miller	Bennett	Atkins (1)	Chapman	Allardyce	Williams (1)	Swann	Jemson	Brazil	Hidersley	Wrightson	Worthington	
Sep 5	Grimsby Town	Div 3	h	1-3	5522	Brown	Miller	Bennett	Atkins	Chapman *	Allardyce	Williams	Swann (1)	Jemson	Brazil	Hidersley	Wrightson	Worthington *	
Sep 12	York City	Div 3	a	1-1	3237	Kelly	Miller	Rathbone	Atkins	Wrightson	Allardyce	Williams	Swann *	Worthington +	Brazil (1)	Branagan	Jemson +	Hidersley *	
Sep 15	Northampton T.	Div 3	h		5179	Kelly	Rathbone	Bennett	Atkins	Wrightson	Allardyce	Miller	Swann	Jemson	Worthington	Hidersley	Branagan	Wilkes	
Sep 19	Rotherham Utd.	Div 3	h	0-0	5124	Kelly	Rathbone	Bennett	Atkins	Wrightson	Allardyce	Miller	Swann	Worthington	Brazil	Hidersley	Branagan	Jemson	
Sep 26	Blackpool	Div 3	a	0-3	8406	Kelly	Rathbone	Bennett +	Atkins	Wrightson	Allardyce	Miller	Swann	Worthington	Jemson	Hidersley	Wilkes +	Chapman	
Sep 29	Brentford	Div 3	h	1-2	4241	Kelly	Rathbone	Bennett	Atkins	Wrightson	Allardyce	Miller *	Swann +	Lowey (1)	Jemson	Hidersley	Worthington +	Chapman *	
Oct 3	Walsall	Div 3	a	1-1	5467	Brown	Rathbone	Bennett	Atkins	Wrightson	Allardyce	Jeffels	Swann	Lowey	Jemson +	Chapman	Worthington +	Miller	
Oct 10	Port Vale	Div 3	h	3-2	6274	Brown	Rathbone	Bennett	Atkins	Jones	Allardyce	Miller +	Mooney +	Ellis (1)	Brazil (2,1p)	Wrightson	Worthington +	Swann *	
Oct 13	Bolton W.	SVT	a	0-0	3478	Brown	Rathbone	Bennett	Atkins	Jones	Allardyce	Williams *	Swann	Ellis +	Mooney	Wrightson	Worthington *	Miller +	
Oct 17	Brighton	Div 3	a	0-0	6043	Brown	Rathbone	Bennett	Atkins	Jones	Allardyce	Joyce	Mooney	Ellis *	Brazil +	Swann	Wrightson +	Jemson *	
Oct 20	Gillingham	Div 3	h	1-1	5676	Kelly	Rathbone	Bennett	Atkins	Jones	Allardyce	Williams (1)	Joyce	Ellis	Mooney	Swann	Wrightson	Jemson	
Oct 24	Bury	Div 3	a	0-4	4316	Kelly	Rathbone +	Bennett	Atkins	Jones	Allardyce	Wrightson	Joyce	Ellis	Mooney	Swann	Worthington +	Chapman	
Oct 27	Stockport Co.	SVT	h	5-2	1968	Kelly	Miller	Wrightson	Atkins	Walker	Lowey	Mooney (1)	Swann (1)	Ellis (1)	Jemson (2)	Hidersley	Chapman	Wilkes	
Oct 31	Chester City	Div 3	h	1-1	5657	Kelly	Rathbone	Bennett	Atkins	Jones	Allardyce	Mooney	Swann (1)	Ellis	Jemson	Hidersley	Miller	Lowey	
Nov 4	Bristol Rovers	Div 3	a	2-1	2804	Kelly	Rathbone	Bennett	Atkins	Jones	Allardyce	Mooney	Swann	Ellis (1)	Jemson (1)	Hidersley	Miller	Lowey	
Nov 7	Mansfield T.	Div 3	h	0-0	3631	Kelly	Miller	Bennett	Atkins	Jones	Allardyce	Mooney	Swann	Ellis	Jemson	Hidersley	Williams	Lowey	
Nov 14	Mansfield T. Rd 1	FAC	h	1-1	7415	Kelly	Rathbone	Bennett	Atkins (1)	Jones	Allardyce	Mooney	Swann	Ellis	Brazil	Hidersley	Miller	Jemson	
Nov 17	Mansfield T. Replay	FAC	a	2-4	4682	Kelly	Rathbone *	Bennett	Atkins	Jones	Allardyce	Mooney	Swann	Jemson (1)	Brazil (1)	Hidersley	Ellis	Miller *	
Nov 21	Doncaster R.	Div 3	h	1-2	5178	Kelly	Rathbone *	Bennett	Atkins	Jones	Allardyce	Mooney	Swann	Jemson	Brazil	Hidersley	Miller * (1)	Ellis	
Nov 28	Fulham	Div 3	h	1-0	5324	Kelly	Rathbone	Bennett	Atkins	Jones	Allardyce	Mooney	Swann	Jemson (1)	Brazil	Hidersley	Miller	Wrightson	
Dec 12	Aldershot	Div 3	h	0-2	4519	Kelly	Rathbone	Bennett	Atkins	Jones	Allardyce	Mooney *	Swann	Jemson	Brazil	Hidersley	Miller	Ellis *	
Dec 19	Notts County	Div 3	a	2-4	5730	Kelly	Rathbone	Bennett	Atkins	Jones *	Allardyce	Mooney	Swann (1)	Jemson (1)	Brazil	Joyce	Miller *	Ellis	
Dec 26	Blackpool	Div 3	h	2-1	11155	Kelly	Rathbone	Bennett	Atkins	Jones	Allardyce	Mooney *	Swann (1)	Ellis	Brazil (1)	Joyce	Hidersley *	Miller	
Dec 28	Sunderland	Div 3	h	1-1	24814	Kelly	Rathbone	Bennett	Atkins	Jones (1)	Allardyce	Mooney	Swann	Ellis	Brazil	Hidersley	Miller	Chapman	
Jan 1	Wigan Ath.	Div 3	a	0-2	6812	Kelly	Miller	Bennett	Atkins	Jones *	Allardyce	Mooney	Swann	Ellis +	Brazil	Hidersley	Jemson +	Chapman *	
Jan 2	York City	Div 3	h	3-0	6302	Brown	Miller	Bennett	Atkins	Chapman	Allardyce	Mooney (1)	Swann	Jemson	Brazil (1)	Joyce	Hidersley	Wrightson	
Jan 9	Bristol City	Div 3	h	2-0	5729	Brown	Rathbone (1) *	Bennett	Atkins	Chapman	Allardyce	Mooney	Swann	Ellis	Brazil (1)	Joyce	Miller *	Wrightson	
Jan 16	Rotherham Utd.	Div 3	a	2-2	4011	Kelly	Rathbone	Bennett	Atkins	Chapman	Allardyce	Mooney	Swann	Ellis	Brazil (2)	Joyce	Miller	Wrightson	
Jan 19	Rochdale	SVT	h	3-1	2983	Brown	Rathbone	Bennett	Atkins (1)	Wrightson	Allardyce	Miller	Swann (1)	Ellis (1)	Brazil	Joyce	Chapman	Jemson	
Jan 27	Northampton T.	Div 3	a	1-0	5052	Brown	Rathbone	Bennett	Atkins	Wrightson	Allardyce	Mooney	Swann	Jemson (1)	Brazil	Joyce	Miller	Chapman	
Jan 30	Southend Utd.	Div 3	h	1-1	6180	Brown	Rathbone	Bennett	Atkins	Wrightson	Allardyce	Mooney (1)	Swann	Jemson	Brazil	Joyce	Miller	Chapman	
Feb 6	Grimsby Town	Div 3	a	1-0	3970	Brown	Rathbone	Bennett	Atkins	Wrightson	Allardyce	Mooney	Swann	Jemson	Brazil (1)	Joyce	Miller	Chapman	
Feb 13	Sunderland	Div 3	a	2-2	10852	Brown	Rathbone	Bennett	Atkins	Wrightson	Allardyce	Mooney (1)	Swann (1)	Jemson	Brazil	Joyce	Miller	Chapman	
Feb 16	Mansfield T. Qtr Final	SVT	h	2-1	5332	Brown	Rathbone	Bennett	Atkins	Wrightson	Chapman	Mooney	Swann	Jemson *	Brazil (2)	Joyce	Miller	Ellis *	
Feb 20	Chesterfield	Div 3	a	0-0	2864	Brown	Rathbone	Bennett	Atkins	Wrightson	Chapman	Mooney	Swann	Jemson *	Brazil	Joyce	Miller	Ellis *	
Feb 27	Walsall	Div 3	h	1-0	6479	Brown	Rathbone	Bennett	Atkins	Wrightson	Chapman	Mooney	Swann	Jemson	Brazil (1p)	Joyce	Miller	Ellis	
Mar 1	Brentford	Div 3	a	0-2	3505	Brown	Rathbone	Bennett *	Atkins	Jones	Chapman	Mooney	Swann	Jemson +	Brazil	Joyce	Miller *	Ellis +	
Mar 5	Brighton	Div 3	h	3-0	5834	Brown	Rathbone *	Bennett	Atkins	Jones	Chapman	Mooney	Swann (2)	Jemson (1)	Brazil	Joyce	Miller *	Ellis	
Mar 9	Hartlepool Utd. Semi/F	SVT	h	2-0	4989	Brown	Miller	Bennett	Atkins (1)	Jones	Chapman	Mooney	Swann	Jemson (1)	Brazil	Joyce	Wrightson	Ellis	
Mar 12	Port Vale	Div 3	a	2-3	4647	Brown	Miller	Wrightson	Atkins	Jones	Allardyce	Mooney	Swann (1)	Jemson	Brazil (1)	Joyce	Chapman	Ellis	
Mar 19	Chester City	Div 3	a	0-1	3724	Brown	Miller	Wrightson	Chapman	Jones	Allardyce	Mooney	Swann	Ellis	Brazil	Williams	Wilkes	Kelly	
Mar 26	Bury	Div 3	h	1-0	6456	Brown	Miller	Rathbone	Atkins	Jones (1)	Wrightson	Mooney	Swann	Ellis	Brazil	Hidersley	Chapman	Allardyce	
Apr 2	Mansfield T.	Div 3	h	1-0	6254	Brown	Miller	Rathbone	Atkins	Jones *	Wrightson	Mooney	Swann (1)	Ellis	Brazil	Hidersley	Allardyce +	Joyce	
Apr 4	Doncaster R.	Div 3	a	2-3	2167	Brown	Miller	Chapman +	Atkins	Wrightson	Allardyce	Mooney	Swann (2)	Ellis *	Brazil	Hidersley	Joyce +	Wilkes *	
Apr 8	Bristol Rovers	Div 3	h	3-1	5386	Brown	Miller	Rathbone	Atkins	Wrightson	Allardyce	Mooney	Swann	Ellis (1)	Brazil (1p)	Hidersley (1)	Joyce	Walker	
Apr 12	Burnley North Final 1L	SVT	a	0-0	15680	Brown	Miller	Rathbone	Atkins	Wrightson	Allardyce	Mooney	Swann	Ellis	Brazil	Hidersley	Joyce	Jones	
Apr 19	Burnley North Final 2L	SVT	a	1-3*	17592	Brown	Miller +	Joyce *	Atkins	Jones	Wrightson	Mooney	Swann	Ellis	Brazil (1)	Hidersley	Williams *	Chapman +	
Apr 23	Gillingham	Div 3	h	0-4	2721	Brown	Wilkes	Joyce	Atkins	Jones	Chapman	Mooney	Swann	Ellis *	Brazil	Hidersley	Williams *	Walker	
Apr 30	Fulham	Div 3	h	1-0	4192	Brown	Miller	Rathbone	Atkins	Jones	Allardyce	Williams	Swann (1)	Ellis *	Brazil (1)	Joyce	Hidersley *	Chapman	
May 2	Aldershot	Div 3	a	0-0	3465	Brown	Miller	Rathbone	Atkins	Wrightson	Allardyce	Mooney +	Swann	Williams	Brazil *	Joyce	Hidersley +	Ellis *	
May 7	Notts County	Div 3	h	1-2	5822	Brown	Miller	Rathbone	Atkins	Hughes	Wrightson	Mooney	Swann	Williams	Ellis (1)	Joyce	Hidersley	Chapman	

(Hill of Bury)

SEASON 1988–1989

The season started badly with defender Mick Bennett breaking his left leg in a pre-season friendly. The results of those games had gone well so it came as a nasty shock when Preston lost their opening league game at home to Port Vale by 3–1. New signings Neil Williams and Mark Patterson made their debuts with Williams scoring North End's goal. As the season panned out results and performances improved although there was little consistency. In the October great wins over Chesterfield, Brentford and Gillingham really excited the fans as the goals flowed freely from the rampant forwards and the defence looked impregnable. This good form continued until the end of November when an FA Cup replay defeat at Tranmere was followed by an awful 6–0 thrashing at Wolverhampton Wanderers, Steve Bull scoring a hat-trick. This led to some mixed results over the next few weeks. Roy Tunks mad a comeback in goal as David Brown's confidence suffered and the team had several other changes, made to it. Other players continued to perform well though with Tony Ellis always dangerous, Bob Atkins still a class act and Patterson ever lively. The star player though was, without doubt, the brilliant Brian Mooney. The Irish ball player showed phenomenal dribbling skills and became a real crowd favourite. In the January the club was hit by the tragic news that their former player, Mick Baxter, still actively involved with the club, had collapsed and died whilst working with some children at Deepdale. It was an awful time for everyone who knew him and tributes flooded in for the popular gentle man. He was just 32. In the aftermath of Mick's passing the mood was subdued at the club but after Christmas Preston made a marvellous challenge for promotion and lost only four of their final 21 games. Playing a quick, inter-passing game, there were many exciting matches and lots of goals for the fans to cheer. For instance, a magnificent demolition of Chesterfield at Deepdale by six goals to nil provided a brilliant hat-trick for Ellis. Gillingham, Brentford and Mansfield were all thrashed and hopes were high that automatic promotion could be achieved. In the end though Preston had to be content with a place in the play-offs. They ended the season as they had begun it by playing against Port Vale. This time over two legs. A draw at Deepdale gave some hope, but as with their first game back in August, Preston lost 3–1 in the return. It deprived the club a place at Wembley which would have been a nice reward for the loyal fans.

DEBUTANTS: (6) Neil Williams, Mark Patterson, Paul Fitzpatrick, Ian Bogie, Tony Philliskirk, Steve Harper

LAST GAMES: (7) McAteer, Brazil, Brown D., Williams O., Jemson, Fitzpatrick, Philliskirk.

Ever presents: None
Hat-tricks: (2) Tony Ellis and Gary Brazil one each
Players used: 23
FA Cup: First Round
Littlewoods Cup: Second Round
Also competed in Sherpa Van Trophy
Manager: John McGrath
Chairman: K.W. Leeming Esq.
Leading scorer: 20 goals – Tony Ellis (all League)
OFFICIAL PLAYER OF THE SEASON: Brian Mooney

Gary Brazil

Trivia Facts:

Tom Finney was the subject of the *This is Your Life* TV programme and many of his former colleagues were there to share Tom's night. Later that year Paul Agnew wrote a biography of North End's best known footballer, which became a bestseller in all the bookshops in Preston. Tom attended many book signings throughout the area and there were queues at each of the venues such was the popularity of the man.

On October 1 1988 the two authors of this book were on opposing sides in a match on the Deepdale plastic which followed the Southend league game. The Lancashire Ambulance XI, for which Ian Rigby was guesting at left-back, took on Mike Payne's Southern Softies XI. Ian had arranged for another guest to play for their side, none other than Alex Bruce! But Mike Payne's goalkeeping proved conclusive as his team ran out easy winners with a 5–1 victory. And no, Brucey didn't score!

Sadly, another former North Ender died at a very young age when Mick Baxter, just 32, died at Deepdale. Mick was the club's community officer at the time and, typically, was working with some children just before his death. A minute's silence was held at both of Preston's next two games. It was a very sad time.

Preston played Hyde United in a re-inactment of the famous FA Cup tie of 1887 when Preston won 26–0. Long shorts and centre partings were the order of the day for the current team!

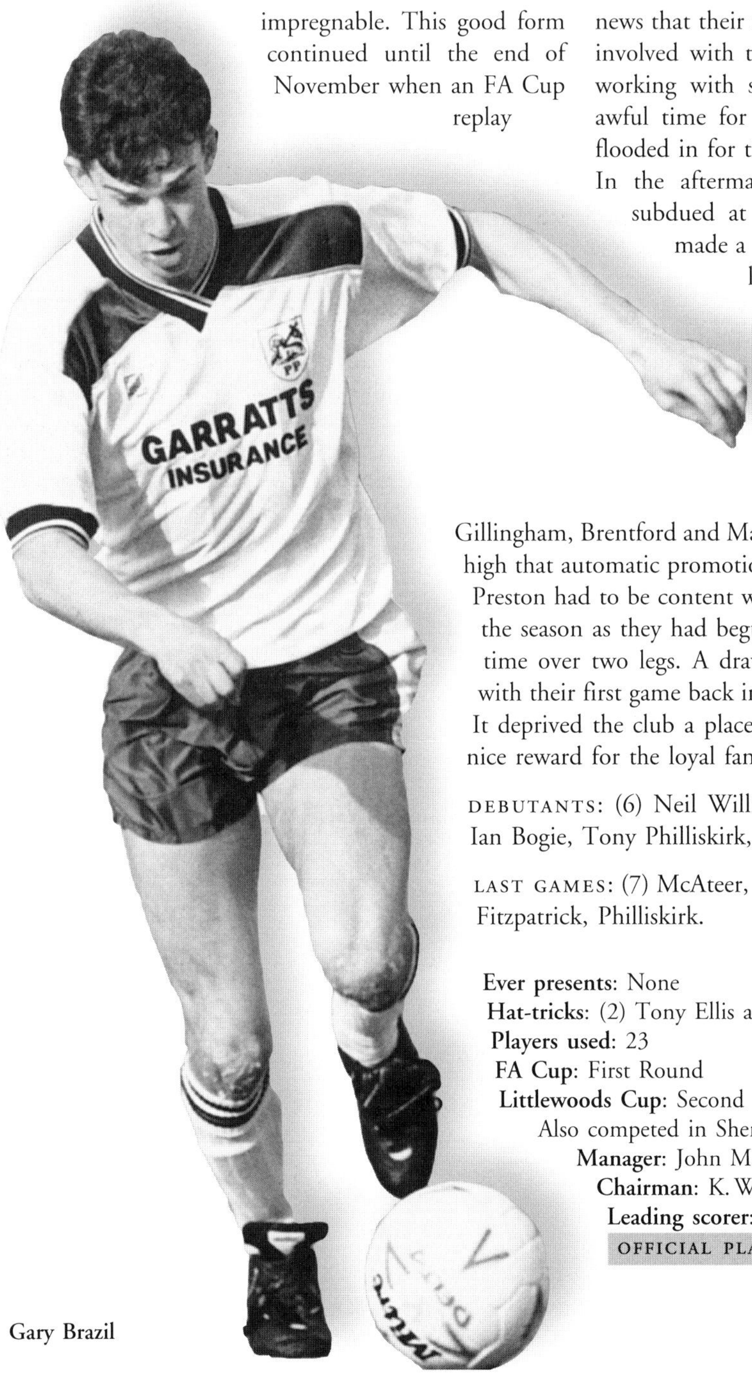

Left to right: *Back row:* W. Joyce, M. Bennett, G. Brazil, G. Swann, D. Brown, A. Kelly, A. McAteer, M. Rathbone, L. Chapman, M. Patterson.
Front row: O. Williams, N. Williams, G. Walker, J. Wrightson, A. Jones, S. Allardyce, R. Atkins, T. Ellis, D. Miller, B. Mooney.

Match Report: Honey From The Bees – 4 Mar 1989 Preston 5 Brentford 3

Having just beaten Chesterfield 6–0 at Deepdale and Gillingham 3–1 in Kent, the Preston fans could hardly have expected another goal feast when Brentford came to Lancashire, but that is exactly what happened. In a ding dong thriller of a match North End continued their incredible goal-scoring run, but it was not before Brentford had tested them to the full. It took only two minutes for the game to burst into life. Philliskirk latched on to a through pass from Ellis and fired home with his trusty left boot. A minute later and a similar move saw Philliskirk's shot cleared off the line. It looked like another six goal haul was on the cards. But the Londoners had other ideas and they were level after ten minutes when Ratcliffe scored from a close range header. Seven minutes later Brentford stunned the crowd further by taking the lead through Bates. A handball decision then gave Patterson the chance to equalise from the penalty spot, but back came Brentford just 28 seconds later! Godfrey was the scorer this time with an unstoppable shot past Tunks. The twists and turns of this amazing game then took another direction. Off went Philliskirk, who was unwell, and on came Joyce as substitute. On 70 minutes Mooney and Patterson combined to send Joyce racing clear and he gleefully clipped the ball over the keeper. The crowd were going wild with excitement by now and six minutes later Deepdale erupted as Patterson beat the offside trap and set up Ellis for goal number four. Just to seal the result Ellis crossed for Joyce and the substitute scored his second goal in the dying moments. A standing ovation, for both sides, greeted the final whistle.

League appearances (46 games)

Allardyce S. 13 + 1, Atkins R. G. 39, Bogie I. 9 + 4, Brazil G. N. 23 + 2, Brown D. J. 23, Ellis A. J. 43 + 2, Fitzpatrick P. J. 2,Harper S. J. 2 + 3, Hughes A. F. S. 22 + 1, Jemson N. B. 6 + 3, Jones A. 29 + 1, Joyce W. G. 35 + 5, McAteer A. 11 + 2, Miller D. B. 9 + 3, Mooney B. J. 38 + 2, Patterson M. A. 42, Philliskirk A. 13 + 1, Rathbone M. J. 32 + 2, Swann G. 16 + 2, Tunks R. W. 23, Williams N. J. F. 40 + 1, Wrightson J. G. 36 + 2.

FA Cup appearances (2 games)

Brown 2, Rathbone 2, Williams N. 2, Allardyce 2, Atkins 2, Wrightson 2, Mooney 2, Brazil 2, Joyce 2, Ellis 2, Patterson 2, McAteer 0 + 1.

Littlewoods Cup appearances (4 games)

Brown 4, Rathbone 4, Miller 2, Williams N. 1 + 1, McAteer 3, Allardyce 3, Swann 3 + 1, Atkins 4, Jones 3 + 1, Wrightson 1, Hughes 1, Mooney 2 + 1, Brazil 3, Joyce 2, Ellis 3, Patterson 4, Williams O. 1.

Sherpa Van Trophy Appearances (3 games)

Tunks 3, Rathbone 1 + 1, Williams N. 3, McAteer 2, Allardyce 1 + 1, Swann 2, Atkins 1, Jones 3, Wrightson 1, Hughes 1, Mooney 2 + 1, Brazil 3, Joyce 3, Ellis 2, Patterson 3.

Goalscorers: 79 League–1 FAC–1 LC–4 SVT–(Total 85)

Ellis 20–0–0–0 (20), Patterson 15 (5 pens)–0–0–1 (16), Brazil 9 (3 pens)–0–1–1 (11), Joyce 9–0–0–1 (10), Mooney 6–0–0–1 (7), Philliskirk 6–0–0–0 (6), Jemson 2–0–0–0 (2), Rathbone 2–0–0–0 (2), Williams N. 2–0–0–0 (2), Swann 2–0–0–0 (2), McAteer 1–0–0–0 (1), Hughes 1–0–0–0 (1), Bogie 1–0–0–0 (1), Atkins 0–1–0–0 (1), Own Goals 3–0–0–0 (3), (Coleman of Mansfield, James of Swansea and Stancliffe of Sheff. Utd.)

Date 1988-9	Opponents	Comp	h or a	Score	Att.	1	2	3	4	5	6	7	8	9	10	11	12	14	Own Goals
Aug 27	Port Vale	Div 3	h	1-3	6718	Brown	Miller	McAteer	Atkins	Jones	Wrightson	N.Williams (1)	Swann	Ellis	Brazil	Patterson *	O.Williams	Rathbone *	
Aug 29	Wigan Ath. Rd 1 1L	LC	a	0-0	4035	Brown	Miller	Rathbone	Atkins	Jones	Allardyce	O.Williams *	Swann	Patterson	Brazil	McAteer	Ellis	N.Williams *	
Sep 3	Huddersfield T.	Div 3	a	0-2	5622	Brown	Miller	Rathbone	Atkins	Jones	Allardyce	Mooney	Swann +	N.Williams *	Brazil	Patterson	Ellis *	Joyce +	
Sep 6	Wigan Ath. Rd 1 2L	LC	h	1-0	4945	Brown	Rathbone	McAteer	Atkins	Jones	Allardyce	Mooney	Joyce	Ellis	Brazil (1)	Patterson	Swann	Wrightson	
Sep 10	Blackpool	Div 3	h	1-0	8779	Brown	Rathbone	McAteer	Atkins	Jones	Wrightson	Miller	Joyce	Ellis	Brazil	Patterson (1)	Swann	N.Williams	
Sep 17	Bristol City	Div 3	a	1-1	7913	Brown	Rathbone (1)	McAteer	Atkins	Jones	Allardyce	Miller	Joyce	Ellis	Brazil	Patterson	Swann	N.Williams	
Sep 20	Chester City	Div 3	h	3-3	5415	Brown	Rathbone	McAteer	Atkins	Jones	Allardyce	Miller *	Joyce	Ellis (1)	Brazil	Patterson (2)	Swann *	N.Williams	
Sep 24	Notts County	Div 3	a	0-0	4965	Brown	Rathbone	McAteer	Atkins	Jones	Allardyce	Miller *	Swann	Ellis	Brazil	Patterson	Mooney *	Wrightson	
Sep 28	Norwich City Rd 2 1L	LC	a	0-2	7484	Brown	Rathbone	McAteer	Atkins	Jones	Allardyce	Miller *	Swann	Ellis	Brazil	Patterson	Mooney *	Wrightson	
Oct 1	Southend Utd.	Div 3	h	3-2	5348	Brown	Rathbone	McAteer (1)	Atkins	Jones	Allardyce	Mooney	Swann	Ellis *	Brazil (2,1p)	Patterson	Miller *	Wrightson	
Oct 5	Bristol Rovers	Div 3	a	0-1	3689	Brown	Miller	Rathbone	Atkins	Jones +	Allardyce	Mooney	Swann *	Ellis	Brazil	Patterson	N.Williams *	Wrightson +	
Oct 8	Bury	Div 3	h	1-0	5863	Brown	Miller *	Rathbone	Atkins	Wrightson	Hughes	Mooney	N.Williams	Ellis (1)	Joyce	Patterson	Jones	Swann *	
Oct 11	Norwich City Rd 2 2L	LC	h	0-3	7002	Brown	N.Williams	Rathbone	Atkins	Wrightson	Hughes *	Mooney	Joyce	Ellis	Swann	Patterson	Jones *	Maloney	
Oct 15	Chesterfield	Div 3	a	3-0	2813	Brown	N.Williams	Rathbone	Atkins	Wrightson	Hughes	Mooney (1)	Joyce	Ellis (1)	Swann (1)	Patterson	Allardyce	Jones	
Oct 22	Brentford	Div 3	a	2-0	5584	Brown	N.Williams	Rathbone	Atkins	Wrightson	Hughes *	Mooney	Joyce	Ellis	Patterson	Swann +	Allardyce *	Brazil + (2)	
Oct 25	Gillingham	Div 3	h	5-0	6390	Brown	N.Williams	Rathbone	Atkins	Wrightson	Allardyce *	Mooney	Joyce (1)	Ellis (1)	Brazil (3,1p)	Miller	Jones *	Hughes	
Oct 29	Swansea City	Div 3	a	1-1	5370	Brown	N.Williams	Rathbone	Atkins	Wrightson	Hughes	Mooney	Joyce	Ellis (1)	Brazil	Patterson *	Miller *	Chapman	
Nov 5	Mansfield T.	Div 3	h	2-0	6434	Brown	N.Williams	Rathbone (1)	Atkins	Wrightson	Hughes	Mooney (1)	Joyce	Ellis	Brazil	Patterson	Miller	Swann	
Nov 8	Wigan Ath.	Div 3	h	2-2	8396	Brown	N.Williams	Rathbone	Atkins	Wrightson	Hughes	Mooney	Joyce	Ellis	Brazil (1p)	Patterson (1)	Chapman	Swann	
Nov 12	Reading	Div 3	a	2-2	6225	Brown	N.Williams	Rathbone	Atkins	Wrightson	Allardyce	Mooney	Joyce	Ellis (1)	Brazil	Patterson (1)	Swann	McAteer	
Nov 19	Tranmere R. Rd 1	FAC	h	1-1	7734	Brown	N.Williams	Rathbone	Atkins (1)	Wrightson	Allardyce	Mooney	Joyce	Ellis	Brazil	Patterson	Swann	McAteer	
Nov 22	Tranmere R. Replay	FAC	a	0-3	7676	Brown	N.Williams	Rathbone *	Atkins	Wrightson	Allardyce	Mooney	Joyce	Ellis	Brazil	Patterson	Swann	McAteer *	
Nov 26	Wolverhampton W.	Div 3	a	0-6	13180	Brown	N.Williams	Rathbone	Atkins	Wrightson *	Allardyce	Mooney	Joyce	Ellis	Brazil	Patterson	Swann	Hughes *	
Dec 3	Cardiff City	Div 3	h	3-3	4926	Tunks	N.Williams	Rathbone	Atkins	Hughes	Allardyce	Brazil (1)	Joyce	Ellis (2)	Fitzpatrick	Patterson	Swann	McAteer	
Dec 6	Bolton W.	SVT	a	0-1	2690	Tunks	N.Williams	McAteer	Atkins +	Jones	Hughes	Brazil	Joyce	Ellis *	Patterson	Swann	Allardyce +	Mooney *	
Dec 13	Bury	SVT	h	4-0	2900	Tunks	N.Williams	McAteer	Jones	Hughes	Allardyce	Mooney (1)	Joyce (1)	Patterson (1)	Brazil (1)	Swann *	Rathbone *	Wrightson	
Dec 17	Fulham	Div 3	a	1-2	3858	Tunks	N.Williams	McAteer	Jones	Hughes	Wrightson	Mooney	Joyce	Brazil	Fitzpatrick	Patterson (1)	Rathbone	Chapman	
Dec 26	Bolton W.	Div 3	h	3-1	12104	Tunks	N.Williams	McAteer	Jones	Wrightson	Hughes (1)	Mooney	Joyce (1)	Ellis (1)	Brazil	Patterson	Fitzpatrick	Rathbone	
Dec 31	Sheffield Utd.	Div 3	h	2-0	11005	Tunks	N.Williams	McAteer	Jones	Wrightson	Hughes	Mooney	Joyce (1)	Ellis	Brazil	Patterson (1)	Rathbone	Miller	
Jan 2	Northampton T.	Div 3	a	0-1	4219	Tunks	N.Williams	McAteer +	Jones	Wrightson	Hughes	Mooney	Joyce	Ellis *	Brazil	Patterson	Rathbone +	Miller *	
Jan 7	Aldershot	Div 3	a	1-2	2135	Tunks	N.Williams	Rathbone +	Jones	Allardyce *	Hughes	Mooney	Joyce (1)	Ellis	Brazil	Patterson	Wrightson *	McAteer +	
Jan 14	Huddersfield T.	Div 3	h	1-0	6959	Tunks	N.Williams	Rathbone	Jones	Wrightson	Hughes	Mooney	Joyce	Ellis	Brazil	Patterson (1)	Miller	McAteer	
Jan 17	Bolton W.	SVT	h	0-1	5569	Tunks	N.Williams	Rathbone	Jones	Wrightson	Hughes	Mooney	Joyce	Ellis	Brazil	Patterson	Swann	McAteer	
Jan 21	Blackpool	Div 3	a	0-1	8951	Tunks	N.Williams	Rathbone *	Jones	Wrightson	Hughes	Mooney	Joyce	Ellis	Brazil	Patterson	Allardyce	McAteer *	
Jan 28	Bristol City	Div 3	h	2-0	6080	Tunks	N.Williams	Rathbone	Jones	Wrightson	Atkins	Mooney (2)	Joyce	Ellis	Brazil	Patterson	Miller	Swann	
Feb 3	Southend Utd.	Div 3	a	1-2	2948	Tunks	N.Williams	Rathbone	Jones	Wrightson	Atkins	Mooney (1)	Joyce	Ellis	McAteer *	Patterson	Brazil *	Swann	
Feb 11	Bristol Rovers	Div 3	h	1-1	7365	Tunks	N.Williams	Rathbone	Jones	Wrightson	Atkins	Mooney (1)	Joyce *	Bogie	Philliskirk	Patterson	Ellis *	Swann	
Feb 18	Bury	Div 3	a	1-1	6977	Tunks	N.Williams (1)	Rathbone	Jones	Wrightson	Atkins	Mooney	Ellis	Bogie	Philliskirk *	Patterson	Allardyce	Joyce *	
Feb 25	Chesterfield	Div 3	h	6-0	7047	Tunks	N.Williams	Rathbone	Jones	Wrightson	Atkins	Mooney *	Ellis (3)	Bogie	Philliskirk (2)	Patterson (1p)	Allardyce	Joyce *	
Feb 28	Gillingham	Div 3	a	3-1	3031	Tunks	N.Williams	Rathbone	Jones	Wrightson	Atkins	Mooney	Ellis (2)	Bogie	Philliskirk	Patterson (1p)	Swann	Joyce	
Mar 4	Brentford	Div 3	h	5-3	8186	Tunks	N.Williams	Rathbone	Jones	Wrightson	Atkins	Mooney	Ellis (1)	Bogie	Philliskirk (1) +	Patterson (1p)	Swann	Joyce + (2)	
Mar 11	Mansfield T.	Div 3	a	3-0	4706	Tunks	N.Williams	Rathbone	Jones	Wrightson	Atkins	Mooney	Ellis (1)	Bogie	Philliskirk (1)	Patterson	Hughes	Joyce	(Coleman)
Mar 14	Swansea City	Div 3	h	1-1	8975	Tunks	N.Williams	Rathbone	Jones	Wrightson	Atkins	Mooney	Ellis	Bogie *	Philliskirk	Patterson	Hughes	Joyce *	(James)
Mar 18	Port Vale	Div 3	a	1-1	8584	Tunks	N.Williams	Rathbone	Jones	Wrightson	Atkins	Mooney	Ellis (1)	Joyce	Philliskirk *	Patterson	Bogie *	Allardyce	
Mar 25	Northampton T.	Div 3	h	3-2	9137	Tunks	N.Williams	Rathbone	Jones	Wrightson	Atkins	Mooney	Ellis	Joyce (2)	Philliskirk	Patterson (1p)	Bogie	Jemson	
Mar 27	Bolton W.	Div 3	a	0-1	10281	Tunks	N.Williams	Rathbone +	Jones	Wrightson	Atkins	Mooney	Ellis	Joyce	Philliskirk *	Patterson	Bogie +	Jemson *	
Apr 1	Fulham	Div 3	h	1-4	8190	Tunks	N.Williams	Allardyce	Jones	Wrightson	Atkins	Mooney +	Ellis	Joyce	Philliskirk (1)	Swann *	Bogie +	Harper *	
Apr 4	Aldershot	Div 3	h	2-2	5977	Tunks	N.Williams	Swann	Jones	Hughes	Atkins	Joyce	Ellis +	Bogie (1) *	Philliskirk (1)	Patterson	Jemson +	Harper *	
Apr 8	Sheffield Utd.	Div 3	a	1-3	12718	Tunks	N.Williams	Swann	Allardyce	Hughes	Atkins	Bogie	Ellis	Joyce	Jemson *	Harper	Mooney *	Miller	(Stancliffe)
Apr 15	Notts County	Div 3	h	3-0	6735	Brown	N.Williams	Swann (1)	Atkins	Wrightson	Hughes	Mooney	Ellis (1)	Joyce (1)	Jemson	Patterson	Bogie	Harper	
Apr 22	Chester City	Div 3	a	1-0	4617	Brown	N.Williams	Swann	Atkins	Wrightson	Hughes	Mooney	Ellis	Joyce	Jemson (1)	Harper *	Bogie *	Miller	
Apr 29	Reading	Div 3	h	2-1	7003	Brown	N.Williams	Swann	Atkins	Wrightson	Hughes	Mooney	Ellis	Joyce	Jemson	Patterson (2,1p)	Miller	Harper	
May 1	Wigan Ath.	Div 3	a	1-1	5671	Brown	N.Williams	Swann	Atkins	Wrightson	Hughes	Mooney	Ellis	Joyce	Jemson (1) *	Patterson	Miller	Harper *	
May 5	Cardiff City	Div 3	a	0-0	3196	Brown	N.Williams	Swann	Atkins	Wrightson	Hughes	Mooney	Ellis	Joyce	Philliskirk *	Patterson	Jemson *	Miller	
May 13	Wolverhampton W.	Div 3	h	3-3	14126	Brown	N.Williams	Swann	Atkins	Wrightson	Hughes	Mooney	Ellis (2)	Joyce	Jemson *	Patterson (1)	Miller	Philliskirk *	

Season 1988–89: Third Division

	P	W	D	L	F	A	Pts
1 Wolves	46	26	14	6	96	49	92
2 Sheffield United	46	25	9	12	93	54	84
3 Port Vale	46	24	12	10	78	48	84
4 Fulham	46	22	9	15	69	67	75
5 Bristol Rovers	46	19	17	10	67	51	74
6 PRESTON	**46**	**19**	**15**	**12**	**79**	**60**	**72**
7 Brentford	46	18	14	14	66	61	68
8 Chester City	46	19	11	16	64	61	68
9 Notts County	46	18	13	15	64	54	67
10 Bolton Wanderers	46	16	16	14	58	54	64
11 Bristol City	46	18	9	19	53	55	63
12 Swansea City	46	15	16	15	51	53	61
13 Bury	46	16	13	17	55	67	61
14 Huddesfield Town	46	17	9	20	63	73	60
15 Manfield Town	46	14	17	15	48	52	59
16 Cardiff City	46	14	15	17	44	56	57
17 Wigan Athletic	46	14	14	18	55	53	56
18 Reading	46	15	11	20	68	72	56
19 Blackpool	46	14	13	19	56	59	54
20 Northampton Town	46	16	6	24	66	76	54
21 Southend United	46	13	15	18	56	75	54
22 Chesterfield	46	14	7	25	51	86	49
23 Gilingham	46	12	4	30	47	81	40
24 Aldershot	46	8	13	25	48	78	37

STAT FACTS:

Best home run without defeat: 17 games
Best away run without defeat: 4 games
Longest run unbeaten: 9 games
Longest run without a win: 5 games
Best home attendance: 14,126 *vs.* Wolves 13.5.89
Worst home attendance: 2,900 *vs.* Bury SVT 13.12.88
Best away attendance: 13,180 *vs.* Wolves 26.11.88
Worst away attendance: 2,135 *vs.* Aldershot 7.1.89
Aggregate and average home attendance: 177,158 – 7,702
Aggregate and average away attendance: 137,253 – 5,967

League position in Division Three: 6th (play-offs) – P46 W19 D15 L12 F79 A60 Pts 72
Home: W14 D7 L2 F56 A31 Away: W5 D8 L10 F23 A29

SEASON 1989–1990

The local Evening Post's Preston North End reporter, Paul Agnew, summed up the mood after the opening day's defeat at Rotherham when he said, " A new soccer season kicked off at 3pm on Saturday, but no-one bothered to tell North End!". In fact the club had another awful start with six defeats and one draw in their first seven league and cup games. What made matters worse was that in each match three goals or more were conceded. It was not until the September that the rot was stopped as Preston, who do nothing by halves, beat Chester 5–0 at Deepdale. In that game Brian Mooney scored a marvellous hat-trick and the skilful Irishman had already made his mark with a series of fine performances. New signing Graham Shaw had also netted a hat-trick, in the 4–3 Littlewoods Cup defeat by Tranmere. Scoring goals was not the problem however, it was stopping them going in at the other end that kept giving manager John McGrath sleepless nights. Eventually Alan Kelly Junior settled down to a regular place in goal and the signing of Mike Flynn in the December was an excellent move. Mind you, his debut was less than memorable as he came on as substitute in an embarrassing FA Cup defeat at non-league minnows Whitley Bay. Back in the league Warren Joyce put his heart and soul into his play and Gary Swann was another who gave so much to the team, playing in a variety of roles and never giving less than 100% effort. Up to Christmas the results gave some concern and the threat of relegation was again a serious one. Everything then came to a head as Preston suffered four defeats on the trot in the January and February. It signalled a sad end to John McGrath's reign as manager as he bowed out leaving Les Chapman in temporary charge. He was given a caretaker role for the next game, away at Reading and he must have wondered what he had let himself in for as North End were humiliated at Elm Park as Reading won 6–0. Funnily enough, a week later Preston beat Cardiff 4–0 at Deepdale and after that, apart from an occasional blip, the results improved. Steve Harper's hat-trick in that Cardiff game lifted the depression and when the fan's favourite, John Thomas returned to Deepdale, it gave everyone hope. But it was a harrowing run-in and it was not until the final day that the relegation fears were ended. The final finishing position of 19th was the best the club could have hoped for after such a difficult year.

DEBUTANTS: (8) Graham Shaw, Andy Gill, Simon Snow, Pat Scully, Mike Flynn, Sammy McIlroy, Steven Anderton, Mike Stowell.

LAST GAMES: (12) Tunks, Atkins, Anderton, Jones A., Bennett, Miller, Patterson, Gill, Snow, Scully, McIlroy, Stowell.

League appearances (46 games)

Anderton S. D. 0 + 1, Atkins R. G. 27 + 1, Bennett M. 10, Bogie I. 30 + 5, Ellis A. J. 17, Flynn M. A. 23, Greenwood N. P. 5, Harper S. J. 28 + 8, Hughes A. F. S. 29 + 6, Jones A. 3, Joyce W. G. 44, Kelly A. T. 42, McIlroy S. B. 20, Miller D. B. 3, Mooney B. J. 44 + 1, Patterson M. A. 12 + 1, Rathbone M. J. 3 + 5, Scully P. J. 13, Shaw G. P. 24 + 7, Snow S. G. 1, Stowell M. 2, Swann G. 46, Thomas J. W. 11, Tunks R. W. 2, Williams N. J. F. 41, Wrightson J. G. 26.

FA Cup appearances (2 games)

Kelly 2, Harper 1 + 1, Joyce 2, Flynn 0 + 1, Hughes 2, Mooney 2, Williams 2, Swann 2, Atkins 2, Bogie 2, Ellis 2, Patterson 2, Shaw 1.

Littlewood Cup appearances (2 games)

Tunks 1, Gill A. 1, Miller 2, Rathbone 1 + 1, Harper 1, Jones 2, Joyce 2, Hughes 1, Mooney 2, Swann 2, Atkins 2, Wrightson 1 + 1, Bogie 1 + 1, Snow 1, Shaw 2.

Leyland Daf Cup appearances (3 games)

Kelly 3, Rathbone 0 + 2, Harper 2, Scully 1, Joyce 2, Flynn 2, Hughes 3, Mooney 1, Williams 3, Swann 3, Bennett 2, Atkins 1, Wrightson 0 + 1, Bogie 3, Ellis 2, Patterson 2, Shaw 3.

Goalscorers: 65 League–1 FAC–4 LC–8 LDC–(Total 78)

Joyce 11–1–0–1 (13), Mooney 10–0–0–1 (11), Shaw 5–0–4 (1pen) 2 (11), Harper 10–0–0–0 (10), Swann 8–0–0–0 (8), Ellis 3–0–0–3 (6), Patterson 4 (2 pens)–0–0–0 (4), Thomas 3–0–0–0 (3), Bogie 3–0–0–0 (3), Williams 3–0–0–0 (3), Hughes 1–0–0–1 (2), Atkins 1–0–0–0 (1), Scully 1–0–0–0 (1), Flynn 1–0–0–0 (1), Own Goals 1–0–0–0 (1) (Foster of Mansfield).

League position in Division Three: 19th – P46 W14 D10 L22 F65 A79 Pts 52
Home: W10 D7 L6 F42 A30   Away: W4 D3 L16 F23 A49

Left to right: *Back row:* J. McGrath (Manager), Hughes, Harper, Ellis, Kelly, Williams, Shaw, Atkins. *Front row:* Swann, Patterson, Bogie, Mooney.

Match Report: The Bees Knees Again – 14 Oct 1989 Preston 4 Brentford 2

After the thrills of this clash the year before the fans could hardly expect a repeat of the excitement of that match, but this was another cracker. Two goals down and struggling for form, North End suddenly came back with avengence in an amazing turnround. In the first 15 minutes Brentford's two recent £100,000 signings, May and Holdsworth, both scored to give the visitors a decisive and deserved lead. Indeed, on 17 minutes Holdsworth should have sewn up the points but Kelly bravely blocked the goal attempt. The first half had seen Preston create very little in attack and at half-time a few harsh words were said in their dressing room. It certainly had an effect because on 59 minutes they began their fightback. Great passing sent Ellis clear and the striker shot low and hard into the corner. With a further 12 minutes gone Preston equalised with superb skill by Ellis setting up skipper Joyce with a well taken goal. If the Preston fans enjoyed that then imagine the mood when Bogie floated in a free-kick to give Harper the merest hint of a chance. The number ten met the ball with a first time volley and Brentford keeper Parkes could only grasp at thin air as the ball sped past him. The atmosphere at Deepdale was by now electric and with just seven minutes to go the result was sealed. Mooney put in a shot which was only parried and in darted Swann to poach an excellent goal. Harper, the all action midfield player, typified Preston's spirit in this match as in one incident he tracked back some 60 yards to spread his body in the way of a shot by the lively Godfrey. Ellis was man of the match though as he gave a brilliant centre-forward's display.

Hat-tricks: (3) Brian Mooney, Graham Shaw and Steve Harper all one each.
Ever presents: (1) Gary Swann   **Players used:** 27
FA Cup: Second Round
Littlewoods Cup: First Round
Also competed in the Leyland Daf Cup
Manager: John McGrath until Jan. 1990, then Les Chapman
Chairman: K. W. Leeming Esq.
Leading scorer: 13 goals – Warren Joyce
(11 League 1 FAC 1 LDC)
OFFICIAL PLAYER OF THE SEASON: Warren Joyce

STAT FACTS:
Best home run without defeat: 5 games
Best away run without defeat: 2 games
Longest run unbeaten: 4 games
Longest run without a win: 5 games
Best home attendance: 9,135 *vs.* Bolton 28.10.89
Worst home attendance: 4,480 *vs.* Leyton Orient 13.2.90
Best away attendance: 11,803 *vs.* Bristol City 1.1.90
Worst away attendance: 1,545 *vs.* Stockport LDC 13.12.89
Aggregate and average home attendance: 145,180 – 6,312
Aggregate and average away attendance: 121,314 – 5,274

Brian Mooney. *Skilful Irishman who originally signed from Liverpool.*

Date 1989-90	Opponents	Comp	h/a	Score	Att.	1	2	3	4	5	6	7	8	9	10	11	12	14	Own Goals
Aug 19	Rotherham Utd.	Div 3	a	1-3	5951	Tunks	Miller	Swann	Atkins	Jones	Hughes	Mooney	Ellis	Joyce	Shaw (1)	Patterson	Bogie	Rathbone	
Aug 22	Tranmere R. Rd 1 1L	LC	h	3-4	4632	Gill	Miller	Swann	Atkins	Jones	Hughes +	Mooney	Bogie *	Joyce	Shaw (3,1p)	Harper	Rathbone *	Wrightson +	
Aug 26	Bury	Div 3	h	2-3	5622	Tunks	Rathbone	Swann	Atkins	Jones	Wrightson	Mooney	Snow *	Joyce	Shaw (1)	Miller	Anderton	Harper * (1)	
Aug 29	Tranmere R. Rd 1 2L	LC	a	1-3	5275	Tunks	Miller	Rathbone	Atkins	Jones	Wrightson	Mooney	Joyce *	Snow	Shaw (1)	Swann	Bogie *	Harper	
Sep 2	Leyton Orient	Div 3	a	1-3	4871	Kelly	Miller *	Rathbone	Atkins	Jones	Hughes	Mooney	Ellis	Joyce	Shaw	Swann	Bogie *	Harper	
Sep 9	Huddersfield T.	Div 3	h	3-3	5822	Kelly	Williams	Swann (1)	Wrightson	Scully	Hughes	Mooney (1)	Ellis *	Joyce	Shaw	Bogie (1)	Rathbone *	Atkins	
Sep 16	Bristol Rovers	Div 3	a	0-3	4350	Kelly	Williams	Swann +	Wrightson *	Scully	Hughes	Mooney	Ellis	Joyce	Shaw	Bogie	Rathbone +	Atkins *	
Sep 23	Chester	Div 3	h	5-0	5230	Kelly	Williams	Swann	Atkins	Scully	Hughes	Mooney (3)	Ellis	Joyce	Harper (2)	Bogie	Rathbone	Snow	
Sep 26	Blackpool	Div 3	a	2-1	8920	Kelly	Williams	Swann	Atkins (1)	Scully	Hughes	Mooney (1)	Ellis	Joyce	Harper	Bogie	Rathbone	Shaw	
Sep 30	Walsall	Div 3	h	0-1	4045	Kelly	Williams	Swann	Atkins	Scully	Hughes	Mooney *	Ellis	Joyce	Harper	Bogie	Shaw *	Wrightson	
Oct 7	Northampton T.	Div 3	a	2-1	3039	Kelly	Williams	Swann	Atkins	Scully	Hughes	Mooney	Ellis (1)	Joyce	Harper (1)	Bogie *	Shaw *	Rathbone	
Oct 14	Brentford	Div 3	h	4-2	5956	Kelly	Williams	Swann (1)	Atkins	Scully	Wrightson	Mooney	Ellis (1)	Joyce (1)	Harper (1)	Bogie	Shaw	Rathbone	
Oct 17	Crewe A.	Div 3	h	0-0	7485	Kelly	Williams	Swann	Atkins	Scully	Hughes	Mooney	Ellis	Joyce	Harper	Bogie	Shaw	Wrightson	
Oct 21	Notts County	Div 3	a	1-2	5284	Kelly	Williams (1)	Swann	Atkins	Scully	Hughes	Mooney	Ellis	Joyce	Harper *	Bogie	Shaw *	Rathbone	
Oct 28	Bolton W.	Div 3	h	1-4	9135	Kelly	Williams	Swann	Atkins	Scully (1)	Hughes *	Mooney	Ellis	Joyce	Harper	Bogie	Shaw *	Rathbone	
Oct 31	Mansfield Town	Div 3	a	2-2	3129	Kelly	Williams	Swann	Atkins	Joyce (1)	Hughes	Mooney (1)	Ellis *	Patterson	Shaw	Bogie	Harper *	Rathbone	
Nov 4	Shrewsbury T.	Div 3	h	2-1	5418	Kelly	Williams	Swann (1)	Atkins	Joyce	Scully	Mooney	Harper	Patterson (1p)	Shaw	Bogie	Rathbone *	Hughes	
Nov 7	Burnley	LDC	h	3-0	5241	Kelly	Williams	Swann	Scully	Joyce (1)	Hughes	Harper	Ellis (2)	Bogie	Shaw	Patterson	Rathbone	Atkins	
Nov 11	Swansea City	Div 3	a	1-2	3843	Kelly	Williams	Swann	Atkins	Joyce	Scully	Harper +	Bogie	Bogie	Shaw *	Patterson (1)	Rathbone *	Hughes +	
Nov 18	Tranmere R. Rd 1	FAC	h	1-0	7521	Kelly	Williams	Swann	Atkins	Joyce (1)	Hughes	Mooney	Ellis	Bogie	Shaw *	Patterson	Harper *	Bennett	
Nov 25	Cardiff City	Div 3	a	0-3	3270	Kelly	Williams	Swann	Atkins	Joyce	Scully +	Mooney	Ellis	Bogie	Patterson	Shaw *	Harper *	Hughes +	
Dec 2	Reading	Div 3	h	1-0	5067	Kelly	Williams	Swann (1)	Atkins	Joyce	Hughes	Mooney	Ellis	Bogie	Shaw	Patterson	Harper	Rathbone	
Dec 9	Whitley Bay Rd2	FAC	h	0-2	4500	Kelly	Williams	Swann	Atkins	Joyce	Hughes	Mooney *	Ellis	Bogie	Patterson	Harper	Rathbone	Flynn *	
Dec 13	Stockport Co.	LDC	a	4-2	1545	Kelly	Williams	Bennett	Atkins	Flynn	Hughes (1)	Bogie *	Ellis (1)	Swann	Shaw (2)	Harper	Rathbone *	Wrightson	
Dec 16	Birmingham City	Div 3	a	1-3	6391	Kelly	Williams	Bennett	Atkins	Flynn	Hughes *	Rathbone	Ellis	Swann +	Shaw	Harper	Mooney *	Patterson + (1p)	
Dec 26	Tranmere R.	Div 3	h	2-2	8300	Kelly	Williams	Bennett	Bogie	Flynn	Hughes	Mooney	Swann (2)	Joyce	Patterson	Harper	Rathbone	Wrightson	
Dec 30	Wigan Ath.	Div 3	h	1-1	7220	Kelly	Williams	Bennett	Bogie	Flynn	Hughes	Mooney	Swann	Joyce	Patterson (1)	Harper	Rathbone	Wrightson	
Jan 1	Bristol City	Div 3	a	1-2	11803	Kelly	Williams	Bennett	Bogie	Flynn	Hughes	Mooney (1)	Swann	Joyce	Patterson	Harper	Rathbone	Wrightson	
Jan 6	Fulham	Div 3	h	1-0	5055	Kelly	Williams	Bennett	Bogie	Flynn	Hughes	Mooney	Swann	Joyce	Patterson	Shaw (1)	Rathbone	Wrightson	
Jan 9	Wigan Ath.	LDC	h	1-2	4539	Kelly	Williams	Bennett *	Bogie	Flynn	Hughes +	Mooney (1)	Swann	Joyce	Patterson	Shaw	Rathbone *	Wrightson +	
Jan 13	Bury	Div 3	a	2-1	4715	Kelly	Williams	Bennett	Swann	Flynn	Hughes	Mooney (1)	Patterson	Joyce (1)	Shaw	Harper	Bogie	Rathbone	
Jan 20	Rotherham	Div 3	h	0-1	6088	Kelly	Williams	Bennett	Swann	Flynn	Hughes	Mooney	Patterson	Joyce *	Shaw	Harper	Bogie *	Rathbone	
Feb 3	Chester	Div 3	a	1-3	2499	Kelly	Williams	Bennett	Swann	Flynn	Hughes *	Mooney	Wrightson	Joyce	Shaw	Greenwood	Harper * (1)	Bogie	
Feb 10	Bristol Rovers	Div 3	h	0-1	5956	Stowell	Williams	Swann	McIlroy	Flynn	Wrightson	Mooney	Greenwood	Joyce	Shaw	Harper	Bogie	Hughes	
Feb 13	Leyton Orient	Div 3	h	0-3	4502	Stowell	Swann	Bennett	McIlroy	Flynn	Wrightson	Mooney	Greenwood	Joyce	Shaw *	Harper	Bogie *	Hughes	
Feb 17	Reading	Div 3	a	0-6	3998	Stowell	Swann	Bennett	Harper	Flynn	Hughes	Mooney	Greenwood	Joyce	McIlroy	Bogie	Wrightson	Shaw	
Feb 24	Cardiff City	Div 3	h	4-0	5716	Kelly	Williams	Swann	McIlroy	Flynn	Wrightson	Mooney	Shaw	Joyce (1)	Thomas	Harper (3)	Bennett	Bogie	
Mar 3	Fulham	Div 3	a	1-3	4207	Kelly	Williams	Swann	McIlroy	Wrightson	Hughes	Mooney	Shaw (1)	Bogie	Thomas	Harper	James	Anderton	
Mar 6	Walsall	Div 3	h	2-0	5210	Kelly	Williams	Swann (1)	McIlroy	Wrightson	Hughes	Mooney	Thomas (1)	Joyce	Harper	Hancock	James		
Mar 10	Blackpool	Div 3	h	2-2	8108	Kelly	Williams	Swann	Wrightson	Joyce	Hughes	Mooney (1)	Shaw (1)	Thomas	Flynn	McIlroy	Harper	Atkins	
Mar 17	Northampton T.	Div 3	h	0-0	5681	Kelly	Williams	Swann	McIlroy	Flynn	Wrightson	Mooney	Shaw	Thomas	Joyce	Harper	Hughes	Atkins	
Mar 20	Brentford	Div 3	a	2-2	4673	Kelly	Williams (1)	Swann	McIlroy	Flynn	Wrightson	Mooney	Hughes	Thomas *	Joyce (1)	Atkins +	Shaw *	Harper +	
Mar 24	Crewe A.	Div 3	a	0-1	4531	Kelly	Williams	Swann	McIlroy	Flynn	Wrightson	Mooney	Hughes	Shaw	Joyce	Atkins	Bogie *	Harper *	
Mar 31	Notts County	Div 3	h	2-4	5810	Kelly	Williams	Swann	McIlroy	Flynn	Wrightson	Mooney	Greenwood	Joyce (2) +	Shaw *	Harper	Bogie *	Hughes +	
Apr 3	Huddersfield T.	Div 3	a	2-0	4381	Kelly	Williams	Swann	McIlroy	Flynn	Wrightson	Mooney	Hughes	Joyce (1)	Atkins	Bogie (1)	Harper	Anderton	
Apr 7	Bolton W.	Div 3	h	1-2	8266	Kelly	Williams	Swann	McIlroy	Flynn	Wrightson	Mooney	Hughes	Joyce	Atkins	Bogie (1)	Bennett	Anderton	
Apr 10	Mansfield Town	Div 3	h	4-0	5035	Kelly	Williams	Swann	McIlroy +	Flynn	Wrightson	Mooney	Hughes (1)	Joyce (2) *	Atkins	Bogie	Harper *	Anderton +	(Foster)
Apr 14	Bristol City	Div 3	h	2-2	7599	Kelly	Williams	Swann	McIlroy	Flynn (1)	Wrightson	Mooney	Hughes	Joyce	Atkins *	Bogie	Harper * (1)	Rathbone	
Apr 16	Tranmere R.	Div 3	a	1-2	10187	Kelly	Williams	Swann	McIlroy	Flynn +	Wrightson	Mooney *	Joyce (1)	Thomas	Atkins	Bogie	Rathbone *	Hughes +	
Apr 21	Birmingham City	Div 3	a	2-2	7680	Kelly	Williams	Swann	McIlroy	Flynn +	Wrightson	Mooney (1)	Joyce	Thomas (1)	Bogie	Harper *	Shaw *	Hughes +	
Apr 24	Wigan Ath.	Div 3	h	1-0	4454	Kelly	Williams	Swann	McIlroy	Atkins	Wrightson	Mooney	Joyce	Thomas (1)	Bogie	Harper	Shaw	Hughes	
Apr 28	Swansea City	Div 3	h	2-0	6695	Kelly	Williams (1)	Swann (1)	McIlroy	Atkins	Wrightson	Mooney	Joyce	Thomas	Bogie	Harper	Shaw	Hughes	
May 5	Shrewsbury T.	Div 3	a	0-2	5319	Kelly	Williams	Swann	McIlroy +	Atkins	Wrightson	Mooney	Joyce	Thomas	Bogie	Harper *	Shaw *	Hughes +	

Mark Patterson

Season 1989–90: Third Division

		P	W	D	L	F	A	Pts
1	Bristol Rovers	46	26	15	5	71	35	93
2	Bristol City	46	27	10	9	76	40	91
3	Notts County	46	25	12	9	73	53	87
4	Tranmere Rovers	46	23	11	12	86	49	80
5	Bury	46	21	11	14	70	49	74
6	Bolton Wanderers	46	18	15	13	59	48	69
7	Birmingham City	46	18	12	16	60	59	66
8	Huddersfield Town	46	17	14	15	61	62	65
9	Rotherham United	46	17	13	16	71	62	64
10	Reading	46	15	19	12	57	53	64
11	Shrewsbury Town	46	16	15	15	59	54	63
12	Crewe Alexandra	46	15	17	14	56	53	62
13	Brentford	46	18	7	21	66	66	61
14	Leyton Orient	46	16	10	20	52	56	58
15	Mansfield Town	46	16	7	23	50	65	55
16	Chester City	46	13	15	18	43	55	54
17	Swansea City	46	14	12	20	45	63	54
18	Wigan Athletic	46	13	14	19	48	64	53
19	PRESTON	46	14	10	22	65	79	52
20	Fulham	46	12	15	19	55	66	51
21	Cardiff City	46	12	14	20	51	70	50
22	Northampton Town	46	11	14	21	51	68	47
23	Blackpool	46	10	16	20	49	73	46
24	Walsall	46	9	14	23	40	72	41

Gary Swann

271

Alex James

George Mutch

Tom Finney

Willie Cunningham

Charlie Wayman

Tommy Thompson

Alan Kelly

Alex Dawson

Alex Bruce

Nobby Lawton

John Thomas

SIR TOM FINNEY
The Pride of Preston

No. 2

BILL SHANKLY

SEASON 1990–1991

Ian Bogie on the attack with Steve Senior in attendance.

from the youth sides, Lee Ashcroft and Lee Cartwright, both acquitted themselves with confidence. After the turn of the year Preston again struggled and it was not until mid-February when they thrashed Burnley 6–1 in the Leyland Daf semi-final cup-tie that they showed signs of an improvement. In the resultant Northern final though, Preston's interest virtually ended after a 4–0 first leg defeat at Tranmere. The league results were better after that as manager Les Chapman changed things around. The away form still left much to be desired and North End were beginning to have a complex about life away from Deepdale. The goalscoring was also limited with only Graham Shaw looking a likely scorer at times. Ronnie Jepson put himself about well and never gave less than 100% in effort, but he probably lacked the finesse that would possibly have suited the team better. Chapman even tried playing with two wingers with Steve Harper and Dave Thompson filling the roles in the latter part of the campaign. Flynn and Wrightson continued to shine in defence and Flynn's long throw was a great attacking weapon. As in many other seasons Preston did well on an individual basis, but as a unit there was often something lacking. It was difficult to put your finger on the problem. In the end the final position of 17th was probably all that the club could have hoped for.

Eighteen goals were conceded in the first six games so it was a baptism of fire for new signings Steve Senior and Simon Farnworth. But eventually things settled down and the recovery began after a 2–1 win at Bolton in mid-September. The defence tightened up and it did become harder to beat Preston, although it was by no means impossible. In fact, too many games were still being lost by the time the FA Cup came round. They had already gone out of the League Cup, sponsored for the first time by Rumbelows, and North End then went out of the FA Cup after a dismal 1–0 home defeat by Mansfield. Only the Leyland Daf competition offered the fans some cheer although it was not until the Northern semi-final of that tournament that the crowd turned out in force. Meanwhile, in the league, Preston found it hard to sustain their better form. Brian Mooney and Ian Bogie showed great skills on the ball in midfield and Gary Swann continued his knack of scoring several important goals. In defence Mike Flynn, Jeff Wrightson and Senior all did well and two youngsters bloodied

DEBUTANTS: (15) Simon Farnworth, Steve Senior, Steven Greaves, Nathan Peel, Martin James, Greg Fee, Lee Ashcroft, Graham Easter, David Thompson, Ronnie Jepson, David Eaves, Lee Cartwright, Matt Lambert, Jason Kerfoot, Matt Jackson.

LAST GAMES: (9) Rathbone, Mooney, Bogie, Harper, Greaves, Peel, Fee, Easter, Jackson.

Trivia Facts:

A video was released about Tom Finney entitled *Tom Finney – The Perfect Player*. It was presented by Jimmy Hill and contributors included Jimmy Armfield, Billy Wright, Tommy Docherty, Nat Lofthouse and Sir Stanley Matthews. Alas, the actual film footage shown was poor and it makes you realise how little film exists of the great man in action.

John Thomas broke his right leg in two places at Bolton as he began the season in the worst possible way. It was the 8th broken leg to hit North End in just 3 years. A few weeks later it was 9 as junior player Gary McCullough broke his leg and then Neil Williams became the 10th victim.

Andy McAteer announced his retirement from the game due to a series of niggly injuries. He decided to concentrate on a career in insurance. Meanwhile, PNE staged a Boxing Night at the Blackburn Moat House.

League position in Division Three: 17th – P46 W15 D11 L20 F54 A67 Pts 56
Home: W11 D5 L7 F33 A29   Away: W4 D6 L13 F21 A38

Left to right: *Back row:*
J. Wrightson, R. Atkins,
A. Hughes, R. Tunks,
A. Kelly, S. Farnworth,
T. Hancock, M. Flynn.
Middle row: W. Joyce,
S. McIlroy, G. Swann,
M. James, N. Greenwood,
N. Williams, M. Rathbone,
Les Chapman (Manager).
Front row: G. Shaw,
J. Thomas, S. Harper,
S. Senior, W. Joyce, I. Bogie,
D. Thompson, S. Anderton.

Ever presents: None
Players used: 29
FA Cup: First Round
Rumbelows Cup: First
Round – Also reached
Northern Final of Leyland
Daf Cup
Manager: Les Chapman
Leading scorer: 15 goals –
Graham Shaw
(10 League 1RC 4 LDC)
Chairman: K. W. Leeming Esq.
Hat-tricks: (1) Ronnie Jepson

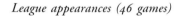

OFFICIAL PLAYER OF THE SEASON: Jeff Wrightson

League appearances (46 games)

Ashcroft L. 6 + 8, Bogie I. 28 + 3, Cartwright L. 13 + 1,
Easter G. P. 1, Eaves D. M. C. 1 + 2, Farnworth S. 23,
Fee G. P. 15, Flynn M. A. 33 + 2, Greaves S. R. 2,
Greenwood N. P. 3 + 2, Harper S. J. 27 + 9,
Hughes A. F. S. 25 + 1, Jackson M. A. 3 + 1, James M. J. 34
+ 3, Jepson R. F. 13 + 1, Joyce W. G. 42, Kelly A. T. 23,
Kerfoot J. J. T. 0 + 1, Lambert M. R. 4 + 1, Mooney B. J. 9,
Peel N. J. 1 + 9, Rathbone M. J. 11 + 2, Senior S. 38,
Shaw G. P. 44, Swann G. 30, Thomas J. W. 5, Thompson
D. S. 21, Williams N. J. F. 11 + 2, Wrightson J. G. 40.

FA Cup appearances (1 game)

Kelly, Senior, Rathbone, Hughes, Flynn, Wrightson,
Swann, Bogie, Greenwood, Shaw and Joyce 1 each and
Harper 0 + 1, Easter 0 + 1.

Match Report: Stalemate at the Junction – 26 December 1990 Crewe 2 Preston 2

When the North End kit was unpacked at Crewe the players found half of it missing and as a result they had to borrow a set of shirts from Crewe. The game was an exciting one and totally absorbing, not even the sending off of Adrian Hughes could dampen the spirits of the travelling fans. Playing into a strong win Preston forced the early pace and they took a deserved lead after only six minutes. Mooney broke down the right and his cross was touched on by Shaw to enable Bogie to shoot into the unguarded net. Preston continued to press forward impressively and the army of fans were delighted with their form. But then, right out of the blue, Crewe scored a stunning equaliser on 17 minutes. When Gardiner gained possession some 30 yards out following a corner there seemed little danger, but he hit a left foot shot as clean as a whistle and the ball flew past Kelly's despairing dive. Play continued to flow from end to end and both sides had chances but on 30 minutes Preston were dealt a cruel blow. Clayton and Hughes tangled for possession and Clayton eventually went down just outside the penalty area. The referee deemed it a professional foul by Hughes and he promptly sent the youngster off. North End continued to show great spirit and Joyce almost scored after a brilliant right wing move. Inside two minutes of the second half Preston were ahead again. An inswinging corner by Bogie bounced off the crossbar and Shaw bundled it in at the far post. The ten men could have gone further ahead as several chances went begging. In the end, as legs began to tire, North End were punished for those misses. Murphy scored after a pass was laid back to him by Sussex and Crewe were level again. It was only fair that such a positive performance gave Preston a point.

Rumbelows Cup appearances (2 games)

Farnworth 2, Senior 2, Williams 2, Bogie 2, Hughes 0 + 1, Thomas 2, Flynn 2, Joyce 2, James 2, Swann 2, Wrightson 2, Harper 0 + 1,
Shaw 1, Peel 1.

Leyland Daf Cup appearances (7 games)

Farnworth 4, Kelly 3, Senior 5, Bogie 1 + 1, Fee 2, Hughes 4, Ashcroft 1 + 2, Eaves 0 + 1, Flynn 6, Rathbone 3, Joyce 6, James 5, Swann 6,
Cartwright 2, Jackson 1, Wrightson 6, Greenwood 1 + 1, Jepson 3, Harper 4 + 1, Shaw 7, Easter 1 + 1, Peel 1 + 1, Mooney 2, Thompson 3.

Goalscorers: 54 League–3 LC–17 LDC–(74)

Shaw 10–1–4 (1 pen) (15), Joyce 9 (1pen)–0–3 (12), Swann 5–2–2 (9), Bogie 8 (1 pen)–0–0 (8), Jepson 3–0–4 (7), Mooney 2–0–2 (4),
Wrightson 3–0–0 (3), Senior 2–0–0 (2), James 2–0–0 (2), Ashcroft 1–0–1 (2), Thompson 2–0–0 (2), Rathbone 1–0–0 (1), Hughes 1–0–0 (1),
Flynn 1–0–0 (1), Peel 1–0–0 (1), Cartwright 1–0–0 (1), Thomas 1(pen)–0–0 (1), Greenwood 1–0–0 (1), Harper 0–0–1 (1).

Trivia Facts:

North End's youth side reached the final of the Lancashire FA Professional Youth Cup Final for the second year running.

When Wigan entertained North End in a reserve fixture Sammy McIlroy Senior played for Preston whilst Sammy McIlroy Junior, his son, played for Wigan.

Season 1990–91: Third Division

		P	W	D	L	F	A	Pts
1	Cambridge United	46	25	11	10	75	45	86
2	Southend United	46	26	7	13	77	51	85
3	Grimsby Town	46	24	11	11	66	44	83
4	Bolton Wanders	46	24	11	11	64	50	83
5	Tranmere Rovers	46	23	9	14	64	46	78
6	Brentford	46	21	13	12	59	47	76
7	Bury	46	20	13	13	67	56	73
8	Bradford City	46	20	10	16	62	54	70
9	Bournemouth	46	19	13	14	58	58	70
10	Wigan Athletic	46	20	9	17	71	54	69
11	Huddersfield Town	46	18	13	15	57	51	67
12	Birmingham City	46	16	17	13	45	49	65
13	Leyton Orient	46	18	10	18	55	58	64
14	Stoke City	46	16	12	18	55	59	60
15	Reading	46	17	8	21	53	66	59
16	Exeter City	46	16	9	21	58	52	57
17	**PRESTON**	**46**	**15**	**11**	**20**	**54**	**67**	**56**
18	Shrewsbury Town	46	14	10	22	61	68	52
19	Chester City	46	14	9	23	46	58	51
20	Swansea City	46	13	9	24	49	72	48
21	Fulham	46	10	16	20	41	56	46
22	Crewe Alexandra	46	11	11	24	62	80	44
23	Rotherham United	46	10	12	24	50	87	87
24	Mansfield Town	46	8	14	24	42	63	38

Date 1990-1	Opponents	Comp	h or a	Score * aet	Att.	1	2	3	4	5	6	7	8	9	10	11	12	14
Aug 25	Grimsby Town	Div 3	h	1-3	6372	Farnworth	Senior	Swann	Greaves	Flynn	Wrightson	Williams	Joyce (1)	Thomas	Shaw	Harper *	Atkins	Peel *
Aug 28	Chester C. Rd 1 1L	RC	h	2-0	3503	Farnworth	Senior	Swann (1)	Bogie	Flynn	Wrightson	Williams	Joyce	Thomas	Shaw (1)	James	Peel	Hughes
Sep 1	Reading	Div 3	a	3-3	4228	Farnworth	Senior (1)	Swann	Bogie	Flynn	Wrightson	Williams *	Peel (1) +	Thomas	Joyce (1)	James	Harper *	Hughes +
Sep 4	Chester C. Rd 1 2L	RC	a	1-5 *	1009	Farnworth	Senior *	Swann (1)	Bogie	Flynn	Wrightson	Williams	Peel +	Thomas	Joyce	James	Harper *	Hughes +
Sep 8	Tranmere R.	Div 3	a	0-4	5648	Farnworth	Senior	Swann	Bogie	Hughes	Wrightson	Williams	Harper *	Thomas	Joyce	James	Peel *	Greaves
Sep 14	Southend Utd.	Div 3	a	2-3	4614	Kelly	Senior *	Williams	Fee	Hughes	Wrightson	Bogie	Swann	Thomas (1p)	Shaw	Joyce (1)	James *	Harper
Sep 18	Bolton W.	Div 3	a	2-1	5844	Farnworth	Williams	James (1)	Fee	Hughes	Wrightson	Joyce	Bogie (1p)	Thomas *	Shaw	Swann	Harper *	Rathbone
Sep 22	Fulham	Div 3	h	1-0	4691	Farnworth	Williams	Rathbone	Fee	Hughes (1)	Wrightson	Joyce	Bogie	Shaw	Swann	James	Harper	Greenwood
Sep 29	Birmingham City	Div 3	h	1-1	7154	Farnworth	Senior	James	Fee	Hughes *	Wrightson	Williams	Bogie (1)	Shaw	Joyce	Swann	Rathbone *	Harper
Oct 2	Brentford	Div 3	h	1-1	5025	Farnworth	Senior	James	Fee	Hughes	Wrightson	Williams *	Bogie	Shaw	Joyce	Swann (1)	Harper *	Rathbone
Oct 6	Exeter City	Div 3	h	1-0	4716	Farnworth	Senior	Rathbone	Fee	Hughes	Wrightson	James	Bogie (1)	Shaw	Joyce	Swann	Williams	Greenwood
Oct 13	Mansfield Town	Div 3	h	1-0	3225	Farnworth	Senior	Rathbone (1)	Fee	Hughes *	Wrightson	James	Bogie	Shaw	Joyce	Swann	Williams * +	Harper +
Oct 20	Rotherham Utd.	Div 3	a	0-1	4599	Farnworth	Senior	James	Fee	Hughes	Wrightson	Harper +	Bogie	Shaw	Joyce	Swann	Greenwood	Flynn +
Oct 23	Chester City	Div 3	h	0-0	5465	Farnworth	Greaves	James	Fee	Flynn	Wrightson	Shaw	Bogie	Hughes *	Joyce	Swann	Greenwood *	Kerfoot
Oct 27	Bournemouth	Div 3	a	0-0	4953	Farnworth	Flynn	James	Fee	Hughes	Wrightson	Shaw	Bogie	Greenwood	Joyce	Swann	Greaves	McCullough
Nov 3	Wigan Ath.	Div 3	a	1-2	4728	Farnworth	Senior	James	Flynn	Hughes +	Wrightson	Shaw	Bogie *	Greenwood (1)	Joyce	Swann	Rathbone *	Peel +
Nov 6	Carlisle Utd.	LDC	a	1-1	1826	Farnworth +	Senior	Rathbone	Joyce	Hughes	Wrightson	James *	Flynn	Greenwood	Shaw (1p)	Swann	Easter *	Peel +
Nov 10	Bradford City	Div 3	a	1-2	7440	Kelly	Senior	Rathbone	Hughes *	Flynn	Wrightson	Swann +	Bogie (1)	Greenwood	Shaw	Joyce	James *	Harper +
Nov 17	**Mansfield Town Rd 1**	FAC	h	0-1	5230	Kelly	Senior	Rathbone	Hughes	Flynn *	Wrightson	Swann +	Bogie	Greenwood	Shaw	Joyce	Harper *	Easter +
Nov 24	Huddersfield T.	Div 3	a	1-2	5844	Kelly	Senior	Rathbone	Joyce (1)	Hughes	Wrightson	Harper +	Bogie	Shaw	Swann	James	Flynn	Peel +
Nov 27	**Rochdale**	LDC	h	3-1	1951	Kelly	Senior	Rathbone	Joyce (2)	Hughes	Wrightson	Harper (1)	Bogie	Shaw	Swann	Easter	Flynn	James
Dec 1	Shrewsbury T.	Div 3	h	4-3	4515	Kelly	Senior	Rathbone	Joyce	Hughes	Wrightson (1)	Mooney	Bogie (2)	Shaw	Swann (1)	Harper	Flynn	Easter
Dec 15	Leyton Orient	Div 3	a	0-1	3287	Kelly	Senior	Rathbone +	Joyce	Hughes	Wrightson	Mooney *	Bogie	Shaw	Swann	Harper	Flynn *	Williams +
Dec 22	Stoke City	Div 3	h	2-0	7532	Kelly	Senior	Williams	Flynn	Hughes	Wrightson	Mooney	Bogie	Joyce	Shaw	Swann (2)	Harper	Peel
Dec 26	Crewe A.	Div 3	a	2-2	4405	Kelly	Senior	Williams	Flynn	Hughes	Wrightson	Mooney	Bogie (1)	Joyce	Shaw (1)	Swann	Harper	Peel
Dec 29	Bury	Div 3	a	1-3	5404	Kelly	Senior	Williams +	Flynn	Hughes *	Wrightson	Mooney (1)	Bogie	Joyce	Shaw	Swann	Harper *	Peel +
Jan 1	Cambridge Utd.	Div 3	h	0-2	5256	Kelly	Senior	Rathbone	Flynn	Hughes *	Wrightson	Mooney	Bogie +	Joyce	Shaw	Swann	Harper *	Peel +
Jan 8	**Darlington**	LDC	h	2-1 *	2418	Kelly	Senior	Rathbone	Flynn	Fee	Wrightson +	Mooney	Peel	Joyce (1)	Shaw	Swann (1)	Greenwood *	Harper +
Jan 12	Reading	Div 3	a	1-2	4470	Kelly	Senior	Rathbone	Flynn	Fee	Wrightson *	Mooney	Easter	Joyce	Shaw +	Swann (1)	Greenwood *	Harper +
Jan 19	Grimsby Town	Div 3	a	1-4	5391	Kelly	Senior	Rathbone	Fee	Flynn	Wrightson	Mooney (1)	Harper	Joyce	Shaw	Swann	Greenwood	James
Jan 26	Southend Utd.	Div 3	h	2-1	4351	Kelly	Rathbone	James	Fee	Flynn	Wrightson (1)	Mooney	Harper	Joyce	Shaw (1)	Swann	Peel	Ashcroft
Jan 29	**Scunthorpe Utd.**	LDC	a	4-1	2155	Farnworth	Joyce	James	Fee	Flynn	Wrightson	Mooney (2)	Harper	Ashcroft	Shaw (1)	Swann (1)	Lambert	Peel
Feb 2	Bolton W.	Div 3	h	1-2	9844	Farnworth	Joyce	James	Fee	Flynn	Wrightson (1)	Thompson *	Harper	Ashcroft	Shaw	Swann	Peel *	Lambert
Feb 5	Fulham	Div 3	a	0-1	2750	Farnworth	Joyce	James	Fee	Flynn	Wrightson	Thompson	Harper +	Ashcroft	Shaw	Swann	Senior	Peel +
Feb 16	Huddersfield T.	Div 3	h	0-1	5504	Farnworth	Senior	Joyce	Hughes	Flynn	Wrightson	Thompson +	Harper *	Jepson	Shaw	Swann	Peel *	James +
Feb 19	**Burnley**	LDC	h	6-1	12016	Farnworth	James	Joyce *	Hughes	Flynn	Wrightson	Thompson	Harper	Jepson (3) +	Shaw (2)	Swann	Easter *	Ashcroft + (1)
Feb 23	Bradford City	Div 3	h	0-3	6878	Farnworth	James	Joyce	Hughes	Flynn	Wrightson	Thompson	Harper *	Jepson	Shaw	Swann	Ashcroft *	Lambert
Mar 2	Shrewsbury T.	Div 3	a	1-0	2989	Farnworth	Senior	James	Hughes	Flynn	Wrightson	Thompson	Cartwright	Jepson	Shaw (1)	Swann	Ashcroft	Lambert
Mar 5	**Tranmere R.**	LDC	a	0-4	8633	Farnworth	Senior	James	Hughes	Flynn	Wrightson	Thompson	Cartwright	Jepson	Shaw	Swann *	Ashcroft *	Lambert
Mar 9	Leyton Orient	Div 3	h	2-1	3651	Farnworth	Senior	James	Hughes	Flynn	Wrightson	Thompson (1)	Cartwright	Jepson *	Shaw (1)	Ashcroft	Harper *	Lambert
Mar 12	Brentford	Div 3	a	0-2	4856	Farnworth	Senior	Lambert +	James	Flynn	Hughes *	Thompson	Cartwright	Eaves	Shaw	Harper	Kerfoot *	Ashcroft +
Mar 16	Birmingham City	Div 3	a	2-0	5334	Farnworth	Senior	James	Joyce (1)	Flynn	Wrightson	Thompson	Cartwright (1)	Jepson	Shaw	Harper	Ashcroft	Lambert
Mar 19	Mansfield Town	Div 3	h	3-1	3245	Farnworth	Senior	James	Joyce (1p)	Flynn	Wrightson	Thompson	Cartwright	Jepson (2)	Shaw	Harper	Ashcroft	Eaves
Mar 23	Exeter City	Div 3	a	0-4	3525	Farnworth	Senior	James	Joyce	Flynn	Wrightson	Thompson +	Bogie +	Jepson	Shaw	Harper	Ashcroft *	Eaves +
Mar 26	Swansea City	Div 3	a	2-0	3491	Kelly	Senior	James	Joyce	Flynn	Wrightson	Thompson	Bogie	Jepson	Shaw (2)	Harper	Cartwright	Eaves
Mar 30	Crewe A.	Div 3	h	5-1	4852	Kelly	Senior	James (1)	Joyce (1)	Flynn	Wrightson *	Thompson (1)	Bogie (1)	Jepson	Shaw (1) +	Harper	Jackson *	Cartwright +
Apr 1	Stoke City	Div 3	a	1-0	11524	Kelly	Senior	James	Joyce	Flynn	Wrightson	Thompson +	Bogie	Cartwright	Shaw (1)	Harper	Jackson	Ashcroft +
Apr 6	Bury	Div 3	h	1-1	5641	Kelly	Senior	James	Joyce	Jackson	Wrightson	Thompson	Bogie	Cartwright	Shaw (1)	Harper	Ashcroft	Eaves
Apr 9	**Tranmere R.**	LDC	h	1-0	5763	Kelly	Senior	James	Joyce	Jackson	Flynn	Thompson *	Cartwright	Jepson (1)	Shaw	Harper	Bogie *	Wrightson
Apr 13	Cambridge Utd.	Div 3	a	1-2	6262	Kelly	Senior	James	Joyce (1)	Flynn	Jackson	Thompson	Cartwright	Jepson	Shaw	Harper	Bogie	Lambert
Apr 16	Swansea City	Div 3	h	1-3	2507	Kelly	Senior (1)	James	Joyce	Jackson +	Flynn	Thompson	Cartwright *	Jepson	Shaw	Harper	Bogie *	Lambert +
Apr 20	Rotherham Utd.	Div 3	a	1-2	4069	Kelly	Senior	James	Joyce	Wrightson	Flynn (1)	Thompson	Bogie	Jepson	Shaw +	Harper	Cartwright	Ashcroft +
Apr 27	Chester City	Div 3	a	1-1	1351	Kelly	Senior	James	Joyce (1)	Wrightson	Jackson	Thompson +	Cartwright	Jepson	Shaw *	Harper	Bogie *	Ashcroft +
May 2	Bournemouth	Div 3	a	0-0	7064	Kelly	Senior	James	Joyce	Flynn	Lambert	Thompson	Cartwright	Ashcroft	Shaw	Harper	Peel	Moylon
May 7	Tranmere R.	Div 3	h	1-2	6006	Kelly	Senior	James	Joyce	Flynn	Lambert	Thompson	Cartwright	Ashcroft (1) *	Shaw +	Harper	Peel *	Bogie +
May 11	Wigan Ath.	Div 3	h	2-1	5917	Kelly	Senior	James	Cartwright	Flynn	Lambert	Thompson	Bogie *	Ashcroft +	Shaw (1)	Harper	Eaves *	Jepson + (1)

278

SEASON 1991-1992

There was a mixed bag of results to open the new campaign with Preston starting their league matches with a defeat at Peterborough. This had come after a good pre-season build up but was to be indicative of the away form which followed. North End could do little right away from Deepdale and they even lost at lowly Scarborough in the Rumbelows Cup. As Preston improved Mike Flynn and Gary Swann looked good and Warren Joyce was playing well until injuries began to hamper his season. The good form at home kept Preston's head above water and later on some exciting cup-ties in both the Autoglass Trophy and the FA Cup gave the fans something to cheer. However, there was some unrest amongst the Preston faithful as they protested against the Board's apparent lack of ambition. The selling on of Ian Bogie and Brian Mooney had particularly angered the fans as once again they saw quality players moving out of Deepdale. Attendances were poor, which was slightly unfair on manager Les Chapman who was working so hard to try to find the right blend. Jeff Wrightson continued to show the form of the previous

year and Lee Ashcroft was a lively raider. Another Lee, Cartwright this time, also showed great promise and loan players, Julian James, Paul Cross and Tim Allpress all did well in their spells with the club. Unfortunately ten days in January saw Preston go out of both remaining cup competitions and over the latter months of the season results went up an down like a yo-yo. Again it was difficult to fault the players individually but the team was capable of going from a great win to an awful defeat in the space of three days as they did in early March, and it was all very frustrating for Chapman. Relegation was certainly a distinct possibility as Preston entered April, but in the end, after a good deal of effort, a win over Birmingham at Deepdale ensured their Third Division survival for another year. Man of the match, Flynn scored one goal and certainly played a big part in a 3–2 win, as he had done all season. Warren Joyce and Graham Shaw also scored and they could both be pleased with their contributions through the year. The signing of Colin Greenall also proved a telling factor as it added some much needed stability to a previously shaky back line. At the last home game, against relegated Bury, the fans expressed their anger at the struggle the club had endured. At the same time the manager announced a clear out of players and made a promise of better things to come. Only time would tell.

DEBUTANTS: (10) George Berry, Julian James, Paul Cross, Tim Allpress, Gareth Ainsworth, Stephen Finney, Neil Whitworth, Lennie Johnrose, Colin Greenall, David Christie.

LAST GAMES: (20) Greenwood, Thomas, Kelly, Swann, Wrightson, Joyce, Hughes, Williams N., Shaw, Senior, Thompson D., Jepson, Lambert, Kerfoot, Berry, James J., Cross, Allpress, Whitworth, Johnrose.

Ever presents: None   **Hat-tricks**: None
Players used: 29   **FA Cup**: Third Round
Manager: Les Chapman
Rumbelows Cup: First Round – Also competed in the Autoglass Trophy
Chairman: K. W. Leeming Esq.
Leading scorer: 17 goals – Graham Shaw (14 League 2 FAC 1 RC)

OFFICIAL PLAYER OF THE SEASON:
Lee Cartwright

Warren Joyce.
Influential midfield player.

League position in Division Three: 17th – P46 W15 D12 L19 F61 A72 Pts 57
Home: W12 D7 L4 F42 A32 Away: W3 D5 L15 F19 A40

Match Report: Brum's Run Undone by North End – 21 Apr 1992 Preston 3 Birmingham 2

In the previous few weeks prior to this game North End had put their fans through agony as the club tried to avoid relegation. In this match they had to suffer all the emotions again before Preston finally won the right to stay up. A goal after just 94 seconds gave the home side the perfect start as Thompson's free-kick found the head of Flynn at the far post. He layed the ball back, Cartwright shot and the ball was deflected home by Joyce. League leaders Birmingham then went two down on 33 minutes as Flynn scored following a Shaw corner. The half-time cup of tea was thoroughly enjoyed by the Preston players but some of them were still thinking about it when the visitors immediately struck back after the restart. Sturridge mis-hit his shot but the ball ran kindly for Gleghorn to fire home. However, good work by Jepson gave Thompson possession and from his chip forward Shaw dribbled round the keeper to make it 3–1. With only 35 minutes left it looked all over but the goal signalled an all out assault by Birmingham and the home fans had to bite their nails. Farnworth pulled off a marvellous save to foil a Rennie header but then the goalkeeper completely messed up a clearance and Rennie was able to pull another goal back. The frantic last 12 minutes were agony for the Preston supporters as Birmingham searched desperately for an equaliser. Eventually though the referee put North End out of their misery and his final whistle brought a huge sigh of relief around the ground. The win was their's and relegation had been staved off again.

League appearances (46 games)

Ainsworth G. 2 + 3, Allpress T.J. 7 + 2, Ashcroft L. 35 + 3, Berry G.F. 4, Cartwright L. 31 + 2, Christie D. 0 + 2, Cross P. 5, Farnworth S. 23, Finney S.K. 0 + 2, Flynn M.A. 43, Greenall C.A. 9, Greenwood N.P. 16 + 4, Hughes A.F.S. 14 + 1, James J.C. 6, James M.J. 36, Jepson R.F. 23 + 1, Johnrose L. 1 + 2, Joyce W.G. 28 + 1, Kelly A.T. 23, Kerfoot J.J.T. 0 + 3, Lambert M.R. 7 + 4, Senior S. 35, Shaw G.P. 45 + 1, Swann G. 28 + 1, Thomas J.W. 8 + 3, Thompson D.S. 18 + 7, Whitworth N.A. 6, Williams N.J.F. 17 + 9, Wrightson J.G. 36 + 1.

FA Cup appearances (3 games)

Farnworth 1, Kelly 2, Senior 3, Swann 3, James M. 2, Wrightson 3, Flynn 3, Joyce 1, Hughes 1, Cartwright 3, Allpress 2, Greenwood 0 + 1, Ashcroft 3, Thomas 3, Shaw 3, Kerfoot 0 + 1.

Rumbelows Cup appearances (2 games)

Farnworth 2, Senior 2, Williams 1, Swann 2, James M. 2, Berry 1 + 1, Wrightson 2, Flynn 2, Joyce 2, Thompson 1 + 1, Ashcroft 1, Jepson 2, Shaw 2.

Autoglass Trophy Appearances (3 games)

Farnworth 1, Kelly 2, Senior 3, Swann 3, James M. 2, Wrightson 3, Cross 1, Lambert 0 + 1, Flynn 3, Joyce 2, Hughes 1, Cartwright 1, Allpress 1, Thompson 0 + 1, Ashcroft 3, Thomas 3, Shaw 3, Ainsworth 1, Finney 0 + 1.

Goalscorers: 61 League–7 FAC–6 RC–5 AT–(Total 79)

Shaw 14–2–1–0 (17), Joyce 6–0–2–2 (10), Swann 5–1–2–0 (8), Greenwood 3–1–0–0 (4) Ashcroft 5–0–0–0 (5), Jepson 5–0–0–0 (5), James M. 4–0–0–0 (4), Flynn 3–1–0–0 (4), Thomas 2–1–0–2 (5), Cartwright 3–0–0–0 (3), Lambert 2–0–0–0 (2), Thompson 2–0–0–0 (2), Senior 1–1–0–0 (2), Wrightson 1–0–1–0 (2), Johnrose 1–0–0–0 (1), Greenall 1–0–0–0 (1), Finney 1–0–0–0 (1), Williams 1–0–0–0 (1), Ainsworth 0–0–0–1 (1) Own Goals 1–0–0–0 (1), (Howard of L. Orient).

STAT FACTS:
Best home run without defeat: 8 games
Best away run without defeat: 2 games
Longest run unbeaten: 6 games
Longest run without a win: 7 games
Best home attendance: 14,337 *vs.* Sheff Wed. FAC 4.1.92
Worst home attendance: 2,152 *vs.* Hull AT 14.1.92
Best away attendance: 16,151 *vs.* Stoke 18.4.92
Worst away attendance: 1,219 *vs.* Chester 2.11.91
Aggregate and average home attendance: 108,759 – 4,729
Aggregate and average away attendance: 119,481 – 5,195

Season 1991–92: Third Division

		P	W	D	L	F	A	Pts
1	Brentford	46	25	7	14	81	55	82
2	Birmingham City	46	23	12	11	69	52	81
3	Huddesfield Town	46	22	12	12	59	38	78
4	Stoke City	46	21	14	11	69	49	77
5	Stockport County	46	22	10	14	75	51	76
6	Peterborough United	46	20	14	12	65	58	74
7	WBA	46	19	14	13	64	49	71
8	Bournemouth	46	20	11	15	52	48	71
9	Fulham	46	19	13	14	57	53	70
10	Leyton Orient	46	18	11	17	62	52	65
11	Hartlepool United	46	18	11	17	57	57	65
12	Reading	46	16	13	17	59	62	61
13	Bolton Wanderers	46	14	17	15	57	56	59
14	Hull City	46	16	11	19	54	54	59
15	Wigan Athletic	46	15	14	17	58	64	59
16	Bradford City	46	13	19	14	62	61	58
17	PRESTON	46	15	12	19	61	72	57
18	Chester City	46	14	14	18	56	59	56
19	Swansea City	46	14	14	18	55	65	56
20	Exeter City	46	14	11	21	57	80	53
21	Bury	46	13	12	21	55	74	51
22	Shrewsbury Town	46	12	11	23	53	68	47
23	Torquay United	46	13	8	25	42	68	47
24	Darlington	46	10	7	29	56	90	37

Jeff Wrightson

Graham Shaw

Steve Senior

Date 1991-2	Opponents	Comp	h or a	Score *aet	Att.	1	2	3	4	5	6	7	8	9	10	11	12	14
Aug 17	Peterborough Utd.	Div 3	a	0-1	6036	Farnworth	Senior	Swann	Wrightson	Flynn	Berry	Thompson	Joyce	Jepson	Shaw	M. James	Williams	Lambert
Aug 20	Scarborough Rd1 1L	RC	h	5-4	2683	Farnworth	Senior	Swann (2)	Wrightson (1)	Flynn	Berry	Thompson	Joyce (1p)	Jepson	Shaw (1)	M. James	Ashcroft	Lambert
Aug 24	Torquay Utd.	Div 3	a	3-0	3654	Farnworth	Senior	M. James	Swann	Flynn	Wrightson	Williams	Joyce	Jepson *	Shaw (1)	Ashcroft (1)	Greenwood * (1)	Lambert
Aug 28	Scarborough Rd1 2L	RC	a	1-3 *	2035	Farnworth	Senior *	M. James	Swann	Flynn	Wrightson	Williams +	Joyce (1)	Jepson	Shaw	Ashcroft	Thompson *	Berry +
Aug 30	Stockport Co.	Div 3	a	0-2	5405	Farnworth	Senior	M. James	Lambert +	Flynn	Wrightson	Berry	Swann *	Jepson	Shaw	Greenwood	Williams *	Ashcroft +
Sep 3	Bournemouth	Div 3	h	2-2	3170	Kelly	Senior	Berry	Joyce	Flynn	Wrightson	Thompson *	Swann	Jepson	Shaw	M. James (1)	Williams	Greenwood * (1)
Sep 7	Bradford City	Div 3	h	1-1	4160	Kelly	Senior	Wrightson	Swann	Flynn	Berry *	Greenwood	Joyce (1p)	Jepson	Shaw	M. James	Ashcroft	Kerfoot
Sep 14	Swansea City	Div 3	a	2-2	3170	Kelly	Senior	Wrightson	Swann	Flynn	J. James	Greenwood	Cartwright *	Jepson	Shaw (2)	M. James	Thompson *	Kerfoot
Sep 17	Leyton Orient	Div 3	a	0-0	3296	Kelly	Senior	M. James	J. James	Flynn	Wrightson	Greenwood *	Joyce	Jepson	Shaw +	Swann	Thompson *	Cartwright *
Sep 21	Stoke City	Div 3	h	2-2	6345	Kelly	Senior	Wrightson	Swann (1)	Flynn	J. James	Greenwood *	Joyce	Jepson (1)	Shaw	M. James	Thompson *	Cartwright
Sep 28	Birmingham City	Div 3	a	1-3	8760	Kelly	Senior	Cross	Swann	Flynn	J. James	Wrightson	Joyce	Jepson	Shaw (1) *	M. James	Cartwright	Thomas *
Oct 1	WBA	Div 3	h	2-0	5293	Kelly	Senior (1)	Cross	Swann (1)	Flynn	J. James	Wrightson	Joyce	Greenwood	Shaw	M. James	Thomas	Cartwright
Oct 12	Bury	Div 3	a	3-2	4265	Kelly	Senior *	Cross +	Swann	Flynn	J. James	Wrightson	Joyce	Greenwood (1)	Shaw (1)	Ashcroft (1)	Williams	Thompson +
Oct 19	Huddersfield T.	Div 3	h	1-0	6866	Kelly	Senior	Cross	Swann	Flynn	Wrightson	Ashcroft	Joyce	Greenwood (1)	Shaw	M. James (1)	Williams	Thompson *
Oct 22	Rochdale	AT	a	1-1	1255	Kelly	Senior	Cross	Swann	Flynn	Wrightson	Ashcroft	Joyce (1)	Thomas	Shaw	M. James *	Williams	Thompson *
Oct 26	Fulham	Div 3	a	0-1	4022	Kelly	Senior	Cross *	Swann	Flynn	Wrightson	Ashcroft	Joyce	Thomas +	Shaw	Cartwright	Williams *	Thompson +
Nov 2	Chester City	Div 3	a	2-3	1219	Kelly	Senior *	Wrightson	Swann (1)	Flynn	Allpress	Ashcroft	Joyce	Thompson	Shaw	M. James +	Williams *	Cartwright +
Nov 5	Wigan Ath.	Div 3	h	3-0	3657	Kelly	Williams	Wrightson	Swann (1)	Flynn	Allpress	Ashcroft	Joyce (2,1p)	Thompson	Shaw	M. James	Thomas	Cartwright
Nov 9	Darlington	Div 3	h	2-1	4643	Kelly	Senior	Wrightson	Swann +	Flynn	Allpress	Ashcroft	Joyce	Thompson *	Shaw (1)	M. James	Williams	Thomas + (1)
Nov 19	Bolton W.	AT	h	2-1	2709	Kelly	Senior	Wrightson	Swann	Flynn	Allpress	Ashcroft	Joyce (1)	Thomas (1)	Shaw	M. James	Williams	Cartwright
Nov 23	Bolton W.	Div 3	a	0-1	7033	Kelly	Senior	Wrightson *	Swann	Flynn	Allpress	Ashcroft	Joyce +	Thomas	Shaw	M. James	Williams	Greenwood +
Nov 27	Mansfield T. Rd 1	FAC	h	1-0	7509	Kelly	Senior	Wrightson	Swann	Flynn	Allpress	Ashcroft	Cartwright	Thomas (1)	Shaw	M. James	Williams	Greenwood
Nov 30	Hull City	Div 3	h	2-2	4280	Kelly	Senior	Wrightson	Swann	Flynn	Allpress	Ashcroft	Cartwright	Thomas (1) *	Shaw (1)	M. James	Greenwood *	Hughes
Dec 7	Witton Albion Rd 2	FAC	h	5-1	6736	Kelly	Senior (1)	Wrightson	Swann (1)	Flynn (1)	Allpress	Ashcroft	Cartwright	Thomas	Shaw (1)	M. James	Greenwood * (1)	Lambert
Dec 14	Hartlepool Utd.	Div 3	h	1-4	5032	Kelly	Senior	Wrightson	Swann	Flynn	Allpress +	Ashcroft (1)	Cartwright	Thomas	Shaw	Greenwood *	Hughes *	Lambert +
Dec 20	Torquay Utd.	Div 3	a	0-1	2183	Kelly	Senior	Wrightson	Hughes	Flynn	Lambert *	Ashcroft	Cartwright	Thomas	Shaw	Greenwood	Allpress *	Eaves
Dec 26	Stockport Co.	Div 3	h	3-2	6782	Kelly	Senior	Wrightson	Swann (1)	Flynn *	Hughes	Ashcroft	Cartwright	Greenwood	Shaw (1p)	M. James (1)	Thomas	Allpress *
Dec 28	Peterborough Utd.	Div 3	h	1-1	5200	Kelly	Senior	Wrightson	Swann	Flynn	Hughes	Ashcroft	Cartwright (1)	Greenwood *	Shaw	M. James	Thomas *	Allpress
Jan 1	Bournemouth	Div 3	a	0-1	5508	Kelly	Senior	Wrightson	Swann	Flynn	Hughes	Ashcroft	Cartwright	Thomas	Shaw *	Allpress +	Kerfoot *	Joyce +
Jan 4	Sheff. Wed. Rd 3	FAC	h	0-2	14337	Farnworth	Senior	Wrightson	Swann	Flynn	Hughes	Ashcroft	Cartwright	Thomas	Shaw	Joyce *	Lambert	Kerfoot *
Jan 11	Shrewsbury T.	Div 3	a	0-2	3154	Farnworth	Senior	Wrightson	Swann	Flynn	Hughes	Ashcroft	Cartwright	Thomas	Shaw *	Ainsworth	Lambert	Kerfoot *
Jan 14	Hull City	AT	h	2-3 *	2152	Farnworth	Senior	Wrightson	Swann	Flynn *	Hughes +	Ashcroft	Cartwright	Thomas (1)	Shaw	Ainsworth (1)	Finney *	Lambert +
Jan 18	Exeter City	Div 3	h	1-3	3585	Farnworth	Senior	Wrightson +	Swann	Whitworth	Hughes	Ashcroft	Cartwright	Thomas	Shaw	Ainsworth	Finney *	Lambert + (1)
Jan 25	Brentford	Div 3	a	0-1	7559	Farnworth	Senior	Lambert	Swann	Whitworth	Hughes	Ashcroft	Cartwright	Johnrose *	Greenwood	M. James	Wrightson	Shaw *
Feb 1	Huddersfield T.	Div 3	a	2-1	6700	Farnworth	Senior +	Flynn	Swann	Whitworth	Hughes	Ashcroft	Cartwright (1)	Greenwood	Shaw (1) *	M. James	Ainsworth *	Williams +
Feb 8	Fulham	Div 3	h	1-2	3878	Farnworth	Senior	Wrightson	Hughes *	Flynn	Whitworth	Ashcroft +	Cartwright	Greenwood	Shaw	Swann	Johnrose * (1)	Williams +
Feb 11	Hull City	Div 3	h	3-1	2932	Farnworth	Senior	Lambert	Wrightson	Flynn	Whitworth	Ashcroft	Cartwright	Jepson (2) *	Shaw	Williams (1)	Johnrose *	Ainsworth
Feb 15	Hartlepool Utd.	Div 3	a	0-2	2140	Farnworth	Senior	Lambert	Wrightson	Flynn	Whitworth	Ashcroft	Cartwright	Greenwood	Shaw	Williams	Swann	Hughes
Feb 22	Shrewsbury T.	Div 3	h	2-2	3342	Farnworth	Senior	M.James (1)	Wrightson (1)	Flynn	Hughes	Ashcroft	Cartwright	Jepson	Shaw	Williams	Lambert	Swann
Feb 29	Reading	Div 3	a	2-2	3390	Kelly	Senior	Lambert (1)	Wrightson	Flynn	Hughes +	Williams *	Cartwright	Jepson	Shaw (1)	M. James	Ashcroft *	Swann +
Mar 3	Exeter City	Div 3	a	1-4	2214	Kelly	Senior	Lambert *	Cartwright	Flynn	Wrightson	Ashcroft (1)	Swann	Jepson +	Shaw	M. James	Williams *	Thompson +
Mar 7	Brentford	Div 3	h	3-2	3548	Farnworth	Senior	Wrightson	Cartwright	Flynn	Hughes	Ashcroft (1)	Joyce	Thompson (1) *	Shaw (1)	M. James	Swann	Williams *
Mar 10	Wigan Ath.	Div 3	a	0-3	3364	Farnworth	Senior	Wrightson	Cartwright *	Flynn	Hughes	Ashcroft	Joyce	Thompson	Shaw	M. James	Lambert *	Ainsworth
Mar 14	Chester City	Div 3	h	0-3	3909	Farnworth	Williams *	Wrightson	Cartwright	Flynn	Hughes	Ashcroft	Joyce	Thompson	Shaw	M. James	Jepson *	Swann
Mar 21	Darlington	Div 3	a	2-0	2270	Farnworth	Williams	M. James	Cartwright	Flynn	Wrightson	Ashcroft	Joyce	Jepson (2)	Shaw	Thompson	Swann	Ainsworth
Mar 28	Bolton W.	Div 3	h	2-1	7327	Farnworth	Williams	M. James	Cartwright	Flynn (1)	Greenwood	Ashcroft	Joyce (1p)	Jepson	Shaw	Thompson	Ainsworth	Lambert
Mar 31	Swansea City	Div 3	h	1-1	3637	Farnworth	Williams	M. James	Cartwright	Flynn	Greenall (1)	Ashcroft	Joyce	Jepson	Shaw *	Thompson	Senior	Ainsworth *
Apr 4	Bradford City	Div 3	h	1-1	6044	Farnworth	Williams	M. James	Cartwright	Flynn	Greenall	Senior *	Joyce	Jepson	Shaw (1) *	Thompson	Swann	Ainsworth *
Apr 11	Leyton Orient	Div 3	h	2-1	3926	Farnworth	Williams	M. James	Cartwright	Flynn (1)	Greenall	Ashcroft *	Joyce	Jepson	Shaw	Thompson	Eaves	Christie	1 og
Apr 14	Reading	Div 3	h	1-1	3203	Farnworth	Williams	M. James	Cartwright (1)	Wrightson	Greenall	Ashcroft	Joyce	Jepson	Shaw	Thompson	Hughes	Eaves
Apr 18	Stoke City	Div 3	a	1-2	16151	Farnworth	Williams	M. James	Cartwright	Flynn	Greenall	Ashcroft	Joyce	Jepson *	Shaw	Thompson (1)	Wrightson	Christie *
Apr 21	Birmingham City	Div 3	h	3-2	7738	Farnworth	Williams	M. James	Cartwright	Flynn (1)	Greenall	Ashcroft	Joyce (1)	Jepson	Shaw (1)	Thompson	Wrightson	Christie
Apr 25	WBA	Div 3	a	0-3	11318	Farnworth	Williams	M. James	Cartwright	Flynn	Greenall	Ashcroft	Joyce	Jepson +	Shaw	Thompson *	Wrightson *	Kerfoot +
May 2	Bury	Div 3	h	2-0	6932	Farnworth	Williams	M. James	Cartwright	Flynn	Greenall	Ashcroft	Joyce (1)	Jepson +	Shaw	Thompson	Wrightson	Finney * (1)

(og) Howard of L.O.

A new division, after the league had been reorganised, five new players in the first league line-up and the possibility of having a Finney in the side again. Not Tom this time alas, but a youngster called Stephen who did well in the pre-season games. The club had a poor start as injuries to key players caused headaches and the results were not good, so much so, that by the end of September the Directors dropped the bombshell that the unlucky Les Chapman would be sacked as manager. It was a devastating blow and the timing, it has to be said, was awful, coming so early and at such a crucial stage of the campaign. Sam Allardyce took over as caretaker boss and initially it was a rocky road. A brilliant hat-trick by Tony Ellis then gave Preston a 3–2 win at local rivals Blackpool and things began to pick up. Ellis was in fact in great form throughout this otherwise dismal year and he was the one bright spot for the fans. Allardyce reigned until Monday December 7 when the Directors announced that the new manager would be John Beck, with his assistant being Gary Peters. They started well! Preston 2 Port Vale 5. It was obvious that Beck had plenty to do and nine players made their debut for the club after his arrival. Mickey Norbury made a goal-scoring start and Glenn Johnstone did well in goal despite playing behind a defence which had more holes than a sieve. Only seven wins after Christmas though put the club in dire need of points as the season reached its climax. With five games left it was still in Preston's own hands, but those five games were all lost and the final relegation curtain

fell at home to Mansfield on May Day. Mayday indeed! Preston actually began well in that game and went 1–0 up through Ellis. But then came the incident that virtually ended the season. North End were awarded a penalty and Norbury missed it. Mansfield then stormed back into the game and tore Preston apart to win 5–1. The last match, at Bolton, produced a carnival atmosphere amongst the oh, so loyal fans but after the inevitable defeat there were many tears from fans and players alike. The supporters deserved so much better than this. Mr Beck would have to change things dramatically but with little money to spend he had to use all his skill in the transfer market, which, to be fair, was his forte. Only time would tell if he could bring Preston up again.

DEBUTANTS: (20) Jon Davidson, Lee Fowler, John Tinkler, Aaron Callaghan, Mark Leonard, Ryan Kidd, David Flitcroft, Simon Burton, Deniol Graham, Colin Taylor, Barry Siddall, Shaun Garnett, Craig Moylon, Richard Lucas, Mickey Norbury, Glenn Johnstone, John Fowler, Neil Whalley, Craig Allardyce, Liam Watson.

LAST GAMES: (21) Allardyce S., Flynn, Farnworth, James M., Eaves, Allardyce C., Finney, Greenall, Christie, Davidson, Fowler L., Tinkler, Leonard, Flitcroft, Graham, Taylor, Siddall, Garnett, Moylon, Johnstone, Fowler J.

Ryan Kidd Concentrates on the job in hand.

STAT FACTS:
Best home run without defeat: 3 games
Best away run without defeat: 2 games
Longest run unbeaten: 4 games
Longest run without a win: 7 games
Best home attendance: 10,403 *vs.* Blackpool 27.2.93
Worst home attendance: 2,852 *vs.* Blackpool A.T. 1.12.92
Best away attendance: 21,720 *vs.* Bolton 8.5.93
Worst away attendance: 1,932 *vs.* Wigan A.T. 6.1.93
Aggregate and average home attendance: 130,651 – 5,680
Aggregate and average away attendance: 154,230 – 6,706

Ever presents: None   **Hat-tricks:** (2) both by Tony Ellis
Players used: 31   **Chairman:** K. W. Leeming   **FA Cup:** First Round
Coca Cola Cup: First round – Also competed in the Autoglass Trophy
Manager: Les Chapman until Sept., then Sam Allardyce as caretaker to Dec., then John Beck.
Leading scorer: 25 goals – Tony Ellis (22 league 1 FAC 1 CCC 1 AT)
OFFICIAL PLAYER OF THE SEASON: Tony Ellis

Lee Ashcroft

		P	W	D	L	F	A	Pts
1	Stoke City	46	27	12	7	73	34	93
2	Bolton Wanderers	46	27	9	10	80	41	90
3	Port Vale	46	26	11	9	79	44	89
4	WBA	46	25	10	11	88	54	85
5	Swansea	46	20	13	13	65	47	73
6	Stockport County	46	19	15	12	81	57	72
7	Leyton Orient	46	21	9	16	69	53	72
8	Reading	46	18	15	13	66	51	69
9	Brighton & Hove A	46	20	9	17	63	59	69
10	Bradford City	46	18	14	14	69	67	68
11	Rotherham United	46	17	14	15	60	60	65
12	Fulham	46	16	17	13	57	55	65
13	Burnley	46	15	16	15	57	59	61
14	Plymouth Argyle	46	16	12	18	59	64	60
15	Huddesfield Town	46	17	9	20	54	61	60
16	Hartlepool United	46	14	12	20	42	60	54
17	Bournemouth	46	12	17	17	45	52	53
18	Blackpool	46	12	15	19	63	75	51
19	Exeter City	46	11	17	18	54	69	50
20	Hull City	46	13	11	22	46	69	50
21	PRESTON	46	13	8	25	65	94	47
22	Mansfield Town	46	11	11	24	52	80	44
23	Wigan Athletic	46	10	11	25	53	72	41
24	Chester City	46	8	5	33	49	102	29

Match Report: Ellis Hat-Trick Seals Derby Win – 10 Oct 1992
Blackpool 2 Preston 3

This was Tony Ellis's match as the North End striker showed all his predatory skills to notch a hat-trick against the old enemy. Within three minutes of the start Preston were a goal up. Flynn's long throw-in landed in the box where everybody missed the ball, everyone that is except Ellis who nodded it past McIlhargey. Eight minutes later a long free-kick by Callaghan was laid off by Leonard to Ashcroft who shot low and hard. The goalkeeper saved but the ball squirted out and Ellis was in like a shot to tap it into the net. The striker then missed another great chance and Preston were also denied a strong penalty claim after Tinkler went down. Blackpool then tried to rally and Leonard headed one effort off the Preston goalline. Other chances in this typically physical derby match came at both ends and the referee added six minutes to the end of the first half. Just before the break a throw-in found Eyres and his well aimed cross was converted by an excellent diving header by Sinclair. Ellis was knocked out straight after the restart and he took a while to recover.

When play restarted Tinkler broke down the right and knocked in a low cross which found Ellis, who was still unsteady. His instincts saw him through though as he swivelled to hit his third goal. As the game progressed Ashcroft missed a great chance and then five players were booked after a free for all when tempers boiled over. Blackpool never gave up and both Eyres and Gouck saw shots blocked before slack marking allowed Briggs to force home a header to give the North End fans a nervous last eight minutes. But for the first time in 31 years Preston held on for a win at Blackpool.

Gareth Ainsworth.
Complete with
tights.

Trivia Fact:

Preston's 'B' team beat Stockport 'A' team 14–0 with left-back Kieran England scoring five goals. The win featured in a run that produced 40 goals for the boys in just five games.

League appearances
(46 games)

Ainsworth G. 26, Allardyce C. S. 0 + 1, Allardyce S. 1 + 2, Ashcroft L. 37 + 2, Burton S. P. 17 + 4, Callaghan A. J. 33 + 2, Cartwright L. 33 + 1, Christie D. 1 + 1, Davidson J. S. 18 + 3, Eaves D. M. C. 1 + 3, Ellis A. J. 34 + 1, Farnworth S. 35, Finney 1 + 3, Flitcroft D. J. 4 + 4, Flynn M. A. 35, Fowler J. A. 5 + 1, Fowler L. E. 29 + 3, Garnett S. M. 10, Graham D. W. T. 8, Greenall C. A. 20, James M. J. 22 + 3, Johnstone G. P. 10, Kidd R. A. 13 + 2, Leonard M. A. 19 + 3, Lucas R. 26, Moylon C. J. 0 + 1, Norbury M. S. 21, Siddall B. 1, Taylor C. 4, Tinkler J. 22 + 2, Watson L. 6 + 2, Whalley D. N. 14.

FA Cup appearances (2 games)

Farnworth 2, Davidson 2, Cartwright 2, Tinkler 0 + 1, Callaghan 2, Fowler L. 2, Flynn 2, Allardyce S. 2, Ashcroft 2, Graham 2, Ellis 2, James 2, Finney 0 + 1.

Coca Cola Cup appearances (2 games)

Farnworth 2, Davidson 2, Cartwright 2, Tinkler 2, Callaghan 2, Fowler L. 2, Eaves 0 + 1, Flynn 2, Flitcroft 0 + 1, Ashcroft 2, Leonard 2, Ellis 2, James 2.

Autoglass Trophy Appearances (2 games)

Farnworth 2, Davidson 2, Cartwright 1, Tinkler 1, Ainsworth 1, Callaghan 2, Lucas 1, Eaves 1, Flynn 2, Flitcroft 0 + 1, Garnett 1, Ashcroft 2, Graham 1, Burton 1, Norbury 1, Ellis 1, Finney 1, James 1 + 1.

Goalscorers: 65 League–5 FAC–2 CCC–2 AT–(Total 74)

Ellis 22–1–1–1 (25), Norbury 8–0–0–1 (9), Ashcroft 7 (1pen)–0–0–0 (7), James 5–0–0–0 (5), Cartwright 3–0–0–0 (3), Burton 3–0–0–0 (3), Watson 3–0–0–0 (3), Fowler L. 2–1–0–0 (3), Tinkler 2–0–1–0 (3), Callaghan 2–1–0–0 (3), Flitcroft 2–0–0–0 (2), Flynn 2–0–0–0 (2), Garnett 2–0–0–0 (2), Davidson 1–1–0–0 (2), Leonard 1–0–0–0 (1), Graham 0–1–0–0 (1).

Date 1992-3	Opponents *New Division Two	Comp	h or a	Score *aet	Att.	1	2	3	4	5	6	7	8	9	10	11	12	14
Aug 15	Bournemouth	Div 2	h	1-1	4756	Farnworth	Davidson	L.Fowler	Tinkler	Flynn	Callaghan	Ashcroft	Cartwright	Leonard	Ellis (1)	James	Eaves	Moylon
Aug 18	Stoke City Rd1 1L	CCC	h	2-1	5581	Farnworth	Davidson	L.Fowler	Tinkler (1)	Flynn	Callaghan	Ashcroft	Cartwright	Leonard	Ellis (1)	James	Eaves	Christie
Aug 22	Fulham	Div 2	a	1-2	3641	Farnworth	Davidson	L.Fowler	Tinkler *	Flynn	Callaghan	Ashcroft	Cartwright	Leonard	Ellis (1)	James +	Eaves *	Flitcroft +
Aug 26	Stoke City Rd1 2L	CCC	a	0-4 *	9745	Farnworth	Davidson *	L.Fowler	Tinkler	Flynn	Callaghan	Ashcroft	Cartwright	Leonard	Ellis +	James	Eaves *	Flitcroft +
Aug 29	Chester City	Div 2	h	4-3	4471	Farnworth	Davidson	L.Fowler	Tinkler *	Flynn (1)	Callaghan	Ashcroft (1)	Cartwright (1)	Leonard (1)	Ellis	James +	Flitcroft *	Christie +
Sep 5	Brighton	Div 2	a	0-2	6026	Farnworth	Davidson	L.Fowler	Eaves	Flynn	Callaghan	Ashcroft	Cartwright	Leonard	Ellis *	Christie +	Burton *	James +
Sep 12	Burnley	Div 2	h	2-0	7209	Farnworth	Davidson	L.Fowler	Tinkler (1)	Flynn	Callaghan +	Ashcroft	Cartwright	Leonard *	Ellis	James	Burton *	Eaves +
Sep 15	Hull City	Div 2	a	4-2	4463	Farnworth	Davidson	L.Fowler	Tinkler	Flynn	Callaghan	Ashcroft (1)	Cartwright (1)	Leonard	Ellis (2)	James	Burton	Eaves
Sep 19	Bradford City	Div 2	a	0-4	5882	Farnworth	Davidson	L.Fowler	Tinkler *	Flynn	Callaghan	Ashcroft	Cartwright	Leonard	Ellis	James	Finney -	
Sep 26	Hartlepool Utd.	Div 2	h	0-2	4347	Farnworth	Davidson	L.Fowler	Tinkler	Flynn	Callaghan *	Ashcroft	Cartwright	Leonard	Ellis	James	Flitcroft *	Kidd
Oct 3	Plymouth Arg.	Div 2	h	1-2	4401	Farnworth	Davidson (1)	L.Fowler	Tinkler	Flynn	Callaghan	Ashcroft	Cartwright	Leonard	Ellis	James	Kidd	Burton
Oct 10	Blackpool	Div 2	a	3-2	7631	Farnworth	Davidson	L.Fowler *	Tinkler	Flynn	Callaghan	Ashcroft	Cartwright	Leonard	Ellis (3) +	James	Kidd *	Finney +
Oct 17	Stoke City	Div 2	h	1-2	8138	Farnworth	Davidson	L.Fowler	Tinkler	Flynn	Callaghan (1)	Ashcroft	Cartwright	Leonard	Ellis	Kidd *	Flitcroft	
Oct 20	Reading	Div 2	h	2-0	3329	Farnworth	Cartwright	L.Fowler	Tinkler	Flynn	Kidd	Ashcroft (1p)	Flitcroft *	Leonard	Ellis	Callaghan	Davidson *	Burton
Oct 24	Mansfield Town	Div 2	a	2-2	3047	Farnworth	Cartwright	L.Fowler (1)	Tinkler	Flynn	Kidd +	Ashcroft	Graham	Leonard *	Callaghan	James (1)	Davidson *	S.Allardyce
Oct 31	Bolton W.	Div 2	h	2-2	7013	Farnworth	Cartwright (1)	L.Fowler	Tinkler	Flynn	Kidd *	Graham	Callaghan	Taylor	Ellis	James (1)	Davidson *	Finney
Nov 3	Stockport Co.	Div 2	a	0-3	4860	Farnworth	Cartwright +	Davidson	Tinkler	Flynn	L.Fowler	Graham *	Callaghan	Taylor	Ellis	James	Eaves *	S.Allardyce +
Nov 7	Wigan Ath.	Div 2	a	2-0	4442	Farnworth	Cartwright	Davidson	Callaghan (1)	Flynn	L.Fowler	Graham	Callaghan	Taylor	Ellis	James (1)	Eaves	S.Allardyce
Nov 14	Bradford City Rd 1	FAC	a	1-1	8553	Farnworth	Cartwright	Davidson	Callaghan	Flynn	L.Fowler (1)	Ashcroft	Graham	S.Allardyce	Ellis *	James	Finney *	Eaves
Nov 21	Rotherham Utd.	Div 2	a	0-1	4246	Farnworth	Cartwright	Davidson	Callaghan	Flynn	L.Fowler	Ashcroft	Graham	S.Allardyce	Taylor *	James	Finney *	Eaves
Nov 25	Bradford City Replay	FAC	h	4-5	7905	Farnworth	Cartwright	Davidson (1)	Callaghan (1)	Flynn	L.Fowler	Ashcroft	Graham (1)	S.Allardyce *	Ellis (1)	James	Tinkler *	Finney
Nov 28	WBA	Div 2	a	1-1	6306	Farnworth	Cartwright	Davidson	Callaghan	Flynn	L.Fowler	Tinkler	Graham	Ashcroft	Ellis (1)	James	Eaves	Taylor
Dec 1	Blackpool	AT	h	1-1	2852	Farnworth	Cartwright	Davidson	Callaghan	Flynn	Eaves	Tinkler	Graham	Ashcroft	Ellis (1)	James	Finney	Critchley
Dec 12	Port Vale	Div 2	h	2-5	6038	Siddall	Davidson	L.Fowler	Callaghan	Flynn	Garnett	Graham	Flitcroft	Ashcroft (1p)	Ellis	James (1)	Tinkler	Burton
Dec 18	Leyton Orient	Div 2	a	1-3	3436	Farnworth	Tinkler +	Davidson	Callaghan	Flynn	Garnett	Graham	Flitcroft	Burton	Ellis	James	Ashcroft * (1)	Moylon +
Dec 28	Exeter City	Div 2	h	2-2	5796	Farnworth	Davidson	Lucas	Callaghan	Flynn	Garnett (1)	Ashcroft	Ainsworth	Norbury (1)	Ellis	Burton	Flitcroft	James
Jan 6	Wigan Ath.	AT	a	1-2	1932	Farnworth	Davidson	Lucas	Callaghan	Flynn	Garnett	Ashcroft *	Ainsworth	Norbury (1)	Finney	Burton +	Flitcroft *	James +
Jan 9	Hull City	Div 2	h	1-2	4719	Farnworth	Tinkler	Lucas	Callaghan	Flynn	Garnett (1)	Ashcroft	Ainsworth	Norbury	Finney *	Burton	Flitcroft	L.Fowler *
Jan 16	Hartlepool Utd.	Div 2	a	0-0	2682	Farnworth	Cartwright	Lucas	Callaghan	Flynn	Garnett	Ashcroft	Ainsworth	Norbury	Ellis	L.Fowler	Flitcroft	Burton
Jan 23	Bradford City	Div 2	h	3-2	5155	Farnworth	Tinkler	Lucas	Callaghan	Flynn	Garnett	Cartwright	Ainsworth	Norbury (1)	Ellis (1)	James (1)	Flitcroft *	Burton
Jan 26	Chester City	Div 2	a	4-2	2901	Farnworth +	Tinkler	Lucas	Callaghan	Flynn (1) *	Garnett	Cartwright	Ainsworth	Norbury (1)	Ellis (1)	James	Flitcroft * (1)	Burton +
Jan 30	Fulham	Div 2	h	1-2	5858	Johnstone	Cartwright	Lucas	Callaghan *	Flitcroft	Garnett	Ashcroft	Ainsworth	Norbury	Ellis (1)	James	Tinkler *	Burton
Feb 6	Bournemouth	Div 2	a	1-2	3601	Johnstone	Cartwright	Lucas	Tinkler (1)	Greenall	Garnett	Ashcroft	Ainsworth	Norbury	Leonard	L.Fowler *	Callaghan	Burton *
Feb 13	Brighton	Div 2	h	1-0	4334	Johnstone	Tinkler	Lucas	Greenall	Flynn	Garnett	Cartwright	Ainsworth	Norbury	Ellis	James *	L.Fowler *	Ashcroft
Feb 16	Burnley	Div 2	a	0-2	12648	Johnstone	Tinkler *	L.Fowler	Lucas	Flynn	Greenall	Cartwright	Ainsworth	Norbury	Ellis	Kidd +	Leonard *	Ashcroft +
Feb 20	Reading	Div 2	a	0-4	3543	Johnstone	Cartwright	L.Fowler	Lucas	Flynn	Greenall	J.Fowler	Ainsworth +	Norbury	Ellis	Ashcroft *	Leonard *	Callaghan +
Feb 27	Blackpool	Div 2	h	3-3	10403	Johnstone	Ainsworth	Lucas	Callaghan	Flynn	Greenall	L.Fowler (1)	J.Fowler	Norbury	Ellis (2)	Ashcroft	Cartwright	James
Mar 6	Plymouth Arg.	Div 2	a	0-4	5201	Johnstone	Ainsworth	Lucas	Whalley	Flynn +	Greenall	Cartwright *	J.Fowler	Norbury	Leonard	Ashcroft	Callaghan *	James *
Mar 9	Swansea City	Div 2	h	1-3	4396	Farnworth	Ainsworth	Lucas	Whalley	Flynn	Greenall	L.Fowler	J.Fowler	Norbury (1)	Burton	Ashcroft	James	Leonard
Mar 12	Wigan Ath.	Div 2	h	3-2	3562	Johnstone	Ainsworth	Lucas	Whalley	Flynn	Greenall	L.Fowler	J.Fowler	Norbury (1) *	Burton (2)	Ashcroft	James *	Callaghan
Mar 17	Huddersfield T.	Div 2	a	0-1	4915	Johnstone	Ainsworth	Lucas	Whalley	Flynn	Greenall	L.Fowler *	Callaghan	Norbury	Burton	Ashcroft	J.Fowler	Ellis +
Mar 20	Stockport Co.	Div 2	h	2-3	5255	Johnstone	Ainsworth	Lucas	Whalley	Flynn	Greenall	Burton	Callaghan	Norbury	Ellis (2)	Ashcroft	J.Fowler	L.Fowler
Mar 24	WBA	Div 2	a	2-3	13217	Farnworth	Ainsworth	Lucas	Whalley	Flynn	Greenall	Burton	Callaghan	Norbury	Ellis (1)	Ashcroft (1)	J.Fowler	L.Fowler
Mar 27	Rotherham Utd.	Div 2	h	5-2	4859	Farnworth	Ainsworth	Lucas	Whalley	Kidd	Greenall	Cartwright	Burton	Norbury (2)	Ellis (3)	Ashcroft	J.Fowler	L.Fowler
Apr 6	Port Vale	Div 2	a	2-2	8271	Farnworth +	Ainsworth	Lucas	Whalley	Kidd	Greenall	Cartwright	Burton *	Watson (1)	Ellis (1)	Ashcroft	C.Allardyce	J.Fowler +
Apr 10	Huddersfield T.	Div 2	h	2-1	7647	Farnworth	Ainsworth	Lucas	Whalley	Kidd	Greenall	Cartwright	Burton	Watson (1)	Ellis (1)	Ashcroft	J.Fowler	Leonard
Apr 12	Exeter City	Div 2	a	1-0	3410	Farnworth	Ainsworth	Lucas	Whalley	Kidd	Greenall	Cartwright	Burton	Watson (1)	Ellis *	Ashcroft	J.Fowler	L.Fowler *
Apr 17	Leyton Orient	Div 2	h	1-4	5890	Farnworth	Ainsworth	Lucas	Whalley	Kidd	Greenall	Cartwright	Burton (1)	Watson	Leonard	Ashcroft	Tinkler	Callaghan
Apr 24	Stoke City	Div 2	a	0-1	18334	Farnworth	Callaghan	Lucas	Ainsworth	Kidd	Greenall	Cartwright *	Leonard	Watson	Burton	Ashcroft	Tinkler	Flitcroft
Apr 27	Swansea City	Div 2	h	0-2	6993	Farnworth	Callaghan	Lucas	Whalley	Kidd	Greenall *	Ainsworth	Burton	Norbury	Leonard +	Ashcroft	Cartwright	Watson +
May 1	Mansfield Town	Div 2	h	1-5	5889	Farnworth	Ainsworth	L.Fowler	Whalley	Kidd	Greenall	Lucas	Watson	Norbury	Ellis (1) *	Burton	Leonard *	Callaghan
May 8	Bolton W.	Div 2	a	0-1	21720	Farnworth	Callaghan	Lucas	Whalley	Kidd	Greenall	L.Fowler *	Ainsworth	Norbury	Burton	Leonard	Watson *	Holland

Lee Cartwright

Ronnie Jepson

League position in Division Two: 21st (Relegated) – P46 W13 D8 L25 F65 A94 Pts 47
Home: W8 D5 L10 F41 A47   Away: W5 D3 L15 F24 A47

SEASON 1993–1994

Another false start and out of the Coca Cola cup at the first hurdle gave Preston fans their usual early season dose of disappointment before a giant pick-me-up then arrived in the form of a 6–1 win over Shrewsbury. Twelve new players had made their debuts before the October was out as manager John Beck continued his policy of clearout followed by an influx of more new blood. Mike Conroy scored a hat-trick in that Shrewsbury game and the goals continued to flow, at both ends mind you, as the season progressed. Nil, nil was a rare scoreline under Beck although, ironically, Preston went out of the Autoglass Trophy at Huddersfield on penalties, after a goalless draw. Beck's reputation as an exponent of direct football was certainly seen in Preston's play, and as the fans quickly found out, you either loved it, or loathed it. Certainly this approach created a hatful of chances and Tony Ellis was at the sharp end. He responded magnificently, scoring 30 league and cup goals as Preston kept up the pressure on the league leaders. Gareth Ainsworth, Paul Raynor, Gavin Nebelling and David Moyes all played well and the consistency of Andy Fensome and Ryan Kidd backed them up. The defence was still prone to the odd lapse or three and other clubs soon knew exactly how North End would play. It was good to see Preston's away form improve this season and the signing of Ian Bryson further helped to strengthen the midfield. Not all new players came from outside as youngsters from the reserves also came into the first team with Farrell Kilbane and Chris Holland making their debuts. In the FA Cup Preston enjoyed a good run which should have been longer but for a shocking defeat at Conference giant killers Kidderminster. The league results continued

to fluctuate but the points gathered were enough to put North End into a play-off position. They played against Torquay in the two-legged semi-final and lost the first leg in Devon, 2–0. But on a great night at Deepdale, and in the last ever game on the plastic pitch, Preston rose to the occasion and produced a memorable 4–1 extra-time win to go through to a Wembley show down with Wycombe Wanderers. The play-off final, against a Wycombe side in their first league season, started well for the Lilywhites and at half-time they led 2–1. After the break, however, Wycombe roared back and scored three more goals without reply. It was a great day out for the success starved Preston fans but the ultimate disappointment was difficult to take.

DEBUTANTS: (18) Kelham O'Hanlon, Chris Sulley, Gavin Nebelling, Paul Raynor, Mike Conroy, Paul Masefield, Trevor Matthewson, David Moyes, Greg Challender, Steve Woods, Chris Holland, Andy Fensome, Ian Bryson, Kevin Magee, Farrell Kilbane, Stuart Hicks, Jamie Squires, Lee Bamber.

LAST GAMES: (15) Ellis, Callaghan, Burton, Lucas, Norbury, Watson, Sulley, Nebelling, Masefield, Matthewson, Challender, Woods, Holland, Bamber and Kilbane F.

Paul Raynor

STAT FACTS:
Best home run without defeat: 11 games
Best away run without defeat: 3 games
Longest run unbeaten: 6 games
Longest run without a win: 6 games
Best home attendance: 12,790 vs. Chester 27.12.93
Worst home attendance: 4,485 vs. Burnley A.T. 19.10.93
Best away attendance: 40,109 at Wembley P/Off final 28.5.94
Worst away attendance: 1,379 vs. Huddersfield A.T. 30.11.93
Aggregate and average home attendance: 154,974 – 7,380
Aggregate and average away attendance: 91,534 – 4,359

Ever presents: None   Hat-tricks: (2) Mike Conroy and Tony Ellis
Players used: 27   FA Cup: Fourth Round
Coca Cola Cup: First Round – Also competed in the Autoglass Trophy
Manager: John Beck   Chairman: K. W. Leeming Esq.
Leading scorer: 30 goals – Tony Ellis (26 League 2 FAC 1 CCC 1 A.T.)
OFFICIAL PLAYER OF THE SEASON: Tony Ellis

League position in Division Three: 5th (Play-offs) – P42 W18 D13 L11 F79 A60 Pts 67
Home: W13 D5 L3 F46 A23   Away: W5 D8 L8 F33 A37

WEMBLEY
STADIUM LIMITED

FOOTBALL LEAGUE CHAMPIONSHIP
Endsleigh
League

Endsleigh
Insurance League

Saturday 28th May
Kick-off 3pm
TURNSTILES OPEN 1PM
TURNSTILE F

BLOCK   ROW   SEAT
204   17   118

£19.00
32100   415 120594 125622A

TO BE RETAINED

3RD DIVISION
3
PLAY-OFF

1994
Division Three
Play-off Final

Memories of the day

Endsleigh
Insurance League

DIVISION THREE
PLAY-OFF FINAL

PRESTON NORTH END v WYCOMBE WANDERERS
SATURDAY 28th MAY 1994
KICK-OFF 3.00pm

Match Report: The Last Goodbye, And How! – May 18 1994. Preston 4 Torquay 1
Play-off semi final a.e.t.

What a way to say goodbye to the Deepdale plastic pitch! A superb night of entertainment for over 11,000 fans saw Preston come back from a 2–0 first leg deficit to snatch victory from the jaws of defeat. The crowd were in a carnival mood and the atmosphere was electric as Preston took an early lead through an Ellis header. It was just the start North End wanted but seven minutes later the crowd were stunned into silence as Goodridge fired home an equaliser and thus restored their two goal cushion. The turning point came in the 36th minute. Torquay's Moore was sent off after he punched Raynor and from then on United were really up against it. Preston's tactics were very basic as they bombarded the visitors with a battery of corners, free-kicks and throw-ins. The pressure had to tell and Torquay eventually cracked with just a minute to go before the break. Moyes headed

Manager John Beck with the playing staff of 1993/94

in Bryson's cross and the noise level rose several decibels. Seven minutes into the second half Raynor took a corner and Hicks headed in to make it 3–1 and the tie was there for the taking. The Torquay boss, former North Ender Don O'Riordan, rallied his troops and at the end of the 90 minutes the scores were still level. Extra-time and the plastic pitch had one more goal to savour, yet another header, Preston's fourth of the night, this time Raynor was the hero, meeting Fensome's cross. As the saying goes, the crowd went wild as a Wembley final beckoned.

League appearances (42 games)

Ainsworth G. 34 + 4, Bamber L.E. 0 + 1, Bryson J.I.C. 24 + 1, Burton S.P. 2 + 1, Callaghan A.J. 1, Cartwright L. 36 + 3, Challender G.L. 5 + 5, Conroy M.K. 28 + 4, Ellis A.J. 36 + 1, Fensome A.B. 31, Hicks S.J. 3 + 1, Holland C.J. 0 + 1, Kidd R.A. 35 + 1, Kilbane F.N. 0 + 1, Lucas R. 21 + 3, Magee K. 5 + 2, Masefield P.D. 6, Matthewson T. 12, Moyes D.W. 29, Nebelling G.M. 22, Norbury M.S. 11 + 10, O'Hanlon K.G. 23, Raynor P.J. 36 + 3, Squires J.A. 4, Sulley C.S. 21, Watson L. 1, Whalley D.N. 17 + 4, Woods S.G. 19 + 1.

FA Cup appearances (4 games)

O'Hanlon 2, Woods 2, Masefield 1, Kidd 4, Moyes 4, Fensome 4, Lucas 4, Nebelling 3, Whalley 1 + 1, Challender 1, Cartwright 3, Raynor 4, Ainsworth 2 + 1, Conroy 4, Bryson 1 + 1, Ellis 4, Norbury 0 + 3.

Coca Cola Cup appearances (2 games)

O'Hanlon 2, Callaghan 1, Masefield 1, Kidd 1, Sulley 2, Nebelling 2, Whalley 2, Cartwright 2, Matthewson 1, Raynor 2, Ainsworth 2, Conroy 1, Ellis 2, Burton 0 + 1, Norbury 1 + 1.

Autoglass Trophy Appearances (3 games)

O'Hanlon 1, Woods 2, Callaghan 1, Masefield 1, Kidd 2, Fensome 2, Lucas 2, Nebelling 2, Whalley 3, Challender 1, Raynor 3, Ainsworth 3, Conroy 2, Moyes 3, Ellis 2, Burton 0 + 1, Norbury 2 + 1, Holland 1.

Goalscorers: 79 League–5 FAC–2 CCC–2 AT–(Total 88)

Ellis 26–2–1–1 (30), Conroy 13–1–0–0 (14), Ainsworth 13–0–0–1 (14), Raynor 6–1–0–0 (7), Norbury 5–0–0–0 (5), Moyes 3–1–0–0 (4), Nebelling 3–0–0–0 (3), Bryson 2–0–0–0 (2), Cartwright 1–0–1–0 (2), Fensome 1–0–0–0 (1), Sulley 1–0–0–0 (1), Kidd 1–0–0–0 (1), Matthewson 1–0–0–0 (1), Challender 1–0–0–0 (1), Own Goals 2–0–0–0 (2), Swailes of Doncaster and Green of Gillingham.

Tony Ellis in action against Crewe Alexandra

Season 1993–94: Third Division

	P	W	D	L	F	A	Pts
1 Shrewsbury Town	42	22	13	7	63	39	79
2 Chester City	42	21	11	10	69	46	74
3 Crewe Alexandra	42	21	10	11	80	61	73
4 Wycombe Wanderers	42	19	13	10	67	53	70
5 PRESTON	**42**	**18**	**13**	**11**	**79**	**60**	**67**
6 Torquay United	42	17	16	9	64	56	67
7 Carlisle United	42	18	10	14	57	42	64
8 Chesterfield	42	16	14	12	55	48	62
9 Rochdale	42	16	12	14	63	51	60
10 Walsall	42	17	9	16	48	53	60
11 Scunthorpe United	42	15	14	13	64	56	59
12 Mansfield Town	42	15	10	17	53	62	55
13 Bury	42	14	11	17	55	56	53
14 Scarborough	42	15	8	19	55	61	53
15 Doncaster Rovers	42	14	10	18	44	57	52
16 Gillingham	42	12	15	15	44	51	51
17 Colchester United	42	13	10	19	56	71	49
18 Lincoln City	42	12	11	19	52	63	47
19 Wigan Athletic	42	11	12	19	51	70	45
20 Hereford United	42	12	6	24	60	79	42
21 Darlington	42	10	11	21	42	64	41
22 Northampton Town	42	9	11	22	44	66	38

Tony Ellis scored all his Deepdale goals on the plastic pitch.

Trivia Fact:

North End's 'B' team won their division of the Lancashire League, Tom Finney wrote the forward for a book on the England football team written by Mike Payne the co-author of this book, Ian Bryson signed for PNE on his 31st birthday and when Mike Conroy scored a hat-trick on his Deepdale debut he received the match ball and promptly presented it to his proud Dad.

Goalkeeper Lee Bamber's league debut came under controversial circumstances as he replaced the sent-off Kelham O'Hanlon, who had fouled an opponent 40 yards from his goal line.

Date 1993-4	Opponents	Comp	h or a	Score * aet	Att.	1	2	3	4	5	6	7	8	9	10	11	12	14	15	
Aug 14	Crewe A.	Div 3	h	0-2	6879	O'Hanlon	Callaghan	Sulley	Nebbeling	Kidd	Raynor	Ainsworth	Whalley	Norbury	Ellis	Burton	Cartwright	Lucas	Bamber	
Aug 17	Burnley Rd1 1L	CCC	h	1-2	6283	O'Hanlon	Callaghan	Sulley	Whalley	Nebbeling	Kidd	Ainsworth	Cartwright	Norbury	Ellis (1)	Raynor	Burton	Lucas	Bamber	
Aug 21	Scarborough	Div 3	a	4-3	2329	O'Hanlon	Masefield	Sulley	Whalley	Nebbeling	Kidd	Ainsworth (2)	Cartwright	Norbury *	Ellis (2)	Raynor	Conroy *	Matthewson	Bamber	
Aug 25	Burnley Rd2 2L	CCC	a	1-4	9346	O'Hanlon	Masefield	Sulley	Whalley	Nebbeling	Matthewson	Ainsworth	Cartwright (1)	Conroy *	Ellis +	Raynor	Burton *	Norbury +	Bamber	
Aug 28	Shrewsbury T.	Div 3	h	6-1	4941	O'Hanlon	Masefield	Sulley	Whalley	Nebbeling (1)	Matthewson	Ainsworth (2)	Cartwright	Conroy (3)	Ellis *	Raynor	Norbury *	Burton	Bamber	
Aug 31	Bury	Div 3	h	3-1	5886	O'Hanlon	Masefield	Sulley	Whalley	Nebbeling (1)	Matthewson	Ainsworth	Cartwright	Conroy (1)	Ellis (1)	Raynor	Norbury	Burton	Bamber	
Sep 4	Lincoln City	Div 3	a	2-0	3793	O'Hanlon	Masefield +	Sulley	Whalley	Nebbeling	Matthewson	Ainsworth	Cartwright	Conroy	Ellis (1)	Raynor (1)	Norbury	Kidd +	Bamber	
Sep 11	Doncaster R.	Div 3	h	3-1	7294	O'Hanlon	Kidd	Sulley	Whalley	Nebbeling	Matthewson (1)	Ainsworth	Cartwright	Conroy (1)	Ellis	Raynor (1)	Norbury	Lucas	Bamber	
Sep 18	Torquay Utd.	Div 3	a	3-4	3912	O'Hanlon	Kidd +	Sulley	Whalley	Nebbeling	Matthewson	Ainsworth (1)	Cartwright	Conroy (1) *	Ellis (1)	Raynor	Norbury *	Lucas +	Bamber	
Sep 25	Mansfield Town	Div 3	a	2-2	3762	O'Hanlon	Moyes	Lucas	Whalley	Nebbeling	Matthewson	Ainsworth	Cartwright	Conroy *	Ellis (2)	Raynor	Norbury	Callaghan	Bamber *	
Sep 28	Carlisle Utd.	AT	a	0-2	3909	O'Hanlon	Masefield	Callaghan	Whalley	Nebbeling	Moyes	Ainsworth	Lucas	Conroy	Norbury	Raynor	Burton	Holland	Bamber	
Oct 2	Colchester Utd.	Div 3	h	1-0	6412	O'Hanlon	Masefield	Sulley	Lucas +	Nebbeling	Matthewson	Ainsworth	Cartwright	Conroy *	Ellis (1)	Raynor	Norbury *	Challender +	Bamber	
Oct 9	Chesterfield	Div 3	h	4-1	6581	Woods	Masefield	Sulley	Challender	Nebbeling	Matthewson	Ainsworth	Cartwright	Conroy	Ellis (3,1p)	Raynor (1)	Norbury	Holland	Bamber	
Oct 16	Wigan Ath.	Div 3	a	2-2	3741	Woods	Fensome	Kidd	Challender	Nebbeling	Matthewson *	Ainsworth (1)	Cartwright	Conroy (1)	Ellis	Raynor	Norbury	Holland *	Bamber	
Oct 19	Burnley	AT	h	2-1	4485	Woods	Fensome	Kidd	Whalley	Nebbeling	Moyes	Ainsworth (1) *	Holland	Norbury	Ellis (1)	Raynor	Challender	Burton *	Bamber	
Oct 23	Rochdale	Div 3	h	2-1	8491	O'Hanlon	Fensome	Kidd	Whalley	Nebbeling	Moyes	Ainsworth +	Cartwright	Conroy *	Ellis (2,1p)	Raynor	Norbury *	Challender +	Woods	
Oct 30	Hereford Utd.	Div 3	a	3-2	3383	O'Hanlon	Fensome	Kidd	Whalley	Nebbeling	Moyes (1)	Conroy	Cartwright	Norbury	Ellis (2)	Raynor	Burton	Challender	Woods	
Nov 2	Walsall	Div 3	a	0-2	4446	O'Hanlon	Fensome	Kidd	Whalley +	Nebbeling	Moyes	Conroy	Cartwright	Norbury *	Ellis	Raynor	Burton *	Challender +	Woods	
Nov 6	Darlington	Div 3	h	3-2	6711	O'Hanlon	Fensome	Kidd	Whalley	Nebbeling (1)	Moyes	Cartwright (1)	Lucas	Conroy (1)	Burton *	Raynor	Norbury *	Holland	Woods	
Nov 13	Mansfield Town Rd 1	FAC	a	2-1	4119	O'Hanlon	Fensome	Kidd	Lucas	Nebbeling	Moyes	Masefield *	Cartwright +	Conroy	Ellis (2,1p)	Raynor	Norbury *	Whalley +	Woods	
Nov 20	Carlisle Utd.	Div 3	a	1-0	10279	O'Hanlon	Fensome	Kidd	Lucas	Nebbeling	Moyes	Ainsworth *	Cartwright	Conroy	Ellis (1)	Raynor	Norbury	Whalley *	Woods	
Nov 27	Wycombe W.	Div 3	h	2-3	9265	O'Hanlon *	Fensome	Kidd	Whalley	Lucas	Moyes	Ainsworth (1)	Challender (1)	Conroy	Ellis	Raynor	Norbury	Cartwright	Woods *	
Nov 30	Huddersfield T. **	AT	a	0-0 *	1379	Woods	Fensome	Kidd	Whalley	Lucas	Moyes	Ainsworth	Challender	Conroy *	Ellis	Raynor	Norbury *	Cartwright	O'Hanlon	
Dec 4	Shrewsbury T. Rd 2	FAC	a	1-0	5018	Woods	Fensome	Kidd	Whalley	Lucas	Moyes	Ainsworth +	Challender	Conroy	Ellis *	Raynor (1)	Bryson *	Norbury +	O'Hanlon	
Dec 11	Scarborough	Div 3	h	2-2	6290	Woods	Fensome	Kidd	Whalley	Lucas	Moyes	Ainsworth	Challender *	Conroy +	Ellis (1p)	Raynor	Bryson * (1)	Norbury +	O'Hanlon	
Dec 17	Crewe A.	Div 3	a	3-4	6035	O'Hanlon	Fensome *	Sulley	Whalley	Kidd	Moyes	Ainsworth (1)	Lucas	Bryson	Ellis +	Raynor (1)	Cartwright *	Conroy + (1)	Woods	
Dec 27	Chester City	Div 3	h	1-1	12790	O'Hanlon	Fensome	Kidd	Whalley +	Nebbeling	Moyes	Ainsworth *	Lucas	Bryson	Ellis (1)	Raynor	Conroy *	Cartwright +	Woods	
Jan 1	Scunthorpe Utd.	Div 3	h	2-2	7669	O'Hanlon	Fensome	Kidd	Cartwright	Nebbeling	Moyes	Bryson	Lucas	Conroy (1)	Ellis *	Raynor	Norbury * (1)	Holland	Woods	
Jan 4	Bury	Div 3	a	1-1	4164	O'Hanlon	Fensome	Kidd	Cartwright	Nebbeling	Moyes	Ainsworth *	Lucas	Conroy	Bryson	Raynor	Norbury * (1)	Whalley	Woods	
Jan 8	Bournemouth Rd 3	FAC	h	2-1	8457	O'Hanlon	Fensome	Kidd	Lucas	Nebbeling	Moyes (1)	Bryson *	Cartwright	Conroy (1)	Ellis	Raynor	Norbury	Ainsworth *	Woods	
Jan 15	Wigan Ath.	Div 3	h	3-0	7728	O'Hanlon	Fensome	Sulley	Lucas	Nebbeling	Moyes	Bryson	Cartwright	Conroy (1)	Ellis (2)	Raynor *	Norbury	Ainsworth *	Woods	
Jan 22	Chesterfield	Div 3	a	1-1	3804	O'Hanlon	Fensome	Kidd	Lucas	Nebbeling	Moyes (1)	Bryson	Cartwright	Conroy	Ellis	Raynor *	Norbury	Ainsworth *	Woods	
Jan 29	Kidderminster Rd 4	FAC	a	0-1	7000	Woods	Fensome	Kidd	Lucas	Nebbeling	Moyes	Ainsworth	Cartwright	Conroy	Ellis *	Raynor	Norbury *	Whalley	O'Hanlon	
Feb 5	Rochdale	Div 3	a	1-2	4317	Woods	Fensome	Kidd	Lucas	Nebbeling +	Moyes	Bryson	Cartwright	Conroy (1)	Ellis	Raynor *	Ainsworth *	Norbury +	O'Hanlon	
Feb 12	Gillingham	Div 3	h	0-0	6167	Woods	Fensome	Sulley	Lucas	Kidd	Moyes	Bryson	Cartwright +	Conroy	Ellis	Raynor *	Ainsworth *	Whalley +	O'Hanlon	
Feb 19	Shrewsbury T.	Div 3	a	0-1	5391	Woods	Fensome	Kidd	Whalley	Lucas	Moyes	Ainsworth	Cartwright	Bryson	Ellis *	Raynor	Conroy *	Kilbane	O'Hanlon	
Feb 26	Lincoln City	Div 3	h	2-0	5941	Woods	Fensome	Sulley	Lucas *	Kidd	Moyes	Ainsworth	Bryson	Conroy (1)	Ellis	Raynor (1)	Magee	Cartwright *	O'Hanlon	
Mar 1	Hereford Utd.	Div 3	h	3-0	6641	Woods	Fensome	Sulley	Cartwright	Kidd	Moyes	Ainsworth	Bryson (1)	Conroy	Ellis (2)	Raynor	Magee	Whalley	O'Hanlon	
Mar 4	Doncaster R.	Div 3	a	1-1	3321	Woods	Fensome	Kidd	Cartwright	Matthewson	Moyes	Ainsworth *	Bryson	Conroy	Watson	Magee +	Raynor *	Whalley +	O'Hanlon	1 o.g.
Mar 12	Torquay Utd.	Div 3	h	3-1	6641	Woods	Kidd	Sulley (1)	Cartwright	Matthewson	Moyes	Ainsworth	Bryson	Norbury *	Ellis (2)	Raynor	Magee	Kilbane *	O'Hanlon	
Mar 15	Northampton T.	Div 3	a	0-2	3845	Woods	Fensome	Kidd	Cartwright	Matthewson +	Moyes	Ainsworth	Bryson	Norbury	Ellis	Raynor *	Magee *	Whalley +	O'Hanlon	
Mar 19	Mansfield Town	Div 3	h	3-1	6747	O'Hanlon	Fensome	Sulley	Cartwright	Kidd	Moyes	Ainsworth (1)	Bryson	Norbury (2)	Ellis	Raynor	Magee	Whalley	Woods	
Mar 26	Colchester Utd.	Div 3	a	1-1	2950	O'Hanlon	Fensome	Sulley	Cartwright	Kidd	Moyes	Ainsworth	Bryson	Norbury (1)	Challender	Magee *	Raynor *	Watson	Woods	
Apr 2	Chester City	Div 3	a	2-3	5638	Woods	Fensome	Sulley	Cartwright	Hicks	Kidd	Ainsworth (1)	Bryson	Norbury	Ellis (1)	Raynor	Lucas	Magee	Bamber	
Apr 4	Northampton T.	Div 3	h	1-1	7517	Woods	Fensome	Sulley	Cartwright	Hicks *	Kidd	Ainsworth (1)	Bryson	Norbury	Ellis	Magee	Watson	Lucas *	Bamber	
Apr 9	Scunthorpe Utd.	Div 3	a	1-3	3790	Woods	Fensome	Sulley	Cartwright	Hicks +	Kidd	Ainsworth (1)	Bryson	Conroy *	Ellis	Magee	Norbury *	Lucas +	Bamber	
Apr 12	Gillingham	Div 3	a	2-2	2453	Woods	Fensome	Sulley *	Cartwright	Kidd	Moyes (1)	Ainsworth	Lucas	Conroy	Ellis	Bryson	Norbury	Magee *	Bamber	1 o.g.
Apr 16	Walsall	Div 3	h	2-0	7020	Woods	Fensome (1)	Squires	Cartwright	Kidd	Moyes	Ainsworth (1)	Lucas	Norbury *	Ellis	Bryson	Raynor *	Challender	Banks	
Apr 23	Darlington	Div 3	a	2-0	2739	Woods	Fensome	Squires	Cartwright	Kidd	Moyes	Ainsworth	Lucas	Conroy *	Raynor (1) +	Bryson	Ellis * (1)	Challender +	Berryman	
Apr 30	Carlisle Utd.	Div 3	h	0-3	11363	Woods	Fensome	Squires	Cartwright	Kidd	Moyes	Ainsworth	Lucas	Raynor	Ellis	Bryson	Conroy	Challender	Berryman	
May 7	Wycombe W.	Div 3	a	1-1	7442	Woods	Fensome	Squires *	Cartwright	Kidd (1)	Moyes	Ainsworth	Lucas	Raynor	Bryson	Magee +	Hicks *	Challender +	Berryman	

** Lost 5-3 on pens.

Own goals: Swailes of Doncaster and Green of Gillingham

SEASON 1994–1995

A more steady start was made to John Beck's second full season in charge of Preston North End. Some good early results did not include the first round of the Coca Cola cup as once again the club went out of the league cup competition early. The first six games were all played away from Deepdale while the grand old stadium was having its playing surface returned to grass after eight seasons of the plastic. One of North End's most loyal servants, groundsman Peter McCallion, lovingly and skilfully relaid the new pitch and on September the third, Preston entertained Lincoln for their first game back on the lush green turf. It was a great occasion, enhanced by a 4–0 win for North End. Two away wins then followed and it looked as though the club were destined for a successful year. But a 3–1 defeat at Darlington then set off a period of poor form. Eight consecutive defeats sent Preston plummeting down the league and the pressure was suddenly on Beck and his team. Mike Conroy scored twice in a win at Mansfield which relieved the pressure a little, and the same player then scored the winner in the televised FA Cup tie against Blackpool. However, there seemed certain amount of unrest within the camp and it was obvious that not everyone was happy with Beck's methods. After the defeat at Chesterfield at the end of November, Beck finally parted company with the club. He had achieved some very positive things at North End but there was also much that the fans and the directors were not happy

with and in the end he had to go. Beck's assistant Gary Peters took charge and was eventually given the job on a permanent basis. Meanwhile, on the field, the players tried hard to overcome all this upheaval and several had good seasons. Andy Fensome was having a particularly fine year, David Moyes was in great form at the heart of the defence and Ian Bryson was consistently strong in midfield. In attack though, Preston lacked an out and out goalscorer, and as a result the goals were shared around the team. One of Peters' first moves was to bring in a young Manchester United reserve player on loan. His name was David Beckham and the youngster quickly made his mark. The player looked good but no-one quite realised at the time just what a brilliant player he was to turn out to be during the next five years. If only he could have stayed at Deepdale. Considering the turmoil through the season Preston and Peters did well to reach the play-offs again although promotion was never really on. However, the promise was there and there was certainly plenty for Peters to build on.

DEBUTANTS: (15) Barry Richardson, Terry Fleming, Neil Trebble, Mark Sale, John Vaughan, Ray Sharp, Graeme Atkinson, Steve Holmes, Dean Emerson, Allan Smart, Stuart Rimmer, Graham Lancashire, Simon Davey, David Beckham, Matt Carmichael.

LAST GAMES: (9) Whalley, Conroy, Hicks, Trebble, Sale, Rimmer, Beckham, Carmichael, Emerson.

Far left: Full-back Andy Fensome in action at Bloomfield Road Blackpool.

Left: Ian Bryson, experienced Scotsman.

Match Report: New Season – Late Start – 13 Aug 1994 Darlington 0 Preston 0

A new season always starts with everyone full of optimism. New players arrive in the summer and the clubs are filled with the excitement of a new challenge. John Beck's side had to travel to Darlington on the opening day of 1994–95

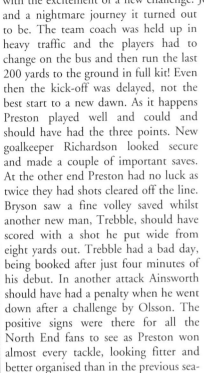

Pre-season photocall.

and a nightmare journey it turned out to be. The team coach was held up in heavy traffic and the players had to change on the bus and then run the last 200 yards to the ground in full kit! Even then the kick-off was delayed, not the best start to a new dawn. As it happens Preston played well and could and should have had the three points. New goalkeeper Richardson looked secure and made a couple of important saves. At the other end Preston had no luck as twice they had shots cleared off the line. Bryson saw a fine volley saved whilst another new man, Trebble, should have scored with a shot he put wide from eight yards out. Trebble had a bad day, being booked after just four minutes of his debut. In another attack Ainsworth should have had a penalty when he went down after a challenge by Olsson. The positive signs were there for all the North End fans to see as Preston won almost every tackle, looking fitter and better organised than in the previous sea-son. The visitors were then given an even better chance as Banks was sent off for the home side after two bookable offences. With ten minutes to go Whalley was very unlucky not to win a penalty when brought down by Gregan, the highly rated Darlington defender. The best chance of the game though came with just five minutes to go as Moyes saw his 15 yard shot cleared off the line. A good start, but North End would have to learn to take their chances.

League appearances (42 games)

Ainsworth G. 16, Atkinson G. 8 + 7, Beckham D. R. J. 4 + 1, Bryson J. I. C. 41, Carmichael M. A. 7 + 3, Cartwright L. 25 + 11, Conroy M. K. 22 + 3, Davey S. 13, Emerson D. 1 + 1, Fensome A. B. 42, Fleming T. M. 20 + 7, Hicks S. J. 8, Holmes S. P. 5, Kidd R. A. 32, Lancashire G. 9 + 8, Magee K. 14, Moyes D. W. 38, Raynor P. J. 34 + 4, Richardson B. 17, Rimmer S. A. 0 + 2, Sale M. D. 10 + 3, Sharp R. 21, Smart A. A. C. 17 + 2, Squires J. A. 11, Trebble N. D. 8 + 11, Vaughan J. 25 + 1, Whalley D. N. 14 + 1.

FA Cup appearances (3 games)

Richardson 3, Fensome 3, Fleming 0 + 1, Whalley 1 + 1, Moyes 3, Ainsworth 1, Cartwright 3, Raynor 3, Trebble 2 + 1, Bryson 3, Sale 0 + 1, Conroy 3, Sharp 3, Holmes 3, Emerson 0 + 2, Smart 2.

Coca Cola Cup appearances (2 games)

Richardson 2, Fensome 2, Fleming 2, Whalley 2, Hicks 2, Moyes 2, Ainsworth 1, Cartwright 2, Raynor 1 + 1, Trebble 1, Bryson 1 + 1, Sale 1 + 1, Kidd 2, Conroy 1 + 1.

Autoglass Trophy Appearances (2 games)

Richardson 1, Fensome 2, Fleming 1 + 1, Moyes 2, Ainsworth 1, Cartwright 1 + 1, Raynor 2, Trebble 2, Bryson 2, Sale 2, Squires 1, Kidd 1, Vaughan 1, Sharp 1, Holmes 1, Whalley 1 + 1.

Goalscorers: 58 League–2 FAC–2 CCC–(62)

Conroy 10–1–0 (11), Smart 6–1–0 (7), Sale 6–0–0 (6), Bryson 5–0–0 (5), Moyes 4–0–1 (5), Trebble 4–0–0 (4), Raynor 3–0–0 (3), Kidd 3–0–0 (3), Davey 3–0–0 (3), Carmichael 3–0–0 (3), Fleming 2–0–0 (2), Beckham 2–0–0 (2), Whalley 1–0–0 (1), Ainsworth 1–0–0 (1), Holmes 1–0–0 (1), Cartwright 1–0–0 (1), Atkinson 1–0–0 (1), Magee 1–0–0 (1), Fensome 0–0–1 (1), Own Goals 1–0–0 (1), Greenall of Lincoln.

League position in Division Three: 5th (Play-offs) – P42 W19 D10 L13 F58 A41 Pts 67
Home: W13 D3 L5 F37 A17   Away: W6 D7 L8 F21 A24

David Beckham before he became a household name, sporting a Preston strip. The main picture shows him being congratulated by Ray Sharp and Simon Davey after scoring from a superb free-kick.

STAT FACTS:

Best home run without defeat: 14 games
Best away run without defeat: 5 games
Longest run unbeaten: 11 games
Longest run without a win: 7 games
Best home attendance: 14,036 *vs.* Blackpool FAC 14.11.94
Worst home attendance: 3,328 *vs.* Chester A.T. 27.9.94
Best away attendance: 10,684 *vs.* Carlisle 14.1.95
Worst away attendance: 1,756 *vs.* Bury A.T. 8.11.94
Aggregate and average home attendance: 178,808 – 8,515
Aggregate and average away attendance: 81,377 – 3,875

Ever presents: (1) Andy Fensome   Hat-tricks: None
Players used: 27   FA Cup: Second Round Replay
Coca Cola Cup: First Round
Also competed in the Autoglass Trophy
Manager: John Beck until November 1994, then Gary Peters
Chairman: B. Gray Esq.
Leading scorer: 11 goals – Mike Conroy (10 League 1 FAC)
OFFICIAL PLAYER OF THE SEASON: Andy Fensome

Season 1994–95: Third Division

		P	W	D	L	F	A	Pts
1	Carlisle United	42	27	10	5	67	31	91
2	Walsall	42	24	11	7	75	40	83
3	Chesterfield	42	23	12	7	62	37	81
4	Bury	42	23	11	8	73	36	80
5	**PRESTON**	**42**	**19**	**10**	**13**	**58**	**41**	**67**
6	Mansfield Town	42	18	11	13	84	59	65
7	Scunthorpe United	42	18	8	16	68	63	62
8	Fulham	42	16	14	12	60	54	62
9	Doncaster Rovers	42	17	10	15	58	43	61
10	Colchester United	42	16	10	16	56	64	58
11	Barnet	42	15	11	16	56	63	56
12	Lincoln City	42	15	11	16	53	54	56
13	Torquay United	42	14	13	15	54	57	55
14	Wigan Athletic	42	14	10	18	53	60	52
15	Rochdale	42	12	14	16	47	74	50
16	Hereford United	42	12	13	17	45	62	49
17	Northampton Town	42	10	14	18	45	67	44
18	Hartlepool United	42	11	10	21	43	69	43
19	Gillingham	42	10	11	21	46	64	41
20	Darlington	42	11	8	23	43	57	41
21	Scarborough	42	8	10	24	49	70	34
22	Exeter City	42	8	10	24	36	70	34

Date 1994-5	Opponents	Comp	h or a	Score	Att.	1	2	3	4	5	6	7	8	9	10	11	12	14	GK	Own Goals
Aug 13	Darlington	Div 3	a	0-0	3315	Richardson	Fensome	Fleming	Whalley	Hicks	Moyes	Ainsworth	Cartwright	Raynor	Trebble	Bryson	Sale	Squires	O'Hanlon	
Aug 17	**Stockport Co. Rd1 1L**	**CCC**	**h***	**1-1**	**2385**	**Richardson**	**Fensome (1p)**	**Fleming**	**Whalley**	**Hicks**	**Moyes**	**Cartwright**	**Kidd**	**Raynor**	**Trebble +**	**Bryson ***	**Conroy ***	**Sale +**	**O'Hanlon**	
Aug 20	Hereford Utd.	Div 3	a	2-0	3039	Richardson	Fensome	Kidd	Whalley	Hicks	Moyes	Ainsworth	Cartwright	Raynor *	Sale (1)	Fleming	Conroy * (1)	Squires	O'Hanlon	
Aug 23	**Stockport Co. Rd1 2L**	**CCC**	**a**	**1-4**	**4547**	**Richardson**	**Fensome**	**Kidd**	**Whalley**	**Hicks**	**Moyes (1)**	**Ainsworth +**	**Cartwright**	**Sale ***	**Conroy**	**Fleming**	**Raynor ***	**Bryson +**	**Vaughan**	
Aug 27	Barnet	Div 3	a	1-2	2441	Richardson	Fensome	Fleming	Whalley	Hicks	Kidd	Ainsworth	Cartwright	Trebble *	Conroy +	Bryson	Sale * (1)	Raynor +	Vaughan	
Aug 30	Bury	Div 3	a	0-0	3623	Richardson	Fensome	Kidd	Whalley	Squires	Moyes	Ainsworth	Bryson	Raynor	Sale	Conroy	Fleming	Cartwright	Vaughan	
Sep 3	Lincoln City	Div 3	h	4-0	8837	Richardson	Fensome	Kidd	Whalley	Squires	Moyes (1)	Ainsworth (1)	Bryson +	Raynor	Sale (1)	Conroy *	Fleming *	Cartwright +	Vaughan	1 o.g.
Sep 10	Fulham	Div 3	a	1-0	5001	Richardson	Fensome	Kidd	Whalley	Hicks	Moyes	Ainsworth +	Bryson	Raynor	Sale	Fleming *	Trebble * (1)	Cartwright +	Vaughan	
Sep 13	Gillingham	Div 3	a	3-2	2555	Richardson	Fensome	Kidd	Whalley +	Hicks	Moyes	Ainsworth	Bryson	Raynor *	Sale (2)	Fleming (1)	Trebble *	Cartwright +	Vaughan	
Sep 17	Darlington	Div 3	h	1-3	8484	Richardson	Fensome	Kidd +	Whalley	Squires	Moyes	Ainsworth	Bryson	Raynor	Sale *	Fleming	Trebble * (1)	Cartwright +	Vaughan	
Sep 24	Doncaster R.	Div 3	a	1-2	3321	Richardson	Fensome	Kidd	Whalley	Squires	Moyes	Ainsworth	Bryson	Fleming (1)	Trebble	Raynor	Hicks	Cartwright	Vaughan	
Sep 27	**Chester City**	**AT**	**h**	**1-1**	**3328**	**Richardson**	**Fensome**	**Kidd**	**Whalley +**	**Squires**	**Moyes**	**Ainsworth**	**Bryson**	**Sale**	**Trebble * (1)**	**Raynor**	**Fleming ***	**Cartwright +**	**Vaughan**	
Oct 1	Walsall	Div 3	h	1-2	7852	Richardson	Fensome	Kidd	Whalley (1)	Squires	Moyes	Ainsworth	Bryson +	Sale	Trebble	Raynor *	Fleming *	Cartwright +	Lucas	
Oct 8	Scunthorpe Utd.	Div 3	h	0-1	6895	Richardson	Fensome	Kidd	Whalley	Hicks	Moyes	Ainsworth	Bryson	Sale *	Fleming	Raynor	Trebble *	Atkinson	Vaughan	
Oct 15	Hartlepool Utd.	Div 3	a	1-3	2002	Vaughan	Fensome	Sharp	Whalley *	Hicks	Kidd	Ainsworth	Bryson	Sale +	Trebble	Atkinson (1)	Cartwright *	Fleming +	Richardson	
Oct 22	Colchester Utd.	Div 3	a	1-3	3015	Vaughan	Fensome	Sharp	Whalley	Hicks	Moyes	Cartwright +	Bryson	Trebble (1)	Conroy *	Atkinson	Sale *	Fleming +	Richardson	
Oct 29	Exeter City	Div 3	h	0-1	6808	Vaughan	Fensome	Sharp	Whalley +	Holmes	Moyes	Fleming	Bryson	Raynor	Conroy *	Atkinson	Sale *	Cartwright +	Richardson	
Nov 5	Mansfield Town	Div 3	a	2-1	2602	Vaughan	Fensome	Sharp	Cartwright	Squires +	Moyes	Fleming	Bryson	Raynor	Conroy (2)	Atkinson	Sale	Whalley +	Richardson	
Nov 8	**Bury**	**AT**	**a**	**0-1**	**1756**	**Vaughan**	**Fensome**	**Sharp**	**Cartwright**	**Holmes**	**Moyes**	**Trebble**	**Bryson**	**Raynor**	**Sale**	**Fleming +**	**Welsh**	**Whalley +**	**Richardson**	
Nov 14	**Blackpool Rd 1**	**FAC**	**h**	**1-0**	**14036**	**Richardson**	**Fensome**	**Sharp**	**Cartwright**	**Holmes**	**Moyes**	**Ainsworth +**	**Bryson**	**Raynor**	**Conroy (1) ***	**Trebble**	**Sale ***	**Whalley +**	**Lucas**	
Nov 19	Northampton T.	Div 3	h	2-0	7297	Richardson	Fensome	Sharp	Cartwright	Holmes	Moyes (1)	Ainsworth	Bryson *	Raynor (1)	Conroy	Trebble +	Emerson *	Fleming +	Lucas	
Nov 26	Chesterfield	Div 3	a	0-1	3191	Richardson	Fensome	Sharp	Cartwright	Holmes	Moyes	Trebble +	Bryson	Smart	Conroy	Kidd	Emerson	Raynor +	Lucas	
Dec 3	**Walsall Rd 2**	**FAC**	**h**	**1-1**	**9767**	**Richardson**	**Fensome**	**Sharp**	**Cartwright**	**Holmes**	**Moyes**	**Trebble +**	**Bryson**	**Smart (1)**	**Conroy**	**Raynor ***	**Emerson ***	**Fleming +**	**Lucas**	
Dec 10	Hereford Utd.	Div 3	h	4-2	6581	Richardson	Fensome	Sharp	Cartwright	Holmes	Moyes	Magee (1) +	Bryson (2p)	Smart *	Conroy (1)	Raynor	Rimmer *	Fleming +	Lucas	
Dec 13	**Walsall Replay**	**FAC**	**a**	**0-4**	**6468**	**Richardson**	**Fensome ***	**Sharp**	**Whalley**	**Holmes**	**Moyes**	**Cartwright**	**Bryson**	**Smart**	**Conroy**	**Raynor +**	**Emerson ***	**Trebble +**	**Lucas**	
Dec 17	Barnet	Div 3	h	1-0	6429	Richardson	Fensome	Sharp	Emerson	Kidd (1)	Moyes	Cartwright	Bryson	Smart *	Conroy	Raynor	Rimmer *	Fleming	Lucas	
Dec 26	Rochdale	Div 3	h	3-0	10491	Richardson	Fensome	Sharp	Cartwright	Kidd (1)	Moyes	Magee +	Bryson	Smart (1) *	Conroy (1)	Raynor	Lancashire *	Atkinson +	Vaughan	
Dec 31	Scarborough	Div 3	h	1-0	8407	Richardson #	Fensome	Sharp +	Cartwright	Kidd	Moyes	Magee	Bryson	Smart (1)	Conroy *	Raynor	Lancashire *	Atkinson +	Vaughan #	
Jan 2	Torquay Utd.	Div 3	a	0-1	3770	Vaughan	Fensome	Fleming	Cartwright	Kidd	Moyes	Ainsworth *	Bryson	Smart +	Lancashire	Atkinson	Trebble *	Conroy +	Lucas	
Jan 10	Colchester Utd.	Div 3	h	2-1	6377	Vaughan	Fensome	Fleming	Cartwright	Kidd	Moyes	Magee +	Bryson	Smart (1) *	Lancashire	Raynor	Trebble * (1)	Atkinson +	Lucas	
Jan 14	Carlisle Utd.	Div 3	a	0-0	10684	Vaughan	Fensome	Fleming	Cartwright	Kidd	Moyes	Magee +	Bryson	Smart *	Lancashire	Raynor	Trebble *	Atkinson +	Richardson	
Jan 21	Mansfield Town	Div 3	h	2-1	8448	Vaughan	Fensome	Fleming	Cartwright	Kidd	Moyes	Magee +	Bryson (1)	Smart (1) *	Lancashire	Raynor	Trebble *	Atkinson +	Richardson	
Jan 24	Wigan Ath.	Div 3	a	1-1	3618	Vaughan	Fensome	Sharp *	Cartwright (1)	Kidd	Moyes	Ainsworth	Bryson	Smart +	Lancashire	Raynor	Trebble *	Fleming +	Richardson	
Feb 4	Chesterfield	Div 3	h	0-0	8544	Vaughan	Fensome	Sharp	Cartwright	Kidd	Moyes	Magee *	Bryson	Smart +	Lancashire	Raynor	Atkinson *	Trebble +	Richardson	
Feb 11	Northampton T.	Div 3	a	1-2	5195	Vaughan	Fensome	Sharp	Cartwright	Kidd	Moyes	Ainsworth +	Bryson	Smart (1)	Atkinson	Raynor	Magee	Trebble +	Richardson	
Feb 18	Carlisle Utd.	Div 3	h	1-0	11867	Vaughan	Fensome	Sharp	Cartwright	Kidd	Moyes	Magee *	Bryson	Smart +	Conroy (1)	Raynor	Atkinson *	Lancashire +	Richardson	
Feb 28	Walsall	Div 3	a	2-2	4492	Vaughan	Fensome	Sharp	Cartwright	Kidd	Moyes	Davey	Bryson	Smart +	Conroy (1)	Raynor (1)	Atkinson	Lancashire +	Richardson	
Mar 4	Doncaster R.	Div 3	h	2-2	9624	Vaughan	Fensome	Sharp	Cartwright	Kidd	Moyes	Davey (1)	Bryson	Lancashire +	Conroy	Raynor *	Beckham * (1)	Smart +	Richardson	
Mar 11	Fulham	Div 3	h	3-2	8601	Vaughan	Fensome	Sharp	Beckham (1)	Kidd	Moyes	Davey	Bryson *	Raynor (1)	Conroy (1)	Magee	Cartwright *	Smart	Richardson	
Mar 18	Bury	Div 3	h	5-0	9626	Vaughan	Fensome	Sharp	Beckham	Kidd	Moyes (1)	Davey	Bryson	Carmichael (2)	Conroy (2)	Magee	Cartwright	Smart	Richardson	
Mar 21	Exeter City	Div 3	a	1-0	2057	Vaughan	Fensome	Sharp	Beckham	Squires	Moyes	Davey	Bryson (1)	Carmichael	Conroy	Magee +	Cartwright	Raynor +	Richardson	
Mar 25	Lincoln City	Div 3	a	1-1	5487	Vaughan	Fensome	Sharp	Beckham	Kidd (1)	Moyes	Davey	Bryson	Carmichael +	Conroy	Magee *	Cartwright *	Raynor +	Richardson	
Apr 1	Gillingham	Div 3	h	1-1	9100	Vaughan	Fensome	Sharp	Raynor	Squires	Moyes	Davey	Bryson	Carmichael (1) +	Atkinson	Magee *	Cartwright *	Smart +	Richardson	
Apr 8	Scarborough	Div 3	a	1-1	4266	Vaughan	Fensome	Fleming	Raynor	Squires	Moyes	Davey	Bryson (1)	Carmichael +	Conroy	Cartwright	Atkinson	Lancashire +	Richardson	
Apr 15	Wigan Ath.	Div 3	h	1-0	10238	Vaughan	Fensome	Fleming	Cartwright	Kidd	Moyes *	Davey	Bryson	Smart (1) +	Conroy	Raynor	Carmichael *	Lancashire +	Richardson	
Apr 17	Rochdale	Div 3	a	1-0	4012	Vaughan	Fensome	Fleming	Cartwright	Kidd	Squires	Davey (1)	Bryson	Smart +	Carmichael *	Raynor	Conroy *	Lancashire +	Richardson	
Apr 22	Torquay Utd.	Div 3	h	0-1	9173	Vaughan	Fensome	Fleming	Cartwright	Kidd +	Squires	Davey	Bryson	Smart	Conroy *	Raynor	Lancashire *	Carmichael +	Richardson	
Apr 29	Hartlepool Utd.	Div 3	h	3-0	9129	Vaughan	Fensome	Fleming	Raynor	Holmes (1)	Moyes (1)	Davey (1)	Bryson	Lancashire	Carmichael	Magee	Sharp	Smart	Richardson	
May 6	Scunthorpe Utd.	Div 3	a	1-2	3691	Vaughan	Fensome +	Fleming	Raynor	Kidd	Moyes	Davey	Bryson	Lancashire	Sale (1) *	Atkinson	Carmichael *	Cartwright +	Richardson	

* Played at Bury   Own Goal: Greenall of Lincoln

The Preston fans noticed a slight difference when returning to Deepdale for the start of the new season, the old West Stand had gone! As part of the ongoing plans for the ground, the stand had been demolished in readiness for a new all-seater stand which was to be built. Chairman Bryan Gray, and his BAXI group were busy attracting sponsors and investors to help raise the funds which would improve facilities and also, hopefully, improve the team. Gary Peters' first full season began with a home defeat, especially disappointing as he had invested in two new strike partners, Andy Saville and Steve Wilkinson who were making their debuts. It took a few games for those lads to settle but as September arrived the team embarked on a great run of results. Dean Barrick and Russ Wilcox came in to tighten the defence and quickly became crowd favourites as they helped turn drawn games into wins, something that was missing in the previous season. Preston had already lost to Sunderland in the Coca Cola Cup and they were soon to go out of the Auto Windscreen Shield. In the league though things went from strength to strength. A great win over Mansfield at Deepdale saw the unique event of two players, Saville and Wilkinson both scoring hat-tricks in the same match, a 6–0 victory. Simon Davey played very well in midfield and weighed in with a number of vital goals, whilst Graeme Atkinson and

Ian Bryson shared the load in the midfield with some great running and passing. The team was playing good, passing football and to complete the picture, by the November, the new stand was taking shape. It was announced that it would be named the Tom Finney Stand. What else could it be? A second round exit in the FA Cup at a foggy Bradford City did not upset the league rhythm and all minds were fixed firmly on the quest for promotion. The key was the excellent away record. Only two games were lost away from Deepdale, a superb record, and one that Preston fans over the years had not been used to. As the season progressed the team looked more and more like champions and as in 1987 they clinched promotion at Leyton Orient's ground where two Saville goals earned a 2–0 win. The next, and penultimate game, was at Hartlepool and another 2–0 win this time gave them the Championship. Peters and his players had been magnificent all season and what a way to celebrate the opening of the superb new stand for the Darlington game. Nearly 19,000 people watched the last game, another 2–0 win, this time against Exeter. The scorers? Who else but Saville and Wilkinson.

DEBUTANTS: (16) Andy Saville, Steve Wilkinson, Michael Brown, Alan Johnson, Dean Barrick, Russ Wilcox, Kevin Kilbane, Neil McDonald, Charlie Bishop, Teuvo Moilanen, Paul Sparrow, Paul Birch, Tony Grant, Gary Bennett, Kevin Gage, David Lucas.

LAST GAMES: (15) Ainsworth, Raynor, Fensome, Magee, Richardson, Fleming, Vaughan, Sharp, Holmes, Lancashire, Smart, Johnson, Bishop, Birch, Grant.

Lee Cartwright, speedy winger in full flow.

Ever presents: None
Hat-tricks: (3) Andy Saville 2, Steve Wilkinson
Players used: 34
FA Cup: Second Round
Coca Cola Cup: First Round
Also competed in the Auto Windscreen Shield
Manager: Gary Peters
Chairman: B. Gray Esq.
Leading scorer: 30 goals – Andy Saville
(29 League 1 AWS)
OFFICIAL PLAYER OF THE SEASON: Andy Saville

League position in Division Three: Champions – P46 W23 D17 L6 F78 A38 Pts 86
Home: W11 D8 L4 F44 A22   Away: W12 D9 L2 F34 A16

Match Report: Irresistible Force Meets Immovable Object – 9 Mar 1996 Gillingham 1 Preston 1

Preston missed a great chance of knocking Gillingham off the top of the Third Division as the division's meanest defence held the division's top scorers. In the context of the season this was a vital game for both sides and the North End travelling army of fans were delighted to see their favourites dominate for long spells. A full house saw Castle go close for the home side early on whilst Davey missed a great chance when he headed over a fine cross by Saville. Gillingham, so impregnable this season were lucky to see their goal still intact as Preston wasted several clear chances. Sparrow and Birch looked impressive for the visitors and Preston seemed in control. It really came as no surprise when they finally broke the deadlock with just three minutes of the second half played. Davey made up for his earlier miss by scoring with a splendid clipped shot over Stannard after good work by Wilkinson on the left. Gillingham were stunned and if Bryson or Wilkinson had put away further clear chances around the hour mark then there would have been no way back for the home side. As it was, on 72 minutes, the referee awarded a free-kick to Gillingham against Sparrow, a decision that incensed Manager Gary Peters. Gillingham, being the dead ball specialists of the division, duly took advantage of this stroke of good fortune and from Naylor's cross, Harris rose to power a header beyond Vaughan in the Preston goal. Tempers became frayed as the game reached its climax and Davey and Barrick were both booked. In the end both sides had to settle for a point.

League appearances (46 games)

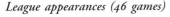

Ainsworth G. 0 + 2, Atkinson G. 42 + 2, Barrick D.A. 39 + 1, Bennett G.M. 5 + 3, Birch P. 11, Bishop C.D. 4, Brown M.A. 6 + 4, Bryson J.I.C. 44, Cartwright L. 22 + 4, Davey 37 + 1, Fensome A.B. 20, Fleming T.M. 5, Gage K.W. 4 + 3, Grant A.J.P. 0 + 1, Holmes S.P. 8, Johnson A.K. 2, Kidd R.A. 23 + 7, Kilbane K.D. 7 + 4, Lancashire G. 2 + 4, Lucas D.A. 1, Magee K. 4 + 1, McDonald N.R. 8 + 3, Moilanen T.J. 2, Moyes D.W. 41, Raynor P.J. 2 + 1, Richardson B. 3, Saville A.V. 44, Sharp R. 1, Smart A.A.C. 0 + 2, Sparrow P. 13, Squires J.A. 3 + 4, Vaughan J. 40, Wilcox R. 27, Wilkinson S.J. 36 + 6.

FA Cup appearances (2 games)

Vaughan 2, Fensome 2, Davey 2, Kidd 1, Moyes 2, Bryson 2, Saville 2, Wilkinson 2, Atkinson 2, Wilcox 1, Cartwright 1 + 1, Barrick 2, McDonald 1.

Coca Cola Cup appearances (2 games)

Vaughan 2, Fensome 1, Fleming 2, Kidd 2, Moyes 2, Raynor 1, Bryson 2, Saville 2, Wilkinson 2, Atkinson 2, Sharp 2, Magee 1 + 1, Ainsworth 0 + 2, Cartwright 1.

Autoglass Trophy Appearances (3 games)

Vaughan 2, Fensome 2, Fleming 0 + 1, Davey 3, Kidd 2 + 1, Moyes 3, Bryson 3, Saville 2, Wilkinson 2, Atkinson 3, Lancashire 0 + 1, Sharp 1, Squires 1 + 1, Cartwright 1 + 2, Brown 1, Richardson 1, Smart 0 + 1, Barrick 2, Wilcox 1, Kilbane 1 + 1, McDonald 2.

Goalscorers: 78 League–3 FAC–3 CCC–3 AT–(Total 87)

Saville 29–0–0–1 (30), Wilkinson 10–1–0–0 (11), Davey 10–0–0–0 (10), Bryson 9–0–1–0 (10), Atkinson 5–0–0–1 (6), Cartwright 3–1–1–0 (5), Moyes 3–0–0–0 (3), Birch 2–0–0–0 (2), Lancashire 2–0–0–0 (2), Wilcox 1–1–0–0 (2), Kidd 0–0–1–1 (2), Squires 1–0–0–0 (1), Brown 1–0–0–0 (1), Kilbane 1–0–0–0 (1), Bennett 1–0–0–0 (1).

STAT FACTS:

Best home run without defeat: 12 games
Best away run without defeat: 10 games
Longest run unbeaten: 21 games
Longest run without a win: 3 games
Best home attendance: 18,700 *vs.* Exeter 4.5.96
Worst home attendance: 5,639 *vs.* Scarborough AWS
Best away attendance: 10,602 *vs.* Gillingham 9.3.96
Worst away attendance: 793 *vs.* Hull AWS 17.10.95
Aggregate and average home attendance: 229,811 – 9,992
Aggregate and average away attendance: 104,411 – 4,540

Season 1995–96: Third Division

	P	W	D	L	F	A	Pts
1 PRESTON	46	23	17	6	78	38	86
2 Gillingham	46	22	17	7	49	20	83
3 Bury	46	22	13	11	66	48	79
4 Plymouth Argyle	46	22	12	12	68	49	78
5 Darlington	46	20	18	8	60	42	78
6 Hereford United	46	20	14	12	65	47	74
7 Colchester United	46	18	18	10	61	51	72
8 Chester City	46	18	16	12	72	53	70
9 Barnet	46	18	16	12	65	45	70
10 Wigan Athletic	46	20	10	16	62	56	70
11 Northampton Town	46	18	13	15	51	44	67
12 Scunthorpe United	46	15	15	16	67	61	60
13 Doncaster Rovers	46	16	11	19	49	60	59
14 Exeter City	46	13	18	15	46	53	57
15 Rochdale	46	14	13	19	57	61	55
16 Cambridge United	46	14	12	20	61	71	54
17 Fulham	46	12	17	17	57	63	53
18 Lincoln City	46	13	14	19	57	73	53
19 Mansfield Town	46	11	20	15	54	64	53
20 Hartlepool	46	12	13	21	47	67	49
21 Leyton Orient	46	12	11	23	44	63	47
22 Cardiff City	46	11	12	23	41	64	45
23 Scarborough	46	8	16	22	39	69	40
24 Torquay United	46	5	14	27	30	84	29

1995–96 Third Division

Left: Captain, Ian Bryson holds the trophy aloft.

Below: Russ Wilcox, Simon Davey and David Moyes after winning promotion at Leyton Orient, 20 April 1996.

Right: North End proudly show off the trophy and their medals.

Champions

Above: Ian Bryson and David Moyes keeping a tight grip of the silverware.

Below: The Championship winning team pictured with the trophy.

Date 1995-6	Opponents	Comp	h or a	Score	Att.	1	2	3	4	5	6	7	8	9	10	11	12	13	14
Aug 12	Lincoln City	Div 3	h	1-2	7813	Vaughan	Fensome +	Fleming	Davey	Kidd	Moyes	Raynor	Bryson	Saville (1)	Wilkinson	Atkinson	Sharp	Lancashire +	Magee
Aug 15	Sunderland Rd1 1L	CCC	h	1-1	6323	Vaughan	Fensome	Sharp	Atkinson	Kidd (1)	Moyes	Fleming #	Bryson	Saville	Wilkinson	Raynor +	Magee	Lancashire +	Ainsworth #
Aug 19	Plymouth Arg.	Div 3	a	2-0	6862	Vaughan	Fensome *	Sharp	Atkinson #	Kidd	Moyes	Fleming	Bryson (1)	Saville	Wilkinson	Magee	Ainsworth *	Lancashire	Squires # (1)
Aug 23	Sunderland Rd1 2L	CCC	a	2-3	7407	Vaughan	Fleming	Sharp	Atkinson	Kidd	Moyes	Cartwright (1)	Bryson (1)	Saville	Wilkinson	Magee *	Ainsworth *	Lancashire	Squires
Aug 26	Wigan Ath.	Div 3	h	1-1	6837	Vaughan	Fleming	Kidd	Atkinson (1)	Holmes	Moyes	Cartwright	Bryson	Saville	Wilkinson	Magee	Ainsworth *	Lancashire	Squires
Aug 29	Bury	Div 3	h	0-0	4682	Vaughan	Fleming	Kidd	Atkinson	Holmes	Moyes	Cartwright	Bryson	Saville	Wilkinson	Magee	Raynor	Lancashire	Squires
Sep 2	Cambridge Utd.	Div 3	h	3-3	7034	Vaughan	Fleming +	Kidd	Atkinson	Holmes	Moyes	Cartwright	Bryson	Saville (1)	Wilkinson (1)	Magee *	Raynor *	Lancashire + (1)	Brown #
Sep 9	Hereford Utd.	Div 3	a	1-0	3124	Richardson	Fensome	Kidd	Atkinson	Squires	Johnson	Cartwright	Bryson	Saville (1)	Wilkinson	Raynor	Magee	Fleming	Brown
Sep 12	Colchester Utd.	Div 3	a	2-2	2869	Richardson	Fensome *	Kidd	Atkinson	Squires	Johnson	Cartwright (1)	Bryson (1)	Saville	Wilkinson +	Brown #	Magee *	Smart +	Barrick #
Sep 16	Scunthorpe Utd.	Div 3	a	2-2	7391	Richardson	Fensome	Barrick	Atkinson (1)	Squires	Kidd	Cartwright +	Bryson	Saville	Wilkinson	Brown #	Johnson	Smart +	Davey #
Sep 23	Fulham	Div 3	a	2-2	5209	Vaughan	Fensome	Barrick	Atkinson	Wilcox	Kidd	Davey (1)	Bryson (1p) #	Saville	Wilkinson	Brown	Squires	Ainsworth	Cartwright #
Sep 30	Chester City	Div 3	h	2-0	8544	Vaughan	Fensome	Barrick	Atkinson	Wilcox	Moyes	Davey	Bryson	Saville (1)	Wilkinson (1)	Brown *	Cartwright *	Smart	Squires
Oct 7	Scarborough	Div 3	h	3-2	7702	Vaughan	Fensome	Barrick	Atkinson	Wilcox *	Moyes	Davey (1)	Bryson	Saville (1)	Wilkinson (1)	Brown #	Kidd *	Kilbane	Cartwright #
Oct 14	Torquay Utd.	Div 3	h	4-0	4058	Vaughan	Fensome	Barrick	Atkinson #	Wilcox	Moyes	Davey	Bryson (2)	Saville (2)	Wilkinson	Cartwright	Kidd *	Richardson	Kilbane #
Oct 17	Hull City	AWS	a	0-1	793	Richardson	Fensome *	Sharp #	Atkinson	Kidd	Moyes	Davey	Bryson	Kilbane	Wilkinson +	Cartwright	Fleming *	Smart +	Squires #
Oct 21	Mansfield Town	Div 3	h	6-0	8989	Vaughan	Fensome	Barrick	Atkinson	Wilcox	Moyes	Davey #	Bryson	Saville (3)	Wilkinson (3)	Cartwright	Kidd	Lancashire	Kilbane #
Oct 28	Doncaster R.	Div 3	a	2-2	4413	Vaughan	Fensome	Barrick	Atkinson	Wilcox *	Moyes	Davey (2)	Bryson	Saville	Wilkinson	Cartwright	Kidd *	Rhodes	Kilbane
Oct 31	Northampton T.	Div 3	a	2-1	4695	Vaughan	Fensome	Barrick	Atkinson	Wilcox (1)	Moyes	Davey	Bryson	Saville (1)	Wilkinson	Cartwright #	Kidd	Rhodes	Kilbane #
Nov 4	Leyton Orient	Div 3	h	4-0	9823	Vaughan	Fensome	Barrick	Atkinson	Wilcox	Moyes	Davey (1)	Bryson	Saville (3)	Wilkinson	Cartwright	Kidd	Rhodes	Kilbane
Nov 7	Scarborough	AWS	h	2-1	5639	Vaughan	Fensome	Barrick	Atkinson (1) #	Wilcox *	Moyes	Davey	Bryson +	Saville	Wilkinson	McDonald	Kidd * (1)	Kilbane +	Cartwright #
Nov 11	Carlisle Utd. Rd 1	FAC	a	2-1	7046	Vaughan	Fensome	Barrick	Atkinson	Wilcox (1)	Moyes	Davey	Bryson	Saville	Wilkinson	Cartwright (1)	Kidd	Lancashire	Brown
Nov 18	Exeter City	Div 3	a	1-1	3550	Vaughan	Fensome	Barrick	Atkinson	Wilcox *	Moyes (1)	Davey	Bryson	Saville	Wilkinson	Cartwright #	Kidd *	Rhodes	McDonald #
Nov 25	Hartlepool Utd.	Div 3	a	3-0	9449	Vaughan	Fensome	Barrick	Atkinson (1)	Kidd	Moyes (1)	Davey	Bryson	Saville (1)	McDonald	Cartwright	Lancashire	Brown
Nov 28	Lincoln City	AWS	a	1-2	1729	Vaughan	Squires	Barrick	Atkinson *	Kidd	Moyes	Davey	Bryson	Saville (1)	Brown +	McDonald	Cartwright *	Lancashire +	Sharp
Dec 2	Bradford City Rd 2	FAC	h	1-2	7602	Vaughan	Fensome *	Barrick	Atkinson	Kidd	Moyes	Davey	Bryson	Saville	Wilkinson (1)	McDonald	Cartwright *	Lancashire	Wilcox
Dec 9	Fulham	Div 3	h	1-1	8422	Vaughan	Fensome #	Barrick	Atkinson	Wilcox	Moyes	Davey	Bryson (1)	Saville	Wilkinson	Cartwright	Kidd	Lancashire	McDonald
Dec 16	Chester City	Div 3	a	1-1	5004	Vaughan	Fensome	Barrick	Atkinson	Wilcox	Moyes	Davey	Bryson	Saville	Wilkinson (1) +	Cartwright	Kidd	Lancashire +	McDonald
Dec 23	Gillingham	Div 3	a	0-0	10669	Vaughan	Fensome	Barrick	Atkinson	Wilcox	Moyes	Davey	Bryson	Saville	Wilkinson	Cartwright	Brown	Kidd	McDonald
Jan 1	Cardiff City	Div 3	h	5-0	8354	Vaughan	Fensome	Barrick	Atkinson (1)	Wilcox #	Moyes	Davey (1)	Bryson	Saville (2)	McDonald	Kidd	Wilkinson	Moilanen	Brown # (1)
Jan 6	Barnet	Div 3	a	0-1	2737	Vaughan	Fensome *	Barrick	Atkinson	Wilcox	Moyes	Davey #	Bryson	Saville	McDonald	Kidd	Cartwright *	Moilanen	Brown #
Jan 13	Plymouth Arg.	Div 3	h	3-2	11126	Vaughan	Bishop	Barrick	Atkinson	Wilcox	Moyes	Davey (1)	Bryson (1)	Saville	McDonald	Cartwright (1)	Wilkinson	Moilanen	Brown
Jan 20	Lincoln City	Div 3	a	0-0	5185	Moilanen	Bishop	Barrick	Atkinson	Wilcox	Moyes	Davey	Bryson *	Saville	McDonald	Cartwright	Wilkinson *	Vaughan	Kidd
Jan 30	Darlington	Div 3	a	2-1	2599	Moilanen	Bishop	Barrick	Atkinson	Wilcox	Moyes	Davey	Kilbane #	Saville (1p)	McDonald *	Cartwright (1)	Wilkinson *	Vaughan	Kidd #
Feb 3	Wigan Ath.	Div 3	a	1-0	5567	Vaughan	Bishop	Barrick	Atkinson	Kidd *	Moyes	Davey	Bryson #	Saville	McDonald	Cartwright	Squires *	Smart	Kilbane # (1)
Feb 10	Barnet	Div 3	h	0-1	9974	Vaughan	Holmes	Barrick	Atkinson *	Wilcox	Moyes	Davey	Kilbane	Saville	McDonald	Cartwright	Wilkinson *	Moilanen	Squires
Feb 17	Colchester Utd.	Div 3	h	2-0	9335	Vaughan	Holmes	Barrick	Atkinson	Kidd	Moyes	Davey	Bryson	Saville (2)	McDonald	Cartwright	McDonald	Lancashire	Squires
Feb 24	Scunthorpe Utd.	Div 3	a	3-1	3638	Vaughan	Holmes	Barrick	Atkinson	Kidd	Moyes	Davey	Bryson	Saville (1)	Wilkinson	Cartwright #	McDonald	Lucas	Lancashire # (1)
Feb 27	Hereford Utd.	Div 3	a	2-2	9761	Vaughan	Holmes	Barrick	Atkinson (1) #	Kidd	Moyes *	Davey	Bryson	Saville (1)	Wilkinson +	Lancashire	Squires *	Brown +	McDonald #
Mar 2	Rochdale	Div 3	h	1-2	9697	Vaughan	Holmes #	Barrick	McDonald	Wilcox	Kidd	Davey	Bryson	Saville (1)	Lancashire *	Brown +	Wilkinson *	Atkinson +	Squires *
Mar 9	Gillingham	Div 3	h	1-1	10602	Vaughan	Sparrow	Barrick	Atkinson	Wilcox	Moyes	Davey (1)	Bryson	Saville	Wilkinson	Birch	Kilbane	Lucas	Squires
Mar 12	Rochdale	Div 3	a	3-0	4597	Vaughan	Sparrow	Barrick	Atkinson	Wilcox	Moyes (1)	Kilbane	Bryson	Saville	Wilkinson (1)	Birch (1)	Kidd	Lucas	Grant
Mar 16	Darlington	Div 3	h	1-1	12070	Vaughan	Sparrow	Barrick	Atkinson	Wilcox	Moyes	Kilbane #	Bryson (1)	Saville	Wilkinson	Birch	Kidd	Lucas	Grant #
Mar 23	Cardiff City	Div 3	a	0-0	3511	Vaughan	Sparrow	Barrick	Atkinson	Wilcox *	Moyes	Davey	Bryson	Saville (1)	Wilkinson	Birch	Kidd *	Kearton	Grant
Mar 26	Bury	Div 3	h	0-0	12260	Vaughan	Sparrow	Barrick	Atkinson	Kidd	Moyes	Davey	Bryson	Saville	Wilkinson	Birch	Squires	Lucas	Grant
Mar 30	Scarborough	Div 3	a	2-1	3771	Vaughan	Sparrow	Barrick	Atkinson	Kidd	Moyes	Davey (1)	Bryson	Bennett (1)	Wilkinson	Birch	Gage	Lucas	Grant
Apr 2	Torquay Utd.	Div 3	h	1-0	11965	Vaughan	Sparrow #	Barrick	Atkinson	Kidd	Moyes	Davey	Bryson	Bennett	Wilkinson (1)	Birch	Grant	Lucas	Gage #
Apr 6	Doncaster R.	Div 3	h	1-0	12773	Vaughan	Sparrow	Barrick	Atkinson	Kidd	Moyes	Davey	Bryson	Bennett	Birch (1)	Wilkinson	Lucas	Gage	
Apr 8	Mansfield Town	Div 3	a	0-0	4661	Vaughan	Sparrow #	Barrick	Atkinson	Kidd	Moyes	Davey	Bryson	Bennett	Birch	Wilkinson *	Kilbane	Gage #	
Apr 13	Northampton T.	Div 3	h	0-3	11774	Vaughan	Sparrow	Barrick	Atkinson #	Kidd	Moyes	Davey	Bryson	Bennett	Birch *	Wilkinson *	Lucas	Gage #	
Apr 16	Cambridge Utd.	Div 3	a	1-2	2831	Vaughan	Gage	Barrick	Atkinson #	Wilcox	Moyes	Davey	Bryson	Saville (1)	Wilkinson	Birch *	Bennett *	Lucas	Kidd #
Apr 20	Leyton Orient	Div 3	a	2-0	5170	Vaughan	Sparrow	Barrick	Kilbane *	Wilcox	Moyes	Davey	Bryson	Saville (2)	Wilkinson	Gage	Bennett *	Lucas	Kidd
Apr 27	Hartlepool Utd.	Div 3	a	2-0	5076	Lucas	Sparrow	Barrick	Kilbane	Wilcox	Moyes	Davey (1)	Bryson	Saville (1)	Wilkinson	Gage	Bennett	Kidd	Atkinson
May 4	Exeter City	Div 3	h	2-0	18700	Vaughan	Sparrow	Barrick	Kilbane *	Wilcox	Moyes	Davey	Bryson	Saville (1)	Wilkinson (1)	Gage #	Bennett *	Kidd	Atkinson

Simon Davey. Contributed ten goals from midfield.

Former school chums David Lucas and Kevin Kilbane, snapped prior to Lucas's debut at Hartlepool.

Steve Wilkinson proved to be an ideal partner with Andy Saville.

SEASON 1996–1997

Over the years the Preston North End football team has put their fans through every emotion possible. During the 1996–7 season they did it again as Gary Peters' men struggled to cope with the demands of a higher division. That they survived relegation was the saving grace of a difficult year. Peters kept faith with the same players that had gained promotion but it was soon obvious that new faces would have to be brought in. Bobby Mimms, Mark Rankine and David Reeves were signed and the latter's arrival meant that Andy Saville was allowed to leave. Rarely, in such a short time at Deepdale, has a player achieved such a cult status as the popular Saville had earned. The mixed results at the start of the season caused Peters headaches but a good draw in the Coca Cola cup gave his team a plum game with Spurs. A very late Michael Holt equaliser gave North End a deserved draw at home but in the second leg Preston were well beaten by 3–0. The team were defending well in general and Dean Barrick and Ryan Kidd were in particularly good form, but too often silly errors were costing Preston goals and points. As soon as it looked as though the team had turned the corner an avoidable defeat set them back again. The manager found it hard to find the right blend, although the November and December saw better results and also progress in the FA Cup. A second round defeat at York was a bitter disappointment though and it was also at York that Preston lost their interest in the Auto Windscreen. Back in the league, results were up and down like a yo-yo with the away form back to 'normal'. Sean Gregan, a terrific signing from Darlington, strengthened the midfield and the later signings of Kurt Nogan and Michael Jackson proved that Peters judgement in the transfer market was very sound. But as the season climaxed North End were in real danger of a quick return to the basement league. A good win over Notts County lifted the spirits though and another against Stockport confirmed that Preston would stay up. The final three games were all won as the relief showed in the play and there was another carnival atmosphere for the last game, at home to Walsall. The fans were able to wave a sentimental goodbye to the Spion Kop which was to be demolished to make way for phase two of the ground improvements. The fans stayed loyal, as ever, and the attendances held up well. The effort was there, few managers had worked as hard as Peters, and the public were appreciative of the work done on the ground and the new players brought in. The club was definitely moving in the right direction.

DEBUTANTS: (13) Michael Holt, John Kay, Bobby Mimms, Mark Rankine, Darren Patterson, David Reeves, Paul McKenna, Sean Gregan, Darren Beckford, Sean Teale, Mark Stallard, Kurt Nogan, Michael Jackson.

LAST GAMES: (10) Saville, Wilkinson, Brown, Bennett, Gage, Kay, Patterson, Beckford, Teale, Stallard.

Sean Gregan, great buy from Darlington at £300,000.

STAT FACTS:
Best home run without defeat: 8 games
Best away run without defeat: 2 games
Longest run unbeaten: 4 games
Longest run without a win: 4 games
Best home attendance: 16,258 *vs.* Spurs CCC 17.9.96
Worst home attendance: 5,767 *vs.* Wigan CCC 3.9.96
Best away attendance: 20,080 *vs.* Spurs CCC 25.9.96
Worst away attendance: 1,169 *vs.* Chesterfield AWS 9.12.96
Aggregate and average home attendance: 216,324 – 9,405
Aggregate and average away attendance: 143,999 – 6,261

Ever presents: None
Hat-tricks: (2) Steve Wilkinson and David Reeves
Players used: 34
FA Cup: Second Round
Coca Cola Cup: Second Round
Also competed in the Auto Windscreen Shield
Manager: Gary Peters
Chairman: B. Gray Esq.
Leading scorer: 14 goals – David Reeves
(11 League 3 FAC)
OFFICIAL PLAYER OF THE SEASON: Sean Gregan

The 1996–97 squad pictured in front of the Tom Finney stand.

Match Report: Ashcroft at the Double – 25 Jan 1997. Burnley 1 Preston 2

Five games without a win and a tough trip to Burnley to face. Hardly anybody expected North End to win this match as they had won only once on their travels all season. So imagine the surprise when, on six minutes, Ashcroft met a Kilbane cross and scored at the second attempt after the keeper had saved his first effort. Burnley struck back immediately, though, as Eyres sent in a curling free-kick. O'Hanlon pushed Swan's header on to the crossbar but could only watch in dismay as Barnes followed up to score. Both sides then missed chances with Bennett the chief culprit for Preston and Nogan for Burnley. For the rest of the game Preston largely dominated the play. Bennett and Ashcroft both missed sitters early in the second half and Nogan then forced O'Hanlon into two full length saves as Burnley struck back. Parkinson blocked a Kilbane rocket and the action continued to entertain … It seemed only a matter of time before the deadlock was broken with Preston looking the more likely. In the 69th minute that break-through came as Barrick sent Cartwright away with a defence-splitting pass. The nippy winger fired in a low shot which Beresford blocked, but the ball ran free and Ashcroft pounced to fire in the rebound. It was a real confidence booster for a Preston side still, even in January, trying to come to terms with life in the higher division after their promotion of the previous season. Several players stood out in this game for North End, with Bryson, Cartwright, Kidd and Ashcroft the pick of the bunch.

League appearances (46 games)

Ashcroft L. 26 + 1, Atkinson G. 12 + 5, Barrick D. A. 30 + 6, Beckford D. R. 0 + 2, Bennett G. M. 10 + 6, Brown M. A. 5 + 1, Bryson J. I. C. 32 + 9, Cartwright L. 14, Davey S. 30 + 7, Gage K. W. 16, Gregan S. M. 21, Holt M. A. 8 + 11, Jackson M. J. 7, Kay J. 7, Kidd 33 + 2, Kilbane K. D. 32 + 4, Lucas D. A. 2, McDonald N. R. 12 + 11, McKenna P. S. 4 + 1, Mimms R. A. 27, Moilanen T. J. 4, Moyes D. W. 26, Nogan K. 5 + 2, O'Hanlon K. G. 13, Patterson D. J. 2, Rankine S. M. 19 + 3, Reeves D. E. 33 + 1, Saville A. V. 12, Sparrow P. 6, Squires J. A. 6 + 3, Stallard M. 4, Teale S. 5, Wilcox R. 35, Wilkinson S. J. 8 + 2.

FA Cup appearances (2 games)

Gage 1, Atkinson 0 + 1, Wilcox 2, Kidd 2, Davey 0 + 1, Bryson 1 + 1, Wilkinson 1, Kilbane 1, Holt 1 + 1, McDonald 2, Squires 0 + 1, Moyes 2, Mimms 2, Ashcroft 2, Rankine 2, Reeves 2, Sparrow 1.

Coca Cola Cup appearances (4 games)

Moilanen 1, Barrick 4, Atkinson 3, Wilcox 4, Kidd 3 + 1, Davey 4, Bryson 3, Saville 4, Wilkinson 2, Holt 2, Kilbane 4, McDonald 0 + 2, Squires 1, Moyes 1, Mimms 2, Rankine 2, Lucas 1, Kay 3, Brown 0 + 1.

Auto Windscreen Shield Appearances (2 games)

Ashcroft 0 + 1, Barrick 1, Atkinson 2, Wilcox 1, Davey 2, Bryson 2, Wilkinson 1, Squires 2, Moyes 0 + 1, Bennett 1, Reeves 1, Sparrow 1, Gregan 1, O'Hanlon 2, McKenna 2, Cartwright 1, Beckford 1, Kidd 1.

Goalscorers: 49 League–6 FAC–8 CCC–2 AWS–(Total 65)

Reeves 11–3–0–0 (14), Ashcroft 8 (1 pen)–3–0–0 (11), Davey 6–0–1–0 (7), Wilkinson 3–0–4–0 (7), Moyes 4–0–0–0 (4), Holt 3–0–1–0 (4), Bennett 3–0–0–1 (4), Bryson 3–0–0–0 (3), Kilbane 2–0–0–0 (2), Atkinson 0–0–1–1 (2), Stallard 1–0–0–0 (1), Gregan 1–0–0–0 (1), Saville 1–0–0–0 (1), McKenna 1–0–0–0 (1), Cartwright 1–0–0–0 (1), McDonald 0–0–1–0 (1), Own Goals 1–0–0–0 (1) Seabury of Shrewsbury.

League position in Division Two: 15th – P46 W18 D7 L21 F49 A55 Pts 61
Home: W14 D5 L4 F33 A19 Away: W4 D2 L17 F16 A36

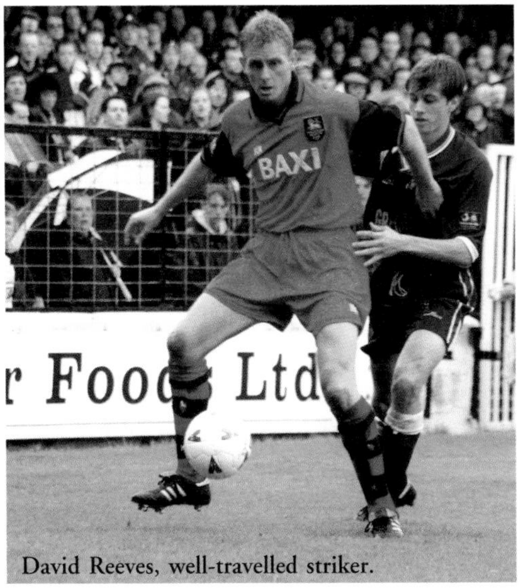

David Reeves, well-travelled striker.

Season 1996–97: Second Division

	P	W	D	L	F	A	Pts
1 Bury	46	24	12	10	62	38	84
2 Stockport Co.	46	23	13	10	59	41	82
3 Luton Town	46	21	15	10	71	45	78
4 Brentford	46	20	14	12	56	43	74
5 Bristol City	46	21	10	15	69	51	73
6 Crewe Alexander	46	22	7	17	56	47	73
7 Blackpool	46	18	15	13	60	47	69
8 Wrexham	46	17	18	11	54	50	69
9 Burnley	46	19	11	16	71	55	68
10 Chesterfield	46	18	14	14	42	39	68
11 Gillingham	46	19	10	17	60	59	67
12 Walsall	46	19	10	17	54	53	67
13 Watford	46	16	19	11	45	38	67
14 Millwall	46	16	13	17	50	55	61
15 PRESTON	**46**	**18**	**7**	**21**	**49**	**45**	**61**
16 Bournemouth	46	15	15	16	43	45	60
17 Bristol Rovers	46	15	11	20	47	50	56
18 Wycombe W	46	15	10	21	51	56	55
19 Plymouth A	46	12	18	16	47	58	54
20 York City	46	13	13	20	47	68	52
21 Peterborough	46	11	14	21	55	73	47
22 Shrewsbury Town	46	11	13	22	49	74	46
23 Rotherham United	46	7	14	25	39	70	35
24 Notts County	46	7	14	25	33	59	35

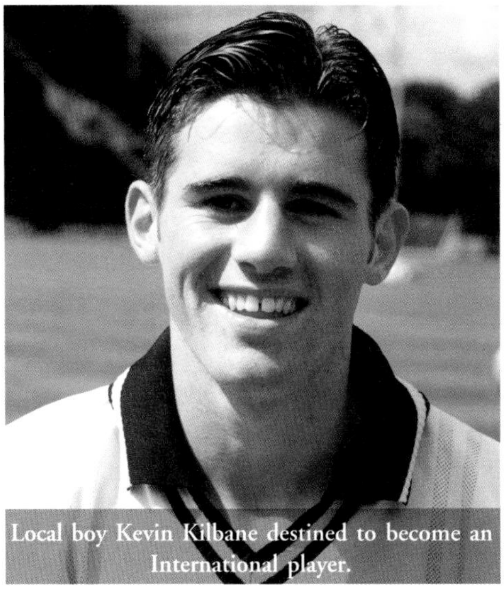
Local boy Kevin Kilbane destined to become an International player.

Date 1996-7	Opponents	Comp	h or a	Score * aet	Att.	1	2	3	4	5	6	7	8	9	10	11	12	13	14
Aug 17	Notts County	Div 2	a	1-2	6879	Moilanen	Gage #	Barrick	Atkinson	Wilcox	Kidd	Davey	Bryson (1)	Saville	Wilkinson	Kilbane *	Holt *	McDonald	Squires #
Aug 20	Wigan Ath. Rd1 1L	CCC	a	3-2	3713	Moilanen	Squires	Barrick	Atkinson	Wilcox	Kidd	Davey	Bryson	Saville	Wilkinson (3)	Kilbane	Holt	McDonald	Brown
Aug 24	Bristol Rovers	Div 2	h	0-0	9752	Moilanen	Kay	Barrick	Atkinson +	Wilcox	Moyes	Davey	Bryson	Saville	Wilkinson	Kilbane #	Holt	McDonald +	Brown #
Aug 27	Crewe A.	Div 2	h	2-1	9498	Moilanen	Kay	Barrick	Atkinson +	Wilcox	Moyes	Davey	Bryson	Saville	Wilkinson (2)	Kilbane	Holt	McDonald +	Brown
Aug 30	Plymouth Arg.	Div 2	a	1-2	9209	Moilanen	Kay	Barrick	Atkinson +	Wilcox	Moyes	Davey	Bryson	Saville	Wilkinson (1)	Kilbane	Kidd	McDonald +	Brown
Sep 3	Wigan Ath. Rd1 2L	CCC	h	4-4 *	5767	Lucas	Kay	Barrick	Atkinson (1)	Wilcox *	Moyes	Davey (1) +	Bryson	Saville	Wilkinson (1)	Kilbane #	Kidd *	McDonald + (1)	Brown #
Sep 7	Bristol City	Div 2	a	1-2	8016	Mimms	Kay	Barrick	McDonald +	Wilcox *	Moyes	Davey	Ashcroft	Saville	Wilkinson	Kilbane (1) #	Kidd *	Atkinson +	Bryson #
Sep 10	York City	Div 2	h	1-0	7608	Mimms	Kay	Barrick	McDonald #	Kidd	Moyes	Davey	Ashcroft (1)	Saville	Atkinson	Kilbane	Holt	Squires	Bryson #
Sep 14	Bournemouth	Div 2	h	0-1	8268	Mimms	Kay	Barrick	McDonald #	Kidd	Moyes	Davey	Ashcroft	Saville	Atkinson *	Kilbane	Holt *	Squires	Bryson #
Sep 17	Tottenham H. Rd2 1L	CCC	h	1-1	16258	Mimms	Kay	Barrick	Rankine	Wilcox	Kidd	Davey	Bryson	Saville	Holt (1)	Kilbane	Atkinson	McDonald	Squires
Sep 21	Wrexham	Div 2	a	0-1	5299	Mimms	Kay	Barrick	Rankine *	Wilcox	Kidd	Davey	Ashcroft	Saville	Holt	Kilbane	Atkinson *	McDonald	Squires
Sep 25	Tottenham H. Rd2 2L	CCC	a	0-3	20080	Mimms	Kay	Barrick	Rankine +	Wilcox	Kidd	Davey	Atkinson	Saville	Holt	Kilbane	Squires	McDonald +	Sharp
Sep 28	Millwall	Div 2	h	2-1	9400	Mimms	Squires	Barrick	Ashcroft	Wilcox	Kidd	Davey	Bryson	Saville (1)	Holt (1) *	Kilbane	Atkinson *	McDonald	Moyes
Oct 1	Watford	Div 2	a	0-1	6434	Mimms	Squires	Barrick	Ashcroft	Wilcox	Kidd	Davey	Bryson	Saville	Holt #	Kilbane *	Atkinson *	McDonald	Bennett #
Oct 5	Peterborough Utd.	Div 2	h	3-4	8874	Mimms	Squires *	Barrick	Patterson	Wilcox	Kidd	Davey	Bryson	Saville	Rankine	Ashcroft (2) +	Holt * (1)	Atkinson +	McDonald
Oct 12	Stockport Co.	Div 2	a	0-1	8405	Mimms	Gage	Barrick	Rankine	Wilcox	Kidd *	Davey	Patterson	Saville	Reeves	Holt #	Bennett *	Sparrow	Bryson #
Oct 15	Walsall	Div 2	a	0-1	3224	Mimms	Gage	Barrick	Rankine	Wilcox	Kidd	Brown	Bryson	Reeves	Bennett	Kilbane	Davey	Sparrow	Holt
Oct 19	Shrewsbury T. ***	Div 2	h	2-1	8333	Mimms	Gage	Barrick	Rankine	Wilcox	Kidd	Brown *	Bryson	Reeves (1)	Bennett #	Kilbane	Davey *	Squires	Holt #
Oct 26	Gillingham	Div 2	a	1-1	6256	Mimms	Gage	Barrick	Rankine	Wilcox	Kidd	Brown	Bryson	Reeves	Bennett *	Kilbane (1)	Holt *	McDonald	Squires
Oct 29	Burnley	Div 2	h	1-1	12652	Mimms	Gage	Barrick	Rankine	Wilcox	Kidd	Brown	Bryson +	Reeves (1)	Bennett *	Kilbane	Holt *	McDonald +	Squires
Nov 2	Rotherham Utd.	Div 2	h	0-0	8867	Mimms	Gage	Barrick #	Rankine	Wilcox	Kidd	Brown +	Bryson	Reeves	Bennett *	Kilbane	Holt *	McDonald +	Squires #
Nov 9	Chesterfield	Div 2	a	1-2	4759	Mimms	Sparrow *	Kidd	Rankine #	Wilcox	Squires	McDonald	Bryson	Reeves (1)	Holt	Kilbane	Wilkinson *	Sharp	Davey #
Nov 16	Altrincham Rd 1	FAC	h	4-1	8286	Mimms	Sparrow	Kidd	Rankine	Wilcox	Moyes	Ashcroft (1) +	McDonald	Reeves (3) #	Wilkinson	Kilbane	Davey	Holt +	Bryson #
Nov 19	Luton Town	Div 2	h	3-2	7004	Mimms	Sparrow	Kidd	Rankine	Wilcox	Moyes (2)	Ashcroft (1)	McDonald	Reeves	Wilkinson +	Kilbane	Davey	Holt +	Bryson
Nov 23	Wycombe W.	Div 2	a	1-0	4920	Mimms	Sparrow	Kidd	Rankine	Wilcox *	Moyes	Ashcroft (1p)	McDonald	Reeves	Wilkinson #	Kilbane	Davey *	Holt	Bryson #
Nov 30	Gillingham	Div 2	h	1-0	9616	Mimms	Sparrow	Kidd #	Rankine *	Wilcox	Moyes	Ashcroft	McDonald	Reeves	Wilkinson +	Kilbane	Davey * (1)	Holt +	Bryson #
Dec 3	Bury	Div 2	a	0-3	5447	Mimms	Sparrow	Kidd +	Rankine *	Wilcox	Moyes	Ashcroft	McDonald	Reeves	Holt #	Kilbane	Davey *	Barrick +	Bryson #
Dec 7	York City Rd 2	FAC	h	2-3	7893	Mimms	Gage +	Kidd	Rankine *	Wilcox	Moyes	Ashcroft (2)	McDonald	Reeves	Holt #	Bryson	Davey *	Squires +	Atkinson #
Dec 9	Chesterfield	AWS	a	2-0	1169	O'Hanlon	Sparrow	Barrick	McKenna	Squires	Gregan	Atkinson (1)	Davey	Bennett (1)	Wilkinson	Bryson	Brown	Holt	Cartwright
Dec 13	Blackpool	Div 2	h	3-0	14626	Mimms	Gage	Barrick	Davey	Kidd	Gregan	Ashcroft	McDonald	Reeves (1)	Atkinson *	Kilbane	Bennett * (2)	Squires	Bryson
Dec 21	Brentford	Div 2	a	0-0	5365	Mimms	Squires	Barrick	Davey	Kidd	Gregan	Ashcroft #	McDonald	Reeves	Bennett *	Kilbane	Rankine *	Moyes	Bryson #
Dec 28	Bristol City	Div 2	h	0-2	10905	Mimms	Gage *	Barrick +	Davey	Kidd	Gregan	Ashcroft	McDonald	Reeves	Bennett	Kilbane	Rankine *	Squires +	Bryson
Jan 11	Millwall	Div 2	a	2-3	7096	Mimms	Squires	Barrick +	Davey (2)	Kidd	Gregan	Atkinson	Rankine	Reeves	Holt *	Kilbane #	Bennett *	McDonald +	Bryson #
Jan 18	Watford	Div 2	h	1-1	8735	Mimms	Gage	Barrick	Kidd	Wilcox	Moyes	Atkinson	Bryson	Reeves	Bennett (1) *	Kilbane +	Beckford *	McKenna +	Cartwright
Jan 21	York City	AWS	a	0-1	1426	O'Hanlon	Cartwright	Kidd	Davey	Wilcox	Squires +	Atkinson	Bryson	Reeves *	Beckford	McKenna	Ashcroft *	Moyes +	Gage
Jan 25	Burnley	Div 2	a	2-1	16186	O'Hanlon	Cartwright	Barrick	Davey	Wilcox	Moyes	Kidd	Bryson	Bennett *	Ashcroft (2)	Kilbane	Reeves *	McKenna	Gage
Feb 1	Chesterfield	Div 2	h	0-1	8681	O'Hanlon	Cartwright	Barrick *	Davey	Wilcox	Gregan	Moyes	Bryson +	Bennett	Ashcroft	Kilbane	Beckford *	McDonald +	Rankine
Feb 8	Rotherham Utd.	Div 2	a	1-0	3556	O'Hanlon	Cartwright #	Teale	Davey	Wilcox	Gregan	Atkinson +	Bryson	Reeves (1)	Ashcroft *	Rankine	Bennett *	McDonald +	Barrick #
Feb 11	Bournemouth	Div 2	a	0-2	4769	O'Hanlon	Sparrow	Barrick +	Teale	Moyes	Gregan	Davey	Bryson	Reeves	Atkinson *	Rankine	Bennett *	Kilbane +	McKenna
Feb 15	Wycombe W.	Div 2	h	2-1	7923	O'Hanlon	Rankine	McKenna (1) #	Teale	Moyes	Gregan	Davey (1)	Bryson	Reeves	Stallard	Kilbane +	Bennett	McDonald +	Barrick #
Feb 22	Luton Town	Div 2	a	1-5	6454	O'Hanlon	Rankine	McDonald +	Teale	Moyes #	Gregan	Davey	Bryson	Reeves (1)	Stallard	McKenna	Bennett	Kilbane +	Barrick #
Feb 25	York City	Div 2	a	1-3	2515	Mimms	Gage	Barrick	Davey	Teale	Gregan	Cartwright (1)	Bryson	Reeves	Stallard +	Atkinson	Wilcox	Kilbane +	McKenna
Mar 1	Bury	Div 2	h	3-1	8749	Mimms	Gage	Barrick	Moyes (1)	Wilcox	Gregan	Cartwright	Bryson	Reeves (1)	Stallard (1)	Davey	Rankine	Kilbane	McKenna
Mar 8	Brentford	Div 2	h	1-0	9489	Mimms	Gage	Barrick	Moyes	Wilcox	Gregan	Cartwright	Bryson (1)	Reeves	Davey	Kilbane	Rankine	Holt	Kidd
Mar 15	Blackpool	Div 2	a	1-2	8017	Mimms	Gage	Barrick	Moyes	Wilcox *	Gregan	Cartwright	Bryson	Reeves	Nogan	Davey (1) +	Kidd *	Ashcroft +	Rankine
Mar 18	Wrexham	Div 2	h	2-1	8271	O'Hanlon	Gage	Kidd	Moyes	Wilcox	Gregan	Cartwright	Ashcroft (1)	Reeves (1)	Nogan	Bryson	Squires	Kilbane	Rankine
Mar 23	Bristol Rovers	Div 2	a	0-1	6405	O'Hanlon	Gage *	Kidd	Moyes	Wilcox	Gregan	Cartwright	Ashcroft	Reeves	Nogan	Bryson	Kilbane *	Squires	Barrick
Mar 29	Notts County	Div 2	h	2-0	9472	O'Hanlon	Kidd	Barrick	Jackson	Moyes (1)	Gregan	Cartwright	Ashcroft	Reeves (1)	Nogan	McKenna	Davey	Atkinson	Rankine
Mar 31	Crewe A.	Div 2	a	0-1	4407	O'Hanlon	Kidd	Wilcox	Jackson	Moyes	Gregan	Rankine #	Ashcroft	Reeves	Bryson	McKenna *	Davey *	Barrick	Wilkinson #
Apr 5	Plymouth Arg.	Div 2	h	1-1	8503	O'Hanlon	Cartwright	Kidd	Jackson	Wilcox	Gregan	Kilbane	Ashcroft	Reeves (1)	Nogan *	Bryson	Davey *	Atkinson	Sparrow
Apr 12	Peterborough Utd.	Div 2	a	0-2	5040	O'Hanlon	Cartwright	Kidd	Jackson	Wilcox +	Gregan	Kilbane *	Ashcroft	Reeves	Davey	Bryson #	Nogan *	Barrick +	Rankine #
Apr 19	Stockport Co.	Div 2	h	1-0	10298	O'Hanlon	Cartwright	Kidd	Jackson	Wilcox	Moyes	Kilbane +	Ashcroft *	Reeves	Davey	Bryson (1)	McDonald *	Holt +	Barrick
Apr 26	Shrewsbury T.	Div 2	a	2-0	5341	Lucas	Moyes	Kidd	Jackson	Wilcox	Gregan (1)	Cartwright +	Ashcroft #	Reeves	Davey (1)	Bryson	McKenna	Holt +	Barrick #
May 3	Walsall	Div 2	h	2-0	10800	Lucas	Moyes	Kidd	Jackson	Wilcox	Gregan	Davey	Ashcroft	Reeves (1)	Holt (1) #	Bryson	McKenna	Barrick	Nogan #

*** 1 Own Goal by Seabury of Shrewsbury

The pre-season had gone well, more quality players had signed for the club and a hard earned point was won at Gillingham in the opening game. What more could a Preston fan want? Jonathan Macken, Michael Appleton and Colin Murdock had joined from Manchester United and a great deal was expected from Fergie's Fledglings, as they were dubbed. North End made a great start losing only one of their first seven league and cup games. David Reeves and Lee Ashcroft were looking sharp and Kurt Nogan at last began to have a little luck in front of goal. A 6–0 thrashing at Blackburn in the Coca Cola Cup was disappointing but on the night Rovers were in a different class, especially in their finishing. North End came back well from that defeat with Sean Gregan, Gary Parkinson and David Moyes playing some skilful and determined football. At the end of the October though Preston hit a goal drought. Bournemouth, Wrexham, Plymouth and York all beat them 1–0 and manager, Gary Peters found it very frustrating. So much so, that he brought in Tony Lormor, a much travelled goalscorer, and he scored on his debut at Luton as Preston won 3–1. Doncaster were beaten in the FA Cup and things suddenly looked brighter. Over the next few weeks North End played some exciting football although the team was still prone to bad defeats. The turn of the year brought some terrific news for all fans of the club. Tom Finney, known for so long by the locals as 'Sir Tom', finally had that accolade bestowed upon him officially as he was given a Knighthood in the New Years Honours List. That was one of the best bits of news ever to come out of Deepdale and a fitting reward for Finney's magnificent

contribution to the history chronicled in this book. Unfortunately, on the field, things took a turn for the worse as results continued to become increasingly poor. It took a toll on Peters and eventually he decided to resign as manager. Rarely has a Preston manager worked as hard to recapture former glories and put things right at Deepdale. But such is life as a football manager and Moyes took over the hot seat, initially temporarily. He desperately searched for his first win, which eventually came at Macclesfield. The team actually looked doomed to relegation as the days went by, a 3–1 home defeat by Carlisle being particularly damaging. Moyes worked hard to instill some fight into the players and a great win at Bournemouth surprised everybody, even Moyes himself. They followed that with a 1–0 home win over Luton and despite a defeat at Plymouth the new spirit was there for all to see. This extra effort was rewarded when Preston clinched their Second Division place for another year with a 1–0 win over Southend, thanks to a Gary Parkinson pile-driver. Moyes was also rewarded, with a full-time contract as the new manager and a great win over runners-up Bristol City in the final game proved what his team were capable of. The outlook was brighter.

DEBUTANTS: (9) Michael Appleton, Julian Darby, David Eyres, Tony Lormor, Jonathan Macken, John Mullin, Colin Murdock, Gary Parkinson, Habib Sissoko.

LAST GAMES: (10) Ashcroft, Atkinson, Barrick, Davey, Lormor, Moyes, Mullin, Reeves, Sissoko, Sparrow.

Match Report: The Completed Jigsaw Puzzle – 18 April 1998. Preston 3 Blackpool 3

The final piece of the jigsaw fell into place after this exciting and yet mistake ridden draw against the old enemy from the coast. In the 50th post-war league game between the two teams Preston needed a result to finally lift the fear of relegation from over their heads. In many ways it was a frustrating day for the home management as silly defensive errors kept allowing Blackpool to stay in the game. A third minute goal by Clarkson threatened to upset Preston but on 23 minutes Eyres was left unmarked to shoot past Banks and score against his old club. When the visitors regained the lead on the stroke of half-time the North End fans were tearing their hair out. Moilanen dropped a corner and Hills said thank you very much and smashed the ball home. Five minutes after the restart a corner by McKenna was cleared but only as far as Parkinson who was stood 30 yards out. The full-back let fly with a ferocious shot that whistled into the Blackpool net for a glorious equaliser. At that point it looked as though there would only be one winner as Preston dominated. That view was enhanced when they took the lead on the hour mark. Rankine's shot was parried and Macken nipped in to score from the rebound. Once again though Preston allowed Blackpool a lifeline as Murdock and Barrick failed to clear and Clarkson was able to shoot past Moilanen. Even then Preston could have won it as Rankine's shot was somehow saved by Banks. But in the end the point was enough and the fans could at last relax, not only because of the recovery against their bitter rivals but also that the relegation threat was over.

STAT FACTS: (Also competed in Auto Windscreen Shield)
Best home run without defeat: 6 games   Best away run without defeat: 3 games   Longest run unbeaten: 5 games
Longest run without a win: 11 games   Best home attendance: 13,500 *vs.* Blackpool 18.4.98
Worst home attendance: 2,703 *vs.* Darlington AWS 9.12.97   Best away attendance: 22,564 *vs.* Blackburn CCC 18.9.97
Worst away attendance: 1,618 *vs.* Mansfield AWS 13.1.98   Aggregate and average home attendance: 217,767 – 9,468
Aggregate and average away attendance: 150,636 – 6,549

League appearances (46 games)

Appleton 31+7, Ashcroft 37, Atkinson 1+2, Barrick 29+4, Cartwright 24+12, Darby 6+6, Davey 17+1, Eyres 26+2, Gregan 33+2, Holt 4+10, Jackson 39+1, Kidd 32+1, Lormor 9+3, Lucas 6, Macken 20+9, McKenna 4+1, Moilanen 40, Moyes 8+1, Mullin 4+3, Murdock 27, Nogan 14+8, Parkinson 44+1, Rankine 34+1, Reeves 12+1, Sissoko 4+3, Sparrow 1.

FA Cup appearances (4 games)

Moilanen 3, Lucas 1, Parkinson 4, Barrick 3, Kidd 4, Murdock 1+1, Jackson 4, Gregan 4, Appleton 4, Ashcroft 3, Lormor 3, Macken 2+1, Rankine 2, Darby 2+1, Eyres 4, Cartwright 0+1, Holt 0+2, Moyes 0+1, Nogan 0+1

Coca Cola Cup appearances (4 games)

Moilanen 4, Parkinson 4, Barrick 3+1, Kidd 4, Murdock 2, Jackson 4, Gregan 3, Appleton 2+1, Cartwright 3+1, Ashcroft 4, Reeves 3 + 1, Macken 2+2, Darby 1+1, Nogan 1+1, Rankine 4, Holt 0+1.

Auto Windscreen Shield (4 games)

Lucas 3, Moilanen 1, Parkinson 4, Barrick 3, Kidd 3, Jackson 4, Gregan 3, Appleton 2, Ashcroft 2, Lormor 3, Murdock 2, Eyres 3, Davey 2, Cartwright 3, Rankine 2, Mullin 1, Nogan 3, Macken 0+3, Darby 0+1, Holt 0+1

Goalscorers: 56 League–8 FAC–6 CCC–5 AWS–(Total 75)

Ashcroft 14 (1p)–2(1p)–0–0 (16), Macken 6–0–2–0 (8), Eyres 4–2–0–2 (8), Parkinson 5–1–0–0 (6), Nogan 5(1p)–0–0–1 (6), Appleton 2–1–0–1 (4), Reeves 1–0–3–0 (4), Lormor 3–0–0–0 (3), Cartwright 2–0–0–1 (3), Gregan 2–1–0–0 (3), Davey 2–0–0–0 (2), Holt 2–0–0–0 (2), Kidd 2–0–0–0 (2), Barrick 1–0–1–0 (2), Jackson 1–0–0–0 (1), Murdock 1–0–0–0 (1), Rankine 1–0–0–0 (1), Moyes 0–1–0–0 (1), Own Goals 2–0–0–0 (2), (Dyche of Bristol City and Cooke of Burnley)

Future players born between August 1997 and July 1998: co-author Mike Payne's grandson, Matthew Carpenter

Ever presents: None
Hat-tricks: (1) Lee Ashcroft
FA Cup: Third Rd.
Coca Cola Cup: Second Rd.
Manager: Gary Peters until January, then David Moyes.
Chairman: B. Gray Esq.
Players used: 26
Leading scorer: 16 goals – Lee Ashcroft (14 League 2 FAC)
OFFICIAL PLAYER OF THE SEASON: Teuvo Moilanen

Season 1997–98: Second Division

	P	W	D	L	F	A	Pts
1 Watford	46	24	16	6	67	30	88
2 Bristol City	46	25	10	11	69	39	85
3 Grimsby Town	46	19	15	12	55	37	72
4 Northampton	46	18	17	11	52	37	71
5 Bristol Rovers	46	20	10	16	70	64	70
6 Fulham	46	20	10	16	60	43	70
7 Wrexham	46	18	16	12	55	51	70
8 Gillingham	46	19	13	14	52	47	70
9 Bournemouth	46	18	12	16	57	42	66
10 Chesterfield	46	16	17	13	46	44	65
11 Wigan Athletic	46	17	11	18	64	66	62
12 Blackpool	46	17	11	18	59	67	62
13 Oldham Athletic	46	15	16	15	62	54	61
14 Wycombe W	46	14	18	14	51	53	60
15 PRESTON	**46**	**15**	**14**	**17**	**56**	**56**	**59**
16 York City	46	14	17	15	52	58	59
17 Luton City	46	14	15	17	60	64	57
18 Millwall	46	14	13	19	43	54	55
19 Walsall	46	14	12	20	43	52	54
20 Burnley	46	13	13	20	55	65	52
21 Brentford	46	11	17	18	50	71	50
22 Plymouth A	46	12	13	21	55	70	49
23 Carlisle United	46	12	8	26	57	73	44
24 Southend United	46	11	10	25	47	79	43

Above: Tuevo Moilanen
Left: Dean Barrick

League position in Division Two: 15th – P46 W15 D14 L17 F56 A56 Pts 59
Home: W10 D6 L7 F29 A26 Away: W5 D8 L10 F27 A30

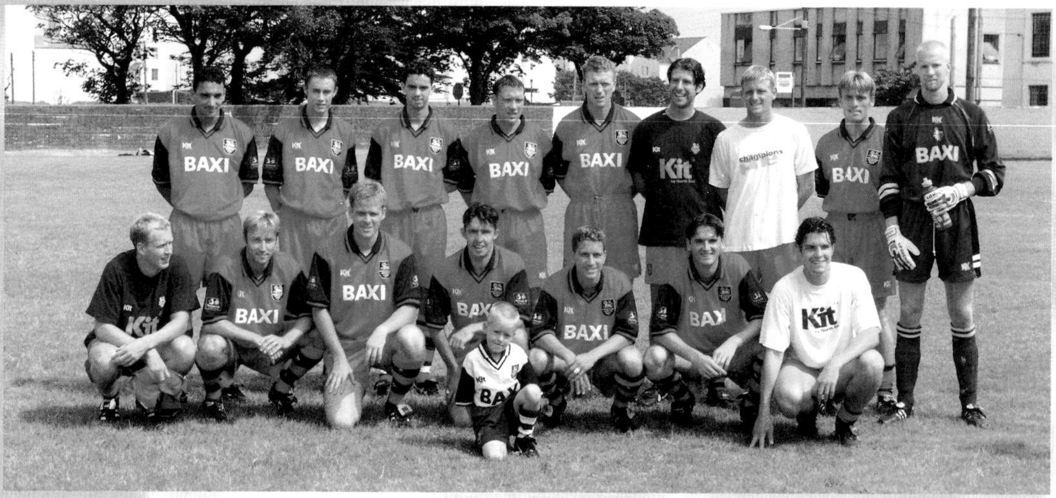

Team group in the Isle of Man. (By kind permission of Island Photographic Co. Ltd, Douglas, Isle of Man)

Date 1997-8	Opponents	Comp	h or a	Score *aet	Att.	1	2	3	4	5	6	7	8	9	10	11	12	13	14
Aug 9	Gillingham	Div 2	a	0-0	6562	Moilanen	Parkinson	Kidd	Murdock	Jackson	Gregan	Cartwright	Ashcroft	Reeves	Macken *	Rankine	Barrick	Nogan *	Darby
Aug 12	**Rotherham Rd 1**	**CCC**	**a**	**3-1**	**2901**	**Moilanen**	**Parkinson**	**Kidd**	**Murdock ***	**Jackson**	**Gregan**	**Cartwright +**	**Ashcroft**	**Reeves (2)**	**Macken (1) #**	**Rankine**	**Nogan #**	**Barrick ***	**Appleton +**
Aug 16	Millwall	Div 2	h	2-1	11486	Moilanen	Parkinson	Kidd	Murdock #	Jackson	Gregan +	Cartwright	Ashcroft (1)	Reeves	Macken (1)	Rankine	Barrick #	Nogan	Appleton +
Aug 23	Chesterfield	Div 2	a	2-3	6288	Moilanen	Parkinson	Barrick (1)	Kidd	Jackson	Gregan #	Cartwright +	Ashcroft	Reeves	Macken *	Rankine (1)	Darby #	Nogan *	Appleton +
Aug 26	**Rotherham Rd 1**	**CCC**	**h**	**2-0**	**9441**	**Moilanen**	**Parkinson**	**Barrick**	**Appleton**	**Jackson**	**Kidd**	**Cartwright #**	**Ashcroft**	**Reeves (1)**	**Nogan ***	**Rankine**	**Darby #**	**Macken * (1)**	**Gregan**
Aug 30	Watford	Div 2	h	2-0	11042	Moilanen	Parkinson	Barrick	Appleton	Jackson	Kidd	Cartwright #	Ashcroft	Reeves	Nogan (2) *	Rankine	Darby #	Macken *	Gregan
Sep 2	Grimsby Town	Div 2	h	2-0	9489	Moilanen	Parkinson	Barrick	Appleton	Jackson	Kidd +	Cartwright #	Ashcroft (1)	Reeves (1)	Nogan	Rankine	Darby #	Macken	Gregan +
Sep 6	Oldham Ath	Div 2	a	0-1	8732	Moilanen	Parkinson	Barrick	Appleton	Jackson	Gregan	Cartwright	Ashcroft	Reeves	Nogan *	Rankine	Darby	Macken *	Moyes
Sep 13	Walsall	Div 2	h	0-0	9092	Moilanen	Parkinson	Barrick	Appleton	Jackson	Gregan	Cartwright	Ashcroft	Reeves +	Nogan *	Rankine	Darby	Macken *	Kidd +
Sep 18	**Blackburn Rvrs Rd 2**	**CCC**	**a**	**0-6**	**22564**	**Moilanen**	**Parkinson**	**Barrick**	**Kidd**	**Jackson**	**Gregan**	**Cartwright**	**Ashcroft**	**Reeves**	**Rankine ***	**Darby**	**Moyes**	**Macken ***	**Atkinson**
Sep 20	Burnley	Div 2	a	1-1	13809	Moilanen	Parkinson	Barrick	Kidd	Jackson	Gregan	Cartwright	Ashcroft	Reeves	Nogan (1) +	Rankine	Darby	Macken	Appleton +
Sep 27	Wycombe W	Div 2	a	0-0	4838	Moilanen	Parkinson	Kidd	Murdock	Jackson	Gregan *	Appleton	Ashcroft	Macken	Rankine	Barrick #	Reeves #	Atkinson *	Darby
Sep 30	**Blackburn Rvrs Rd 2**	**CCC**	**h**	**1-0**	**11472**	**Moilanen**	**Parkinson**	**Kidd**	**Murdock**	**Jackson**	**Gregan ***	**Appleton**	**Ashcroft**	**Macken**	**Rankine**	**Barrick (1)**	**Reeves**	**Holt ***	**Cartwright**
Oct 4	Brentford	Div 2	h	2-1	8804	Moilanen	Parkinson	Kidd +	Murdock (1)	Jackson	Gregan	Appleton	Ashcroft (1)	Reeves *	Rankine	Barrick	Darby	Holt *	Cartwright +
Oct 11	Bournemouth	Div 2	h	0-1	8531	Lucas	Parkinson	Kidd	Murdock	Jackson *	Appleton	Cartwright	Ashcroft	Holt	Rankine	Barrick	Darby	Atkinson * +	Nogan +
Oct 17	Carlisle Utd	Div 2	a	2-0	6541	Moilanen	Parkinson (1)	Kidd	Murdock	Moyes	Appleton	Cartwright	Ashcroft (1)	Reeves	Rankine	Barrick	Darby	O'Hanlon	Holt
Oct 21	Bristol City + 1 o.g.	Div 2	a	1-2	9039	Moilanen	Parkinson	Kidd	Murdock	Moyes	Appleton	Cartwright	Ashcroft	Reeves	Rankine	Barrick	Darby	O'Hanlon	Holt
Oct 25	Wrexham	Div 2	h	0-1	9098	Moilanen	Parkinson	Kidd	Murdock	Moyes	Appleton	Cartwright #	Ashcroft	Reeves	Rankine	Atkinson +	Darby #	Lucas	Holt +
Nov 1	Plymouth Arg	Div 2	h	0-1	8405	Moilanen	Parkinson +	Kidd	Murdock	Moyes	Darby	Macken #	Ashcroft	Nogan *	Rankine	Eyres	Gregan #	Holt *	Cartwright +
Nov 4	York City	Div 2	a	0-1	3370	Moilanen	Parkinson	Kidd	Murdock #	Moyes	Gregan	Macken *	Ashcroft	Nogan +	Rankine	Eyres	Appleton #	Holt *	Cartwright +
Nov 8	Luton Town	Div 2	a	3-1	5767	Moilanen	Parkinson	Barrick	Kidd	Jackson	Gregan	Appleton	Ashcroft (1) *	Lormor (1)	Rankine	Eyres (1)	Darby	Macken *	Cartwright
Nov 15	**Doncaster Rvrs Rd 1**	**FAC**	**h**	**3-2**	**7953**	**Moilanen**	**Parkinson**	**Barrick #**	**Kidd**	**Jackson**	**Gregan (1)**	**Appleton (1)**	**Ashcroft**	**Lormor**	**Rankine ***	**Eyres (1)**	**Murdock #** **Macken**	**Darby *** **Holt**	**Lucas**
Nov 18	Bristol Rvrs	Div 2	h	1-2	7798	Moilanen	Parkinson	Kidd +	Murdock	Jackson (1)	Gregan	Appleton	Ashcroft *	Lormor	Rankine	Eyres	Darby	Holt *	Barrick +
Nov 22	Wigan Ath	Div 2	a	4-1	5649	Moilanen	Parkinson	Barrick	Kidd (1)	Jackson	Gregan	Appleton	Ashcroft (1)	Lormor	Rankine	Cartwright (2) #	Darby #	Holt	Murdock
Nov 29	Fulham	Div 2	h	3-1	9723	Moilanen	Parkinson	Barrick	Kidd	Jackson	Gregan	Appleton	Ashcroft (3,1p) #	Lormor	Rankine	Cartwright	Holt #	O'Hanlon	Murdock
Dec 2	Southend Utd	Div 2	a	2-3	2307	Moilanen	Parkinson	Barrick	Kidd	Jackson	Gregan	Appleton	Ashcroft	Lormor (2)	Darby	Cartwright #	Holt #	Lucas	Murdock
Dec 6	**Notts County Rd 2**	**FAC**	**h**	**2-2**	**7583**	**Lucas**	**Parkinson (1)**	**Barrick**	**Kidd**	**Jackson**	**Gregan**	**Appleton**	**Ashcroft (1)**	**Lormor**	**Darby ***	**Eyres**	**Holt** **O'Hanlon**	**Macken *** **Atkinson**	**Murdock**
Dec 9	**Darlington Rd 1**	**AWS**	**h**	**3-2 ***	**2703**	**Lucas**	**Parkinson**	**Barrick**	**Kidd**	**Jackson**	**Gregan**	**Appleton (1)**	**Ashcroft**	**Lormor #**	**Murdock +**	**Eyres (2)**	**Macken #**	**O'Hanlon**	**Darby +**
Dec 13	Northampton Town	Div 2	h	1-0	7448	Moilanen	Parkinson	Barrick	Kidd	Jackson	Gregan	Appleton	Darby	Lormor	Macken (1) +	Eyres	Murdock	O'Hanlon	Holt +
Dec 16	**Notts Co. Rd 2 Replay**	**FAC**	**a**	**2-1***	**3052**	**Moilanen**	**Parkinson**	**Barrick**	**Kidd**	**Jackson**	**Gregan**	**Appleton**	**Darby**	**Lormor #**	**Macken +**	**Eyres (1)**	**Holt #** **O'Hanlon**	**Moyes * (1)** **Rankine**	**Nogan +**
Dec 20	Blackpool	Div 2	a	1-2	8342	Moilanen	Parkinson	Barrick #	Kidd	Jackson	Gregan	Appleton	Darby +	Lormor *	Macken	Eyres	Moyes #	Holt * (1)	Cartwright +
Dec 26	Oldham Ath	Div 2	h	1-1	13441	Moilanen	Parkinson +	Barrick #	Murdock	Moyes	Gregan	Appleton	Cartwright	Holt (1)	Macken +	Eyres	Jackson #	Lormor *	Darby +
Dec 28	Grimsby Town	Div 2	a	1-3	6725	Moilanen	Jackson	Barrick	Murdock	Moyes *	Gregan (1)	Appleton	Cartwright	Holt #	Darby +	Eyres	Lormor #	Parkinson *	Rankine +
Jan 3	**Stockport Co. Rd 3**	**FAC**	**h**	**1-2**	**12180**	**Moilanen**	**Parkinson #**	**Kidd**	**Murdock**	**Jackson**	**Gregan**	**Appleton**	**Ashcroft (1) ***	**Macken**	**Rankine**	**Eyres**	**Cartwright #** **Barrick**	**Holt *** **Lormor**	**Lucas**
Jan 10	Gillingham	Div 2	h	1-3	7776	Lucas	Darby *	Kidd	Murdock	Jackson	Gregan (1)	Appleton	Rankine	Macken	Holt +	Eyres	Barrick	Cartwright *	Nogan +
Jan 13	**Macclesfield Rd 2**	**AWS**	**a**	**1-0**	**1618**	**Lucas**	**Parkinson**	**Barrick**	**Davey**	**Jackson**	**Kidd**	**Cartwright (1)**	**Rankine**	**Lormor**	**Nogan ***	**Eyres**	**Appleton**	**Holt ***	**Murdock**
Jan 17	Watford	Div 2	a	1-3	10182	Lucas	Parkinson (1)	Barrick *	Davey	Jackson	Kidd	Cartwright	Rankine	Lormor	Nogan	Eyres	Appleton	Macken *	Murdock
Jan 24	Chesterfield	Div 2	h	0-0	8231	Lucas	Parkinson	Kidd	Davey	Jackson	Gregan	Cartwright	Rankine	Lormor *	Nogan	Eyres	Appleton	Macken *	Murdock
Jan 27	**Mansfield Qtr-Final**	**AWS**	**h**	**1-0**	**3609**	**Lucas**	**Parkinson**	**Kidd**	**Davey**	**Jackson**	**Gregan**	**Cartwright**	**Rankine**	**Lormor ***	**Nogan (1)**	**Eyres**	**Appleton**	**Macken ***	**Murdock**
Jan 31	Walsall	Div 2	a	1-1	5377	Lucas	Parkinson	Kidd	Davey	Jackson	Gregan	Cartwright	Rankine	Macken *	Nogan (1p)	Eyres #	Appleton #	Lormor *	Murdock
Feb 7	Burnley + 1 o.g.	Div 2	h	2-3	12263	Lucas	Parkinson	Kidd	Davey	Jackson	Gregan	Cartwright	Rankine	Ashcroft	Nogan (1)	Eyres #	Appleton #	Macken	Murdock
Feb 14	Brentford	Div 2	a	0-0	4952	Moilanen	Parkinson	Kidd *	Murdock	Jackson	Gregan	Cartwright	Ashcroft	Mullin #	Nogan	Appleton	Eyres #	Barrick *	Davey
Feb 17	**Burnley Area Semi-Fin**	**AWS**	**a**	**0-1**	**10079**	**Moilanen**	**Parkinson**	**Barrick**	**Murdock**	**Jackson**	**Gregan**	**Cartwright**	**Ashcroft**	**Mullin**	**Nogan ***	**Appleton**	**Eyres**	**Macken ***	**Davey**
Feb 21	Wycombe W	Div 2	h	1-1	7665	Moilanen	Parkinson	Barrick	Murdock	Jackson	Gregan	Cartwright	Ashcroft	Mullin +	Nogan *	Appleton	Eyres	Macken * (1)	Sissoko +
Feb 24	Carlisle Utd.	Div 2	h	0-3	8985	Moilanen	Parkinson	Barrick	Moyes	Jackson	Gregan	Cartwright #	Ashcroft +	Mullin *	Sissoko	Appleton	Davey #	Macken *	Eyres +
Feb 28	Bournemouth	Div 2	a	2-0	5009	Moilanen	Parkinson	Kidd	Murdock	Jackson	Gregan	Appleton (1)	Davey (1)	Ashcroft +	Sissoko	Eyres	Rankine	Cartwright	Mullin +
Mar 3	Luton Town	Div 2	h	1-0	6992	Moilanen	Parkinson	Kidd (1)	Murdock	Jackson	Gregan	Appleton	Davey	Ashcroft	Sissoko +	Eyres	Rankine	Cartwright	Mullin +
Mar 7	Plymouth Arg	Div 2	a	0-2	4201	Moilanen	Parkinson	Kidd *	Murdock	Jackson	Gregan	Appleton	Davey	Ashcroft	Sissoko +	Eyres	Rankine	Cartwright *	Mullin +
Mar 14	York City	Div 2	h	3-2	7664	Moilanen	Parkinson (1)	Barrick	Murdock	Jackson	Gregan	Appleton (1)	Davey +	Ashcroft	Mullin #	Eyres (1)	Macken #	Cartwright	Sissoko +
Mar 21	Bristol Rvrs	Div 2	a	2-2	5278	Moilanen	Parkinson	Kidd	Murdock	Jackson	Rankine #	Appleton	Davey (1)	Ashcroft (1)	Macken +	Eyres	Cartwright #	Barrick	Nogan +
Mar 25	Millwall	Div 2	a	1-0	5888	Moilanen	Parkinson	Kidd *	Murdock	Jackson	Rankine	Appleton	Davey	Ashcroft (1) +	Macken #	Eyres	Cartwright #	Barrick *	Nogan +
Mar 28	Wigan Ath	Div 2	h	1-1	10171	Moilanen	Parkinson	Barrick	Murdock	Jackson	Rankine	Appleton	Davey	Ashcroft (1)	Macken *	Eyres #	Cartwright #	Sissoko *	Nogan
Apr 4	Fulham	Div 2	a	1-2	8814	Moilanen	Parkinson	Barrick	Murdock	Jackson	Rankine	Appleton #	Davey	Nogan	Macken (1) *	Eyres	Cartwright #	Holt *	Moyes
Apr 11	Southend Utd.	Div 2	h	1-0	8096	Moilanen	Parkinson (1)	Barrick	Murdock	Jackson	Gregan #	Rankine *	Davey	Ashcroft	Macken	Eyres	Cartwright #	McKenna *	Nogan
Apr 13	Northampton Town	Div 2	a	2-2	5664	Moilanen	Parkinson	Barrick	Murdock	Jackson	McKenna	Rankine	Davey #	Ashcroft (1)	Macken (1)	Eyres +	Cartwright #	Moyes	Nogan +
Apr 18	Blackpool	Div 2	h	3-3	13500	Moilanen	Parkinson (1)	Barrick	Murdock	McKenna	Gregan	Rankine	Davey	Ashcroft	Macken (1)	Eyres (1) +	Moyes	Holt	Nogan +
Apr 25	Wrexham	Div 2	a	0-0	7302	Moilanen	Parkinson	Sparrow	McKenna	Jackson	Gregan	Rankine	Davey	Ashcroft	Macken	Eyres #	Appleton #	Moyes	Nogan
May 2	Bristol City	Div 2	h	2-1	12067	Moilanen	Parkinson	Barrick	McKenna	Jackson	Gregan	Rankine	Davey	Ashcroft (1)	Macken	Eyres (1)	Sparrow	Appleton	Nogan

* **Own goals:** Dyche v Bristol City & Cooke v Burnley

North End, unusually, made a great start to the new campaign with David Moyes working hard on the fitness of the players in the pre-season games. With only a couple of fresh faces coming in it was important that the potential of some of the youngsters in the team was realised. Only one game was lost in the opening ten league games and results away from Deepdale were especially encouraging. By the middle of October Preston were on top of the division and deservedly so. Some brilliant cameo performances by supersub Jason Harris won North End several points and the youngster was desperate to prove himself. There were several games which ended in a draw, and it was usually in games where Preston had done enough to win. These dropped points were to prove vital in the final reckoning, although to be fair North End made a habit of snatching some late goals. A romantic tie against minnows Ford United from the Ryman league in the FA Cup kept the season rolling along and a second round win over Walsall gave Preston a dream home draw with the mighty Arsenal. What a night that was, but alas, the Londoners proved just a little too strong over the 90 minutes. Apart from a home defeat by Fulham the league form up until Christmas still gave the fans plenty to enjoy and at the turn of the year the club was buzzing. A rare defeat, at Bournemouth, was then offset by a wonderful all round team effort at Wrexham where North End hit five without reply. Other good results

kept the pot boiling but injuries and suspensions were beginning to stretch the squad to the limits. Steve Basham's arrival on loan proved an excellent move by Moyes and the former Premier striker was soon amongst the goals. Unfortunately points began to be lost more frequently and the late goals went against Preston rather than for them as they had done earlier in the - season. Defeats against Macclesfield, Blackpool and Bournemouth were particularly damaging on the run in and Preston's record over their last ten games cost them dearly. With Fulham running away with the title and Walsall looking good for the runners-up spot, it was a question of whether Preston could make the play-offs. This they managed, comfortably in the end, but in their match they came up against Gillingham. In the two games little went right for the North Enders and the players were resigned to another season of Division Two football. The late signing of Graham Alexander certainly added some quality to the team but maybe a little more speculation in the transfer market around Christmas time may have been what the Doctor ordered.

DEBUTANTS: (11) Graham Alexander, Steve Basham, Darren Byfield, Neil Clement, Andy Gray, Jason Harris, Craig Harrison, Dominic Ludden, Paul McGregor, Mark Wright, Stuart King.

LAST GAMES: (7) Byfield, Clement, Gray, Harris, Harrison, Holt, McGregor.

League appearances (46 games)

Alexander G. 10, Appleton M.A. 13 + 12, Basham S.B. 15 + 2, Byfield D. 3 + 2, Cartwright L. 14 + 13, Clement N. 4, Darby J.T. 12 + 8, Eyres D. 33 + 1, Gray A. 5, Gregan S.M. 40 + 1, Harris J.A.S. 9 + 25, Harrison C. 6, Holt M.A. 0 + 3, Jackson M.J. 44, Kidd R.A. 27 + 1, Lucas D.A. 31, Ludden 26 + 6, Macken J.P. 30 + 12, McGregor P. 1 + 3, McKenna P.S. 31 + 5, Moilanen T.J. 15, Murdock C.J. 28 + 5, Nogan K. 39 + 3, Parkinson G.A. 27, Rankine S.M. 42, Wright M.S. 1.

FA Cup appearances (3 games)

Appleton 1 + 1, Cartwright 3, Darby 0 + 1, Eyres 1, Gregan 3, Harris 2 + 1, Jackson 2, Kidd 3, Lucas 3, Ludden 2, Macken 1 + 1, McKenna 1 + 1, Murdock 2, Nogan 3, Parkinson 3, Rankine 3, Wright 0 + 1.

Worthington Cup appearances (2 games)

Appleton 2, Cartwright 0 + 1, Eyres 2, Gregan 2, Holt 0 + 1, Jackson 2, Kidd 1, Ludden 1, Macken 2, McKenna 1, Moilanen 2, Murdock 1, Nogan 2, Parkinson 2, Rankine 2.

Auto Windscreen Shield Appearances (2 games)

Appleton 1, Byfield 1, Cartwright 1, Darby 2, Gregan 1, Harris 2, Harrison 1, Jackson 2, Kidd 1, King S.S.D. 0 + 1, Lucas 2, Macken 2, McKenna 2, Murdock 2, Nogan 0 + 1, Parkinson 2, Wright 0 + 1.

Goalscorers: 78 League–7 FAC–3 AWS–(Total 88)

Nogan 18–3–0 (21), Basham 10–0–0 (10), Macken 8–0–1 (9), Eyres 8–0–0 (8), Jackson 8–0–0 (8), Harris 6–1–0 (7), Cartwright 4–0–0 (4), Rankine 3–1–0 (4), Kidd 3–0–0 (3), Gregan 3–0–0 (3), Darby 1–1–1 (3), Parkinson 1p–0–1p (2), Appleton 2–0–0 (2), Byfield 1–0–0 (1), Murdock 1–0–0 (1), McKenna 0–1–0 (1). Own Goals 1–0–0 (1) (Hill of Northampton)

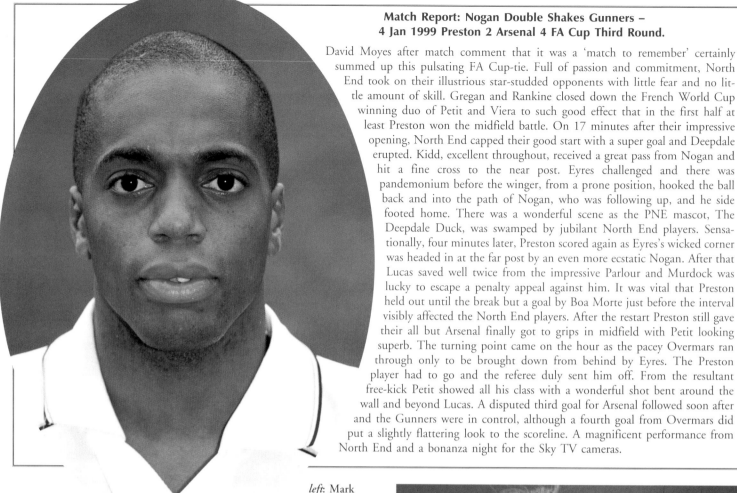

Match Report: Nogan Double Shakes Gunners – 4 Jan 1999 Preston 2 Arsenal 4 FA Cup Third Round.

David Moyes after match comment that it was a 'match to remember' certainly summed up this pulsating FA Cup-tie. Full of passion and commitment, North End took on their illustrious star-studded opponents with little fear and no little amount of skill. Gregan and Rankine closed down the French World Cup winning duo of Petit and Viera to such good effect that in the first half at least Preston won the midfield battle. On 17 minutes after their impressive opening, North End capped their good start with a super goal and Deepdale erupted. Kidd, excellent throughout, received a great pass from Nogan and hit a fine cross to the near post. Eyres challenged and there was pandemonium before the winger, from a prone position, hooked the ball back and into the path of Nogan, who was following up, and he side footed home. There was a wonderful scene as the PNE mascot, The Deepdale Duck, was swamped by jubilant North End players. Sensationally, four minutes later, Preston scored again as Eyres's wicked corner was headed in at the far post by an even more ecstatic Nogan. After that Lucas saved well twice from the impressive Parlour and Murdock was lucky to escape a penalty appeal against him. It was vital that Preston held out until the break but a goal by Boa Morte just before the interval visibly affected the North End players. After the restart Preston still gave their all but Arsenal finally got to grips in midfield with Petit looking superb. The turning point came on the hour as the pacey Overmars ran through only to be brought down from behind by Eyres. The Preston player had to go and the referee duly sent him off. From the resultant free-kick Petit showed all his class with a wonderful shot bent around the wall and beyond Lucas. A disputed third goal for Arsenal followed soon after and the Gunners were in control, although a fourth goal from Overmars did put a slightly flattering look to the scoreline. A magnificent performance from North End and a bonanza night for the Sky TV cameras.

left: Mark Rankine
Right: Steve Basham

STAT FACTS:
Best home run without defeat: 6 games
Best away run without defeat: 7 games
Longest run unbeaten: 7 games
Longest run without a win: 5 games
Best home attendance: 21,099 *vs.* Arsenal FAC 4.1.99
Worst home attendance: 5,650 *vs.* Grimsby WC 18.8.98
Best away attendance: 28,779 *vs.* Man. City 12.10.98
Worst away attendance: 1,205 *vs.* Hartlepool AWS 19.1.99
Aggregate and average home attendance: 274,403 – 11,931
Aggregate and average away attendance: 203,213 – 8,835

Ever presents: None
Hat-tricks: None
FA Cup: Third Rd.
Worthington Cup: Second Rd.
Manager: David Moyes
Chairman: B. Gray Esq.
Players used: 26
North End also competed in the Auto Windscreen Shield
Leading scorer: 21 goals – Kurt Nogan (18 League 3 FAC)

OFFICIAL PLAYER OF THE SEASON: Michael Jackson

League position in Division Two: 5th (Reached Play-offs) – P46 W22 D13 L11 F78 A50 Pts 79
Home: W12 D6 L5 F46 A23   Away: W10 D7 L6 F32 A27

David Eyres

Season 1998–99: Second Division

	P	W	D	L	F	A	Pts
1 Fulham	46	31	8	7	79	32	101
2 Walsall	46	26	9	11	63	47	87
3 Man City	46	22	16	8	69	33	82
4 Gillingham	46	22	14	10	75	44	80
5 PRESTON	**46**	**22**	**13**	**11**	**68**	**50**	**79**
6 Wigan Athletic	46	22	10	14	75	48	76
7 Bournemouth	46	22	13	12	63	41	76
8 Stoke City	46	21	6	19	59	63	69
9 Chesterfield	46	17	13	19	46	44	64
10 Millwall	46	17	11	9	52	59	62
11 Reading	46	16	11	18	54	63	61
12 Luton Town	46	16	10	20	51	60	58
13 Bristol Rovers	46	13	17	16	65	56	56
14 Blackpool	46	14	14	18	44	54	56
15 Burnley	46	13	16	17	54	73	55
16 Notts County	46	14	12	20	52	61	54
17 Wrexham	46	13	14	19	43	62	53
18 Colchester United	46	12	16	18	52	70	52
19 Wycombe W	46	13	12	21	52	58	51
20 Oldham Athletic	46	14	9	23	48	66	51
21 York City	46	13	11	22	56	80	50
22 Northampton	46	10	18	18	43	57	48
23 Lincoln City	46	13	7	26	42	74	46
24 Macclesfield Town	46	11	10	25	43	63	43

Jonathan Macken

Date 1998-9	Opponents	Comp	h or a	Score	Att.	1	2	3	4	5	6	7	8	9	10	11	12	13	14
Aug 8	York City	Div 2	h	3-0	8656	Moilanen	Parkinson	Kidd	Murdock	Jackson	Gregan +	Appleton (1) #	Rankine (1)	Nogan (1)	Macken	Eyres *	Ludden *	Holt +	McKenna #
Aug 12	**Grimsby T. Rd1 1L**	**WC**	**a**	**0-0**	**3008**	**Moilanen**	**Parkinson**	**Ludden**	**Murdock**	**Jackson**	**Gregan**	**Appleton**	**Rankine**	**Nogan**	**Macken**	**Eyres**	**Lucas Holt**	**Cartwright McKenna**	**Moyes**
Aug 15	Luton Town	Div 2	a	1-1	5392	Moilanen	Parkinson	Ludden	Murdock	Jackson	Gregan	Appleton	Rankine	Nogan +	Macken (1) *	Eyres	Cartwright *	Holt +	McKenna
Aug 18	**Grimsby T. Rd1 2L**	**WC**	**h**	**0-0 ***	**5650**	**Moilanen**	**Parkinson**	**Kidd**	**McKenna**	**Jackson**	**Gregan**	**Appleton**	**Rankine**	**Nogan**	**Macken ***	**Eyres +**	**Lucas Holt ***	**Cartwright + Darby**	**Moyes**
Aug 22	Stoke City	Div 2	h	3-4	11587	Moilanen	Parkinson	Kidd	McKenna	Jackson	Gregan	Appleton	Rankine	Nogan (2)	Macken +	Eyres (1)	Cartwright	Holt +	Murdock
Aug 29	Lincoln City	Div 2	a	4-3	4130	Moilanen	Parkinson *	Kidd	Murdock	Jackson	Gregan	McKenna *	Rankine	Nogan (1)	Macken (2)	Eyres (1) +	Cartwright *	Ludden +	Harris #
Aug 31	Chesterfield	Div 2	h	2-0	9249	Moilanen	Parkinson	Kidd (1)	Murdock	Jackson	Gregan	McKenna	Rankine *	Nogan #	Macken +	Eyres	Cartwright *	Ludden +	Harris # (1)
Sep 5	Bristol Rovers	Div 2	a	2-2	6702	Moilanen	Parkinson	Ludden	Kidd	Jackson (1)	Gregan	McKenna *	Rankine	Nogan +	Macken	Eyres #	Cartwright *	Darby +	Harris # (1)
Sep 8	Wycombe W.	Div 2	a	1-0	3800	Moilanen	Parkinson	Ludden	Kidd	Jackson	Gregan	McKenna	Rankine	Nogan (1) *	Macken #	Eyres	Cartwright *	Appleton	Harris #
Sep 12	Reading	Div 2	h	4-0	9836	Moilanen	Parkinson	Ludden	Kidd	Jackson (2) +	Gregan	McKenna	Rankine *	Nogan	Macken #	Eyres (2)	Cartwright *	Appleton +	Harris #
Sep 19	Oldham Ath.	Div 2	a	1-0	8205	Moilanen	Parkinson	Ludden	Kidd +	Jackson	Appleton (1)	McKenna	Rankine	Nogan *	Macken #	Eyres	Cartwright *	Murdock +	Harris #
Sep 26	Gillingham	Div 2	h	1-1	10506	Moilanen	Parkinson	Ludden	Murdock	Jackson	Gregan	McKenna *	Rankine	Nogan	Macken #	Eyres	Cartwright *	Appleton	Harris # (1)
Oct 3	Walsall	Div 2	a	0-1	5802	Moilanen	Parkinson	Ludden	Murdock	Jackson	Gregan	McKenna *	Rankine +	Nogan	Macken	Eyres #	Cartwright *	Appleton +	Harris #
Oct 12	Manchester City	Div 2	a	1-0	28779	Moilanen	Parkinson (1p)	Ludden	Murdock	Jackson	Gregan	McKenna *	Rankine	Nogan #	Harris +	Eyres	Cartwright *	Macken +	Appleton #
Oct 17	Colchester Utd.	Div 2	h	2-0	10483	Moilanen	Parkinson	Ludden	Murdock	Kidd	Gregan	McKenna	Rankine	Nogan (1)	Macken	Eyres (1)	Cartwright	Darby	Appleton
Oct 20	Macclesfield T.	Div 2	h	2-2	10316	Moilanen	Parkinson *	Ludden	Murdock	Jackson (1)	Gregan +	McKenna	Rankine	Nogan	Macken #	Eyres	Kidd *	Cartwright +	Harris # (1)
Oct 24	Northampton T. ++	Div 2	a	1-1	6085	Moilanen	Parkinson	Ludden	Kidd	Jackson	Gregan	McKenna	Rankine	Nogan	Harris	Eyres	Cartwright	Appleton +	Murdock
Nov 7	Burnley	Div 2	h	4-1	15888	Lucas	Parkinson	Ludden	Kidd	Jackson	Appleton	McKenna	Rankine (1) *	Nogan (1)	Byfield (1) +	Eyres (1)	Cartwright *	Macken +	Murdock
Nov 10	Millwall	Div 2	h	0-1	10228	Lucas	Parkinson	Ludden	Kidd	Jackson	Appleton +	McKenna *	Rankine	Nogan	Byfield	Eyres #	Cartwright *	Gregan +	Harris #
Nov 14	**Ford United Rd 1**	**FAC**	**h**	**3-0**	**10167**	**Lucas**	**Parkinson**	**Ludden**	**Murdock**	**Kidd**	**Gregan**	**Cartwright**	**Rankine (1) +**	**Nogan ***	**Harris (1)**	**Appleton**	**McKenna Macken ***	**Eyres Darby + (1)**	**O'Hanlon**
Nov 21	Blackpool	Div 2	a	0-0	10868	Lucas	Parkinson	Ludden	Kidd	Jackson	Gregan	Cartwright	Rankine	Nogan	Macken #	McKenna	Murdock	Darby	Harris #
Nov 28	Wigan Ath.	Div 2	h	2-2	11562	Lucas	Parkinson +	Ludden	Kidd	Jackson	Gregan	Cartwright	Rankine (1)	Nogan	Harris	McKenna	Murdock	Macken + (1)	Darby
Dec 5	**Walsall Rd 2**	**FAC**	**h**	**2-0**	**8488**	**Lucas**	**Parkinson**	**Ludden**	**Kidd**	**Jackson**	**Gregan**	**Cartwright**	**Rankine**	**Nogan (1)**	**Harris**	**McKenna (1)**	**Murdock Macken**	**Wright + Darby**	**O'Hanlon**
Dec 8	**Burnley**	**AWS**	**a**	**1-0**	**3366**	**Lucas**	**Parkinson**	**Kidd**	**Murdock**	**Jackson**	**Darby**	**Cartwright**	**Byfield**	**Macken (1)**	**Harris ***	**McKenna**	**Wright ***	**Nogan**	**Moyes**
Dec 12	Notts County	Div 2	a	3-2	5096	Lucas	Parkinson	Ludden	Kidd	Jackson	Gregan (1)	Cartwright (1) *	Rankine	Nogan #	Harris (1)	Darby +	Murdock *	Macken +	Byfield #
Dec 19	Fulham	Div 2	h	0-1	12321	Lucas	Parkinson	Ludden #	Kidd	Jackson	Gregan	Cartwright	Rankine	Nogan *	Harris	Darby +	Byfield *	Macken +	Appleton #
Dec 26	Stoke City	Div 2	a	1-0	23272	Lucas	Parkinson	Kidd	Murdock	Jackson (1)	Gregan	Cartwright	Rankine	Macken #	Byfield *	Eyres	Nogan *	Appleton	Harris #
Dec 28	Wrexham	Div 2	h	3-1	12106	Lucas	Parkinson	Kidd	Murdock	Jackson	Gregan	Cartwright (2)	Rankine	Nogan (1)	Macken #	Eyres +	McKenna *	Appleton +	Harris # *
Jan 4	**Arsenal Rd 3**	**FAC**	**h**	**2-4**	**21099**	**Lucas**	**Parkinson**	**Kidd**	**Murdock**	**Jackson**	**Gregan +**	**Cartwright**	**Rankine**	**Nogan (2) #**	**Macken ***	**Eyres**	**McKenna * Appleton +**	**Harris # Darby**	**O'Hanlon**
Jan 9	York City	Div 2	a	1-0	5744	Lucas	Parkinson	Kidd #	Murdock	Jackson	Appleton	McKenna	Rankine	Nogan (1)	Macken	Eyres	Moyes	Darby	Harris #
Jan 16	Luton Town	Div 2	h	2-1	11034	Lucas	Parkinson	Harrison	Murdock	Jackson	Gregan	McKenna	Rankine	Nogan (1) *	Macken #	Eyres +	Darby *	Appleton +	Harris # (1)
Jan 19	**Hartlepool Utd.**	**AWS**	**a**	**2-2 ***	**1205**	**Lucas**	**Parkinson (1p)**	**Harrison**	**Murdock**	**Jackson**	**Gregan**	**McKenna ***	**Darby (1)**	**Macken**	**Harris**	**Appleton +**	**Nogan ***	**King +**	**Rankine**
Jan 23	Chesterfield	Div 2	a	1-0	6138	Lucas	Parkinson +	Harrison	Kidd (1)	Jackson	Gregan	Cartwright	Rankine	Nogan *	Macken #	McKenna	Murdock *	Darby +	Harris #
Jan 26	Bournemouth	Div 2	a	1-3	6170	Lucas	Darby	Harrison	Kidd	Jackson	Gregan	Cartwright	Rankine	Nogan (1)	Macken #	McKenna +	Murdock	Ludden +	Harris #
Jan 30	Wrexham	Div 2	a	5-0	6394	Lucas	Darby	Harrison	Kidd (1)	Jackson (1)	Gregan #	Cartwright	Rankine	Nogan (1) *	Macken (1) +	Eyres (1)	McKenna *	Harris +	Ludden #
Feb 6	Bristol Rovers	Div 2	h	2-2	12170	Lucas	Darby	Harrison	Kidd	Jackson	Gregan	Cartwright (1)	Rankine	Nogan (1)	Macken *	Eyres #	Basham *	McKenna	Harris #
Feb 13	Wycombe W.	Div 2	h	2-1	10686	Lucas	Darby	Harrison	Murdock	Kidd	Gregan	Cartwright	Rankine	Nogan +	Basham (2) #	Eyres *	McKenna *	Ludden +	Harris #
Feb 20	Reading	Div 2	a	1-2	10937	Lucas	Parkinson +	Ludden *	Kidd	Jackson	Gregan	Cartwright	Rankine	Nogan	Basham (1)	McKenna #	Murdock *	Darby +	Harris #
Feb 23	Lincoln City	Div 2	h	5-0	9849	Lucas	Darby	Ludden	Kidd *	Jackson	Gregan	Cartwright +	Rankine	Nogan (2)	Basham (2) #	Gray	Murdock *	Macken + (1)	Harris #
Feb 27	Oldham Ath.	Div 2	h	2-1	12965	Lucas	Darby	Ludden	Murdock	Jackson (1)	Gregan	Gray	Rankine	Nogan (1)	Basham #	Wright +	Morgan	Macken +	Harris #
Mar 6	Gillingham	Div 2	a	1-1	9581	Lucas	Darby	Ludden	Murdock	Jackson	Gregan (1)	Gray	Rankine	Nogan	Basham +	Eyres	Appleton	Macken +	Harris
Mar 14	Burnley	Div 2	a	1-0	11561	Lucas	Darby	Ludden	Murdock	Jackson	Gregan *	Gray	Rankine	Nogan (1)	Basham #	Eyres +	Appleton *	Macken +	Harris #
Mar 20	Bournemouth	Div 2	h	0-1	12882	Lucas	Darby	McKenna	Murdock	Jackson	Appleton #	Gray +	Rankine	Nogan	Basham	Eyres	Morgan	Macken *	Harris #
Mar 27	Northampton T.	Div 2	h	3-0	10686	Lucas	Alexander	Eyres	Murdock	Jackson	Appleton	Macken (1)	Rankine +	Nogan	Basham (2) *	McKenna	McGregor *	Darby +	Winstanley
Apr 2	Colchester Utd.	Div 2	a	0-1	5644	Lucas	Alexander	Clement	Murdock	Jackson	Gregan	Macken #	Rankine	Nogan	Basham	Appleton *	McKenna *	Darby	Eyres #
Apr 5	Manchester City	Div 2	h	1-1	20857	Lucas	Alexander	Clement	Murdock	Jackson	Gregan	McKenna	Rankine #	Nogan +	Basham (1)	Eyres	McGregor	Macken +	Appleton #
Apr 10	Macclesfield T.	Div 2	a	2-3	4325	Lucas	Alexander	Clement #	Murdock	Jackson	Gregan	McGregor +	McKenna	Nogan	Basham (2)	Eyres	Darby	Macken +	Appleton #
Apr 13	Wigan Ath.	Div 2	a	2-2	5396	Lucas	Alexander	Clement	Murdock (1)	Jackson	Gregan	Cartwright	Rankine #	Macken +	Basham	Eyres (1)	Darby	Appleton +	Nogan #
Apr 17	Blackpool	Div 2	h	1-2	15337	Lucas	Alexander	Ludden	Murdock	Jackson	Gregan	McKenna *	Rankine +	Macken #	Basham	Eyres	Darby *	Appleton +	Nogan # (1)
Apr 20	Walsall	Div 2	h	1-0	13337	Lucas	Alexander	Ludden	Murdock	Jackson	Gregan (1)	McKenna	Appleton	Macken	Harris *	Eyres	Darby *	McGregor	Clement
Apr 24	Millwall	Div 2	a	2-2	6016	Lucas	Alexander	Ludden	Murdock	Jackson (1)	Gregan	McKenna	Darby (1)	Macken	Basham	Harris +	Wright	McGregor +	Clement
May 1	Notts County	Div 2	h	1-1	11862	Lucas	Alexander	Ludden	Murdock	Jackson	Gregan	McKenna	Appleton	Macken (1)	Basham	Harris +	Darby	McGregor +	Clement
May 8	Fulham	Div 2	a	0-3	17176	Lucas	Alexander	Kidd	Murdock	Jackson	Gregan	McKenna	Rankine +	Macken	Harris *	Appleton	Basham *	Darby +	McGregor

++ Own goal by Hill of Northampton

*Lost to Grimsby 6-7 on penalties in WC and to Hartlepool 3-4 on penalties in AWS, both a.e.t.

SEASON 1999–2000

Trivia Facts:

A pre-season friendly at Bolton had to be abandoned when a 'fearsome' electrical storm hit the Reebok Stadium. A bolt of lightening struck with such power that it put out all the floodlights so the referee abandoned the match.

The FA Cup replay vs. Enfield was played at Clarence Park, home of St Alban's, where Enfield were ground sharing that season.

Deepdale Duck, alias Simon Nash, made the National papers after his antics during the games landed him in hot water, and PNE's reserves played the majority of their home games at Bamber Bridge's Irongate ground, mainly to protect Deepdale's newly laid pitch.

The first £100,000 spent in the summer of 1999 proved to be a fine investment. No, it wasn't spent on a player, but on the Deepdale pitch. The whole ground was dug up and a completely new and revolutionary grass surface was laid. And how it paid off for the club, as David Moyes led his men to an incredible season of triumph. From pre-season training, through the autumn and winter and on to a glorious spring the manager left no stone unturned to organise success. North End hit the top of the division after just two games and stayed there or thereabouts throughout the campaign. The players responded to Moyes superbly, and everyone at the club gave their utmost. But there had to be stars and during this season the men who took the most plaudits were Sean Gregan, a captain fantastic, and Jonathan Macken, a striker to rival some of his illustrious predecessors. Graham Alexander was outstanding, Rob Edwards partnered him to great effect and Michael Jackson was awesome at the heart of the defence. There was also the magnificent efforts of the veterans in midfield, Mark Rankine and David Eyres. The key to the season was the ability of the team to cleverly put unbeaten runs together, 18 league games in one of them, and that put great pressure on the other teams. Preston's away record was tremendous and they didn't lose a league game on their travels until January 2000. And there was also a remarkable number of clean sheets, 24 in the league and six games in a row at the most crucial last stage of the season. No wonder Tepi Moilanen, North End's 'Flying Fin' was named Division Two goalkeeper of the year! As with all sides selected by Moyes, it was very much the 'team' ethic that carried North End through and every one of the players who took part in the eventual Championship victory could be proud of their contribution. As for Moyes, well, he could do no wrong. Bringing in Brett Angell for the final run-in added a little extra punch to the attack for those vital last 15 games. And just to add to the excitement of a wonderful campaign, North End had good runs in both the main cup competitions. The fans were able to enjoy a great day out at Goodison Park against Everton in the FA Cup 5th Round and although Preston lost 2–0 they gave an excellent account of themselves. Maybe the Everton chiefs were impressed with Preston's manager that day? For the final home game 19,407 people turned up at Deepdale to see Preston race into a 3–0 lead over Millwall before half-time and the partying began. The visitors did pull two goals back after the break but nothing was going to spoil North End's celebrations and when Gregan lifted the Division Two trophy the place erupted! And the pitch still looked magnificent too!

DEBUTANTS: (10) Iain Anderson, Brett Angell, Brian Barry Murphy, Mark Beesley, David Beresford, Faroud Diaf, Adam Eaton, Rob Edwards, Bjarki Gunnlaugsson, Alex Mathie.

LAST GAMES: (8) Angell, Beesley, Beresford, Darby, Diaf, King, Mathie, Nogan.

STAT FACTS:
Best home run without defeat: 12 games
Best away run without defeat: 12 games
Longest run unbeaten: 18 games
Longest run without a win: 3 games
Best home attendance: 19,407 vs. Millwall 29.4.2000
Worst home attendance: 3,306 vs. Wrexham AWS 7.12.1999
Best away attendance: 37,846 vs. Everton FAC 29.1.2000
Worst away attendance: 1,808 vs. Enfield FAC 30.11.1999
Aggregate and average home attendance: 294,837 – 12,819
Aggregate and average away attendance: 187,359 – 8,146

Ever presents: (2) Alexander and Jackson
Hat-tricks: (1) Gunnlaugsson (AWS vs. Wrexham)
FA Cup: Fifth Rd.
Worthington Cup: Third Rd. North End also competed in the Auto Windscreen Shield
Manager: David Moyes
Chairman: B. Gray Esq.
Players used: 30
Leading scorer: 25 goals – Jonathan Macken
(22 League, 1 FAC, 2 W.Cup)
OFFICIAL PLAYER OF THE SEASON: Sean Gregan

Michael Appleton

League position in Division Two: Champions – P46 W28 D11 L7 F74 A37 Pts 95
Home: W15 D4 L4 F37 A23   Away: W13 D7 L3 F37 A14

Bjarki
Gunnlaugsson

	P	W	D	L	F	A	Pts
1 Preston	46	28	11	7	74	37	95
2 Burnley	46	25	13	8	69	47	88
3 Gillingham	46	25	10	11	79	48	85
4 Wigan Ath.	46	22	17	7	72	38	83
5 Millwall	46	23	13	10	76	50	82
6 Stoke City	46	23	13	10	68	42	82
7 Bristol Rovers	46	23	11	12	69	45	80
8 Notts County	46	18	11	17	61	55	65
9 Bristol City	46	15	19	12	59	57	64
10 Reading	46	16	14	16	57	63	62
11 Wrexham	46	17	11	18	52	61	62
12 Wycombe W.	46	16	13	17	56	53	61
13 Luton Town	46	17	10	19	61	65	61
14 Oldham Ath.	46	16	12	18	50	55	60
15 Bury	46	13	18	15	61	64	57
16 AFC Bournemouth	46	16	9	21	59	62	57
17 Brentford	46	13	13	20	47	61	52
18 Colchester	46	14	10	22	59	82	52
19 Cambridge Utd.	46	12	12	22	64	65	48
20 Oxford Utd.	46	12	9	25	43	73	45
21 Cardiff City	46	9	17	20	45	67	44
22 Blackpool	46	8	17	21	49	77	41
23 Scunthorpe Utd.	46	9	12	25	40	74	39
24 Chesterfield	46	7	15	24	34	63	36

Trivia Facts:

1999–2000 was the first season where the players wore squad numbers on their shirts. The original list read like this: 1 Lucas, 2 Alexander, 3 Ludden, 4 Kidd, 5 Jackson, 6 Gregan, 7 Cartwright, 8 Rankine, 9 Nogan, 10 Basham, 11 Eyres, 12 Parkinson, 13 Not allocated, 14 Murdock, 15 Edwards, 16 McKenna, 17 Macken, 18 Appleton, 19 Not allocated, 20 Morgan, 21 Moilanen, 22 Eaton, 23 M.Wright, 24 Diaf, 25 Darby, 26 King, 27 Beesley, 28 Barry Murphy.

North End received a further £85,000 because of a sell-on clause after Alan Kelly Junior moved from Sheffield United to Blackburn Rovers.

League appearances (46 games)

Alexander G. 46, Anderson I. 11 + 1, Angell B. 9 + 6, Appleton M. 21 + 5, Barry Murphy B. 0 + 1, Basham S. 11 + 13, Beesley M. 0 + 1, Beresford D. 1 + 3, Cartwright L. 22 + 8, Darby J. 2 + 1, Diaf F. 1 + 2, Edwards R. 37 + 4, Eyres D. 26 + 15, Gregan S. 33, Gunnlaugsson B. 12 + 13, Jackson M. 46, Kidd, R. 28 + 1, Lucas D. 6, Ludden D. 3, Macken J. 40 + 4, Mathie A. 5 + 7, McKenna P. 17 + 7, Moilanen T. 40 + 1, Murdock C. 29 + 4, Nogan K. 16 + 6, Parkinson G. 0 + 1, Rankine M. 44, Wright M. 0+2

Goalscorers: 74 League – 9 FAC – 7 WC – 5 AWS – (Total 95)

Macken 22–1–2–0 (25), Alexander 6–3–1–0 (10), Angell 8–0–0–0 (8), Eyres 7–1–0–0 (8), Gunnlaugsson 1–1–0–4 (6), Jackson 5–0–0–0 (5), Nogan 4–0–0–0 (4), Appleton 3–0–1–0 (4), Mathie 2–0–2–0 (4), Gregan 3–0–0–0 (3), Basham 2–0–1–0 (3), Edwards 2–0–0–1 (3), McKenna 2–1–0–0 (3), Anderson 2–0–0–0 (2), Murdock 2–0–0–0 (2), Cartwright 1–0–0–0 (1). Own goals 2–2–0–0 (4)

Match Report: Old Boy Eyres – The Main Man. 18 December 1999
Preston 3 Blackpool 0 Divison Two

It took a long time, but Preston North End finally breached the stubborn Blackpool defence when one of their old boys, David Eyres, broke the deadlock. In the 71st minute Paul Beesley brought down Alex Mathie 30 yards from goal. Up stepped Eyres to crash home an unstoppable drive that flew in off the crossbar. It was the breakthrough North End wanted and just three minutes later Michael Appleton hit another shot that deflected up off a defender. Appleton reacted swiftly and followed up to head wide of the keeper to make it 2–0. Earlier Blackpool had worked hard and only a great save by Tepi Moilanen stopped Phil Clarkson from scoring. The goalkeeper then made an even better stop from Junior Bent. However, North End also had their moments, most notably when Eyres, the star of the show, hit a fierce low shot along the ground which cannoned back off the post with Tony Caig beaten. Six minutes before the opening goal Eyres put in a crashing header that came back off the crossbar and it looked as though it might be one of those games for Eyres. The probable turning point of the game came after manager David Moyes had taken off Bjarki Gunnlaugsson and Jon Macken, and put on Alex Mathie and Kurt Nogan. The new forwards gave the Blackpool defenders a torrid time and questions that they couldn't answer. After the two goals Preston were rampant and if Eyres' first goal was a bit special, his second four minutes from the end was out of this world. He won the ball some 30 yards from goal, strode forward, looked up and then calmly placed the ball into the corner of the net. A superb finish! In the end North End won comfortably but their all round team effort earlier in the game had paved the way to the three points.

Worthington Cup appearances (5 games)

Alexander 5, Appleton 2, Barry Murphy 0+1, Basham 1+1, Cartwright 3, Edwards 5, Eyres 1+2, Gregan 4, Gunnlaugsson 0+1, Jackson 5, Kidd 3+1, Lucas 1, Ludden 1, Macken 5, Mathie 2, McKenna 5, Moilanen 4, Murdock 3, Nogan 1+2, Rankine 4

FA Cup appearances (6 games)

Alexander 6, Appleton 3, Basham 0+1, Beresford 0+1, Cartwright 2+1, Darby 2, Diaf 0+1, Edwards 6, Eyres 5, Gregan 6, Gunnlaugsson 3+3, Jackson 6, Kidd 3, Lucas 1, Macken 5+1, Mathie 1+2, McKenna 1+1, Moilanen 5, Murdock 3+1, Nogan 3+2, Rankine 5

Auto Windscreen Shield Appearances (2 games)

Alexander 1, Appleton 2, Barry Murphy 1, Beesley 0+1, Beresford 1, Cartwright 0+1, Darby 2, Diaf 2, Eaton A. 0+1, Edwards 2, Gunnlaugsson 2, Kidd 2, King S. 0+1, Lucas 1, Ludden 1, Macken 2, Mathie 1, McKenna 0+1, Moilanen 1, Murdock 1, Nogan 0+1

Date 1999-2000	Opponents	Com.	h or a	Score	Att.	1	2	3	4	5	6	7	8	9	10	11	12	13	14	15	16
Aug 7	Oldham Ath.	Div 2	a	1-0	9437	Lucas	Alexander	Ludden *	Murdock	Jackson	Gregan	Appleton	Rankine	Nogan +	Macken (1)	Eyres	Moilanen	Edwards *	Basham +	Wright	McKenna
Aug 10	Wrexham Rd 1 1L	WC	h	1-0	4930	Lucas	Alexander	Edwards	Murdock	Jackson	Gregan	Appleton (1)	Rankine	Nogan #	Macken	McKenna	Moilanen	B'Murphy	Eyres	Basham #	Darby
Aug 14	Stoke City	Div 2	h	2-1	11465	Lucas	Alexander	Kidd	Murdock (1)	Jackson	Gregan	Appleton	Rankine	Nogan (1)	Macken *	Eyres +	Moilanen	B'Murphy	Basham *	Wright	McKenna +
Aug 21	Wycombe W.	Div 2	a	1-1	5091	Lucas	Alexander	Kidd	Murdock	Jackson	Gregan	Appleton	Rankine	Nogan (1) *	Macken	Eyres +	Moilanen	B'Murphy	Basham *	Darby	McKenna +
Aug 24	Wrexham Rd 1 2L	WC	a	2-0	2911	Moilanen	Alexander	Kidd	Murdock	Jackson	Gregan	Appleton #	Edwards *	Macken (1) +	Basham (1)	McKenna	Lucas	B'Murphy *	Eyres #	Rankine	Nogan +
Aug 28	Wigan Ath.	Div 2	h	1-4	13889	Lucas	Alexander	Kidd	Murdock	Jackson	Gregan #	Appleton	Rankine	Macken +	Basham (1)	Eyres *	Moilanen *	Edwards	Nogan +	Cartwright #	McKenna
Sep 1	Reading	Div 2	a	2-2	7628	Lucas	Alexander	Kidd *	Murdock	Jackson	Gregan	Appleton	Rankine	Macken	Basham (1)	Eyres (1) +	Moilanen	Edwards *	Nogan	Cartwright +	McKenna
Sep 4	Chesterfield	Div 2	h	0-2	8506	Lucas	Alexander	Ludden	Murdock	Jackson	Edwards	Cartwright	Rankine	Nogan	Basham	Eyres *	Moilanen	Appleton	Macken *	Eaton	McKenna
Sep 11	Burnley	Div 2	h	0-0	13708	Moilanen	Alexander	Ludden	Murdock	Jackson	McKenna +	Cartwright	Rankine	Nogan	Basham	Eyres *	O'Hanlon	Appleton +#	Macken *	Edwards #	B'Murphy
Sep 14	Sheffield Utd. Rd 2 1L	WC	a	0-2	5350	Moilanen	Alexander	Ludden *	Murdock	Jackson	McKenna	Cartwright	Rankine	Edwards	Macken	Eyres	Lucas	Kidd *	Eaton	Wright	Darby
Sep 18	Gillingham	Div 2	a	2-0	6610	Moilanen	Alexander	Edwards	Kidd	Jackson	Gregan (1)	Cartwright *	Rankine	Mathie	Macken (1)	Eyres	Lucas	Eaton	McKenna *	Beesley	Darby
Sep 21	Sheffield Utd. Rd 2 2L	WC	h	3-0	5658	Moilanen	Alexander (1)	Edwards	Kidd	Jackson	Gregan	Cartwright	Rankine	Mathie (2)	Macken	McKenna	Lucas	Murdock	Beesley	Eyres	Darby
Sep 25	Brentford	Div 2	a	2-2	7100	Moilanen	Alexander	Edwards	Kidd	Jackson	Gregan	Cartwright *	Rankine	Mathie	Macken (1)	McKenna (1)	Lucas	Murdock	Nogan *	Eyres	Darby
Oct 2	Cambridge Utd.	Div 2	h	2-1	9522	Moilanen	Alexander	Edwards	Kidd +	Jackson	Gregan	Cartwright	Rankine	Mathie #	Macken (2)	McKenna *	Lucas	Murdock +	Nogan	Eyres *	Gun'sson #
Oct 9	Bristol City	Div 2	h	1-0	10042	Moilanen	Alexander	Edwards	Kidd	Jackson	Gregan	Cartwright	Rankine	Mathie (1) +	Macken	McKenna *	Lucas	Murdock	Nogan +	Eyres *	Gun'sson
Oct 12	Arsenal Rd 3	WC	a	1-2	15236	Moilanen	Alexander	Edwards	Kidd	Jackson	Gregan	Cartwright	Rankine	Mathie +	Macken (1) #	McKenna *	Lucas	Murdock	Nogan #	Eyres *	Gun'sson +
Oct 16	Scunthorpe Utd.	Div 2	a	1-1	5536	Moilanen	Alexander	Edwards	Murdock	Jackson	Gregan	Cartwright	Rankine	Mathie *	Macken (1)	McKenna +	Lucas	Diaf	Nogan *	Eyres +	Gun'sson
Oct 19	Millwall (og by Nethercott)	Div 2	a	2-0	6355	Moilanen	Alexander	Edwards	Murdock	Jackson	Gregan	Cartwright (1)	Rankine	Nogan *	Macken +	McKenna	Lucas	Diaf	Mathie +	Eyres *	Gun'sson
Oct 23	Brentford (og by Marshall)	Div 2	h	2-1	10382	Moilanen	Alexander (1p)	Edwards	Murdock	Jackson	Gregan	Cartwright #	Rankine	Nogan +	Macken	McKenna *	Lucas	Kidd	Mathie +	Eyres *	Gun'sson
Oct 31	Bristol Rovers Rd 1	FAC	a	1-0	6145	Moilanen	Alexander	Edwards	Murdock	Jackson	Gregan	Cartwright	Rankine	Nogan	Macken*	McKenna (1)	Lucas	Kidd	Diaf	Darby	Gun'sson *
Nov 3	AFC Bournemouth	Div 2	h	3-0	9630	Moilanen	Alexander (1p)	Edwards	Murdock	Jackson	Gregan	Cartwright	Rankine	Nogan #	Macken (1) *	McKenna (1) +	Lucas	Kidd	Diaf #	Mathie +	Gun'sson *
Nov 6	Colchester Utd.	Div 2	a	2-2	3818	Moilanen	Alexander	Edwards	Murdock	Jackson	Gregan	Cartwright *	Rankine	Nogan (1)	Macken	Diaf +	Lucas	Kidd	Darby	Mathie + (1)	Gun'sson *
Nov 12	Notts County	Div 2	h	2-0	14226	Moilanen	Alexander	Edwards	Murdock	Jackson	Gregan	Cartwright	Rankine	Nogan *	Macken (2) #	Eyres +	Lucas	Kidd +	Darby	Mathie *	Wright #
Nov 20	Enfield Rd 2	FAC	h	0-0	11566	Lucas	Alexander	Edwards	Kidd	Jackson	Gregan	Cartwright #	Rankine	Mathie *	Gunn'sson	Eyres	Moilanen	Ludden	Macken *	Nogan #	McKenna
Nov 23	Luton	Div 2	a	2-0	5124	Moilanen	Alexander	Edwards	Kidd	Jackson	Gregan	Cartwright	Rankine	Nogan	Macken	Eyres (2)	Lucas	Murdock	Mathie	Appleton	Gun'sson
Nov 27	Bury	Div 2	a	3-1	6469	Moilanen	Alexander	Edwards	Kidd	Jackson (1)	Gregan (1)	Cartwright *	Rankine	Nogan	Macken (1) +	Eyres #	Lucas	Murdock	Mathie +	Appleton*	Gun'sson #
Nov 30	Enfield Rd 2 Replay	FAC*	a	3-0	1808	Moilanen	Alexander (1p)	Edwards	Kidd	Jackson *	Gregan	Darby	Appleton	Nogan	Macken *	Eyres (1) #	Lucas	Murdock *	Mathie +	Diaf	Gun'sson#(1)
Dec 4	Oldham Ath.	Div 2	h	2-0	10970	Moilanen	Alexander	Edwards	Kidd	Jackson	Appleton	Darby	Rankine	Nogan #	Macken (2)	Eyres	Lucas	Murdock	Mathie	Diaf	Gun'sson #
Dec 7	Wrexham Rd 1	AWS	h	4-1	3306	Moilanen	Alexander +	Edwds (1)#	Kidd	Darby	Appleton	Diaf	B'Murphy	Mathie	Macken *	Gunn'sson (3)	O'Hanlon	Eaton #	King +	Eyres	Nogan *
Dec 11	Oldham Ath. Rd 3	FAC	h	2-1	9940	Moilanen	Alexander (1p)	Edwards	Kidd	Jackson	Gregan	Darby +	Rankine	Gunn'sson #	Macken (1) #	Eyres	Lucas	B'Murphy	Diaf +	Mathie #	Nogan *
Dec 18	Blackpool	Div 2	h	3-0	16821	Moilanen	Alexander	Edwards	Kidd	Jackson	Gregan	Beresford #	Rankine	Gunn'sson +	Macken *	Eyres (2)	Lucas	Murdock	Mathie +	Nogan *	Appleton # (1)
Dec 26	Wrexham	Div 2	a	0-0	7872	Moilanen	Alexander	Edwards	Kidd	Jackson	Gregan	Darby +	Appleton	Gunn'sson #	Macken *	Eyres	Lucas	Murdock	Diaf +	Nogan *	Basham #
Dec 28	Bristol Rovers	Div 2	h	2-1	16680	Moilanen	Alexander (1p)	Edwards	Kidd #	Jackson	Gregan	Appleton	Rankine	Nogan	Macken (1)	Eyres +	Lucas	Murdock#	Beresford +	Basham	Gun'sson
Jan 3	Cardiff City	Div 2	a	4-0	10142	Moilanen	Alexander (2,1p)	Edwards (1)	Murdock	Jackson	Gregan	Appleton	Rankine	Nogan (1)	Macken #	Eyres +	Lucas	Kidd	Ludden	Beresford +	Gun'sson #
Jan 8	Plymouth Arg. Rd 4 *	FAC	a	3-0	10824	Moilanen	Alexander (1p)	Edwards	Murdock	Jackson	Gregan	Appleton	Rankine	Nogan *	Macken *	Eyres	Lucas	Kidd	Ludden	Beresford *	Gun'sson #
Jan 10	Hartlepool Rd 2	AWS	h	1-2	3635	Lucas	Darby	Ludden	Murdock	Kidd	Edwards #	Beresford	Appleton +	Gunn'sson (1)	Macken *	Diaf	O'Hanlon	Parkinson	MKenna+	Cartwright #	Beesley *
Jan 14	Stoke City	Div 2	a	1-2	10285	Moilanen	Alexander (1p)	Edwards	Murdock	Jackson	Gregan	Appleton #	Rankine	Nogan	Macken	Eyres +	Lucas	Kidd	Diaf	Beresford +	Gun'sson #
Jan 22	Wycombe W.	Div 2	h	3-2	10969	Moilanen	Alexander	Edwards	Murdock (1)	Jackson	Gregan	Cartwright +	Rankine	Gunn'sson	Macken (2)	Appleton	Lucas	Kidd	McKenna +	Beresford	Wright
Jan 29	Everton Rd 5	FAC	a	0-2	37846	Moilanen	Alexander	Edwards	Murdock	Jackson	Gregan	Appleton +	Rankine	Gunn'sson	Macken	Eyres #	Lucas	Kidd	MKenna *	C'twright #*	Basham +
Feb 1	Oxford Utd.	Div 2	a	4-0	5164	Moilanen	Alexander	Edwards	Murdock	Jackson	Gregan +	Appleton (1)	Rankine	Basham *	Macken (2) #	Eyres (1)	Lucas	Kidd	McKenna +	Wright #	Beesley *
Feb 5	Reading	Div 2	h	2-2	12618	Moilanen	Alexander	Edwards	Murdock	Jackson (1)	Gregan	Appleton	Rankine	Basham *	Macken (1)	Eyres	Lucas	Kidd	McKenna	Wright	Gun'sson *
Feb 12	Chesterfield	Div 2	a	1-0	4726	Moilanen	Alexander	Edwards	Murdock	Jackson	Gregan (1)	Appleton	McKenna +	Gunn'sson *	Macken	Eyres	Lucas	Kidd	Ludden	Darby *	Basham +
Feb 19	Bury	Div 2	h	1-1	13901	Moilanen	Alexander	Edwards	Murdock	Jackson	Gregan	Appleton	Rankine	Gunn'sson	Macken (1)	Eyres +	Lucas	McKenna	Ludden	Darby	Basham +
Feb 26	Gillingham	Div 2	h	0-2	13246	Moilanen	Alexander	Edwards	Murdock	Jackson	Gregan	Appleton +	Rankine	Gunn'sson #	Macken	Anderson *	Lucas	Eyres +	McKenna	Basham *	Angell #
Mar 4	Burnley	Div 2	a	3-0	22310	Moilanen	Alexander	Kidd	Murdock	Jackson (1)	Gregan #	Edwards (1)	Rankine	Basham	Macken (1) +	Anderson *	Lucas	Eyres *	C'twright #	Gun'sson	Angell +
Mar 7	Colchester Utd.	Div 2	h	2-3	11323	Moilanen	Alexander *	Kidd	Murdock	Jackson	Edwards	Cartwright	Rankine	Basham +	Macken	Anderson #	Lucas	Eyres #	Appleton	Gun'sson *	Angell # (2)
Mar 11	AFC Bournemouth	Div 2	a	1-0	5317	Moilanen	Alexander	Kidd	Murdock	Jackson	Edwards #	Cartwright	Rankine	Angell (1) *	Macken	Eyres +	Lucas	McKenna #	Appleton +	Gun'sson	Basham *
Mar 14	Oxford Utd.	Div 2	h	3-1	12008	Moilanen	Alexander	Kidd	Murdock	Jackson	McKenna	Cartwright #	Rankine	Angell (2) +	Macken (1) *	Eyres	Lucas	Anderson #	Appleton	Gun'sson +	Basham *
Mar 18	Luton	Div 2	h	1-0	13731	Moilanen	Alexander	Kidd	Murdock	Jackson	Gregan	Anderson (1) +	Rankine	Angell	Macken *	Eyres #	Lucas	Edwards #	C'twright +	Gun'sson	Basham *
Mar 21	Notts County	Div 2	a	0-1	6401	Moilanen	Alexander	Kidd *	Murdock	Jackson	Edwards	Cartwright	Rankine	Angell	Basham #	Anderson +	Lucas	McKenna	Eyres +	Gun'sson #	Macken *
Mar 25	Wrexham	Div 2	h	1-0	12481	Moilanen	Alexander	Kidd	Murdock	Jackson	Gregan	Cartwright #	Rankine	Angell	Basham +	Anderson (1) *	Lucas	Appleton #	Eyres	Gun'sson +	McKenna *
Apr 1	Blackpool	Div 2	a	0-0	9042	Moilanen	Alexander	Edwards	Kidd	Jackson	Gregan	Cartwright	Rankine	Angell	Macken +	Anderson #	Lucas	Basham	Eyres #	Gun'sson +	McKenna
Apr 4	Wigan Ath.	Div 2	a	1-0	15593	Moilanen	Alexander	Edwards	Kidd	Jackson (1)	Gregan +	McKenna	Rankine	Gunn'sson #	Macken	Anderson +	Lucas	Basham *	Eyres #	Angell	Cartwright +
Apr 8	Cardiff City	Div 2	h	0-0	13794	Moilanen	Alexander	Edwards	Kidd	Jackson	McKenna	Basham #	Rankine	Gunn'sson	Macken +	Anderson	Lucas	Appleton	Eyres #	Angell +*	Cartwright *
Apr 15	Bristol Rovers	Div 2	a	2-0	10111	Moilanen	Alexander	Edwards	Kidd	Jackson	McKenna	Appleton	Rankine	Gunn'sson (1) +	Macken (1) #	Anderson *	Lucas	Murdock	Eyres #	Angell +	Cartwright *
Apr 22	Scunthorpe Utd.	Div 2	h	1-0	15518	Moilanen	Alexander	Edwards	Kidd	Jackson	McKenna *	Appleton	Rankine	Gunn'sson	Macken #	Anderson +	Lucas	Murdock	Eyres +	Angell # (1)	Cartwright *
Apr 24	Cambridge Utd.	Div 2	a	0-2	6068	Moilanen	Alexander #	Edwards	Kidd	Jackson	Appleton +	Cartwright *	Rankine	Gunn'sson	Angell	McKenna	Lucas	Murdock *	Eyres +	Basham #	Parkinson
Apr 29	Millwall	Div 2	h	3-2	19407	Moilanen	Alexander	Edwards *	Kidd	Jackson (1)	Appleton	McKenna	Rankine	Gunn'sson #	Angell (1)	Eyres (1)	Lucas	Murdock *	Macken #	Basham	Cartwright
May 6	Bristol City	Div 2	a	2-0	11160	Moilanen	Alexander	Edwards	Murdock	Jackson	Appleton (1)	McKenna	Rankine	Angell (1)	Macken	Eyres #	Lucas	Basham *	Cartwright	B'Murphy #	Parkinson +
	* 1 own goal by O'Sullivan and 1 own goal by Beswetherwick	* At St. Albans																			

SEASON 2000–2001

Preston North End's first season back in the second highest division in 20 years, now called Division One, was a big challenge for David Moyes and his men. In fact it was a big challenge for all at the club as it was new territory for a whole generation. It turned out to be a roller coaster of excitement, frustration and yet ultimate disappointment. Again the team started the season well, it was getting to be a habit, and up to the middle of October it looked very good indeed. Only two defeats and some excellent away performances, always a clue as to how well North End will fare in a season. The problems arrived in the autumn and through Christmas. Some bad defeats, injuries and suspensions, and some poor defending had Moyes and the fans tearing their hair out. Jon Macken was still the main goal threat but he had a poor first half of the season. Steve Basham suffered an horrendous leg break and Moyes decided to bring in Erik Meijer on loan from Liverpool. The move failed as the big Dutch striker never scored once in his nine games. It was not until the New Year that the team finally turned the corner. Moyes had brought in David Healy just before Christmas from Manchester United reserves and he immediately began to repay the manager's faith. The big turning point came in January 2001 after the club had had a three week mid-season break. It gave the manager time to take stock, and when the season resumed, at Portsmouth on February 3, the whole side looked fresh, eager and ready for a determined push up the table. Healy's goal won the game at Fratton Park and then QPR were demolished 5–0 at Deepdale in the next game. In those final 18 games North End's record read: P18 W11 D4 L3 F29 A13 Pts 37. It was definitely promotion form! There was a new confidence in the team, not seen in the weeks leading up to Christmas and after Preston had beaten WBA 3–0 at home in the final game it was on to their biggest games in 40 years. The play-off semi-final against Birmingham was unbelievable, with the second leg giving a night of drama that rivalled anything that Deepdale had ever seen before in its 120 year history. The penalty shoot-out victory sent the fans wild and the club was off to a final at the Millennium Stadium Cardiff. Sadly, the match against Bolton proved a game too far for the Lilywhites as former North End old boy Sam Allardyce led his Wanderers team to the promised land of the Premiership. The sight of Sean Gregan slumped crestfallen on the Welsh turf summed up everyone's feelings. Preston had come within 90 minutes of the Premier League and only time would tell if the players would ever get over the bitter disappointment. But, oh such unbelievable memories.

Jon Macken

League position in Division One: 4th (Reached the play-offs) – P46 W23 D9 L14 F64 A52 Pts 78
Home: W12 D6 L5 F32 A18 Away: W11 D3 L9 F32 A34

Date 2000-1	Opponents	Comp	h or a	Score	Att.	1	2	3	4	5	6	7	8	9	10	11	12	13	14	15	16
Aug 12	Grimsby Town	Div1	a	2-1	5755	Moilanen	Alexander	Edwards	Gregan	Murdock	McKenna	Anderson*	Rankine	Basham+	Macken(1)	Appleton(1)	Lucas	Eyres+	Wright	Robinson*	Bry Murphy
Aug 19	Sheffield United	Div 1	h	3-0	13948	Moilanen	Alexander	Edwards	Gregan	Murdock	Robinson	Anderson	Rankine	Basham	Macken(2)	Appleton(1)	Lucas	Cartwright	Ludden	Robinson	Bry Murphy
Aug 22	Shrewsbury Rd 1	WC	a	0-1	2445	Lucas	Alexander	Edwards	Morgan	Murdock	Robinson	Bry Murphy	Bry Murphy	Basham	Macken	McKenna	O'Hanlon	Appleton	Parkinson	Ludden	Anderson
Aug 26	Bolton	Div 1	h	0-2	19954	Moilanen	Alexander+	Edwards	Jackson	Murdock	Appleton	Anderson	Rankine	Basham	Macken	McKenna*	Lucas	Eyres	Robinson*	Cartwright	Bry Murphy
Aug 28	Wimbledon	Div 1	h	1-1	13519	Moilanen	Parkinson	Edwards	Jackson+	Murdock	Gregan	Appleton(1)	Rankine	Basham(1)#	Macken	McKenna	Lucas	Eyres+	Robinson	Cartwright+	Anderson+
Sep 2	Portsmouth	Div 1	h	1-0	13343	Moilanen	Alexander	Edwards	Jackson	Murdock	Appleton	Anderson +	Rankine	Basham(1)#	Macken*	McKenna	Lucas	Eyres*	Robinson#	Cartwright+	Parkinson
Sep 5	Shrewsbury Rd 1	WC	h	4-1	5451	Lonergan	Alexander(1)	Edwards	Gregan	Gregan	Gregan#	Anderson*	Robinson	Basham*	Macken(3)+	Anderson*	Moilanen	Eyres+	Rankine#	Bry Murphy#	Parkinson
Sep 9	QPR	Div 1	a	0-0	11092	Lucas	Alexander	Edwards	Gregan	Murdock	Appleton	Anderson*	Rankine	Basham	Macken+	McKenna	O'Hanlon	Jackson	Cartwright*	Robinson	Eyres*
Sep 12	Birmingham	Div 1	a	1-3	16464	Lucas	Alexander	Edwards	Gregan	Murdock	Appleton	Cartwright+	Rankine(1)	Basham#	Macken*	McKenna	O'Hanlon	Jackson+	Eyres*	Robinson#	Gun'sson*
Sep 16	Stockport Co.	Div 1	h	1-1	12735	Lucas+	Alexander	Edwards	Gregan	Murdock	Appleton	Cartwright	Rankine	McBride	Basham*	McKenna(1)#	O'Hanlon+	Jackson	Eyres*	Robinson	Parkinson
Sep 19	Coventry C. Rd 2	WC	a	1-3	10770	Lucas	Alexander(1p)	Edwards	Gregan	Murdock	Appleton	Cartwright	Rankine	McBride+	Basham*	McKenna	O'Hanlon	Jackson	Eyres	Robinson	Parkinson
Sep 23	Sheffield Wed. +	Div 1	h	3-1	17379	Lucas	Alexander(1)	Edwards	Gregan	Murdock	Appleton	Cartwright#	Rankine(1)	Basham*	Basham*	McKenna#	O'Hanlon	Jackson	Eyres*	Robinson	Anderson(1)#
Sep 27	Coventry C. Rd 2	WC	a	1-4	7425	Lonergan	Alexander	Edwards	Jackson	Gregan	Gregan	Cartwright#	Rankine(1)	Basham*	Robinson	Anderson(1)*	Moilanen	Kidd+	Eyres*	Appleton	Anderson*
Sep 30	Crystal Palace	Div 1	h	2-0	13028	Lucas	Alexander	Edwards	Jackson	Gregan	Appleton	Cartwright	Rankine	Basham(1)+	Robinson(1)+	McKenna(1)*	Moilanen	Kidd	Eyres*	Robinson#	Bry Murphy
Oct 14	Tranmere	Div 1	a	1-0	14511	Lucas	Alexander	Edwards	Gregan	Murdock	Appleton	Cartwright	Rankine	Basham(1)#	Robinson	McKenna	Moilanen	Kidd	Anderson*	Gun'sson	Bry Murphy
Oct 17	Norwich	Div 1	h	1-0	13002	Lucas	Alexander	Edwards	Gregan	Murdock	Appleton	Cartwright	McKenna	Meijer	Robinson	Anderson+	Moilanen	Kidd	Jackson	Gun'sson(1)+	Bry Murphy
Oct 21	Huddersfield	Div 1	h	0-0	13161	Lucas	Alexander	Edwards	Gregan	Murdock	Appleton	Cartwright+	Rankine	Meijer	Robinson	McKenna*	Moilanen	Kidd	Jackson	Gun'sson	Anderson
Oct 24	Fulham	Div 1	a	1-0	14354	Moilanen	Alexander	Edwards	Gregan	Murdock	Appleton(1)	Cartwright*	Rankine	Meijer	Macken(1)	McKenna	Moilanen	Robinson+	Jackson	Gun'sson	Anderson
Oct 27	Barnsley	Div 1	h	1-2	13566	Lucas	Alexander	Edwards	Gregan	Murdock	Appleton	Cartwright*	Rankine	Meijer+	Macken(1)	McKenna	Moilanen	Robinson	Jackson*	Gun'sson	Anderson+
Nov 4	Nottm Forest	Div 1	a	1-3	19504	Lucas	Alexander	Edwards	Gregan	Murdock	Appleton(1)	Anderson*	Rankine	Meijer+	Macken(1)#	McKenna	Moilanen	Cartwright	Jackson*	Gun'sson	Robinson+
Nov 10	Crewe Alex.	Div 1	h	2-1	12632	Lucas	Parkinson	Kidd	Gregan	Murdock	Appleton(1)	Anderson	Rankine(1)	Meijer+	Macken*	McKenna	Moilanen	Cartwright	Ludden	Gun'sson	Robinson+
Nov 18	Watford	Div 1	h	3-2	13066	Lucas	Parkinson*	Kidd#	Gregan	Jackson	Appleton	Anderson(1)*	Rankine(1)	Meijer	Macken(1)+	McKenna	Moilanen	Cartwright*	Edwards#	Gun'sson*	Robinson*
Nov 25	WBA	Div 1	a	1-1	20043	Lucas	Parkinson*	Edwards	Gregan	Jackson	Appleton	Anderson+	Rankine	Meijer	Macken	McKenna	Moilanen	Cartwright*	Kidd	Gun'sson	Robinson*
Dec 2	Fulham	Div 1	h	1-1	16047	Lucas	Parkinson	Edwards	Gregan	Murdock	Robinson*	Anderson+	Rankine	Meijer#	Macken	McKenna	Moilanen	Cartwright+	Ludden*	Robinson+	Bry Murphy
Dec 9	Burnley	Div 1	a	2-1	17355	Lucas	Alexander(1)	Edwards	Jackson	Murdock	Gregan	Cartwright	Rankine	Gu'sson+	Macken(1)	McKenna	Moilanen	Kidd	Ludden	Robinson+	Bry Murphy
Dec 16	Grimsby	Div 1	a	0-4	8198	Lucas	Alexander	Edwards	Jackson*	Murdock	Appleton	Cartwright*	Rankine	Gu'sson+	Macken(1)	Anderson+	Lonergan	Parkinson	Appleton	Robinson+	Ludden
Dec 23	Gillingham	Div 1	h	1-2	14667	Moilanen	Parkinson	Edwards	Jackson	Gregan	Appleton	Cartwright*	Rankine#	Robinson#	Macken	McKenna	Lonergan	Murdock*	Ludden#	Robinson+	Bry Murphy
Dec 26	Wolves	Div 1	a	1-0	24306	Lucas	Alexander+	Edwards	Jackson	Gregan	Appleton	Anderson(1)*	Rankine(1)	Robinson#	Macken	McKenna	Moilanen	Murdock*	Ludden#	Cartwright+	Bry Murphy*
Dec 30	Sheffield United	Div 1	a	2-3	22316	Lucas	Parkinson	Edwards+	Jackson	Murdock*	Appleton	Cartwright#	Appleton	McBride	Healy(1)+	McKenna	Moilanen	Kidd*	Robinson#	Anderson#	Bry Murphy*
Jan 1	Bolton W.	Div 1	h	0-1	15863	Lucas	Parkinson+	Kidd	Jackson	Murdock*	Gregan	Bry Murphy	Rankine	McBride*	Macken+	McKenna	Moilanen	Healy+	Robinson*	Rankine*	Cartwright
Jan 6	Stockport Co. Rd3	FAC	h	0-1	9975	Lucas	Parkinson+	Eaton	Jackson	Kidd	Appleton	Bry Murphy	Rankine	McBride*	Healy	McKenna	Moilanen	Macken*	Robinson*	Morgan	Cartwright+
Jan 10	Blackburn Rvrs	Div 1	a	2-3	23983	Lucas	Parkinson#	Kidd+	Jackson	Gregan	Appleton	Cartwright	Rankine	Healy(1p)	Macken(1)*	McKenna	Moilanen	McBride*	Robinson	Murdock#	Bry Murphy#
Jan 13	Wimbledon	Div 1	a	1-3	7242	Lucas	Cartwright*	Kidd	Jackson	Murdock	Appleton	Robinson(1)	Rankine	Healy	Macken	Edwards	Moilanen	McKenna*	Morgan	Parkinson	Bry Murphy+
Feb 3	Portsmouth	Div 1	h	1-0	13331	Moilanen	Parkinson	Edwards	Jackson	Murdock	McKenna	Cartwright	Rankine	Healy(1)*	Macken	Healy(1)+	Lucas	Eaton	Anderson	Gun'sson+	Bry Murphy+
Feb 10	QPR	Div 1	a	5-0	14423	Moilanen	Alexander	Edwards	Jackson	Murdock	McKenna*	Cartwright*	Rankine#	McBride(1)*	Macken(2)+	Healy(1)+	Lucas	Kidd	Anderson(1)*	Gun'sson	Bry Murphy#
Feb 13	Stockport	Div 1	h	1-0	7590	Moilanen	Alexander	Edwards	Jackson	Murdock	McKenna	Cartwright	Rankine#	McBride	Macken	Healy(1)	Moilanen	Kidd	Anderson	Gun'sson	Bry Murphy#
Feb 20	Birmingham	Div 1	h	0-2	14864	Moilanen	Parkinson	Edwards	Jackson	Murdock	McKenna	Cartwright#	Rankine+	McBride	Healy	Anderson*	Lucas	Alexander	Gregan+	Gun'sson*	Bry Murphy#
Feb 24	Sheffield Wed.	Div 1	h	2-0	14379	Moilanen	Alexander(1p)	Edwards	Jackson	Murdock	McKenna(1)	Cartwright	Rankine	Healy+	Macken(1)	Gun'sson*	Lucas	Kidd	Gregan*	Anderson	Bry Murphy*
Mar 3	Crystal Palace	Div 1	a	2-0	15160	Moilanen	Alexander(1p)	Edwards	Jackson	Murdock	Gregan	Cartwright	Rankine	Healy(1)+	Macken(1)	McKenna	Lucas	Kidd	Gun'sson	Anderson	Bry Murphy+
Mar 6	Tranmere	Div 1	h	1-1	10335	Moilanen	Alexander	Edwards	Jackson	Murdock	Gregan	Cartwright	Rankine	Healy+	Macken(1)	McKenna	Lucas	Kidd	Gun'sson	Anderson	Bry Murphy+
Mar 14	Wolves	Div 1	h	2-0	15457	Moilanen	Alexander	Edwards	Jackson	Murdock*	Gregan(1)	Cartwright#	Rankine	Healy+	Macken+	McKenna(1)	Lucas	Kidd	Gun'sson	Anderson	Cresswell(1)*
Mar 17	Norwich City	Div 1	a	2-1	16282	Moilanen	Alexander	Edwards	Jackson	Gregan	Gregan(1)	Cartwright#	Rankine	Healy(1)	Macken(2)	McKenna	Lucas	Alexander	Gun'sson*	Cresswell	Bry Murphy#
Mar 31	Gillingham	Div 1	a	0-0	13550	Moilanen	Alexander	Edwards	Jackson	Murdock	Gregan	Anderson+	Rankine	Cresswell	Macken	McKenna	Lucas	Murdock	Gun'sson	Anderson*	Healy+
Apr 7	Burnley	Div 1	h	0-3	16591	Lucas	Alexander	Edwards	Gregan	Murdock	McKenna	Cartwright*	Rankine	Cresswell	Macken*	Cresswell	Lucas+	Kidd	Gun'sson	Anderson*	Bry Murphy*
Apr 10	Huddersfield	Div 1	a	0-0	13185	Lucas	Alexander	Edwards	Kidd	Murdock	Gregan	Cartwright*	Rankine#	Cresswell	Healy+	McKenna	Lonergan	Macken	Anderson*	Anderson#	Bry Murphy#
Apr 14	Nottm Forest	Div 1	h	1-1	16842	Lucas	Alexander	Edwards	Kidd	Murdock	Gregan	Anderson+	Rankine	Healy(1)*	Macken	McKenna	Lonergan	Morgan	Gun'sson	Anderson#	Wright+
Apr 16	Barnsley	Div 1	a	4-0	16361	Lucas	Alexander	Edwards	Kidd	Murdock	Gregan	Cartwright	Rankine#	Healy#	Macken(1)*	McKenna(1)	Lonergan	Cartwright	Gun'sson	Cresswell(1)#	Bry Murphy+
Apr 21	Watford	Div 1	h	3-2	14071	Lonergan	Alexander(1p)	Edwards	Kidd	Murdock	Gregan	Anderson+	Rankine	Healy(1)*	Macken(2)	McKenna	O'Hanlon	Cartwright+	Gun'sson	Cresswell	Bry Murphy#
Apr 28	Crewe Alex.	Div 1	a	3-1	9415	Lucas	Alexander	Edwards	Jackson#	Kidd	Gregan	Anderson+	Rankine	Healy(1)*	Macken(2)	McKenna	Lonergan	Cartwright+	Gun'sson#	Anderson*	Bry Murphy#
May 2	Blackburn Rvrs	Div 1	h	0-1	16975	Lucas	Alexander	Eaton	Kidd	Gregan	Bry Murphy	Cartwright	Rankine+	Cresswell	Macken	Anderson#	Lonergan	Eaton	Keane+	Healy*	Keane+
May 6	WBA	Div 1	h	2-1	16226	Lucas	Alexander(1p)	Eaton#	Kidd	Jackson	Gregan(1)+	Cartwright	Bry Murphy	Cresswell	Healy	Gun'sson*	Lonergan	Abbott	Keane+	Anderson+	Murdock#

+ Own Goal by Walker

Match Report: McKenna's Gold – Thursday 17 May 2001. Preston 2 Birmingham 1
Divison One play-off semi-final (Agg. 2–2, PNE won 4–2 on penalties)

This game had everything and rarely has Deepdale seen a night like it in all its glorious history. Trailing 1–0 from the first leg, Preston had it all to do but they attacked the Midlanders from the first whistle. North End swept forward in wave after wave and only some heroic defending by Darren Purse and Michael Johnson kept the home side out. But that defence could only hold out for 24 minutes as that was when David Healy hammered in an unstoppable shot after Graham Alexander's throw had deflected to him. Deepdale went wild but this was just the start of the drama and Birmingham were certainly not going to lie down without a fight. David Lucas had to be at his best to deny McCarthy and Marcello in quick succession, and just after the break Sonner's header crashed against the crossbar. The pressure on Preston intensified as Birmingham sought the goal they needed. On the hour it came as Horsfield shot home from a left-wing cross. Lucas then made another save as Birmingham went in for the kill. Then, out of the blue, with 11 minutes to go, Preston were given a penalty after Sonner handled a corner from Rob Edwards. 'Penalty King' Alexander stepped forward having already scored four from the spot in the season. The fans held their breath and then watched in horror as Alexander's kick crashed against the bar and was cleared. With four minutes of stoppage time left Lazaridis all but settled the match when his shot rolled along the goalline, but stayed the right side from North End's point of view. Edwards gained possession and played it forward down the left to Macken. Preston's star striker found his partner Healy and he burst through for a shot at goal. Keeper Bennett parried the ball but couldn't hold it and there was Mark Rankine to bundle the ball home. The ground erupted as extra-time was forced by this last second goal. There was plenty of excitement in the extra period but no further score, so it was down to a penalty shoot-out. Trevor Francis, Birmingham's manager, did his side no favours by objecting when the referee decided to take the kicks towards the Fulwood End instead of the now derelict Town End. Francis threw all his toys out of his pram, even taking his players off in protest, and delayed the spot-kicks for 15 minutes. When they did finally start Alexander, what a brave decision, elected to take the first. 1–0. Lucas then brilliantly saved from Marcello and Healy sent Bennett the wrong way, 2–0! Purse then hit a post and Sean Gregan blasted his kick home to make it 3–0. Lazaridis, at last, then put Birmingham on the scoresheet but all it needed was for Edwards to score, Bennett guessed right and saved and Nicky Eaden put the pressure back on Preston to make it 3–2. The atmosphere was electric as Paul McKenna, the local boy from Chorley, stepped forward. Some fans could not watch, they thought it was all over. IT WAS NOW! GOAL!!. McKenna's shot went in and the celebrations began. What a night, what a game; bring on Bolton!

Goalscorers: 64 League – 6 WC – 2 P/Offs – (Total 72) (None scored in FAC)

Macken 19–3–0 (22), Healy 9–0–1 (10), Alexander 5–2–0 (7), Anderson 6–0–0 (6), Rankine 4–1–1 (6), Appleton 5–0–0 (5), McKenna 5–0–0 (5), Basham 2–0–0 (2), Cresswell 2–0–0 (2), Gregan 2–0–0 (2), Gunnlaugsson 1–0–0 (1), Jackson 1–0–0 (1), McBride 1–0–0 (1), Robinson 1–0–0 (1), Own Goals 1–0–0 (1) (Walker of Sheff.Wed.).

League appearances (46 games)

Alexander G. 34, Anderson I. 19+12, Appleton M. 25+1, Barry Murphy B. 2+12, Basham S. 11, Cartwright L. 29+8, Cresswell R. 5+6, Eaton A. 1, Edwards R. 41+1, Eyres D. 0+5, Gregan S. 40+2, Gunnlaugsson B. 5+14, Healy D. 19+3, Jackson M. 26+2, Keane M. 0+2, Kidd R. 13+2, Lonergan A. 1, Lucas D. 28+1, Ludden D. 0+2, Macken J. 37+1, McBride B. 8+1, McKenna P. 43+1, Meijer E. 9, Moilanen T. 17, Murdock, C. 33+4, O'Hanlon K. 0+1, Parkinson G. 11, Rankine M. 43+1, Robinson S. 6+16, Wright M. 0+1.

FA Cup appearances (1 games)

Appleton 1, Barry Murphy 1, Cartwright 0+1, Eaton 1, Healy 1, Jackson 1, Kidd 1, Lucas 1, Macken 0+1, McBride 1, McKenna 1, Parkinson 1, Rankine 1.

Division One Play-Offs (3 games)

Alexander 3, Anderson 1+2, Cartwright 3, Cresswell 1+2, Edwards 3, Gregan 3, Healy 3, Kidd 3, Lucas 3, Macken 3, McKenna 2+1, Murdock 3, Rankine 2.

Worthington Cup appearances (4 games)

Alexander 4, Anderson 2, Appleton 1, Barry Murphy 1+2, Basham 4, Cartwright 4, Edwards 4, Eyres 0+2, Gregan 3, Jackson 2, Kidd 0+1, Lonergan 1, Lucas 3, Macken 2, McBride 1, McKenna 2, Morgan P. 1, Murdock 4, Rankine 2+1, Robinson 3.

Season 2000–01: Division One

		P	W	D	L	F	A	Pts
1	Fulham	46	30	11	5	90	32	101
2	Blackburn Rovers	46	26	13	7	76	39	91
3	Bolton W.	46	24	15	7	76	45	87
4	Preston	46	23	9	14	64	52	78
5	Birmingham	46	23	9	14	59	48	78
6	WBA	46	21	11	14	60	52	74
7	Burnley	46	21	9	16	50	54	72
8	Wimbledon	46	17	18	11	71	50	69
9	Watford	46	20	9	17	76	67	69
10	Sheffield Utd.	46	19	11	16	52	49	68
11	Nottm. Forest	46	20	8	18	55	53	68
12	Wolverhampton W.	46	14	13	19	45	48	55
13	Gillingham	46	13	16	17	61	66	55
14	Crewe Alex.	46	15	10	11	47	62	55
15	Norwich City	46	14	12	20	46	58	54
16	Barnsley	46	15	9	22	49	62	54
17	Sheffield Wed.	46	15	8	23	52	71	53
18	Grimsby Town	46	14	10	22	43	62	52
19	Stockport Co.	46	11	18	17	58	65	51
20	Portsmouth	46	10	19	17	47	59	49
21	Crystal Palace	46	12	13	21	57	70	49
22	Huddersfield	46	11	15	20	48	57	48
23	QPR	46	7	19	20	45	75	40
24	Tranmere R.	46	9	11	26	46	77	38

DEBUTANTS: (8) Richard Cresswell, David Healy, Michael Keane, Andy Lonergan, Brian McBride, Erik Meijer, Paul Morgan, Steve Robinson.

LAST GAMES: (10) Appleton, Eyres, Gunnlaugsson, Ludden, McBride, Meijer, Morgan, O'Hanlon, Parkinson, Wright.

Trivia Facts:

The Town End was demolished through the spring and summer of 2001 ready for a new stand to be built.

Willie Cunningham, PNE's former Scotland captain, died in November 2000 and George Mutch, Preston's 1938 FA Cup final hero died in April 2001.

Thieves stole valuables and his Alfa Romeo car from Jon Macken just prior to the play-off final.

When Paul Williams was sent off playing for Coventry at Deepdale he incurred a bill of £3,700 after he kicked the fourth official's electronic number board on his way to the dressing rooms and damaged it beyond repair. He agreed to pay the cost.

SEASON 2001–2002

Two major decisions made during the 2001–02 season threatened to undo all the good work of the previous few years. First, in early October, Chairman Brian Gray, of BAXI, decided to stand down. It was a big blow as Gray had been a huge influence at Deepdale, and he can be very proud of his achievements. Not many Chairman can say they won two Championships. Then in March 2002 the inevitable happened as David Moyes was snapped up by a Premiership club. After the excitement of reaching the play-offs the season before the 2001–02 campaign turned out to be a bit disappointing. There was never any danger of relegation and there were many highlights but there was also an air of uncertainty about Moyes from day one and it was all a little unsettling for fans and players alike. For the first time for a while North End made a bad start to a new season. An away match at Gillingham is never Preston's most popular venue, but to travel the long road to Kent and return having been hammered 5–0 posed some immediate questions for manager, players and fans alike. There were no wins in the first five league games, but slowly and surely Moyes began to turn things around and during the autumn an excellent run of results lifted everyone's spirits. The 6–0 rout of Stockport more than avenged the FA Cup defeat the previous January, with David Healy scoring his first hat-trick for the club. But once again the season was full of ups and downs. Chris Lucketti came in from Huddersfield to stiffen up the defence whilst Alexander, Edwards, Gregan and McKenna continued to show their impressive consistency. But something was missing and the fans sensed that there were changes afoot. After a chirpy run in the FA Cup which again took North End to the 5th round, it became clear that Moyes was unsettled. One of his last acts as manager was to sell Jon Macken to Manchester City for £5 million but over the past three years Moyes had been linked with virtually every managerial position that became vacant in the Premiership and in the end the pull of that division proved too much for the talented young manager to resist. When Everton signed him it was only confirming the inevitable to regular Deepdale fans. Those fans were appeased to some extent by the fact that the clubs agreed a compensation fee that reportedly would be one million pounds, subject to certain clauses. To their professional credit though the players knuckled down under caretaker manager Kelham O'Hanlon and finished the season with four wins in the last six games. In the circumstances the final position of 8th in the table was commendable. The end of the season saw the players backing O'Hanlon's claim for the job, but the Board had other ideas and chose 61–year-old former Scotland manager, Craig Brown to take the reins for 2002–3. Time would tell if they had made the right choice.

DEBUTANTS: (8) Dickson Etuhu, Kevin Gallacher, Thordur Gudjonsson, Colin Hendry, Chris Lucketti, Paul Reid, Eric Skora, Clyde Wijnhard.

LAST GAMES: (11) Ainsworth, Basham, Gallacher, Gregan, Gudjonsson, Hendry, Kidd, Macken, Reid, Robinson, Wijnhard.

David
Healy

League position in Division One: 8th – P46 W20 D12 L14 F71 A59 Pts 72
Home: W13 D7 L3 F45 A21 Away: W7 D5 L11 F26 A38

Match Report: Gregan, Captain Fantastic! Boxing Day 2001.
Wolves 2 Preston 3. Division One

Molineux has not often been a ground where Preston North End have gained points, but this Boxing Day fixture against Wolves proved a massive confidence booster for the rest of the season for them. With Colin Murdock injured, manager David Moyes had to move Sean Gregan into the back four and bring in Paul McKenna to partner former Wolves player Mark Rankine in midfield. A great start by the home side had North End at full stretch, but the first real chance of the match fell to Jon Macken after 14 minutes. McKenna sent him away with a great pass but Macken blazed wide when he really should have done better. Five minutes later Wolves made Preston pay for that miss by taking the lead. Paul Sturridge reacted quickly to lob the ball perfectly over David Lucas following Alex Rae's free-kick. In the 37th minute Wolves almost made it 2–0 for the home side but this time Lucas came to the rescue with a brilliant save from Nathan Blake's header. Obviously some choice words were said in the Preston dressing room at half-time because the Lilywhites came out with a much more determined look after the break. Within 92 seconds they were level! Graham Alexander's mishit cross found David Healy standing in the D. He chested the ball down and spun round to beat Michael Oakes with an excellent right-foot shot. Seven minutes later North End turned the match around completely with a marvellous goal from Iain Anderson. Healy's pass found the winger wide on the left. Shades of Tom Finney as Anderson dropped his shoulder, cut inside, and curled a terrific shot into the far corner with Oakes hopelessly beaten. In the 65th minute a terrible combined blunder by Gregan and Lucas gave the home side an equaliser. Gregan should have cleared it, instead passed to Lucas, and Blake nipped in to charge down the clearance. To Lucas's horror the ball landed in the back of the net. Luckily for the goalkeeper, and for Gregan, the skipper made amends almost immediately. Alexander sent in a corner, Healy headed it goalwards and there was Gregan to deflect the ball past Oakes. The final 18 minutes saw some heavy pressure from Wolves but North End defended like lions and one magnificent block by Gregan saved a certain goal. The captain had certainly led by example as he did throughout his Preston career.

Richard Cresswell,
leading goalscorer

Ever presents: None
Hat-tricks: (1) Healy *vs.* Stockport home league
FA Cup: Fifth Rd.
Worthington Cup: Second Rd.
Manager: David Moyes until March 2002, then Kelham O'Hanlon
as caretaker until the end of season
Chairman: B. Gray Esq. then D. Shaw Esq. (acting)
Players used: 29
Leading scorer: 16 goals – Richard Cresswell
(13 league, 2 FAC, 1 W.Cup)
OFFICIAL PLAYER OF THE SEASON: Richard Cresswell

STAT FACTS:
Best home run without defeat: 9 games
Best away run without defeat: 5 games
Longest run unbeaten: 11 games
Longest run without a win: 5 games
Best home attendance: 21,013 *vs.* Man City 21.10.01
Worst home attendance: 11,371 *vs.* Millwall 15.9.01
Best away attendance: 34,220 *vs.* Man City 10.2.02
Worst away attendance: 2,227 *vs.* Kidderminster
21.8.01
Aggregate and average home attendance:
342,417 – 14,888
Aggregate and average away attendance:
353,677 – 15,377

Season 2001–02: Division One

	P	W	D	L	F	A	Pts
1 Man. City	46	31	15	9	108	52	99
2 WBA	46	27	8	11	61	29	89
3 Wolverhampton W.	46	25	11	10	76	43	86
4 Millwall	46	22	11	13	69	48	77
5 Birmingham	46	21	13	12	70	49	76
6 Norwich City	46	22	9	15	60	51	75
7 Burnley	46	21	12	13	70	62	75
8 Preston	46	20	12	14	71	59	72
9 Wimbledon	46	18	13	15	63	57	67
10 Crystal Palace	46	20	6	20	70	62	66
11 Coventry City	46	20	6	20	59	53	66
12 Gillingham	46	18	10	18	64	67	64
13 Sheffield Utd.	46	15	15	16	53	54	60
14 Watford	46	16	11	19	62	56	59
15 Bradford City	46	15	10	21	69	76	55
16 Nottm. Forest	46	12	18	16	50	51	54
17 Portsmouth	46	13	14	19	60	72	53
18 Walsall	46	13	12	21	51	71	51
19 Grimsby Town	46	12	14	20	50	72	50
20 Sheffield Wed.	46	12	14	20	49	71	50
21 Rotherham Utd.	46	10	19	17	52	66	49
22 Crewe Alex.	46	12	13	21	47	76	49
23 Barnsley	46	11	15	20	59	86	48
24 Stockport Co.	46	6	8	32	42	102	26

League appearances (46 games)

Ainsworth G. 3+2, Alexander G. 45, Anderson I. 17+15, Barry Murphy B. 2+2, Basham S. 0+16, Cartwright L. 34+2, Cresswell R. 27+15, Eaton A. 6+6, Edwards R. 36, Etuhu D. 16, Gallacher K. 1+4, Gregan S. 40+1, Gudjonsson T. 4+3, Healy D. 34+9, Hendry C. 2, Jackson M. 12+1, Keane M. 17+3, Kidd R. 5+1, Lucas D. 23+1, Lucketti C. 40, Macken J. 28+3, McKenna P. 37+1, Moilanen T. 23+1, Murdock C. 22+1, Rankine M. 24+2, Reid P. 0+1, Robinson S. 0+2, Skora E. 2+2, Wijnhard C. 6

FA Cup appearances (3 games)

Alexander 2, Anderson 2, Barry Murphy 0+1, Basham 1+1, Cartwright 1+1, Cresswell 1+1, Edwards 3, Gregan 2, Gudjonsson 0+1, Healy 2+1, Keane 3, Lucas 1, Lucketti 3, Macken 2+1, McKenna 2, Moilanen 2, Murdock 2, Robinson 0+1, Skora 2

Worthington Cup appearances (2 games)

Alexander 2, Anderson 2, Basham 0+1, Cartwright 1, Cresswell 1+1, Eaton 1, Edwards 1, Gallacher 0+1, Gregan 2, Healy 2, Jackson 1, Keane 0+1, Kidd 1, Lucas 1, Lucketti 1, Macken 1, McKenna 1, Moilanen 1, Murdock 2, Rankine 1, Robinson 0+1

Goalscorers: 71 League – 4 FAC – 2 W.Cup – (Total 77)

Cresswell 13–2–1 (16), Healy 10–0–0 (10), Macken 8–1–1 (10), Alexander 6–1–0 (7), Anderson 5–0–0 (5), McKenna 4–0–0 (4), Rankine 4–0–0 (4), Etuhu 3–0–0 (3), Wijnhard 3–0–0 (3), Edwards 2–0–0 (2), Keane 2–0–0 (2), Lucketti 2–0–0 (2), Murdock 2–0–0 (2), Ainsworth 1–0–0 (1), Basham 1–0–0 (1), Cartwright 1–0–0 (1), Gallacher 1–0–0 (1), Gregan 1–0–0 (1), Reid 1–0–0 (1), Own Goals 1–0–0 (1) (Purse of Birmingham)

Date 2001-2	Opponents	Comp	h or a	Score	Att.	1	2	3	4	5	6	7	8	9	10	11	12	13	14	15	16
Aug 11	Gillingham	Div 1	a	0-5	9412	Lucas	Alexander	Edwards	Jackson	Murdock	Gregan	Cartwright	Rankine	Healy	Macken	Cresswell	Moilanen	Keane	Robinson	Anderson	McKenna
Aug 18	Walsall	Div 1	h	1-1	11402	Lucas	Alexander	Edwards	Jackson	Murdock (1)	Gregan	Cartwright	Rankine	Healy *	Macken +	McKenna #	Moilanen	Gallacher +	Cresswell *	Keane	Anderson #
Aug 21	Kidderminster Rd 1	WC	a	3-2*	2227	Lucas	Alexander	Eaton	Jackson (1)	Murdock	Gregan	Cartwright *	Rankine #	Healy	Macken (1)	Anderson +	Moilanen	Galachr *(1)	Cresswell+	Keane #	B'Murphy
Aug 25	Grimsby Town	Div 1	a	2-2	5789	Lucas	Alexander	B'Murphy	Murdock (1)	Lucketti	Gregan	Cartwright	Keane *	Healy (1)	Macken +	Gallacher #	Moilanen	Jackson	Cresswell +	Rankine *	Anderson #
Aug 27	Wimbledon	Div 1	h	1-1	13359	Lucas *	Alexander	B'Murphy	Murdock	Lucketti	Gregan	Cartwright	Keane (1)	Healy	Cresswell +	Rankine #	Moilanen *	Basham +	Jackson	Robinson #	Anderson
Sep 8	Wolverhampton W	Div 1	h	1-2	14381	Lucas	Alexander	Kidd	Murdock	Lucketti (1)	Gregan	McKenna	Keane +	Healy #	Cresswell	Anderson *	Moilanen	Basham #	Jackson	Robinson +	Cartwrit *
Sep 12	Tranmere Rd 2	WC	a	1-4	5143	Moilanen	Alexander	Kidd *	Murdock	Lucketti	Gregan	McKenna	Anderson +	Healy	Cresswell (1)	Edwards	Lucas	Basham *	Jackson	Robinson +	Cartwrigt
Sep 15	Millwall	Div 1	h	1-0	11371	Moilanen	Alexander	Edwards	Murdock	Lucketti	Gregan	Anderson (1)*	McKenna	Healy +	Cresswell	Cartwright	Lucas	Gallacher *#	Kidd #	Keane	Macken +
Sep 18	WBA	Div 1	a	0-2	18289	Moilanen	Alexander	Edwards	Murdock	Lucketti	Gregan	Cartwright	McKenna	Cresswell	Macken	Kidd *	Lucas	Anderson	Healy *	Jackson	B'Murphy
Sep 23	Birmingham	Div 1	a	1-0	23004	Moilanen	Alexander	Edwards (1)	Murdock	Lucketti	Gregan	Cartwright	McKenna	Healy	Macken	Rankine	Lucas	Anderson	Cresswell	Jackson	B'Murphy
Sep 26	Norwich City	Div 1	h	4-0	12014	Moilanen	Alexander(1p)	Edwards (1)	Jackson	Lucketti	McKenna	Cartwright	Rankine	Healy +	Macken (2)	Anderson *	Lucas	Kidd	Cresswell +	McKinlay	B'Murphy*
Sep 30	Watford	Div 1	a	1-1	18911	Moilanen	Alexander	Edwards	Jackson	Lucketti	Gregan	Cartwright	Rankine	Healy *	Macken (1)	McKenna	Lucas	Murdock	Cresswell *	Anderson	B'Murphy
Oct 13	Crewe Alex.	Div 1	a	1-2	7746	Moilanen	Alexander	Edwards	Jackson	Lucketti	Gregan	Cartwright	Rankine (1)	Healy +	Macken *	McKenna	Lucas	Murdock	Cresswell *	Anderson +	Keane
Oct 16	Sheffield Wed.	Div 1	a	2-1	15592	Moilanen	Alexander	Edwards	Jackson	Lucketti	Gregan	Cartwright	Rankine (1)	Healy +	Macken (1)	Anderson *	Lucas	Murdock	Cresswell +	Gallacher	McKenna *
Oct 21	Man. City	Div 1	h	2-1	21013	Moilanen	Alexander	Edwards	Jackson	Lucketti	Gregan	Cartwright	Rankine	Healy (1) *	Macken (1)	McKenna	Lucas	Murdock	Cresswell *	Gallacher	Anderson
Oct 23	Sheffield Utd.	Div 1	h	3-0	14027	Moilanen	Alexander	Edwards *	Jackson	Lucketti	Gregan	Cartwright	Rankine	Healy (1) +	Macken (1) #	McKenna	Lucas	Murdock *	Cresswell +	Gallacher *(1)	Anderson
Oct 26	Portsmouth	Div 1	a	1-0	15402	Moilanen	Alexander	Murdock	Jackson *	Lucketti	Gregan	Cartwright (1)	Rankine	Healy +	Macken	McKenna	Lucas	Eaton *	Cresswell +	Gallacher	Anderson
Oct 29	Coventry	Div 1	a	2-2	18755	Moilanen	Alexander	Kidd	Murdock	Lucketti (1)	Gregan	Cartwright	Rankine	Healy +	Macken	McKenna	Lucas	Eaton	Creswell+(1)	Gallacher	Anderson
Nov 3	Stockport Co.	Div 1	h	6-0	13776	Moilanen *	Alexander	Kidd	Murdock	Lucketti (1)	Gregan	Cartwright	Rankine	Healy (3) #	Macken +	McKenna (1)	Lucas *	Eaton	Cresswell#(1)	Gallacher +	Anderson
Nov 8	Barnsley	Div 1	h	2-2	19042	Lucas	Alexander	Kidd *	Murdock	Lucketti	Gregan	Cartwright +	Rankine (1)	Healy #	Macken	McKenna	O'Hanlon	Eaton *	Cresswell#(1)	Gallacher	Anderson +
Nov 17	Nottm. Forest	Div 1	a	1-1	21020	Lucas	Alexander	Eaton	Murdock	Lucketti	Gregan	Cartwright	Rankine	Cresswell (1)	Macken *	McKenna	Lonergan	Basham *	Anderson	Keane	B'Murphy
Nov 20	Bradford City	Div 1	h	1-1	13763	Lucas	Alexander (1p)	Edwards	Murdock	Lucketti	Gregan *	Cartwright	Rankine	Cresswell	Healy	McKenna	Lonergan	Basham	Anderson *	Keane	Eaton
Nov 24	Crystal Palace	Div 1	h	2-1	15264	Lucas	Alexander (1p)	Edwards	Murdock	Lucketti	Gregan	Cartwright	Rankine	Cresswell (1)	Healy *	McKenna	Lonergan	Basham *	Anderson	Keane	Eaton
Dec 1	Sheffield Utd.	Div 1	a	2-2	16720	Lucas	Alexander	Edwards	Murdock	Lucketti	Gregan	Cartwright	Rankine	Cresswell (1)	Healy (1) *	McKenna	Lonergan	Basham	Macken *	Keane	Eaton
Dec 9	Burnley	Div 1	h	2-3	20370	Lucas	Alexander (1p)	Edwards	Murdock	Lucketti	Gregan	Cartwright +	Macken	Cresswell *	Healy	McKenna (1)	Lonergan	Anderson +	Basham *	Keane	Eaton
Dec 15	Rotherham Utd	Div 1	a	0-1	6558	Lucas	Alexander	Edwards	Murdock #	Lucketti	Gregan	Cartwright *	Rankine +	Healy	Macken	McKenna	Moilanen	Anderson #	Basham *	Keane +	Eaton
Dec 22	Grimsby Town	Div 1	h	0-0	14667	Lucas	Alexander	Edwards	Murdock	Lucketti	Gregan	Anderson *	Rankine	Healy	Macken	McKenna	Moilanen	Cartwright	Basham *	Keane	Eaton
Dec 26	Wolverhampton W	Div 1	a	3-2	24024	Lucas	Alexander	Edwards	Anderson (1)*	Lucketti	Gregan (1)	Cartwright	Rankine	Healy (1)	Macken +	McKenna	Moilanen	Skora	Basham +	Keane	Eaton *
Dec 29	Wimbledon	Div 1	a	0-2	6051	Lucas	Alexander	Edwards	Murdock	Lucketti	McKenna	Cartwright #	Rankine	Healy	Macken *	Anderson +	Moilanen	Cresswell *	Basham #	Keane	Eaton +
Jan 12	Walsall	Div 1	a	2-1	6314	Lucas	Alexander	Edwards	Murdock	Lucketti	Skora *	Keane	Anderson (1)	Healy	Macken	McKenna	Moilanen	B'Murphy	Basham*(1)	Robinson	Eaton
Jan 15	Brighton Rd 3	FAC	a	2-0	6548	Lucas	Alexander	Edwards	Murdock	Lucketti	Skora (1)	Keane	Anderson +	Healy #	Macken (1) *	McKenna	Moilanen	B'Murphy +	Basham *	Robinson #	Eaton
Jan 19	Gillingham	Div 1	h	0-2	13289	Moilanen	Alexander	Edwards	Murdock *	Lucketti	Skora	Keane +	Anderson	Healy	Macken	McKenna	Lonergan	Gregan *	Basham +	Cartwright	Eaton
Jan 26	Sheffield Utd. Rd 4	FAC	h	2-1	13068	Moilanen	Alexander (1p)	Edwards	Murdock	Lucketti	Gregan	Keane	Anderson	Healy	Basham +	Skora *	Lonergan	Macken *	Creswel*(1)	Cartwrigt	B'Murphy
Jan 29	Bradford City	Div 1	a	1-0	15217	Moilanen	Alexander	Edwards	Etuhu	Lucketti	Gregan	Cartwright	Keane (1)	Healy	Cresswell *	Anderson	Lonergan	Macken *	Basham	B'Murphy	Eaton
Jan 31	Watford	Div 1	h	1-1	12749	Moilanen	Alexander (1)	Eaton	Etuhu	Lucketti	Gregan	Cartwright #	Keane	Healy *	Macken +	Cresswell	Lonergan	Skora	Basham +	B'Murph*	Anderson #
Feb 5	Sheffield Wed.	Div 1	h	4-2	14038	Moilanen	Alexander	Edwards	Etuhu (1)	Eaton	Gregan *	Cartwright	Keane	Cresswell	Macken (1)	Anderson +	Lonergan	Skora	Healy + (1)	Sow	Reid * (1)
Feb 10	Man. City	Div 1	a	2-3	34220	Moilanen	Alexander	Edwards	Etuhu	Lucketti	Gregan	Cartwright *	Keane	Cresswell +	Macken (1)	Healy	Lucas	Skora	Andrson+(1)	Eaton	Gudjonson*
Feb 17	Chelsea Rd 5	FAC	a	1-3	28133	Moilanen	Alexander	Edwards	Anderson *	Lucketti	Gregan	Cartwrit +	Keane	Cresswell (1)	Macken	McKenna	Lucas	Skora	Healy *	Eaton	Gudjnsn +
Feb 22	Norwich City	Div 1	a	0-3	19506	Moilanen	Alexander	Edwards	Etuhu	Lucketti	Gregan	Anderson *	Keane #	Cresswell	Healy	McKenna +	Lucas	Skora #	Basham +	Eaton	Gudjonson*
Feb 26	WBA	Div 1	h	1-0	14487	Lucas	Edwards	Edwards	Etuhu (1)	Lucketti	Gregan	Gudjonsson +	Keane	Cresswell	Macken *	McKenna	Moilanen	Skora +	Basham	Healy *	Anderson
Mar 2	Birmingham (1 og*)	Div 1	h	1-0	15543	Lucas	Alexander	Edwards	Hendry	Lucketti	Gregan	Gudjonsson #	Etuhu	Cresswell +	Macken *	McKenna	Moilanen	Keane +	Eaton	Healy *	Anderson #
Mar 5	Millwall	Div 1	a	1-2	11071	Lucas	Alexander	Edwards	Etuhu	Lucketti	Hendry #	Gudjonsson +	Keane *	Cresswell	Healy (1)	McKenna	Moilanen	Cartwright	Basham +	Eaton #	Anderson *
Mar 9	Rotherham Utd	Div 1	h	2-1	14579	Lucas	Alexander	Edwards	Etuhu	Lucketti	Eaton	Gudjonsson +	Anderson *	Cresswell (2)	Healy	McKenna	Moilanen	Cartwright +	Basham *	Reid	Keane
Mar 17	Burnley	Div 1	a	1-2	18388	Lucas	Alexander	Edwards	Etuhu #	Lucketti	Gregan	Cartwright *	Rankine	Cresswell	Healy +	Keane	Moilanen	Anderson *(1)	Basham +	Eaton	Gudjonson#
Mar 20	Crewe Alex.	Div 1	h	2-2	13396	Lucas	Alexander	Edwards	Etuhu	Lucketti	Gregan	Cartwright	McKenna (1)	Cresswell (1)	Healy *	Anderson	Moilanen	Keane	Basham *	Eaton	Gudjonson
Mar 23	Stockport Co.	Div 1	a	2-0	6139	Lucas	Alexander	Edwards	Etuhu	Lucketti	Gregan	Cartwright	McKenna (1)	Cresswell (1)	Wijnhard *	Anderson	Moilanen	Keane	Rankine	Eaton	Healy *
Mar 30	Portsmouth	Div 1	h	2-0	16832	Moilanen	Alexander (1p)	Edwards *	Etuhu	Lucketti	Gregan	Cartwright +	McKenna	Cresswell	Wijnhard (1) #	Anderson	O'Hanlon	Ainsworth +	Rankine	Eaton *	Healy #
Apr 1	Barnsley	Div 1	a	1-2	14188	Moilanen	Alexander	Eaton	Rankine #	Lucketti *	Gregan	Cartwright +	McKenna	Cresswell	Wijnhard (1)	Keane	O'Hanlon	Ainsworth +	Etuhu	Jackson *	Healy #
Apr 6	Coventry	Div 1	h	4-0	15665	Moilanen	Alexander	Edwards	Etuhu (1)	Jackson	Gregan	Ainsworth (1)*	McKenna	Cresswell (1)	Wijnhard (1)	Keane	Lucas	Anderson *	Eaton	Rankine	Healy
Apr 13	Crystal Palace	Div 1	a	0-2	21361	Moilanen	Alexander	Edwards	Etuhu	Jackson	Gregan	Ainsworth *	McKenna	Cresswell	Wijnhard	Keane +	Lucas	Anderson +	Eaton	Rankine	Healy *
Apr 21	Nottm. Forest	Div 1	h	2-1	17390	Moilanen	Alexander	Edwards	Etuhu *	Jackson	Gregan	Ainsworth	McKenna	Cresswell (1)	Wijnhard +	Keane #	Lucas	Anderson *	Eaton	Rankine#(1)	Healy +
	* Own goal by Purse																				

SEASON 2002–2003

Once again Preston North End had a season of ups and downs, cementing their position as a solid Division One side but making no real attack on promotion. Newly installed manager Craig Brown worked hard, tried some new ideas and won plenty of friends with his commonsense approach. However, it must be said that North End lacked inspiration for much of the season and in the end the games sort of drifted away. There was another poor start with only one win in the first eight games and Brown chopped and changed his team selections to try and find the right balance. He centred his selections around the new star forward Ricardo Fuller, a Jamaican with power and pace, and an eye for goal. The big striker did well early on and created quite an impression but at the end of November 2002 he was unluckily injured and it was so bad that he was out for the rest of the season. It was a bitter blow to Brown and the team and they had to regroup after hearing the news. Richard Cresswell continued to give his all and again was the main source of goals, but scoring goals was not the main problem, stopping them was. Brown brought in former Scotland goalkeeper Jonathan Gould but still too many goals were conceded and that was what was hindering any chance of progress. Chris Lucketti, now captain, played his heart out and Graham Alexander and Paul McKenna were models of consistency, in fact Alexander was even second highest goalscorer, hitting 9 penalties in his 11 goals from his full-back position. Several new players were brought in as the season developed but of these

only Eddie Lewis looked likely to be a long term success. The results deteriorated and for the first time for a long time the Preston manager's work was being questioned by fans and it made for some uncomfortable days at Deepdale. Too many games were being lost, and Brown came across as making excuses: before, during and after games. There was no doubting that he was an honest and hard-working manager but unfortunately the rigours of day-to-day management seemed to prove difficult for him. But he soldiered on determinedly and North End did produce some good performances, especially at home. The team was certainly taking on the look of the League of Nations. In the last game of the season North End had, in their 16 man squad, 2 Scots, 8 Englishman, a Welshman, an American, a Nigerian, a Canadian, a Frenchman and a Pole! Luckily – apart from the Scots of course – they all spoke English! A miserable Christmas, defeat against Rochdale in the FA Cup and a mid-table finish left the North End fans largely undecided about Craig Brown, but to be fair he had a hard act to follow. It was not all gloom as a lot of people were willing him to succeed.

DEBUTANTS: (10) Pawel Abbott, John Bailey, Marlon Broomes, Ricardo Fuller, Jonathan Gould, George Koumantarakis, Eddie Lewis, Simon Lynch, Tyrone Mears, Brian O'Neil.

LAST GAMES: (7) Anderson, Bailey, Barry Murphy, Eaton, Rankine, Moilanen, Murdock.

Colin Murdock

Pawell Abbott

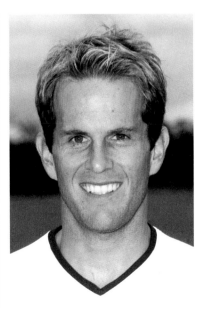

Eddie Lewis

League position in Division One: 12th – P46 W16 D13 L17 F68 A70 Pts 61
Home: W11 D7 L5 F44 A29 Away: W5 D6 L12 F24 A41

Match Report: 'Is There Anybody There?' Wimbledon 2 Preston 0 April 21 2003 Division One

This match, watched by the lowest league gate to see a Preston North End game since official records began, was one of those games that will be instantly forgettable for virtually everyone connected with the club. Less than 1,000 fans turned up, although the official attendance was given as 1,053, but that included season ticket holders, whether they showed up or not! It was one of those days for the Preston forwards too, as they didn't turn up either! Time after time chances were created only for the young players like Simon Lynch and Pawel Abbott to snatch at shots when they needed to show a little composure. Good tackling robbed Eddie Lewis three times when he tried to burst through and Eric Skora forced a couple of good interceptions by Kelvin Davis in the home goal. There was no doubt that North End were in control, all they needed was a goal. The first half remained goalless but Preston continued to dominate after the restart. But on the hour mark the inevitable happened as completely against the run of play Wimbledon took the lead. A rare mistake by Brian O'Neil lost Preston's possession and the ball was sent out to Patrick Agyemang (remember the name) out on the right. He crossed into the box and Neil Shipperley picked his spot. It was a bitter blow for the visitors but five minutes later the same player made it 2–0 as he tapped in after Jonathan Gould had failed to hold a shot by Alex Tapp. How often, over the years, have we seen an away performance like this from Preston, being let down by a lack of finishing? It was not as though they could look to the crowd to lift them, although the 281 hardy souls who had made the long trip to London did their best to spur them on. Chances were still being created, and still being missed. Abbott was put through by Etuhu but was foiled by Davis, and the goalkeeper then made an even better save from Etuhu's header. At the other end Gould made a fine save from David Connolly near the end. That could have been 3–0 and a complete travesty. But as the old football maxim goes, if you don't score you don't win matches, and never has this been truer than at Wimbledon in April 2003. The game would probably be memorable for only one player as John Bailey was given his North End debut by Craig Brown when the youngster came on as a late substitute. As Brown pointed out it was a very young Preston side with six players 20 years old or less. Having said that it was still a bad defeat and very, very frustrating.

League appearances (46 games)

Abbott P. 6+10, Alexander G. 45, Anderson I. 0+8, Bailey J. 0+1, Barry Murphy B. 2, Broomes M. 21+7, Cartwright L. 13+9, Cresswell R. 42, Eaton A. 0+1, Edwards R. 26, Etuhu D. 33+6, Fuller R. 18, Gould J. 13+1, Healy D. 12+12, Jackson M. 21+1, Keane M. 1+4, Koumantarakis G. 10, Lewis E. 34+4, Lucas D. 19+2, Lucketti C. 43, Lynch S. 6+11, McKenna P. 39+2, Mears T. 11+11, Moilanen T. 14+1, Murdock C. 24, O'Neil B. 12+3, Rankine M. 11+8, Skora E. 30+6

FA Cup appearances (1 game)

Abbott 1, Alexander 1, Anderson 0+1, Broomes 1, Cartwright 0+1, Etuhu 1, Healy 1, Lewis 1, Lucketti 1, McKenna 1, Mears 0+1, Moilanen 1, Murdock 1, Skora1

Worthington Cup appearances (4 games)

Alexander 4, Anderson 1, Broomes 3, Cartwright 0+2, Cresswell 3+1, Eaton 1, Edwards 2, Etuhu 4, Fuller 1+1, Healy 4, Jackson 1, Keane 1, Lewis 3+1, Lucas 4, Lucketti 4, McKenna 3, Mears 1+1, Moilanen 0+1, Murdock 1+1, Rankine 1+3, Skora 2

Goalscorers: 68 League – 1 FAC – 5 W.Cup – (Total 74)

Cresswell 16–0–0 (16), Alexander 10 (8p)–0–1(1p) (11(9p)), Fuller 9–0–2 (11), Etuhu 6–0–0 (6), Lewis 5–0–1 (6), Healy 5–0–0 (5), Abbott 4–0–0 (4), Koumantarakis 3–0–0 (3), McKenna 3–0–0 (3), Lucketti 2–0–0 (2), Cartwright 1–0–0 (1), Jackson 1–0–1 (2), Lynch 1–0–0 (1), Mears 1–0–0 (1), Anderson 0–1–0 (1), Skora 0–0–1 (1) Own Goals 1–0–0 (1) (Own Goal by Ashby of Gillingham)

Colin Murdock,
PNE's Northern Ireland
international defender.

Date 2002-3	Opponents	Comp	h or a	Score	Att.	1	2	3	4	5	6	7	8	9	10	11	12	13	14	15	16
Aug 10	Crystal Palace	Div 1	h	1-2	14663	Moilanen	Alexander	Edwards #	Jackson	Lucketti	Murdock	McKenna +	Rankine	Fuller (1) *	Cresswell	Skora	Lucas	Broomes	Healy *	Etuhu +	Anderson #
Aug 14	Nottm Forest	Div 1	a	2-2	18065	Moilanen	Alexander	Edwards	Jackson	Lucketti	Murdock	Etuhu (1) *	Rankine	Fuller (1)	Cresswell	Skora	Lucas	McKenna	Healy	Keane *	Cartwright
Aug 17	Rotherham	Div 1	a	0-0	6885	Moilanen	Alexander	Edwards	Jackson	Lucketti	Murdock	Etuhu	Rankine	Fuller	Cresswell *	Skora	Lucas	Broomes	Healy *	McKenna	Anderson
Aug 24	Stoke City	Div 1	h	4-3	15422	Moilanen	Alexander	Edwards	Etuhu *	Lucketti	Murdock	McKenna	Rankine	Fuller (1)	Cresswell (1)	Healy (2) +	Lucas	Broomes	Jackson	Keane *	Cartwrit +
Aug 26	Gillingham	Div 1	a	1-1	7785	Moilanen	Alexander	Edwards	Jackson	Lucketti	Broomes *	McKenna	Skora +	Fuller	Cresswell (1)	Healy	Lucas	Murdock	Etuhu *	Keane +	Cartwright
Aug 31	Ipswich Town	Div 1	h	0-0	15357	Moilanen	Alexander	Edwards	Skora	Lucketti	Murdock	McKenna	Rankine	Fuller	Cresswell	Healy *	Lucas	Etuhu *	Jackson	Keane	Cartwright
Sep 11	Scunthorpe Rd 1	WC	h	2-1*	5594	Lucas	Alexndr (1p)	Edwards	Etuhu +	Lucketti	Broomes	McKenna	Keane	Healy *	Cresswell	Lewis #	Moilanen	Rankine +	Jackson	Fuller * (1)	Cartwrit #
Sep 14	Sheffield Wed.	Div 1	h	2-2	13632	Moilanen	Alexander	Edwards *	Skora	Lucketti	Murdock	McKenna	Rankine #	Fuller (1)	Cresswell (1)	Lewis +	Lonergan	Broomes *	Keane	Healy +	Etuhu #
Sep 17	Watford	Div 1	h	1-1	12408	Moilanen	Alexander	Broomes	Skora	Lucketti	Murdock	McKenna	Etuhu	Fuller	Cresswell (1)	Keane *	Lucas	Jackson	Lewis	Healy *	Rankine
Sep 21	Derby County	Div 1	a	2-0	29257	Moilanen	Alexander	Edwards *	Skora	Lucketti	Murdock #	McKenna	Etuhu (1)	Fuller +	Cresswell	Broomes	Lonergan	Jackson	Lewis *	Healy + (1)	Rankine #
Sep 24	Wolverhampton W.	Div 1	a	0-4	23695	Moilanen	Alexander	Broomes	Skora +	Lucketti	Murdock	McKenna	Etuhu #	Fuller	Cresswell	Jackson *	Lonergan	Keane	Lewis *	Healy +	Rankine #
Sep 28	Norwich City	Div 1	h	1-2	13550	Moilanen	Alexander	Broomes	Skora *	Lucketti	Murdock	McKenna	Etuhu+	Fuller	Cresswell (1)	Lewis	Lucas	Jackson	Rankine +	Healy *	Cartwright
Oct 1	Macclesfield Rd 2	WC	a	2-1	2036	Lucas *	Alexander	Broomes	Skora (1)	Lucketti	Etuhu	Anderson	Rankine +	Healy	Cresswell	Jackson (1)	Moilanen *	McKenna	Bry Murph	Keane	Lewis +
Oct 5	Bradford City	Div 1	a	1-1	13215	Moilanen	Alexndr (1p)	Broomes	Skora	Lucketti	Murdock	McKenna	Etuhu *	Fuller	Cresswell +	Lewis	Lonergan	Jackson	Healy +	Rankine	Anderson *
Oct 19	Walsall	Div 1	a	3-3	6332	Moilanen	Alexander (1)	Broomes	Skora	Lucketti (1)	Murdock +	McKenna	Etuhu *	Healy (1)	Cresswell	Rankine	Lucas	Jackson	Eaton	Mears +	Anderson *
Oct 26	Reading	Div 1	h	1-0	13021	Lucas	Alexander	Broomes	Skora	Lucketti	Murdock	McKenna	Rankine	Healy *	Creswell (1) #	Lewis +	Moilanen	Abbott *	Etuhu	Broomes +	Mears #
Oct 29	Portsmouth	Div 1	a	2-3	18637	Lucas	Alexndr (1p)	Edwards *	Broomes	Lucketti	Murdock	McKenna	Skora	Lewis #	Cresswell (1)	Rankine +	Moilanen	Jackson *	Abbott #	Healy	Etuhu +
Nov 2	Burnley	Div 1	h	3-1	16046	Lucas	Alexander	Edwards	Skora #	Lucketti	Murdock	McKenna (1)	Etuhu	Fuller (2) *	Cresswell	Lewis +	Moilanen	Abbott	Rankine #	Broomes +	Healy *
Nov 5	Birmingham Rd 3	WC	a	2-0	17241	Lucas	Alexander	Edwards	Broomes	Lucketti #	Mears *	McKenna	Etuhu	Fuller (1) +	Healy	Lewis (1)	Moilanen	Cresswell *	Rankine +	Murdock #	Jackson
Nov 9	Millwall	Div 1	a	1-2	7554	Lucas	Alexander	Edwards	Skora *	Murdock	Broomes	McKenna	Etuhu	Fuller (1)	Cresswell	Lewis	Moilanen	Abbott	Rankine	Healy *	Jackson
Nov 16	Grimsby	Div 1	a	3-3	5774	Moilanen	Alexndr (1p)	Edwards	Skora *	Jackson	Broomes	McKenna	Etuhu (1)	Fuller	Cresswell (1)	Lewis	Lonergan	Abbott	Rankine	Healy *	Cartwright
Nov 23	Brighton	Div 1	h	2-2	13068	Lucas	Alexander	Edwards	Skora *	Lucketti (1)	Murdock	McKenna	Etuhu	Fuller	Cresswell (1)	Lewis	Moilanen	Broomes	Rankine *	Healy	Cartwright
Nov 26	Leicester	Div 1	h	2-0	13048	Lucas	Alexander	Edwards	Skora	Lucketti	Murdock	McKenna	Etuhu	Fuller (2) +	Cresswell	Lewis *	Moilanen	Broomes *	Rankine	Healy	Cartwrit +
Nov 30	Coventry	Div 1	a	2-1	13313	Lucas	Alexander	Edwards	Skora #	Lucketti	Murdock	McKenna	Etuhu	Fuller *	Cresswell (1)	Lewis (1) +	Moilanen	Broomes	Rankine #	Healy *	Cartwrit +
Dec 4	Aston Villa Rd 4	WC	a	0-5	23042	Lucas	Alexander	Eaton	Skora #	Lucketti	Murdock	McKenna +	Etuhu *	Healy	Cresswell	Lewis	Moilanen	Broomes	Rankine +	Mears #	Cartwrit +
Dec 7	Wimbledon	Div 1	h	3-5	12415	Lucas	Alexndr (1p)	Edwards	Skora	Lucketti	Broomes	McKenna (1)	Etuhu *	Healy	Abbott (1)	Lewis	Moilanen	Murdock	Rankine *	Mears	Cartwright
Dec 14	Grimsby	Div 1	h	3-0	12420	Lucas	Alexndr (1p)	Edwards	Skora *	Lucketti	Murdock	McKenna +	Etuhu	Healy (1) #	Cresswell (1)	Lewis	Moilanen	Broomes	Rankine +	Mears *	Abbott #
Dec 21	Sheffield Utd	Div 1	a	0-1	16342	Lucas	Alexander	Broomes *	Mears	Lucketti	Murdock	Rankine	Etuhu	Healy	Cresswell	Lewis	Moilanen	Anderson *	Bailey	McCormck	O'Neil
Dec 26	Rotherham	Div 1	h	0-2	15452	Lucas	Alexander	Edwards *	Skora +	Lucketti	Broomes	McKenna	Etuhu	Healy	Cresswell	Lewis #	Moilanen	Anderson +	Rankine	Mears *	Abbott #
Dec 28	Crystal Palace	Div 1	a	0-2	18484	Lucas	Alexander	Broomes	Skora #	Lucketti	Murdock	McKenna	Etuhu +	Healy *	Cresswell	Mears	Moilanen	Anderson *	Rankine	Lewis #	Abbott +
Jan 1	Stoke City	Div 1	a	1-2	14862	Lucas *	Alexander	Bry Murph	Rankine	Lucketti	Broomes	McKenna	Etuhu #	Healy	Cresswell +	Lewis	Moilanen *	Anderson	Mears #	Skora	Abbott (1)+
Jan 4	Rochdale Rd 3	FAC	h	0-1	8762	Moilanen	Alexander	Broomes	Skora *	Lucketti	Murdock	McKenna	Etuhu +	Healy	Abbott	Lewis #	O'Hanlon	Andrsn(1)#	Mears +	O'Neil	Cartwrit *
Jan 18	Ipswich Town	Div 1	a	0-3	24666	Gould	Mears *	Broomes	Skora	Murdock	Bry Murphy	O'Neil	Cartwright	Healy	Abbott +	Lewis #	Lonergan	Eaton *	Lynch +	McCormck	Anderson #
Jan 25	Nottm Forest	Div 1	h	1-1	13508	Gould	Alexander	Mears	O'Neil	Lucketti	McKenna	Lewis #	Cartwright	Lynch (1)	Kumntrks +	Murdock	Lonergan	Rankine	Jackson	Abbott +	Anderson #
Feb 1	Gillingham *1 o.g.	Div 1	h	3-0	12121	Gould	Alexndr (1p)	Broomes #	Jackson	Lucketti	McKenna	Lewis (1)	Cartwright	Cresswell	Kumntrks *	O'Neil +	Lucas	Rankine	Lynch *	Skora +	Mears #
Feb 8	Millwall	Div 1	h	2-1	13117	Gould	Alexander	Edwards	Jackson	Lucketti	Etuhu	Lewis (1) #	Cartwrit (1)	Cresswell	Kumntrks +	O'Neil	Lucas	Rankine	Lynch +	Skora	Mears #
Feb 22	Wolverhampton W.	Div 1	h	0-2	16070	Gould	Alexander	Edwards	Jackson	Lucketti	McKenna	Lewis	Cartwright *	Cresswell	Kumntrks +	O'Neil	Lucas	Rankine	Lynch +	Skora *	Mears
Mar 1	Sheffield Wed.	Div 1	a	1-0	18912	Gould	Alexander	Edwards +	Jackson	Lucketti	McKenna	Lewis #	Cartwright *	Cresswell (1)	Kumntrks	O'Neil	Lucas	Broomes +	Lynch *	Skora	Mears #
Mar 4	Watford	Div 1	a	1-0	11101	Gould	Alexndr (1p)	Broomes	Jackson	Lucketti	McKenna +	Lewis	Cartwright *	Cresswell	Kumntrks	O'Neil	Lucas	Rankine	Lynch	Skora +	Mears *
Mar 9	Derby County	Div 1	h	4-2	14003	Gould #	Alexander (1)	Broomes	Jackson	Lucketti	McKenna +	Lewis	Cartwright	Cresswell (1)	Kumntrks (1)*	Etuhu (1)	Lucas #	Keane +	Lynch *	Murdock	Mears
Mar 15	Leicester	Div 1	a	1-2	30713	Gould +	Alexander	Broomes *	Jackson	Lucketti	McKenna	Lewis (1)	Cartwright	Cresswell	Kumntrks	Etuhu #	Lucas +	Edwards	Lynch #	Skora *	Mears
Mar 18	Walsall	Div 1	h	5-0	11170	Lucas	Alexndr (1p)	Edwards	Jackson *	Lucketti	McKenna #	Lewis +	Cartwright	Cresswell (1)	Kumntrks (2)	Etuhu (1)	Lonergan	Broomes *	Lynch +	Skora	Mears #
Mar 22	Portsmouth	Div 1	h	1-1	16665	Lucas	Alexander	Edwards	Broomes #	Lucketti	McKenna (1)	Lewis	Cartwright *	Cresswell	Kumntrks +	Etuhu	Lonergan	O'Neil #	Lynch +	Skora	Mears *
Apr 5	Coventry	Div 1	h	2-2	13026	Lucas	Alexander	Edwards *	Jackson	Lucketti	McKenna	Lewis	Cartwright +	Cresswell (1)	Lynch	Etuhu	Lonergan	O'Neil +	Abbott (1) *	Skora	Mears
Apr 8	Burnley	Div 1	a	0-2	12245	Lucas	Alexander	Mears	Jackson	Lucketti	McKenna	Lewis #	O'Neil	Cresswell	Lynch *	Etuhu +	Lonergan	Cartwrit +	Abbott *	Burley	Skora #
Apr 12	Brighton	Div 1	a	2-0	6669	Lucas	Alexander	Mears	Jackson (1)	Lucketti	McKenna	Lewis +	O'Neil	Cresswell (1)	Abbott	Skora *	Gould	Cartwrit +	Lynch	Edwards	Etuhu *
Apr 15	Reading	Div 1	a	1-5	14012	Lucas	Alexander	Mears (1)	Jackson	Lucketti	McKenna +	Cartwright	Etuhu #	Cresswell	Lynch *	Skora	Gould +	O'Neil #	Abbott	Edwards	Lewis *
Apr 19	Sheffield Utd	Div 1	h	2-0	14793	Gould	Alexander	Mears	Jackson	Lucketti	O'Neil	Lewis (1) #	Etuhu (1)	Cresswell *	Abbott	Skora +	Lucas	Bailey	Lynch *	Cartwrit #	McKenna +
Apr 21	Wimbledon	Div 1	a	0-2	1053	Gould	Alexander	Mears	Jackson	Lucketti	O'Neil *	Lewis	Etuhu	Abbott +	Lynch	Skora #	Lucas	Broomes	Bailey +	Cartwrit #	McKenna *
Apr 26	Bradford City	Div 1	h	1-0	13652	Gould	Alexander	Mears	Jackson	Lucketti	O'Neil	Lewis *	Etuhu	Cresswell	Abbott (1) #	McKenna +	Lucas	Broomes	Lynch #	Cartwrit *	Skora +
May 4	Norwich City	Div 1	a	0-2	20232	Gould	Alexander	Mears	Lucketti	Edwards +	McKenna	Lewis *	Etuhu	Cresswell	Lynch	Skora #	Lonergan	Broomes +	Abbott #	Cartwrit *	Bailey
	* O.G. by Ashby			* aet																	

Trivia Facts:

In April 2003 a statue was unveiled to commemorate the famous 'Splash' picture of Tom Finney. It incorporated a fountain and will stand outside the entrance to the National Football Museum.

Preston North End's youth side won the North West Youth Alliance league having the record of: P18 W13 D3 L2 F50 A24. The side also won the Lancashire FA Youth cup.

STAT FACTS:

Best home run without defeat: 6 games
Best away run without defeat: 4 games
Longest run unbeaten: 8 games
Longest run without a win: 6 games
Best home attendance: 16,665 *vs.* Portsmouth 22.3.03
Worst home attendance: 5,594 *vs.* Scunthorpe 11.9.02
Best away attendance: 30,713 *vs.* Leicester 15.3.03
Worst away attendance: 1,053 *vs.* Wimbledon 21.4.03
Aggregate and average home attendance: 318,627 – 13,853
Aggregate and average away attendance: 339,803 – 14,774

Ever presents: None
Hat-tricks: None
FA Cup: Third Rd.
Worthington Cup: Fourth Rd.
Manager: Craig Brown
Chairman: D. Shaw Esq.
Players used: 28
Leading scorer:
16 goals – Richard Cresswell (All league)

OFFICIAL PLAYER OF THE SEASON: Chris Lucketti

Season 2002–03: Division One

		P	W	D	L	F	A	Pts
1	Portsmouth	46	29	11	6	97	45	98
2	Leicester City	46	26	14	6	73	40	92
3	Sheffield Utd.	46	23	11	12	72	52	80
4	Reading	46	25	4	17	61	46	79
5	Wolverhampton W.	46	20	16	10	81	44	76
6	Nottm. Forest	46	20	14	12	82	50	74
7	Ipswich Town	46	19	13	14	80	64	70
8	Norwich City	46	19	12	15	60	49	69
9	Millwall	46	19	9	18	59	69	66
10	Wimbledon	46	18	9	18	76	73	65
11	Gillingham	46	16	14	16	56	65	62
12	Preston	46	16	13	17	68	70	61
13	Watford	46	17	9	20	54	70	60
14	Crystal Palace	46	14	17	15	59	52	59
15	Rotherham Utd.	46	15	14	17	62	62	59
16	Burnley	46	15	10	21	65	89	55
17	Walsall	46	15	9	22	57	69	54
18	Derby Co.	46	15	7	24	55	74	52
19	Bradford City	46	14	10	22	51	73	52
20	Coventry City	46	12	14	20	46	62	50
21	Stoke City	46	12	14	20	45	69	50
22	Sheffield Wed.	46	10	16	20	56	73	46
23	Brighton	46	11	12	23	49	67	45
24	Grimsby Town	46	9	12	25	48	85	39

SEASON 2003–2004

A quote from one of the *Evening Post* match reports sort of summed up the 2003–04 season after another disappointing year of 'What-ifs, maybes and hard luck stories.' North End had another dreadful start to the campaign, losing four of the first five games, including going out of the Coca Cola Cup to lowly Notts County after a penalty shoot-out. After that it was yet another roller coaster of emotions as the team gave the fans the usual mix of ups and downs. Each time the team started to put a run together, a bad mistake, or a refereeing error, or the poltergeist that Craig Brown had obviously upset in a former life, came back to seek revenge! Thank goodness for the form at Deepdale. Preston lost the first two, both live on television and both times unluckily, but then lost only three more at home all season. It was just as well as on their travels North End found it hard to pick up points and only four times came back with all three. As we have said many times before in this book, the key to a successful season for North End, are the results away from Deepdale. To be fair to Brown, he tried everything he knew to lift the players but was let down at times by his own men. Richard Cresswell, leading scorer for the past two seasons, could not buy a goal. David Healy showed patchy form and Ricardo Fuller had a good first half of the season but then the goals dried up almost completely in the second half. At the back too many sloppy goals were conceded, although Michael Jackson made a strong comeback and Chris Lucketti and Graham Alexander continued to show their considerable experience. In midfield the problem was finding the right balance and in many games North End were outplayed in that area. It was not all doom and gloom however and there were some outstanding days to enjoy as well. The 5–3 win over Burnley just before Christmas was an amazing match and saw Fuller at his best as he notched a hat-trick. Preston knocked Reading out of the FA Cup with a thrilling replay victory at their Madjeski Stadium, and other wins over Coventry, Rotherham, Crystal Palace and WBA were all outstanding games. But each time the fans were lifted by wins like this it was followed by a poor performances, most notably when the team lost at Swansea in the FA Cup 4th round. Before the season was over Brown had brought in former Motherwell manager Billy Davis as his assistant, and the pair still had plenty of work to do. The summer months of 2004 would be crucial for the likeable Scots and everyone hoped that things would be put right by the August. The biggest problem they faced was the high expectancy levels the fans now had, and Brown could blame David Moyes for that.

DEBUTANTS: (7) Lee Briscoe, Craig Burley, Claude Davis, Scot Gemmill, Mark Jackson, Alan McCormack, Jeff Smith.

LAST GAMES: (11) Abbott, Briscoe, Burley, Cartwright, Edwards, Gemmill, Mike Jackson, Keane, Koumantarakis, Lucas, Smith.

Action from Deepdale

League position in Division One: 15th – P46 W15 D14 L17 F69 A71 Pts 59
Home: W11 D7 L5 F43 A29 Away: W4 D7 L12 F28 A42

Match Report: Cue Etuhu, Palace Boo Hoo – Preston 4 Crystal Palace 1. 6 December 2003. Division One

Having drawn against Crystal Palace four weeks earlier in London, Preston were looking to go one better in the return fixture at Deepdale. It was a strange game, however, as North End squandered chance after chance in a first half they dominated. David Healy missed two great openings, Brian O'Neil saw his header crash against a post and Chris Lucketti and Michael Jackson both put in headers just off target. On top of all that Paul McKenna twice shot straight at goalkeeper Thomas Myhre and Dickson Etuhu should have scored with another gilt-edged chance. It was incredible that the scoreline was still blank at the break and manager Craig Brown must have been tearing his hair out. But the first-half was completely forgotten as Preston had cause to celebrate after the interval. Only two minutes had gone when Healy's shot was beaten out by Myrhe only for Etuhu, at last, to give the home side the lead they deserved. If that was one pivotal moment, then two minutes later there was another. Ricardo Fuller looked through on goal only for him to be yanked back by Palace player-boss Kit Symons. The referee gave Preston a penalty and sent Symons off. Graham Alexander slammed home the spot-kick and it was 2–0. As so often happens, going down to 10 men inspired the visitors to their best spell, working really hard to overcome their handicap. They even managed to pull a goal back on 70 minutes when Shaun Derry punished some slack defending to beat Jonathan Gould with a neat finish. But Preston dispelled any thoughts of a famous comeback by scoring a third and restoring the two-goal margin. Fuller crossed from the right, Etuhu dummied and Eddie Lewis shot home via a deflection. Richard Cresswell was having a torrid time in front of goal at the time and he must have been delighted when a simple chance presented itself to him. But, great professional that he is, he resisted the temptation to shoot and instead squared the ball to an even better placed Healy who a simple tap-in to score. It was a marvellous example of a player putting the team first and Cresswell's part in the goal was loudly applauded. On another day Preston could have had a hatful of goals and 4–1 was a poor reward for the overall supremacy against a much-fancied side.

Trivia Facts:

Lee Cartwright's 13-year stay at Deepdale finally came to an end when he signed for Stockport County in January 2004. He leaves holding the record of most substitute appearances for North End of 97.

The pre-season games saw plenty of goals with five each against Chorley and Team Bath, four against Yeovil and three against Bamber Bridge.

In November 2003 England Ladies beat Scotland Ladies 5–0 in an international at Deepdale watched by a crowd of 6,779.

Season 2003–4: Division One

	P	W	D	L	F	A	Pts
1 Norwich City	46	28	10	8	79	39	94
2 WBA	46	25	11	10	64	42	86
3 Sunderland	46	22	13	11	62	45	79
4 West Ham	46	19	17	10	67	45	74
5 Ipswich Town	46	21	10	15	84	72	73
6 Crystal Palace	46	21	10	15	72	61	73
7 Wigan Ath.	46	18	17	11	60	45	71
8 Sheffield Utd.	46	20	11	15	65	56	71
9 Reading	46	20	10	16	55	57	70
10 Millwall	46	18	15	13	55	48	69
11 Stoke City	46	18	12	16	58	55	66
12 Coventry City	46	17	14	15	67	54	65
13 Cardiff City	46	17	14	15	68	58	65
14 Nottm. Forest	46	15	15	16	61	58	60
15 Preston	46	15	14	17	69	71	59
16 Watford	46	15	12	19	54	68	57
17 Rotherham Utd.	46	13	15	18	53	61	54
18 Crewe Alex.	46	14	11	21	57	66	53
19 Burnley	46	13	14	19	60	77	53
20 Derby Co.	46	13	13	20	53	67	52
21 Gillingham	46	14	9	23	48	67	51
22 Walsall	46	13	12	21	45	65	51
23 Bradford City	46	10	6	30	38	69	36
24 Wimbledon	46	8	5	33	41	89	29

STAT FACTS:
Best home run without defeat: 11 games
Best away run without defeat: 4 games
Longest run unbeaten: 7 games
Longest run without a win: 6 games
Best home attendance: 19,161 *vs.* Wigan 17.1.04
Worst home attendance:
5,016 *vs.* Notts County 12.8.03
Best away attendance: 28,777 *vs.* West Ham 10.1.04
Worst away attendance:
2,866 *vs.* Wimbledon 10.4.04
Aggregate and average home attendance:
325,943 – 14,171
Aggregate and average away attendance:
360,216 – 15,662

League appearances (46 games)

Abbott P. 2+7, Alexander G. 45, Briscoe L. 2, Broomes M. 30, Burley C. 1+3, Cartwright L. 2+10, Cresswell R. 41+4, Davis C. 16+6, Edwards R. 16+8, Etuhu D. 23+8, Fuller R. 37+1, Gemmill S. 7, Gould J. 37, Healy D. 27+11, Jackson Mark 0+1, Jackson Michael 41+2, Keane M. 21+9, Koumantarakis G. 1+6, Lewis E. 26+7, Lonergan A. 8, Lucas D. 1+1, Lucketti C. 37, Lynch S. 6+13, McCormack A. 2+3, McKenna P. 39, Mears T. 11+1, O'Neil B. 27+2, Skora E. 0+2, Smith J. 0+5

FA Cup appearances (3 games)

Abbott 0+3, Alexander 3, Broomes 1, Cresswell 1, Davis 2, Edwards 1, Etuhu 2, Fuller 2, Gould 3, Healy 3, Jackson Michael 1, Keane 2, Koumantarakis 2, Lewis 2, Lucketti 1, McKenna 3, Mears 1, O'Neil 3

Worthington Cup appearances (1 game)

Abbott 0+1, Alexander 1, Cartwright 1, Cresswell 1, Edwards 1, Etuhu 1, Fuller 1, Gould 1, Healy 0+1, Jackson Michael 1, Keane 1, Lucketti 1, Mears 0+1, Skora 1

Ever presents: None
Hat-tricks: (1)
Fuller *vs.* Burnley home in the League
FA Cup: Fourth Rd.
Coca Cola Cup: First Rd.
Manager: Craig Brown
Chairman: D. Shaw Esq.
Players used: 29
Leading scorer: 19 goals – Ricardo Fuller
(17 league, 2 FAC)

OFFICIAL PLAYER OF THE SEASON:
David Healy

Goalscorers: 69 League – 6 FAC – (Total 75) (No goals in the Worthington Cup)

Fuller 17–2 (19), Healy 15–0 (15), Alexander 9(8p)–0 (9), Lewis 6–0 (6), McKenna 6–0 (6), Etuhu 3–1 (4), Cresswell 2–1 (3), Abbott 2–0 (2), Koumantarakis 1–1 (2), O'Neil 1–1 (2), Davis 1–0 (1), Gemmill 1–0 (1), Keane 1–0 (1), Lucketti 1–0 (1), Lynch 1–0 (1), Mears 1–0 (1), Own Goals 1–0 (1) (Mawene of Derby)

Date 2003-4	Opponents	Comp	h or a	Score	Att.	1	2	3	4	5	6	7	8	9	10	11	12	13	14	15	16
Aug 9	West Ham	Div 1	h	1-2	18246	Gould	Alexander	Edwards	Jackson	Lucketti	O'Neil	Lewis (1)	Etuhu *	Fuller	Cresswell	Healy	Lucas	Abbott	Keane	Lynch	Skora *
Aug 12	Notts County Rd 1	C Cup	h	0-0 *	5016	Gould	Alexander	Edwards +	Jackson	Lucketti	Skora #	Cartwright *	Etuhu	Fuller	Cresswell	Keane	Lucas	Abbott +	Mears *	Lynch	Healy #
Aug 16	Wigan Ath.	Div 1	a	1-1	12073	Gould	Alexander	Edwards	Jackson	Lucketti	O'Neil	Lewis *	Etuhu +	Fuller (1)	Cresswell	Keane *	Lucas	Abbott	Davis	Cartwrit +	Healy *
Aug 23	Sunderland	Div 1	h	0-2	14080	Gould	Alexander	Edwards #	Jackson	Lucketti	Etuhu	Lewis	McKenna+	Fuller	Cresswell	Keane *	Lucas	O'Neil *	Davis	Lynch #	Healy +
Aug 25	WBA	Div 1	a	0-1	24402	Gould	Alexander *	Broomes	Davis #	Lucketti	O'Neil *	Lewis	McKenna	Fuller	Cresswell +	Keane	Lucas *	Etuhu #	Jackson #	Edwards	Healy +
Aug 30	Stoke City	Div 1	h	1-0	12965	Gould	Alexander	Broomes	Jackson	Lucketti	O'Neil	Lewis	McKenna +	Fuller (1)	Cresswell +	Keane	Lucas	Etuhu *	Jackson #	Edwards	Healy *
Sep 13	Bradford City	Div 1	a	1-2	11243	Lucas	Alexander	Broomes	Davis #	Lucketti	O'Neil *	Lewis	McKenna +	Fuller (1)	Cresswell +	Etuhu *	Lonergan	Etuhu *	Cartwright	Edwards	Healy *
Sep 16	Coventry	Div 1	a	4-2	11886	Gould	Alexander	Broomes	Jackson	Lucketti	O'Neil *	Lewis +	McKenna	Fuller (2)	Cresswell (1) #	Etuhu *	Lucas	Keane + (1)	Cartwrit *	Lynch #	Healy
Sep 20	Rotherham	Div 1	h	4-1	12340	Gould	Alexander (1p) *	Broomes	Jackson	Lucketti	O'Neil (1) #	Keane +	McKenna	Fuller (1)	Cresswell (1)	Edwards	Lucas	Etuhu	Cartwrit *	Lynch #	Healy
Sep 27	Walsall	Div 1	h	1-2	6981	Gould	Mears	Broomes +	Jackson	Lucketti	O'Neil	Keane *	McKenna	Fuller (1)	Cresswell	Edwards *	Lucas	Skora	Cartwrit *	Lynch	Healy *
Oct 1	Nottm Forest	Div 1	a	1-0	22278	Gould	Alexander	Broomes	Jackson	Lucketti	O'Neil	Keane *	McKenna	Abbott (1) #	Healy +	Cartwright	Lonergan	Etuhu *	Edwards #	Cresswell *	Abbott #
Oct 4	Wimbledon	Div 1	h	1-0	13801	Gould	Alexander	Broomes	Jackson	Lucketti	O'Neil *	Keane *	McKenna	Fuller (1)	Healy #	Lewis	Lonergan	Etuhu *	Cartwright *	Cresswell *	Cartwrit
Oct 14	Millwall	Div 1	h	1-0	8015	Gould	Alexander	Broomes	Jackson	Lucketti	O'Neil	Keane *	McKenna (1)	Fuller	Cresswell +	Lewis +	Lonergan	Healy	Edwards #	Davis *	Cartwrit *
Oct 18	Reading	Div 1	a	2-3	13130	Gould	Alexander (1p)	Broomes	Jackson	Lucketti	O'Neil *	Keane +	McKenna	Fuller (1)	Cresswell *	Lewis #	Lonergan	Etuhu - (1)	Cartwrit *	Edwards #	Etuhu
Oct 21	Crewe Alex.	Div 1	h	1-1	7012	Gould	Alexander	Broomes	Jackson	Lucketti	O'Neil *	Keane +	McKenna	Fuller	Cresswell	Keane	Lonergan	Etuhu - (1)	Cartwrit	Edwards	Healy
Oct 25	Ipswich Town	Div 1	a	1-2	14863	Gould	Alexander (1p)	Broomes	Jackson	Lucketti	O'Neil #	Cartwright *	McKenna	Fuller (1)	Cresswell +	Healy (1) #	Lonergan	Edwards	Lynch	Abbott +	Lewis #
Nov 1	Derby County	Div 1	h	3-0	12839	Gould	Alexander (1p) *	Davis	Jackson	Lucketti	O'Neil #	Cartwright *	McKenna	Fuller (1)	Cresswell +	Healy (1) *	Lonergan	Cartwrit	Cartwrit	Lynch +	Lewis +
Nov 4	Watford	Div 1	h	2-1	11572	Gould	Alexander	Broomes *	Jackson	Lucketti	Keane	Lewis	McKenna	Healy (1) +	Cresswell	Etuhu	Lucas	Abbott * (1)	Cartwright	Lynch	Davis +
Nov 8	Crystal Palace	Div 1	a	1-1	14608	Gould	Alexander	Edwards	Jackson	Lucketti	Keane *	Lewis +	McKenna	Healy (1)	Cresswell	O'Neil #	Lucas	Etuhu *	Cartwrit +	Abbott	Lynch *
Nov 22	Norwich City	Div 1	a	0-0	14775	Gould	Alexander	Edwards #	Jackson	Lucketti	Broomes	Etuhu	McKenna	Healy	Cresswell *	O'Neil #	Lucas	Abbott +	Lewis -	Lynch #	Davis
Nov 29	Sheffield Utd	Div 1	a	0-2	21003	Gould	Alexander	Edwards #	Jackson	Davis	Broomes	Etuhu +	McKenna	Fuller	Cresswell	O'Neil *	Lucas	Abbott *	Cartwright	Healy +	Lewis #
Dec 6	Crystal Palace	Div 1	h	4-1	12836	Gould	Alexander (1p) +	Broomes	Jackson	Lucketti #	O'Neil *	Etuhu (1) *	McKenna	Fuller	Healy (1)	Lewis (1)	Lucas	Abbott	Cartwrit +	Davis +	Cresswell *
Dec 9	Cardiff City	Div 1	a	2-2	13703	Gould	Alexander	Broomes	Jackson	Lucketti	O'Neil	Etuhu	McKenna #	Fuller	Cresswell +	Lewis #	Lucas	Lynch *	Cartwright	Davis #	Healy +
Dec 13	Gillingham	Div 1	h	2-0	7602	Gould	Alexander	Broomes	Jackson	Lucketti	O'Neil	Etuhu	McKenna	Fuller (1)	Cresswell +	Healy +	Lonergan	Keane	Cartwright	Abbott	Healy +
Dec 20	Burnley	Div 1	h	5-3	18802	Gould	Alexander	Broomes	Jackson	Lucketti	O'Neil *	Lewis	McKenna	Fuller (3)	Cresswell #	Lewis (1)	Lonergan	Keane	Abbott +	Davis *	Healy * (1)
Dec 26	Stoke City	Div 1	a	1-1	20216	Gould	Alexander	Davis	Jackson	Lucketti	O'Neil *	Lewis	McKenna	Fuller +	Cresswell *	Healy (1)	Lonergan	Keane	Abbott *	Abbott *	Etuhu *
Dec 28	Crewe Alex.	Div 1	h	3-3	15830	Gould	Alexander	Davis	Jackson	Lucketti	O'Neil	Lewis	Etuhu *	Fuller +	Healy	Abbott +	Lonergan	Cartwright	Mears	Skora *	Cresswell *
Jan 3	Reading Rd 3	FAC	h	3-3	9840	Gould	Alexander	Davis	Jackson *	Lucketti *	O'Neil	Lewis	McKenna	Fuller (2) *	Healy	Keane	Lonergan	Cartwrigt	Mears	Etuhu	Abbott +
Jan 10	West Ham	Div 1	a	2-1	28777	Gould	Alexander	Mears	Davis *	Lucketti	O'Neil	Keane +	McKenna	Fuller (1)	Cresswell	Healy (1)	Lonergan	Cartwrigt	Etuhu *	Abbott	Koumntk +
Jan 13	Reading Rd 3 Rep.	FAC	a	2-1	9314	Gould	Alexander (1p)	Edwards	Mears	O'Neil	Etuhu	Keane	McKenna	Healy	Cresswell (1) *	Koumntrks (1)	Lonergan	Cartwright	Abbott *	Skora	McCormak
Jan 17	Wigan Ath.	Div 1	h	2-4	19161	Gould	Alexander (1p)	Mears *	Broomes	Lucketti	Davis *	Etuhu (1)	McKenna	Fuller	Cresswell	Davis	Lonergan	Cartwright	Skora	Cartwright	Koumntk +
Jan 24	Swansea City Rd 4	FAC	a	1-2	10201	Gould	Broomes	Broomes	Davis	O'Neil	Etuhu (1) +	Lewis	McKenna	Fuller	Koumntrkis *	Healy	Lonergan	Keane	Abbott *	Cartwright	Mears
Feb 7	WBA	Div 1	h	3-0	16569	Lonergan	Alexander (1p)	Broomes #	Jackson	Mears	Healy (1)	Etuhu *	McKenna #	Fuller	Cresswell	Lewis (1) +	Gould	Keane #	Abbott	Burley #	Edwards +
Feb 14	Watford	Div 1	a	0-2	12675	Lonergan	Alexander	Broomes #	Jackson	Mears	Healy	Lewis	McKenna *	Fuller	Cresswell	Keane +	Gould	Edwards #	Burley +	Davis	O'Neil +
Feb 21	Millwall	Div 1	a	0-2	12903	Gould	Alexander	Mears	Jackson	Davis (1)	O'Neil *	Lewis	Healy +	Fuller	Cresswell +	Keane	Lonergan	Lucketti	Burley +	McCormak	Lynch #
Feb 28	Ipswich Town	Div 1	a	0-2	23359	Gould	Alexander	Mears *	Jackson	Lucketti	O'Neil	Lewis #	McKenna +	Fuller	Cresswell	Burley	Lonergan	Lucketti	Burley +	McCormak	Lynch
Mar 2	Reading	Div 1	h	2-1	11745	Gould	Alexander (1p)	Edwards	Jackson +	Davis *	Lucketti	Healy (1)	McKenna	Fuller +	Cresswell #	Lewis *	Lucas	Lewis *	Mears +	McCormak	Smith
Mar 6	Burnley	Div 1	a	1-3	15847	Gould	Alexander (1p)	Edwards	Jackson	Lucketti *	Etuhu +	Keane #	McKenna	Fuller (1)	Cresswell	Mears	Lucas	McCormk	Lewis *	Lynch #	Smith
Mar 10	Sunderland	Div 1	a	1-1	27181	Lonergan	Alexander	Edwards	Mike Jackson	Mears (1)	McCormack *	Keane #	Healy	Fuller	Cresswell *	Lynch	Lucas	Briscoe	Smith +	Mark Jackson	Armstrong
Mar 13	Gillingham	Div 1	h	0-0	13111	Lonergan	Alexander	Mears	Jackson	Lucketti	Edwards	Gemmill	McKenna	Fuller	Cresswell *	Lynch	Lucas	McCormak	Lynch +	Keane +	Koumntk +
Mar 17	Coventry	Div 1	h	1-4	13142	Lonergan	Alexander	Mears *	Jackson	Davis	McKenna	Gemmill	Healy	Fuller (1)	Cresswell *	Mears	Lucas	McCormak	Keane *	Lynch #	Smith
Mar 20	Walsall	Div 1	a	0-1	11551	Gould	Alexander (1p)	Edwards #	Jackson	Lucketti	Etuhu	Gemmill +	Healy	Fuller +	Cresswell +	Lynch	Gould	Edwards +	Briscoe	Smith * +	Koumntk +
Mar 27	Rotherham	Div 1	a	0-1	6268	Gould	Alexander	Broomes	Jackson	Broomes	Etuhu	Gemmill (1) #	Healy	Healy	Cresswell	McKenna	Lonergan	Briscoe *	Keane #	Keane	Koumntk
Apr 3	Bradford City	Div 1	h	1-0	12367	Gould	Alexander	Broomes	Jackson	Lucketti	Davis *	Gemmill (1) #	Etuhu	Fuller	Cresswell	McKenna	Lonergan	McCormak	Briscoe	Keane	Keane
Apr 10	Wimbledon	Div 1	a	3-3	2866	Gould	Alexander	Broomes *	Jackson	Lucketti	Etuhu #	Gemmill	Healy	Fuller (1)	Cresswell	McKenna	Lonergan	Edwards	Keane #	Smith	Smith
Apr 12	Nottm Forest	Div 1	h	3-3	15117	Gould	Alexander	Broomes	Mike Jackson	Lucketti (1)	Etuhu #	Gemmill #	McKenna (1)	Lynch (1)	Koumntrkis *	Edwards +	Lonergan	Smith +	McCormak	Lynch #	Koumnt * (1)
Apr 17	Derby County (1o.g*)	Div 1	a	1-5	24162	Gould	Alexander	Broomes	Mike Jackson	Lucketti (1)	Etuhu +	McCormack	Briscoe +	Fuller	Koumntrkis *	McKenna (1)	Lonergan	Smith +	Keane #	Lynch #	Cresswell #
Apr 24	Cardiff City	Div 1	h	2-2	11972	Gould	Alexander	Broomes	Mike Jackson	Lucketti	Etuhu *	Lewis (1) +	Healy	Fuller	Cresswell	McKenna (1)	Lucas	Mark Jackson +	Lynch -	Eebert	Armstrong
May 1	Norwich City	Div 1	a	2-3	23673	Gould	Alexander	Broomes	Davis	Lucketti	Etuhu *	Lewis	Healy	Lynch +	Cresswell +	McKenna (1)	Lucas	Briscoe	Smith -	Davis	McCormk
May 9	Sheffield Utd	Div 1	h	3-3	16612	Gould	Alexander (1)	Broomes	Mike Jackson	Lucketti	Etuhu *	Lewis	Healy (1)	Fuller (1)	Cresswell *	McKenna +	Lucas	Koumntr +	Smith	McCormk *	Mike Jackso *

* Lost aet 7-6 on pens
* o.g. by Mawene

SEASON 2004–2005

Craig Brown was full of optimism at the start of the 2004–05 season, especially after an opening-day victory at home to Watford. Before the month of August was over, though, Brown had been sacked and the club was in turmoil! It was not the best way to start a new campaign, so what happened subsequently was nothing short of miraculous. Derek Shaw and his Board decided to promote Brown's assistant Billy Davies, and the former Motherwell manager accepted the job. He knew it would not be easy and he quickly observed that new blood was needed to boost the players. Results fluctuated, as did the performances, with the home form remaining strong, but away from Deepdale North End struggled. There was a mini-run in the Carling Cup and by the start of December Davies was beginning to exert his influence. Patrick Agyemang was signed from Gillingham to add pace and strength to the attack and Chris Sedgwick came from Rotherham to stiffen up the midfield. A 5–0 defeat at Wigan early in the December left Preston struggling at the bottom end of the table, but then an amazing turnaround began. After a 2–1 home win over West Ham on December 18 the next 20 league games brought just one defeat! The rise up the table was astonishing and suddenly Preston had found a rhythm and a confidence not seen since David Moyes' time. They say confidence is the key in football and as Preston's confidence grew then so did their results reflect it. The decision by Davies to bring in his good friend David 'Ned' Kelly as his assistant should not be underestimated and soon the management was getting the best out of the players. Richard Cresswell scored regularly, especially at Deepdale, Paul McKenna was outstanding in midfield and at the back Preston's summer signing Youl Mawene oozed class and skill. When Davies then signed a 19 year old from Bury called David Nugent for £100,000 the manager struck gold. Nugent was a quick and lively forward, brimful of confidence and with a natural eye for a goal. Suddenly Preston were making people sit up and take notice as wins over Sunderland, QPR and the double over West Ham especially impressed. The one problem position was goalkeeper. Andy Lonergan suffered an horrendous injury and Davies had to bring in Chris Day on loan, before signing Carlo Nash from Middlesbrough. Altogether six goalkeepers were used during the season. At the beginning of December the thought of the play-offs was but a distant dream but the final position of fifth meant that they had to beat Derby for the right to make the Millennium Stadium final. This they did with aplomb and it was off to Cardiff to meet West Ham, a side they had already beaten twice. All the omens looked good but alas, yet again it proved a game too far for the men from Lancashire as on the day they played poorly. The thing that probably upset the fans most was that West Ham were there for the taking, as they too played poorly, and if the team had reproduced just a fraction of the form showed in February and March then surely we would be writing that North End were now a Premiership club. As it is they are consigned to another year in Division One. The fans should be so proud of the team's achievements during the season, and they are, but it is also so galling that we came within a whisker of making it to the top flight for the first time in 44 years. It was a bitter pill to swallow and may take some getting over.

League appearances (46 games)

Agyemang P. 15+12, Alexander G. 41+1, Broomes M. 8+2, Cresswell R. 46, Curtis J. 12, Daley O. 1+13, Davidson C. 6+3, Davis C. 21+11, Day C. 6, Etuhu D. 22+13, Folly Y. 0+2, Fuller R. 2, Gould J. 4, Healy D. 11, Hill M. 11+3, Jackson M. 0+2, Kozluk R. 0+1, Langmead K. 0+1, Lewis 37+3, Lonergan A 23, Lucketti C. 41, Lynch S. 2+6, Mawene Y. 46, McCormack A. 0+3, McKenna P. 37+2, Mears T. 1+3, Nash C. 7, Ndumbu-Nsungu G. 4+2, Neal C. 0+1, Nugent D. 13+5, Oliveira 1+4, O'Neil B. 40+3, O'Neill J. 0+2, Sedgwick C. 24, Skora E. 5+4, Smith A. 3+11, Ward G. 6+1.

FA Cup appearances (1 game)

Agyemang, 1, Alexander 1, Etuhu 1, Jackson 0+1, Kozluk 1, Lewis 1, Lonergan 1, Lucketti 1, Mawene 1, McKenna 1, Mears 0+1, O'Neill J. 1, Sedgwick 1.

Carling Cup appearances (3 games)

Alexander 3, Broomes 1, Cresswell 3, Daley 1+2, Davidson 1+1, Davis 3, Etuhu 3, Healy 1, Jackson 1+2, Lewis 2, Lonergan 2, Lucketti 1, Lynch 0+1, Mawene 3, McCormack 0+1, McKenna 2, O'Neil B. 3, Skora 0+1, Smith 2+1, Ward 1.

Goalscorers: League 67 – Carling Cup 7 – (Total) (74)

Cresswell 16(1p)–4 (20), Nugent 8–0 (8), Alexander 7(6p)–1 (8), Healy 5–0 (5), Lucketti 4–0 (4), Lewis 4–0 (4), Agyemang 4–0 (4), Etuhu 3–0 (3), McKenna 3–0(3), O'Neil B. 3–0 (3), Sedgwick 3–0 (3), Mawene 2–0 (2), Fuller 1–0 (1), Davidson 1–0 (1), Lonergan 1–0 (1), Daley 0–1(1), Lynch 0–1 (1) Own Goals 2–0 (2).

Date 2004-5	Opponents	Cmp	h or a	Score	Att.	Goalkeeper	Defender	Defender	Defender	Defender	Midfield	Midfield	Midfield	Midfield	Forward	Forward	Sub	Sub	Sub	Sub	Sub
Aug 7	Watford	LC	h	2-1	12208	Lonergan	O'Neil	Mawene	Lucketti	Davis	Skora *	Etuhu	Healy (1p)	Lewis	Fuller +	Cresswell (1)	Ward	McCormk+	Daley	Smith *	Brown
Aug 11	Wolverhampton W	LC	a	2-2	26115	Lonergan	Alexander	Mawene	Lucketti (1)	Davis +	Skora	Etuhu	O'Neil	Lewis	Healy (1) *	Cresswell	Ward	McCormk+	Daley	Smith *	Brown
Aug 14	Gillingham	LC	a	1-2	7073	Lonergan	Alexander	Mawene	Lucketti	Davis	Broomes *	McKenna #	Healy	Lewis	Fuller (1) #	Cresswell	Ward	Skora +	O'Neil #	Smith	Davidson*
Aug 20	Sheffield Utd	LC	h	0-1	12084	Lonergan	Alexander	Mawene	Lucketti	Davis *	Skora +	McKenna	O'Neil	Lewis	Healy	Cresswell	Ward	Broomes *	Daley	Smith	Lynch +
Aug 28	Brighton	LC	a	0-1	5996	Lonergan	Broomes	Mawene *	Lucketti	Davis	Skora +	McKenna	O'Neil	Lewis	Healy	Cresswell	Ward	McCormk	Daley *	Smith +	Davidson
Aug 30	Rotherham	LC	h	2-0	11439	Lonergan	Broomes	Mawene	Lucketti	Davis	Etuhu (2)	McKenna	O'Neil	Lewis #	Healy +	Cresswell *	Ward	McCormk	Daley #	Smith +	Lynch *
Sep 11	Stoke City	LC	h	3-0	12759	Lonergan	Alexander	Mawene	Lucketti	Curtis	Etuhu	McKenna	O'Neil +	Healy (1) #	Lynch *	Cresswell (2)	Ward	Skora +	Daley	Smith *	Jackson #
Sep 14	Reading	LC	a	1-3	11857	Lonergan	Alexander	Mawene	Lucketti	Curtis	Etuhu	McKenna *	O'Neil	Lewis	Healy (1)	Cresswell	Ward	Skora *	Daley	Smith	Lynch
Sep 18	Sunderland	LC	a	1-3	24264	Lonergan	Alexander (1p)	Mawene	Lucketti *	Curtis	Etuhu	Skora +	O'Neil	Lewis	Healy #	Cresswell	Ward	McCormk	Davidson *	Smith +	Lynch #
Sep 21	Mansfield Rd 1	CC	a	4-0	3028	Lonergan	Alexander (1)	Mawene	Davis	Davidson	Etuhu	Daley (1) #	O'Neil +	Lewis	Smith *	Cresswell (1)	Ward	McCormk+	Lyng	Jackson #	Lynch*(1)
Sep 25	Crewe Alex	LC	h	1-0	11823	Lonergan	Alexander	Mawene	Davis	Curtis	Etuhu	O'Neil +	Davidson (1)	Lewis	Smith *	Cresswell	Ward	McCormk+	Daley	Jackson	Lynch *
Sep 28	Plymouth A.	LC	h	1-1	11445	Lonergan	Alexander	Mawene	Davis	Curtis	Etuhu	O'Neil #	Davidson +	Lewis	Ndumbu-N *	Cresswell (1)	Ward	McCormk	Daley +	Jackson *	McKena#
Oct 2	Leicester	LC	a	1-1	21249	Lonergan (1)	Alexander	Mawene	Davis	Broomes	Etuhu	O'Neil	Curtis	Davidson +	Ndumbu-N *	Cresswell	Ward	Lewis +	Daley	Smith *	McKenna
Oct 4	Leicester Rd 2	CC	a	3-2*	6751	Lonergan	Alexander +	Mawene	Davis	Broomes	Etuhu	O'Neil	McKenna	Lewis #	Jackson *	Cresswell (3, 1p)	Ward	Brown	Daley +	Smith *	Davidson#
Oct 16	Leeds Utd	LC	a	0-1	30458	Lonergan	Alexander	Mawene	Lucketti	Broomes #	Etuhu	Curtis	McKenna	Davidson +	Healy *	Cresswell	Ward	O'Neil	Ndumbu *	Smith +	Lewis #
Oct 19	QPR	LC	h	2-1	10548	Lonergan *	Alexander +	Mawene	Lucketti (1)	Davis	Etuhu	O'Neil	McKenna	Lewis	Healy (1)	Cresswell (1)	Ward *	Lynch	Ndumbu	Smith	Daley +
Oct 23	Nottm Forest	LC	h	3-2	12439	Ward	Alexander	Mawene	Lucketti	Curtis	Etuhu (1)	Davis	McKenna (1)	Lewis #	Ndumbu-N *	Cresswell +	Gould	Lynch +	O'Neil	Smith *	Daley #
Oct 27	Everton Rd 3	CC	a	0-2	33922	Ward	Alexander #	Mawene	Lucketti	Davis *	Etuhu	O'Neil	McKenna	Smith +	Healy	Cresswell	Gould	Lynch	Skora *	Jackson #	Daley +
Oct 30	Ipswich	LC	a	0-3	23745	Ward	Alexander	Mawene	Lucketti	Curtis #	Etuhu	O'Neil *	McKenna	Lewis	Ndumbu-N +	Cresswell	Gould	Lynch +	Skora *	Smith	Daley #
Nov 3	Coventry	LC	a	1-1	12478	Ward	Alexander	Mawene	Lucketti	Davis	Etuhu	O'Neil +	McKenna	Lewis (1)	Smith *	Cresswell	Gould	Lynch	Skora	Ndumbu *	Daley +
Nov 6	Leeds Utd	LC	h	2-4	18531	Ward	Alexander	Mawene +	Lucketti	Curtis	Etuhu	Davis	McKenna	Lewis	Smith *	Cresswell (2)	Gould	Lynch	O'Neil *	Broomes	Daley +
Nov 13	Millwall	LC	h	1-1	10339	Gould	Alexander	Mawene	Lucketti	Curtis	Etuhu	Daley	McKenna	Lewis (1)	Lynch *	Cresswell	Ward	Skora	O'Neil	Broomes	Langmead *
Nov 19	Cardiff	LC	a	1-0	10950	Gould	Alexander	Mawene (1)	Lucketti	Curtis *	Broomes	O'Neil	McKenna	Lewis	Agyemang +	Cresswell	Ward	J.O'Neill	McCormk	Daley *	Davidson +
Nov 27	Derby County	LC	h	3-0	12702	Gould	Alexander (2,1p)	Mawene	Lucketti	Broomes	Sedgwick +	O'Neil	McKenna *	Lewis	Agyemang	Cresswell (1) #	Ward	Etuhu *	Davis	Daley +	Lynch #
Dec 5	Wigan Ath	LC	a	0-5	10565	Gould	Alexander	Mawene *	Lucketti	Broomes	Sedgwick	O'Neil	Etuhu	Davis	Agyemang	Cresswell	Ward	Davidson	Lewis *	Daley	Lynch
Dec 11	Burnley	LC	a	0-2	15318	Ward	Davis	Mawene	Lucketti	Davidson	Etuhu	O'Neil *	McKenna	Lewis	Agyemang	Cresswell	Neal	Alexander	Broomes	Daley *	Lynch
Dec 18	West Ham	LC	h	2-1	13451	Lonergan	Davis	Mawene	Lucketti	Davidson *	Sedgwick	O'Neil (1) +	McKenna	Lewis (1)	Agyemang #	Cresswell	Ward	Alexander *	Etuhu +	Oliveira #	J.O'Neill
Dec 26	Stoke City	LC	a	0-0	20350	Lonergan	Alexander	Mawene	Davis	Davidson +	Oliveira *	O'Neil	McKenna	Lewis	Agyemang	Cresswell	Ward	Brooms + *	Etuhu *	Daley #	J.O'Neill
Dec 28	Reading * 1 og	LC	h	3-0	12795	Lonergan	Alexander	Mawene	Lucketti	Davis	Sedgwick +	O'Neil	McKenna *	Lewis (1)	Agyemang (1)	Cresswell #	Ward	Oliveira +	Etuhu *	Daley	J.O'Neill #
Jan 1	Sunderland	LC	h	3-2	16940	Lonergan	Alexander	Mawene	Lucketti	Davis	Sedgwick #	O'Neil *	McKenna	Lewis	Agyemang +	Cresswell (3)	Ward	Oliveira #	Etuhu *	Daley +	J.O'Neill
Jan 3	Crewe Alex	LC	a	2-0	8667	Lonergan	Alexander	Mawene	Lucketti	Davis *	Sedgwick (1)	O'Neil (1)	McKenna	Lewis	Agyemang +	Cresswell	Ward	Oliveira	Etuhu *	Daley	J.O'Neill +
Jan 8	WBA Rd 3	FAC	h	0-2	13005	Lonergan	Alexander	Mawene	Lucketti	Kozluk	Sedgwick +	Etuhu	McKenna	Lewis	Agyemang	J.O'Neill *	Ward	Jackson *	McCormk	Davis	Mears +
Jan 15	Leicester	LC	h	1-1	12677	Lonergan	Alexander	Mawene	Lucketti	Hill	Sedgwick +	Etuhu	McKenna (1)	O'Neil	Agyemang *	Cresswell	Ward	Kozluk	Daley	Nugent *	Oliveira +
Jan 22	Plymouth A.	LC	a	2-0	13663	Lonergan	Alexander	Mawene	Lucketti	Hill	Sedgwick (1) *	O'Neil +	McKenna	Lewis	Agyemang(1) #	Cresswell	Ward	Kozluk *	Davis	Nugent #	Etuhu +
Feb 5	Coventry	LC	h	3-2	13691	Lonergan	Alexander (1p)	Mawene	Lucketti (1)	Hill	Sedgwick *	O'Neil	Etuhu	Lewis	Agyemang #	Cresswell (1) +	Ward	Davidson	Davis *	Nugent +	Smith #
Feb 12	QPR	LC	a	2-1	15620	Lonergan	Alexander #	Mawene	Lucketti (1)	Hill	Sedgwick	O'Neil	Etuhu +	Lewis	Agyemang *	Cresswell	McKenna +	Davidson	Davis #	Nugent* (1)	Smith
Feb 18	Ipswich	LC	h	1-1	14418	Ward #	Alexander	Mawene	Lucketti	Hill	Sedgwick	O'Neil	McKenna	Davidson *	Nugent (1) +	Cresswell	Neal #	Etuhu *	Davis	Agyemng +	Smith
Feb 23	Nottm Forest	LC	a	0-2	19209	Day	Alexander	Mawene	Lucketti	Hill	Sedgwick	O'Neil	McKenna	Lewis	Nugent	Cresswell	Neal	Davidson	Davis *	Agyemng +	Smith
Feb 26	Burnley	LC	h	1-0	18202	Day	Alexander (1p) *	Mawene	Lucketti	Davidson	Sedgwick	O'Neil	McKenna	Lewis	Nugent	Cresswell +	Hill	Etuhu	Davis *	Agyemng +	Smith
Mar 5	West Ham	LC	a	2-1	26442	Day	Alexander	Mawene	Lucketti	Hill	Sedgwick	O'Neil #	McKenna	Lewis +	Nugent (1) *	Cresswell	Ward	Etuhu	Davis +	Agyemng*(1)	Etuhu #
Mar 12	Wolverhampton W	LC	h	2-2	16296	Day	Alexander (1p)	Mawene	Lucketti	Davidson	Sedgwick	O'Neil *	McKenna #	Lewis +	Nugent	Cresswell (1)	Ward	Etuhu *	Davis #	Agyemng +	Mears
Mar 15	Sheffield Utd	LC	a	1-1	18647	Day	Alexander	Mawene	Lucketti	Davidson	Sedgwick	O'Neil	McKenna +	Lewis #	Nugent *	Cresswell (1)	Ward	Folly	Davis #	Agyemng *	Hill +
Mar 19	Watford	LC	a	2-0	19649	Day	Alexander	Mawene	Lucketti	Davidson	Sedgwick #	O'Neil	McKenna (1)	Lewis *	Nugent (1) +	Cresswell	Ward	Folly	Davis #	Agyemng +	Hill *
Apr 2	Gillingham +1 og	LC	h	1-1	15054	Nash	Alexander	Mawene	Lucketti	Davidson	Sedgwick +	O'Neil	McKenna	Lewis *	Nugent #	Cresswell	Ward	Folly +	Davis *	Agyemng #	Hill
Apr 5	Brighton	LC	h	3-0	14234	Nash	Alexander (1p) +	Mawene	Lucketti	Davidson	Sedgwick *	O'Neil #	McKenna	Lewis	Nugent (1)	Cresswell (1)	Ward	Folly #	Davis +	Agyemng *	Hill
Apr 9	Rotherham	LC	a	2-1	6312	Nash	Alexander	Mawene (1)	Lucketti	Davidson	Sedgwick (1) +	O'Neil	McKenna	Lewis *	Nugent	Cresswell #	Ward	Etuhu	Davis +	Agyemng #	Hill *
Apr 16	Cardiff	LC	h	3-0	15141	Nash	Alexander	Mawene	Lucketti	Hill	Sedgwick +	O'Neil *	McKenna	Lewis	Nugent (2) #	Cresswell (1)	Ward	Etuhu *	Davis	Agyemng #	Mears +
Apr 24	Millwall	LC	a	1-2	11417	Nash	Alexander	Mawene	Lucketti	Hill #	Sedgwick *	O'Neil	McKenna	Agyemang +	Nugent (1)	Cresswell	Ward	Etuhu +	Davis	Smith #	Mears *
Apr 30	Wigan Ath	LC	h	1-1	20221	Nash	Alexander	Mawene	Lucketti	Hill	Sedgwick	O'Neil (1) #	McKenna	Davidson *	Nugent +	Cresswell	Ward	Etuhu *	Davis	Agyemng +	Mears #
May 8	Derby County	LC	a	1-3	31237	Nash	Alexander	Mawene *	Davis	Hill	Mears	Etuhu	McKenna	Sedgwick +	Agyemang (1)	Cresswell #	Ward	O'Neil +	Lucketti	Nugent #	Broomes *
	*Hughes of Reading +Brown of Gillingham			*aet																	

Season 2004–05: Division One

		P	W	D	L	F	A	Pts
1	Sunderland	46	29	7	10	76	41	94
2	Wigan Ath.	46	25	12	9	79	35	87
3	Ipswich Town	46	24	13	9	85	56	85
4	Derby Co.	46	22	10	14	71	60	76
5	Preston	46	21	12	13	67	58	75
6	West Ham	46	21	10	15	66	56	73
7	Reading	46	19	13	14	51	44	70
8	Sheffield Utd.	46	18	13	15	57	56	67
9	Wolverhampton W.	46	15	21	10	72	59	66
10	Millwall	46	18	12	16	51	45	66
11	QPR	46	17	11	18	54	58	62
12	Stoke City	46	17	10	19	36	38	61
13	Burnley	46	15	15	16	38	39	60
14	Leeds Utd.	46	14	18	14	49	52	60
15	Leicester City	46	12	21	13	49	46	57
16	Cardiff City	46	13	15	18	48	51	54
17	Plymouth Argyle	46	14	11	21	52	64	53
18	Watford	46	12	16	18	52	59	52
19	Coventry City	46	13	13	20	61	73	52
20	Brighton	46	13	12	21	40	65	51
21	Crewe Alex.	46	12	14	20	66	86	50
22	Gillingham	46	12	14	20	45	66	50
23	Nottm. Forest	46	9	17	20	42	66	44
24	Rotherham Utd.	46	5	14	27	35	69	29

League position in Division One: : 5th – P46 W21 D12 L13 F67 A58 Pts 75
Home: W14 D7 L2 F44 A22 Away: W7 D5 L11 F23 A36

Match Report: Christmas, Pressy's Day, New Year, Cressy's Day –
Preston 3 Sunderland 2. 1 January 2005. Division One

A cracking match, in sodden conditions heralded a New Year in the best possible style for Preston North End fans. The star of the proceedings was Richard Cresswell, whose first-half hat-trick was a superb lesson in the art of finishing. Patrick Agyemang's early header which flashed narrowly past a post set the scene for Preston and they pushed forward at every opportunity. The fans did not have to wait long for a breakthrough though. Eddie Lewis fired in a free-kick to the far post where Brian O'Neil stretched to turn it back inside. Cresswell was there to touch home his first goal, his 50th for the club. Preston were rampant as Cresswell, twice, Chris Sedgwick and Lewis all went close to adding to their lead. On 31 minutes the second goal arrived, this time with a brilliant breakaway following a Sunderland corner. Eventually the ball fell for Cresswell in the centre circle and he had a long, clear run for goal. Defenders pounded after him but Cressy kept his cool and beat Thomas Myrhe with a clinical shot. The striker then almost scored again after he chipped the keeper only for the ball to fall just the wrong side of the crossbar. But with two minutes of the half left Cresswell completed a brilliant hat-trick as a superbly worked free-kick routine between Sedgwick and Lewis gave Cresswell the chance to lash the ball home. Needless to say the Preston players received a standing ovation as they left the field at the break. It probably would have been better had the half-time interval not

happened because the Sunderland manager was able to have a few choice words with his team. In the second half they responded with a spirited late comeback. Both sides had chances before Sunderland pulled a goal back on 73 minutes when Elliott curled a shot around Andy Lonergan's dive. Nine minutes later the visitors set the home nerves jangling when the lively Sean Thornton pulled another goal back. North End had to dig deep in the final 11 minutes, three of which was stoppage time, but they defended well and in the end they thoroughly deserved their win. The final shot total of 15–5 underlined Preston's overall supremacy but credit Sunderland for the late fightback which so nearly salvaged a point.

STAT FACTS:
Best home run without defeat: 9 games
Best away run without defeat: 4 games
Longest run unbeaten: 10 games
Longest run without a win: 4 games
Best home attendance: 20,315 v Derby 15.5.05
Worst home attendance: 10339 v Millwall 13.11.04
Best away attendance: 70,275 v West Ham
Play-off Final
Worst away attendance: 3028 v Mansfield 21.9.04
Aggregate and average home attendance:
319,437—13,889
Aggregate and average away attendance:
391,101—17,004

DEBUTANTS: (19) Patrick Agyemang, John Curtis, Omar Daley, Callum Davidson, Chris Day, Yoann Folly, Matthew Hill, Rob Kozluk, Kelvin Langmead, Youl Mawene, Carlo Nash, Guylain Ndumbu-Nsungu, Chris Neal, David Nugent, Felipe Oliveira, Joe O'Neill, Chris Sedgwick, Andy Smith and Gavin Ward.

LAST GAMES: (13 known) Curtis, Daley, Day, Folly, Kozluk, Langmead, Ndumbu-Nsungu, Oliveira, O'Neill, Gould, Healy, Fuller, Lynch.

Ever presents: (2) Mawene and Cresswell
Hat-tricks: (2) Cresswell (2)
FA Cup: Third Rd.
Carling Cup: Third Rd.
Manager: Craig Brown until August 2004, then Billy Davies
Chairman: D. Shaw Esq.
Players used: 29
Leading scorer: Richard Cresswell 20 goals (17 Lg 4 L.Cup)

OFFICIAL PLAYER OF THE SEASON:
Youl Mawene

David Nugent in full flow

The Play-offs

The end of season play-offs began for the first time at the end of the 1986–87 campaign but Preston North End's first involvement in them came at the end of their Division 3 season of 1988–89. Their complete record in these matches now reads:

P15 W3 D3 L9 F13 A21

Here is a brief match report of each game.

Division 3 Play-off Semi-final 1st Leg played at Deepdale on 22 May 1989.
Preston North End 1 Port Vale 1.

The best crowd of the season, 14,321, a balmy spring night, FA Cup final referee Joe Worrall in charge and a great atmosphere at Deepdale. Everything was set for a big night, but alas the game fell flat. North End had started well and took the lead after just 15 minutes. Nigel Jemson latched on to a fine through ball and although goalkeeper Mark Grew blocked his first attempt the striker rammed in the rebound. The bright start continued for a while with Grew making excellent saves from Tony Ellis, twice. After the break though Port Vale had the better as Preston faded. On 67 minutes they gained a deserved equaliser when Robbie Earle scored and after that they held the disappointing home team with ease.

Division 3 Play-off Semi-final 2nd Leg played at Vale Park on 25 May 1989.
Port Vale 3 Preston North End 1.

The second leg played in the potteries was a cracker of a match but ended in tears for the visitors after Port Vale powered their way to the final. A lively first 15 minutes saw both sides go close with Nigel Jemson and Neil Williams unlucky not to score. And just as it seemed that Vale were buckling they then opened the scoring when Darren Beckford nudged home a knockdown by Ron Futcher. Preston hit back immediately and a glorious goal by Mark Patterson put them level. A terrible decision by the referee then gave Port Vale a penalty but much to the travelling fans delight David Brown made a fine save from the spot-kick. The sides were therefore still level at the interval but within six minutes of the restart the turning point of the match arrived. A mistake by Williams allowed John Jeffers to centre for Beckford to slide home his second goal. Then, with 14 minutes left, Beckford scored a killer third goal to claim his hat-trick, although it was helped by a huge deflection by Brown.

Division 3 Play-off Semi-final 1st Leg played at Plainmoor on 15 May 1994.
Torquay 2 Preston North End 0.

North End's dream of a trip to Wembley Stadium seemed to die in the sea mist that fell on the Devon coastal town of Torquay. Preston were lacklustre throughout and a goal in each half from Duane Darby and Darren Moore settled the match. All through North End had struggled to put their game together and it could have been far worse for the visitors. With ten minutes to go Tony Ellis almost pulled back an away goal lifeline but home goalkeeper Ashley Bayes pulled off the save of the match. At the other end Steve Woods also had to make late saves to keep the score respectable and Preston were left with it all to do in the second leg.

Division 3 Play-off Semi-final 2nd Leg played at Deepdale on 18 May 1994.
Preston North End 4 Torquay 1 a.e.t.

What a night and what a result! The last ever game on plastic turned out to be a thrilling and exhilarating match which saw Preston come back from the dead. For much of the night North End were trying to come from behind. Tony Ellis had scored with a header on 8 minutes but Torquay then equalised through Gregory Goodridge and the two goal margin was restored. All Preston could do was pound the Torquay defence for the rest of the game, which they did. They were also helped when Darren Moore was sent off for punching Paul Raynor. A minute before the break David Moyes headed number two and seven minutes after half-time Stuart Hicks made it 3–1 with another header, and 3–3 on aggregate. It was bedlam at Deepdale as the frenzied crowd urged North End forward. Torquay grittily held on and, indeed, created a couple of good chances themselves. The match went into extra-time and with just four minutes of that left Andy Fensome's cross was headed home by Raynor. Deepdale went wild with delight and they chanted 'Wemberlee, Wemberlee' as the plans were made to visit the famous old Stadium in London.

7

Division 3 Play-off Final played at Wembley Stadium on 28 May 1994.
Wycombe Wanderers 4 Preston North End 2.

At half-time it looked good for North End. They were leading 2–1 in the final at Wembley and although not at their best they deserved the lead. But after the break it all went wrong as Martin O'Neill's Wycombe side dominated and scored three goals. Earlier, on 32 minutes a brilliant overhead kick by Ian Bryson put North End ahead but within 30 seconds Jamie Squires put through his own goal after a cross by Steve Thompson. Five minutes later Tony Ellis sent in a cross and Paul Raynor scored with a fine header. Preston had the edge now but within two minutes of the restart Simon Garner clinically equalised and the tide turned dramatically. From then on Wycombe gained control and after 57 minutes Dave Carroll made it 3–2. With 18 minutes left Carroll scored an excellent second goal for himself and the fourth goal for his team. It was all over and O'Neill led his side to promotion.

Date	Opponents Play-off fixtures	Comp	h or a	Score	Att.	1	2	3	4	5	6	7	8	9	10	11	12	14	15	16	17
1988-9																					
22.5.89	Port Vale S/F 1st Leg	Div 3	h	1-1	14321	Brown	Williams	Swann	Atkins	Wrightson	Hughes	Mooney	Ellis	Joyce	Jemson (1)	Patterson	Rathbone	Miller			
25.5.89	Port Vale S/F 2nd Leg	Div 3	a	1-3	13416	Brown	Williams	Swann	Atkins	Wrightson	Hughes	Mooney +	Ellis	Joyce	Jemson *	Patterson (1)	Rathbone *	Miller +			
	Aggregate 2-4																				
1993-4																					
15.5.94	Torquay Utd. S/F 1st Leg	Div 3	a	0-2	4440	Woods	Fensome	Sulley	Cartwright	Matthewson	Moyes	Ainsworth	Lucas *	Raynor	Ellis	Bryson	Conroy *	Challender	Berryman		
18.5.94	Torquay Utd. S/F 2nd Leg*	Div 3	h	4-1	11442	Woods	Fensome	Kidd	Cartwright	Hicks (1)	Moyes (1)	Ainsworth	Whalley	Raynor (1) *	Ellis (1) +	Bryson	Lucas *	Challender +	Berryman		
	Aggregate 4-3																				
28.5.94	Wycombe W. Final *	Div3	n	2-4	40109	Woods	Fensome	Kidd	Cartwright	Squires	Moyes	Ainsworth	Whalley	Raynor (1)	Ellis	Bryson (1)	Conroy	Lucas	Berryman		
	* Played at Wembley																				
1994-5																					
14.5.95	Bury S/F 1st Leg	Div 3	h	0-1	13297	Vaughan	Fensome	Fleming	Raynor +	Kidd	Moyes	Davey	Bryson	Lancashire	Sale *	Magee	Conroy *	Cartwright +	Richardson		
17.5.95	Bury S/F 2nd Leg	Div 3	a	0-1	9094	Vaughan	Fensome +	Fleming	Raynor	Kidd	Moyes	Davey	Bryson	Smart	Sale *	Cartwright	Conroy *	Ainsworth +	Richardson		
	Aggregate 0-2																				
1998-9																					
16.5.99	Gillingham S/F 1st Leg	Div 2	h	1-1	18584	Lucas	Alexander	Ludden	Murdock	Jackson	Gregan	Cartwright	Rankine	Nogan *	Macken	Eyres (1)	Appleton *	Kidd	Harris #		
19.5.99	Gillingham S/F 2nd Leg	Div 2	a	0-1	10505	Lucas	Alexander	Ludden #	Murdock *	Jackson	Gregan	Cartwright	Appleton	Macken +	Rankine	Eyres	Darby *	Nogan +	Harris #		
	Aggregate 1-2																				
2000-1																					
13.5.01	Birmingham S/F 1st Leg	Div 1	a	0-1	29072	Lucas	Alexander	Edwards	Murdock	Kidd	Gregan	Cartwright	McKenna	Cresswell	Macken *	Healy	Moilanen	Anderson *	Bry Murpy	Collins	Gunlagso
1.5.01	Birmingham S/F 2nd Leg*	Div 1	h	2-1	16928	Lucas	Alexander	Edwards	Murdock	Kidd	Gregan	Cartwright	Rankine (1)	Healy (1)	Macken +	Anderson *	Moilanen	Cresswell *	Bry Murpy	McKenna *	Gunlagso
28.5.01	Bolton P/Off Final +	Div 1	n	0-3	54328	Lucas	Alexander	Edwards	Murdock	Kidd	Gregan	Cartwright +	Rankine	Healy	Macken	McKenna *	Moilanen	Cresswell	Bry Murpy	Anderson +	Jackson
	* Agg 2-2 Won 4-2 on pens																				
	+Played at Millenium Stadium Cardiff																				
2004-5																					
15.5.05	Derby Co. S/F 1st Leg	Champ	h	2-0	20315	Nash	Mawene	Lucketti	Davis	Hill	Sedgwick	O'Neil *	McKenna	Lewis #	Cresswell (1)	Nugent (1) *	Ward	Mears	Etuhu *	Agyemng *	Broomes #
19.5.05	Derby Co. S/F 2nd Leg	Champ	a	0-0	31310	Nash	Mawene	Lucketti	Davis	Hill	Sedgwick	O'Neil *	McKenna	Lewis #	Cresswell	Nugent +	Ward	Mears	Etuhu *	Agyemng +	Broomes #
30.5.05	West Ham P/Off Final +	Champ	n	0-1	70275	Nash	Mawene #	Lucketti	Davis	Hill	Sedgwick +	O'Neil *	McKenna	Lewis	Cresswell	Nugent	Ward	Broomes	Etuhu *	Agyemng +	Alexander +
	+ Played at the Millennium Stadium, Cardiff																				

Division 3 Play-off Semi-final 1st Leg played at Deepdale on 14 May 1995.
Preston North End 0 Bury 1.

For the second year running Preston reached the play-offs but for the second year running it was also a very disappointing experience. But if you don't score then you don't win matches and Bury came to do a job, did the business and gained the bonus of an away goal. They returned to Gigg Lane over the moon with their night's work. The decisive goal came in the first half when David Pugh, unmarked, was able to turn and shoot past John Vaughan. The second half was one-way traffic as Preston pushed forward relentlessly. Ian Bryson, Simon Davey, Mark Sale and Graham Lancashire all came close to equalising and Bury goalkeeper Gary Kelly excelled on other occasions. David Moyes missed two easy chances with headers from corners but the best chance of the night fell to Bury's Phil Stant, but he failed to convert from 3 yards! A difficult tie for North End and it left them with a lot to do in the second leg.

Division 3 Play-off Semi-final 2nd Leg played at Gigg Lane on 17 May 1995.
Bury 1 Preston North End 0.

Doomed to another year in Division Three, that was the verdict after a disappointing second leg at Bury. Defences dominated this scrappy match with Preston failing to find the necessary guile or invention to unlock the home rearguard. When North End did create a worthwhile chance they found goalkeeper Gary Kelly, son of the Preston legend, in top form. One save he made in the 67th minute from Ian Bryson's header was out of this world. Ryan Kidd missed a great chance and Simon Davey had one effort hoofed off the line. Preston needed a goal to settle them down and had they scored there was no doubt that they could still have gone on to win the tie. With three minutes left the tie was finally settled when Tony Rigby snatched a goal for the home side. Bury deserved to go through as Preston never found the form they needed.

Division Two Play-off Semi-final 1st Leg played at Deepdale on 16 May 1999.
Preston North End 1 Gillingham 1.

A tragic mistake by goalkeeper David Lucas dealt a body blow to Preston after they had worked hard to forge a lead. In a scrappy first-half Gillingham put up a defensive barrier and Preston struggled to break them down. Lee Cartwright, playing only his second game in three months, missed the best chance on the half hour when he nodded a great cross by David Eyres wide when it seemed easier to score. A goalmouth scramble almost led to Mark Rankine bundling the ball home and Sean Gregan's follow up was desperately hacked away. Finally, on 55 minutes, Eyres headed in Graham Alexander's cross and Deepdale went wild. Lucas then made a fine save, but four minutes later, in the 76th minute, he allowed a weak shot from Robert Taylor to squirm under his body to give Gillingham an equaliser. It was very disappointing but North End deserved no more than a draw.

Division Two Play-off Semi-final 2nd Leg played at the Priestfield Stadium on 19 May 1999.
Gillingham 1 Preston North End 0.

It took Gillingham just 64 seconds to score what proved to be the decisive goal in this second leg tie, and it ended North End's Wembley dream. The winning goal was scored by Andy Hessenthaler, after the ball was laid off by Carl Asaba. After that Preston huffed and puffed, created a few good chances, but the forwards were unable to find the necessary finish. Jon Macken, Dominic Ludden, Sean Gregan and Michael Jackson all went close as the visitors pushed forward. It was all Preston for long spells but try as they might they could not break down a stubborn and resolute Gillingham defence. Ludden, in particular, had a fine game for North End and it was all so very frustrating to miss out on another chance of a final.

Division One Play-off Semi-final 1st Leg played at St Andrews on 13 May 2001.
Birmingham 1 Preston North End 0.

Nearly 30,000 people packed St Andrews and watched in frenzied excitement as Birmingham pounded the Preston goal. It was a real backs-to-the-wall performance by the Lilywhites but they defended superbly and set themselves up for a fighting chance in the return at Deepdale. The noise from the home crowd was deafening but the North End lads refused to be intimidated. David Lucas had a busy night and made several fine saves and it was not until the 55th minute that Birmingham made a breakthrough. A free-kick pinged about in the area before finding Nicky Eaden, who was left with time and space to pick his spot. Lucas then made a brilliant save from Geoff Horsfield and try as they might Birmingham could not add to their total.

Division One Play-off Semi-final 2nd Leg played at Deepdale on May 17 2001
Preston North End 2 Birmingham 1 – a.e.t. Preston won 4–2 on penalties.

This was an unbelievable night of high drama and excitement at Deepdale, that ended in triumph for David Moyes and his boys. Trailing by one goal from the first leg, Preston equalised after just 24 minutes with a well taken strike by David Healy. But on the hour mark Birmingham regained the initiative by equalising on the night and taking an aggregate lead. When Graham Alexander, of all people, missed a penalty with 11 minutes to go it looked as though Preston had lost their chance. But in injury time, with the match drifting away, Mark Rankine latched on to a rebound from Healy's shot to force the ball home. Deepdale went 'bananas' and eventually the match went to extra-time and then the dreaded penalty shoot-out. Nerves were jangling, on and off the pitch, the atmosphere was electric, but North End came through when local lad Paul McKenna scored from the decisive kick. It was difficult for all North End fans to describe their emotions at that particular moment!

Division One Play-off Final played at the Millennium Stadium Cardiff on 28 May 2001.
Bolton Wanderers 3 Preston North End 0.

It proved to be a game too far for David Moyes and his team as their Lancashire rivals Bolton won through after a strong performance. The score flattered Bolton somewhat, with two of the goals coming right at the end as Preston pushed forward desperately in search of an equaliser. A 14th minute shot by Gareth Farrelly found the net via a deflection and from that moment Preston were playing catch-up. The first-half was controlled by the Wanderers, but after a half-time pep talk from Moyes, North End showed a little more of their capabilities. Mark Rankine saw a fine effort fly just wide and when Jon Macken set up David Healy it looked odds on an equaliser. Unfortunately for North End Matt Clarke pulled off the save of the match, tipping the ball around a post. If one incident was the turning point of the match, that was it. The Preston players continued to work their socks off but they just could not find a route to goal. In the end, as Preston pushed forward, they were caught when with two minutes to go Michael Ricketts broke clear and coolly slotted home goal number two. To rub salt in the wound Ricardo Gardiner scored again in stoppage time. It was a cruel blow and the North End players slumped to the ground in tears at the end of a tough match. It was so near and yet so far.

Billy Davies
PNE manager

Championship Play-off Semi-final 1st Leg played at Deepdale on 15 May 2005.
Preston North End 2 Derby County 0.

A big crowd, lots of expectation and a determined Preston side gave Deepdale another game to remember. It was a hard-working display by Preston and Derby rarely featured as an attacking force. It was no more than North End deserved when they took the lead on 38 minutes. Richard Cresswell and Chris Sedgwick combined to give David Nugent a chance. He burst past two defenders before flicking a great shot past the Derby keeper. The first-half performance warranted more goals such was North End's dominance and that was the only worry for Billy Davies's men. But the second-half was much the same pattern with Preston pushing forward and Derby struggling to get going. However, the visitors defended stubbornly and it looked as though Preston would have to settle for the one goal lead. Then with just two minutes left on the clock, a fluke goal by leading scorer Cresswell gave Preston another score and the second leg would be even more difficult for Derby.

Agyemang P.	0+3	Gregan S.M.	5	Mooney B.J.	2	
Ainsworth G.	3+1	Harris J.A.S.	0+2	Moyes D.W.	5	
Alexander G.	5+1	Healy D.	3	Murdock C.J.	5	
Anderson I.	1+2	Hicks S.J.	1	Nash C.	3	
Appleton M.A.	1+1	Hill M.	3	Nogan K.	1+1	
Atkins R.G.	2	Hughes A.F.S.	2	Nugent D.	3	
Broomes M.	0+2	Jackson M.J.	2	O'Neil B.	3	
Brown D.J.	2	Jemson N.B.	2	Patterson M.A.	2	
Bryson J.I.C.	5	Joyce W.G	2	Rankine S.M.	4	
Cartwright L.	9+1	Kidd R.A.	7	Rathbone M.J.	0+1	
Challender G.L.	0+1	Lancashire G.	1	Raynor P.J.	5	
Conroy M.K.	0+3	Lewis E.	3	Sale M.D.	2	
Cresswell R.	4+2	Lucas D.A.	5	Sedgwick C.	3	
Darby J.T.	0+1	Lucas R.	1+1	Smart A.A.C.	1	
Davey S.	2	Lucketti C.	3	Squires J.A.	1	
Davis C.	3	Ludden D.	2	Sulley C.S.	1	
Edwards R.	3	Macken J.P.	5	Swann G.	2	
Ellis A.J.	5	Magee K.	1	Vaughan J.	2	
Etuhu D.	0+3	Matthewson T.	1	Whalley D.N.	2	
Eyres D.	2	Mawene Y.	3	Williams N.J.F.	2	
Fensome A.B.	5	McKenna P.	5+1	Woods S.G.	3	
Fleming T.M.	2	Miller D.B.	0+1	Wrightson J.G.	2	

Goalscorers: Raynor 2, Jemson, Patterson, Ellis, Hicks, Bryson, Moyes, Eyres, Healy, Rankine, Nugent and Cresswell all one each.

In the one penalty shoot out so far, against Birmingham in 2000-1, Alexander, Healy, Gregan and McKenna scored and Edwards missed as Preston won 4-2.

Championship Play-off Semi-final 2nd Leg played at Pride Park on 19 May 2005.
Derby County 0 Preston North End 0.

Not the most thrilling of matches but, instead, a thoroughly professional performance by the men from Deepdale. They came to do a job and did it magnificently. The North End players defended brilliantly and rarely did Derby threaten Carlo Nash's goal. Preston were in total control in the first half with Chris Lucketti, Claude Davis, Youl Mawene and Matt Hill a solid yellow brick wall that Derby had no answer to. After the break it was more of the same although there was one big scare with 8 minutes to go. The referee made an awful decision in penalising Lucketti for a challenge on Rasiak, who went down theatrically. The ref gave a penalty but justice was seen to be done when Rasiak hit the post with his kick and the ball was cleared. Nash made a good save diving to his right but Preston themselves could have wrapped up the game with a couple of late chances and in the end ran out deserved winners.

Championship Play-off Final played at the Millennium Stadium Cardiff on 30 May 2005.
West Ham United 1 Preston North End 0.

Preston North End became the first team to lose three play-off finals after this so disappointing defeat against an equally unimpressive West Ham side. In truth Preston were very poor on the day and never looked like reproducing the form they showed in February and March. They had already beaten West Ham twice in the regular season and all the omens looked good for the men from Lancashire. But several of their players just could not find their form and once again it proved a match too far. West Ham had the better of the chances but only because Preston failed to compete in the right areas. Claude Davis had an excellent game and captain Chris Lucketti also played his part with his usual steadiness. But in the midfield Paul McKenna and Brian O'Neil had poor games, not at their influential best at all. The decisive goal sort of summed up Preston's match. The Hammer's danger-man Matthew Etherington centred from the left and both Davis and Matt Hill slipped at the vital moment to let in Bobby Zamora whose scuffed shot found the net. David Nugent and Richard Cresswell were given nothing to latch on to by their midfield and Preston rarely had a shot, let alone look like scoring. It was bitterly disappointing, but at least the southern press were happy, as they had totally written North End off before the play-offs had even started!

Roll of Honour

Internationals while playing for Preston North End FC, including substitute appearances (up to June 2005)

ENGLAND
W. C. Rose 1 cap 1886
F. Dewhurst 9 caps 1886–89 11 goals
J. Goodall 4 caps 1888–89 3 goals
R. howarth 4 caps 1887–91
R. Holmes 7 caps 1888–95
F. Becton 1 cap 1895 2 goals
R. Bond 5 caps 1905–06 2 goals
J. McCall 5 caps 1913–21 1 goal
A. Rawlings 1 cap 1921
W. T. Roberts 2 caps 1924 2 goals
H. Holdcroft 2 caps 1937
T. Finney 76 caps 1946–58 30 goals
T. Thompson 1 cap 1957

SCOTLAND
P. McBride 6 caps 1904–09
A. James 4 caps 1926–29 2 goals
F. O'Donnell 4 caps 1937–8 2 goals
A. Beattie 7 caps 1937–39
G. Mutch 1 cap 1938
T. Smith 1 cap 1938
W. Shankly 5 caps 1938–39
R. Beattie 1 cap 1939
J. Dougal 1 cap 1939 1 goal
A. McLaren 3 caps 1947 4 goals
T. Docherty 22 caps 1952–58 1 goal
W. Cunningham 8 caps 1954–55
G. Alexander 17 caps 2002–05
B. O'Neil 1 cap 2005

WALES
Dr Mills-Roberts 2 caps 1888
J. Trainer 19 caps 1888–99
R. Roberts 1 cap 1892
S. Davies 3 caps 1920 3 goals
R. John 2 caps 1935
B. Godfrey 3 caps 1964–65 2 goals

EIRE
F. O'Farrell 2 caps 1957–59
J. O'Neill 1 cap 1960
J. Fullam 1 cap 1960
A. Kelly 45 caps 1962–73
R. Treacy 8 caps 1974–6 1 goal
M. Lawrenson 1 cap 1977
P. McGee 6 caps 1979–80 2 goals
J. Anderson 5 caps 1997–99

NORTHERN IRELAND
A. Gara 3 caps 1902 3 goals
J. McKnight 1 cap 1912 1 goal
W. Irvine 3 caps 1968–69 2 goals
C. Murdock 17 caps 2000–02
D. Healy 32 caps 2001–04 11 goals
A. Smith 7 caps 2004–05

FINLAND
T. Moilanen 3 caps 1997–2000

ICELAND
B. Gunnlaugsson 2 caps 2000 1 goal

JAMAICA
R. Fuller 10 caps 2002–04 2 goals
C. Davis 13 caps 2003–05
O. Daley 3 caps 2005 *

SOUTH AFRICA
G. Koumantarakis 1 cap 2003

UNITED STATES OF AMERICA
B. McBride 2 caps 2001 1 goal †
E. Lewis 21 caps 2003–05 5 goals

* Daley on loan from Portmore United (Jamaica)
† McBride on loan from Columbus Crew (USA)

Postscript

The incredible journey made by Preston North End over the past 127 years has left a remarkable legacy for the people of the famous old Lancashire city. It has been an unbelievable roller-coaster ride of every conceivable emotion, and we hope you will agree with us that it has been a magnificent story which epitomises all that is great about being involved with an English league football team. This book proves that it is vitally important that the town clubs of this country should survive and flourish, as there are few other institutions which create the same fervour and commitment as the 'local team'.

The fans of North End, no matter what age they are, will have a host of memories to cherish, and there are few clubs in the country that can match the history of the Lilywhites. The special atmosphere of Deepdale is unforgettable and when the final side of the ground is developed then it will be one of the best stadiums in the league. North End have from day one been a pioneering side, playing a huge part in the growth and development of the sport in this country. They have been led, both on and off the field, by an array of astute and forward-thinking men.

Some of the greatest players in the world have proudly worn the famous white shirt, led by the one and only Tom Finney. When you read the story of the club, it is evident that Sir Tom epitomises all that is good about Preston North End. He has been Mr Preston North End for over 60 years now and the proud President for several of them.

Ian Rigby and I have supported the club for a total of almost 100 years between us, and throughout that time we have suffered, along with everyone else, when North End have had a poor year. But the good memories and highlights far outweigh the downside of supporting our team. We are sure that over the next few years there will be many more twists and turns to add to the story so far … We can't wait!

Everyone connected with Preston North End can be proud of the achievements of the club, from the pioneering Old Invincibles through to last season's team that reached the Division One Play-off final, just one tiny step from the Premiership. It is also a club that the fans can be proud to be associated with. Hopefully our united dream of making it to the big time once again will soon be fulfilled and we offer our sincere best wishes to the Chairman, the Manager and the players for the future.

Mike Payne

Ian Rigby